Getting Started is as EASY as 1, 2, 3 . . . 4!

1. Sign Up

Instructors register with myBusinessCourse.com

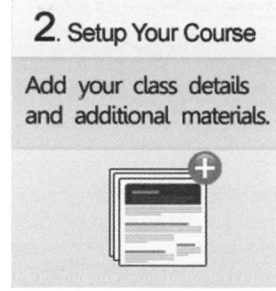

2. Setup Your Course

Add your class details and additional materials.

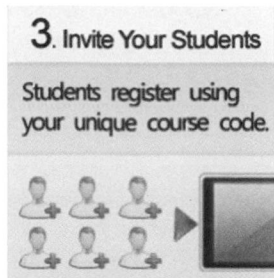

3. Invite Your Students

Students register using your unique course code.

4. Manage Your Course

Study, test, and grade assignments. It's simple!

Provide Instruction and Practice 24/7

◆ Assign **homework** from your Cambridge Business Publishers textbook and have myBusinessCourse grade it for you automatically.

◆ With our **eLectures**, your students can revisit accounting topics as often as they like or until they master the topic.

◆ **Guided Examples** show students how to solve select problems.

◆ Make homework due before class to ensure students enter your classroom prepared.

◆ Additional practice and **exam preparation** materials are available to help students achieve better grades and content mastery.

STUDENT SELF-STUDY OPTION

Not all instructors choose to incorporate **myBusinessCourse** into their course. In such cases, students can access the Self-Study option for MBC. The Self-Study option provides most of the learning tools available in the Instructor-Led courses, including:

◆ eLectures
◆ Guided Examples
◆ Practice Quizzes

The Self-Study option does not include homework assignments from the textbook. Only the Instructor-Led option includes homework assignments.

Want to learn more about myBusinessCourse?

Contact your sales representative or visit **www.mybusinesscourse.com**.

STUDENTS: Find your access code on the myBusinessCourse insert on the following pages. If you have a used copy of this textbook, you can purchase access online at **www.mybusinesscourse.com**.

Cambridge Business Publishers
Series in Accounting

Computerized Accounting
- **QuickBooks Online**, by Williams
- **Computerized Accounting with QuickBooks® 2015**, by Williams
- **Computerized Accounting with QuickBooks® 2018**, by Williams

Financial Accounting
- **Financial Accounting for Undergraduates, 3e** by Wallace, Nelson, Christensen, and Ferris
- **Financial Accounting, 5e** by Dyckman, Hanlon, Magee, and Pfeiffer
- **Financial Accounting for MBAs, 7e** by Easton, Wild, Halsey, and McAnally
- **Financial Accounting for Executives & MBAs, 4e** by Simko, Ferris, and Wallace
- **Cases in Financial Reporting, 8e** by Drake, Engel, Hirst, and McAnally

Financial Accounting Using IFRS
- **Financial Accounting, 2e** by Wong, Dyckman, Hanlon, Magee, and Pfeiffer

Managerial Accounting
- **Managerial Accounting for Undergraduates, 1e** by Christensen, Hobson, and Wallace
- **Managerial Accounting, 8e** by Hartgraves & Morse
- **Cases in Managerial and Cost Accounting, 1e** by Allen, Brownlee, Haskins, and Lynch

Combined Financial & Managerial Accounting
- **Financial & Managerial Accounting for Undergraduates, 1e** by Wallace, Nelson, Christensen, Hobson, and Ferris
- **Financial & Managerial Accounting for Decision Makers, 3e** by Dyckman, Hanlon, Magee, Pfeiffer, Hartgraves, and Morse
- **Financial & Managerial Accounting for MBAs, 5e** by Easton, Halsey, McAnally, Hartgraves, and Morse

Intermediate Accounting
- **Intermediate Accounting, 1e** by Hanlon, Hodder, Nelson, and Roulstone
- **Guide to Intermediate Accounting Research, 1e** by Collins
- **Cases in Financial Reporting, 8e** by Drake, Engel, Hirst, and McAnally

Cost Accounting
- **Cases in Managerial and Cost Accounting, 1e** by Allen, Brownlee, Haskins, and Lynch

Auditing
- **Alpine Cupcakes Audit Case** by Dee, Durtschi, and Mindak

Financial Statement Analysis & Valuation
- **Financial Statement Analysis & Valuation, 5e** by Easton, McAnally, Sommers, and Zhang
- **Corporate Valuation, 2e** by Holthausen & Zmijewski

Advanced Accounting
- **Advanced Accounting, 4e** by Hamlen
- **Advanced Accounting, 3e** by Halsey & Hopkins

Governmental and Not-For-Profit Accounting
- **Accounting for Governmental and Nonprofit Organizations, 1e** by Patton, Patton, and Ives
- **Governmental and Not-for-Profit Accounting: An Active Learning Workbook** by Convery

FASB Codification and eIFRS
- **Skills for Accounting Research: Text & Cases, 3e** by Collins

my BusinessCourse

FREE WITH NEW COPIES OF THIS TEXTBOOK*

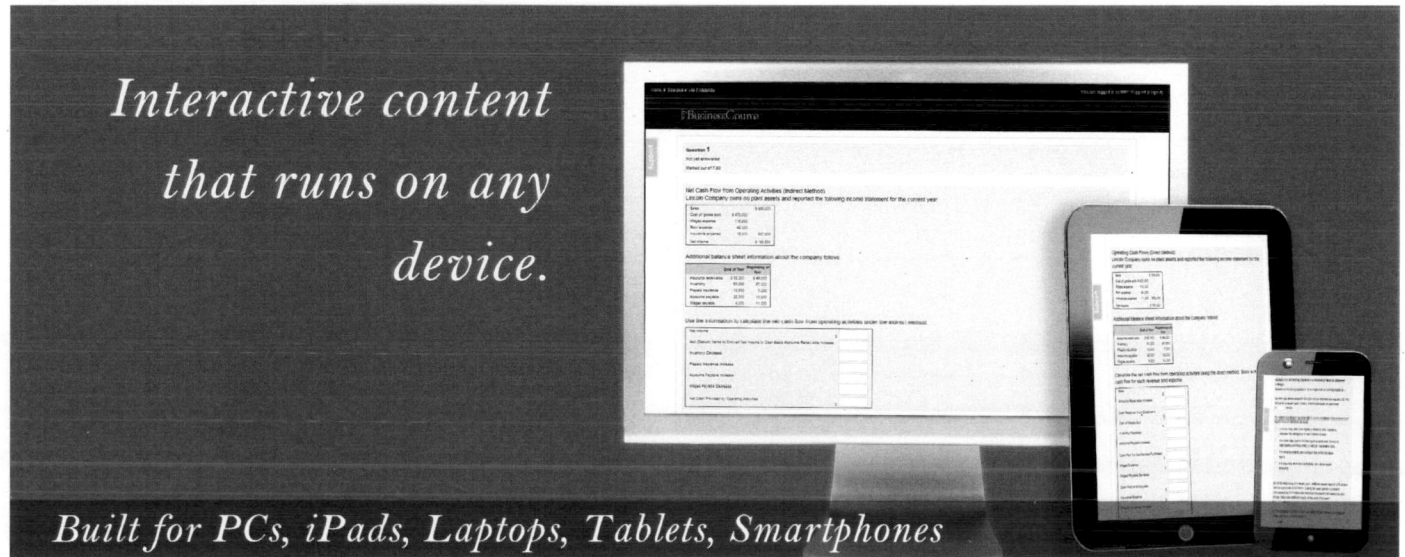

Financial & Managerial Accounting
for Undergraduates

First Edition

James S. Wallace
The Peter F. Drucker and Masatoshi Ito
Graduate School of Management
Claremont Graduate University

Karen K. Nelson
M.J. Neeley School of Business
Texas Christian University

Theodore E. Christensen
Terry College of Business
University of Georgia

L. Scott Hobson
The Marriott School of Management
Brigham Young University

Kenneth R. Ferris
W.P. Carey School of Business
Arizona State University

Permissions Statement:

Materials from the Certified Management Accountant Examinations, Copyright © 2015 by the Institute of Certified Management Accountants, are reprinted and/or adapted with permission.

All Fezzari photos courtesy of Fezzari Bicycles.

Bookstores & Faculty: To order this book, contact the company via email customerservice@cambridgepub.com or call 800-619-6473.

Students & Retail Customers: To order this book, please visit the book's Website and order directly online.

Printed in the Canada.
10 9 8 7 6 5 4 3 2 1

About the Authors

JAMES S. WALLACE is an Associate Professor at The Peter F. Drucker and Masatoshi Ito Graduate School of Management at The Claremont Graduate University. He received his B.A. from the University of California, Santa Barbara, his M.B.A. from the University of California, Davis, and his Ph.D. from the University of Washington. Professor Wallace also holds a CPA certification from the state of California. He previously served on the faculty of the University of California, Irvine and has served as a visiting professor at the University of California, San Diego. Professor Wallace's work has appeared in leading academic journals including the *Journal of Accounting and Economics*, the *Journal of Corporate Finance*, and *Information Systems Research*, along with leading applied journals such as the *Journal of Applied Corporate Finance*, the *Journal of Accountancy*, *Issues in Accounting Education* and *Accounting Horizons*. Prior to his career in academics, Professor Wallace worked in public accounting and in industry with a Fortune 500 company. He has done consulting work with numerous companies in multiple industries.

KAREN K. NELSON is the M.J. Neeley Professor of Accounting at Texas Christian University. She previously served on the faculty at Rice University, and Stanford University, and as a visiting professor at the University of Michigan. She earned her Ph.D. at the University of Michigan and a bachelor's degree (summa cum laude) from the University of Colorado. She also holds a CPA license from the state of Colorado. Professor Nelson's research focuses on financial reporting and disclosure issues, including the role of regulators, auditors, and private securities litigation in monitoring financial reporting quality. She has held research seminars at over 50 leading business schools in the U.S. and abroad, and published in a variety of leading academic journals including *The Accounting Review*, *Journal of Accounting and Economics*, *Journal of Accounting*, and *Review of Accounting Studies*. Her research has been featured in the financial press in publications such as *The Wall Street Journal*, *Business Week,* and *Forbes*. She is an active member of the American Accounting Association and serves on the Editorial Board of *The Accounting Review*. She has taught financial accounting at all levels, and her students have honored her with numerous awards for teaching excellence. She is a member of the Standing Advisory Group of the Public Company Accounting Oversight Board.

THEODORE E. CHRISTENSEN is director and Terry Distinguished Chair of Business in the J. M. Tull School of Accounting at the University of Georgia. Prior to coming to UGA, he was on the faculty at Brigham Young University from 2000–2015 and at Case Western Reserve University from 1995–2000. He was a visiting professor at the University of Michigan (2013–2014) and the University of Utah (2012), and has taught at Santa Clara University in a summer program since 2005. He received a B.S. degree in accounting at San Jose State University, a M.Acc. degree in tax at Brigham Young University, and a Ph.D. in accounting from the University of Georgia. Professor Christensen has authored and coauthored articles published in many journals including *The Accounting Review, Journal of Accounting and Economics, Journal of Accounting Research, Review of Accounting Studies, Contemporary Accounting Research, Accounting Organizations and Society*, the *Journal of Business Finance & Accounting*, the *Journal of Accounting, Auditing, and Finance, Accounting Horizons*, and *Issues in Accounting Education*. He is also the author of an advanced financial accounting textbook. Professor Christensen has taught financial accounting at all levels, financial statement analysis, business valuation, both introductory and intermediate managerial accounting, and corporate taxation. He is the recipient of numerous awards for both teaching and research. He has been active in serving on various committees of the American Accounting Association and is a CPA.

L. SCOTT HOBSON is a Teaching Professor of Accounting at Brigham Young University (BYU), where he joined the faculty in 2003. He received his B.S. in accounting and Master of Accountancy degrees from BYU in 1983. Prior to his career in academics, Professor Hobson was the founder and owner of Hilton Farnkopf & Hobson (now HFH Consultants), a management consulting firm headquartered in Walnut Creek, California, for 14 years. He also worked in public accounting at Price Waterhouse for 5.5 years in both audit and consulting. While at Price Waterhouse, he taught for 2 years as an adjunct faculty at San Jose State University. He has taught accounting at all levels, from principles to M.B.A. courses, including managerial accounting, financial accounting, governmental and not-for-profit accounting, and management consulting. Professor Hobson is licensed as a CPA (inactive) in California. Professor Hobson has published a case titled "Managing the CPA Firm at Dodge Company" in *Issues in Accounting Education*.

KENNETH R. FERRIS is a Professor in the W.P. Carey School of Business at Arizona State University. He received a B.B.A. and an M.B.A. from The George Washington University and an M.A. and a Ph.D. from The Ohio State University. He previously served on the faculties of Northwestern University, The Claremont Graduate University, Southern Methodist University, and Thunderbird School of Global Management, In addition, he has taught at numerous academic institutions in Australia, Hong Kong, Japan, and New Zealand. Professor Ferris is the author or co-author of eleven books, over fifty academic and professional publications, and over eighty case studies. He previously served as a director of several NYSE listed companies and is active in executive education programs around the world.

Welcome to *Financial & Managerial Accounting for Undergraduates*. We wrote this book to satisfy the needs of students taking an introductory course in financial and managerial accounting by providing a **high quality, contemporary, and engaging textbook at an affordable price**. *Financial & Managerial Accounting for Undergraduates* is written for students who want to understand how financial statements are prepared and how the information in published financial reports is used. It will also introduce students to management accounting concepts and decision making tools that will help them become effective managers in an increasingly competitive global market. The publication of this text has benefited from extensive feedback and suggestions from focus groups, market surveys, manuscript reviews, and interviews with faculty from across the country.

TARGET AUDIENCE

Financial & Managerial Accounting for Undergraduates is intended for use in the financial and managerial accounting courses at the undergraduate level; courses that balance the development of financial statements and management accounting tools with their interpretation and use in decision making. This book teaches students how to read, analyze, and interpret financial and managerial accounting data to make informed business decisions.

We believe students become more engaged in the course when they see how the content pertains to their future careers. Once engaged in the course, students perform much better and enjoy the class more. Furthermore, we believe accounting is a discipline best learned by doing. Unlike some other disciplines, accounting needs to be practiced. Consequently, we took great care to incorporate a number of pedagogical devices and real examples that illustrate the relevance of financial and managerial accounting to professional careers.

RELEVANCE

"Why do I need to study accounting?"

Students frequently ask this or similar questions. The extent to which they feel accounting is relevant to their daily lives will often determine how much effort they put into the course. The following features are used throughout the book to convey the relevance of accounting to their lives and society.

Real Data and Examples

Today's students must be skilled in using real financial statements and accounting information to make business decisions. Through their exposure to various financial statements, students will learn that, while financial statements do not all look the same, they can readily understand and interpret them to make business decisions. In each financial accounting chapter, we incorporate a wide range of examples using real companies that students know. In addition, the **Extending Your Knowledge** section in the assignments of each financial accounting chapter requires students to use the financial statements of **Columbia Sportswear Company** and **Under Armour Corporation**.

The managerial accounting chapters of the text also incorporate a wide range of examples using real companies such as **Microsoft**, **Amazon** and **Google**. The **Service Industry in Focus** section in the assignments of each managerial accounting chapter requires the students to use the financial and operational data of a fictitious consulting company, Environmental Business Consultants, LLC, to address real business issues. Most managerial accounting chapters also include real-world examples from **Fezzari**, a custom bike manufacturer.

Environmental Business Consultants

FEZZARI
BICYCLES

Accounting in Practice

These boxed inserts help bridge the gap between the classroom and what students encounter in the real world. **Accounting In Practice** illustrations document situations a reader is likely to encounter and present the choices that companies face in reporting financial results and making decisions.

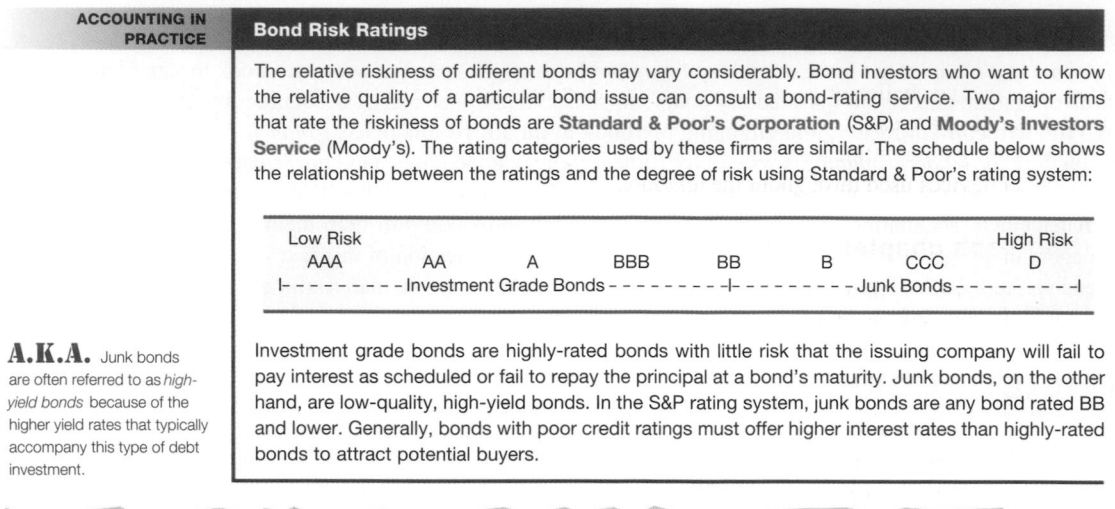

ACCOUNTING IN PRACTICE

Bond Risk Ratings

The relative riskiness of different bonds may vary considerably. Bond investors who want to know the relative quality of a particular bond issue can consult a bond-rating service. Two major firms that rate the riskiness of bonds are **Standard & Poor's Corporation** (S&P) and **Moody's Investors Service** (Moody's). The rating categories used by these firms are similar. The schedule below shows the relationship between the ratings and the degree of risk using Standard & Poor's rating system:

Low Risk   High Risk

AAA   AA   A   BBB   BB   B   CCC   D

⊢ – – – – – – – Investment Grade Bonds – – – – – – – ⊣– – – – – – – Junk Bonds – – – – – – – ⊣

A.K.A. Junk bonds are often referred to as *high-yield bonds* because of the higher yield rates that typically accompany this type of debt investment.

Investment grade bonds are highly-rated bonds with little risk that the issuing company will fail to pay interest as scheduled or fail to repay the principal at a bond's maturity. Junk bonds, on the other hand, are low-quality, high-yield bonds. In the S&P rating system, junk bonds are any bond rated BB and lower. Generally, bonds with poor credit ratings must offer higher interest rates than highly-rated bonds to attract potential buyers.

Corporate Social Responsibility

Increasingly, companies have found that "doing good" leads to a more successful, profitable enterprise. These boxed inserts help students understand how corporate social responsibility is being embraced by forward-thinking enterprises as part of their long-term business models.

Standards of Professionalism

CORPORATE SOCIAL RESPONSIBILITY

The opening vignette of this chapter discusses how the California State Bar Association determines the reasonable costs of pursuing action against disciplined lawyers. Because of the extraordinary responsibility society places upon the attorneys within our democracy, it is critical that groups such as the California State Bar Association maintain the highest ethical standards for its members. Just how does the Association see this responsibility? The following is quoted from the California Attorney Guidelines of Civility and Professionalism:

"As officers of the court with responsibilities to the administration of justice, attorneys have an obligation to be professional with clients, other parties and counsel, the courts and the public. This obligation includes civility, professional integrity, personal dignity, candor, diligence, respect, courtesy, and cooperation, all of which are essential to the fair administration of justice and conflict resolution."

Additional Features

Additional features included throughout the text emphasize the relevance of the current environment of business on accounting concepts.

Features included in the financial accounting chapters:

- **Principle Alert** boxes discuss upcoming or new accounting pronouncements and changes in accounting principles.
- **Forensic Accounting** boxes highlight how financial accounting knowledge can help aid in the prevention of errors and fraud.
- **Thinking Globally** boxes emphasize the similarities and differences in business practices between companies in the U.S. and companies in other countries.
- **IFRS Alert** boxes examine issues related to similarities and differences in the reporting standards under U.S. GAAP and IFRS.

Features included in the managerial accounting chapters:

- **Service Industry** margin callouts identify the sections of the text that apply managerial accounting concepts to the service industry.

- **Service Industry in Focus** cases provide students an opportunity to apply what they learned within a service industry situation.
- **Decision Time** boxes help students look beyond the accounting numbers to see the importance of other business information in making the best decision.

SUCCESS

Accounting can be challenging—especially for students lacking business experience or previous exposure to business courses. To help students succeed in their accounting courses, we provide a wealth of resources through our online learning and homework systems, myBusinessCourse (MBC), and through pedagogical devices used throughout the textbook.

Putting each chapter in context

Often, students lose sight of the big picture. The Past/Present/Future feature provides students with an overview of where the chapter fits within the whole course.

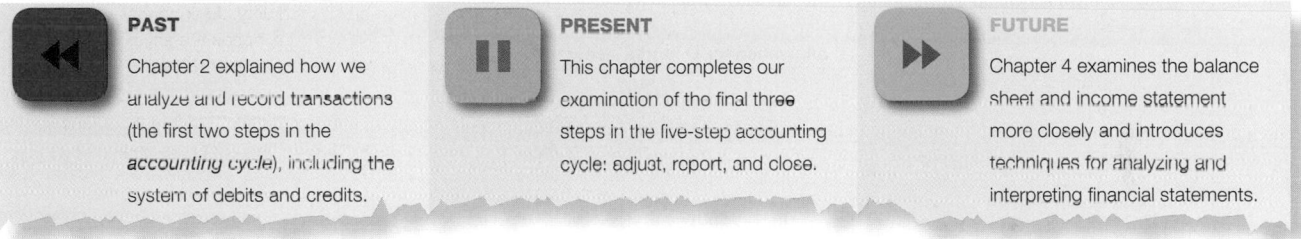

PAST

Chapter 2 explained how we analyze and record transactions (the first two steps in the *accounting cycle*), including the system of debits and credits.

PRESENT

This chapter completes our examination of the final three steps in the five-step accounting cycle: adjust, report, and close.

FUTURE

Chapter 4 examines the balance sheet and income statement more closely and introduces techniques for analyzing and interpreting financial statements.

Mapping each chapter

Each chapter begins with an overview that visually depicts the layout of the chapter.

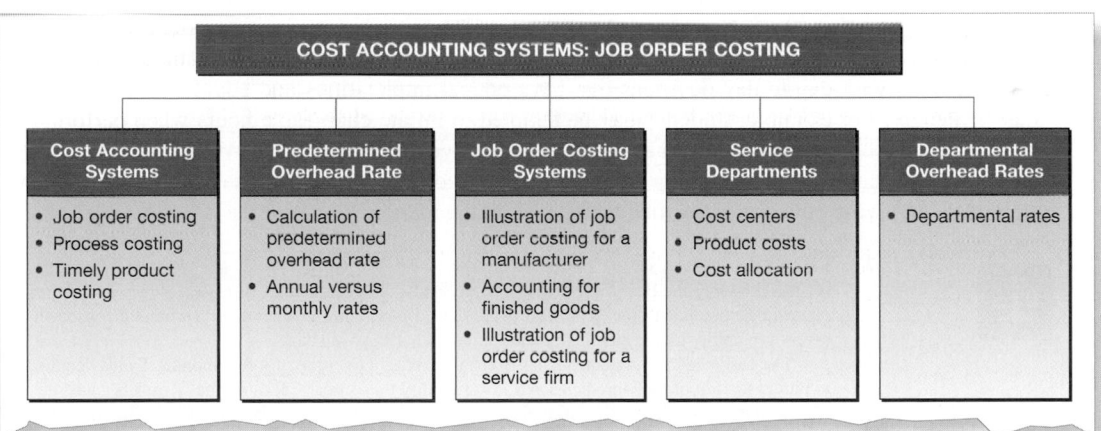

COST ACCOUNTING SYSTEMS: JOB ORDER COSTING

Cost Accounting Systems	Predetermined Overhead Rate	Job Order Costing Systems	Service Departments	Departmental Overhead Rates
• Job order costing • Process costing • Timely product costing	• Calculation of predetermined overhead rate • Annual versus monthly rates	• Illustration of job order costing for a manufacturer • Accounting for finished goods • Illustration of job order costing for a service firm	• Cost centers • Product costs • Cost allocation	• Departmental rates

Your Turn!

Your Turn boxes are integrated throughout each chapter as a means of reinforcing the material just presented. Solutions are provided at the end of the chapter so students can check their work.

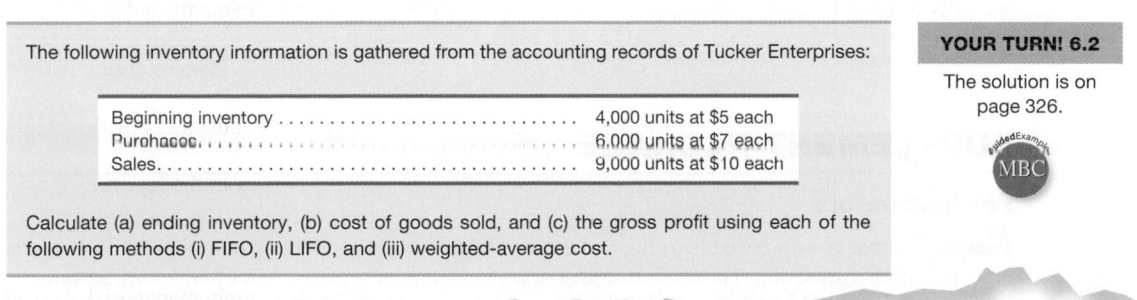

The following inventory information is gathered from the accounting records of Tucker Enterprises:

Beginning inventory	4,000 units at $5 each
Purchases	6,000 units at $7 each
Sales	9,000 units at $10 each

Calculate (a) ending inventory, (b) cost of goods sold, and (c) the gross profit using each of the following methods (i) FIFO, (ii) LIFO, and (iii) weighted-average cost.

YOUR TURN! 6.2

The solution is on page 326.

MBC

A.K.A. Boxes

A.K.A. (Also Known As) boxes inform students of commonly used alternative terms that they may encounter.

> **A.K.A.** Manufacturing overhead has several other names that are commonly used in practice, such as **factory overhead**, factory burden, or indirect manufacturing costs.

3. **Manufacturing overhead** consists of all manufacturing costs not included in direct material and direct labor. Manufacturing overhead includes indirect material, indirect labor, factory supplies used, factory payroll tax and fringe benefits costs, factory utilities, and factory building and machinery costs (such as depreciation, insurance, property taxes, and repairs and maintenance). Manufacturing overhead specifically *excludes* selling and non-factory administrative expenses because these expenses are not incurred in the manufacturing process.

Hints

Helpful suggestions are inserted in the margin as **Hints** to help students understand difficult concepts.

This entry brings the credit balance in the Allowance for Doubtful Accounts account to the required amount—$1,560, as shown below:

Allowance for Doubtful Accounts		
	400	Beg.
	1,160	Dec. 31
	1,560	Bal.

Hint: In contrast to the percentage of net sales method, the accounts receivable aging method takes into account the beginning balance of the Allowance for Doubtful Accounts.

ETHICS

Enron, WorldCom, Waste Management, Bernie Madoff, and other high-profile incidents of fraud highlight the consequences of unethical decisions made by real people facing difficult challenges in businesses today. Although most students will not face such significant decisions, they will certainly be confronted with day-to-day decisions that have ethical implications and could lead to more serious challenges. For example, students may be tempted to inflate chargeable hours when performance evaluations and bonuses are based on achieving a target level of chargeability. We discuss ethics where appropriate in the textbook, including an assignment in most chapters that raises an ethical issue. Assignments involving ethics are identified by the icon in the margin.

>
>
> **EYK2-3. Ethics Case** Great Cakes is a large bakery known for its quality "boxed cake" products. Its motto is "We Use Only the Best Ingredients." Ralph Sands, the purchasing supervisor, is responsible for ordering the ingredients for all the bakery products. He is being considered for a promotion based on his proven ability to purchase ingredients at the best price available.
>
> The cost of all the ingredients has risen substantially over the past few months. Sands decides to purchase 25% of the ingredients at a lower quality than Great Cakes normally uses because the cost is significantly less. Without relying on the company's test kitchens, he believes this substitution will not be noticed by the customers and the lower cost will counterbalance the increased costs of the other ingredients.
>
> Sands explains this decision to his friend, Lynn Pall, the company's accountant, one day at lunch. He also tells her that he does not intend to inform management of the inclusion of the lower-quality ingredients in the bakery's products.
>
> *Required*
> What ethical considerations arise from Ralph Sands' decisions? What problems face Lynn Pall because of his actions?

SUPPLEMENT PACKAGE

For Instructors

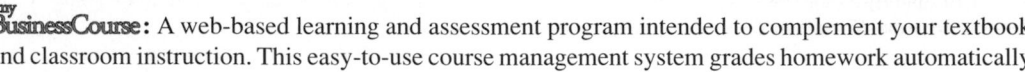

myBusinessCourse: A web-based learning and assessment program intended to complement your textbook and classroom instruction. This easy-to-use course management system grades homework automatically and provides students with additional help when you are not available. In addition, detailed diagnostic tools assess class and individual performance. myBusinessCourse is ideal for online courses or traditional face-to-face courses for which you want to offer students more resources to succeed. Assignments with the in the margin are available in myBusinessCourse.

Instructor CD-ROM: This convenient supplement provides the text's ancillary materials on a portable CD-ROM. All the faculty supplements that accompany the textbook are available, including Power-Point, Solutions Manual, Test Bank, and Computerized Test Bank.

Solutions Manual: Created by the authors, the *Solutions Manual* contains complete solutions to all the assignment material in the text.

PowerPoint: The PowerPoint slides outline key elements of each chapter.

Test Bank: The Test Bank includes multiple-choice items, matching questions, short essay questions, and problems.

Website: All instructor materials are accessible via the book's Website (password protected) along with other useful links and marketing information: **www.cambridgepub.com**

For Students

myBusinessCourse: A web-based learning and assessment program intended to complement your textbook and faculty instruction. This easy-to-use program grades homework automatically and provides you with additional help when your instructor is not available. Assignments with the in the margin are available in myBusinessCourse. Access is free with new copies of this textbook (look for page containing the access code towards the front of the book). If you buy a used copy of the book, you can purchase access at **www.mybusinesscourse.com**.

Website: Practice quizzes and other useful links are available to students free of charge on the book's Website.

ACKNOWLEDGMENTS

This book benefited greatly from the valuable feedback of focus group attendees, reviewers, students, and colleagues. We are extremely grateful to them for their help in making this project a success.

Wagdy Abdallah, *Seton Hall University*

Ira Abdullah, *Robert Morris University*

Nasrollah Ahadiat, *California State Polytechnic University*

Markus Ahrens, *St. Louis Community College*

James Aitken, *Central Michigan University*

Dave Alldredge, *Salt Lake Community College*

Natalie Allen, *Texas A&M University*

Michael Alles, *Rutgers University*

Bam Alling, *University of North Carolina—Wilmington*

David Ambrosini, *Cabrillo College*

Bridget Anakwe, *Delaware State University*

Matthew Anderson, *Michigan State University*

Adam Baker, *Minnesota State Community Technical College—Moorehead*

Lisa Banks, *Mott Community College*

James Bannister, *University of Hartford*

Richard Barnhart, *Grand Rapids Community College*

Gerhard Barone, *Gonzaga University*

Sara Barritt, *Northeast Community College*

Nancy Batch, *Mountain View College*

Vernon Bell, *Marshall University*

James Benjamin, *Texas A&M University*

Debbie Benson, *Kennesaw State University*

Jason Bergner, *University of Nevada—Reno*

Swati Bhandarkar, *University of Georgia*

Diane Biagioni, *Indiana University*

Timothy Biggart, *Berry College*

Lydia Botsford, *DeAnza College*

Amy Bourne, *Oregon State University*

Rada Brooks, *University of California, Berkeley*

Marilyn Brooks-Lewis, *Warren County Community College*

Amy Browning, *Ivy Tech Community College*

Eugene Bryson, *University of Alabama—Huntsville*

Ian Burt, *Niagara University*

Marci Butterfield, *University of Utah*

Sandra Byrd, *Missouri State University*

Jeffrey Byrne, *Indiana University—Southeast*

Jennifer Cainas, *University of South Florida*

Michael Calegari, *Santa Clara University*

Mike Campbell, *Montana State University*

James Cannon, *Iowa State University*

John Capka, *Cuyahoga Community College*

Rodney Carmack, *Arkansas State University*

Tommy Carnes, *Berry College*

Jackie Casey, *University of North Carolina—Wilmington*

John Cergnul, *St. Mary's College—IN*

Melissa Chadd, *Victoria College*
Christy Chauvin , *Delgado Community College*
Betty Chavis, *California State University—Fullerton*
Yu Chen, *Texas A&M International*
Julie Chenier, *Louisiana State University*
Alan Cherry, *Loyola Marymount University*
Catherine Chiang, *Elon University*
Alice Chu, *Golden West College*
Lawrence Chui, *University of St. Thomas*
Leslie Cohen, *University of Arizona*
Scott Collins, *Penn State University*
Carolyn Conn, *St. Edwards University*
Sue Convery, *Michigan State University*
David Cook, *Calvin College*
Erin Cornelsen, *University of South Dakota*
Nancy Coster, *Loyola Marymount University*
John Coulter, *Western New England College*
Timothy Creel, *Tennessee State University*
Cheryl Crespi, *Central Connecticut State University*
James Crumbacher, *West Liberty University*
Richard Culp, *Ball State University*
Emmanuel Danso, *Palm Beach State College*
Somnath Das, *University of Illinois—Chicago*
Judy Daulton, *Piedmont Technical College*
Annette Davis, *Glendale Community College*
Rosemond Desir, *Colorado State University*
Tom Determan, *University of Wisconsin—Parkside*
Patricia Doherty, *Boston University*
Vicky Dominguez, *College of Southern Nevada*
Pamela Donahue, *Northern Essex Community College*
Chan Du, *University of Massachusetts—Dartmouth*
Peggy Eaton, *Jackson Community College*
Jeanne Eibes, *Creighton University*
Jerrilyn Eisenhauer, *Tulsa Community College*
Ahmed El-Zayaty, *The University of Findlay*
Raymond Elson, *Valdosta State University*
James Emig, *Villanova University*
Lili Eng, *Missouri University of Science & Technology*
Cole Engel, *Fort Hayes State University*
Michael Fagan, *Raritan Valley Community College*
Connie Fajardo, *National University*
Alan Falcon, *Loyola Marymount University*
Kurt Fanning, *Grand Valley State University*
Lucile Faurel, *Arizona State University*
Charles Fazzi, *St. Vincent College*
Bud Fennema, *Florida State University*
Cathy Finger, *Saint Mary's College of California*
Julie Finnegan, *Mendocino College*
Linda Flaming, *Monmouth University*
David Folsom, *Lehigh University*
Gary Ford, *Tompkins Cortland Community College*
David Forcster, *Haywood Community College*
Jackie Franklin, *Spokane Falls Community College*
Mitchell Franklin, *Syracuse University*
Carolyn Galantine, *Pepperdine University*

Dennis George, *University of Dubuque*
Julie Gilbert, *Triton College*
Lisa Gillespie, *Loyola University*
Brian Gilligan, *Morton College*
Julie Gittelman, *Salisbury University*
Alan Glazer, *Franklin & Marshall College*
Marina Grau, *Houston Community College*
Lisa Gray, *Valencia College*
Glen Greencorn, *St. Mary's University Canada*
Thomas Guarino, *Plymouth State University*
Wendy Gunn, *St. Louis Community College*
Bruce Gunning, *Kent State University—East Liverpool*
Lorna Hardin, *University of Washington—Bothell*
David Harr, *American University*
Judy Harris, *Nova Southeastern University*
Patricia Hart-Timm, *Northwood University*
Bob Hartman, *University of Iowa*
Rosemary Hayward, *Cabrillo College*
Haihong He, *California State University—Los Angeles*
Hassan Hefzi, *California State Polytechnic University*
Cassy Henderson, *Sam Houston State University*
Joshua Herbold, *University of Montana*
Merrily Hoffman, *San Jacinto College*
Cynthia Hollenbach, *University of Denver*
Steven Hornik, *Central Florida University*
Jana Hosmer, *Blue Ridge Community College*
Maggie Houston, *Wright State University*
Marsha Huber, *Youngstown State University*
Carol Hughes, *Asheville-Buncombe Technical Community College*
Kathy Hurley, *Boise State University*
Connie Hylton, *George Mason University*
Laura Ilcisin, *University of Nebraska at Omaha*
Stephen Jablonsky, *Colorado State University*
Sharon Jackson, *Samford University*
Shirin Jahanian, *Temple University*
Marianne James, *California State University—Los Angeles*
Ching-Lih Jan, *California State University—Northridge*
Mark Jasonowicz, *Grand Rapids Community College*
Bill Jefferson, *Metropolitan Community College*
Catherine Jeppson, *California State University—Northridge*
Gene Johnson, *University of Hawaii*
Randy Johnston, *University of Colorado*
Mark Judd, *University of San Diego*
Thomas Kam, *Hawaii Pacific University*
Kathryn Kapka, *University of Texas—Tyler*
Jocelyn Kauffunger, *University of Pittsburgh*
Sara Kern, *Gonzaga University*
Suzanne Kiess, *Jackson College*
Christine Kloezeman, *Glendale Community College*
Dennis Knutson, *University of Wisconsin—Eau Claire*
John Koeplin, *University of San Francisco*
Phillip Korb, *University of Baltimore*
Paul Koulakov, *Nashville State Community College*
Elida Kraja, *St. Louis Community College*
Mary-Jo Kranacher, *York College*

Lynn Krausse, *Bakersfield College*

Christopher Kwak, *De Anza College*

Donald Ladd, *University of Southern Maine*

Steven LaFave, *Augsburg College*

Benjamin Lansford, *Rice University*

Cathy Larson, *Middlesex Community College*

Doug Larson, *Salem State University*

Greg Lauer, *North Iowa Area Community College*

Gary Laycock, *Ivy Tech Community College*

Ron Lazer, *University of Houston*

Joan Lee, *Fairfield University*

Charles Leflar, *University of Arkansas*

Jennifer LeSure, *Ivy Tech Community College*

Elliott Levy, *Bentley College*

Christine Li, *College of Marin*

Siyi Li, *University of Illinois*

Zining Li, *Southern Methodist University*

Lihong Liang, *Syracuse University*

Emily Lindsay, *American University*

Sara Linton, *Roosevelt University*

John Long, *Jackson College*

Debbie Luna, *El Paso Community College*

Heather Lynch, *Northeast Iowa Community College*

Nancy Lynch, *West Virginia University*

Susan Lynn, *University of Baltimore*

Lois Mahoney, *Eastern Michigan University*

David Manifold, *Caldwell Community College & Technical Institute*

Joe Manzo, *Lehigh University*

Ariel Markelevich, *Suffolk University*

Thomas Marsh, *Northern Virginia Community College*

Dawn Massey, *Fairfield University*

Michele Matherly, *Xavier University*

Clarice McCoy, *Brookhaven College*

Annie McGowan, *Texas A&M University*

Michele McGowan, *King's College*

Allison McLeod, *University of North Texas*

Jeff McMillan, *Clemson University*

Casey McNellis, *University of Montana*

Cathryn Meegan, *Chipola College*

Sara Melendy, *Gonzaga University*

Michael Meyer, *University of Notre Dame*

Linda Miller, *Northeast Community College*

Sue Minke, *Indiana University Purdue University—Fort Wayne*

April Mohr, *Jefferson Community and Technical College*

Michelle Moshier, *SUNY—Albany*

Sheila Muller, *Northern Essex Community College*

Johnna Murray, *University of Missouri, St. Louis*

Patricia Naranjo , *Rice University*

Tammie Neeley, *Salt Lake Community College*

Joshua Neil, *Colorado University—Boulder*

Bruce Neumann, *University of Colorado—Denver*

Monica Newman, *Western State Colorado University*

Joseph Nicassio, *Westmoreland County Community College*

Micki Nickla, *Ivy Tech Community College*

Wayne Nix, *Jackson State University*

Tracie Nobles, *Austin Community College*

Hossein Noorian, *Wentworth Institute of Technology*

Lisa Novak, *Mott Community College*

Sarah Nutter, *George Mason University*

Barbara Nyden, *Missouri State University—West Plains*

Roshelle Overton, *Central New Mexico Community College*

Ken O'Brien, *Farmingdale State University*

Kalpana Pai, *Texas Wesleyan University*

Angela Pannell, *Mississippi State University*

Abbie Gail Parham, *Georgia Southern University*

Keith Patterson, *Brigham Young University—Idaho*

Paige Paulsen, *Salt Lake Community College*

Sy Pearlman, *California State University—Long Beach*

Mary Pearson, *Southern Utah University*

Ron Pearson, *Bay College*

Aaron Pennington, *University of Cincinnati*

Kimberly Perkins, *Austin Community College*

Julie Petherbridge, *Mercer University*

Marietta Peytcheva, *Lehigh University*

Robert Picard, *Idaho State University*

Elizabeth Pierce, *Saginaw Valley State University*

Gary Pieroni, *University of California—Berkeley*

Ronald Premuroso, *University of Montana*

Jean Price, *Marshall University*

Claudia Qi, *University at Buffalo*

Allan Rabinowitz, *Pace University*

Kamala Raghavan, *Texas Southern University*

Ann Randolph, *Xavier University*

Kathleen Rankin, *Duquesne University*

Melinda Ratliff, *Mountain View College*

Paul Recupero, *Newbury College*

Aaron Reeves, *St. Louis Community College—Forest Park*

Vernon Richardson, *University of Arkansas*

Shani Robinson, *Sam Houston State University*

Reed Roig, *Queens University of Charlotte*

Gregg Romans, *Ivy Tech Community College*

Lydia Rosencrants, *LaGrange College*

Mark Ross, *Western Kentucky University*

John Rossi, *Moravian College*

Pamela Rouse, *Butler University*

Maria Roxas, *Central Connecticut State University*

Bernadette Ruf, *Delaware State University*

Ron Sabado, *Highline College*

John Sanders, *University of Southern Maine*

Albert Schepanski, *University of Iowa*

Arnold Schneider, *Georgia Tech University*

Robert Schweikle, *Blackburn College*

Barbara Scofield, *Washburn University*

Steve Sefcik, *University of Washington*

Jamie Seitz, *University of Southern Indiana*

Daniel Selby, *University of Richmond*

Randy Serrett, *University of Houston Downtown*

Dan Sevall, *Hult International University*

Cathy Sevigny, *Bridgewater State University*

Tracy Sewell, *Gulf Coast State College*
Ray Shaffer, *Youngstown State University*
Carol Shaver, *Louisiana Tech University*
Dennis Shea, *Southern New Hampshire University*
Regina Shea, *Community College of Baltimore County*
Mehdi Sheikholeslami, *Bemidji State University*
John Shon, *Fordham University*
Gregory Sinclair, *San Francisco State University*
Ken Sinclair, *Lehigh University*
Eric Slayter, *Cal Poly—San Luis Obispo*
Gene Smith, *Eastern New Mexico University*
Gerald Smith, *University of Northern Iowa*
James Smith, *University of San Diego*
Nancy Snow, *University of Toledo*
Robin Soffer, *Northwestern University*
Liang Song, *University of Massachusetts—Dartmouth*
Marilyn Stansbury, *Calvin College*
George Starbuck, *McMurry University*
Randall Stone, *East Central University*
Ronald Stone, *California State University—Northridge*
Jeff Strawser, *Sam Houston State University*
Rick Street, *Spokane Community College*
John Suckow, *Lansing Community College*
Stephanie Swaim, *North Lake College*
Kent Swift, *University of Montana*
Aida Sy, *Marist College*
Mary Sykes, *University of Houston*
Ted Takamura, *Eastern Oregon University*
Robert Tallo, *Pitt Community College*
Kim Tan, *California State University—Stanislaus*
Diane Tanner, *University of North Florida*
Linda Tarrago, *Hillsborough Community College*
Jenny Teruya, *University of Hawaii—Manoa*

Randall Thomas, *Upper Iowa University*
Robin Thomas, *North Carolina State University*
Dalton Tong, *University of Baltimore; Johns Hopkins University*
Sheri Trumpfheller, *University of Colorado—Colorado Springs*
Michael Tydlaska, *Mountain View College*
Eric Typpo, *University of the Pacific*
Joan Van Hise, *Fairfield University*
Marcia Viet, *University of Central Florida*
George Violette, *University of Southern Maine*
Marcia Vorholt, *Xavier University*
Robert Walsh, *University of Dallas*
Doris Warmflash, *SUNY Westchester Community College*
Brian Watkins, *Brigham Young University—Hawaii*
Randi Watts, *Jackson College*
Debra Webb, *Blinn College*
Andrea Weickgenannt, *Xavier University*
Donna Whitten, *Purdue University North Central*
Monica Widdig, *University of Cincinnati Blue Ash College*
Idalene Williams, *Metropolitan Community College*
Valerie Williams, *Duquesne University*
Jim Williamson, *San Diego State University*
Paula Wilson, *University of Puget Sound*
Douglas Woods, *The University of Akron Wayne College*
Maef Woods, *Heidelberg University*
Daryl Woolley, *University of Idaho*
Susan Wright, *DeKalb Technical College*
Jia Wu, *University of Massachusetts—Dartmouth*
Rong Yang, *SUNY—Brockport*
Kathryn Yarbrough, *University of North Carolina—Charlotte*
Robert Yu, *University of Wisconsin—Whitewater*
Amy Yurko, *Duquesne University*
Judith Zander, *Grossmont College*
Jian Zhou, *University of Hawaii at Manoa*

In addition, we are extremely grateful to George Werthman, Lorraine Gleeson, Dana Vinyard, Jill Sternard, Marnee Fieldman, Jocelyn Mousel, Katie Jones-Aiello, Beth Gilgen Nodus, Debbie McQuade, Terry McQuade, and the entire team at Cambridge Business Publishers for their encouragement, enthusiasm, and guidance. Feedback is always welcome. Please feel free to contact us with your suggestions or questions.

Jim Wallace   Karen Nelson   Ted Christensen   Scott Hobson   Ken Ferris

January 2018

Brief Contents

Chapter 1 Financial Accounting and Business Decisions **2**

Chapter 2 Processing Accounting Information **58**

Chapter 3 Accrual Basis of Accounting **120**

Chapter 4 Understanding Financial Statements **188**

Chapter 5 Accounting for Merchandising Operations **232**

Chapter 6 Accounting for Inventory **274**

Chapter 7 Internal Control and Cash **330**

Chapter 8 Accounting for Receivables **380**

Chapter 9 Accounting for Long-Lived and Intangible Assets **424**

Chapter 10 Accounting for Liabilities **468**

Chapter 11 Stockholders' Equity **528**

Chapter 12 Statement of Cash Flows **576**

Chapter 13 Analysis and Interpretation of Financial Statements **628**

Chapter 14 Overview of Managerial Accounting **694**

Chapter 15 Managerial Accounting Concepts and Cost Flows **710**

Chapter 16 Cost Accounting Systems: Job Order Costing **750**

Chapter 17 Cost Accounting Systems: Process Costing **796**

Chapter 18 Activity-Based Costing **844**

Chapter 19 Cost-Volume-Profit Relationships **882**

Chapter 20 Variable Costing: A Tool for Decision Making **926**

Chapter 21 Relevant Costs and Short-Term Decision Making **948**

Chapter 22 Planning and Budgeting **982**

Chapter 23 Standard Costing and Variance Analysis **1024**

Chapter 24 Flexible Budgets, Segment Reporting, and Performance Analysis **1060**

Chapter 25 Capital Budgeting **1108**

Appendix A Columbia Sportswear Company **A-1**

Appendix B Financial Statements for Under Armour **B-1**

Appendix C Financial Statements for LVMH Moet Hennessy - Louis Vuitton **C-1**

Appendix D Accounting for Investments and Consolidated Financial Statements **D-1**

Appendix E Accounting and the Time Value of Money **E-1**

Index **I-1**

Contents

About the Authors **iii**

Preface **v**

CHAPTER 1

Financial Accounting and Business Decisions 2

Business Organization 4
    Your Turn! 1.1 **5**

Activities of a Business 5
    Financing Activities 5
    Investing Activities 6
    Operating Activities 6
    Your Turn! 1.2 **6**

Accounting Information and Its Use 6
    External Users of Accounting 7
    Internal Users of Accounting 8
    Your Turn! 1.3 **8**
    Ethics and Accounting 8
    Your Turn! 1.4 **9**

The Accounting Process 10
    Generally Accepted Accounting Principles **10**
    International Financial Reporting Standards **11**
    Your Turn! 1.5 **12**

Financial Statements 12
    Balance Sheet 13
    Income Statement **14**
    Statement of Stockholders' Equity **15**
    Statement of Cash Flows **17**
    Relations Among the Financial Statements **18**
    Your Turn! 1.6 **19**

Other Annual Report Components 20
    Notes to Financial Statements 20
    Independent Auditor's Report 20
    Management's Discussion and Analysis 21
    Your Turn! 1.7 **21**

Careers in Accounting 22

Comprehensive Problem 23

Appendix 1A: FASB's Conceptual Framework 25
Summary of Learning Objectives 28
Key Terms 30
Assignments 31
Serial Problem: Kate's Cards 51
Answers to Self-Study Questions: 55
Your Turn! Solutions 56

CHAPTER 2

Processing Accounting Information 58

Accounting Cycle 60
    Your Turn! 2.1 **61**

Analyzing Transactions 61
    Accounting Equation Expanded **62**
    Transactions and the Accounting Equation: An Illustration **62**
    Transaction Summary **66**
    Your Turn! 2.2 **67**

The "Account" System 68
    Chart of Accounts **68**
    System of Debits and Credits **68**
    Your Turn! 2.3 **69**
    Your Turn! 2.4 **70**

Recording Transactions 70
    General Journal **71**
    Posting Journal Entries to the General Ledger **72**
    Illustration of the Recording Process **72**
    Summary Illustration of Journalizing and Posting Transactions **76**
    Your Turn! 2.5 **78**

Trial Balance 79
    Your Turn! 2.6 **80**

Comprehensive Problem 80
Summary of Learning Objectives 82
Key Terms 83
Assignments 84
Serial Problem: Kate's Cards 112
Answers to Self-Study Questions: 117
Your Turn! Solutions 118

CHAPTER 3

Accrual Basis of Accounting 120

Accrual Basis of Accounting 122
    Revenue Recognition Principle **122**
    Expense Recognition (Matching) Principle **124**
    Your Turn! 3.1 **125**

Adjusting Accounts 125
    Unadjusted Trial Balance **125**
    Types of Adjustments **126**
    Your Turn! 3.2 **126**

Deferral Adjusting Entries 126
    Allocating Previously Recorded Assets to Expenses **126**

Allocating Previously Recorded Unearned Revenue to Revenue 128
Your Turn! 3.3 129

Accrual Adjusting Entries 129
Recording Previously Unrecorded Expenses 129
Recording Previously Unrecorded Revenues 130
Summary of Accounting Adjustments 131
Your Turn! 3.4 133

Adjusted Trial Balance and Financial Statements 133
Preparing the Adjusted Trial Balance 133
Preparing Financial Statements 134
Income Statement 134
Statement of Stockholders' Equity 134
Balance Sheet 135
Statement of Cash Flows 135
Your Turn! 3.5 136

Closing Process 137
Your Turn! 3.6 137
Journalizing and Posting the Closing Entries 137
Summary of the Accounting Cycle 139
Your Turn! 3.7 140

Quality of Accounting Numbers 140
Comprehensive Problem 141
Appendix 3A: Closing Process--Using Income Summary Account 144
Your Turn! 3A.1 145
Your Turn! 3A.2 148
Appendix 3B: Using a Worksheet 148
Summary of Learning Objectives 151
Key Terms 153
Assignments 153
Serial Problem: Kate's Cards 180
Answers to Self-Study Questions: 184
Your Turn! Solutions 184

CHAPTER 4

Understanding Financial Statements 188
Balance Sheet Classification and Analysis 190
Current Assets 190
Long-Term Assets 191
Current Liabilities 192
Long-Term Liabilities 193
Stockholders' Equity 193
Presentation Format 193
Your Turn! 4.1 195

Income Statement Classification and Analysis 195

Your Turn! 4.2 198

Working with Financial Statements 198
Analysis Based on Ratios 198
Working with the Balance Sheet 199
Your Turn! 4.3 201
Working with the Income Statement 201
Your Turn! 4.4 203
Working with the Statement of Stockholders' Equity 203
Working with the Statement of Cash Flows 204
Your Turn! 4.5 206

Comprehensive Problem 207
Summary of Learning Objectives 209
Key Terms 210
Assignments 211
Serial Problem: Kate's Cards 225
Answers to Self-Study Questions: 228
Your Turn! Solutions 229

CHAPTER 5

Accounting for Merchandising Operations 232
The Nature of Merchandising 234
Operating Cycle of a Merchandising Firm 235
Cost Flows 236
Inventory Systems 236
Your Turn! 5.1 237

Accounting for Purchases of Merchandise 237
Transportation Costs 237
Purchase Returns and Allowances 238
Purchase Discounts 239
Your Turn! 5.2 241

Accounting for Sales of Merchandise 241
Sales Returns and Allowances 242
Sales Discounts 243
Net Sales 244
Your Turn! 5.3 245

Profitability Analysis 245
Gross Profit Percentage 245
Return on Sales Ratio (Profit Margin) 246
Your Turn! 5.4 247

Comprehensive Problem 248
Appendix 5A: Periodic Inventory System 249
Your Turn! 5A.1 250
Your Turn! 5A.2 251
Your Turn! 5A.3 252
Appendix 5B: The New Revenue Recognition Standard 253
Your Turn! 5B.1 254
Summary of Learning Objectives 254

Key Terms 256
Assignments 256
Serial Problem: Kate's Cards 267
Answers to Self-Study Questions: 271
Your Turn! Solutions 271

CHAPTER 6

Accounting for Inventory 274

Inventory Categories and Concepts 276
  Categories of Inventory 276
  Concepts of Inventory Management 277
Inventory Ownership and Physical Count 278
  Ownership of Inventory 278
  Physical Count of Inventory 279
  Your Turn! 6.1 280
Inventory Costing Methods 280
  Goods Flow vs. Cost Flow 281
  Data for Illustration of Cost Flow
    Assumptions 281
  Specific Identification Method 282
  First-In, First-Out (FIFO) Method 282
  Last-In, First-Out (LIFO) Method 283
  Weighted-Average Cost Method 284
  Your Turn! 6.2 285
  Comparative Analysis of Inventory Costing
    Methods 285
  Selecting Inventory Methods 285
  Analysis of Costing Methods and Gross
    Profit 287
  Your Turn! 6.3 291
Lower-of-Cost-or-Market Method 291
  Net Realizable Value 291
  Lower-of-Cost-or-Market Method 291
  Your Turn! 6.4 293
Inventory Analysis 293
  Inventory Turnover and Days' Sales in
    Inventory 293
  Your Turn! 6.5 294
Comprehensive Problem 295
Appendix 6A: Inventory Costing Methods and the
  Perpetual Inventory System 296
  Your Turn! 6A.1 302
Appendix 6B: LIFO Reserve 302
  Your Turn! 6B.1 303
Summary of Learning Objectives 303
Key Terms 305
Assignments 305
Serial Problem: Kate's Cards 323
Answers to Self-Study Questions: 326
Your Turn! Solutions 326

CHAPTER 7

Internal Control and Cash 330

Fraud 332
  Fraud Triangle 332
Internal Control 333
  COSO Framework 333
  Control Failures 338
  The Sarbanes-Oxley Act 338
  Your Turn! 7.1 339
Accounting for Cash 339
  Reporting Cash 339
  Cash and Cash Equivalents 340
Internal Control of Cash Receipts
  Transactions 341
  Cash Received on Account 341
  Cash Received from Retail Cash Sales 343
  Checks 345
  Using Electronic Funds Transfer 346
  The Petty Cash Fund 346
  Your Turn! 7.2 347
  The Bank Statement 347
  The Bank Reconciliation 347
  Your Turn! 7.3 352
Effective Cash Management 352
  Monitoring Cash 352
  Primary Activities of Effective Cash
    Management 353
Comprehensive Problem 354
Appendix 7A: Auditing and Internal Control 355
  Your Turn! 7A.1 357
Summary of Learning Objectives 357
Key Terms 359
Assignments 359
Serial Problem: Kate's Cards 373
Answers to Self-Study Questions: 377
Your Turn! Solutions 378

CHAPTER 8

Accounting for Receivables 380

Receivables 382
Accounts Receivable 382
Accounting for Bad Debts 383
  Allowance Method 384
  Your Turn! 8.1 387
Estimating Credit Losses 387
  Percentage of Net Sales Method 388
  Your Turn! 8.2 388
  Accounts Receivable Aging Method 388
  Your Turn! 8.3 391

Credit Card Sales 392
    Your Turn! 8.4 392
Notes Receivable 393
    Interest on Notes Receivable 393
    Adjusting Entry for Interest 395
    Reporting Notes Receivable on the Balance
        Sheet 396
    Your Turn! 8.5 396
Analyzing and Managing Receivables 396
    Your Turn! 8.6 397
    Factoring and Discounting 397
Comprehensive Problem 398
Appendix 8A: Direct Write-Off Method 400
    Your Turn! 8A.1 400
Summary of Learning Objectives 401
Key Terms 402
Assignments 402
Serial Problem: Kate's Cards 419
Answers to Self-Study Questions: 423
Your Turn! Solutions 423

CHAPTER 9

Accounting for Long-Lived and Intangible Assets 424

Overview of Long-Lived Assets 426
Accounting for Long-lived Assets
    (Cost Determination) 427
    Acquisition Cost of Long-Lived Assets 427
    Expenditures Related to Land 429
    Your Turn! 9.1 430
Nature of Depreciation 430
    Allocation versus Valuation: Depreciation
        Accounting 431
    Calculating Depreciation Expense 431
    A Comparison of Alternative Depreciation
        Methods 435
    Depreciation Method Estimate Changes 436
    Your Turn! 9.2 439
Revenue Versus Capital Expenditures 439
    Revenue Expenditures 439
    Capital Expenditures 439
    Your Turn! 9.3 440
Disposals of Plant Assets 441
    Sale of Plant Assets 441
    Your Turn! 9.4 442
Intangible Assets 442
    Measurement of Intangible Assets (Cost
        Determination) 443
    Amortization of Intangibles 443
Examples of Intangible Assets 444

    Patents 444
    Copyright 444
    Franchises 444
    Trademarks 445
    Goodwill 445
    Your Turn! 9.5 446
Balance Sheet Presentation 446
Return on Assets and Asset Turnover 446
    Your Turn! 9.6 448
Comprehensive Problem 448
Summary of Learning Objectives 449
Key Terms 450
Assignments 450
Serial Problem: Kate's Cards 463
Answers to Self-Study Questions: 467
Your Turn! Solutions 467

CHAPTER 10

Accounting for Liabilities 468

Current Liabilities 470
    Accounts Payable 470
    Notes Payable and Interest 470
    Interest Payable 472
    Current Portion of Long-Term Debt 472
    Sales and Excise Taxes Payable 472
    Payroll-Related Liabilities 473
    Your Turn! 10.1 475
    Income Taxes Payable 475
    Advance Payments—Unearned Revenue 476
Long-Term Liabilities 476
    Long-Term Notes (Term Loans) 477
    Types of Bonds 478
    Bond Prices 479
    Recording Bonds 481
    Your Turn! 10.2 485
    Advantages and Disadvantages of Long-Term
        Bonds and Notes 485
Contingent Liabilities 486
    Examples of Contingent Liabilities 487
    Summary of Accounting Treatment for
        Liabilities 489
    Your Turn! 10.3 490
Analyzing Liabilities 490
    Current Ratio and Quick Ratio 490
    Times-Interest-Earned Ratio 491
    Your Turn! 10.4 492
Comprehensive Problem 493
Appendix 10A: Bond Pricing 493
    Your Turn! 10A.1 502
Appendix 10B: Leases 502

Your Turn! 10B.1　**503**
Summary of Learning Objectives　**503**
Key Terms　**505**
Assignments　**505**
Serial Problem: Kate's Cards　**522**
Answers to Self-Study Questions:　**525**
Your Turn! Solutions　**526**

CHAPTER 11

Stockholders' Equity　**528**

Nature and Formation of a Corporation　**530**
　Advantages of the Corporate Form of
　　Organization　**530**
　Disadvantages of the Corporate Form of
　　Organization　**532**
　Accounting for Stockholders' Equity in
　　Alternative Organizational Forms　**533**
　Your Turn! 11.1　**533**
Par Value Stock and No-Par Value Stock　**533**
Types of Capital Stock　**534**
　Common Stock　**534**
　Preferred Stock　**535**
　Your Turn! 11.2　**537**
Stock Issuances for Cash　**538**
　Issuing Stock at a Premium　**538**
　Issuing No-Par Stock　**538**
　Noncash Stock Issuances　**539**
　Your Turn! 11.3　**539**
Stock Splits　**540**
　Your Turn! 11.4　**540**
Treasury Stock　**540**
　Accounting for Treasury Stock　**541**
　Your Turn! 11.5　**542**
Cash Dividends and Stock Dividends　**542**
　Cash Dividends　**543**
　Stock Dividends　**544**
　Your Turn! 11.6　**546**
Retained Earnings and the Statement of
　Stockholder's Equity　**546**
　Statement of Stockholders' Equity　**547**
　Your Turn! 11.7　**547**
Analyzing Stockholders' Equity　**548**
　Return on Common Stockholders' Equity　**548**
　Dividend Yield and Dividend Payout Ratio　**548**
Comprehensive Problem　**550**
　Your Turn! 11.8　**550**
Summary of Learning Objectives　**551**
Key Terms　**553**
Assignments　**553**
Serial Problem: Kate's Cards　**570**

Answers to Self-Study Questions:　**574**
Your Turn! Solutions　**574**

CHAPTER 12

Statement of Cash Flows　**576**

Cash and Cash Equivalents　**578**
Activity Classifications in the Statement of Cash
　Flows　**579**
　Operating Activities　**580**
　Investing Activities　**580**
　Financing Activities　**580**
　An Illustration of Activity Classification
　　Usefulness　**581**
Noncash Investing and Financing Activities　**582**
Using the Statement of Cash Flows　**582**
Cash Flow from Operating Activities　**583**
　Your Turn! 12.1　**584**
Preparing the Statement of Cash Flows Using the
　Indirect Method　**584**
　Five Steps to Preparing a Statement of Cash
　　Flows　**585**
　Your Turn! 12.2　**591**
Analyzing Cash Flows　**592**
　Free Cash Flow　**592**
　Operating-Cash-Flow-to-Current-Liabilities
　　Ratio　**592**
　Operating-Cash-Flow-to-Capital-Expenditures
　　Ratio　**593**
　Your Turn! 12.3　**594**
Comprehensive Problem　**595**
Appendix 12A: Preparing the Statement of Cash
　Flows Under the Direct Method　**597**
　Your Turn! 12A.1　**599**
Summary of Learning Objectives　**599**
Key Terms　**600**
Assignments　**601**
Serial Problem: Kate's Cards　**620**
Answers to Self-Study Questions:　**624**
Your Turn! Solutions　**624**

CHAPTER 13

Analysis and Interpretation of Financial Statements　**628**

Persistent Earnings and the Income
　Statement　**630**
　Discontinued Operations　**632**
　Changes in Accounting Principles　**632**
　Comprehensive Income　**633**
　Your Turn! 13.1　**634**

Sources of Information 634
    Analytical Techniques 634
Horizontal Analysis 635
Trend Analysis 637
    Your Turn! 13.2 639
Vertical Analysis 639
    Your Turn! 13.3 640
Ratio Analysis 641
    Analyzing Firm Profitability 641
    Your Turn! 13.4 645
    Analyzing Short-Term Firm Liquidity 645
    Your Turn! 13.5 650
    Analyzing Long-Term Firm Solvency 650
    Your Turn! 13.6 652
    Financial Ratios for Common Stockholders 653
    Your Turn! 13.7 655
Limitations of Financial Statement Analysis 656
Comprehensive Problem 657
Appendix 13A: Financial Statement
    Disclosures 658
Summary of Learning Objectives 661
Summary of Financial Statement Ratios 662
Key Terms 664
Assignments 665
Serial Problem: Kate's Cards 685
Answers to Self-Study Questions: 692
Your Turn! Solutions 692

CHAPTER 14

Overview of Managerial Accounting 694
Introduction To Managerial Accounting 696
    Managerial Accounting versus Financial
        Accounting 696
    Objectives of Managerial Accounting 697
Types of Business Entities 697
    Your Turn! 14.1 698
Major Trends in Business and Managerial
    Accounting 698
    Outsourcing 698
    Factory Automation 699
    Just-in-Time Inventory Systems 699
    Lean Manufacturing 700
    Customer Profitability 700
    Big Data and Predictive Analytics 701
Introducing Two New Companies 701
    Fezzari—A U.S. Bicycle Manufacturer and
        Distributor 701
    Environmental Business Consultants, LLC—A
        U.S. Service Firm 702
Careers In Managerial Accounting 703

    Alternative Career Paths 703
    Work/Life Balance 704
Professional Certifications 705
    Certified Public Accountant (CPA) 705
    Certified Management Accountant (CMA) 705
    Other Professional Certifications 705
Summary of Learning Objectives 706
Key Terms 707
Assignments 707
Your Turn! Solutions 709

CHAPTER 15

Managerial Accounting Concepts and Cost
Flows 710
Key Objectives of a Managerial Accounting
    System 712
    Product Costing in a Manufacturing
        Environment 712
    Your Turn! 15.1 715
    Product Costing in a Service and Merchandising
        Environment 715
    Cost Control 716
Inventories and Cost Categories 716
    Inventories 716
    Manufacturing Product Cost Categories 717
    Your Turn! 15.2 718
Product Cost Flows 719
    Raw Materials 719
    Labor 720
    Manufacturing Overhead 721
    Cost of Goods Manufactured 722
    Cost of Goods Sold 723
Illustration of Product Cost Accumulation 723
    Introduction of T-Accounts 723
    Real-World Manufacturing Example 724
    Schedule of Cost of Goods Manufactured 724
    Decision Time 15.1 726
    Calculating Cost of Goods Sold 726
    Income Statement for a Manufacturing
        Firm 727
Illustration of Product Cost Journal Entries 727
    Cost Flows 729
    Financial Statements 730
Comprehensive Problem 736
Summary of Learning Objectives 737
Key Terms 737
Assignments 738
Certified Management Accountant (CMA®) Exam
    Sample Questions 746
Answers to Self-Study Questions: 748
Your Turn! Solutions 748

Decision Time Solution   748

CHAPTER 16

Cost Accounting Systems: Job Order Costing   750

Cost Accounting Systems   752
  Two Basic Types of Cost Accounting
    Systems   752
  Your Turn! 16.1   753
  Timely Product Costing   753
  Your Turn! 16.2   754
Predetermined Overhead Rates   755
  Calculation of Predetermined Overhead
    Rate   755
  Your Turn! 16.3   756
  Annual versus Monthly Rates   756
Job Order Costing Systems   757
  Illustration of Job Order Costing for a
    Manufacturer   758
  Decision Time   766
  Illustration of Job Order Costing for a Service
    Firm   767
Accounting for Service Departments   768
  Service Departments as Cost Centers   768
  Service Department Costs as Product
    Costs   768
  Method of Cost Allocation   769
  Choosing an Allocation Basis   770
Departmental Overhead Rates   771
  Departmental Overhead Rates   771
  Your Turn! 16.4   772
Comprehensive Problem   774
Summary of Learning Objectives   774
Key Terms   776
Assignments   776
Certified Management Accountant (CMA®) Exam
  Sample Questions   791
Answers to Self-Study Questions: 794
Your Turn! Solutions   795
Decision Time Solution   795

CHAPTER 17

Cost Accounting Systems: Process Costing   796

Introduction to Process Costing   798
  Job Order Costing Review   798
  Process Costing   799
Characteristics of Process Costing   800
  Manufacturing Departments   801

Basic Processing Patterns   801
Process Costing Steps   802
  Step 1: Visualize the Physical Flow of the
    Units   804
  Step 2: Calculate the Equivalent Units   805
  Your Turn! 17.1   807
  Step 3: Determine the Per-Unit Costs   807
  Step 4: Calculate the Cost of Goods
    Manufactured   808
  Step 5: Calculate the Ending Work in Process
    Inventory   809
The Product Cost Report   809
  Companies with Multiple Production
    Processes   811
Journal Entries Illustrated   811
  Material   811
  Labor   811
  Manufacturing Overhead   811
  Your Turn! 17.2   812
Comprehensive Problem   814
Appendix 17A: Process Costing Using FIFO
  Method   816
  Your Turn! 17.3   820
  Your Turn! 17.4   825
Summary of Learning Objectives   825
Key Terms   827
Assignments   827
Certified Management Accountant (CMA®) Exam
  Sample Questions   840
Answers to Self-Study Questions: 842
Your Turn! Solutions   843

CHAPTER 18

Activity-Based Costing   844

Understanding Indirect Costs Using Activity-
  Based Costing   846
  Changing Cost Environment   847
Activity-Based Costing   848
  ABC Product Costing Model   850
Traditional Product Costing and ABC
  Compared   851
  Your Turn! 18.1   854
  Limitations of ABC Illustration   855
  Comparing Traditional and Activity-Based
    Costing   855
ABC Implementation Issues   855
ABC and Customer Profitability Analysis   857
  Customer Profitability Profile   857
Activity-Based Management   859
  Customer Profitability Analysis   860

Summary of Learning Objectives　861
Key Terms　862
Assignments　863
Certified Management Accountant (CMA®) Exam
　Sample Questions　878
Answers to Self-Study Questions:　881
Your Turn! Solution　881

CHAPTER 19

Cost-Volume-Profit Relationships　882

Cost Behavior Analysis　884
　Selecting the Activity Basis　884
　Cost-Volume Graphs　885
　Classifications of Cost Behavior Patterns　886
Relevant Range　887
Analyzing Cost Behavior　888
　Scattergraph Method　888
　Your Turn! 19.1　889
　High-Low Method　889
　Your Turn! 19.2　891
　Least Squares Regression Method　891
　Analyzing Costs in Practice　892
　Service and Merchandising　892
Cost-Volume-Profit (CVP) Analysis　893
　Break-Even Analysis　893
　Contribution Margin Analysis　895
Planning For Profit　897
　Desired Profit　897
　Decision Time　899
　Margin of Safety　900
　Operating Leverage　900
　Your Turn! 19.3　904
　Using Cost-Volume-Profit Relationships　904
　Break-Even Analysis and Multiple Products　905
　Cost-Volume-Profit Analysis for Retail
　　Businesses　906
　Service and Merchandising　906
　Service and Merchandising　908
Comprehensive Problem　909
Summary of Learning Objectives　910
Key Terms　912
Assignments　912
Certified Management Accountant (CMA®) Exam
　Sample Questions　923
Answers to Self-Study Questions:　925
Your Turn! Solutions　925
Decision Time Solution　925

CHAPTER 20

Variable Costing: A Tool for Decision Making　926

Treatment of Product Costs　928
　Absorption Costing　928
　Variable Costing　928
　Appropriate Use of Absorption Costing and
　　Variable Costing　930
Variable Costing Income Statement　930
　Income Statement Preparation　930
　Income Reconciliation　932
　Your Turn! 20.1　933
Advantages and Disadvantages of Variable
　Costing　934
　Advantages　934
　Disadvantages　935
Comprehensive Problem　938
Summary of Learning Objectives　939
Key Terms　939
Assignments　940
Certified Management Accountant (CMA®) Exam
　Sample Questions　944
Answers to Self-Study Questions:　946
Your Turn! Solution　946

CHAPTER 21

Relevant Costs and Short-Term Decision Making　948

Management and the Decision-Making
　Process　950
　Who Makes Decisions?　950
　Phases of Decision Making　952
Relevant Costs and Differential Analysis　953
　Decision Time 21.1　955
Illustrations of Differential Analysis　955
　The Special Order　955
　Your Turn! 21.1　956
　Make or Buy?　957
　Dropping Unprofitable Segments　958
　Service and Merchandising　958
　Decision Time 21.2　959
　Sell or Process Further?　959
　Constrained Resources　963
　Your Turn! 21.2　964
　Service and Merchandising　964
Summary of Learning Objectives　965
Key Terms　966
Assignments　966

Certified Management Accountant (CMA®) Exam
  Sample Questions   977
Answers to Self-Study Questions: 981
Your Turn! Solutions   981
Decision Time Solutions   981

CHAPTER **22**

Planning and Budgeting   982
The Planning Process   984
  Strategic Planning   985
  Your Turn! 22.1   986
  Operational Planning   986
  Progress Measurement and Reporting   987
The Budgeting Process   987
  Advantages of Budgeting   988
  Decision Time 22.1   988
  Elements of Effective Budgeting   989
  Zero-Base Budgeting   990
The Framework of the Master Budget   991
Illustration of a Master Budget and its
  Components   992
  Sales Budget   992
  Production Budget   993
  Direct Material Budget   994
  Direct Labor Budget   995
  Manufacturing Overhead Budget   995
  Selling and Administrative Expense Budget   997
  Capital Expenditures Budget   997
  Cash Budget   998
  Your Turn! 22.2   999
  Illustration of a Service Firm's Budgets   999
  Budgeted Financial Statements   1001
Comprehensive Problem   1005
Summary of Learning Objectives   1008
Key Terms   1010
Assignments   1010
Certified Management Accountant (CMA®) Exam
  Sample Questions   1020
Answers to Self-Study Questions: 1022
Decision Time Solution   1023
Your Turn! Solutions   1023

CHAPTER **23**

Standard Costing and Variance
Analysis   1024
Standard Costs   1026
  Uses of Standard Cost Accounting   1027
Determining Standard Costs   1028
  Direct Material Standards   1028

  Direct Labor Standards   1028
  Variable Overhead Standards   1029
  Total Standard Costs   1030
Cost Variances   1031
  Direct Materials Variances   1032
  Fezzari's Direct Materials Variances   1034
  Your Turn! 23.1   1035
  Direct Labor Variances   1036
  Fezzari's Direct Labor Variances   1037
  Your Turn! 23.2   1038
  Variable Overhead Variances   1039
Fezzari's Variable Overhead Variances   1040
  Your Turn! 23.3   1041
  Decision Time 23.1   1041
Standard Costs In Financial Statements   1041
Appendix 23A: Cost Variance Journal Entries
  Illustrated   1043
  Your Turn! 23.4   1044
  Your Turn! 23.5   1045
Comprehensive Problem   1045
Summary of Learning Objectives   1047
Key Terms   1048
Assignments   1048
Certified Management Accountant (CMA®) Exam
  Sample Questions   1055
Answers to Self-Study Questions: 1058
Decision Time Solution   1058
Your Turn! Solutions   1058

CHAPTER **24**

Flexible Budgets, Segment Reporting, and
Performance Analysis   1060
Static Budgets   1062
Flexible Budgets   1063
  Flexible Budgets in a Manufacturing
    Environment   1063
  Flexible Budgets in a Service Environment   1066
  Service and Merchandising   1066
Internal Reporting of Segment Operations   1069
  Decentralized Organizations   1069
  Segment Reporting   1070
  Types of Business Segments   1070
  Your Turn! 24.1   1071
Performance Reporting   1072
  Departmental Operations   1074
  Contribution Margin Income Statement   1074
  Segment Performance Evaluation   1074
Service Company Segment Reporting
  Illustration   1075
  Office Margin   1075

Service and Merchandising   **1075**
Your Turn! 24.2   **1079**
Performance Analysis   **1079**
Return on Investment   **1079**
Return on Sales   **1080**
Asset Utilization   **1081**
Residual Income   **1081**
Balanced Scorecard   **1082**
Decision Time 24.1   **1083**
Service and Merchandising   **1084**
Appendix 24A: Transfer Pricing   **1086**
Comprehensive Problem   **1092**
Summary of Learning Objectives   **1093**
Key Terms   **1095**
Assignments   **1095**
Certified Management Accountant (CMA®) Exam
Sample Questions   **1104**
Answers to Self-Study Questions   **1106**
Your Turn! Solutions   **1106**
Decision Time Solution   **1106**

CHAPTER 25

Capital Budgeting   1108

Elements Of Capital Budgeting   **1110**
Capital Budgeting Phases   **1110**
Capital Expenditure Analysis   **1111**
Required Rates of Return and the Time Value of
Money   **1112**
Cost of Capital   **1112**
Your Turn! 25.1   **1113**
Time Value of Money   **1114**
Performing Net Present Value Calculations   **1115**
Single-Sum Cash Flows   **1115**
Your Turn! 25.2   **1116**
Annuity Flows   **1116**
Your Turn! 25.3   **1117**
Measurement of Investments and Returns   **1117**
Cash Flows   **1117**
After-Tax Cash Flows   **1118**
Depreciation Tax Shield   **1118**
Illustration of After-Tax Cash Flows   **1119**
Summary of Concerns Underlying Capital
Budgeting   **1121**
Net Present Value Analysis   **1121**
Basic Steps   **1121**
Illustration of Net Present Value Analysis   **1122**
Decision Time 25.1   **1126**
Liquidation Proceeds   **1126**
Your Turn! 25.4   **1127**
Excess Present Value Index   **1127**

Other Capital Budgeting Analyses   **1128**
Cash Payback Analysis   **1128**
Average Rate of Return Analysis   **1129**
Capital Budgeting: A Complex Subject   **1131**
Service and Merchandising   **1131**
Comprehensive Problem   **1133**
Summary of Learning Objectives   **1134**
Key Terms   **1135**
Assignments   **1135**
Certified Management Accountant (CMA®) Exam
Sample Questions   **1144**
Answers to Self-Study Questions: **1147**
Your Turn! Solutions   **1147**
Decision Time Solution   **1147**

APPENDIX A

Columbia Sportswear Company   A-1

Report of Independent Auditors   **A-2**
Financial Statements   **A-3**
Notes To Financial Statements   **A-7 (On Book Website)**
Earnings Per Share Data   **A-22 (On Book Website)**
Supplemental Information   **A-23 (On Book Website)**
Report On Internal Control   **A-25 (On Book Website)**

APPENDIX B

Financial Statements for Under Armour   B-1

APPENDIX C

Financial Statements for LVMH Moet Hennessy - Louis Vuitton   C-1

APPENDIX D (On Book Website)

Accounting for Investments and Consolidated Financial Statements   D-1

Investments   **D-2**
Debt and Equity Securities   **D-2**
Investment Categories   **D-2**
Investments in Debt Securities   **D-3**
Purchase   **D-4**
Recognition of Interest Income   **D-5**
Balance Sheet Valuation   **D-5**
Sale or Redemption at Maturity   **D-7**
Investments in Equity Securities   **D-8**
Purchase   **D-8**

Recognition of Investment Income   **D-9**
Balance Sheet Valuation   **D-9**
Sale   **D-11**
Current and Noncurrent Classifications   **D-12**
Parent-Subsidiary Relationship   **D-12**
Consolidated Financial Statements   **D-12**
Limitations of Consolidated Statements   **D-13**
Summary of Learning Objectives   **D-14**
Key Terms   **D-15**
Self-Study Questions   **D-15**
Questions   **D-17**
Exercises—Set A   **D-17**
Exercises—Set B   **D-19**
Problems—Set A   **D-21**
Problems—Set B   **D-23**
Answers to Self-Study Questions   **D-26**

APPENDIX **E**

Accounting and the Time Value of Money   **E-1**

Time Value of Money Concept   **E-2**
Time Value of Money: Simple Interest Model   **E-2**
Time Value of Money: Compound Interest Model   **E-2**
Future Value of an Amount   **E-3**
Future Value of an Annuity   **E-5**
Present Value of an Amount   **E-6**
Present value of an Annuity   **E-9**
Calculations Using a Calculator and a Spreadsheet   **E-10**
Summary of Learning Objectives   **E-10**
Glossary of Key Terms   **E-10**
Self-Study Questions   **E-11**
Exercises—Set A   **E-11**
Exercises—Set B   **E-12**
Answers to Self-Study Questions: **E-14**

Index   **I-1**

1

Financial Accounting and Business Decisions

Learning Objectives *identify the key learning goals of the chapter.*

PRESENT

This chapter explains business formation, the uses and users of accounting, the types of activities companies pursue, and financial statements that report on business.

FUTURE

The next chapters more fully explain financial statements, including how they are prepared, constructed, analyzed, and interpreted.

Past/Present/Future *provides an overview of where the chapter fits within the whole course.*

LEARNING OBJECTIVES

1. **Explain** business organization and its three forms. *(p. 4)*

2. **Describe** business activities. *(p. 5)*

3. **Indicate** who uses accounting information. *(p. 6)*

4. **Explain** the accounting process and generally accepted accounting principles. *(p. 10)*

5. **Describe** the accounting equation and each financial statement. *(p. 12)*

6. **Explain** additional disclosures that accompany financial statements. *(p. 20)*

7. **Describe** careers in accounting. *(p. 22)*

8. Appendix 1A: **Discuss** FASB's conceptual framework. *(p. 25)*

WHAT THE NUMBERS MEAN

If it's true that accounting is the language of business, then an understanding of the material in this textbook is crucial to your future livelihood. All of us confront accounting issues in our daily lives. We must control our cash and other assets; we must monitor our paychecks and our expenses; we must purchase items that fit within our budgets; and we must use accounting data in making business decisions.

It is no surprise then that accounting knowledge ranks near the top of what employers look for when hiring new workers. It is also no surprise that students with accounting knowledge perform better than those that do not understand the basics of accounting. This book provides fundamental financial accounting knowledge for future success in business and life.

*A **Focus Company** introduces each chapter and illustrates the relevance of accounting in everyday business.*

Columbia Sportswear Company (Columbia.com), a maker of clothing for dedicated lovers of the greater outdoors, must also rely upon accounting for its success. It uses financial reports to judge its performance and that of its managers. It uses accounting controls to monitor its inventory. It uses accounting data to assess the wisdom of payments, and their amounts, to shareholders. Consequently, accounting not only impacts our lives, but also the business activities of all companies worldwide. We even witness national and international politicians using accounting data to justify or reject key economic and governmental policies.

This first chapter introduces us to many basic relations and principles underlying financial accounting reports. It also identifies many key users of accounting information and how that information is useful in businesses globally.

FINANCIAL ACCOUNTING AND BUSINESS DECISIONS

Business Organization	Activities of a Business	Accounting Information and Its Use	Information Dissemination	Other Annual Report Components	FASB Conceptual Framework (Appendix 1A)
• Sole proprietorship • Partnership • Corporation	• Financing • Investing • Operating	• External users • Internal users • Ethics and accounting	• Accounting process • Generally Accepted Accounting Principles • International Financial Reporting Standards • Financial statements	• Notes to financial statements • Independent auditor's report • Management's Discussion and Analysis	• Objectives • Elements • Characteristics • Recognition and Measurement

BUSINESS ORGANIZATION

The first decision every business faces is deciding what form of organization it will take. The three principal forms of business organization are the sole proprietorship, the partnership, and the corporation. Although each of these organizational forms is treated as an accounting entity, only the corporation is viewed under the law as a legal entity separate and distinct from its owners. A corporation has an unlimited life, which means that it will continue to exist indefinitely unless it is formally dissolved. The life of a sole proprietorship or partnership is limited by the participation of the existing owners. If an owner dies or withdraws, the business typically ends as well.

A **sole proprietorship** is a business owned by one person; it is the most common of the three forms of business organization. The primary advantage of the sole proprietorship is its ease of formation. As the only owner, the sole proprietor makes all of the decisions affecting the business. This organizational form also enjoys certain income tax advantages relative to a corporation in that the income of that business is not taxed; instead, its income is included as part of the owner's income that is reported to the taxation authorities.

A **partnership** is a voluntary association of two or more persons for the purpose of conducting a business. Partnerships and sole proprietorships differ principally with respect to the number of owners. Partnerships can be as small as two people or as large as the biggest accounting or legal firms, which have hundreds or even thousands of partners. Partnerships are also easy to establish. Because a partnership involves multiple owners, the partners should establish the rights and obligations of each partner to avoid any misunderstandings that might lead to disputes and lawsuits. An advantage of the partnership form over the sole proprietorship is the broader skill set that multiple partners can bring to a business. Partnerships also enjoy the same income tax advantage as sole proprietorships.

A **corporation**, on the other hand, is a legal entity created under the laws of a state or the federal government. A corporation can have as few as one owner but most have many owners. The owners of a corporation receive shares of stock as evidence of their ownership interest in the business, and consequently, they are referred to as **stockholders** (or *shareholders*). Since corporations are a separate legal entity, they must pay income taxes on any earned profits. This leads to a situation of double taxation because the income of the corporation is taxed and stockholders also pay taxes on dividends they receive from the corporation. The corporation is the dominant organizational form in terms of the volume of business activity conducted in the United States and worldwide.

While most businesses start off as either a sole proprietorship or as a partnership, some outgrow these organizational forms and convert to the corporate form. For example, the **Columbia Sportswear Company** was incorporated in 1961 after beginning as a sole proprietorship in 1938. Two primary reasons for converting a sole proprietorship or a partnership to the corporate form of business are the relative ease of raising capital to grow the business and the protection afforded to stockholders against personal liability. A third advantage of the corporate form is the relative ease of selling ownership shares. For example, stock exchanges, such as the **New York Stock Exchange (NYSE)**, exist to enable stockholders to readily buy and sell their ownership shares. No such exchanges exist for sole proprietors or partners, and thus, selling an ownership interest in a sole proprietorship or a partnership is a more difficult, time-consuming event.

Proprietorship	**Partnership**	**Corporation**
• One owner controlled	• Shared owner control	• All types of owner control
• Business not taxed, but owner taxed	• Business not taxed, but owners taxed	• Business taxed **and** owners taxed
• Not legal entity	• Not legal entity	• Separate legal entity
• Limited life	• Limited life	• Unlimited life

Your Turn! boxes reinforce the material just presented with self-study questions. To aid learning, solutions are provided at the end of the chapter.

YOUR TURN! 1.1

The solution is on page 56.

Identify three characteristics for each of the principal forms of business organizations.

1. sole proprietorship
2. partnership
3. corporation

ACTIVITIES OF A BUSINESS

Every business, regardless of its organizational form, its industry, or its size, is involved in three types of business activities—financing, investing, and operating.

LO2 Describe business activities.

Financing Activities

Before a company can begin operations, a company must acquire money to support its operations. Employees need to be hired, buildings constructed, raw materials purchased, and machinery put in place. Companies can obtain the necessary funds to undertake these activities in several ways. These **financing activities** are generally categorized as either debt financing or equity financing.

Debt financing involves borrowing money from sources such as a bank by signing a note payable or directly from investors by issuing bonds payable. The individuals or financial institutions that lend money to companies are called their **creditors**. Debt financing involves an obligation to repay a creditor both the amount initially borrowed, called the **principal**, and an interest fee for the use of the funds.

Equity financing involves selling shares of stock to investors. In contrast to creditors who lend money to a business and expect to receive that money back with interest, investors that purchase shares of stock are buying an ownership interest in the company. Investors hope that their stock will increase in value so that they can earn a profit when they sell their shares. The owners of a company's stock may also receive dividend payments when the company decides to distribute some of its net income.

Investing Activities

For a company to undertake its business, it needs to purchase certain long-term resources necessary to conduct its business, such as a printing press purchased by a printing company. The purchase of these resources is known as **investing activities**. Companies can obtain the money needed to make an investment in such items as land, buildings, and equipment from either the financing activities discussed above or from any excess cash accumulated from running the business profitably.

Investing activities involve acquisition and disposition of items such as factories, office furniture, computer and data systems, and delivery vehicles, to carry out the business plans. These items are referred to as *assets*. Investing decisions regarding these assets are known as *asset management*.

Operating Activities

The day-to-day activities of producing and selling a product or providing a service are referred to as **operating activities**. Operating activities are critical for a business because if a company is unable to generate income from its operations it is very likely that the business will fail. If creditors and stockholders do not believe that a company will be able to generate a profit, they are unlikely to provide the financing needed to start, or maintain, its operations.

Exhibit 1-1 provides a summary of the three types of business activities. Arrows are pointing both toward, and away from, operating activities. This is because financing and investing activities are necessary to carry out a company's operating activities; however, if a company's operating activities generate excess cash, then the excess cash can be used to either finance additional investments, repay the company's creditors, or pay dividends to shareholders.

Exhibit 1-1	Business Activities

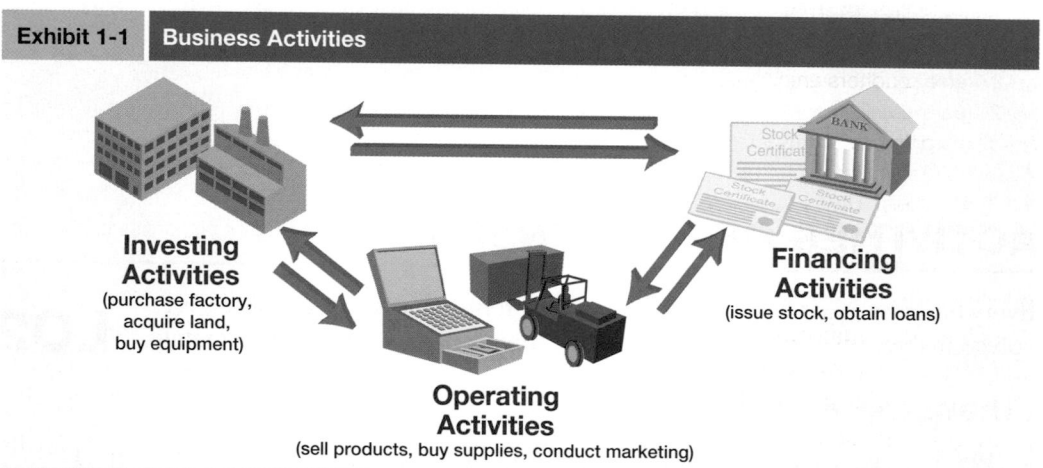

Investing Activities (purchase factory, acquire land, buy equipment)

Financing Activities (issue stock, obtain loans)

Operating Activities (sell products, buy supplies, conduct marketing)

YOUR TURN! 1.2

The solution is on page 56.

Classify each of the following activities as a financing, investing, or operating activity.

1. Receiving a loan from a bank.
2. Selling merchandise online.
3. Purchasing a delivery truck.
4. Purchasing merchandise for resale to customers.
5. Issuing shares of stock in exchange for cash.
6. Paying employee salaries.

ACCOUNTING INFORMATION AND ITS USE

LO3 **Indicate** who uses accounting information.

In today's society, many individuals and agencies are involved in the economic life of a business. The information needs of these parties are fulfilled, in part, by accounting information. Information users are classified by their relation to a business as either *external users* or *internal users*.

External Users of Accounting

An important function of the accounting process is to accumulate and report accounting information that details a business's results of operations, cash flows, and financial position. By U.S. law, publicly owned businesses must publish financial statements annually and quarterly. The subset of accounting that produces these publicly available financial statements is referred to as **financial accounting**. Financial accounting is the focus of the first thirteen chapters of this book.

Financial accounting information serves a variety users. Potential investors and investment professionals need financial data to compare prospective investments to determine which, if any, should be invested in, and at what price. Creditors must consider the financial strength of a business before lending it funds, and stockholders must evaluate whether to remain invested in a business, buy more shares, or sell their existing shares of stock.

The financial statements issued by a company are the main source of financial information for these external users. Because financial statements are often used to evaluate the management team running the business, their objectivity is sometimes called into question because the reports are prepared by the management team itself. To establish the validity of financial statements, most businesses have their financial data audited by an independent public accountant. Publicly owned businesses are required to have their financial statements audited. The independent public accountant, or independent auditor, examines the financial statements and recommends any changes or improvements that are warranted. The independent auditor then expresses a professional opinion as to whether the financial statements are fairly presented "in conformity with generally accepted accounting principles." External users have greater confidence in financial statements that have been audited by an independent, certified public accountant.

The Big Four

Independent auditors are licensed by the state in which they do their auditing work and are identified as **certified public accountants (CPAs)**. To qualify as a CPA, an individual must pass a rigorous examination that is administered nationally and must meet the educational and work experience requirements set by each state to ensure high standards of accounting and auditing performance. The four largest U.S. public accounting firms, referred to as the *Big Four*, have offices located throughout the world and employ thousands of auditors. These firms are **Deloitte & Touche**, **Ernst & Young**, **KPMG, LLP**, and **PricewaterhouseCoopers**.

ACCOUNTING IN PRACTICE

Accounting In Practice *boxes describe how accounting is used in real companies.*

There are many other external users of a company's accounting information. For example, a business's customers may want information to help them determine if a company like **Whirlpool** will be able to honor its product warranties. Labor unions require information to determine the level of pay raises that they can demand from companies like **United Parcel Service**. **Exhibit 1-2** illustrates the kind of accounting information that is required by a company's external users.

Real Companies *and* **Institutions** *are highlighted in bold, blue font.*

Exhibit 1-2	Accounting Information Needs of External Users	
User Group		**Accounting Information Needed to Answer Questions such as:**
Potential investors and stockholders		How does the profitability of **Target** compare to that of **WalMart**? How does **Bank of America Corporation** compare with **Wells Fargo & Company** in terms of firm size?
Creditors and lenders		Will **Delta Airlines** be able to repay its creditors in a timely fashion? Is it safe to provide a bank loan to the **Federal Express Corporation**?
Taxation authorities and regulators		Is **Time Warner Inc.** reporting the proper amount of taxable income? Is **Duke Energy**'s rate hike justified by its operating costs?

Internal Users of Accounting

A major function of accounting is to provide the internal management of a company with the data needed for decision making and the efficient management of the business. While managers have an interest in the information reported to external users, managers also require various other types of information, such as the cost of its products, estimates of the income to be earned from a sales campaign, cost comparisons of alternative courses of action, and long-range budgets. Because of the strategic nature of much of this information, it is usually only available to a company's top-level management. The process of generating and analyzing such data is referred to as **managerial accounting** and is the focus of the last twelve chapters of this book. **Exhibit 1-3** illustrates the various types of accounting information that are required by a company's internal users.

Exhibit 1-3	Accounting Information Needs of Internal Users
User Group	**Accounting Information Needed to Address Questions such as:**
Marketing Department	What is the optimal price to sell the **Samsung** Galaxy phone to maximize the company's sales revenue?
	Was the promotional campaign by **Lionsgate** successful in promoting the company's *Hunger Game* series?
Management Team	How much is the Olive Garden restaurant chain contributing to the overall profitability of its parent company, the **Darden Restaurant Group**?
	What is the projected profitability of the **General Motors'** Chevrolet brand for the coming year?
Finance Department	Is there sufficient cash available for **Hewlett Packard** to buy back a large amount of its outstanding common stock?
	Will **General Electric** have sufficient cash flow to pay its short-term expenses?

YOUR TURN! 1.3

The solution is on page 56.

1. Are financial statements the primary output of managerial or financial accounting? Explain.
2. Identify at least two internal users and explain why they need accounting information.
3. Identify at least two external users and explain why they need accounting information.

Ethics and Accounting

Ethics deals with the values, rules, and justifications that govern one's way of life. Although fundamental ethical concepts such as right and wrong, good and evil, justice and morality are abstract, many issues in our daily lives have ethical dimensions. The way that we respond to these issues defines our ethical profile. In both our personal and professional lives, our goal is to act ethically and responsibly.

Ethical behavior has not always been the rule in business. Business history reveals unethical activities such as price gouging of customers, using inside information for personal gain, paying bribes to government officials for favors, ignoring health and safety regulations, selling arms and military equipment to aggressor governments, polluting the environment, and issuing misleading financial information. Well-known accounting scandals at such companies as **Enron, WorldCom,** and **AIG** have again brought ethics to the forefront.

Increasingly, business managers recognize the importance and value of ethical behavior by their employees. It is now commonplace for businesses to develop a written code of ethics to help guide the behavior of employees. Similarly, professional organizations of accountants have written ethics codes. The **American Institute of Certified Public Accountants (AICPA)**, for example, has a professional code of ethics to guide the conduct of its member CPAs. Similarly, the **Institute of Management Accountants (IMA)** has written standards of ethical conduct for accountants employed in the private sector.

Unethical behavior that results in misleading financial statements such as those at Enron and WorldCom has the potential to erode public confidence and trust in accounting information. In response to this decline in public confidence, the U.S. Congress passed the **Sarbanes-Oxley Act** in 2002 with the goal of restoring investor trust by reducing the likelihood of future accounting scandals. Among the many changes required by this legislation is that a company's top management must certify in writing the accuracy of its reported financial statement information, and these executives risk criminal prosecution for fraudulent certification. In addition, companies must now report on the internal controls put into place to help deter errors in the financial reporting process and to detect them should they occur.

A.K.A. The *Sarbanes-Oxley Act* of 2002 is often referred to as SarBox or SOX.

	FORENSIC ACCOUNTING
Accountant as Detective—CSI in Real Life	

 Law enforcement personnel are not the only people who perform criminal investigations. A branch of accounting known as **forensic accounting** is vitally important in many types of criminal investigations, from financial statement fraud, to money laundering, to massive investment frauds such as the one perpetrated by Bernard Madoff (who is currently serving a 150-year prison sentence). Unlike law enforcement personnel, forensic accountants are involved both before and after the commission of a crime.

Forensic Accounting *boxes highlight how financial accounting knowledge can help aid in the prevention of errors and fraud.*

Accountants face several unique ethical dimensions as a result of their work. These dimensions include the following:

1. The output produced by accountants has financial implications for individuals, as well as businesses. These situations generate considerable pressure on the accountant to "improve" the reported results. The amount of income taxes to be paid by an individual or business, the amount of a bonus to be received by an employee, the price to be paid by a customer, and the amount of money to be distributed to a business's owners are examples of situations in which the financial implications can lead to efforts to influence the outcome. *Ethical behavior mandates that accountants ignore these pressures.*

2. Accountants have access to confidential, sensitive information. Tax returns, salary data, details of financial arrangements, planned acquisitions, and proposed price changes are examples of this type of information. *Ethical behavior mandates that accountants respect the confidentiality of information.*

3. A criticism of U.S. business practices is that they are too "bottom-line" (that is, short-term profit) oriented. This orientation can lead to unethical actions by management to increase reported short-term profits. Because accountants measure and report a firm's profit, they must be particularly concerned about these ethical breakdowns. *Both accountants and management must recognize the importance of a long-run perspective.* Studies indicate that, over the long term, successful companies and ethical practices go hand in hand.

As an accountant for the Madoff Corporation, you are responsible for measuring and reporting the company's net income. It appears that actual results are going to be less than was expected by Wall Street analysts. Your supervisor has asked that you report some of next period's sales revenue early so that the current period's net income will be in line with analyst expectations. You know that reporting revenue like this represents a violation of generally accepted accounting principles. He states that you will not really be doing anything wrong because the sales revenues are real—the company will just be reporting the revenue earlier than accounting guidelines allow. What should you do?

YOUR TURN! 1.4

The solution is on page 56.

THE ACCOUNTING PROCESS

LO4 Explain the accounting process and generally accepted accounting principles.

Accounting is *the process of measuring economic activity of an entity in monetary terms and communicating results to users.* The accounting process consists of two principal activities—measurement and communication.

The measurement process must (1) identify the relevant economic activities of a business, (2) quantify these economic activities, and (3) record the resulting measures in a systematic manner. Measurement is done in monetary terms. In the United States, measurements are stated in U.S. dollars. In other countries, measurements are expressed in the local currency. In Mexico, for example, measurements are stated in pesos, and in most European countries, they are stated in euros.

The purpose of accounting is to provide useful financial information, and the communication process is extremely important. Accordingly, the accounting process (1) prepares financial reports to meet the needs of the user and (2) helps interpret the financial results for that user. To provide reports that serve users effectively, managers must be aware of how these users are likely to apply the reports. The needs of the various users differ; as such, there are different types of accounting reports. Managers employ various techniques to help users interpret the content of reports. These techniques include the way the report is formatted, the use of charts and graphs to highlight trends, and the calculation of ratios to emphasize important financial relations.

Thinking Globally *boxes emphasize the similarities and differences in business practices between companies in the U.S. and companies in other countries.*

THINKING GLOBALLY

Companies measure their operating performance using the currency of their principal place of business. The **Johnson & Johnson Company**, a well-known maker of baby shampoo and Band-Aids, is headquartered in New Jersey, and reports its financial results using the U.S. dollar. On the other hand, **Moet Hennessy Louis Vuitton**, the luxury goods manufacturer, is headquartered in Paris, France, and reports its financial results using the euro. Some companies prepare "convenience translations" of their financial statements in the currency and language of other countries so that potential foreign investors can more readily understand the company's financial performance and condition.

Generally Accepted Accounting Principles

It is important that financial statements be prepared under a set of rules that is understood by the users of reports. Imagine if every business were free to determine exactly how it measured and communicated its financial health and operating performance. How would a user of this information be able to compare one company's results to another if each played by a different set of rules? Financial statement users who rely on accounting data expect that all companies will follow the same standards and procedures when preparing their statements. These standards and procedures are called **generally accepted accounting principles (GAAP)**.

Generally accepted accounting principles are guides to action that can (and do) change over time. Sometimes specific accounting principles must be altered or new principles formulated to fit a changing set of economic circumstances or changes in business practices. For instance, there existed no generally accepted accounting principles to account for the emerging dot.com companies; and consequently, the business community had to create a set of guidelines for companies such as **Amazon.com** and **eBay** to measure and communicate their financial results.

A.K.A. *Generally accepted accounting principles are often referred to as GAAP (pronounced like the clothing store "Gap").*

Financial Accounting Oversight

Organizations such as the **Financial Accounting Standards Board (FASB)**, the American Institute of Certified Public Accountants (AICPA), and the **U.S. Securities and Exchange Commission (SEC)** are instrumental in the development of generally accepted accounting principles in the United States. As a federal agency, the SEC's primary focus is to regulate the interstate sale of stocks and bonds. The SEC requires companies under its jurisdiction to submit audited annual financial statements to the agency which it then makes available to the general public. The SEC has the power to set the accounting principles used by these companies, but the agency has largely delegated that principle-setting responsibility to the FASB.

The FASB is a nongovernmental entity whose pronouncements establish U.S. GAAP.[1] The FASB consists of a seven-member board and follows a process that allows for input from interested parties as it considers a new or changed accounting principle (see the appendix to this chapter for additional information on the conceptual framework the FASB has developed to formulate accounting standards). A new or changed principle requires the support of at least a majority of the board members. More recently, the **Public Company Accounting Oversight Board (PCAOB)** was established. The PCAOB is empowered to approve auditing standards, known as **generally accepted auditing standards (GAAS)**, and monitor the quality of financial statements and audits. **Exhibit 1-4** illustrates the structure of financial accounting oversight in the United States.

Exhibit 1-4	Financial Accounting Oversight

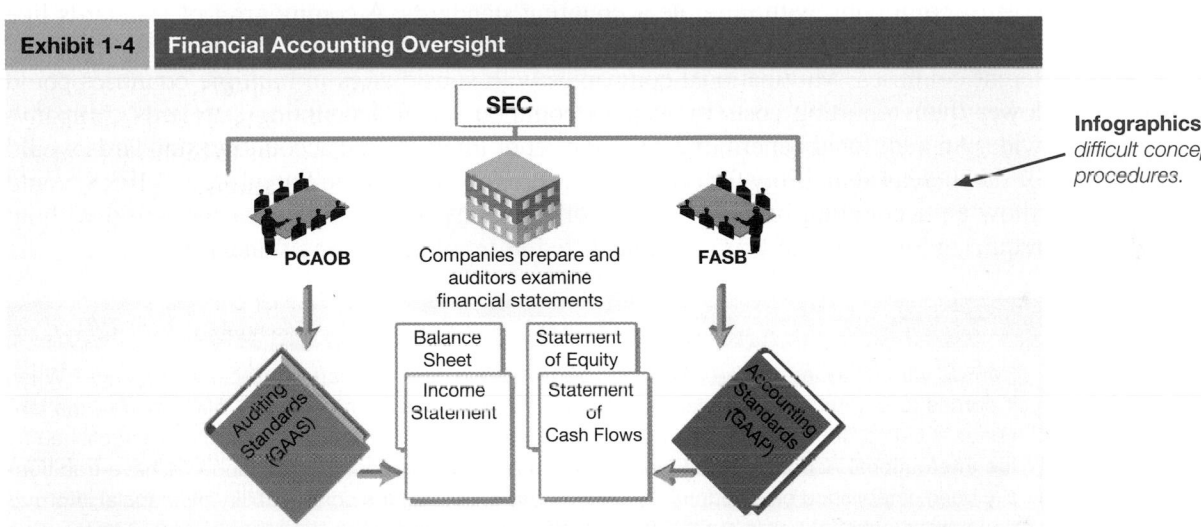

Infographics illustrate difficult concepts and procedures.

Accounting principles, however, do differ among countries of the world. Energized by the continuing growth of international business, efforts are underway to create greater uniformity in worldwide accounting principles. The FASB completed a major restructuring, called the FASB Accounting Standards Codification, in 2009 concerning how GAAP is organized and communicated. This codification represents the authoritative U.S. GAAP for non-governmental entities and is easily researched through an online database maintained by the FASB. A major justification for the codification project was to ease the convergence of U.S. GAAP and international standards.

International Financial Reporting Standards

The past few decades have witnessed a steady acceptance for the need for international financial reporting standards. This acceptance coincides with the increasing globalization of business. Although several organizations are working to increase international harmonization in accounting, the organization that has taken the lead in formulating international accounting principles is the **International Accounting Standards Board (IASB)**. The accounting standards formulated by the IASB are referred to as the **International Financial Reporting Standards (IFRS)**. Approximately 120 nations or reporting jurisdictions either require or permit the use of IFRS. This includes the European Union, Australia, New Zealand, Israel, and Canada. Other large economies including the United States, Japan, China, India, and Russia are working hard to converge their national standards with IFRS.

A.K.A. *International financial reporting standards are often referred to as IFRS (pronounced "eye furs")*

---

[1] Paralleling the FASB structure, the **Governmental Accounting Standards Board (GASB)** was organized in 1984 to formulate the generally accepted accounting principles for state and local governments.

The SEC has assumed a leadership role, dating back several decades, in the development of a strong set of international reporting standards. In 1988 the SEC issued a policy statement supporting the establishment of international accounting standards. In 2002 the SEC announced support for the FASB and the IASB to work toward the convergence of U.S. GAAP and IFRS. In 2007 the SEC voted to accept foreign issuers of financial statements prepared using IFRS to file in the United States without reconciliation to U.S. GAAP. In 2008 the SEC proposed a roadmap for moving U.S. companies to IFRS. In 2009, the SEC approved 110 U.S. firms as potential early adopters of IFRS. The SEC in its 2014–2018 strategic plan wrote, "Due to the increasingly global nature of the capital markets, the agency will work to promote higher quality financial reporting worldwide and will consider, among other things, whether a single set of high-quality global accounting standards is achievable."

The arguments for the need for international financial reporting standards revolve around the increase in companies raising capital in more than one country and the high cost of complying with multiple accounting standards. A common set of standards like IFRS will aid investors in comparing the financial performance of companies from different countries. Multinational companies with subsidiaries in multiple countries could lower their reporting costs by using a common set of accounting standards company-wide. An additional benefit of a common set of international accounting standards would be the increased mobility for accounting professionals. A solid knowledge of IFRS would allow an accounting professional to work in many different parts of the world without requiring him or her to learn a whole different set of accounting standards.

IFRS Alert boxes *examine issues related to similarities and differences in the reporting standards under U.S. GAAP and IFRS.*

IFRS ALERT

How do you get a German, an Italian, and a Spaniard to communicate in the same language? When it comes to communicating financial information, that decision has already been made—the language is called "IFRS." IFRS refers to *International Financial Reporting Standards* as established by the International Accounting Standards Board (IASB). While accounting standards have traditionally been established on a country-by-country basis, making the comparability of financial information across national borders difficult, the IASB was established to "harmonize" global accounting practices. Many countries have now replaced their national GAAP with the International Financial Reporting Standards (IFRS) issued by the IASB.

YOUR TURN! 1.5

The solution is on page 56.

Match the items from column 1 with the correct item in column 2.

1. Accounting
2. Generally Accepted Accounting Principles (GAAP)
3. Public Company Accounting Oversight Board (PCAOB)
4. International Accounting Standards Board (IASB)

a. Guides to action for financial reporting
b. Responsible for formulating international accounting standards
c. The process of measuring economic activity of an entity in monetary terms and communicating the results to users
d. The organization empowered to approve auditing standards

FINANCIAL STATEMENTS

LO5   **Describe** the accounting equation and each financial statement.

There are four basic financial statements: the balance sheet, the income statement, the statement of stockholders' equity, and the statement of cash flows. Each financial statement begins with a heading. The heading provides the name of the company, the name of the financial statement, and the date or time period of the statement.

Balance Sheet

The **balance sheet** is a listing of a firm's assets, liabilities, and stockholders' equity as of a given date, usually the end of an accounting period. The balance sheet depicts a framework called the **accounting equation**. The accounting equation states that the sum of a business's economic resources must equal the sum of any claims on those resources. That is, a business obtains resources that it utilizes in its operations from outside sources, principally creditors and stockholders, who maintain claims on those resources. Consequently, the accounting equation can be written as:

$$\text{Resources of a company} = \text{Claims on resources}$$

Assets refer to a company's resources, liabilities refer to creditor claims on those resources, and stockholders' equity refers to owner claims on those resources. Using these terms, the accounting equation can be reformulated as:

$$\text{Assets} = \text{Liabilities} + \text{Stockholders' equity}$$

This equation states that the firm's assets equals the sum of its liabilities plus its stockholders' equity—see **Exhibit 1-5**. Throughout the accounting process, the accounting equation must always remain in balance.

Exhibit 1-5	Accounting Equation for a Business				
Economic Terms	Resources	=	Creditor claims on resources	+	Stockholder (owner) claims on resources
Business Terms	Assets	=	Liabilities	+	Stockholders' equity

Assets are the economic resources of a business that can be expressed in monetary terms. Assets take many forms. Cash is an asset, as are claims to receive cash payments from customers for goods or services provided, called accounts receivable. Other types of assets include inventory, supplies, land, buildings, and equipment. The key characteristic of any asset is that it represents a probable future economic benefit to a business.

Liabilities are the obligations or debts that a business must pay in cash or in goods and services at some future time as a consequence of past transactions or events. For example, a business can borrow money and sign a promissory note agreeing to repay the borrowed amount in six months. The business reports this obligation as a liability called notes payable. Similarly, if a business owes money to various suppliers for goods or services already provided, it is called accounts payable, or if it owes wages to its employees for work already performed, it is called wages payable. The business reports these obligations on its balance sheet.

Stockholders' equity refers to the ownership (stockholder) claims on the assets of the business. Stockholders' equity represents a *residual claim* on a business's assets; that is, it is a claim on the assets of a business that remain after all liabilities to creditors have been satisfied. For this reason, stockholders' equity is sometimes referred to as a business's **net assets**, where net assets equal the difference between the total assets and total liabilities. In equation format,

Hint: Only resources that can be expressed in monetary terms are included among the assets reported on the balance sheet. There exist some assets that cannot be expressed in monetary terms, such as the value of a company's workforce, and, therefore, are not reported on a balance sheet.

Hints help explain difficult concepts.

$$\text{Assets} - \text{Liabilities} = \text{Stockholders' equity}$$

and,

$$\text{Net assets} = \text{Stockholders' equity}$$

Columbia's balance sheet is shown in **Exhibit 1-6** and reports the company's assets, liabilities, and stockholders' equity. (All Columbia Sportswear amounts are in thousands of dollars.) Columbia's assets totaled $1,792,209 at year-end 2014, with the largest asset being cash of $413,558 followed by inventories of $384,650. Total assets ($1,792,209) are equal to the sum of liabilities ($436,975) and stockholders' equity ($1,355,234). This equality must always exist as required by the accounting equation.

Real financial data for focus companies illustrate key concepts of each chapter.

Hint: Final totals in the financial statements are double underlined. Follow this format whenever asked to prepare a financial statement.

Exhibit 1-6	Columbia Sportswear Balance Sheet

COLUMBIA SPORTSWEAR COMPANY
Balance Sheet
December 31, 2014
(In thousands)

Assets

Cash.	$ 413,558
Investments	27,267
Accounts receivable.	344,390
Inventories	384,650
Prepaid expenses and other current assets.	96,176
Property, plant, and equipment, net	291,563
Other assets.	234,605
Total assets	$1,792,209

Liabilities and Stockholders' Equity
Liabilities

Accounts payable.	$ 214,275
Income taxes payable.	23,776
Other liabilities	198,924
Total liabilities	436,975
Stockholders' Equity	
Common stock.	72,700
Retained earnings.	1,282,534
Total stockholders' equity.	1,355,234
Total liabilities and stockholders' equity	$1,792,209

Columbia's balance sheet indicates that the company principally depends on stockholders' equity to finance its operations since liabilities totaled only $436,975 at 2014 year-end, or approximately 24 percent of total assets. Columbia has been quite profitable in the past and its board of directors has chosen not to distribute much of its net income.

Takeaways summarize the key concepts before proceeding to the next topic.

TAKEAWAY 1.1	Concept	Method	Assessment
	What mix of financing does a company use?	The balance sheet provides information regarding the various forms of financing, both debt financing and equity financing. Compare the amount of liabilities appearing on the balance sheet to the amount of equity appearing on the balance sheet.	A higher ratio of liabilities to equity implies a higher use of creditor financing, and vice versa. Creditor financing is viewed by users as more risky.

Income Statement

A.K.A. *The income statement is also called the statement of operations, the statement of income, and the earnings statement.*

The **income statement** reports the results of operations for a business for a given time period, usually a quarter or a year. The income statement lists the revenues and expenses of the business. **Sales revenue** are increases to a company's resources that result when goods or services are provided to customers. The amount of sales revenue earned is measured by the value of the assets received in exchange for the goods or services delivered.

Expenses are decreases in a company's resources from generating revenue. Expenses are generally measured by the value of the assets used up or exchanged as a result of a business's operating activities. Common examples of expenses include the cost of the items sold, referred to as cost of goods sold, selling expenses, marketing expenses, administrative expenses, interest expense, and income taxes. When total revenue exceeds total expenses, the resulting amount is called **net income**; when total expenses exceed sales revenue, the resulting amount is called a **net loss**.

Columbia's income statement is presented in **Exhibit 1-7**. The statement begins with the business's name, statement title, and time period to which the statement applies. For Columbia, total revenue in 2014 is reported to be $2,108,550 (remember amounts are rounded to the nearest $1,000). Next, Columbia subtracts a series of expenses totaling $1,971,377, yielding net income of $137,173.

A.K.A. *Sales revenue* is also referred to as revenue, sales, net sales, or net revenue.

A.K.A. *Net income* is also referred to as net earnings or net profit.

Exhibit 1-7	Columbia Sportswear Income Statement

COLUMBIA SPORTSWEAR COMPANY
Income Statement
For Year Ended December 31, 2014
(In thousands)

Revenue	
Sales.	$2,100,590
Other revenue.	7,960
Total revenue.	2,108,550
Expenses	
Cost of sales.	1,145,639
Selling, general, and administrative expense.	769,076
Income tax expense	56,662
Total expenses	1,971,377
Net income.	$ 137,173

Concept ➔	Method ➔	Assessment	TAKEAWAY 1.2
Is a company profitable?	The income statement reports a company's performance for a given period of time. Compare reported sales revenue to reported expenses.	Sales revenue in excess of expenses yields net income, implying a profitable company. If expenses exceed revenue, the company has a net loss.	

Statement of Stockholders' Equity

The **statement of stockholders' equity** reports the events causing an increase or decrease in a business's stockholders' equity during a given time period, including both the changes in a company's common stock and changes in its retained earnings. The statement of stockholders' equity consists of two parts—contributed capital and earned capital. **Contributed capital** is a measure of the capital contributed by the stockholders of a company when they purchase ownership shares in the company. Ownership shares are called *common shares* or *common stock*. **Earned capital** is a measure of the capital that is earned by the company, reinvested in the business, and not distributed to its stockholders—that is, its *retained earnings*.

Retained earnings are increased when operations produce net income and decreased when operations produce a net loss. Retained earnings also decrease when a company pays a dividend to its stockholders.

Note: According to a 2011 survey of 500 companies, nearly 98% (489 out of 500) of the companies surveyed issue a Statement of Stockholders' Equity, while only 1% issue a separate Statement of Retained Earnings. Source: Accounting Trends & Techniques, 2011.

A company's retained earnings for a period is determined as follows (sometimes called *statement of retained earnings*):

Retained earnings, beginning of period	$1,200,539
Add: Net income (loss)	137,173
Less: Dividends and other	(55,178)
Retained earnings, end of period	$1,282,534

Columbia's statement of stockholders' equity appears in **Exhibit 1-8**. We focus here on Columbia's retained earnings from its statement of stockholders' equity to emphasize two important concepts: (1) the relation between the income statement and the balance sheet and (2) the components of retained earnings. Columbia's statement of stockholders' equity in **Exhibit 1-8** begins with its ending retained earnings from 2013 of $1,200,539. Its net income of $137,173 from 2014 is added. Can you find this amount on Columbia's income statement in **Exhibit 1-7**? Next, the portion of these earnings that was distributed to Columbia's stockholders in 2014 as a dividend ($55,178) is subtracted to yield an ending retained earnings balance of $1,282,534 as of December 31, 2014. Can you find this amount on Columbia's balance sheet in **Exhibit 1-6**?

Exhibit 1-8	Columbia Sportswear Statement of Stockholders' Equity

COLUMBIA SPORTSWEAR COMPANY
Statement of Stockholders' Equity
For Year Ended December 31, 2014

(In thousands)	Common Stock	Retained Earnings	Total
Balance, December 31, 2013	$52,325	$1,200,539	$1,252,864
Add: Common stock issued	35,375		35,375
Net income		137,173	137,173
Less: Common stock repurchased	(15,000)		(15,000)
Dividends and other		(55,178)	(55,178)
Balance, December 31, 2014	$72,700	$1,282,534	$1,355,234

TAKEAWAY 1.3	Concept ⟶	Method ⟶	Assessment
	What portion of a company's current period net income is distributed to its stockholders, and what portion is retained?	The statement of stockholders' equity reports both a company's net income and the amount of dividends distributed to stockholders. Compare the company's dividends to its net income.	A higher ratio of dividends to net income implies that a company is distributing more of its net income to its stockholders, whereas a lower ratio implies it is retaining more of its income for purposes such as growing its business.

CORPORATE SOCIAL RESPONSIBILITY

Corporate Social Responsibility boxes showcase how forward-thinking companies are embracing CSR as part of their long-term business models.

Reporting on Triple Bottom Line

Companies worldwide are focused on more than just the bottom line. Research shows that financial responsibility goes hand in hand with social responsibility. This is labeled a "virtuous cycle" because financial success provides the means to act socially responsible, and acting socially responsible increases a company's financial performance. Financial statements are not well suited for measuring social performance. To aid in the pursuit of socially responsible behavior, accountants have developed a **triple bottom line** framework in which the single bottom line of financial performance is supplemented with a social bottom line and an environmental bottom line. The triple bottom line standard for urban and community accounting has been ratified by the United Nations and has become widely used in public sector accounting.

Statement of Cash Flows

The **statement of cash flows** reports a business's cash inflows and cash outflows during a given period of time. The cash flows are grouped into the three business activities of operating, investing, and financing. The cash flow from operating activities includes the cash received from the sale of goods and services and the cash spent on operating expenses. The cash flow from investing activities includes the cash payments and receipts when a business buys and sells certain assets that it uses in its operations. The cash flow from financing activities reports the issuances and repurchases of shares in a business and the amounts borrowed and repaid to creditors.

Columbia's statement of cash flows is in **Exhibit 1-9**. This statement shows that Columbia's cash balance decreased during 2014 by $23,931 from $437,489 on December 31, 2013, to $413,558 on December 31, 2014. Columbia's operating activities provided $185,783 in cash while Columbia's investing activities used $184,027 and Columbia's financing activities used $25,687. Adding the changes in cash for the three types of activities produces the decrease of $23,931. The statement of cash flows always concludes with this reconciliation of the cash balance from the beginning of the year to the end of the year. Can you find the ending cash balance on Columbia's balance sheet in **Exhibit 1-6**?

Exhibit 1-9	Columbia Sportswear Statement of Cash Flows

COLUMBIA SPORTSWEAR COMPANY
Statement of Cash Flows
For Year Ended December 31, 2014
(In thousands)

Cash flows from operating activities	$185,783
Cash flows from investing activities.	(184,027)
Cash flows from financing activities.	(25,687)
Net increase (decrease) in cash	(23,931)
Cash at beginning of year	437,489
Cash at end of year	$413,558

Concept ➝	Method ➝	Assessment	TAKEAWAY 1.4
What are the major sources and uses of a company's cash?	The statement of cash flows reports a company's sources and uses of cash separated into three activities: operating, investing, and financing. Identify a company's sources and uses of cash as reported in the statement of cash flows.	Sources of cash are reported as positive numbers and uses of cash as negative numbers. Larger positive numbers represent major cash sources and larger negative numbers represent major cash uses.	

Relations Among the Financial Statements

The income statement, the statement of stockholders' equity, the balance sheet, and the statement of cash flows are linked to one another. That is, the financial statements *articulate*. To illustrate the linkages, refer to the financial statements of Columbia Sportswear in **Exhibit 1-10**. Observe that Ⓐ, the company's net income (or net loss) for a period is an input to the statement of stockholders' equity, and that Ⓑ, the ending common stock,

Exhibit 1-10	Financial Statements for Columbia Sportswear Company

Columbia Sportswear Company
Income Statement
For Year Ended December 31, 2014

Revenue	
Sales.	$2,100,590
Other revenue.	7,960
Total revenue	2,108,550
Expenses	
Cost of sales.	1,145,639
Selling, general, and administrative	769,076
Income tax expense.	56,662
Total expenses.	1,971,377
Net income.	$ 137,173

Columbia Sportswear Company
Statement of Stockholders' Equity
For Year Ended December 31, 2014

	Common Stock	Retained Earnings	Total
Balance, December 31, 2013. .	$52,325	$1,200,539	$1,252,864
Add: Common stock issued .	35,375		35,375
Net income		137,173	137,173
Less: Common stock repurchased	(15,000)		(15,000)
Dividends and other . . .		(55,178)	(55,178)
Balance, December 31, 2014. .	$72,700	$1,282,534	$1,355,234

Columbia Sportswear Company
Balance Sheet
December 31, 2014

Assets		Liabilities	
Cash	$ 413,558	Accounts payable.	$ 214,275
Investments	27,267	Income taxes payable	23,776
Accounts receivable.	344,390	Other liabilities	198,924
Inventories	384,650	Total liabilities.	436,975
Prepaid expenses and other current assets. .	96,176	**Stockholders' Equity**	
Property, plant, and equipment, net	291,563	Common stock.	72,700
Other assets.	234,605	Retained earnings	1,282,534
		Total stockholders' equity	1,355,234
Total assets	$1,792,209	Total liabilities and stockholders' equity .	$1,792,209

Columbia Sportswear Company
Statement of Cash Flows
For Year Ended December 31, 2014

Cash flows from operating activities	185,783
Cash flows from investing activities.	(184,027)
Cash flows from financing activities	(25,687)
Net increase in cash.	(23,931)
Cash at beginning of year	437,489
Cash at end of year	$413,558

retained earnings, and total equity are inputs to the balance sheet. The statement of cash flows Ⓒ explains the change in the cash balance on the balance sheet for a period.

When financial statements are prepared, the sequence suggested by these relations is customarily followed; that is, (1) the income statement is prepared first, followed by (2) the statement of stockholders' equity, then (3) the balance sheet, and finally (4) the statement of cash flows.

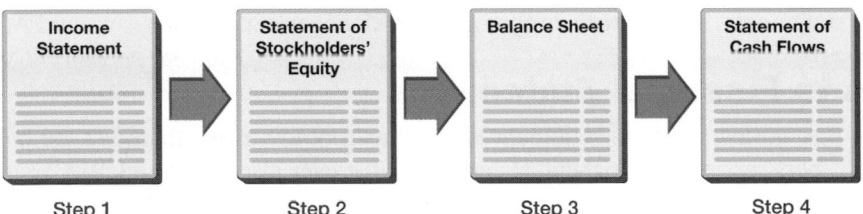

Three of these financial statements present information covering a specific period of time: the income statement, the statement of stockholders' equity, and the statement of cash flows. For this reason, these financial statements are referred to as **period-of-time statements**. In contrast, the balance sheet reports information as of a specific date. The balance sheet, therefore, is referred to as a **point-in-time statement**.

Exhibit 1-11	Financial Statement Links Across Time

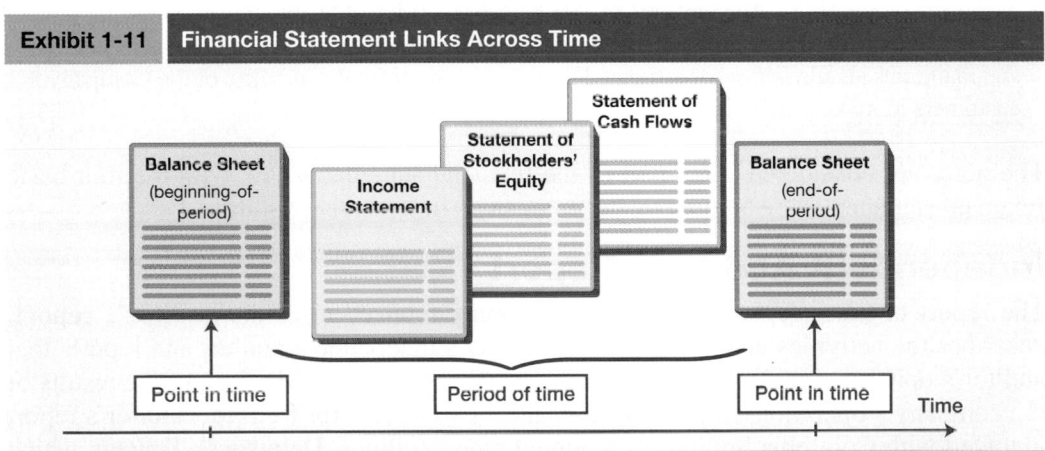

Kanzu Corporation started business on January 1, 2016. The following information was compiled by Kanzu as of December 31, 2016.

Sales revenue.............	$20,000	Accounts payable.....................	$ 4,000
Expenses	12,000	Notes payable	33,000
Dividends	3,000	Common stock......................	20,000
Cash.....................	1,500	Retained earnings	?
Accounts receivable.........	2,500	Cash flow from operating activities	6,500
Inventory.................	3,000	Cash flow from investing activities.........	(55,000)
Equipment	15,000	Cash flow from financing activities.........	50,000
Building	40,000		

Prepare the company's year-end financial statements: an income statement, a statement of stockholders' equity, a balance sheet, and a statement of cash flows.

YOUR TURN! 1.6

The solution is on pages 56–57.

Guided Example icons denote the availability of a demonstration video in **myBusinessCourse** (MBC). See the Preface for more on MBC.

OTHER ANNUAL REPORT COMPONENTS

Columbia Sportswear Company, like all publicly traded companies in the United States, must file an **annual report** called a **Form 10-K** with the U.S. Securities and Exchange Commission (SEC). Some companies also mail a less detailed version of their annual report to their stockholders. The four financial statements explained in this chapter are essential components of this report. Additional components of the annual report are the notes to the financial statements, the auditor's report, and the Management's Discussion and Analysis.

Notes to Financial Statements

LO6 **Explain** additional disclosures that accompany financial statements.

A skilled financial statement user wants to know more than just the bare numbers reported in financial statements. That user also wants to know assumptions and estimates that were used in preparing the statements, the measurement procedures that were followed, and the details behind certain summary numbers. **Notes to the financial statements**, which are quantitative as well as qualitative, provide a great deal more information than just the numbers alone. For example, notes usually contain a description regarding how the company determined the value of its inventory, a detailed chart to explain the property, plant, and equipment account, and a description of any pending lawsuits. No analysis of the annual report is complete without a careful reading of the notes to the financial statements. The following is a short excerpt from Columbia's notes:

Excerpts *from recent financial statements and notes are used to illustrate and reinforce concepts.*

Accounts receivable   Accounts receivable have been reduced by an allowance for doubtful accounts. The Company makes ongoing estimates of the collectability of accounts receivable and maintains an allowance for estimated losses resulting from the inability of the Company's customers to make required payments.

The notes are considered a key part of the financial statements and, with the four basic financial statements, are audited by the company's independent auditor.

Independent Auditor's Report

The report of the independent auditor, commonly referred to as the **auditor's report**, describes the activities undertaken by a company's independent auditor and reports that auditor's opinion regarding whether the financial statements fairly present the results of the company's operations and financial health. A short excerpt from the auditor's report included with Columbia Sportswear's annual report follows. **Deloitte & Touche**, which is Columbia's independent auditor, reports that the financial statements of Columbia are, in its opinion, fairly presented. The independent auditor has intentionally avoided using language such as the statements are "correctly presented" or are "exactly correct." As we will see in subsequent chapters, the financial statements are prepared only after the management team makes a number of assumptions, estimates, and accounting policy decisions. As a consequence, it is inappropriate to describe the statements as being right or wrong since the reported numbers are dependent on the accounting policies selected and the assumptions and estimates made by management.

Report of Independent Registered Public Accounting Firm
In our opinion, such consolidated financial statements present fairly, in all material respects, the financial position of Columbia Sportswear Company and subsidiaries as of December 31, 2014 and 2013, and the results of their operations and their cash flows for each of the three years in the period ended December 31, 2014, in conformity with accounting principles generally accepted in the United States of America. Also, in our opinion, such a financial statement schedule, when considered in relation to the basic consolidated financial statements taken as a whole, presents fairly, in all material respects, the information set forth therein.
DELOITTE & TOUCHE LLP

Management's Discussion and Analysis

In addition to the financial statements and footnotes, the SEC requires companies to provide other information, such as a description of its business, the properties it owns, and the risks it faces. Unlike the financial statements and footnotes, however, this information is not audited by the company's independent auditor. An important component of this other information is the **Management's Discussion and Analysis**, or MD&A, which contains management's interpretation of the company's recent performance and financial condition. This interpretation helps financial statement users gain a context within which to place their own analysis and interpretation of the numbers that appear in the financial statements.

The MD&A is also where a company's management provides its opinion regarding what the future holds for its business. Discussions of future opportunities and risks are called "forward-looking" and are helpful to any financial statement user interested in learning about such things as potential new markets for the company's products or potential new competitors. Obviously these forward-looking statements are subjective in nature, and the statement users must do an independent analysis of the financial statements.

The following is a short excerpt from Columbia's MD&A.

Business Outlook

The global business climate continues to present us with a great deal of uncertainty, making it difficult to predict future results. Factors that could significantly affect our full year 2015 outlook include:

- Unseasonable weather conditions or other unforeseen factors affecting consumer demand and the resulting effect on order cancellations, sales returns, customer accommodations, reorders, direct-to-consumer sales and suppressed demand in subsequent seasons;
- Macroeconomic trends affecting consumer traffic and spending in brick and mortar retail channels;
- The rate of new store expansion and performance of our existing stores and e-commerce sites in our global direct-to-consumer operations;
- Changes in mix and volume of full price sales in relation to closeout product sales and promotional sales activity;
- Production capacity constraints and associated risks, including timely delivery, quality and non-compliance;
- Costs and business interruption risks related to our supply chain, including work slowdowns and stoppages due to labor disputes at west coast ports in the United States;
- Risks associated with information technology infrastructure investments and projects, including our multi-year global ERP system implementation;
- Our ability to effectively manage operating costs;
- Continued political and economic uncertainty, which is creating headwinds in key global markets; and
- Fluctuating foreign currency exchange rates.

These factors and others may have a material effect on our financial condition, results of operations or cash flows, particularly with respect to quarterly comparisons.

Match each of the items in the left column with the appropriate annual report component where we would find that item, from the right column.

1. An opinion regarding the fair presentation of financial statements.
2. Information regarding the procedures followed to value a company's assets.
3. A discussion of new markets that a company plans to enter.

    a. Management Discussion and Analysis
    b. Notes to the Financial Statements
    c. Auditor's report

YOUR TURN! 1.7

The solution is on page 57.

CAREERS IN ACCOUNTING

LO7 Describe careers in accounting.

Without a doubt one of the primary considerations students have when selecting a major are the job prospects after graduation. The good news for accounting majors is that the present is very good and the future looks even brighter. According to the Bureau of Labor Statistics, accounting jobs are expected to grow by 13 percent annually through 2022, assuring accounting majors will be in demand for the foreseeable future.

ACCOUNTING IN PRACTICE | **Job Openings at Columbia Sportswear**

Attaining a solid understanding of accounting will lead to job opportunities, even for those who do not want to be accountants. For example, a recent search on Columbia Sportswear's website resulted in 191 open positions. Fifteen percent of those open positions mentioned accounting skills in the job requirements. The open positions ranged from traditional accounting jobs, such as Senior Account Analyst, to sales and marketing jobs, such as Store Manager. In today's competitive job market, accounting knowledge can be the competitive advantage that helps you secure a good job.

Accounting opportunities are present in multiple areas. **Exhibit 1-12** lists some typical job titles in (1) private accounting; (2) public accounting; and (3) government. Accountants working in the private sector work for a particular company, whereas an accountant working in public accounting spends most of their time working for clients of their employer.

Accounting professionals are not just in high demand, they are also held in high regard by the public. Accounting professionals often earn various certificates in order to further distinguish themselves. The most sought after certification is the Certified Public Accountant (CPA) certificate. This certification requires both education and professional experience, passing an examination, and the highest ethical standards. Three other important certifications are the Certified Management Accountant (CMA), the Certified Internal Auditor (CIA), and the Certified Fraud Examiner (CFE) certificates.

Exhibit 1-12	**Careers in Accounting**		
	Private Accounting	**Public Accounting**	**Government Accounting**
Typical Positions	Internal audit Tax Financial reporting Analyst Budgeting Cost accounting	Auditor Tax Consulting Strategy	Auditor Tax Budgeting Criminal investigation

One of the reasons that accounting graduates find great opportunities upon graduation is because the accounting courses provide specific skills that can be applied immediately on the job. It is therefore quite apparent that when one compares the advantages and disadvantages of an accounting career, the positive job outlook and the high salaries are often listed. Accountants also have a great deal of mobility and upward advancement potential.

According to the U.S. Bureau of Labor Statistics, the 2013 median pay for the 1.2 million accounting jobs in their database was $72,500. **Exhibit 1-13** compares the 2015 salaries of starting accountants, accountants with a couple years of experience, and more senior accountants in both public accounting and in large corporations.

Accounting Career Resources   **ACCOUNTING IN PRACTICE**

Careers in accounting are both numerous and varied. You can learn more about accounting careers by visiting the following Websites:

The American Institute of Certified Public Accountants (AICPA) www.aicpa.org
The American Association of Finance & Accounting (AAFA) www.aafa.com
The National Society of Accountants (NSA) www.nsacct.org
The Accounting Degree Guide www.myaccountingdegree.org
Accounting Coach www.accountingcoach.com
Robert Half www.roberthalf.com

COMPREHENSIVE PROBLEM

You have been approached by Janet Jones about helping her assemble a set of December 31 financial statements for her new business. Janet began the operations of her bakery shop on January 1, 2016. Janet decided that she did not want to risk any personal liability resulting from operating the business; consequently, she organized the bakery, called Sweet Pleasures, as a corporation.

Required
Use the format of **Exhibits 1-6** through **1-9** to prepare an income statement, statement of stockholders' equity, balance sheet, and statement of cash flows for Sweet Pleasures as of December 31, 2016. Use the account titles and balances provided below. Be sure to use proper underlining and double underlining.

Sales of goods	$200,000	Dividends	$ 10,000
Cash.	99,000	Bank loan payable	20,000
Rent expense	16,000	Accounts receivable.	40,000
Interest payable	1,600	Cash received from operating activities.	160,000
Cash received from issuance of common stock . . .	50,000	Cash payments for operating activities	94,000
Insurance expense.	20,000	Salary expense.	40,000
Purchase of equipment	27,000	Cash received from borrowing from bank . . .	20,000
Equipment	27,000	Interest expense.	1,600
Common stock.	50,000	Administrative expense	18,000
Cash dividends paid.	10,000		

Solution

SWEET PLEASURES CORPORATION
Income Statement
For Year Ended December 31, 2016

Revenue		
Sales of goods		$200,000
Expenses		
Rent expense	$16,000	
Insurance expense	20,000	
Salary expense	40,000	
Administrative expense	18,000	
Interest expense	1,600	
Total expenses		95,600
Net income		$104,400

SWEET PLEASURES CORPORATION
Statement of Stockholders' Equity
For Year Ended December 31, 2016

	Common Stock	Retained Earnings	Total
Balance, January 1, 2016	$ 0	$ 0	$ 0
Add: Common stock issued	50,000		50,000
Net income		104,400	104,400
Less: Dividends		(10,000)	(10,000)
Balance, December 31, 2016	$50,000	$ 94,400	$144,400

SWEET PLEASURES CORPORATION
Balance Sheet
December 31, 2016

Assets		Liabilities	
Cash	$ 99,000	Bank loan payable	$ 20,000
Accounts receivable	40,000	Interest payable	1,600
Equipment	27,000	Total liabilities	21,600
		Stockholders' Equity	
		Common stock	50,000
		Retained earnings	94,400
		Total stockholders' equity	144,400
Total assets	$166,000	Total liabilities and stockholders' equity	$166,000

SWEET PLEASURES CORPORATION
Statement of Cash Flows
For Year Ended December 31, 2016

Cash flow from operating activities		
Cash received from operating activities	$160,000	
Cash payments for operating activities	(94,000)	
Cash provided by operating activities		$66,000
Cash flow from investing activities		
Purchase of equipment	(27,000)	
Cash used by investing activities		(27,000)
Cash flow from financing activities		
Borrowing from bank	20,000	
Issuance of common stock	50,000	
Cash dividends paid	(10,000)	
Cash provided by financing activities		60,000
Net increase of cash		99,000
Cash at January 1, 2016		0
Cash at December 31, 2016		$99,000

APPENDIX 1A: FASB's Conceptual Framework

The FASB has developed a conceptual framework, in coordination with the International Accounting Standards Board, to guide the formulation of U.S. generally accepted accounting principles. The **conceptual framework** is a cohesive set of interrelated objectives and fundamentals for external financial reporting whose purpose is to guide the formulation of specific U.S. accounting principles. This framework, outlined in **Exhibit 1A-1**, consists of (1) financial reporting objectives, (2) financial statement elements, (3) qualitative characteristics of accounting information, and (4) recognition and measurement criteria for financial statements. A recurrent theme in the conceptual framework is the importance of providing information that is useful to financial statement users.

LO8 Appendix 1A: **Discuss** FASB's conceptual framework.

Exhibit 1A-1	Summary of Conceptual Framework

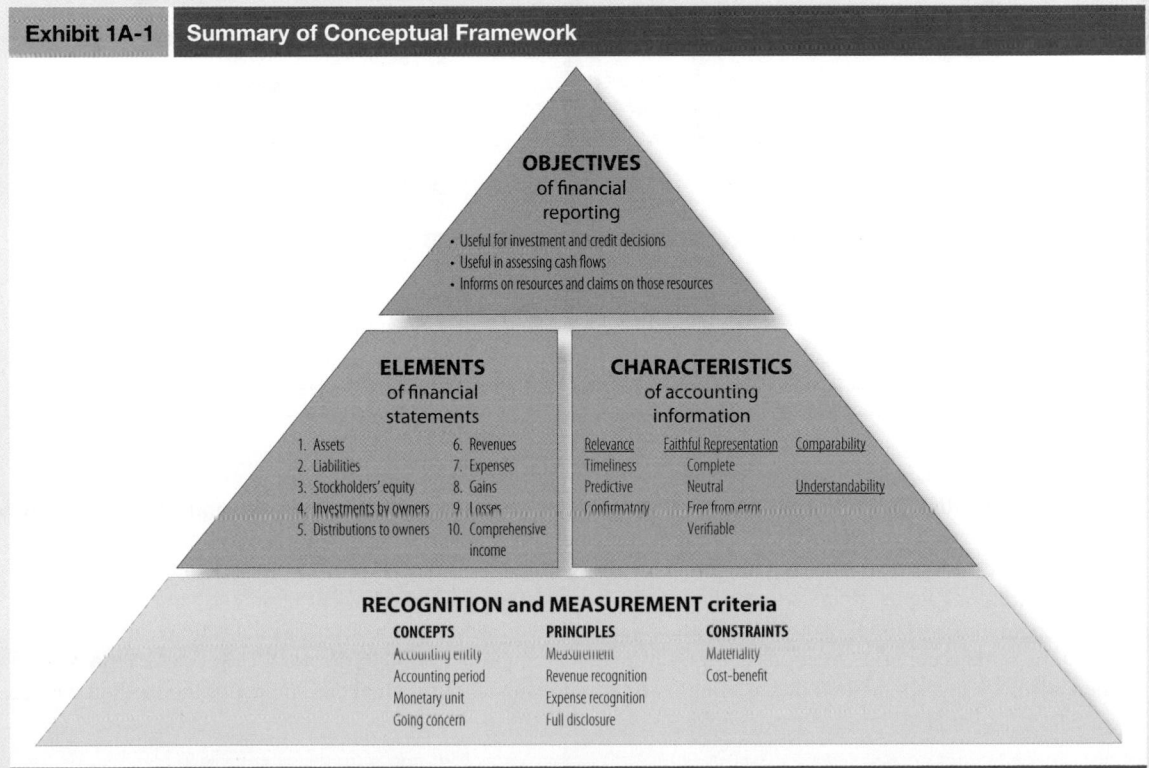

Financial Reporting Objectives

The **financial reporting objectives** of the conceptual framework focus on information useful to investors and creditors. Accordingly, financial statements have the principal objective of providing information that is (1) useful in making investment, credit, and similar decisions and (2) helpful in assessing the ability of enterprises to generate future cash flows. Financial statements should also (3) contain information about a company's economic resources, the claims on those resources, and the effects of events that change those resources and claims. This helps to identify a company's financial strengths and weaknesses, predict future performance, and evaluate earlier expectations.

Financial Statement Elements

The **financial statement elements** of the conceptual framework are the components of financial statements. These elements include assets, liabilities, stockholders' equity, investments by owners, distributions to owners, revenues, expenses, gains, losses, and comprehensive income.

Qualitative Characteristics

The **qualitative characteristics of accounting information** are depicted in **Exhibit 1A-2**. These qualities are intended to contribute to decision usefulness. The two primary qualities are **relevance** and **faithful representation**. To be relevant, accounting information must make a difference in a user's decisions. Relevant information must be timely and contribute to the predictive and evaluative decisions made by investors and creditors. Faithful representation has the characteristics of being complete, neutral, free from error, and verifiable.

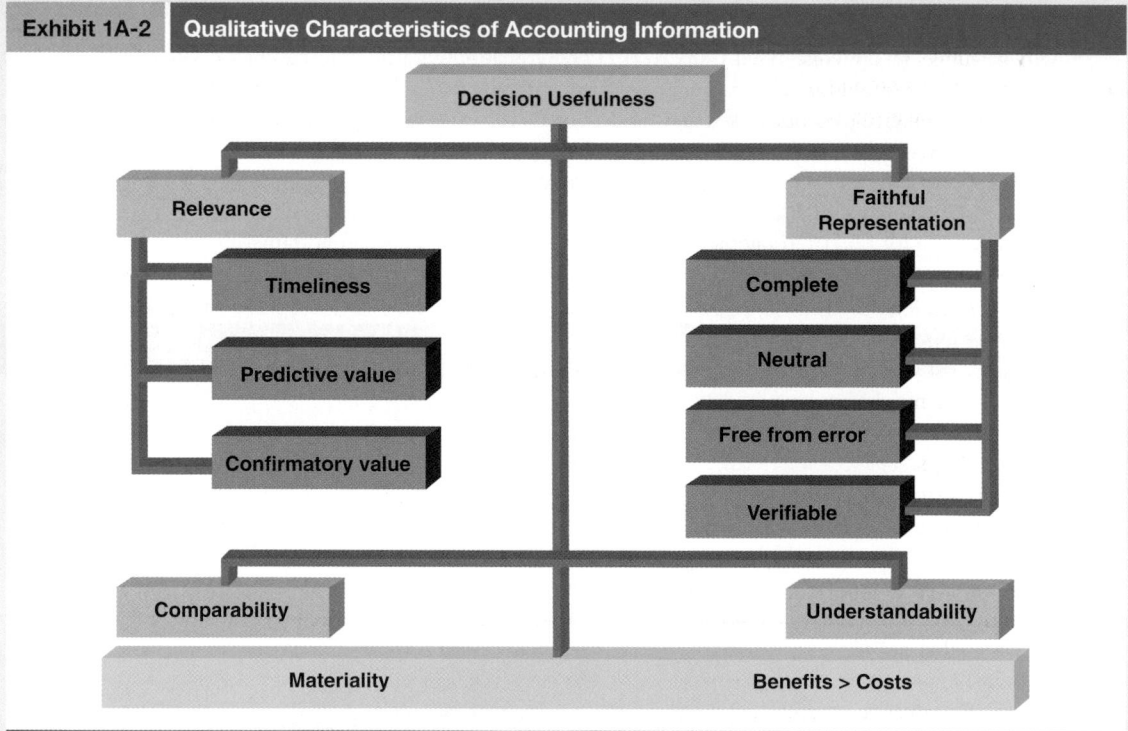

Exhibit 1A-2 **Qualitative Characteristics of Accounting Information**

Additional enhancing qualitative characteristics of accounting information are comparability and understandability. In order to enable users to most effectively compare financial results across companies, U.S. GAAP requires that companies disclose in the notes to financial statements the accounting policy choices they elected to use in the preparation of their financial statements. **Comparability** aids users to understand similarities and differences among items. Related to comparability is **consistency**, although they are not the same. Comparability relates to making comparisons among more than one item, whereas consistency relates to a single item and means the same accounting methods are used from one accounting period to the next. U.S. GAAP requires that when a firm changes a method of reporting its financial results that the financial impact of the method change be revealed in its notes to financial statements. **Understandability** is enhanced if information is classified, characterized, and presented clearly and concisely.

Recognition and Measurement Criteria

The **recognition and measurement criteria** of the framework specify the conditions that must be satisfied before a particular asset, liability, revenue, or expense can be recorded in the financial records. An item under consideration must meet the definition of an element and be measurable, and information about the item must achieve the primary qualitative characteristics of accounting information. The recognition and measurement criteria consist of four concepts, four principles, and two constraints.

Concepts

A fundamental concept in accounting is the entity. An **accounting entity** is an economic unit with identifiable boundaries for which we accumulate and report financial information. Before we can analyze and report activities, we must identify the particular entity. Each sole proprietorship, partnership, and corporation is an entity, and separate accounting records must be maintained for each unit. In accumulating financial information, we maintain a record of the activities of the accounting entity separately from the economic and personal activities of its owners. The operations of most businesses are virtually continuous. Yet, the economic life of a company can be divided into specific periods of time, known as the **accounting period**, which is typically one year for purposes of preparing financial statements. Although the division of the total life of a business into segments based on annual periods is artificial, the concept of the accounting period is useful for financial reporting. The **monetary unit concept** specifies that a monetary unit (for example, the dollar in the United States and the euro in the European Union) is to be used to measure and record an entity's economic activity. Only items that can be expressed in these monetary units are included in the financial statements. When all assets, liabilities, and stockholders' equity are stated in monetary terms, they can be added or subtracted to prepare financial statements. Also, relations among financial statement components can be calculated and presented to help interpret the statements. In the absence of evidence to the contrary, a business is assumed to have an indefinite life. The **going concern concept** presumes that an enterprise will continue to operate indefinitely and will not be sold or otherwise liquidated.

Principles

Four principles frame financial accounting information: measurement, revenue recognition, expense recognition, and full disclosure. U.S. GAAP is a mixed measurement system. It is primarily founded on the **cost principle**, meaning assets and liabilities are initially recorded at the amount paid or obligated to pay. Historical acquisition cost is considered the proper initial measurement because, for example, at the time an asset is acquired, it represents the fair value of the asset as agreed upon by both the buyer and seller. However, the fair value principle is sometimes applied after acquisition, which is a "market-based" measurement system for assets and liabilities. The **revenue recognition principle** states that sales revenue should be recorded when services are performed or goods are sold. The revenue recognition principle requires two conditions to exist before sales revenue is recorded on the income statement: (1) the revenue must be earned and (2) it must be realized or realizable. Normally, both conditions are not met until services are performed or goods are sold.[2] To the extent feasible, all expenses related to a company's earned sales revenue should be recognized (matched) with, or deducted from, that revenue in the determination of net income. The **expense recognition (matching) principle** states that net income is determined by linking any expenses incurred with the related earned sales revenues. Thus, expenses are recorded in the period that they help to generate the revenues.

Together, the revenue recognition principle and the expense recognition principle define the accrual basis of accounting. Under the **accrual basis of accounting**, sales revenue is recognized when it is both earned and realized (revenue recognition principle) and expenses are recorded in the period in which they help to generate the earned revenue (expense recognition principle). It is important to observe that recording revenues and expenses do not depend upon the receipt or payment of cash. The accrual basis of accounting is widely used. Under the **cash basis of accounting**, revenues are recorded when cash is received from operating activities and

---

[2] In 2014, the FASB and IASB issued a joint revenue recognition standard that is intended to improve financial reporting by providing consistent principles for recognizing revenue regardless of the company's industry or geography. The new rule replaces a patchwork of previous standards, and is based on a five-step process that broadly considers when goods or services are transferred from the seller to the buyer. For U.S. GAAP, the new guidance will generally be effective after December 15, 2017.

expenses are recorded when cash payments are made for operating activities. Net income, therefore, becomes the difference between operating cash receipts and operating cash payments. The cash basis is not considered generally accepted.

All information necessary for a user's understanding of financial statements should be disclosed in a company's annual report. The purpose of accounting is to provide useful information to those parties interested in a firm's financial health. Sometimes, facts or conditions exist that, although not specifically part of the data in the accounting system, have considerable influence on a full understanding and interpretation of financial statements. To properly inform financial statement users, the **full disclosure principle** requires that a business disclose all significant financial facts and circumstances.

Constraints

Two factors constrain the qualitative characteristics of accounting information: materiality and cost-benefit. Applying accounting procedures requires effort and costs money. When amounts involved are too small to affect the financial picture, the application of theoretically correct accounting procedures is hardly worth its cost. The concept of **materiality** permits a firm to expense the cost of such assets as small tools, office equipment, and furniture when acquired because their cost is "immaterial" in amount. The **cost-benefit constraint** requires that the benefit derived from the information outweighs the cost of providing it.

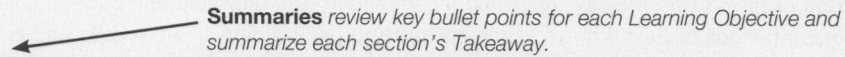

Summaries *review key bullet points for each Learning Objective and summarize each section's Takeaway.*

SUMMARY OF LEARNING OBJECTIVES

LO1   Explain business organization and its three forms. (p. 4)

- There are three primary organizational forms that a business can take. They are the sole proprietorship, the partnership, and the corporation.
- A sole proprietorship consists of a single owner. It is the most common form of business and the easiest to establish.
- A partnership is similar to a sole proprietorship except that there is more than one owner. Partnerships are also relatively easy to establish. An advantage of the partnership form over the sole proprietorship is the broader set of skills and resources that multiple partners can bring to an enterprise.
- A corporation is the most complex of the three organizational forms. The advantages of the corporate form of business include the ease of transferring ownership interests and the ease of raising funds. Another advantage is the limited liability protection it offers its owners. A disadvantage of the corporate form is the possibility of double taxation of the company's net income.

LO2   Describe business activities. (p. 5)

- Companies engage in three types of business activities: operating, investing, and financing.
- Operating activities consist of selling products or providing services to generate sales revenue and using economic resources to manufacture goods or provide services.
- Investing activities consist of those activities needed to provide the infrastructure to run a company's operations. Also included in this activity category are investments of excess cash.
- Financing activities consist of both debt financing and equity financing. Debt financing involves the procurement of a bank loan, whereas equity financing involves the sale of shares of stock to investors.

LO3   Indicate who uses accounting information. (p. 6)

- Accounting information is important to both internal and external users.
- Financial accounting produces publicly available financial statements for external users including investors, creditors, taxation authorities, regulatory agencies, labor unions, and customers.
- The process of generating and analyzing data for internal management use is referred to as managerial accounting.
- Business leaders recognize the importance of ethical behavior.

LO4   Explain the accounting process and generally accepted accounting principles. (p. 10)

- Accounting is the process of measuring the economic activities of an enterprise in monetary terms and communicating the results to interested parties.
- The basic purpose of accounting is to provide financial information that is useful in making economic decisions.
- The Financial Accounting Standards Board (FASB) is a private sector organization that has responsibility for formulating generally accepted accounting principles in the United States.

- Generally accepted accounting principles (GAAP) are the standards and procedures that guide the preparation of financial statements.
- The International Accounting Standards Board (IASB) has taken the lead role in formulating International Accounting Reporting Standards (IFRS).
- The SEC has strongly supported the establishment of international accounting standards.
- A common set of standards such as IFRS benefits multinational companies, investors, and accounting professionals.

Describe the accounting equation and each financial statement. (p. 12)   LO5

- The accounting equation, Assets = Liabilities + Stockholders' Equity, is the fundamental framework within which accounting analysis takes place.
  - Assets are the economic resources of a business that can be expressed in monetary terms.
  - Liabilities are the obligations that a business must pay in money or services in the future as a consequence of past transactions or events.
  - Stockholders' equity is the residual interest of the owners in the assets of a business.
- The *income statement* presents a company's sales revenues and expenses for a period of time.
- The *statement of stockholders' equity* reports the financial events causing a change in stockholders' equity during a period of time, and includes retained earnings and common stock.
- The *balance sheet* presents a company's assets, liabilities, and stockholders' equity as of a given date.
- The *statement of cash flows* reports a company's cash inflows and outflows during a period of time.

Explain additional disclosures that accompany financial statements. (p. 20)   LO6

In addition to the basic financial statements, the annual report includes notes to the financial statements, an independent auditor's report, and Management's Discussion and Analysis.

- The notes to the financial statements provide both a quantitative and a qualitative description of a company's financial statements and explain the numbers reported in those financial statements.
- The independent auditor's report provides a degree of assurance that a company's financial statements are presented fairly and can be relied upon for decision-making purposes.
- The Management's Discussion and Analysis (MD&A) provides management with an opportunity to both analyze past performance and discuss future opportunities and concerns involving a company.

Describe careers in accounting. (p. 22)   LO7

- Accounting graduates are in high demand and can anticipate bright employment prospects.
- Accountants can find jobs in public accounting, private corporations, or the government.

Appendix 1A: Discuss FASB's conceptual framework. (p. 25)   LO8

- The conceptual framework provides a guide to the formulation of U.S. generally accepted accounting principles.
- The framework consists of interrelated objectives, elements, characteristics, and recognition and measurement criteria.
- The financial reporting objectives of the conceptual framework focus on information useful to investors and creditors.
- The financial statement elements of the conceptual framework are the components of financial statements.
- The qualitative characteristics of accounting information are intended to contribute to decision usefulness.
- The recognition and measurement criteria of the framework specify the conditions that must be satisfied before a particular asset, liability, revenue, or expense can be recorded in the financial records.

Concept ⟶	Method ⟶	Assessment	**SUMMARY**
What mix of financing does a company use?	The balance sheet provides information regarding the various forms of financing, both debt financing and equity financing. Compare the amount of liabilities appearing on the balance sheet to the amount of equity appearing on the balance sheet.	A higher ratio of liabilities to equity implies a higher use of creditor financing, and vice versa. Creditor financing is viewed by users as more risky.	**TAKEAWAY 1.1**

SUMMARY	Concept ⟶	Method ⟶	Assessment
TAKEAWAY 1.2	Is a company profitable?	The income statement reports a company's performance for a given period of time. Compare reported sales revenue to reported expenses.	Sales revenue in excess of expenses yields net income, implying a profitable company. If expenses exceed revenue, the company has at a net loss.
TAKEAWAY 1.3	What portion of a company's current period net income is distributed to its stockholders, and what portion is retained?	The statement of stockholders' equity reports both a company's net income and the amount of dividends distributed to stockholders. Compare the company's dividends to its net income.	A higher ratio of dividends to net income implies that a company is distributing more of its net income to it stockholders, whereas a lower ratio implies that it is retaining more of its income for purposes such as growing its business.
TAKEAWAY 1.4	What are the major sources and uses of a company's cash?	The statement of cash flows reports a company's sources and uses of cash separated into three activities: operating, investing, and financing. Identify a company's sources and uses of cash as reported in the statement of cash flows.	Sources of cash are reported as positive numbers and uses of cash as negative numbers. Larger positive numbers represent major cash sources and larger negative numbers represent major cash uses.

KEY TERMS ⟵

Key Terms *are listed for each chapter with references to page numbers within the chapter.*

Accounting (p. 10)

Accounting entity (p. 27)

Accounting equation (p. 13)

Accounting period (p. 27)

Accrual basis of accounting (p. 27)

American Institute of Certified Public Accountants (AICPA) (p. 9)

Annual report (p. 20)

Assets (p. 13)

Auditor's report (p. 20)

Balance sheet (p. 13)

Cash basis of accounting (p. 27)

Certified public accountants (CPAs) (p. 7)

Comparability (p. 26)

Conceptual framework (p. 25)

Consistency (p. 26)

Contributed capital (p. 15)

Corporation (p. 4)

Cost-benefit constraint (p. 28)

Cost principle (p. 27)

Creditors (p. 5)

Debt financing (p. 5)

Earned capital (p. 15)

Equity financing (p. 5)

Ethics (p. 8)

Expense recognition (matching) principle (p. 27)

Expenses (p. 15)

Faithful representation (p. 26)

Financial accounting (p. 7)

Financial Accounting Standards Board (FASB) (p. 10)

Financial reporting objectives (p. 26)

Financial statement elements (p. 26)

Financing activities (p. 5)

Forensic accounting (p. 9)

Form 10-K (p. 20)

Full disclosure principle (p. 28)

Generally accepted accounting principles (GAAP) (p. 10)

Generally accepted auditing standards (GAAS) (p. 11)

Going concern concept (p. 27)

Governmental Accounting Standards Board (GASB) (p. 11)

Income statement (p. 14)

Institute of Management Accountants (p. 9)

International Accounting Standards Board (IASB) (p. 11)

International Financial Reporting Standards (IFRS) (p. 11)

Investing activities (p. 6)

Liabilities (p. 13)

Management's Discussion and Analysis (p. 21)

Managerial accounting (p. 8)

Materiality (p. 28)

Monetary unit concept (p. 27)

Net assets (p. 13)

Net income (p. 15)

Net loss (p. 15)

New York Stock Exchange (NYSE) (p. 5)

Notes to the financial statements (p. 20)

Operating activities (p. 6)

Partnership (p. 4)

Period-of-time statements (p. 19)

Point-in-time statement (p. 19)

Principal (p. 5)

Public Company Accounting Oversight Board (PCAOB) (p. 11)

Qualitative characteristics of accounting information (p. 26)

Recognition and measurement criteria (p. 27)

Relevance (p. 26)

Retained earnings (p. 15)

Revenue recognition principle (p. 27)

Sales revenue (p. 14)

Sarbanes-Oxley Act (p. 9)

Sole proprietorship (p. 4)

Statement of cash flows (p. 17)

Statement of stockholders' equity (p. 15)

Stockholders (p. 4)

Stockholders' equity (p. 13)

Triple bottom line (p. 16)

Understandability (p. 27)

U.S. Securities and Exchange Commission (SEC) (p. 10)

→ **Self-Study Questions** *in multiple choice format with answers provided at the end of each chapter.*

Assignments with the 🔵 **logo in the margin are available in** ^my^ BusinessCourse.
See the Preface of the book for details.

SELF-STUDY QUESTIONS

(Answers to Self-Study Questions are at the end of this chapter.)

1. Which form of business organization is characterized by limited liability?   LO1

   a. Sole proprietorship

   b. Partnership

   c. Corporation

   d. Both sole proprietorship and partnership

> **Homework** *icons indicate which assignments are available in* **myBusinessCourse** *(MBC). This feature is only available when the instructor incorporates MBC in the course.*

2. Which of the following processes best defines accounting?   LO4

   a. Measuring economic activities

   b. Communicating results to interested parties

   c. Preventing fraud

   d. Both a and b.

3. Generally accepted accounting principles are: LO4

   a. A set of guidelines to aid in the financial reporting process

   b. A set of laws to prevent financial fraud

   c. A set of standards for ethical conduct

   d. A set of voluntary "best business practices"

4. To which area of accounting are generally accepted accounting principles primarily relevant?   LO3

   a. Managerial accounting

   b. Financial accounting

   c. Tax accounting

   d. Financial reporting to all regulatory agencies

5. Which of the following is not one of the three types of business activities?   LO2

   a. Investing

   b. Financing

   c. Marketing

   d. Operating

6. If assets total $90,000 and liabilities total $50,000, how much are net assets?   LO5

   a. $40,000

   b. $90,000

   c. $140,000

   d. $50,000

LO5 7. **What are increases in resources that a firm earns by providing goods or services to its customers?**
  a. Assets
  b. Revenues
  c. Expenses
  d. Liabilities

LO6 8. **Which of the following items is not required to be included as part of a company's annual report?**
  a. Notes to the financial statements
  b. Management discussion and analysis
  c. Detailed history of the company
  d. Auditor's report

LO3 9. **Which of the following situations presents ethical challenges to accountants?**
  a. Pressure by superiors to produce a "good" number
  b. Avoiding the disclosure of confidential information
  c. An emphasis on short-term results
  d. All the above present ethical challenges to accountants

LO1 10. **Match the following organizational attributes in the left column with the organizational form in the right column that the attribute is most often associated with.**

  1. Tax advantages   *a.* Sole proprietorship
  2. Unlimited liability   *b.* Partnership
  3. Shared control   *c.* Corporation
  4. Most complex to set up
  5. Easiest to raise a large amount of funds
  6. Single owner

LO5 11. **The financial statements of Power Company contain the following. How much is net income?**

Accounts payable.	$12,000
Revenues	19,000
Accounts receivable.	10,000
Expenses	8,000
Cash.	7,000

  a. $6,000   *c.* $19,000
  b. $11,000   *d.* $17,000

LO5 12. **If Chandler Company reports its year-end total liabilities to be $85,000, and its year-end stockholders' equity to be $100,000, how much are Chandler Company's year-end total assets?**
  a. $15,000
  b. $185,000
  c. $100,000
  d. Cannot be determined from the given information

LO5 13. **Huff Company began the year with a retained earnings balance of $30,000, reported net income for the year of $45,000, and reported ending retained earnings of $60,000. How much dividends did Huff Company report for the year?**
  a. $135,000   *c.* $15,000
  b. $35,000   *d.* $30,000

QUESTIONS

1. Define *accounting*. What is the basic purpose of accounting?

2. What is the distinction between *financial* accounting and *managerial* accounting?

3. Who are some of the outside groups that may be interested in a company's financial data and what are their particular interests?

4. What are *generally accepted accounting principles* and what organization has primary responsibility for their formulation in the United States?

5. What are the main advantages and disadvantages of the corporate form of business?

6. What role does financial accounting play in the allocation of society's financial resources?

7. What is the accounting equation? Define *assets, liabilities,* and *stockholders' equity.*

8. What are the three principal business activities and how do they differ?

9. What is meant by corporate social responsibility?

10. What is the difference between generally accepted accounting principles (GAAP) and international financial reporting standards (IFRS)?

11. What are *revenues* and *expenses*?

12. What is the purpose of an income statement? The statement of stockholders' equity? The balance sheet? The statement of cash flows?

13. What is a *period-of-time statement*? Give three examples.

14. What is a *point-in-time statement*? Give one example.

15. On December 31, the Mill Company had $800,000 in total assets and owed $250,000 to creditors. If the corporation's common stock amounted to $400,000, what amount of retained earnings should appear on its December 31 balance sheet?

16. What are three aspects of the accounting environment that may create ethical pressure on an accountant?

17. What type of information might you find in the Management's Discussion and Analysis (MD&A) section of the annual report?

18. What is the purpose of having the financial statements audited by an independent auditor?

19. Determine whether the following statements are true or false and explain why:

    a. The accounting process is only interested in communicating economic activity.
    b. There are few potential users of financial accounting information.
    c. Financial accounting is primarily used to communicate to outside users.
    d. Auditors ensure the validity of a company's financial statements.

20. Why did the FASB develop a conceptual framework?

21. What are two primary qualities of accounting information that contribute to decision usefulness?

22. How would you describe, in one sentence, each of the following accounting principles, concepts and constraints?

Accounting entity	Consistency
Accounting period	Revenue recognition
Monetary unit	Expense recognition (matching)
Cost-benefit	Materiality
Going concern	Full disclosure

23. Which of the following is a primary qualitative characteristic of accounting information?
    a. Relevance
    b. Faithful representation
    c. Comparability
    d. All of the above are important characteristics.

SHORT EXERCISES

SE1-1. Forms of Business Organization Match the following forms of business organization with the set of attributes that best describes that form of business: sole proprietorship, partnership, or corporation.

    a. Shared control, unlimited liability, tax advantages, increased skills and resources
    b. Best for raising large amounts of funds, double taxation, limited liability, easiest to transfer ownership interests
    c. Sole ownership, easiest to establish, tax advantages, unlimited liability

LO1

LOs *link assignments to the Learning Objectives of each chapter.*

LO4 **SE1-2.** **Accounting Processes** Identify the following processes as either measuring or communicating.

    a. Prepare financial statements for the entity

    b. Identify relevant economic activities of the entity

    c. Record relevant economic activities of the entity

    d. Interpret financial results of the entity

    e. Quantify relevant economic activities of the entity

LO3 **SE1-3.** **Types of Statements** Match the following type of report with the most likely statement user: management, taxation authority, regulatory agency, or investor.

    a. Financial statements

    b. Tax return

    c. Annual budget

    d. Special report on a bank's financial health

LO4 **SE1-4.** **Accounting Organizations** Match the following organizations with the set of accounting guidelines: Financial Accounting Standards Board (FASB), International Accounting Standards Board (IASB).

    a. Generally accepted accounting principles (GAAP)

    b. International financial reporting standards (IFRS)

LO2 **SE1-5.** **Business Activities** Match the following activities with the type of activity: Operating, Investing, Financing.

    a. Day-to-day business activities

    b. Purchase of land for a new warehouse

    c. Sale of merchandise inventory

    d. Obtain a new bank loan

    e. Payment of dividends

    f. Invest excess cash

    g. Purchase office supplies

    h. Sell old equipment that is no longer needed

LO5 **SE1-6.** **Financial Statement Items** Identify the financial statement (or statements) in which each of the following items would appear: income statement (IS), statement of stockholders' equity (SSE), balance sheet (BS), or statement of cash flows (SCF).

    a. Assets

    b. Revenues

    c. Cash flow from investing activities

    d. Stockholders' equity

    e. Expenses

    f. Net change in cash

    g. Net income

    h. Liabilities

LO6 **SE1-7.** **Annual Report Components** Which of the following would not be part of the notes to the financial statements in a company's annual report?

    a. Qualitative information about potential lawsuits

    b. Additional information about the reported total of notes payable

    c. Details about potential new products to be introduced during the next year

    d. Details of estimates used to compute the expected amount of warranty expense

LO3 **SE1-8.** **Sarbanes-Oxley Act** The Sarbanes-Oxley Act of 2002 was enacted to help restore confidence in financial reporting. Which of the following was not part of the legislation?

    a. Severe penalties for fraudulent reporting

    b. A requirement for certification of the financial statements by top management

    c. A new statement of social responsibility

    d. A report on controls to help prevent and detect errors in the reporting process

SE1-9. Financial Accounting and Generally Accepted Accounting Principles Answer the following multiple-choice questions: **LO4**

1. What is not a primary function of financial accounting in society?
   a. Provide comedy material for late-night talk shows.
   b. Aid in the proper allocation of financial resources in a free enterprise economic system.
   c. Aid users to make better investing decisions.
2. IFRS refers to:
   a. A random set of letters.
   b. A set of standards and procedures that form guidelines for international financial accounting.
   c. A set of standards and procedures that form guidelines for international managerial accounting.
3. GAAP:
   a. Is the distance between two objects.
   b. Is a set of guidelines for preparing managerial reports in the United States.
   c. Is a set of guidelines for preparing financial reports in the United States.

SE1-10. Cash Flow Activity Classification Classify each activity as financing, investing, or operating: **LO2**

1. Repay a loan from a bank.
2. Sell merchandise from a storefront operation.
3. Dispose of an old delivery truck.
4. Pay rent on a company warehouse.
5. Repurchase shares of stock from stockholders.
6. Pay utilities.

SE1-11. Using the Basic Accounting Equation Use the basic accounting equation to answer the following: **LO5**

a. Perkins Company has total assets of $150,000 and total liabilities of $90,000. How much is the company's total stockholders' equity?
b. Gassol Company has total liabilities of $170,000 and total stockholders' equity of $95,000. How much total assets does the company have?
c. If Brown Company's total assets increased by $35,000 during the year, and its total liabilities decreased during the same year by $5,000, what was the change in the company's total stockholders' equity?

SE1-12. Using the Basic Accounting Equation Henderson Company had beginning-of-the-year total assets of $300,000 and total liabilities of $180,000.   **LO5**

a. If during the year total assets increased by $15,000 and total liabilities increased by $40,000, what is the end-of-year total stockholders' equity?
b. If during the year total assets increased by $60,000 and total liabilities decreased by $5,000, what is the end-of-year total stockholders' equity?
c. If during the year total liabilities increased by $40,000 and total stockholders' equity increased by $35,000, what are the end-of-year total assets?

SE1-13. Financial Statements Indicate which statement (or statements) you would examine to locate the following items: balance sheet (BS), income statement (IS), statement of stockholders' equity (SSE), or statement of cash flows (SCF).   **LO5**

a. Expenses for the period
b. Cash at year-end
c. Cash used to purchase new equipment
d. Dividends for the period

SE1-14. Financial Statements Indicate which statement (or statements) you would examine to locate the following items: balance sheet (BS), income statement (IS), statement of stockholders' equity (SSE), or statement of cash flows (SCF).   **LO5**

a. Revenues for the period
b. Cash at year-end
c. Cash used to pay back borrowings
d. Dividends for the period

LO4 **SE1-15. International Accounting Principles** The worldwide acceptance of a global set of international accounting principles will provide certain benefits.

    a. Which group has taken the lead in developing a set of international accounting principles?

    b. Identify and briefly discuss two major benefits that would result from the adoption of a global set of international accounting principles.

LO8
(Appendix 1A)

SE1-16. Principles of Accounting Which of the following accounting principles applies to the statement of cash flows?

    a. Materiality

    b. Conservatism

    c. Accrual basis of accounting

    d. Cash basis of accounting

LO8
(Appendix 1A)

SE1-17. Generally Accepted Accounting Principles Select the best answer to each of the following questions:

    1. Accounting rules are developed to provide:
        a. Simplicity
        b. Useful information
        c. Complexity
        d. Ability to change over time

    2. The conceptual framework consists of each of the following except:
        a. Financial reporting objectives
        b. Financial statement elements
        c. Ratio analysis guidelines for analysts
        d. Recognition criteria for financial statement items

    3. Which of the following is a financial statement element?
        a. Income statement
        b. Liabilities
        c. Balance sheet
        d. Statement of cash flows

LO8
(Appendix 1A)

SE1-18. Basic Accounting Principles Match the following list of accounting concepts, principles, and assumptions with the definitions below:

Accounting period concept	Consistency	Cost principle
Going concern concept	Materiality constraint	Full disclosure principle
	Comparability	

    1. Ability to compare the financial performance of different companies.

    2. Assumption that a company will continue to operate beyond the current period.

    3. Only items large enough to make a difference to a user must be disclosed in the financial statements.

    4. Prepare financial statements at set time intervals.

    5. Record assets on the balance sheet at an amount equal to what was paid for them.

    6. A company prepares its financial statements using the same methods used in prior periods.

    7. All items of importance to the users of financial statements should be disclosed in the annual report.

LO4 **SE1-19. FASB Codification** A major reason for the codification project completed by the FASB in 2009 was to:

    a. ease the convergence between financial and managerial accounting

    b. ease the convergence between U.S. GAAP and IFRS

    c. ease the convergence between financial and tax accounting

    d. ease the convergence between U.S. GAAP and GASB

SE1-20. Basic Accounting Principles Which of the following is not considered a qualitative characteristic of accounting information?

LO8
(Appendix 1A)

    a. faithful representation
    b. comparability
    c. assets must equal liabilities and stockholders' equity
    d. relevance

SE1-21. Basic Accounting Principles Identify whether the following statements are true or false.

LO8
(Appendix 1A)

    1. Together the revenue recognition principle and the expense recognition (matching) principle define the accrual basis of accounting.
    2. The cash basis of accounting is only used in the preparation of the statement of cash flows.
    3. The accrual basis of accounting is used in the preparation of the income statement and the balance sheet.

EXERCISES—SET A

E1-1A. Forms of Business Organization Match the following organizational attributes in the left column with the organizational form in the right column. More than one organizational form may be associated with a given attribute.

LO1

    1. Unlimited liability
    2. Full control
    3. Business income combined with owner(s) income for income tax purposes
    4. Relatively more difficult to establish
    5. Easier to raise funds

    a. Sole proprietorship
    b. Partnership
    c. Corporation

E1-2A. Accounting Process Establish the correct sequence of steps in the accounting measurement process.

LO4

    a. Record in a systematic fashion
    b. Identify relevant economic activity
    c. Quantify economic activity

E1-3A. Types of Accounting Identify the type of accounting associated with each type of report: Managerial, Financial, Tax, or some combination as needed.

LO3

    a. Budget for internal use by management
    b. Tax return for state income taxes
    c. Audited financial statements
    d. Special reports for regulators of a public utility

E1-4A. Corporate Social Responsibility Which of the following is not part of the triple bottom line reporting framework?

LO5

    a. Economic bottom line
    b. Social bottom line
    c. Competitive bottom line
    d. Environmental bottom line

E1-5A. Generally Accepted Accounting Principles Identify whether the following statements are true or false:

LO4

    a. U.S. GAAP is universally accepted in all countries in the world.
    b. U.S. GAAP is established by the IASB.
    c. Once established, U.S. GAAP is rarely, if ever, modified.
    d. The international counterpart to the FASB is the IASB.

E1-6A. Business Activities Identify each of the following activities as operating (O), investing (I), or financing (F):

LO2

    a. Payment of employee salaries
    b. Repayment of a loan
    c. Issuance of common stock
    d. Purchase of equipment to manufacture a company's products
    e. Sale of merchandise inventory
    f. Investment of excess cash in the shares of another company

LO5 **E1-7A.** **The Accounting Equation** Determine the missing amount in each of the following cases:

Assets	Liabilities	Stockholders' Equity
$175,000	$62,000	?
?	$47,000	$31,000
$115,000	?	$49,000

LO5 **E1-8A.** **Determining Net Income** The beginning and ending balances of retained earnings for the year were $50,000 and $65,000, respectively. If dividend payments during the year were $4,000, determine the net income or net loss for the year.

    a. $19,000 net loss
    b. $19,000 net income
    c. $15,000 net income
    d. $11,000 net income

LO5 **E1-9A.** **Determining Retained Earnings and Net Income** The following information appears in the records of Bock Corporation at year-end:

Accounts receivable.	$ 28,000	Retained earnings	$?
Accounts payable.	12,000	Supplies	8,000
Cash.	7,000	Equipment, net.	145,000
Common stock.	115,000		

    a. Calculate the balance in retained earnings at year-end.
    b. If the amount of the retained earnings at the beginning of the year was $38,000, and $13,000 in dividends is paid during the year, calculate net income for the year.

LO5 **E1-10A.** **Determining Stockholders' Equity and Assets** Determine the following:

    a. The stockholders' equity of a corporation that has assets of $550,000 and liabilities of $306,000.
    b. The assets of a corporation that has liabilities of $250,000, common stock of $100,000, and retained earnings of $85,000.

LO5 **E1-11A.** **Financial Statements** Karl Flury operates a golf driving range. For each of the following financial items related to his business, indicate the financial statement (or statements) in which the item would be reported: balance sheet (BS), income statement (IS), statement of stockholders' equity (SSE) or statement of cash flows (SCF).

    a. Accounts receivable
    b. Cash received from the sale of land
    c. Net income
    d. Cash invested in the business by Flury
    e. Notes payable
    f. Supplies expense
    g. Land
    h. Supplies

LO5 **E1-12A.** **Omitted Financial Statement Data** For the following four unrelated situations, A through D, calculate the unknown amounts appearing in each column:

	A	B	C	D
Beginning				
Assets......................................	$45,000	$32,000	$53,000	?
Liabilities..................................	28,000	15,000	29,000	19,000
Ending				
Assets......................................	50,000	30,000	41,000	52,000
Liabilities..................................	22,000	?	20,000	24,000
During Year				
Sales revenue.............................	?	26,000	31,000	27,000
Expenses	12,000	22,000	12,000	19,000
Dividends	2,000	3,000	?	4,000

E1-13A. Other Components of the Annual Report Identify where the following items will appear in a company's annual report: Management's Discussion and Analysis (MD&A), notes to the financial statements, or the auditor's report, or indicate that the item is not disclosed.

LO6

a. A comment that the financial statements appear to be fairly presented
b. A discussion about new competition likely to occur next year
c. A quantitative summary of notes payable appearing on the balance sheet
d. The "secret" ingredients in the company's special sauce

E1-14A. Ethics In each of the following cases, (a) identify the aspect of the accounting environment primarily responsible for the ethical pressure on the accountant as pressure to achieve a favorable outcome, to disclose confidential information, or to report good short-term results, and (b) indicate the appropriate behavioral response for the accountant.

LO3

Ethics *assignments are denoted by this icon.*

1. James Jehring, a tax accountant, is preparing an income tax return for a client. The client asks Jehring to take a sizable deduction on the tax return for business-related travel even though the client states that he has no documentation to support the deduction. "I don't think the IRS will audit my return," declares the client.
2. Willa English, an accountant for Dome Construction Company, has just finished putting the numbers together for a construction project on which the firm is going to submit a bid next month. At a social gathering that evening, a friend casually asks English what Dome's bid is going to be. Ms. English knows that the friend's brother works for a competitor of Dome.
3. The manager of Cross Department Store is ending his first year with the firm. December's business was slower than expected, and the firm's annual results are trailing last year's results. The manager instructs Kyle Tarpley, the store accountant, to include sales revenues from the first week of January in the December data. "This way, we'll show an increase over last year," declares the manager.

E1-15A. International Accounting Principles Identify whether the following statements are true or false.

LO4

1. One argument for IFRS is that companies raise capital in more than one country.
2. IFRS is accepted as GAAP in every country of the world.
3. The SEC allows foreign companies to file their annual reports using IFRS.

E1-16A. The Conceptual Accounting Framework The Financial Accounting Standards Board worked many years to develop a conceptual framework for U.S. GAAP.

LO8
(Appendix 1A)

a. What is the purpose of a conceptual framework?
b. Identify the financial reporting objectives that are specified in the conceptual framework.

E1-17A. Recognition and Measurement Criteria Indicate the accounting concepts, principles, or constraints that underlie each of the following independent situations: accounting entity concept, going concern concept, cost-benefit constraint, expense recognition (matching principle), materiality constraint, revenue recognition principle, full disclosure principle, cost principle.

LO8
(Appendix 1A)

a. Dr. Kline is a practicing pediatrician. Over the years, she has accumulated a personal investment portfolio of securities, virtually all of which have been purchased from her earnings as a pediatrician. The investment portfolio is not reflected in the accounting records of her medical practice.

  b. A company purchases a desk tape dispenser for use by the office secretary. The tape dispenser cost $10 and has an estimated useful life of 15 years. The purchase is immediately expensed on the company's income statement.

  c. A company sells a product that has a two-year warranty covering parts and labor. In the same period that revenues from product sales are recorded, an estimate of future warranty costs is recorded on the company's income statement.

  d. A company is sued for $1 million by a customer claiming that a defective product caused an accident. The company believes that the lawsuit is without merit. Although the case will not be tried for a year, the company adds a note describing the lawsuit to its current financial statements.

LO8
(Appendix 1A)

E1-18A. Revenue Recognition Principle For each of the following situations, determine whether the criteria for revenue recognition have been met by December 31, 2015.

  a. A manufacturing company received $50,000 cash on December 31, 2015, as an advance payment on a special order for a piece of equipment. The equipment will be manufactured by March 31, 2016.

  b. A television dealer acquired six new high-definition television sets for $8,400 cash on December 31, 2015, and advertised their availability, at $2,000 each, in that evening's newspaper.

  c. A snow removal service signed a contract on November 15, 2015, with a shopping mall to clear its parking lot of all snowfalls over 1 inch during the months of December 2015 through March 2016. The cost is $600 per month and payment is due in two $1,200 installments: January 2, 2016, and February 1, 2016. By December 31, 2015, no snowfall over 1 inch had occurred.

LO5, 8
(Appendix 1A)

MBC

E1-19A. Accrual Basis of Accounting versus Cash Basis of Accounting On December 31, Sawyer Patterson completed his first year as a financial planner. The following data are available from his accounting records:

Fees billed to clients for services rendered	$131,000	Rent expense for year just ended	$12,000
Cash received from clients.	111,000	Utility expenses incurred	5,100
Supplies purchased for cash	7,100	Utility bills paid	3,300
Supplies used during the year	6,100	Salary earned by assistant	39,400
Cash paid for rent (rent is paid through Mar. of next year)	15,000	Salary paid to assistant	35,100

  a. Compute Sawyer's net income for the year just ended using the accrual basis of accounting.

  b. Compute Sawyer's net income for the year just ended using the cash basis of accounting.

  c. Which net income amount is computed in accordance with generally accepted accounting principles?

LO8
(Appendix 1A)

E1-20A. Recognition and Measurement Criteria The following are unrelated accounting practices:

  1. Vine Company purchased a new $18 snow shovel that is expected to last six years. The shovel is used to clear the firm's front steps during the winter months. The shovel's cost is recorded on the company's balance sheet as an asset.

  2. Filene Corporation has been named as the defendant in a $40 million pollution lawsuit. Because the lawsuit will take several years to resolve and the outcome is uncertain, Filene's management decides not to mention the lawsuit in the current year financial statements.

Required

For each of the given practices, indicate which accounting concepts, principles, or constraints apply and whether they have been applied appropriately. For each inappropriate accounting practice, indicate the proper accounting procedure.

EXERCISES—SET B

E1-1B. Forms of Business Organization Match the following organizational attributes in the left column   **LO1**
with the organizational form in the right column. More than one organizational form may be associated with a given attribute.

1. Limited liability	*a.* Sole proprietorship
2. Shared control	*b.* Partnership
3. Double taxation	*c.* Corporation
4. Easiest to form	
5. Easier to transfer ownership	

E1-2B. The Accounting Process Establish the correct sequence of steps in the accounting measurement   **LO4**
process.

a. Quantify economic activity
b. Identify relevant economic activity
c. Record in a systematic fashion

E1-3B. Types of Accounting Identify the type of accounting associated with each type of report: Managerial,   **LO3**
Financial, Tax, or some combination as needed.

a Cost report for a new product
b. Tax return for federal income taxes
c. Unaudited financial statements requested for a bank loan
d. Special report for banking regulators

E1-4B. Corporate Social Responsibility Which of the following is not part of the triple bottom line reporting framework?   **LO5**

a. Social bottom line
b. Environmental bottom line
c. Economic bottom line
d. Efficiency bottom line

E1-5B. Generally Accepted Accounting Principles Identify whether the following statements are true or   **LO4**
false.

a. GAAP can differ from one country to another
b. U.S. GAAP is established by the FASB.
c. U.S. GAAP is a guide to action that may change over time.
d. At this time there is no international counterpart to the FASB.

E1-6B. Business Activities Identify each of the following activities as operating (O), investing (I), or financing (F).   **LO2**

a. Payment of rent on the company headquarters
b. Repurchase of the company's common stock
c. Obtain a long-term bank loan
d. Sale of an empty warehouse
e. Delivery of consulting service
f. Sale of short-term investments

E1-7B. The Accounting Equation Determine the missing amount in each of the following cases: **LO5**

Assets	Liabilities	Stockholders' Equity
$350,000	?	$210,000
$130,000	$95,000	?
?	$65,000	$ 59,000

LO5   **E1-8B.**   **Determining Net Income** The beginning and ending balances of retained earnings for the year were $55,000 and $82,000, respectively. If dividend payments during the year were $8,000, determine the net income or net loss for the year.

    a. $14,000 net loss
    b. $27,000 net income
    c. $35,000 net income
    d. $14,000 net income

LO5   **E1-9B.**   **Determining Retained Earnings and Net Income** The following information appears in the records of Boco Corporation at year-end:

Accounts receivable...............	$ 42,000	Retained earnings	$?
Accounts payable.................	21,000	Supplies	30,000
Cash...........................	18,000	Equipment, net...................	105,000
Common stock...................	125,000		

    a.   Calculate the amount of retained earnings at year-end.
    b.   If the amount of the retained earnings at the beginning of the year was $25,000, and $10,000 in dividends is paid during the year, calculate net income for the year.

LO5   **E1-10B.**   **Determining Stockholders' Equity and Assets** Determine the following:

    a.   The stockholders' equity of a corporation that has assets of $850,000 and liabilities of $310,000.
    b.   The assets of a corporation that has liabilities of $195,000, common stock of $110,000, and retained earnings of $80,000.

LO5   **E1-11B.**   **Financial Statements** Kattie Klein operates a bakery. For each of the following financial statement items related to her business, indicate the financial statement (or statements) in which the item would be reported: balance sheet (BS), income statement (IS), statement of stockholders' equity (SSE) or statement of cash flows (SCF).

    a.   Accounts payable
    b.   Cash received from the sale of equipment
    c.   Net loss
    d.   Cash invested in the business by Klein
    e.   Notes receivable
    f.   Rent expense
    g.   Building
    h.   Inventory

LO5   **E1-12B.**   **Omitted Financial Statement Data** For the following four unrelated situations, A through D, calculate the unknown amounts appearing in each column:

	A	B	C	D
Beginning				
Assets............................	$38,000	$22,000	$38,000	?
Liabilities.........................	28,000	15,000	29,000	19,000
Ending				
Assets............................	40,000	36,000	44,000	50,000
Liabilities.........................	22,000	?	20,000	24,000
During Year				
Sales revenue.....................	?	26,000	31,000	27,000
Expense	12,000	22,000	12,000	19,000
Dividends	2,000	3,000	?	4,000

LO6   **E1-13B.**   **Other Components of the Annual Report** Identify where the following items will appear in a company's annual report: Management's Discussion and Analysis (MD&A), notes to the financial statements, or the auditor's report, or indicate that the item is not disclosed.

    a.   A comment that the statements are presented in conformity with generally accepted accounting principles
    b.   A discussion about new products to be introduced next year
    c.   A quantitative summary of property, plant, and equipment appearing on the balance sheet
    d.   The salaries of every employee

E1-14B. Ethics In each of the following cases, (a) identify the aspect of the accounting environment primarily responsible for the ethical pressure on the accountant as pressure to achieve a favorable outcome, to disclose confidential information, or to report good short-term results, and (b) indicate the appropriate behavioral response for the accountant.

LO3

1. Jenny Jones, a tax accountant, is preparing an income tax return for a client. The client asks Jones to omit some income she received for consulting services because the amount was paid in cash. "I don't think the IRS will audit my return," declares the client. "And even if they do, what are the chances they would catch this?"
2. Fred French, an accountant for Top Electronics Company, has just finished estimating the cost for a new iPod device that the company plans to introduce. Cost estimates help the company to determine the price they can charge for new products. At a social gathering that evening, a friend casually asks Fred what Top's cost for the iPod device came out to be. Fred knows that the friend's brother works for a competitor of Top Electronics.
3. The manager of Jazz Department Store is ending his first year with the firm. December's business was slower than expected, and the firm's annual results are below Wall Street's expectations. The manager instructs Chris Green, store accountant, to record some of December's expenses in the following year. "This way, we'll meet Wall Street's expectations," declares the manager.

E1-15B. International Accounting Principles Although there are obstacles to the worldwide acceptance of a global set of international accounting principles, the potential benefits appear significant.

Identify and briefly discuss three potential benefits to the worldwide acceptance of a global set of international accounting principles.

LO4

E1-16B. The Conceptual Framework The Financial Accounting Standards Board worked many years to develop a conceptual framework for U.S. GAAP.

LO8
(Appendix 1A)

a. Identify the financial statement elements that are specified in the conceptual framework.
b. Before a financial statement element may be recorded in the accounts, certain recognition criteria must be met. What are those recognition criteria?

E1-17B. Recognition and Measurement Criteria Indicate the accounting concepts, principles, or constraints that underlie each of the following independent situations: accounting entity concept, going concern concept, cost-benefit constraint, expense recognition (matching principle), materiality constraint, revenue recognition principle, full disclosure principle, cost principle.

LO8
(Appendix 1A)

a. Ford Motor Company reports in its annual report to stockholders that revenues from automotive sales "are recorded by the company when products are shipped to dealers."
b. The annual financial report of Chrysler Corporation and subsidiaries includes the financial data of its significant subsidiaries, including Chrysler Financial Corporation (which provides financing for dealers and customers), Chrysler Technologies Corporation (which manufactures high-technology electronic products), and Pentastar Transportation Group, Inc. (which includes Thrifty Rent-A-Car System, Inc., and Dollar Rent A Car Systems, Inc.).
c. A company purchased a parcel of land several years ago for $65,000. The land's estimated current market value is $80,000. The Land account balance is not increased but remains at $65,000.
d. A company has a calendar-year fiscal year-end. On January 8, 2013, a tornado destroyed its largest warehouse, causing a $1,800,000 loss. This information is reported in a footnote to the 2012 financial statements.

E1-18B. Revenue Recognition Principle For each of the following situations, determine whether the criteria for revenue recognition have been met by December 31, 2015.

LO8
(Appendix 1A)

a. A manufacturing company received $70,000 cash on December 31, 2015, as an advance payment on a special order for a piece of equipment. The equipment will be manufactured by March 31, 2016.
b. An appliance dealer acquired ten new washer/dryer sets for $7,800 cash on December 31, 2015, and advertised their availability, at $1,000 for each set, in that evening's newspaper.
c. A yard maintenance service signed a contract on October 15, 2015, with an apartment complex to maintain its grounds during the months of November 2015 through June 2016. The cost is $500 per month and payment is due in two $2,000 installments: December 15, 2015 and March 15, 2016.

LO5, 8
(Appendix 1A)

E1-19B. Accrual Basis of Accounting versus Cash Basis of Accounting On December 31, Hermani Patterson completed his first year as a financial planner. The following data are available from his accounting records:

Fees billed to clients for services rendered	$137,000	Rent expense for year just ended	$12,000
Cash received from clients.................	115,000	Utility expense incurred	5,200
Supplies purchased for cash	7,500	Utility bills paid	3,200
Supplies used during the year	6,800	Salary earned by assistant...............	39,000
Cash paid for rent (rent is paid through		Salary paid to assistant	35,000
Feb. of next year)	14,000		

    a.   Compute Hermani's net income for the year just ended using the accrual basis of accounting.

    b.   Compute Hermani's net income for the year just ended using the cash basis of accounting.

    c.   Which net income amount is computed in accordance with generally accepted accounting principles?

LO8
(Appendix 1A)

E1-20B. Recognition and Measurement Criteria The following are unrelated accounting practices:

    1.   A recession has caused a slowing of business activity and lower profits for Balke Company. Consequently, the firm delays making its payments for December's rent and utilities until January and does not record either of these expenses in December.

    2.   Gail Derry, a consultant operating as a sole proprietorship, used her business car for a personal, month-long vacation. A full year's gas and oil expenditures on the car are charged to the firm's gas and oil expense account.

Required

For each of the given practices, indicate which accounting concepts, principles, or constraints apply and whether they have been applied appropriately. For each inappropriate accounting practice, indicate the proper accounting procedure.

PROBLEMS—SET A

LO1

P1-1A. Forms of Business Organization Presented below are four independent situations:

    a.   Kali Kane, a senior in college looking for summer employment, decided to start a dog-walking business. Each morning and evening she picks up a group of dogs and walks them around the city park.

    b.   Brothers Joe and Jay Simmons each owned a separate electronics repair shop. They decided to combine their talents and resources in order to expand the amount of business they could undertake.

    c.   Three chemists at a large engineering company decided to start their own business based on an experimental chemical process they had developed outside the company. The process had the potential to be very successful; however, it was quite dangerous and could result in large legal problems.

    d.   Jack Prince ran a small, but successful holistic healing spa. The spa has gained a strong reputation beyond the community where it is located. Jack decided to open a chain of similar spas across the state to capitalize on his reputation. This will require a substantial investment in supplies and employee training. In addition, since Jack will not be able to closely supervise each location, he is worried about potential liability.

Required

Explain the form of organization that would be best in each situation—sole proprietorship, partnership, or corporation. Explain what factors you considered important in each situation.

LO5

P1-2A. Financial Statements While each of the financial statements is likely to aid in any business decision, it is often the case that a particular financial statement may be best suited to help in a particular decision. Consider each decision below independently:

    a.   You are trying to determine whether a particular firm is a good investment. You understand that share price increases are impacted heavily by a company's earnings potential.

b. You are employed in the lending department of a large bank. You are trying to determine if you should lend to a potential customer. If you do make the loan you are especially concerned that the company will have sufficient collateral in the event that it is unable to repay the loan.

c. You wish to invest in a firm that provides you with a steady source of income. You especially want a firm that pays out a large part of its net income as dividends.

d. You are trying to determine if a particular firm will have sufficient cash flow in order to keep expanding without relying too heavily on external sources of financing.

Required

Determine which of the financial statements contains the most useful information to help in your decision. Explain what information you used from each statement to help you make your decision.

P1-3A. Balance Sheet The following balance sheet data are for Normandy Catering Service, a corporation, at May 31, 2016: **LO5**

Accounts receivable.	$27,300	Accounts payable.	10,200
Notes payable	29,000	Cash.	14,200
Equipment, net.	61,000	Common stock.	41,500
Supplies.	16,400	Retained earnings	?

Required

Prepare a balance sheet for Normandy as of May 31, 2016.

P1-4A. Statement of Stockholders' Equity and Balance Sheet The following is balance sheet information for Lynch Janitorial Service, Inc., at the end of 2016 and 2015: **LO5**

	December 31, 2016	December 31, 2015
Accounts payable.	$ 6,000	$ 9,000
Cash.	25,000	22,000
Accounts receivable.	39,000	31,000
Land.	46,000	46,000
Building, net.	250,000	260,000
Equipment, net.	44,000	46,000
Mortgage payable	93,000	103,000
Supplies.	18,000	16,000
Common stock.	225,000	225,000
Dividends.	12,000	0
Retained earnings	?	?

Required

a. Prepare a balance sheet as of December 31 of each year.

b. Prepare a statement of stockholders' equity for 2016. (*Hint:* The increase in retained earnings is equal to the net income less the dividend.)

P1-5A. Statement of Stockholders' Equity and Balance Sheet The following is balance sheet information for House Janitorial Service, Inc., at the end of 2016 and 2015: **LO5**

	December 31, 2016	December 31, 2015
Accounts payable.	$ 12,000	$ 18,000
Cash.	50,000	44,000
Accounts receivable.	78,000	62,000
Land.	92,000	92,000
Building, net.	500,000	520,000
Equipment, net.	75,000	77,000
Mortgage payable	175,000	205,000
Supplies.	27,000	30,000
Common stock.	420,000	420,000
Dividends.	20,000	0
Retained earnings	?	?

Required

a. Prepare a balance sheet as of December 31 of each year.

b. Prepare a statement of stockholders' equity for 2016. (*Hint:* The increase in retained earnings is equal to the net income less the dividend.)

LO5   **P1-6A.**   **Income Statement and Balance Sheet**   On March 1, 2016, Amy Dart began Dart Delivery Service, which provides delivery of bulk mailings to the post office, neighborhood delivery of weekly newspapers, data delivery to computer service centers, and various other delivery services using leased vans. On February 28, Dart invested $20,000 of her own funds in the firm and borrowed $8,000 from her father on a six-month, non-interest-bearing note payable. The following information is available at March 31:

Accounts receivable	$10,700	Delivery fees earned	$23,300
Rent expense	2,500	Cash	12,700
Advertising expense	1,100	Supplies inventory	15,800
Supplies expense	2,500	Notes payable	8,000
Accounts payable	1,400	Insurance expense	900
Salaries expense	6,200	Common stock	20,000
Miscellaneous expense	300	Retained earnings	?

Required

a. Prepare an income statement for the month of March.

b. Prepare a balance sheet as of March 31, 2016.

LO5   **P1-7A.**   **Statement of Cash Flows**   Shown below is selected information from the financial records of Mantle Corporation as of December 31:

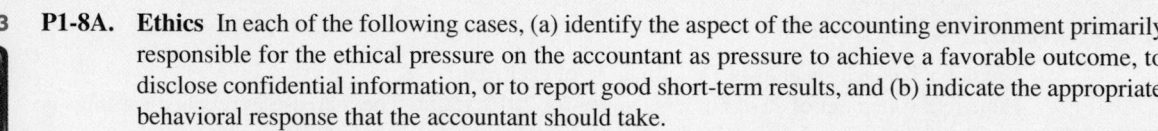

Inventory	$165,000	Cash purchase of equipment	$ 29,000
Cash collected from customers	350,000	Buildings, net	810,000
Equipment, net	355,000	Sales revenue	910,000
Retained earnings	480,000	Cash paid for operating activities	205,000
Cash dividends paid	38,000	Principal payments on existing note payable	41,000
Salary expense	215,000	Common stock	529,000

Required

a. Determine which of the above items will appear on the statement of cash flows and then prepare the statement for Mantle Corporation for the year ended December 31, 2016.

b. Comment on the adequacy of Mantle's operations to provide cash for its investing and financing activities.

LO3   **P1-8A.**   **Ethics**   In each of the following cases, (a) identify the aspect of the accounting environment primarily responsible for the ethical pressure on the accountant as pressure to achieve a favorable outcome, to disclose confidential information, or to report good short-term results, and (b) indicate the appropriate behavioral response that the accountant should take.

1. Patricia Kelly, an accountant for Wooden Company, is reviewing the costs charged to a government contract that Wooden worked on this year. Wooden is manufacturing special parts for the government and is allowed to charge the government for its actual manufacturing costs plus a fixed fee. Kelly notes that $75,000 worth of art objects purchased for the president's office is buried among the miscellaneous costs charged to the contract. Upon inquiry, the firm's vice president replies, "This sort of thing is done all the time."

2. Barry Marklin, accountant for Smith & Wesson partnership, is working on the 2016 year-end financial data. The partnership agreement calls for Smith and Wesson to share the firm's 2016 net income equally. In 2017, the partners will share the net income 60 percent to Smith and 40 percent to Wesson. Wesson plans to cut back his involvement in the firm. Smith wants Marklin to delay recording sales revenue from work done at the end of 2016 until January 2017. "We haven't received the cash yet from those services," declares Smith.

3. The St. Louis Wheelers, a professional football franchise, just signed its first-round draft pick to a multiyear contract that is reported in the newspapers as a four-year, $20 million contract. Johanna Factor, the Wheelers' accountant, receives a call from an agent of another team's first-round pick.

"Just calling to confirm the contract terms reported in the papers," states the agent. "My client should receive a similar contract, and I'm sure you don't want him to get shortchanged."

P1-9A.   Financial Statements and Other Components   Match each of the items in the left column with the appropriate annual report component from the right column: **LO5, 6**

1. The company's total liabilities	a. Income Statement
2. The sources of cash during the period	b. Balance Sheet
3. An opinion about whether the financial statements are fairly stated	c. Statement of Cash Flows
	d. Statement of Stockholders' Equity
4. The amount of dividends that are distributed to the company's stockholders	e. Notes to the Financial Statements
	f. Management's Discussion and Analysis (MD&A)
5. A discussion of potential new products to be introduced the next year	g. Auditor's report
6. Information regarding accounting methods used	
7. The company's total revenue for the period	

P1-10A.   Income Statement, Statement of Stockholders' Equity, and Balance Sheet   Napolean Corporation   **LO5**
started business on January 1, 2016. The following information was compiled by Napolean's accountant on December 31, 2016:

Sales revenue.	$32,000	Equipment, net.	$28,000
Expenses	20,000	Building, net.	59,000
Dividends	5,000	Accounts payable.	7,000
Cash.	3,250	Notes payable	50,500
Accounts receivable.	2,750	Common stock.	33,000
Inventory.	4,500	Retained earnings	?

Required

a.   You have been asked to assist the accountant for the Napolean Corporation in preparing year-end financial statements. Use the above information to prepare an income statement, statement of stockholders' equity, and a balance sheet as of December 31, 2016.

b.   Comment on the decision to pay a $5,000 dividend.

P1-11A.   Recognition and Measurement Criteria   The following are unrelated accounting situations and the   **LO8**
accounting treatment that was followed in each firm's records: **(Appendix 1A)**

1. Martin Company mounts a $600,000 year-long advertising campaign on a national cable television network. The firm's annual accounting period is the calendar year. The television network required full payment in December at the beginning of the campaign. Accounting treatment is
     Increase Advertising Expense, $600,000
     Decrease Cash, $600,000

2. Because of a local bankruptcy, machinery worth $200,000 was acquired at a "bargain" purchase price of $180,000. Accounting treatment is
     Increase Machinery, $180,000
     Decrease Cash, $180,000

3. Tim Vagly, a consultant operating a sole proprietorship, withdrew $20,000 from the business and purchased stocks as an investment gift to his wife. Accounting treatment is
     Increase Investments, $20,000
     Decrease Cash, $20,000

4. Sioux Company received a firm offer of $96,000 for a parcel of land it owns that cost $68,000 two years ago. The offer was refused, but the indicated gain was recorded in the accounts. Accounting treatment is
     Increase Land, $28,000
     Increase Revenue from Change in Land Value, $28,000

Required

In each of the given situations, indicate which accounting concepts, principles or constraints apply and whether they have been applied appropriately. If you decide the accounting treatment is not generally accepted, discuss the effect of the departure on the balance sheet.

PROBLEMS—SET B

LO1   **P1-1B.**   **Forms of Business Organization**

Presented below are four independent situations:

a.   Dino Owens, a photography major in college, decided to start a photography business specializing in weddings and similar occasions. Dino is still able to go to school full-time as all of his jobs are on weekends or holidays.

b.   Joe Thursday and Jay Lightfoot each owned a separate detective agency. They decided to combine their talents and resources in order to expand the amount of business they could undertake.

c.   Three business school professors at a large university decided to start their own consulting business based on their combined talents. They feel that the insurance they can obtain will satisfy any possible legal issues they may face. They plan to use one professor's home office to meet clients, so start-up costs should be minimal.

d.   Vera Gold runs a small, but successful beauty salon. The salon has gained a strong reputation beyond the community where it is located. Vera has decided to open a chain of similar salons across the state to capitalize on her reputation. This will require a substantial investment in facilities and supplies. In addition, since Vera will not be able to closely supervise each location, she is worried about potential liability.

Required

Explain the form of organization that would be best in each situation—sole proprietorship, partnership, or corporation. Explain what factors you considered important in each situation.

LO5   **P1-2B.**   **Financial Statements**   While each of the financial statements is likely to aid in any business decision, it is often the case that a particular financial statement may be best suited to help in a particular decision. Consider each decision below independently:

a.   You are trying to determine whether a particular firm is a good investment. You want to invest in a firm that has strong revenue growth.

b.   You are employed as a financial analyst for a large investment firm. You are trying to assess the riskiness of a particular investment opportunity. You understand that the more debt a firm has relative to its stockholders' equity, the riskier the firm is.

c.   You are trying to determine how much of a firm's net income it distributes to its stockholders.

d.   You are trying to determine how a particular firm was able to finance its large expansion during the year.

Required

Determine which of the financial statements contains the most useful information to help in your decision. Explain what information you used from each statement to help you make your decision.

LO5   **P1-3B.**   **Balance Sheet**   The following balance sheet data are for Bettis Plumbing Contractors, Inc., a corporation, at May 31, 2016:

Accounts payable.	$ 9,900	Common stock.	$101,000
Cash	15,700	Retained earnings	?
Equipment, net	100,000	Notes payable	31,000
Supplies	28,500	Accounts receivable.	9,200
Land	25,000		

Required

Prepare a balance sheet for Bettis as of May 31, 2016.

P1-4B. **Statement of Stockholders' Equity and Balance Sheet** The following is balance sheet information   **LO5**
for Jordon Packaging Service at the end of 2016 and 2015:

	December 31, 2016	December 31, 2015
Accounts payable.	$ 2,800	$ 2,600
Cash.	11,000	12,000
Accounts receivable.	23,800	19,500
Equipment, net.	33,000	28,000
Notes payable	21,000	21,000
Supplies .	5,700	5,200
Common stock.	6,000	6,000
Dividends .	13,000	0
Retained earnings	?	?

Required
a.   Prepare a balance sheet as of December 31 of each year.
b.   Prepare a statement of stockholders' equity for 2016. (*Hint:* The increase in retained earnings is equal to the net income less the dividend.)

P1-5B. **Statement of Stockholders' Equity and Balance Sheet** The following is balance sheet information   **LO5**
for Jackson Packaging Service at the end of 2016 and 2015:

	December 31, 2016	December 31, 2015
Accounts payable.	$ 16,000	$ 14,000
Cash.	53,000	47,000
Accounts receivable.	80,000	64,000
Equipment, net.	76,000	78,000
Notes payable	175,000	175,000
Supplies .	29,000	31,000
Common stock.	30,000	30,000
Dividends .	15,000	0
Retained earnings	?	?

Required
a.   Prepare a balance sheet as of December 31 of each year.
b.   Prepare a statement of stockholders' equity for 2016. (*Hint:* The increase in retained earnings is equal to the net income less the dividend.)

P1-6B. **Income Statement and Balance Sheet** The first year records of R. Levy, Interior Decorator, show   **LO5**
the following information for the year-end December 31, 2016:

Notes payable	$ 6,000	Supplies	$ 9,500
Decorating fees earned	57,600	Cash.	6,200
Insurance expense.	1,600	Accounts receivable.	8,600
Supplies expense.	8,100	Advertising expense.	700
Miscellaneous expense	1,200	Salaries expense	33,000
Common stock.	7,000	Rent expense.	4,500
Retained earnings	?	Accounts payable.	2,800

Required
a.   Prepare an income statement for the year.
b.   Prepare a balance sheet as of December 31, 2016.

LO5 **P1-7B.** **Statement of Cash Flows** Shown below is selected information from the financial records of Mays Corporation as of December 31, 2016:

Inventory	$145,000	Cash purchase of equipment	$129,000
Cash collected from customers	670,000	Buildings, net	860,000
Equipment, net	255,000	Sales revenue	940,000
Retained earnings	580,000	Cash paid for operating activities	425,000
		Principal payments on existing	
Cash dividends paid	85,000	note payable	128,000
Salary expense	226,000	Common stock	329,000

Required

a. Determine which of the above items will appear on the statement of cash flows and then prepare the statement for Mays Corporation for the year ended December 31, 2016.

b. Comment on the adequacy of Mays' operations to provide cash for its investing and financing activities.

LO3 **P1-8B.** **Ethics** In each of the following cases, (a) identify the aspect of the accounting environment primarily responsible for the ethical pressure on the accountant as pressure to achieve a favorable outcome, to disclose confidential information, or to report good short-term results, and (b) indicate the appropriate behavioral response that the accountant should take:

1. Kenneth Mills, an accountant for the Riley Company, is reviewing costs charged to a big government contract to supply logistical support. The contract specifies that Riley is entitled to its cost plus 10 percent extra for profit. Kenneth notices that gardening services at the home of the company president, Stu Riley, are included under miscellaneous expenses. The company's vice president, Slick Lowe, tells you not to worry about this since the government expects a little bit of fancy accounting to be included in all of its contracts.

2. Sergio Salles, an accountant for the law partnership Dewy and Suem, is working on the year-end financial statements. Currently the two partners, Dewy and Suem, each receive one-half of the firm's net income. Next year the allocation will change to a two-thirds, one-third split since Suem will be taking considerable time off to do pro bono work, something Dewy never does. Dewy suggested to Salles that he delay booking a large partial settlement the partnership received in December until January of next year when they will receive the final cash payment. Dewy commented that it would be "cleaner" to keep it all together.

3. Pete Freely is the accountant for a large professional services firm. Part of his responsibility is to complete payroll tax reports based on the salaries paid to all the employees. Pete received a call from a friend at a search firm that specializes in personnel such as those employed at Pete's place of employment. Pete's friend casually asked how much certain employees were making, explaining he wanted to be able to calibrate market wages for work he was doing.

LO5, 6 **P1-9B.** **Financial Statements and Other Components** Match each of the items in the left column with the appropriate annual report component from the right column:

1. The company's total assets
2. An opinion regarding whether the financial statements followed GAAP
3. Information regarding the estimates used in the financial statements
4. The use of cash during the period
5. The company's total expenses for the period
6. A discussion of potential risks that a company may encounter in the future
7. The amount of a company's earnings that are distributed to the company's stockholders

a. Income Statement
b. Statement of Stockholders' Equity
c. Balance Sheet
d. Statement of Cash Flows
e. Management's Discussion and Analysis (MD&A)
f. Notes to the Financial Statements
g. Auditor's report

P1-10B. Income Statement, Statement of Stockholders' Equity, and Balance Sheet Prag Corporation **LO5** started business on January 1, 2016. The following information was compiled by Prag's accountant on December 31, 2016:

Sales revenue.	$52,000	Equipment, net.	$27,000
Expenses	41,000	Building, net.	49,000
Dividends	8,000	Accounts payable.	8,000
Cash.	5,250	Notes payable	49,500
Accounts receivable.	6,750	Common stock.	33,000
Inventory.	5,500	Retained earnings	?

Required

a. You have been asked to assist the accountant for the Prag Corporation in preparing year-end financial statements. Use the above information to prepare an income statement, statement of stockholders' equity, and a balance sheet as of December 31, 2016.

b. Comment on the decision to pay an $8,000 dividend.

P1-11B. Recognition and Measurement Criteria The following are unrelated accounting situations and the **LO8** accounting treatment that was followed in each firm's records: **(Appendix 1A)**

1. The Baldwin Company mounts an $800,000 year-long advertising campaign on a new national cable television network. The firm's annual accounting period is the calendar year. The television network required full payment in December at the beginning of the campaign. Accounting treatment is
   Increase Advertising Expense, $800,000
   Decrease Cash, $800,000

2. Because of a local bankruptcy, machinery worth $300,000 was acquired at a "bargain" purchase price of $150,000. Accounting treatment is
   Increase Machinery, $150,000
   Decrease Cash, $150,000

3. J.P. Smith, a consultant operating a sole proprietorship, withdrew $40,000 from the business and purchased stocks as an investment gift to his wife. Accounting treatment is
   Increase Investments, $40,000
   Decrease Cash, $40,000

4. Morongo Company received a firm offer of $106,000 for a parcel of land it owns that cost $75,000 two years ago. The offer was refused, but the indicated gain was recorded in the accounts. Accounting treatment is
   Increase Land, $31,000
   Increase Revenue from Change in Land Value, $31,000

Required

In each of the given situations, indicate which accounting concepts, principles or constraints apply and whether they have been applied appropriately. If you decide the accounting treatment is not generally accepted, discuss the effect of the departure on the balance sheet.

SERIAL PROBLEM: KATE'S CARDS

SP1. Kate Collins has always been good at putting together rhymes for any occasion. Recently, Kate's financial assistance for college was cut back due to budget problems in the state where she lives. Kate determined that the best way to raise enough money to stay in school and still have enough time for her studies was to start a greeting card business. She feels that this will not only help her to raise money, but it will supplement what she is learning at school as a business major.

Kate decided that she would start small and work out of her dorm room, designing the cards on a new Apple iMac that she was planning to purchase. Kate also decided to offer classes in greeting card design to other aspiring greeting card producers. After much thought, Kate decided to name her business "Kate's Cards."

Kate's Cards is a continuous problem that requires students to apply the concepts from the current chapter. There is a Kate's Cards assignment in each of the financial accounting chapters of the text.

Required

a. What form of business—sole proprietorship, partnership, or corporation—should Kate choose? Discuss why the organizational form that you selected is most appropriate for Kate.

b. What accounting information will Kate need to run her business?

c. What balance sheet accounts—assets, liabilities, and stockholders' equity—and income statement accounts—revenues and expenses—will Kate likely need to use?

d. Should Kate use her personal bank account or open a separate business bank account?

Extending Your Knowledge *assignments require use of the real-world financial statements and critical thinking skills.*

EXTENDING YOUR KNOWLEDGE

REPORTING AND ANALYSIS

COLUMBIA SPORTSWEAR COMPANY

EYK1-1. **Financial Reporting Problem: Columbia Sportswear Company** Financial statements for the **Columbia Sportswear Company** are reported in Appendix A at the end of the textbook.

Required
Refer to Columbia Sportswear's financial statements to answer the following questions:

a. How much did Columbia's total assets increase or decrease from December 31, 2013, to December 31, 2014?

b. How much did Columbia's cash and cash equivalents increase or decrease from December 31, 2013, to December 31, 2014, and how much cash did Columbia report on its December 31, 2014, balance sheet?

c. How much accounts receivable and accounts payable did Columbia report on December 31, 2014?

d. Did Columbia experience revenue growth in 2014?

e. Was Columbia profitable in 2014? How does the company's 2014 profit compare to 2013?

COLUMBIA SPORTSWEAR COMPANY

UNDER ARMOUR

EYK1-2. **Comparative Analysis Problem: Columbia Sportswear Company vs. Under Armour, Inc.** Simplified financial statements for the **Columbia Sportswear Company** are reported in **Exhibit 1-11** and **Under Armour**'s financial statements are presented in **Appendix B** at the end of this book.

Required
1. Based on the information in these financial statements, compare the following for each company as of December 31, 2014:
   a. Total assets
   b. Sales
   c. Net income
   d. Cash flow from operations
2. From this information, what can you conclude about the relative size and operating performance of each company?

EYK1-3. **Business Decision Problem** Paul Seale, a friend of yours, is negotiating the purchase of an exterminating company called Total Pest Control. Seale has been employed by a national pest control service and knows the technical side of the business. However, he knows little about accounting, so he asks for your assistance. The owner of Total Pest Control, Greg Krey, provided Seale with income statements for the past three years, which showed an average net income of $72,000 per year. The latest balance sheet shows total assets of $285,000 and liabilities of $45,000. Seale brings the following matters to your attention:

1. Krey is asking $300,000 for the firm. He told Seale that because the firm has been earning a 30 percent return on stockholders' equity, the price should be higher than the net assets reported on the balance sheet. (Note: The return on stockholders' equity is calculated as net income divided by total stockholders' equity.)

2. Seale noticed that there was no salary expense reported for Krey on the income statements, even though he worked half-time in the business. Krey explained that, because he had other income, he withdrew only $18,000 each year from the firm for personal use. If he purchases the firm, Seale will hire a full-time manager to run the firm at an annual salary of $36,000.

3. Krey's tax returns for the past three years report a lower net income for the firm than the amounts shown in the financial statements. Seale is skeptical about the accounting principles used in preparing the company's financial statements.

Required

a. If Seale accepts Krey's average annual income figure of $72,000, what would Seale's return on stockholders' equity be, assuming that the net income remained at the same level and that the firm was purchased for $300,000?

b. Should Krey's withdrawals of $18,000 per year affect the net income reported in the financial statements? What will Seale's percentage return be if he takes into consideration the $36,000 salary he plans to pay a full-time manager?

c. Could there be legitimate reasons for the difference between net income as shown in the financial statements and net income as reported on the tax returns, as mentioned in point 3? How might Seale obtain additional assurances about the propriety of the company's financial statements?

EYK1-4. **Financial Analysis Problem** Todd Jansen is deciding among several job offers. One job offer he is considering is in the marketing department at Columbia Sportswear. Before he makes his decision, he decides to review the financial reports of the company.

Required

Use the Columbia Sportswear annual report located in Appendix A at the end of this book to answer the following questions:

a. Were the financial statements of Columbia audited? If so, what firm performed the audit?

b. What was the amount of Columbia's 2014 net income? How does this compare with 2013 net income?

c. How much cash was provided or used for investing activities? What were the major sources and uses of cash from investing activities?

d. How much were accrued liabilities in 2014? What makes up this balance?

e. What are some of the more significant estimates used in the preparation of the company's financial statements?

f. To what amount are the financial statements rounded?

CRITICAL THINKING

EYK1-5. **Accounting Research Problem** Go to this book's Website and locate the annual report of General Mills, Inc. for the year ending May 25, 2014 (fiscal year 2014).

GENERAL MILLS, INC.

Required

a. Refer to the company's balance sheet.
   1. What form of business organization does General Mills use? What evidence supports your answer?
   2. What is the date of the most recent balance sheet?
   3. For the most recent balance sheet, what is the largest asset reported? The largest liability?

b. Refer to the company's income statement.
   1. What time period is covered by the fiscal year 2014 statement of earnings?
   2. What total amount of sales revenue did General Mills generate in the most recent period? What is the change in sales revenues from last year to the current report year?
   3. What is the net income (i.e., net earnings, including earnings attributable to noncontrolling interests) for the most recent period?

c. Refer to the company's statement of cash flows.
   1. For the most recent period, what is the amount and trend of the cash flow from operating activities?
   2. For the most recent period, what is the amount and trend of the cash flow from investing activities?
   3. For the most recent period, what is the amount and trend of the cash flow from financing activities?

EYK1-6. **Accounting Communication Activity** Jasper Simmons is an intern for the Newby Company. He knows the company's balance sheet is supposed to balance, but he is not having much luck getting it to balance. Jasper knows that you are taking a course in accounting so he asks for your help. Jasper provides you with the following balance sheet that is currently out of balance:

NEWBY COMPANY				
Balance Sheet				
December 31, 2016				
Assets			**Liabilities**	
Cash....................	15,000	Inventory...........................	20,000	
Accounts receivable...........	30,000	Notes payable	38,000	
Equipment, net...............	28,000	**Stockholders' Equity**		
Accounts payable............	(22,000)	Dividends...........................	(11,000)	
		Common stock.....................	10,000	
		Retained earnings, beginning of year......	10,000	
Total.....................	51,000	Total...............................	67,000	

In addition, Jasper provides you with a correct income statement that reports a net income for 2016 of $24,000.

Required
a. Prepare a corrected balance sheet for the Newby Company.
b. Write a memo to Jasper explaining what he did wrong.
c. In the memo explain the purpose of the balance sheet.

EYK1-7. **Accounting Ethics Case** Jack Hardy, CPA, has a brother, Ted, in the retail clothing business. Ted ran the business as a sole proprietor for 10 years. During this 10-year period, Jack helped Ted with various accounting matters. For example, Jack designed the accounting system for the company, prepared Ted's personal income tax returns (which included financial data about the clothing business), and recommended various cost control procedures. Ted paid Jack for all of these services. A year ago, Ted expanded the business and incorporated. Ted is president of the corporation and also chairs the corporation's board of directors. The board of directors has overall responsibility for corporate affairs. When the corporation was formed, Ted asked Jack to serve on its board of directors. Jack accepted. In addition, Jack now prepares the corporation's income tax returns and continues to advise his brother on accounting matters.

Recently, the corporation applied for a large bank loan. The bank wants audited financial statements for the corporation before it will decide on the loan request. Ted asked Jack to perform the audit. Jack replied that he cannot do the audit because the code of ethics for CPAs requires that he be independent when providing audit services.

Required
Why is it important that a CPA be independent when providing audit services? Which of Jack's activities or relationships impair his independence?

EYK1-8. **Ethics** As the accountant for Minkow Corporation, you are responsible for reporting the company's profit. It appears that the company's actual results are much better than was expected by Wall Street analysts. Your supervisor has requested that you report some of next period's expenses now so that this period's profits will be in line with analyst expectations. He states that you are not really doing anything wrong since the reported results will be more conservative. In addition, this will make it easier to make next year's numbers. What should you do?

COLUMBIA
SPORTSWEAR
COMPANY

EYK1-9. **Corporate Social Responsibility Problem** Go to the **Columbia Sportswear Company** Website and find the section on their commitment to corporate and environmental responsibility. These sections can be found near the bottom of their home page under the section "About Us."

Required
Answer the following questions.
a. How does Columbia describe the company's efforts at corporate responsibility?
b. How is the Higg Index used by Columbia's environmental responsibility efforts?

    c. What featured initiative has Columbia embarked upon?

    d. Why do you think that Columbia makes these efforts to be a good corporate citizen? Why do you think they devote so much space on their Website to promote these efforts?

EYK1-10. Forensic Accounting Problem Go to the Association of Certified Fraud Examiners Website and find their description of a forensic accountant. This can be found under the Career tab, Career Paths, then click on Accounting followed by Forensic Accountant (www.acfe.com/career-path-forensic-accountant.aspx).

Forensic Accounting *assignments are denoted by this icon.*

Required

Answer the following questions.

    a. What do forensic accountants do?

    b. What skills and abilities should a forensic accountant possess?

    c. How might the knowledge learned from this course help you to become a forensic accountant?

EYK1-11. Analyzing IFRS Financial Statements The 2014 financial statements of LVMH Moet Hennessey-Louis Vuitton S.A. are presented in Appendix C at the end of this book. LVMH is a Paris-based holding company and one of the world's largest and best-known luxury goods companies. As a member of the European Union, French companies are required to prepare their consolidated (group) financial statements using International Financial Reporting Standards (IFRS). After reviewing LVMH's consolidated financial statements, consider the following questions:

    a. What is LVMH's largest asset account on its 2014 balance sheet? What percentage of total assets does this asset represent?

    b. Is LVMH principally debt financed or equity financed in 2014? What percentage of LVMH's assets is financed with debt?

    c. Is LVMH profitable in 2014? What percentage of the company's sales revenue in 2014 is represented by its "profit for the year," or its net income?

    d. How much is LVMH's cash flow from operating activities in 2014? How does LVMH's profit for the year (net income) compare with its cash flow from operating activities?

EYK1-12. Working with the Takeaways You have just learned that you inherited a large sum of money. You know that it is important to invest this money wisely, and you have decided to invest in the shares of several different companies. One of those companies is the Columbia Sportswear Company.

Required

Answer the following questions regarding your potential investment in Columbia Sportswear shares:

    a. Should you request financial statements from the company, and if so, which ones?

    b. Is it important that the financial statements be audited by an independent auditor? Explain.

    c. What does each of the four financial statements tell you about Columbia's financial health or operating performance?

ANSWERS TO SELF-STUDY QUESTIONS:

1. c, (pp. 4–5) 2. d, (p. 10) 3. a, (p. 10) 4. b, (pp. 7–8) 5. c, (pp. 5–6) 6. a, (p. 13) 7. b, (p. 14) 8. c, (pp. 20–21) 9. d, (pp. 8–9) 10. (pp. 4–5)

    1. Sole proprietorship and partnership

    2. Sole proprietorship and partnership

    3. Partnership

    4. Corporation

    5. Corporation

    6. Sole proprietorship

11. b, (p. 15) 12. b, (pp. 13–14) 13. c, (pp. 15–16)

YOUR TURN! SOLUTIONS

Solution 1.1

Sole proprietorship: Easiest to set up, owner controlled, and tax advantages.

Partnership: Relatively easy to establish, larger skill set, and tax advantages.

Corporations: Easiest to raise capital, easiest to transfer ownership, and protection against personal liability.

Solution 1.2

1. Financing
2. Operating
3. Investing
4. Operating
5. Financing
6. Operating

Solution 1.3

1. The financial statements are the primary output of financial accounting. External users require information on a business's performance and financial position. This is the type of information provided by the financial statements. Managerial accounting involves the process of generating and analyzing financial data to use for internal decision making and management of the business.
2. Internal users include management, the marketing department, and the finance department, among others. Each of these groups require data to help them run their departments and make good business decisions.
3. External users include, among others, investors, lenders, and regulators. These external groups require accounting information to help them make decisions regarding a company's performance and financial position.

Solution 1.4

Your supervisor is asking you to participate in the preparation of fraudulent financial statements. This is not only unethical it is also illegal and could subject you to criminal prosecution. By reporting the sales revenue early, the financial statements will mislead users into thinking the company is doing better than it actually is. This in turn may lead them to make erroneous investment decisions. You should not follow your supervisor's request. Instead you should explain to your supervisor why reporting sales revenue prior to when it is earned is unethical. If your supervisor continues to pressure you, you should report your supervisor's request to a higher level of management in the company.

Solution 1.5

1. c
2. a
3. d
4. b

Solution 1.6

KANZU CORPORATION Income Statement For Year Ended December 31, 2016	
Sales revenue.	$20,000
Expenses	12,000
Net income.	$ 8,000

KANZU CORPORATION
Statement of Stockholders' Equity
For Year Ended December 31, 2016

	Common Stock	Retained Earnings	Total
Balance, January 1, 2016.	$ 0	$ 0	$ 0
Add: Common stock issued.	20,000		20,000
Net income.		8,000	8,000
Less: Dividends		(3,000)	(3,000)
Balance, December 31, 2016.	$20,000	$5,000	$25,000

KANZU CORPORATION
Balance Sheet
December 31, 2016

Assets			**Liabilities**		
Cash.	$ 1,500		Accounts payable.	$ 4,000	
Accounts receivable.	2,500		Notes payable	33,000	
Inventory.	3,000		Total liabilities.		$37,000
Building	40,000		**Stockholders' Equity**		
Equipment	15,000		Common stock.	20,000	
Total assets	$62,000		Retained earnings	5,000	
			Total stockholders' equity		25,000
			Total liabilities and stockholders' equity . . .		$62,000

KANZU CORPORATION
Statement of Cash Flows
For Year Ended December 31, 2016

Cash flow from operating activities	$ 6,500
Cash flow from investing activities.	(55,000)
Cash flow from financing activities.	50,000
Net increase in cash.	1,500
Cash at January 1, 2016	0
Cash at December 31, 2016	$ 1,500

Solution 1.7

1. c
2. b
3. a

2 Processing Accounting Information

PAST

Chapter 1 described the environment of financial accounting. It also introduced the financial statements and how they are related.

PRESENT

This chapter explains the accounting system, including transaction analysis, the system of debits and credits, and the journalizing of transactions.

FUTURE

Chapter 3 describes accounting adjustments, the construction of financial statements, and the period-end closing process.

LEARNING OBJECTIVES

1. **Identify** the five major steps in the accounting cycle. *(p. 60)*

2. **Analyze** and **record** transactions using the accounting equation. *(p. 61)*

3. **Explain** the nature, format, and purpose of an account. *(p. 68)*

4. **Describe** the system of debits and credits and its use in recording transactions. *(p. 68)*

5. **Explain** the process of journalizing and posting transactions. *(p. 70)*

6. **Describe** the trial balance. *(p. 79)*

A "QUICK" WAY TO DO ACCOUNTING

While not everyone is familiar with the company **Intuit Inc.**, nearly everyone that works in the business world is familiar with some of its products. Intuit is a software company based in Mountain View California that develops the popular financial and tax preparation software QuickBooks, Quicken, and TurboTax.

Quicken was founded in 1983 by Scott Cook and Tom Prouix. At that time Mr. Cook realized that personal computers would eventually replace pencil-and-paper based accounting systems if proper software was available.

Mr. Cook's notion has been proven correct, and Intuit now has over $4.5 billion in annual sales with net income of nearly $1 billion. The company is quite valuable with a market capitalization of nearly $25 billion. Intuit is consistently ranked in *Fortune's* "Top 100 Best Companies to Work For." Certainly the company can put its software to good use accounting for all this financial activity.

While software such as QuickBooks certainly makes accounting for transactions a lot easier by automating the process, the basic accounting remains the same as a manual pencil-and-paper system. This chapter describes the details of the accounting system of debits and credits. That system is applied throughout the world in all business settings. This chapter also explains the process of journalizing and posting transactions so that financial statements can be prepared for both internal and external users of accounting. The system described in this chapter also provides the foundation for accounting software used on computers. In addition, a knowledge of accounting can prove very helpful for not only working at a company like Intuit, but for nearly every company.

PROCESSING ACCOUNTING INFORMATION				
Accounting Cycle	**Analyzing Transactions**	**The Account**	**Recording Transactions**	**Trial Balance**
• Five major steps • Accounting period	• Using the accounting equation • Expanding the accounting equation • Transaction analysis: An illustration	• Chart of accounts • T-account • System of debits and credits	• General journal • Posting journal entries to general ledger • Illustration of recording process	• Purpose of trial balance • Limitations of trial balance

ACCOUNTING CYCLE

LO1 Identify the five major steps in the accounting cycle.

Businesses engage in economic activities. The role of accounting is to analyze these activities for their impact on a company's accounting equation, and then enter the results of that analysis in the company's accounting system. When a company's management team needs financial data for decision-making purposes and for reports to external parties, the company's financial statements are prepared and communicated. At the end of the accounting period, the "books are closed," a process that prepares the accounting records for the next accounting period. The accounting activities described constitute major steps in the **accounting cycle**—a sequence of activities undertaken by accountants to accumulate and report the financial information of a business. Stated succinctly, these steps are analyze, record, adjust, report, and close. **Exhibit 2-1** shows the sequence of the major steps in the accounting cycle.

Exhibit 2-1	Five Major Steps in the Accounting Cycle

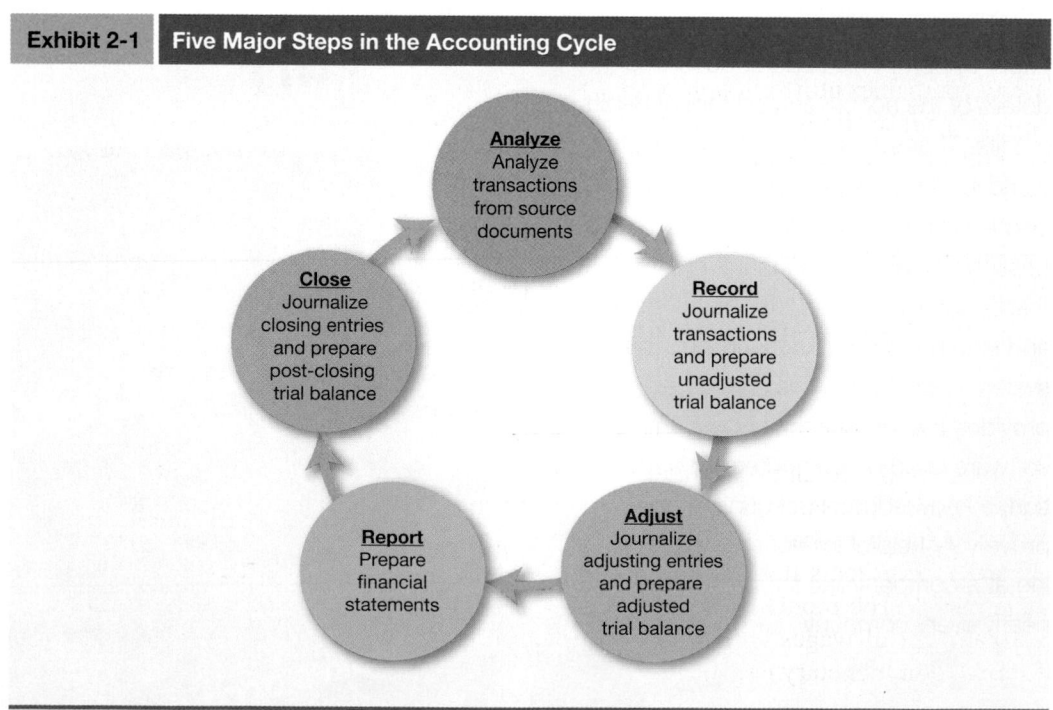

The five steps in the accounting cycle do not occur with equal frequency. A business analyzes and records financial transactions daily during the accounting period. It adjusts and reports accumulated financial data whenever management needs financial information, usually at weekly, monthly, or quarterly intervals, but at least annually. Closing the books occurs just once, at the end of the accounting period. This chapter focuses on the first two steps of the accounting cycle—analyze and record. In Chapter 3, we examine the final three steps of the cycle.

It is important to know that the steps in the accounting cycle are undertaken whether a business uses a manual accounting system or a computer based system like QuickBooks by **Intuit**. This chapter explains the accounting cycle using a manual system for Web-Work, a Website development and consulting business launched on December 1, 2016.

Accounting Periods	ACCOUNTING IN PRACTICE

The annual accounting period is known as a **fiscal year**. Businesses with fiscal year-ends on December 31, are said to be on a **calendar year**. About 60 percent of U.S. businesses are on a calendar year. Many companies prefer to have their accounting year coincide with their "natural" year—that is, at a point in time when business activity is at a low point. For example, many retailers conclude their fiscal year when inventory quantities are low and easier to count, as year-end accounting procedures are more efficiently accomplished when there is less inventory. The "natural" year does not necessarily coincide with the calendar year. For example, **Gap**, a retailer, ends its fiscal year on the Friday nearest January 31. The company's busiest period is November through January, when its customers are holiday shopping. Similarly, the **Boston Celtics**, a professional basketball team, concludes its fiscal year on June 30, following completion of the NBA finals.

Place the following five major steps in the accounting cycle in the proper order:

a) Report   c) Close   e) Adjust

b) Record   d) Analyze

YOUR TURN! 2.1

The solution is on page 118.

ANALYZING TRANSACTIONS

Many companies utilize a computer-based accounting system to record their financial transactions. You may have some personal experience using accounting software programs like QuickBooks by **Intuit**. While these computer-based accounting systems are not as sophisticated as the systems used by major corporations, they work in much the same way. Similarly, manual systems might lack the sophistication of large accounting systems utilized by companies like **Ford Motor Company**, but the basic process remains the same.

LO2 Analyze and **record** transactions using the accounting equation.

The accounting equation is written as:

Assets = Liabilities + Stockholders' equity

This accounting equation provides a convenient way to analyze and summarize a company's financial transactions and data. The first step in the accounting cycle—analyze—is to determine just what information (if any) must be recorded in a company's accounting records. Only items that can be expressed in monetary terms are recorded in financial statements. (The monetary unit concept was discussed in Appendix 1A.) For example, the payment of wages to Tim Cook, the CEO of **Apple**, is recorded because it can be expressed in monetary terms.

An **accounting transaction** is an economic event that must be recorded in the company's accounting records. In general, any event that affects any of the elements of the accounting equation—assets, liabilities, or stockholders' equity—must be recorded in a company's accounting records. Some activities—for example, ordering supplies, bidding on a contract, or negotiating the purchase of an asset—may represent a business activity, but an accounting transaction does not occur until such activities result in a change in an asset, liability, or stockholders' equity account.

An accounting transaction affects at least two elements of the accounting equation, but the equation must always remain in balance. This is where the term **double-entry accounting** comes from. For example, if an asset account such as Cash is increased, one of the following financial events must also occur to keep the accounting equation in balance:

a. Another asset, such as Accounts Receivable, must decrease; or
b. A liability, such as Notes Payable, must increase; or
c. Stockholders' equity, such as Common Stock, must increase.

IFRS ALERT

Both the FASB in the United States and the FASB's international counterpart, the IASB, are working hard to "harmonize" remaining differences between U.S. GAAP and IFRS. One area that these organizations do not need to worry about is how double-entry accounting works. The same process that is described in this chapter, using debits and credits, is universally followed.

Accounting Equation Expanded

Stockholders' equity has two components—the amount invested by stockholders (common stock) and the cumulative net income of the business that has not yet been distributed to stockholders as a dividend (retained earnings). Common stock is increased when the company issues shares of stock. Retained earnings is increased by revenues and decreased by expenses (revenues and expenses are the elements of a company's net income or net loss). Retained earnings is also decreased by a company's payment of dividends. Incorporating these two components into stockholders' equity, the *expanded accounting equation* is illustrated in **Exhibit 2-2**.

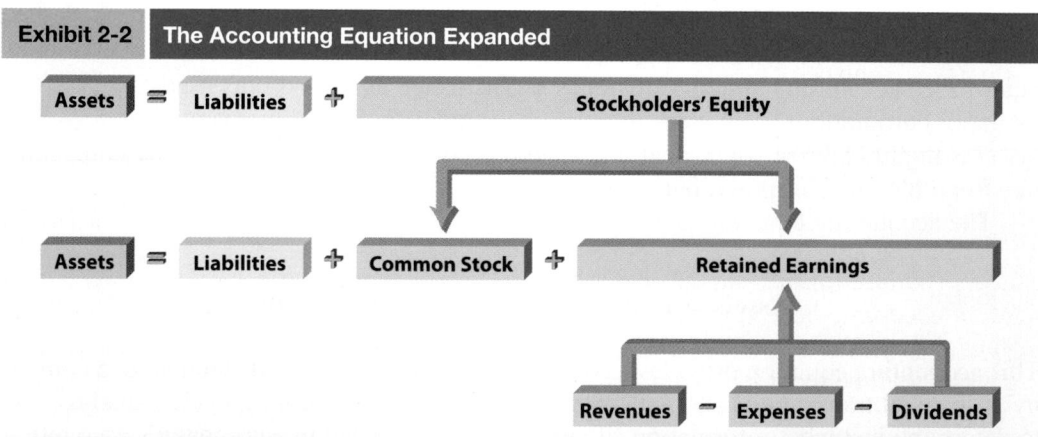

Exhibit 2-2 **The Accounting Equation Expanded**

Transactions and the Accounting Equation: An Illustration

We now consider the transactions of WebWork, Inc., a developer of web-based applications, to illustrate how various economic activities and events lead to financial statements.

Steve Gates first established WebWork on December 1, 2016. The company's transactions for December, the first month of operations, are analyzed on the following pages. The accounting equation for WebWork is shown after each transaction so that the financial effects of each transaction can be examined. The accounting equation remains in balance following each transaction. This is not a coincidence; it is the result of the fundamental structure of the accounting system.

The following pages illustrate eleven transactions that occurred at WebWork during December 2016. Avoid the temptation to skip any of these transactions because each transaction is included to illustrate a particular concept or approach to recording an economic event utilizing the accounting equation.

Transaction 1. Issued Stock

On December 1, 2016, Steve Gates invested $30,000 cash in exchange for all of the company's common stock. This transaction increased the company's assets, Cash, by $30,000 and increased its stockholders' equity, Common Stock, by $30,000, as illustrated below using the accounting equation. (For each transaction that impacts stockholders' equity, we add a brief description—in this case "Issued stock.")

	Assets	=	Liabilities	+	Stockholders' Equity	
	Cash	=			Common Stock	
(1)	+30,000	=			+30,000	Issued stock
	$30,000				$30,000	

It is important to verify the equality of the accounting equation following each transaction. After the above transaction is recorded, both sides of the equation total $30,000.

Transaction 2. Paid Rent in Advance

On December 1, WebWork prepaid its office rent for the next six months, December 2016 through May 2017. WebWork's rent is $1,800 per month; meaning it paid a total of $10,800 cash (6 × $1,800). This transaction decreased Cash by $10,800 and increased Prepaid Rent by $10,800.

	Assets			=	Liabilities	+	Stockholders' Equity
	Cash	+	Prepaid Rent	=			Common Stock
Balance	30,000						30,000
(2)	−10,800		+10,800				
	19,200	+	10,800				30,000
		$30,000		=			$30,000

The expenditure for prepaid rent is recorded as an asset because the advance payment is a future economic benefit to the company. This outlay of cash has value to the business beyond the current accounting period, but any rent that is used up in the current accounting period will be recorded as an expense for the month of December.

Transaction 3. Purchased Office Supplies on Account

On December 1, WebWork purchased office supplies on account totaling $2,850. Businesses often extend credit to their customers. Credit allows businesses to pay for goods or services at a later date. When credit is used to purchase goods or services, the purchase is said to be made *on account*. This transaction increased Office Supplies by $2,850 and increased Accounts Payable by the same amount.

	Assets			=	Liabilities	+	Stockholders' Equity
	Cash	+ Office Supplies	+ Prepaid Rent	=	Accounts Payable	+	Common Stock
Balance	19,200		10,800				30,000
(3)		+2,850			+2,850		
	19,200 +	2,850	+10,800 =		2,850	+	30,000
		$32,850		=			$32,850

Office supplies are recorded as an asset because they are expected to be used by the business in future periods beyond the current accounting period. Any supplies that are used up in the current accounting period will be recorded as an expense for the month of December. Following the purchase of office supplies, WebWork's assets total $32,850, which is equal to the sum of total liabilities of $2,850 plus stockholders' equity of $30,000.

Transaction 4. Signed Bank Note in Exchange for Cash

On December 1, WebWork obtained a two-year bank loan in the amount of $36,000, after signing a note payable. Annual interest charges on the note amount to 10 percent and are due each November 30. As a consequence of this loan, the company's Cash account increased by $36,000 and the Notes Payable account, a liability, increased by $36,000.

	Assets			=	Liabilities		+	Stockholders' Equity
	Cash	+ Office Supplies	+ Prepaid Rent	=	Accounts Payable	+ Notes Payable	+	Common Stock
Balance	19,200	2,850	10,800		2,850			30,000
(4)	+36,000					+36,000		
	55,200 +	2,850	+ 10,800 =		2,850	+ 36,000	+	30,000
		$68,850				$68,850		

Transaction 5. Purchased Equipment With Cash

On December 2, WebWork used cash to purchase office equipment costing $32,400. This transaction decreased Cash by $32,400 and increased Office Equipment by the same amount. The accounting equation remains in balance because an equal amount, $32,400, is added to one asset (Equipment) and subtracted from another asset (Cash).

	Assets				=	Liabilities		+	Stockholders' Equity
	Cash	+ Office Supplies	+ Prepaid Rent	+ Equipment	=	Accounts Payable	+ Notes Payable	+	Common Stock
Balance	55,200	2,850	10,800			2,850	36,000		30,000
(5)	−32,400			+32,400					
	22,800 +	2,850	+ 10,800 +	32,400 =		2,850	+ 36,000 +		30,000
		$68,850					$68,850		

Transaction 6. Received Customer Prepayment

On December 5, WebWork received a prepayment in the amount of $3,000 for services to be performed over the next few months. Because WebWork has not yet performed the services, it does not record the $3,000 payment as revenue. This practice follows the revenue recognition principle discussed in Appendix 1A. Instead, a liability account, **Unearned Revenue**, is increased by $3,000, and the Cash account is increased by $3,000. Unearned revenue is a liability because the company accepted payment for goods or services that have not yet been provided and, therefore, the amount cannot be recorded as earned revenue.

A.K.A. Unearned revenue is also called *deferred revenue.*

	Assets			=	Liabilities			+ Stockholders' Equity
Cash +	Office Supp. +	Prepd. Rent +	Equip-ment =	Accts. Pay. +	Unearned Revenue +	Notes Pay. +	Common Stock	
Bal. 22,800	2,850	10,800	32,400	2,850		36,000	30,000	
(6) +3,000					+3,000			
25,800 +	2,850 +	10,800 +	32,400 =	2,850 +	3,000 +	36,000 +	30,000	

$71,850 $71,850

Transaction 7. Provided Services to Customers for Cash

On December 6, WebWork performed services for several customers and was paid $13,510 cash. This transaction increased Cash by $13,510 and increased Fee Revenue by the same amount.

	Assets			=	Liabilities			+	Stockholders' Equity	
									Retained Earnings	
Cash +	Office Supp. +	Prepd Rent +	Equip-ment =	Accts. Pay. +	Unearned Revenue +	Notes Pay. +	Comm. Stock +		Rev. −Exp.−Div.	
Bal. 25,800	2,850	10,800	32,400	2,850	3,000	36,000	30,000			
(7) +13,510								+13,510		Fee revenue
39,310+	2,850 +	10,800+	32,400 =	2,850 +	3,000	+36,000+	30,000 +	13,510		

$85,360 $85,360

This transaction is recorded as earned revenue because WebWork has performed the services for which it was paid.

Transaction 8. Provided Services for Cash and on Account

On December 8, WebWork performed $4,740 of services and received $1,000 in cash with the remaining $3,740 to be paid to WebWork by customers within 90 days. As previously noted in transaction 3 above, businesses often extend credit to customers, allowing them to pay for goods or services at a later date. Under accrual accounting, revenue must be recorded when earned, regardless of when payment is received. Consequently, this transaction increased Cash by $1,000, and Accounts Receivable by $3,740, and it increased Fee Revenue by the total amount of $4,740. The accounting equation remains in balance because both sides of the equation are increased by $4,740.

A.K.A. Delivering goods or services in advance of payment is referred to as providing goods or services "on account" or "on credit."

	Assets				=	Liabilities			+	Stockholders' Equity	
										Retained Earnings	
Cash +	Accts. Rec. +	Office Supp. +	Prepd. Rent +	Equip-ment =	Accts. Pay. +	Unearned Revenue +	Notes Pay. +	Comm. Stock +		Rev. −Exp.−Div.	
Bal. 39,310		2,850	10,800	32,400	2,850	3,000	36,000	30,000	13,510		
(8) +1,000	+3,740								+4,740		Fee revenue
40,310+	3,740+	2,850+	10,800+	32,400 =	2,850 +	3,000	+36,000+	30,000 +	18,250		

$90,100 $90,100

Non-Accounting Transaction. Hired an Employee

On December 9, WebWork hired an employee to provide administrative help in the office. The employee will be paid $1,620 every two weeks and begins work Monday, December 12. At the time the employee is hired there is no immediate financial effect on the assets, liabilities, or stockholders' equity of the company. There is only an employment agreement between the employee and the company. The employee has not yet performed any work, nor has the employee received any wages.

Transaction 9. Paid Employee Wages

On December 23, WebWork paid the employee after she completed her first two weeks on the job. This transaction decreased Cash by $1,620, and increased Wage Expense by $1,620. By definition, an increase in expenses decreases stockholders' equity.

			Assets			=		Liabilities		+		Stockholders' Equity		
Cash	+ Accts. Rec.	+ Office Supp.	+ Prepd. Rent	+ Equip- ment		= Accts. Pay.	+ Unearned Revenue	+ Notes Pay.	+ Comm. Stock	+		Retained Earnings		
											Rev.	− Exp.	−Div.
Bal. 40,310	3,740	2,850	10,800	32,400		2,850	3,000	36,000	30,000		18,250		
(9) −1,620												−1,620	Wage expense
38,690 + 3,740 + 2,850 + 10,800 + 32,400 = 2,850 + 3,000 + 36,000 + 30,000 + 18,250 − 1,620

$88,480 $88,480

Transaction 10. Received Payment on Account from Customer

On December 27, WebWork received a payment of $2,400 cash from a customer that had previously received services performed on account (see Transaction 8). This transaction increased Cash by $2,400, and decreased Accounts Receivable by $2,400.

			Assets			=		Liabilities		+		Stockholders' Equity		
Cash	+ Accts. Rec.	+ Office Supp.	+ Prepd. Rent	+ Equip- ment		= Accts. Pay.	+ Unearned Revenue	+ Notes Pay.	+ Comm. Stock	+		Retained Earnings		
											Rev.	− Exp.	− Div.
Bal. 38,690	3,740	2,850	10,800	32,400		2,850	3,000	36,000	30,000		18,250	1,620	
(10) +2,400	−2,400												
41,090 + 1,340 + 2,850 + 10,800 + 32,400 = 2,850 + 3,000 + 36,000 + 30,000 + 18,250 − 1,620

$88,480 $88,480

After recording this transaction, the balance in Accounts Receivable is $1,340. This represents the amount still owed to WebWork for services that were previously performed on account but remain unpaid.

Transaction 11. Paid Cash Dividend

On December 30, WebWork paid a cash dividend. Dividends are not a business expense, and are not included in the calculation of net income. Rather, dividends are a distribution of the company's accumulated net income to its stockholders. Payment of the dividend decreased Cash by $500 and increased Dividends by $500. (By definition, an increase in dividends causes a decrease in stockholders' equity.)

			Assets			=		Liabilities		+		Stockholders' Equity		
Cash	+ Accts. Rec.	+ Office Supp.	+ Prepd. Rent	+ Equip- ment		= Accts. Pay.	+ Unearned Revenue	+ Notes Pay.	+ Comm. Stock	+		Retained Earnings		
											Rev.	− Exp.	− Div.
Bal. 41,090	1,340	2,850	10,800	32,400		2,850	3,000	36,000	30,000		18,250	1,620	
(11) −500													−500 Dividends
40,590 + 1,340 + 2,850 + 10,800 + 32,400 = 2,850 + 3,000 + 36,000 + 30,000 + 18,250 − 1,620 − 500

$87,980 $87,980

Transaction Summary

Exhibit 2-3 provides a summary of the eleven accounting transactions for WebWork, for the month of December. The exhibit illustrates the financial effect of each transaction using the accounting equation. It is important that the accounting equation remains in balance at all times, and that the equality between total assets and the sum of total liabilities and stockholders' equity is maintained following each transaction.

Exhibit 2-3	Summary of December Transactions and Their Effect on the Expanded Accounting Equation

	Assets					=	Liabilities			+	Stockholders' Equity				
	Cash +	Accts. Rec. +	Office Supp. +	Prepd. Rent +	Equip- ment	=	Accts. Pay. +	Unearned Revenue +	Notes Pay.	+	Comm. Stock +	Retained Earnings			
												Rev. −	Exp. −	Div.
(1)	+30,000										+30,000				
(2)	−10,800			+10,800											
(3)			+2,850				+2,850								
(4)	+36,000								+36,000						
(5)	−32,400				+32,400										
(6)	+3,000							+3,000							
(7)	+13,510											+13,510			
(8)	+1,000	+3,740										+4,740			
(9)	−1,620													−1,620	
(10)	+2,400	−2,400													
(11)	−500														−500
	40,590 +	1,340 +	2,850 +	10,800 +	32,400	=	2,850 +	3,000 +	36,000	+	30,000 +	18,250 −	1,620 −	500	
			$87,980								$87,980				

Concept	→	Method	→	Assessment	TAKEAWAY 2.1
When should an event be recorded in a company's accounting records?		Review the event details. Does the event affect the company's assets, liabilities, or stockholders' equity?		If the event affects any of the elements of the accounting equation, it must be recorded in a company's accounting records.	

Ford Aerobics Studio, Inc., operates as a corporation. The firm rents studio space (including a sound system) and specializes in offering aerobics classes to individuals and groups. On January 1, the assets, liabilities, and stockholders' equity of the business were as follows: Cash, $5,000; Accounts Receivable, $5,200; Accounts Payable, $1,000; Notes Payable, $2,500; Common Stock, $5,500; and Retained Earnings, $1,200. The January business activities for the studio were as follows:

YOUR TURN! 2.2

The solution is on page 118.

1. Paid $600 cash on accounts payable.
2. Paid January rent of $3,600 cash.
3. Billed clients for January classes in the amount of $11,500.
4. Received a $500 invoice from a supplier for T-shirts given free to January's class members as an advertising promotion.
5. Collected $10,000 cash on account from clients for prior aerobics classes.
6. Paid employee wages of $2,400 cash.
7. Received a $680 invoice for January's utilities.
8. Paid $20 cash to the bank as January interest on an outstanding note payable.
9. Paid $900 cash in dividends to stockholders.
10. Paid $4,000 cash on January 31 to purchase a sound system to replace the rented system.

Required

a. Set up an expanded accounting equation in columnar form with the following individual assets, liabilities, and stockholders' equity accounts: Cash, Accounts Receivable, Equipment, Accounts Payable, Notes Payable, Common Stock, and Retained Earnings. Enter the January 1 balances below each account. (The beginning balance in the Equipment account is $0.)

b. Record the financial impact (increase or decrease) of each transaction (l) through (l0) on the beginning account balances. Then total the columns to demonstrate that total assets equal the sum of total liabilities plus stockholders' equity as of January 31.

THE "ACCOUNT" SYSTEM

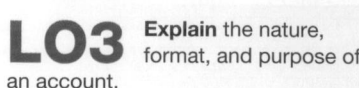

LO3 Explain the nature, format, and purpose of an account.

The basic component of an accounting system is the **account**, which is an individual record of the increases and decreases in a specific asset, liability, or stockholders' equity item. An account is created for each individual asset, liability, and stockholders' equity item on a company's financial statements. Some common account titles are Cash, Accounts Receivable, Notes Payable, Fee Revenue, and Rent Expense.

Chart of Accounts

Businesses maintain a chart of accounts to facilitate the analysis of a company's business activities. A **chart of accounts** is a list of the titles of all accounts in a business's accounting system. Account titles are grouped by, and in the order of, the five major components of the expanded accounting equation: assets, liabilities, stockholders' equity, revenues, and expenses. **Exhibit 2-4** shows the chart of accounts for WebWork and indicates the account numbers that will be used throughout this illustration. (Each company maintains its own unique set of accounts and its own numbering system.)

Exhibit 2-4	Chart of Accounts for WebWork

Assets	Equity
110 Cash	310 Common Stock
120 Accounts Receivable	320 Retained Earnings
130 Office Supplies	330 Dividends
150 Prepaid Rent	
170 Office Equipment	**Revenues**
175 Accumulated Depreciation— Office Equipment	410 Fee Revenue
	Expenses
Liabilities	510 Supplies Expense
210 Accounts Payable	520 Wage Expense
220 Interest Payable	530 Rent Expense
230 Wages Payable	540 Depreciation Expense— Office Equipment
250 Unearned Revenue	550 Interest Expense
260 Notes Payable	

System of Debits and Credits

LO4 Describe the system of debits and credits and its use in recording transactions.

One basic characteristic of all accounts is that data entries separately record the increases and decreases to an account. The method of recording data entries in the accounts is a matter of convention; that is, a simple set of rules is followed, which involves debits and credits.

A **T-account** is a simplified form of an account which is used to capture these effects. T-accounts are so named because they resemble the letter "T" as shown below:

Account Title (e.g., Cash)

Debit	Credit
Always the left side	Always the right side

The terms **debit** and **credit** refer to the left side and the right side, respectively, of an account. Regardless of what amount is recorded in an account, any entry made on the left side is a debit to the account while any entry recorded on the right side is a credit to the account. The words *debit* and *credit* are abbreviated *dr.* (from the Latin *debere*) and *cr.* (from the Latin *credere*), respectively.

The system of debits and credits identifies which side of the account, debit or credit, is used to increase the account and which side of the account is used to decrease the account. **Exhibit 2-5** summarizes these rules for each of the six primary categories of accounts: assets, liabilities, stockholders' equity, revenues, expenses, and dividends.

Observe the following relations in **Exhibit 2-5**:

1. Debit always refers to the left side of an account; credit always refers to the right side.

2. The pattern of increases and decreases in accounts derives from the accounting equation. Assets are on the left side of the accounting equation and increase with debit (or left side) entries. Assets decrease with credit entries.

3. Liabilities and stockholders' equity are on the right side of the accounting equation and increase with credit (or right side) entries. Liabilities decrease with debit entries.

4. The **normal balance** of an account is the side on which increases to the account are recorded. This is because increases in an account are usually greater than, or equal to, decreases in an account. Asset accounts normally have debit balances while liability and stockholders' equity accounts normally have credit balances.

5. Revenue, expense, and dividends are temporary subdivisions of retained earnings. The pattern of increases and decreases in these accounts derives from their relation to retained earnings. Revenues increase earnings, and just like the retained earnings account, revenue accounts increase with credit entries and decrease with debit entries. On the other hand, expenses decrease earnings, and so have the opposite pattern as retained earnings; expense accounts increase with debit entries and decrease with credit entries.

6. Dividends are distributions of retained earnings to shareholders, and like expense accounts have the opposite pattern as retained earnings; dividends increase with debit entries and decrease with credit entries.

Exhibit 2-5	System of Increases and Decreases, Debits and Credits, and Normal Balances

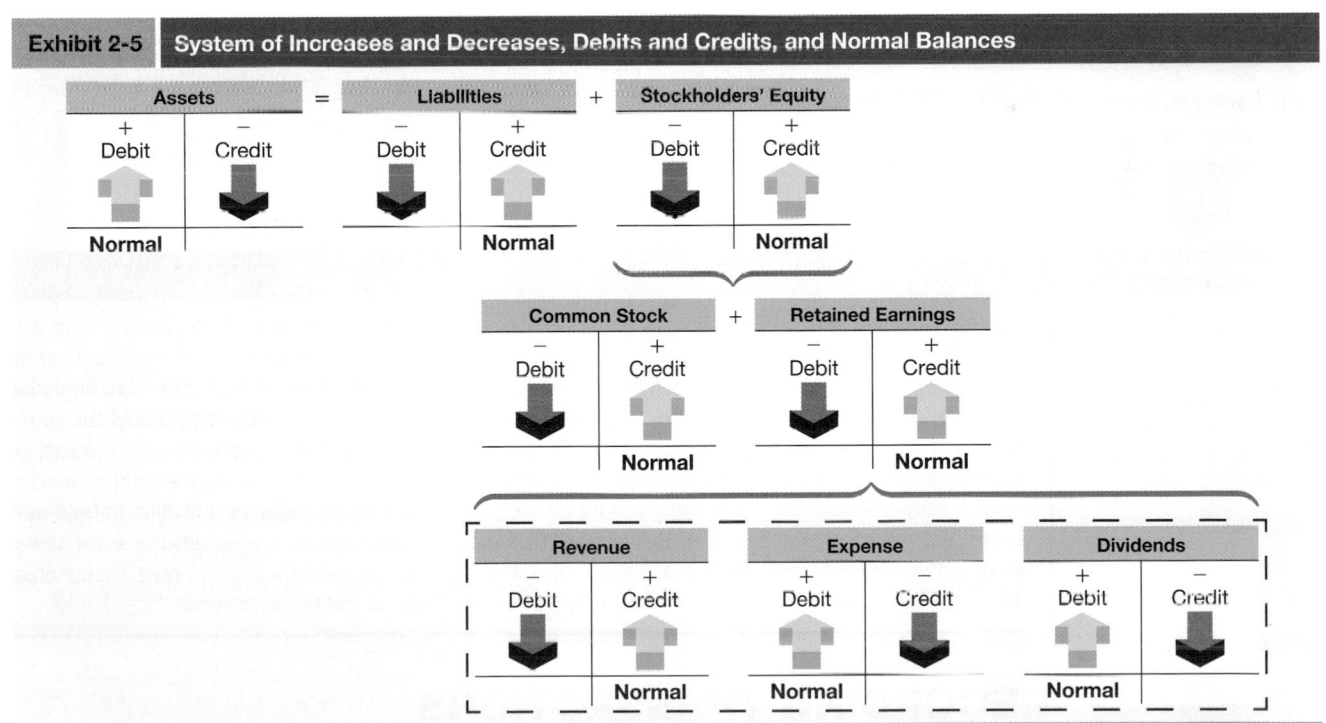

For each of the following accounts, identify whether the account's normal balance is a debit or a credit.

a. Cash
c. Wage expense
e. Dividends
g. Inventory

b. Common stock
d. Notes payable
f. Sales revenue

YOUR TURN! 2.3

The solution is on page 118.

As an example, the Cash T-account with the December transactions for WebWork is presented in **Exhibit 2-6**.

Exhibit 2-6	Cash T-account

Cash

(1)	30,000	10,800	(2)
(4)	36,000	32,400	(5)
(6)	3,000	1,620	(9)
(7)	13,510	500	(11)
(8)	1,000		
(10)	2,400		
	85,910	45,320	
Bal.	40,590		

To compute the T-account balance, sum the numbers in each column and subtract the smaller total from the larger total. In this example, subtract 45,320 from 85,910 to compute the 40,590 balance.

Note that amounts are not indicated with either a plus (+) or minus (-) sign in a T-account because, as shown in **Exhibit 2-5**, the type of the account and whether the data entry is a debit or credit to that account tell us if the amount is an increase or decrease. Because Cash is an asset, increases are always shown on the left as debits and decreases on the right as credits.

A T-account consists of: (1) the account title (such as Cash), (2) amounts reflecting increases and decreases, and (3) cross-references to other accounting records. It is customary to reference (or link) the data entries in a T-account with a number or a letter to identify the related accounting transaction that originated the data. This permits a systematic review of the data entries in the event of a recording error. It also enables a company, and its independent auditor, to review the company's set of accounts and match the account information with the related accounting transactions. The numerical references in the Cash T-account above are the ones used to identify the December transactions for WebWork from **Exhibit 2-3**.

YOUR TURN! 2.4

The solution is on page 118.

Using the information in **Exhibit 2-3**, construct the T-account for Accounts Receivable in proper form.

CORPORATE SOCIAL RESPONSIBILITY

What to Record?

An important element of the conceptual framework discussed in Appendix 1A in Chapter 1 is the monetary unit concept, which states that only those items that can be expressed in monetary terms are reported in financial statements. This causes many items of interest to be excluded from financial statements. Reporting of a company's social responsibility activities, for example, would be compromised if it were constrained to the activities that can be expressed in monetary terms. Reporting guidelines established by the Global Reporting Initiative, the organization that pioneered the world's most widely-used sustainability reporting framework, allow for a wider range of activities to be measured and reported. For example, **Bayer Group**, a global healthcare company, reports such items as greenhouse emissions, net water usage, and employee safety records in its annual sustainable development report. Bayer's sustainability report can be found at the Bayer Website.

RECORDING TRANSACTIONS

LO5 **Explain** the process of journalizing and posting transactions.

Earlier in this chapter we analyzed the transactions of WebWork using the accounting equation. This approach enabled us to see how accounting transactions affect a company's financial position and operations. This approach is not feasible, however, for even a modest-sized business because of the large number of transactions. Consequently, we now explain the process of analyzing and recording accounting information in an actual accounting system.

An initial step in the analysis and recording process is to identify evidence of a business transaction. This usually comes in the form of a source document. **Source documents** are printed forms or computer records that are generated when a firm engages in a business transaction. At a minimum, a source document usually specifies the dollar amount involved, the date of the transaction, and possibly the party dealing with the firm. Some examples of source documents include (1) a supplier's invoice showing evidence of a purchase of supplies on account, (2) a bank check indicating the payment of an obligation, (3) a deposit slip showing the amount of cash deposited in a bank, and (4) a cash receipt indicating the amount of cash received from a customer for services rendered. An example of an invoice follows. Regardless of its form, the source document serves as the basis for the analysis of the underlying business event.

WebWork, Inc.

INVOICE

137 Technology Lane
Irvine, CA. 92614
Phone (949) 727-3555

INVOICE # [**100**]
DATE: DECEMBER 10, 2016

TO:
Pick Enterprises
1055 Kinrose Ave
Los Angeles, CA 90024
(310) 208-5570

FOR:
Web design

DESCRIPTION	HOURS	RATE	AMOUNT
Design work for Website, including motion graphics	17.5	$125	$2,187.50
		TOTAL	$2,187.50

Make all checks payable to WebWork, Inc.
Total due in 15 days. Overdue accounts subject to a service charge of 1% per month.

Thank you for your business!

Once the source document has been analyzed to determine the accounts affected and the amounts involved, we then record the transaction. All accounting transactions are initially recorded in a journal. A **journal**, or *book of original entry,* is a tabular record in which a business's activities are reflected in terms of debits and credits and recorded in chronological order. A journal organizes information by date, and thus, serves as a chronological diary of a company's business activities. The word *journalize* means to record a transaction in a journal. An entry in a journal is called a **journal entry**.

General Journal

The **general journal** is a record with enough flexibility that any type of business transaction can be recorded in it. Like all journals in an accounting system, the general journal is a book of original entry in which accounting data are entered into a company's accounting system. **Exhibit 2-7** shows the first transaction as it is recorded in WebWork's general journal. The procedure for recording entries in the general journal follows:

❶ Indicate the year, month, and date of entry. (Usually the year and month are rewritten only at the top of each page of the journal or at the point in the journal where the year and month change.)

A.K.A. A company's journals are also referred to as its "*books.*"

A.K.A. Another term often used to describe the recording of a transaction is to "*book*" the transaction.

❷ Enter the titles of accounts affected (from the chart of accounts) in the Description column. Accounts to receive debits are entered close to the left margin and are recorded first. Accounts to receive credits are recorded next and indented slightly to the right.

❸ Enter dollar amounts in the left (Debit) and right (Credit) columns.

❹ Record an explanation of the transaction below the account titles; it should be brief, disclosing information necessary to understand the event recorded.

Exhibit 2-7	General Journal with First Entry of WebWork		
	GENERAL JOURNAL		
Date	**Description**	**Debit**	**Credit**
2016			
❶ Dec. 1	Cash ❷	30,000 ❸	
	Common stock		30,000
	Issued stock in exchange for cash. ❹		

A journal entry that involves more than two accounts is called a **compound journal entry**. (As shown below, the journal entry for Transaction 8 is an example of a compound journal entry involving three accounts.) Any number of accounts can appear in a compound entry; but, regardless of how many accounts are used, the sum of the debit amounts always equals the sum of the credit amounts. Accordingly, each transaction entered in the general journal is recorded with equal dollar amounts of debits and credits. The account titles cited in the Description column should correspond to those from the chart of accounts. (To delineate between journal entries made in the general journal, we leave a blank line between each transaction entry.)

Posting Journal Entries to the General Ledger

After an accounting transaction is journalized in the general journal, the debits and credits in each journal entry are immediately transferred to another component of the accounting system called the general ledger. While the general journal organizes transactions in chronological order, the general ledger organizes transactions by account. This makes it easier to determine the balance of each account, which in turn facilitates the preparation of the company's financial statements. Although businesses can use various ledgers to accumulate detailed accounting information, all firms have a general ledger. A **general ledger** is a listing of each account of a company and the amounts making up each account.

The process of transferring the debit and credit information from the general journal to the general ledger is called **posting**. It is important to be able to trace each data entry appearing in a general ledger account to the general journal location from which it was posted; consequently, both the general journal and general ledger accounts have a **posting reference** code. The posting reference of the general journal indicates the account to which the related debit or credit has been posted. The posting references in the general journal and ledger accounts are entered when the journal entries are posted to the ledger accounts (automatically when computerized, or by hand for a manual system). We will use the transaction number as the posting reference in the examples that follow.

Illustration of the Recording Process

We now apply the recording process to the transactions of WebWork, that were summarized in **Exhibit 2-3**. For each transaction, we **(1) analyze** the transaction using the accounting equation, **(2) journalize** the transaction, and **(3) post** journal entries to the general ledger (for simplicity, we use the T-account structure for each ledger account).

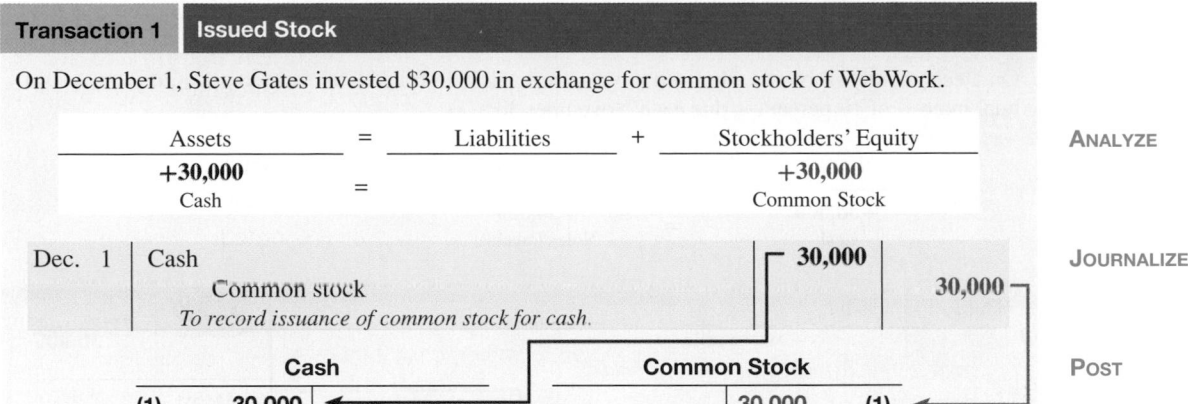

Transaction 1 | **Issued Stock**

On December 1, Steve Gates invested $30,000 in exchange for common stock of WebWork.

Assets	=	Liabilities	+	Stockholders' Equity	ANALYZE
+30,000	=			+30,000	
Cash				Common Stock	

Dec. 1 | Cash 30,000
     Common stock 30,000
     To record issuance of common stock for cash. — JOURNALIZE

Cash   **Common Stock** — POST
(1) 30,000   30,000 (1)

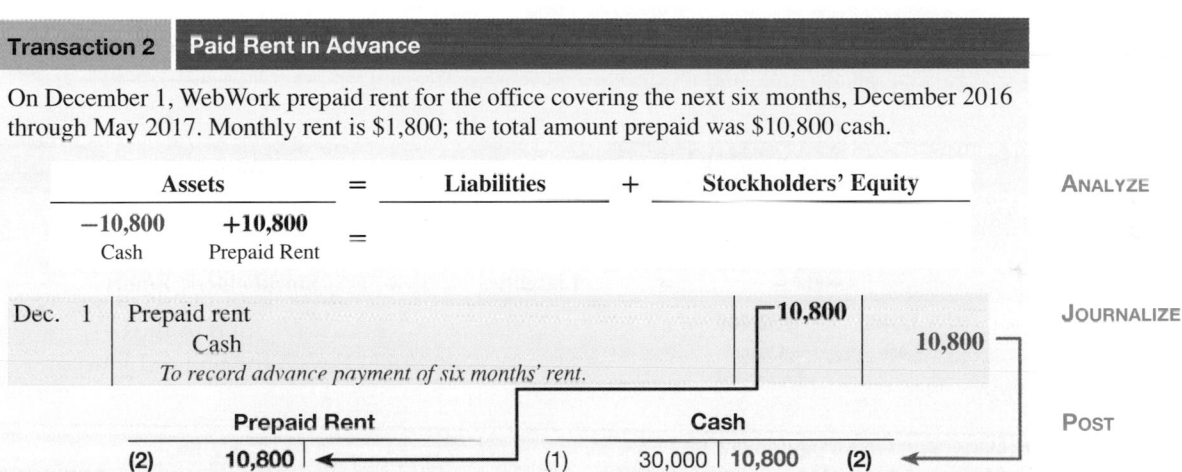

Transaction 2 | **Paid Rent in Advance**

On December 1, WebWork prepaid rent for the office covering the next six months, December 2016 through May 2017. Monthly rent is $1,800; the total amount prepaid was $10,800 cash.

Assets	=	Liabilities	+	Stockholders' Equity	ANALYZE
−10,800 +10,800	=				
Cash Prepaid Rent					

Dec. 1 | Prepaid rent 10,800
     Cash 10,800
     To record advance payment of six months' rent. — JOURNALIZE

Prepaid Rent   **Cash** — POST
(2) 10,800   (1) 30,000 | 10,800 (2)

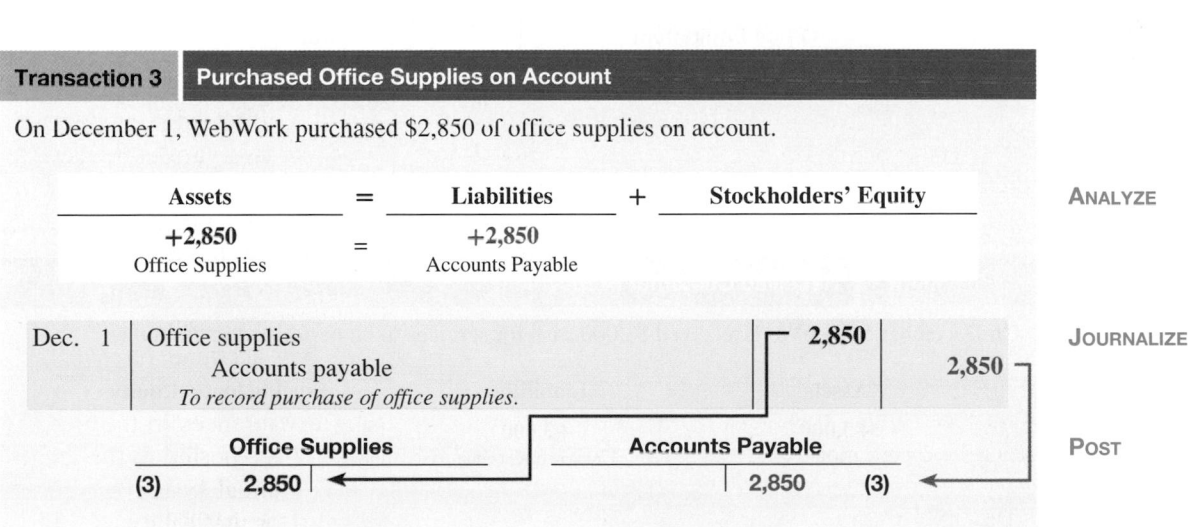

Transaction 3 | **Purchased Office Supplies on Account**

On December 1, WebWork purchased $2,850 of office supplies on account.

Assets	=	Liabilities	+	Stockholders' Equity	ANALYZE
+2,850	=	+2,850			
Office Supplies		Accounts Payable			

Dec. 1 | Office supplies 2,850
     Accounts payable 2,850
     To record purchase of office supplies. — JOURNALIZE

Office Supplies   **Accounts Payable** — POST
(3) 2,850   2,850 (3)

Transaction 4 | **Signed Bank Note in Exchange for Cash**

On December 1, WebWork obtained a two-year bank loan for $36,000, signing a note payable. Annual interest of 10 percent is due each November 30.

ANALYZE

Assets	=	Liabilities	+	Stockholders' Equity
+36,000	=	+36,000		
Cash		Notes Payable		

JOURNALIZE

Dec.	1	Cash	36,000	
		Notes payable		36,000
		To record borrowing of funds.		

POST

	Cash					Notes Payable		
(1)	30,000	10,800	(2)			36,000	(4)	
(4)	**36,000**							

Transaction 5 | **Purchased Equipment with Cash**

On December 2, WebWork used cash to purchase $32,400 of office equipment.

ANALYZE

Assets		=	Liabilities	+	Stockholders' Equity
−32,400	+32,400	=			
Cash	Office Equipment				

JOURNALIZE

Dec.	2	Office equipment	32,400	
		Cash		32,400
		To record purchase of office equipment.		

POST

	Office Equipment			Cash		
(5)	32,400		(1)	30,000	10,800	(2)
			(4)	36,000	**32,400**	(5)

Transaction 6 | **Received Customer Prepayment**

On December 5, WebWork received $3,000 cash for services to be performed in the future.

ANALYZE

Assets	=	Liabilities	+	Stockholders' Equity
+3,000	=	+3,000		
Cash		Unearned Revenue		

JOURNALIZE

Dec.	5	Cash	3,000	
		Unearned revenue		3,000
		To record advance payment from a customer.		

POST

	Cash				Unearned Revenue		
(1)	30,000	10,800	(2)		3,000	(6)	
(4)	36,000	32,400	(5)				
(6)	**3,000**						

Transaction 7 | **Provided Services to Customers for Cash**

On December 6, WebWork performed services for several customers and was paid $13,510 cash.

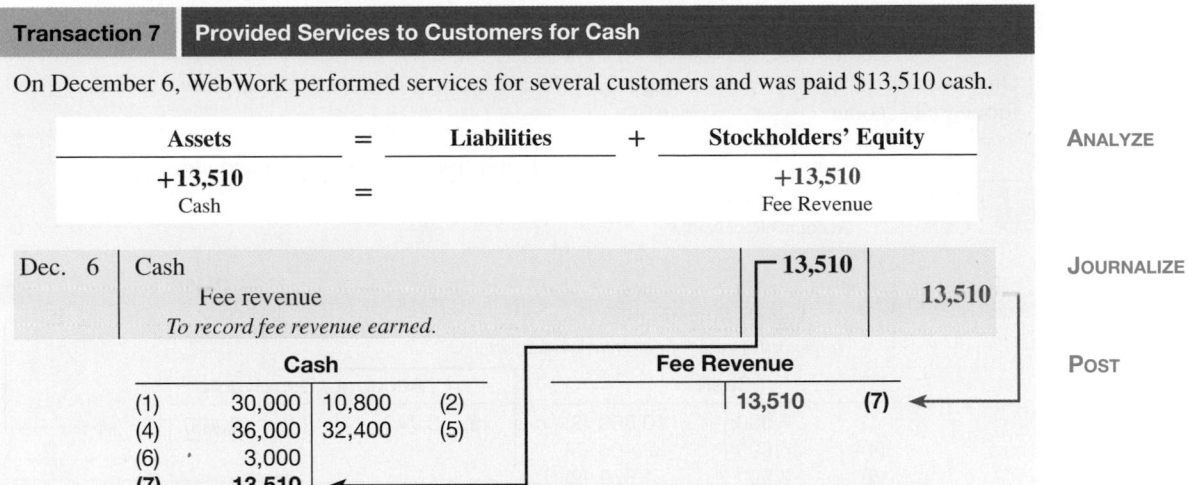

ANALYZE

JOURNALIZE

POST

Transaction 8 | **Provided Services for Cash and on Account**

On December 8, WebWork performed $4,740 of services for which it received $1,000 cash with the remaining $3,740 to be paid in the future.

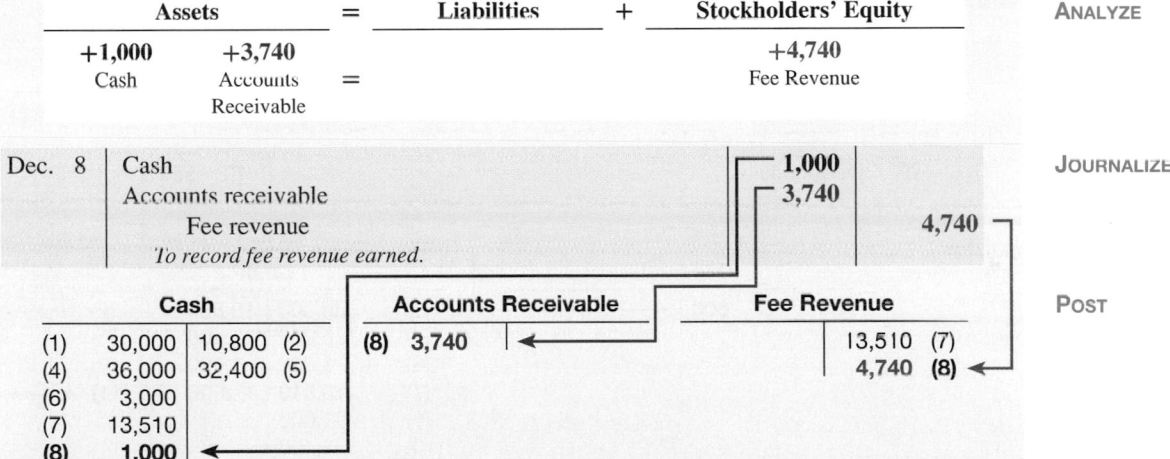

ANALYZE

JOURNALIZE

POST

Transaction 9 | **Paid Employee Wages**

On December 23, WebWork paid its employee $1,620 cash upon completion of her first two weeks on the job.

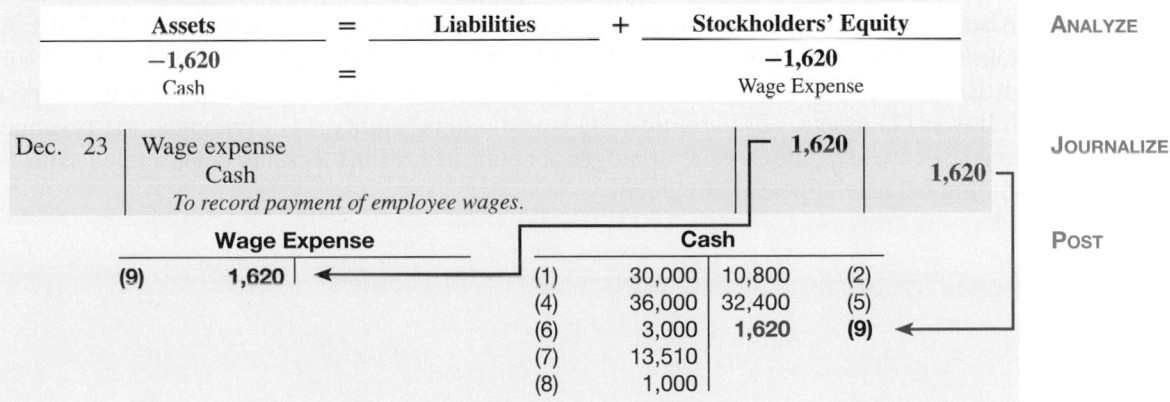

ANALYZE

JOURNALIZE

POST

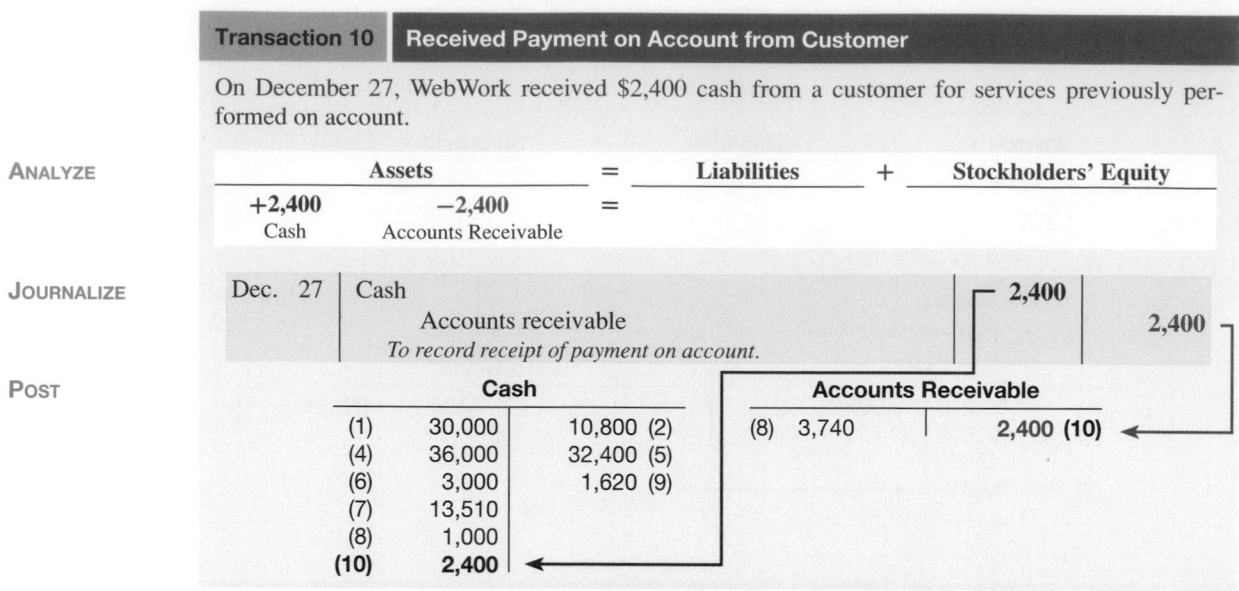

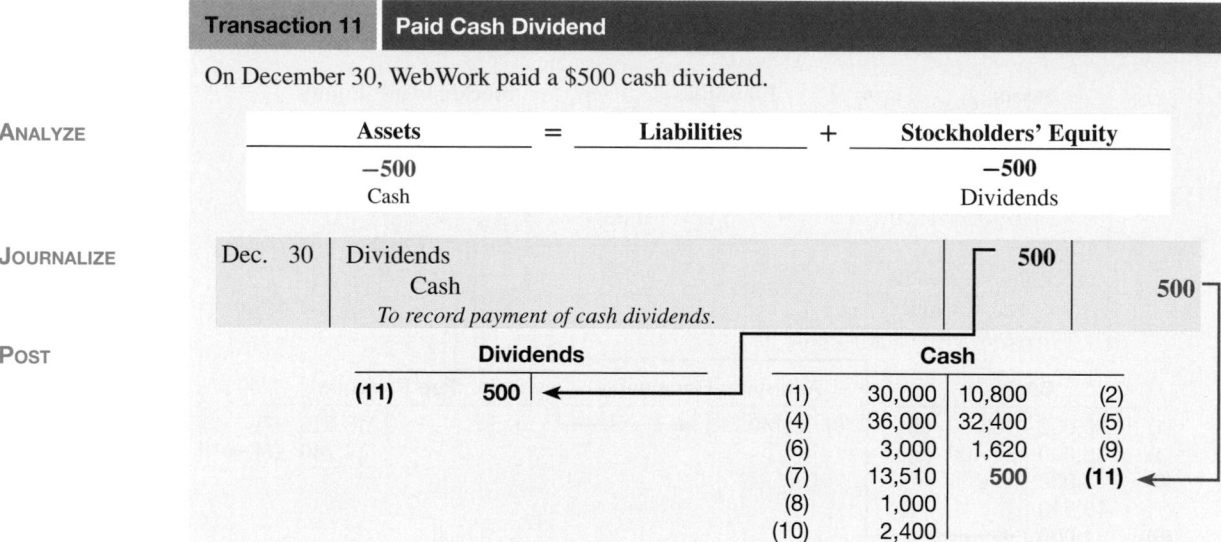

Summary Illustration of Journalizing and Posting Transactions

Exhibit 2-8 presents the general journal for WebWork for the month of December 2016. Also, **Exhibit 2-9** presents the general ledger for WebWork as of December 31, 2016. All journal entries appearing in **Exhibit 2-8** have been posted to the general ledger accounts in **Exhibit 2-9**. The accounts in WebWork's general ledger are grouped by category as follows: (1) assets, (2) liabilities, (3) stockholders' equity, (4) dividends, (5) revenues, and (6) expenses. Each general ledger account in **Exhibit 2-9** has been totaled with the ending balance appearing in green.

Exhibit 2-8	General Journal for WebWork

General Journal

	Date	Account Titles and Explanation	Debit	Credit

(1)	2016
	Dec. 1
		Cash
		    Common stock
		    To record issuance of common stock for cash.
			30,000	30,000

(2)	1	Prepaid rent
		    Cash
		    To record advance payment of six months' rent.
			10,800	10,800

(3)	1	Office supplies
		    Accounts payable
		    To record purchase of office supplies.
			2,850	2,850

(4)	1	Cash
		    Notes payable
		    To record a bank loan, with a signed note payable.
			36,000	36,000

(5)	2	Office equipment
		    Cash
		    To record purchase of office equipment.
			32,400	32,400

(6)	5	Cash
		    Unearned revenue
		    To record a prepayment from a customer.
			3,000	3,000

(7)	6	Cash
		    Fee revenue
		    To record fee revenue earned.
			13,510	13,510

(8)	8	Cash
		Accounts receivable
		    Fee revenue
		    To record fee revenue earned.
			1,000
			3,740
				4,740

(9)	23	Wage expense
		    Cash
		    To record payment of employee wages.
			1,620	1,620

(10)	27	Cash
		    Accounts receivable
		    To record receipt of payment on account.
			2,400	2,400

(11)	30	Dividends
		    Cash
		    To record payment of cash dividends.
			500	500

Exhibit 2-9	General Ledger for WebWork

General Ledger

Assets   =   **Liabilities**   +   **Stockholders' Equity**

Cash

(1)	30,000	10,800	(2)
(4)	36,000	32,400	(5)
(6)	3,000	1,620	(9)
(7)	13,510	500	(11)
(8)	1,000		
(10)	2,400		
Bal.	40,590		

Accounts Receivable

(8)	3,740	2,400	(10)
Bal.	1,340		

Office Supplies

(3)	2,850	
Bal.	2,850	

Prepaid Rent

(2)	10,800	
Bal.	10,800	

Office Equipment

(5)	32,400	
Bal.	32,400	

Accounts Payable

		2,850	(3)
		2,850	Bal.

Unearned Revenue

		3,000	(6)
		3,000	Bal.

Notes Payable

		36,000	(4)
		36,000	Bal.

Common Stock

		30,000	(1)
		30,000	Bal.

Dividends

(11)	500	
Bal.	500	

Fee Revenue

		13,510	(7)
		4,740	(8)
		18,250	Bal.

Wage Expense

(9)	1,620	
Bal.	1,620	

Assets = $87,980   =   **Liabilities = $41,850**   +   **Stockholders' Equity = $46,130**

YOUR TURN! 2.5

The solution is on pages 118–119.

For each of the transactions below, complete the following requirements.

1. Record the effect of each transaction using the accounting equation.
2. Prepare journal entries for each transaction.
3. Post the journal entries for each transaction to the appropriate T-accounts.

Transactions:

a. The company received $1,300 cash from clients for services rendered.
b. The company paid $2,400 cash for wages to employees.
c. The company collected $600 cash from clients on account.
d. The company paid a $400 cash dividend.
e. The company purchased $700 of office supplies on account.
f. The company billed clients $900 for services rendered, which were unpaid.
g. The company paid $500 cash to suppliers on account.

ACCOUNTING IN PRACTICE	Careers at Intuit

A company like Intuit obviously needs employees with a strong knowledge of accounting. However, understanding accounting and how accounting is used at Intuit and other companies is important for many career paths that might surprise you. For example, sales and marketing uses accounting to track and forecast sales activity, human resources uses accounting in employee performance evaluation, and corporate strategy uses accounting to research investment opportunities and communicate with corporate stakeholders. Clearly, knowledge of accounting will help you go far whatever your chosen career.

TRIAL BALANCE

A **trial balance** is a listing of all accounts from the general ledger with their respective debit or credit balance. A trial balance is prepared at the end of an accounting period after all transactions have been recorded. **Exhibit 2-10** shows a trial balance for WebWork, Inc., as of December 31, 2016. The sequence of the accounts and the dollar amounts are taken directly from the general ledger T-accounts in **Exhibit 2-9** (which follow the order of the account numbering system in WebWork's chart of accounts). The debit and credit columns from the trial balance are in balance; that is, the $90,100 sum of the debit account balances equals the $90,100 sum of the credit account balances.

LO6 **Describe** the trial balance.

The two principal reasons for preparing a trial balance are:

1. To serve as a check on whether the sum of the debit balances and the sum of the credit balances from the general ledger accounts are equal. If the totals are not equal, it would indicate the presence of some type of recording error.

2. To show all general ledger account balances in one location, which facilitates the preparation of financial statements. The trial balance, however, is *not* a financial statement.

A trial balance must be dated. In **Exhibit 2-10**, the trial balance of WebWork, Inc., was prepared as of December 31, 2016.

While it is required that a trial balance be in balance—that is, that the total of the debit column equal the total of the credit column—this equality does not guarantee that the accounting data is error-free. Potential data errors could still exist as a consequence of (1) transactions not being journalized, (2) journal entries not being posted, (3) journal entries being posted in the wrong amount, and (4) journal entries being posted to the wrong accounts.

Exhibit 2-10	Unadjusted Trial Balance for WebWork	
WEBWORK, INC. **Unadjusted Trial Balance** **December 31, 2016**		
	Debit	**Credit**
Cash.	$40,590	
Accounts receivable.	1,340	
Office supplies	2,850	
Prepaid rent	10,800	
Office equipment	32,400	
Accounts payable.		$ 2,850
Unearned revenue		3,000
Notes payable		36,000
Common stock.		30,000
Dividends	500	
Fee revenue		18,250
Wage expense	1,620	
Totals	$90,100	$90,100

TAKEAWAY 2.2	Concept	⟶	Method	⟶	Assessment
	Is the trial balance in balance?		Ending balances for all of the general ledger accounts entered on the trial balance. Total the debit column and the credit column on the trial balance.		Verify the equality of the sum of the debit account balances and the sum of the credit account balances.

YOUR TURN! 2.6

The solution is on page 119.

Each of the following accounts from the Devin Company has a normal balance. The unadjusted balances are as of December 31, 2016, the end of Devin's first year of operations:

Cash...........................	1,500	Common stock...............	7,500	
Accounts receivable................	4,500	Sales revenue.................	12,000	
Inventory.......................	3,750	Salary expense................	4,500	
Property, plant, and equipment........	11,250	Administrative expenses	750	
Accounts payable.................	2,250	Dividends	1,500	
Notes payable	6,000			

Prepare an unadjusted trial balance for the Devin Company as of December 31, 2016.

FORENSIC ACCOUNTING

Fraudulent Reporting

Verifying that the sum of the debit account balances from the general ledger is equal to the sum of the credit account balances is not sufficient to guarantee accuracy of financial records. The infamous accounting scandal at **WorldCom** provides a case in point. To inflate its net income, WorldCom improperly "capitalized expenses"—that is, they inappropriately debited property, plant, and equipment, an asset account, when they should have debited an expense account. While the sum of the debit account balances on WorldCom's books did equal the sum of the credit account balances, assets were overstated and expenses were understated by almost $7 billion. WorldCom's CEO Bernard Ebbers, the mastermind of this fraudulent accounting scheme, was convicted of conspiracy to commit fraud, securities fraud, and making false filings with the SEC. Mr. Ebbers was sentenced to 25 years in prison.

COMPREHENSIVE PROBLEM

Juan Rios acted upon his entrepreneurial spirit and started a graphic design business called Juan's Designs. Based on an excellent business plan, Juan was able to raise sufficient capital to begin operations in October 2016. During the month of October, the following events occurred related to the business.

1. Stockholders invested $40,000 cash in the business in exchange for common stock.
2. Paid $2,500 cash for rent on an office suite for the month of October.
3. Purchased two desktop computers, software, and a printer for $10,000 cash.
4. Purchased miscellaneous supplies for $500 that will be used during the month, all on account.
5. Purchased an advertisement in a local newspaper for $300 cash, announcing the opening of his new business.
6. Performed $5,500 of design work on account.
7. Received $3,500 cash from customers for design work previously completed.
8. Paid $350 cash toward the company's accounts payable balance.
9. Paid $2,500 cash for wages of Juan Rios.

Required

a. Use the following accounts to create a general ledger using T-accounts.

Cash	Common Stock	Wage Expense
Accounts Receivable	Service Revenue	Advertising Expense
Equipment	Supplies Expense	Rent Expense
Accounts Payable		

Prepare journal entries and post the above accounting transactions to their general ledger T-accounts.

b. Prepare an unadjusted trial balance as of October 31, 2016.

Solution

Date	Description	Post Ref.	Debit	Credit
October	Cash	1	40,000	
	Common stock	1		40,000
	Owner purchased shares for cash.			
	Rent expense	2	2,500	
	Cash	2		2,500
	Paid rent for office suite.			
	Equipment	3	10,000	
	Cash	3		10,000
	Purchased office equipment.			
	Supplies expense	4	500	
	Accounts payable	4		500
	Purchased supplies on account to be used in current month.			
	Advertising expense	5	300	
	Cash	5		300
	Purchased advertising.			
	Accounts receivable	6	5,500	
	Service revenue	6		5,500
	Performed design work on account.			
	Cash	7	3,500	
	Accounts receivable	7		3,500
	Received cash from previously billed work.			
	Accounts payable	8	350	
	Cash	8		350
	Paid cash towards accounts payable.			
	Wage expense	9	2,500	
	Cash	9		2,500
	Paid wages.			

Cash

(1)	40,000	2,500	(2)
(7)	3,500	10,000	(3)
		300	(5)
		350	(8)
		2,500	(9)
Bal.	27,850		

Accounts Receivable

(6)	5,500	3,500	(7)
Bal.	2,000		

Accounts Payable

(8)	350	500	(4)
		150	Bal.

Equipment

(3)	10,000	

Service Revenue

		5,500	(6)

Common Stock

		40,000	(1)

Wage Expense

(9)	2,500	

Supplies Expense

(4)	500	

Rent Expense

(2)	2,500	

Advertising Expense

(5)	300	

JUAN'S DESIGNS
Unadjusted Trial Balance
October 31, 2016

	Debit	Credit
Cash.	$27,850	
Accounts receivable.	2,000	
Equipment	10,000	
Accounts payable.		$ 150
Common stock.		40,000
Service revenue		5,500
Supplies expense.	500	
Wage expense.	2,500	
Advertising expense.	300	
Rent expense.	2,500	
Totals	$45,650	$45,650

SUMMARY OF LEARNING OBJECTIVES

LO1   Identify the five major steps in the accounting cycle. (p. 60)

- Five major steps in the accounting cycle are:
  1. Analyze.
  2. Record.
  3. Adjust.
  4. Report.
  5. Close.

LO2   Analyze and record transactions using the accounting equation. (p. 61)

- The accounting equation provides a convenient way to summarize the recording of financial information.
- The initial step in the accounting process—analyze—is to determine which transactions (if any) need to be recorded.
- An *accounting transaction* is an economic event that requires accounting recognition. An event that affects any of the elements of the basic accounting equation (assets, liabilities, or stockholders' equity) must be recorded.

Explain the nature, format, and purpose of an account. (p. 68)   LO3

■   An account is an individual record of the increases and decreases in specific assets, liabilities, stockholders' equity, dividends, revenues, or expenses.

■   Information provided by the account includes its title, amounts reflecting increases and decreases, cross-references to other accounting records, and dates and descriptive notations.

Describe the system of debits and credits and its use in recording transactions. (p. 68)   LO4

■   The left side of an account is always the debit side; the right side of an account is always the credit side.

■   Increases in assets, dividends, and expenses are debit entries; increases in liabilities, stockholders' equity, and revenues are credit entries. Decreases are the opposite.

■   The normal balance of any account appears on the account side used for recording account increases.

■   For each accounting transaction, the sum of the debit amounts must always equal the sum of the credit amounts.

■   All accounting transactions are analyzed using one or more of the basic account categories: (1) assets, (2) liabilities, (3) stockholders' equity, (4) dividends, (5) revenues, and (6) expenses.

Explain the process of journalizing and posting transactions. (p. 70)   LO5

■   Source documents provide the basis for analyzing business transactions.

■   Accounting entries are initially recorded in a journal in chronological order; the journal is a book of original entry and acts like a diary of a business's activities.

■   A general ledger is a grouping of all of the accounts that are used to prepare the basic financial statements.

■   Posting is the transfer of information from a journal to the general ledger accounts.

■   Posting references are used to cross-reference the information in journals and the general ledger accounts.

Describe the trial balance. (p. 79)   LO6

■   A trial balance is a list of the accounts in the general ledger with their respective debit or credit balance.

■   A trial balance is prepared after all transactions have been recorded for an accounting period.

■   A trial balance serves as a mechanical check to evaluate the equality of the sum of the debit account balances and the sum of the credit account balances.

■   A trial balance facilitates the preparation of the financial statements by showing all account balances in one concise record.

Concept ➡	Method ➡	Assessment	SUMMARY
When should an event be recorded in a company's accounting records?	Review the event details. Does the event affect the company's assets, liabilities, or stockholders' equity?	If the event affects any of the elements of the accounting equation, it must be recorded in a company's accounting records.	TAKEAWAY 2.1
Is the trial balance in balance?	Ending balances for all of the general ledger accounts entered on the trial balance. Total the debit column and the credit column on the trial balance.	Verify the equality of the sum of the debit account balances and the sum of the credit account balances.	TAKEAWAY 2.2

KEY TERMS

Account (p. 68)	**Deferred revenue** (p. 64)	**Posting** (p. 72)
Accounting cycle (p. 60)	**Double-entry accounting** (p. 62)	**Posting reference** (p. 72)
Accounting transaction (p. 62)	**Fiscal year** (p. 61)	**Source documents** (p. 71)
Calendar year (p. 61)	**General journal** (p. 71)	**T-account** (p. 68)
Chart of accounts (p. 68)	**General ledger** (p. 72)	**Trial balance** (p. 79)
Compound journal entry (p. 72)	**Journal** (p. 71)	**Unearned revenue** (p. 64)
Credit (p. 68)	**Journal entry** (p. 71)	
Debit (p. 68)	**Normal balance** (p. 69)	

Assignments with the ⊕ logo in the margin are available in ᵐʸBusinessCourse.
See the Preface of the book for details.

SELF-STUDY QUESTIONS

(Answers to Self-Study Questions are at the end of this chapter.)

LO2   1. **Which of the following transactions does not affect the balance sheet totals?**
   a.   Purchased $500 supplies on account
   b.   Paid off a $3,000 note payable
   c.   Received $4,000 cash from a bank after signing a note payable
   d.   Ordered a new machine that will be paid for upon its delivery in two months

LO2   2. **Tobias Company purchased inventory on account. This transaction will affect:**
   a.   Only the balance sheet
   b.   Only the income statement
   c.   The income statement and the statement of retained earnings
   d.   The income statement, balance sheet, and statement of retained earnings

LO2   3. **If assets increase by $100 and liabilities decrease by $30, stockholders' equity must:**
   a.   Remain unchanged
   b.   Increase by $130
   c.   Decrease by $70
   d.   Decrease by $130

LO3   4. **A T-account consists of how many parts?**
   a.   One
   b.   Two
   c.   Three
   d.   Four

LO4   5. **Which of the following is true?**
   a.   The debit is on the right side of an asset account
   b.   The debit is on the left side of an asset account
   c.   The credit is on the left side of a liability account
   d.   The debit is on the right side of an expense account

LO4   6. **Which of the following accounts has a normal debit balance?**
   a.   Accounts Payable
   b.   Notes Payable
   c.   Common Stock
   d.   Advertising Expense

LO4   7. **Which of the following accounts is increased by a credit?**
   a.   Accounts Receivable
   b.   Sales Revenue
   c.   Dividends
   d.   Advertising Expense

LO4   8. **Which of the following is true?**
   a.   A debit will increase a liability account
   b.   A credit will increase an asset account
   c.   A credit will increase a revenue account
   d.   A debit will decrease an expense account

LO4   9. **In applying the rules of debits and credits, which of the following statements is correct?**
   a.   The word *debit* means to increase and the word *credit* means to decrease
   b.   Asset, expense, and common stock accounts are debited for increases
   c.   Liability, revenue, and common stock accounts are debited for increases
   d.   Asset, expense, and dividends are debited for increases

LO4   10. **Which of these accounts has a normal debit balance?**
   a.   Assets, expenses, dividends
   b.   Assets, revenues, common stock
   c.   Liabilities, revenues, common stock
   d.   Assets, liabilities, dividends

11. **The general ledger includes accounts for all but which of the following?** LO5
    a. Assets
    b. Expenses
    c. Dividends
    d. All of the above are in the general ledger

12. **Which of the following will cause a trial balance to be out of balance?** LO6
    a. Mistakenly debiting an asset account instead of an expense account
    b. Posting $123 as $213 to both a debit and a credit account
    c. Posting the same transaction twice by mistake
    d. Posting only the debit part of a transaction

13. **A journal entry that contains more than just two accounts is called:** LO5
    a. A posted journal entry
    b. An adjusting journal entry
    c. An erroneous journal entry
    d. A compound journal entry

14. **Posting refers to the process of transferring information from:** LO5
    a. A journal to the general ledger accounts
    b. General ledger accounts to a journal
    c. Source documents to a journal
    d. A journal to source documents

15. **Which of the following is not one of the five steps in the accounting cycle?** LO1
    a. Analyze
    b. Adjust
    c. Eliminate
    d. Report

16. **The purchase of $500 of supplies on account will:** LO2
    a. Increase both assets and stockholders' equity by $500
    b. Increase assets and decrease liabilities by $500
    c. Increase assets and decrease stockholders' equity by $500
    d. Increase both assets and liabilities by $500

17. **Matching steps in the accounting cycle to their definitions.** LO1

1. Analyze	a. Prepare financial statements
2. Record	b. Analyze transactions from source documents
3. Adjust	c. Journalize closing entries and prepare post-closing trial balance
4. Report	d. Journalize adjusting entries and prepare adjusted trial balance
5. Close	e. Journalize transactions and prepare unadjusted trial balance

QUESTIONS

1. List the five major steps in the accounting cycle in their proper order.
2. Define the term *fiscal year*.
3. Provide three examples of source documents that underlie business transactions.
4. Provide an example of a transaction that would:
    a. Increase one asset account but not change the amount of total assets.
    b. Decrease an asset account and a liability account.
    c. Decrease an asset account and increase an expense account.
    d. Increase an asset account and a liability account.

5. Explain the financial effect (increase, decrease, or no effect) of each of the following transactions on stockholders' equity:

   a. Purchased supplies for cash.
   b. Paid an account payable.
   c. Paid salaries.
   d. Purchased equipment for cash.
   e. Invested cash in business.
   f. Rendered services to customers, on account.
   g. Rendered services to customers, for cash.

6. The retained earnings on a balance sheet are $80,000. Without seeing the rest of the balance sheet, can you conclude that stockholders should be able to receive a dividend in the amount of $80,000 cash from the business? Justify your answer.

7. On December 31, the Miller Company had $900,000 in total assets and owed $300,000 to creditors. If the corporation's common stock amounted to $250,000, what amount of retained earnings should appear on the company's December 31, balance sheet?

8. Some accounting students believe that debits are good and credits are bad. Explain why this is not an accurate way to think about debits and credits.

9. What is an account?

10. What information is recorded in an account?

11. What does the term *debit* mean? What does the term *credit* mean?

12. What type of account—asset, liability, stockholders' equity, dividend, revenue, or expense—is each of the following accounts? Indicate whether a debit entry or a credit entry increases the balance of the account.

Professional Fees Earned	Common Stock
Accounts Receivable	Advertising Expense
Accounts Payable	Supplies
Cash	Dividends

13. How is the normal side of an account determined?

14. What is the normal balance (debit or credit) of each of the accounts in Discussion Question 12?

15. Describe the nature and purpose of a general journal.

16. What is the justification for the use of posting references?

17. Describe a compound journal entry.

18. What is a chart of accounts?

19. Explain the terms *general ledger* and *trial balance*. What are the primary reasons for preparing a trial balance?

20. Explain how it is possible for a trial balance to be in balance but still be in error.

21. What is a T-account and how is it used?

22. Is it possible for an accounting transaction to only affect the left side of the accounting equation and still leave the equation in balance? If so, provide an example.

23. Would a company record a transaction in its general ledger when an order is placed for the purchase of a machine that will be paid for at the time of its delivery in three months? Explain your answer.

SHORT EXERCISES

LO4   **SE2-1.   Normal Balances** Indicate for each of the following accounts whether the normal balance is a debit or a credit:

   a. Accounts Receivable
   b. Accounts Payable
   c. Dividends
   d. Wage Expense
   e. Inventory
   f. Interest Income
   g. Retained Earnings

SE2-2. **Debit and Credit Effects** Indicate the account that will be debited for each of the following **LO4** transactions:

    a. Issued common stock for cash
    b. Borrowed money from a bank
    c. Provided services on account
    d. Purchased inventory on account
    e. Collected cash from customers that owed a balance due

SE2-3. **Debit and Credit Effects** Indicate the account that will be credited for each of the following **LO4** transactions:

    a. Issued common stock for cash
    b. Borrowed money from a bank
    c. Provided services on account
    d. Purchased inventory on account
    e. Collected cash from customers that owed a balance due

SE2-4. **Determine a Transaction** The Pearce Company recorded a transaction by debiting Accounts **LO4** Receivable and crediting Sales Revenue. What event was being recorded?

SE2-5. **Determine the Cash Balance** The beginning-of-the-period cash balance for the Travis Company **LO4** was a $12,000 debit. Cash sales for the month were $6,000 and sales on account were $8,000. The company paid $2,500 cash for current-period purchases and also paid $3,000 cash for amounts due from last month. What is the ending debit or credit balance in the Cash account?

SE2-6. **Recording Transactions with the Accounting Equation** During the year, the Decker Company expe- **LO2** rienced the following accounting transactions:

    1. Issued common stock in the amount of $100,000
    2. Paid a $30,000 cash dividend
    3. Borrowed $25,000 from a bank
    4. Made a principal payment of $2,500 on an outstanding bank loan
    5. Made an interest payment of $1,200 on an outstanding bank loan

Using the accounting equation, record each of the transactions in columnar format using the following template:

Assets	=	Liabilities	+	Stockholders' Equity		
Cash	=	Notes Payable	+	Common Stock	+	Retained Earnings

SE2-7. **Posting Transactions to T-accounts** Using the data from short exercise SE2-6, prepare journal en- **LO5** tries and post your transaction analysis to the appropriate T-accounts.

SE2-8. **Prepare a Trial Balance** The following balances were taken from the general ledger of Howser **LO6** Corporation as of December 31. All balances are normal. Prepare a trial balance.

Cash.	$ 6,000	Accounts receivable.	$10,800
Accounts payable.	6,000	Common stock.	36,000
Equipment	30,000	Dividends	2,400
Utilities expense.	2,000	Administrative expense	8,000
Sales revenue.	17,200		

SE2-9. **Prepare a Corrected Trial Balance** The following trial balance for Magill Company has errors that **LO6** cause it to be out of balance. Prepare a corrected version of the trial balance for Magill Company.

MAGILL COMPANY Unadjusted Trial Balance December 31, 2016	Debit	Credit
Cash	$ 20,000	
Inventory.		$ 85,000
Accounts receivable.	30,000	
Accounts payable.		12,000
Common stock.		40,000
Retained earnings		58,000
Sales revenue.	100,000	
Cost of goods sold.	60,000	
Selling expenses	15,000	
Totals	$225,000	$195,000

LO1   **SE2-10.** **The Accounting Cycle** The following is the correct order of the five steps in the accounting cycle:

a.   Analyze; adjust; record; report; close
b.   Analyze; record; adjust; report; close
c.   Analyze; record; adjust; close; report
d.   Analyze; report; adjust; record; close

LO3   **SE2-11.** **The Account** Which of the following is not part of the T-account?

a.   Title
b.   Amount
c.   Cross-reference
d.   Analysis

EXERCISES—SET A

LO2   **E2-1A.** **Accounting Equation** Determine the missing amount in each of the following cases:

	Assets	Liabilities	Stockholders' Equity
a.	$320,000	$175,000	?
b.	?	$61,000	$42,000
c.	$121,000	?	$71,000

LO2   **E2-2A.** **Transaction Analysis** Following the example shown in (a) below, indicate the accounting effects of the listed transactions on the assets, liabilities, and stockholders' equity of Martin & Company, a corporation:

a.   Purchased, for cash, a desktop computer for use in the office.
     ANSWER: Increase assets (Office Equipment)
             Decrease assets (Cash)
b.   Rendered services and billed the client.
c.   Paid rent for the month.
d.   Rendered services to a client for cash.
e.   Received amount due from a client in Transaction (b).
f.   Purchased an office desk on account.
g.   Paid employees' salaries for the month.
h.   Paid for desk purchased in Transaction (f).
i.   The company paid a dividend.

E2-3A. Analysis of Accounts Calculate the unknown amount in each of the following five independent situations. The answer to situation *(a)* is given as an example. **LO2**

	Account	Beginning Balance	Ending Balance	Other Information
a.	Cash.................	$ 7,000	$ 5,250	Total cash disbursed, $5,400.
b.	Accounts receivable.....	9,000	9,300	Services on account, $16,500.
c.	Notes payable	17,500	20,000	Borrowed funds by issuing a note, $30,000.
d.	Accounts payable.......	2,500	1,720	Payments on account, $2,900.
e.	Stockholders' equity	29,000	46,000	Capital contribution, $5,000.

	Unknown Amounts Required	
a.	Total cash received	$3,650
b.	Total cash collected from credit customers..............	_____
c.	Notes payable repaid during the period.................	_____
d.	Goods and services received from suppliers on account	_____
e.	Net income, assuming that no dividends were paid	_____

E2-4A. Transaction Analysis The accounts below are from the general ledger of The Bast Company. For each letter given in the T-accounts, describe the type of business transaction(s) or event(s) that would most likely be reflected by entries on that side of the account. For example, the answer to (a) is amounts for services performed for clients on account. **LO2, 5**

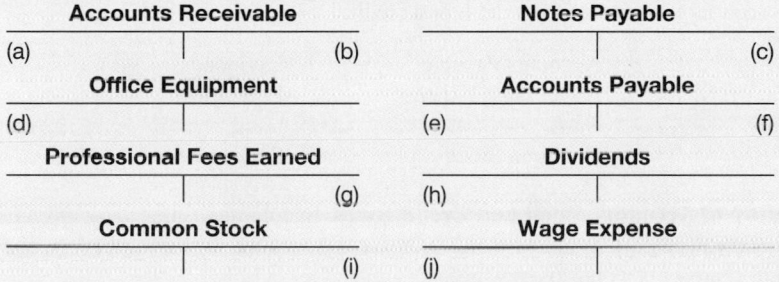

E2-5A. Transaction Analysis Match each of the following transactions of Lesch & Company with the appropriate letters, indicating the debits and credits to be made. The key for the letters follows the list of transactions. The correct answer for Transaction (1) is given as an illustration: **LO4**

		Answer
1.	Purchased supplies on account.	*a, d*
2.	Paid interest on note payable.	_____
3.	Paid cash dividend to stockholders.	_____
4.	Returned some defective supplies and received a reduction in the amount owed.	_____
5.	Made payment to settle note payable.	_____
6.	Received an invoice for utilities used.	_____
7.	Received payment in advance from client for work to be done next month.	_____
8.	Received additional capital contribution from stockholders.	_____

Financial Effect of Transaction

a.	Debit an asset	*g.*	Debit dividends
b.	Credit an asset	*h.*	Credit dividends
c.	Debit a liability	*i.*	Debit a revenue
d.	Credit a liability	*j.*	Credit a revenue
e.	Debit common stock	*k.*	Debit an expense
f.	Credit common stock	*l.*	Credit an expense

LO5 **E2-6A.** **Transaction Entries** Creative Designs, a firm providing art services for advertisers, began business on June 1. The following accounts in its general ledger are needed to record the transactions for June: Cash; Accounts Receivable; Supplies; Office Equipment; Accounts Payable; Common Stock; Dividends; Service Fees Earned; Rent Expense; Utilities Expense; and Salaries Expense.

    a. Using the accounting equation, record each of the transactions in columnar format.

    b. Use journal entries to record the following transactions for June in the general journal.

June	1	Lisa Ryan invested $8,000 cash to begin the business; she received common stock for her investment.
	2	Paid rent for June, $450.
	3	Purchased office equipment on account, $3,500.
	6	Purchased art materials and other supplies costing $2,500; paid $900 down with the remainder due within 30 days.
	11	Billed clients for services, $4,750.
	17	Collected $2,100 from clients on account.
	19	Paid $2,000 on account to office equipment company (see June 3 transaction).
	25	Lisa Ryan received a $750 dividend.
	30	Paid utility bill for June, $450.
	30	Paid salaries for June, $2,750.

LO5 **E2-7A.** **Source Documents** For each transaction in E2-6A, indicate the related source document or documents that provide evidence supporting the transaction.

LO4, 5 **E2-8A.** **Nature of Accounts, Debit and Credit Rules** For each of the accounts listed below, indicate whether the account is increased by a debit or a credit:

Accounts Payable	Dividends
Advertising Expense	Equipment
Cash	Land
Common Stock	Service Fees Earned

LO4, 5 **E2-9A.** **Nature of Accounts, Debit and Credit Rules** In columns, enter *debit* or *credit* to describe the journal entry necessary to increase and decrease the account shown on the left, and which side of the account represents its normal balance.

	Increase	Decrease	Normal Balance
Asset...........................	_____	_____	_____
Liability.........................	_____	_____	_____
Common stock..................	_____	_____	_____
Dividends......................	_____	_____	_____
Revenue.......................	_____	_____	_____
Expense.......................	_____	_____	_____

LO4, 5 **E2-10A.** **Nature of Accounts, Debit and Credit Rules** For each of the accounts listed below, indicate whether the account is increased by a debit or a credit:

Accounts Receivable	Notes Payable
Advertising Revenue	Retained Earnings
Building	Supplies
Common Stock	Utilities Expense

LO2, 4 **E2-11A.** **Transaction Analysis** Match each of the following transactions of L. Boyd & Company with the appropriate letters, indicating the debits and credits to be made. The key for the letters follows the list of transactions. The correct answer for Transaction 1 is given as an illustration.

		Answer
1.	Stockholders contributed cash to the business.	_a,f_
2.	Purchased equipment on account.	_____
3.	Received and immediately paid advertising bill.	_____
4.	Purchased supplies for cash.	_____
5.	Borrowed money from a bank, giving a note payable.	_____
6.	Billed customers for services rendered.	_____
7.	Made a partial payment on account for equipment.	_____
8.	Paid employee's salary.	_____
9.	Collected amounts due from customers billed in Transaction 6.	_____

Financial Effect of Transaction

a.	Debit an asset	*f.*	Credit common stock
b.	Credit an asset	*g.*	Debit a revenue
c.	Debit a liability	*h.*	Credit a revenue
d.	Credit a liability	*i.*	Debit an expense
e.	Debit common stock	*j.*	Credit an expense

E2-12A. Transaction Analysis and Trial Balance Make T-accounts for the following accounts that appear in the general ledger of Daniel Kelly, an attorney: Cash; Accounts Receivable; Office Equipment; Legal Database Subscription; Accounts Payable; Common Stock; Dividends; Legal Fees Earned; Salaries Expense; Rent Expense; and Utilities Expense. Using the accounting equation, record each of the transactions in columnar format. Prepare journal entries and record the following October transactions in the T-accounts and key all entries with the number identifying the transaction. Determine the balance in each account and prepare a trial balance sheet as of October 31. **LO5, 6**

Oct. 1 Kelly started his law practice by contributing $21,500 cash to the business on October 1, receiving shares of common stock in the company.
     2 Purchased office equipment on account, $11,400.
     3 Paid office rent for October, $900.
     4 Paid $9,750 to access online legal database for two years.
     5 Billed clients for services rendered, $11,500.
     6 Made $6,000 payment on account for the equipment purchased on October 2.
     7 Paid legal assistant's salary, $2,800.
     8 Collected $8,400 from clients previously billed for services.
     9 Received invoice for October utilities, $190; it will be paid in November.
    10 Paid stockholders $2,000 as a cash dividend.

E2-13A. Transaction Analysis and Trial Balance Make T-accounts for the following accounts that appear in the general ledger of Mead Pet Hospital, owned by R. Mead, a veterinarian: Cash; Accounts Receivable; Supplies; Office Equipment; Accounts Payable; Common Stock; Dividends; Professional Fees Earned; Salaries Expense; and Rent Expense. Using the accounting equation, record each of the transactions in columnar format. Prepare journal entries and record the following December transactions in the T-accounts and key all entries with the number identifying the transaction. Finally, determine the balance in each account and prepare a trial balance as of December 31. **LO5, 6**

Dec. 1 Mead opened a checking account on December 1 at United Bank in the name of Mead Pet Hospital and deposited $25,000 cash. Mead received common stock for his investment.
     2 Paid rent for December, $1,100.
     3 Purchased office equipment on account, $2,900.
     4 Purchased supplies for cash, $2,500.
     5 Billed clients for services rendered, $8,500.
     6 Paid secretary's salary, $1,950.
     7 Paid $1,500 on account for the equipment purchased on December 3.
     8 Collected $6,000 from clients previously billed for services.
     9 Paid stockholders $2,500 as a cash dividend.

LO3   **E2-14A. The Account** The following transactions occurred during December, the first month of operations for Harris Company. Prepare journal entries and create a T-account for accounts payable that includes the following five transactions.

1. Purchased $750 of inventory on account.
2. Purchased $200 of inventory on account.
3. Paid suppliers $600.
4. Purchased $500 of inventory on account.
5. Paid suppliers $300.

LO2   **E2-15A. Recording Transactions with the Accounting Equation** During the year, the Decker Company experienced the following accounting transactions:

1. Purchased equipment with cash in the amount of $150,000
2. Purchased supplies on account in the amount of $15,000
3. Collected $17,500 cash from customers
4. Paid a cash dividend of $11,000

Using the accounting equation, record each of the transactions in columnar format using the following template:

Assets				=	Liabilities	+	Stockholders' Equity
Cash +	Accounts Receivable	+ Supplies +	Equipment =		Accounts Payable	+	Retained Earnings

LO5   **E2-16A. Posting Transactions to T-accounts** Using the data from short exercise E2-15A, prepare journal entries and post your transaction analysis to the appropriate T-accounts.

EXERCISES—SET B

LO2   **E2-1B. Accounting Equation** Determine the missing amount in each of the following cases:

	Assets	Liabilities	Stockholders' Equity
a.	$425,000	$109,000	?
b.	?	$ 79,000	$31,000
c.	$161,000	?	$93,000

LO2   **E2-2B. Transaction Analysis** Following the example shown in (a) below, indicate the effects of the listed transactions on the assets, liabilities, and stockholders' equity of John Dallmus, certified public accountant, a corporation:

a. Purchased, for cash, a desktop computer for use in the office.
    ANSWER: Increase assets (Office Equipment)
            Decrease assets (Cash)
b. Rendered accounting services and billed client.
c. Paid utilities for month.
d. Rendered tax services to client for cash.
e. Received amount due from client in Transaction (b).
f. Purchased a copying machine on account.
g. Paid employees' salaries for month.
h. Paid for copying machine purchased in Transaction (f).
i. The company paid a dividend.

LO2   **E2-3B. Analysis of Accounts** Compute the unknown amount required in each of the following five independent situations. The answer to situation (a) is given as an illustration:

	Account	Beginning Balance	Ending Balance	Other Information
a.	Cash.................	$ 8,100	$ 5,250	Total cash disbursed, $6,100.
b.	Accounts receivable.....	10,500	8,900	Services on account, $17,000.
c.	Notes payable	17,000	18,500	Borrowed funds by issuing a note, $33,000.
d.	Accounts payable.......	5,280	1,750	Payments on account, $4,000.
e.	Stockholders' equity	34,000	41,000	Capital contribution, $6,100.

	Unknown Amounts Required	
a.	Total cash received	$3,250
b.	Total cash collected from credit customers.................	_____
c.	Notes payable repaid during the period....................	_____
d.	Goods and services received from suppliers on account	_____
e.	Net income, assuming that no dividends were paid	_____

E2-4B. **Transaction Analysis** The accounts below are from the general ledger of Andrew Miller &   **LO2, 5**
Company, an architectural firm. For each letter given in the T-accounts, describe the type of business
transaction(s) or event(s) that would most likely be reflected by entries on that side of the account. For
example, the answer to (a) is amounts for services performed for clients on account.

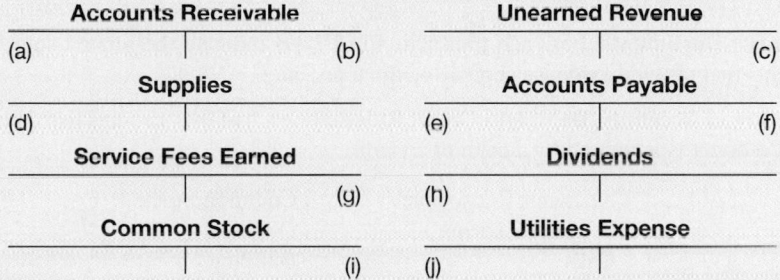

E2-5B. **Transaction Analysis** Match each of the following transactions of Ardon Peralta & Company, a   **LO4**
landscape design firm, with the appropriate letters, indicating the debits and credits to be made. The
key for the letters follows the list of transactions. The correct answer for Transaction 1 is given as an
illustration:

		Answer
1.	Purchased supplies on account.	*a, d*
2.	Paid interest on a bank loan.	_____
3.	The business paid the stockholders a dividend.	_____
4.	Returned some defective supplies and received a reduction in the amount owed.	_____
5.	Made payment to repay bank loan.	_____
6.	Received an invoice for supplies used.	_____
7.	Received payment in advance from client for work to be done next month.	_____
8.	Paid employee's salary.	_____
9.	Peralta contributed additional capital to the business.	_____

Financial Effect of Transaction

a.	Debit an asset	g.	Debit dividends
b.	Credit an asset	h.	Credit dividends
c.	Debit a liability	i.	Debit a revenue
d.	Credit a liability	j.	Credit a revenue
e.	Debit common stock	k.	Debit an expense
f.	Credit common stock	l.	Credit an expense

LO5   E2-6B.   Transaction Entries Thoro Clean, a firm providing house-cleaning services, began business on April 1. The following accounts in its general ledger are needed to record the transactions for April: Cash; Accounts Receivable; Supplies; Prepaid Van Lease; Equipment; Accounts Payable; Notes Payable; Common Stock; Retained Earnings; Dividends; Cleaning Fees Earned; Wage Expense; Advertising Expense; and Fuel Expense.

a.   Using the accounting equation, record each of the transactions in columnar format.

b.   Use journal entries to record the following transactions for April in the general journal.

April   1   Randy Storm invested $11,500 cash to begin the business; he received common stock for his investment.

2   Paid six months' lease on a van, $2,850.

3   Borrowed $10,000 from a bank and signed a note payable agreeing to repay the $10,000 in one year plus 10 percent interest.

3   Purchased $5,500 of cleaning equipment; paid $3,500 down with the remainder due within 30 days.

4   Purchased cleaning supplies for $4,300 cash.

7   Paid $350 for newspaper advertisements to run during April.

21   Billed customers for services, $3,500.

23   Paid $1,500 on account to cleaning equipment firm (see April 3 transaction).

28   Collected $2,300 from customers on account.

29   Randy Storm received a $1,000 cash dividend.

30   Paid wages for April, $1,750.

30   Paid service station for gasoline used during April, $255.

LO5   E2-7B.   Source Documents For each transaction in E2-6B indicate the related source document or documents that provide evidence supporting the transaction.

LO4, 5   E2-8B.   Nature of Accounts, Debit and Credit Rules For each of the accounts listed below, indicate whether the account is increased by a debit or a credit:

Accounts Receivable	Common Stock
Supplies Expense	Dividends
Cash	Building
Equipment	Professional Fees Earned

LO4, 5   E2-9B.   Nature of Accounts, Debit and Credit Rules In the three columns, enter *debit* or *credit* to describe the journal entry necessary to increase and decrease the account shown to the left, and indicate which side of the account represents its normal balance.

	Increase	Decrease	Normal Balance
Cash............................	_____	_____	_____
Accounts payable..................	_____	_____	_____
Common stock....................	_____	_____	_____
Retained earnings	_____	_____	_____
Fee revenue	_____	_____	_____
Wage expense	_____	_____	_____

LO4, 5   E2-10B.   Nature of Accounts, Debit and Credit Rules For each of the accounts listed below, indicate whether the account is increased by a debit or a credit:

Accounts Receivable	Notes Payable
Sales Revenue	Retained Earnings
Equipment	Inventory
Common Stock	Rent Expense

LO2, 4   E2-11B.   Transaction Analysis Match each of the following transactions of R. Couche & Company, a printing company, with the appropriate letters, indicating the debits and credits to be made. The key for letters follows the list of transactions. The correct answer for Transaction (1) is given as an illustration:

		Answer
(1)	Stockholders contributed cash to the business.	*a, f*
(2)	Purchased inventory on account.	_____
(3)	Received and immediately paid a utility bill.	_____
(4)	Purchased supplies for cash.	_____
(5)	Borrowed money from a bank, giving a note payable.	_____
(6)	Billed customers for services rendered.	_____
(7)	Made a partial payment on account.	_____
(8)	Paid employee's salary.	_____
(9)	Collected amounts due from customers billed in Transaction 6.	_____

Financial Effect of Transaction

a.	Debit an asset	*f.*	Credit common stock
b.	Credit an asset	*g.*	Debit a revenue
c.	Debit a liability	*h.*	Credit a revenue
d.	Credit a liability	*i.*	Debit an expense
e.	Debit common stock	*j.*	Credit an expense

E2-12B. Transaction Analysis and the Trial Balance Make T-accounts for the following accounts that appear in the general ledger of Matthew Thomas, an attorney: Cash; Accounts Receivable; Office Equipment; Legal Database Subscription; Accounts Payable; Common Stock; Dividends; Legal Fees Earned; Salaries Expense; Rent Expense; and Utilities Expense. Using the accounting equation, record each of the transactions in columnar format. Prepare journal entries and record the following October transactions in the T-accounts and key all entries with the number identifying the transaction. Determine the balance in each account and prepare a trial balance as of October 31. **LO5, 6**

Oct. 1 Thomas started his law practice by contributing $17,500 cash to the business on October 1; he received common stock for his investment.
2 Purchased office equipment on account, $14,000.
3 Paid office rent for October, $700.
4 Paid $11,600 to access online legal database for two years.
5 Billed clients for services rendered, $11,300.
6 Made $6,000 payment on account for the equipment purchased on October 2.
7 Paid legal assistant's salary, $3,100.
8 Collected $9,400 from clients previously billed for services.
9 Received invoice for October utilities, $180; it will be paid in November.
10 The firm paid stockholders $1,500 cash as a dividend.

E2-13B. Transaction Analysis and Trial Balance Make T-accounts for the following accounts that appear in the general ledger of The Dog & Cat Hospital, owned by Kate Miller, a veterinarian: Cash; Accounts Receivable; Supplies; Office Equipment; Accounts Payable; Common Stock; Dividends; Professional Fees Earned; Salaries Expense; and Rent Expense. Using the accounting equation, record each of the transactions in columnar format. Prepare journal entries and record the following December transactions in the T-accounts and key all entries with the number identifying the transaction. Finally, determine the balance in each account and prepare a trial balance as of December 31. **LO5, 6**

Dec. 1 Miller opened a checking account on December 1 at Biltmore Bank in the name of The Dog & Cat Hospital and deposited $31,000 cash; Miller received common stock for her investment.
2 Paid rent for December, $2,400.
3 Purchased office equipment on account, $2,900.
4 Purchased supplies for cash, $2,500.
5 Billed clients for services rendered, $8,300.
6 Paid secretary's salary, $1,950.
7 Paid $1,700 on account for the equipment purchased on December 3.
8 Collected $6,100 from clients previously billed for services.
9 The firm paid stockholders $1,500 cash as a dividend.

E2-14B. The Account The following transactions occurred during January, the first month of operations for Ruby Corporation. Prepare journal entries and create a T-account for inventory that includes the **LO3**

following five transactions. (*Hint:* When inventory is sold, it should be expensed to a Cost of Goods Sold expense account.)

1. Purchased $950 of inventory on account.
2. Purchased $1,800 of inventory on account.
3. Sold inventory with an original cost of $450.
4. Purchased $1,100 of inventory on account.
5. Sold inventory with an original cost of $1,500.

LO2   **E2-15B. Recording Transactions with the Accounting Equation** During the year, the Decker Company experienced the following accounting transactions:

1. Purchased equipment with cash in the amount of $130,000
2. Purchased supplies on account in the amount of $15,000
3. Collected $37,000 cash from customers
4. Paid a cash dividend of $25,000

Using the accounting equation, record each of the transactions in columnar format using the following template:

Assets				=	Liabilities	+	Stockholders' Equity
Cash +	Accounts Receivable	+ Supplies +	Equipment =		Accounts Payable	+	Retained Earnings

LO5   **E2-16B. Posting Transactions to T-accounts** Using the data from E2-15B, (a) prepare journal entries and (b) post your transactions to the appropriate T-accounts.

PROBLEMS—SET A

LO2   **P2-1A.   Transaction Analysis** The accounting equation of L. Chen & Company as of the beginning of the accounting period is given below, followed by seven transactions whose effects on the accounting equation are shown. Describe each transaction that occurred. Of the transactions affecting Retained Earnings, transaction (e) had no effect on net income for the period.

	Cash	+	Accounts Receivable	+ Supplies	=	Accounts Payable	+	Notes Payable	+	Common Stock	+	Retained Earnings
Balance	$4,100	+	$9,000	+ $700	=	$800	+	$2,500	+	$2,000	+	$8,500
(a)	+6,500		−6,500									
(b)	−400			+400								
(c)			+7,000									+7,000
(d)	−800					−800						
(e)	−4,900											−4,900
(f)	−300			+300								
(g)	+1,200							+1,200				

LO2   **P2-2A.   Transaction Analysis** An analysis of the transactions of Hewitt Detective Agency for the month of May appears below. Line 1 summarizes the company's accounting equation data as of May 1; lines 2–10 represent the transactions for May:

	Cash	+	Accounts Receivable	+	Supplies	+	Equipment	=	Accounts Payable	+	Notes Payable	+	Common Stock	+	Retained Earnings
(1)	$2,400	+	$7,600	+	$500	+	$8,000	=	$300	+	$5,000	+	$10,000	+	$3,200
(2)	+2,000										+2,000				
(3)	+6,100		−6,100												
(4)					+980				+980						
(5)			+6,800												+6,800
(6)	−300								−300						
(7)	+1,500														+1,500
(8)	−800														−800
(9)	−750						+750								
(10)	−2,500										−2,500				

Required

a. Show that assets equal liabilities plus stockholders' equity as of May 1.

b. Describe the apparent transaction indicated by each line. (For example, line 2: Borrowed $2,000, giving a note payable.) If any line could reasonably represent more than one type of transaction, describe each type.

c. Show that assets equal liabilities plus stockholders' equity as of May 31.

P2-3A. **Transaction Analysis** Grant Appraisal Service provides commercial and industrial appraisals **LO2** and feasibility studies. On January 1, the assets and liabilities of the business were the following: Cash, $10,700; Accounts Receivable, $15,800; Accounts Payable, $600; and Notes Payable, $3,500. Common Stock had a balance of $18,400. Assume that Retained Earnings as of January 1, were $4,000. The following transactions occurred during the month of January:

Jan. 1 Paid rent for January, $950.
2 Received $8,800 payment on customers' accounts.
3 Paid $750 on accounts payable.
4 Received $1,700 for services performed for cash customers.
5 Borrowed $5,000 from a bank and signed a note payable for that amount.
6 Billed the city $6,200 for a feasibility study performed; billed various other credit customers, $1,900.
7 Paid the salary of an assistant, $3,500.
8 Received invoice for January utilities, $410.
9 Paid $6,000 cash for employee salaries.
10 Purchased a van (on January 31) for business use, $8,800.
11 Paid $150 to bank as January interest on the outstanding notes payable.

Required

a. Set up an accounting equation in columnar form with the following individual assets, liabilities, and stockholders' equity accounts: Cash, Accounts Receivable, Van, Accounts Payable, Notes Payable, Common Stock, and Retained Earnings. Enter the January 1 balances below each item. (*Note:* The beginning Van account balance is $0.)

b. Show the impact (increase or decrease) of transactions 1–11 on the beginning balances, and total the columns to show that assets equal liabilities plus stockholders' equity as of January 31.

P2-4A. **Transaction Analysis** On June 1, a group of bush pilots in Thunder Bay, Ontario, Canada, formed **LO2** the Outpost Fly-In Service, Inc., by selling $65,000 of common stock for cash. The group then leased several amphibious aircraft and docking facilities, equipping them to transport campers and hunters to outpost camps owned by various resorts. The following transactions occurred during June:

June 1 Sold common stock for cash, $65,000.
2 Paid June rent for aircraft, dockage, and dockside office, $3,500.
3 Received invoice for the cost of a reception the firm gave to entertain resort owners, $1,600.
4 Paid for June advertising in various sports magazines, $800.
5 Paid insurance premium for June, $1,800.
6 Rendered fly-in services for various groups for cash, $24,200.

Required

a. Set up an accounting equation in columnar form with the following individual assets, liabilities, and stockholders' equity accounts: Cash, Accounts Receivable, Equipment, Accounts Payable, Notes Payable, Common Stock, and Retained Earnings. Enter the January 1 balances below each item. (*Note:* The beginning Equipment account balance is $0.)

b. Show the impact (increase or decrease) of the January transactions on the beginning balances, and total all columns to show that assets equal liabilities plus stockholders' equity as of January 31.

LO2   P2-11A. Transaction Analysis On December 1, Peter Allen started Career Services Inc., providing career and vocational counseling services. The following transactions took place during the month of December:

Dec. 1 Allen invested $7,000 in the business, receiving common shares.
      2 Paid rent for December on furnished office space, $1,750.
      3 Received invoice for December advertising, $500.
      4 Borrowed $16,000 from a bank and signed a note payable for that amount.
      5 Received $1,200 for counseling services rendered for cash.
      6 Billed certain governmental agencies and other clients for counseling services, $6,800.
      7 Paid secretary's salary, $2,200.
      8 Paid December utilities, $910.
      9 Paid stockholders a dividend of $900 cash.
     10 Purchased land for cash to use as a site for a new facility, $13,000.
     11 Paid $900 to the bank as December interest on a note payable.

Required

a. Set up an accounting equation in columnar form with the following column headings: Cash, Accounts Receivable, Land, Accounts Payable, Notes Payable, Common Stock, and Retained Earnings.

b. Show how the December transactions affect the items in the accounting equation, and total all columns to show that assets equal liabilities plus stockholders' equity as of December 31.

LO4, 5, 6   P2-12A. Transaction Analysis and the Effect of Errors on the Trial Balance The following T-accounts contain numbered entries for the May transactions of Carol Marsh, a market analyst, who opened her business on May 1, 2016:

Cash				Common Stock		
(1)	13,000	4,800	(2)		13,000	(1)
(9)	3,700	810	(4)			
		1,950	(6)			
		600	(8)			

Accounts Receivable				Dividends		
(5)	6,400	3,700	(9)	(8)	600	

Office Supplies				Professional Fees Earned		
(3)	2,800				6,400	(5)

Office Equipment				Rent Expense		
(2)	4,800			(4)	810	

Accounts Payable				Utilities Expense		
(6)	1,950	2,800	(3)	(7)	270	
		270	(7)			

Required

a. Give a description of each of the nine numbered transactions entered in the above T-accounts. Example: (1) Carol Marsh invested $13,000 of her personal funds in her business.

b. The following trial balance, prepared from Marsh's data as of May 31, contains several errors. Itemize the errors and indicate the correct totals for the trial balance.

CAROL MARSH & COMPANY
Unadjusted Trial Balance
May 31, 2016

	Debit	Credit
Cash	$ 8,450	
Accounts receivable.	3,700	
Office supplies	2,800	
Office equipment	4,800	
Accounts payable.		$ 1,120
Common stock		13,000
Dividends		600
Professional fees earned		6,400
Rent expense	810	
Totals	$20,560	$21,120

P2-13A. Transaction Analysis and Trial Balance Pam Brown owns Art Graphics, a firm providing designs for advertisers and market analysts. On July 1, the business's general ledger showed the following normal account balances: **LO4, 5, 6**

Cash	$ 6,800	Accounts payable.	$ 2,100
Accounts receivable.	9,800	Notes payable	3,300
		Common stock.	2,000
		Retained earnings	9,200
Total Assets	$16,600	Total Liabilities and Stockholders' Equity	$16,600

The following transactions occurred during the month of July:

July 1 Paid July rent, $510.
2 Collected $7,100 on account from customers.
3 Paid $1,800 installment due on the $3,300 noninterest-bearing note payable.
4 Billed customers for design services rendered on account, $16,550.
5 Rendered design services and collected from cash customers, $1,200.
6 Paid $1,400 to creditors on account.
7 Collected $12,750 on account from customers.
8 Paid a delivery service for delivery of graphics to commercial firms, $650.
9 Paid July salaries, $4,600.
10 Received invoice for July advertising expense, to be paid in August, $600.
11 Paid utilities for July, $250.
12 Paid stockholders a dividend of $2,000 cash.
13 Received invoice for supplies used in July, to be paid in August, $2,260.
14 Purchased computer for $6,300 cash to be used in the business starting next month.

Required

a. Set up accounts for the general ledger accounts with July 1 balances and enter the beginning balances. Also provide the following accounts: Equipment; Service Fees Earned; Rent Expense; Salaries Expense; Delivery Expense; Advertising Expense; Utilities Expense; Supplies Expense; and Dividends. Prepare journal entries and record the listed transactions in the appropriate T-accounts.
b. Prepare a trial balance as of July 31.

P2-14A. Transaction Analysis and Trial Balance Outpost Fly-In Service, Inc., operates leased amphibious aircraft and docking facilities, equipping the firm to transport campers and hunters from Vancouver, Canada, to outpost camps owned by various resorts. On August 1, 2016, the firm's trial balance was as follows: **LO4, 5, 6**

OUTPOST FLY-IN SERVICE, INC. Unadjusted Trial Balance August 1, 2016		
	Debit	Credit
Cash	$48,600	
Accounts receivable	23,200	
Accounts payable		$ 1,700
Notes payable		3,000
Common stock		50,000
Retained earnings		17,100
Totals	$71,800	$71,800

During the month of August, the following transactions occurred:

Aug. 1 Paid August rental cost for aircraft, dockage, and dockside office, $5,000.
     2 Paid insurance premium for August, $900.
     3 Paid for August advertising in various sports magazines, $1,000.
     4 Rendered fly-in services for various groups for cash, $13,750.
     5 Billed the Canadian Ministry of Natural Resources for services in transporting mapping personnel, $4,400.
     6 Received $17,400 on account from clients.
     7 Paid $1,750 on accounts payable.
     8 Billed various clients for services, $16,400.
     9 Paid interest on a note payable for August, $25.
   10 Paid August wages, $12,800.
   11 Received invoice for the cost of fuel used during August, $3,800.
   12 Paid a cash dividend, $5,000 (debit Retained Earnings).

Required

a. Set up accounts for each item in the August 1 trial balance and enter the beginning balances. Also provide accounts for the following items: Service Fees Earned, Wage Expense, Advertising Expense, Rent Expense, Fuel Expense, Insurance Expense, and Interest Expense. Prepare journal entries and record the transactions for August in the appropriate T-accounts, using the dates given.

b. Prepare a trial balance as of August 31.

LO4, 5, 6   **P2-15A. Transaction Analysis and Trial Balance** Mary Aker opened a tax practice on June 1. The following accounts will be needed to record her transactions for June: Cash; Accounts Receivable; Office Supplies; Tax Library; Office Furniture and Fixtures; Accounts Payable; Notes Payable; Common Stock; Dividends; Professional Fees Earned; Rent Expense; Salaries Expense; Advertising Expense; Utilities Expense; and Interest Expense. The following transactions occurred during the month of June:

June 1 Aker opened a business checking account at a local bank, investing $13,500 in her practice in exchange for common stock.
     2 Purchased office furniture and fixtures for $9,800, paid $2,800 cash, and gave a note payable for the balance.
     3 Purchased books and software for a tax library on account, $3,700.
     4 Purchased office supplies for cash, $950.
     5 Paid rent for June, $750.
     6 Returned $300 of books with defective bindings. The return reduced the amount owed to the supplier.
     7 Billed clients for professional services rendered, $8,500.
     8 Paid $1,700 on account for the library items purchased on June 3.
     9 Collected $5,900 on account from clients billed on June 7.
   10 Paid June salaries, $3,100.
   11 Received invoice for June advertising, to be paid in July, $300.
   12 Paid stockholders $800 cash as a dividend.
   13 Paid utilities for June, $160.
   14 Paid interest for June on note payable, $250.

Required

a. Prepare journal entries and record the above transactions in T-accounts, and key entries with the number of the transactions.

b. Prepare a trial balance as of June 30.

P2-16A. Transaction Analysis and the Effect of Errors on the Trial Balance　　　　　LO4, 5, 6

The following T-accounts contain numbered entries for the May transactions of Flores Corporation, an architectural firm, which opened its offices on May 1:

Cash				Accounts Payable			
(1)	20,000	1,400	(4)	(5)	310	1,530	(3)
(10)	5,200	5,950	(7)	(8)	1,000	290	(9)
		1,000	(8)				

Accounts Receivable				Common Stock			
(6)	8,750	5,200	(10)			20,000	(1)

Supplies				Professional Fees Earned			
(3)	1,530	310	(5)			8,750	(6)

Office Equipment				Rent Expense			
(2)	5,000			(4)	1,400		

Notes Payable				Utilities Expense			
		5,000	(2)	(9)	290		

Salaries Expense			
(7)	5,950		

Required

a. Give a description of each of the 10 numbered transactions entered in the above accounts. Example: (1) Flores Corporation issued common stock for cash, $20,000.

b. The following trial balance, prepared for Flores Corporation as of May 31, contains several errors. Itemize the errors, and indicate the correct totals for the trial balance.

FLORES CORPORATION Unadjusted Trial Balance May 31, 2016	Debit	Credit
Cash...	$61,850	
Accounts receivable......................................	3,550	
Supplies	1,220	
Office equipment		$ 5,000
Accounts payable...		510
Notes payable		50,000
Common stock...		2,000
Professional fees earned		8,570
Rent expense..	1,400	
Utilities expense..	290	
Salaries expense	5,950	
Totals	$74,260	$66,080

P2-17A. Transaction Analysis and Trial Balance James Behm, electrical contractor, began business on May　　LO5, 6
1. The following transactions occurred during the month of May:

May　1　Behm invested $15,500 of his personal funds in the business in exchange for common stock.

　　　2　Purchased equipment on account, $4,200.

　　　3　Returned $1,200 of equipment that was not satisfactory. The return reduced the amount owed to the supplier.

　　　4　Purchased supplies on account, $860.

May 5 Purchased a truck for $9,500. Behm paid $7,000 cash and gave a note payable for the balance.
    6 Paid rent for May, $875.
    7 Paid fuel cost for truck, $90.
    8 Billed customers for services rendered, $13,700.
    9 Paid $3,000 on account for equipment purchased on May 2.
   10 Paid utilities for May, $210.
   11 Received invoice for May advertising, to be paid in June, $350.
   12 Paid employees' wages, $3,350.
   13 Collected $8,600 on accounts receivable.
   14 Paid stockholders $1,500 cash as a dividend.
   15 Paid interest for May on an outstanding note payable, $30.

Required

a. Prepare journal entries and record the above transactions in T-accounts, and key entries with the numbers of the transactions. The following accounts will be needed to record the transactions for May: Cash; Accounts Receivable; Supplies; Equipment; Truck; Accounts Payable; Notes Payable; Common Stock; Dividends; Service Revenue; Rent Expense; Wages Expense; Utilities Expense; Truck Expense; Advertising Expense; and Interest Expense.

b. Prepare a trial balance as of May 31.

PROBLEMS—SET B

LO2 **P2-1B.** **Transaction Analysis** The accounting equation of Matthew Thomas, attorney, at the beginning of an accounting period is given below, followed by seven transactions whose effects on the accounting equation are shown. Describe each transaction that occurred. Of the transactions affecting retained earnings, transaction (e) had no effect on net income for the period.

	Cash	+	Accounts Receivable	+	Supplies	=	Accounts Payable	+	Notes Payable	+	Common Stock	+	Retained Earnings
Balance	$4,100	+	$9,000	+	$900	=	$1,000	+	$2,500	+	$7,500	+	$3,000
(a)	+7,500		−7,500										
(b)					+400		+400						
(c)			+8,000										+8,000
(d)	−800						−800						
(e)	−4,900												−4,900
(f)	−300				+300								
(g)	+3,200								+3,200				

LO2 **P2-2B.** **Transaction Analysis** An analysis of the transactions of Likert Shipping Services for the month of May appears below. Line 1 summarizes Likert's accounting equation data as of May 1; lines 2–10 represent the transactions for the month of May:

	Cash	+	Accounts Receivable	+	Supplies	+	Equipment	=	Accounts Payable	+	Notes Payable	+	Common Stock	+	Retained Earnings
(1)	$3,500	+	$6,700	+	$900	+	$9,000	=	$700	+	$6,000	+	$3,200	+	$10,200
(2)	+2,000										+2,000				
(3)	+5,200		−5,200												
(4)					+870				+870						
(5)			+4,600												+4,600
(6)	−300								−300						
(7)	+1,900														+1,900
(8)	−800														−800
(9)	−750						+750								
(10)	−2,500										−2,500				

Required

a. Show that assets equal liabilities plus stockholders' equity as of May 1.

b. Describe the apparent transaction indicated by each line. (For example, line 2: Borrowed $2,000, giving a note payable.) If any line could reasonably represent more than one type of transaction, describe each type.

c. Show that assets equal liabilities plus stockholders' equity as of May 31.

P2-3B. Transaction Analysis Smith Appraisal Service provides commercial and industrial appraisals and feasibility studies. On January 1, the assets and liabilities of the business were the following: Cash, $8,700; Accounts Receivable, $18,800; Accounts Payable, $4,600; and Notes Payable, $6,500. Assume that Retained Earnings as of January 1, were $1,000. The balance of Common Stock was $15,400. The following transactions occurred during the month of January: **LO2**

Jan. 1 Paid rent for January, $1,000.
   2 Received $9,800 on customers' accounts.
   3 Paid $900 on accounts payable.
   4 Received $900 for services performed for cash customers.
   5 Borrowed $8,000 from a bank and signed a note payable for that amount.
   6 Billed the city $7,800 for a feasibility study performed; billed various other credit customers, $4,000.
   7 Paid salary of assistant, $4,500.
   8 Received invoice for January utilities, $610.
   9 Paid $6,000 cash for employees salaries.
   10 Purchased a van (on January 31) for business use, $9,800 cash.
   11 Paid $375 to the bank as January interest on an outstanding note payable.

Required

a. Set up an accounting equation in columnar form with the following individual assets, liabilities, and stockholders' equity accounts: Cash, Accounts Receivable, Van, Accounts Payable, Notes Payable, Common Stock, and Retained Earnings. Enter January 1 balances below each item. (*Note.* The beginning Van amount is $0.)

b. Show the impact (increase or decrease) of transactions 1–11 on the beginning balances, and total the columns to show that assets equal liabilities plus stockholders' equity as of January 31.

P2-4B. Transaction Analysis On June 1, a group of bush pilots in British Columbia, Canada, formed the BC Back-Country Airlines, Inc., by selling $51,000 of common stock for cash. The group then leased several aircraft and docking facilities, equipping them to transport campers and hunters to outpost camps owned by various resorts. The following transactions occurred during June: **LO2**

June 1 Sold common stock for cash, $51,000.
   2 Paid June rent for aircraft, dockage, and dockside office, $5,500.
   3 Received invoice for the cost of a reception the firm gave to entertain resort owners, $3,100.
   4 Paid for June advertising in various sports magazines, $1,900.
   5 Paid insurance premium for June, $3,500.
   6 Rendered services for various groups for cash, $25,000.
   7 Billed the Canadian Ministry of Natural Resources for transporting mapping personnel, $4,900, and billed various firms for services, $15,000.
   8 Paid $1,500 on accounts payable.
   9 Received $14,200 on account from clients.
   10 Paid June wages, $16,000.
   11 Received an invoice for the cost of fuel used during June, $3,500.
   12 Paid a cash dividend, $6,000.

Required

a. Set up an accounting equation in columnar form with the following column headings: Cash, Accounts Receivable, Accounts Payable, Common Stock, and Retained Earnings.

b. Show how the June transactions affect the items in the accounting equation, and total all columns to show that assets equal liabilities plus stockholders' equity as of June 30.

LO2 **P2-5B.** **Accounting Equation** Determine the following:

    a.   The stockholders' equity of a company that has assets of $480,000 and liabilities of $330,000.

    b.   The retained earnings of a company that has assets of $675,000, liabilities of $225,000, and common stock of $165,000.

    c.   The assets of a corporation that has liabilities of $500,000, common stock of $300,000, and retained earnings of $255,000.

LO2 **P2-6B.** **Transaction Analysis** Following the example shown in (a) below, indicate the effects of the listed transactions on the assets, liabilities, and stockholders' equity of McKay & Company:

    a.   Rendered services to clients for cash.
         ANSWER: Increase assets (Cash)
               Increase stockholders' equity (increase Revenue)

    b.   Invested cash in the firm in exchange for common stock.

    c.   Purchased a document scanner on account.

    d.   Borrowed cash from a bank and signed a nine-month note.

    e.   Paid amount due on account for scanner purchased in (*c*).

    f.   Rendered services and billed clients.

    g.   Paid stockholders a cash dividend.

    h.   Paid interest on note payable to bank.

    i.   Received payment from clients billed in (*f*).

LO2 **P2-7B.** **Transaction Analysis** On October 1, Deloitte & Coopers started a consulting firm. The asset, liability, and stockholders' equity account balances **after** each of the firm's first six transactions are shown below. Describe each of these six transactions.

	Cash	+	Accounts Receivable	+	Supplies	+	Equipment	=	Notes Payable	+	Common Stock	+	Retained Earnings
(a)	$7,000	+	$ 0	+	$ 0	+	$ 0	=	$ 0	+	$7,000	+	$ 0
(b)	4,500	+	0	+	2,500	+	0	=	0	+	7,000	+	0
(c)	7,500	+	0	+	2,500	+	0	=	3,000	+	7,000	+	0
(d)	2,500	+	0	+	2,500	+	5,000	=	3,000	+	7,000	+	0
(e)	2,500	+	2,000	+	2,500	+	5,000	=	3,000	+	7,000	+	2,000
(f)	3,500	+	1,000	+	2,500	+	5,000	=	3,000	+	7,000	+	2,000

LO2 **P2-8B.** **Determination of Omitted Financial Statement Data** For the four unrelated situations, A–D, below, calculate the unknown amounts indicated by the letters appearing in each column:

	A	B	C	D
Beginning				
Assets.	$38,000	$12,000	$28,000	$ (d)
Liabilities.	18,600	5,000	10,000	9,000
Ending				
Assets.	30,000	36,000	41,000	37,000
Liabilities.	17,300	(b)	15,000	15,000
During the Year				
Common stock	2,000	6,100	(c)	3,500
Revenues	(a)	28,000	18,000	24,000
Dividends	5,000	1,500	2,000	6,500
Expenses	9,500	21,000	11,000	17,000

LO2 **P2-9B.** **Transaction Analysis** Appearing below is an analysis of the June transactions for Carlton Communications Company. Line 1 summarizes Carlton's accounting equation data as of June 1; lines 2–10 are the transactions for June:

	Cash	+	Accounts Receivable	+	Supplies	+	Equipment	=	Accounts Payable	+	Notes Payable	+	Common Stock	+	Retained Earnings
(1)	$3,500	+	$5,200	+	$820	+	$12,000	=	$600	+	$3,000	+	$10,920	+	$7,000
(2)					+670				+670						
(3)							+6,000				+6,000				
(4)	+4,200		−4,200												
(5)			+7,800												+7,800
(6)	−600								−600						
(7)	−200				+200										
(8)	−4,600														−4,600
(9)	+3,000										+3,000				
(10)	−750						+750								

Required

a. Show that assets equal liabilities plus stockholders' equity as of June 1.

b. Describe the apparent transaction indicated by each line. For example, line 2: Purchased supplies on account, $670. If any line could reasonably represent more than one type of transaction, describe each type.

c. Show that assets equal liabilities plus stockholders' equity as of June 30.

P2-10B. Transaction Analysis Torrey Mann began the Mann Word Processing Service in December 2015. **LO2** The firm provides word-processing services for businesses and is currently operating with leased equipment. On January 1, 2016, the assets and liabilities of the business were: Cash, $6,400; Accounts Receivable, $7,500; Accounts Payable, $900; and Notes Payable, $3,500. Assume that Retained Earnings as of January 1, 2016, were zero. Common Stock balance was $9,500. The following transactions occurred during the month of January:

Jan.   1 Paid rent on office and equipment for January, $900.
       2 Collected $8,200 on account from clients.
       3 Borrowed $5,000 from a bank and signed a note payable for that amount.
       4 Billed clients for work performed on account, $9,150.
       5 Paid $400 on accounts payable.
       6 Received invoice for January advertising, $750.
       7 Paid January salaries, $3,750.
       8 Paid January utilities, $230.
       9 Paid stockholders a dividend in the amount of $2,600.
      10 Purchased fax machine (on January 31) for business use, $1,750.
      11 Paid $150 to bank as January interest on the outstanding notes payable.

Required

a. Set up an accounting equation in columnar form with the following individual assets, liabilities, and stockholders' equity accounts: Cash, Accounts Receivable, Equipment, Accounts Payable, Notes Payable, Common Stock, Retained Earnings. Enter the January 1 balances below each item. (*Note:* The beginning Equipment amount is $0.)

b. Show the impact (increase or decrease) of the January transactions on the beginning balances, and total all columns to show that assets equal liabilities plus stockholders' equity as of January 31.

P2-11B. Transaction Analysis On December 1, Judy Johnson started Adult Career Services, which provided **LO2** career and vocational counseling services to individuals. The following transactions took place during the month of December:

Dec.   1 Johnson invested $10,000 in the business in exchange for common stock.
       2 Paid rent for December on furnished office space, $1,250.
       3 Received invoice for December advertising, $800.
       4 Borrowed $27,000 from a bank and signed a note payable for that amount.

Dec. 5 Received $4,200 for counseling services rendered for cash.
       6 Billed certain governmental agencies and other clients for counseling services, $9,800.
       7 Paid secretary's salary, $3,400.
       8 Paid December utilities, $370.
       9 Paid stockholders a dividend in the amount of $900.
      10 Purchased land for cash to use as a site for the company's future offices, $22,000.
      11 Paid $100 to the bank as December interest on the outstanding note payable.

Required

a. Set up an accounting equation in columnar form with the following column headings: Cash, Accounts Receivable, Land, Accounts Payable, Notes Payable, Common Stock, and Retained Earnings.

b. Show how the December transactions affect the items in the accounting equation, and total all columns to show that assets equal liabilities plus stockholders' equity as of December 31.

LO4, 5, 6 **P2-12B. Transaction Analysis and the Effect of Errors on the Trial Balance** The following T-accounts contain numbered entries for the May transactions of Valerie Rankine who opened a consulting services business on May 1:

Cash				Common Stock			
(1)	20,000	4,800	(2)			20,000	(1)
(9)	3,700	810	(4)				
		1,950	(6)				
		600	(8)				

Accounts Receivable				Dividends			
(5)	6,400	3,700	(9)	(8)	600		

Office Supplies			Professional Fees Earned			
(3)	2,800				6,400	(5)

Office Equipment			Rent Expense		
(2)	4,800		(4)	810	

Accounts Payable				Utilities Expense		
(6)	1,950	2,800	(3)	(7)	270	
		270	(7)			

Required

a. Give a description of each of the nine numbered transactions entered in the above accounts. Example: (1) Valerie Rankine invested $20,000 of her personal funds in the business in exchange for common stock.

b. The following trial balance, prepared for Rankine's firm as of May 31, contains several errors. Itemize the errors and indicate the correct totals for the trial balance.

RANKINE CONSULTING SERVICES Unadjusted Trial Balance May 31, 2016		
	Debit	Credit
Cash.	$15,450	
Accounts receivable.	3,700	
Office supplies	2,800	
Office equipment	4,800	
Accounts payable.		$ 1,120
Common stock		20,000
Dividends		600
Professional fees earned		6,400
Rent expense	810	
Totals	$27,560	$28,120

P2-13B. Transaction Analysis and Trial Balance Ashley Somers owns San Diego Art Company, a firm LO4, 5, 6 providing designs for advertisers, market analysts, and others. On July 1, the business's general ledger showed the following normal account balances:

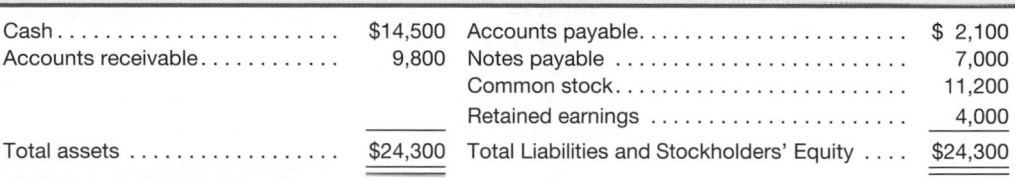

Cash.	$14,500	Accounts payable.	$ 2,100
Accounts receivable.	9,800	Notes payable	7,000
		Common stock.	11,200
		Retained earnings	4,000
Total assets	$24,300	Total Liabilities and Stockholders' Equity	$24,300

The following transactions occurred during the month of July:

July 1 Paid July rent, $670.
2 Collected $8,100 on account from customers.
3 Paid $3,500 installment due on the $7,000 noninterest-bearing note payable to a relative.
4 Billed customers for design services rendered on account, $19,550.
5 Rendered design services and collected from cash customers, $1,400.
6 Paid $1,900 to creditors on account.
7 Collected $16,500 on account from customers.
8 Paid a delivery service for delivery of graphics to commercial firms, $400.
9 Paid July salaries, $4,600.
10 Received invoice for July advertising expense, to be paid in August, $800.
11 Paid utilities for July, $350.
12 The business paid a $2,000 cash dividend.
13 Received invoice for supplies used in July, to be paid in August, $2,260.
14 Purchased a computer for $4,300 cash to be used in the business starting next month.

Required
a. Set up accounts for the general ledger accounts with July 1 balances and enter the beginning balances. Also provide the following accounts: Equipment; Dividends; Service Fees Earned; Rent Expense; Salaries Expense; Delivery Expense; Advertising Expense; Utilities Expense; and Supplies Expense. Prepare journal entries and record the listed transactions in the appropriate T-accounts.
b. Prepare a trial balance as of July 31.

P2-14B. Transaction Analysis and Trial Balance BC Back-Country Airlines, Inc., operates leased amphibi- LO4, 5, 6 ous aircraft and docking facilities, equipping the firm to transport campers and hunters from British Columbia, Canada, to outpost camps owned by various resorts. On August 1, the firm's trial balance was as follows:

BC BACK-COUNTRY AIRLINES, INC. Unadjusted Trial Balance August 1, 2016		
	Debit	**Credit**
Cash.	$ 88,600	
Accounts receivable.	23,200	
Accounts payable.		$ 1,700
Notes payable		6,000
Common stock.		83,000
Retained earnings		21,100
Totals	$111,800	$111,800

During August the following transactions occurred:

Aug. 1 Paid August rental cost for aircraft, dockage, and dockside office, $7,500.
2 Paid the insurance premium for August, $2,800.
3 Paid for August advertising in various sports magazines, $1,500.
4 Rendered services for various groups for cash, $16,750.

Aug. 5 Billed the Canadian Ministry of Natural Resources for services in transporting mapping personnel, $5,100.

6 Received $20,400 on account from clients.

7 Paid $1,700 on accounts payable.

8 Billed various clients for services, $19,400.

9 Paid interest on an outstanding note payable for August, $95.

10 Paid August wages, $14,800.

11 Received invoice for the cost of fuel used during August, $5,600.

12 Paid a cash dividend, $2,500 (debit Retained Earnings).

Required

a. Set up accounts for each item in the August 1 trial balance and enter the beginning balances. Also provide similar accounts for the following items: Service Fees Earned, Wages Expense, Advertising Expense, Rent Expense, Fuel Expense, Insurance Expense, and Interest Expense. Create journal entries and record the transactions for August in the appropriate T-accounts, using the dates given.

b. Prepare a trial balance as of August 31, 2016.

LO4, 5, 6 **P2-15B. Transaction Analysis and Trial Balance** William Groff opened a tax practice, (William Groff, Tax Accounting, Inc.), on June 1. The following accounts will be needed to record the business's transactions for June: Cash; Accounts Receivable; Office Supplies; Tax Library; Office Furniture and Fixtures; Accounts Payable; Notes Payable; Common Stock; Dividends; Professional Fees Earned; Rent Expense; Salaries Expense; Advertising Expense; Utilities Expense; and Interest Expense. The following transactions occurred in June:

June 1 Groff opened a business checking account at a local bank, investing $25,000 in his practice in exchange for common stock.

2 Purchased office furniture and fixtures for $9,800, paid $4,800 cash, and gave a note payable for the balance.

3 Purchased books and software for a tax library on account, $6,700.

4 Purchased office supplies for cash, $660.

5 Paid rent for June, $850.

6 Returned $300 of books with defective bindings. The return reduced the amount owed to the supplier.

7 Billed clients for professional services rendered, $18,600.

8 Paid $1,700 on account for the library items purchased on June 3.

9 Collected $15,900 on account from clients billed on June 7.

10 Paid June salaries, $4,900.

11 Received an invoice for June advertising, to be paid in July, $400.

12 The business paid stockholders a cash dividend of $800.

13 Paid utilities for June, $160.

14 Paid interest for June on an outstanding note payable, $160.

Required

a. Prepare journal entries and record the above transactions in T-accounts, and key entries with the numbers of the transactions.

b. Prepare a trial balance from the general ledger as of June 30.

LO4, 5, 6 **P2-16B. Transaction Analysis and the Effect of Errors on the Trial Balance**

The following T-accounts contain numbered entries for the May transactions of the Claremont Corporation, an architectural firm, which opened its offices on May 1:

Cash				Accounts Payable			
(1)	50,000	1,400	(4)	(5)	310	1,530	(3)
(10)	5,200	5,950	(7)	(8)	1,000	290	(9)
		1,000	(8)				

Accounts Receivable				Common Stock			
(6)	8,750	5,200	(10)			50,000	(1)

Supplies				Professional Fees Earned			
(3)	1,530	310	(5)			8,750	(6)

Office Equipment		Rent Expense	
(2)	5,000	(4)	1,400

Notes Payable		Utilities Expense	
	5,000 (2)	(9)	290

Salaries Expense	
(7)	5,950

Required

a.   Give a description of each of the 10 numbered transactions entered in the above accounts. Example: (1) Claremont Corporation issued common stock for cash, $50,000.

b.   The following trial balance, prepared for Claremont Corporation as of May 31, contains several errors. Itemize the errors, and indicate the correct totals for the trial balance.

CLAREMONT CORPORATION Unadjusted Trial Balance May 31, 2016		
	Debit	**Credit**
Cash.	$ 91,850	
Accounts receivable.	3,550	
Supplies	1,220	
Office equipment		$ 5,000
Accounts payable.		510
Notes payable		50,000
Common stock.		50,000
Professional fees earned		8,570
Rent expense.	1,400	
Utilities expense.	290	
Salaries expense	5,950	
Totals	$104,260	$114,080

P2-17B.   Transaction Analysis and Trial Balance   Walsh & Company, Electrical Contractors began operations on May 1. The following transactions occurred during the month of May: **LO5, 6**

May   1   Stockholders invested $60,000 in the business in exchange for common stock.
   2   Purchased equipment on account, $4,200.
   3   Returned $200 of equipment that was not satisfactory. The return reduced the amount owed to the supplier.
   4   Purchased supplies on account, $860.
   5   Purchased a truck for $12,500. Walsh paid $5,500 cash and gave a note payable for the balance.
   6   Paid rent for May, $875.
   7   Paid fuel cost for truck, $60.
   8   Billed customers for services rendered, $15,700.
   9   Paid $5,000 on account for equipment purchased on May 2.
   10   Paid utilities for May, $210.
   11   Received invoice for May advertising, to be paid in June, $280.
   12   Paid employees' wages, $5,350.
   13   Collected $8,600 on accounts receivable.
   14   Walsh paid stockholders a dividend of $2,500 cash.
   15   Paid interest for May on an outstanding note payable, $80.

Required

a.   Create journal entries and record the above transactions in T-accounts, and key entries with the numbers of the transactions. The following accounts will be needed to record the transactions for May: Cash; Accounts Receivable; Supplies; Equipment; Truck; Accounts Payable; Notes Payable; Common Stock; Dividends; Service Revenue; Rent Expense; Wages Expense; Utilities Expense; Truck Expense; Advertising Expense; and Interest Expense.

b.   Prepare a trial balance as of May 31.

SERIAL PROBLEM: KATE'S CARDS

(Note: This is a continuation of the Serial Problem: Kate's Cards from Chapter 1.)

SP2.   In September 2016, Kate incorporated Kate's Cards after investigating different organizational forms, and began the process of getting her business up and running. The following events occurred during the month of September 2016:

1. Kate deposited $10,000 that she had saved into a newly opened business checking account. She received common stock in exchange.
2. Kate designed a brochure that she will use to promote her greeting cards at local stationery stores.
3. Kate paid Fred Simmons $50 to critique her brochure before undertaking her final design and printing.
4. Kate purchased a new iMac computer tablet, specialized graphic arts software, and commercial printer for the company, paying $4,800 in cash. She decided to record all of these items under the same equipment account.
5. Kate purchased supplies such as paper and ink for $350 at the local stationery store. She opened a business account with the store and was granted 30 days credit on all purchases, including the one she just made.
6. Kate designed her first 5 cards and prepared to show them to potential customers.
7. The owner of the stationery store where Kate opened her account was impressed with Kate's work and ordered 1,000 of each of the five card designs at a cost of $1 per card, or $5,000 total. Kate tells the customer that she will have them printed and delivered within the week.
8. Kate purchased additional supplies, on account, in the amount of $1,500.
9. Kate delivered the 5,000 cards. Because the owner knows that Kate is just starting out, he paid her immediately in cash. He informed her that if the cards sell well that he will be ordering more, but would expect a 30-day credit period like the one he grants to his own business customers.
10. The cost to Kate for the order was $1,750 of the supplies she had purchased. (*Hint:* This cost should be recorded as a debit to an expense called Cost of Goods Sold.)
11. Kate paid her balance due for the supplies in full.
12. Kate decided that she should have special renters' insurance to cover the business equipment she now owns. She purchased a one-year policy for $1,200, paying the entire amount in cash. (*Hint:* Two accounts will need to be debited here, one for the current month expense and one for the prepaid amount.)
13. Kate determined that all of her equipment will have a useful life of 4 years (48 months) at which time it will not have any resale or scrap value. (*Hint:* Kate will expense 1/48th of the cost of the equipment each month to Depreciation Expense. The credit will be to Accumulated Depreciation.)
14. Kate paid herself a salary of $1,000 for the month.

Required

a. Prepare a general ledger with the following accounts: Cash; Accounts Receivable; Supplies Inventory; Prepaid Insurance; Equipment; Accumulated Depreciation; Accounts Payable; Common Stock; Retained Earnings; Sales Revenue; Cost of Goods Sold; Consulting Expense; Insurance Expense; Depreciation Expense; Wages Expense. Prepare journal entries for the above transactions using these accounts.
b. Post the accounting transactions for the month of September 2016 to the general ledger T-accounts.
c. Prepare a trial balance for Kate's Cards as of September 30, 2016.

EXTENDING YOUR KNOWLEDGE

REPORTING AND ANALYSIS

COLUMBIA
SPORTSWEAR
COMPANY

EYK2-1.   Financial Reporting Problem: Columbia Sportswear Company The financial statements for the **Columbia Sportswear Company** can be found in Appendix A at the end of this book. The following selected accounts, in thousands, are from those statements:

Common stock.	$ 72,700
Accounts payable.	214,275
Accounts receivable.	344,390
Inventories	384,650
Prepaid expenses and other current assets.	39,175
Property, plant, and equipment	291,563
Net sales.	2,100,590

Required

a. For each of these accounts, indicate whether a debit or a credit is required to increase its balance.

b. What other account is likely involved when:
   1. Accounts receivable is increased?
   2. Accounts payable is decreased?
   3. Net sales are increased?

EYK2-2.   **Comparative Analysis Problem: Columbia Sportswear Company vs. Under Armour, Inc.**
The financial statements for the **Columbia Sportswear Company** can be found in Appendix A and **Under Armour, Inc.**'s financial statements can be found in Appendix B at the end of this book.

COLUMBIA
SPORTSWEAR
COMPANY

UNDER ARMOUR,
INC.

Required

a. Each of the following accounts is listed in the company's financial statements:

Columbia Sportswear		Under Armour, Inc.	
1	Accounts receivable	1	Inventories
2	Property, plant, and equipment	2	Provision for income taxes
3	Accounts payable	3	Long term debt
4	Common stock	4	Retained earnings
5	Interest income	5	Cost of goods sold

Determine the normal balance (debit or credit) for each of the accounts listed above.

b. Identify the probable other account involved when:
   1. Cost of goods sold is increased.
   2. Interest income is increased.
   3. Accounts receivable is decreased.
   4. Income taxes payable is increased.

EYK2-3.   **Business Decision Problem**
Sarah Penney operates the Wildlife Picture Gallery, selling original art and signed prints received on consignment (rather than purchased) from recognized wildlife artists throughout the country. The firm receives a 30 percent commission on all art sold and remits 70 percent of the sales price to the artist. All art is sold on a cash basis.

Sarah began the business on March 1, 2016. She received a $10,000 loan from a relative to help her get started. Sarah signed a note agreeing to repay the loan in one year. No interest is being charged on the loan, but the relative does expect to receive a set of financial statements each month. On April 1, 2016, Sarah asks for your help in preparing the financial statements for the first month.

Sarah has carefully kept the firm's checking account up to date and provides you with the following complete listing of the cash receipts and disbursements for March 2016:

Cash Receipts	
Original investment by Sarah Penney in exchange for common stock	$ 6,500
Loan from relative	10,000
Sales of art	95,000
Total cash receipts	$111,500
Cash Disbursements	
Payments to artists for sales made	$ 54,000
Payment of March rent for gallery space	900
Payment of March staff wages	4,900
Payment of airfare for personal vacation of Sarah Penney (vacation will be taken in April)	500
Total cash disbursements	60,300
Cash balance, March 31, 2016	$ 51,200

Sarah also gives you the following documents she has received:

1. A $350 invoice for March utilities; payment is due by April 15, 2016.
2. A $1,700 invoice from Careful Express for the shipping of the artwork sold during March; payment is due by April 10, 2016.
3. The one-year lease she signed for the gallery space; as an incentive to sign the lease, the landlord reduced the first month's rent by 25 percent; the monthly rent starting in April is $1,200.

In your discussions with Sarah, she tells you that she has been so busy that she is behind in sending artists their share of the sales proceeds. She plans to catch up within the next week.

Required

From the above information, prepare the following financial statements for Wildlife Picture Gallery: (a) income statement for the month of March 2016; (b) statement of stockholders' equity for the month of March 2016; and (c) balance sheet as of March 31, 2016. To obtain the data needed, you may wish to use T-accounts to construct the company's accounts.

EYK2-4. **Financial Analysis Problem** Tim Johnson runs a local photography studio, Action Images, Inc. Action Images is organized as a corporation. Tim's primary sources of revenue are from the events he is contracted to photograph, mostly sporting events, and from photography lessons given at a local community college. Most of Tim's photographic event customers pay him soon after they receive an invoice from Tim, approximately one week after the event, although in some cases Tim receives payment on the day of the event. The community college pays Tim at the end of each month that he teaches a class. Tim maintains the following accounts to account for these revenue transactions: Cash, Accounts Receivable, Photographic Revenue, Teaching Revenue.

Tim leases the studio where he does most of his work. He owns all his equipment, which consists of cameras, lenses, lighting, a computer, printer, furniture, and miscellaneous office equipment. These assets are accounted for in the following accounts: Photographic Equipment, Office Equipment, and Furniture.

Tim does most of the work himself, but he does employ part-time help on days of his photo events, and he also employs a part-time bookkeeper. Most months Tim has expenses for the studio rent, utilities, advertising, supplies, and insurance. The following accounts are used to account for these expenses: Rent Expense, Utilities Expense, Salaries Expense, Advertising Expense, Supplies Expense, and Insurance Expense.

Tim pays himself a monthly salary. In addition, if his business does well, he will receive a dividend from Action Images. The following stockholders' equity accounts are maintained by Tim: Common Stock and Retained Earnings.

During the month of November, Tim hired a new bookkeeper while his regular bookkeeper was away on vacation. The new bookkeeper was inexperienced, and Tim is concerned that things may not have been recorded correctly. He has asked you to review the following transactions. For each transaction, Tim provides you with the account, the amount either debited or credited, and an explanation for the transaction. In each case, the explanation is correct.

	Account	Debit	Credit
1	Cash	5,000	
	Photographic revenue		5,000
	Issued common stock in exchange for cash.		
2	Cash	2,000	
	Teaching revenue		2,000
	Received $2,000 from the community college for course taught.		
3	Cash	4,500	
	Accounts receivable		5,400
	Received $4,500 from customers for work done last month.		
4	Photographic equipment	1,600	
	Cash		1,600
	Purchase of a new camera for $1,600.		
5	Utilities expense	3,000	
	Cash		3,000
	To pay the month's rent on the studio		
6	Supplies expense	150	
	Accounts receivable		150
	Purchased printing supplies on account.		
7	Salaries expense	3,000	
	Cash		3,000
	Paid the salaries for the month.		

Required

a. For each entry, state if it is correct. If the entry is in error, make the necessary correction.

b. Will any of the errors cause the trial balance to be out of balance?

c. What effect did the errors have on Tim's net income for November?

CRITICAL THINKING

EYK2-5. **Accounting Research Problem** Go to this book's Website and locate the annual report of General Mills, Inc. for the year ending May 25, 2014 (fiscal year 2014).

GENERAL MILLS, INC.

Required

1. For each of the income statement accounts, indicate the normal balance.
2. For each of the balance sheet accounts, indicate the normal balance.

EYK2-6. **Accounting Communication Activity** Fred Jones is struggling with some accounting concepts and has come to you for help. In particular he does not understand what is meant by a debit and a credit. He was especially confused when he learned that sometimes debits result in account increases and sometimes debits result in account decreases.

Required

Write a short memorandum to Fred that explains what is meant by debits and credits as it applies to accounts used by a company.

EYK2-7. **Accounting Ethics Case** Andy Frame and his supervisor are sent on an out-of-town assignment by their employer. At the supervisor's suggestion, they stay at the Spartan Inn, across the street from the Luxury Inn. After three days of work, they settle their lodging bills and leave. On the return trip, the supervisor gives Andy what appears to be a copy of a receipt from the Luxury Inn for three nights of lodging. Actually, the supervisor indicates that he prepared the Luxury Inn receipt on his office computer and plans to complete his expense reimbursement request using the higher lodging costs from the Luxury Inn.

Required

What are the ethical considerations that Andy faces when he prepares his expense reimbursement request?

EYK2-8. **Corporate Social Responsibility Problem** The Global Reporting Initiative (GRI) is a network-based organization that has pioneered the development of the world's most widely used sustainability reporting framework. The GRI Website is located at http://www.globalreporting.org/. Sustainability reporting differs from financial reporting in several areas. One difference that is readily apparent is that sustainability reports contain performance metrics that are measured in units other than dollars. For example, greenhouse emissions may be measured in metric tons and employee in-kind volunteering may be measured in hours.

Required
Go to the GRI Website and near the bottom, left of the page, under Useful Pages, select Disclosure Database. Use the Search feature in the middle of the page to select a report of one of the listed firms. What are some of the areas that the company reports on, and what measures do they use?

EYK2-9. **Forensic Accounting Problem** Accrual accounting is based on the idea that revenue should be recognized when earned and that any resources consumed in the revenue-generating process (expenses) should be matched with those revenues in the same period. Another basic principle on which GAAP is based is that of the accounting period. This principle sets the time period for which the revenues and expenses are to be measured and matched. For many firms, this date is December 31. Revenues earned after December 31 are to be reported in the following period, and expenses in the following period are then matched to those revenues. One way that companies have been found to misrepresent their reported performance is to violate these principles by "holding the books open" beyond December 31. In other words, the firm will improperly record revenue earned after year-end as if it were earned in the current year, and at the same time, fail to properly match the expenses associated with those revenues. How might a forensic accountant who has been hired to investigate improper financial reporting catch this type of activity?

EYK2-10. **IFRS Financial Statements** Thomson Reuters is a global information company created by the 2008 merger of the Thomson Corporation, a Canadian company, with the Reuters Company, a United Kingdom-based company. The company operates in over 100 countries and has over 50,000 employees. The company provides financial, legal, scientific, and tax information services to the public on a fee basis. The shares of Thomson Reuters are listed on the New York Stock Exchange and the Toronto Stock Exchange. The company prepares its financial statements using IFRS but also reconciles this information to various non-IFRS measures. You can view the company's financial statements and the Canadian GAAP-IFRS reconciliation at www.thomsonreuters.com.

Required
1. What are the advantages of having a single, global set of accounting standards like IFRS?
2. A competitor of Thomson Reuters is U.S.-based Bloomberg L.P, a closely held financial software, news and data company founded by Michael Bloomberg, former mayor of New York City. Bloomberg prepares its financial statements using U.S. GAAP. What constraints would you face in trying to compare the financial results of Thomson Reuters to Bloomberg?

EYK2-11. **Working with the Takeaways**

Part A
Each of the following accounts from the Furst Company has a normal balance as of December 31, 2016, the end of Furst's first year of operations.

Cash	$100	Common stock	$500
Accounts receivable	300	Dividends	100
Inventory	250	Sales revenue	800
Property, plant, and equipment	750	Selling expenses	300
Accounts payable	150	Administrative expenses	50
Notes payable	400		

Required
Prepare a trial balance for Furst Company as of December 31, 2016.

Part B

Lampe Distributors was formed to serve as a distributor of fine furnishings imported from overseas manufacturers. Assume the following trial balance was prepared as of December 31, 2016, at the end of Lampe's first year of operations:

LAMPE DISTRIBUTORS Unadjusted Trial Balance December 31, 2016		
	Debit	Credit
Cash	$ 23,000	
Accounts receivable.	4,500	
Buildings.	72,000	
Equipment	20,500	
Inventory.	38,000	
Accounts payable.		$ 5,500
Notes payable		47,750
Common stock.		42,000
Dividends	6,000	
Sales revenue.		280,250
Wage expense	100,000	
Selling expenses	31,000	
Rent expense	23,000	
Administrative expenses	15,750	
Tax expense.	23,000	
Totals	$356,750	$375,500

It is apparent that there is an error somewhere in the company's accounts since the sum of the debit account balances ($356,750) does not equal the sum of the credit account balances ($375,500). After further research, we learn the following:

1. A cash purchase of $20,000 in inventory, occurring near year-end, was not recorded.
2. By mistake, $5,000 that should have been recorded as Accounts Payable was recorded as Notes Payable.
3. A credit of $26,000 was accidentally recorded in the Wage Expense account rather than in Sales Revenue.
4. A sale on account of $18,750 was correctly recorded as Sales Revenue, but the other side of the entry was mistakenly never recorded.

Required
a. Which of the four errors, if any, is the reason that the trial balance is not in balance?
b. Which of the errors, if any, must be corrected?
c. Prepare a corrected trial balance.

ANSWERS TO SELF-STUDY QUESTIONS:

1. d, (pp. 61–66) 2. a, (pp. 61–66) 3. b, (pp. 61–66) 4. c, (p. 70) 5. b, (p. 69) 6. d, (p. 69)
7. b, (p. 69) 8. c, (p. 69) 9. d, (p. 69) 10. a, (p. 69) 11. d, (p. 72) 12. d, (p. 79) 13. d, (p. 72)
14. a, (p. 72) 15. c, (p. 60) 16. d, (pp. 61–62) 17. 1. (b), 2. (e), 3. (d), 4. (a), 5. (c), (p. 60)

YOUR TURN! SOLUTIONS

Solution 2.1

d, b, e, a, c

Solution 2.2

		Cash	+	Accounts Receivable	+	Equipment	=	Accounts Payable	+	Notes Payable	+	Common Stock	+	Retained Earnings
a.		$ 5,000	+	$ 5,200	+	$ 0	=	$1,000	+	$2,500	+	$5,500	+	$1,200
b.	(1)	−600						−600						
	(2)	−3,600												−3,600
	(3)			+11,500										+11,500
	(4)							+500						−500
	(5)	+10,000		−10,000										
	(6)	−2,400												−2,400
	(7)							+680						−680
	(8)	−20												−20
	(9)	−900												−900
	(10)	−4,000				+4,000								
		$ 3,480	+	$ 6,700	+	$4,000	=	$1,580	+	$2,500	+	$5,500	+	$4,600

$14,180 $14,180

Solution 2.3

a. Debit
b. Credit
c. Debit
d. Credit
e. Debit
f. Credit
g. Debit

Solution 2.4

Accounts Receivable

(8)	3,740	2,400	(10)
Bal.	1,340		

Solution 2.5

1.		Assets					Liabilities		Equity			
										Retained Earnings		
		Cash	+	Accounts Receivable	+	Office Supplies	=	Accounts Payable	+	Revenues − Expenses − Dividends		
a.		$ 1,300								$1,300		Service revenue
b.		−2,400								−2,400		Wages expense
c.		600		−600								
d.		−400								−400		Dividends
e.						700		700				
f.				900						900		Service revenue
g.		−500						−500				

2. a.

Cash	1,300	
Service revenue		1,300
Revenue payment for services rendered.		

b.

Wages expense	2,400	
Cash		2,400
Paid employee wages.		

c.

Cash	600	
Accounts receivable		600
Received payment from clients.		

d.

Dividends	400	
Cash		400
Paid cash dividend.		

e.

Office supplies	700	
Accounts payable		700
Purchased office supplies on account.		

f.

Accounts receivable	900	
Service revenue		900
Billed clients for services rendered.		

g.

Accounts payable	500	
Cash		500
Paid suppliers.		

3.

Cash

(a)	1,300	2,400	(b)	
(c)	600	400	(d)	
		500	(g)	

Accounts Receivable

(f)	900	600	(c)

Office Supplies

(e)	700

Accounts Payable

(g)	500	700	(e)

Service Revenue

	1,300	(a)
	900	(f)

Wages Expense

(b)	2,400

Dividends

(d)	400

Solution 2.6

Devin Company
Unadjusted Trial Balance
December 31, 2016

	Debit	Credit
Cash.	$ 1,500	
Accounts receivable.	4,500	
Inventory.	3,750	
Property, plant, and equipment	11,250	
Accounts payable.		$ 2,250
Notes payable		6,000
Common stock.		7,500
Dividends	1,500	
Sales revenue.		12,000
Salary expense.	4,500	
Administrative expenses	750	
Totals	$27,750	$27,750

3

Accrual Basis of Accounting

PAST

Chapter 2 explained how we analyze and record transactions (the first two steps in the *accounting cycle*), including the system of debits and credits.

PRESENT

This chapter completes our examination of the final three steps in the five-step accounting cycle: adjust, report, and close.

FUTURE

Chapter 4 examines the balance sheet and income statement more closely and introduces techniques for analyzing and interpreting financial statements.

LEARNING OBJECTIVES

1. **Explain** the accrual basis of accounting and contrast it with the cash basis with reference to revenue and expense recognition. *(p. 122)*

2. **Describe** the adjusting process. *(p. 125)*

3. **Illustrate** deferral adjustments. *(p. 126)*

4. **Illustrate** accrual adjustments. *(p. 129)*

5. **Explain** the adjusted trial balance and use it to prepare financial statements. *(p. 133)*

6. **Describe** the closing process and **summarize** the accounting cycle. *(p. 137)*

7. Appendix 3A: **Describe** the process of closing to the Income Summary account and **summarize** the accounting cycle. *(p. 144)*

8. Appendix 3B: **Explain** how to use a worksheet in the adjusting and closing process. *(p. 148)*

MAKING DOUGH

Krispy Kreme is similar to other companies when it comes to the end-of-year accounting process. As it closes its books for the year, its employees must get the accounting information organized to prepare the financial statements for its annual report. That process normally requires several accounting adjustments to properly determine how well a company performed and its financial condition.

Many estimates, assumptions, and judgments make up these accounting adjustments. Krispy Kreme's recent annual report had a fiscal year-end of February 2. However, because of those adjustments and other year-end procedures, it did not file its audited financial statements until April 3, two months later.

Accounting adjustments are important to investors and others that rely on financial statements for valuing company stock. Not long ago, Krispy Kreme was a high-flying company with a stock price of nearly $50 per share. Today, its stock is selling for less than half of that price.

What precipitated such a dramatic drop in its stock price? One reason suggested by Wall Street pundits is Krispy Kreme's accounting methods. It appears that some adjustments that Krispy Kreme made propped up its earnings much like the yeast in its donuts. When investors began to question the "quality" of Krispy Kreme's earnings, a sharp sell-off of its stock followed as worried stockholders moved their money to alternative investments.

Why are accounting adjustments so important? This chapter focuses on that question. It explains the importance of those adjustments for financial statements. It also shows how companies account for adjustments and how financial statements are prepared from final adjusted numbers.

ACCRUAL BASIS OF ACCOUNTING				
Accrual Accounting	**Accounting Adjustments**	**Adjusted Trial Balance and Financial Statements**	**Closing Process**	**Assessing the Accounting Numbers**
• Revenue recognition • Expense recognition	• Allocating prepaid assets to expense • Allocating deferred revenue to revenue • Accruing expenses • Accruing revenue	• Adjusted trial balance • Preparing financial statements from adjusted trial balance	• Closing the accounts and closing entries • Post-closing trial balance • Accounting cycle • Closing to the Income Summary account (Appendix 3A) • Using a worksheet (Appendix 3B)	• Quality of earnings concept • Conservative versus aggressive accounting

eLectures
MBC

ACCRUAL BASIS OF ACCOUNTING

LO1 **Explain** the accrual basis of accounting and contrast it with the cash basis with reference to revenue and expense recognition.

Most individuals, and some small businesses, measure their financial performance by looking at their cash flow. For example, an individual who pays for all of her purchases from a checking account is likely to evaluate her financial well-being in terms of her available cash. If she ends the period with a higher cash balance than she started with, she is likely to conclude that she generated a profit.

The cash basis of accounting is not considered generally accepted for most businesses. Generally accepted accounting principles require that companies use the accrual basis of accounting. The accrual basis of accounting requires a business to measure and report its operating performance regardless of whether all revenues have been collected in cash and all expenses have been paid with cash.

Revenue Recognition Principle

Under the cash basis of accounting, the receipt and payment of cash is the determining factor for when sales revenue is recognized and when expenses are deducted. Under the accrual basis of accounting, sales revenue is recognized when it is earned, regardless of when the related cash is collected; and, expenses are recognized when incurred, regardless of whether cash has been paid. For most businesses, this means that its sales revenue is recognized at the time that goods and services are delivered to a customer. Revenue may be recognized before, after, or at the same time that cash is received.

Revenue Earned *When* Cash Is Received

For most sales, **Krispy Kreme** will receive cash at the same time that the customer receives donuts. Under these circumstances, accrual accounting recognizes sales revenue at the same time that the company receives payment for its product. As a consequence, Krispy Kreme will debit Cash and credit Sales Revenue.

	April 30	Cash	100	
A = L + SE +100 + 100 Rev.		Sales revenue		100
		To record revenue at time of cash receipt.		

Revenue Earned *Before* Cash Is Received

Safeway purchases large quantities of Krispy Kreme donuts for resale in their grocery stores. Assume that Safeway agrees to pay for the donuts in thirty days following each purchase. Even though Krispy Kreme has not received any payment for the delivered donuts, the company has earned the right to receive the cash, and consequently, Krispy Kreme must recognize the sales revenue prior to cash collection. In this case, it will debit Accounts Receivable and credit Sales Revenue at the time of the sale. The subsequent collection of cash on the account does not result in sales revenue being recognized.

April 30	Accounts receivable	100		
	Sales revenue		100	A = L + SE
	To recognize revenue earned.			+100 + 100 Rev.
May 30	Cash	100		
	Accounts receivable		100	A = L + SE
	To recognize cash received.			+100
				−100

Revenue Earned *After* Cash Is Received

Assume that **Albertsons** prepays for its donut purchases by giving Krispy Kreme a cash payment prior to receiving any donuts. Even though Krispy Kreme has received cash, it has not earned the revenue, and thus, will defer the recognition of any sales revenue until earned, which is at the time of product delivery. Krispy Kreme will record a liability account, Unearned Revenue, until such time as the donuts are delivered to Albertsons and it earns the revenue.

April 30	Cash	100		
	Unearned revenue		100	A = L + SE
	To recognize the receipt of cash prior to revenue being earned.			+100 +100
May 30	Unearned revenue	100		
	Sales revenue		100	A = L + SE
	To recognize earned revenue.			−100 + 100 Rev.

As these examples demonstrate, it is the earning of sales revenue that determines when revenue is recognized by a company under the accrual basis of accounting, and not the timing of the cash collection.

Concept ⟶	Method ⟶	Assessment	TAKEAWAY 3.1
When should sales revenue be recognized?	Understand the nature of a company's earning process. Record revenue when it is earned.	Early recognition of revenue overstates current period revenue; recognizing revenue too late understates current period revenue.	

Revenue Recognition   **PRINCIPLE ALERT**

In May of 2014, the FASB and IASB jointly issued a new revenue recognition standard. Revenue must still be earned to be recognized; however, the new standard requires a five-step process based on the core principle that a company should recognize revenue to depict the transfer of promised goods or services to a customer in an amount that reflects the consideration that the company expects to receive in exchange for those goods or services. The five-step process consists of:

Step 1.   Identify the contract with a customer.
Step 2.   Identify the separate performance obligations in the contract.
Step 3.   Determine the transaction price.
Step 4.   Allocate the transaction price to the separate performance obligations in the contract.
Step 5.   Recognize revenue when or as the entity satisfies a performance obligation.

It remains to be seen how the new standard will affect companies financial statements, but the effects will likely vary across industries and could significantly change the timing of revenue recognition, accelerating it in some cases and delaying it in others. We discuss the new standard in more detail in Appendix 5B in Chapter 5.

Expense Recognition (Matching) Principle

Accounting requires that the expenses incurred to generate revenues be recognized (matched) in the same period. In other words, business expenses are recognized (matched) with sales revenues so that they are reported on the same income statement. Like the recognition of revenue, the recognition of expenses can occur prior to, simultaneously with, or subsequent to the receipt of cash. It is the recognition of revenue, and not the payment of cash, that determines when expenses are recognized under the accrual basis of accounting.

Referring again to Krispy Kreme, assume the company pays $50 cash to acquire baking materials for its donuts. A cash purchase is not considered to be a business expense until Krispy Kreme sells the donuts it produces. The cash purchase of materials prior to sale would be accounted for as a reduction of cash and an increase in supplies, both assets.

A = L + SE	May 15	Baking supplies	50	
+50		Cash		50
−50		*To record cash payment for supplies*		

The cash payment precedes the revenue recognition and the matching of expense. But what happens if the materials are purchased on account and used in donuts sold before the baking materials are paid for? In this case, the accrual basis of accounting dictates the recognition of expense prior to the cash payment for the materials so that the expense is properly matched with the earned revenue in the same accounting period.

A = L + SE	May 15	Baking supplies	50	
+50 +50		Accounts payable		50
		To record purchase of supplies on account		

In each of the above cases the expense is recognized when the donuts are sold with the following journal entry:

A = L + SE	May 15	Cost of goods sold	50	
−50 −50		Baking supplies		50
		To record cost of product sold		

The key point is that under accrual accounting the recognition of expense is matched to the recognition of revenue in the same period. This may occur after the cash expenditure, before the cash expenditure, or at the same time as the cash expenditure. In addition, it should be stressed that the purpose of accrual accounting is to adjust cash flows such that revenues and expenses are recognized in the period the revenue is earned and the corresponding resources to earn the revenue are used up. Such matching would not necessarily occur under the cash basis of accounting. Ultimately both cash-basis accounting and accrual-basis accounting will yield the same results; however, the results will likely differ period by period.

TAKEAWAY 3.2	Concept ⟶	Method ⟶	Assessment
	When should expenses be recognized?	Understand the nature of the company's earning process.	Early recognition of expenses overstates current period expenses; recognizing expenses too late understates current period expenses.
		Expenses should be recognized with the related revenue in the same accounting period.	

Prepare journal entries for Sawyer Enterprises for each of the following accrual accounting adjustments on June 30.

1. Sawyer Enterprises sells $600 of merchandise to Apollo Inc. with terms of cash due in 30 days.
2. Apollo Inc. prepays Sawyer Enterprises $700 for merchandise that will be delivered in 30 days.
3. Sawyer Enterprises purchases and receives inventory of $400 from its supplier Adamo Co. The terms are cash due in 45 days.

ADJUSTING ACCOUNTS

LO2 Describe the adjusting process.

In Chapter 2, we analyzed a series of accounting transactions for WebWork, Inc., that occurred during the month of December. We prepared journal entries for those transactions and recorded them in the general journal. We then posted the company's journal entry data to the general ledger, which we set up in T account form. Many of the general ledger account balances from Chapter 2, however, require an end-of-period adjustment to bring them to the correct balance for the preparation of WebWork's financial statements. For example, WebWork prepaid six months of rent for its office space on December 1. By December 31, one month's rent has expired. The prepaid rent account must be adjusted so that the account balance reflects the remaining amount of rent that is still prepaid and rent expense is recognized for the month of December. When it is time to prepare a company's financial statements, the company must review account balances and make any necessary end-of-period adjustments to bring those (unadjusted) accounts to their proper balance.

Unadjusted Trial Balance

The end-of-period adjustment process begins with the preparation of a trial balance of all general ledger accounts. Because this trial balance reports the account balances before any adjustments have been made, it is referred to as the **unadjusted trial balance**. An unadjusted trial balance is prepared to insure that the general ledger is in balance before the end-of-period adjusting process begins. Accumulating all general ledger account balances in one location makes it easier to review the accounts and determine which account balances must be adjusted. The unadjusted trial balance of WebWork, Inc., as of December 31 is in **Exhibit 3-1**.

Exhibit 3-1	Unadjusted Trial Balance for WebWork, Inc.	

WEBWORK, INC.
Unadjusted Trial Balance
December 31, 2016

	Debit	Credit
Cash.	$40,590	
Accounts receivable.	1,340	
Office supplies	2,850	
Prepaid rent	10,800	
Office equipment	32,400	
Accounts payable.		$ 2,850
Unearned revenue		3,000
Notes payable		36,000
Common stock.		30,000
Dividends.	500	
Fee revenue		18,250
Wage expense	1,620	
Totals	$90,100	$90,100

Types of Adjustments

There are four types of accounting adjustments made at the end of an accounting period:

Prepaid Expenses	Unearned Revenues	Accrued Expenses	Accrued Revenues
Allocating previously recorded assets to expenses to reflect the proper expenses incurred during that period.	Allocating previously recorded unearned revenue to earned revenue to reflect revenues earned during the period.	Recording operating expenses that have not yet been paid or recorded to reflect expenses incurred during the period.	Recording revenues that have not yet been received or recorded to reflect revenue earned during the period.

Journal entries to record accounting adjustments are known as **adjusting entries**. Each adjusting entry affects one or more balance sheet accounts (an asset or liability account) and one or more income statement accounts (an expense or revenue account).

Adjustments in the first two categories—allocating "prepaid" assets to expense, and allocating "unearned" revenues to revenue—are referred to as **deferrals**. The distinguishing characteristic of a deferral is that the adjustment deals with an amount that has previously been recorded in a balance sheet account. The adjusting entry, in effect, decreases the balance sheet account and increases an income statement account. Adjustments in the last two categories—increasing expenses and increasing revenues—are referred to as **accruals**. The unique characteristic of an accrual is that the adjustment deals with an amount that has not previously been recorded in an account. Consequently, the adjusting entry increases both a balance sheet account and an income statement account.

YOUR TURN! 3.2

The solution is on page 185.

Match the transaction from the first column with the type of accounting adjustment from the second column.

1. Record depreciation for the month on buildings
2. Record rental income for the month on equipment rented on a long-term rental agreement. Payment will be received next month.
3. Record rental income at month-end on amounts that had been prepaid at the beginning of the month.
4. Record utility expense at the end of the month for amounts that had previously been paid in advance and recorded as an asset.

a. Prepaid expenses
b. Unearned revenue
c. Accrued expenses
d. Accrued revenues

DEFERRAL ADJUSTING ENTRIES

LO3 Illustrate deferral adjustments.

Allocating Previously Recorded Assets to Expenses

Prepaid Expenses

Many expenditures benefit multiple accounting periods. These expenditures must be allocated over the periods benefited. Common examples include purchases of buildings, equipment, and supplies; prepayments of rent and advertising; and payments of insurance premiums covering more than one year. Outlays for these expenditures are normally debited to an asset account at the time of payment. Then, at the end of each accounting period, the estimated portion of the expenditure that has expired, or that has been used up, during the period is transferred from the asset account to an expense account to achieve a proper recognition of revenue and expenses.

These adjustments are commonly identified by inspecting the unadjusted trial balance for costs that benefit multiple accounting periods. For example, by looking at the

December 31 trial balance of WebWork (**Exhibit 3-1**), we observe that adjustments are required to allocate costs of the purchased office supplies, the prepaid rent, and the office equipment to the current period (December) and subsequent accounting periods that benefit from these expenditures. The next three sections illustrate those adjustments.

Office Supplies

WebWork purchased office supplies on account and recorded the expenditure in an asset account, Office Supplies, as follows:

Dec. 1	Office supplies	2,850	
	Accounts payable		2,850
	To record the purchase of office supplies.		

$$A = L + SE$$
$$+2,850 \quad +2,850$$

During December, office supplies were used up as services were provided. The cost of office supplies used is an expense for December that reduces the amount of supplies available. It is unnecessary to record an expense as each individual supply item, such as a copier cartridge or LCD cleaner, is used up. Instead, at the end of December, the company physically counts the supplies still available and then subtracts that amount from the total amount purchased to determine the amount used up. For example, assume that a physical count of the office supplies reveals that $1,530 worth of WebWork's office supplies are available at the end of the month. This implies that $1,320 ($2,850 − $1,530) worth of supplies were used up during December. An adjusting entry is needed to transfer this amount to an expense account, Supplies Expense, as follows:

Dec. 31	Supplies expense	1,320	
	Office supplies		1,320
	To record expense of office supplies used in December.		

$$A = L + SE$$
$$-1,320 \qquad -1,320$$
$$\text{Exp.}$$

When this adjusting entry is posted, it properly shows the $1,320 December expense for office supplies and reduces the asset account, Office Supplies, to $1,530, the actual amount of the asset remaining as of December 31.

Office Supplies			
Unadjusted	2,850		
		1,320	(a)
Adjusted	1,530		

Supplies Expense			
Unadjusted	0		
(a)	1,320		
Adjusted	1,320		

Prepaid Rent

On December 1, WebWork paid six months' rent in advance and debited the $10,800 payment to Prepaid Rent, an asset account. As each day passes and the rented space is occupied, rent expense is being incurred, and the balance of the prepaid rent is decreasing. It is unnecessary to record rent expense on a daily basis because financial statements are not prepared daily; however, at the end of the accounting period, an adjusting entry is necessary to recognize the correct amount of rent expense for the period and to decrease the Prepaid Rent account. Specifically, on December 31, one month of WebWork's prepaid rent has been used up; consequently, WebWork will transfer $1,800 ($10,800/6 months) from the Prepaid Rent account to the Rent Expense account, as follows:

Dec. 31	Rent expense	1,800	
	Prepaid rent		1,800
	To record rent expense for December.		

$$A = L + SE$$
$$-1,800 \qquad -1,800$$
$$\text{Exp.}$$

The posting of this adjusting entry shows the correct rent expense ($1,800) for December in the Rent Expense account and reduces the Prepaid Rent account balance to the correct balance ($9,000) that remains prepaid as of December 31. (Examples of other prepaid expenses for which similar adjustments are made include prepaid insurance and prepaid advertising.)

Prepaid Rent			
Unadjusted	10,800		
		1,800	(b)
Adjusted	9,000		

Rent Expense			
Unadjusted	0		
(b)	1,800		
Adjusted	1,800		

Depreciation

The process of allocating the cost of buildings, equipment, and vehicles to the periods benefiting from their use is called **depreciation**. Because these long-lived assets help generate revenue for a company over many years, each accounting period in which the assets are used must reflect a portion of their cost as an expense. The allocation of the cost of revenue-generating assets over the many periods that they help produce revenues is an application of the expense recognition principle. This periodic expense is known as *depreciation expense*.

There is no exact way to measure the amount by which these assets are used up each period, which means that the periodic depreciation expense is an estimate. The procedure used in this chapter estimates the annual amount of depreciation expense by dividing the acquisition cost of the asset by its estimated useful life in years. This method is called **straight-line depreciation**. (We will explore other depreciation methods in a later chapter.)

Hint: A contra account is increased and decreased in the opposite way of its controlling account. Also, the normal balance of a contra account is opposite to the normal balance of its controlling account.

When recording depreciation expense, the asset account is not reduced directly. Instead, the reduction is recorded in a contra account called **Accumulated Depreciation**. **Contra accounts** are so named because they are used to record reductions in, or offsets against, a controlling account. In this case, the Accumulated Depreciation contra account offsets the controlling account, Office Equipment, which has a normal debit balance. Accumulated depreciation therefore has a normal credit balance and appears in the balance sheet as a deduction against Office Equipment. Use of the contra account Accumulated Depreciation allows the original cost of the related asset to be reported in the company's balance sheet, followed by the accumulated amount of depreciation taken to date. Users of financial statements want to see both of these amounts so that they can estimate how much of an asset has been used up and how much remains to benefit the business in future periods.

To illustrate, assume that the office equipment purchased by WebWork for $32,400 is expected to last six years. Straight-line depreciation is $5,400 per year ($32,400/6 years), or $450 per month ($5,400/12 months). At the end of December, WebWork would make the following adjusting entry:

A = L + SE
−450   −450
          Exp

Accumulated Depreciation—Office Equipment		
	0	Unadjusted
	450	(c)
	450	Adjusted

Depreciation Expense		
Unadjusted	0	
(c)	450	
Adjusted	450	

A.K.A. Book value is also called *carrying value*.

Dec. 31	Depreciation expense	450	
	Accumulated depreciation—Office equipment		450
	To record December depreciation.		

When the preceding adjusting entry is posted, it shows the estimated cost of using the asset during December, and shows the estimated expense ($450) in the company's December income statement. On the balance sheet, the accumulated depreciation is subtracted from the related asset account (Office Equipment). The resulting balance (acquisition cost less accumulated depreciation) is called the asset's **book value** and represents the unexpired asset cost to be applied as an expense against future periods. For example, the December 31, 2016, balance sheet shows WebWork's office equipment with a book value of $31,950, presented as follows:

Office equipment	$32,400
Less: Accumulated depreciation	450
Office equipment, net.	$31,950

Unearned Revenues

Allocating Previously Recorded Unearned Revenue to Revenue

Sometimes a business receives fees for services or products before the services or products are rendered. Such transactions are initially recorded by debiting the Cash account and crediting a liability account called **Unearned Revenue**. The Unearned Revenue account is also called **Deferred Revenue** and represents an obligation to perform a service, or provide a product, in the future. Once the service or product is provided, the revenue is earned. The required adjusting entry is a debit to the Unearned Revenue account, which reduces the liability account, and a credit to the Revenue account for the amount of revenue earned in the current period.

Deferred Service Revenue

On December 5, WebWork signed a four-month contract to perform work for $750 per month, with the entire contract price of $3,000 received in advance. The journal entry made on December 5 was:

Dec. 5	Cash	3,000	
	Unearned revenue		3,000
	Received $3,000 advance payment on a four-month contract.		

A = L + SE
+3,000 +3,000

On December 31, the following adjusting entry transfers $750, the revenue earned in December, to Fee Revenue and it reduces the liability Unearned Revenue by the same amount:

Dec. 31	Unearned revenue	750	
	Fee revenue		750
	To record portion of advance earned in December.		

A = L + SE
−750 +750 Rev.

Unearned Revenue			
		3,000	Unadjusted
(d)	750		
		2,250	Adjusted

Fee Revenue			
		18,250	Unadjusted
		750	(d)
		19,000	Adjusted

After the journal entry is posted to the general ledger accounts, the liability account shows a balance of $2,250, the amount of future services still owed by WebWork and the Fee Revenue account reflects the $750 earned in December.

Other examples of revenues received in advance include rental prepayments by real estate management companies, insurance premiums received in advance by insurance companies, subscription revenues received in advance by magazine and newspaper publishers, and membership fees received in advance by health and fitness clubs. In each case, a liability account is established when the prepayment is initially received. Later, an adjusting entry is made to reflect the revenues earned from the services provided or products delivered during the current accounting period.

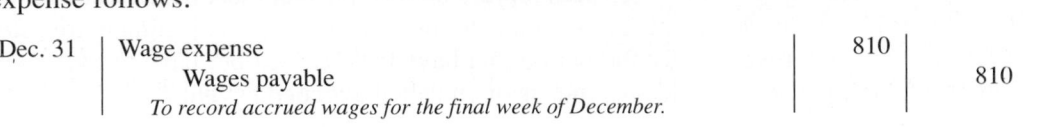

Prepare journal entries for each of the following end-of-year accounting adjustments.

1. Record depreciation expense adjustment of $700 on the company's buildings.
2. Record $1,500 for rent expense that was previously recorded as part of a $2,000 advance rent payment to the company's landlord.

YOUR TURN! 3.3

The solution is on page 185.

ACCRUAL ADJUSTING ENTRIES

Recording Previously Unrecorded Expenses

A company often incurs expenses before paying for them. Employee wages, utilities, and income taxes are all examples of expenses that are typically incurred by a business before payment is made. Usually the cash payments are made at regular time intervals, such as weekly, monthly, quarterly, or annually. If the accounting period ends on a date that does not coincide with a scheduled cash payment date, an adjusting entry must be recorded to reflect the expense incurred during the period. Such expenses are referred to as **accrued expenses**. WebWork has two such adjustments to make on December 31, one for its employee wages and the other for interest on its bank loan.

LO4 Illustrate accrual adjustments.

Accrued Expenses

Accrued Wages

WebWork's employee is paid every two weeks at the rate of $810 per week. The employee was paid $1,620 on Friday, December 23. At the close of business on Friday, December 30, the employee has worked one week during December for which wages are not paid until January. Because the employee's wages are $810 per week, an additional wage expense of $810 must be reflected in WebWork's income statement for December. The adjusting entry at the end of December to accrue one week of wage expense follows:

A = L + SE
+ 810 −810
Exp

Dec. 31	Wage expense	810	
	Wages payable		810
	To record accrued wages for the final week of December.		

Wages Payable			
		0	Unadjusted
		810	(e)
		810	Adjusted

Wage Expense		
Unadjusted	1,620	
(e)	810	
Adjusted	2,430	

This adjustment enables WebWork's December income statement to show the cost of all wages *incurred* during the month rather than just the wages *paid*. Also, its balance sheet will correctly show a liability for unpaid wages at the end of December.

When the employee is paid on the next regular payday in January, WebWork must insure that the one week of accrued wages for December are not again charged to expense. When the employee is paid $1,620 on Friday, January 6, the following entry is made:

A = L + SE
−1,620 −810   −810
              Exp.

Jan. 6	Wages payable	810	
	Wage expense	810	
	Cash		1,620
	To record two weeks wages paid.		

This entry eliminates the liability recorded in Wages Payable at the end of December and debits January Wage Expense for only those wages earned by the employee in January.

Accrued Interest

On December 1, 2016, WebWork obtained a bank loan in the amount of $36,000 and signed a two-year note payable. The annual interest rate on the note is 10 percent, with interest payable each November 30. The amount of interest expense must be reflected in net income for the period. Interest expense (or interest revenue) is computed based on three factors: (1) the principal amount of the money borrowed (or loaned); (2) the rate of interest expressed as an annual rate; and (3) the amount of time in the calculation. The first year's interest of $3,600 ($36,000 × 10 percent) is due on November 30, 2017. Because interest accumulates as time passes, an adjusting entry is needed on December 31, 2016, to reflect the interest expense for December. December's interest is $300 ($3,600/12 months), and the adjusting entry at December 31 follows:

A = L + SE
      +300   −300
              Exp

Dec. 31	Interest expense	300	
	Interest payable		300
	To record accrued interest expense for December.		

Interest Payable

		0	Unadjusted
		300	(f)
		300	Adjusted

Interest Expense

Unadjusted	0	
(f)	300	
Adjusted	300	

When this adjusting entry is posted to the general ledger, the correct interest expense for December is shown as well as a liability for one month's interest that has accrued as of December 31.

When the first year's interest of $3,600 is paid on November 30, 2017, WebWork must remember that $300 of that amount relates to 2016. On November 30, 2017, the following entry records the interest payment:

A = L + SE
−3,600 −300 −3,300
              Exp.

Nov. 30	Interest payable	300	
	Interest expense	3,300	
	Cash		3,600
	To record payment of annual interest.		

This entry eliminates the interest payable that was accrued on December 31, 2016, and debits the Interest Expense account for $3,300 ($300 times 11 months), the correct interest expense for the first 11 months of 2017.

| **Accrued Revenues** |

Recording Previously Unrecorded Revenues

Revenues from selling a product or providing a service must be recognized in the period in which the goods are sold or the services are performed. A company, however, may provide services during a period that are neither paid for by customers nor billed at the end of the period. The value of these services represents revenue that must be included in the current period income statement. To accomplish this, end-of-period adjusting entries are made to reflect any revenues for the period that have been earned but have not yet been paid or billed. Such accumulated revenue is often called **accrued revenue**.

Accrued Fees

WebWork entered into a contract with a local company on December 2 that requires a December 31 adjusting entry to accrue revenue. Under the one-year contract, WebWork agreed to maintain that company's Website in exchange for a monthly fee of $150, payable at the end of every three months. By December 31, WebWork has earned one month of fee revenue, and the following adjusting entry is made:

Dec. 31	Accounts receivable	150	
	Fee revenue		150
	To record accrued fee revenue earned in December.		

A   = L +   SE
+150   +150 Rev.

Accounts Receivable

Unadjusted	1,340	
(g)	150	
Adjusted	1,490	

Fee Revenue

	18,250	Unadjusted
	750	(d)
	150	(g)
	19,150	Adjusted

When WebWork receives the first $450 payment on February 28, 2017, the company must remember that $150 was previously earned and recorded in 2016. The following entry records the payment received on that date:

Feb. 28	Cash	450	
	Accounts receivable		150
	Fee revenue		300
	To record receipt of quarterly payment.		

A   = L +   SE
+450   +300 Rev.
150

This entry eliminates the accounts receivable established on December 31, 2016, and records $300 of fee revenue earned for the first two months of 2017.

Accrued Interest

Another example of accrued revenue involves a company that has loaned money to another entity on which interest has been earned but that has not yet been collected at the end of the accounting period. Assume WebWork loaned $2,000 to James Corporation on November 1, 2016, with annual interest at the rate of 6 percent. The loan balance, along with interest, is to be repaid one year later. On December 31, 2016, WebWork would make the following adjusting entry:

Dec. 31	Interest receivable	20	
	Interest income		20
	To record interest earned on note.		

A   = L +   SE
+20 | 20

The $20 interest is computed as follows:

Principal Amount of Note	×	Annual Interest Rate	×	Time as a fraction of a year	=	Interest
$2,000	×	6%	×	2/12	=	$20

Since WebWork did not actually have a loan to James Corporation, the adjustment calculated above will not be posted to the general ledger.

Summary of Accounting Adjustments

Exhibit 3-2 summarizes the adjusting entries for WebWork as recorded in its general journal. These adjustments would be posted to the company's general ledger.

    Exhibit 3-3 lists the four types of accounting adjustments and also shows (1) examples of how each type of adjustment arises, (2) the generic adjusting entry for each type of adjustment, and (3) what accounts are overstated or understated *prior to* any adjustment. As we explained, each adjustment affects at least one balance sheet (asset or liability) account and at least one income statement account (expense or revenue).

Exhibit 3-2	**Adjusting Entries for WebWork, Inc.**		

GENERAL JOURNAL

Date	Description	Debit	Credit	
2016				
Dec. 31	Supplies expense	1,320		(a)
	Office supplies		1,320	
	To record expense of office supplies used in December.			
Dec. 31	Rent expense	1,800		(b)
	Prepaid rent		1,800	
	To record rent expense for December.			
Dec. 31	Depreciation expense	450		(c)
	Accumulated depreciation—Office equipment		450	
	To record December depreciation.			
Dec. 31	Unearned revenue	750		(d)
	Fee revenue		750	
	To record portion of advance earned in December.			
Dec. 31	Wage expense	810		(e)
	Wages payable		810	
	To record accrued wages for the final week of December.			
Dec. 31	Interest expense	300		(f)
	Interest payable		300	
	To record accrued interest expense for December.			
Dec. 31	Accounts receivable	150		(g)
	Fee revenue		150	
	To record accrued fee revenue earned in December.			

Exhibit 3-3	**Four Types of Accounting Adjustments**

Accounting Adjustment	Examples	Adjusting Entry	Financial Effects If *Not* Adjusted	
			Balance Sheet	**Income Statement**
Deferrals				
Prepaid expenses	Expiration of prepaid rent, insurance, and advertising; depreciation of buildings and equipment	Dr. Expense Cr. Asset (or contra asset)	Asset overstated Equity overstated	Expense understated
Unearned revenues	Use of prepayments on customer orders, gift cards, and subscriptions	Dr. Liability Cr. Revenue	Liability overstated Equity understated	Revenue understated
Accruals				
Accrued expenses	Incurred but not yet paid cash for wages, interest, and tax expenses	Dr. Expense Cr. Liability	Liabilty understated Equity overstated	Expense understated
Accrued revenues	Earned but not yet received cash for service, sales, and interest revenues	Dr. Asset Cr. Revenue	Asset understated Equity understated	Revenue understated

TAKEAWAY 3.3	Concept →	Method →	Assessment
	When should an adjusting entry be made?	Individual account balances and transaction details such as contracts and agreements. Knowledge of the proper account balance is needed. Adjustments involve (1) allocating assets to expense, (2) allocating unearned revenue to revenue, (3) accruing expenses, or (4) accruing revenues.	Record an adjusting entry so that accounts are correctly reported; otherwise income and assets (and/ or liabilities) are incorrectly reported.

Prepare journal entries for each of the following end-of-year accounting adjustments.

1. Record $400 of revenue earned that was previously recorded as unearned revenue due to an advance payment from a customer.
2. Record $500 of accrued interest expense that applies to the company's bank loan. The $500 is part of the company's annual cash interest payment that is due next period.

YOUR TURN! 3.4

The solution is on page 185.

MBC

ADJUSTED TRIAL BALANCE AND FINANCIAL STATEMENTS

After the end-of-period adjustments are recorded in the general journal and posted to the general ledger, the company prepares an adjusted trial balance. The company then uses the adjusted trial balance to prepare financial statements.

eLectures
MBC

Preparing the Adjusted Trial Balance

LO5 Explain the adjusted trial balance and use it to prepare financial statements.

The **adjusted trial balance** lists all the general ledger account balances after the end-of-period adjustments have been posted. **Exhibit 3-4** presents Web-Work's adjusted trial balance as of December 31 in the two right-hand columns of the exhibit. This exhibit begins with the unadjusted trial balance, shown in the two left-hand columns, and lists the seven adjustments in the middle columns. For example, the first adjusting entry adjusted office supplies for the $1,320 of supplies used in December. This adjustment is highlighted in **Exhibit 3-4**. Office Supplies has a $2,850 debit balance in the unadjusted trial balance column. The adjustment of a $1,320 credit appears in the credit column of the adjustments. This leads to a $1,530 debit balance in the adjusted trial balance.

Exhibit 3-4	Adjusted Trial Balance for WebWork, Inc.						

WEBWORK, INC.
Adjusted Trial Balance
December 31, 2016

	Unadjusted Trial Balance		Adjustments		Adjusted Trial Balance	
	Debit	**Credit**	**Debit**	**Credit**	**Debit**	**Credit**
Cash.	$40,590				$40,590	
Accounts receivable.	1,340		(g) $ 150		1,490	
Office supplies	2,850			(a) $1,320	1,530	
Prepaid rent	10,800			(b) 1,800	9,000	
Office equipment	32,400				32,400	
Accumulated depreciation—						
Office equipment				(c) 450		$ 450
Accounts payable.		$ 2,850				2,850
Interest payable				(f) 300		300
Wages payable.				(e) 810		810
Unearned revenue		3,000	(d) 750			2,250
Notes payable		36,000				36,000
Common stock.		30,000				30,000
Dividends	500				500	
Fee revenue		18,250		(d) 750		19,150
				(g) 150		
Supplies expense.			(a) 1,320		1,320	
Wage expense	1,620		(e) 810		2,430	
Rent expense			(b) 1,800		1,800	
Depreciation expense.			(c) 450		450	
Interest expense.			(f) 300		300	
Totals	$90,100	$90,100	$5,580	$5,580	$91,810	$91,810

The adjusting entry also affects supplies expense, as shown in the exhibit. Supplies expense has a zero balance in the unadjusted trial balance. The adjustment appears as a $1,320 debit in the adjustments column, leading to a $1,320 debit balance in the adjusted trial balance for supplies expense. Using this presentation, managers can readily see the adjustments made and their impact on the financial accounting numbers. (Another common format for the adjusted trial balance is to only show the two right-hand columns as shown in **Exhibit 3-5**—either format is acceptable.)

ACCOUNTING IN PRACTICE

Getting a Loan

Because of the size of many corporations like **McDonald's Corp.** and **Amazon.com Inc.**, it is easy to believe that corporations are the primary form of businesses in the United States. In reality, sole proprietorships, with a single owner, comprise about 70 percent of U.S. businesses according to the Small Business Administration (SBA). A common form of financing for these businesses is a 7(a) loan guaranteed by the SBA. While the procedures learned in this chapter needed to produce financial statements may seem like something only an accountant would need to know, this skill set is very useful for anybody applying for a loan. Listed near the top of the 7(a) loan application checklist is the preparation of personal and business financial statements.

Preparing Financial Statements

The adjusted trial balance is used to prepare the income statement, the statement of stockholders' equity, and the balance sheet. (It is also helpful in preparing the statement of cash flows although other information is also necessary to complete this financial statement.) We illustrate the preparation of financial statements for WebWork in **Exhibit 3-5**. Recall from Chapter 1 that financial statements are prepared in the following sequence: (1) the income statement, (2) the statement of stockholders' equity, (3) the balance sheet, and (4) the statement of cash flows.

Income Statement

The income statement presents a company's revenues and expenses and shows whether the company operated at a profit or a loss. WebWork's adjusted trial balance contains one revenue account and five expense accounts. The revenue and expense accounts are reported in WebWork's income statement located in the lower right side of **Exhibit 3-5**. The income statement shows its net income for December is $12,850.

Statement of Stockholders' Equity

The statement of stockholders' equity reports the transactions and events causing a company's stockholders' equity to increase or decrease during an accounting period. The middle right side of **Exhibit 3-5** presents WebWork's statement of stockholders' equity for December. The stockholders' equity accounts in the general ledger provides some of the information for this statement, including the common stock and retained earnings balances at the beginning of the period, new common stock issuances, and dividends during the period. Since December was the first month of operations for WebWork, the beginning retained earnings balance is zero. The net income (or net loss) amount is obtained from the company's income statement.

Balance Sheet

The balance sheet reports a company's assets, liabilities, and stockholders' equity. The assets and liabilities for WebWork as of December 31, 2016, shown in the upper right side of **Exhibit 3-5**, come from the adjusted trial balance. The $12,350 amount reported as retained earnings is taken from the statement of stockholders' equity as of December 31.

Statement of Cash Flows

The statement of cash flows reports information regarding a company's cash inflows and outflows. The statement of cash flows classifies cash flows into three activity categories: operating, investing, and financing. The procedures for preparing a statement of cash flows are discussed in Chapter 12.

Exhibit 3-5	Financial Statements Prepared From the Adjusted Trial Balance

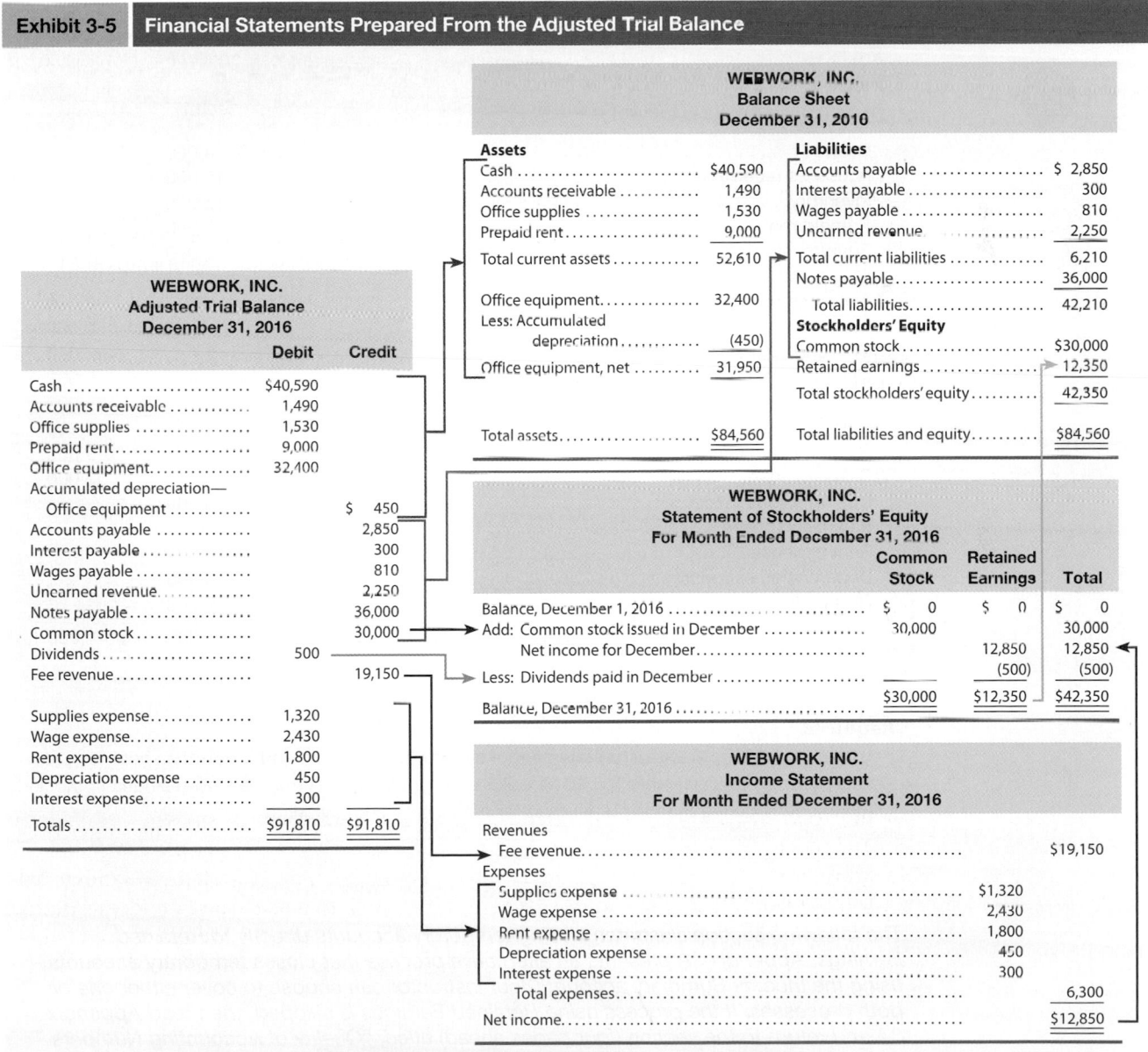

The income statement, the statement of stockholders' equity, and the statement of cash flows are financial statements covering periods of time. These statements illustrate the *accounting period concept* that useful financial statements can be prepared for arbitrary time periods within a company's total life span. Since a company does not complete all of its transactions by the end of an accounting period, accounting principles must provide a process to account for a company's continuing transactions. The end-of-period adjusting procedures provided by the accrual basis of accounting are that process. A major purpose of adjusting entries is to ensure that correct amounts of revenue and expense are reported for each accounting period.

YOUR TURN! 3.5

The solution is on pages 185–186.

Cassi Company prepared the following adjusted trial balance to assist in the preparation of its December 31, 2016, financial statements.

CASSI COMPANY Adjusted Trial Balance December 31, 2016	Debit	Credit
Cash.	$ 4,000	
Accounts receivable.	15,000	
Inventory.	18,000	
Prepaid rent	5,000	
Equipment	50,000	
Accumulated depreciation		$ 10,000
Accounts payable.		8,000
Salaries payable		9,000
Dividends payable		2,000
Unearned revenue		5,000
Long-term debt		35,000
Common stock.		15,000
Retained earnings		5,000
Sales revenue.		52,000
Cost of goods sold.	30,000	
Salaries expense	5,000	
Rent expense	6,000	
Depreciation expense.	6,000	
Dividends	2,000	
Totals	$141,000	$141,000

Required
Prepare an income statement, a statement of stockholders' equity, and a balance sheet for Cassi Company using its December 31, 2016, adjusted trial balance. There were no changes in stockholders' equity during the year other than for net income and dividends.

The following section illustrates closing temporary accounts directly to Retained Earnings. Appendix 3A presents an alternative process that closes temporary accounts using the Income Summary account. Your instructor can choose to cover either one or both processes. If the process using Retained Earnings is skipped, then read Appendix 3A and return to the section (four pages ahead) titled, "Quality of Accounting Numbers."

CLOSING PROCESS

All accounts can be identified as either permanent accounts or temporary accounts. **Permanent accounts** are the accounts presented on the balance sheet. They consist of the asset, liability, and stockholders' equity accounts. The distinguishing feature of a permanent account is that any balance in the account at the end of an accounting period is carried forward to the following accounting period. **Temporary accounts** are used to gather information for a particular accounting period. Revenue, expense, and dividend accounts are temporary subdivisions of stockholders' equity. At the end of the accounting period, temporary account balances are transferred to Retained Earnings, which is a permanent stockholders' equity account. The process of transferring the balances in temporary accounts to Retained Earnings is referred to as the **closing process** or **closing procedures**.

LO6 **Describe** the closing process and **summarize** the accounting cycle.

A temporary account is *closed* when an entry is made that changes its account balance to zero—that is, the entry is equal in amount to the account's ending balance but is opposite to the balance as a debit or credit. An account that is closed is said to be closed *to* the account that receives the offsetting debit or credit. Thus, a closing entry simply transfers the balance of one account to another account. Because closing entries bring temporary account balances to zero, the temporary accounts are then ready to start accumulating data for the next accounting period. In essence, closing the temporary accounts prevents information from the current accounting period from being carried forward to a subsequent period, which enables financial statement users to make meaningful comparisons of revenue and expenses from one period to the next. The following summarizes the classification of permanent and temporary accounts.

A.K.A. Closing procedures are also known as **closing the books**.

Permanent Accounts	Temporary Accounts
Assets	Revenues
Liabilities	Expenses
Common Stock	Dividends
Retained Earnings	

YOUR TURN! 3.6

The solution is on page 186.

For each of the following accounts, identify whether the account is either a permanent account or a temporary account:

a. Cash
b. Common Stock
c. Wage Expense
d. Notes Payable
e. Dividends
f. Sales Revenue
g. Inventory
h. Prepaid Expense

Journalizing and Posting the Closing Entries

The Retained Earnings account is used to close the temporary revenue, expense, and Dividends accounts. The closing entries occur only at the end of an accounting period and consist of three steps, which are graphically shown below.

1. **Close the revenue accounts.** Debit each revenue account for an amount equal to its current credit balance, and credit the Retained Earnings account for the total amount of earned revenue.

2. **Close the expense accounts.** Credit each expense account for an amount equal to its current debit balance, and debit the Retained Earnings account for the total amount of expenses.

3. **Close the Dividends account.** Debit the Retained Earnings account and credit the Dividends account for an amount equal to the balance in the Dividends account.

Closing Process for WebWork

Exhibit 3-6 illustrates the closing entries for WebWork as recorded in the company's general journal. The financial information in these entries is posted to the appropriate general ledger accounts, which is represented using T-accounts.

Exhibit 3-6	Closing Revenue, Expense, and Dividends Accounts—WebWork, Inc.		
	GENERAL JOURNAL		
Date	**Description**	**Debit**	**Credit**
2016			
1 Dec. 31	Fee revenue	19,150	
	Retained earnings		19,150
	To close the revenue account.		
2 Dec. 31	Retained earnings	6,300	
	Supplies expense		1,320
	Wage expense		2,430
	Rent expense		1,800
	Depreciation expense		450
	Interest expense		300
	To close the expense accounts.		
3 Dec. 31	Retained earnings	500	
	Dividends		500
	To close the dividends account.		

The financial effect of posting these entries on the general ledger is diagrammed below.

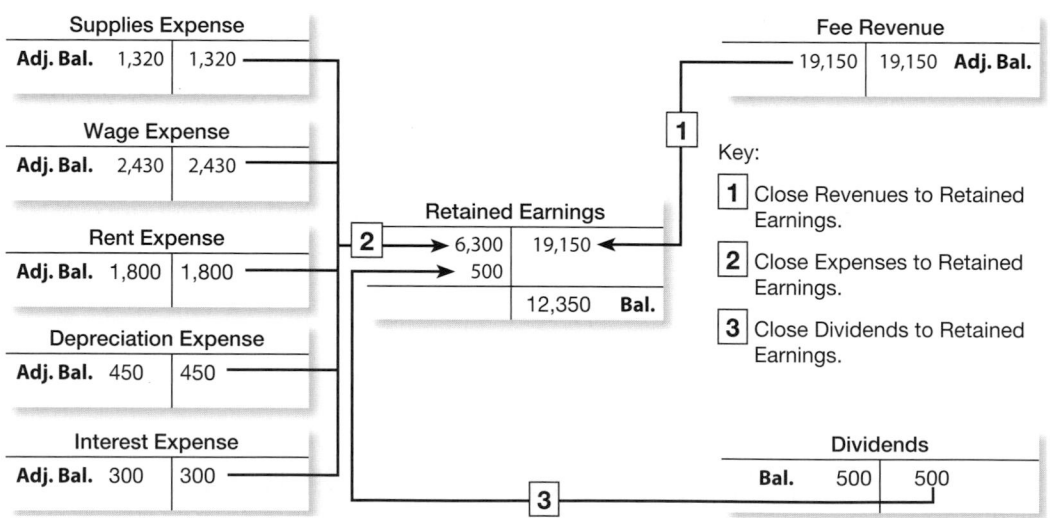

Preparing the Post-Closing Trial Balance

After closing entries are recorded in the general journal and posted to the general ledger, all of the temporary accounts have zero balances. At this point a **post-closing trial balance** is prepared. The post-closing trial balance provides evidence that an equality of debits and credits has been maintained in the general ledger throughout the adjusting and closing processes, and that the general ledger is in balance to start the next accounting period. Because the temporary accounts have been closed, only the balance sheet (or permanent) accounts appear in the post-closing trial balance. **Exhibit 3-7** presents the post-closing trial balance for WebWork.

Exhibit 3-7	Post-Closing Trial Balance for WebWork, Inc.

WEBWORK, INC.
Post-Closing Trial Balance
December 31, 2016

	Debit	Credit
Cash.	$40,590	
Accounts receivable.	1,490	
Office supplies	1,530	
Prepaid rent	9,000	
Office equipment	32,400	
Accumulated depreciation—Office equipment		$ 450
Accounts payable.		2,850
Interest payable		300
Wages payable.		810
Unearned revenue		2,250
Notes payable		36,000
Common stock.		30,000
Retained earnings		12,350
Totals	$85,010	$85,010

Summary of the Accounting Cycle

The sequence of accounting procedures known as the *accounting cycle* occurs each fiscal period and represents a systematic process for accumulating and reporting the financial data of a business. **Exhibit 3-8** summarizes the five major steps in the accounting cycle as described in this and the preceding chapter.

Exhibit 3-8	The Accounting Cycle: A Summary

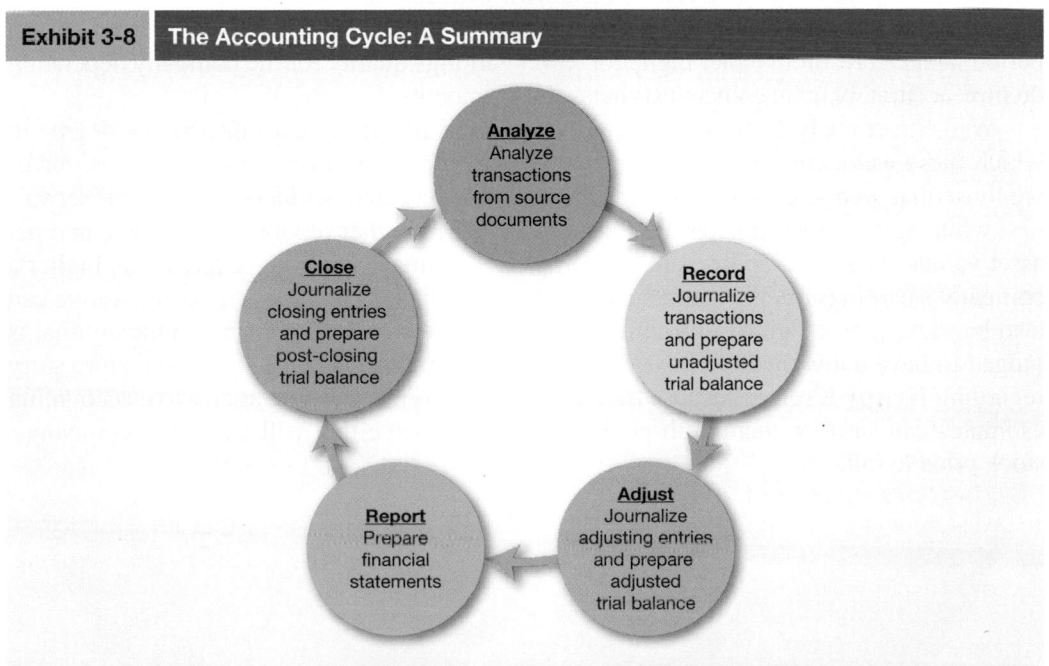

YOUR TURN! 3.7

The solution is on
page 186.

Prior to closing its books, the Morgan Company has the following balances in its temporary accounts as of December 31.

	Debit	Credit
Sales revenue.		$79,000
Cost of goods sold.	$41,000	
Wage expense	22,000	
Rent expense	3,000	
Depreciation expense.	2,000	
Interest expense.	4,000	
Dividends	5,000	

Required
Prepare closing entries as of December 31 for the Morgan Company.

For readers skipping the closing process using Retained Earnings, please resume reading here.

QUALITY OF ACCOUNTING NUMBERS

Earnings quality is a phrase used to characterize the degree to which a company's financial statements reflect its true financial condition and performance. The better the statements represent the company's actual financial condition and performance, the higher a company's earnings quality is assumed to be.

While many end-of-period adjustments discussed in this chapter are based on direct calculations, such as the time remaining for a prepaid insurance policy or the interest rate on an outstanding loan, many other adjustments that we discuss in later chapters involve judgments on the part of the company's management. Examples of judgments leading to adjusting entries are the amount of future warranty work associated with a company's product, the amount of a company's accounts receivable that will not be collected, and the estimated depreciable lives of a company's plant and equipment. Each of these items involves estimates of future events that cannot be known with certainty. Consequently, each of these estimates can have a material affect on a company's reported financial results in any given period, and can result in either higher or lower earnings quality for the company depending on how accurately management estimates these amounts.

Wall Street analysts often evaluate a company's quality of earnings by the degree to which these estimates are considered conservative or aggressive. Conservative estimates are those that are more pessimistic, leading to lower reported net income and net asset values, while aggressive estimates are those that result in higher reported net income and net asset values. The more conservative a company's estimates are judged to be, the higher a company's earnings quality is often assumed to be, although being overly conservative can also be viewed as a sign of low earnings quality. Investors may punish a company that is judged to have a low quality of earnings, as we saw in this chapter's opening feature story regarding **Krispy Kreme**, because they worry that a company using aggressive accounting estimates can surprise them with poor future performance that will cause the company's stock price to fall.

COMPREHENSIVE PROBLEM

Balke Laboratory began operations on July 1, 2014, and provides diagnostic services for physicians and medical clinics. The company's fiscal year ends on June 30, and the accounts are adjusted annually on this date. Balke's unadjusted trial balance as of June 30, 2016, is as follows:

BALKE LABORATORY Unadjusted Trial Balance June 30, 2016		
	Debit	**Credit**
Cash.	$ 1,000	
Accounts receivable.	9,200	
Prepaid insurance	6,000	
Supplies	31,300	
Laboratory equipment	270,000	
Accumulated depreciation—Laboratory equipment		$ 30,000
Accounts payable.		3,100
Diagnostic fees received in advance		4,000
Common stock.		90,000
Retained earnings		50,000
Diagnostic fees revenue.		220,400
Wage expense	58,000	
Rent expense	22,000	
Totals	$397,500	$397,500

The following information is also available:

1. The Prepaid Insurance account balance represents a premium paid on January 1, 2016, for two years of fire and casualty insurance coverage. Before 2016, Balke Laboratory had no insurance protection.
2. The supplies were physically counted at June 30, 2016. The count totaled $6,300.
3. All laboratory equipment was purchased on July 1, 2014. It is expected to last nine years.
4. Balke Laboratory received a $4,000 cash payment on April 1, 2016, from Boll Clinic for diagnostic services to be provided uniformly over the four months beginning April 1, 2016. Balke credited the payment to Diagnostic Fees Received in Advance. The services for April, May, and June have been provided to Boll Clinic.
5. Unpaid wages at June 30, 2016, were $600.
6. Balke Laboratory rents facilities for $2,000 per month. Because of cash flow problems, Balke was unable to pay the rent for June 2016. The landlord gave Balke permission to delay the payment until July.

Required
a. Make the necessary adjusting entries as of June 30, 2016.
b. Prepare the adjusted trial balance as of June 30, 2016.
c. Prepare the Income Statement, Balance Sheet, and Statement of Stockholders' Equity for Balke Laboratory at June 30, 2016.
d. Make the necessary closing entries as of June 30, 2016.
e. Prepare the post-closing trial balance as of June 30, 2016.

Solution

a.	June 30	Insurance expense	1,500	
		Prepaid insurance		1,500
		To record 6 months' insurance expense.		
		($6,000/4 = $1,500).		
	30	Supplies expense	25,000	
		Supplies		25,000
		To record supplies expense for the year.		
		($31,300 − $6,300 = $25,000).		
	30	Depreciation expense—Laboratory equipment	30,000	
		Accumulated depreciation—Laboratory equipment		30,000
		To record depreciation for the year.		
		($270,000/9 years = $30,000).		
	30	Diagnostic fees received in advance	3,000	
		Diagnostic fees revenue		3,000
		To record portion of advance payment that has been earned.		
		($4,000 × 3/4 = $3,000).		
	30	Wage expense	600	
		Wages payable		600
		To record unpaid wages at June 30.		
	30	Rent expense	2,000	
		Rent payable		2,000
		To record rent expense for June.		

b.

Balke Laboratory
Adjusted Trial Balance
June 30, 2016

	Unadjusted Trial Balance		Adjustments				Adjusted Trial Balance	
	Debit	Credit		Debit		Credit	Debit	Credit
Cash	$ 1,000						$ 1,000	
Accounts receivable	9,200						9,200	
Prepaid insurance	6,000		1		$ 1,500		4,500	
Supplies	31,300		2		25,000		6,300	
Laboratory equipment	270,000						270,000	
Accumulated depreciation—Laboratory equipment		$ 30,000	3		30,000			$ 60,000
Accounts payable		3,100						3,100
Wages payable			5		600			600
Rent payable			6		2,000			2,000
Diagnostic fees received in advance		4,000	4	$ 3,000				1,000
Common stock		90,000						90,000
Retained earnings		50,000						50,000
Diagnostic fees revenue		220,400	4		3,000			223,400
Wage expense	58,000		5	600			58,600	
Rent expense	22,000		6	2,000			24,000	
Insurance expense			1	1,500			1,500	
Supplies expense			2	25,000			25,000	
Depreciation expense—Laboratory equipment			3	30,000			30,000	
Totals	$397,500	$397,500		$62,100		$62,100	$430,100	$430,100

c.

Balke Laboratory
Income Statement
For the year ended June 30, 2016

Revenues		
Diagnostic fees revenue		$223,400
Expenses		
Wage expense	58,600	
Rent expense	24,000	
Insurance expense	1,500	
Supplies expense	25,000	
Depreciation expense	30,000	
Total expenses		139,100
Net income		$ 84,300

Balke Laboratory
Statement of Stockholders' Equity
For the year ended June 30, 2016

	Common Stock	Retained Earnings	Total
Balance, June 30, 2015	$90,000	$ 50,000	$140,000
Net income		84,300	84,300
Balance, June 30, 2016	$90,000	$134,300	$224,300

Balke Laboratory
Balance Sheet
June 30, 2016

Assets		Liabilities	
Cash	$ 1,000	Accounts payable	$ 3,100
Accounts receivable	9,200	Wages payable	600
Prepaid insurance	4,500	Rent payable	2,000
Supplies	6,300	Diagnostic fees received in advance	1,000
Total current assets	21,000	Total liabilities	6,700
		Stockholders' equity	
Laboratory equipment	270,000	Common stock	90,000
Less: Accumulated depreciation	(60,000)	Retained earnings	134,300
Laboratory equipment, net	210,000	Total stockholders' equity	224,300
Total assets	$231,000	Total liabilities and stockholders' equity	$231,000

d. June 30 | Diagnostic fees revenue | 223,400 |
| 　　Retained earnings | | 223,400 |
| *To close the revenue account* | | |

Retained earnings	139,100
Wage expense		58,600
Rent expense		24,000
Insurance expense		1,500
Supplies expense		25,000
Depreciation expense—Laboratory equipment		30,000
To close the expense accounts		

e.

Balke Laboratory
Post-Closing Trial Balance
June 30, 2016

	Debit	Credit
Cash	$ 1,000	
Accounts receivable	9,200	
Prepaid insurance	4,500	
Supplies	6,300	
Laboratory equipment	270,000	
Accumulated depreciation—Laboratory equipment		$ 60,000
Accounts payable		3,100
Wages payable		600
Rent payable		2,000
Diagnostic fees received in advance		1,000
Common stock		90,000
Retained earnings		134,300
Totals	$291,000	$291,000

APPENDIX 3A: Closing Process—Using Income Summary Account

All accounts can be identified as either permanent accounts or temporary accounts. **Permanent accounts** are the accounts presented on the balance sheet. They consist of the asset, liability, and stockholders' equity accounts. The distinguishing feature of a permanent account is that any balance in the account at the end of an accounting period is carried forward to the following accounting period. **Temporary accounts** are used to gather information for a particular accounting period. Revenue, expense, and dividend accounts are temporary subdivisions of stockholders' equity. At the end of the accounting period, temporary account balances are transferred to retained earnings, which

LO7 **Appendix 3A:** **Describe** the process of closing to the Income Summary account and **summarize** the accounting cycle.

is a permanent stockholders' equity account. The process of transferring the balances in temporary accounts to retained earnings is referred to as the **closing process** or **closing procedures**.

A temporary account is *closed* when an entry is made that changes its account balance to zero—that is, the entry is equal in amount to the account's ending balance but is opposite to the balance as a debit or credit. An account that is closed is said to be closed *to* the account that receives the offsetting debit or credit. Thus, a closing entry simply transfers the balance of one account to another account. Because closing entries bring temporary account balances to zero, the temporary accounts are then ready to start accumulating data for the next accounting period. In essence, closing the temporary accounts prevents information from the current accounting period from being carried forward to a subsequent period, which enables financial statement users to make meaningful comparisons of revenue and expenses from one period to the next. The following summarizes the classification of permanent and temporary accounts.

A.K.A.
Closing procedures are also known as **closing the books**.

Permanent Accounts	Temporary Accounts
Assets	Revenues
Liabilities	Expenses
Common Stock	Dividends
Retained Earnings	Income Summary

YOUR TURN! 3A.1

The solution is on page 186.

For each of the following accounts, identify whether the account is either a permanent account or a temporary account:

a. Cash
b. Common Stock
c. Wage Expense
d. Notes Payable

e. Dividends
f. Sales Revenue
g. Inventory
h. Prepaid Expense

Journalizing and Posting the Closing Entries

A summary account is traditionally used to close the temporary revenue and expense accounts. We use an account titled Income Summary (alternative titles for this account include Revenue and Expense Summary, Income and Expense Summary, and Profit and Loss Summary). The closing entries occur only at the end of an accounting period and consist of four steps, which are graphically shown as follows.

1. **Close the revenue accounts.** Debit each revenue account for an amount equal to its current credit balance, and credit the Income Summary account for the total amount of earned revenue.
2. **Close the expense accounts.** Credit each expense account for an amount equal to its current debit balance, and debit the Income Summary account for the total amount of expenses.

After steps 1 and 2, the balance of the Income Summary account equals the current period net income (if a credit balance) or net loss (if a debit balance).

3. **Close the Income Summary account.** In the case of net income, debit the Income Summary account and credit the Retained Earnings account for an amount equal to net income. In the case of a net loss, debit the Retained Earnings account and credit the Income Summary account for an amount equal to the net loss.
4. **Close the Dividends account.** Debit the Retained Earnings account and credit the Dividends account for an amount equal to the balance in the Dividends account.

Closing Process for WebWork

Exhibit 3A-1 illustrates the closing entries for the revenue and expense accounts for WebWork as recorded in the company's general journal. The financial information in these entries is posted to the appropriate general ledger accounts, which is represented using T-accounts.

Exhibit 3A-1	Closing Revenue and Expense Accounts—WebWork, Inc.

GENERAL JOURNAL

	Date	Description	Debit	Credit
	2016			
1	Dec. 31	Fee revenue	19,150	
		Income summary		19,150
		To close the revenue account.		
	Dec. 31	Income summary	6,300	
		Supplies expense		1,320
		Wage expense		2,430
2		Rent expense		1,800
		Depreciation expense		450
		Interest expense		300
		To close the expense accounts.		

After steps 1 and 2, the Income Summary account has a credit balance equal to WebWork's net income of $12,850. Steps 3 and 4 close the Income Summary account and the Dividends account to the Retained Earnings account. These two entries are recorded in WebWork's general journal in **Exhibit 3A-2**. The financial effect of posting these entries on the general ledger is diagrammed below.

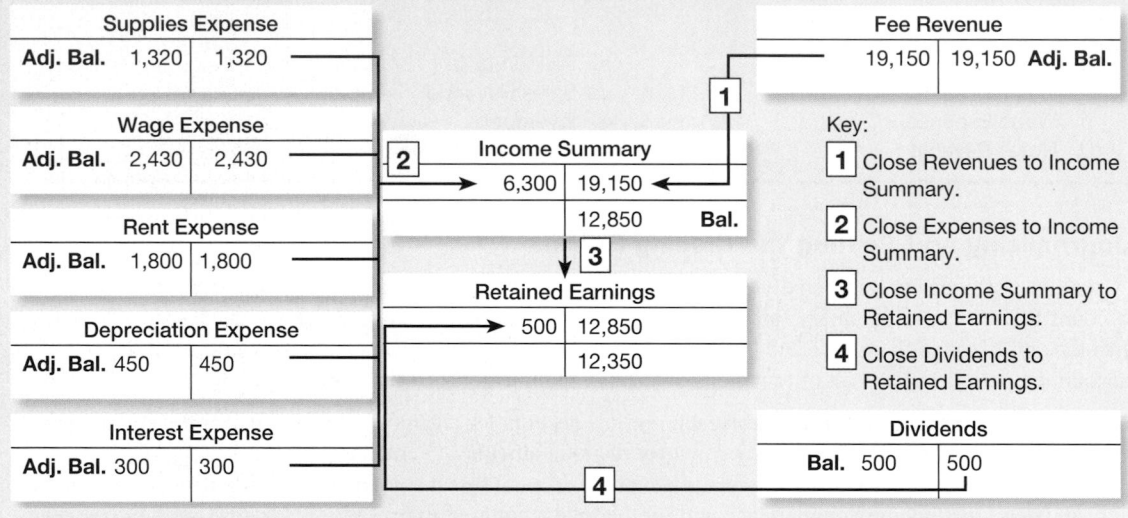

Exhibit 3A-2	Closing the Income Summary and Dividends Accounts—WebWork, Inc.

GENERAL JOURNAL

	Date	Description	Debit	Credit
	2016			
3	Dec. 31	Income summary	12,850	
		Retained earnings		12,850
		To close the Income Summary account.		
4	Dec. 31	Retained earnings	500	
		Dividends		500
		To close the Dividends account.		

Preparing the Post-Closing Trial Balance

After closing entries are recorded in the general journal and posted to the general ledger, all of the temporary accounts have zero balances. At this point a **post-closing trial balance** is prepared. The post-closing trial balance provides evidence that an equality of debits and credits has been maintained in the general ledger throughout the adjusting and closing processes, and that the general ledger is in balance to start the next accounting period. Because the temporary accounts have been closed, only the balance sheet (or permanent) accounts appear in the post-closing trial balance. **Exhibit 3A-3** presents the post-closing trial balance for WebWork.

Exhibit 3A-3	Post-Closing Trial Balance for WebWork, Inc.		

WebWork, Inc.
Post-Closing Trial Balance
December 31, 2016

	Debit	Credit
Cash.	$40,590	
Accounts receivable.	1,490	
Office supplies	1,530	
Prepaid rent	9,000	
Office equipment	32,400	
Accumulated depreciation—Office equipment		$ 450
Accounts payable.		2,850
Interest payable		300
Wages payable.		810
Unearned revenue		2,250
Notes payable		36,000
Common stock.		30,000
Retained earnings		12,350
Totals	$85,010	$85,010

Summary of the Accounting Cycle

The sequence of accounting procedures known as the *accounting cycle* occurs each fiscal period and represents a systematic process for accumulating and reporting the financial data of a business. **Exhibit 3A-4** summarizes the five major steps in the accounting cycle as described in this and the preceding chapter.

Exhibit 3A-4	The Accounting Cycle: A Summary

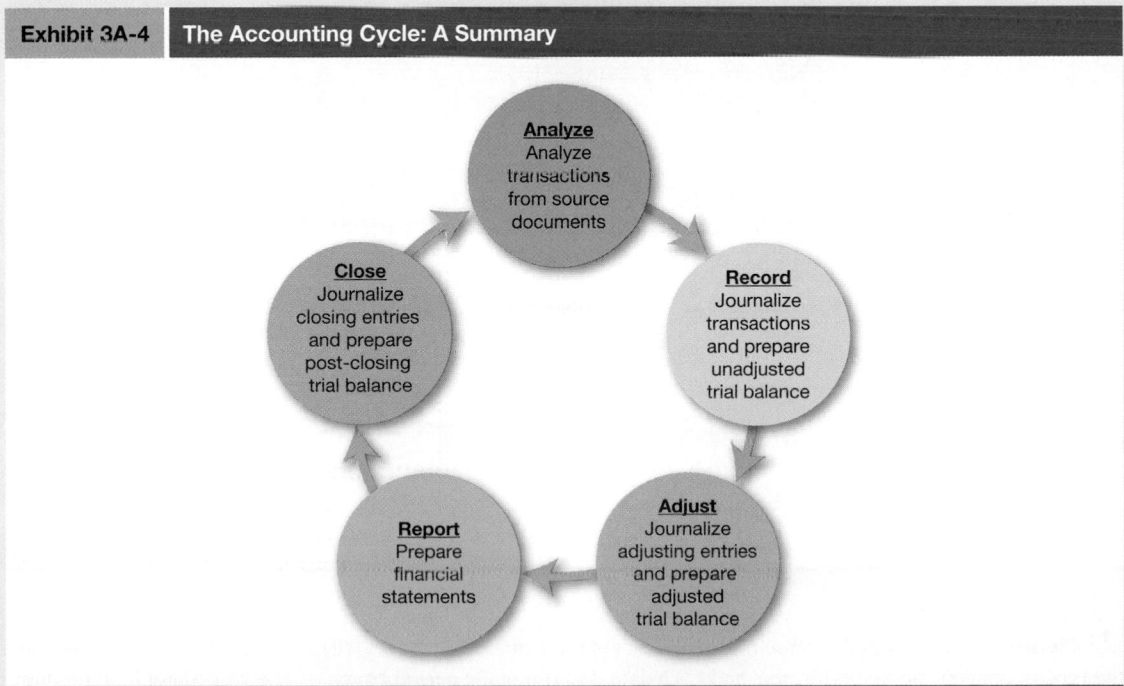

YOUR TURN!
3A.2

The solu-
tion is on
page 187.

Prior to closing its books, the Morgan Company has the following balances in its temporary accounts as of December 31.

	Debit	Credit
Sales revenue...		$79,000
Cost of goods sold...	$41,000	
Wage expense	22,000	
Rent expense	3,000	
Depreciation expense.....................................	2,000	
Interest expense..	4,000	
Dividends	5,000	

Required

Prepare closing entries as of December 31 for the Morgan Company.

APPENDIX 3B: Using a Worksheet

A worksheet can be used to facilitate the adjusting and closing processes, and ultimately, the preparation of a company's financial statements. A **worksheet** is an informal document that helps accumulate the accounting information needed to prepare the financial statements. A worksheet is a tool; it is not part of a company's formal accounting records. In this section, we explain how a worksheet can be used to help compile information for a set of financial statements. Computer programs such as Microsoft Excel can simplify the preparation of a worksheet.

LO8 Appendix 3B: **Explain** how to use a worksheet in the adjusting and closing process.

Preparing a Worksheet

A worksheet is prepared at that stage in the accounting cycle when it is time to adjust the accounts and prepare the financial statements. The basic structure of a worksheet is illustrated in **Exhibit 3B-1**, which includes an explanation of the format used. The worksheet is prepared in the order indicated by the red colored numbers in the exhibit.

Exhibit 3B-1

	1

(HEADING FOR WORKSHEET)

Description	Unadjusted Trial Balance		Adjustments		Adjusted Trial Balance		Income Statement		Balance Sheet	
	Debit	Credit	Debit	Credit	Debit	Credit	Debit	Credit	Debit	Credit

2
Unadjusted trial balance

Accounts that arise for adjustments

3
Adjustment amounts

4
Adjusted account balances

5
Classify adjusted balances into either the income statement or balance sheet columns

6
Balancing of columns for each statement

1 **Heading**   The worksheet *heading* includes (1) the name of the entity, (2) the term *Worksheet* to indicate the type of analysis being performed, and (3) a date describing the period covered. The worksheet includes both income statement data (for the period described) and balance sheet data (for the end of the period described).

Exhibit 3B-2 illustrates the heading for WebWork's worksheet. The worksheet has a description column and 10 amount (monetary) columns. A set of Debit and Credit columns is provided for each of the five headings: Unadjusted Trial Balance, Adjustments, Adjusted Trial Balance, Income Statement, and Balance Sheet.

2 Unadjusted Trial Balance The unadjusted trial balance is the starting point for the accounting analysis on the worksheet. It is entered in the worksheet's description column and the first pair of monetary columns. Once the trial balance is entered in the worksheet and double-ruled, it reflects the general ledger at the time the worksheet is prepared. **Exhibit 3B-2** shows the worksheet placement of WebWork's unadjusted trial balance as of December 31, 2016.

3 Adjustments *When a worksheet is used, all adjustments are first entered on the worksheet.* This procedure permits the adjustments to be reviewed for completeness and accuracy. To adjust accounts already appearing in the unadjusted trial balance, we simply enter the amounts in the appropriate side (debit or credit) of the adjustments columns on the lines containing the accounts. When accounts not appearing in the unadjusted trial balance require adjustment, their titles are listed as needed in the Description column below the accounts already listed. Adjustments entered on the worksheet are not yet journalized; journalizing the adjustments occurs later. The adjustments recorded on WebWork's worksheet in **Exhibit 3B-2** are identical to those illustrated in the chapter (see **Exhibit 3-2**). After recording all the adjusting entries on the worksheet, we total the adjustments columns to verify that the sum of the debit entries equals the sum of the credit entries.

4 Adjusted Trial Balance Once the adjustments have been entered on the worksheet, there is sufficient information available to complete an adjusted trial balance. The adjusted figures are determined by combining horizontally, line by line, the amounts in the first four money columns— that is, the unadjusted trial balance and the adjustments. We review the calculations for two lines of **Exhibit 3B-2** to illustrate this process. The first line shows the Cash account with a debit amount of $40,590 in the unadjusted trial balance. Because Cash is not affected by any of the adjustments, the $40,590 appears in the debit column of the adjusted trial balance. On the third line, the Office Supplies account begins with a debit of $2,850 in the unadjusted trial balance and then shows a credit of $1,320 in the adjustments column. The $1,320 credit is subtracted from the $2,850 debit, and the remaining $1,530 is shown as a debit in the adjusted trial balance.

Exhibit 3B-2

WEBWORK, INC.
Worksheet
For Month Ended December 31, 2016

	Unadjusted Trial Balance Debit	Credit	Adjustments Debit	Credit	Adjusted Trial Balance Debit	Credit	Income Statement Debit	Credit	Balance Sheet Debit	Credit
Cash................	$40,590				$40,590				$40,590	
Accounts receivable....	1,340		(g) $ 150		1,490				1,490	
Office supplies	2,850			(a) $1,320	1,530				1,530	
Prepaid rent	10,800			(b) 1,800	9,000				9,000	
Office equipment	32,400				32,400				32,400	
Accumulated depreciation—										
Office equipment				(c) 450		$ 450				$ 450
Accounts payable......		$ 2,850				2,850				2,850
Interest payable				(f) 300		300				300
Wages payable........				(e) 810		810				810
Unearned revenue		3,000	(d) 750			2,250				2,250
Notes payable		36,000				36,000				36,000
Common stock........		30,000				30,000				30,000
Dividends	500				500				500	
Fee revenue		18,250		(d) 750		19,150		$19,150		
				(g) 150						
Wage expense	1,620		(e) 810		2,430		2,430			
Supplies expense......			(a) 1,320		1,320		$ 1,320			
Rent expense			(b) 1,800		1,800		1,800			
Depreciation expense...			(c) 450		450		450			
Interest expense.......			(f) 300		300		300			
Totals	$90,100	$90,100	$5,580	$5,580	$91,810	$91,810	6,300	19,150	85,510	72,660
Net income...........							12,850			12,850
Totals							$19,150	$19,150	$85,510	$85,510

After calculating the adjusted trial balance amounts for all accounts on the worksheet, we total the two columns of the adjusted trial balance to verify that they are equal and that our worksheet is in balance.

5 **Extension of the Adjusted Trial Balance**   The amounts in the adjusted trial balance columns are extended into the two remaining pairs of columns as follows:

Expenses	→ Debit column of income statement
Revenues	→ Credit column of income statement
Assets and cash dividends	→ Debit column of balance sheet
Liabilities, Common Stock, Retained Earnings, and contra assets	→ Credit column of balance sheet

Expense and revenue account balances are extended to the income statement columns because these accounts will be used to prepare the income statement. Similarly, asset, contra asset, liability, and stockholders' equity accounts are balance sheet accounts, so their balances are extended to the balance sheet columns. In addition, the Dividends debit balance is extended to the balance sheet debit column, and the credit balances in the Common Stock and Retained Earnings accounts are extended to the balance sheet credit column. **Exhibit 3B-2** shows the extension of WebWork's adjusted trial balance to the worksheet's income statement and balance sheet columns. Once the proper extensions are made, the worksheet is complete except for balancing the two pairs of statement columns containing the adjusted balances.

6 **Balancing the Worksheet**   The first step in balancing is to add each of the income statement and balance sheet columns and record their respective totals on the same line as the totals of the adjusted trial balance columns. The difference between the total debits and total credits in the income statement columns is the difference between total revenues and total expenses—that is, the net income or net loss for the period. The net income or net loss must be the amount by which the debit and credit columns for the balance sheet differ. This is true because the Retained Earnings account balance, as extended, does not yet reflect the net income or net loss for the current period.

When revenues exceed expenses, we balance the two pairs of statement columns by adding the net income figure to both the debit column of the income statement and the credit column of the balance sheet. **Exhibit 3B-2** illustrates this balancing situation with WebWork's net income for December of $12,850. If expenses exceed revenues, we add the amount of net loss to the credit column of the income statement and to the debit column of the balance sheet. After we have added the net income (or loss) to the proper columns, we total and double-rule the four columns. The worksheet is now complete.

A completed worksheet aids in the last three steps of the accounting cycle—adjust, report, and close.

Adjust: The adjusting entries to be journalized and posted can be taken from the information in the adjustments columns. Because adjustments have first been entered on the worksheet, they can be reviewed for their financial effects before being journalized. Thus, the likelihood of incorrect adjustments appearing in the formal accounting records is reduced.

Report: The income statement can be prepared from the data in the income statement columns. Two pieces of information for the statement of stockholders' equity are available in the worksheet—the net income (or net loss) and dividends. The assets and liabilities needed for the balance sheet are available in the balance sheet columns (the ending Retained Earnings balance for the balance sheet is obtained from the statement of stockholders' equity).

Close: The closing entries to be journalized and posted can be prepared from data in the worksheet because it displays all of the temporary account balances. The revenue and expense account balances are shown in the income statement columns and the cash dividends account balance is shown in the balance sheet debit column.

SUMMARY OF LEARNING OBJECTIVES

Explain the accrual basis of accounting and contrast it with the cash basis with reference to revenue and expense recognition. (p. 122)   LO1

- Revenue is recognized on an accrual basis at the time that it is earned. This may be prior to the receipt of cash, at the same time as the receipt of cash, or following the receipt of cash.
- Expenses are matched against revenues in the same accounting period that the associated revenue is recognized. This may be prior to cash payment, at the same time as cash payment, or following cash payment.
- Revenue recognition and the corresponding matching of expenses may differ in timing on an accrual basis versus on a cash basis.

Describe the adjusting process. (p. 125)   LO2

- Adjusting entries are made to achieve the appropriate recognition of revenues and matching of expenses with revenues, and consist of four general types of adjustments:
  1. Allocating previously recorded assets to operating expenses to reflect the total expenses incurred during the period.
  2. Allocating previously recorded unearned revenue to revenue to reflect revenues earned during the period.
  3. Recording operating expenses to reflect expenses incurred during the period that have not yet been paid or recorded.
  4. Recording revenues to reflect revenue earned during the period that has not yet been received or recorded.

Illustrate deferral adjustments. (p. 126)   LO3

- Deferral adjustments deal with amounts that have previously been recorded on the balance sheet and require adjustment to their correct amounts.
- The adjustment decreases the balance sheet amount and increases an income statement amount.
- Deferral adjustments include adjustments to prepaid expenses and adjustments to unearned revenues.

LO4 **Illustrate accrual adjustments. (p. 129)**
- Accrual adjustments deal with amounts that have not been previously recorded in an account.
- The adjustment increases both a balance sheet account and an income statement account.
- Accrual adjustments include adjustments to accrue expenses and adjustments to accrue revenues.

LO5 **Explain the adjusted trial balance and use it to prepare financial statements. (p. 133)**
- An income statement, statement of stockholders' equity, balance sheet, and statement of cash flows may be prepared from an adjusted trial balance and other information.
- The stockholders' equity accounts may need to be reviewed to obtain information regarding the beginning balances and additional capital contributions during the period for the statement of stockholders' equity.

LO6 **Describe the closing process and summarize the accounting cycle. (p. 137)**
- *Closing the books* means closing the revenue, expense, and dividend accounts by transferring the balances to the Retained Earnings account.

LO7 **Appendix 3A: Describe the process of closing to the Income Summary account and summarize the accounting cycle. (p. 144)**
- *Closing the books* means closing the revenue, expense, and other temporary accounts. Revenue and expense account balances are transferred to the Income Summary account. The balances of the Income Summary account and the Dividends account are then transferred to the Retained Earnings account.

LO8 **Appendix 3B: Explain how to use a worksheet in the adjusting and closing process. (p. 148)**

A worksheet is an informal document that helps in compiling the information needed for the preparation of the financial statements. A worksheet is a tool of the accountant; it is not part of a company's formal accounting records. The worksheet consists of a heading, along with the following columns:
- *a.* Unadjusted trial balance
- *b.* Adjustments
- *c.* Adjusted trial balance
- *d.* Income statement
- *e.* Balance sheet

A completed worksheet aids in the last three steps of the accounting cycle: adjust, report, and close.

SUMMARY	Concept →	Method →	Assessment
TAKEAWAY 3.1	When should sales revenue be recognized?	Understand the nature of a company's earning process. Record revenue when it is earned.	Early recognition of revenue overstates current period revenue; recognizing revenue too late understates current period revenue.
TAKEAWAY 3.2	When should expenses be recognized?	Understand the nature of the company's earning process. Expenses should be recognized with the related revenue in the same accounting period.	Early recognition of expenses overstates current period expenses; recognizing expenses too late understates current period expenses.
TAKEAWAY 3.3	When should an adjusting entry be made?	Individual account balances and transaction details such as contracts and agreements. Knowledge of the proper account balance is needed. Adjustments involve (1) allocating assets to expense, (2) allocating unearned revenue to revenue, (3) accruing expenses, or (4) accruing revenues.	Record an adjusting entry so that accounts are correctly reported; otherwise income and assets (and/or liabilities) are incorrectly reported.

KEY TERMS

Accruals (p. 126)

Accrued expenses (p. 129)

Accrued revenue (p. 130)

Accumulated
   depreciation (p. 128)

Adjusted trial balance (p. 133)

Adjusting entries (p. 126)

Book value (p. 128)

Carrying value (p. 128)

Closing procedures (p. 137, 145)

Closing process (p. 137, 145)

Closing the books (p. 137, 145)

Contra accounts (p. 128)

Deferrals (p. 126)

Deferred revenue (p. 128)

Depreciation (p. 127)

Earnings quality (p. 140)

Permanent accounts (p. 137,
   144)

Post-closing trial
   balance (p. 138, 146)

Straight-line
   depreciation (p. 128)

Temporary accounts (p. 137,
   144)

Unadjusted trial
   balance (p. 125)

Unearned revenue (p. 128)

Worksheet (p. 148)

Assignments with the ⬤ logo in the margin are available in BusinessCourse.
See the Preface of the book for details.

SELF-STUDY QUESTIONS

(Answers to the Self-Study Questions are available at the end of the chapter.)

1. **Which of the following is an example of an adjusting entry?**   LO3
   a. Recording the purchase of supplies on account
   b. Recording depreciation expense on a truck
   c. Recording the billing of customers for services rendered
   d. Recording the payment of wages to employees

2. **An adjusting entry to record utilities used during a month for which no bill has yet been received is**   LO4
   an example of
   a. Allocating assets to expense to reflect the actual operating expenses incurred during the accounting
       period
   b. Allocating revenues received in advance to revenue to reflect actual revenues earned during the
       accounting period
   c. Accruing expenses to reflect expenses incurred during the accounting period that are not yet paid or
       recorded
   d. Accruing revenues to reflect revenues earned during the accounting period that are not yet received
       or recorded

3. **Which of the following is not an example of a closing entry?**   LO6
   a. Close each revenue account to the Retained Earnings account
   b. Close each expense account to the Retained Earnings account
   c. Close the Dividends account to the Retained Earnings account
   d. Close Unearned Revenue to Retained Earnings

4. **Which of the following transactions does not affect total assets, total liabilities, or total**   LO1
   stockholders' equity on the balance sheet?
   a. Purchasing $500 supplies on account
   b. Paying a $3,000 note payable
   c. Collecting $4,000 from customers on account
   d. Payment of an $800 dividend

5. **The beginning and ending balances of retained earnings for the year were $30,000 and $35,000,**   LO6
   respectively. If yearly dividends totaled $3,000, what was the net income or net loss for the year?
   a. $8,000 net loss
   b. $14,000 net income
   c. $2,000 net income
   d. $8,000 net income

LO2 **6.** The ending balance of the Accounts Receivable account was $12,000. Services billed to customers for the period were $21,500, and collections on account from customers were $23,600. What was the beginning balance of Accounts Receivable?

    a. $33,500   *c.* $9,900

    b. $14,100   *d.* $33,100

LO1 **7.** Kelly Corporation received an advanced payment of $20,000 in 2015 from Rufus Company for consulting services. Kelly performed half of the consulting in 2015 and the remainder in 2016. Kelly reports using the accrual basis of accounting. How much revenue from this consulting project will Kelly report in 2015?

    a. $20,000   *c.* $0

    b. $10,000   *d.* $15,000

QUESTIONS

1. Why is the adjusting step of the accounting cycle necessary?

2. What four different types of adjustments are frequently necessary at the close of an accounting period? Provide an example of each type.

3. On January 1, Prepaid Insurance was debited with the cost of a two-year premium in the amount of $1,872. What adjusting entry should be made on January 31 before the January financial statements are prepared?

4. What is a contra account? What contra account is used in reporting the book value of a depreciable asset?

5. At the beginning of January, the first month of the accounting year, the Supplies account had a debit balance of $825. During January, purchases of $260 of supplies were debited to the account. Although only $630 of supplies was on hand at the end of January, the necessary adjusting entry was omitted. How will the omission affect (a) the income statement for January and (b) the balance sheet prepared as of January 31?

6. The publisher of *International View*, a monthly magazine, received two-year subscriptions totaling $9,720 on January 1. (a) What entry should be made to record the receipt of the $9,720? (b) What entry should be made at the end of January before financial statements are prepared for the month?

7. Globe Travel Agency pays an employee $475 in wages each Friday for a five-day work week ending on that day. The last Friday of January falls on January 27. What adjusting entry should be made on January 31, the fiscal year-end?

8. The Bayou Company earns interest amounting to $360 per month on its investments. The company receives the interest every six months, on December 31 and June 30. Monthly financial statements are prepared. What adjusting entry should be made on January 31?

9. Define *permanent account*. Provide an example.

10. Define *temporary account*. Provide an example.

11. Which group of accounts is closed at the end of the accounting year? Why?

12. What is the purpose of a post-closing trial balance? Which of the following accounts should not appear in the post-closing trial balance: Cash, Unearned Revenue, Dividends, Depreciation Expense, Utilities Payable, Supplies Expense, Retained Earnings?

SHORT EXERCISES

LO1 **SE3-1.** **Steps in the Accounting Cycle** Listed below, out of order, are the steps in an accounting cycle.

    1. Prepare the unadjusted trial balance.

    2. Post journal entries to general ledger accounts.

    3. Analyze transactions from source documents.

    4. Journalize and post adjusting entries.

    5. Prepare the financial statements.

    6. Record transactions in a journal.

    7. Prepare the post-closing trial balance.

    8. Prepare the adjusted trial balance.

    9. Journalize and post closing entries.

(a) Place the numbers from the above list in the order in which the steps in the accounting cycle are performed, and (b) identify the steps in the accounting cycle that occur daily.

SE3-2. **Accrual Accounting** Evan Corporation provided consulting services for Kensington Company **LO1**
in 2015. Evan incurred costs of $60,000 associated with the consulting and billed Kensington
$90,000. Evan paid $40,000 of its costs in 2015 and the remaining $20,000 in 2016. Evan received
$45,000 of its billing in 2015. Kensington paid the remaining $45,000 in 2016. Evan reports on the
accrual basis of accounting. How much is Evan's 2015 and 2016 profit related to the Kensington
consulting?

SE3-3. **Adjusting Accounts** MacKenzie Enterprises includes the following accounts in its general ledger. **LO2**
Explain why each of these accounts may need to be adjusted.

  a. Rent Payable
  b. Unearned Revenue
  c. Prepaid Subscriptions
  d. Depreciation Expense

SE3-4. **Adjusting Entry for Depreciation** Cowley Company just completed its first year of operations. **LO3**
The December 31 equipment account has a balance of $20,000. There is no balance in the Accumu-
lated Depreciation—Equipment account or in the Depreciation Expense account. The accountant
estimates the yearly equipment depreciation to be $4,000. Prepare the required adjusting entry to
record the yearly depreciation for equipment.

SE3-5. **Adjusting Entry for Prepaid Insurance** Cooper Inc. recorded the purchase of a three-year insur- **LO3**
ance policy on July 1 in the amount of $3,600 by debiting Prepaid Insurance and crediting Cash.
Prepare the necessary December 31 year-end adjusting entry.

SE3-6. **Accrual Adjusting Entries** Prepare adjusting journal entries for Sparky Electronics for the follow- **LO3, 4**
ing items:

  a. Salaries for employees in the amount of $2,500 have not been paid.
  b. Interest expense of $1,200 for an outstanding note.
  c. Work performed but not yet billed for $3,500.

SE3-7. **Analyze an Adjusted Trial Balance** The trial balance of Fisher Supplies contains the following **LO3, 4**
balance sheet accounts that require adjustment. Identify the likely income statement account that
will be used to adjust these accounts.

  a. Prepaid Insurance
  b. Accumulated Depreciation
  c. Supplies
  d. Unearned Revenue
  e. Interest Payable

SE3-8. **Prepare an Income Statement from an Adjusted Trial Balance** The Century Company's ad- **LO5**
justed trial balance contains the following balances as of December 31: Retained Earnings $8,500;
Dividends $2,000; Sales $20,000; Cost of Goods Sold $8,000; Selling and Administrative Expenses
$3,000; Interest Expense $1,500. Prepare an income statement for the year.

SE3-9. **Prepare Closing Entries to Retained Earnings** Use the data from SE3-8 to prepare the closing **LO6**
entries for The Century Company. Close the temporary accounts straight to retained earnings. The
balance of $8,500 in the retained earnings account is from the beginning of the year. What is the
ending retained earnings balance after posting the closing entries?

SE3-10. **Identify Financial Statements from Adjusted Trial Balance Accounts** Trownel Corp reports the **LO5**
following accounts in its adjusted trial balance. Identify which financial statement each account
would appear on:

  a. Cash   d. Unearned Revenue
  b. Sales   e. Retained Earnings
  c. Accounts Payable   f. Interest Income

SE3-11. **Prepare Closing Entries Using the Income Summary Account** Use the data from SE3-8 to pre- **LO7**
pare the closing entries for The Century Company. Close the temporary accounts to income sum- **(Appendix 3A)**
mary. The balance of $8,500 in the retained earnings account is from the beginning of the year.
What is the ending retained earnings balance after posting the closing entries?

LO8
(Appendix 3B)

SE3-12. The Accounting Worksheet The adjusted trial balance section of Menlo Company's worksheet shows a $1,500 debit balance in utility expense. At the end of the accounting period the accounting manager accrues an additional $300 of utility expense for the last week of the period. This will result in the following amounts appearing on Menlo's worksheet for utilities expense:

    a. $300 debit adjustment; $1,800 debit adjusted trial balance; $1,800 debit balance sheet

    b. $300 debit adjustment; $1,800 debit adjusted trial balance; $1,800 debit income statement

    c. $300 credit adjustment; $1,200 debit adjusted trial balance; $1,800 debit income statement

    d. $300 credit adjustment; $1,800 debit adjusted trial balance; $1,800 debit income statement

EXERCISES—SET A

LO4

E3-1A. Transaction Entries and Adjusting Entries Deluxe Building Services offers janitorial services on both a contract basis and an hourly basis. On January 1, Deluxe collected $30,000 in advance on a six-month contract for work to be performed evenly during the next six months.

    a.   Provide the general journal entry on January 1 to record the receipt of $30,000 for contract work.

    b.   Provide the adjusting entry to be made on January 31, for the contract work done during January.

    c.   At January 31, a total of 35 hours of hourly rate janitor work was unbilled. The billing rate is $25 per hour. Provide the adjusting entry needed on January 31. (*Note:* The firm uses the account Fees Receivable to reflect amounts due but not yet billed.)

LO3, 4

E3-2A. Adjusting Entries Selected accounts of Ideal Properties Inc., a real estate management firm, are shown below as of January 31, before any adjusting entries have been made:

	Debit	Credit
Prepaid insurance	$6,840	
Supplies	2,100	
Office equipment	6,240	
Unearned rent revenue		$ 5,550
Salaries expense	3,250	
Rent revenue		16,000

Monthly financial statements are prepared. Using the following information, record in a general journal the adjusting entries necessary on January 31:

    a.   Prepaid Insurance represents a three-year premium paid on January 1.

    b.   Supplies of $975 were on hand January 31.

    c.   Office equipment is expected to last eight years. Depreciation is recorded monthly.

    d.   On January 1, the firm collected six months' rent in advance from a tenant renting space for $925 per month.

    e.   Accrued salaries not recorded as of January 31 are $510.

LO3, 4

E3-3A. Adjusting Entries For each of the following unrelated situations, prepare the necessary adjusting entry in general journal form:

    a.   Unrecorded depreciation on equipment is $750.

    b.   The Supplies account has a balance of $3,100. Supplies on hand at the end of the period totaled $1,200.

    c.   On the date for preparing financial statements, an estimated utilities expense of $425 has been incurred, but no utility bill has been received.

    d.   On the first day of the current month, rent for four months was paid and recorded as a $2,800 debit to Prepaid Rent and a $2,800 credit to Cash. Monthly statements are now being prepared.

    e.   Nine months ago, Solid Insurance Company sold a one-year policy to a customer and recorded the receipt of the premium by debiting Cash for $624 and crediting Unearned Premium Revenue for $624. No adjusting entries have been prepared during the nine-month period. Annual financial statements are now being prepared.

    f.   At the end of the accounting period, employee wages of $1,050 have been incurred but not paid.

    g.   At the end of the accounting period, $350 of interest has been earned but not yet received on notes receivable that are held.

E3-4A. **Statement of Stockholders' Equity** On January 1, the credit balance of the Retained Earnings account was $51,000. The company's Common Stock account had an opening balance of $65,000, and $7,000 in new capital contributions were made during the year. On December 31, at year-end, the Dividends account had a debit balance of $10,500 before closing. The income statement shows net income of $30,500. Prepare a statement of stockholders' equity for Strife & Company, architectural design firm.   **LO5**

E3-5A. **Closing Entries** The adjusted trial balance prepared as of December 31, for Phyllis Howell & Company, Consultant, contains the following revenue and expense accounts: **LO6**

	Debit	Credit
Service fees earned		$80,500
Rent expense	$20,800	
Salaries expense	52,000	
Supplies expense.	5,600	
Depreciation expense.	11,300	
Retained earnings		72,000
Dividends	10,000	

Prepare journal entries to close the accounts directly to Retained Earnings. After these entries are posted, what is the balance in the Retained Earnings account?

E3-6A. **Revenue Recognition** Identify the proper point to recognize revenue for each of the following transactions.   **LO1**

   a.   Napoleon Industries sells a machine in January with terms of no payment due until six months later.

   b.   Emma Company collects an advance deposit of $700 in July toward the purchase of a $3,000 piece of equipment that is delivered to the customer the following September.

   c.   Ashley Corporation receives payment in October at the time of delivery of a rebuilt engine for a tractor.

E3-7A. **Expense Matching** Identify the proper point to recognize expense for each of the following transactions.   **LO1**

   a.   Katharina Inc. purchases on credit six custom sofas for $800 each in June. Two of the sofas are sold for $1,200 each in June. One of the sofas is sold for $1,000 in July and the remaining three sofas are sold for $1,500 each in August. All sales are for cash. Katharina pays its supplier in July.

   b.   Kuyu Co. purchases $500 of supplies in January. Half the supplies are used in January with the remaining half used in February.

   c.   Jane Co. purchases $1,000 of inventory for cash in September. The entire inventory is sold in November.

E3-8A. **Closing Entries** In the midst of closing procedures, Echo Corporation's accountant became ill and was hospitalized. You have volunteered to complete the closing of the books. You find that all the revenue and expense accounts have zero balances. The Dividends account has a debit balance of $19,000. The Retained Earnings account has a beginning credit balance of $125,000. Expenses totaled $308,500, and revenues totaled $347,400. Prepare journal entries to complete the closing procedures as of year-end directly to Retained Earnings. After these entries are posted, what is the balance in the Retained Earnings account?   **LO6**

E3-9A. **Analysis of Adjusted Data** Selected T-account balances for Coyle Company are shown below as of January 31; adjusting entries have already been posted. The firm uses a calendar-year accounting period and makes monthly adjustments.   **LO3, 4**

Supplies	Supplies Expense
Jan. 31 . . . . . Bal. 800	Jan. 31 . . . . . Bal. 960

Prepaid Insurance	Insurance Expense
Jan. 31 . . . . . Bal. 492	Jan. 31 . . . . . . Bal. 82

Wages Payable	Wages Expense
Bal. 650 . . . . . Jan. 31	Jan. 31 . . . . Bal. 3,200

Truck	Accumulated Depreciation—Truck
Jan. 31 . . . . Bal. 8,700	Bal. 2,610 . . . . Jan. 31

a.   If the amount in Supplies Expense represents the January 31 adjustment for the supplies used in January, and $750 worth of supplies were purchased during January, what was the January 1 balance of Supplies?

b.   The amount in the Insurance Expense account represents the adjustment made at January 31 for January insurance expense. If the original insurance premium was for one year, what was the amount of the premium and on what date did the insurance policy start?

c.   If we assume that no balance existed in Wages Payable or Wages Expense on January 1, how much cash was paid as wages during January?

d.   If the truck has a useful life of five years, what is the monthly amount of depreciation expense and how many months has Coyle owned the truck?

LO3, 4   **E3-10A. Analysis of the Impact of Adjustments on Financial Statements** At the end of the first month of operations, the Bradley Company's accountant prepared financial statements that showed the following amounts:

Assets.	$60,000
Liabilities.	20,000
Stockholders' equity	40,000
Net income.	9,000

In preparing the statements, the accountant overlooked the following items:

a.   Depreciation for the month, $850.
b.   Service revenue earned but unbilled at month-end, $1,500.
c.   Employee wages earned but unpaid at month-end, $375.

Determine the correct amounts of assets, liabilities, and stockholders' equity at month-end and net income for the month.

LO6   **E3-11A. Closing Entries** The adjusted trial balance of the Rose Corporation, prepared as of December 31, contains the following accounts:

	Debit	Credit
Service fees earned		$92,500
Interest income.		2,600
Salaries expense	$41,800	
Advertising expense.	4,300	
Depreciation expense.	8,700	
Income tax expense.	11,000	
Common stock.		75,000
Retained earnings		61,000
Cash dividends.	15,000	

Prepare journal entries to close the accounts directly to Retained Earnings. After these entries are posted, what is the ending balance in the Retained Earnings account?

LO7
(Appendix 3A)   **E3-12A. Closing Entries** Use the information provided in E3-5A to prepare journal entries to close the accounts using the Income Summary account. After these entries are posted, what is the balance in the Retained Earnings account?

LO7
(Appendix 3A)   **E3-13A. Closing Entries** In the midst of closing procedures, Echo Corporation's accountant became ill and was hospitalized. You have volunteered to complete the closing of the books, and you find that all revenue and expense accounts have zero balances and that the Income Summary account has a single debit entry for $311,000 and a single credit entry for $352,000. The Dividends account has a debit balance of $19,000, and the Retained Earnings account has a credit balance of $120,000. Prepare journal entries to complete the closing procedures as of year-end.

E3-14A. Worksheet Identify each of the 10 amount columns of the worksheet and indicate to which column the adjusted balance of the following accounts would be extended:

LO8
(Appendix 3B)

a.	Accounts Receivable	*f.*	Rent Receivable
b.	Accumulated Depreciation	*g.*	Prepaid Insurance
c.	Dividends	*h.*	Service Fees Earned
d.	Wages Payable	*i.*	Common Stock
e.	Depreciation Expense	*j.*	Retained Earnings

E3-15A. Closing Entries Use the information provided in E3-11A to prepare journal entries to close the accounts using the Income Summary account. After these entries are posted, what is the balance in the Retained Earnings account?

LO7
(Appendix 3A)

E3-16A. Worksheet The adjusted trial balance columns of a worksheet for Bonn Corporation are shown below. The worksheet is prepared for the year ended December 31.

LO8
(Appendix 3B)

	Adjusted Trial Balance	
	Debit	**Credit**
Cash.	$ 6,000	
Accounts receivable.	6,500	
Equipment	78,000	
Accumulated depreciation		$ 14,000
Notes payable		12,500
Common stock.		43,000
Retained earnings		20,600
Cash dividends.	8,000	
Service fees earned		71,900
Rent expense	18,000	
Salaries expense	38,500	
Depreciation expense.	7,000	
Totals	$162,000	$162,000

Complete the worksheet by (a) entering the adjusted trial balance, (b) putting in the worksheet income statement and balance sheet columns, (c) extending the adjusted trial balance to the income statement and balance sheet columns, and (d) balancing the worksheet.

EXERCISES—SET B

E3-1B. Transaction Entry and Adjusting Entries Beale Building Services offers janitorial services on both a contract basis and an hourly basis. On January 1, Beale collected $60,000 in advance on a six-month contract for work to be performed evenly during the next six months.

LO4

a. Provide the general journal entry on January 1 to record the receipt of $60,000 for contract work.
b. Provide the adjusting entry to be made on January 31, for the contract work done during January.
c. At January 31, a total of 35 hours of hourly rate janitor work was unbilled. The billing rate is $28 per hour. Provide the adjusting entry needed on January 31. (*Note:* The firm uses the account Fees Receivable to reflect amounts due but not yet billed.)

E3-2B. Adjusting Entries Judy Brock began Brock Refinishing Service on July 1. Selected accounts are shown below as of July 31, before any adjusting entries have been made:

LO3, 4

	Debit	Credit
Prepaid rent	$5,700	
Prepaid advertising.	930	
Supplies	3,000	
Unearned refinishing fees.		$ 900
Refinishing fees revenue		2,500

Using the following information, record in a general journal the necessary adjusting entries on July 31:

a. On July 1, the firm paid one year's rent of $5,700.

b. On July 1, $930 was paid to a local newspaper for an advertisement to run daily for the months of July, August, and September.

c. Supplies on hand at July 31 total $1,100.

d. At July 31, refinishing services of $975 have been performed but not yet billed to customers. The firm uses the account Fees Receivable to reflect amounts due but not yet billed.

e. One customer paid $900 in advance for a refinishing project. At July 31, the project is one-half complete.

LO3, 4   **E3-3B.**   **Adjusting Entries** For each of the following unrelated situations, prepare the necessary adjusting entry in general journal form:

a. Unrecorded depreciation on equipment is $1,850.

b. The Supplies account has a balance of $4,000. Supplies on hand at the end of the period total $2,500.

c. On the date for preparing financial statements, an estimated utilities expense of $610 has been incurred, but no utility bill has been received.

d. On the first day of the current month, rent for four months was paid and recorded as a $2,800 debit to Prepaid Rent and a $2,800 credit to Cash. Monthly statements are now being prepared.

e. Nine months ago, Macke Insurance Company sold a one-year policy to a customer and recorded the receipt of the premium by debiting Cash for $624 and crediting Unearned Premium Revenue for $624. No adjusting entries have been prepared during the nine-month period. Annual financial statements are now being prepared.

f. At the end of the accounting period, employee wages of $635 have been incurred but not paid.

g. At the end of the accounting period, $725 of interest has been earned but not yet received on notes receivable that are held.

LO5   **E3-4B.**   **Statement of Stockholders' Equity** On January 1, the credit balance of the Retained Earnings account was $50,000. The company's common stock account had an opening balance of $85,000 and new contributions during the year totaled $9,000. On December 31, at year-end, the Dividends account had a debit balance of $6,500. The income statement shows net income of $31,000. Prepare a statement of stockholders' equity for A. Miller & Company, architectural design firm.

LO6   **E3-5B.**   **Closing Entries** The adjusted trial balance prepared December 31, for Cheryl Fontaine & Company, shipping agent, contains the following accounts:

	Debit	Credit
Commissions earned		$94,900
Wages expense	$36,000	
Insurance expense	1,900	
Utilities expense	9,500	
Depreciation expense	9,800	
Dividends	12,000	
Common stock		60,000
Retained earnings		22,100

Prepare journal entries to close the accounts directly to Retained Earnings. After these entries are posted, what is the ending balance in the Retained Earnings account?

LO1   **E3-6B.**   **Revenue Recognition** Identify the proper point to recognize revenue for each of the following transactions.

a. Apollo Industries sells a machine in January with terms of 50 percent due on delivery in January and the remaining balance due three months later.

b. Mia Company collects an advance deposit of $850 in May toward the purchase of a $4,000 piece of equipment that is delivered to the customer the following month.

c. Beckett Corporation receives payment in March at the time of delivery of a rebuilt engine for a forklift.

E3-7B. Expense Matching Identify the proper point to recognize expenses for each of the following **LO1** transactions.

a. Garner Inc. purchases for cash five custom dining tables for $1,000 each in March. Three tables are later sold for $1,750 each in April, and the remaining two tables are sold for $1,500 each in May.

b. Peyton Company purchases $300 of office supplies that are both paid for and used in August.

c. Kerra Company purchases $500 of inventory on account in July. The inventory is sold for $650 in August. Kerra pays its suppliers the $500 due in September.

E3-8B. Closing Entries In the midst of closing procedures, Claremont Corporation's accountant became ill **LO6** and was hospitalized. You have volunteered to complete the closing of the books. You find that all the revenue and expense accounts have zero balances. The Dividends account has a debit balance of $31,000. The Retained Earnings account has a beginning credit balance of $191,000. Expenses totaled $318,800, and revenues totaled $347,400. Prepare journal entries to complete the closing procedures as of year-end directly to Retained Earnings. After these entries are posted, what is the balance in the Retained Earnings account?

E3-9B. Analysis of Adjusted Data Selected T-account balances for the Parris Company are shown below as **LO3, 4** of January 31; adjusting entries have already been posted. The firm uses a calendar-year accounting period and makes monthly adjustments.

Supplies	Supplies Expense
Jan. 31 ... Bal. 950	Jan. 31 .. Bal. 2,540

Prepaid Insurance	Insurance Expense
Jan. 31 ... Bal. 910	Jan. 31 ... Bal. 182

Wages Payable	Wages Expense
Bal. 650 ... Jan. 31	Jan. 31 .. Bal. 3,200

Truck	Accumulated Depreciation—Truck
Jan. 31 .. Bal. 8,700	Bal. 2,610 .. Jan. 31

a. If the amount in Supplies Expense represents the January 31 adjustment for the supplies used in January, and $635 worth of supplies were purchased during January, what was the January 1 balance of Supplies?

b. The amount in the Insurance Expense account represents the adjustment made at January 31 for January insurance expense. If the original insurance premium was for one year, what was the amount of the premium and on what date did the insurance policy start?

c. If we assume that no balance existed in Wages Payable or Wages Expense on January 1, how much cash was paid as wages during January?

d. If the truck has a useful life of five years, what is the monthly amount of depreciation expense and how many months has Parris owned the truck?

E3-10B. Analysis of the Impact of Adjustments on Financial Statements At the end of the first month of **LO3, 4** operations, the Omar Company's accountant prepared financial statements that showed the following amounts:

Assets.	$80,000
Liabilities.	30,000
Stockholders' equity	50,000
Net income.	11,000

In preparing the statements, the accountant overlooked the following items:

a. Depreciation for the month, $4,500.

b. Service revenue earned but unbilled at month-end, $1,700.

c. Employee wages earned but unpaid at month-end, $450.

Determine the correct amounts of assets, liabilities, and stockholders' equity at month-end and net income for the month.

E3-11B. Closing Entries The adjusted trial balance of the Matthews Corporation, prepared December 31, **LO6** contains the following accounts:

	Debit	Credit
Service fees earned		$102,500
Interest income.		6,500
Salaries expense	$49,800	
Advertising expense.	4,300	
Depreciation expense.	9,500	
Income tax expense.	9,900	
Common stock.		80,000
Retained earnings		57,700
Cash dividends.	17,000	

Prepare journal entries to close the accounts directly to Retained Earnings. After these entries are posted, what is the ending balance in the Retained Earnings account?

LO7
(Appendix 3A)

E3-12B. Closing Entries Use the information provided in E3-5B to prepare journal entries to close the accounts using the Income Summary account. After these entries are posted, what is the balance in the Retained Earnings account?

LO7
(Appendix 3A)

E3-13B. Closing Entries In the midst of closing procedures, Claremont Corporation's accountant became ill. You have volunteered to complete the closing of the books, and you find that all revenue and expense accounts have zero balances and that the Income Summary account has a single debit entry for $318,800 and a single credit entry for $357,400. The Cash Dividends account has a debit balance of $16,000, and the Retained Earnings account has a credit balance of $117,000. Prepare journal entries to complete the closing procedures as of year-end.

LO8
(Appendix 3B)

E3-14B. Worksheet Identify each of the 10 amount columns of the worksheet and indicate to which column the adjusted balance of the following accounts would be extended:

a.   Accounts Receivable
b.   Accumulated Depreciation
c.   Dividends
d.   Salaries Payable
e.   Wages Expense

f.   Interest Receivable
g.   Prepaid Rent
h.   Service Fees Earned
i.   Common Stock
j.   Retained Earnings

LO7
(Appendix 3A)

E3-15B. Closing Entries Use the information provided in E3-11B to prepare journal entries to close the accounts using the Income Summary account. After these entries are posted, what is the balance in the Retained Earnings account?

LO8
(Appendix 3B)

E3-16B. Worksheet The adjusted trial balance columns of a worksheet for Frankfurt Corporation are shown below. The worksheet is prepared for the year ended December 31.

	Adjusted Trial Balance	
	Debit	Credit
Cash.	$ 14,000	
Accounts receivable.	18,500	
Equipment	78,000	
Accumulated depreciation		$ 24,000
Notes payable		13,000
Common stock.		43,000
Retained earnings		20,600
Cash dividends.	8,000	
Service fees earned		82,000
Rent expense	18,000	
Salaries expense	37,100	
Depreciation expense.	9,000	
Totals	$182,600	$182,600

Complete the worksheet by (a) entering the adjusted trial balance, (b) putting in the worksheet income statement and balance sheet columns, (c) extending the adjusted trial balance to the income statement and balance sheet columns, and (d) balancing the worksheet.

PROBLEMS—SET A

P3-1A. **Transaction Entries, Posting, Trial Balance, and Adjusting Entries** Mark Ladd opened Ladd **LO3, 4**
Roofing Service on April 1. Transactions for April are as follows:

April 1 Ladd contributed $13,500 of his personal funds in exchange for common stock to begin
the business.
2 Purchased a used truck for $6,100 cash.
3 Purchased ladders and other equipment for a total of $3,100, paid $1,000 cash, with the
balance due in 30 days.
4 Paid two-year premium on liability insurance, $3,000.
5 Purchased supplies on account, $1,200.
6 Received an advance payment of $1,800 from a customer for roof repair work to be done
during April and May.
7 Billed customers for roofing services, $5,500.
8 Collected $6,500 on account from customers.
9 Paid bill for truck fuel used in April, $75.
10 Paid April newspaper advertising, $100.
11 Paid assistants' wages, $4,500.
12 Billed customers for roofing services, $5,000.

Required

a. Set up a general ledger with the following accounts: Cash; Accounts Receivable; Supplies; Prepaid Insurance; Trucks; Accumulated Depreciation—Trucks; Equipment; Accumulated Depreciation—Equipment; Accounts Payable; Unearned Roofing Fees; Common Stock; Roofing Fees
Earned; Fuel Expense; Advertising Expense; Wages Expense; Insurance Expense; Supplies Ex-
pense; Depreciation Expense—Trucks; and Depreciation Expense—Equipment.
b. Record these transactions in the general journal and post to the ledger accounts.
c. Prepare an unadjusted trial balance as of April 30.
d. Prepare the journal entries to adjust the books for insurance expense, supplies expense, depreciation expense on the truck, depreciation expense on the equipment, and roofing fees earned. Supplies on hand on April 30 amounted to $800. Depreciation for April was $155 on the truck and
$35 on the equipment. One-fourth of the roofing fee received in advance was earned by April 30.
Post the adjusting entries.

P3-2A. **Transaction Entries, Posting, Trial Balance, and Adjusting Entries** The Wellness Catering Ser- **LO3, 4**
vice had the following transactions in July, its first month of operations:

July 1 Kelly Foster contributed $18,000 of personal funds to the business in exchange for
common stock.
2 Purchased the following items for cash from a catering firm that was going out of business
(make a compound entry): delivery van, $3,780; equipment, $3,240; and supplies, $1,700.
3 Paid premium on a one-year liability insurance policy, $2,160.
4 Entered into a contract with a local service club to cater weekly luncheon meetings for one
year at a fee of $750 per month. Received eight months' fees in advance.
5 Paid rent for July, August, and September, $2,340.
6 Paid employee's two weeks' wages (five-day week), $1,700.
7 Billed customers for services rendered, $5,000.
8 Purchased supplies on account, $3,400.
9 Paid employee's two weeks' wages, $1,800.
10 Paid July bill for gas, oil, and repairs on delivery van, $850.
11 Collected $3,700 from customers on account.
12 Billed customers for services rendered, $4,800.
13 Foster received a $2,000 dividend.

Required

a. Set up a general ledger that includes the following accounts: Cash; Accounts Receivable; Sup-
plies; Prepaid Rent; Prepaid Insurance; Delivery Van; Accumulated Depreciation—Delivery
Van; Equipment; Accumulated Depreciation—Equipment; Accounts Payable; Wages Payable;
Unearned Catering Fees; Common Stock; Dividends; Catering Fees Revenue; Wages Expense;

Rent Expense; Supplies Expense; Insurance Expense; Delivery Van Expense; Depreciation Expense—Delivery Van; and Depreciation Expense—Equipment.

b. Record July transactions in the general journal and post to the ledger accounts.

c. Prepare an unadjusted trial balance as of July 31.

d. Record adjusting journal entries in the general journal and post to the ledger accounts. The following information is available on July 31:

> Supplies on hand, $1,600
> Accrued wages, $525
> Estimated life of delivery van, three years
> Estimated life of equipment, six years

Also, make any necessary adjusting entries for insurance, rent, and catering fees indicated by the July transactions.

LO3, 4 **P3-3A.** **Trial Balance and Adjusting Entries** Photomake, Inc., a commercial photography studio, has just completed its first full year of operations on December 31. The general ledger account balances before year-end adjustments follow. No adjusting entries have been made to the accounts at any time during the year. Assume that all balances are normal.

Cash	$ 2,150	Accounts payable	$ 1,710
Accounts receivable	3,600	Unearned photography fees	2,600
Prepaid rent	12,600	Common stock	24,000
Prepaid insurance	2,970	Photography fees earned	34,480
Supplies	4,250	Wages expense	11,000
Equipment	22,800	Utilities expense	3,420

An analysis of the firm's records discloses the following items:

1. Photography services of $1,450 have been rendered, but customers have not yet been billed. The firm uses the account Fees Receivable to reflect amounts due but not yet billed.

2. The equipment, purchased January 1, has an estimated life of 10 years.

3. Utilities expense for December is estimated to be $650, but the bill will not arrive until January of next year.

4. The balance in Prepaid Rent represents the amount paid on January 1, for a two-year lease on the studio.

5. In November, customers paid $2,600 in advance for pictures to be taken for the holiday season. When received, these fees were credited to Unearned Photography Fees. By December 31, all fees are earned.

6. A three-year insurance premium paid on January 1, was debited to Prepaid Insurance.

7. Supplies on hand at December 31 are $1,750.

8. At December 31, wages expense of $500 has been incurred but not paid.

Required

a. Prove that the sum of the debits equals the sum of the credits for Photomake's unadjusted account balances by preparing an unadjusted trial balance as of December 31.

b. Record adjusting entries in the general journal.

LO3, 4 **P3-4A.** **Adjusting Entries** Dole Carpet Cleaners ended its first month of operations on June 30. Monthly financial statements will be prepared. The unadjusted account balances are as follows:

DOLE CARPET CLEANERS Unadjusted Trial Balance June 30, 2015		
	Debit	Credit
Cash	$ 1,180	
Accounts receivable	450	
Prepaid rent	3,100	
Supplies	2,520	
Equipment	4,440	
Accounts payable		$ 760
Common stock		2,500
Retained earnings		5,000
Dividends	200	
Service fees earned		4,650
Wages expense	1,020	
	$12,910	$12,910

The following information is also available:

1. The balance in Prepaid Rent was the amount paid on June 1 for the first two months' rent.
2. Supplies on hand at June 30 were $950.
3. The equipment, purchased June 1, has an estimated life of five years.
4. Unpaid wages at June 30 were $450.
5. Utility services used during June were estimated at $650. A bill is expected early in July.
6. Fees earned for services performed but not yet billed on June 30 were $380. The firm uses the account Fees Receivable to reflect amounts due but not yet billed.

Required

Prepare the adjusting entries needed at June 30 for the general journal.

P3-5A. Adjusting Entries The following information relates to December 31 adjustments for Finest Print, a printing company. The firm's fiscal year ends on December 31. **LO3, 4**

1. Weekly salaries for a five-day week total $2,520, payable on Fridays. December 31 of the current year is a Tuesday.
2. Finest Print has $25,000 of notes payable outstanding at December 31. Interest of $250 has accrued on these notes by December 31, but will not be paid until the notes mature next year.
3. During December, Finest Print provided $1,000 of printing services to clients who will be billed on January 2. The firm uses the account Fees Receivable to reflect amounts due but not yet billed.
4. Starting December 1, all maintenance work on Finest Print's equipment is handled by Prompt Repair Company under an agreement whereby Finest Print pays a fixed monthly charge of $125. Finest Print paid six months' service charge in advance on December 1, debiting Prepaid Maintenance for $750.
5. The firm paid $900 on December 15 for a series of radio commercials to run during December and January. One-third of the commercials have aired by December 31. The $900 payment was debited to Prepaid Advertising.
6. Starting December 16, Finest Print rented 400 square feet of storage space from a neighboring business. The monthly rent of $0.80 per square foot is due in advance on the first of each month. Nothing was paid in December, however, because the neighbor agreed to add the rent for one-half of December to the January 1 payment.
7. Finest Print invested $7,500 in securities on December 1 and earned interest of $62 on these securities by December 31. No interest will be received until January.
8. The annual depreciation on the firm's equipment is $2,425. No depreciation has been recorded during the year.

Required

Prepare the required December 31 adjusting entries in the general journal.

LO3, 4 **P3-6A.** **Adjusting Entries** The following selected accounts appear in the Shaw Company's unadjusted trial balance as of December 31, the end of the fiscal year (all accounts have normal balances):

Prepaid advertising.	$ 1,200	Unearned service fees	$ 5,400
Wages expense	43,800	Service fees earned	87,000
Prepaid insurance	3,420	Rental income	4,900

Required

Prepare the necessary adjusting entries in the general journal as of December 31, assuming the following:

1. Prepaid advertising at December 31 is $950.
2. Unpaid wages earned by employees in December are $1,600.
3. Prepaid insurance at December 31 is $2,750.
4. Unearned service fees at December 31 are $2,800.
5. Rent revenue of $1,300 owed by a tenant is not recorded at December 31.

LO3, 4 **P3-7A.** **Adjusting Entries** The following selected accounts appear in the Birch Company's unadjusted trial balance as of December 31, the end of the fiscal year (all accounts have normal balances):

Prepaid maintenance	$2,700	Commission fees earned	$86,000
Supplies	9,400	Rent expense	10,800
Unearned commission fees	8,500		

Required

Prepare the necessary adjusting entries in the general journal as of December 31, assuming the following:

1. On September 1, the company entered into a prepaid equipment maintenance contract. Birch Company paid $2,700 to cover maintenance service for six months, beginning September 1. The $2,700 payment was debited to Prepaid Maintenance.
2. Supplies on hand at December 31 are $3,200.
3. Unearned commission fees at December 31 are $4,000.
4. Commission fees earned but not yet billed at December 31 are $3,500. (*Note:* Debit Fees Receivable.)
5. Birch Company's lease calls for rent of $900 per month payable on the first of each month, plus an annual amount equal to 1 percent of annual commissions earned. This additional rent is payable on January 10 of the following year. (*Note:* Be sure to use the adjusted amount of commissions earned in computing the additional rent.)

LO5, 6 **P3-8A.** **Financial Statements and Closing Entries** The adjusted trial balance shown below is for Fine Consulting Service as of December 31. Byran Fine made no capital contributions during the year.

	Adjusted Trial Balance	
	Debit	Credit
Cash	$ 2,700	
Accounts receivable	3,270	
Supplies	5,060	
Prepaid insurance	1,500	
Equipment	6,400	
Accumulated depreciation—Equipment		$ 1,080
Accounts payable		845
Long-term notes payable		7,000
Common stock		3,000
Retained earnings		5,205
Dividends	2,900	
Service fees earned		62,400
Rent expense	15,000	
Salaries expense	33,400	
Supplies expense	4,700	
Insurance expense	3,250	
Depreciation expense—Equipment	720	
Interest expense	630	
Totals	$79,530	$79,530

Required

a. Prepare an income statement and a statement of stockholders' equity for the year, and a balance sheet as of December 31.

b. Prepare closing entries directly to Retained Earnings in general journal form.

P3-9A. **Closing Entries** The adjusted trial balance shown below is for Bayou, Inc., at December 31: **LO6**

	Adjusted Trial Balance	
	Debit	Credit
Cash...	$ 3,500	
Accounts receivable..	8,000	
Prepaid insurance	3,600	
Equipment	75,000	
Accumulated depreciation...................................		$ 12,000
Accounts payable...		600
Common stock..		30,000
Retained earnings		14,100
Cash dividends...	7,500	
Service fees earned		102,200
Miscellaneous income		4,200
Salaries expense	42,800	
Rent expense	12,900	
Insurance expense..	1,800	
Depreciation expense.......................................	8,000	
Income tax expense...	8,800	
Income tax payable		8,800
Totals	$171,900	$171,900

Required

a. Prepare closing entries directly to Retained Earnings in general journal form.

b. After the closing entries are posted, what is the ending balance in the Retained Earnings account?

c. Prepare a post-closing trial balance.

P3-10A. **Balance Sheet and Net Income** At the beginning of 2015, Flynn's Parking Lots had the following balance sheet: **LO5**

Assets		**Liabilities**	
Cash............................	$ 4,800	Accounts payable..................	$12,000
Accounts receivable...............	14,700		
Land............................	67,000	**Stockholders' Equity**	
		Common stock....................	27,000
		Retained earnings	47,500
		Total Liabilities and	
Total Assets	$86,500	Stockholders' Equity.............	$86,500

a. At the end of 2015, Flynn had the following assets and liabilities: Cash, $9,800; Accounts Receivable, $17,400; Land, $67,000; and Accounts Payable, $7,500; and Common Stock, $27,000. Prepare a year-end balance sheet for Flynn's Parking Lots.

b. Assume that stockholders did not invest any money in the business during the year but received $10,000 as a dividend; what was Flynn's net income or net loss for 2015?

P3-11A. **Determination of Retained Earnings and Net Income** The following information appears in the records of Bock Corporation at the end of 2015: **LO5**

Accounts receivable...............	$ 25,000	Retained earnings	$?
Accounts payable..................	11,000	Supplies	9,000
Cash.............................	8,000	Equipment	138,000
Common stock....................	115,000		

a.   Calculate the amount of retained earnings at the end of 2015.

b.   Using your answer from part *a*, if the amount of the retained earnings at the beginning of 2015 was $30,000, and $19,000 in dividends were paid during 2015, what was the company's net income for 2015?

LO3, 4, 5   **P3-12A. Transaction Analysis, Trial Balance, and Financial Statements** Angela Mehl operates the Mehl Dance Studio. On June 1, the business's general ledger contained the following information:

Cash.........................	$ 5,930	Accounts payable.................	$ 480
Accounts receivable..............	8,000	Notes payable	3,580
		Common stock...................	7,870
		Retained earnings	2,000
	$13,930		$13,930

The following transactions occurred during the month of June:

June 1   Paid June rent for practice studio, $975.
      2   Paid June piano rental, $240 (Rent Expense).
      3   Collected $5,320 from students on account.
      4   Borrowed $1,500 and signed a promissory note payable due in six months.
      5   Billed students for June instructional fees, $7,500.
      6   Paid interest for June on notes payable, $30.
      7   Paid $350 for advertising ballet performances.
      8   Paid costume rental, $550 (Rent Expense).
      9   Collected $2,100 admission fees from ballet performances given during the month.
    10   Paid $480 owed on account.
    11   Received invoice for June utilities, to be paid in July, $465.
    12   Paid stockholders $900 cash as a dividend.
    13   Purchased piano for $5,000 cash, to be used in business starting in July.

Required

a.   Set up accounts for the general ledger with June 1 balances and enter the beginning balances. Also provide the following accounts: Piano; Dividends; Instructional Fees Earned; Performance Revenue; Rent Expense; Utilities Expense; Advertising Expense; and Interest Expense. Record the listed transactions in the accounts.

b.   Prepare a trial balance as of June 30.

c.   Prepare an income statement for the month of June.

d.   Prepare a statement of stockholders' equity for the month of June.

e.   Prepare a balance sheet as of June 30.

f.   Prepare closing entries.

g.   Prepare a post-closing trial balance.

LO3, 4, 5, 6   **P3-13A. Transaction Analysis, Trial Balance, and Financial Statements** On December 1, a group of individuals formed a corporation to establish the *Beeper,* a neighborhood weekly newspaper featuring want ads of individuals and advertising of local firms. The free paper will be mailed to about 8,000 local residents; revenue will be generated from advertising and want ads. The December transactions are summarized as follows:

Dec.   1   Sold common stock of Beeper, Inc., for cash, $35,000.
      2   Paid December rent on furnished office, $1,200.
      3   Purchased for $750, on account, T-shirts displaying company logo. The T-shirts were distributed at a grand opening.
      4   Paid to creditor on account, $750.
      5   Collected "Help wanted" ad revenue in cash, $4,500.
      6   Paid post office for cost of bulk mailing, $910.
      7   Billed various firms for advertising in the first two issues of the newspaper, $5,600.
      8   Paid Acme Courier Service for transporting newspapers to post office, $50.
      9   Paid for printing newspaper, $2,900.
    10   Collected "Help wanted" ad revenue in cash, $2,570.
    11   Received invoice for December utilities, to be paid in January, $610.

Dec. 12 Paid for printing newspaper, $2,900.
13 Paid December salaries, $4,100.
14 Billed various firms for advertising in two issues of the newspaper, $8,850.
15 Paid post office for cost of bulk mailing, $930.
16 Paid Acme Courier Service for transporting newspapers to post office, $350.
17 Collected $5,100 on accounts receivable.
18 Purchased fax machine for office in exchange for a six-month note payable, $1,400.

Required

a.   Set up accounts for the following items: Cash, Accounts Receivable, Office Equipment, Accounts Payable, Notes Payable, Common Stock, Advertising Revenue, Want Ad Revenue, Printing Expense, Advertising Expense, Utilities Expense, Salaries Expense, Rent Expense, and Delivery Expense. Prepare journal entries in a general journal and record the foregoing transactions in the accounts.

b.   Prepare a trial balance as of December 31.

c.   Prepare an income statement for the month of December.

d.   Prepare a balance sheet as of December 31. (*Note:* In this problem, the net income for December becomes the amount of retained earnings at December 31.)

P3-14A. Balance Sheets for a Corporation The following balance sheet data are given for Normandy Catering Service, a corporation, as of May 31:   LO5

Accounts receivable.	$20,300	Accounts payable.	$ 5,200
Notes payable	20,000	Cash.	12,200
Equipment	55,000	Common stock.	42,500
Supplies	19,400	Retained earnings	?

Assume that on June 1, the following transactions occurred:

June 1 Purchased additional equipment costing $18,000, giving $3,000 cash and a $15,000 note payable.
1 Paid a cash dividend of $9,000.

Required

a.   Prepare a balance sheet as of May 31.

b.   Prepare a balance sheet as of June 2.

P3-15A. Determination of Net Income and Retained Earnings The following selected income statement and balance sheet information is available for Lloyd Appraisers at the end of the current month: LO5

Supplies	$ 6,500	Accounts payable.	$ 4,000
Accounts receivable.	18,000	Salaries expense	17,000
Utilities expense.	700	Appraisal fees earned.	31,000
Supplies expense.	1,400	Common stock	10,000
Rent expense	2,500	Retained earnings (beginning)	10,000
Cash.	3,600		

a.   Calculate the net income or net loss for the month.

b.   If Mr. Lloyd made no additional investment in the business during the month but received $8,000 as a dividend, what is the balance in Retained Earnings at the end of the month?

P3-16A. Trial Balance and Financial Statements The following account balances were taken (out of order) from the general ledger of R. Ladd & Company as of January 31. Ladd trains dogs for competitive championship field trials. The firm's accounting year began on January 1. All accounts have normal balances.   LO5

Land	$21,000	Office rent expense	$ 800
Maintenance expense	860	Supplies expense	760
Supplies	1,200	Utilities expense	200
Advertising expense	380	Fees earned	18,400
Common stock	18,000	Accounts receivable	8,200
Retained earnings	9,000		
Cash	7,300	Salaries expense	4,480
Accounts payable	880	Dividends	1,100

Required

a. Prepare a trial balance from the given data.

b. Prepare an income statement for the month of January.

c. Prepare a statement of stockholders' equity for the month of January.

d. Prepare a balance sheet as of January 31.

LO5 **P3-17A. Trial Balance and Financial Statements** The following account balances, in alphabetical order, are from the general ledger of Morgan's Waterproofing Service at January 31. The firm began business on January 1. All accounts have normal balances.

Accounts payable	$ 3,500	Notes payable	$ 4,000
Accounts receivable	21,000	Rent expense	1,700
Advertising expense	1,420	Salaries expense	8,000
Cash	10,400	Service fees earned	25,760
Common stock	29,740	Supplies	8,860
Dividends	1,000	Supplies expense	10,250
Interest expense	50	Utilities expense	320

Required

a. Prepare a trial balance from the given data.

b. Prepare an income statement for the month of January.

c. Prepare a statement of stockholders' equity for the month of January.

d. Prepare a balance sheet as of January 31.

LO5, 7
(Appendix 3A)

P3-18A. Financial Statements and Closing Entries Use the information provided in P3-8A.

Required

a. Prepare an income statement, a statement of stockholders' equity, and a balance sheet as of December 31.

b. Prepare closing entries using the Income Summary account.

LO7
(Appendix 3A)

P3-19A. Closing Entries Use the information provided in P3-9A.

Required

a. Prepare closing entries in general journal form using the Income Summary account.

b. After the closing entries are posted, what is the ending balance in the Retained Earnings account?

c. Prepare a post-closing trial balance.

P3-20A. Worksheet The following unadjusted trial balance was prepared as of March 31:

FOCUS TRAVEL AGENCY Unadjusted Trial Balance March 31		
	Debit	Credit
Cash	$ 2,400	
Commissions receivable	8,000	
Supplies	1,750	
Prepaid insurance	1,800	
Equipment	16,000	
Accumulated depreciation		$ 7,600
Accounts payable		550
Unearned commissions		700
Common stock		4,000
Retained earnings		9,000
Dividends	900	
Commissions earned		18,990
Salaries expense	6,500	
Rent expense	1,870	
Advertising expense	1,000	
Utilities expense	620	
Totals	$40,840	$40,840

Focus Travel Agency's fiscal year ends on March 31. The following additional information is available:

1. Depreciation for the year is $1,500.
2. Supplies on hand at March 31 amount to $820.
3. By March 31, $600 of the unearned commissions was earned. The remainder will be earned in the next year.
4. Insurance expense for the year is $1,200.
5. Accrued salaries payable total $800 at March 31.

Required

Enter the trial balance on a worksheet and complete the worksheet using the adjustment data given above.

PROBLEMS—SET B

P3-1B. Transaction Entries, Posting, Trial Balance, Adjusting Entries Huang Karate School began business on June 1. Transactions for June were as follows:

June 1 Po Huang contributed $10,000 of his personal funds in exchange for common stock to begin the business.
2 Purchased equipment for $4,750, paying $750 cash, with the balance due in 30 days.
3 Paid six months' rent, $6,450.
4 Paid one-year premium on liability insurance, $876.
5 Paid June newspaper advertising, $525.
6 Billed participants for karate lessons to date, $2,200.
7 Received $855 from a local company to conduct a special three-session class on self-defense for its employees. The three sessions will be held on June 29, July 6, and July 13, at $285 per session.
8 Collected $2,800 on account from participants
9 Paid $275 to repair damage to wall caused by an errant kick.
10 Billed participants for karate lessons to date, $2,000.
11 Paid assistant's wages, $950.

Required

a. Set up a general ledger with the following accounts: Cash; Accounts Receivable; Prepaid Rent; Prepaid Insurance; Equipment; Accumulated Depreciation—Equipment; Accounts Payable; Utilities Payable; Unearned Karate Fees; Common Stock; Karate Fees Earned; Advertising Expense; Repairs Expense; Wages Expense; Rent Expense; Insurance Expense; Depreciation Expense—Equipment; and Utilities Expense.

b. Record these transactions in general journal form and post to the ledger accounts.

c. Prepare an unadjusted trial balance as of June 30.

d. Prepare the adjusting entries for rent expense, insurance expense, depreciation expense, utilities expense, and karate fees earned. Depreciation expense for June is $150, and estimated utilities expense for June is $320. Post the adjusting entries.

LO3, 4   P3-2B.   Transaction Entries, Posting, Trial Balance, and Adjusting Entries Market-Probe, a market research firm, had the following transactions in June, its first month of operations.

June   1   J. Witson invested $28,000 of personal funds in the firm in exchange for common stock.

2   The firm purchased the following from an office supply company: office equipment, $11,040; office supplies, $2,840. Terms called for a cash payment of $4,000, with the remainder due in 60 days. (Make a compound entry.)

3   Paid June rent, $1,275.

4   Contracted for four months' advertising in a local newspaper at $325 per month and paid for the advertising in advance.

5   Signed a six-month contract with an electronics firm to provide research consulting services at a rate of $3,200 per month. Received two months' fees in advance. Work on the contract started immediately.

6   Billed various customers for services rendered, $7,500.

7   Paid two weeks' salaries (five-day week) to employees, $3,600.

8   Paid J. Witson's travel expenses to business conference, $1,440.

9   Paid $520 cash for postage to mail questionnaire.

10   Paid two weeks' salaries to employees, $3,600.

11   Billed various customers for services rendered, $7,200.

12   Collected $7,800 from customers on account.

13   J. Witson received a $2,500 cash dividend.

Required

a. Set up a general ledger that includes the following accounts: Cash; Accounts Receivable; Office Supplies; Prepaid Advertising; Office Equipment; Accumulated Depreciation—Office Equipment; Accounts Payable; Salaries Payable; Unearned Service Fees; Common Stock; Dividends; Service Fees Earned; Salaries Expense; Advertising Expense; Supplies Expense; Rent Expense; Travel Expense; Depreciation Expense—Office Equipment; and Postage Expense.

b. Record June transactions in general journal form and post to the ledger accounts.

c. Prepare an unadjusted trial balance as of June 30.

d. Record adjusting journal entries in general journal form, and post to the ledger accounts. The following information is available on June 30:

Office supplies on hand, $1,830.

Accrued salaries, $925.

Estimated life of office equipment, eight years.

Also, make any necessary adjusting entries for advertising and for service fees indicated by the June transactions.

LO3, 4   P3-3B.   Trial Balance and Adjusting Entries Deliverall, a mailing service, has just completed its first full year of operations on December 31, 2015. The firm's general ledger account balances before year-end adjustments are given below. No adjusting entries have been made to the accounts at any time during the year. Assume that all balances are normal.

Cash	$ 2,600	Accounts payable	$ 2,700
Accounts receivable	5,120	Common stock	7,530
Prepaid advertising	1,680	Mailing fees earned	86,000
Supplies	6,570	Wages expense	38,800
Equipment	42,240	Rent expense	4,700
Notes payable	8,500	Utilities expense	3,020

An analysis of the firm's records reveals the following:

1. The balance in Prepaid Advertising represents the amount paid for newspaper advertising for one year. The agreement, which calls for the same amount of space each month, covers the period from February 1, 2015, to January 31, 2016. Deliverall did not advertise during its first month of operations.
2. The equipment, purchased January 1, has an estimated life of eight years.
3. Utilities expense does not include expense for December, estimated at $525. The bill will not arrive until January 2016.
4. At year-end, employees have earned $1,500 in wages that will not be paid until January.
5. Supplies on hand at year-end amounted to $1,720.
6. At year-end, unpaid interest of $450 has accrued on the notes payable.
7. The firm's lease calls for rent of $525 per month payable on the first of each month, plus an amount equal to ½ percent of annual mailing fees earned. The rental percentage is payable within 15 days after the end of the year.

Required

a. Demonstrate that the sum of the debits equals the sum of the credits for the unadjusted account balances shown above by preparing an unadjusted trial balance as of December 31, 2015.
b. Record adjusting entries in general journal form.

P3-4B.   Adjusting Entries The Wheel Place, Inc., began operations on March 1 to provide automotive wheel alignment and balancing services. On March 31, 2015, the unadjusted balances of the firm's accounts are as follows: **LO3, 4**

THE WHEEL PLACE, INC. Unadjusted Trial Balance March 31, 2015	Debit	Credit
Cash	$ 1,900	
Accounts receivable	5,820	
Prepaid rent	4,770	
Supplies	3,700	
Equipment	36,180	
Accounts payable		$ 4,510
Unearned service revenue		1,500
Common stock		38,400
Service revenue		12,360
Wages expense	4,400	
Totals	$56,770	$56,770

The following information is also available.

1. The balance in Prepaid Rent was the amount paid on March 1 to cover the first six months' rent.
2. Supplies on hand on March 31 amounted to $1,920.
3. The equipment has an estimated life of nine years.
4. Unpaid wages at March 31 were $660.
5. Utility services used during March were estimated at $590. A bill is expected early in April.

6. The balance in Unearned Service Revenue was the amount received on March 1 from a new car dealer to cover alignment and balancing services on all new cars sold by the dealer in March and April. The Wheel Place agreed to provide the services at a fixed fee of $750 each month.

Required

Prepare the adjusting entries needed at March 31 in general journal form.

LO3, 4   P3-5B.   Adjusting Entries The following information relates to the December 31 adjustments for Water Barrier, a firm providing waterproofing services for commercial and residential customers. The firm's fiscal year ends December 31; no adjusting entries have been made during the year.

1. The firm paid a $3,000 premium for a three-year insurance policy, coverage to begin October 1. The premium payment was debited to Prepaid Insurance.
2. Weekly wages for a five-day work week total $1,250, payable on Fridays. December 31 is a Thursday.
3. Water Barrier received $4,800 in November for services to be performed during December through February of the following year. When received, this amount was credited to Unearned Service Fees. By December 31, one-third of this amount was earned.
4. Water Barrier receives a 5 percent commission from the manufacturer on sales of a waterproofing agent to Water Barrier's customers. By December 31, Water Barrier had sales of $10,000 (during November and December) for which no commissions had been received or recorded.
5. During December, fuel oil costs of $650 were incurred to heat the firm's buildings. Because the monthly bill from the oil company has not yet arrived, no entry has been made for this amount (fuel oil costs are charged to Utilities Expense).
6. The Supplies account has a balance of $17,500 on December 31. A count of supplies on December 31 indicates that $3,500 worth of supplies are still on hand.
7. On December 1, Water Barrier borrowed $10,000 from the bank, giving a note payable. Interest is not payable until the note is due near the end of the following January. However, the interest for December is $95.
8. Water Barrier rents parking spaces in its lot to firms in the office building next door. On December 1, Water Barrier received $8,000 as advance payments to cover parking privileges in the lot for December through March of the following year. When received, the $8,000 was credited to Unearned Parking Fees.

Required

Prepare the necessary December 31 adjusting entries in general journal form.

LO3, 4   P3-6B.   Adjusting Entries The following selected accounts appear in the Albany Company's unadjusted trial balance as of December 31, the end of the fiscal year (all accounts have normal balances):

Prepaid advertising.	$ 3,200	Unearned service fees	$ 5,400
Wages expense	45,800	Service fees earned	88,000
Prepaid insurance	6,420	Rental income	4,900

Required

Make the necessary adjusting entries in general journal form as of December 31 assuming the following:

a.   Prepaid advertising at December 31 is $900.
b.   Unpaid wages earned by employees in December are $1,700.
c.   Prepaid insurance at December 31 is $2,380.
d.   Unearned service fees at December 31 are $2,500.
e.   Rent revenue of $4,000 owed by a tenant is not recorded at December 31.

LO3, 4   P3-7B.   Adjusting Entries The following selected accounts appear in the Burns Company's unadjusted trial balance as of December 31, the end of the fiscal year (all accounts have normal balances):

Prepaid maintenance	$ 6,000	Commission fees earned	$97,000
Supplies	10,400	Rent expense	10,800
Unearned commission fees	10,700		

Required

Make the necessary adjusting entries in general journal form at December 31, assuming the following:

1. On September 1, the company entered into a prepaid equipment maintenance contract. The Burns Company paid $6,000 to cover maintenance service for six months, beginning September 1. The $6,000 payment was debited to Prepaid Maintenance.
2. Supplies on hand at December 31 are $3,500.
3. Unearned commission fees at December 31 are $5,000.
4. Commission fees earned but not yet billed at December 31 are $3,800. (*Note:* Debit Fees Receivable.)
5. The Burns Company's lease calls for rent of $900 per month payable on the first of each month, plus an annual amount equal to 2 percent of annual commissions earned. This additional rent is payable on January 10 of the following year. (*Note:* Be sure to use the adjusted amount of commissions earned in calculating the additional rent.)

P3-8B. **Financial Statements and Closing Entries** Outdoors, Inc., publishes magazines for skiers and hikers. The firm has the following adjusted trial balance at December 31:   **LO5, 6**

OUTDOORS, INC. Adjusted Trial Balance December 31		
	Debit	**Credit**
Cash.	$ 5,400	
Accounts receivable.	18,600	
Supplies	4,200	
Prepaid insurance	930	
Office equipment	70,000	
Accumulated depreciation.		$ 13,000
Accounts payable.		16,100
Unearned subscription revenue.		10,000
Salaries payable.		3,500
Common stock.		21,000
Retained earnings		23,220
Subscription revenue.		188,300
Advertising revenue		49,700
Salaries expense	120,230	
Printing and mailing expense.	85,600	
Rent expense.	4,800	
Supplies expense.	6,100	
Insurance expense.	1,860	
Depreciation expense.	5,500	
Income tax expense.	1,600	
Totals	$324,820	$324,820

Required

a. Prepare an income statement for the year and a balance sheet as of December 31.
b. Prepare closing entries directly to Retained Earnings in general journal form.

LO6   P3-9B.   Closing Entries The adjusted trial balance for Okay Moving Service as of December 31 is as follows:

	Adjusted Trial Balance	
	Debit	Credit
Cash.	$ 4,800	
Accounts receivable.	5,250	
Supplies	5,300	
Prepaid advertising.	3,000	
Trucks.	30,300	
Accumulated depreciation—Trucks.		$ 10,000
Equipment	7,600	
Accumulated depreciation—Equipment		2,100
Accounts payable.		1,200
Unearned service fees		6,700
Common stock.		10,000
Retained earnings		16,050
Dividends	7,500	
Service fees earned		80,500
Wages expense	29,800	
Rent expense	10,200	
Insurance expense.	4,900	
Supplies expense.	5,100	
Advertising expense.	8,000	
Depreciation expense—Trucks	4,000	
Depreciation expense—Equipment	800	
Totals	$126,550	$126,550

Required
a.   Prepare the closing entries at December 31 directly to Retained Earnings in general journal form.
b.   After the closing entries are posted, calculate the ending balance in the Retained Earnings account.
c.   Prepare a post-closing trial balance.

LO5   P3-10B. Balance Sheet and Net Income Determination At the beginning of 2015, Luxury Parking Services had the following balance sheet:

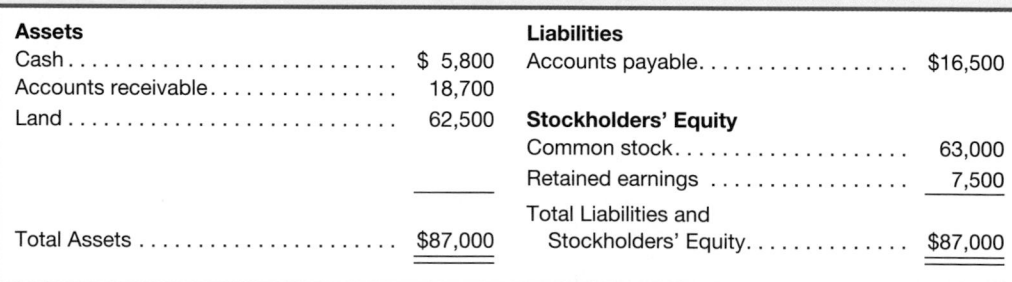

Assets		**Liabilities**	
Cash.	$ 5,800	Accounts payable.	$16,500
Accounts receivable.	18,700		
Land	62,500	**Stockholders' Equity**	
		Common stock.	63,000
		Retained earnings	7,500
		Total Liabilities and	
Total Assets	$87,000	Stockholders' Equity.	$87,000

a.   At the end of 2015, Luxury Parking Services had the following assets and liabilities: Cash, $8,800; Accounts Receivable, $18,400; Land, $62,500; and Accounts Payable, $11,500. Prepare a year-end balance sheet for Luxury Parking Services assuming that no additional stock was issued.
b.   Assuming that stockholders did not invest any money in the business during the year but received a $15,000 dividend, what was the company's net income or net loss for 2015?

P3-11B. Determination of Retained Earnings and Net Income The following information appears in the **LO5** records of the Wellington Corporation at year-end 2015:

Accounts receivable.............	$ 36,000	Retained earnings	$?
Accounts payable................	10,000	Supplies	9,000
Cash..........................	7,000	Equipment	140,000
Common stock..................	130,000		

   a. Calculate the amount of retained earnings at the end of 2015.

   b. Using your answer to part *a*, if the amount of the retained earnings at the beginning of 2015 was $30,000, and $9,000 in dividends were paid during 2015, what was the net income for 2015?

P3-12B. Transaction Analysis, Trial Balance, and Financial Statements Kate Miller operates the Miller **LO3, 4, 5, 6** Dance Studio. On June 1, the studio's general ledger contained the following information:

Cash..........................	$10,930	Accounts payable.................	$ 480
Accounts receivable..............	17,420	Notes payable	3,000
		Common stock..................	11,870
		Retained earnings	13,000
	$28,350		$28,350

The following transactions occurred during the month of June:

June   1 Paid June rent for practice studio, $2,075.
         2 Paid June piano rental, $800 (Rent Expense).
         3 Collected $14,320 from students on account.
         4 Borrowed $6,500 and signed a promissory note payable due in six months.
         5 Billed students for June instructional fees, $9,600.
         6 Paid interest for June on the outstanding notes payable, $90.
         7 Paid $550 for advertising ballet performances.
         8 Paid costume rental, $800 (Rent Expense).
         9 Collected $6,100 admission fees from ballet performances given during June.
       10 Paid $780 owed on account.
       11 Received invoice for June utilities, to be paid in July, $480.
       12 The studio paid stockholders a cash dividend of $850.
       13 Purchased piano for $6,000 cash, to be used in business starting in July.

Required

   a. Set up accounts for the general ledger with June 1 balances and enter the beginning balances. Also provide the following accounts: Piano; Dividends; Instructional Fees Earned; Performance Revenue; Rent Expense; Utilities Expense; Advertising Expense; and Interest Expense. Record the listed transactions in the accounts.

   b. Prepare a trial balance as of June 30.

   c. Prepare an income statement for the month of June.

   d. Prepare a statement of stockholders' equity for the month of June.

   e. Prepare a balance sheet as of June 30.

   f. Prepare closing entries.

   g. Prepare a post-closing trial balance.

P3-13B. Transaction Analysis, Trial Balance, and Financial Statements On December 1, a group of in- **LO3, 4, 5, 6** dividuals formed a corporation to establish the *Arcadia News,* a neighborhood newspaper featuring "Help wanted" ads by individuals and advertising by local firms. The free paper will be mailed to about 20,000 local residents; revenue will be generated from advertising and the want ads. The December transactions are summarized below:

Dec. 1 Sold common stock for cash, $60,000.

2 Paid December rent on furnished office, $5,000.

3 Purchased for $550, on account, T-shirts displaying company logo. The T-shirts were distributed at a grand opening.

4 Paid to creditor on account, $350.

5 Collected want ad revenue in cash, $2,800.

6 Paid post office for cost of bulk mailing, $710.

7 Billed various firms for advertising in the first two issues of the newspaper, $6,300.

8 Paid Tucson Courier Service for transporting newspapers to the post office, $70.

9 Paid for printing newspaper, $3,900.

10 Collected want ad revenue in cash, $4,570.

11 Received invoice for December utilities, to be paid in January, $510.

12 Paid for printing newspaper, $4,900.

13 Paid December salaries, $6,100.

14 Billed various firms for advertising in two issues of the newspaper, $8,950.

15 Paid post office for cost of bulk mailing, $630.

16 Paid Tucson Courier Service for transporting newspapers to the post office, $60.

17 Collected $5,100 on accounts receivable.

18 Purchased fax machine for the office in exchange for a six-month note payable, $3,100.

Required

a. Set up accounts for the following: Cash, Accounts Receivable, Office Equipment, Accounts Payable, Notes Payable, Common Stock, Advertising Revenue, Want Ad Revenue, Printing Expense, Advertising Expense, Utilities Expense, Salaries Expense, Rent Expense, and Delivery Expense. Prepare journal entries in a general journal and record the foregoing transactions in the accounts.

b. Prepare a trial balance as of December 31.

c. Prepare an income statement for the month of December.

d. Prepare a balance sheet as of December 31. (*Note:* In this problem, the net income for December becomes the amount of retained earnings at December 31.)

LO5 **P3-14B. Balance Sheets** The following balance sheet data are given for Cornell Catering Service, a corporation, at May 31:

Accounts receivable..............	$30,300	Accounts payable.................	$ 5,200
Notes payable	20,000	Cash............................	12,200
Equipment	55,000	Common stock...................	62,500
Supplies	16,400	Retained earnings	?

Assume that on June 1, the following transactions occurred:

June 1 Purchased additional equipment costing $26,000, giving $3,000 cash and a $23,000 note payable.

2 Paid a cash dividend of $9,000.

Required

a. Prepare a balance sheet as of May 31.

b. Prepare a balance sheet as of June 2.

LO5 **P3-15B. Determination of Net Income and Stockholders' Equity** The following selected income statement and balance sheet information is available for Zerbst Land Appraisers at the end of the current month:

Supplies	$ 6,900	Accounts payable.................	$ 4,000
Accounts receivable..............	18,000	Salaries expense	15,000
Utilities expense..................	700	Appraisal fees earned.............	31,000
Supplies expense.................	1,300	Common stock...................	15,000
Rent expense....................	3,500	Retained earnings (beginning)	5,000
Cash............................	3,600		

a. Calculate the net income or net loss for the month.

b. If stockholders made no additional investment during the month but received $7,000 as a dividend, what is the amount of retained earnings at the end of the month?

P3-16B. Trial Balance and Financial Statements The following account balances were prepared (out of order) from the general ledger of The Dog Whisperer, Inc. as of January 31. The company trains dogs having behavioral problems. The firm's business began on January 1. All accounts have normal balances.

LO5

Facilities	$34,000	Office rent expense	$ 800
Maintenance expense	460	Supplies expense	760
Supplies	1,640	Utilities expense	200
Advertising expense	550	Fees earned	18,470
Common stock	41,600	Accounts receivable	8,200
Cash	7,300	Salaries expense	4,480
Accounts payable	420	Dividends	2,100

Required
a. Prepare a trial balance from the given data.
b. Prepare an income statement for the month of January.
c. Prepare a statement of stockholders' equity for the month of January.
d. Prepare a balance sheet as of January 31.

P3-17B. Trial Balance and Financial Statements The following account balances, in alphabetical order, are from the general ledger of The Columbus Service Company at January 31. The firm's business began on January 1. All accounts have normal balances.

LO5

Accounts payable	$ 7,200	Notes payable	$12,000
Accounts receivable	42,000	Rent expense	2,900
Advertising expense	640	Salaries expense	16,000
Cash	20,800	Service fees earned	51,520
Common stock	59,480	Supplies	17,920
Dividends	8,000	Supplies expense	20,500
Interest expense	800	Utilities expense	640

Required
a. Prepare a trial balance from the given data.
b. Prepare an income statement for the month of January.
c. Prepare a statement of stockholders' equity for the month of January.
d. Prepare a balance sheet as of January 31.

P3-18B. Financial Statements and Closing Entries Use the information provided in P3-8B.

LO5, 7
(Appendix 3A)

Required
a. Prepare an income statement for the year and a balance sheet as of December 31.
b. Prepare closing entries in general journal form using the Income Summary account.

P3-19B. Closing Entries Use the information provided in P3-9B.

LO7
(Appendix 3A)

Required
a. Prepare closing entries at December 31 in general journal form using the Income Summary account.
b. After the closing entries are posted, calculate the ending balance in the Retained Earnings account.
c. Prepare a post-closing trial balance.

LO8
(Appendix 3B)

P3-20B. Worksheet The July 31 unadjusted trial balance of Sharp Outfitters, a firm renting various types of equipment to canoeists and campers, follows.

SHARP OUTFITTERS Unadjusted Trial Balance July 31	Debit	Credit
Cash	$ 3,750	
Supplies	8,600	
Prepaid insurance	3,200	
Equipment	97,000	
Accumulated depreciation		$ 16,500
Accounts payable.		3,500
Unearned rental fees		8,850
Common stock.		33,000
Retained earnings		9,000
Dividends	1,200	
Rental fees earned		78,150
Wages expense	28,800	
Rent expense	3,300	
Advertising expense.	2,300	
Travel expense	850	
	$149,000	$149,000

Sharp Outfitters' fiscal year ends on July 31. The following additional information is available:

1. Supplies on hand at July 31 amount to $4,300.
2. Insurance expense for the year is $1,600.
3. Depreciation for the year is $9,250.
4. The unearned rental fees consist of deposits received from customers in advance when reservations are made. During the year, $4,850 of the unearned rental fees were earned. The remaining deposits apply to rentals for August and September.
5. At July 31, revenue from rental services earned during July but not yet billed or received amounts to $2,500. (*Note:* Debit Fees Receivable.)
6. Accrued wages payable for equipment handlers and guides amounts to $700 at July 31.

Required
Enter the trial balance in a worksheet and complete the worksheet using the adjustment data given above.

SERIAL PROBLEM: KATE'S CARDS

(Note: This is a continuation of the Serial Problem: Kate's Cards from Chapters 1 and 2.)

SP3. Getting ready for the upcoming holiday season is traditionally a busy time for greeting card companies, and it was no exception for Kate. The following transactions occurred during the month of October:

1. Hired an assistant at an hourly rate of $10 per hour to help with some of the computer layouts and administrative chores.
2. Supplements her business by teaching a class to aspiring card designers. She charges and receives a total of $450.
3. Delivers greeting cards to several new customers. She bills them a total of $1,500.
4. Pays a utility bill in the amount of $250 that she determines is the business portion of her utility bill.

5. Receives an advance deposit of $500 for a new set of cards she is designing for a new customer.
6. Pays her assistant $200 for the work done this month.
7. Determines that the assistant has worked 10 additional hours this month that have not yet been paid.
8. Ordered and receives additional supplies in the amount of $1,000. These were paid for during the month.
9. Counts her remaining inventory of supplies at the end of the month and determines the balance to be $300. Don't forget to consider the supplies inventory balance at September 30, from Chapter 2. (*Hint:* This expense will be a debit to Cost of Goods Sold.)
10. Records the adjusting entries for depreciation and insurance expense for the month.
11. Pays herself a salary of $1,000.
12. Deciding she needs a little more cash, Kate pays herself a $500 dividend.
13. Receives her next utility bill during December and determines $85 applies to October's operations.

Required

Using the information that you gathered and the general ledger accounts that you prepared through Chapter 2, plus the new information above, complete the following:

a. Journalize the above transactions and adjusting entries.
b. Post the October transactions and adjusting entries. (Use the general ledger accounts prepared in Chapter 2 and add any new accounts that you may need.)
c. Prepare a trial balance as of October 31, 2015.
d. Prepare an income statement and a statement of stockholders' equity for the two-month period ending October 31, 2015, and a balance sheet as of October 31, 2015.
e. Prepare the closing entries as of October 31, 2015.
f. Prepare a post-closing trial balance.

EXTENDING YOUR KNOWLEDGE

REPORTING AND ANALYSIS

EYK3-1.   Financial Reporting Problem: Columbia Sportswear Company The financial statements for the Columbia Sportswear Company can be found in Appendix A at the end of this book.

Required

Answer the following questions using Columbia's Consolidated Financial Statements and the Notes to the consolidated financial statements:

a. Identify an item that likely requires adjusting entries for prepayments.
b. Identify an item that likely requires an adjusting accrual.
c. Examine the statement of cash flows and identify the amount of depreciation and amortization expense for 2014. Where on the balance sheet was this accrual likely also shown?
d. Identify the items that will require closing entries. What account will they be ultimately closed to?

EYK3-2.   Comparative Analysis Problem: Columbia Sportswear Company vs. Under Armour, Inc. The financial statements for the Columbia Sportswear Company can be found in Appendix A, and Under Armour, Inc.'s financial statements can be found in Appendix B at the end of this book.

Required

a. Examine the balance sheet of Columbia Sportswear and identify three items that indicate that the company uses the accrual method of accounting. In each case, identify the likely income statement account that is affected by these accruals.
b. Examine the balance sheet of Under Armour, Inc. and identify three items that indicate the company uses the accrual method of accounting. In each case, identify the likely income statement account that is affected by these accruals.

EYK3-3. **Business Decision Problem** Wyland Consulting Services, a firm started three years ago by Bruce Wyland, offers consulting services for material handling and plant layout. The balance sheet prepared by the firm's accountant at the close of 2015 is shown here.

WYLAND CONSULTING SERVICES Balance Sheet As of December 31, 2015					
Assets			**Liabilities**		
Cash.......................		$ 3,400	Notes payable		$30,000
Accounts receivable............		22,875	Accounts payable..........		4,200
Supplies		13,200	Unearned consulting fees....		11,300
Prepaid insurance		4,500	Wages payable............		400
Equipment	$68,500		Total Liabilities		45,900
Less: Accumulated depreciation ...	(23,975)	44,525	**Stockholders' Equity**		
			Common stock............		20,000
			Retained earnings		22,600
			Total Stockholders' Equity ...		42,600
			Total Liabilities and		
Total Assets		$88,500	Stockholders' Equity......		$88,500

Earlier in the year, Wyland obtained a bank loan of $30,000 for the firm. One of the provisions of the loan is that the year-end debt-to-equity ratio (ratio of total liabilities to total stockholders' equity) shall not exceed 1.0. Based on the above balance sheet, the ratio at the end of 2015 is 1.08 ($45,900/$42,600).

Wyland is concerned about being in violation of the loan agreement and asks your assistance in reviewing the situation. Wyland believes that his rather inexperienced accountant may have overlooked some items at year-end.

In discussions with Wyland and the accountant, you learn the following:

1. On January 1, 2015, the firm paid a $4,500 insurance premium for two years of coverage. The amount in Prepaid Insurance has not been adjusted.
2. Depreciation on the equipment should be 10 percent of cost per year. The accountant inadvertently recorded 15 percent for 2015.
3. Interest on the bank loan has been paid through the end of 2015.
4. The firm concluded a major consulting engagement in December, doing a plant layout analysis for a new factory. The $6,000 fee has not been billed or recorded in the accounts.
5. On December 1, 2015, the firm received an $11,300 advance payment from Croy Corporation for consulting services to be rendered over a two-month period. This payment was credited to the Unearned Consulting Fees account. One-half of this fee was earned by December 31, 2015.
6. Supplies costing $4,800 were on hand on December 31. The accountant filed the record of the count but made no entry in the accounts.

Required

a. What is the correct debt-to-equity ratio at December 31, 2015? Is the firm in violation of the loan agreement? Prepare a schedule to support your computation of the correct total liabilities and total stockholders' equity as of December 31, 2015.

b. Why might the loan agreement have contained the debt-to-equity provision?

EYK3-4. **Financial Analysis Problem** Purpose: To learn more about the Financial Accounting Standards Board (FASB)

Address: http://www.fasb.org

Required

Use the information on the FASB site to answer the following questions:

a. When was the FASB established?

b. What is the mission of the FASB?

c. Who has oversight responsibility for the FASB?

d. What are some of the current projects of the FASB?

CRITICAL THINKING

EYK3-5. **Accounting Research Problem** Refer to the annual report of **General Mills, Inc.** for the year ending May 25, 2014 (fiscal year 2014), available on this book's Website. Review the consolidated balance sheets.

GENERAL MILLS, INC.

Required
  a. Identify two assets listed in the consolidated balance sheets that indicate that General Mills uses the accrual basis of accounting. Which income statement accounts of General Mills are affected by adjustments to these assets accounts?
  b. Identify two liabilities listed in the consolidated balance sheets that indicate that General Mills uses the accrual basis of accounting. Which income statement accounts of General Mills are affected by these adjustments?

EYK3-6. **Accounting Communications Activity** Many people do not understand the concept of accrual accounting and how it differs from accounting on a cash basis. In particular, they are confused as to why a company's results in any one accounting period can differ so much between the two methods of accounting. Because the cash basis is understood to a far larger degree, many people argue that the cash basis should be the primary basis of accounting.

Required
Write a short memorandum that explains the difference between accrual accounting and the cash basis of accounting. In your memo give a simple example of how the accrual basis can give a clearer picture of a company's performance in a given period.

EYK3-7. **Accounting Ethics Case** It is the end of an accounting year for Juliet Kravetz, controller of a medium-sized, publicly held corporation specializing in toxic waste cleanup. Within the corporation, only Kravetz and the president know that the firm has been negotiating for several months to land a very large contract for waste cleanup in Western Europe. The president has hired another firm with excellent contacts in Western Europe to help with the negotiations. The outside firm charges an hourly fee plus expenses, but has agreed not to submit a bill until the negotiations are in their final stages (expected to occur in another three to four months). Even if the contract falls through, the outside firm is entitled to receive payment for its services. Based upon her discussion with a member of the outside firm, Kravetz knows that its charge for services provided to date will be $150,000. This is a material amount for the company.

Kravetz knows that the president wants the negotiations to remain as secret as possible so that competitors will not learn of the European contract that the company is pursuing. Indeed, the president recently stated to her, "This is not the time to reveal our actions in Western Europe to other staff members, our auditors, or readers of our financial statements; securing this contract is crucial to our future growth." No entry has been made in the accounting records for the cost of the contract negotiations. Kravetz now faces an uncomfortable situation. The company's outside auditor has just asked her if she knows of any year-end adjustments that have not yet been recorded.

Required
What are the ethical considerations that Kravetz faces in answering the auditor's question? How should she respond to the question?

EYK3-8. **Corporate Social Responsibility Problem** Unlike financial reporting that requires all reported amounts to be expressed in monetary terms, Corporate Social Responsibility (CSR) reporting is often more qualitative than quantitative. This has caused some individuals to discount the CSR reports as too subjective.

Required
  a. Can you identify any subjective areas within a financial statement prepared under GAAP?
  b. Discuss the reasons both financial reporting, and to a larger extent CSR reporting, allow subjective estimates to be part of the report.

EYK3-9. **Forensic Accounting Problem** Most employees that choose to commit fraud against their employers feel justified in doing so. For example, a demotion with a corresponding pay cut can pro-

vide motivation to produce what is called "wages in kind," where the employee creates his or her own wages.

Required

What actions might an organization take to prevent "wages in kind"?

EYK3-10. Analyzing IFRS Financial Statements The 2014 financial statements of LVMH Moet Hennessey-Louis Vuitton S.A. are presented in Appendix C at the end of this book. LVMH is a Paris-based holding company and one of the world's largest and best-known luxury goods companies. As a member of the European Union, French companies are required to prepare their consolidated (group) financial statements using International Financial Reporting Standards (IFRS). After reviewing LVMH's consolidated financial statements, consider the following questions.

Required

a. Identify two assets listed in the group balance sheets that indicate that LVMH uses the accrual basis of accounting. Which income statement accounts of LVMH are affected by adjustments to these assets accounts?

b. Identify two liabilities listed in the group balance sheets that indicate that LVMH uses the accrual basis of accounting. Which income statement accounts of LVMH are affected by these adjustments?

EYK3-11. Working with the Takeaways The Aspen Company has the following items that require adjustments as of December 31.

a. Service revenue of $600 had been received prior to work being performed. This amount was properly recorded as unearned revenue. At year-end, $400 of the services have now been performed.

b. Interest expense of $750 has not been recorded.

c. Services in the amount of $800 have been performed but not yet billed.

d. A physical count determined that supplies still available were $250. The Supplies asset account shows a balance of $700.

Required

Provide the adjusting entry needed to correct the balance in each of the affected accounts.

ANSWERS TO SELF-STUDY QUESTIONS:

1. b, (pp. 126–127) 2. c, (pp. 129–130) 3. d, (pp. 137–138) 4. c, (p. 123) 5. d, (pp. 134–135)
6. b, (pp. 122–123) 7. b, (pp. 122–123)

YOUR TURN! SOLUTIONS

Solution 3.1

1.	June 30	Accounts receivable	600	
		Sales revenue		600
		To recognize revenue earned.		
2.	June 30	Cash	700	
		Unearned revenue		700
		To recognize cash prior to revenue being earned.		
3.	June 30	Inventory	400	
		Accounts payable		400
		To record the purchase of inventory on account.		

Solution 3.2

1. c,   2. d,   3. b,   4. a

Solution 3.3

1.	Dec. 31	Depreciation expense	700	
		Accumulated depreciation—Buildings		700
		To record depreciation on buildings.		

2.	Dec. 31	Rent expense	1,500	
		Prepaid rent		1,500
		To record rent expense.		

Solution 3.4

1.	Dec. 31	Unearned revenue	400	
		Revenue		400
		To recognize revenue earned on a previously recorded advance payment from a customer.		

2.	Dec. 31	Interest expense	500	
		Interest payable		500
		To accrue interest expense.		

Solution 3.5

THE CASSI COMPANY
Income Statement
For the Year Ended December 31, 2016

Sales revenues		$52,000
Expenses		
Cost of goods sold	$30,000	
Salaries expense	5,000	
Rent expense	6,000	
Depreciation expense	6,000	
Total expenses		47,000
Net income		$ 5,000

THE CASSI COMPANY
Statement of Stockholders' Equity
For the Year Ended December 31, 2016

	Common Stock	Retained Earnings	Total
Balance, December 1, 2016	$15,000	$5,000	$20,000
Add: Net income for December		5,000	5,000
Less: Dividends in December		(2,000)	(2,000)
Balance, December 31, 2016	$15,000	$8,000	$23,000

THE CASSI COMPANY Balance Sheet As of December 31, 2016					
Assets			**Liabilities**		
Current assets			Current liabilities		
Cash....................	$ 4,000		Accounts payable.......	$ 8,000	
Accounts receivable.........	15,000		Salaries payable........	9,000	
Inventory..................	18,000		Dividends payable	2,000	
Prepaid rent	5,000		Unearned service	5,000	
Total current assets		$42,000	Total current liabilities..		$24,000
			Long-term debt		35,000
Equipment	50,000		Total liabilities..........		59,000
Less: Accumulated					
depreciation	(10,000)	40,000	**Stockholders' Equity**		
			Common stock.........	15,000	
			Retained earnings	8,000	
			Total stockholders'		
			equity		23,000
Total Assets		$82,000	Total Liabilities and		
			Stockholders' Equity...		$82,000

Solution 3.6

a. Permanent
b. Permanent
c. Temporary
d. Permanent

e. Temporary
f. Temporary
g. Permanent
h. Permanent

Solution 3.7

Dec. 31	Sales revenue	79,000	
	Retained earnings		79,000
	To close the revenue account.		
Dec. 31	Retained earnings	72,000	
	Cost of goods sold		41,000
	Wage expense		22,000
	Rent expense		3,000
	Depreciation expense		2,000
	Interest expense		4,000
	To close the expense accounts.		
Dec. 31	Retained earnings	5,000	
	Dividends		5,000
	To close the dividends account.		

Solution 3A.1

a. Permanent
b. Permanent
c. Temporary
d. Permanent

e. Temporary
f. Temporary
g. Permanent
h. Permanent

Solution 3A.2

Dec. 31	Sales revenue	79,000	
	Income summary		79,000
	To close the revenue account.		
Dec. 31	Income summary	72,000	
	Cost of goods sold		41,000
	Wage expense		22,000
	Rent expense		3,000
	Depreciation expense		2,000
	Interest expense		4,000
	To close the expense accounts.		
Dec. 31	Income summary	7,000	
	Retained earnings		7,000
	To close the Income Summary account.		
Dec. 31	Retained earnings	5,000	
	Dividends		5,000
	To close the Dividends account.		

4

Understanding Financial Statements

PAST

Chapters 1 through 3 explained the five-step accounting cycle: analyze, record, adjust, report, and close.

PRESENT

This chapter introduces classified financial statements and some key ratios computed from those statements.

FUTURE

Later chapters expand on ratios used in analyzing financial statements, starting in Chapter 5, which focuses on analyzing and recording merchandising transactions.

LEARNING OBJECTIVES

1. **Describe** a classified balance sheet. *(p. 190)*

2. **Describe** a single-step and multi-step income statement. *(p. 195)*

3. **Discuss** use of a balance sheet and ratios to assess liquidity and solvency. *(p. 199)*

4. **Discuss** use of the income statement and ratios to assess profitability. *(p. 201)*

5. **Explain** the components of the statement of stockholders' equity. *(p. 203)*

6. **Explain** use of the statement of cash flows to help assess solvency. *(p. 204)*

IDENTIFYING A WIN-WIN COMPANY

After a visit to one of **Apple**'s many retail stores, you will likely find it hard to believe that the company ever faced financial difficulties. The company has a cult-like following for its products including its Macintosh computer, the iPod, the iPhone, the iPad, and the Watch. Business has not always been so good for the company that was established by Steve Jobs, Steve Wozniak, and Ronald Wayne. In fact, Apple suffered crippling financial losses and record low stock prices in the mid-1990s. Steve Jobs, who left the company in 1985 to start another business, was brought back to Apple in 1997 as chief executive officer (CEO). Over the next few years, Jobs was able to return the company to profitability.

Being a profitable company has allowed Apple to benefit from what some refer to as a virtuous cycle in which the company is able to both do good financially and do good socially. The company's solid financial resources provide the ability to do good, whereas doing good helps the company do well financially.

Apple realizes that a win-win situation can be obtained through its commitment to social responsibility. For example, Apple's Website explains how important it is to follow sound environmental policies to conserve natural resources. An example of this philosophy is its packaging for the iPhone 5, which is 42 percent smaller than the packing used for the original iPhone. The smaller packaging allows 80 percent more iPhone boxes to fit on each shipping pallet, which in turn enables more phones to fit on each boat and plane. Fitting more phones on each boat and plane results in fewer boats and planes used, which lowers the overall CO_2 emissions required by the shipping of the iPhone.

But what if we decide to consider investing in a company like Apple? How should we go about determining whether Apple is a good investment? We first want to do some research to determine if the company is profitable and financially sound. In this, and future chapters, we will begin to accumulate the financial skills needed to evaluate the financial health and operating performance of companies such as Apple.

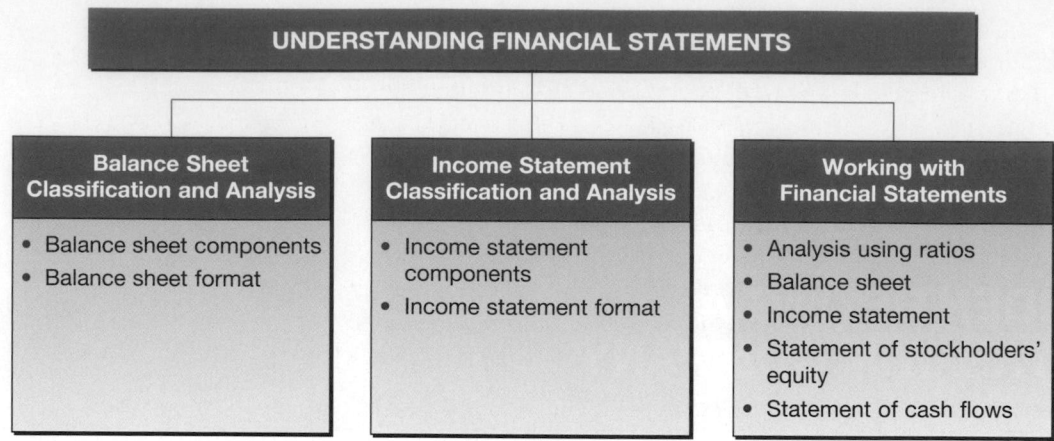

BALANCE SHEET CLASSIFICATION AND ANALYSIS

LO1 Describe a classified balance sheet.

A **classified balance sheet** presents the assets and liabilities of a business in separate sub-groups. Such classification aids our financial analysis and business decision making. **Exhibit 4-1** presents a list of the typical components of a classified balance sheet. A company need not use all of the components, and each company will use only those components necessary to report its financial position. **Exhibit 4-1** shows that a company's assets are commonly classified into two subgroups: current assets and long-term assets. Similarly, liabilities are classified into two subgroups: current liabilities and long-term liabilities. Classified balance sheets are presented by most businesses.

Exhibit 4-1	Typical Components of a Classified Balance Sheet

Assets

Current Assets
(will be consumed or turned into cash within one year)
- Cash and cash equivalents
- Accounts receivable
- Inventory
- Other current assets

Non-current Assets
- Property, plant, and equipment
- Intangible assets
- Other long-term assets

Current Liabilities
(will require payment within one year)
- Accounts payable
- Accrued expenses payable
- Short-term notes payable
- Other current liabilities

Long-Term Liabilities
- Long-term notes payable
- Other long-term liabilities

Liabilities

Contributed Capital

Retained Earnings

Stockholders' Equity

Current Assets

Current assets consist of cash and other assets that will be converted into cash or used up within the normal operating cycle of a business or one year, whichever is longer. The **normal operating cycle** of a business is the average period of time between the use of cash to deliver a service or to buy goods for resale and the subsequent collection of cash from customers who purchase those services or products. For most businesses, the normal operating cycle is less than one year. For example, the normal operating cycle for a grocery store chain like **Safeway** might be as short as a week or two, on average, and even only a day or two for perishable products like bread and fresh sliced vegetables.

Current assets are listed on a classified balance sheet in the order of their expected liquidity. **Liquidity** is determined by the ability of an asset to be readily converted into cash. **Exhibit 4-1** lists five examples of current assets in the order of their expected liquidity: cash, short-term marketable securities, accounts receivable, inventory, and other current assets. Short-term marketable securities represent short-term investments in the securities of other firms that can be quickly sold for cash. Accounts receivable and inventory are converted into cash as part of the normal operations of a business; that is, inventory is sold for cash or on credit (accounts receivable) that is subsequently collected as cash from customers. Other current assets, such as supplies, are consumed during the normal operating cycle rather than converted into cash, and thus, represent the least liquid of the current assets. The following excerpt shows the current asset section of **Apple**.

APPLE INC. Balance Sheet (Partial) September 27, 2014 (in millions)	
Current assets	
Cash	$13,844
Short-term investments	11,233
Accounts receivable	27,219
Inventory	2,111
Other current assets	14,124
Total current assets	$68,531

Long-Term Assets

Long-term assets are assets that the company does not expect to convert into cash within the next year or use up during the course of the normal operating cycle, whichever is longer. Long-term assets include property, plant, and equipment, intangible assets, and other long-term assets.

Property, Plant, and Equipment

Property, plant, and equipment consists of the land, buildings, equipment, vehicles, furniture, and fixtures that a company uses in its day-to-day operations. Investments into property, plant, and equipment, or PP&E, are often referred to as *capital expenditures* or capital investments. The following excerpt shows the PP&E section of **Apple**.

APPLE INC. Balance Sheet (Partial) September 27, 2014 (in millions)		
Property, plant, and equipment		
Land and buildings	$ 4,863	
Equipment	29,639	
Leasehold improvements	4,513	$39,015
Less: accumulated depreciation and amortization		18,391
Total property, plant, and equipment		$20,624

Intangible Assets

Intangible assets consist of brand names, copyrights, patents, and trademarks that a company acquires. These assets are referred to as "intangible" because, unlike buildings and equipment, they lack a physical presence. But, like buildings and equipment, intangible assets enable a company to generate revenue from its customers who recognize the quality associated with products bearing a brand name or trademark. The following excerpt shows the intangible asset section of **Apple**.

APPLE INC. Balance Sheet (Partial) September 27, 2014 (in millions)	
Intangible assets	
Goodwill	$4,616
Acquired technology	4,142
	$8,758

Other Long-Term Assets

Other long-term assets consist of resources that a company consolidates into a single miscellaneous category for purposes of presentation on the balance sheet. We discuss and illustrate the various types of assets that comprise this category of assets in later chapters. The following excerpt shows the other asset section of **Apple**.

APPLE INC. Balance Sheet (Partial) September 27, 2014 (in millions)	
Other long-term assets	
Long-term marketable securities	$130,162
Other assets	3,764
	$133,926

Current Liabilities

Current liabilities consist of liabilities that must be settled within the normal operating cycle or one year, whichever is longer. **Exhibit 4-1** lists four types of current liabilities: accounts payable, accrued expenses payable, short-term notes payable, and other current liabilities. Accounts payable reflects the amounts owed for inventory that was purchased from suppliers on credit. Accrued expenses payable include wages, utilities, interest, income tax, and property taxes that are legally owed by a company but which have not yet been paid. Short-term notes payable represent amounts owed that are specified in a formal contract called a note. Other current liabilities consist of current obligations that the company aggregates into a single miscellaneous category. One example is the advance payments received from customers (deferred revenue), such as for goods under a layaway plan that will be earned as revenue within the normal operating cycle or one year, whichever is longer. The following excerpt shows the current liabilities section of **Apple**.

APPLE INC. Balance Sheet (Partial) September 27, 2014 (in millions)	
Current liabilities	
Accounts payable	$30,196
Accrued expenses	18,453
Deferred revenue	8,491
Short-term loans	6,308
Total current liabilities	$63,448

Long-Term Liabilities

Long-term liabilities consist of debt obligations not due to be settled within the normal operating cycle or one year. Long-term notes payable and bonds payable are two examples of long-term liabilities. Other long-term liabilities include unfunded employee retirement plans that will be funded by the company in the future. The following excerpt shows the long-term liabilities section of **Apple**.

A.K.A. Long-term liabilities are also referred to as *noncurrent liabilities*.

APPLE INC. Balance Sheet (Partial) September 27, 2014 (in millions)	
Long-term liabilities	
Deferred revenue	$ 3,031
Long-term debt.	28,987
Other long-term liabilities	24,826
Total long-term liabilities.	$56,844

Stockholders' Equity

Stockholders' equity is the residual ownership interest in the assets of a business after its liabilities have been paid off. The stockholders' equity of a corporation is divided into two main categories: amounts invested by stockholders (common stock) and the cumulative net income of a business that has not yet been distributed to its stockholders as a dividend (retained earnings). The following excerpt shows the stockholders' equity section of **Apple**.

A.K.A. Stockholders' equity is also referred to as *shareholders' equity*.

APPLE INC. Balance Sheet (Partial) September 27, 2014 (in millions)	
Stockholders' equity	
Common stock	$ 23,313
Retained earnings.	87,152
Other equity	1,082
Total stockholders' equity.	$111,547

Presentation Format

There are two generally accepted formats for presenting a classified balance sheet—the account form and the report form. For the **account form**, assets are displayed on the left side and liabilities and stockholders' equity are displayed on the right side. For the **report form**, assets are displayed at the top, with liabilities displayed below the assets, and stockholders' equity displayed below liabilities. Apple's 2014 and 2013 balance sheets in report form are presented in **Exhibit 4-2**. The report form is the more widely used format.

Hint: According to Accounting Trends and Techniques, a recent survey of 600 large U.S. companies shows that 88% use the report form for their balance sheet while 12% use the account form.

Exhibit 4-2	Report Form of a Classified Balance Sheet

APPLE INC.
Balance Sheet
September 27, 2014, and September 28, 2013

(in millions)	2014	2013
Assets		
Current assets		
Cash	$ 13,844	$ 14,259
Short-term investments	11,233	26,287
Accounts receivable.	27,219	20,641
Inventory.	2,111	1,764
Other current assets.	14,124	10,335
Total current assets.	68,531	73,286
Long-term assets		
Property, plant and equipment.	20,624	16,597
Intangible assets.	8,758	5,756
Other long-term assets.	133,926	111,361
Total long-term assets	163,308	133,714
Total assets	$231,839	$207,000
Liabilities		
Current liabilities		
Accounts payable.	$ 30,196	$ 22,367
Other current liabilities	33,252	21,291
Total current liabilities.	63,448	43,658
Long-term liabilities	56,844	39,793
Total liabilities	120,292	83,451
Stockholders' Equity		
Common stock.	23,313	19,764
Retained earnings	87,152	104,256
Other equity	1,082	(471)
Total stockholders' equity	111,547	123,549
Total liabilities and stockholders' equity	$231,839	$207,000

IFRS ALERT

Go to Appendix C at the end of this book and review the classified balance sheet of LVMH Moet Hennessy, Louis Vuitton. LVMH is a Paris-based holding company and one of the world's largest and best-known luxury goods companies. As a member of the European Union, French companies are required to prepare their consolidated (group) financial statements using International Financial Reporting Standards (IFRS). After reviewing LVMH's balance sheet, prepare a list of differences between LVMH's IFRS balance sheet and Apple's U.S. GAAP balance sheet in **Exhibit 4-2**. Differences include: (1) LVMH presents noncurrent assets before its current assets—that is, it lists the company's assets in reverse order of liquidity; (2) LVMH presents shareholders' equity before liabilities; (3) LVMH presents noncurrent liabilities before current liabilities; and (4) LVMH uses slightly different labeling for some of its balance sheet accounts, for instance common stock is referred to as "share capital."

YOUR TURN! 4.1

The solution is on page 229.

The President of Musicland Company requests that you prepare a classified balance sheet in report form for the company. The following financial data are available from the company's accounting records as of December 31, 2016.

Other current liabilities	$ 2,000	Other current assets	$ 1,500
Long-term notes payable	20,000	Inventory	12,200
Stockholders' equity	17,500	Property, plant, & equipment, net	25,000
Accounts payable	2,500	Accounts receivable	3,000
Cash	300		

INCOME STATEMENT CLASSIFICATION AND ANALYSIS

A **single-step income statement** is the simplest form of an income statement. The name originates from the way the statement is constructed. The sum of the expenses is subtracted from the sum of the revenues in a single step to arrive at net income. An example of a single-step income statement for Apple Inc. for the years ended September 27, 2014, and September 28, 2013, is in **Exhibit 4-3**.

LO2 **Describe** a single-step and multi-step income statement.

Exhibit 4-3	Single-Step Income Statement for Apple Inc.	

APPLE INC.
Income Statement
For Years Ended September 27, 2014, and September 28, 2013

(in millions)	2014	2013
Revenues		
Net sales	$182,795	$170,910
Other income	980	1,156
Total revenues	183,775	172,066
Expenses		
Cost of goods sold	112,258	106,606
Research and development expenses	6,041	4,475
Selling, general and administrative	11,993	10,830
Income tax expense	13,973	13,118
Total expenses	144,265	135,029
Net income	$ 39,510	$ 37,037

Specifically, Apple's 2014 revenues are totaled, yielding $183,775 million. Next, Apple's 2014 expenses of $144,265 million are totaled and subtracted from total revenues to yield Apple's 2014 net income of $39,510 million.

A **multi-step income statement** presents revenues and expenses in distinct categories to facilitate financial analysis and management decision making. A multi-step income statement provides financial statement users with more information, and thus, enables them to make better and more informed decisions about a business. A multi-step income statement is divided into two main sections; the operating section and the non-operating section. The operating section contains revenues and expenses related to the principal business activities of the company. The non-operating section contains revenues and expenses that are incidental to the company's principal business activities, such as gains or losses on the sale of equipment and interest revenue or expense.

The format of a multi-step income statement will differ somewhat depending on whether the company is a service firm or a merchandising firm. The difference in format between

A.K.A A multi-step income statement is also known as a *classified income statement*.

service firms and merchandising firms results because service firms do not sell a physical product and therefore do not have cost of goods sold. Examples of service companies include accounting firms, health care providers, and architects. In contrast, merchandising companies sell goods to customers. We discuss merchandisers in more detail in Chapter 5.

For a service company, its total operating expenses are subtracted from its service revenues to determine its income from operations. Operating expenses are those expenses that relate to the primary operating activities of a business. Operating expenses are commonly classified as selling, general and administrative expenses. Revenue and expense items that do not relate to the primary operating activities of the company appear in a separate category called *Other Income and Expense*. The net amount of other income and expense is either added to or subtracted from income from operations to determine pretax income.

A.K.A. Gross profit is often referred to as *gross margin*.

For a merchandising company, the cost of goods sold is subtracted from the firm's net sales to determine its gross profit on sales. **Gross profit**, or gross profit on sales, is defined as the difference between net sales and cost of goods sold and reveals the amount of sales revenue remaining after subtracting the cost of products sold. **Net sales** are total sales less an estimate of **sales returns and allowances** and **sales discounts**. Sales returns and allowances represent the expected amount given to the customer for the return of merchandise or in lieu of a return. Sales discounts represent an expected amount allowed to the buyer for early payment. These items will be discussed further in Chapter 5. Gross profit also reveals how much sales revenue remains to cover a business's operating expenses. The remainder of the structure of a merchandising company's multi-step income statement (following gross profit) is the same as the structure of the service company's multi-step income statement.

A.K.A. Income before income tax is also known as *pretax income*.

Exhibit 4-4 presents a multi-step income statement for **Apple Inc.** Apple's multi-step income statement provides more detail to the financial statement user with four measures of company performance: gross profit on sales, income from operations, income before income taxes, and net income. Gross profit on sales indicates just how well the company performed in terms of purchasing goods, warehousing those goods, and pricing the goods for sale. Income from operations reports Apple's performance after considering the cost of running its stores, paying its employees, advertising to its customers, and administering the business. The income before income taxes reports the company's performance after considering various nonoperating items like interest expense and interest income but before subtracting the expected cost

Exhibit 4-4	Multi-Step Income Statement for a Merchandising Company	

APPLE INC. Income Statement For Years Ended September 27, 2014 and September 28, 2013		
(in millions)	2014	2013
Net sales.	$182,795	$170,910
Less cost of goods sold	112,258	106,606
Gross profit on sales	70,537	64,304
Operating expenses		
Research and development expenses	6,041	4,475
Selling, general and administrative.	11,993	10,830
Total operating expenses	18,034	15,305
Income from operations.	52,503	48,999
Other income and expenses	980	1,156
Income before income taxes.	53,483	50,155
Income tax expense.	13,973	13,118
Net income	$ 39,510	$ 37,037

A multi-step income statement for a service firm will not have cost of goods sold nor will it have a subtotal for gross profit on sales

of income taxes. Income tax is then subtracted from income before income taxes in order to compute net income. Income tax is computed as a percentage of income before income taxes.

Net sales for Apple consists primarily of sales of hardware, software, digital content, and support contracts. Apple records reductions from these amounts for future product returns. Cost of goods sold represents the cost to Apple for the items sold. Cost of goods sold is typically the largest expense for a retail company such as Apple. Cost of goods sold is subtracted directly from net sales to highlight the gross profit on sales. The gross profit on sales is an important financial indicator for investment professionals who follow retail companies like Apple. Analysts compare the gross profit on sales between retailers as a way to assess the effectiveness of the retailer's pricing and purchasing policies.

The operating expenses section includes those expenses that relate to the primary operating activities of a business. Operating expenses consist primarily of selling expenses and administrative expenses. Examples of Apple's selling, general and administrative expenses include sales salaries expense, delivery expense, advertising expense, depreciation expense, rent expense, office salaries expense, and supplies expense.

The other income and expense section of the income statement is sometimes labeled nonoperating activities. Examples of revenues and expenses that do not relate to the primary operating activities of a merchandising firm include:

Other Expenses and Losses	Other Revenues and Gains
• Interest expense • Losses on asset sales	• Interest revenue • Gains on asset sales • Dividend income

These items are reported in the other income and expense section that follows the financial information regarding a business's primary operating activities.

Net income measures Apple's bottom-line performance—that is after all costs of running the business are subtracted. Net income is the same whether the company uses a single-step or multi-step income statement format.

Exhibit 4-5 presents the components of a multi-step income statement for Webwork (a service company) and for Apple (a merchandising company). We see the absence of the cost of goods sold section, including the gross profit subtotal, in the service company's income statement. Otherwise, the income statements follow the same format.

Exhibit 4-5	Classified Income Statements for Service and Merchandising Companies

WEBWORK, INC. Income Statement For Year Ended December 31, 2016		APPLE INC. Income Statement For Year Ended September 27, 2014	
Revenues	$19,150	Net sales.	$182,795
		Less cost of goods sold.	112,258
		Gross profit on sales	70,537
Operating expenses		Operating expenses	
Wage, rent and supplies expenses. . . .	5,550	Research and development expenses	6,041
Depreciation and interest expenses . . .	750	Selling, general and administrative	11,993
Total operating expenses	6,300	Total operating expenses	18,034
Income from operations	12,850	Income from operations	52,503
Other income and expenses	—	Other income and expense	980
Income before income taxes	12,850	Income before income taxes	53,483
Income tax expense	3,855	Income tax expense	13,973
Net income	$ 8,995	Net income	$ 39,510

IFRS ALERT

Appendix C at the end of this book presents the multi-step income statement for LVMH Moet Hennessy, Louis Vuitton. LVMH is a Paris-based holding company and one of the world's largest and best-known luxury goods companies. As a member of the European Union, French companies are required to prepare their consolidated (group) financial statements using International Financial Reporting Standards (IFRS). Make a list of the similarities and any differences between LVMH's multi-step income statement and Apple's multi-step income statement in **Exhibit 4-4**. Like Apple, LVMH reports several measures of company performance: gross margin, profit from recurring operations, operating profit, net financial income (expense). Differences include (1) LVMH including more subsections; (2) LVMH uses the word "profit" instead of "income"; (3) LVMH separates out minority interest (less than 100 percent owned subsidiaries that are consolidated with the parent LVMH); (4) LVMH refers to its interest expense as "cost of financial debt." Other than these labeling differences, LVMH's multi-step income statement under IFRS is strikingly similar to Apple's U.S. GAAP multi-step income statement.

YOUR TURN! 4.2

The solution is on page 229.

MBC

Musicland provides the following information and requests that we prepare a multi-step income statement for the year ended December 31, 2016. Musicland pays income tax at the rate of 30 percent of income.

Selling, general and administrative expenses...	$25,000	Cost of goods sold	$ 45,000
Research & development expense..........	10,000	Net sales	100,000
Interest expense	5,000		

WORKING WITH FINANCIAL STATEMENTS

Chapter 1 introduced the basic financial statements. We now extend that discussion by demonstrating how financial statements are used to address questions about a company's operating performance and financial health.

Analysis Based on Ratios

If Apple's net income in 2014 totaled $39,510 million, would we conclude that the company had a good year or a bad year? While $39,510 million is a large number, some frame of reference is needed before we can conclude that this amount represents a good, bad, or mediocre level of operating performance. For example, $39,510 million is a phenomenal performance if the company had only $1 million in assets to operate with during the year. But it is not as exceptional if the company had $100,000 million in assets to operate with during the year.

Investment professionals use a variety of methods to get a better understanding of how to interpret a net income number like $39,510 million. One such method involves ratio analysis. **Ratio analysis** expresses the relation of one relevant accounting number to another relevant accounting number through the process of division. The result of the division is expressed as a percentage, a rate, or as a proportion.

To illustrate how a ratio can provide additional meaning to Apple's net income of $39,510 million, we can divide Apple's net income by its total assets of $231,839 million, which is known as its **return on assets (ROA)**.

$$\text{Return on Assets (ROA)} = \frac{\text{Net income}}{\text{Total Assets}}$$

The result is 17.0 percent and tells us that Apple earned a rate of return of 17.0 percent on each dollar of assets invested in the business in 2014.

Although a single number like Apple's net income is difficult to interpret in isolation, a single ratio is also difficult to interpret without some point of reference or benchmark. Business professionals often use one of two techniques to further their understanding of ratios. **Trend analysis** compares a company's results, or the results of a ratio, over time. This technique helps the financial statement user identify any readily observable trends in a company's performance. **Benchmarking analysis** compares a company's performance, or a ratio, to that of its competitors, or to an industry average. Under benchmarking analysis, we are trying to compare, or benchmark, a company's performance against similar companies, or against an industry standard. Trend analysis and benchmarking analysis are powerful tools to place a company's results into a meaningful context.

Working with the Balance Sheet

LO3 Discuss use of a balance sheet and ratios to assess liquidity and solvency.

The balance sheet helps users evaluate the financial health of a company. The balance sheet also provides information on how the company finances the acquisition of its assets, with debt or with equity. **Exhibit 4-2** presented a simplified version of Apple's balance sheet.

Terms such as liquidity and solvency refer to the financial well-being of a company. For a company to remain in business it must be able to pay its bills when they come due. Before a bank such as **Bank of America** will commit to extend a loan to a company like Apple, it needs to assess the likelihood that it will be repaid the amount borrowed and be paid the interest due on the amount borrowed, both in a timely manner. This assessment involves evaluating Apple's *liquidity*, the ability to pay obligations that come due in the current year, and *solvency*, the ability to pay obligations over the long term.

Liquidity

Liquidity refers to a company's ability to pay its short-term financial obligations. It depends on several factors, including the level of cash a company has and how quickly it can generate cash from operations or its assets.

Current Ratio   One widely-used measure of a company's liquidity is the **current ratio**. The current ratio is defined as current assets divided by current liabilities. Current assets provide a measure of the cash available and expected to be generated in the current period. Current liabilities provide a measure of the cash that will be needed in the current period to pay existing or expected obligations.

$$\text{Current ratio} = \frac{\text{Current assets}}{\text{Current liabilities}}$$

A current ratio greater than one implies that a company has more cash and current assets than needed to pay off its current obligations, and a ratio less than one implies the opposite. While this interpretation is overly simplistic, it does provide an easily understood assessment of a company's liquidity. In general, the greater the current ratio, the more liquid a company is, and the less concern a lender has in extending a loan to the company.

One of Apple's competitors is **Hewlett-Packard Inc.**, an online retailer of personal computers. The current ratios for both Apple and for Hewlett-Packard are shown in **Exhibit 4-6**. Both companies report current ratios greater than one in 2014 and 2013; however, Apple reports a lower current ratio than does Hewlett-Packard in 2014 and a higher ratio in 2013. Based on this ratio, we would conclude that Apple is less liquid than Hewlett-Packard in 2014 and more liquid than Hewlett-Packard in 2013, although each company appears to be sufficiently liquid to satisfy currently due obligations.

Exhibit 4-6	Current Ratio		
(in millions)		**2014**	**2013**
Apple		$\dfrac{\$68{,}531}{\$63{,}448} = 1.08{:}1$	$\dfrac{\$73{,}286}{\$43{,}658} = 1.68{:}1$
Hewlett-Packard.		$\dfrac{\$50{,}145}{\$43{,}735} = 1.15{:}1$	$\dfrac{\$50{,}364}{\$45{,}521} = 1.11{:}1$

TAKEAWAY 4.1	Concept →	Method →	Assessment
	Can a company meet its short-term obligations?	Current assets and current liabilities from the balance sheet. $\text{Current ratio} = \dfrac{\text{Current assets}}{\text{Current liabilities}}$	A larger current ratio implies greater liquidity and a greater ability to pay short-term obligations.

Solvency

Lenders often provide loans that have repayment terms that extend over several years. In such cases the lender is interested in evaluating a company's solvency. **Solvency** refers to a company's ability to pay its long-term financial obligations. It depends on several factors, including the level of assets a company has. Solvency, therefore, is a measure of a company's ability to survive over the long term. (Both liquidity and solvency are important indicators of financial health but, a company must first be liquid. If a company is unable to pay its bills in the short term, it is irrelevant whether it is solvent in the long term.)

Debt-to-Total-Assets Ratio In general, the more debt a company uses to finance its assets and day-to-day operations, the riskier it is. This follows because the amount borrowed and the interest on that amount must be paid on a regular schedule. If a company is unable to meet the cash outflows required to satisfy its debt repayment schedule or meet its regular interest payments, a lender can legally demand immediate repayment of a loan, potentially forcing a company into bankruptcy if it is unable to repay that amount. The **debt-to-total-assets ratio**, calculated as total liabilities divided by total assets, provides a measure of this risk and is one ratio used to assess a company's solvency.

$$\textbf{Debt-to-total-assets ratio} = \frac{\textbf{Total liabilities}}{\textbf{Total assets}}$$

The greater the debt-to-total-assets ratio, the greater is a company's risk of not being able to pay its interest payments or principal repayments on a timely basis, and the lower is the company's solvency. Like the current ratio, the debt-to-total-assets ratio should not be used in isolation. There are many factors that must be considered when judging a company's solvency.

Exhibit 4-7 shows the debt-to-total-assets ratios for Apple and Hewlett-Packard. This exhibit reveals that in both 2014 and 2013, Hewlett-Packard used considerably more debt to finance its assets than did Apple (74.1 percent versus 51.9 percent in 2014). Consequently, Hewlett-Packard would be considered a riskier, less solvent company. A lender such as **Citibank** would likely be more concerned about the solvency of Hewlett-Packard than the solvency of Apple.

Exhibit 4-7	Debt-to-Total-Assets Ratio		
(in millions)		**2014**	**2013**
Apple		$\dfrac{\$120,292}{\$231,839} = 51.9\%$	$\dfrac{\$83,451}{\$207,000} = 40.3\%$
Hewlett-Packard.		$\dfrac{\$76,475}{\$103,206} = 74.1\%$	$\dfrac{\$78,407}{\$105,676} = 74.2\%$

Concept ⟶	Method ⟶	Assessment	TAKEAWAY 4.2
Can a company meet its long-term obligations?	Total assets and total liabilities from the balance sheet. $\text{Debt-to-total-assets ratio} = \dfrac{\text{Total liabilities}}{\text{Total assets}}$	A larger ratio implies reduced solvency and a reduced ability to repay outstanding obligations over the long term.	

The following information is available from the financial statements of the Philips Company

YOUR TURN! 4.3

The solution is on pages 229-230.

	2016	2015
Net sales.	$120,000	$110,000
Net income	20,000	15,000
Cash provided by operating activities	25,000	22,000
Expenditures on property, plant, and equipment.	7,000	6,000
Current assets	75,000	65,000
Current liabilities.	50,000	45,000
Total assets	220,000	190,000
Total liabilities.	$150,000	$145,000

Compute the current ratio and the debt-to-total-assets ratio and comment on any trends observed between 2015 and 2016.

Working with the Income Statement

Apple generates income by selling computers, iPads, iPods, iPhones, peripherals, and downloads from its iTunes store. The company's income statement provides a report detailing how much net income Apple was able to generate from these activities. A review of a company's income and its components is called profitability analysis. Apple's net income of $39,510 million for the year ended September 27, 2014, indicates that Apple was able to sell these products at a price that exceeded the cost of manufacturing. Apple's income statement, presented in **Exhibit 4-4**, also shows that the company's profitability increased from 2013 to 2014.

LO4 Discuss use of the income statement and ratios to assess profitability.

Apple's net income increased by $2,473 million, from $37,037 million in 2013 to $39,510 million in 2014. During a similar period, Hewlett-Packard's net income decreased by $100 million, from $5,113 million to $5,013 million. This suggests that Apple outperformed one of its leading competitors during this period. How was that possible? Perhaps Apple's success reflects its superior product line or possibly its greater product focus. Alternatively, it might reflect the superior operating acumen of Apple's management team.

Measures for Profitability Analysis

There are many ways to measure a company's success. One such measure is profitability. Profitability indicates whether or not a company is able to bring its products or services to the market efficiently, and whether it produces products or services that are valued by the market. The more profitable a company is, the better are its long-term prospects. Consistently unprofitable companies are on a path to failure.

A.K.A. Return on sales is often referred to as *profit margin*.

Return on Sales Ratio (Profit Margin) It is somewhat unfair, and potentially misleading, to compare two companies of differing size on the basis of net income. A larger company is expected to generate a larger net income. But a large net income does not necessarily indicate that a company is performing more efficiently than a company with a smaller net income. One measure that facilitates a comparison of the profitability between companies of different size is the return on assets ratio, which we already explained. Another useful measure is the **return on sales (ROS) ratio**, calculated as net income divided by net sales.

$$\text{Return on sales ratio} = \frac{\text{Net income}}{\text{Net sales}}$$

Exhibit 4-8 shows the calculation of return on sales for both Apple and Hewlett-Packard. Apple is a bit larger than Hewlett-Packard based on sales generated in 2014 ($182,795 million for Apple versus $111,454 million for Hewlett-Packard). Apple also generates much more net income than Hewlett-Packard ($39,510 million for Apple versus $5,013 million for Hewlett-Packard in 2014). Together, this translates into a much higher return on sales for Apple (21.6 percent for Apple versus 4.5 percent for Hewlett-Packard in 2014). An ROS of 21.6 percent indicates Apple has 21.6 cents left over for each dollar of sales revenue after subtracting all of its expenses. This is nearly five times as much as Hewlett-Packard, which generates just 4.5 cents for each dollar of sales revenue. This result suggests that Apple is a more profitable company than Hewlett-Packard, possibly because it is able to command a premium price for its products and/or because it runs a more efficient operation than does Hewlett-Packard.

Exhibit 4-8	Return on Sales			
(in millions)		**2014**		**2013**
Apple		$\frac{\$39,510}{\$182,795} = 21.6\%$		$\frac{\$37,037}{\$170,910} = 21.7\%$
Hewlett-Packard..........................		$\frac{\$5,013}{\$111,454} = 4.5\%$		$\frac{\$5,113}{\$112,298} = 4.6\%$

ACCOUNTING IN PRACTICE

Using Accounting to Bolster Savings

Do you know somebody that lives paycheck to paycheck? Chances are the answer is yes since statistics show that 4 out of 10 Americans have essentially no savings. In fact many have negative savings when you consider all their credit card debt. What is the best way to avoid this situation? The answer is to apply some accounting basics such as using a budget to identify every expense and keep good records tracking your spending. Next analyze your spending. Chances are you will find many places you can reduce or eliminate wasteful spending and add to your savings.

Concept ⟶	Method ⟶	Assessment	TAKEAWAY 4.3
How much net income does a company generate from each dollar of sales revenue?	Net sales and net income from the income statement. $\text{Return on sales ratio} = \dfrac{\text{Net income}}{\text{Net sales}}$	A larger ratio indicates that a company is more profitable on each sales dollar because it commands a premium price for its products and/or is more operationally efficient.	

The following information is available from the financial statements of the Philips Company.

YOUR TURN! 4.4

The solution is on page 230.

	2016	2015
Net sales.	$120,000	$110,000
Net income.	20,000	15,000
Cash provided by operating activities	25,000	22,000
Expenditures on property, plant, and equipment.	7,000	6,000
Current assets	75,000	65,000
Current liabilities.	50,000	45,000
Total assets	220,000	190,000
Total liabilities.	$150,000	$145,000

Compute the return on sales ratio and comment on any trends observed between 2015 and 2016.

Working with the Statement of Stockholders' Equity

Chapter 1 introduced the statement of stockholder's equity, which summarizes the changes in a company's stockholders' equity during the period. The statement of stockholders' equity consists of two parts—contributed capital and earned capital. **Contributed capital** is a measure of the capital contributed by the stockholders of a company when they purchase ownership shares in the company. Ownership shares are called common shares or common stock. **Earned capital** is a measure of the capital that is earned by the company, reinvested in the business, and not distributed to its stockholders—that is, its retained earnings. Retained earnings at the end of a fiscal period is calculated as retained earnings at the start of the period, plus net income for the period, less any dividends paid during the period.

LO5 Explain the components of the statement of stockholders' equity.

> **Retained earnings, beginning of period**
> **+ Net income**
> **− Dividends**
> _____
> **Retained earnings, end of period**

    Exhibit 4-9 presents the statement of stockholders' equity for Apple. The column labeled Common Stock represents the change in Apple's contributed capital during the period covered by the statement. The change to common stock resulted from the issuance of additional shares to Apple's existing stockholders, to new stockholders, or possibly to Apple's employees.

    The column labeled Retained Earnings in **Exhibit 4-9** represents Apple's earned capital. The primary adjustments in this column are Apple's net income and the dividends Apple distributes to its shareholders.

Exhibit 4-9	Statement of Stockholders' Equity

APPLE INC.
Statement of Stockholders' Equity

(in millions)	Common Stock	Retained Earnings	Other Equity	Total Equity
Balance at September 29, 2012........	$16,422	$101,289	$499	$118,210
Issuance of common stock	2,253			2,253
Net income........................		37,037		37,037
Dividends		(10,676)		(10,676)
Other adjustments	1,089	(23,394)	(970)	(23,275)
Balance at September 28, 2013........	19,764	104,256	(471)	123,549
Issuance of common stock	2,863			2,863
Net income........................		39,510		39,510
Dividends		(11,215)		(11,215)
Other adjustments	686	(45,399)	1,553	(43,160)
Balance at September 27, 2014........	$23,313	$ 87,152	$1,082	$111,547

CORPORATE SOCIAL RESPONSIBILITY	Investing with a Social Conscience

Not all investors are singularly focused on the financial performance of businesses they invest in. For a segment of the investing community, corporate social responsibility goes hand in hand with financial performance in choosing an investment. **Socially responsible investing (SRI)**, also known as sustainable investing, considers a firm's environmental stewardship, consumer protection, human rights, and diversity, along with its financial performance. Investments in SRI funds are near $3 trillion and have grown in recent years at a pace almost six times greater than the growth of professionally managed investments.

eLectures
MBC

Working with the Statement of Cash Flows

LO6 Explain use of the statement of cash flows to help assess solvency.

A common refrain heard from business people is that we do not pay bills with net income, we pay bills with cash! While net income is eventually converted into cash, it is the cash available that a company uses to run its business and pay its bills. Where can we find information about a company's cash resources? The answer is the statement of cash flows, which provides information on a company's sources and uses of cash.

The statement of cash flows aids us in understanding the change in cash reported by a company over a period of time. The statement explains the change in the cash reported between two balance sheet dates. The statement of cash flows is segmented into three activity categories: (1) cash flow from operating activities, (2) cash flow from investing activities, and (3) cash flow from financing activities. The separation into these three activities increases the statement's usefulness. For example, knowing that cash increased is not as useful as knowing that cash increased because of increased operating cash flow or because of a bank loan.

Exhibit 4-10 shows a simplified version of Apple's statement of cash flows. Apple reported a decrease of $415 million in cash in 2014, decreasing from $14,259 million in 2013 to $13,844 million in 2014. These cash balances are on Apple's balance sheet in

Exhibit 4-2. Most of Apple's cash flow in 2014 was generated from operating activities ($59,713 million). Apple used much of its cash flow in its investing activities, with a net of $9,017 million used for purchase of investments and $9,571 used to purchase additional property, plant, and equipment. Apple also used a significant amount of cash in its financing activities. The largest of these financing activities was the repurchase of $45,000 million of common stock.

Exhibit 4-10	Statement of Cash Flows		
APPLE INC. **Statement of Cash Flows** **For Years Ended September 27, 2014, and September 28, 2013**			
(in millions)		**2014**	**2013**
Cash flow provided by operating activities			
Cash receipts less cash disbursements from operating activities . . .		$59,713	$53,666
Net cash provided by operations		59,713	53,666
Cash flow provided by investing activities			
Net purchases of investments		(9,017)	(24,042)
Net payments for property, plant, and equipment		(9,571)	(8,165)
Other cash payments		(3,991)	(1,567)
Net cash used by investing.		(22,579)	(33,774)
Cash flow provided by financing activities			
Net cash from issuance of debt		18,266	16,896
Payment of dividends.		(11,126)	(10,564)
Repurchase of common stock		(45,000)	(22,860)
Other receipts.		311	149
Net cash used by financing.		(37,549)	(16,379)
Net increase (decrease) in cash.		(415)	3,513
Cash at beginning of year		14,259	10,746
Cash at year-end		$13,844	$14,259

Free Cash Flow

The level of cash flow provided by operating activities is valuable information on a company's ability to generate cash from its day-to-day operations. One measure of cash flow health is **free cash flow**. Free cash flow is often calculated by subtracting a company's capital expenditures for PP&E from its cash flow provided by operating activities. A company's free cash flow is an indicator of its ability to expand operations, repay lenders, or pay stockholders a dividend after replacing the value of any property, plant and equipment used in operations. In general, the larger a company's free cash flow, the healthier a company is in terms of operating cash flow.

Hint: When calculating a firm's free cash flow, "capital expenditures" amount is the cash spent for purchases of PP&E less the cash proceeds received from sale of PP&E. Both amounts are reported on a statement of cash flows.

Free cash flow = Cash flow from operations − Capital expenditures

We calculate Apple's free cash flow in 2014 and 2013 with information reported in Apple's statement of cash flows in **Exhibit 4-10**.

(in millions)	2014	2013
Cash flow provided by operating activities	$59,713	$53,666
Less: Expenditures on property, plant, and equipment.........	(9,571)	(8,165)
Free cash flow	$50,142	$45,501

Apple's free cash flow of $50,142 in 2014 and $45,501 in 2013 indicates that it generates a healthy free cash flow. It also suggests that Apple should have no trouble financing future purchases of property, plant, and equipment, repaying its lenders, or paying dividends to its stockholders, using its operating cash flow.

TAKEAWAY 4.4	Concept ⟶	Method ⟶	Assessment
	How much free cash flow does a company generate?	Cash provided by operating activities less cash expended on purchases of property, plant, and equipment. Cash provided by operations – Capital expenditures ――――――――――― = Free cash flow	Larger free cash flow indicates a greater ability to expand operations, repay debt, or pay dividends without external financing.

YOUR TURN! 4.5

The solution is on page 230.

The following information is available from the financial statements of the Philips Company.

	2016	2015
Net sales.	$120,000	$110,000
Net income.	20,000	15,000
Cash provided by operating activities	25,000	22,000
Expenditures on property, plant, and equipment.	7,000	6,000
Current assets	75,000	65,000
Current liabilities.	50,000	45,000
Total assets	220,000	190,000
Total liabilities.	150,000	145,000

Compute the free cash flow and comment on any trends observed between 2015 and 2016.

FORENSIC ACCOUNTING

Accountant as Detective—Cash Fraud Schemes

Frauds involving cash are the most common frauds, and are more common than corruption or fraudulent financial statements. The more common cash schemes include (1) skimming, where an employee accepts cash from a customer but does not record a sales transaction, (2) cash larceny, where an employee steals cash from the daily receipts before they are deposited in a bank, (3) check tampering, where an employee steals blank company checks and makes them out to themselves or an accomplice, and (4) cash register disbursement, where an employee fraudulently voids a sale on his or her cash register and steals the cash.

COMPREHENSIVE PROBLEM

Following are items reported on the financial statements of **Microsoft Corporation** as of June 30, 2014. (Some of the reported accounts have been combined for simplicity.) Amounts given are in millions of dollars.

Cash flow provided by operating activities	$32,231
Cash at June 30, 2013	3,804
Cash at June 30, 2014	8,669
Net revenue	86,833
Cash flow from investing activities	(18,833)
Inventory	2,660
Accounts receivable	21,485
Cost of goods sold	26,934
Cash flow from financing activities	(8,533)
Other current assets	81,432
Property, plant, and equipment	13,011
Operating expenses	32,140
Other income	61
Intangible assets	27,108
Other long-term assets	18,019
Income tax expense	5,746
Accounts payable	13,569
Other current liabilities	32,056
Long-term liabilities	36,975
Common stock	68,366
Retained earnings	17,710
Other stockholders' equity	3,708

a. Prepare a multi-step income statement, a classified balance sheet, and a statement of cash flows using the accounts listed above.

b. Compute the following ratios:
    Current ratio
    Debt-to-total-assets ratio
    Return on sales ratio

Solution

a.

MICROSOFT CORPORATION	
Income Statement	
For Year Ended June 30, 2014 (in millions)	

Net sales	$86,833
Less cost of goods sold	26,934
Gross profit on sales	59,899
Operating expenses	32,140
Income from operations	27,759
Other income	61
Income before income taxes	27,820
Income tax expenses	5,746
Net income	$22,074

MICROSOFT CORPORATION
Balance Sheet
June 30, 2014 (in millions)

Assets

Current assets

Cash	$ 8,669	
Accounts receivable	21,485	
Inventory	2,660	
Other current assets	81,432	
Total current assets		$114,246
Property, plant, and equipment		13,011
Intangible assets		27,108
Other long-term assets		18,019
Total assets		$172,384

Liabilities and Stockholders' Equity

Current liabilities

Accounts payable	$13,569	
Other current liabilities	32,056	
Total current liabilities		$45,625
Long-term liabilities		36,975
Total liabilities		82,600

Stockholders' equity

Common stock	68,366	
Retained earnings	17,710	
Other stockholders' equity	3,708	
Total stockholders' equity		89,784
Total liabilities and stockholders' equity		$172,384

MICROSOFT CORPORATION
Statement of Cash Flows
For Year Ended June 30, 2014 (in millions)

Cash flow provided by operating activities	$32,231
Cash flow used by investing activities	(18,833)
Cash flow used by financing activities	(8,533)
Net increase in cash	4,865
Cash at June 30, 2013	3,804
Cash at June 30, 2014	$ 8,669

b.

Current ratio	$\dfrac{\$114,246}{\$45,625} = 2.50:1$
Debt-to-total-assets ratio	$\dfrac{\$82,600}{\$172,384} = 47.9\%$
Return on sales ratio	$\dfrac{\$22,074}{\$86,833} = 25.4\%$

SUMMARY OF LEARNING OBJECTIVES

Describe a classified balance sheet. (p. 190)   **LO1**

- A classified balance sheet contains two subgroups of assets (current assets and long-term assets) and two subgroups of liabilities (current liabilities and long-term liabilities).
- A classified balance sheet can be presented in account form or report form.

Describe a single-step and multi-step income statement. (p. 195)   **LO2**

- A multi-step income statement classifies items into subgroups in order to facilitate analysis and decision making.
- A multi-step income statement for a merchandising firm often includes one section for sales revenue; two sections for expenses: cost of goods sold and operating expenses; and a section for other income and expenses.
- A multi-step income statement for a service firm is similar, but does not have a section for cost of goods sold.

Discuss use of a balance sheet and ratios to assess liquidity and solvency. (p. 199)   **LO3**

- Ratio analysis involves expressing the relation of one relevant accounting number with another relevant accounting number through the process of division. This process helps to provide a context to interpret a particular number.
- Two techniques that are often used in ratio analysis are (1) trend analysis where ratios are examined over time and (2) benchmarking analysis where a company's ratios are compared to those of another company or to an average of an industry as a whole.
- Liquidity refers to a company's ability to pay those obligations that are expected to come due in the next year.
- The current ratio, or current assets divided by current liabilities, provides a measure of a company's liquidity.
- Solvency refers to a company's ability to repay its debts over the long term.
- The debt-to-total-assets ratio, calculated as total debt divided by total assets, provides one measure of a company's solvency.

Discuss use of the income statement and ratios to assess profitability. (p. 201)   **LO4**

- Return on sales, or net income divided by net sales, provides a measure of a company's profitability by indicating how much net income a company earns on each dollar of sales revenue.

Explain the components of the statement of stockholders' equity. (p. 203)   **LO5**

- Stockholders' equity comprises two parts: (1) contributed capital and (2) earned capital.
- Contributed capital is the capital contributed to a firm by stockholders when they purchase ownership shares in the company.
- Earned capital represents the net income that has been earned by a company and not distributed to stockholders as a dividend.

Explain use of the statement of cash flows to help assess solvency. (p. 204)   **LO6**

- The statement of cash flows provides information regarding a company's sources and uses of cash.
- Free cash flow, calculated as cash provided from operating activities less cash expended on property, plant, and equipment, provides information regarding management's ability to expand operations, repay debt, or make distributions to stockholders, using a firm's operating cash flow.

SUMMARY	Concept ⟶	Method ⟶	Assessment
TAKEAWAY 4.1	Can a company meet its short-term obligations?	Current assets and current liabilities from the balance sheet. $$\text{Current ratio} = \frac{\text{Current assets}}{\text{Current liabilities}}$$	A larger current ratio implies greater liquidity and a greater ability to pay short-term obligations.
TAKEAWAY 4.2	Can a company meet its long-term obligations?	Total assets and total liabilities from the balance sheet. $$\text{Debt-to-total-assets ratio} = \frac{\text{Total liabilities}}{\text{Total assets}}$$	A larger ratio implies reduced solvency and a reduced ability to repay outstanding obligations over the long term.
TAKEAWAY 4.3	How much net income does a company generate from each dollar of sales revenue?	Net sales and net income from the income statement. $$\text{Return on sales ratio} = \frac{\text{Net income}}{\text{Net sales}}$$	A larger ratio indicates that a company is more profitable on each sales dollar because it commands a premium price for its products and/or is more operationally efficient.
TAKEAWAY 4.4	How much free cash flow does a company generate?	Cash provided by operating activities less cash expended on purchases of property, plant, and equipment. $$\begin{array}{l} \text{Cash provided by operations} \\ \underline{-\ \text{Capital expenditures}} \\ \text{Free cash flow} \end{array}$$	Larger free cash flow indicates a greater ability to expand operations, repay debt, or pay dividends without external financing.

KEY TERMS

Account form (p. 193)

Benchmarking analysis (p. 199)

Classified balance sheet (p. 190)

Contributed capital (p. 203)

Current assets (p. 190)

Current liabilities (p. 192)

Current ratio (p. 199)

Debt-to-total-assets ratio (p. 200)

Earned capital (p. 203)

Free cash flow (p. 205)

Gross profit (Gross margin) (p. 196)

Intangible assets (p. 191)

Liquidity (p. 191, 199)

Long-term liabilities (Noncurrent liabilities) (p. 193)

Multi-step income statement (Classified income statement) (p. 195)

Net sales (p. 196)

Normal operating cycle (p. 190)

Property, plant, and equipment (p. 191)

Ratio analysis (p. 198)

Report form (p. 193)

Return on assets (ROA) (p. 198)

Return on sales (ROS) ratio (profit margin) (p. 202)

Sales discounts (p. 196)

Sales returns and allowances (p. 196)

Single-step income statement (p. 195)

Socially responsible investing (SRI) (p. 204)

Solvency (p. 200)

Stockholders' equity (Shareholders' equity) (p. 193)

Trend analysis (p. 199)

Assignments with the ⓂⒷⒸ logo in the margin are available in ᵐʸBusinessCourse.
See the Preface of the book for details.

SELF-STUDY QUESTIONS

(Answers to Self-Study Questions are at the end of this chapter.)

1. **Which of the following items will not be reported on a classified balance sheet?**   **LO1**
   a.   Current assets
   b.   Net income
   c.   Total liabilities
   d.   Common stock

2. **Which of the following would not be considered a current asset?**   **LO1**
   a.   Inventory
   b.   Accounts receivable
   c.   Property, plant, and equipment
   d.   Cash

3. **For the balance sheet to be in balance, the following must exist:**   **LO1**
   a.   Total assets must be greater than total liabilities
   b.   Total assets must be less than total liabilities
   c.   Total assets must equal total liabilities plus stockholders' equity
   d.   Total liabilities must equal total stockholders' equity

4. **Which of the following would be considered an intangible asset?**   **LO1**
   a.   Cash
   b.   Land
   c.   Accounts payable
   d.   Patents

5. **Which of the following would most likely be classified as a long-term liability?**   **LO1**
   a.   Accounts payable
   b.   Notes payable
   c.   Accounts receivable
   d.   Common stock

6. **Ratio analysis always involves which type of arithmetic operation?**   **LO3**
   a.   Addition
   b.   Subtraction
   c.   Multiplication
   d.   Division

7. **Which of the following is not a true statement?**   **LO3**
   a.   Benchmarking analysis involves comparing a company to its industry's averages.
   b.   Benchmarking analysis involves comparing a company to its competitors.
   c.   Trend analysis involves comparing a company's ratios over time.
   d.   Benchmarking analysis involves comparing a company's ratios over time.

8. **A company reported net income of $200 on net sales of $2,000. The company's return on sales is:**   **LO4**
   a. $1,800
   b.   10 percent
   c.   0.1 percent
   d.   None of the above

9. **The return on sales ratio does *not* provide insight on which of the following:**   **LO4**
   a.   A company's net income per dollar of sales.
   b.   A measure of a company's financial performance.
   c.   A measure of a company's cash flow flexibility.
   d.   A measure of a company's operating efficiency.

10. **Which of the following is not shown on the statement of stockholders' equity?**   **LO5**
    a.   Contributed capital.
    b.   Retained earnings.
    c.   Common stock.
    d.   Total liabilities.

LO3 **11.** **The following data appear in the financial statements of a company. Calculate its current ratio.**

Current assets	$10,000
Current liabilities.	$5,000

    a. 2:1
    b. 1:2
    c. $5,000
    d. ($5,000)

LO5 **12.** **The following data pertains to Smith Consulting, Inc. for 2013. Compute its ending retained earnings.**

Beginning-of-year retained earnings	$120,000
Net income.	37,500
Dividends paid	5,000

    a. $157,500
    b. $152,500
    c. $162,500
    d. $115,000

LO2 **13.** **A merchandising company's multi-step income statement differs from that of a service company in what way?**
    a. There is no difference.
    b. A service company does not include a line for cost of goods sold.
    c. A service company has a line for selling expenses whereas a merchandising company does not.
    d. A merchandising company will have a line for income from operations whereas a service company will not.

QUESTIONS

1. List three subgroups of assets that may be found in the asset section of a classified balance sheet.

2. Define *current asset* and *normal operating cycle*.

3. Which of the following are current assets: land, cash, prepaid expense, building, accounts receivable, inventory, equipment?

4. What is meant by corporate social responsibility?

5. Define the following ratios: current ratio, debt-to-total-assets ratio, and return on sales ratio.

6. What is meant by socially responsible investing?

7. Which of the following measures are best computed using a classified balance sheet?
    a. Liquidity
    b. Solvency
    c. Free cash flow
    d. Both a. and b.

8. Which of the following is a correct statement?
    a. The current ratio is a measure of firm solvency.
    b. The current ratio is a measure of firm liquidity.
    c. The debt-to-total-assets ratio is a measure of firm liquidity.
    d. None of the above is correct.

9. Free cash flow is measured using information from which financial statement?
    a. Balance sheet
    b. Income statement
    c. Statement of cash flows
    d. Statement of retained earnings

10. Socially responsible investing
    a. Means making as much money on your investments as you can as your only goal.
    b. Means investing in companies that adhere to environmental and social policies in their operations.
    c. Is too small of a concept to matter much.

SHORT EXERCISES

SE4-1. **Preparing a Classified Balance Sheet** Dino Company, a merchandising firm, reports the following   **LO1**
data as of January 31, 2016:

Stockholders' equity	$ 4,700
Property, plant, and equipment	10,000
Inventory.	2,500
Accounts receivable.	1,200
Other current liabilities	600
Accounts payable.	800
Long-term notes payable.	8,000
Cash.	400

Prepare a classified balance sheet for Dino Company as of January 31, 2016.

SE4-2. **Evaluating Firm Profitability** The following financial information is taken from the annual reports   **LO4**
of the Smith Company and the Wesson Company:

	Smith	Wesson
Net income.	$10,000	$100,000
Net sales.	50,000	400,000

Calculate the return on sales ratio for each company and determine which firm is more profitable.

SE4-3. **Evaluating Firm Liquidity** The following financial information is taken from the balance sheets of   **LO3**
the Drucker Company and the Ito Company:

	Drucker	Ito
Current assets	$250,000	$50,000
Current liabilities.	100,000	15,000

Calculate the current ratio for each company and determine which firm has the higher level of liquidity.

SE4-4. **Evaluating Firm Solvency** The following financial information is taken from the balance sheets of   **LO3**
the Lambeth Company and the Maritza Company:

	Lambeth	Maritza
Total debt.	$350,000	$ 850,000
Total assets	550,000	1,000,000

Calculate the debt-to-total-assets ratio and determine which firm has the higher level of solvency.

SE4-5. **Calculating Free Cash Flow** The following financial information is taken from the annual reports of   **LO6**
the Jackson Company and the Pearce Company:

	Jackson	Pearce
Cash flow from operating activities	$250,000	$750,000
Cash investment in property & equipment.	75,000	240,000

Calculate the free cash flow for each company and determine which firm has better cash flow health.

LO6   **SE4-6.**   **Statement of Cash Flows** Which of the following would not appear on a company's statement of cash flows?

  a.   Cash flow from operating activities
  b.   Net change in cash
  c.   Total assets
  d.   Cash flow for investing activities

LO3   **SE4-7.**   **Debt-to-Total-Assets Ratio** Ruby Company's balance sheet reports the following totals: Assets = $40,000; Liabilities = $25,000; Stockholders' Equity = $15,000. Determine the company's debt-to-total-assets ratio.

  a.   37.5%
  b.   62.5%
  c. $15,000
  d.   166.7%

LO6   **SE4-8.**   **Free Cash Flow** Lester Linens reports the following items on its statement of cash flows:

  Cash flow provided by operating activities = $100,000
  Cash flow used by investing activities = $50,000
  Cash flow used by financing activities = $25,000
  Capital expenditures = $40,000

  Determine Lester's free cash flow:

  a. $40,000
  b. $5,000
  c.   40%
  d. $60,000

LO4   **SE4-9.**   **Return on Sales** The following data are from the financial statements of Burkee Wines, Inc. Compute Burkee's return on sales ratio for 2016.

  Total revenues for 2016: $3,500,000
  Total expenses for 2016: $2,800,000

  a.   125%
  b.   80%
  c.   25%
  d.   20%

LO2   **SE4-10.**   **The Multi-step Income Statement** Dino Company, a merchandising firm, reports the following data for the month ended January 31:

Operating expenses	$ 3,000
Cost of goods sold	4,000
Net sales	10,000
Income tax expense	1,200
Other income	500

Prepare a multi-step income statement for Dino Company for the month of January.

LO6   **SE4-11.**   **Statement of Cash Flows** Identify whether the following statements are true or false.

  a.   The statement of cash flows provides information about whether a firm is "rich" or not.
  b.   The statement of cash flows provides information about a firm's financial health.
  c.   The statement of cash flows provides information about a firm's liquidity.
  d.   The statement of cash flows provides information about a firm's solvency.

EXERCISES—SET A

E4-1A. Preparing a Classified Balance Sheet From the following accounts, listed in alphabetical order, prepare a classified balance sheet for Berkly Wholesalers as of December 31, 2016. All accounts have normal balances.

LO1

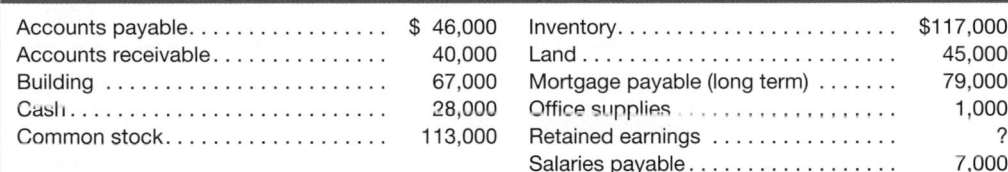

Accounts payable.	$ 46,000	Inventory.	$117,000
Accounts receivable.	40,000	Land	45,000
Building	67,000	Mortgage payable (long term)	79,000
Cash.	28,000	Office supplies	1,000
Common stock.	113,000	Retained earnings	?
		Salaries payable.	7,000

E4-2A. Multi-step Income Statement From the following accounts, listed in alphabetical order, prepare a multi-step income statement for Karlman Distributors for the year ended December 31. All accounts have normal balances.

LO2

Selling, general and administrative expense	$196,000	Sales revenue.	$560,000
Cost of goods sold.	335,000	Income tax expense.	10,000
Interest expense.	5,000		

E4-3A. Evaluating the Liquidity and Solvency of a Company Identify whether the following statements are true or false.

LO3, 4, 6

a. The current ratio is a measure of a firm's liquidity.
b. Free cash flow is a measure of a firm's solvency.
c. The return on sales ratio is a measure of a firm's liquidity.
d. The debt-to-total-assets ratio is a measure of a firm's liquidity.

E4-4A. Classified Balance Sheet The Werthman Company collected the following information for the preparation of its December 31, 2016, classified balance sheet:

LO1

Accounts receivable.	$17,000	Property, plant, and equipment	$200,000
Cash.	17,000	Inventory.	68,000
Other current assets.	25,000	Other long-term assets	40,000
Accounts payable.	25,000	Common stock.	92,000
Long-term liabilities	55,000	Retained earnings	?
Other current liabilities	19,000		

Prepare a classified balance sheet for Werthman Company.

E4-5A. Profitability, Liquidity, and Solvency Ratios Shannon Corporation gathered the following information from its 2016 financial statements:

LO3, 4, 6

Net sales.	$185,000
Net income.	35,200
Cash provided by operating activities	35,000
Expenditures on property, plant, and equipment.	15,000
Current assets	40,500
Current liabilities.	27,000
Total assets	135,000
Total liabilities.	97,500

Using the above data, calculate the following: (1) return on sales ratio, (2) current ratio, (3) debt-to-total-assets ratio, and (4) free cash flow.

LO3 **E4-6A.** **Return on Assets** The following information was taken from **Apple Inc.**'s 2014 financial statements. Numbers are in millions.

APPLE INC.
AAPL

	2014	2013
Net income	$ 39,510	$ 37,037
Total assets	231,839	207,000

Required

a. What was Apple's return on assets for 2014 and 2013?

b. Based on your answer from part *a.*, how did the company's performance change from 2013 to 2014?

LO5 **E4-7A.** **Statement of Stockholders' Equity** You have been asked to assist with the preparation of a statement of stockholders' equity for Maxx Company for the year ended December 31, 2016. You determine the following balances:

Common stock at December 31, 2015	$8,000
Retained earnings at December 31, 2015	7,500
Net income during 2016	4,500
Dividends during 2016	750
Issuance of common stock during 2016	600

Required

Prepare a statement of stockholders' equity for Maxx Company for 2016.

LO4 **E4-8A.** **Return on Sales** Kuyu Co.'s sales rose 12 percent over prior year sales of $100,000; however, net income increased by only 6 percent over the prior year's net income. If Kuyu's prior year return on sales ratio was 8 percent, what is the current year return on sales ratio?

LO6 **E4-9A.** **Free Cash Flow** Kat Co. reports the following financial data for the current year:

Cash flow from operating activities	$21,500
Cash flow from investing activities	(10,555)
Cash flow from financing activities	4,250
Cash disbursed for capital expenditures	(4,325)

Compute Kat's free cash flow.

LO5 **E4-10A.** **Statement of Stockholders' Equity** Prag Co. reported the following financial data for its most current year:

Beginning-of-year common stock	$ 95,000
Beginning-of-year retained earning	175,400
Net income	33,400
Dividends paid	10,500
Issuance of common stock	16,000

Compute Prag's end-of-year total stockholders' equity.

EXERCISES—SET B

LO1 **E4-1B.** **Preparing a Classified Balance Sheet** From the following accounts, listed in alphabetical order, prepare a classified balance sheet for Balford Wholesalers as of December 31, 2016. All accounts have normal balances.

Accounts payable..................	$ 55,000	Inventory......................	$142,000
Accounts receivable................	54,000	Land........................	58,000
Building and equipment.............	87,000	Mortgage payable (long-term).....	85,000
Cash.......................	40,000	Office supplies	2,000
Common stock....................	125,000	Retained earnings	?
		Salaries payable...............	8,000

E4-2B. **Multi-step Income Statement** From the following accounts, listed in alphabetical order, prepare a multi-step income statement for Kokomo Wholesale for the year ended December 31. All accounts have normal balances.   **LO2**

Sellling, general, and administrative expenses ...	$260,000	Sales revenue...........	$580,000
Cost of goods sold........................	275,000	Income tax expense......	8,000
Interest expense.........................	5,000		

E4-3B. **Evaluating the Liquidity and Solvency of a Company** Identify whether the following statements are true or false.   **LO3, 4, 6**

a. The current ratio is a measure of a firm's solvency.
b. Free cash flow is a measure of a firm's liquidity.
c. The return on sales ratio is a measure of a firm's solvency.
d. The debt-to-total-assets ratio is a measure of a firm's solvency.

E4-4B. **Classified Balance Sheet** The Cambridge Company collected the following information for the preparation of its December 31, 2016, classified balance sheet: **LO1**

Accounts receivable................	$26,000	Property, plant, and equipment......	$200,000
Cash.......................	20,000	Inventory......................	65,000
Other current assets...............	32,000	Other long-term assets	40,000
Accounts payable.................	21,000	Common stock..................	115,000
Long-term liabilities ,..............	60,000	Retained earnings	?
Other current liabilities	18,000		

Prepare a classified balance sheet for Cambridge Company.

E4-5B. **Profitability, Liquidity, and Solvency Ratios** O'Neill Corporation gathered the following information from its 2016 financial statements: **LO3, 4, 6**

Net sales....................................	$280,000	Current assets	$ 50,000
Net income................................	80,000	Current liabilities.........	25,000
Cash provided by operating activities	100,000	Total assets	140,000
Expenditures on property, plant, and equipment...	17,000	Total liabilities...........	99,500

Using the above data, calculate the following: (1) return on sales ratio, (2) current ratio, (3) debt-to-total-assets ratio, and (4) free cash flow.

E4-6B. **Return on Assets** Daisy Company reports the following information in its financial statements. Numbers are in thousands.   **LO3**

	2016	2015
Net sales...	$41,300	$44,100
Net income...	12,500	16,250
Total assets	63,900	87,400

There were 4,000 outstanding shares at December 31, 2016.

Required

a.   What was Daisy's return on assets ratio for 2016 and 2015?

b.   Based on your answer from part a., how did the company's performance change from 2015 to 2016?

LO5   **E4-7B.**   **Statement of Stockholders' Equity**   You have been asked to assist with the preparation of a statement of stockholders' equity for Palatin Company for the year ended December 31, 2016. You determine the following balances:

Common stock at December 31, 2015	$47,000
Retained earnings at December 31, 2015	18,750
Net income during 2016	23,400
Dividends during 2016	9,100
Issuance of common stock during 2016	5,000

Required

Prepare a statement of stockholders' equity for Palatin Company for 2016.

LO4   **E4-8B.**   **Return on Sales**   Bomont Co.'s sales rose 8 percent over prior year sales of $300,000, however net income increased by 6 percent over the prior year's net income. If Bomont's prior year return on sales ratio was 25 percent, what is the current year return on sales ratio?

LO6   **E4-9B.**   **Free Cash Flow**   Bern Co. reports the following financial data for the current year:

Cash flow from operating activities	$41,500
Cash flow from investing activities	27,455
Cash flow from financing activities	21,175
Cash disbursed for capital expenditures	(11,425)

Compute Bern's free cash flow.

LO5   **E4-10B.**   **Statement of Stockholders' Equity**   Stuart Co. reported the following financial data for its most current year:

Beginning-of-year common stock	$130,000
Beginning-of-year retained earnings	325,500
Net income	10,500
Dividends paid	7,000
Issuance of common stock	15,000

Compute Stuart's end-of-year total stockholders' equity.

PROBLEMS—SET A

LO1   **P4-1A.**   **Preparing a Classified Balance Sheet**   The following financial data for Crane Distributors was collected as of December 31, 2016. All accounts have normal balances.

Accounts payable	$ 70,000	Accounts receivable	$120,200
Delivery equipment	80,000	Accumulated depreciation	55,000
Inventory	114,000	Cash	15,200
Retained earnings	?	Common stock	110,000
Supplies	6,400	Prepaid insurance	4,000

Required

Prepare a classified balance sheet as of December 31, 2016, for Crane Distributors.

P4-2A. Preparing a Classified Balance Sheet The following financial data for the Marshall Corporation **LO1** was collected as of December 31, 2016. All accounts have normal balances.

Furniture and equipment	$107,000	Accumulated depreciation—furniture and equipment	$ 48,800
Cash	50,400	Accounts receivable	95,200
Common stock	190,000	Accounts payable	18,400
Prepaid insurance	300	Inventory	93,000
Retained earnings	?		

Required
Prepare a classified balance sheet as of December 31, 2016.

P4-3A. Multi-step Income Statements The adjusted trial balance of Crane Distributors on December 31, **LO2** 2016, is shown below.

CRANE DISTRIBUTORS
Adjusted Trial Balance
December 31, 2016

	Debit	Credit
Cash	$ 20,200	
Accounts receivable	110,200	
Inventory	94,000	
Prepaid insurance	2,400	
Supplies	6,400	
Delivery equipment	85,000	
Accumulated depreciation		$ 35,000
Accounts payable		90,000
Common stock		105,000
Retained earnings		42,000
Sales revenue		785,800
Cost of goods sold	513,400	
Salaries expense	123,000	
Rent expense	40,000	
Supplies expense	6,400	
Utilities expense	4,000	
Depreciation expense	16,000	
Insurance expense	6,800	
Income tax expense	30,000	
	$1,057,800	$1,057,800

Required
Prepare a multi-step income statement for the year ended December 31, 2016. Combine all the operating expenses into one line on the income statement for selling, general and administrative expenses.

P4-4A. Preparing the Financial Statements Listed below are items reported on the financial statements of **LO1, 6** the Huntington Company as of June 30, 2016:

Cash flow provided by operating activities	$39,000	Other long-term assets	$17,500
Cash at June 30, 2015	6,000	Cash flow from financing activities	1,300
Cash at June 30, 2016	36,000	Current liabilities	22,000
Inventory	5,500	Long-term liabilities	16,250
Accounts receivable	15,200	Intangible assets	9,500
Cash flow from investing activities	(10,300)	Common stock	60,000
Other current assets	1,500	Retained earnings	?
Property, plant and equipment	50,000		

Required

Prepare a classified balance sheet as of June 30, 2016, and statement of cash flows for 2016.

LO3, 4 **P4-5A.** **Assessing a Firm's Profitability, Liquidity and Solvency** Presented below is financial data for the Forrester Company as of year-end 2015 and 2016:

	2015	2016
Current assets	$ 55,000	$ 60,000
Total assets	100,000	130,000
Current liabilities.	27,500	40,000
Total liabilities.	75,000	80,000
Net sales.	140,000	190,000
Net income.	21,000	26,000

Required

Calculate Forrester's current ratio, debt-to-total-assets ratio, and return on sales ratio. Comment on the trend in the company's profitability, liquidity, and solvency from 2015 to 2016.

LO2, 4 **P4-6A.** **Profitability and the Income Statement** Presented below is income statement data for Longo & Company as of year-end 2016:

Income tax expense.	$ 5,400	Net revenue	$58,500
Cost of goods sold.	14,300	Operating expenses.	27,000
Other expenses	900		

Required

Prepare a multi-step income statement for 2016 and calculate the company's return on sales ratio. If Longo's return on sales was 16 percent in 2015, is the company's profitability improving or declining?

P4-7A. **Preparing the Statement of Stockholders' Equity** Presented below is financial data for Likert & Co. as of year-end 2016:

Cash.	$ 7,500	Accumulated depreciation	$(14,000)
Retained earnings, Jan. 1, 2016.	15,000	Net income.	35,000
Intangible assets	25,000	Stockholders' equity, Jan. 1, 2016.	65,000
Common stock.	50,000	Retained earnings, Dec. 31, 2016	37,000
Accounts payable.	4,000	Stockholders' equity, Dec. 31, 2016 . . .	87,000
Dividends paid	13,000		

Required

Prepare a statement of stockholders' equity for Likert & Co. as of December 31, 2016.

LO3, 4 **P4-8A.** **Interpreting Liquidity, Solvency, and Profitability Ratios** Presented below are financial data for two retail companies:

	Company A	Company B
Return on sales ratio	15.5%	13.9%
Current ratio	0.5	2.0
Debt-to-total-assets.	65%	30%

Required

Consider the financial ratio data for the two companies. Which company represents the better investment opportunity in your view and why?

P4-9A. Ratio Analysis The following balances were reported in the financial statements for Nafooz   **LO3, 4**
Company.

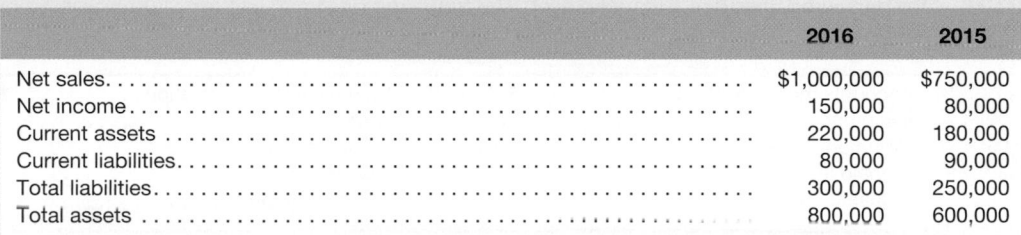

	2016	2015
Net sales.	$1,000,000	$750,000
Net income.	150,000	80,000
Current assets	220,000	180,000
Current liabilities.	80,000	90,000
Total liabilities.	300,000	250,000
Total assets	800,000	600,000

Required
1. Compute the following ratios for 2016 and 2015 for Nafooz Company.
   a. Return on sales ratio
   b. Current ratio
   c. Debt-to-total-assets ratio
2. Comment on changes to Nafooz Company's profitability, liquidity, and solvency.

P4-10A. Multi-step Income Statement and Adjusting Entries The Boston Trading Company, whose ac-   **LO2**
counting year ends on December 31, had the following normal balances in its general ledger at December 31:

Cash.	$15,000	Sales revenue.	$610,000
Accounts receivable.	56,600	Cost of goods sold.	394,000
Inventory.	74,000	Utilities expense.	4,800
Prepaid insurance	3,000	Sales salaries expense.	77,000
Office supplies.	4,200	Delivery expense	10,800
Furniture and fixtures	21,000	Advertising expense.	5,600
Accumulated depreciation—		Rent expense.	9,400
furniture and fixtures.	7,000	Office salaries expense	56,000
Delivery equipment.	86,000	Income tax expense.	9,000
Accumulated depreciation—			
delivery equipment	12,000		
Accounts payable.	43,000		
Long-term notes payable.	28,000		
Common stock.	70,000		
Retained earnings	56,400		

During the year, the accounting department prepared monthly statements but no adjusting entries were
made in the journals and ledgers. Data for the year-end procedures are as follows:

1. Prepaid insurance, December 31, was $1,500
2. Depreciation expense on furniture and fixtures for the year was $2,000
3. Depreciation expense on delivery equipment for the year was $11,000
4. Salaries payable, December 31, ($1,800 sales and $1,200 office) was $3,000
5. Unused office supplies on December 31 were $1,200

Required
a. Record the necessary adjusting entries at December 31.
b. Prepare a multi-step income statement for the year. Combine all the operating expenses into one
line on the income statement for selling, general and administrative expenses.

PROBLEMS—SET B

LO1 **P4-1B.** **Preparing a Classified Balance Sheet** The following financial data for McKensie & Company was collected as of December 31, 2016. All accounts have normal balances.

Accounts receivable.	$223,000	Accumulated depreciation	$110,000
Inventory.	268,000	Cash	32,400
Common stock.	200,000	Accounts payable.	150,000
Prepaid insurance	5,800	Supplies	12,800
Retained earnings	?	Delivery equipment.	160,000

Required
Prepare a classified balance sheet as of December 31, 2016, for McKensie & Company.

LO1 **P4-2B.** **Preparing a Classified Balance Sheet** The following financial data for the St. John Corporation was collected as of December 31, 2016. All accounts have normal balances.

Accounts receivable.	$195,400	Furniture and equipment	$196,000
Accounts payable.	36,800	Cash	92,800
Prepaid insurance	600	Accumulated Depreciation—	
Common stock.	400,000	furniture and equipment	77,600
Retained earnings	?	Inventory.	175,000

Required
Prepare a classified balance sheet as of December 31, 2016.

LO2 **P4-3B.** **Multi-step Income Statement** The adjusted trial balance of Marshall Corporation on December 31, 2016, is shown below.

Marshall Corporation
Adjusted Trial Balance
December 31, 2016

	Debit	Credit
Cash.	$ 50,400	
Accounts receivable.	95,200	
Inventory.	87,000	
Prepaid insurance	1,300	
Furniture and fixtures	32,000	
Accumulated depreciation—furniture and fixtures.		$ 6,800
Delivery equipment.	66,000	
Accumulated depreciation—delivery equipment		34,000
Accounts payable.		17,400
Common stock.		208,000
Retained earnings		59,600
Sales revenue.		371,200
Cost of goods sold.	214,800	
Salaries expense	97,000	
Rent expense.	20,800	
Utilities expense.	6,800	
Insurance expense.	1,500	
Depreciation expense—furniture and fixtures	3,200	
Depreciation expense—delivery equipment	18,000	
Income tax expense.	3,000	
	$697,000	$697,000

Required

Prepare a multi-step income statement for the year ended December 31, 2016. Combine all the operating expenses into one line on the income statement for selling, general and administrative expenses.

P4-4B. **Preparing the Financial Statements** Listed below are items reported on the financial statements of the Manhattan Company as of June 30, 2016: LO1, 6

Cash flow provided by operating activities	$ 45,000	Other long-term assets	$ 35,000
Cash at June 30, 2015	18,000	Cash flow from financing activities.	2,600
Cash at June 30, 2016	35,000	Current liabilities.	44,000
Inventory.	12,000	Long-term liabilities	36,500
Accounts receivable.	24,400	Intangible assets	19,000
Cash flow from investing activities.	(30,600)	Common stock.	102,000
Other current assets.	3,000	Retained earnings	?
Property, plant and equipment.	85,000		

Required

Prepare a classified balance sheet as of June 30, 2016, and statement of cash flows for 2016.

P4-5B. **Assessing a Firm's Profitability, Liquidity and Solvency** Presented below is financial data for the Miller Company as of year-end 2015 and 2016: LO3, 4

	2015	2016
Current assets	$ 80,000	$120,000
Total assets	250,000	350,000
Current liabilities.	60,000	140,000
Total liabilities.	160,000	230,000
Net sales	265,000	375,000
Net income	36,000	51,500

Required

Calculate Miller's current ratio, debt-to-total-assets ratio, and return on sales ratio. Comment on the trend in the company's profitability, liquidity, and solvency from 2015 to 2016.

P4-6B. **Profitability and the Income Statement** Presented below are income statement data for VanPool & Company for 2016: LO2, 4

Income tax expense.	$11,000	Sales revenue	$118,000
Cost of goods sold.	25,000	Operating expenses.	52,000
Other expenses	2,000		

Required

Prepare a multi-step income statement for 2016 and calculate the company's return on sales ratio. If VanPool's return on sales was 26 percent in 2015, did the company's profitability increase or decrease in 2016?

P4-7B. **Preparing a Statement of Stockholders' Equity** Presented below is financial data for Thomas & Co. as of December 31, 2016: LO5

Cash.	$ 19,000	Inventory.	$ 14,000
Retained earnings, Jan. 1, 2016.	26,000	Net income.	60,000
Building	50,000	Stockholders' equity, Jan. 1, 2016.	146,000
Common stock.	120,000	Retained earnings, Dec. 31, 2016	?
Accrued expenses payable	8,000	Stockholders' equity, Dec. 31, 2016 . . .	181,000
Dividends paid	25,000		

Required

Prepare a statement of stockholders' equity as of December 31, 2016.

LO3, 4   P4-8B.   Interpreting Profitability, Liquidity, and Solvency Ratios Presented below is financial data for two furniture manufacturing companies:

	Company B	Company D
Return on sales ratio	9.0%	10.9%
Current ratio	1.9	1.0
Debt-to-total-assets ratio	41%	59%

Required

Consider the financial data of the two companies. Which company represents the better investment opportunity in your opinion and why?

LO3, 4   P4-9B.   Ratio Analysis The following balances were reported in the financial statements for Ruby Company.

	2016	2015
Net sales	$1,650,000	$1,750,000
Net income	170,000	205,000
Current assets	410,000	535,000
Current liabilities	170,000	210,000
Total liabilities	500,000	675,000
Total assets	1,550,000	2,450,000

Required

1. Compute the following ratios for 2016 and 2015 for Ruby Company.
    a.   Return on sales ratio
    b.   Current ratio
    c.   Debt-to-total-assets ratio
2. Comment on changes to Ruby Company's profitability, liquidity, and solvency.

LO2   P4-10B.   Multi-step Income Statement and Adjusting Entries Oregon Distributors, whose accounting year ends on December 31, had the following normal balances in its ledger accounts at December 31:

Cash	$ 45,750	Common stock	$ 125,000
Accounts receivable	92,000	Retained earnings	42,000
Inventory	84,400	Sales revenue	1,165,000
Prepaid insurance	7,200	Cost of goods sold	822,200
Office supplies	4,800	Utilities expense	5,600
Furniture and fixtures	28,000	Sales salaries expense	108,000
Accumulated depreciation—		Delivery expense	36,800
furniture and fixtures	10,800	Advertising expense	28,200
Delivery equipment	70,000	Rent expense	30,000
Accumulated depreciation—		Office salaries expense	72,000
delivery equipment	24,400		
Accounts payable	69,400		
Long-term notes payable	30,000		
Income tax expense	12,000		

During the year, the accounting department prepared monthly statements, but no adjusting entries were made in the journals and ledgers. Data for the year-end procedures are as follows:

1. Prepaid insurance, December 31, was $2,600
2. Depreciation expense on furniture and fixtures for the year was $3,000
3. Depreciation expense on delivery equipment for the year was $10,000
4. Salaries payable, December 31, ($2,000 sales and $800 office) was $2,800
5. Office supplies on hand, December 31, were $1,800

Required

a. Record the necessary adjusting entries in general journal form at December 31.

b. Prepare a multi-step income statement for the year. Combine all the operating expenses into one line on the income statement for selling, general and administrative expenses.

SERIAL PROBLEM: KATE'S CARDS

(Note: This is a continuation of the Serial Problem: Kate's Cards from Chapter 3.)

SP4. In order to learn more about the industry and to meet people who could give her advice, Kate attended several industry trade shows. At the most recent trade show, Kate was introduced to Fred Abbott, operations manager of "Sentiments," a national card distributor. After much discussion, Fred asked Kate to consider being one of Sentiments' card suppliers. He provided Kate with a copy of the company's recent financial statements. Fred indicated that he expects that Kate will need to supply Sentiments with approximately 50 card designs per month. Kate is to send Sentiments a monthly invoice, and she will be paid approximately 30 days from the date the invoice is received in Sentiments' corporate office. Naturally, Kate was thrilled with this offer, since this will certainly give her business a big boost.

Required

Kate has several questions. Answer the following questions for Kate.

a. What type of information does each of Sentiments' financial statements provide to Kate?

b. What financial statements would Kate need to evaluate whether Sentiments will have enough cash to meet its current liabilities? Explain what to look for.

c. What financial statement would Kate need to evaluate whether Sentiments will be able to survive over a long period of time? Explain what to look for.

d. What financial statement would Kate need to evaluate Sentiments' profitability? Explain what to look for.

e. Where can Kate find out whether Sentiments has outstanding debt? How can Kate determine whether Sentiments will be able to meet its interest and principal payments on any debts that it has?

f. How could Kate determine whether Sentiments pays a dividend?

g. In deciding whether to go ahead with this opportunity, are there other areas of concern that Kate should be aware of?

EXTENDING YOUR KNOWLEDGE

REPORTING AND ANALYSIS

EYK4-1. **Financial Reporting Problem: Columbia Sportswear Company** The financial statements for **Columbia Sportswear** can be found in Appendix A at the end of this textbook.

Required

Answer the following questions using the Consolidated Balance Sheet and the Notes to the consolidated financial statements:

a. What were the combined totals of Columbia's liabilities and stockholders' equity for 2014 and 2013?

b. How do these amounts compare with Columbia's total assets for each year?

c. What was the largest, in dollar value, of Columbia's assets each year? What does this asset represent?

d. What is the balance of accrued liabilities made up of?

EYK4-2. **Comparative Analysis Problem: Columbia Sportswear Company vs. Under Armour, Inc.** The financial statements for **Columbia Sportswear** can be found in Appendix A and **Under Armour**'s financial statements can be found in Appendix B at the end of this textbook.

Required

a. Calculate for each company the following ratios for 2014:
    1. Current ratio
    2. Debt-to-total-assets ratio
    3. Return on sales ratio
b. Comment on the companies' relative profitability, liquidity, and solvency.

EYK4-3. **Business Decision Problem** Diskman, a maker of computer memory devices, reports the following information in its financial statements. Assume that you are a loan officer at a major bank and have been assigned the task of evaluating whether to extend a loan for a plant expansion to the company.

(in millions)	2016	2015	2014
Current assets	$ 4,356	$4,033	$2,915
Total assets	10,175	8,777	6,002
Current liabilities	1,093	960	871
Total liabilities	3,114	2,997	2,093
Retained earnings	1,797	813	(487)
Net sales	5,662	4,827	3,567
Cost of goods sold	3,223	2,565	2,282
Net income	987	1,300	415
Cash flow from operating activities	1,054	1,452	488
Cash flow from investing activities	(667)	(2,715)	(375)
Cash flow from financing activities	(48)	991	25
Expenditures for property, plant, and equipment	(193)	(108)	(60)

Required

a. Calculate the company's current ratio, debt-to-total-assets ratio, return on sales ratio, and free cash flow for each year.
b. Comment on Diskman's liquidity, solvency, and profitability.
c. Based on what you have learned about Diskman, would you recommend offering the company a loan?

EYK4-4. **Financial Analysis Problem** As part of your internship at Walleys Inc. you have been assigned the job of developing a few important ratios from the company's financial statements. This information is intended to be used by the company to help Walleys obtain a large bank loan. In particular, the data will need to convince the bank that Walleys is a good loan risk based on its liquidity, solvency, and profitability. Below are the data you pulled together:

	2016	2015
Current ratio	2.2:1	1.5:1
Debt-to-total-assets ratio	57 percent	63 percent
Return on sales ratio	9.3 percent	9.1 percent
Free cash flow	Up 17 percent	Up 19 percent
Net income	Up 15 percent	Down 12 percent

Required

Prepare brief comments that discuss how each of these items can be used to support the argument that Walleys is showing improving financial health.

CRITICAL THINKING

GENERAL MILLS, INC.

EYK4-5. **Accounting Research Problem** Go to this book's Website and locate the annual report of **General Mills, Inc.** for the year ending May 25, 2014 (fiscal year 2014).

Required

1. Calculate the company's return on sales for 2012, 2013, and 2014. What is the trend?
2. Calculate the company's current asset ratio for 2013 and 2014. What is the trend?

3. Calculate the company's debt-to-total-assets ratio for 2013 and 2014. What is the trend?

4. Calculate the company's free cash flow for 2012, 2013, and 2014. What is the trend?

EYK4-6. **Accounting Communication Activity** V. J. Simmons is the President of Forward Engineering Associates. He is a very good engineer, but his accounting knowledge is quite limited.

Required

V. J. has heard that ratio analysis can help him determine the financial condition of his company. In particular, he would like you to explain to him in a memo how to calculate and interpret the following three ratios: (1) return on sales ratio, (2) current ratio, and (3) debt-to-total-assets ratio. Prepare a memo for V.J.

EYK4-7. **Accounting Ethics Case** In the post-Enron environment, and with the enactment of the Sarbanes-Oxley legislation, many firms are proactively portraying themselves as being "ethical." Ethical behavior is, for example, part of the Corporate Social Responsibility movement. This behavior includes many dimensions, from the ethical treatment of employees and the environment, to ethical financial reporting. Academic research has found a positive correlation between a firm's reputation and its financial performance. Do you feel that strong ethics makes good business sense? Why do you think that there is a positive correlation between ethical behavior and successful corporate financial performance?

EYK4-8. **Corporate Social Responsibility Problem** Many investors consider past performance, fees, and investment objectives as the sole criteria for selecting a mutual fund for investment purposes. A growing number of investors are also asking about the actions and philosophies of the companies that form a fund's underlying investment portfolio. Socially responsible mutual funds have been developed to fill this need. These funds are designed for investors who want to align their investments with their religious, political, or social convictions.

Because there is no universally accepted definition as to what makes a company responsible or an investment a socially responsible investment, socially responsible funds are quite diverse. Not surprisingly different funds may take opposite positions on certain controversial issues such as family planning, gay rights, or animal testing.

For the most part, socially responsible funds select their underlying investment firms through either a negative filter or a positive filter. A negative filter is used to screen out firms that are not considered acceptable to the positions advocated by the fund. Examples of firms that may be screened out include firms that are involved in gambling, alcohol, tobacco, or weapons. A positive filter is used to include firms that are seen to be leaders in areas advocated by the fund, such as environmental, diversity, or human rights records.

Required

a. Go to the Websites of three socially responsible mutual funds
1. Calvert Signature Funds: http://www.calvertgroup.com/sri-signature.html
2. Domini Social Equity Fund: http://www.domini.com/domini-funds/Domini-Social-Equity-Fund/index.htm
3. Green Century Balanced Fund: http://www.greencentury.com/funds/Green-Century-Balanced-Fund

b. Compare the screening criteria used by each fund. How do they differ and how are they alike?

EYK4-9. **Forensic Accounting Problem** Debra Day, a business major at a local college, was recently hired for the summer at Sweet Delights, a popular ice cream parlor near the campus. Debra spent most of her time tending the cash register where she noticed that most of the customers paid in cash and never seemed to care about getting a receipt. Debra soon figured out that she could ring up a much lesser amount on the register, charge the customer the full amount, then toss the receipt. For example, on a $7 order she would charge and collect the full $7 from the customer, but only ring up $5. She would then deposit $5 in the register so that it would agree with the register tape and pocket the $2.

Required

a. What type of fraud is Debra committing?

b.   The store manager recently hired you as a forensic accountant to critique the controls at Sweet Delights. He has noticed that while the store seems as busy as ever, and the cash in the register agrees with the tapes, the store is not as profitable as it previously was. What control would you recommend to help prevent the type of fraud being committed by Debra?

LOGITECH INTERNATIONAL

EYK4-10.   Working with the Takeaways   Throughout this chapter we have considered the financial statements of Apple Inc. and have undertaken select financial analysis using the Takeaways. Utilize these same tools to analyze the financial data of **Logitech International**, a manufacturer of computer peripherals. The following information was reported by Logitech in the company's financial statements as of year-end March 31, 2014 and 2013:

March 31 (in millions)	2014	2013
Current assets	$ 933	$ 847
Total assets	1,451	1,382
Current liabilities	455	462
Total liabilities	647	660
Net sales	2,128	2,099
Net income	74	(228)
Cash provided by operating activities	205	122
Expenditures on property, plant, and equipment	47	54

Required

1.   Calculate the return on sales ratio for each year and comment on Logitech's profitability.
2.   Calculate the current ratio for each year and comment on Logitech's liquidity.
3.   Calculate the debt-to-total-assets ratio for each year and comment on Logitech's solvency.
4.   Calculate the free cash flow for each year and comment on what this means for Logitech.
5.   Apple's fiscal year-end occurs near the end of September, whereas Logitech uses a March year-end. How might this affect a comparison of the financial results of the two companies?

EYK4-11.   Evaluating Firm Liquidity, Solvency, Profitability and Free Cash Flow: IFRS Financial Statements   The 2014 financial statements of LVMH Moet Hennessey-Louis Vuitton S.A. are presented in Appendix C at the end of this book. LVMH is a Paris-based holding company and one of the world's largest and best-known luxury goods companies. As a member of the European Union, French companies are required to prepare their consolidated (group) financial statements using International Financial Reporting Standards (IFRS). Using this financial data, calculate the company's (a) return on sales ratio using net profit, group share, (b) current ratio, (c) debt-to-total-assets ratio, and (d) free cash flow for 2013 and 2014. Comment on the trend in LVMH's liquidity, solvency, profitability, and free cash flow from 2013 to 2014.

ANSWERS TO SELF-STUDY QUESTIONS:

1. b, (pp. 190–193) 2. c, (pp. 190–191) 3. c, (p. 190) 4. d, (pp. 192–193) 5. b, (p. 193) 6. d, (p. 198)
7. d, (p. 199) 8. b, (p. 202) 9. c, (p. 202) 10. d, (p. 203) 11. a, (p. 199) 12. b, (p. 203) 13. b, (pp. 195–196)

YOUR TURN! SOLUTIONS

Solution 4.1

MUSICLAND COMPANY BALANCE SHEET DECEMBER 31, 2016	
Assets	
Current assets	
Cash	$ 300
Accounts receivable	3,000
Inventory	12,200
Other current assets	1,500
Total current assets	17,000
Property, plant, & equipment, net	25,000
Total assets	$42,000
Liabilities and Stockholders' Equity	
Current liabilities	
Accounts payable	$ 2,500
Other current liabilities	2,000
Total current liabilities	4,500
Long-term notes payable	20,000
Total liabilities	24,500
Stockholders' equity	17,500
Total liabilities and stockholders' equity	$42,000

Solution 4.2

Musicland Company Income Statement For Year Ended December 31, 2016	
Net sales	$100,000
Less Cost of goods sold	45,000
Gross profit on sales	55,000
Operating expenses	
Selling, general and administrative	25,000
Research and development expenses	10,000
Total operating expenses	35,000
Income from operations	20,000
Other income and expense	
Interest expense	5,000
Income before income taxes	15,000
Income tax expense	4,500
Net income	$ 10,500

Solution 4.3

	2016	2015
Current ratio	$\dfrac{75,000}{50,000} = 1.50:1$	$\dfrac{65,000}{45,000} = 1.44:1$
Debt-to-total-assets ratio	$\dfrac{150,000}{220,000} = 68.2\%$	$\dfrac{145,000}{190,000} = 76.3\%$

The Philips Company has improved its performance on both measures. Both its liquidity as reflected by the current ratio and its solvency as reflected by the debt-to-total-assets ratio are trending in a positive direction (the current ratio is increasing and the debt-to-total assets ratio is decreasing).

Solution 4.4

	2016	2015
Return on sales	$\dfrac{20,000}{120,000} = 16.7\%$	$\dfrac{15,000}{110,000} = 13.6\%$

The Philips Company has improved its performance from 2015 to 2016. The company is earning a higher amount of net income on every dollar of sales revenue as indicated by its return on sales ratio.

Solution 4.5

	2016	2015
Free cash flow	$25,000 - 7,000 = 18,000$	$22,000 - 6,000 = 16,000$

The Philips Company has improved its performance from 2015 to 2016. The company has more cash for a possible plant expansion as seen in its increasing free cash flow.

5 Accounting for Merchandising Operations

PAST

Chapters 1 through 4 explained the five-step accounting cycle: analyze, record, adjust, report, and close.

PRESENT

This chapter focuses on analyzing and recording merchandising transactions.

FUTURE

Chapter 6 describes the accounting for inventory, including cost assumptions, the lower of cost or market approach, and inventory analysis.

LEARNING OBJECTIVES

1. **Explain** the operations of a merchandising company and **contrast** that with the operations of a service company. *(p. 234)*

2. **Describe** the accounting for purchases of merchandise. *(p. 237)*

3. **Describe** the accounting for sales of merchandise. *(p. 241)*

4. **Define** the gross profit percentage and the return on sales ratio, and **explain** their use in profitability analysis. *(p. 245)*

5. Appendix 5A: **Describe** and **illustrate** a periodic inventory system. *(p. 249)*

6. Appendix 5B: **Describe** and **illustrate** the new revenue recognition standard. *(p. 253)*

TARGET

Target Corporation is one of the largest merchandising companies in the world with almost 1,800 stores and with sales of over $70 billion. Target sells products, often referred to as *inventory*. However, Target does not manufacture or make its inventory. Instead, it buys this inventory from manufacturers such as **Sony** and **Panasonic**, and then resells that inventory to consumers. Some refer to companies such as Target as "middlemen."

Target's recent balance sheet reports that it carries nearly $9 billion in inventory, which is about 62 percent of its total current assets. Further, Target's income statement shows that its cost of goods (or inventory) sold of $51 billion makes up 75 percent of its total operating expenses. Target must track all of these purchases and sales of its inventory.

This chapter describes the most common inventory system that merchandisers apply in today's business world. This system *perpetually* tracks all purchases and sales of inventory. Such tracking is important for managers to effectively manage this key asset and to regularly compute measures that report on management's ability to generate profit from inventory.

ACCOUNTING FOR MERCHANDISING OPERATIONS					
Merchandising	**Accounting for Purchases of Merchandise**	**Accounting for Sales of Merchandise**	**Profitability Analysis**	**Periodic Inventory System (Appendix 5A)**	**New Revenue Recognition Standard (Appendix 5B)**
• Operating cycle • Cost flows • Inventory systems—perpetual and periodic	• Transportation costs • Purchase returns and allowances • Purchase discounts • Credit period	• Sales returns and allowances • Sales discounts • Net sales	• Gross profit percentage • Return on sales ratio	• Purchases of merchandise • Sales of merchandise • Comparing periodic and perpetual systems • Cost of good sold using a periodic system	• Sales discounts • Sales returns and allowances

eLectures
MBC

THE NATURE OF MERCHANDISING

LO1 **Explain** the operations of a merchandising company and **contrast** that with the operations of a service company.

Manufacturers, wholesalers, and retailers are companies that sell products rather than services. Wholesalers and retailers are both merchandising firms. **Merchandising firms** buy finished products, warehouse and display the products for varying periods of time, and then resell the products. Merchandising firms do not manufacture products nor do they consume the products that they purchase. Merchandising firms provide additional services to their customers, but their primary business is the resale of goods produced by other companies. **Exhibit 5-1** illustrates the typical relationship among these three types of companies and the final consumer.

Exhibit 5-1	**Distribution of Products to Individual Consumers**

Manufacturer   Wholesaler and/or Retailer   Consumer

These are *Merchandising companies.*
They resell; they do not manufacture
or consume products as part of their
business activities.

Manufacturers convert raw materials and component parts into a finished product through the application of skilled labor and machine operations. **Ford Motor Company**, for example, converts raw materials such as sheets of steel and components such as tires into automobiles and trucks. Similarly, **Del Monte** converts raw materials such as fresh peaches and components such as metal cans into canned peaches. Manufacturers typically only sell their products to wholesale distributors. This process is referred to as a business-to-business or "B2B" transaction.

Wholesalers buy finished products from manufacturing firms in large quantities. The wholesale distributor then sells and ships the product to various retailers in smaller quantities to satisfy the local demand for the product. Some wholesalers handle the products of only one manufacturer, while others handle the products of many manufacturers. **Retailers** typically buy products from wholesale distributors and resell the finished products to individual consumers in what is referred to as a business-to-consumer transaction (a B2C transaction). Retailers often have multiple store locations, including the Internet, where they display the products they are offering for sale, enabling customers to view and buy the products. Radio, television, newspaper, and online advertisements inform potential customers of product availability and price. Retailers may range in size from small, with only one store location, to large, with thousands of store locations along with an online Website, such as **Target.com**.

Operating Cycle of a Merchandising Firm

Exhibit 5-2 presents the operating cycle of a merchandising firm. There are three primary transactions involved in a merchandising firm's operating cycle: ❶ the purchase of merchandise and its placement in inventory; ❷ the removal of merchandise from inventory when sold and delivered to the customer; and ❸ the receipt of cash from the customer in payment for a cash-and-carry or prior credit purchase. These transactions involve three current asset accounts: cash, accounts receivable, and inventory. The purchased merchandise becomes part of the retailer's inventory until sold; an account receivable is created when the inventory is sold to a customer on credit; and, cash is received when the customer pays for the previously purchased goods. In cases where a customer pays immediately with cash for the purchased merchandise, no accounts receivable is created.

Exhibit 5-2	Comparison of Operating Cycle for a Merchandising Firm and a Service Firm

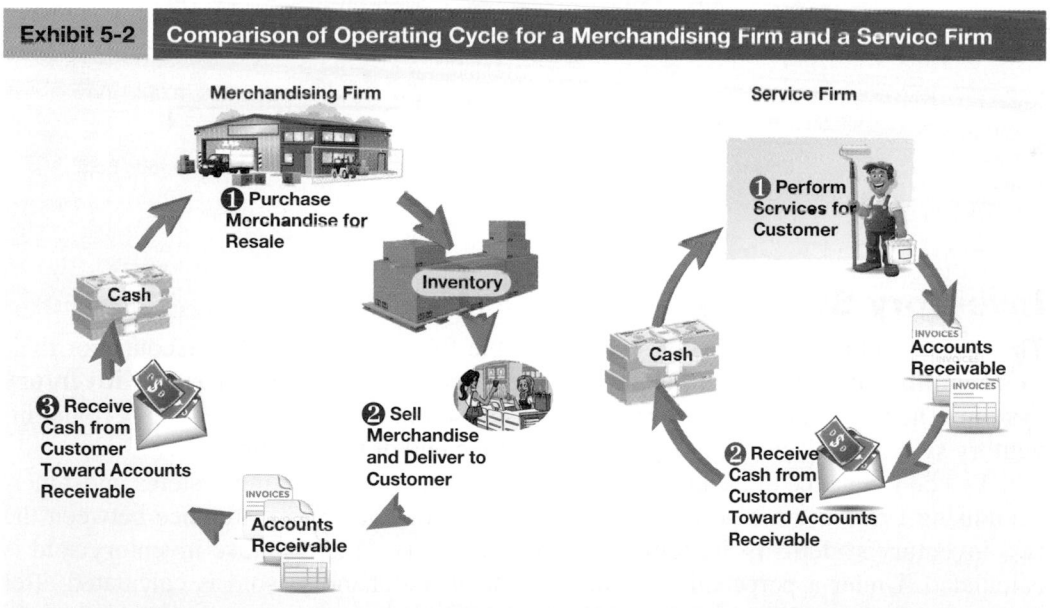

In contrast, there are only two primary transactions involved in the operating cycle of a service firm: ❶ performing a service, and ❷ receiving cash from the customer. Service firms have no inventory to warehouse or display, and consequently, the length of their operating cycle is typically much shorter than that of a merchandising firm.

The three primary transactions for a merchandising firm repeat frequently, creating the cycle depicted in **Exhibit 5-2**. The timing of the cash collection depends upon the credit terms associated with the sale. When a wholesaler sells to a retailer, a B2B transaction, the sale is usually concluded on a credit basis. That is, the retailer is allowed some period of time following the sale, frequently 30 days or more, to pay the wholesaler for the purchased goods. Some retailers call a credit sale a **sale on account** (also referred to as **sale on credit**). "On account" means on a credit basis.

When retailers such as **Nordstrom** sell to individual consumers, the consumer can (1) pay cash at the time of the sale; (2) use a credit card such as **Discover**, **MasterCard**, or **Visa**; or (3) use an "open account" with the retailer. An **open account** is a charge account provided by a retailer for its customers. Many retailers such as Nordstrom have their own branded credit card to facilitate open account sales. If a customer pays cash, the retailer receives cash immediately. If the customer uses a major credit card issued by a financial institution like **Citibank**, the retailer transmits the credit card information to the card-issuing financial institution and collects the cash either on the same day or within a few days following the credit-sale transaction. If the customer uses an open account, the retailer may not collect the cash from the customer for 30 to 60 days or longer, depending upon the length of the credit terms allowed by the retailer.

Cost Flows

The costs of inventory for merchandisers all flow through its accounting system as diagrammed below. Specifically, a company records its *costs of goods purchased* and adds this to any *beginning inventory* it might have. These two components make up the company's *cost of goods available for sale*. From that total, a company either sells part or all of this inventory, which is recorded in *cost of goods sold*, or carries some of its inventory into the next period, referred to as its *ending inventory*.

The mathematical representation of this cost flow relation is:

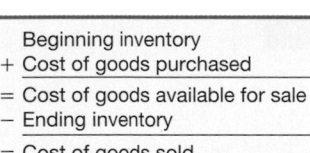

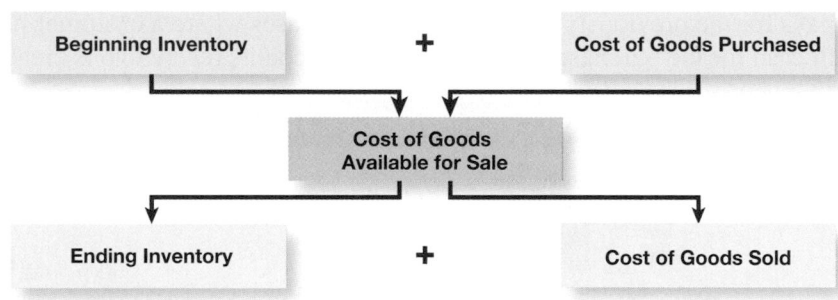

Inventory Systems

There are two basic inventory systems available for merchandisers to account for their **merchandise inventory**: the **perpetual inventory system** and the **periodic inventory system**. The perpetual inventory system is discussed in this chapter, and the periodic inventory system is discussed in Appendix 5A at the end of this chapter.

As a consequence of the growing use of computerized accounting systems, most merchandising firms use the perpetual inventory system. The main difference between the two inventory systems is the timing of when the cost of merchandise inventory sold is calculated. Under a perpetual system, the cost of merchandise sold is calculated after every sale, and consequently, the inventory balance is kept "perpetually" up-to-date. In contrast, under a periodic system, the cost of merchandise sold is only calculated "periodically" when a physical count of the inventory is done. A physical inventory count is time consuming and usually occurs only at the end of a fiscal period. As a consequence, the actual inventory balance remains unknown until the end of a fiscal period.

A major advantage of the perpetual system is the increased control it provides over the inventory. Since the inventory is being continuously updated, management is able to determine whether current inventory levels are adequate to satisfy pending or expected sales. In addition, having a record of exactly how much inventory is available allows management to compare these amounts to a physical count of the inventory. Management can then investigate any difference between the amounts to identify the presence of theft or spoilage (in the case of perishable goods).

Which of the following statements is false?

a. There are three primary transactions involved in a merchandising firm's operating cycle.

b. The sum of beginning inventory plus the cost of goods purchased is equal to the cost of goods sold.

c. The two basic inventory systems are the perpetual inventory system and the periodic inventory system.

d. Manufacturers convert raw materials and component parts into finished goods.

YOUR TURN! 5.1

The solution is on page 271.

ACCOUNTING FOR PURCHASES OF MERCHANDISE

When a company using the perpetual inventory system purchases merchandise, it debits the Inventory account for the acquisition cost of the merchandise purchased to reflect an increase in the amount of inventory and credits the Accounts Payable account to reflect an increase in the amount owed to the supplier. For example, the Barton Wholesale Electronics' purchase invoice for inventory shown in **Exhibit 5-3** requires Barton to record the company's purchase of merchandise from Malibu Manufacturing on November 10 with the following journal entry:

LO2 **Describe** the accounting for purchases of merchandise.

Nov. 10	Inventory	21,000	
	Accounts payable		21,000
	To record the purchase of 100 disk drives from Malibu Manufacturing with credit terms of 2/10, n/30.		

A = L + SE
+21,000 +21,000

Transportation Costs

Transportation Costs Incurred by Buyer

Transportation costs are sometimes incurred by a merchandising company when it acquires goods, and this cost is included as part of the acquisition cost of the inventory. When the buyer is responsible for shipping costs, it is referred to as **FOB shipping point**. An example of an invoice that specifies the shipping and payment terms is shown in **Exhibit 5-3**. (Shipping terms are explained further in Chapter 6.) Assume Barton (buyer) pays $126 to a freight company on November 11, for transportation costs on the 100 disk drives purchased from Malibu Manufacturing (seller). Barton makes the following journal entry to record the payment of $126:

Nov. 11	Inventory	126	
	Cash		126
	To record the payment of $126 of transportation costs for the purchase of 100 disk drives.		

A = L + SE
+126

−126

| Exhibit 5-3 | Invoice for Inventory Purchase |

INVOICE

Malibu Manufacturing
100 Computer Way
Claremont, CA 91711
909-607-6064
Fax 909-610-1234
sales@malibu.com

Date: November 10, 2016
Invoice # 1050

SHIP TO: George Jones
Barton Wholesale Electronics
100 Main Street
Anytown, CA 91234
123-456-7890
Customer ID ABC12345

SALESPERSON	SHIPPING METHOD	SHIPPING TERMS	DELIVERY DATE	PAYMENT TERMS
Kate Kanzu	UPS	FOB Shipping Point	Nov 12, 2016	2/10, n/30

QUANTITY	ITEM #	DESCRIPTION	UNIT PRICE	DISCOUNT	LINE TOTAL
100	A30	1.5 TB Disk Drives	210		$21,000
				Total	$21,000

Make all checks payable to Malibu Manufacturing.
Thank you for your business.

| PRINCIPLE ALERT | **Cost Principle** |

The inclusion of transportation cost in the acquisition cost of inventory is consistent with the *cost principle*. The cost principle states that an asset is initially recorded at the amount paid to acquire the asset. There can be multiple expenditures associated with an asset acquisition, and all expenditures that are reasonable and necessary to acquire an asset are added to the asset's initial recorded cost.

Transportation Costs Incurred by Seller

When the seller is responsible for shipping costs, it is referred to as **FOB destination**. Instead of the shipping terms stated in the invoice above, assume that the seller, Malibu Manufacturing, is responsible for and paid the $126 transportation costs. In this case the transportation cost would be considered an operating expense of the seller, and Malibu Manufacturing would debit an expense account titled Freight-out Expense as follows:

A	=	L	+	SE			
−126				−126 Exp			

Nov. 11	Freight-out expense	126	
	Cash		126
	To record payment for the transportation cost for goods sold.		

Malibu paid the freight charges on the Barton purchase of disk drives, and it will attempt to pass on this cost to the buyer in the form of a higher sales price for the items purchased.

Purchase Returns and Allowances

Occasionally, a purchaser is dissatisfied with some or all of the merchandise purchased because the merchandise was, for example, manufactured poorly, the wrong merchandise was shipped, or the merchandise was damaged during shipping. When such circumstances are encountered, the purchaser and the seller can remedy the problem by agreeing to treat the value of the unwanted items either as a purchase return or as a purchase allowance.

With a **purchase return**, the purchaser ships the unsatisfactory merchandise back to the seller and receives a credit against the amount due equal to the **invoice price** of the returned merchandise. With a **purchase allowance**, the purchaser retains the merchandise, and the seller reduces the amount that the purchaser owes the seller for the shipment, in effect reducing the sales price.

As an example of a purchase return, assume that on November 15, Barton returns 10 of the 100 disk drives purchased on November 10. Barton has not yet paid Malibu Manufacturing for the goods purchased. Accordingly, Barton makes the following journal entry on November 15 to record the purchase return:

Nov. 15	Accounts payable	2,100		
	Inventory		2,100	A = L + SE
	To record a purchase return of 10 disk drives at an invoice price of			−2,100 −2,100
	$210 each to Malibu Manufacturing.			

This entry reduces the Inventory account balance and reduces the amount owed. When the purchaser and seller reach agreement on how to handle a purchase return, they also must agree on which party pays the freight charges on the returned merchandise. (Usually the seller pays freight charges when goods are returned, in an attempt to maintain a positive customer relationship and to increase the likelihood of future repeat business.)

Bar Codes ACCOUNTING IN PRACTICE

Merchandisers often use bar codes with computerized inventory systems to account for inventory. The merchandiser prints bar codes on the outside of cartons containing the merchandise, enabling clerks with bar code scanners or robots with built-in scanners to read the codes to identify and trace the contents of cartons as they move into and out of warehouses and trucks.

1234567890

Purchase Discounts

Credit Period

When merchandise is sold on credit, the **credit period** is the maximum amount of time, often stated in days, that a purchaser can take to pay a seller for the purchased items. A typical credit period for a wholesale distributor is 30 days. The credit period is frequently described as the *net credit period*, or net terms. Merchandisers use the notation "**n/**" followed by the number of days in the credit period to designate the time period that a customer can take before paying cash for purchased goods. For example, **n/30** indicates a credit period of 30 days, and n/45 indicates a credit period of 45 days.

To encourage the early payment of unpaid bills, many firms offer their customers a cash discount if payment is made within a designated discount period. A **cash discount**, or **sales discount**, is the amount that the seller deducts from the invoice price if payment is made within the allowed discount period. Some refer to the cash discount offered to credit customers as a "quick-pay incentive." Sellers usually state cash discounts as a percent of the invoice price. The **discount period** is the maximum amount of time, stated in days, that a purchaser has to pay the seller if the purchaser wants to claim the cash discount. The discount period is always shorter than the credit period. Most merchandisers use the format "cash discount percent/discount period" to designate the cash discount and the discount period. For example, 1/10 indicates a cash discount of one percent of the invoice price and a discount period of ten days following the invoice date. Finally, merchandisers usually combine the notation for the cash discount and the discount period with the notation for the credit period. For example, 1/10, n/30 represents a cash discount of one percent if paid within ten days of the sale with a total credit period of 30 days following the date of the sale.

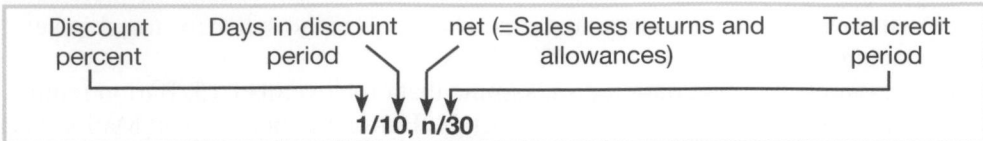

To illustrate, let's return to the Barton example in which Malibu Manufacturing and Barton agree on terms of 2/10, n/30, for the sale on November 10. Barton deducts two percent of the $21,000 invoice price ($420) if it pays Malibu by November 20. In that case, Barton pays $20,580 cash [computed as $21,000 \times (1 - 0.02)$]. If Barton pays Malibu after November 20 but no later than December 10, the amount that Barton must pay is $21,000. After December 10, the $21,000 amount would become overdue and often incurs additional interest cost depending on the invoice terms. **Exhibit 5-4** illustrates this example.

Discounts are normally attractive to merchandisers. For instance, if Barton did not take the discount offered by Malibu, this is like Barton paying an interest rate of 2 percent on the $21,000 for 20 days (30-day credit period − 10-day discount period). This is similar to paying an annual interest rate of 36.5 percent, computed as 2 percent $\times$ 365/20. Barton can borrow money at lower rates.

Exhibit 5-4	**Purchase Discounts**

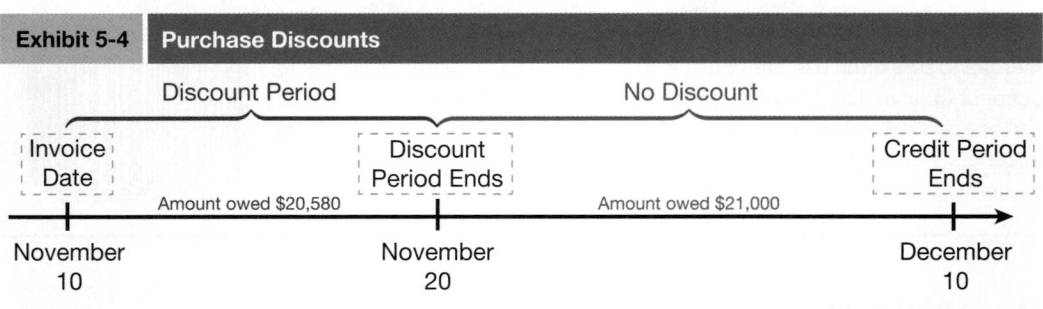

Accounting for Discounts

Let's extend the prior example where Barton owes $18,900 to Malibu Manufacturing; recall that Barton made a $21,000 purchase, then had a $2,100 purchase return, yielding an amount owed of $18,900. See T-account in the margin.

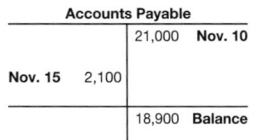

Pay Within Discount Period   Assume that Barton makes a cash payment to Malibu on November 20, the last day of the discount period. (November 11, the first day following the date of sale, is the first day of the discount period, and November 20 is the tenth or last day of the discount period.) Barton records the cash payment, less the cash discount, with the following journal entry:

A = L + SE	Nov. 20	Accounts payable	18,900	
−378 −18,900		Inventory		378
−18,522		Cash		18,522
		To record the purchase discount and payment to Malibu		
		Manufacturing within the discount period.		

This entry reduces to zero the amount that Barton owes Malibu Manufacturing. It also records the purchase discount of two percent ($18,900 $\times$ 2 percent = $378) as a reduction of the cost in the Inventory account. The entry reveals that $18,522 in cash was paid by Barton to Malibu Manufacturing ($18,900 − $378 = $18,522). Two aspects of this transaction should be noted. First, the cash discount applies only to the cost of the merchandise and not to the transportation cost. Second, the invoice price of the returned merchandise is subtracted from the total invoice price before the cash discount is calculated.

The net total cost reflected in Barton's Inventory account for the disk drives follows:

	Inventory				
Purchase (+100 units)	Nov 10	21,000			
Freight-in	Nov 11	126			
			2,100	Nov 15	Purchase return (−10 units)
			378	Nov 20	Purchase discount
	Balance	18,648			

A total cost of $18,648 is assigned to the 90 disk drives in Barton's inventory (100 purchased − 10 returned). This results in an average cost per disk drive of $207.20 ($18,648/90).

Pay After Discount Period If Barton made a cash payment to Malibu sometime between November 21 and December 10, after the discount period expired, Barton is not eligible to receive the two percent purchase discount. Consequently, Barton would record a full cash payment on November 25 with the following journal entry:

Nov. 25	Accounts payable	18,900	
	Cash		18,900
	To record full payment to Malibu Manufacturing following expiration of the discount period.		

A = L + SE
−18,900 −18,900

When Barton makes the payment to Malibu outside of the allowed discount period, the net total cost in Barton's Inventory account for the 90 disk drives is:

	Inventory				
Purchase (+100 units)	Nov 10	21,000			
Freight-in	Nov 11	126			
			2,100	Nov 15	Purchase return (−10 units)
	Balance	19,026			

A total cost of $19,026 is assigned to the 90 disk drives in Barton's inventory, resulting in an average cost per disk drive of $211.40 ($19,026/90). The cost per disk drive is higher in this situation because Barton did not make the payment for the inventory in a timely fashion to make it eligible for the cash discount.

On June 1, Musicland Inc. purchases 125 CDs at $4.08 each on account from its distributor for a total of $510. The credit terms of the purchase were 2/10 n/30. Also on June 1, Musicland paid freight charges of $22.18 cash for delivery of the CDs. On June 4, Musicland returned 15 defective CDs for an account credit of $61.20. On June 8, Musicland paid for the remaining 110 CDs. Record these transactions in journal entry form for Musicland.

YOUR TURN! 5.2

The solution is on page 271.

ACCOUNTING FOR SALES OF MERCHANDISE

Manufacturing firms and merchandising firms credit Sales Revenue when they sell products, regardless of whether the sales transaction is on credit or for cash. The Sales Revenue account has a normal credit balance.

LO3 Describe the accounting for sales of merchandise.

Let's return to our example and assume that Barton sells 15 disk drives purchased from Malibu Manufacturing (the assumed cost per unit = $18,648/90 disk drives = $207.20 per disk drive) to The Computer Outlet Store at a sales price of $280 per unit. Barton makes the credit sale on December 12, with terms of 1/10, n/15, and The

Computer Outlet Store pays shipping cost. Barton makes the following *two* journal entries to record the sale:

	A = L + SE			
	+4,200 +4,200 Rev			

Dec. 12	Accounts receivable		4,200	
	Sales revenue			4,200
	To record sale of 15 disk drives at a sales price of $280 each to The Computer Outlet Store with credit terms of 1/10, n/15.			

| | A = L + SE | | | |
| | −3,108 −3,108 Exp | | | |

Dec. 12	Cost of goods sold		3,108	
	Inventory			3,108
	To record sale of 15 disk drives with a unit cost of $207.20 to The Computer Outlet Store.			

A.K.A. Sales revenue is also referred to as *revenue*.

Revenue Side   The first journal entry records $4,200 of sales revenue ($280 × 15 disk drives) from the sale to Computer Outlet. The debit to Accounts Receivable increases the amount due from customers, and the credit to Sales Revenue increases the total revenue from sales of merchandise during the accounting period.

A.K.A. Cost of goods sold is often referred to as *COGS*.

A.K.A Cost of goods sold is also referred to as *cost of sales*.

Cost Side   The second journal entry transfers the $3,108 cost of merchandise sold ($207.20 × 15 disk drives) from the Inventory account, an asset account, to the Cost of Goods Sold account, an expense account. The debit to Cost of Goods Sold increases the total cost of merchandise sold during the accounting period, and the credit to Inventory removes the cost of the merchandise sold from the Inventory account. **Cost of goods sold** is the total cost of merchandise sold to customers during the accounting period.

After recording this sale, the net cost in Barton's Inventory account related to the disk drives is $15,540, as follows:

	Inventory				
Purchase (+100 units)	Nov 10	21,000	2,100	Nov 15	Purchase return (−10 units)
Freight-in	Nov 11	126	378	Nov 20	Purchase discount
			3,108	Dec 12	Cost of goods sold (−15 units)
	Balance	15,540			

The $15,540 cost relates to the 75 disk drives (100 purchased − 10 returned − 15 sold) remaining in inventory. The average cost per disk drive remains $207.20 ($15,540/75 disk drives).

PRINCIPLE ALERT	**Revenue and Expense Recognition**

The entry to record sales revenue when 15 disk drives are sold to The Computer Outlet Store illustrates the *revenue recognition principle*. For a merchandising firm, the revenue recognition principle states that revenue is recorded when goods are sold. Normally, this is the earliest point in time that the revenue is both earned (the company has delivered the goods) and realized (the company has received payment or has a claim to receive payment for the goods sold). The entry to record the cost of goods sold illustrates the *expense recognition (matching) principle*. Expense recognition states that expenses should be recorded in the same accounting period as the revenues they help generate.

Sales Returns and Allowances

When buyers have returns and allowances, there are sellers that must record those same returns and allowances. With a sales return, the customer ships the merchandise back to the seller and the customer receives a reduction in the amount due to the seller. For example, textbook publishers often allow college bookstores to return any unsold textbooks to publishers at the conclusion of a term. With a sales allowance, the customer retains the merchandise, and the seller reduces the amount the customer owes, in effect reducing the sales price.

Accounting for **sales returns** requires two journal entries. The first entry offsets the sales revenue generated from the transaction and reduces the amount owed by the customer. The second entry transfers the cost of merchandise from Cost of Goods Sold back to the Inventory account. In the case of a **sales allowance**, the goods are not returned to the seller. As a result, only the first of these two entries is required.

Extending the previous example, assume that on December 15, The Computer Outlet Store returned five of the disk drives that it had purchased on December 12. Computer Outlet returned the units because it ordered five units too many; there is nothing wrong with the disk drives. Barton records the sales return by making the following two journal entries:

Dec. 15	Sales returns and allowances	1,400	
	Accounts receivable		1,400
	To record the return of 5 disk drives by The Computer Outlet Store, with a sales price of $280 each.		

$$A \;=\; L \;+\; SE$$
$$ 1,400$$
$$-1,400 \text{Contra-Rev}$$

Dec. 15	Inventory	1,036	
	Cost of goods sold		1,036
	To record the return of 5 disk drives with a unit cost of $207.20 from The Computer Outlet Store.		

$$A \;=\; L \;+\; SE$$
$$ +1,036$$
$$+1,036 \text{Exp}$$

The first entry offsets the revenue generated from the sale by debiting Sales Returns and Allowances and it reduces the amount the customer owes by crediting Accounts Receivable. The Sales Returns and Allowances account is a *contra-revenue account* and is subtracted from gross sales revenue on the income statement.

The second journal entry transfers the cost of the merchandise from Cost of Goods Sold back to the Inventory account by debiting Inventory (increasing it) and by crediting Cost of Goods Sold (decreasing it). After recording the transfer from Cost of Goods Sold to Inventory, the net total cost in Barton's Inventory account related to the disk drives is:

Hint: *Contra accounts, such as the contra-revenue account, are useful because they provide more information than if the related account were used by itself. For example, by using both the revenue and the contra-revenue accounts, it is possible to track how much of the original sales have had associated returns or allowances.*

Inventory						
Purchase (+100 units)	Nov 10	21,000	2,100	Nov 15	Purchase return (−10 units)	
Freight-in	Nov 11	126	378	Nov 20	Purchase discount	
Sales return (+5 units)	Dec 15	1,036	3,108	Dec 12	Cost of goods sold (−15 units)	
	Balance	16,576				

The $16,576 total cost relates to 80 units (100 purchased − 10 purchase return − 15 sold + 5 sales return); and, the average cost of the inventory remains $207.20 ($16,576/80).

ACCOUNTING IN PRACTICE

Monitoring Sales Returns and Allowances

Companies accumulate sales revenue in one account and sales returns and allowances in another account so that they can separately monitor both types of activities. A high ratio of sales returns and allowances to sales revenue is undesirable, often indicating a problem in the quality of the merchandise or its packaging. A company can compare the ratio for the current year to prior-year ratios, or to a target ratio set for the current year, to determine how well the company is managing its product and packaging quality.

Sales Discounts

When making a cash payment for purchased goods, a customer is entitled to take a cash discount only if the payment is made during the allowed discount period. If a cash discount is taken, the seller records it in a separate account called Sales Discounts.

Pay Within Discount Period

Returning to the previous example, assume that The Computer Outlet Store agrees to terms of 1/10, n/15, and it then pays the amount due Barton after deducting the 1 percent cash discount on December 22, the last day of the cash discount period. (December 13 is the first day of the discount period, and December 22 is the tenth or last day of the discount period.) Barton makes the following journal entry to record the cash received from Computer Outlet:

A = L + SE
+2,772   −28
            Contra-
−2,800   Rev

Dec. 22	Cash	2,772	
	Sales discounts	28	
	Accounts receivable		2,800
	To record the sales discount and cash payment from The Computer Outlet Store within the allowed discount period.		

This entry reduces the amount the customer, Computer Outlet, owes the seller, Barton, to zero. The total undiscounted amount due from The Computer Outlet Store was $2,800 ($4,200 sale − $1,400 sales return). With terms of 1/10, n/15, the sales discount is $28 ($2,800 × 1 percent) and the cash collected is $2,772 ($2,800 − $28).

Companies accumulate sales discounts in a separate account. This enables management to monitor the dollar amount of sales discounts being taken by customers. Sales Discounts is a *contra-revenue account* like Sales Returns and Allowances. Both accounts are contra to, or subtracted from, gross Sales Revenue on the income statement. There are two important aspects of the sales discount calculation. First, the cash discount applies only to the sales price of the merchandise sold and not to any transportation cost. Second, the sales price of any merchandise returned must be subtracted from the total amount before calculating the cash discount.

Pay After Discount Period

If The Computer Outlet Store makes a cash payment after December 22 (after the discount period has expired), the cash discount does not apply. For example, if cash is received in full payment from Computer Outlet on December 27, Barton would record the following journal entry:

A = L + SE
+2,800

−2,800

Dec. 27	Cash	2,800	
	Accounts receivable		2,800
	To record cash received from The Computer Outlet Store outside the allowed discount period.		

| PRINCIPLE ALERT | **Revenue Recognition** |

In May of 2014, the FASB and IASB jointly issued a new revenue recognition standard that will go into effect after December 15, 2017. Revenue must still be earned to be recognized; however, the new standard requires that a company recognize revenue to depict the transfer of promised goods or services to a customer in an amount that reflects the consideration that the company expects to receive in exchange for those goods or services. We discuss the new standard in more detail in Appendix 5B at the end of this chapter.

Net Sales

Net sales is the gross sales revenue generated through merchandise sales less any sales returns and allowances and any sales (cash) discounts. A company calculates its net sales for the period by subtracting the balances of the Sales Returns and Allowances account (normal debit balance) and the Sales Discounts account (normal debit balance) from the balance of the Sales Revenue account (normal credit balance).

Gross sales revenue
– Sales returns and allowances
– Sales discounts
= Net sales

YOUR TURN! 5.3

The solution is on
pages 271–272.

On June 15, a customer buys 75 CDs on account from Musicland for $10 each, for a total of $750. The **list price** of the CDs is $12 each, but Musicland gave the customer a $2 per CD discount because of the large order. On June 20, the customer returned, unopened, five of the CDs and was given a purchase credit of $50. The customer paid its full balance of $700 on June 25. Record these transactions in journal entry form for Musicland. The unit cost of the CDs in inventory is $4.20 each.*

*$4.20 is calculated from the prior Your Turn! as follows:
Inventory cost = $510.00 + $22.18 − $61.20 − $8.98 = $462.00
Inventory quantity = 125 − 15 = 110
Cost per unit = $462.00/110 = $4.20

PROFITABILITY ANALYSIS

Gross Profit Percentage

Managers, investment professionals, and stockholders closely monitor a company's gross profit on sales. They know that if gross profit on sales declines from one year to the next, net income for the current and following year is also likely to decline. A declining gross profit can indicate problems in a company's purchasing activities or problems selling its goods at an acceptable price. For a merchandising company, the Cost of Goods Sold is subtracted from the firm's net sales to determine its gross profit on sales. **Gross profit**, or **gross profit on sales**, is defined as the difference between Net Sales and Cost of Goods Sold and reveals the amount of sales revenue remaining after subtracting the cost of products sold. (Recall that net sales equals gross sales revenue less any sales returns and allowances and sales discounts.)

Financial statement users who monitor a company's gross profit are also usually interested in its **gross profit percentage**—that is, the rate at which a company earns gross profit on its sales revenue. A merchandising company measures its gross profit percentage as follows:

LO4 Define the gross profit percentage and the return on sales ratio, and **explain** their use in profitability analysis.

A.K.A. Gross profit is often referred to as *gross margin*.

$$\text{Gross profit percentage} = \frac{\text{Gross profit on sales}}{\text{Net sales}}$$

Using the data in **Exhibit 5-5**, the 2014 gross profit percentage for **Target** is 29.4 percent.

Financial analysis of the gross profit percentage frequently involves comparing the company against its performance in prior years and against the performance of competitor companies. Gross profit percentages for a two-year period are presented in **Exhibit 5-5** for both **Target Corporation** and one of its chief competitors, **Walmart Corporation**.

Exhibit 5-5	Gross Profit Percentage for Target Corporation and Walmart Corporation	
(in millions)	**2014**	**2013**
Target.....	$\dfrac{\$21,340}{\$72,618} = 29.4\,\text{percent}$	$\dfrac{\$21,240}{\$71,279} = 29.8\,\text{percent}$
Walmart ...	$\dfrac{\$115,007}{\$473,076} = 24.3\,\text{percent}$	$\dfrac{\$113,307}{\$465,604} = 24.3\,\text{percent}$

Target's gross profit percentage decreased 0.4 percent, from 29.8 percent in 2013 to 29.4 percent in 2014; however, in both years Target has a higher gross profit percentage than Walmart. Walmart's gross profit percentage is only 24.3 percent in both 2013 and 2014. One explanation for the large difference between the gross profit percentages of the two companies is their different business strategies. Target attempts to sell higher-quality products at a reasonable price, whereas Walmart focuses more on low prices and less on product quality.

ACCOUNTING IN PRACTICE	**A Taxing Situation**

One of the troubles with getting a good job and earning a big paycheck is that others will want to share in your good fortune. While you can simply tell your friends no, you do not want to lend them money, you cannot tell the I.R.S. that you would prefer not to pay your taxes. Filing a tax return, even if you hire a professional to help, requires you to maintain records of your expenses and income. The better you are at recordkeeping, the better chance you will have at making sure you maximize your deductions and save on the amount of taxes you pay. In addition, if you are ever audited, excellent recordkeeping will prove invaluable to your defense.

TAKEAWAY 5.1	Concept ⟶	Method ⟶	Assessment
	Is a company able to maintain prices on its goods consistent with changes in the cost of its inventory?	Gross profit and net sales Gross profit percentage $= \dfrac{\text{Gross profit on sales}}{\text{Net sales}}$	A higher ratio suggests the company has market power to command higher retail prices. A lower ratio suggests competitive pressures on price setting.

Return on Sales Ratio (Profit Margin)

A.K.A. Return on sales is often referred to as *profit margin*.

First introduced in Chapter 4, the **return on sales ratio** reveals the net income earned on each dollar of net sales and is computed by dividing net income by net sales:

$$\text{Return on sales ratio} = \frac{\text{Net income}}{\text{Net sales}}$$

Return on sales ratios for **Target Corporation** and **Walmart Corporation** are presented in **Exhibit 5-6**. Target's return on sales ratio for 2014 is (2.3) percent. Target discontinued operating its stores in Canada in 2014, and the expenses associated with this decision, like severance pay and other costs of winding down the business, were reflected in their income for the year. Excluding these expenses, Target's earnings for 2014 were $2,449, and their return on sales ratio was 3.4 percent. A company has a number of ways to improve its return on sales ratio, for example, by raising its retail prices or by purchase discounts from buying in larger quantities. It could also reduce operating expenses by reducing salaries, administrative costs, or selling and marketing costs, or, like Target, discontinuing poorly performing segments of the business. Analysts like to compare return on sales ratios for a company over time to detect any trends. They also like to compare the ratio with those of competitors.

Exhibit 5-6	Return on Sales Ratios for Target Corporation and Walmart Corporation	
(in millions)	**2014**	**2013**
Target	$\dfrac{\$(1,636)}{\$72,618} = (2.3)$ percent	$\dfrac{\$1,971}{\$71,279} = 2.8$ percent
Walmart . . .	$\dfrac{\$16,022}{\$473,076} = 3.4$ percent	$\dfrac{\$16,999}{\$465,604} = 3.7$ percent

Walmart's return on sales ratio for 2014 indicates that they earned 3.4 cents for each dollar of sales. The return on sales ratio allows us to compare a company's ability to earn profits on its sales regardless of company size. Walmart generates over six times the sales revenue as does Target ($72,618 million for Target versus $473,076 for Walmart), yet Walmart has a return on sales ratio that is similar to Target's (after excluding the costs of discontinuing their Canadian operations). The return on sales for both companies decreased from 2013 to 2014, although Walmart's declined less.

Concept	→	Method	→	Assessment	**TAKEAWAY 5.2**
Is a company able to maintain prices on its goods consistent with changes in its total expenses?		Net income and net sales $\text{Return on sales ratio} = \dfrac{\text{Net income}}{\text{Net sales}}$		A higher ratio suggests the company is providing a higher net income on each dollar of net sales.	

The President of Musicland has asked for help to evaluate the company's performance during the current year. In particular, we are requested to calculate Musicland's gross profit and its return on sales ratio and then explain what these measures indicate. The following information is from Musicland's financial statements:

Net sales.	$100,000
Cost of goods sold.	45,000
Net income.	10,500

YOUR TURN! 5.4

The solution is on page 272.

Governance and Conflicts of Interest

CORPORATE SOCIAL RESPONSIBILITY

An important component of good corporate responsibility is strong corporate governance. **Target** publishes a Business Conduct Guide for its employees as part of its governance program. Included in this handbook are guidelines concerning conflicts of interest. The list below provides examples of potential conflicts of interest:

- Owning a substantial amount of stock in any competing business or in any organization that does business with us.
- Serving as a director, manager, consultant, employee or independent contractor for any organization that does business with us, or is a competitor—except with our company's specific prior knowledge and consent.
- Accepting or receiving gifts of any value or favors, compensation, loans, excessive entertainment or similar activities from any individual or organization that does business or wants to do business with us, or is a competitor.
- Representing the company in any transaction in which you or a related person has a substantial interest.
- Disclosing or using for your benefit confidential or non-public information about Target or other organizations with which we do business.
- Taking personal advantage of a business opportunity that is within the scope of Target's business—such as by purchasing property that Target is interested in acquiring.

COMPREHENSIVE PROBLEM

Williams Distributing Company is a merchandising company. Williams uses the perpetual inventory system. Record each of the following transactions related to the company's purchasing and selling of merchandise:

March   1   Purchased merchandise on account for $6,000; terms were 2/10, n/30.
            3   Paid $200 cash for freight on the March 1 purchase.
            6   Returned merchandise costing $300 (part of the $6,000 purchase).
         10   Paid for merchandise purchased on March 1.
         12   Sold merchandise on account costing $8,000 for $10,000; terms were 2/10, n/30.
         15   Accepted returned and undamaged merchandise from a customer costing $400 that had been sold on account for $500 (part of the $10,000 sale).
         20   Received payment from customer for merchandise sold on March 12.

Solution

March	1	Inventory	6,000	
		Accounts payable		6,000
		Purchased merchandise with 2/10, n/30 terms.		
	3	Inventory	200	
		Cash		200
		Paid freight on March 1 purchase.		
	6	Accounts payable	300	
		Inventory		300
		Returned merchandise from March 1 purchase.		
	10	Accounts payable	5,700	
		Inventory		114
		Cash		5,586
		Paid for merchandise purchased on March 1 within the discount period [($6,000 − $300) × 2% = $114].		
	12	Accounts receivable	10,000	
		Sales revenue		10,000
		To record revenue from sale of merchandise.		
	12	Cost of goods sold	8,000	
		Inventory		8,000
		To record cost of merchandise sold and to reduce inventory.		
	15	Sales returns and allowances	500	
		Accounts receivable		500
		To record revenue lost from return by customer.		
	15	Inventory	400	
		Cost of goods sold		400
		To record cost of goods returned by customer.		
	20	Cash	9,310	
		Sales discounts	190	
		Accounts receivable		9,500
		To record receipt of cash from customer within the discount period [($10,000 −$500) × 2% = $190].		

APPENDIX 5A: Periodic Inventory System

An alternative to the perpetual inventory system is the periodic inventory system. The **periodic inventory system** does not update the Inventory account or the Cost of Goods Sold account as merchandise transactions occur during the year. Instead, the Inventory account and the Cost of Goods Sold account are updated only at the end of the accounting period when a physical count of the inventory on hand is undertaken. The periodic inventory system is unacceptable for most companies because up-to-date inventory amounts are not available during the year for managerial decision making. The following section illustrates the journal entries that Barton Wholesale Electronics would make if it used the periodic inventory system. We utilize the same data used in the chapter to illustrate the perpetual inventory system to facilitate an easy comparison of the two systems.

LO5 Appendix 5A: **Describe** and **illustrate** a periodic inventory system.

Accounting for Purchases of Merchandise

When a company uses the periodic inventory system, it records the purchase of merchandise by debiting the cost of the merchandise to the Purchases account, rather than the Inventory account, and crediting the cost to Accounts Payable. (The Purchases account has a normal debit balance.) On November 10, Barton records the purchase of 100 disk drives with a list price of $210 each and terms of 2/10, n/30 by making the following journal entry:

Nov. 10	Purchases	21,000	
	Accounts payable		21,000
	To record the purchase of 100 disk drives from Malibu with 2/10, n/30 terms.		

A = L + SE
+21,000 −21,000

Transportation Costs

When a purchaser using the periodic inventory system bears the cost of transporting the merchandise from the seller, the purchaser records the transportation cost in the Freight In account, rather than in the Inventory account. (The Freight In account has a normal debit balance.) Barton makes the following journal entry on November 12 to record payment of $126 of transportation costs on the purchase of 100 disk drives:

Nov. 12	Freight in	126	
	Cash		126
	To record the payment of $126 of transportation costs on the purchase of 100 disk drives.		

A = L + SE
−126 −126

Purchase Returns and Allowances

If a purchaser is dissatisfied with merchandise that was purchased and a purchase return or allowance is granted, the purchaser records the purchase return or allowance using the Purchase Returns and Allowances account, rather than the Inventory account. (Purchase Returns and Allowances is a contra-purchases account with a normal credit balance.) On November 15, Barton records the return of 10 disk drives to Malibu Manufacturing by making the following journal entry:

Nov. 15	Accounts payable	2,100	
	Purchase returns and allowances		2,100
	To record the return of 10 disk drives at a list price of $210.		

A = L + SE
−2,100 +2,100

Purchase Discounts

If a purchaser makes a cash payment to the seller before the end of the allowed discount period, the purchaser deducts a cash discount. Otherwise, the purchaser pays the full invoice price. When a purchaser takes a cash discount, the purchaser credits the Purchase Discounts account, rather than the Inventory account. (Purchase Discounts is a contra-purchases account with a normal credit balance.) Barton makes the following journal entry on November 20 to record its cash payment to Malibu Manufacturing after deducting the cash discount:

				Nov. 20	Accounts payable	18,900	
A	=	L	+	SE			
−18,522		−18,900		+378	Purchase discounts		378
					Cash		18,522
					To record the payment to Malibu Manufacturing within the allowed		
					discount period.		

If Barton makes payment between November 21 and December 10, after the discount period has expired, the cash discount does not apply. In this case, Barton records a cash payment on November 25 with the following journal entry:

				Nov. 25	Accounts payable	18,900	
A	=	L	+	SE			
−18,900		−18,900			Cash		18,900
					To record the payment to Malibu Manufacturing outside the allowed		
					discount period.		

YOUR TURN! 5A.1

The solution is on page 272.

Assume that Musicland uses the *periodic system*. On June 1, Musicland purchased 125 CDs at $4.08 each on account from its distributor for $510. The terms of the purchase were 2/10, n/30. Also on June 1, Musicland paid in cash a freight charge of $22.18 for delivery of the CDs. On June 4, Musicland returned 15 defective CDs for a credit of $61.20. On June 8, Musicland paid for the remaining 110 CDs. Record the transactions in journal entry form for Musicland.

Accounting for Sales of Merchandise

Under the periodic inventory system, a seller makes only one journal entry to record a sale of merchandise. The entry records an account receivable (or Cash) from the customer and the sales revenue from the sale by debiting Accounts Receivable and crediting Sales Revenue. Barton records the December 12 sale of 15 disk drives to The Computer Outlet Store at a sales price of $280 each with terms of 1/10, n/15 by making the following entry:

				Dec. 12	Accounts receivable	4,200	
A	=	L	+	SE			
+4,200				+4,200	Sales revenue		4,200
				Rev	*To record the sale of 15 disk drives at a sales price of $280 each to*		
					The Computer Outlet Store with credit terms of 1/10, n/15.		

The same journal entry is made under the perpetual inventory system. Under the periodic inventory system, however, there is no concurrent entry to transfer the cost of merchandise sold from the Inventory account to the Cost of Goods Sold account.

Sales Returns and Allowances

Under the periodic inventory system, only one journal entry is used to record a sales return or allowance. The entry records the reduction of the revenue from the sale and the reduction of the account receivable from the customer by debiting Sales Returns and Allowances and crediting Accounts Receivable. Barton records the December 15 return by The Computer Outlet Store of five disk drives by making the following journal entry:

				Dec. 15	Sales returns and allowances	1,400	
A	=	L	+	SE			
−1,400				−1,400	Accounts receivable		1,400
				Rev	*To record the return of 5 disk drives by The Computer Outlet Store;*		
					sales price was $280 each.		

This entry is the same as the first journal entry under the perpetual inventory system; however, Barton does not make the second journal entry that was made under the perpetual inventory system. Under the periodic inventory system, there is no immediate reinstatement of the returned merchandise to the Inventory account or corresponding reduction in the Cost of Goods Sold account.

Sales Discounts

The journal entry to record the receipt of a cash payment from a customer is exactly the same under either the perpetual inventory system or the periodic inventory system. If the payment is made within the allowed discount period, the entry includes a debit to Sales Discounts, a contra-sales account. Barton records the cash received from The Computer Outlet Store on December 22 (within the discount period) as follows:

Dec. 22	Cash	2,772	
	Sales discounts	28	
	Accounts receivable		2,800
	To record the cash payment from The Computer Outlet Store within		
	the discount period.		

A = L + SE
+2,772 −28
−2,800 Rev

If The Computer Outlet Store makes its cash payment any time between December 13 and December 27 (after the discount period), the cash discount does not apply. Barton records the cash received from Computer Outlet on December 27 with the following journal entry:

Dec. 27	Cash	2,800	
	Accounts receivable		2,800
	To record the cash payment from The Computer Outlet Store outside		
	the discount period.		

A = L + SE
+2,800
−2,800

Assume Musicland uses the *periodic system*. On June 15, a customer buys on account 75 CDs from Musicland for $10 each, for a total of $750. The list price of the CDs is $12 each, but Musicland provided the customer with a $2 per CD discount because of the large order. On June 20, the customer returned, unopened, five of the CDs and was given a credit of $50. The customer paid its full balance of $700 on June 25. Record these transactions on Musicland's books. The unit cost of the CDs in inventory is $4.20 each.*

*$4.20 is computed from Your Turn 5.1 as follows:
   Inventory cost = $510.00 + $22.18 − $61.20 − $8.98 = $462.00
   Inventory quantity = 125 − 15 = 110
   Cost per unit = $462.00/110 = $4.20

YOUR TURN! 5A.2

The solution is on page 272.

Comparison of Entries Under the Perpetual and Periodic Systems

Exhibit 5A-1 summarizes all key journal entries under both the perpetual and periodic inventory systems for purchases and sales of merchandise.

Exhibit 5A-1	Comparison of Journal Entries under the Perpetual and Periodic Systems				
Date	**Transaction**	**Perpetual Inventory System**		**Periodic Inventory System**	

Nov 10	Purchase of merchandise on credit	Inventory
		   Accounts payable
			21,000
			21,000
				Purchases
				   Accounts payable
					21,000
					21,000

Nov 11	Freight cost	Inventory
		   Cash
			126
			126
				Freight In
				   Cash
					126
					126

Nov 15	Purchase returns	Accounts payable
		   Inventory
			2,100
			2,100
				Accounts payable
				   Purchase returns
					2,100
					2,100

Nov 20	Purchase discount and payment	Accounts payable
		   Inventory
		   Cash
			18,900
			378
			18,522
				Accounts payable
				   Purchase discounts
				   Cash
					18,900
					378
					18,522

Dec 12	Sale of merchandise on credit	Accounts receivable
		   Sales revenue
			4,200
			4,200
				Accounts receivable
				   Sales revenue
					4,200
					4,200

		Cost of goods sold Inventory	3,108 3,108	No entry	

Dec 15	Return of sales merchandise	Sales returns and allowances
		   Accounts receivable
			1,400
			1,400
				Sales returns and allowances
				   Accounts receivable
					1,400
					1,400

		Inventory Cost of goods sold	1,036 1,036	No entry	

Dec 22	Sales discount and payment	Cash
		Sales discounts
		   Accounts receivable
			2,772
			28
			2,800
				Cash
				Sales discounts
				   Accounts receivable
					2,772
					28
					2,800

Cost of Goods Sold Using a Periodic System

If a firm uses a periodic system rather than a perpetual system, it does not record cost of goods sold at the time sales revenue is recorded. Instead, cost of goods sold is calculated periodically at the end of the accounting period when the inventory is physically counted. Cost of goods sold is then backed into by subtracting the ending inventory from the **cost of goods available for sale**, which represents the total inventory that was available to be sold. The calculation of cost of goods sold using the periodic method is shown in **Exhibit 5A-2**.

Exhibit 5A-2	Cost of Goods Sold Computation Using the Periodic Method

	Beginning inventory
+	Cost of goods purchased during the period
=	Cost of goods available for sale
−	Ending inventory
=	Cost of goods sold

One additional difference between the periodic method and the perpetual method is how a company keeps track of items that affect the Inventory account. Under the perpetual system, items such as transportation charges, purchase returns, and purchase discounts, are recorded directly to the Inventory account. Under the periodic system, separate accounts are used for each of these items, which are then added to beginning inventory to arrive at the cost of goods available for sale. An illustration of this is shown in **Exhibit 5A-3**, assuming that there was no beginning inventory.

Exhibit 5A-3	Cost of Goods Sold Illustration Using the Periodic Method

BARTON WHOLESALE ELECTRONICS
Cost of Goods Sold
For Year Ended December 31, 2016

Inventory, January 1...			$ 0
Purchases..		$21,000	
Less: Purchase returns and allowances	$2,100		
Purchase discounts	378	2,478	
Net purchases		18,522	
Add: Freight-in		126	
Cost of goods purchased......................................			18,648
Cost of goods available for sale...............................			18,648
Less: Inventory, December 31			16,576
Cost of goods sold..			$ 2,072

**YOUR
TURN! 5A.3**

The solution is on
page 273.

Assume that Musicland uses a periodic inventory system. Prepare a schedule of cost of goods sold as of December 31, 2015, using the following information:

Inventory, January 1, 2015..	$10,000
Purchases...	50,000
Purchase returns and allowances	2,000
Freight-in	200
Purchase discounts	1,000
Inventory, December 31, 2015..	12,200

APPENDIX 5B: The New Revenue Recognition Standard

The FASB and IASB have issued a new revenue recognition standard in an effort to create more consistency in the recognition of revenue across various industries. The core principle behind the new standard is that a company should recognize revenue when it transfers goods or services to a customer, and the amount of revenue that the company recognizes should reflect the consideration that the entity expects to receive in exchange for those goods or services. For U.S. GAAP, the new standard will generally be effective for fiscal years beginning after December 15, 2017.

LO6 Describe and illustrate the new revenue recognition standard.

Learning objective 3 (LO3) on pages 241–245 of this chapter illustrates the accounting for the sale of merchandise under the current accounting standard, which applies until the new standard goes into effect. Under the current standard, a company may record revenue at the gross amount of the sale and then later reduce this gross amount for both sales discounts and sales returns and allowances *if and when* these events occur. However, the new standard only permits a company to recognize revenue at *the net amount it expects to receive*. Consequently, end-of-period adjusting entries are used to reduce the gross amounts to the net amounts that the company expects to receive after sales discounts are taken and returns and allowances are made. A company must use its judgment to estimate the amount of sales discounts that will be taken and sales returns and allowances that will be made in future periods for sales that occur in the current period. It is reasonable to assume that nearly all customers will take the sales discounts because of the financial benefits of doing so. It is also likely that companies will use past experience to estimate sales returns and allowances.

The following illustrates the accounting for sales of merchandise for Barton Wholesale Electronics under the new revenue recognition standard. Barton's fiscal year-end is December 31.

Assume that during the year Barton sells merchandise on account totaling $500,000. Further assume the cost to Barton of this merchandise was $400,000. The following two journal entries summarize Barton's credit sales during the year, along with the associated cost of goods sold.

Various dates	Accounts receivable	500,000	
	Sales revenue		500,000
	To record sale of merchandise on account.		
Various dates	Cost of goods sold	400,000	
	Inventory		400,000
	To record cost of goods sold.		

The new revenue recognition standard requires Barton to estimate the amount of both sales discounts and sales returns and allowances. Below we illustrate three adjusting journal entries made at year-end to comply with the new revenue recognition standard. The first adjusting journal entry applies to estimated sales discounts, and the other two adjusting journal entries apply to estimated sales returns and allowances.

Adjusting Journal Entry for Sales Discounts

Barton offers credit terms of 1/10, n/15 to encourage early payment. At year-end, Barton recognizes that there are $9,000 of sales on account still eligible for the 1 percent discount. Barton believes that all companies will pay within the discount period to receive the 1 percent discount. Barton makes the following adjusting journal entry at the year-end to provide for these estimated sales discounts:

Dec. 31	Sales discounts	90	
	Allowance for sales discounts		90
	To record the estimated sales discount taken of 1 percent on credit		
	sales still eligible for discount at year-end ($9,000 × 0.01).		

This adjusting journal entry debits Sales discounts for the amount of discounts Barton estimates will be taken. The Sales discounts account is a contra account to Sales revenue. The credit in this entry is to the Allowance for sales discounts, which is a contra account to Accounts receivable.

Adjusting Journal Entry for Sales Returns and Allowances

Barton allows a 60-day return privilege for the merchandise it sells. At year-end, Barton estimates there remain $100,000 of sales (with a cost to Barton of $80,000) that are still within the 60-day return period and that, from past experience, 10 percent of this merchandise will be returned. Barton makes the following adjusting journal entries at year-end to provide for these estimated returns.

Dec. 31	Sales returns and allowances	10,000	
	Sales refunds payable		10,000
	To record the estimated return of 10 percent of the merchandise sold		
	that is still eligible for return at year-end ($100,000 × 0.10).		
Dec. 31	Estimated inventory return	8,000	
	Cost of goods sold		8,000
	To record the estimated return of 10 percent of the merchandise sold		
	that is still eligible for return at year-end ($80,000 × 0.10).		

The first adjusting journal entry debits Sales returns and allowances for the amount of merchandise that Barton estimates will be returned within the return period. Sales returns and allowance represents a contra account to Sales revenue. The credit in this entry is to Sales refunds payable, a liability account representing the refund that will be due upon the return of the merchandise.

The second adjusting journal entry debits Estimated inventory return for the amount of inventory Barton estimates will be returned. Estimated inventory return is an asset account.

In subsequent periods, management will assess these three important accounts: Allowance for Sales Discounts, Sales Refunds Payable, and Estimated Inventory Return. Management would adjust upward or downward as necessary during the year-end adjustment process to report balances for these accounts that reflect economic circumstances. All other entries during the period for returns, allowances, and discounts are identical to those described in the chapter.

YOUR TURN! 5B.1

The solution is on page 273.

WikiTech's fiscal year-end is December 31. Assume that during the year, WikiTech sells merchandise on account totaling $1,000,000. Further assume the cost to WikiTech of this merchandise was $300,000. WikiTech offers credit terms of 2/10, n/30 to encourage early payment. At year-end, WikiTech recognizes that there are $150,000 of sales on account still eligible for the 2 percent discount. WikiTech believes that all companies will pay within the discount period to receive the 2 percent discount. In addition, WikiTech allows a 90-day return privilege for the merchandise it sells. At year-end, WikiTech estimates there remain $200,000 of sales (with a cost to WikiTech of $60,000) that are still within the 90-day return period and that, from past experience, 7.5 percent of this merchandise is expected to be returned. Prepare the period-end adjusting journal entries needed for WikiTech to comply with the new revenue recognition standard.

SUMMARY OF LEARNING OBJECTIVES

LO1   **Explain the operations of a merchandise company and contrast that with the operations of a service company. (p. 234)**

- Merchandise inventory is a stock of products that a company buys from another company and makes available for sale to its customers.
- Merchandising firms sell merchandise. There are two types of merchandising firms: wholesale distributors and retailers.
- Manufacturing companies convert raw materials and components into finished products through the application of skilled labor and machine operations; wholesale distributors buy finished product from manufacturing firms in large quantities and sell smaller quantities to retailers; retailers sell the products to individual consumers.
- The operating cycle of a merchandising firm consists of three types of transactions: purchase merchandise for resale and warehouse the inventory, remove goods from inventory and ship to the customer at sale, and receive cash from the customer.
- The primary revenue source for a service firm is from providing services to customers, rather than manufacturing or selling a physical product.

LO2   **Describe the accounting for purchases of merchandise. (p. 237)**

- The perpetual inventory system records the cost of merchandise in the Inventory account at the time of purchase and updates the Inventory account for subsequent transactions as they occur.
- When the perpetual inventory system is used, the Inventory account is affected by merchandise transactions as follows:
  - Debited for the invoice price of purchases.
  - Debited for transportation costs.

- Credited for the cost of purchase returns and allowances.
- Credited for cash discounts taken.
- Credited for the cost of the merchandise sold.
- Debited for the cost of any sales returns.

Describe the accounting for sales of merchandise. (p. 241)   **LO3**

■ When a perpetual inventory system is used, the following procedure is followed to account for the sale of merchandise:
- Credit Sales Revenue at the time of the sale, and debit Cash or Accounts Receivable.
- Debit Cost of Goods Sold and credit Inventory at the time of sale to match expenses with revenue and to update the inventory balance.

Define the gross profit percentage and the return on sales ratio, and explain their use in profitability analysis. (p. 245)   **LO4**

■ The gross profit percentage is the rate at which a company earns gross profit on net sales.
■ The gross profit percentage is calculated as net sales less the cost of goods sold, all divided by net sales.
■ The return on sales ratio reveals how much of each dollar of net sales is earned by the company after subtracting all expenses.
■ The return on sales ratio is calculated by dividing net income by net sales.

Appendix 5A: Describe and illustrate a periodic inventory system. (p. 249)   **LO5**

■ The periodic inventory system updates both the Inventory account and the Cost of Goods Sold account at the end of the accounting period when a physical count of the inventory is taken.
■ Under the periodic inventory system separate accounts are used to record merchandise purchases, transportation costs, purchase returns and allowances, and purchase discounts, rather than recording these items to the Inventory account.
■ The periodic inventory system does not update the Inventory account or the Cost of Goods Sold account as merchandise transactions occur during the year. Instead, the Inventory account and the Cost of Goods Sold account are updated only at the end of the accounting period when a physical count of the inventory is taken. Other accounts are used to record purchases, transportation costs, purchase returns and allowances, and purchase discounts.
■ Cost of goods sold is calculated by subtracting the remaining inventory on hand from the cost of goods available for sale, which represents the aggregate inventory that was available to be sold.
■ The basic formula for calculating the cost of goods sold under the periodic system is to calculate goods available for sale consisting of beginning inventory plus net purchases during the period, less purchase returns and allowances and less purchase discounts, and then subtract ending inventory from this amount.

Appendix 5B: The new revenue recognition standard (p. 253)   **LO6**

■ The FASB and IASB have issued a new revenue recognition standard with the aim of creating more consistency in the recognition of revenue across industries.
■ The core principle underlying the new standard is that a company should recognize revenue in the amount of consideration it expects to receive in exchange for the transfer of goods or services to a customer.

SUMMARY	Concept	Method	Assessment
TAKEAWAY 5.1	Is a company able to maintain prices on its goods consistent with changes in the cost of its inventory?	Gross profit and net sales $\text{Gross profit percentage} = \dfrac{\text{Gross profit on sales}}{\text{Net sales}}$	A higher ratio suggests the company has market power to command higher retail prices. A lower ratio suggests competitive pressures on price setting.
TAKEAWAY 5.2	Is a company able to maintain prices on its goods consistent with changes in its total expenses?	Net income and net sales $\text{Return on sales ratio} = \dfrac{\text{Net income}}{\text{Net sales}}$	A higher ratio suggests the company is providing a higher net income on each dollar of net sales.

KEY TERMS

Cash discount (p. 239)	Invoice price (p. 239)	Purchase allowance (p. 239)
Cost of goods available for sale (p. 252)	List price (p. 245)	Purchase return (p. 239)
Cost of goods sold (cost of sales) (p. 242)	Manufacturers (p. 234)	Retailers (p. 235)
	Merchandise inventory (p. 236)	Return on sales ratio (profit margin) (p. 246)
Credit period (p. 239)	Merchandising firms (p. 234)	
Discount period (p. 239)	Net sales (p. 244)	Sale on account (p. 236)
FOB destination (p. 238)	Open account (p. 236)	Sale on credit (p. 236)
FOB shipping point (p. 237)	Operating cycle (p. 235)	Sales allowance (p. 243)
Gross profit (gross margin) (p. 245)	Periodic inventory system (p. 236)	Sales discount (p. 239)
Gross profit on sales (p. 245)	Perpetual inventory system (p. 236)	Sales returns (p. 243)
Gross profit percentage (p. 245)		Wholesalers (p. 235)

Assignments with the ⓜ logo in the margin are available in BusinessCourse.
See the Preface of the book for details.

SELF-STUDY QUESTIONS

(Answers to Self-Study Questions are at the end of this chapter.)

LO2

1. **On March 1, Troy Company purchased merchandise with an invoice price of $2,700 and 2/10, n/30 terms. On March 3, Troy pays $100 transportation cost on the purchased goods. On March 10, Troy pays for the merchandise. What is Troy's total cost of the purchased merchandise?**
   a. $2,700
   b. $2,744
   c. $2,746
   d. $2,800

LO2

2. **Newman Company started business on January 1. During the year, the company purchased merchandise with an invoice price of $500,000. Newman also paid $20,000 freight on the merchandise. During the year, Newman also returned $80,000 of the merchandise to its suppliers. All purchases were paid for in a timely manner, and a $10,000 cash discount was taken. $418,000 of the merchandise was sold for $627,000. What is the December 31, balance in the Inventory account?**
   a. $82,000
   b. $32,000
   c. $12,000
   d. $2,000

LO2

3. **Saber Company uses the perpetual inventory system. Saber purchased merchandise with an invoice price of $800, terms 2/10, n/30. If Saber returns merchandise with an invoice price of $200 to the supplier, what should the journal entry to record the return include?**
   a. Debit to Inventory of $200
   b. Debit to Inventory of $196
   c. Credit to Inventory of $200
   d. Credit to Inventory of $100

LO4

4. **Ira Company reports net sales of $500, cost of sales of $300, and net income of $50. What is the gross profit percentage and return on sales ratio for Ira?**
   a. Gross profit percentage is 10 percent and return on sales ratio is 40 percent.
   b. Gross profit percentage is 60 percent and return on sales ratio is 10 percent.
   c. Gross profit percentage is 40 percent and return on sales ratio is 10 percent.
   d. Gross profit percentage is 40 percent and return on sales ratio is 25 percent.

LO2

5. **Smith & Sons purchased $5,000 of merchandise from the Claremont Company with terms of 3/10, n/30. How much discount is Smith & Sons entitled to take if it pays within the allowed discount period of 10 days?**
   a. $50
   b. $100
   c. $150
   d. $300

LO2

6. **Moonitz Inc. purchased merchandise with a list price of $6,000 from the Sprague Company. Sprague offers its customers credit terms of 2/10, n/30. What amount should Moonitz pay if the cash discount is taken?**
   a. $5,940
   b. $6,060
   c. $6,120
   d. $5,880

7. The Arcadia Company is a merchandiser and reports the following data at year-end:

Net sales.	$100,000
Cost of goods sold.	60,000
Net income.	15,000

What is the company's gross profit percentage?
- a. 40 percent
- b. 60 percent
- c. 15 percent
- d. None of the above

8. Using the data in Question 7, what is The Arcadia Company's return on sales ratio?

- a. 40 percent
- b. 60 percent
- c. 15 percent
- d. None of the above

9. Which of the following statements regarding cost flows is true?

- a. Cost of goods available for sale is equal to beginning inventory minus cost of goods purchased.
- b. Cost of goods available for sale is equal to beginning inventory plus cost of goods purchased.
- c. CGAS = beginning inventory minus ending inventory.
- d. CGAS − cost of goods sold minus cost of goods purchased.

10. Denald Co. uses the periodic inventory system. When goods are purchased, Denald will:

- a. debit freight costs to Inventory.
- b. debit purchase returns and allowance for returned items.
- c. debit the Purchases account for purchases on account.
- d. debit the Inventory account for purchases on account.

11. Kali Company began the period with $20,000 in inventory. The company also purchased an additional $20,000 of inventory and returned $2,000 for a full credit. A physical count of the inventory at year-end revealed an inventory on hand of $16,000. What was Kali's cost of goods sold for the period?

- a. $16,000
- b. $22,000
- c. $48,000
- d. $50,000

QUESTIONS

1. Describe the differences between (a) a manufacturer, (b) a wholesale distributor, and (c) a retailer.
2. Describe the three primary transactions in the operating cycle of a merchandising firm.
3. What is the difference between a credit period and a discount period? What is a cash discount?
4. Sprague Company purchased merchandise with a list price of $2,000 from the Thompson Company. Thompson offers a two percent cash discount if payment is received within 10 days. What is the payment amount if the cash discount is taken?
5. Krane Company purchased $4,000 of merchandise and paid $250 in transportation costs to deliver the merchandise. Krane then returned $1,000 of the merchandise before paying the supplier within the discount period. Krane was entitled to a two percent cash discount. How much did Krane pay the supplier?
6. What is the primary difference between a merchandise return and a merchandise allowance?
7. Define the *return on sales ratio*. What does this ratio measure?
8. Define *gross profit on sales*.
9. Define *gross profit percentage*. How is this percentage used by analysts and investors?
10. When merchandisers and manufacturers prepare income statements for their annual reports to shareholders, they usually begin the statement with net sales. For internal reporting purposes, however, the income statements will show gross sales and the related contra-revenue accounts of sales returns and allowances and sales discounts. What might explain this difference in the financial information disclosed to external parties and management? Do you consider the more limited disclosure in the annual reports to be inconsistent with the full disclosure principle? Briefly explain your point of view.

SHORT EXERCISES

LO1 **SE5-1.** **Merchandising versus Service Firm** For each of the following accounts, indicate whether it would be found in the records of a merchandising firm, a service firm, or both.

   a. Cost of goods sold.
   b. Service revenue.
   c. Purchase returns and allowances.
   d. Inventory.
   e. Accounts receivable.
   f. Accounts payable.
   g. Sales revenue.
   h. Freight-out.

LO2 **SE5-2.** **Accounting for Purchase Transactions** Debra Company began operations on June 1. The following transactions took place in June:

   a. Purchases of merchandise on account were $600,000.
   b. The cost of freight to receive the inventory was $20,000. This was paid in cash.
   c. Debra returned $10,000 of the merchandise due to an ordering error. Debra received a full credit for the return.
   d. Debra paid the remaining balance for the merchandise.

   Calculate the dollar amount that Debra will have in inventory at the end of the month. Assume Debra uses the perpetual inventory system and there were no sales.

LO2 **SE5-3.** **Accounting for Purchase Transactions** Use the data from SE5-2 and prepare the journal entries to record the June transactions.

LO2 **SE5-4.** **Accounting for Purchase Discounts** Ken Company purchased $5,000 of merchandise from Marilyn Company with terms of 3/10 n/45. What percent discount will Ken Company get if it pays within the allowed discount period? If Ken Company fails to pay within the discount period, how many days does Ken Company have from the date of purchase before the payment is considered to be late?

LO2 **SE5-5.** **Accounting for Purchase Discounts** Using the information in SE5-4, what amount will Ken Company pay to Marilyn Company if Ken Company takes advantage of the purchase discount?

LO3 **SE5-6.** **Accounting for Sales Transactions** Kate Company uses the perpetual inventory system. Record the journal entries for the following transactions:

   a. On July 16, Kate sold $600 of merchandise with terms of 2/10 n/30. The cost of the merchandise was $360.
   b. On July 19, the customer returned $100 of the merchandise from (a). The cost of the merchandise was $60.
   c. On July 22, the customer paid the entire balance due to Kate.

LO4 **SE5-7.** **Gross Profit Percentage** Using the data below, compute Dino's gross profit percentage for the month of January.

Net sales.	$10,000
Cost of goods sold.	4,000
Operating expenses.	3,000
Other income.	500
Income tax expense.	1,200

LO4 **SE5-8.** **Return on Sales Ratio** Using the data in SE5-7, compute Dino's return on sales ratio for the month of January.

LO5 **SE5-9.** **Cost of Goods Sold and the Periodic System** Kanzu Company uses the periodic inventory system. (Appendix 5A) Kanzu started the period with $10,000 in inventory. The Company purchased an additional $25,000 of merchandise, and returned $1,000 for a full credit. A physical count of inventory at the end of the period revealed that there was an ending inventory balance of $8,000. What was Kanzu's cost of goods sold during the period?

SE5-10. Cost of Goods Sold and the Periodic System Hermani Company uses the periodic inventory system. Hermani started the period with $20,000 in inventory. The Company purchased an additional $25,000 of merchandise and returned $3,000 for a full credit. If Hermani's cost of goods sold during the period was $35,000, what must have been the total of the physical inventory count?

LO5
(Appendix 5A)

SE5-11. Journalize Periodic Inventory Entries Prepare the journal entries to record the following transactions for the Walbright Company using a periodic inventory system.

a. On June 2, Walbright purchased $350,000 of merchandise from the Ferway Company with terms, 3/15, n/30.
b. On June 5, Walbright returned $50,000 of the merchandise purchased on June 2.
c. On June 13, Walbright paid the balance due to Ferway.

LO5
(Appendix 5A)

SE5-12. New Revenue Recognition Standard—Adjusting Journal Entry–Sales Discounts McDowell Corporation reports it sold merchandise on account for a total of $800,000 for the current year. The cost to McDowell for the merchandise was $300,000. To encourage early payment, McDowell offers its customers credit terms of 1/10, n/30. At year-end, there is $125,000 of sales on account still eligible for the 1 percent discount. McDowell believes that all customers will pay within the discount period to receive the discount. Prepare the adjusting journal entry needed for McDowell Corporation to comply with the new revenue recognition standard. Assume McDowell's fiscal year-end is December 31.

LO6
(Appendix 5B)

SE5-13. New Revenue Recognition Standard—Adjusting Journal Entries–Sales Returns and Allowances During the year, Reed Company sells merchandise on account totaling $2,000,000 (the cost to Reed for this merchandise was $800,000). Reed allows a 60-day return privilege for the merchandise it sells. At year-end, Reed estimates there remain $350,000 of sales (with a cost to Reed of $140,000) that are still within the 60-day return period. Based on past experience, Reed expects 5 percent of this merchandise to be returned. Prepare the period-end adjusting journal entries needed for Reed Company to comply with the new revenue recognition standard. Reed's fiscal year-end is December 31.

LO6
(Appendix 5B)

EXERCISES—SET A

E5-1A. Cash Discount Calculations On June 1, Forest Company sold merchandise with a list price of $30,000. For each of the sales terms below, determine the proper amount of cash received:

LO3

	Credit Terms	Date Paid
1.	2/10, n/30	June 8
2.	1/10, n/30	June 15
3.	1/15, n/30	June 14
4.	n/30	June 28

E5-2A. Journal Entries for Sale, Return, and Remittance—Perpetual System On September 13, Brady Company sold merchandise with an invoice price of $1,100 ($600 cost), with terms of 2/10, n/30, to Dalton Company. On September 17, $250 of the merchandise ($100 cost) was returned because it was the wrong model. On September 23, Brady Company received a check for the amount due from Dalton Company.

LO3

Required
Prepare the journal entries made by Brady Company for these transactions. Brady uses the perpetual inventory system.

E5-3A. Journal Entries for Purchase, Return, and Remittance—Perpetual System On April 13, the Kesselman Company purchased $25,000 of merchandise from the Krausman Company, with terms of 1/10, n/30. On April 15, Kesselman paid $500 to Ace Trucking Company for freight on the shipment. On April 18, Kesselman Company returned $800 of merchandise for credit. Final payment was made to Krausman on April 22. Kesselman Company records purchases using the perpetual inventory system.

LO2

Required
Prepare the journal entries that Kesselman Company should make on April 13, 15, 18, and 22.

LO2, 3   E5-4A.   Journal Entries for Merchandise Transactions on Seller's and Buyer's Books—Perpetual System The following are selected transactions for Lamont, Inc., during the month of June:

June 21   Sold and shipped on account to Lowery Company, $3,000 ($2,000 cost) of merchandise, with terms of 2/10, n/30.

28   Lowery Company returned defective merchandise billed at $300 on June 21 ($210 cost).

30   Received from Lowery Company a check for full settlement of the June 21 transaction.

Required

Prepare the necessary journal entries for (a) Lamont, Inc., and (b) Lowery Company. Both companies use the perpetual inventory system.

LO2   E5-5A.   Recording Purchases—Perpetual System On July 1, Alvarez, Inc. purchased merchandise for $2,500, with terms of 2/10, n/30. On July 5, the firm returned $800 of the merchandise to the seller. Payment of the account occurred on July 8. Alvarez uses the perpetual inventory system.

Required

a.   Prepare the journal entries for July 1, July 5, and July 8.

b.   Assuming that the account was paid on July 14, prepare the journal entry for payment on that date.

LO4   E5-6A.   Profitability Analysis Shannon Enterprises reports the following information on its year-end income statement:

Net sales	$180,000	Operating expenses	$40,000
Cost of goods sold	110,000	Other income	25,000

Required

Calculate Shannon's gross profit percentage and return on sales ratio.

LO5   E5-7A.   Journal Entries for Sale, Return, and Remittance—Periodic System On June 8, Stevens Com-
(Appendix 5A)   pany sold merchandise listing for $1,850 to Dalton Company, terms 2/10, n/30. On June 12, $550 worth of the merchandise was returned because it was the wrong color. On June 18, Stevens Company received a check for the amount due.

Required

Record the journal entries made by Stevens Company for these transactions. Stevens uses the periodic inventory system.

LO5   E5-8A.   Journal Entries for Purchase, Return, and Remittance—Periodic System On March 10, Hor-
(Appendix 5A)   ton Company purchased $19,000 worth of merchandise from James Company, terms 1/10, n/30. On March 12, Horton paid $210 freight on the shipment. On March 15, Horton returned $300 of merchandise for credit. Final payment was made to James on March 19. Horton Company uses the periodic inventory system.

Required

Prepare the journal entries that Horton should make on March 10, March 12, March 15, and March 19.

**LO5   E5-9A.   Journal Entries for Merchandise Transactions on Seller's and Buyer's Records—Periodic Sys-
(Appendix 5A)   tem** The following are selected transactions for Franklin, Inc., during the month of April:

April   20   Sold and shipped on account to Lind Stores merchandise for $3,000, with terms of 2/10, n/30.

27   Lind Stores returned defective merchandise billed at $250 on April 20.

29   Received from Lind Stores a check for full settlement of the April 20 transaction.

Required

Prepare the necessary journal entries for (a) Franklin, Inc., and (b) Lind Stores. Both companies use the periodic inventory system.

LO6   E5-10A.   New Revenue Recognition Standard—Adjusting Journal Entries SourceOne sold $4,000,000 of
(Appendix 5B)   merchandise on account during the current year. The cost for this merchandise to SourceOne was $1,400,000. To encourage early payment from its customers, SourceOne offers credit terms of 2/10, n/30. At year-end, SourceOne recognizes that there are $375,000 of sales on account still eligible for the 2 percent discount. SourceOne believes that all customers will pay within the discount period to

receive this discount. In addition, SourceOne allows a 60-day return privilege for the merchandise it sells. At year-end, SourceOne estimates there remain $700,000 of sales (with a cost to SourceOne of $245,000) that are still within the 60-day return period and that, based on past experience, 4 percent of this merchandise is expected to be returned. Prepare the period-end adjusting journal entries needed for SourceOne to comply with the new revenue recognition standard. Assume SourceOne's fiscal year-end is December 31.

E5-11A. New Revenue Recognition Standard—Adjusting Journal Entries During the year, Fischer Company sells merchandise on account totaling $10,000,000 with a cost of merchandise to Fischer of $4,000,000. Fischer offers its customers credit terms of 1/15, n/30. Fischer recognizes that there are $820,000 of sales on account still eligible for the 1 percent discount at year-end and believes that all customers will pay within the discount period. Additionally, Fischer allows a 90-day return privilege for the merchandise it sells. At year-end, Fischer estimates sales of $2,500,000 (with a cost to Fischer of $1,000,000) remain that are still within the 90-day return period. From past experience, 8 percent of this merchandise is expected to be returned. Prepare the period-end adjusting journal entries needed for Fischer Company to comply with the new revenue recognition standard. Fischer's fiscal year-end is December 31.

LO6
(Appendix 5B)

EXERCISES—SET B

E5-1B. Cash Discount Calculations On April 1, the Fitzgerald Company sold merchandise with a list price of $60,000. For each of the sales terms below, determine the proper amount of cash received:

LO3

	Credit Terms	Date Paid
1.	1/15, n/30...	April 14
2.	n/30	April 28
3.	2/10, n/30...	April 8
4.	1/10, n/30...	April 15

E5-2B. Journal Entries for Sale, Return, and Remittance—Perpetual System On October 14, the Patrick Company sold merchandise with an invoice price of $1,200 ($750 cost), with terms of 2/10, n/30, to the Baxter Company. On October 18, $300 of merchandise ($150 cost) was returned because it was the wrong size. On October 24, the Patrick Company received a check for the amount due from the Baxter Company.

LO3

Required
Prepare the journal entries for the Patrick Company using the perpetual inventory system.

E5-3B. Journal Entries for Purchase, Return, and Remittance—Perpetual System On May 15, Monique Company purchased $40,000 of merchandise from the Terrell Company, with terms of 1/10, n/30. On May 17, Monique paid $310 to Swift Trucking Company for freight on the shipment. On May 20, Monique Company returned $800 of merchandise for credit. Final payment was made to Terrell on May 24. Monique Company records purchases using the perpetual inventory system.

LO2
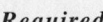

Required
Prepare the journal entries that Monique Company should make on May 15, 17, 20, and 24.

E5-4B. Journal Entries for Merchandise Transactions on Seller's and Buyer's Books—Perpetual System The following are selected transactions of Candello, Inc., during the month of June:

LO2, 3

June 18 Sold and shipped on account to Dante Company $6,000 ($3,000 cost) of merchandise, with terms of 2/10, n/30.
25 Dante Company returned merchandise billed at $800 on June 18 ($300 cost).
27 Received from Dante Company a check for full settlement of the June 18 transaction.

Required
Prepare the necessary journal entries for (a) Candello, Inc., and (b) Dante Company. Both companies use the perpetual inventory system.

LO2   E5-5B.   Recording Purchases—Perpetual System On September 12, Evans, Inc., purchased merchandise for $4,500, with terms of 2/10, n/30. On September 16, the firm returned $500 of the merchandise to the seller. Payment of the account occurred on September 19. Evans uses the perpetual inventory system.

Required
a.   Prepare the journal entries for September 12, September 16, and September 19.
b.   Assuming that the account was paid on September 25, prepare the journal entry for payment on that date.

LO4   E5-6B.   Profitability Analysis Alex Enterprises reports the following information on its year-end income statement:

Net sales	$190,000	Operating expenses	$20,000
Cost of goods sold	130,000	Other income	10,000

Required
Calculate Alex's gross profit percentage and return on sales ratio.

LO5
(Appendix 5A)   E5-7B.   Journal Entries for Sale, Return, and Remittance—Periodic System On March 10, the Sharon Company sold merchandise listing for $2,500 to the Dillard Company with terms of 2/10, n/30. On March 14, $100 of merchandise was returned because it was the wrong size. On March 20, Sharon Company received a check for the amount due.

Required
Prepare the journal entries made by Sharon Company for these transactions. Sharon uses the periodic inventory system.

LO5
(Appendix 5A)   E5-8B.   Journal Entries for Purchase, Return, and Remittance—Periodic System On August 15, the Harris Company purchased $16,500 of merchandise from Jason Company with terms of 2/10, n/30. On August 17, Harris paid $350 freight on the shipment. On August 20, Harris returned $500 worth of the merchandise for credit. Final payment was made to Jason on August 24. Harris Company records purchases using the periodic inventory system.

Required
Prepare the journal entries that Harris should make on August 15, August 17, August 20, and August 24.

LO5
(Appendix 5A)   E5-9B.   Journal Entries for Merchandise Transactions on Seller's and Buyer's Books—Periodic System The following are selected transactions of Fenton, Inc., during the month of January:

Jan.   20   Sold and shipped on account to Lawrence Stores merchandise listing for $2,500 with terms of 2/10, n/30.
        27   Lawrence Stores was granted a $700 allowance on goods shipped January 20.
        29   Received from Lawrence Stores a check for full settlement of the January 20 transaction.

Required
Prepare journal entries for (a) Fenton, Inc., and (b) Lawrence Stores. Both companies use the periodic inventory system.

LO6
(Appendix 5B)   E5-10B.   New Revenue Recognition Standard—Adjusting Journal Entries PrimeTech sold $2,000,000 of merchandise on account during the current year. The cost for this merchandise to PrimeTech was $600,000. To encourage early payment from its customers, PrimeTech offers credit terms of 2/10, n/30. At year-end, PrimeTech recognizes that there are $200,000 of sales on account still eligible for the 2 percent discount. PrimeTech believes that all customers will pay within the discount period to receive this discount. In addition, PrimeTech allows a 60-day return privilege for the merchandise it sells. At year-end, PrimeTech estimates there remain $450,000 of sales (with a cost to PrimeTech of $135,000) that are still within the 60-day return period and that, based on past experience, 7 percent of this merchandise is expected to be returned. Prepare the period-end adjusting journal entries needed for PrimeTech to comply with the new revenue recognition standard. Assume PrimeTech's fiscal year-end is December 31.

LO6
(Appendix 5B)   E5-11B.   New Revenue Recognition Standard—Adjusting Journal Entries During the year, Butler Corporation sells merchandise on account totaling $5,000,000 with a cost of merchandise to Butler of $2,000,000. Butler offers its customers credit terms of 1/15, n/30. Butler recognizes that there are

$410,000 of sales on account still eligible for the 1 percent discount at year-end and believes that all companies will pay within the discount period. Additionally, Butler allows a 90-day return privilege for the merchandise it sells. At year-end, Butler estimates sales of $1,200,000 (with a cost to Butler of $480,000) remain that are still within the 90-day return period. From past experience, 6 percent of this merchandise is expected to be returned. Prepare the period-end adjusting journal entries needed for Butler Corporation to comply with the new revenue recognition standard. Butler Corporation's fiscal year-end is December 31.

PROBLEMS—SET A

P5-1A. **Journal Entries for Merchandise Transactions on Seller's and Buyer's Books—Perpetual System**   LO2, 3
The following transactions occurred between the Decker Company and Mann Stores, Inc., during March:

Mar. 8 Decker sold $14,000 worth of merchandise ($9,600 cost) to Mann Stores with terms of 2/10, n/30.
  10 Mann Stores paid freight charges on the shipment from Decker Company, $500.
  12 Mann Stores returned $2,000 of the merchandise ($1,600 cost) shipped on March 8.
  17 Decker received full payment for the net amount due from the March 8 sale.
  20 Mann Stores returned goods that had been billed originally at $800 ($600 cost). Decker issued a check for $784.

Required
Prepare the necessary journal entries for (a) the books of Decker Company and (b) the books of Mann Stores, Inc. Assume that both companies use the perpetual inventory system.

P5-2A. **Journal Entries for Merchandise Transactions—Perpetual System** Rockford Corporation, which   LO2, 3
began business on August 1, sells on terms of 2/10, n/30. Credit terms for its purchases vary with the supplier. Selected transactions for August are given below. Unless noted, all transactions are on account and involve merchandise held for resale. The perpetual inventory system is used.

Aug. 1 Purchased merchandise from Norris, Inc., $4,000, terms 2/10, n/30.
  5 Paid freight on shipment from Norris, Inc., $220.
  7 Sold merchandise to Denton Corporation, $5,500 ($4,100 cost).
  7 Paid $300 freight on August 7 shipment and billed Denton for the charges.
  9 Returned $800 worth of the merchandise purchased August 1 from Norris, Inc., because it was defective. Norris approved the return.
  9 Received $750 of returned merchandise ($500 cost) from Denton Corporation. Rockford approved the return.
  10 Paid Norris, Inc., the amount due.
  14 Purchased from Chambers, Inc., goods with a price of $9,000. Terms 1/10, n/30.
  15 Paid freight on shipment from Chambers, Inc., $320.
  17 Received the amount due from Denton Corporation.
  18 Sold merchandise to Weber, Inc., $9,600 ($6,600 cost).
  20 Paid $350 freight on August 18 shipment and billed Weber for the charges.
  24 Paid Chambers, Inc., the amount due.
  28 Received the amount due from Weber, Inc.

Required
Prepare journal entries for these transactions for Rockford Corporation.

P5-3A. **Effects of Transactions on the Inventory Account—Perpetual System** Watt Wholesale Company   LO2, 3
purchases merchandise from a variety of manufacturers and sells the merchandise to a variety of retailers. All sales are subject to a cash discount (2/10, n/30). Watt uses a perpetual inventory system. The May 1 balance in Watt's Inventory account was a $70,000 debit. The following transactions occurred during May:

May 2 Purchased $5,500 of merchandise from Ajax Manufacturing; terms are 1/10, n/30.
  4 Paid $200 freight on the May 2 purchase.
  12 Paid Ajax for the May 2 purchase.
  14 Purchased $4,000 of merchandise from Baker Manufacturing; terms are 2/10, n/45.
  16 Received a $300 allowance on the May 14 purchase since some of the merchandise was the wrong color. All of the merchandise is salable at regular prices.

May 18 Purchased $2,500 of merchandise from Charles Industries; terms are 2/10, n/30.
    19 Sold merchandise with a list price of $2,000 ($1,200 cost) to Daytime Industries.
    22 Daytime Industries returned 40 percent of the merchandise from the May 19 sale.
    26 Paid Baker Manufacturing for the May 14 purchase.
    29 Paid Charles Industries for the May 18 purchase.

Required

Prepare a schedule that shows the impact of these transactions on Watt's Inventory account. Use the following headings:

Date	Transaction	Debit Amount	Credit Amount	Account Balance

LO2, 3 **P5-4A.** **Journal Entries for Merchandise Transactions—Perpetual System** Cushing Distributing Company uses the perpetual inventory system. Cushing had the following transactions related to merchandise during the month of June:

June 1 Purchased on account merchandise for resale for $10,000; terms were 2/10, n/30.
    3 Paid $550 cash for freight on the June 1 purchase.
    7 Returned merchandise costing $600 (part of the $10,000 purchase).
    10 Paid for merchandise purchased on June 1.
    13 Sold merchandise on account costing $8,000 for $10,000; terms were 2/10, n/30.
    16 Customer returned merchandise costing $750 that had been sold on account for $1,000 (part of the $10,000 sale).
    22 Received payment from customer for merchandise sold on June 13.

Required

Prepare journal entries for each of the transactions for the Cushing Distributing Company.

LO4 **P5-5A.** **Profitability Analysis** Kolby Enterprises reports the following information on its income statement:

Net sales.	$250,000	Administrative expenses	$10,000
Cost of goods sold.	150,000	Other income	15,000
Selling expenses	50,000	Other expense	10,000

Required

Calculate Kolby's gross profit percentage and return on sales ratio. Explain what each ratio tells us about Kolby's performance. Kolby is planning to add a new product and expects net sales to be $45,000 and cost of goods to be $38,000. No other income or expenses are expected to change. How will this affect Kolby's gross profit percentage and return on sales ratio? What do you advise regarding the new product offering?

LO5
(Appendix 5A) **P5-6A.** **Journal Entries for Merchandise Transactions on Seller's and Buyer's Books—Periodic System** The following transactions occurred between Southwick Company and Mann Stores, Inc., during March:

Mar. 8 Southwick sold $7,100 worth of merchandise to Mann Stores, terms 2/10, n/30.
    10 Mann Stores paid freight charges on the shipment from Southwick Company, $200.
    12 Mann Stores returned $700 of the merchandise shipped on March 8.
    17 Southwick received full payment for the net amount due from the March 8 sale.
    20 Mann Stores returned goods that had been billed originally at $400. Southwick issued a check for $392.

Required

Prepare the necessary journal entries for (a) the books of Southwick Company and (b) the books of Mann Stores, Inc. Assume that both companies use the periodic inventory system.

LO5
(Appendix 5A) **P5-7A.** **Journal Entries for Merchandise Transactions—Periodic System** The Malvado Corporation sells goods on terms of 2/10, n/30. Credit terms for its purchases vary with the supplier. Selected transactions for August are given below. Unless noted, all transactions are on account and involve merchandise held for resale. The periodic inventory system is used.

Aug. 1 Purchased merchandise from Norris, Inc., $2,500; terms 2/10, n/30.
    5 Paid freight on shipment from Norris, Inc., $120.

Aug. 7 Sold merchandise to Denton Corporation, $3,100.

7 Paid freight on shipment to Denton Corporation, $150, and billed Denton for the charges.

9 Returned $400 worth of the merchandise purchased August 1 from Norris, Inc., because it was defective. Norris approved the return.

9 Received $500 of returned merchandise from Denton Corporation.

10 Paid Norris, Inc., the amount due.

14 Purchased from Chambers, Inc., goods with a price of $4,500. Terms 1/10, n/30.

15 Paid freight on shipment from Chambers, Inc., $160.

17 Received the amount due from Denton Corporation.

18 Sold merchandise to Weber, Inc., $4,800.

20 Paid freight on August 18 shipment to Weber, Inc., $160 and billed Weber.

24 Paid Chambers, Inc., the amount due.

28 Received the amount due from Weber, Inc.

Required

Prepare the necessary journal entries for the Malvado Corporation.

PROBLEMS—SET B

P5-1B. Journal Entries for Merchandise Transactions on Seller's and Buyer's Books—Perpetual System LO2, 3
Riggs Distributing Company had the following transactions with Arlington, Inc., during the month of November:

Nov. 10 Riggs sold and shipped $7,000 worth of merchandise ($4,500 cost) to Arlington, terms 2/10, n/30.

12 Arlington, Inc., paid freight charges on the shipment from Riggs Company, $450.

14 Riggs received $600 of merchandise returned by Arlington ($420 cost) from the November 10 sale.

19 Riggs received payment in full for the net amount due on the November 10 sale.

24 Arlington returned goods that had originally been billed at $400 ($280 cost). Riggs issued a check for $392.

Required

Prepare the necessary journal entries (a) on the books of Riggs Distributing Company and (b) on the books of Arlington, Inc. Assume that both companies use the perpetual inventory system.

P5-2B. Journal Entries for Merchandise Transactions—Perpetual System Webster Company was established on July 1. Its sales terms are 2/10, n/30. Credit terms for its purchases vary with the supplier. Selected transactions for the first month of operations are given below. Unless noted, all transactions are on account and involve merchandise held for resale. Webster Company uses the perpetual inventory system. LO2, 3

July 1 Purchased goods from Dawson, Inc., $2,500; terms 1/10, n/30.

2 Purchased goods from Penn Company, $4,500; terms 2/10, n/30.

3 Paid freight on shipment from Dawson, $300.

5 Sold merchandise to Ward, Inc., $1,400 ($1,100 cost).

5 Paid freight on shipment to Ward, Inc., $90. (*Hint:* debit Delivery Expense)

8 Returned $500 worth of the goods purchased July 1 from Dawson, Inc., because some goods were damaged. Dawson approved the return.

9 Received returned goods from Ward, Inc., worth $200 ($150 cost).

10 Paid Dawson, Inc., the amount due.

10 Purchased goods from Dorn Company with a list price of $2,600. Terms 2/10, n/30.

11 Paid freight on shipment from Dorn Company, $150.

15 Received the amount due from Ward, Inc.

15 Sold merchandise to Colby Corporation, $3,200 ($2,400 cost).

16 Mailed a check to Penn Company for the amount due on its July 2 invoice.

18 Received an allowance of $200 from Dorn Company for defective merchandise purchased on July 10.

19 Paid Dorn Company the amount due.

25 Received the amount due from Colby Corporation.

Required

Prepare the necessary journal entries for the Webster Company.

LO2, 3   P5-3B.   Effects of Transactions on the Inventory Account—Perpetual System Rand Wholesale Company purchases merchandise from a variety of manufacturers and sells the merchandise to a variety of retailers. All sales are subject to a cash discount (2/10, n/30). Rand has a perpetual inventory system. The February 1 balance in Rand's Inventory account was a $50,000 debit. The following transactions occurred during February:

Feb. 2 Purchased $8,600 of merchandise from Sweet Manufacturing; terms are 1/10, n/30.
  5 Paid $270 freight on the February 2 purchase.
  11 Paid Sweet for the February 2 purchase.
  13 Purchased $6,000 of merchandise from Tayler Manufacturing; terms are 2/10, n/45.
  16 Received a $300 allowance on the February 13 purchase since some of the merchandise was the wrong size. All of the merchandise is salable at regular prices.
  17 Purchased $5,200 of merchandise from Zorn Industries; terms are 2/10, n/30.
  20 Sold merchandise with a list price of $3,000 ($1,200 cost) to Valley Mart.
  22 Valley Mart returned 20 percent of the merchandise from the February 20 sale.
  23 Paid Tayler Manufacturing for the February 13 purchase.
  28 Paid Zorn Industries for the February 17 purchase.

Required
Prepare a schedule that shows the impact of these transactions on Rand's Inventory account. Use the following headings:

Date	Transaction	Debit Amount	Credit Amount	Account Balance

LO2, 3   P5-4B.   Journal Entries for Merchandise Transactions Janetto Distributing Company uses the perpetual inventory system. Janetto had the following transactions related to merchandise during the month of August:

Aug. 10 Purchased on account merchandise for resale for $9,000; terms were 2/10, n/30.
  12 Paid $350 cash for freight on the August 10 purchase.
  16 Returned merchandise costing $800 (part of the $9,000 purchase).
  19 Paid for merchandise purchased on August 10.
  22 Sold merchandise on account costing $8,000 for $10,000; terms were 2/10, n/30.
  25 Customer returned merchandise costing $750 that had been sold on account for $900 (part of the $10,000 sale).
  31 Received payment from customer for merchandise sold on August 22.

Required
Record each of the transactions related to purchasing and selling merchandise for the Janetto Distributing Company.

LO4   P5-5B.   Profitability Analysis Ashley Enterprises reports the following information on its income statement:

Net sales.	$300,000	Administrative expenses	$20,000
Cost of goods sold.	170,000	Other income	15,000
Selling expenses	50,000	Other expense	10,000

Required
Compute Ashley's gross profit percentage and return on sales ratio. Explain what each ratio tells us about Ashley's performance. Ashley is planning to add a new product and expects net sales to be $32,000 and cost of goods to be $26,000. No other income or expenses are expected to change. How will this affect Ashley's gross profit percentage and return on sales ratio? What do you advise regarding the new product offering?

LO5   P5-6B.   Journal Entries for Merchandise Transactions on Seller's and Buyer's Books—Periodic System
(Appendix 5A) Fortune Distributing Company had the following transactions with Arlington, Inc., during November:

Nov. 10 Fortune sold and shipped $8,500 worth of merchandise to Arlington, terms 2/10, n/30.
  12 Arlington, Inc., paid freight charges on the shipment from Fortune Company, $450.
  14 Fortune received $900 of merchandise returned by Arlington from the November 10 sale.
  19 Fortune received payment in full for the net amount due on the November 10 sale.
  24 Arlington returned goods that had originally been billed at $700. Fortune issued a check for $686.

Required

Prepare the necessary journal entries (a) on the books of Fortune Distributing Company and (b) on the books of Arlington, Inc. Assume that both companies use the periodic inventory system.

P5-7B. **Journal Entries for Merchandise Transactions—Periodic System** Polidor Company was established on July 1. Its sales terms are 2/10, n/30. Credit terms for its purchases vary with the supplier. Selected transactions for the first month of operations are given below. Unless noted, all transactions are on account and involve merchandise held for resale. All purchases are recorded using the periodic inventory system.

LO5
(Appendix 5A)

July	1	Purchased goods from Dawson, Inc., $2,500; terms 1/10, n/30.
	2	Purchased goods from Penn Company, $5,100; terms 2/10, n/30.
	3	Paid freight on shipment from Dawson, $100.
	5	Sold merchandise to Ward, Inc., $1,700.
	5	Paid freight on shipment to Ward, Inc., $80. (*Hint:* debit Delivery Expense)
	8	Returned $300 worth of the goods purchased July 1 from Dawson, Inc., because some goods were damaged. Dawson approved the return.
	9	Received returned merchandise from Ward, Inc., $200.
	10	Paid Dawson, Inc., the amount due.
	10	Purchased goods from Dorn Company with a price of $1,900. Terms 2/10, n/30.
	11	Paid freight on shipment from Dorn Company, $130.
	15	Received the amount due from Ward, Inc.
	15	Sold merchandise to Colby Corporation, $3,500.
	16	Mailed a check to Penn Company for the amount due on its July 2 invoice.
	18	Received an allowance of $100 from Dorn Company for defective merchandise purchased on July 10.
	19	Paid Dorn Company the amount due.
	25	Received the amount due from Colby Corporation.

Required

Prepare the necessary journal entries for Polidor Company.

SERIAL PROBLEM: KATE'S CARDS

(Note: This is a continuation of the Serial Problem: Kate's Cards from Chapters 1 through 4.)

SP5. Kate was a little worried about some of the practices of Fred Abbott, the CEO of Sentiments, and decided that an association with Sentiments could damage the reputation of her own company. Kate is very concerned that her business be viewed as socially responsible and any damage to her reputation at this early stage could prove very difficult to overcome. She therefore decided to concentrate her efforts on producing a quality product that consumers would be proud to purchase and send to their loved ones.

As expected, November saw a boom in Kate's greeting card business. She invested in additional computer graphics equipment, which she partially funded with a bank loan of $15,000 and an additional investment of her own funds into the business. The loan carries an interest rate of six percent with interest payments required semiannually. The entire principal balance is due in one balloon payment in two years. Kate uses a perpetual inventory system. As of December 2, 2015, Kate's Cards had the following account balances:

Cash	$11,900	Accumulated depreciation	$ 1,600
Accounts receivable	16,800	Accounts payable	13,800
Inventory	16,000	Other current liabilities	900
Other current assets	3,600	Long-term note payable	15,000
Computer equipment	38,900	Common stock	25,000
		Retained earnings	30,900

The company had the following transactions during December 2015:

Dec. 7 Paid $1,800 to employees. Of this amount, $900 was for an amount owed from November. Salaries due to employees at the end of each month are recorded as Other Current Liabilities.

9 Received $5,400 from customers as payment on account.

12 Sold, for cash, $9,000 of greeting cards. This merchandise had cost $6,000 to produce.

14 Purchased additional inventory totaling $7,000 on account with terms of 2/10, n/45.

15 Paid cash for supplies (listed as Other Current Assets) in the amount of $600.

19 Sold, on account with terms of 2/10, n/30, greeting cards totaling $6,000. The merchandise had cost $4,000 to produce.

21 Paid additional salaries of $1,400.

25 Paid the total owed for the merchandise that was purchased on December 14.

28 Received payment in full from the customer that purchased the merchandise on December 19.

31 Depreciation for the month totaled $900.

31 A physical count of inventory and supplies revealed that $13,000 and $2,000, respectively, were on hand at year-end. Assume that Other Current Assets consists only of the cost of supplies.

Required
a. Prepare journal entries for the December transactions.
b. Prepare a classified income statement for the month of December 2015.
c. Calculate Kate's gross profit percentage and return on sales ratio for December 2015.

EXTENDING YOUR KNOWLEDGE

REPORTING AND ANALYSIS

COLUMBIA
SPORTSWEAR
COMPANY

EYK5-1. **Financial Reporting Problem: The Columbia Sportswear Company** The financial statements for the **Columbia Sportswear Company** are in Appendix A at the end of this book.

Required
Using the company's Consolidated Statement of Operations (which is another name for Income Statement), answer the following questions.

a. What was the change in net sales and in net income from 2013 to 2014?
b. What was the gross profit percentage in each of the three years, 2012 through 2014? Comment on the trend in this ratio.
c. What was the return on sales ratio in each of the three years, 2012 through 2014? Comment on the trend in this ratio.

COLUMBIA
SPORTSWEAR
COMPANY

UNDER ARMOUR,
INC.

EYK5-2. **Comparative Analysis Problem: The Columbia Sportswear Company vs. Under Armour, Inc.** The financial statements for the **Columbia Sportswear Company** and **Under Armour, Inc.** are in Appendix A and B, respectively, at the end of this book.

Required
a. Based on the information you find in these financial statements, determine the following values for each company:
  1. Gross profit for 2014
  2. Gross profit percentage for 2014
  3. Net income for 2014
  4. Return on sales ratio for 2014
b. Based on this information, what can you say about the relative performance of these two companies?

EYK5-3. **Business Decision Problem** Northwestern Corporation started a retail clothing business on July 1, 2015. During 2015, Northwestern Corporation had the following summary transactions related to merchandise inventory:

	Purchases	Sales
July	$240,000	$ 360,000
August	384,000	696,000
September	312,000	576,000
October	360,000	660,000
November.	900,000	1,020,000
December.	264,000	1,344,000

On average, Northwestern's cost of goods sold is 50 percent of sales. Assume that there were no sales returns and allowances or purchases returns and allowances during this six-month time period.

Required
a. Calculate the ending merchandise inventory for each of the six months.
b. Northwestern's purchases peaked during November; its sales peaked during December. Did Northwestern plan its purchases wisely? Should Northwestern expect a similar pattern in future years?

EYK5-4. **Financial Analysis Problem** Johnson & Johnson is a worldwide manufacturer of health care products, including Band-Aid bandages and Mylanta antacid. It reported the following results for three recent years (Year 3 is the most recent):

JOHNSON & JOHNSON

(in millions)	Year 3	Year 2	Year 1
Net sales.	$63,747	$61,095	$53,324
Cost of goods sold.	18,511	17,751	15,057

Assume that similar-sized companies in the same basic industries have experienced an average gross profit percentage of 70 percent each year.

Required
a. Calculate the gross profit percentage for Johnson & Johnson for the three years.
b. Compare the three-year trend in gross profit percentage for Johnson & Johnson to the assumed industry average. Analyze the trend and evaluate the performance of Johnson & Johnson compared to the assumed industry average.

CRITICAL THINKING

EYK5-5. **Accounting Research Problem** Refer to the fiscal year 2014 annual report of General Mills, Inc., available on this book's Website.

GENERAL MILLS, INC.

Required
a. How much sales revenue did General Mills report in 2013 and 2014?
b. What was the company's gross profit percentage in 2013 and 2014?
c. How much net income did the company earn in 2013 and 2014?
d. What was the company's return on sales for 2013 and 2014? What can we conclude about the company's performance over the two-year period?

EYK5-6. **Accounting Communication Activity** Nobel Company produces custom machinery that has few competitors. As such, Nobel is able to charge a large markup that is reflected in its large gross profit percentage. Recently the marketing director proposed offering a new set of products that are more generic in nature, and therefore will not allow large markups. The accounting department has, however, determined the products will add to Nobel's overall net income. The following table provides estimates of Nobel's profitability both with and without the new product:

	Without New Product	With New Product
Net sales..	$250,000	$350,000
Cost of goods sold...................................	125,000	210,000
Net income..	25,000	31,500

Required

The President of Nobel, Jack Towne, has asked you to write a memo answering the following questions.

a.   How will the new product line affect the company's profitability as measured by its gross profit percentage and the return on sales ratio?

b.   How is it possible for net income to improve, while at the same time these profitability ratios may deteriorate?

c.   Should the company expand by offering this new product line?

EYK5-7.   Accounting Ethics Case   During the last week of 2014, George Connors, controller of We 'R' Appliances, received a memorandum from the firm's president, Jane Anderson. The memorandum stated that Anderson had negotiated a very large sale with a new customer and directed Connors to see that the order was processed and the goods shipped before the end of the year. Anderson noted that she had to depart from the usual credit terms of n/30 and allow terms of n/60 to clinch the sale. Although the credit terms were unusual for the company, Connors was particularly pleased with the news because business had been somewhat slow. The goods were shipped on December 29 and the sale was incorporated into the 2014 financial data.

It is now mid-February 2015, and two events have occurred recently that, together, cause concern for Connors. First, he was inadvertently copied on a letter from the firm's bank to Anderson. The letter stated that the bank had reconsidered its decision to deny a loan to the company and is now granting the loan based on the new, and favorable, sales data supplied by the president. The bank was "particularly impressed with the sales improvement shown in December." Although Connors had been involved in the initial loan application that was denied, he had been unaware that the president had reapplied for the loan.

The second event was that all of the goods shipped on December 29, 2014, to the new customer had just been returned.

Required

What are the ethical considerations George Connors faces as a result of the recent events?

TARGET   **EYK5-8.   Corporate Social Responsibility Problem   Target** is one of a large growing number of companies that publish an annual corporate social responsibility report. Go to the Target Website and navigate to the section on corporate responsibility to download Target's latest corporate responsibility report. Discuss some of the ways that Target documents its good citizenship.

EYK5-9.   Analyzing IFRS Financial Statements   The 2014 financial statements of LVMH Moet Hennessey-Louis Vuitton S.A. are presented in Appendix C at the end of this book. LVMH is a Paris-based holding company and one of the world's largest and best-known luxury goods companies. As members of the European Union, French companies are required to prepare their consolidated (group) financial statements using International Financial Reporting Standards (IFRS). Using the company's financial statements, calculate the company's (a) gross profit percentage and (b) return on sales ratio for 2013 and 2014. Comment on the trend in the company's profitability over the two-year period.

COSTCO   **EYK5-10.   Working with the Takeaways   Costco Wholesale Corporation** is the largest membership warehouse club chain in the world based on sales volume. It is the fifth largest general retailer in the United States. Costco is also one of the fastest growing retailers, having grown to over 600 locations since its start in 1983. A look at Costco's income statement reveals the following data:

COSTCO WHOLESALE CORPORATION		
(in millions)	2014	2013
Net sales.	$110,212	$102,870
Cost of goods sold.	98,458	91,948
Net income.	2,058	2,039

Required

Evaluate Costco's performance in terms of gross profit percentage and return on sales ratio. How does Costco compare to Target and Walmart? (See **Exhibits 5-5** and **5-6** on pages 245 and 246.)

ANSWERS TO SELF-STUDY QUESTIONS:

1. c, (pp. 237–241) 2. c, (pp. 237–241) 3. c, (pp. 238–241) 4. c, (pp. 245–247) 5. c, (pp. 239–241)
6. d, (pp. 239–241) 7. a, (pp. 245–247) 8. c, (p. 246) 9. b, (p. 236) 10. c, (p. 249)
11. h, (pp. 250–251)

YOUR TURN! SOLUTIONS

Solution 5.1

b) is false. The sum of beginning Inventory plus the cost of goods purchased is equal to the cost of goods available for sale. This would be equal to the cost of goods sold only if all available inventory was sold.

Solution 5.2

June 1	Inventory	510.00	
	Accounts payable		510.00
	To record merchandise purchased on account (125 CDs @ $4.08 each)		

June 1	Inventory	22.18	
	Cash		22.18
	To record payment of freight charges on merchandise purchased.		

June 4	Accounts payable	61.20	
	Inventory		61.20
	To record the return of defective merchandise (15 units @ $4.08 per unit).		

June 8	Accounts payable	448.80	
	Cash		439.82
	Inventory		8.98
	To record full payment within discount period. Cash discount earned = $8.98.		

Solution 5.3

June 15	Accounts receivable	750.00	
	Sales revenue		750.00
	To record the sale of 75 CDs on account.		

June 15	Cost of goods sold	315.00	
	Inventory		315.00
	To record cost of goods sold for 75 CDs.		

June 20	Sales returns and allowances	50.00	
	Accounts receivable		50.00
	To record the return of 5 CDs for credit.		

June 20	Inventory	21.00	
	Cost of goods sold		21.00
	To record the return of 5 CDs for credit		

June 25	Cash	700.00	
	Accounts receivable		700.00
	To record cash payment from customer.		

Solution 5.4

Gross profit percentage = ($100,000 − $45,000)/$100,000 = 55 percent
Return on sales ratio = $10,500/$100,000 = 10.5 percent

A gross profit percentage of 55 percent indicates that Musicland was able to earn 55 cents for each dollar of net sales after considering just its cost of goods sold. In other words, Musicland still has 55 cents available from each dollar of net sales to cover its remaining expenses and to earn a net profit.

A return on sales ratio of 10.5 percent indicates that Musicland was able to earn 10.5 cents in net income from each dollar of net sales after subtracting all of the business's expenses.

Solution 5A.1

June 1	Purchases	510.00	
	Accounts payable		510.00
	To record merchandise purchased on account (125 @ $4.08 each).		

June 1	Freight in	22.18	
	Cash		22.18
	To record payment of freight charge on merchandise purchase.		

June 4	Accounts payable	61.20	
	Purchase returns and allowances		61.20
	To record the return of defective merchandise (15 units).		

June 8	Accounts payable	448.80	
	Cash		439.82
	Purchase discounts		8.98
	To record payment for merchandise purchased.		

Solution 5A.2

June 15	Accounts receivable	750.00	
	Sales revenue		750.00
	To record the sale of 75 CDs on account.		

June 20	Sales returns and allowances	50.00	
	Accounts receivable		50.00
	To record the return of 5 CDs for credit.		

June 25	Cash	700.00	
	Accounts receivable		700.00
	To record cash payment from customer.		

Solution 5A.3

MUSICLAND COMPANY Cost of Goods Sold For Year Ended December 31, 2015			
Cost of goods sold			
Inventory, January 1			$10,000
Purchases		$50,000	
Less: Purchase returns and allowances	$2,000		
Purchase discounts	1,000	3,000	
Net purchases		47,000	
Add: Freight-in		200	
Cost of goods purchased			47,200
Cost of goods available for sale			57,200
Less: Inventory, December 31			12,200
Cost of goods sold			$45,000

Solution 5B.1

Adjusting Journal Entry for Sales Discount

Dec. 31	Sales discounts	3,000	
	Allowance for sales discounts		3,000
	To record the estimated sales discount taken of 2 percent on credit sales still eligible for discount at year-end ($150,000 × 0.02).		

Adjusting Journal Entry for Sales Returns

Dec. 31	Sales returns and allowances	15,000	
	Sales refunds payable		15,000
	To record the estimated return of 7.5 percent of the merchandise sold that is still eligible for return at year-end ($200,000 × 0.075).		
Dec. 31	Estimated inventory return	4,500	
	Cost of goods sold		4,500
	To record the estimated return of 7.5 percent of the merchandise sold that is still eligible for return at year-end ($60,000 × 0.075).		

6

Accounting for Inventory

PAST

Chapter 5 focused on accounting for merchandising transactions.

PRESENT

This chapter explains the accounting for inventory and the cost flow assumptions we make to simplify computations.

FUTURE

Chapter 7 focuses on fraud risks faced by businesses and internal controls used to combat fraud and errors.

LEARNING OBJECTIVES

1. **Explain** inventory concepts and modern inventory practices. *(p. 276)*
2. **Describe** inventory costing under specific identification, weighted-average cost, FIFO, and LIFO. *(p. 280)*
3. **Analyze** the financial effects of different inventory costing methods on company profit. *(p. 285)*
4. **Apply** the lower-of-cost-or-market method. *(p. 291)*
5. **Define** *inventory turnover* and *days' sales in inventory* and **explain** the use of these ratios. *(p. 293)*
6. Appendix 6A: **Describe** inventory costing under a perpetual inventory system using specific identification, weighted-average cost, FIFO, and LIFO. *(p. 296)*
7. Appendix 6B: **Define** the LIFO reserve and **explain** how it is used to compare the performance of companies using different inventory costing methods. *(p. 302)*

BEST BUY

The period following the financial crisis of 2008 will likely be remembered as some of the most difficult years ever in the retail industry. Retail company bankruptcies during this time period include **Linens 'n Things**, **Mervyn's**, **Sharper Image**, **Steve and Barry's**, and **Wickes Furniture**. However, the bankruptcy of **Circuit City** was perhaps the biggest surprise. Circuit City had over 500 stores throughout the United States that were full of the latest flat screen TVs and electronics. What could explain the failure of Circuit City when the company's biggest rival, **Best Buy**, reported nearly $5 million in profits during the same time period? One key explanation, according to *Time* magazine, was ineffective inventory management.

Circuit City was unable to sell its existing inventory quickly enough, thereby failing to generate the necessary cash flow to enable the company to pay off its huge debt load and creating a backlog that prevented the company from ordering the newer models that consumers preferred. Best Buy, on the other hand, spent considerable time and effort revamping its supply chain and inventory management system to avoid such a fate. The Vice President of Logistics and Transportation with Best Buy observed that "Without better inventory management, Best Buy would have been a thing of the past."

With inventory comprising over one-third of Best Buy's assets, it is readily apparent why effective inventory management is so crucial to its financial health (and that of Circuit City). But how is Best Buy's inventory valued and recorded on its balance sheet? What measures exist for management and financial statement users to evaluate how effectively those inventories are being managed? We discuss answers to both of these important questions and others in this chapter.

Source: "Why Circuit City Busted, While Best Buy Boomed," by Anita Hamilton, Time.com, November 11, 2008; Best Buy 10-K report; Circuit City 10-K report.

To illustrate shrinkage (the usual situation), assume that the December 31 balance of the Inventory account (including all items) is $120,600. Also assume that a physical count of the inventory produced a total cost at December 31 of $120,000. The following period-end adjusting entry is required at December 31 to adjust the balance in the Inventory account from $120,600 to $120,000:

A	=	L	+	SE				

−600				−600
				Exp
					Dec. 31	Cost of Goods Sold
						    Inventory
						    To adjust the inventory account balance to the total cost determined by
						    a physical inventory count in a perpetual inventory system.
							600	600

YOUR TURN! 6.1

The solution is on page 326.

The Counter Company just completed the year-end physical count of its inventory. The total value of inventory was determined to be $300,000. The following additional information came to light following the conclusion of the physical count:

1. The company included $20,000 of inventory that was shipped F.O.B. destination.
2. The company included $15,000 of inventory that was shipped F.O.B. shipping point.
3. The company did not include $25,000 of inventory that was being sold on consignment by Johnson Sales, a consignment dealer. The inventory is located at Johnson Sales, but it was still owned by The Counter Company at the time of its physical count of inventory.

Discuss how this additional information affects the $300,000 value that The Counter Company initially determined to be the value of its ending inventory.

INVENTORY COSTING METHODS

LO2 **Describe** inventory costing under specific identification, weighted-average cost, FIFO, and LIFO.

In general, the value of a company's inventory is entered into the accounting records at its acquisition cost. Inventory costing is simple when the acquisition cost remains constant. For example, assume that the Fletcher Motor Company purchased electric motors four times during the year, as shown in **Exhibit 6-2**.

Exhibit 6-2	Illustration of Cost Flows When Prices Do Not Change
February 10 purchase	100 motors at $180 each
April 25 purchase	150 motors at $180 each
July 16 purchase	150 motors at $180 each
October 8 purchase	200 motors at $180 each
December 31 ending inventory	40 motors at $ _?_ each

The December 31 ending inventory for Fletcher Motor Company includes 40 electric motors, some from the July 16 purchase and some from the October 8 purchase. In this case, it is easy to determine the cost to be assigned to the 40 motors ($40 \times \$180 = \$7,200$) since all of the inventory purchases were made at the exact same purchase price of $180. In real business situations, however, the purchase price of an item of inventory often changes. The trend is usually toward increasing prices, but some purchase prices may actually decline. When purchase prices change during the year, a company must either keep track of the acquisition cost of each specific unit or make an assumption about which units have been sold and which units remain in inventory. Most companies choose the latter option and make an assumption about which units have been sold and which are still available because the cost of keeping track of exactly which units are sold can be prohibitively expensive.

Goods Flow vs. Cost Flow

Two concepts that are helpful in understanding the problem of assigning a cost to inventory when purchase prices are changing are goods flow and cost flow. **Goods flow** describes the actual physical movement of inventory through a business. **Cost flow** is the assumed assignment of costs to goods sold and to ending inventory. The cost flow need not, and often does not, reflect the actual goods flow through a business.

Generally accepted accounting principles permit businesses to use a cost flow that does not reflect the company's actual goods flow. For example, the goods flow in a grocery store chain like Safeway will almost always be such that the goods brought in first will be the first goods to be sold. This physical goods flow results in the least amount of loss due to spoilage. However, just because Safeway operates with this physical goods flow through its stores does not mean that the company is required to adopt a similar cost flow to calculate the value of its inventory. The *cost flow assumption* adopted could be one in which the most recent goods added to inventory are assumed to be the first goods sold.

The following sections on inventory costing use the periodic system. Appendix 6A uses the perpetual system. Your instructor can choose to cover either one or both systems. If the following periodic system is skipped, then read Appendix 6A and return to the section (on page 288) titled "Income Tax Effects."

Data for Illustration of Cost Flow Assumptions

In this section, we introduce and illustrate four generally accepted methods of costing inventories: (1) specific identification, (2) first-in, first-out (FIFO), (3) last-in, first-out (LIFO), and (4) weighted average cost. Following an illustration of the four methods, a comparative analysis of the financial results of the methods is presented. To facilitate a comparison of their results, we use a common set of data. Assume that Claremont Company's purchases and sales of inventory during the year are as shown in **Exhibit 6-3**.

Exhibit 6-3	Purchases and Sales for Application of Inventory Methods			
Date	**Event**	**No. of Units**	**Unit Cost**	**Total Cost**
Jan. 1	Beginning inventory	60	@ $10 =	$ 600
Mar. 27	Purchase inventory.	90	@ $11 =	$ 990
May 2	**Sell inventory**	(130)		
Aug. 15	Purchase inventory.	100	@ $13 =	$1,300
Nov. 6	Purchase inventory.	50	@ $16 =	$ 800
Dec. 10	**Sell inventory**	(90)		
Dec. 31	Ending inventory.	80		

The four inventory costing methods differ in the way they assign costs to the 80 units in ending inventory and the 220 units in cost of goods sold. Under the periodic inventory system, the Inventory account and the Cost of Goods Sold account are updated only at the end of the period, following a physical count of the ending inventory. Once the total cost of ending inventory is determined, the ending inventory amount is subtracted from cost of goods available for sale to derive the period's cost of goods sold.

Specific Identification Method

The **specific identification method** involves (1) keeping track of the purchase cost of each specific unit available for sale and (2) costing the ending inventory at the actual costs of the specific units not sold. Assume that the 80 unsold units consist of 10 units from beginning inventory, 20 units from the August 15 purchase, and all 50 of the units purchased on November 6. The cost assigned to the ending inventory and cost of goods sold is shown in **Exhibit 6-4**. Observe that the entire $3,690 of cost of the goods available for sale is assigned as either ending inventory or as cost of goods sold.

This information is used to compute ending inventory

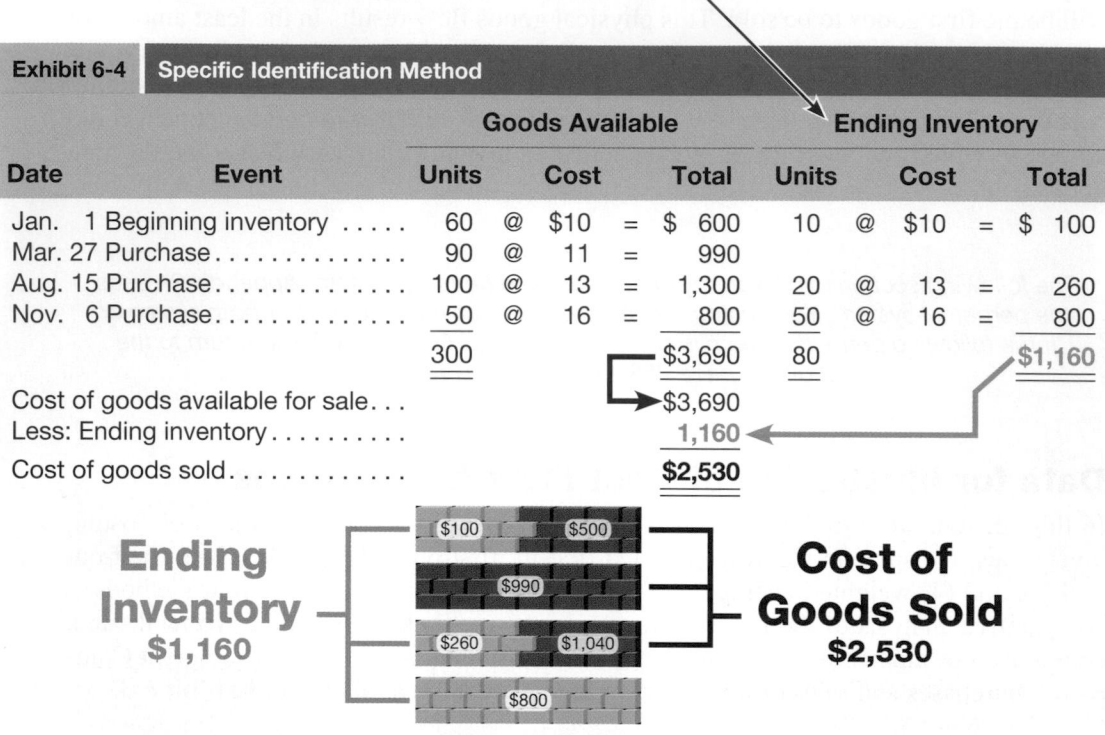

Exhibit 6-4	Specific Identification Method							
		Goods Available			**Ending Inventory**			
Date	**Event**	**Units**	**Cost**	**Total**	**Units**	**Cost**		**Total**
Jan. 1 Beginning inventory		60 @	$10 =	$ 600	10 @	$10	=	$ 100
Mar. 27 Purchase..............		90 @	11 =	990				
Aug. 15 Purchase..............		100 @	13 =	1,300	20 @	13	=	260
Nov. 6 Purchase..............		50 @	16 =	800	50 @	16	=	800
		300		$3,690	80			$1,160

Cost of goods available for sale. . . $3,690
Less: Ending inventory. 1,160
Cost of goods sold. $2,530

Ending Inventory $1,160

$100 $500
$990
$260 $1,040
$800

Cost of Goods Sold $2,530

First-In, First-Out (FIFO) Method

The **first-in, first-out (FIFO) method** assumes that the oldest goods (or earliest purchased) are sold first. This implies that ending inventory is *always* made up of the most recent purchases. FIFO results in the cost allocations as shown in **Exhibit 6-5**. This method assumes the first 220 units acquired are sold first and that the last 80 units purchased are those remaining.

| Exhibit 6-5 | First-In, First-Out Method | | | | | | | | | |

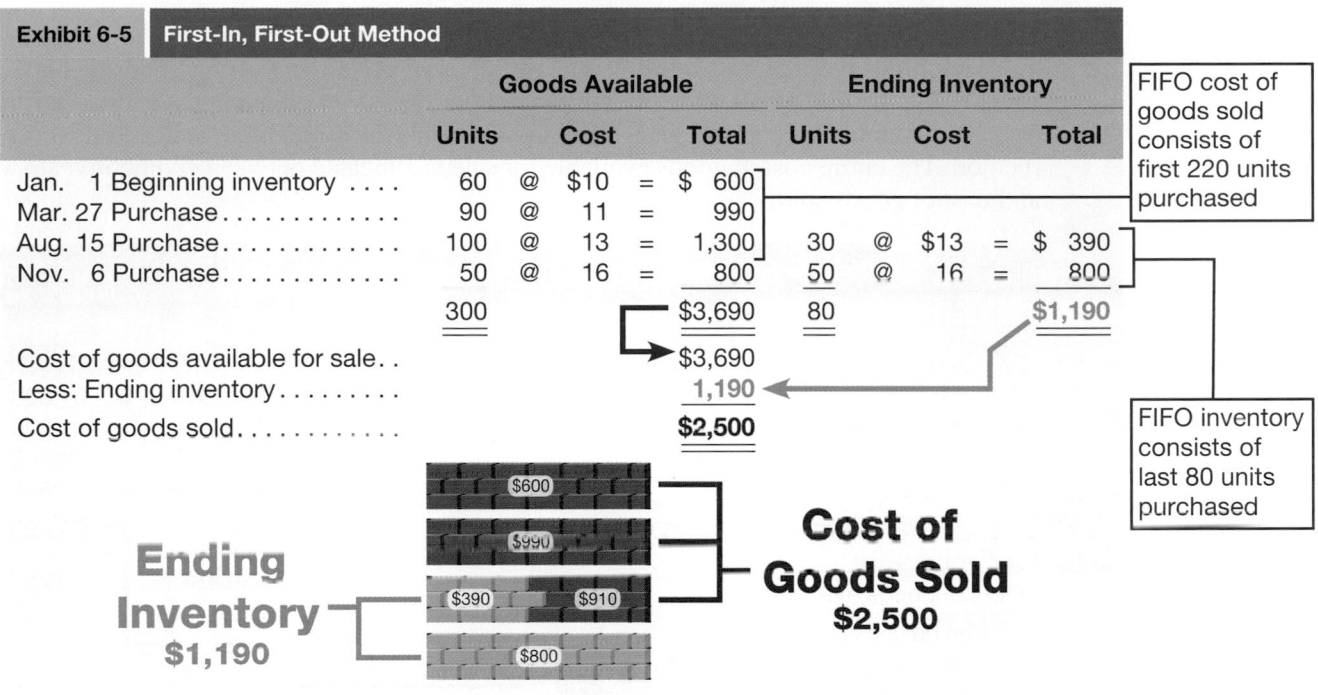

	Goods Available			Ending Inventory							FIFO cost of goods sold consists of first 220 units purchased
	Units	Cost		Total	Units	Cost		Total			
Jan. 1 Beginning inventory	60	@ $10	=	$ 600							
Mar. 27 Purchase.............	90	@ 11	=	990							
Aug. 15 Purchase.............	100	@ 13	=	1,300	30	@ $13	=	$ 390			
Nov. 6 Purchase.............	50	@ 16	=	800	50	@ 16	=	800			
	300			$3,690	80			$1,190			

Cost of goods available for sale.. $3,690
Less: Ending inventory......... 1,190
Cost of goods sold........... **$2,500**

FIFO inventory consists of last 80 units purchased

Ending
Inventory
$1,190

$600
$990
$390 $910
$800

**Cost of
Goods Sold
$2,500**

Last-In, First-Out (LIFO) Method

The **last-in, first-out (LIFO) method** assumes that the most recent purchases are sold first. **Exhibit 6-6** illustrates the calculation of LIFO cost of goods sold. LIFO assumes that the 220 units last (most recently) purchased are sold first, and that the 80 oldest units available for sale remain at the end of the period.

| Exhibit 6-6 | Last-In, First-Out Method | | | | | | | | | |

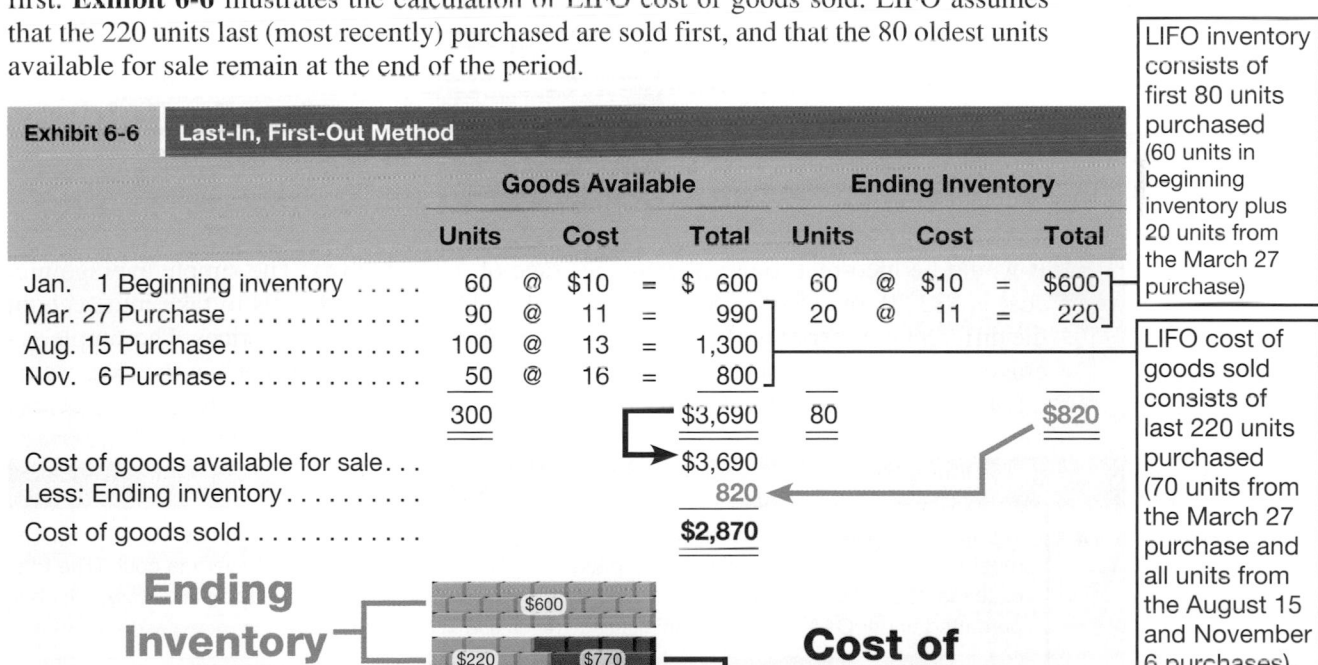

	Goods Available			Ending Inventory							LIFO inventory consists of first 80 units purchased (60 units in beginning inventory plus 20 units from the March 27 purchase)
	Units	Cost		Total	Units	Cost		Total			
Jan. 1 Beginning inventory	60	@ $10	=	$ 600	60	@ $10	=	$600			
Mar. 27 Purchase..............	90	@ 11	=	990	20	@ 11	=	220			
Aug. 15 Purchase..............	100	@ 13	=	1,300							
Nov. 6 Purchase..............	50	@ 16	=	800							
	300			$3,690	80			$820			

Cost of goods available for sale... $3,690
Less: Ending inventory.......... 820
Cost of goods sold............. **$2,870**

LIFO cost of goods sold consists of last 220 units purchased (70 units from the March 27 purchase and all units from the August 15 and November 6 purchases).

Ending
Inventory
$820

$600
$220 $770
$1,300
$800

**Cost of
Goods Sold
$2,870**

Weighted-Average Cost Method

A.K.A. The weighted-average cost method is often referred to as the *average cost method.*

The **weighted-average cost method** spreads the total dollar cost of the goods available for sale equally among all units. In our illustration, the weighted-average cost per unit is $12.30, computed as $3,690/300. **Exhibit 6-7** diagrams the assignment of costs under this method. The entire cost of goods available for sale is allocated between ending inventory and cost of goods sold.

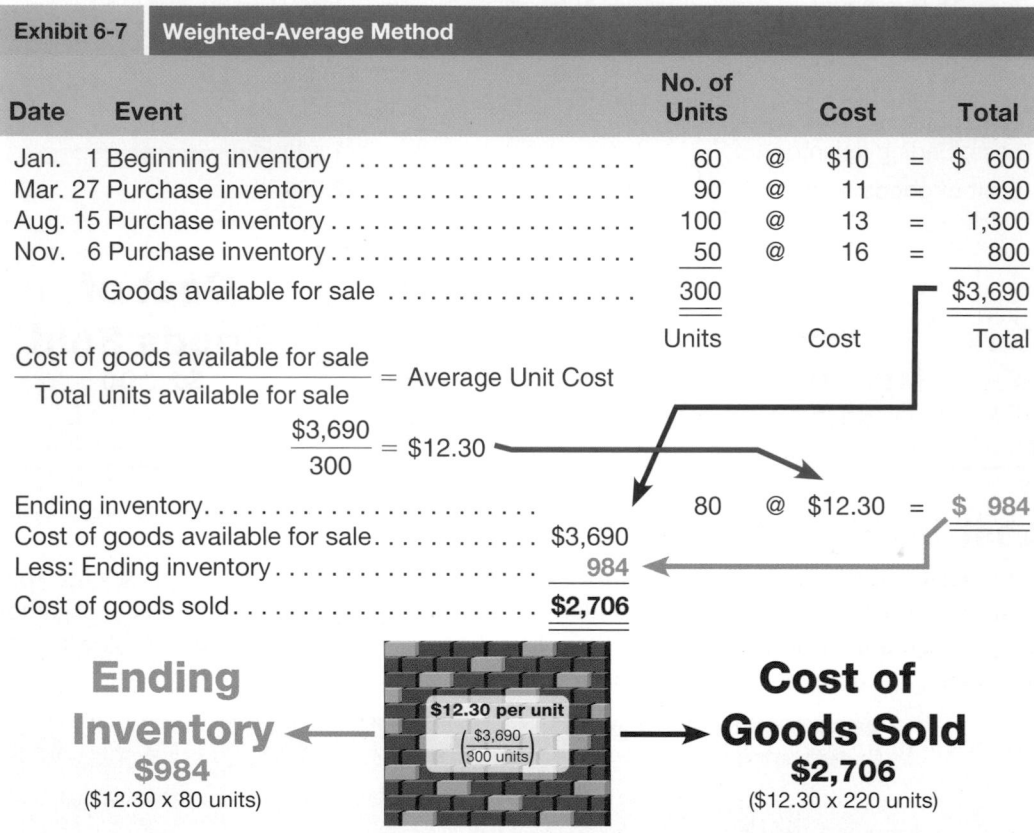

Exhibit 6-7	Weighted-Average Method					
Date	**Event**	**No. of Units**		**Cost**		**Total**
Jan. 1	Beginning inventory	60	@	$10	=	$ 600
Mar. 27	Purchase inventory	90	@	11	=	990
Aug. 15	Purchase inventory	100	@	13	=	1,300
Nov. 6	Purchase inventory	50	@	16	=	800
	Goods available for sale	300				$3,690
		Units		Cost		Total

$$\frac{\text{Cost of goods available for sale}}{\text{Total units available for sale}} = \text{Average Unit Cost}$$

$$\frac{\$3,690}{300} = \$12.30$$

Ending inventory........................	80 @ $12.30	=	$	984
Cost of goods available for sale........... $3,690				
Less: Ending inventory................... 984				
Cost of goods sold..................... **$2,706**				

Ending Inventory
$984
($12.30 x 80 units)

$12.30 per unit
$\frac{\$3,690}{300 \text{ units}}$

Cost of Goods Sold
$2,706
($12.30 x 220 units)

It would be incorrect to use a *simple* average of the unit costs. The simple average unit cost is $12.50, or $[(\$10 + \$11 + \$13 + \$16)/4]$. This figure fails to take into account the different number of units purchased and available at the various prices. The simple average cost yields the same result as the weighted-average cost only when the exact same number of units is purchased at each unit price.

ACCOUNTING IN PRACTICE

Inventory Costing Methods

The following chart identifies the inventory costing method used by a sample of 600 U.S. firms. The most frequently used method is FIFO, followed by LIFO and then weighted-average cost. (The total exceeds 100% because some firms use more than one method to value their inventory, which is permitted under GAAP.) [Source: Accounting Trends and Techniques]

70%	
60%	
50%	
40%	
30%	
20%	
10%	
0%	FIFO LIFO Weighted-average Other

The following inventory information is gathered from the accounting records of Tucker Enterprises:

Beginning inventory	4,000 units at $5 each
Purchases.	6,000 units at $7 each
Sales.	9,000 units at $10 each

Calculate (a) ending inventory, (b) cost of goods sold, and (c) the gross profit using each of the following methods (i) FIFO, (ii) LIFO, and (iii) weighted-average cost.

YOUR TURN! 6.2

The solution is on page 326.

Comparative Analysis of Inventory Costing Methods

The purchase price data used in the Claremont Company illustration has an important characteristic: the purchase price of the inventory increased each time that a purchase was made, from $11 per unit to $13 per unit to $16 per unit. Increasing inventory prices are frequently encountered in the real world where price inflation is common and price deflation is uncommon. **Exhibit 6-8** summarizes the results of applying the four inventory costing methods to the Claremont Company data and reveals that the FIFO method produces the lowest cost of goods sold ($2,500), while the LIFO method produces the highest cost of goods sold ($2,870). The exhibit also reveals that FIFO produces the highest year-end value of ending inventory ($1,190), while LIFO produces the lowest year-end value of ending inventory ($820). Specific identification and weighted-average cost produce ending inventory values and cost of goods sold values that fall in between the results obtained using FIFO and LIFO.

LO3 Analyze the financial effects of different inventory costing methods on company profit.

These results, however, are highly dependent on the purchase prices for the inventory. If the inventory's purchase price had been decreasing rather than increasing, the financial effects would have been just the opposite, with LIFO producing the lowest cost of goods sold and FIFO the highest. If the purchase prices had been perfectly stable, there would be no difference between the cost of goods sold or the ending inventory for any of the four methods.

Exhibit 6-8	Results of Different Inventory Costing Methods			
	Specific Identification	FIFO	LIFO	Weighted-Average
Cost of goods sold.	$2,530	$2,500	$2,870	$2,706
Ending inventory.	1,160	1,190	820	984

Selecting Inventory Methods

Under generally accepted accounting principles, a company is permitted to select one or more of the four methods for purposes of assigning cost to its ending inventory and its cost of goods sold. Which method (or methods, since a company may elect to value some of its inventory using FIFO, some using LIFO, and some using weighted-average cost) is selected by a company depends upon a number of factors—the type of product, the cost of the product, whether the product is perishable, whether the company desires to report a high or a low net income, and income tax considerations.

Specific Identification Method

Companies might choose to use specific identification for unique items with small volume and high unit cost, such as fine art or jewelry, that would justify the cost of tracking the specific unit cost of each inventory item. Specific identification is usually not cost-justified for inventories that have a low unit cost or involve high volumes of similar products.

FIFO Method

Many companies, especially those with perishable, time-dated, or style-affected merchandise, attempt to sell their oldest merchandise first. This is especially true for companies that sell food products, chemicals, and drugs. For these types of companies, the cost flow produced by the FIFO method most closely matches the actual goods flow. However, a company is not required to use the cost flow assumption that most closely matches its actual goods flow. When costs are rising, FIFO will result in the lowest cost of goods sold, and therefore, the highest net income. The desire to show a higher net income by some companies partly explains the popularity of the FIFO method.

LIFO Method

Although LIFO does not reflect the actual goods flow for most businesses, its popularity is likely linked to the potential income tax savings associated with its use. We illustrate the income tax advantages of the LIFO method in the next section. For some industries, however, LIFO does depict the actual goods flow. For example, in industries that extract natural resources, such as mining, the product is frequently dumped onto a storage pile from an overhead trestle, and sold inventory is taken from the top of the pile. One disadvantage of using LIFO when beginning inventories have been maintained or increased is that a firm's ending inventory can be substantially undervalued since old purchase prices tend to be retained on a company's books under the LIFO method. This, in turn, will cause a firm's current assets and total assets to likewise be undervalued.

Weighted-Average Cost Method

Weighted-average cost is best suited for businesses that warehouse a large volume of undifferentiated goods in a common area. Liquid fuels, grains, and other commodities are examples. Weighted-average cost typically generates a cost of goods sold amount that is neither high nor low as compared to the other methods, as is revealed in **Exhibit 6-8**.

Summary

We can broadly summarize the choice among the cost flow assumptions as follows:

1. Specific identification most closely identifies the actual cost of goods sold and ending inventory but can be costly to implement.

2. FIFO approximates the actual physical flow of goods for most firms.

3. LIFO is popular because of the income tax savings associated with its use.

4. Weighted-average cost is most often associated with businesses in which undifferentiated goods are commingled in a common area like a warehouse.

ACCOUNTING IN PRACTICE | **Geek Squad Accountant**

Thought you had to be a technology geek to work for Best Buy's Geek Squad? Think again. Accounting skills could be your path to geek stardom. A recent job posting at Best Buy seeks an Accounting Analyst—Geek Squad Retail Services. The job description states the Accounting Analysts will "provide controllership support for Retail Services within the Geek Squad portfolio and additionally ECC (Enterprise Customer Care)." In addition "this role will provide reporting and analysis of monthly results, along with identifying and documenting business risks and opportunities." And who says accountants can't hold their own among the geeks?

Analysis of Costing Methods and Gross Profit

To illustrate the financial effects of the different inventory costing methods, assume that the 220 units sold by the Claremont Company were sold for $20 each, producing sales of $4,400 ($20 × 220). **Exhibit 6-9** shows the difference in gross profit under each of the four inventory costing methods. Remember that the difference in reported gross profit results from the assumptions made about cost flow, not from any difference in the physical flow of goods. In each case, 220 units were sold and 80 units remained. Each of the inventory costing methods is in accord with generally accepted accounting principles, yet the methods have different financial affects on gross profit and net income.

Exhibit 6-9	Gross Profit Using Alternative Inventory Costing Methods			
	Specific Identification	FIFO	LIFO	Weighted-Average
Sales (220 units @ $20)	$4,400	$4,400	$4,400	$4,400
Cost of goods sold.	2,530	2,500	2,870	2,706
Gross profit.	$1,870	$1,900	$1,530	$1,694
Increased gross profit compared with LIFO. .	$ 340	$ 370		$ 164

Income Statement and Balance Sheet Effects

As **Exhibit 6-9** reveals, LIFO results in the smallest gross profit ($1,530), with FIFO producing the highest ($1,900) gross profit. This result occurs because the purchase price of inventory was increasing throughout the year, from $11 per unit to $13 per unit to $16 per unit. When costs are rising, FIFO tends to overstate gross profit (and income) because older, lower unit costs are included in the cost of goods sold and matched with current sales prices. In other words, in the illustration, the units sold are charged to costs of goods sold under FIFO at unit costs of $10, $11, and $13. If the latest purchase price reflects the inventory's current acquisition cost, the units sold must be replaced by units costing $16 (or more if costs continue to rise).

It is frequently argued that LIFO provides a better matching of current costs with current revenues since the cost of the most recent purchases constitutes the LIFO cost of goods sold. While LIFO associates the current, higher unit costs with cost of goods sold, it assigns costs to ending inventory using the older, lower unit costs. As a consequence, the value of the LIFO ending inventory on the balance sheet is often undervalued in terms of the inventory's current value. When inventory quantities are maintained or increased, the LIFO method prevents older costs from appearing in the cost of goods sold. No doubt, some firms still carry LIFO inventories at unit costs that existed more than 10 years ago. Under FIFO, the ending inventory is measured at relatively recent costs, which means the ending inventory reflects relatively current costs.

Consistency and Full Disclosure

PRINCIPLE ALERT

Inventory costing requires the application of *consistency* and *full disclosure*. Because of the possible variation in gross profit and ending inventory values that result from the use of different inventory costing methods, it is important that a firm use the same inventory costing method from one fiscal period to the next. This application of consistency enhances the comparability of a firm's cost of goods sold, gross profit, net income, inventory, current assets, and total assets over time. In addition, a firm should disclose which inventory costing method it is using, either in its financial statements or in the notes to the statements. This information is required by the full disclosure principle and is important to users who compare financial data across firms.

For readers skipping the periodic system, please resume reading here.

Income Tax Effects

During periods of rising purchase prices, LIFO results in a lower gross profit than any of the alternative inventory costing methods. A lower gross profit, and net income, means that lower amounts of income taxes need to be paid. Hence, the desire to reduce current income tax payments is a major reason for widespread use of LIFO.

To illustrate LIFO's income tax advantage, assume that the Huntington Corporation has beginning inventory of 10 units costing $500 each, and that only two transactions occur. In the first transaction, it purchases 10 more units costing $630 each, for a total cash purchase price of $6,300. In the second transaction, it sells 10 units for $700 each, for a total cash sale of $7,000. Both transactions are for cash and, for simplicity, we assume that the company's operating expenses are zero and the applicable income tax rate is 35 percent. **Exhibit 6-10** presents the income statements and cash flows for Huntington under both FIFO and LIFO.

Exhibit 6-10	FIFO vs. LIFO Comparison: Phantom Profit Effect and Tax Benefit			
	FIFO		**LIFO**	
	Income Statement	**Cash In (Out)**	**Income Statement**	**Cash In (Out)**
Sales (10 @ $700)...............	$ 7,000	$7,000	$ 7,000	$7,000
Cost of goods sold				
Beginning inventory (10 @ $500)	5,000		5,000	
Purchases (10 @ $630).............	6,300	(6,300)	6,300	(6,300)
Goods available (20 units)...........	11,300		11,300	
Ending inventory				
10 @ FIFO	6,300			
10 @ LIFO			5,000	
Cost of goods sold..................	5,000		6,300	
Pretax income	2,000		700	
Income tax (at 35%)................	700	(700)	245	(245)
Net income.......................	$ 1,300		$ 455	
Net cash proceeds		$ 0		$ 455

Under FIFO, Huntington reports $1,300 of net income, but cash from sales ($7,000) is only enough to replace the inventory sold ($6,300) and pay the income tax ($700) on the $2,000 in FIFO pretax net income. The net income of $1,300 is not realized in cash, and consequently, is unavailable to pay dividends or be reinvested in the business or replace the sold inventory. As a consequence, FIFO net income is sometimes referred to as *phantom profit.*

Under LIFO, Huntington reports net income of $455 as a consequence of its higher cost of goods sold ($6,300). With a lower net income, it incurs a smaller cash outflow ($245) for income taxes. The attractiveness of LIFO during periods of rising inventory purchase prices is evidenced by LIFO's more favorable net cash flow ($455) as compared with FIFO ($0). Use of LIFO during times of falling inventory purchase prices, however, has the opposite income tax effect.

Management is usually free to select different accounting treatments for financial reporting to shareholders and for income tax reporting to the Internal Revenue Service (IRS). For example, it is acceptable for a business to use different methods of computing depreciation when reporting under GAAP on the income statement and for reporting under income tax regulations on a company's income tax return. This situation has led some individuals to correctly infer that U.S. corporations effectively maintain two sets of financial records—one for reporting to shareholders and one for reporting to the IRS. An exception to this flexibility occurs when a company chooses to use LIFO for income tax reporting to benefit from the lower income taxes that result from the use of LIFO when purchase prices are rising. A U.S. federal tax regulation known as the **LIFO conformity rule** requires any company that selects LIFO for income tax reporting to also use LIFO for financial reporting to shareholders. It is currently not possible to report lower taxable income to the IRS using LIFO while also reporting higher net income to shareholders using FIFO. (The elimination of LIFO for income tax purposes has been discussed during budget debates in an effort to generate additional tax revenues to help close the U.S. budget deficit.)

Errors in the Inventory Count

A physical count of inventory is necessary to determine the value of a company's ending inventory regardless of what inventory method is used. Unfortunately, errors in the inventory count, for example failing to count some items or counting some items twice, can occur. These errors affect not only the value of ending inventory reported on the balance sheet in the period of the error, but also cost of goods sold and gross profit. Further, the error is not limited to only the current period—cost of goods sold and gross profit in the following period are also affected. To illustrate, assume that the Arrow Company began operations in 2014. **Exhibit 6-11** summarizes Arrow's 2014 and 2015 transactions.

Exhibit 6-11	Inventory Transactions for Arrow Company	Inventory Units	Inventory Balance
2014	Beginning inventory	0	0
	Purchased 1,000 units of merchandise inventory for $3 per unit	1000	$3,000
	Sold 400 units of merchandise inventory	(400)	(1,200)*
	Ending inventory	600	$1,800
2015	Beginning inventory	600	$1,800
	Purchased 2,000 units of merchandise inventory for $3 per unit	2,000	6,000
	Sold 1,500 units of merchandise inventory	(1,500)	(4,500)*
	Ending inventory	1,100	$3,300

* Cost of goods sold.

Assume that Arrow Company made an error in its physical count of inventory at the end of 2014, mistakenly double-counting 40 units of inventory, and consequently, overstating ending inventory by $120 (40 units × $3). As illustrated in **Exhibit 6-12**, both the value of ending inventory and cost of goods sold in 2014 are affected. Further, because ending inventory in 2014 becomes beginning inventory in 2015, cost of goods sold in 2015 is also misstated. **Exhibit 6-12** illustrates these effects on both the 2014 and 2015 Arrow Company income statements.

Exhibit 6-12	Inventory Error Effects					
Cost of goods sold		=	**Beginning Inventory**	+ **Purchases**	−	**Ending Inventory**
2014: $1,080 (instead of $1,200).		=	$ 0	+ $3,000	−	$1,920**
2015: $4,620 (instead of $4,500).		=	$1,920	+ $6,000	−	$3,300

Key figures		**No Error**	**With Error**
2014			
Cost of goods sold		$1,200	$1,080 ↓
Gross profit (under)/over stated			$ 120
2015			
Cost of goods sold		$4,500	$4,620 ↑
Gross profit (under)/over stated			$ (120)

** ($1,800 + $120)

In sum, an error in the ending inventory account in the current year affects the value of ending inventory in the current year, as well as current year gross profit through cost of goods sold. The error also affects, in an opposite direction, gross profit in the following year (through its effect on cost of goods sold). To show this, and using the company in **Exhibit 6-12**, notice that the combined cost of goods sold for both years is $5,700, without the error ($1,200 + $4,500) or with the error ($1,080 + $4,620). Further, we see that ending inventory was overstated in 2014 by $120, which resulted in: 2014 ending inventory being overstated by $120, 2014 cost of goods sold being understated by $120, and 2014 gross profit being overstated by $120. The same $120 error is carried through to 2015 where it causes cost of goods sold to be overstated by $120 (because of the overstatement of beginning inventory), and gross profit to be understated by $120.

FORENSIC ACCOUNTING | **Fraudulent Reporting**

Most errors in inventory result from honest mistakes; however, there are inventory counts that have been intentionally overstated. One such case involved a retail company called **Crazy Eddie**, which was a discount electronics store. Court records indicate that Eddie, the founder, hired his nephew, Sammy, who had earned a degree in accounting, to inflate sales by $15 to $20 million per year, and falsified inventories to justify the inflated figures. The U.S. Securities and Exchange Commission ultimately charged Eddie with securities fraud and he was sentenced to 8 years in prison and ordered to pay more than $150 million in fines.

YOUR TURN! 6.3

The solution is on page 327.

Assume Pointer Company began operations in 2015. The table below summarizes Pointer's 2015 and 2016 transactions. For simplicity assume that cost of goods sold is the only expense that occurs.

		Inventory Units	Inventory Balance	Sales
2015	Beginning inventory	0	0	
	Purchased 2,000 units of merchandise for $5 per unit	2,000	$10,000	
	Sold 1,500 units of merchandise for $10 per unit	(1,500)	(7,500)	$15,000
	Ending inventory.	500	$ 2,500	
2016	Beginning inventory	500	$ 2,500	
	Purchased 3,000 units of merchandise for $5 per unit	3,000	$15,000	
	Sold 2,500 units of merchandise for $10 per unit	(2,500)	(12,500)	$25,000
	Ending inventory.	1,000	$ 5,000	

Assume that Pointer made an error in its physical count of Inventory at the end of 2015, mistakenly omitting 100 units of inventory, and consequently, understating ending inventory by $500 (100 units × $5). Determine Pointer's 2015 and 2016 ending inventory without the error. Also compute Pointer's sales, cost of goods sold, and net income for 2015 and 2016 both with and without the error.

LOWER-OF-COST-OR-MARKET METHOD

LO4 Apply the lower-of-cost-or-market method.

In general, inventory is valued at its acquisition cost using the common inventory costing methods explained in this chapter. However, it can be necessary to report inventory at a lower value if there is evidence that the inventory's utility to a business—that is, the inventory's revenue-generating ability—has fallen below its acquisition cost. Such *inventory write-downs* can occur when (1) merchandise must be sold at reduced prices because it is damaged or otherwise not in normal salable condition or when (2) the cost of replacing the ending inventory has declined below the inventory's recorded acquisition cost.

Net Realizable Value

Damaged, physically deteriorated, or obsolete merchandise should be measured and reported at its net realizable value on the balance sheet when this value is less than the inventory's acquisition cost. **Net realizable value** is an item's estimated selling price less the expected cost of disposal. For example, assume that an inventory item cost $300 but can be sold for only $200 because it is damaged. If the related selling costs are estimated to be $20, the inventory should be written down to $180 ($200 estimated selling price less $20 estimated disposal cost) and a $120 inventory write-down loss ($300 − $180) should be reported on the income statement for the current period.

Lower-of-Cost-or-Market Method

The **lower-of-cost-or-market (LCM)** method provides for the recognition of an inventory write-down loss when the inventory's replacement cost declines below its recorded acquisition cost. Under LCM, a loss is reported in the period when the inventory's replacement cost declines, rather than during a subsequent period when the actual sale of the inventory takes place. Market, for purposes of applying the LCM method, is defined as the current replacement cost of the inventory. This procedure assumes that decreases in the replacement cost of inventory will be accompanied by proportionate decreases in the selling price of the inventory. The LCM method values the ending inventory at its lower (replacement) market value. Consequently, income decreases by the amount that the ending inventory is written down. When the ending inventory becomes part of the cost of goods sold in a future period, its reduced carrying value helps maintain normal profit margins in the period when sold.

To illustrate, assume that an inventory item that cost $80 has been selling at a retail price of $100, yielding a gross profit percentage of 20 percent. Assume also that by year-end, the item's replacement cost has declined to $60—a 25 percent decline—and a proportionate reduction in its selling price from $100 to $75 is expected in the following period. In this case, the inventory is written down to its $60 replacement cost, reducing the current period's net income by a $20 write-down loss ($80 − $60 = $20). When the inventory is sold in a subsequent period for $75, the normal gross profit percentage of 20 percent on sales is reported ($75 − $60 = $15 gross profit). The LCM method is applied to each individual item in inventory. It can also be applied to different categories of inventory.

In **Exhibit 6-13**, LCM is applied on an *individual item-by-item* basis, and the value of ending inventory is $6,820. Inventory replacement costs are in such sources as current catalogs, purchase contracts with suppliers, and other forms of price quotations.

Exhibit 6-13	Application of the Lower-of-Cost-or-Market					
		Per Unit		**Total**		**LCM**
Inventory Item	**Quantity**	**Cost**	**Market**	**Cost**	**Market**	**Individual Item**
Cameras						
Model V70.........	40	$80	$75	$3,200	$3,000	$3,000
Model V85.........	30	60	64	1,800	1,920	1,800
Subtotal.........				$5,000	$4,920	—
Calculators						
Model C20	90	13	15	$1,170	$1,350	1,170
Model C40	50	20	17	1,000	850	850
Subtotal.........				$2,170	$2,200	—
Total				$7,170	$7,120	$6,820

YOUR TURN! 6.4

The solution is on
page 327.

The Images Company sells three types of video equipment—DSLR cameras, Point and Shoot cameras, and Camcorders. The cost and market value of its inventory of video equipment follow:

	Cost	Market
DSLR	$110,000	$125,000
Point and Shoot	73,000	92,000
Camcorders	57,000	48,000

Compute the value of the Images Company's ending inventory under the lower-of-cost-or-market method applied on an item-by-item basis.

INVENTORY ANALYSIS

Inventory Turnover and Days' Sales In Inventory

The **inventory turnover ratio** indicates how many times a year, on average, a firm sells its inventory, and it is calculated as:

LO5 Define *inventory turnover* and *days' sales in inventory* and **explain** the use of these ratios.

$$\text{Inventory turnover} = \frac{\text{Cost of goods sold}}{\text{Average inventory}}$$

This ratio relates data from two financial statements: the income statement and the balance sheet. Cost of goods sold is taken from the income statement, while the average inventory is calculated from balance sheet data—that is, the beginning and ending inventories are summed and the total is divided by two.

In general, the faster a company can turn over its inventory, the more profitable the company will be. Further, the higher the inventory turnover ratio, the less time a firm has its funds tied up in its inventory and the less risk the firm faces from trying to sell out-of-date merchandise. What is considered to be a satisfactory inventory turnover varies from industry to industry. A grocery store chain like **Safeway**, for example, should have a much higher inventory turnover than a jewelry store like **Zales**.

To illustrate the inventory turnover ratio, **Best Buy** reported the following financial data:

($ millions)	2014	2013
Cost of goods sold	$31,292	$31,212
Beginning inventory	5,376	6,571
Ending inventory	5,174	5,376

Best Buy's inventory turnover in 2014 is 5.93, computed as $31,292/[($5,376 + $5,174)/2]. A similar calculation reveals that Best Buy's inventory turnover was 5.23 in 2013, indicating an improvement from 2013 to 2014.

The inventory turnover ratio can be influenced by a firm's choice of inventory costing method. Inventory amounts calculated using LIFO, for example, will typically be smaller than the same inventory calculated using FIFO. An investor comparing inventory turnover ratios between different firms will need to verify that the firms are using the same inventory costing method; otherwise, any ratio comparisons will be apples-to-oranges rather than apples-to-apples.

An extension of the inventory turnover ratio is the **days' sales in inventory**, calculated as:

$$\text{Days' sales in inventory} = \frac{365}{\text{Inventory turnover}}$$

A.K.A. The days' sales in inventory ratio is also referred to as the *days' inventory-on-hand ratio* and the *inventory-on-hand period.*

This ratio indicates how many days it takes, on average, for a firm to sell its inventory. During 2014, for example, Best Buy's days' sales in inventory was 61.6 days, or 365/5.93; that is, Best Buy took over 61 days to sell its inventory. Similar calculations reveal it took an average of 69.8 days for Best Buy to sell its inventory in 2013. Do these ratio results indicate that Best Buy is doing a good job of managing its investment in inventory? Without comparable ratio data from a competitor like Target Corporation, it is difficult to conclude whether a days' sales in inventory ratio of 61.6 days indicates that Best Buy is doing a good or bad job of managing its inventory.

TAKEAWAY 6.1	Concept ➡	Method ➡	Assessment
	How long, on average, does it take to sell the inventory?	Cost of goods sold, beginning inventory, and ending inventory $$\text{Inventory turnover} = \frac{\text{Cost of goods sold}}{\text{Average inventory}}$$ $$\text{Days' sales in inventory} = \frac{365}{\text{Inventory turnover}}$$	A higher inventory turnover or a lower days' sales in inventory indicates that the company is able to sell its inventory more quickly.

YOUR TURN! 6.5

The solution is on page 327.

Flip Company installed a new inventory management system at the beginning of 2016. Shown below are financial data from the company's accounting records:

	2015	2016
Sales revenue.	$4,000,000	$4,400,000
Cost of goods sold.	2,000,000	2,300,000
Beginning inventory	450,000	430,000
Ending inventory.	430,000	320,000

Calculate the inventory turnover and days' sales in inventory for 2015 and 2016. Discuss your findings.

CORPORATE SOCIAL RESPONSIBILITY

Best Buy and an Ethical Supply Chain

Many businesses strive to not only do well financially, but also to do good environmentally and socially. **Best Buy** serves as the ultimate seller of many products manufactured by other companies, such as TVs by **Sony**, cameras by **Nikon**, and computers by **Dell**. Best Buy also sells its exclusive brands. As the manufacturer of these products, Best Buy faces decisions on how and where these products are produced. Best Buy's Corporate Responsibility Report states, "While manufacturing expertise, lower labor costs and an efficient global supply chain make production in southeastern Asia a viable proposition, our operations there have not been without challenges." Best Buy meets these challenges through their ethical manufacturing program that includes supplier compliance standards that embody standards of the Fair Labor Association Workplace Code of Conduct and the core labor standards of the International Labor Organization. Best Buy also has a factory audit program to identify environmental and social problems at its suppliers.

The Montclair Corporation had the following inventory transactions for its only product during 2015:

Purchases	
February 15.	2,000 units @ $27.00 each
April 20	3,000 units @ $28.40 each
October 25	1,200 units @ $31.25 each
Sales	
March 1.	1,200 units @ $50.00 each
June 12.	2,000 units @ $52.00 each
August 10	1,000 units @ $53.00 each
December 14	1,600 units @ $55.00 each

The Montclair Corporation had 1,000 units in its January 1, 2015, beginning inventory with a unit cost of $24 each. Montclair uses the periodic inventory system.

Required

a. Determine the cost assigned to Montclair's December 31, 2015, ending inventory and Montclair's cost of goods sold for 2015 under each of the following inventory costing methods:
   1. Weighted-average cost
   2. FIFO
   3. LIFO
b. Determine Montclair's gross profit for 2015 under each of the following inventory costing methods:
   1. Weighted-average cost
   2. FIFO
   3. LIFO
c. Determine Montclair's inventory turnover and days' sales in inventory for 2015 under each of the following inventory costing methods:
   1. Weighted-average cost
   2. FIFO
   3. LIFO

Solution

a. Units available:

1,000 units @ $24.00 =	$ 24,000
2,000 units @ $27.00 =	54,000
3,000 units @ $28.40 =	85,200
1,200 units @ $31.25 =	37,500
7,200	$200,700

1. **Weighted-average cost:**

   Weighted-average unit cost: $200,700/7,200 units = $ 27.875

   Ending inventory: 1,400 units × $27.875 = $ 39,025

   Cost of goods sold: $200,700 − $39,025 = $161,675

2. **FIFO:**

   Ending inventory:

1,200 units @ $31.25 =	$ 37,500
200 units @ $28.40 =	5,680
1,400	$ 43,180

   Cost of goods sold: $200,700 − $43,180 = $157,520

3. **LIFO:**

   Ending inventory:

1,000 units @ $24.00 =	$ 24,000
400 units @ $27.00 =	10,800
1,400	$ 34,800

   Cost of goods sold: $200,700 − $34,800 = $165,900

b. Sales revenue:

$$
\begin{array}{lll}
1,200 \text{ units @ } \$50.00 = & \$\ 60,000 \\
2,000 \text{ units @ } \$52.00 = & 104,000 \\
1,000 \text{ units @ } \$53.00 = & 53,000 \\
1,600 \text{ units @ } \$55.00 = & 88,000 \\
\hline
5,800 & \$305,000 \\
\end{array}
$$

1. Weighted-average gross profit = $305,000 − $161,675 = $143,325
2. FIFO gross profit = $305,000 − $157,520 = $147,480
3. LIFO gross profit = $305,000 − $165,900 = $139,100

c.

	Inventory Turnover	Days' Sales in Inventory
Weighted-average cost	5.13	71.15 days
FIFO	4.69	77.83 days
LIFO	5.64	64.72 days

APPENDIX 6A: Inventory Costing Methods and the Perpetual Inventory System

eLectures

MBC

This appendix illustrates the accounting for inventories using the perpetual inventory system under the four costing methods of: (1) specific identification; (2) first-in, first-out; (3) last-in, first-out; and (4) weighted-average cost. All four methods are illustrated using the following data for Claremont Company.

LO6 **Describe** inventory costing under a perpetual inventory system using specific identification, weighted-average cost, FIFO, and LIFO.

Date	Event	No. of Units		Unit Cost		Total Cost
Jan. 1	Beginning inventory	60	@	$10	=	$ 600
Mar. 27	Purchase inventory.	90	@	11	=	990
	Goods available for sale.	150				$1,590
May 2	**Sell inventory**	(130)				
Aug. 15	Purchase inventory.	100	@	13	=	1,300
Nov. 6	Purchase inventory.	50	@	16	=	800
	Goods available for sale.	170				$3,690
Dec. 10	**Sell inventory**	(90)				
Dec. 31	Ending inventory.	80				

Under all four inventory costing methods, the Inventory account is increased each time a purchase occurs for the amount of the purchase and is decreased each time a sale occurs by an amount equal to the cost of goods sold. The methods differ only in the computation of cost of goods sold, consisting of 220 units (130 + 90 = 220), and the year-end Inventory account balance, consisting of 80 units remaining.

Specific Identification Method

Under the **specific identification method**, the actual cost of the specific units sold is identified and used to compute the cost of goods sold. To illustrate, assume that (1) 50 of the 130 units sold on May 2 came from the beginning inventory of 60 units and the remaining 80 units sold (50 + 80 = 130) came from the purchase of 90 units on March 27, and that (2) 10 of the 90 units sold on December 10 came from the purchase of 90 units on March 27 and the remaining 80 units sold (10 + 80 = 90) came from the purchase of 100 units on August 15. **Exhibit 6A-1** illustrates the calculation of cost of goods sold and ending inventory using specific identification. The cost of goods sold is $2,530 (sum of the Sold Total column), and the ending inventory of 80 units is valued at $1,160 (final amount in the Inventory Balance Total column).

Exhibit 6A-1	Specific Identification Method (Perpetual Inventory System)								
	Purchased			Sold			Inventory Balance		
Date	Units	Unit Cost	Total	Units	Unit Cost	Total	Units	Unit Cost	Total
Jan. 1							60	$10	$ 600
Mar. 27	90	$11	$ 990				60	10	1,590
							90	11	
May 2				50	$10	$ 500	10	10	210
				80	11	880	10	11	
Aug. 15	100	13	1,300				10	10	1,510
							10	11	
							100	13	
Nov. 6	50	16	800				10	10	2,310
							10	11	
							100	13	
							50	16	
Dec. 10				10	11	110	10	10	1,160
				80	13	1,040	20	13	
							50	16	
Total						$2,530			

First-In, First-Out (FIFO) Method

Under the **first-in, first-out (FIFO) method**, each time that a sale is made the cost of the oldest goods are charged to cost of goods sold. Visually, the FIFO method appears like a conveyor belt. Items of inventory are placed on the belt and then move along to the end. As items reach the end of the conveyor belt, they are assumed to be sold. Those items still on the belt (which are the last items placed on the belt) are assumed to remain in inventory until they reach the end of the conveyor belt. This visualization is illustrated in **Exhibit 6A-2**.

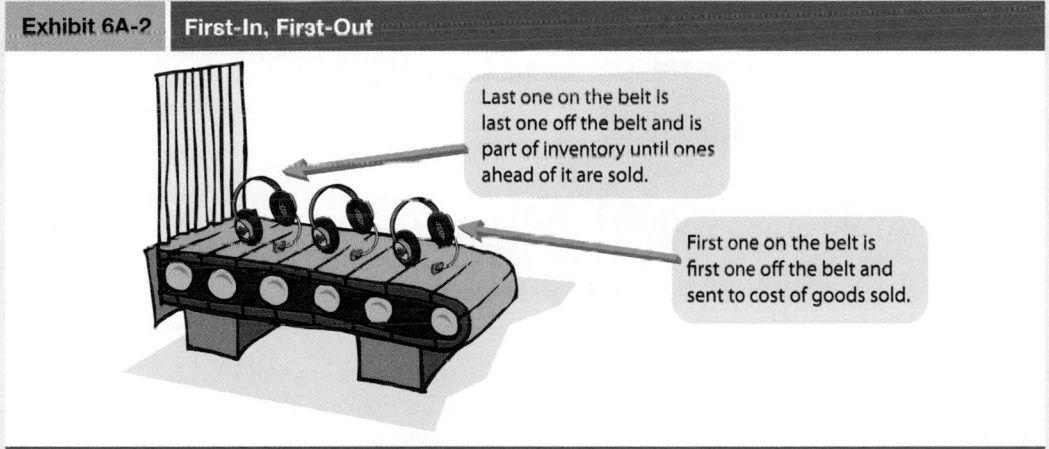

Exhibit 6A-2   First-In, First-Out

Last one on the belt is last one off the belt and is part of inventory until ones ahead of it are sold.

First one on the belt is first one off the belt and sent to cost of goods sold.

Results of the FIFO method are in **Exhibit 6A-3**. FIFO handles the May 2 sale of 130 units as follows: The oldest units are the units in the January 1 beginning inventory. These are the first 60 units assumed to be sold. The next oldest units are the units purchased on March 27 and 70 units are needed from this purchase (130 sold − 60 from January 1) to provide all of the units sold on May 2. After the May 2 sale, only 20 units remain, all from the March 27 purchase.

The December 10 sale of 90 units is handled in a similar manner. The oldest units at December 10 are the 20 units remaining from the March 27 purchase. These are the first units assumed to be sold. The next oldest units are the 100 units purchased on August 15 and 70 additional units are needed for the sale (90 sold − 20 from the March 27 purchase). Therefore, 70 of the 100 units purchased on August 15 are assumed to be included in the units sold on December 10. After the December 10 sale, 30 units remain from the August 15 purchase and 50 units remain from the November 6 purchase.

Cost of goods sold using the FIFO method is $2,500 (sum of the Sold Total column), and the ending inventory is $1,190 (final amount in the Inventory Balance Total column).

Exhibit 6A-3 — First-In, First-Out Method (Perpetual Inventory System)

Date	Purchased Units	Unit Cost	Total	Sold Units	Unit Cost	Total	Inventory Balance Units	Unit Cost	Total
Jan. 1							60	$10	$ 600
Mar. 27	90	$11	$ 990				60 / 90	10 / 11	1,590
May 2				60 / 70	$10 / 11	$ 600 / 770	20	11	220
Aug. 15	100	13	1,300				20 / 100	11 / 13	1,520
Nov. 6	50	16	800				20 / 100 / 50	11 / 13 / 16	2,320
Dec. 10				20 / 70	11 / 13	220 / 910	30 / 50	13 / 16	1,190
Total						$2,500			

Last-In, First-Out (LIFO) Method

When the **last-in, first-out (LIFO) method** is used, the cost of the most recent inventory purchased is charged to cost of goods sold when a sale occurs. Visually, the LIFO method appears like a stack of bricks. Each new brick entered into inventory is placed on top of the existing stack of bricks. When a brick is sold, the last brick placed on the stack is pulled from the top of the stack and given to the customer. The bricks at the bottom of the stack are assumed to remain in inventory until the newer bricks from the top of the stack are first sold. This visualization is illustrated in **Exhibit 6A-4**.

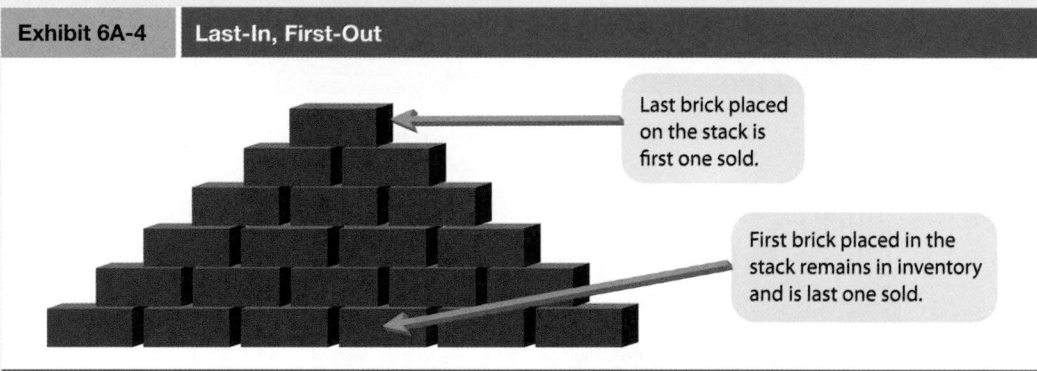

Exhibit 6A-4 — Last-In, First-Out

Last brick placed on the stack is first one sold.

First brick placed in the stack remains in inventory and is last one sold.

Exhibit 6A-5 illustrates the results using LIFO. The LIFO method handles the May 2 sale of 130 units as follows: The most recently purchased units (newest units) are the units from the March 27 purchase. These are the first 90 units assumed to be sold. The next newest units are the units in the January 1 beginning inventory and 40 units from the January 1 units are needed (130 sold − 90 from the March 27 purchase) to provide all of the units sold on May 2. After the May 2 sale, only 20 units remain, all from the January 1 beginning inventory.

The December 10 sale of 90 units is handled in a similar manner. The newest units at December 10 are the 50 units purchased on November 6. These are the first units assumed to be sold. The next newest units are the 100 units purchased on August 15 and 40 additional units are needed for the sale (90 sold − 50 from the November 6 purchase). Therefore, 40 of the 100 units purchased on August 15 are assumed to be included in the units sold on December 10. After the sale, 20 units remain from the January 1 inventory and 60 units remain from the August 15 purchase.

Cost of goods sold using LIFO is $2,710 (sum of the Sold Total column), and the ending inventory is $980 (final amount in the Inventory Balance Total column).

| Exhibit 6A-5 | Last-In, First-Out Method (Perpetual Inventory System) | | | | | | | | |

	Purchased			Sold			Inventory Balance		
Date	Units	Unit Cost	Total	Units	Unit Cost	Total	Units	Unit Cost	Total
Jan. 1							60	$10	$ 600
Mar. 27	90	$11	$ 990				60	10	1,590
							90	11	
May 2				90	$11	₵ 990			
				40	10	400	20	10	200
Aug. 15	100	13	1,300				20	10	1,500
							100	13	
Nov. 6	50	16	800				20	10	2,300
							100	13	
							50	16	
Dec. 10				50	16	800	20	10	980
				40	13	520	60	13	
Total						$2,710			

Weighted-Average Cost Method

When the **weighted-average cost method** is used, a new weighted-average unit cost is calculated for the goods (**total cost divided by total units**) each time that goods are purchased and added to inventory. The cost of goods sold for each sale is calculated by multiplying the weighted-average unit cost at the time of sale by the number of units sold. **Exhibit 6A-6** illustrates the calculation of cost of goods sold and ending inventory under the weighted-average cost method. The weighted-average unit cost is calculated three times in **Exhibit 6A-6**. On March 27, 90 units were purchased at a unit cost of $11, and the updated weighted-average unit cost on this date is:

$$[\$600 + \$990]/[60 \text{ Units} + 90 \text{ Units}] = \$10.60$$

On August 15, 100 units were purchased at a unit cost of $13. The updated weighted-average unit cost on this date is:

$$[\$212 + \$1,300]/[20 \text{ Units} + 100 \text{ Units}] = \$12.60$$

On November 6, 50 units were purchased at a unit cost of $16. The updated weighted-average unit cost on this date is:

$$[\$1,512 + \$800]/[120 \text{ Units} + 50 \text{ Units}] = \$13.60$$

The cost of goods sold is $2,602 (sum of the Sold Total column), and the ending inventory is $1,088 (final amount in the Inventory Balance Total column).

| Exhibit 6A-6 | Weighted-Average Cost Method (Perpetual Inventory System) | | | | | | | | |

	Purchased			Sold			Inventory Balance		
Date	Units	Unit Cost	Total	Units	Unit Cost	Total	Units	Unit Cost	Total
Jan. 1							60	$10.00	$ 600
Mar. 27	90	$11	$ 990				150	10.60	1,590
May 2				130	$10.60	$1,378	20	10.60	212
Aug. 15	100	13	1,300				120	12.60	1,512
Nov. 6	50	16	800				170	13.60	2,312
Dec. 10				90	13.60	1,224	80	13.60	1,088
Total						$2,602			

Comparative Analysis of Inventory Costing Methods

The purchase price data used in the Claremont Company illustration has an important characteristic: the purchase price of the inventory increased each time that a purchase was made, from $11 per unit to $13 per unit to $16 per unit. Increasing inventory prices are frequently encountered in the real world where price inflation is common and price deflation is uncommon. **Exhibit 6A-7** summarizes the results of applying the four inventory costing methods to the Claremont Company data and reveals that the FIFO method produces the lowest cost of goods sold ($2,500), while the LIFO method produces the highest cost of goods sold ($2,710). The exhibit also reveals that FIFO produces the highest year-end value of ending inventory ($1,190), while LIFO produces the lowest year-end value of ending inventory ($980). Specific identification and weighted-average cost produce ending inventory values and cost of goods sold values that fall in between the results obtained using FIFO and LIFO.

These results, however, are highly dependent on the purchase prices for the inventory. If the inventory's purchase price had been decreasing rather than increasing, the financial effects would have been just the opposite, with LIFO producing the lowest cost of goods sold and FIFO the highest. If the purchase prices had been perfectly stable, there would be no difference between the cost of goods sold or the ending inventory for any of the four methods.

Exhibit 6A-7	Results of Different Inventory Costing Methods			
	Specific Identification	FIFO	LIFO	Weighted-Average
Cost of goods sold.	$2,530	$2,500	$2,710	$2,602
Ending inventory.	1,160	1,190	980	1,088

Selecting Inventory Methods

Under generally accepted accounting principles, a company is permitted to select one or more of the four methods for purposes of assigning cost to its ending inventory and its cost of goods sold. Which method (or methods, since a company may elect to value some of its inventory using FIFO, some using LIFO, and some using weighted-average cost) is selected by a company depends upon a number of factors—the type of product produced, the cost of producing the product, whether the product is perishable, whether the company desires to report a high or a low net income, and income tax considerations.

Specific Identification Method

Companies might choose to use specific identification for unique items with small volume and high unit cost, such as fine art or jewelry, that would justify the cost of tracking the specific unit cost of each inventory item. Specific identification is usually not cost-justified for inventories that have a low unit cost or involve high volumes of similar products.

FIFO Method

Many companies, especially those with perishable, time-dated, or style-affected merchandise, attempt to sell their oldest merchandise first. This is especially true for companies that sell food products, chemicals, and drugs. For these types of companies, the cost flow produced by the FIFO method most closely matches the actual goods flow. However, a company is not required to use the cost flow assumption that most closely matches its actual goods flow. When costs are rising, FIFO will result in the lowest cost of goods sold, and therefore, the highest net income. The desire to show a higher net income by some companies partly explains the popularity of the FIFO method.

LIFO Method

Although LIFO does not reflect the actual goods flow for most businesses, its popularity is likely linked to the potential income tax savings associated with its use. We illustrate the income tax advantages of the LIFO method on p. 288. For some industries, however, LIFO does depict the actual goods flow. For example, in industries that extract natural resources, such as mining, the product is frequently dumped onto a storage pile from an overhead trestle, and sold inventory is taken from the top of the pile. One disadvantage of using LIFO when beginning inventories have been maintained or increased is that a firm's ending inventory can be substantially undervalued since old purchase prices tend to be retained on a company's books under the LIFO method. This, in turn, will cause a firm's current assets and total assets to likewise be undervalued.

Weighted-Average Cost Method

Weighted-average cost is best suited for businesses that warehouse a large volume of undifferentiated goods in a common area. Liquid fuels, grains, and other commodities are examples. Weighted-average cost typically generates a cost of goods sold amount that is neither high nor low as compared to the other methods, as is revealed in **Exhibit 6A-7**.

Summary

We can broadly summarize the choice among the cost flow assumptions as follows:

1. Specific identification most closely identifies the actual cost of goods sold and ending inventory but can be costly to implement.
2. FIFO approximates the actual physical flow of goods for most firms.
3. LIFO is popular because of the income tax savings associated with its use.
4. Weighted-average cost is most often associated with businesses in which undifferentiated goods are commingled in a common area like a warehouse.

Analysis of Costing Methods and Gross Profit

To illustrate the financial effects of the different inventory costing methods, assume that the 220 units sold by the Claremont Company were sold for $20 each, producing sales of $4,400 ($20 × 220). **Exhibit 6A-8** shows the difference in gross profit under each of the four inventory costing methods. Remember that the difference in reported gross profit results from the assumptions made about cost flow, not from any difference in actual goods flow. In each case, 220 units were sold and 80 units remained. Each of the inventory costing methods is in accord with generally accepted accounting principles, yet the methods have different financial effects on gross profit and net income.

Exhibit 6A-8	Gross Profit Using Alternative Inventory Costing Methods			
	Specific Identification	FIFO	LIFO	Weighted-Average
Sales (220 units @ $20)	$4,400	$4,400	$4,400	$4,400
Cost of goods sold.	2,530	2,500	2,710	2,602
Gross profit.	$1,870	$1,900	$1,690	$1,798
Increased gross profit compared with LIFO.	$ 180	$ 210		$ 108

Income Statement and Balance Sheet Effects

As **Exhibit 6A-8** reveals, LIFO results in the smallest gross profit ($1,690) with FIFO producing the highest ($1,900) gross profit. This result occurs because the purchase price of inventory was increasing throughout the year, from $11 per unit to $13 per unit to $16 per unit. Most agree that when costs are rising, FIFO tends to overstate gross profit (and income) because older, lower unit costs are included in the cost of goods sold and matched with current sales prices. In other words, in the illustration, the units sold are charged to costs of goods sold under FIFO at unit costs of $10, $11, and $13. If the latest purchase price reflects the inventory's current acquisition cost, the units sold must be replaced by units costing $16 (or more if costs continue to rise).

It is frequently argued that LIFO provides a better matching of current costs with current revenues since the cost of the most recent purchases constitutes the LIFO cost of goods sold. While LIFO associates the current, higher unit costs with cost of goods sold, it assigns costs to ending inventory using the older, lower unit costs. As a consequence, the value of the LIFO ending inventory on the balance sheet is often undervalued in terms of the inventory's current value. When inventory quantities are maintained or increased, the LIFO method prevents older costs from appearing in the cost of goods sold. No doubt, some firms still carry LIFO inventories at unit costs that existed more than 10 years ago. Under FIFO, the ending inventory is measured at relatively recent costs.

Comparison of Inventory Costing Methods

Exhibit 6A-9 summarizes the results of applying the periodic and perpetual costing methods to the same Claremont data. The specific identification method and the FIFO method yield the exact same results for ending inventory and cost of goods sold regardless of whether the periodic or the perpetual method is being used. Only LIFO and weighted-average methods produce different results under the periodic and perpetual systems.

Exhibit 6A-9	Summary Results of Different Inventory Costing Methods		
Costing Method		Ending Inventory	Cost of Goods Sold
Specific identification			
Periodic....................................		$1,160	$2,530
Perpetual.................................		1,160	2,530
FIFO			
Periodic....................................		1,190	2,500
Perpetual.................................		1,190	2,500
LIFO			
Periodic....................................		820	2,870
Perpetual.................................		980	2,710
Average			
Periodic....................................		984	2,706
Perpetual.................................		1,088	2,602

Choice of a periodic versus perpetual system does *not* affect specific identification or FIFO

Choice of a periodic versus perpetual system does affect LIFO and weighted-average results

YOUR TURN! 6A.1

The solution is on pages 327–328.

The following information applies to the Kensington Company.

Jan. 1 Beginning inventory 1,000 units at $5 each

Jan. 5 Purchased 600 units at $6 each

Jan. 15 Sold 200 units

Jan. 17 Purchased 300 units at $7 each

Jan. 25 Sold 400 units

Kensington Company utilizes a perpetual inventory system. Calculate the cost of goods sold and ending inventory using the following methods.

a. FIFO

b. LIFO

c. Weighted-average

APPENDIX 6B: LIFO Reserve

As shown in this chapter, the LIFO inventory costing method can produce significantly different results relative to other inventory costing methods for both ending inventory and cost of goods sold, and therefore gross profit and net income. The difference is greatest when compared to results obtained using FIFO. When costs are rising, FIFO will result in higher reported ending inventory, lower cost of goods sold, and higher net income relative to LIFO.

LO7 **Define** the LIFO reserve and **explain** how it is used to compare the performance of companies using different inventory costing methods.

To make comparisons between companies using LIFO and companies using FIFO, we need to use the **LIFO inventory reserve**, or simply *LIFO reserve*. Companies that use LIFO are required under generally accepted accounting principles to report the difference between ending inventory using LIFO and the inventory that would have been reported under FIFO. This difference is called the LIFO inventory reserve and is disclosed in notes to financial statements.

Referring again to **Exhibit 6-8**, FIFO ending inventory is valued at $1,190 and LIFO ending inventory at $820. The LIFO reserve is $370 ($1,190 − $820). Use of LIFO can have a material impact on many ratios, and one way to compensate for these effects is to use the LIFO reserve to restate the reported inventory. To illustrate, assume that Claremont Company, whose inventory costing method results are contrasted in **Exhibit 6-8**, has current assets of $2,100 and current liabilities of $1,400 under the LIFO method. **Exhibit 6B-1** calculates the current ratio (current assets divided by current liabilities) under both LIFO and FIFO. (The current ratio is discussed in Chapter 2.)

Exhibit 6B-1	Impact of the LIFO Inventory Reserve on the Current Ratio	
	LIFO	**FIFO**
Current ratio	$\dfrac{\$2,100}{\$1,400} = 1.50$	$\dfrac{(\$2,100 + \$370)}{\$1,400} = 1.76$

Hint: *The LIFO reserve is also used to restate the LIFO cost of goods sold to that under FIFO. The LIFO cost of good sold minus the change in the LIFO reserve from the beginning to the end of the period equals FIFO cost of goods sold.*

As shown in **Exhibit 6B-1**, the current ratio is much higher under FIFO (1.76) than under LIFO (1.50). Differences occur between LIFO and FIFO companies for many ratios, with FIFO resulting in more favorable ratios in most cases since FIFO generally results in higher inventory values and higher net earnings. For some ratios, however, LIFO produces more favorable results. Two examples are the inventory turnover ratio and the days' sales in inventory ratio. Because LIFO results in lower inventory values, the inventory turnover (and consequently, the days' sales in inventory) under LIFO appears higher (lower) than it does under FIFO. (The LIFO reserve also affects cost of goods sold and therefore the numerator of the inventory turnover ratio; in most cases the adjustment to cost of goods sold is much smaller than the adjustment to average inventory, leading to a higher inventory turnover under LIFO than under FIFO.)

Concept ⟶	Method ⟶	Assessment	TAKEAWAY 6.2
What effect does the use of LIFO have on ending inventory relative to the use of FIFO?	Ending inventory and the LIFO inventory reserve The value of LIFO ending inventory + the LIFO inventory reserve = The value of FIFO ending inventory	If the LIFO reserve is material it can have a significant impact on many ratios when compared to FIFO. The calculation of these ratios can be adjusted using the LIFO inventory reserve to provide a more comparable set of results.	

Adams Inc. reports ending Inventory under the LIFO method at $165,000. Adams also discloses a LIFO reserve of $20,000. What would Adams have reported for ending inventory if it had used FIFO rather than LIFO?.

YOUR TURN! 6B.1

The solution is on page 328.

SUMMARY OF LEARNING OBJECTIVES

Explain inventory concepts and modern inventory practices. (p. 276)

LO1

- Merchandise inventory is a stock of goods that a merchandising company buys from a manufacturer and makes available for sale to its customers.
- A manufacturing firm maintains three different inventory categories: raw materials inventory, work-in-process inventory, and finished goods inventory.
- Traditionally, manufacturers have maintained just-in-case inventories of raw materials and components to provide for unplanned production or delayed raw material shipments, resulting in high levels of inventory carrying costs.
- Today, many manufacturers have adopted the just-in-time (JIT) manufacturing philosophy which is designed to eliminate or minimize raw materials, work-in-process, and finished goods inventories. The key to JIT manufacturing is careful inventory order planning and sophisticated production management.
- Ownership of goods in transit depends on the shipping terms. The buyer assumes ownership of goods in transit shipped F.O.B. shipping point, whereas the seller maintains ownership of goods shipped F.O.B. destination until the buyer assumes possession at delivery.
- Consignment goods are goods held for sale by parties other than the seller. The seller maintains legal ownership of these inventory items while they are held for sale by the consignment seller.
- The year-end physical count of inventory is taken to verify the inventory balance. It consists of three steps:
  - Count the number of individual items of merchandise on hand at the end of the year.
  - Determine the unit cost of each individual item and multiply the unit cost times the quantity on hand to obtain the total cost for each individual item of merchandise.
  - Add together the total cost of all the individual items to obtain the total cost of the inventory on hand.

LO2 **Describe inventory costing under specific identification, weighted-average cost, FIFO, and LIFO. (p. 280)**

- To assign cost to units sold (cost of goods sold) and units available (inventory), a company must either keep track of the cost of each specific unit (specific identification method) or make an assumption about which units have been sold (weighted-average cost, FIFO, and LIFO methods).
- The weighted-average cost method assumes that a mix of the goods available is sold; the FIFO method assumes that the oldest goods are sold first; and, the LIFO method assumes that the newest goods are sold first.

LO3 **Analyze the financial effects of different inventory costing methods on company profit. (p. 285)**

- Each of the alternative inventory costing methods produces a different cost of goods sold and gross profit unless purchase prices have been perfectly stable.
- When costs are rising, the LIFO method does the best job of matching current costs with revenues; LIFO also produces a lower gross profit and lower income taxes than either weighted-average cost or FIFO.

LO4 **Apply the lower-of-cost-or-market method. (p. 291)**

- Damaged, physically deteriorated, or obsolete merchandise should be valued and reported at its net realizable value—that is, its estimated selling price less the expected cost of disposal.
- The lower-of-cost-or-market method provides for inventory write-downs to be recorded in the period that the replacement cost of inventory declines below the inventory's acquisition cost.

LO5 **Define *inventory turnover* and *day's sales in inventory* and explain the use of these ratios. (p. 293)**

- Inventory turnover and days' sales in inventory indicate, respectively, how many times on average during the year a firm sells its inventory and how many days on average it takes a firm to sell its inventory.
- Inventory turnover and days' sales in inventory provide evidence regarding a firm's ability to sell its inventory and its ability to effectively manage its investment in inventory.

LO6 **Appendix 6A: Describe inventory costing under a perpetual inventory system using specific identification, weighted-average cost, FIFO, and LIFO. (p. 296)**

- To assign cost to units sold (cost of goods sold) and units available (inventory), a company must either keep track of the cost of each specific unit (specific identification method) or make an assumption about which units have been sold (weighted-average cost, FIFO, and LIFO methods).
- The weighted-average cost method assumes that a mix of the goods available is sold; the FIFO method assumes that the oldest goods are sold; and, the LIFO method assumes that the newest goods are sold.
- The specific identification method and the FIFO method yield the exact same results for ending inventory and for cost of goods sold regardless of whether the periodic or the perpetual method is being used. Only LIFO and weighted-average methods produce different results.

LO7 **Appendix 6B: Define the LIFO reserve and explain how it is used to compare the performance of companies using different inventory costing methods. (p. 302)**

- The LIFO inventory reserve represents the difference between the value of LIFO ending inventory and what the value of ending inventory would have been under FIFO.
- The LIFO inventory reserve can cause a material effect on many ratios. These ratios should be adjusted for the LIFO inventory reserve when comparing a company using LIFO with a FIFO company.

SUMMARY	Concept ⟶	Method ⟶	Assessment
TAKEAWAY 6.1	How long, on average, does it take to sell the inventory?	Cost of goods sold, beginning inventory, and ending inventory $$\text{Inventory turnover} = \frac{\text{Cost of goods sold}}{\text{Average inventory}}$$ $$\text{Days' sales in inventory} = \frac{365}{\text{Inventory turnover}}$$	A higher inventory turnover or a lower days' sales in inventory indicates that the company is able to sell its inventory more quickly.
TAKEAWAY 6.2	What effect does the use of LIFO have on ending inventory relative to the use of FIFO?	Ending inventory and the LIFO inventory reserve The value of LIFO ending inventory + the LIFO inventory reserve = The value of FIFO ending inventory	If the LIFO reserve is material it can have a significant impact on many ratios when compared to FIFO. The calculation of these ratios can be adjusted using the LIFO inventory reserve to provide a more comparable set of results.

KEY TERMS

Consignment goods (p. 278)

Cost flow (p. 281)

Days' sales in inventory
(days' inventory on hand
ratio; inventory on hand
period) (p. 294)

Finished goods
inventory (p. 277)

First-in, first-out (FIFO)
method (p. 282, 297)

F.O.B. destination (p. 278)

F.O.B. shipping point (p. 278)

Goods flow (p. 281)

Goods in transit (p. 278)

Inventory carrying
costs (p. 277)

Inventory overage (p. 279)

Inventory shrinkage (p. 279)

Inventory turnover
ratio (p. 293)

Just-in-case inventory (p. 277)

Just-in-time (JIT)
manufacturing (p. 277)

Last-in, first-out (LIFO)
method (p. 283, 298)

LIFO conformity rule (p. 289)

LIFO inventory reserve (p. 302)

Lower-of-cost-or-market
(LCM) (p. 291)

Net realizable value (p. 291)

Physical count of
inventory (p. 279)

Quick response system (p. 277)

Raw materials
inventory (p. 276)

Specific identification
method (p. 282, 296)

Weighted-average cost
method (average cost
method) (p. 284, 299)

Work-in-process
inventory (p. 276)

Assignments with the ⬤ logo in the margin are available in ᵐʸBusinessCourse.
See the Preface of the book for details.

SELF-STUDY QUESTIONS

(Answers to Self-Study Questions are at the end of this chapter.)

1. **Which of the following concepts relates to the elimination or minimization of inventories by a manufacturing firm?**   LO1
   a. Quick response
   b. Just-in-time
   c. Just-in-case
   d. Specific identification

2. **Which inventory costing method assumes that the most recently purchased merchandise is sold first?**   LO2
   a. Specific identification
   b. Weighted-average cost
   c. FIFO
   d. LIFO

3. **Which inventory costing method results in the highest-valued ending inventory during a period of rising unit costs?**   LO3
   a. Specific identification
   b. Weighted-average cost
   c. FIFO
   d. LIFO

4. **Under which of the following freight terms does the seller retain ownership of the shipped goods?**   LO1
   a. F.O.B. shipping point
   b. F.O.B. destination

5. **When should ending inventory be written down below its acquisition cost on the balance sheet?**   LO4
   a. When units are damaged, physically deteriorated, or obsolete.
   b. When the inventory's replacement cost exceeds its acquisition cost.
   c. When the inventory's replacement cost is below its acquisition cost.
   d. Both a and c.

6. **Which inventory costing method results in the highest net income during a period of rising unit prices?**   LO3
   a. Specific identification
   b. Weighted-average cost
   c. FIFO
   d. LIFO

LO3   7. **Which inventory costing method is expensive to implement?**
    a.   Specific identification
    b.   Weighted-average cost
    c.   FIFO
    d.   LIFO

LO3   8. **Which inventory costing method is frequently used when undifferentiated units are stored in a common area?**
    a.   Specific identification
    b.   Weighted-average cost
    c.   FIFO
    d.   LIFO

LO3   9. **Which inventory costing method results in the lowest net income during a period of rising unit prices?**
    a.   Specific identification
    b.   Weighted-average cost
    c.   FIFO
    d.   LIFO

LO4   10. **Which inventory costing method does not require the use of the lower-of-cost-or-market method?**
    a.   Specific identification
    b.   Weighted-average cost
    c.   FIFO
    d.   All methods require the use of LCM.

LO5   11. **Tracker Corp. reported annual cost of goods sold of $30,000 and average inventory on hand during the year of $3,750. What was Tracker's inventory turnover?**
    a.   0.125 times
    b.   8.0 times
    c. $26,250
    d.   8.0%

LO7
(Appendix 6B)   12. **The Avner Company reports ending inventory under the LIFO method of $15,000. Had Avner used FIFO, the ending inventory would have been reported as $16,500. Avner's LIFO inventory reserve is:**
    a. $31,500
    b. $15,000
    c. $1,500
    d.   91%

LO6
(Appendix 6A)   13. **The periodic inventory system differs from the perpetual inventory system:**
    a.   because the periodic system is not compatible with modern technology.
    b.   because the perpetual system continually updates inventory, while the periodic inventory system only updates inventory at the end of the period.
    c.   because the periodic system continually updates inventory, while the perpetual inventory system only updates inventory at the end of the period.
    d.   because the periodic system is more complex and costly.

QUESTIONS

1. What are the three inventory accounts maintained by a manufacturing firm? Define each.
2. ShopMart Stores uses point-of-sale equipment at its checkout counters to read universal bar codes. It also uses a quick response system. What is a quick response system?
3. What are *just-in-case inventory* and *inventory carrying costs?*
4. What is the *just-in-time manufacturing philosophy?* Describe it.
5. What is meant by *goods flow* and *cost flow?*
6. Describe how each of the following inventory costing methods is used with the perpetual inventory system: (a) Specific identification; (b) Weighted-average cost; (c) First-in, first-out; and (d) Last-in, first-out.

7. Describe the type of inventory for which the goods flow would most naturally correspond to the cost flow for each of the inventory costing methods: (i) Specific identification, (ii) Weighted-average cost, (iii) FIFO, and (iv) LIFO.

8. Why do relatively stable purchase prices reduce the significance of the choice of an inventory costing method?

9. What is the nature of FIFO *phantom profits* during periods of rising inventory purchase prices?

10. If costs have been rising, which inventory costing method—weighted-average cost; first-in, first-out; or last-in, first-out—yields (a) the lowest ending inventory value? (b) the lowest net income? (c) the largest ending inventory value? (d) the largest net income?

11. Even though it does not represent their goods flow, why might firms adopt last-in, first-out inventory costing during periods when inventory costs are rising?

12. Describe two situations in which merchandise may be valued on the balance sheet at an amount less than its acquisition cost.

13. Which of the following is not an inventory costing method?
    a. Specific identification
    b. Weighted-average cost
    c. Just-in-time manufacturing
    d. FIFO

14. What is the effect on reported net income of applying the lower-of-cost-or-market method to ending inventory?

15. How do the accounting principles of consistency and full disclosure apply to inventory costing?

16. Which party, the seller or the buyer, bears the freight cost when the terms are F.O.B. shipping point? When the terms are F.O.B. destination?

17. What is a LIFO inventory reserve and how can it be useful to an analyst?

18. Moyer Company has an inventory turnover of 4.51. What is Moyer's days' sales in inventory?

19. In an annual report, Craftmade International, Inc., describes its inventory accounting policies as follows:

> Inventories are stated at the lower-of-cost-or-market, with inventory cost determined using the first-in, first-out (FIFO) method. The cost of inventory includes freight-in and duties on imported goods.

Also in an annual report, Kaiser Aluminum Corporation made the following statement in discussing its inventories:

> The Company recorded pretax charges of approximately $19.4 million because of a reduction in the carrying values of its inventories caused principally by prevailing lower prices for alumina, primary aluminum, and fabricated products.

What accounting principle did Craftmade International follow when it included the costs of freight-in and duties on imported goods in its Inventory account? Briefly describe how a firm determines which costs to include in its inventory account. What accounting principle did Kaiser Aluminum follow when it recorded the $19.4 million pretax charge? Briefly describe the rationale for this principle.

20. What are the three steps that make up the year-end physical count of inventory?

SHORT EXERCISES

SE6-1. Departures from Acquisition Cost At year-end, The Appliance Shop has a refrigerator that has been used as a demonstration model. The refrigerator cost $350 and sells for $500 when new. In its present condition, the refrigerator will be sold for $325. Related selling costs are an estimated $15. At what amount should the refrigerator be carried in inventory?

LO4

    a. $350   c. $325
    b. $335   d. $310

LO2 **SE6-2.** **Inventory Costing Methods** Which inventory costing method requires that a company keep track of the cost of each specific unit of inventory?

    a. Specific identification

    b. Lower-of-cost-or-market method

    c. LIFO

    d. All of the above

LO1 **SE6-3.** **Identify Goods to Be Included in Inventory** Patterson Company has the following items at year-end. Identify which items should be included in Patterson's year-end inventory count.

    1. Goods held on consignment by Sell For You Company.

    2. Goods held by Patterson on consignment that will be sold for another company.

    3. Goods in transit sent to a client F.O.B. shipping point.

    4. Goods in transit sent to a client F.O.B. destination.

LO4 **SE6-4.** **Lower-of-Cost-or-Market Method** The Claremont Company's ending inventory is composed of 50 units that had cost $20 each and 100 units that had cost $15 each. If the company can replace all 150 units at a price of $16 each, what value should be assigned to the company's ending inventory assuming that it applies LCM?

LO4 **SE6-5.** **Lower-of-Cost-or-Market Method** The McQuenny Company's ending inventory is composed of 100 units that had an acquisition cost of $25 per unit and 50 units that had an acquisition cost of $30 per unit. If the company can replace all 150 units at a replacement cost of $27 per unit, what value should be assigned to the company's ending inventory assuming that it applies the LCM method?

LO5 **SE6-6.** **Inventory Turnover and Days' Sales in Inventory** W. Glass & Company reported the following information in its recent annual report:

	2015	2016
Cost of goods sold.	$4,000,000	$4,600,000
Beginning inventory	900,000	860,000
Ending inventory.	860,000	640,000

Calculate the company's inventory turnover and days' sales in inventory for both years.

LO5 **SE6-7.** **Inventory Turnover and Days' Sales in Inventory** Herberger & Company disclosed the following information in its recent annual report:

	2015	2016
Cost of goods sold.	$16,000,000	$20,000,000
Beginning inventory	2,000,000	4,000,000
Ending inventory.	4,000,000	5,000,000

Calculate the company's inventory turnover and days' sales in inventory for both years.

LO2 **SE6-8.** **Inventory Costing Methods and the Periodic Method** Lambeth Company experienced the following events in January:

Date	Event	Units		Unit Cost	Total Cost
Jan. 10	Purchased inventory.	100	@	$12	$1,200
Jan. 20	Purchased inventory.	200	@	14	2,800
Jan. 30	Sold inventory	150			

If the Lambeth Company uses the FIFO inventory costing method, calculate the company's cost of goods sold and its ending inventory as of January 31 assuming the periodic method.

SE6-9. **Inventory Costing Methods and the Periodic Method** Lambeth Company experienced the following events in February:

LO2

Date	Event	Units		Unit Cost	Total Cost
Feb. 1	Purchased inventory..........................	100	@	$20	$2,000
Feb. 4	Sold inventory	50			
Feb. 9	Purchased inventory..........................	100	@	$22	$2,200
Feb. 27	Sold inventory	100			

If the Lambeth Company uses the LIFO inventory costing method, calculate the company's cost of
goods sold and ending inventory as of February 28 assuming the periodic method.

SE6-10. **Errors in Inventory Count** Bow Corp. accidentally overstated its 2015 ending inventory by $750.
Assume that ending 2016 inventory is accurately counted. The error in 2015 will have what effect on
Bow Corp.?

LO3

a. 2015 net income is understated by $750.
b. 2015 net income is overstated by $750.
c. 2016 net income is understated by $750.
d. Both b and c are correct.

SE6-11. **Inventory Costing Methods and the Periodic Method** McKay & Company experienced the following events in March:

LO2

Date	Event	Units		Unit Cost	Total Cost
Mar. 1	Purchased inventory..........................	100	@	$15	$1,500
Mar. 3	Sold inventory	60			
Mar. 15	Purchased inventory..........................	100	@	$18	$1,800
Mar. 20	Sold inventory	40			

If McKay & Company uses the weighted-average cost method, calculate the company's cost of goods
sold and ending inventory as of March 31 assuming the periodic method.

SE6-12. **Inventory Costing Methods and the Perpetual Method** Refer to the information in SE6-11 and
assume the perpetual inventory system is used. Use the weighted-average inventory costing method
to calculate the company's cost of goods sold and ending inventory as of March 31. Round your final
answers to the nearest dollar.

LO6
(Appendix 6A)

SE6-13. **Inventory Costing Methods and the Perpetual Method** Refer to the information in SE6-9 and as
sume the perpetual inventory system is used. Use the LIFO inventory costing method to calculate the
company's cost of goods sold and ending inventory as of February 28.

LO6
(Appendix 6A)

SE6-14. **LIFO Inventory Reserve** Lamil Company reports ending inventory of $150,000 on a LIFO basis
and also reports a LIFO inventory reserve of $27,000. If Lamil had used FIFO rather than LIFO, end-
ing inventory would have been:

LO7
(Appendix 6B)

a. $123,000.
b. $150,000.
c. $177,000.
d. $182,500.

EXERCISES—SET A

E6-1A. **Just-in-Time Inventories** Raymond Manufacturing Company uses the perpetual inventory system
and plans to use raw materials costing $900,000 in manufacturing its products. Raymond will operate
its factory 300 days during the year. Currently, Raymond follows the just-in-case philosophy with its
raw materials inventory, keeping raw materials costing $12,000 in its raw materials inventory. Ray-
mond plans to switch to the just-in-time manufacturing philosophy by keeping only the raw materials
needed for the next two days of production. Calculate the new raw materials inventory level after
Raymond implements the just-in-time manufacturing philosophy in its factory.

LO1

LO2 **E6-2A.** **Inventory Costing Methods—Periodic Method** The Lippert Company uses the periodic inventory system. The following July data are for an item in Lippert's inventory:

July   1 Beginning inventory, 30 units @ $9 per unit.
       10 Purchased 50 units @ $10 per unit.
       15 Sold 60 units.
       26 Purchased 25 units @ $11 per unit.

Calculate the cost of goods sold for July and ending inventory at July 31 using (a) first-in, first-out, (b) last-in, first-out, and (c) the weighted-average cost methods. Round your final answers to the nearest dollar.

LO1 **E6-3A.** **Year-End Physical Inventory** The December 31 inventory for the Hayes Company included five products. The year-end physical count revealed the following:

Product	Quantity Available
A	26
B	50
C	64
D	75
E	55

The related unit costs were: A, $10; B, $6; C, $9; D, $8; and E, $7.

Required
Calculate the total cost of the December 31 physical inventory.

LO2 **E6-4A.** **Inventory Costing Methods—Periodic Method** Archer Company is a retailer that uses the periodic inventory system. On August 1, it had 80 units of product A at a total cost of $1,600. On August 5, Archer purchased 100 units of A for $2,116. On August 8, it purchased 200 units of A for $4,416. On August 11, it sold 165 units of A for $4,800. Calculate the August cost of goods sold and the ending inventory at August 31 using (a) first-in, first-out, (b) last-in, first-out, and (c) the weighted-average cost methods. Round your final answers to the nearest dollar.

LO3 **E6-5A.** **Errors in Inventory Counts** The following information was taken from the records of Taylor Enterprises:

	2016	2015
Beginning inventory	$ 60,000	$ 50,000
Cost of goods purchased	420,000	400,000
Cost of goods available for sale	480,000	450,000
Ending inventory	55,000	60,000
Cost of goods sold	$425,000	$390,000

The following two errors were made in the physical inventory counts:
1. 2015 ending inventory was understated by $7,000.
2. 2016 ending inventory was overstated by $3,000.

Compute the correct cost of goods sold for both 2015 and 2016.

LO4 **E6-6A.** **Departures from Acquisition Cost** Determine the proper total inventory value for each of the following items in Viking Company's ending inventory:

a. Viking has 500 video games in stock. The games cost $36 each, but their year-end replacement cost is $30. Viking has been selling the games for $60, but competitors are now selling them for $50. Viking plans to drop its price to $50. Viking's normal gross profit on video games is 40 percent.

b. Viking has 400 rolls of camera film that are past the expiration date marked on the film's box. The films cost $1.65 each and are normally sold for $3.30. New replacement films still cost

$1.65. To clear out these old films, Viking will drop their selling price to $1.40. There are no related selling costs.

c. Viking has seven cameras in stock that have been used as demonstration models. The cameras cost $180 and normally sell for $280. Because these cameras are in used condition, Viking has set the selling price at $160 each. Expected selling costs are $10 per camera. New models of the camera (on order) will cost Viking $200 and will be priced to sell at $320.

E6-7A. Inventory Costing Methods—Periodic Method The following information is for the Bloom Company; the company sells just one product:

LO2

		Units	Unit Cost
Beginning inventory		200	$10
Purchases:	Feb. 11	500	14
	May 18	400	16
	October 23	100	20

At year-end, there was an ending inventory of 340 units. Assume the use of the periodic inventory method. Calculate the value of ending inventory and the cost of goods sold for the year using (a) first-in, first-out, (b) last-in, first-out, and (c) the weighted average cost method.

E6-8A. Inventory Costing Methods—Periodic Method The following data are for the Bloom Company, which sells just one product:

LO2

		Units	Unit Cost
Beginning inventory, January 1		200	$10
Purchases:	February 11	500	14
	May 18	400	16
	October 23	100	18
Sales	March 1	400	
	July 1	380	

Calculate the value of ending inventory and cost of goods sold using the periodic method and (a) first-in, first-out, (b) last-in, first-out, and (c) weighted-average cost method. Round your final answers to the nearest dollar.

E6-9A. Applying IFRS LVMH is a Paris-based manufacturer of luxury goods that prepares its financial statements using IFRS. During the year, the management of the company undertook a review of the fair value of its inventory and found that the inventory had appreciated above its book value of 12 million euros. According to the company's management, the inventory was undervalued by 2 million euros. Prepare the journal entry to revalue the company's inventory. How would the revaluation immediately affect the company's (a) current ratio, (b) inventory turnover, and (c) days' sales in inventory?

LO4, 5

E6-10A. Lower-of-Cost-or-Market (LCM) Method The following data are taken from the Browning Corporation's inventory accounts:

LO4

Item Code	Quantity	Unit Cost	Replacement Cost
ACE	100	$27	$24
BDF	300	29	31
GHJ	400	22	18
MBS	200	24	27

Calculate the value of the company's ending inventory using the lower-of-cost-or-market method applied to each item of inventory.

E6-11A. Inventory Turnover and Days' Sales in Inventory The Southern Company installed a new inventory management system at the beginning of 2015. Shown below are data from the company's accounting records as reported out by the new system:

LO5

	2015	2016
Sales revenue..	$8,000,000	$11,000,000
Cost of goods sold...	4,000,000	4,800,000
Beginning inventory...	510,000	530,000
Ending inventory...	530,000	600,000

Calculate the company's (a) inventory turnover and (b) days' sales in inventory for 2015 and 2016. Comment on your results.

LO4

E6-12A. Lower-of-Cost-or-Market (LCM) Method The following data refer to the Flemming Company's ending inventory:

Item Code	Quantity	Unit Cost	Replacement Cost
ABX.........................	80	$50	$55
TYG	150	40	42
JIL..........................	175	28	25
GGH	90	44	38

Calculate the value of the company's ending inventory by using the lower-of-cost-or-market applied to each item of inventory.

LO7
(Appendix 6B)

E6-13A. The LIFO Inventory Reserve Midwestern Steel Company uses the LIFO inventory costing method to value its ending inventory. The following data were obtained from the company's accounting records:

Current assets (under FIFO)...	$8,000,000
Current liabilities..	6,000,000
Inventory under LIFO	2,200,000
Inventory under FIFO	2,700,000

Calculate the company's (a) LIFO inventory reserve and (b) the current ratio assuming (i) FIFO and (ii) LIFO.

LO6
(Appendix 6A)

E6-14A. Inventory Costing Methods—Perpetual Method Refer to the information in E6-2A and assume the perpetual inventory system is used. Calculate the cost of goods sold for the July 15 sale using (a) first-in, first-out, (b) last-in, first-out, and (c) the weighted-average cost methods. Round your final answers to the nearest dollar.

LO6
(Appendix 6A)

E6-15A. Inventory Costing Methods—Perpetual Method Refer to the information in E6-4A and assume the perpetual inventory system is used. Calculate the inventory cost of item A on August 11 (after the sale) using (a) first-in, first-out, (b) last-in, first-out, and (c) the weighted-average cost methods. Round your final answers to the nearest dollar.

LO6
(Appendix 6A)

E6-16A. Inventory Costing Methods—Perpetual Method Refer to the information in E6-8A and assume the perpetual inventory system is used. Calculate the value of ending inventory and cost of goods sold using the perpetual method and (a) first-in, first-out, (b) last-in, first-out, and (c) weighted-average cost method.

EXERCISES—SET B

LO1

E6-1B. Just-in-Time Inventories Carson Manufacturing Company uses the perpetual inventory system and plans to use raw material costing $1,650,000 in making its products. Carson will operate its factory 300 days during the year. Currently, Carson follows the just-in-case philosophy with its raw materials inventory, keeping raw materials costing $20,000 in its raw materials inventory. Carson plans to switch to the just-in-time manufacturing philosophy by keeping only the raw materials needed for the next two days of production. Calculate the new raw materials inventory level after Carson implements the just-in-time manufacturing philosophy.

E6-2B. **Inventory Costing Methods—Periodic Method** Merritt Company uses the periodic inventory system. The following May data are for an item in Merritt's inventory: **LO2**

May   1 Beginning inventory, 150 units @ $30 per unit.
     12 Purchased 100 units @ $35 per unit.
     16 Sold 180 units.
     24 Purchased 170 units @ $38 per unit.

Calculate the cost of goods sold for May and ending inventory at May 31 using (a) first-in, first-out, (b) last-in, first-out, and (c) the weighted-average cost method. Round your final answers to the nearest dollar.

E6-3B. **Year-End Physical Inventory** The December 31, inventory for the Simmons Company included five products. The year-end physical count revealed the following quantities on hand: **LO1**

Product	Quantity Available
K	40
L	42
M	60
N	50
P	55

The related unit costs K, $7; L, $10; M, $9; N, $5; and P, $4.

Required
Calculate the total cost of the December 31, physical inventory.

E6-4B. **Inventory Costing Methods—Periodic Method** Spangler Company is a retailer that uses the periodic inventory system. On March 1, it had 100 units of product M at a total cost of $1,590. On March 6, Spangler purchased 200 units of M for $3,600. On March 10, it purchased 125 units of M for $3,000. On March 15, it sold 180 units of M for $5,400. Calculate the March cost of goods sold and the ending inventory at March 31 using (a) first-in, first-out, (b) last-in, first-out, and (c) the weighted-average cost method. Round your final answers to the nearest dollar.   **LO2**

E6-5B. **Errors in Inventory Counts** The following information was taken from the records of Spencer Enterprises: **LO3**

	2016	2015
Beginning inventory	$ 55,000	$ 75,000
Cost of goods purchased.	540,000	500,000
Cost of goods available for sale.	595,000	575,000
Ending inventory.	85,000	55,000
Cost of goods sold.	$510,000	$520,000

The following two errors were made in the physical inventory counts:

1. 2015 ending inventory was overstated by $30,000.
2. 2016 ending inventory was understated by $18,000.

Compute the correct cost of goods sold for both 2015 and 2016.

E6-6B. **Departures from Acquisition Cost** Determine the proper total inventory value for each of the following items in Packer Company's ending inventory: **LO4**

a. Packer has 60 model X3 cameras in stock. The cameras cost $160 each, but their year-end replacement cost is only $140. Packer has been selling the cameras for $210, but competitors are now selling them for $170. Packer plans to match the selling price at $170. Packer's normal gross profit on cameras is 35 percent.

b. Packer has 550 rolls of film that are past the expiration date since film is now a slow moving item. The film cost $2.00 each and normally sells for $4.00. New replacement film still costs

$2.00. Packer has put the expired film on clearance and is selling it for $1.50 per roll. There are no related selling costs.

c. Packer has four computers in stock that have been used as demonstration models. These computers cost $400 and normally sell for $550. Because they are used, Packer is selling them for $350 each. Expected selling costs are $10 per computer. New models of the computer (on order Z) will cost Packer $420 and will be priced to sell at $590.

LO2 E6-7B. Inventory Costing Methods—Periodic Method The Toon Company, which uses the periodic inventory system, has the following records:

		Units	Unit Cost
Beginning inventory		100	$49
Purchases:	Jan. 6	650	42
	July 15	550	38
	Dec. 28	200	36

Ending inventory was 360 units. Compute the ending inventory and the cost of goods sold for the year using (a) first-in, first out, (b) weighted-average cost, and (c) last-in, first-out.

LO2 E6-8B. Inventory Costing Methods—Periodic Method The following data are for the Miller Corporation, which sells just one product:

		Units	Unit Cost
Beginning inventory, January 1		200	$12
Purchases	February 11	500	13
	May 18	400	15
	October 23	100	17
Sales	March 1	350	
	July 1	400	

Calculate the value of ending inventory and cost of goods sold using the periodic method and (a) first-in, first-out, (b) last-in, first-out, and (c) weighted-average cost method. Round your final answers to the nearest dollar.

LO4, 5 E6-9B. Applying IFRS The French Petroleum Company is a Paris-based oil and gas company that prepares its financial statements using IFRS. During the year, the management of the company undertook a review of the fair value of its oil and gas inventory and found that the inventory had appreciated above its book value of 55 million euros. According to the company's management, the oil and gas inventory was undervalued by 6 million euros. Prepare the journal entry to revalue the company's inventory. How would the revaluation immediately affect the company's (a) current ratio, (b) inventory turnover, and (c) days' sales in inventory?

LO4 E6-10B. Lower-of-Cost-or-Market (LCM) Method The following data are taken from the Smith & Wesson Corporation's inventory accounts:

Item Code	Quantity	Unit Cost	Replacement Cost
ZKE.	100	$22	$18
XYF.	300	33	35
MNJ	400	23	20
UBS	220	33	37

Calculate the value of the company's ending inventory using the lower-of-cost-or-market method applied to each item of inventory.

LO5 E6-11B. Inventory Turnover and Days' Sales in Inventory The Northern Company installed a new inventory management system at the beginning of 2015. Shown below are data from the company's accounting records as reported by the new system:

	2015	2016
Sales revenue.	$10,000,000	$12,000,000
Cost of goods sold.	5,000,000	5,900,000
Beginning inventory	610,000	630,000
Ending inventory.	630,000	750,000

Calculate the company's (a) inventory turnover and (b) days' sales in inventory for 2015 and 2016. Comment on your results.

E6-12B. Lower-of-Cost-or-Market (LCM) Method The following data refer to the Froning Company's ending inventory:

LO4

Item Code	Quantity	Unit Cost	Unit Market
LXC.	60	$40	$48
KWT	210	38	34
MOR.	300	25	20
NES	100	26	32

Calculate the value of the company's ending inventory by using the lower-of-cost-or-market method applied to each item of inventory.

E6-13B. The LIFO Inventory Reserve Midwestern Steel Company uses the LIFO inventory costing method to value its ending inventory. The following data were obtained from the company's accounting records:

LO7
(Appendix 6B)

Current assets (under LIFO).	$9,500,000
Current liabilities.	7,500,000
Inventory under LIFO	3,800,000
Inventory under FIFO	4,700,000

Calculate the company's (a) LIFO inventory reserve and (b) current ratio assuming (i) FIFO and (ii) LIFO.

E6-14B. Inventory Costing Methods—Perpetual Method Refer to the information in E6-2B and assume the perpetual inventory system is used. Calculate the cost of goods sold for the May 16 sale using (a) first-in, first-out, (b) last-in, first-out, and (c) the weighted-average cost method. Round your final answers to the nearest dollar.

LO6
(Appendix 6A)

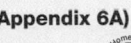

E6-15B. Inventory Costing Methods—Perpetual Method Refer to the information in E6-4B and assume the perpetual inventory system is used. Calculate the ending inventory cost of item M on March 15 (after the sale) using (a) first-in, first-out, (b) last-in, first-out, and (c) the weighted-average cost method. Round your final answers to the nearest dollar.

LO6
(Appendix 6A)

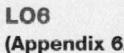

E6-16B. Inventory Costing Methods—Perpetual Method Refer to the information in E6-8B and assume the perpetual inventory system is used. Calculate the value of ending inventory and cost of goods sold using the perpetual method and (a) first-in, first-out, (b) last-in, first-out, and (c) weighted-average cost method. Round your final answers to the nearest dollar.

LO6
(Appendix 6A)

PROBLEMS—SET A

P6-1A. Just-in-Time Inventory The Dixon Manufacturing Company uses the perpetual inventory system with its raw material inventory. Dixon plans to include raw material costing $2,000,000 in the products that it manufactures. John Dixon, president of the company, wants to adopt the just-in-time manufacturing philosophy for the raw materials inventory. He wants to have only the raw material needed for the next day's production at the end of each day. The factory operates 250 days each year. Historically, the raw materials inventory balance at the end of the day has averaged $40,000 cost. Dixon has an annual inventory carrying cost equal to 20 percent of total inventory cost.

LO1

Required

a. What is the anticipated inventory carrying cost (in dollars) if Dixon does not adopt the just-in-time manufacturing philosophy?

b. Calculate the average level (in dollars) for the raw materials inventory if Dixon adopts the just-in-time manufacturing philosophy.

c. Calculate the reductions in the raw materials inventory level and the raw materials inventory annual carrying cost if Dixon adopts the just-in-time manufacturing philosophy.

d. What other factors or situations should Dixon consider before deciding to have only one day's supply of raw material? (*Hint:* Consider factors and situations related to environment, supplier problems, labor problems, etc.)

LO2   P6-2A.   Inventory Costing Methods—Periodic Method Fortune Stores uses the periodic inventory system for its merchandise inventory. The April 1 inventory for one of the items in the merchandise inventory consisted of 120 units with a unit cost of $330. Transactions for this item during April were as follows:

April   9 Purchased 40 units @ $345 per unit.
        14 Sold 80 units @ $550 per unit.
        23 Purchased 20 units @ $350 per unit.
        29 Sold 40 units @ $550 per unit.

Required

a. Calculate the cost of goods sold and the ending inventory cost for the month of April using the weighted-average cost method. Round your final answers to the nearest dollar.

b. Calculate the cost of goods sold and the ending inventory cost for the month of April using the first-in, first-out method.

c. Calculate the cost of goods sold and the ending inventory cost for the month of April using the last-in, first-out method.

LO4   P6-3A.   Lower-of-Cost-or-Market (LCM) Method The following data are taken from the Simpson Corporation's inventory accounts:

Item Code	Quantity	Unit Cost	Replacement Cost
Product 1			
ZKE....................................	100	$22	$18
ZKF....................................	300	33	36
Product 2			
MNJ	400	22	19
MNS	250	33	37

Calculate the value of the company's ending inventory using the lower-of-cost-or-market method applied to each item of inventory.

LO2, 3   P6-4A.   Inventory Costing Methods—Periodic Method Chen Sales Corporation uses the periodic inventory system. On January 1, 2015, Chen had 1,000 units of product A with a unit cost of $20 per unit. A summary of purchases and sales during 2015 follows:

	Unit Cost	Units Purchased	Units Sold
Feb. 2			400
Apr. 6	$22	1,800	
July 10			1,600
Aug. 9..	25	800	
Oct. 23			800
Dec. 30..	29	1,400	

Required

a. Assume that Chen uses the first-in, first-out method. Compute the cost of goods sold for 2015 and the ending inventory balance at December 31, 2015, for product A.

b. Assume that Chen uses the last-in, first-out method. Compute the cost of goods sold for 2015 and the ending inventory balance at December 31, 2015, for product A.

c. Assume that Chen uses the weighted-average cost method. Compute the cost of goods sold for 2015 and the ending inventory balance at December 31, 2015, for product A.

d. Assuming that Chen's products are perishable items, which of the three inventory costing methods would you choose to:
   1. Reflect the likely goods flow through the business?
   2. Minimize income taxes for the period?
   3. Report the largest amount of net income for the period?
   Explain your answers.

P6-5A. Inventory Turnover and Days' Sales in Inventory The Eastern Corporation installed a new inventory management system at the beginning of 2015. Eastern reported an inventory turnover of 2.80 in 2015. Shown below are data from the company's accounting records as reported by the new system:

LO5

	2015	2016
Sales revenue.	$19,000,000	$20,000,000
Cost of goods sold.	8,500,000	8,000,000
Beginning inventory	2,500,000	2,530,000
Ending Inventory.	2,530,000	2,600,000

Calculate the company's (a) inventory turnover and (b) days' sales in inventory for 2015 and 2016. Comment on your results.

P6-6A. Goods in Transit The Cardinal Wholesale Company sells merchandise to a variety of retailers. Cardinal uses different freight terms with its various customers and suppliers. All sales are made on account. LO1

Required

For each of the following transactions, indicate which company has ownership of the goods in transit:

a. Cardinal sold merchandise to X-Mart Stores, with shipping terms of F.O.B. shipping point.

b. Cardinal purchased merchandise from Zendo Manufacturing Company, with shipping terms of F.O.B. destination.

c. Cardinal sold merchandise to Mary's Boutique, with shipping terms of F.O.B. destination.

d. Sunshine Manufacturing Company sold merchandise to Cardinal, with shipping terms of F.O.B. shipping point.

e. Cardinal purchased merchandise from Warfield Manufacturing Company, with freight terms of F.O.B. shipping point.

f. Stevenson Stores purchased merchandise from Cardinal, with shipping terms of F.O.B. shipping point.

P6-7A. Lower-of-Cost-or-Market (LCM) Method The Venner Company had the following inventory at year-end:

LO4

		Unit Price	
	Quantity	Cost	Market
Fans			
Model X1.	300	$18	$19
Model X2.	250	23	24
Model X3.	450	29	26
Heaters			
Model B7	500	24	28
Model B8	290	35	32
Model B9	100	41	37

Required

a. Determine the value of ending inventory after applying the lower-of-cost-or-market method to each item of inventory.

b.   Would the net income be lower under the cost method or the lower-of-cost-or-market method?

LO2   P6-8A.   Inventory Costing Methods—Periodic Method The following data are for the Portet Corporation, which sells just one product:

		Units	Unit Cost
Beginning inventory, January 1		1,200	$ 8
Purchases	February 11	1,500	9
	May 18	1,400	10
	October 23	1,100	14
Sales	March 1	1,400	
	July 1	1,400	
	October 29	1,200	

Calculate the value of ending inventory and cost of goods sold at year-end using the periodic method and (a) first-in, first-out, (b) last-in, first-out, and (c) weighted-average cost method. Round the cost per unit to 3 decimal places and round your final answers to the nearest dollar. If the replacement cost of the inventory at year-end is $15, how will the cost of goods sold under each method be affected?

LO1   P6-9A.   Physical Inventory Calculation Apache Stores conducted a physical inventory at December 31. The items counted during the physical inventory are listed below. Apache's accountant provided the unit costs.

	December 31	
Item Description	Count	Unit Cost
Colorado wool sweaters.	48	$32
Magnum wool sweaters	27	34
Johnson jackets	50	30
Magnum caps.	45	12
Evans caps.	26	10
Colorado shirts.	72	20
Johnson shirts	68	15
Magnum boots.	45	60

Required

Prepare a schedule to determine the total cost of each item in the inventory and the total cost of the complete inventory at December 31.

LO6   P6-10A.   Inventory Costing Methods—Perpetual Method Refer to the information in P6-2A and assume the
(Appendix 6A)   perpetual inventory system is used.

Required

a.   Calculate the cost of goods sold and the ending inventory cost for the month of April using the weighted-average cost method.

b.   Calculate the cost of goods sold and the ending inventory cost for the month of April using the first-in, first-out method.

c.   Calculate the cost of goods sold and the ending inventory cost for the month of April using the last-in, first-out method.

LO6   P6-11A.   Inventory Costing Methods—Perpetual Method Refer to the information in P6-4A and assume the
(Appendix 6A)   perpetual inventory system is used.

Required

a.   Assume that Chen uses the first-in, first-out method. Compute the cost of goods sold for 2015 and the ending inventory balance at December 31, 2015, for product A.

b.   Assume that Chen uses the last-in, first-out method. Compute the cost of goods sold for 2015 and the ending inventory balance at December 31, 2015, for product A.

c.   Assume that Chen uses the weighted-average cost method. Compute the cost of goods sold for 2015 and the ending inventory balance at December 31, 2015, for product A.

    d. Assuming that Chen's products are perishable items, which of the three inventory costing methods would you choose to:

        1. Reflect the likely goods flow through the business?

        2. Minimize income taxes for the period?

        3. Report the largest amount of net income for the period?

        Explain your answers.

P6-12A. The LIFO Inventory Reserve Waterloo Manufacturing Company uses the LIFO inventory costing method to value its ending inventory. The following data were obtained from the company's accounting records:

LO7
(Appendix 6B)

Current assets (under FIFO)...	$20,000,000
Current liabilities..	15,000,000
Inventory under LIFO...	6,500,000
Inventory under FIFO...	7,700,000

Calculate the company's (a) LIFO inventory reserve and (b) current ratio assuming (i) FIFO and (ii) LIFO. If the company's LIFO gross profit was $10,000,000 and the change in the LIFO inventory reserve was $1,400,000, calculate the company's gross profit under FIFO.

P6-13A. Inventory Costing Methods—Perpetual Method Using the data in P6-8A, assume that Portet Corporation uses the perpetual inventory system. Calculate the value of ending inventory and cost of goods sold at year-end using the perpetual method and (a) first-in, first-out, (b) last-in, first-out, and (c) weighted-average cost method. Round the cost per unit to 3 decimal places and round your final answers to the nearest dollar. If the replacement cost of the inventory at year-end is $15, how will the cost of goods sold under each method be affected?

LO6
(Appendix 6A)

PROBLEMS—SET B

P6-1B. Just-in-Time Inventory The Field Manufacturing Company uses the perpetual inventory system for its raw materials inventory. Field plans to include raw material costing $2,500,000 in the products that it manufactures. Henry Field, president of the company, wants to adopt the just-in-time manufacturing philosophy for the raw materials inventory. He wants to have only the raw material needed for the next day's production at the end of each day. The factory operates 280 days each year. Historically, the raw materials inventory balance at the end of the day has averaged $55,000 cost. Field has an annual inventory carrying cost equal to 22 percent of total inventory cost.

LO1

Required

    a. What is the anticipated annual inventory carrying cost (in dollars) if Field does not adopt the just-in-time manufacturing philosophy?

    b. Calculate the average level (in dollars) for the raw materials inventory if Field adopts the just-in-time manufacturing philosophy.

    c. Calculate the reduction in the raw materials inventory level and the raw materials inventory annual carrying cost if Field adopts the just-in-time manufacturing philosophy.

    d. What other factors or situations should Field consider before deciding to have only one day's supply of material? (*Hint:* Consider factors and situations related to environment, supplier problems, labor problems, etc.)

P6-2B. Inventory Costing Methods—Periodic Method The Shiloh Company uses the periodic inventory system for its merchandise inventory. The June 1 inventory for one of the items in the merchandise inventory consisted of 60 units with a unit cost of $45. Transactions for this item during June were as follows:

LO2

June   5 Purchased 40 units @ $50 per unit.

       13 Sold 50 units @ $95 per unit.

       25 Purchased 30 units @ $53 per unit.

       29 Sold 20 units @ $100 per unit.

Required

    a. Compute the cost of goods sold and the ending inventory cost for the month of June using the weighted-average cost method. Round the cost per unit to 3 decimal places and round your final answers to the nearest dollar.

b. Compute the cost of goods sold and the ending inventory cost for the month of June using the first-in, first-out method.

c. Compute the cost of goods sold and the ending inventory cost for the month of June using the last-in, first-out method.

LO4   P6-3B. Lower-of-Cost-or-Market (LCM) Method The following data are taken from the Smithfield Corporation's inventory accounts:

Item Code	Quantity	Unit Cost	Replacement Cost
Product 1			
XKE.....................................	100	$32	$30
XKF.....................................	400	43	44
Product 2			
ZNJ.....................................	400	32	29
ZNS.....................................	300	43	47

Calculate the value of the company's ending inventory using the lower-of-cost-or-market method applied to each item of inventory.

LO2, 3   P6-4B. Inventory Costing Methods—Periodic Method The Gleem Sales Corporation uses the periodic inventory system. On January 1, 2015, Gleem had 2,600 units of product B with a unit cost of $40 per unit. A summary of purchases and sales during 2015 follows:

	Unit Cost	Units Purchased	Units Sold
Jan. 3			1,600
Mar. 8...	$44	3,000	
June 13...			2,000
Sept. 19	46	800	
Nov. 23...	48	1,200	
Dec. 28...			1,800

Required

a. Assume that Gleem uses the first-in, first-out method. Compute the cost of goods sold for 2015 and the ending inventory balance at December 31, 2015, for product B.

b. Assume that Gleem uses the last-in, first-out method. Compute the cost of goods sold for 2015 and the ending inventory balance at December 31, 2015, for product B.

c. Assume that Gleem uses the weighted-average cost method. Compute the cost of goods sold for 2015 and the ending inventory balance at December 31, 2015, for product B.

d. Assuming that Gleem sells items that quickly become obsolete, which of these three inventory costing methods would you choose to:
   1. Reflect the likely goods flow through the business?
   2. Minimize income tax for the period?
   3. To report the largest amount of net income for the period?
   Explain your answers.

LO5   P6-5B. Inventory Turnover and Days' Sales in Inventory The Western States Corporation installed a new inventory management system at the beginning of 2015. The company reported an inventory turnover of 1.80 in 2015. Shown below are data from the Western States' accounting records as reported by the new system:

	2015	2016
Sales revenue...	$49,000,000	$42,000,000
Cost of goods sold...	30,000,000	29,500,000
Beginning inventory	16,250,000	16,500,000
Ending inventory...	16,500,000	20,600,000

Calculate the company's (a) inventory turnover and (b) days' sales in inventory for 2015 and 2016. Comment on your results.

P6-6B. **Goods in Transit** Marshall Distributors sells merchandise to a variety of retailers. Marshall uses dif- **LO1**
ferent freight terms with its various customers and suppliers. All sales are made on account.

Required

For each of the following transactions, indicate which company has ownership of the goods in transit:

a. Marshall sold merchandise to Clay Boutique, with shipping terms of F.O.B. destination.
b. Marshall purchased merchandise from Campbell Manufacturing Company, with freight terms of F.O.B. shipping point.
c. Marshall sold merchandise to Save-A-Lot Stores, with shipping terms of F.O.B. shipping point.
d. Marshall purchased merchandise from Central Manufacturing Company, with shipping terms of F.O.B. destination.
e. Levinson Stores purchased merchandise from Marshall, with shipping terms of F.O.B. shipping point.
f. Connor Manufacturing Company sold merchandise to Marshall, with shipping terms of F.O.B. shipping point.

P6-7B. **Lower-of-Cost-or-Market (LCM) Method** The Crane Company had the following inventory at **LO4**
year-end:

		Unit Price	
	Quantity	Cost	Market
Desks			
Model 9001	70	$190	$215
Model 9002	45	310	268
Model 9003	20	345	360
Cabinets			
Model 7001	120	60	68
Model 7002	80	95	85
Model 7003	50	135	126

Required

a. Determine the value of the ending inventory after applying the lower-of-cost-or-market method to each item of inventory.
b. Would the net income be lower under the cost method or the lower-of-cost-or-market method?

P6-8B. **Inventory Costing Methods—Periodic Method** The following data are for the Graham Corpora- **LO2**
tion, which sells just one product:

		Units	Unit Cost
Beginning inventory, January 1		1,200	$18
Purchases	February 11	1,500	19
	May 18	1,400	21
	October 23	1,100	23
Sales	March 1	1,400	
	July 1	1,400	
	October 29	1,000	

Calculate the value of ending inventory and cost of goods sold for the year using the periodic method and (a) first-in, first-out, (b) last-in, first-out, and (c) weighted-average cost method. Round the cost per unit to 3 decimal places and round your final answers to the nearest dollar. If the replacement cost of the inventory at year-end is $25, how will the cost of goods sold under each method be affected?

P6-9B. **Physical Inventory Calculation** Furniture City conducted a physical inventory at December 31. The **LO1**
items counted during the physical inventory are listed below. Furniture City's accountant provided the unit costs.

Item Description	December 31 Count	Unit Cost
Taylor sofas	10	$250
Georgia sofas	8	300
Taylor chairs	22	175
Taylor recliners	16	200
Georgia recliners	4	210
Carolina lamps	16	30
Chicago lamps	18	28
Georgia tables	10	155

Required

Prepare a schedule to determine the total cost of each item in the inventory and the total cost of the complete inventory at December 31.

LO6
(Appendix 6A)

P6-10B. Inventory Costing Methods—Perpetual Method Refer to the information in P6-2B and assume the perpetual inventory system is used.

Required

a.　Compute the cost of goods sold and the ending inventory cost for the month of June using the weighted-average cost method.

b.　Compute the cost of goods sold and the ending inventory cost for the month of June using the first-in, first-out method.

c.　Compute the cost of goods sold and the ending inventory cost for the month of June using the last-in, first-out method.

LO6
(Appendix 6A)

P6-11B. Inventory Costing Methods—Perpetual Method Refer to the information in P6-4B and assume the perpetual inventory system is used.

Required

a.　Assume that Gleem uses the first-in, first-out method. Compute the cost of goods sold for 2015 and the ending inventory balance at December 31, 2015, for product B.

b.　Assume that Gleem uses the last-in, first-out method. Compute the cost of goods sold for 2015 and the ending inventory balance at December 31, 2015, for product B.

c.　Assume that Gleem uses the weighted-average cost method. Compute the cost of goods sold for 2015 and the ending inventory balance at December 31, 2015, for product B.

d.　Assuming that Gleem sells items that quickly become obsolete, which of these three inventory costing methods would you choose to:

1.　Reflect the likely goods flow through the business?

2.　Minimize income tax for the period?

3.　To report the largest amount of net income for the period?

Explain your answers.

LO7
(Appendix 6B)

P6-12B. The LIFO Inventory Reserve The Peoria Manufacturing Company uses the LIFO inventory costing method to value its ending inventory. The following data were obtained from the company's accounting records:

Current assets (under LIFO)	$47,500,000
Current liabilities	36,000,000
Inventory under LIFO	16,000,000
Inventory under FIFO	18,700,000

Calculate the company's (a) LIFO inventory reserve and (b) current ratio assuming (i) FIFO and (ii) LIFO. If the company's LIFO gross profit was $18,000,000 and the change in the LIFO inventory reserve was $2,500,000, calculate the company's gross profit under FIFO.

P6-13B. Inventory Costing Methods—Perpetual Method Using the data in P6-8B, assume that Graham **LO6** Corporation uses the perpetual inventory system. Calculate the value of ending inventory and cost of **(Appendix 6A)** goods sold for the year using the perpetual method and (a) first-in, first-out, (b) last-in, first-out, and (c) weighted-average cost method. Round the cost per unit to 3 decimal places and round your final answers to the nearest dollar. If the replacement cost of the inventory at year-end is $25, how will the cost of goods sold under each method be affected?

SERIAL PROBLEM: KATE'S CARDS

(Note: This is a continuation of the Serial Problem: Kate's Cards from Chapters 1 through 5.)

SP6.   As expected, the holiday season was very busy for Kate and her greeting card company. In fact, most of her supplies were fully depleted by year-end, necessitating a restocking of inventory. Assume that Kate uses the periodic method of accounting for inventory and that her January beginning inventory was $0. The following transactions occurred for Kate's Cards during January of the New Year:

Purchases	Units		Unit Cost	Total Cost
Jan. 10	400	@	$3.00 per unit	$1,200
Jan. 17	500	@	$3.50 per unit	1,750
Jan. 23	300	@	$4.00 per unit	1,200
Total	1,200			$4,150

Sales	Units
Jan. 15	360
Jan. 21	420
Jan. 27	380
Total	1,160

Required
a.   Calculate the company's cost of goods sold and value of ending inventory for the month of January using (1) FIFO, (2) LIFO, and (3) the weighted-average cost method. Round the cost per unit to 3 decimal places and round your final answers to the nearest dollar.
b.   If the replacement cost of Kate's inventory is $4.00 per unit on January 31, what value should be reported for her ending inventory on the January 31 balance sheet under each of the three inventory costing methods?

EXTENDING YOUR KNOWLEDGE

REPORTING AND ANALYSIS

EYK6-1.   Financial Reporting Problem: The Columbia Sportswear Company The financial statements for the **Columbia Sportswear Company** can be found in Appendix A at the end of this textbook.

COLUMBIA
SPORTSWEAR
COMPANY

Required
Answer the following questions using Columbia's Consolidated Financial Statements:
a.   How much inventory does Columbia carry on its balance sheet? What percentage of Columbia's total assets does inventory represent in 2014 and 2013?
b.   Compute the inventory turnover and days' sales in inventory for 2014 and 2013. Inventory at December 31, 2012, was $363.3 million.
c.   Is Columbia's inventory management improving?

COLUMBIA
SPORTSWEAR
COMPANY

UNDER ARMOUR,
INC.

EYK6-2.   **Comparative Analysis Problem: Columbia Sportswear Company vs Under Armour, Inc.** The financial statements for **Columbia Sportswear Company** can be found in Appendix A at the end of this textbook, and the financial statements of **Under Armour, Inc.** can be found in Appendix B.

Required
a. Compare the dollar value of inventory carried on the balance sheet by each company in 2014 and 2013. Which company carries the greatest dollar amount of inventory? Compare the ratio of inventory divided by total assets for each company for 2014 and 2013. Which company carries the largest relative investment in inventory?
b. Calculate the inventory turnover and days' sales in inventory for 2014 and 2013 for each company. Inventory at December 31, 2012, for Columbia and Under Armour, Inc. was $363.3 million and $319.3 million, respectively.
c. Which company appears to be doing the better job of managing its investment in inventory?

EYK6-3.   **Business Decision Problem** Mackenzie Company is a wholesaler that uses the perpetual inventory system. On January 1, 2015, Mackenzie had 3,000 units of its product at a cost of $5 per unit. Transactions related to inventory during 2015 were as follows:

Purchases				Sales			
Feb. 5	9,000 units	@	$6	March 8	8,000 units	@	$ 9
May 19	20,000 units	@	7	June 21.	19,000 units	@	10
Dec. 15.	3,000 units	@	9	Dec. 28.	4,000 units	@	12

Mackenzie is trying to decide whether to use the first-in, first-out (FIFO) inventory costing method or the last-in, first-out (LIFO) inventory costing method.

Required
a. Assume that Mackenzie decides to use the FIFO inventory costing method.
  1. What would gross profit be for 2015?
  2. How would Mackenzie's gross profit and ending inventory for 2015 change if the December 15, 2015, purchase had been made on January 3, 2016, instead?
  3. How would Mackenzie's gross profit and ending inventory for 2015 change if the December 15, 2015, purchase had been for 6,000 units instead of 3,000 units?
b. Assume that Mackenzie decides to use the LIFO inventory costing method.
  1. What would gross profit be for 2015?
  2. How would Mackenzie's gross profit and ending inventory for 2015 change if the December 15, 2015, purchase had been made on January 3, 2016, instead?
  3. How would Mackenzie's gross profit and ending inventory for 2015 change if the December 15, 2015, purchase had been for 6,000 units instead of 3,000 units?
c. Which inventory costing method should Mackenzie choose and why?

EYK6-4.   **Financial Analysis Problem** Purpose: To use annual financial report filings to learn about how a company accounts for its inventory.

Select any publicly traded company not discussed in this chapter and go to its Website. Find the section on investor information and download its latest annual report (you may download its 10K report rather than the annual report).

Required
Using this report, answer the following questions.
a. What is the name of the company you chose and what is the primary industry that it operates in?
b. Does the company list inventory on its balance sheet? If so, where on the balance sheet does it appear?
c. Does the company have a separate note in the notes to the financial statements that provides a more detailed breakdown of the amount of inventory listed? If so, what is that breakdown?
d. What inventory method does the company use?
e. Calculate the inventory turnover ratio and days' sales in inventory for the most current year shown.

CRITICAL THINKING

EYK6-5. **Accounting Research Problem** The fiscal year 2014 annual report of **General Mills, Inc.** is available on this book's Website.

GENERAL MILLS, INC.

Required

a. What percentage of total assets are represented by General Mills' investment in inventory in 2014 and 2013?

b. Compute the inventory turnover and days' sales in inventory for General Mills for 2014 and 2013. In 2012, the ending inventory was $1,478.8 million.

c. Is the company doing a better job of managing its investment in inventory in 2014?

d. What inventory costing method does General Mills use?

e. What is the value of the company's LIFO reserve at year-end 2014? General Mills labels its LIFO reserve as the "Excess of FIFO over LIFO cost" in Note 17. (Appendix 6B)

EYK6-6. **Accounting Communications Activity** **Pactiv Corporation** is a leader in the consumer and foodservice packaging market. In December 2009 the company announced a change in the accounting for inventories. www.businesswire.com/news/home/20091221005622/en/ Pactiv-Announces-Inventory-Accounting-Change-LIFO-FIFO

PACTIV CORPORATION

Required

Sarah Jenkins, CEO of a competing firm, read this announcement, but was confused about what exactly Pactiv was doing. She asked that you write a memo explaining the following items.

a. What about its accounting for inventory was Pactiv changing?

b. Why does Pactiv believe the new method is preferable?

c. What benefit does Pactiv believe will be realized from the change?

EYK6-7. **Accounting Ethics Case** Reed Kohler is in his final year of employment as controller for Quality Sales Corporation; he hopes to retire next year. As a member of top management, Kohler participates in an attractive company bonus plan. The overall size of the bonus is a function of the firm's net income before bonus and income taxes—the larger the net income, the larger the bonus.

Due to a slowdown in the economy, Quality Sales Corporation has encountered difficulties in managing its cash flow. To improve its cash flow by reducing cash payments for income taxes, the firm's auditors have recommended that the company change its inventory costing method from FIFO to LIFO. This change would cause a significant increase in the cost of goods sold for the year. Kohler believes the firm should not switch to LIFO this year because its inventory quantities are too large. He believes that the firm should work to reduce its inventory quantities and then switch to LIFO (the switch could be made in a year or two). After expressing this opinion to the firm's treasurer, Kohler is stunned when the treasurer replies: "Reed, I can't believe that after all these years with the firm, you put your personal interests ahead of the firm's interests."

Explain why Kohler may be viewed as holding a position that favors his personal interests. What can Kohler do to increase his credibility when the possible change to LIFO is discussed at a meeting of the firm's top management next week?

EYK6-8. **Corporate Social Responsibility Problem** The Corporate Social Responsibility highlight in this chapter discussed how **Best Buy** is working to make sure its supply chain complies with the company's high ethical standards. One of the ways this is done is for Best Buy's Global Sourcing team to work with their Social and Environmental Responsibility team.

BEST BUY

Go to the Best Buy Website and its page on Corporate Responsibility & Sustainability (https://corporate.bestbuy.com/sustainability/) and locate Best Buy's Fiscal Year 2015 Sustainability Report. Open the report and scroll down to the section entitled: "Supply Chain Sustainability Program." The Supply Chain Sustainability (SCS) Program seeks to control risk, enhance the partnership with suppliers (by building their capacity for responsible business practices), and to create value for all stakeholders. The supplier code of conduct and the audit methodology are intended to create business value by improving working and environmental conditions in the supply chain. Explain the six parts of the code of conduct and the factory audit program utilized in the SCS program.

CRAZY EDDIE

COMPTRONIX
CORPORATION

LESLIE FAY
COMPANY

LARIBEE
MANUFACTURING
COMPANY

PHAR-MOR

EYK6-9. **Forensic Accounting Problem** The chapter highlights an inventory fraud case at **Crazy Eddie**. Unfortunately there have been many other serious inventory frauds where the auditors were fooled by illegal acts. A few of these cases include (1) **Comptronix Corporation**, (2) **Leslie Fay Company**, (3) **Laribee Manufacturing Company**, and (4) **Phar-Mor** drug stores.

Do a computer search of one of these cases and explain how inventory was used to commit the fraud. List some ways the auditors can lessen the chance such frauds could go undetected.

LO5

EYK6-10. **Inventory Turnover and Days' Sales in Inventory: IFRS Financial Statements** The 2014 financial statements of LVMH Moet Hennessey-Louis Vuitton S.A. are presented in Appendix C at the end of this book. LVMH is a Paris-based holding company and one of the world's largest and best-known luxury goods companies. As a member of the European Union, French companies are required to prepare their consolidated (group) financial statements using International Financial Reporting Standards (IFRS). LVMH's IFRS financial statements are presented in Appendix C at the end of this textbook. Using these financial statements, calculate the company's (a) inventory turnover and (b) days' sales in inventory for 2013 and 2014. Comment on the company's trend in inventory management effectiveness.

LO7
(Appendix 6B)

EYK6-11. **Working with the Takeaways** Felix Company uses the LIFO inventory costing method to value inventory. The following financial data was obtained from its accounting records for the current year:

Current assets (including inventory)	$4,000
Current liabilities	2,000
Inventory under LIFO	575
Inventory under FIFO	775

Compute (a) the current ratio assuming (i) LIFO and (ii) FIFO and (b) the LIFO inventory reserve.

ANSWERS TO SELF-STUDY QUESTIONS:

1. b, (p. 277) 2. d, (p. 283) 3. c, (pp. 285–286) 4. b, (p. 278) 5. d, (p. 291) 6. c, (p. 286)
7. a, (pp. 285–286) 8. b, (p. 286) 9. d, (pp. 286–287) 10. d, (pp. 291–292) 11. b, (p. 293)
12. c, (pp. 302–303) 13. b, (p. 281)

YOUR TURN! SOLUTIONS

Solution 6.1

The $15,000 of goods shipped F.O.B. shipping point should be deducted from the inventory valuation, and the $25,000 of consignment goods should be included in the inventory valuation. The corrected ending inventory total should be $310,000 ($300,000 − $15,000 + $25,000).

Solution 6.2

a. Ending inventory using:

   i. FIFO: 1,000 × $7 = $7,000
   ii. LIFO: 1,000 × $5 = $5,000
   iii. Weighted-average cost: 1,000 × [(4,000 × $5) + (6,000 × $7)]/10,000 = 1,000 × $6.20 = $6,200

b. Cost of goods sold using:

   i. FIFO: (4,000 × $5) + (5,000 × $7) = $55,000
   ii. LIFO: (6,000 × $7) + (3,000 × $5) = $57,000
   iii. Weighted-average cost: 9,000 × [(4,000 × $5) + (6,000 × $7)]/10,000 = 9,000 × $6.20 = $55,800

c. Gross profit using:

   i. FIFO: $90,000 − $55,000 − $35,000
   ii. LIFO: $90,000 − $57,000 = $33,000
   iii. Weighted-average cost: $90,000 − $55,800 = $34,200

Solution 6.3

	Cost of Goods Sold	Beginning Inventory		Purchases		Ending Inventory
2015	$7,000 (instead of $7,500)	$ —	+	$10,000	−	$3,000
2016	$13,000 (instead of $12,500)	$ 3,000	+	$15,000	−	$5,000

		With Error	Without Error
2015			
	Sales.	$15,000	$15,000
	Cost of goods sold.	7,500	7,000
	Net income.	$ 7,500	$ 8,000
2016			
	Sales.	$25,000	$25,000
	Cost of goods sold.	12,500	13,000
	Net income.	$12,500	$12,000

Solution 6.4

The lowest value for each inventory item is: DSLR $110,000, Point and Shoot $73,000, and Camcorders $48,000. The total of the inventory is therefore valued under LCM at $231,000 ($110,000 + $73,000 + $48,000).

Solution 6.5

	2015	2016
Inventory turnover	$\dfrac{\$2,000,000}{(\$450,000 + \$430,000)/2} = 4.55$	$\dfrac{\$2,300,000}{(\$430,000 + \$320,000)/2} = 6.13$
Days' sales in inventory	365/4.55 = 80.22 days	365/6.13 = 59.54 days

The company increased its sales by $400,000 from 2015 to 2016, and at the same time, decreased its average inventory by $65,000 ($440,000 − $375,000) as a consequence of improved inventory management. This resulted in a significantly improved inventory turnover (6.13 versus 4.55) and 20.68 (80.22 − 59.54) less days' sales in inventory. It appears that the new inventory management system is a financial success.

Solution 6A.1

FIFO

		Purchased			Sold Unit		Inventory Balance		
Date	Units	Unit Cost	Total	Units	Cost	Total	Units	Unit Cost	Total
Jan. 1							1,000	$5.00	$5,000
Jan. 5	600	$6.00	$3,600				1,000	5.00	8,600
							600	6.00	
Jan. 15 . . .				200	$5.00	$1,000	800	5.00	7,600
							600	6.00	
Jan. 17 . . .	300	7.00	2,100				800	5.00	9,700
							600	6.00	
							300	7.00	
Jan. 25 . . .				400	5.00	2,000	400	5.00	7,700
							600	6.00	
							300	7.00	
						$3,000			

LIFO

Date	Units	Purchased Unit Cost	Total	Units	Sold Unit Cost	Total	Units	Unit Cost	Total
								Inventory Balance	
Jan. 1							1,000	$5.00	$5,000
Jan. 5	600	$6.00	$3,600				1,000	5.00	8,600
							600	6.00	
Jan. 15 . . .				200	$6.00	$1,200	1,000	5.00	7,400
							400	6.00	
Jan. 17 . . .	300	7.00	2,100				1,000	5.00	9,500
							400	6.00	
							300	7.00	
Jan. 25 . . .				300	7.00		1,000	5.00	6,800
				100	6.00	2,700	300	6.00	
						$3,900			

Weighted Average

Date	Units	Purchased Unit Cost	Total	Units	Sold Unit Cost	Total	Units	Unit Cost	Total
								Inventory Balance	
Jan. 1							1,000	$5.000	$5,000
Jan. 5	600	$6.00	$3,600				1,600	5.375	8,600
Jan. 15 . . .				200	$5.375	$1,075	1,400	5.375	7,525
Jan. 17 . . .	300	7.00	2,100				1,700	5.662	9,625
Jan. 25 . . .				400	5.662	2,265	1,300	5.662	7,360
						$3,340			

Solution 6B.1
$165,000 + $20,000 = $185,000

7

Internal Control and Cash

PAST

Chapter 6 explained the accounting for inventory. We described and applied the costing methods of specific identification, FIFO, LIFO, and weighted-average.

PRESENT

In this chapter, we focus our attention on another current asset, cash. In addition, we study how internal control can be used to prevent errors and fraud associated with assets such as cash and inventory.

FUTURE

Chapter 8 explains the accounting for accounts and notes receivable. We will explain the reporting of uncollectible accounts and how managers monitor such accounts.

LEARNING OBJECTIVES

1. **Define** the three elements of fraud. *(p. 332)*

2. **Discuss** how the COSO framework helps prevent fraud, **identify** potential internal control failures, and **discuss** SOX regulations. *(p. 333)*

3. **Define** cash and **discuss** the accounting for cash. *(p. 339)*

4. **Describe** the internal controls for cash. *(p. 341)*

5. **Illustrate** the bank reconciliation process. *(p. 347)*

6. **Describe** the four primary activities of effective cash management. *(p. 352)*

7. Appendix 7A: **Describe** financial statement audits and operational audits. *(p. 355)*

REAL LIFE CSI

If you were given the list of checks shown in the table to the right and were asked if you noticed anything unusual, what would you say? The list represents the checks that a manager at the Arizona State Treasurer wrote to embezzle funds for his own use. All the vendors to whom these checks were written were fictitious.[1]

If you were a forensic accountant trained in such techniques as Benford's Law (see Forensic Accounting box on page 336 of this chapter), you would have had no trouble noticing that the amounts on these checks were made to look random, but were anything but random. In fact, the pattern of the check amounts is almost the direct opposite of what Benford's Law would predict.

Benford's Law is one of many techniques forensic accountants use to catch fraud. It is estimated that the typical organization loses 5 percent of its revenue to fraud each year. According to the Association of Certified Fraud Examiners, this percentage loss translates to nearly $4 trillion worldwide. Although detecting fraud is important, it is far better to keep fraud from occurring in the first place. Developing a knowledge of the elements of fraud and understanding how internal controls can prevent fraud are critical to all organizations.

Date of Check	Amount
October 9	$ 1,927.48
	27,902.31
October 14	86,241.90
	72,117.46
	81,321.75
	97,473.96
October 19	93,249.11
	89,658.17
	87,776.89
	92,105.83
	79,949.16
	87,602.93
	96,879.27
	91,806.47
	84,991.67
	90,831.83
	93,766.67
	88,338.72
	94,639.49
	83,709.28
	96,412.21
	88,432.86
	71,552.16
TOTAL	**$1,878,687.58**

In this chapter, we study internal controls. Perhaps this discussion will inspire some of you to embark on a career in forensic accounting to help bring the fraud epidemic under control. Who knows, you may even inspire a new television series, "CSI Accounting!"

---

[1] Mark J. Nigrini, I've Got Your Number, *Journal of Accountancy*, April 30, 1999.

INTERNAL CONTROL AND CASH

Fraud	Internal Control	Accounting for Cash	Internal Controls for Cash	Cash Management	Auditing and Internal Control (Appendix 7A)
• The fraud triangle • Pressure • Rationalization • Opportunity	• The COSO framework • Control failures • The Sarbanes-Oxley Act	• Defining cash • Reporting cash • Defining cash equivalents	• Cash received on account • Cash received from cash sales • Bank reconciliation	• Monitoring cash • Effective cash management	• Auditing and financial statements • Audit procedures as controls • Audit report • Operational audits

FRAUD

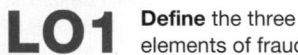 **LO1** **Define** the three elements of fraud.

Infamous stories of fraud involving **Enron Corporation** and **Madoff Investment Securities LLC** illustrate the potential cost that fraud can have on so many people. Unfortunately, it is nearly impossible to completely prevent fraud; however, we do know much about why fraud is committed and what can be done to lower the risk of it occurring. Research has shown that any individual, under the right circumstances, can commit fraud. This does not mean, however, that everyone will commit fraud. What it does mean is that it is very difficult to determine prior to the commission of a fraud exactly which employee will be the one to commit fraud.

Fraud refers to any act by the management or employees of a business involving an intentional deception for personal gain. Fraud may include, among other acts, embezzlement of a business's cash, theft of assets, filing false insurance claims, filing false health claims, and financial statement fraud. Fraud is a punishable crime and is also a violation of civil law.

Fraud Triangle

Research has shown that three elements are almost always present when a fraud occurs. These elements are often referred to as the **fraud triangle** and include (1) a perceived pressure, (2) some way to rationalize the fraudulent act, and (3) a perceived opportunity. Reducing or suppressing any of the three elements of the fraud triangle reduces the likelihood of fraud occurring in a business.

Unfortunately, the fraud triangle is not well understood. Because of this, nearly all fraud prevention efforts by businesses are devoted to the third element—reducing the opportunity to commit fraud. Too often, little effort is expended on the other elements of fraud even though it has been shown that efforts in any one area can reduce the effort needed in the other two areas.

Pressure

Pressure can be divided into several categories, but research has shown that nearly all frauds are committed by individuals who feel perceived pressure from some sort of financial need. Financial pressure could come from living beyond one's means and being unable to pay one's bills, experiencing large medical bills, or the financial pressure from vices like gambling, drugs or alcohol. The latter pressure is sometimes referred to as vice pressure.

Financial statement fraud, such as the overstatement of revenues or the understatement of expenses, usually occurs because of pressure on management to "make the numbers," either to satisfy Wall Street analyst expectations or to attain a company-sponsored monetary bonus.

While it is not possible to completely eliminate this element of fraud, numerous methods have proven successful at lowering the risk of financial statement fraud. An obvious action is to perform careful personnel screening before hiring any employee to reduce the likelihood of employing individuals with known histories of fraud.

Rationalization

Very few individuals want to commit fraud since they recognize that it is wrong. In order to overcome this tremendous feeling of guilt, most employees need to come up with some form of rationalization so that they can live with the knowledge of what they did. Common rationalizations include such attitudes as (1) I am underpaid and the company owes it to me; (2) Everyone else is doing it; or (3) I am only borrowing the money and I will pay it back later.

The best way to reduce this element of fraud is to create an environment in which it is difficult to rationalize unethical behavior. A company that promotes a culture of honesty and integrity, within which unethical behavior is considered unacceptable, is much less likely to encounter fraudulent behavior by management or its employees. The key to building organization-wide attitudes regarding ethical behavior starts with the "tone at the top"—that is, the behaviors and attitudes displayed by a company's CEO or president.

Opportunity

The third element of the fraud triangle is perceived opportunity. An individual will only attempt to commit a fraud if he or she perceives that there is an opportunity to succeed. Of course this element is related to the other two elements. For example, if an employee is under tremendous pressure either at work or outside the workplace, he may attempt to commit a fraud even if he perceives only a small chance of success, while an individual under much less pressure will likely only attempt the fraud if it is perceived to be easy to commit.

INTERNAL CONTROL

Reducing the opportunity to commit fraud often involves implementing a system of internal control, including such measures as physical control over cash and proper authorization over cash disbursements.

LO2 Discuss how the COSO framework helps prevent fraud, **identify** potential internal control failures, and **discuss** SOX regulations.

COSO Framework

In 1992, the Committee on Sponsoring Organizations of the Treadway Commission (COSO) released a framework to help companies structure and evaluate their internal controls. Twenty years later, in 2013, COSO updated their framework to reflect changes in business environments brought about by developments such as technological advancements and increasing globalization.

The COSO framework identifies five internal control components: (1) the control environment, (2) risk assessment, (3) control activities, (4) information and communication, and (5) monitoring activities.

1. Control Environment

The **control environment** sets the tone of the organization. An environment of ethical values and integrity is crucial to keeping employees from feeling that it is acceptable to commit fraud. The control environment provides the foundation for all other components of internal control. Included in the control environment are management's philosophy and management style; the organizational structure and assignment of authority and responsibility; the process for attracting and developing competent employees; and the rewards to drive accountability for performance.

CORPORATE SOCIAL RESPONSIBILITY	**Governance and Conflicts of Interest**

Much of what was done at **Enron** was perfectly legal. Enron's management became very skilled at staying within the letter of the law, even if it meant violating the spirit of the law. Examples include the use of specialized accounting rules that allowed Enron to mask the true level of its debt so that financial statement users would be unable to obtain a transparent view of the company's financial position. Top executives at Enron created a culture of deceit within the company that provided employees with an easy rationalization for their own misdeeds. Corporate Social Responsibility, by way of contrast, espouses the notion that not only is it important to make money, but it is important to do so in a responsible way. Cutting corners and playing fast and loose with the rules may work in the short term, but it is not sustainable as the Enron saga reveals. Creating a culture of ethical behavior within a business is perhaps the most important internal control that exists to not only prevent fraud, but to provide a foundation for a sustainable enterprise.

2. Risk Assessment

Every organization faces a variety of different risks from both internal and external sources. Risk is defined as the possibility that an event will occur that has a negative impact on the organization's objectives. **Risk assessment** involves identifying and analyzing relevant risks to an organization's objectives. Because items external to the organization such as the economic conditions, industry competitors, and regulations, along with internal items such as operating conditions are constantly changing, risk assessment must be an ongoing dynamic and iterative process.

3. Control Activities

The accounting system represents a cornerstone of the control environment that is necessary to reduce the opportunity for, and success of, fraudulent behavior. A critical aspect of the accounting system is a strong system of internal controls. **Internal controls** are the measures undertaken by a business to ensure the reliability of its accounting data, protect its assets from theft or unauthorized use, ensure that employees are following the company's policies and procedures, and evaluate the performance of employees, departments, divisions, and the company as a whole. Management is responsible for designing, installing, and monitoring internal controls throughout the business with the intent of attaining "reasonable assurance," rather than "absolute assurance," that the controls will meet their objectives.

Control activities are the specific policies and procedures designed to reduce risk. A control activity can be either a prevention control or a detection control. A **prevention control** is intended to deter a problem or fraud before it can arise. A **detection control**, on the other hand, is designed to discover any problems or fraud shortly after it arises. Prevention controls are generally more desirable and preferred than detection controls, reflecting the old saying that "an ounce of prevention is worth a pound of detection."

A company should incorporate the following elements when it designs its prevention and detection controls:

- Establish clear lines of authority and responsibility.
- Implement segregation of duties.
- Hire competent personnel.

- Use control numbers on all business documents.
- Develop plans and budgets.
- Maintain adequate accounting records.
- Provide physical and electronic controls.

We consider each of these elements in the following paragraphs and provide examples of their use.

Establish Clear Lines of Authority and Responsibility

The organizational structure of a company defines the lines of authority and responsibility within the company. It informs employees about who is in charge of which functions and to whom each person reports.

The existence of an identified supervisor is a prevention control. Employees know that the supervisor is evaluating their performance; consequently, they are more likely to perform according to a company's established policies and rules. Supervision is also a detection control. A supervisor is likely to discover errors or irregularities when he or she reviews the work performance of employees.

Implement Segregation of Duties

Segregation of duties requires that when allocating various duties within the accounting system, management should make sure that no employee is assigned too many different responsibilities. As a general rule, no individual employee should be able to perpetrate and conceal irregularities in the transaction processing system. To accomplish this, management must separate three functions: the authorization function, the recording function, and the custody function.

When an employee prepares a purchase order to buy merchandise, that employee is effectively "authorizing" the transaction. When the merchandise is received, a second employee should prepare the receiving report when he or she gains "custody" of the merchandise. And, neither of these two employees should be allowed to "record" the purchase order, the receipt of the merchandise, or the payment of cash for the goods in the accounting records. Separating the work functions in this manner will reduce the likelihood of fraud occurring because committing a fraud when work duties are separated requires collusion among multiple employees. Proper segregation of duties is a prevention control.

Hire Competent Personnel

Because people are the most important element of an accounting system, it is vital that a company hire competent personnel. Management must screen each job applicant to determine that he or she has sufficient education, training, and experience to qualify for the job. After hiring an employee, the company should provide specific formal training so that the employee is able to complete all of the tasks that the job requires. The training should refer to written policy statements, procedure manuals, and job descriptions so that the employee can become familiar with all aspects and expectations of his or her job. Hiring and training employees is a prevention control.

Some companies routinely rotate personnel among various jobs. For example, a company might switch jobs between an employee working exclusively with the accounts receivable and an employee working exclusively with accounts payable. This rotation may disclose errors or irregularities resulting from over-familiarity with a job or just carelessness. Requiring employees to take vacations of at least one week in duration may also disclose errors or irregularities when another employee performs the vacationing employee's duties. These personnel policies act as a detection control.

Job Rotation and Mandatory Vacations as Internal Controls

Job rotation and mandatory vacations is one of the best internal controls for uncovering fraud. For many frauds, it is necessary for the perpetrator to actively cover up his or her misdeeds through the falsification of accounting records. Requiring job rotation and vacations allows another employee to perform these job responsibilities, often leading to the discovery of fraud. And you thought your employer was only giving you that vacation to be nice!

Source: Association of Certified Fraud Examiners 2008 Report.

Use Control Numbers on All Business Documents

All business documents such as purchase orders, sales invoices, credit memos, and checks should have **control numbers** preprinted on them. Each control number should be unique for that type of document. For example, the bank checks that you use to pay your personal expenses have control numbers on them, usually in the upper right-hand corner of the check, referred to as a *check number*. These numbers act as a detection control enabling you to track each check written, and to ensure that no one has written an improper check against your account.

Develop Plans and Budgets

Top management should initiate the planning and budgeting process to establish forward thinking about the business and to provide a basis for evaluating department and employee performance. Every company should prepare an annual operating plan and budget. These items provide guidance for all levels of management regarding how to respond to various situations. The **budget** also provides a basis for comparing actual operating results to planned results when management evaluates operating unit performance. An example of evaluating performance involves comparing the actual advertising expense to the budgeted advertising expense. When variances between actual and budgeted amounts are observed, those variances should be investigated by management. This type of control activity is both a prevention control and a detection control.

Benford's Law Aids Accounting Sleuths

 How often should the number 9 appear as the first digit of an amount reported on a financial statement? If you say one out of ten times you, like most people, would be wrong. It turns out the number 9 should appear less than five percent of the time, whereas the number 1 will appear as the first digit of a reported amount over thirty percent of the time! This numerical phenomenon, known as Benford's Law, was discovered by Frank Benford while working as a physicist at the GE Research Laboratories.

An intuitive explanation of Benford's Law appeared in the *Journal of Accountancy* in the article "I've Got Your Number" written by Mark Nigrini. Nigrini offered an explanation that considered "the total assets of a mutual fund that is growing at 10 percent per year. When the total assets are $100 million, the first digit of total assets is 1. The first digit will continue to be 1 until total assets reach $200 million. This will require a 100 percent increase (from 100 to 200), which, at a growth rate of 10 percent per year, will take about 7.3 years (with compounding). At $500 million the first digit will be 5. Growing at 10 percent per year, the total assets will rise from $500 million to $600 million in about 1.9 years, significantly less time than assets took to grow from $100 million to $200 million. At $900 million, the first digit will be 9 until total assets reach $1 billion, or about 1.1 years at 10 percent. Once total assets are $1 billion the first digit will again be 1, until total assets again grow by another 100 percent. The persistence of a 1 as a first digit will occur with any phenomenon that has a constant (or even an erratic) growth rate."

Benford's Law has been applied to the detection of fraudulent financial statements by forensic accountants with some success. The reasoning is simply that when somebody makes up numbers to produce a fraudulent financial statement they are more likely to choose numbers more randomly than the pattern identified by Benford's Law.

Maintain Adequate Accounting Records

In previous chapters, we discussed a number of detection controls that help ensure that a business has adequate accounting records. These controls include using the double-entry approach to record transactions (debits must equal credits), preparing trial balances (total debits must equal total credits), and taking a physical count of the inventory on hand (physical inventory total should equal perpetual inventory total).

Many control activities related to maintaining accurate accounting records involve comparisons of various amounts. For instance, each business should periodically make a physical inspection of its plant assets to compare the data in the plant assets' ledger account to the plant assets actually in use. This inspection identifies any missing assets and any assets not recorded in the asset account. Similarly, a business should periodically confirm the amounts owed to suppliers (Accounts Payable) and the amounts due from customers (Accounts Receivable) by contacting the suppliers and customers to verify any amounts owed or to be received. This internal control process is known as accounts receivable confirmation and accounts payable confirmation.

Provide Physical and Electronic Controls

Physical and electronic controls are prevention controls that take many forms. Locked doors are an important physical control. Locked doors help prevent the theft of assets and protect the integrity of the accounting system. Many companies install safes and vaults to store cash prior to depositing it in a bank and to hold important business documents such as mortgages and securities. Any installed safes and vaults should be of sufficient quality that they can withstand fire and such natural disasters as flooding and tornados. Fencing off company property and assigning security guards at the gates are other commonly used physical controls.

Electronic controls are also widely used by businesses. Merchandising firms use electronic cash registers to ensure that each salesperson records each transaction as it occurs and that the salesperson stores cash in a locked drawer. Retailers, convenience stores, and banks use observation cameras to monitor their operations. Retailers also attach special plastic tags to merchandise, which activate electronic sensors and set off alarms if an individual attempts to leave a store without having the plastic tag removed by a salesperson.

4. Information and Communication

The fourth control component of the COSO framework involves communication. It is important that individuals receive a clear message from senior management that control responsibilities must be taken seriously. To do this management must obtain or generate relevant and quality information from both internal and external sources. This information must then be communicated in a continual and iterative process of providing, sharing, and then obtaining new information.

5. Monitoring Activities

It is necessary for the internal control system to be monitored in order to assess the quality of the system's performance over time. **Monitoring activities** involve ongoing evaluations, special evaluations, or some combination of each. Ongoing evaluations are built into the business processes at various levels of the organization and provide timely information. Special evaluations are conducted periodically and vary in scope and frequency based on risk assessments, results from ongoing evaluations, and other management considerations.

Internal Audits

Internal audits are one type of monitoring activity. In a small company, internal auditing is a function typically assigned to an employee who has other duties as well. In a large company, internal auditing is an activity assigned to an independent department that reports to top management or the board of directors of the corporation. **Internal auditing** is a company function that provides independent appraisals of the company's financial statements, its internal control, and its operations.

The evaluation of a company's internal control involves two phases. First, the internal auditor determines whether sufficient internal controls are in place. Second, the internal auditor determines whether the internal controls in place are actually functioning as planned. After completing the appraisal, the internal auditor makes recommendations to management regarding additional controls that are needed or improvements that are required for existing controls.

Control Failures

Occasionally, internal controls fail. For example, an employee may forget to lock an exterior door and a thief will steal some merchandise. Or, an employee with custody responsibilities steals cash received from customers. A company cannot completely prevent these types of incidents from occurring. Consequently, many businesses purchase insurance to compensate the company if any of these types of incidents do occur. Casualty insurance provides financial compensation to a business for losses from fire, natural disasters, and theft. A **fidelity bond** is an insurance policy that provides financial compensation for theft by employees specifically covered by the insurance.

Another reason that internal controls fail is **employee collusion**. When two or more employees work together to circumvent or avoid prescribed internal controls, this act is known as *employee collusion*. For example, an employee with custody of an asset (like cash) can work with an employee with recording responsibilities to steal the asset and cover up the theft in the accounting records. Employee collusion is difficult to prevent or detect. Hiring high-quality employees and paying them market wages is the best approach to avoid collusion. Close employee supervision is also important.

THINKING GLOBALLY

While it might appear that financial fraud occurs only in the United States, that is far from the truth. For example, in 2008, India's leading software services firm, **Satyam Computer Services**, was found to have defrauded stockholders for over a decade by overstating the company's revenues and its cash by over $1 billion. The company's independent auditors, **PricewaterhouseCoopers**, were arrested shortly thereafter on charges of being an accomplice to the financial fraud.

As with employee collusion, senior management can often circumvent internal controls. Additionally, in small companies where proper segregation of duties is not possible, the owner must serve as the mitigating control. This requires the owner to be present most of the time and also provides opportunity for the owner to circumvent internal controls.

The Sarbanes-Oxley Act

For public companies, strong internal controls like those described above are no longer simply a matter of good business practice; they are required by law. Following the **Enron** and **WorldCom** accounting scandals, the U.S. Congress passed landmark legislation called the Sarbanes-Oxley Act (SOX). This Act mandates that all publicly traded U.S. corporations maintain an adequate system of internal controls. Further, top management must ensure the reliability of these controls and outside independent auditors must attest to the adequacy of the controls. Failing to do so can result in prison sentences of up to 20 years and/or monetary fines of up to $5 million.

Concept	→	Method	→	Assessment	TAKEAWAY 7.1
Are the internal controls adequate?		The COSO framework identifies five internal control components: (1) the control environment, (2) risk assessment, (3) control activities, (4) information and communication, and (5) monitoring activities.		Monitoring activities include appraisals of the company's internal control system. If weaknesses are reported, be cautious in relying on the reported financial statements.	

YOUR TURN! 7.1

The solution is on page 378.

Identify which internal control concept is being violated and explain how this may cause an opportunity for fraud to occur within a business:

1. The supervisor for the purchasing department has not taken a vacation in three years.
2. Inventory is left in a receiving area at the back of the store by an open door.
3. The purchasing supervisor has the authority to order a purchase and also to receive the merchandise, record its receipt, and authorize the accounting department to issue a check.

ACCOUNTING FOR CASH

Cash includes coins, currency (paper money), checks, money orders, traveler's checks, and funds on deposit at a financial institution in a company's checking accounts and savings accounts. An item is considered to be an element of cash if (1) it is accepted by a bank or other financial institution (brokerage firm or credit union) for deposit, and (2) it is free from restrictions that would prevent its use for paying debts.

LO3 Define cash and **discuss** the accounting for cash.

Many near-cash items such as certificates of deposit, postdated checks, not-sufficient-funds checks, and IOUs are not considered to be cash. **Certificates of deposit** (CDs) are securities issued by a bank when cash is invested for a short period of time, typically three months to one year. CDs pay a fixed rate of interest on any deposited funds. A **postdated check** is a check from another person or company with a date that is later than the current date. A postdated check does not become equivalent to cash until the actual calendar date on the check. A **not-sufficient-funds check** (NSF check) is a check from an individual or company that had an insufficient cash balance in the bank when the holder of the check presented it to the bank for payment. IOU is a slang term for a note receivable—that is, a written document that states that one party promises to pay another party a certain amount of cash on a certain date. CDs are accounted for as investments, whereas postdated checks, NSF checks, and IOUs are accounted for as Other Receivables.

Reporting Cash

A company may have only one Cash account in the general ledger or it may have multiple cash accounts, such as Cash in Bank, Cash on Hand, and Petty Cash. Cash in Bank includes any cash held in a company's checking and savings accounts, while Cash on Hand includes cash items not yet deposited in the bank. Petty Cash is an example of cash on hand that is used for small disbursements and is maintained at the company's business location.

When a company has several bank accounts, it may maintain a separate general ledger account for each account or use a single Cash in Bank account. Although a company may prepare for internal use only a balance sheet that shows each individual bank account separately, the balance sheet that the company prepares for external users typically shows the combined balances of all bank accounts and other cash accounts under a single heading of Cash. Management is likely to want to see the detail involving the multiple cash accounts that the company maintains so that it can monitor and control the various accounts and on hand amounts. Most external users, however, are only interested in the total amount of cash and its relationship to other items on the balance sheet.

Balance Sheet Title for Cash

Cash is cash, or is it? Companies often include many other items, such as certificates of deposit, that are very similar to cash in their Cash account. Companies also vary in the title they use for their Cash account on their balance sheet. In fact, Cash is not the most common term used. Cash and Cash Equivalents is by far the most commonly used label. The following table identifies the label used by a sample of 600 large U.S. firms for their Cash account on the balance sheet:

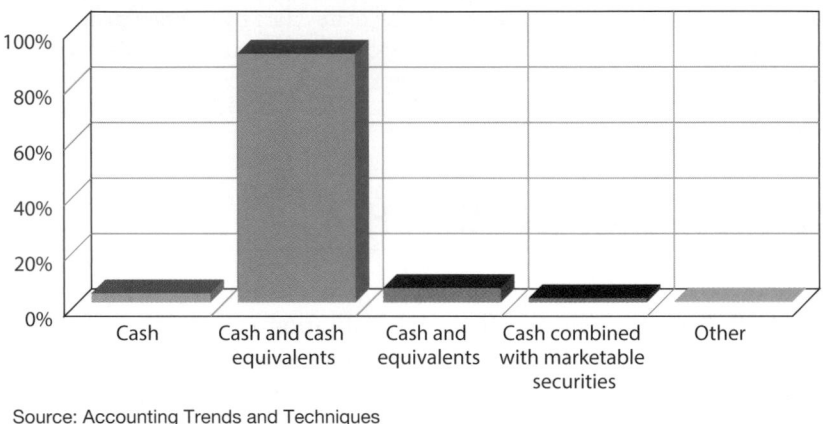

Source: Accounting Trends and Techniques

Cash is a current asset and is shown first in the balance sheet listing of assets. Some of a company's cash may be **restricted cash**, in which case it is restricted for a special purpose. For example, a company may have a restriction on its cash to cover a litigation settlement. Restricted cash should be reported separately on the balance sheet as either a current or noncurrent asset depending on the length of the restriction. Sometimes a company's total cash includes one or more compensating balances. A **compensating balance** is a minimum cash balance that a bank requires a firm to maintain in its bank account as part of a borrowing arrangement. Compensating balances related to short-term borrowings are current assets, which, if significant, are reported separately from the cash amount among the current assets. Compensating balances related to long-term borrowings are reported as long-term assets.

Cash and Cash Equivalents

A company may combine certain short-term, highly liquid investments with cash and present a single amount called **cash and cash equivalents** on the balance sheet. Cash equivalents are highly liquid, short-term investments of 90 days maturity or less in such risk-free securities as U.S. Treasury bills and money market funds. A company presents this combined amount on the balance sheet so that it reconciles with the change in cash and cash equivalents appearing on the company's statement of cash flows. The statement of cash flows explains the changes in a firm's total cash and cash equivalents during an accounting period.

Concept	Method	Assessment	TAKEAWAY 7.2
Are there any restrictions on a company's use of its cash and cash equivalents?	Balance sheet and the notes to the financial statements. Are there any restrictions to cash or compensating cash balances reported?	Any assessments of liquidity should consider any existing cash restrictions.	

INTERNAL CONTROL OF CASH RECEIPTS TRANSACTIONS

Most companies develop elaborate internal controls to protect their cash because it is their most liquid asset, and in all likelihood, an important operating asset. Cash is highly desirable, easily taken and concealed, and quickly converted into other assets. In addition, a high percentage of a company's transactions involve cash. Cash is received from customers following a sale and cash is paid to suppliers and employees for goods and services. A company receives cash from customers, for example, as payment on account and as payment for cash sales. The following sections describe cash handling procedures and the related internal controls for these two types of cash receipts.

LO4 **Describe** the internal controls for cash.

Cash Received on Account

A company receives cash through the mail from customers who are making payments on their accounts receivable balance. Four departments play major roles in processing cash receipts that arrive via the mail: the mailroom, the treasurer's department, the controller's department, and the internal audit department. **Exhibit 7-1** and the following paragraphs describe the role that each department plays in processing mailed cash receipts.

Mailroom

A company often sets up a separate post office box and requests that its customers mail any cash payments on account to that post office box. All other mail and company correspondence are directed to another company address or a different post office box. This approach automatically sorts a company's mail into two groups: (1) cash receipts from customers and (2) all other mail.

Mailroom employees open the envelopes containing cash receipts from customers. Each envelope should contain two items: a check and a remittance advice. A **remittance advice** is a form that accompanies a check to inform the company receiving the check about the purpose of the check. The remittance advice includes the customer's name, the amount paid, and such reference numbers as the invoice number and the customer account number.

Mailroom employees ensure that the dollar amount on each check and the related remittance advice are the same and then place the two documents in separate piles. An employee then endorses each check "For Deposit Only" so that no one can cash the check. The mailroom employees also prepare a remittance list. A **remittance list** is a list of all of the checks received on a given day. For each check, the remittance list includes the customer name and/or account number, the check number, and the amount received.

A separate mailroom employee compares the remittance list total to a list totaling the checks and another list totaling the remittance advices to ensure that the check amounts are listed correctly and that they agree with the remittance advices. The mailroom then sends the checks to the treasurer's department and the remittance list and the remittance advices to the controller's department.

Exhibit 7-1	Processing Cash Received on Account Through the Mail

Mailroom

1. Opens mail from separate post office box.
2. Compares checks to remittance advices.
3. Endorses checks.
4. Prepares remittance list and compares it to total of checks.
5. Sends checks to treasurer.
6. Sends remittance list and remittance advices to controller.

Treasurer (Custody)

1. Prepares deposit slip.
2. Sends deposit slips and checks to bank.
3. Sends copy of deposit slip to controller.
4. Files a copy of the deposit slip.

Controller (Recording)

1. Compares deposit slip from treasurer to remittance list total.
2. Uses the total on the remittance list to prepare the journal entry to record the cash receipt.
3. Uses the remittance advices to post to the accounts receivable subsidiary ledger.
4. Files the remittance list, remittance advices, and deposit slip copy.

Internal Audit

1. Receives monthly bank statement directly from the bank through the mail.
2. Prepares bank reconciliation.
3. Prepares adjusting entries.

Treasurer

The treasurer's department is a *custodial* department. It maintains custody of the received customer checks. It has no responsibilities for any recording or posting activities. The duties of this department include preparing a bank deposit slip (original plus two copies) for each batch of checks received and sending the original deposit slip and the customer checks to the bank. One copy of the deposit slip is forwarded to the controller's department, and the treasurer's department files the second copy for future reference.

Controller

The controller's department is a *recording* department. It records the cash receipts in a journal and posts the cash receipts to the company's general ledger and the Accounts Receivable account. The controller's department never has access to, or custody of, the received customer checks.

Before recording and posting the cash receipts, the controller's department compares the total on the deposit slip copy from the treasurer's department to the remittance list obtained from the mailroom to ensure that the treasurer's department deposited all of the checks sent from the mailroom. The controller's department then prepares a journal entry (debit Cash and credit Accounts Receivable) to record the cash receipts. The dollar amount of the debit and credit is the total from the deposit slip.

The controller's department uses the individual remittance advices to post the cash payments to the Accounts Receivable account of each individual customer. After processing, the remittance list, the remittance advices, and the deposit slip copy are filed in the controller's department for future reference.

Internal Audit

Internal audit is an independent department; it has no recurring custody, recording, or authorization duties related to accounting transactions. Once each month, the internal audit department performs its independent review and **reconciliation** duties related to the cash received. The internal auditor receives the monthly bank statement directly from the bank through the mail. This ensures that no one can alter the information returned with the bank statement. The internal audit department uses the bank statement to prepare the monthly bank reconciliation and create any needed journal entries. The preparation of the bank reconciliation and related journal entries are discussed later in this chapter.

Cash Received from Retail Cash Sales

A retailer receives cash from customers when the retailer sells merchandise. The retailer must design internal controls to protect any cash received. Five groups play major roles in collecting, protecting, processing, and recording cash received from retail customers: the retail sales area, the retail sales supervisor, the treasurer's department, the controller's department, and the internal audit department. **Exhibit 7-2** and the following paragraphs describe the role that each group plays.

Retail Sales Area

Sales associates use cash registers to record cash sales and to control and protect the cash collected from customers. Each sales associate uses a unique **password** or key to identify him or herself to the cash register. Each associate should have a separate cash drawer for collecting cash from customers and making change. Each sales associate begins each business day with a fixed amount of change in his or her cash drawer. The sales associates enter details of each sale into the cash register and place any cash received from customers into the assigned cash drawer. The cash register prints a paper tape listing the description and price of the items sold and the total amount due. The cash register also records this information either in the memory of the cash register or in a computer memory that the cash register accesses.

Retail Sales Supervisor

The retail sales supervisor oversees the retail sales operations of a business. Throughout the day, the supervisor approves any unusual transactions such as merchandise returns. At the end of the day, the supervisor counts the contents of each cash drawer. He or she compares the amount of cash in each drawer in excess of the beginning amount to the sales total accumulated by the cash register for each sales associate. The supervisor then prepares a written report (three copies) to document the total sales and the total cash received.

The supervisor delivers the cash in excess of the initial change amount and a copy of the written report to the treasurer's department. The cash register tape and another copy of the written report are taken to the controller's department. The supervisor files the third copy of the written report for future use if needed.

Exhibit 7-2	Processing Cash Received from Retail Cash Sales

Retail Sales Area

1. Begin each day with a fixed amount of change in drawer of each cash register.
2. Sales associate enters details of each sale into a cash register and places cash received from the customer into the cash register drawer assigned to that sales associate.

Retail Sales Supervisor

1. Observes the sales operation during the day.
2. Approves any unusual transactions during the day.
3. At the end of the day, counts the contents of each drawer with the sales associate responsible for the drawer.
4. Compares the amount in the drawer in excess of the beginning amount to the sales total accumulated by the cash register for that sales associate.
5. Prepares written report of sales and cash received.
6. Sends cash and a copy of the written report to the treasurer.
7. Sends cash register tape and a copy of the report to the controller.

Treasurer (Custody)

1. Prepares deposit slip.
2. Sends deposit slip and cash to bank.
3. Sends copy of deposit slip to controller.
4. Files a copy of the deposit slip.

Controller (Recording)

1. Compares deposit slip from treasurer to written report and cash register tape.
2. Uses the written report to prepare the journal entry to record cash sales.
3. Files written report and deposit slip.

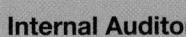
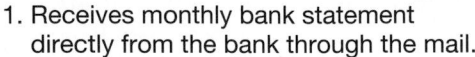

Internal Auditor

1. Receives monthly bank statement directly from the bank through the mail.
2. Prepares bank reconciliation.
3. Prepares adjusting entries.

Treasurer

The treasurer's department takes custody of any cash from the retail sales supervisor after signing a receipt that the supervisor retains as proof of the cash delivery. Employees of the treasurer's department count the cash and prepare a deposit slip (original plus two copies). The employees then send the original deposit slip and cash to the bank for deposit. One copy of the deposit slip is sent to the controller's department, and the treasurer's department files the final copy for future reference.

Controller

The controller's department is responsible for recording cash sales. The controller's department never has access to or custody of the cash. Before recording and posting the cash receipts, the controller's department compares the total on the deposit slip copy from the treasurer's department to the written report from the retail sales supervisor to ensure that the treasurer's department deposited all of the cash received. The controller's department then prepares a journal entry to record the cash sales. This entry also reflects any shortage or overage of cash, should this occur.

Internal Audit

The duties of the internal audit department with respect to cash received from retail sales are identical to its duties with respect to cash received on account. Note again that the bank sends the monthly bank statement directly to a company's internal auditor. If a company does not have an internal auditor, the bank sends the monthly bank statement to an appropriate person designated by the company, usually someone who does not have custody or recording responsibilities for cash. The internal audit department prepares a bank reconciliation statement and makes any needed journal entries.

Checks

When a company opens a checking account at a bank, the bank requires each company employee who will sign checks to sign a signature card. Occasionally, a bank employee compares the signatures on the checks presented for payment by various parties to the authorized signatures on the signature cards. This comparison provides an internal control for the bank that it is not cashing a check written by an unauthorized employee. The bank is responsible for any amounts erroneously paid out of a company's checking account.

A **check** is a written order signed by a checking account owner (also known as the *maker*) directing the bank (called the *payer*) to pay a specified amount of money to the person or company named on the check (called the *payee*). A check is a negotiable instrument; it can be transferred to another person or company by writing "pay to the order of" and the name of the other person or company on the back of the check and then signing the back of the check.

| Magnetic Characters on Checks | ACCOUNTING IN PRACTICE |

The routing number on a check tells the various banks handling the check how to route it through the U.S. Federal Reserve System to properly transfer the cash between bank accounts. The routing number has two formats: the fraction format (Item 3 in **Exhibit 7-3**) and the MICR format (item 4 in **Exhibit 7-3**). Both formats are printed on each check. In the fraction format in **Exhibit 7-3**, the number 79 represents the state in which the bank is located, the number 123 represents the number of the bank where the checking account is located, and the number 759 represents the Federal Reserve District and bank through which the check must clear. In the MICR format, the number 0759 identifies the Federal Reserve District and bank, the number 0123 identifies the specific bank, and the number 8 is the check digit.

Exhibit 7-3 presents a sample check. As noted previously, proper internal control requires that business documents such as checks be prenumbered in numerical sequence. The printed check number appears in two locations in **Exhibit 7-3**: in standard type in the upper right corner ❶ and in MICR (magnetic ink character recognition) form on the bottom of the check ❷. Also printed twice on the check are alternative formats of the routing number for the check, a fraction format ❸ and an MICR format ❹. (See Accounting in Practice, Magnetic Characters on Checks, above.) The check printer also places the customer's account number on the check in MICR form ❺. When the check is processed by the banking system, the MICR check amount ❻ is added at the bottom right of the check. Banks use special equipment that reads MICR codes directly into computer files.

Exhibit 7-3	Sample Check

Using Electronic Funds Transfer

Many companies receive payments from customers or make payments to suppliers using electronic funds transfer rather than writing and mailing checks. **Electronic funds transfer**, commonly known as EFT, involves sending an electronic message from one computer to another to cause a transfer of money from one financial institution to another, or directly to a company. Actually, two electronic messages are sent. To illustrate, assume that a company wants to use EFT to transfer money to a second company to pay an invoice. The paying company has its computer send a message to its bank's computer to request the funds transfer. This is known as *retail EFT*. Then, the paying company's bank uses EFT to transfer funds to the receiving company's bank. This is known as *wholesale EFT* or *bank-to-bank EFT*. Wholesale EFT usually involves a central bank (such as a Federal Reserve Bank) that acts as an automated clearinghouse by increasing the balance of one bank and decreasing the balance of the other bank.

The Petty Cash Fund

Most businesses find it inconvenient and expensive to write checks for small expenditures. Instead, these businesses establish a petty cash fund. A **petty cash fund** is a small amount of cash, for example $300, that is placed in a secure location on a business's premises to be used to pay for small expenditures such as postage, delivery service charges, and minor purchases of supplies. The size of the petty cash fund depends on how often it is used and the amount of the disbursements. Firms often select an amount that will last for three or four weeks.

Although the use of a petty cash fund violates the rule that all cash payments should be made by check or EFT, control can be maintained by handling the fund on an imprest basis with documented procedures. An imprest fund contains a fixed amount of cash. A business establishes a petty cash fund by writing a check against the firm's checking account and cashing the check at the bank. All replenishments of the petty cash fund are also made by check. As a result, all expenditures are ultimately controlled by check, providing a paper trail of all cash transfers to the petty cash fund.

Match the internal control function from the left-hand column with the area of responsibility in the right-hand column:

1. Prepares deposit receipt.
2. Approves unusual transactions.
3. Prepares remittance list.
4. Prepares bank reconciliation.
5. Compares deposit receipt to remittance list.

a. Retail sales supervisor
b. Mailroom
c. Treasurer's department
d. Controller's department
e. Internal audit department

YOUR TURN! 7.2

The solution is on page 378.

The Bank Statement

At the end of each month, a company's bank prepares a bank statement for each checking account that the company maintains and then sends the statement to the internal audit department of the company that owns the checking account. **Exhibit 7-4** is the bank statement from Anchor National Bank for the Wilson Corporation's checking account as of November 30, 2016.

In the body of the bank statement, the bank lists Wilson's deposits and other credits on the left, Wilson's checks (in numerical order) and other debits in the center, and Wilson's daily account balance on the right. The daily account balance is the balance in the account as of the end of each day listed. The bank presents a summary calculation of Wilson's ending account balance near the bottom of the statement.

The bank defines a series of code letters at the bottom of the statement. These code letters identify debits and credits not related to paying checks or making deposits. These code letters are not standard from bank to bank. In **Exhibit 7-4**, EC identifies corrections of errors made by the bank; DM (debit memo) identifies automatic loan payments and bank charges for items such as collecting notes; CM (credit memo) identifies amounts collected by the bank for the depositor; SC (service charge) identifies fees charged by the bank for the checking account; OD (overdraft) indicates a negative balance in the account; RT (returned item) identifies items such as posted checks and NSF checks for which the bank could not collect cash; and IN (interest earned) identifies interest added to the account. The bank statement for the Wilson Corporation does not show any interest because federal regulations do not allow corporate checking accounts to earn interest.

The Bank Reconciliation

The internal audit department prepares a bank reconciliation as of the end of each month. A **bank reconciliation** is a schedule that (1) accounts for all differences between the ending cash balance on the bank statement and the ending cash balance in the Cash account in the company's general ledger and (2) determines the reconciled cash balance as of the end of the month. The internal audit department employee preparing the bank reconciliation needs access to the bank statement, the general ledger, cash receipts records, and cash disbursements records to prepare the reconciliation.

LO5 Illustrate the bank reconciliation process.

Exhibit 7-4	Bank Statement of Wilson Corporation

ANCHOR NATIONAL BANK
123 Center Street
Madison, Wisconsin 53701

Wilson Corporation
1847 Elmwood Avenue
Madison, Wisconsin 53712

Account Number   27-31020558
Statement Date   November 30, 2016

Deposits and Credits		Checks and Debits			Daily Balance	
Date	Amount	Number	Date	Amount	Date	Amount
Nov. 01	420.00	149	Nov. 02	125.00	Nov. 01	6,060.30
Nov. 02	630.00	154	Nov. 03	56.25	Nov. 02	6,565.30
Nov. 07	560.80	155	Nov. 10	135.00	Nov. 03	6,509.05
Nov. 10	480.25	156	Nov. 08	315.10	Nov. 07	6,801.19
Nov. 14	525.00	157	Nov. 07	233.26	Nov. 08	6,486.09
Nov. 17	270.25	158	Nov. 11	27.14	Nov. 10	6,831.34
Nov. 21	640.20	159	Nov. 18	275.00	Nov. 11	6,804.20
Nov. 26	300.00CM	160	Nov. 15	315.37	Nov. 14	7,329.20
Nov. 26	475.00	161	Nov. 17	76.40	Nov. 15	7,013.83
Nov. 30	471.40	162	Nov. 21	325.60	Nov. 17	7,207.68
		163	Nov. 21	450.00	Nov. 18	6,932.68
		164	Nov. 23	239.00	Nov. 21	6,731.58
		165	Nov. 21	65.70	Nov. 23	6,492.58
		166	Nov. 28	482.43	Nov. 26	7,262.58
		169	Nov. 28	260.00	Nov. 28	6,520.15
		170	Nov. 30	122.50	Nov. 30	6,488.95
		171	Nov. 30	370.10		
			Nov. 07	35.40RT		
			Nov. 26	5.00DM		
			Nov. 30	10.00SC		

Beginning Balance	+	Deposits and Credits	−	Checks and Debits	=	Ending Balance
$5,640.30	+	$4,772.90	−	$3,924.25	=	$6,488.95

Item Codes: EC: Error Correction   DM: Debit Memo   CM: Credit Memo
SC: Service Charge   OD: Overdraft   RT: Returned Item
IN: Interest Earned

ACCOUNTING IN
PRACTICE

Debits or Credits?

Debit and credit terminology may seem backward on a bank statement. Debits decrease a bank account balance and credits increase a bank account balance. To understand this, realize that bank statements are prepared from the perspective of the bank, not the customer of the bank. In other words, when a company deposits cash in its checking account, the bank debits Cash and credits a liability account called a Customer Deposit. The bank statement sent to a company each month is a statement of its Customer Deposit account held by the bank. As with any liability, debits decrease its balance and credits increase its balance.

Bank Reconciliation Structure

Exhibit 7-5 outlines the structure of a company's bank reconciliation. The bank reconciliation is really two schedules prepared side by side. The schedule on the left includes bank items, and the schedule on the right includes items related to the company's general ledger.

Exhibit 7-5	Structure of a Company's Bank Reconciliation

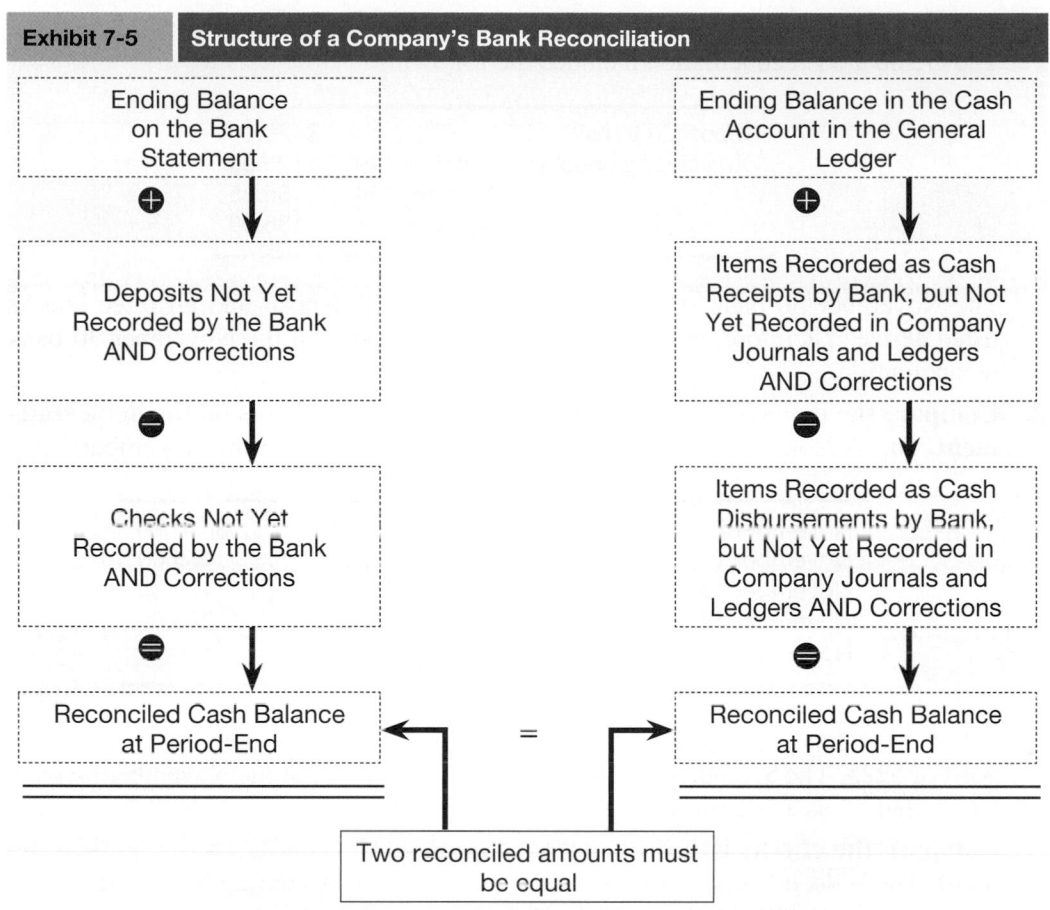

The schedule on the left begins with the ending cash balance from the bank statement (the month-end balance according to the bank's records). The internal audit department employee preparing the reconciliation adds (1) deposits not yet recorded by the bank, called **deposits in transit**, and (2) any corrections not yet made by the bank that will increase the bank balance. The preparer then subtracts (1) checks not yet recorded by the bank, called **outstanding checks**, and (2) any corrections not yet made by the bank that will decrease the bank balance. The resulting total is the reconciled cash balance at the end of the month.

The schedule on the right begins with the ending balance in the Cash account in the company's general ledger. The internal audit department employee adds (1) items recorded as cash receipts by the bank but not yet recorded in the company's journals and (2) any corrections not yet made by the company that will increase the general ledger cash balance. The preparer subtracts (1) items recorded as cash disbursements by the bank but not yet recorded in the company's journals and (2) any corrections not yet made by the company that will decrease the general ledger cash balance. The resulting total is the reconciled cash balance at the end of the month. The totals of the two schedules should be the same.

Bank Reconciliation Illustrated   Assume that the internal auditor of the Wilson Corporation is preparing the November 30, 2016, bank reconciliation. She uses the following procedures to reconcile the November 30 bank statement balance of $6,488.95 to the November 30 general ledger Cash account balance of $5,322.69:

1. **Trace outstanding items on the bank reconciliation for the previous month to the current bank statement.** Any items on the previous bank reconciliation that have

still not been processed by the bank must appear on the current bank reconciliation. The October 31 reconciliation included the following:

Deposit in transit		$420.00
Outstanding checks:	Number 149	$125.00
	Number 154	56.25
	Number 155	135.00

The November 30 bank statement includes the $420 deposit and all three checks listed above. Therefore, none of these items will appear on the November 30 bank reconciliation.

2. **Compare the deposits made during the month to the deposits on the bank statement.** The Wilson Corporation made the following deposits during November:

November 2	$630.00	November 21	$640.20
November 7	560.80	November 26	475.00
November 10	480.25	November 29	471.40
November 14	525.00	November 30	225.00
November 17	270.25		

All of these deposits appear on the bank statement except for the November 30 deposit of $225. The $225 deposit will appear on the left side of the November 30 bank reconciliation as a deposit in transit.

3. **Compare the checks issued during the month to the checks on the bank statement.** The Wilson Corporation issued the following checks during November:

Number 156	$315.10	Number 165	$ 65.70
Number 157	233.26	Number 166	482.43
Number 158	27.14	Number 167	301.66
Number 159	275.00	Number 168	149.50
Number 160	315.37	Number 169	260.00
Number 161	76.40	Number 170	122.50
Number 162	325.60	Number 171	370.10
Number 163	450.00	Number 172	450.00
Number 164	239.00	Number 173	240.50

Four of the checks—numbers 167, 168, 172, and 173—do not appear on the bank statement. These four checks will appear on the left side of the November 30 bank reconciliation as outstanding checks.

4. **Scan the bank statement for charges and credits not yet reflected in the general ledger.** The Wilson Corporation's bank statement contains a charge of $35.40 for a returned item, a debit memo of $5.00, and a service charge of $10.00 in the checks and other debits column. The deposits and other credits column contains a credit memo for $300.00. Supplemental information sent by the bank with the bank statement reveals that the bank charged a $35.40 NSF check against Wilson's account, collected a $300.00 note for Wilson and charged a $5.00 collection fee, and that the service charge for the month of November was $10.00. These four items have not yet been recorded by Wilson Corporation. Therefore, they must be listed on the right side of the bank reconciliation.

5. **Check for errors.** The Wilson Corporation recorded check number 159 as $725.00. The correct amount of $275.00 appears on the bank statement. The check was written to pay for office supplies. The correction of the transposition in the amount of $450 must be listed on the right side of the bank reconciliation.

After the five preceding procedures have been completed, the November 30 bank reconciliation for the Wilson Corporation appears as shown in **Exhibit 7-6**. Note that both the left side and the right side of the reconciliation end with a reconciled cash balance and that the two amounts are the same. This reconciled cash balance is the amount that will appear on the November 30 balance sheet for the company.

Exhibit 7-6	November 30, 2016, Bank Reconciliation for Wilson Corporation

WILSON CORPORATION
Bank Reconciliation
November 30, 2016

Ending balance from bank statement ...		$6,488.95	Balance from general ledger			$4,872.69
Add: Deposits in transit		225.00	Add: Check 159 for $275			
			recorded as $725			450.00
			Collection of note	$300.00		
		6,713.95	Less: Collection fee	5.00		295.00
						5,617.69
Less: Outstanding checks:						
No. 167	$301.66		Less: NSF check		35.40	
No. 168	149.50		Service charge		10.00	45.40
No. 172	450.00					
No. 173	240.50	1,141.66				
Reconciled cash balance		$5,572.29	Reconciled cash balance			$5,572.29

Before the Wilson Corporation prepares its financial statements for November, Wilson must make journal entries to bring the balance in the Cash account into agreement with the reconciled cash balance on the bank reconciliation. These entries incorporate the items on the company's side of the bank reconciliation as follows:

Nov. 30	Cash	450.00		A = L + SE	
	Office supplies expense		450.00	+450.00	+450.00 Exp
	To correct recording error on check number 159.				
Nov. 30	Cash	295.00		A = L + SE	
	Miscellaneous expense	5.00		+295.00	−5.00 Exp
	Notes receivable		300.00	−300.00	
	To record a note collected by the bank, less a collection fee.				
Nov. 30	Accounts receivable	35.40		A = L + SE	
	Cash		35.40	+35.40	
	To reclassify an NSF check as an account receivable.			−35.40	
Nov. 30	Miscellaneous expense	10.00		A = L + SE	
	Cash		10.00	−10.00	−10.00 Exp
	To record bank service charge for November.				

YOUR TURN! 7.3

The solution is on page 378.

Match the reconciling items from the left-hand column with the proper reconciling action from the right-hand column:

1. Deposits in transit
2. Outstanding checks
3. Bank service charge
4. Cash collected by bank on note

a. Add to bank statement balance
b. Subtract from bank statement balance
c. Add to cash general ledger account
d. Subtract from cash general ledger account

EFFECTIVE CASH MANAGEMENT

LO6   **Describe** the four primary activities of effective cash management.

Cash is typically one of a company's most important assets. Without cash, a company would be unable to pay its employees or its suppliers. In short, a company would be unable to continue operating. As a consequence, managers spend considerable time and effort managing and monitoring this key asset. Similarly, investors and lenders spend considerable time understanding where a company's cash came from and how the company spent it.

Monitoring Cash

The most effective tool for external parties to monitor a company's cash is the statement of cash flows.[2] As discussed in Chapter 1, the statement of cash flows identifies a company's cash inflows and cash outflows, segmenting them into the three business activities of operating, investing, and financing. **Exhibit 7-7** presents the statement of cash flows for WebWork Inc. for the month ended December 31, 2016.

The positive numbers on the statement of cash flows represent a company's cash inflows and the negative numbers represent a company's cash outflows. WebWork's primary cash inflows involved the sale of stock ($30,000) and its bank borrowings ($36,000). The company's primary uses of cash involved the purchase of office equipment ($32,400) and the payment of rent ($10,800). Not only does the statement of cash flows identify the sources and uses of cash, but it also identifies whether a company's cash balance increased or decreased for the period. **Exhibit 7-7** reveals that WebWork's cash account increased by $40,590 for the month of December.

While having some cash on hand is important to enable a company to pay its employees and its suppliers on a timely basis, having too much cash on hand may indicate

---

[2] The statement of cash flows provides an after-the-fact monitoring of cash sources and uses. Many companies use a cash budget in order to plan anticipated cash inflows and outflows so that they are able to manage the amount of cash on hand at an appropriate level. Cash budgets are covered in most managerial accounting textbooks.

that a company is not maximizing the return on its assets. Thus, it is important for managers to not only monitor a company's cash but also to manage it effectively to ensure that the company is earning an adequate return on this key asset.

Exhibit 7-7	Statement of Cash Flows for WebWork, Inc.

WEBWORK, INC.
Statement of Cash Flows
For Month Ended December 31, 2016

Cash flow from operating activities		
Cash received from clients.	$19,910	
Cash paid to employees and suppliers	(1,620)	
Cash paid for rent.	(10,800)	
Cash provided by operating activities		$ 7,490
Cash flow from investing activities		
Purchase of office equipment.	(32,400)	
Cash used by investing activities		(32,400)
Cash flow from financing activities		
Stock issued.	30,000	
Borrowing from bank	36,000	
Cash dividends.	(500)	
Cash provided by financing activities.		65,500
Net increase in cash.		40,590
Cash at December 1, 2016		0
Cash at December 31, 2016		$40,590

Primary Activities of Effective Cash Management

Effective cash management generally involves four primary activities:

1. **Manage accounts receivable.** Since accounts receivable rarely include interest charges for late payment, the sooner that cash from sales can be collected, the sooner the cash can be used to pay suppliers, pay debt, or be invested in operations. Thus, managers should try to increase the rate at which accounts receivable are collected.

2. **Manage inventory levels.** Inventory should be maintained at levels that allow a company to satisfy customer needs while, at the same time, avoid having too much of the company's resources tied up in inventory for extended periods of time. Thus, managers should try to keep inventory levels as low as possible without losing any sales.

3. **Manage accounts payable.** Since accounts payable rarely include an interest charge for late payment, the longer a manager takes to pay off these accounts, the longer a company can use its cash to fund operations. Thus, managers should delay the payment of accounts payable. However, they should not be delayed beyond the point at which suppliers are no longer willing to do business with the company on reasonable terms. Where accounts payable have credit terms that provide a discount for prompt payment, managers must evaluate the trade-off involved by delaying the payment of accounts payable versus the reduced purchase price that results from timely payment.

4. **Invest excess cash.** Since cash on hand or in a bank account yields a very low rate of return, it is important to invest any excess cash. Thus, an important management activity is forecasting a company's cash needs by constructing a cash budget each period. Only a sufficient amount of cash necessary to cover a company's day-to-day needs should be kept on hand; any excess amounts should be invested in an effort to earn an adequate rate of return on this asset.

COMPREHENSIVE PROBLEM

At December 31, 2016, the Cash account in the Tyler Company's general ledger had a debit balance of $18,434.27. The December 31, 2016, bank statement showed a balance of $19,726.40. In reconciling the two amounts, you discover the following:

1. Bank deposits made by Tyler on December 31 amounting to $2,145.40 do not appear on the bank statement.
2. A non-interest-bearing note receivable from the Smith Company for $2,000, left with the bank for collection, was collected by the bank at the end of December. The bank credited the proceeds, less a $5 collection charge, on the bank statement. Tyler Company has not recorded the collection.
3. Accompanying the bank statement is a debit memorandum indicating that John Miller's check for $450 was charged against Tyler's bank account on December 30 because of insufficient funds.
4. Check No. 586, written for advertising expense of $869.10, was recorded as $896.10 by Tyler Company.
5. A comparison of the paid checks returned by the bank with the recorded disbursements revealed that the following checks are still outstanding as of December 31:

No. 561.............	$306.63	No. 591.............	$190.00
No. 585.............	440.00	No. 592.............	282.50
No. 588.............	476.40	No. 593.............	243.00

6. The bank mistakenly charged Tyler Company's account for check printing costs of $30.50, which should have been charged to Taylor Company.
7. The bank charged Tyler Company's account $42.50 for the rental of a safe deposit box. No entry has been made in Tyler's records for this expense.

Required
a. Prepare a bank reconciliation as of December 31, 2016.
b. Prepare any necessary journal entries at December 31, 2016.

Solution
a.

TYLER COMPANY
Bank Reconciliation
December 31, 2016

Ending balance from bank statement		$19,726.40	Balance from general ledger		$18,434.27
Add: Deposits not credited by bank......		2,145.40	Add: Collection of note.............	$2,000.00	
Error by bank (Check printing			Less: Collection charge	5.00	1,995.00
charge of Taylor Co.)		30.50	Error in recording check No. 586		27.00
		21,902.30			20,456.27
Less: Outstanding checks:			Less:		
No. 561.........................	$306.63		NSF check	450.00	
No. 585.........................	440.00		Charge for safe deposit box........	42.50	492.50
No. 588.........................	476.40				
No. 591.........................	190.00				
No. 592.........................	282.50				
No. 593.........................	243.00	1,938.53			
Reconciled cash balance..............		$19,963.77	Reconciled cash balance............		$19,963.77

b.	Dec. 31	Cash	1,995.00		A = L + SE	
		Miscellaneous expense	5.00		+1,995.00	−5.00
		Notes receivable—Smith Company		2,000.00	−2,000.00	
		To record collection of Smith Company's note by bank, less				
		collection charge.				
	31	Cash	27.00		A = L + SE	
		Advertising expense		27.00	+27.00	+27.00
		To correct error in recording advertising expense.				
	31	Accounts receivable—John Miller	450.00		A = L + SE	
		Cash		450.00	+450.00	
		To reclassify NSF check as an account receivable.			−450.00	
	31	Miscellaneous expense	42.50		A = L + SE	
		Cash		42.50	−42.50	−42.50
		To record rental expense of safety deposit box.				

APPENDIX 7A: Auditing and Internal Control

One of the internal control concepts previously discussed is conducting internal company audits. Internal audits provide appraisals of a company's financial statements, its internal control, and its operations. Internal auditors, who are employees of the company that they audit, conduct internal audits under the direction of top management or a company's board of directors.

Parties outside the company, such as bankers and stockholders, prefer independent appraisals of a company's performance. These parties are usually unwilling to accept an audit report prepared by company-employed internal auditors because of possible bias and conflicts of interest. Consequently, creditors and stockholders usually require that an independent, professional auditing firm conduct an audit of the annual financial statements. Moreover, U.S. securities law requires that all corporations whose common stock is publicly traded have an independent firm of certified public accountants (CPAs) audit the company's annual financial statements.

LO7 Appendix 7A
Describe financial statement audits and operational audits.

Not Your Ordinary Audit

FORENSIC ACCOUNTING

The financial statement audit is performed to enable the independent auditor to express an opinion regarding whether the financial statements present fairly, in all material respects, the financial position and results of operations of a company. In so doing, the independent auditor is looking for material errors, whether the errors are a result of unintentional misstatement or fraud. To perform the audit, the auditor will perform statistical sampling of the reported transactions to make judgments regarding the fairness of the reported statements. The auditor is not specifically looking for fraud, and likely will not find it even if present, because the financial statement audit is not designed to uncover fraud. The forensic accountant, by way of contrast, is specifically looking for fraud. Forensic accountants concentrate their efforts where fraud is likely to occur or is suspected, rather than on the financial statements as a whole. The forensic accountant will also utilize additional investigative techniques and follow leads suggested by what appear to be immaterial items. The forensic accountant will often have additional skills not common to financial statement auditors, such as surveillance tactics and interviewing and interrogation skills.

Financial Statement Audits

A **financial statement audit** is an examination of a company's annual financial statements by a firm of independent certified public accountants. (The quarterly financial reports of U.S. publicly traded companies are "reviewed" by an independent audit firm but they are not subject to a full audit like the annual financial statements.) The independent audit firm conducts this examination so it can prepare a report that expresses an opinion regarding whether (or not) the financial statements fairly present the results of operations, cash flows, and financial position of a company.

Going Concern Concept

The *going concern concept* assumes that a business entity will continue to operate indefinitely. As part of the annual audit, a company's independent auditors must assess the likelihood that the company that they are auditing will continue as a going concern for a reasonable period. Events such as recurring losses, pending litigation, and the loss of a major customer or supplier may raise concern about a firm's ability to maintain its going-concern status. In such cases, the independent auditors should assess management's response to the problem and the type of financial statement disclosure being made about the problem. When substantial doubt exists about a company's going-concern status, the independent auditors may include a paragraph in the audit report expressing their concern regarding this issue.

Audit Procedures

The independent audit firm conducts the annual financial statement audit according to standards established by the **Public Company Accounting Oversight Board (PCAOB)**, a quasi-governmental agency established by the Sarbanes-Oxley Act. The PCAOB is responsible for establishing auditing standards, inspecting the auditing practices of independent audit firms, and disciplining those firms that fail to maintain acceptable audit standards and practices.

The annual financial statement audit includes many different stages of work. During the early stage of an audit, the independent auditor reviews and evaluates the internal controls imbedded in a company's accounting system and other systems. This review and evaluation help the auditor determine what additional investigative steps, if any, should be included in the audit. The auditor then collects and analyzes data that substantiate the amounts in the financial statements. The auditor obtains most of these data from accounting records (such as journals and ledgers), business documents (such as purchase orders, sales invoices, and payment approval forms), and outside sources (such as banks, insurance companies, and suppliers).

The Audit Report

The **audit report** that the independent auditor issues following the annual audit specifies the financial statements that were audited, summarizes the audit process, and states the auditor's opinion regarding the financial statement data. The opinion usually states that the financial statements "fairly present" the results of operations, cash flow, and financial position of the company. The independent auditor does not conduct the audit to determine whether the financial statements are absolutely correct. Instead, the audit is conducted to determine whether the financial statements are a fair representation of operating results, cash flow, and financial position.

The primary purpose of the annual financial statement audit is *not* the discovery of fraudulent acts by management or employees of the company. Many audit procedures use statistical samples of transactions and data rather than examining the complete population of transactions. The auditors use samples to minimize the time required to conduct the audit, and consequently, to minimize its cost. As a result, there is the possibility that some errors or irregularities will exist in the transactions and data that the auditor does not review or evaluate. However, the independent auditor carefully designs the sampling procedures to detect errors and irregularities that are material in relation to the financial statements.

Report of Independent Registered Public Accounting Firm

In our opinion, such consolidated financial statements present fairly, in all material respects, the financial position of the Company as of December 31, 2014 and 2013, and the results of its operations and its cash flows for each of the three years in the period ended December 31, 2014, in conformity with accounting principles generally accepted in the United States of America. Also, in our opinion, such a financial statement schedule, when considered in relation to the basic consolidated financial statements taken as a whole, presents fairly, in all material respects, the information set forth therein.

DELOITTE & TOUCHE LLP

Operational Audits

Both internal audit departments and independent audit firms perform operational audits. An **operational audit** is an evaluation of activities, systems, and internal controls within a company to determine their efficiency, effectiveness, and economy. Operational auditing goes beyond accounting records and financial statements to obtain a full understanding of the operations of a company. Companies dedicated to continuous quality improvement often use operational audits to identify specific areas where they need to improve the quality of their operations or products.

Auditors design operational audits to assess the quality and efficiency of operational performance, identify opportunities for improvement, and develop specific recommendations for improvement. The scope of an operational audit can be very narrow, such as a review and evaluation of the procedures for processing cash receipts, or quite broad, such as a review and evaluation of all of the internal controls in a computerized accounting system.

Match the description in the left-hand column with the type of audit in the right-hand column:

1. Conducted by company employees
2. Conducted by independent auditors
3. Conducted by both independent auditors and internal auditors
4. Primary purpose is to report on the fairness of a company's financial statements
5. Evaluation of the efficiency and effectiveness of company activities

a. Internal audit
b. Financial statement audit
c. Operational audit

YOUR TURN! 7A.1

The solution is on page 378.

SUMMARY OF LEARNING OBJECTIVES

Define the three elements of fraud. (p. 332)

LO1

■ The fraud triangle consists of three parts: (1) pressure, (2) rationalization, and (3) opportunity.

Discuss how the COSO framework helps prevent fraud, identify potential internal control failures, and discuss SOX regulations. (p. 333)

LO2

■ The COSO framework identifies five internal control components; (1) the control environment; (2) risk assessment; (3) control activities; (4) information and communication; and (5) monitoring activities.

■ Internal controls are the measures undertaken by a company to ensure the reliability of its accounting data, protect its assets from theft or unauthorized use, ensure that employees follow the company's policies and procedures, and evaluate the performance of employees, departments, divisions, and the company as a whole.

■ A prevention control is designed to deter problems before they arise. A detection control is designed to discover problems soon after they arise. Prevention controls are generally more desirable than detection controls.

■ A company should incorporate the following concepts when it designs its internal control:
  • Establish clear lines of authority and responsibility.
  • Implement segregation of duties.
  • Hire competent personnel.
  • Use control numbers on all business documents.
  • Develop plans and budgets.
  • Maintain adequate accounting records.
  • Provide physical and electronic controls.

■ The internal control system must be monitored in order to assess the quality of the system's performance over time. One type of monitoring activity is an internal audit.

■ Occasionally, internal controls fail. To compensate, many businesses purchase a fidelity bond, an insurance policy that provides financial compensation for theft by employees specifically covered by the insurance.

■ For public companies, strong internal controls are required by law. The Sarbanes-Oxley Act (SOX) mandates that all publicly traded U.S. corporations maintain an adequate system of internal controls, that top management ensures the reliability of these controls, and that outside independent auditors attest to the adequacy of the controls. Failing to do so can result in prison sentences of up to 20 years and/or monetary fines of up to $5 million.

LO3 **Define cash and discuss the accounting for cash. (p. 339)**

- Cash includes coins, currency (paper money), checks, money orders, traveler's checks, and funds on deposit at a financial institution in a company's checking accounts and savings accounts.
- A company can have one or more cash accounts in its general ledger. Cash is a current asset.
- A company may combine certain short-term, highly liquid investments with cash and present a single amount called *cash and cash equivalents*.
- Not all of the company's cash may be available for general use. Restricted cash represents cash that has been restricted for specific uses. A compensating balance is an amount that a company must maintain in a bank account as part of a loan agreement.

LO4 **Describe the internal controls for cash. (p. 341)**

- Companies develop elaborate internal controls to protect cash, their most liquid asset.
- Four departments play major roles in processing cash received on account: the mailroom (open mail, endorse checks, list checks), the treasurer's department (deposit checks), the controller's department (update general ledger accounts), and the internal audit department (reconcile bank statement).
- Five departments play major roles in processing cash received from retail sales: the retail sales area (enter sales in cash register and place cash in drawer), the retail sales supervisor (count cash and prepare reports), the treasurer's department (deposit cash), the controller's department (update general ledger), and the internal audit department (reconcile bank statement).
- Many companies receive payments from customers or make payments to suppliers using electronic funds transfer (EFT) rather than writing and mailing checks. EFT involves sending an electronic message from one computer to another to cause a transfer of money from one financial institution to another, or directly to a company.
- A petty cash fund is a small amount of cash placed in a secure location on a company's premises to be used to pay for small expenditures such as postage and delivery service.

LO5 **Illustrate the bank reconciliation process. (p. 347)**

- A bank reconciliation is a schedule that (1) accounts for all differences between the ending cash balance of the bank statement and the ending cash balance of the Cash account in a company's general ledger and (2) determines the reconciled cash balance as of the end of the month.
- The procedure used to prepare the bank reconciliation involves four steps:
  - Trace outstanding items on the bank reconciliation from the previous month to the current bank statement.
  - Compare the deposits made during the month to the deposits on the bank statement.
  - Compare the checks issued during the month to the checks on the bank statement.
  - Scan the bank statement for charges and credits not yet reflected in the general ledger.
  - Check for errors.

LO6 **Describe the four primary activities of effective cash management. (p. 352)**

- Effective cash management includes monitoring and managing accounts receivable, inventory, and accounts payable, and investing any excess cash.
- Cash should be monitored using the statement of cash flows.

LO7 **Appendix 7A: Describe financial statement audits and operational audits. (p. 355)**

- A financial statement audit is an examination of a company's financial statements by a firm of independent certified public accountants. The firm issues an audit report upon completion of the audit.
- An operational audit is an evaluation of activities, systems, and internal controls within a company to determine their efficiency, effectiveness, and economy.

SUMMARY	Concept ⟶	Method ⟶	Assessment
TAKEAWAY 7.1	Are the internal controls adequate?	The COSO framework identifies five internal control components: (1) the control environment, (2) risk assessment, (3) control activities, (4) information and communication, and (5) monitoring activities.	Monitoring activities include appraisals of the company's internal control system. If weaknesses are reported, be cautious in relying on the reported financial statements.

Are there any restrictions on a company's use of its cash and cash equivalents?	Balance sheet and the notes to the financial statements. Are there any restrictions to cash or compensating cash balances reported?	Any assessments of liquidity should consider any existing cash restrictions.	TAKEAWAY 7.2

KEY TERMS

Audit report (p. 356)
Bank reconciliation (p. 347)
Budget (p. 336)
Cash (p. 339)
Cash and cash equivalents (p. 340)
Certificates of deposit (p. 339)
Check (p. 345)
Compensating balance (p. 340)
Control activities (p. 334)
Control environment (p. 333)
Control numbers (p. 336)
Deposits in transit (p. 349)
Detection control (p. 334)

Electronic funds transfer (p. 346)
Employee collusion (p. 338)
Fidelity bond (p. 338)
Financial statement audit (p. 355)
Fraud (p. 332)
Fraud triangle (p. 332)
Internal auditing (p. 338)
Internal controls (p. 334)
Monitoring activities (p. 337)
Not-sufficient-funds check (p. 339)
Operational audit (p. 357)

Outstanding checks (p. 349)
Password (p. 343)
Petty cash fund (p. 346)
Postdated check (p. 339)
Prevention control (p. 334)
Public Company Accounting Oversight Board (PCAOB) (p. 356)
Reconciliation (p. 343)
Remittance advice (p. 341)
Remittance list (p. 341)
Restricted cash (p. 340)
Risk assessment (p. 334)
Segregation of duties (p. 335)

Assignments with the ⓜ logo in the margin are available in BusinessCourse.
See the Preface of the book for details.

SELF-STUDY QUESTIONS

(Answers to the Self-Study Questions are at the end of the chapter.)

1. **Which of the following is not one of the three elements of the fraud triangle?**
   a. Pressure
   b. Rationalization
   c. Embezzlement
   d. Opportunity

2. **Which of the following is not a common internal control concept?**
   a. Establish clear lines of responsibility
   b. Provide physical and electronic controls
   c. Collusion among employees
   d. Separate work functions

3. **Which of the following are considered good internal control practice?**
   a. Job rotation
   b. Required vacations
   c. Only promoting from within
   d. Both *a* and *b*

4. **Burton Company should utilize all except one of the following concepts related to placing control numbers on business documents. Which concept should Burton not use?**
   a. Write the control number on the document when it is used.
   b. Place control numbers on all business documents.
   c. Use the documents in strict numerical sequence.
   d. Periodically account for all numbers used.

5. **An operational audit is:**
   a. Just another word for a financial statement audit
   b. Only performed by independent auditors
   c. Used to assess the quality and efficiency of operational performance
   d. Usually reported to the public along with the financial statements

6. **Which of the following statements is correct regarding the reporting of cash?**
   a. Restricted cash is always shown as a noncurrent asset.
   b. Cash is shown as the first asset on the balance sheet.
   c. Restricted cash is usually combined with unrestricted cash on the balance sheet.
   d. If a company maintains more than one bank account, each must be shown separately on the balance sheet.

7. **The treasurer is responsible for each of the following except:**
   a. Prepare the deposit slip.
   b. Send deposit slips and checks to the bank.
   c. Prepare the bank reconciliation.
   d. File a copy of the deposit receipt.

8. **What is a bank reconciliation?**
   a. A formal financial statement that lists all of a firm's bank account balances
   b. A merger of two banks that previously were competitors
   c. A statement sent monthly by a bank to a depositor that lists all deposits, checks paid, and other credits and charges to the depositor's account for the month
   d. A schedule that accounts for differences between a firm's cash balance as shown on its bank statement and the balance shown in its general ledger Cash account

9. **In a bank reconciliation, outstanding checks are:**
   a. Deducted from the bank balance
   b. Added to the bank balance
   c. Deducted from the general ledger balance
   d. Added to the general ledger balance

10. **Which of the following statements about a petty cash fund is not true?**
    a. The fund is managed on an imprest basis.
    b. The fund is used to pay for minor items such as postage and delivery charges.
    c. The fund should have a balance large enough to support one replenishment per year.
    d. All replenishments are made by check.

QUESTIONS

1. Describe the three elements of the fraud triangle and how they relate to each other.
2. Explain why supervision is an important internal control.
3. Define and contrast prevention controls and detection controls. Which are more desirable?
4. Yates Company is reviewing its internal procedures to try to improve the company's internal control. It specifically wants to separate work functions. What three types of work functions must be separated to improve internal control?
5. Janet Jones is considered one of the rising stars at Finch Company. Janet is very hard working and has not taken a vacation in three years. Explain why this is a violation of good internal control.
6. Why does the control environment provide the foundation for the entire internal control system?
7. In what way did the Sarbanes-Oxley Act impact the need for internal control?
8. How are a financial statement audit and an operational audit similar and different?
9. What types of items are included in cash? What are the two important characteristics of an item of cash?
10. Which of the following are considered to be cash: paper money, certificates of deposit, postdated checks, traveler's checks, funds in a checking account, and money orders?
11. What is a remittance advice? What types of data are included on a remittance advice?
12. What is electronic funds transfer (EFT)? What are retail EFT and wholesale EFT?
13. What is the purpose of a bank reconciliation?

14. In preparing a bank reconciliation, how should you determine (a) deposits not recorded in the bank statement and (b) outstanding checks?

15. Indicate whether the following bank reconciliation items should be (1) added to the bank statement balance, (2) deducted from the bank statement balance, (3) added to the ledger account balance, or (4) deducted from the ledger account balance:

a. Bank service charge

b. NSF check

c. Deposit in transit

d. Outstanding check

e. Bank error charging company's account with another company's check

f. Difference of $270 in amount of check written for $410 but recorded by the company as $140

16. Which of the items listed in Discussion Question 15 require a journal entry on the company's books?

17. What is an imprest petty cash fund? How is such a fund established and replenished?

18. Carter Manufacturing Company makes a variety of consumer products. For the year just ended (and the two prior years), sales of private-label product to Mega-Mart (1,200 stores nationwide) have made up 60 to 65 percent of total sales. On December 31 of the year just ended, Mega-Mart informed Carter that it would be buying all private-label products from another manufacturer under a five year contract. Losing this business will result in a 50 to 55 percent reduction in total gross profit for Carter.

a. What is the going concern concept and how does it apply to this situation?

b. How should the full disclosure principle be applied when preparing the annual report for the year just ended?

c. What is the independent auditor's responsibility in this situation?

SHORT EXERCISES

SE7-1. **The Fraud Triangle** Each of the following is part of the fraud triangle except: LO1

    a. pressure.

    b. opportunity.

    c. concealment.

    d. rationalization.

SE7-2. **Segregation of Duties** Having one person responsible for the related activities of ordering merchandise, receiving the merchandise, and paying for the merchandise: LO2

    a. provides increased security over the firm's assets.

    b. is an example of good internal control.

    c. is a good example of segregation of duties.

    d. increases the potential of fraud.

SE7-3. **Internal Control** Internal controls do each of the following except: LO2

    a. protect assets from theft.

    b. evaluate the performance of employees.

    c. guarantee the accuracy of the accounting records.

    d. increase the likelihood that any errors will be caught.

SE7-4. **Auditors** Which of the following is true? LO2, 7

    a. Internal auditors are independent of the company they audit.

    b. Internal audits provide appraisals of a company's internal control.

    c. The company being audited cannot pay the external auditing firm since this would violate their independence.

    d. Outside parties prefer appraisals by internal auditors over those of external auditors since they know more about the company being audited.

SE7-5. **The COSO framework identifies five internal control components** Which of the following is not one of the five components: LO2

    a. segregation of duties

    b. risk assessment

    c. monitoring activities

    d. control activities

LO3   **SE7-6.**   **Cash**   Cash includes each of the following except:
- *a.*   a postdated check.
- *b.*   currency.
- *c.*   money orders.
- *d.*   funds in a checking account.

LO3   **SE7-7.**   **Restricted Cash**   Restricted cash:
- *a.*   must be shown as a current asset.
- *b.*   must be shown as a noncurrent asset.
- *c.*   is shown as a liability.
- *d.*   is reported separate from unrestricted cash.

LO4   **SE7-8.**   **Electronic Funds Transfer**   Electronic funds transfer (EFT) involves transferring cash from one location to another using:
- *a.*   armored trucks.
- *b.*   computers.
- *c.*   bicycle messengers.
- *d.*   the mail service.

LO4   **SE7-9.**   **Cash Internal Control**   Good internal control over cash received on account involves the mailroom doing each of the following activities except:
- *a.*   Open the mail.
- *b.*   Prepare the deposit receipt.
- *c.*   Prepare the remittance list.
- *d.*   Send checks to the treasurer.

LO6   **SE7-10.**   **Cash Management**   Effective cash management involves all the following except:
- *a.*   Manage accounts receivable.
- *b.*   Manage inventory.
- *c.*   Invest excess cash.
- *d.*   Conduct internal audits.

EXERCISES—SET A

LO2   **E7-1A.**   **Internal Control**   Explain how each of the following procedures strengthens a company's internal control:
- *a.*   After preparing a check for a cash disbursement, the accountant for Travis Lumber Company cancels the supporting business documents (purchase order, receiving report, and invoice) by stamping them PAID.
- *b.*   The salespeople for Davis Department Store give each customer a cash register receipt along with the proper change. A sign on each cash register states that no refunds or exchanges are allowed without the related cash register receipt.
- *c.*   The ticket-taker at the Esquire Theater tears each admission ticket in half and gives one half back to the ticket purchaser. The seat number is printed on each half of the ticket.
- *d.*   John Renaldo's restaurant provides servers with prenumbered customers' checks. The servers are to void checks with mistakes on them and issue new ones rather than make corrections on them. Voided checks must be given to the manager every day.

LO4   **E7-2A.**   **Internal Controls for Cash Received on Account**   Hudson Company sells supplies to restaurants. Most sales are made on open account (credit sales). Hudson has requested your help in designing procedures for processing checks received from its customers. Briefly describe the procedures that should be used in each of the following departments:
- *a.*   Mailroom
- *b.*   Treasurer's department
- *c.*   Controller's department

LO5   **E7-3A.**   **Bank Reconciliation**   Use the following information to prepare a bank reconciliation for Young Company at June 30:
1. Balance per Cash account, June 30, $7,039.80.
2. Balance per bank statement, June 30, $7,300.25.

3. Deposits not reflected on bank statement, $950.
4. Outstanding checks, June 30, $1,260.45.
5. Service charge on bank statement not recorded in books, $35.
6. Error by bank—Yertel Company check charged on Young Company's bank statement, $375.
7. Check for advertising expense, $260, incorrectly recorded in books as $620.

E7-4A.   Bank Reconciliation Components Identify the requested amount in each of the following situations: **LO5**

a.   Munsing Company's May 31 bank reconciliation shows deposits in transit of $1,200. The general ledger Cash in Bank account shows total cash receipts during June of $55,600. The June bank statement shows total cash deposits of $54,300 (and no credit memos). What amount of deposits in transit should appear in the June 30 bank reconciliation?

b.   Sandusky Company's August 31 bank reconciliation shows outstanding checks of $1,900. The general ledger Cash in Bank account shows total cash disbursements (all by check) during September of $49,800. The September bank statement shows $49,200 of checks clearing the bank. What amount of outstanding checks should appear in the September 30 bank reconciliation?

c.   Fremont Corporation's March 31 bank reconciliation shows deposits in transit of $700. The general ledger Cash in Bank account shows total cash receipts during April of $41,000. The April bank statement shows total cash deposits of $37,100 (including $1,100 from the collection of a note; the note collection has not yet been recorded by Fremont). What amount of deposits in transit should appear in the April 30 bank reconciliation?

E7-5A.   Internal Control Explain how each of the following actions strengthens a company's system of   **LO2**
internal control:

a.   Separate work functions.
b.   Hire competent personnel.
c.   Develop plans and budgets.
d.   Use control numbers on all business documents.

E7-6A.   Effective Cash Management Explain how each of the following activities can improve a company's   **LO6**
cash management:

a.   Manage accounts receivable.
b.   Manage inventory.
c.   Manage accounts payable.
d.   Invest excess cash.

E7-7A.   Cash and Cash Equivalents Identify each of the following items as either cash (C), cash equivalents   **LO3**
(CE), or neither (N):

a.   Coin
b.   U.S. treasury bills
c.   Checks
d.   Six-month certificate of deposit
e.   Currency

E7-8A.   External versus Internal Audit Explain why parties outside the company, such as bankers and   **LO7**
stockholders, prefer an independent appraisal of the company's financial results rather than relying on   **(Appendix 7A)**
the work of internal auditors.

E7-9A.   Operational Audits Explain the nature of an operational audit.   **LO7**
  (Appendix 7A)

EXERCISES—SET B

E7-1B.   Internal Control Explain how each of the following procedures strengthens a company's internal   **LO2**
control:

a.   Western Corporation's photocopy machines are activated by keying a code number. Each employee is assigned a different, confidential code number. Each copy machine keeps track of the number of copies run under each employee number.

b. Picket Company's bank requires a signature card on file for each Picket Company employee who is authorized to sign checks.

c. Fast Stop Convenience Stores have programmed their cash registers to imprint a blue star on every 300th receipt printed. A sign by each cash register states that the customer will receive $2 if his or her receipt has a blue star on it.

d. Wilson Corporation has a policy that every employee must take two weeks of vacation each year.

LO4 **E7-2B.** **Internal Controls for Cash Received from Retail Sales** Edwards Company operates a retail department store. Most customers pay cash for their purchases. Edwards has asked you to help it design procedures for processing cash received from customers for cash sales. Briefly describe the procedures that should be used in each of the following departments:

a. Retail sales departments
b. Retail sales supervisor
c. Treasurer's department
d. Controller's department

LO5 **E7-3B.** **Bank Reconciliation** Use the following information to prepare a bank reconciliation for Dillon Company at April 30:

1. Balance per Cash account, April 30, $6,042.10.
2. Balance per bank statement, April 30, $6,553.28.
3. Deposits not reflected on bank statement, $450.
4. Outstanding checks, April 30, $1,340.18.
5. Service charge on bank statement not recorded in books, $19.
6. Error by bank—Dillard Company check charged on Dillon Company's bank statement, $450.
7. Check for advertising expense, $120, incorrectly recorded in books as $210.

LO5 **E7-4B.** **Bank Reconciliation Components** Identify the requested amount in each of the following situations:

a. Howell Company's August 31 bank reconciliation shows deposits in transit of $2,250. The general ledger Cash in Bank account shows total cash receipts during September of $87,750. The September bank statement shows total cash deposits of $87,000 (and no credit memos). What amount of deposits in transit should appear in the September 30 bank reconciliation?

b. Wright Corporation's March 31 bank reconciliation shows deposits in transit of $1,400. The general ledger Cash in Bank account shows total cash receipts during April of $64,600. The April bank statement shows total cash deposits of $63,100 (including $500 from the collection of a note; the note collection has not yet been recorded by Wright). What amount of deposits in transit should appear in the April 30 bank reconciliation?

c. Braddock Company's October 31 bank reconciliation shows outstanding checks of $2,200. The general ledger Cash in Bank account shows total cash disbursements (all by check) during November of $69,300. The November bank statement shows $67,200 of checks clearing the bank. What amount of outstanding checks should appear in the November 30 bank reconciliation?

LO2 **E7-5B.** **Internal Control** Explain how each of the following items strengthens a company's system of internal control:

a. Conduct internal audits.
b. Establish clear lines of authority and responsibility.
c. Maintain adequate accounting records.
d. Provide physical and electronic controls.

LO6 **E7-6B.** **Effective Cash Management** Presented below is the statement of cash flows for Smith & Sons for the month ended December 31. Identify (a) the major sources of cash, (b) the major uses of cash, and (c) the change in the cash balance during the month.

SMITH & SONS
Statement of Cash Flows
For the Month Ended December 31

Cash flows from operating activities		
Cash receipts from customers		$13,275
Cash payments for operating activities		(11,131)
Cash provided by operating activities		2,144
Cash flows from investing activities		
Net purchases of investments		(140)
Net capital expenditures		(30,000)
Cash used by investing activities		(30,140)
Cash flows for financing activities		
Repurchase of common stock		(7,300)
Cash dividends paid		(6,000)
Cash used in financing activities		(13,300)
Net decrease in cash		(41,296)
Cash at beginning of month		95,000
Cash at end of month		$53,704

E7-7B. Cash and Cash Equivalents Identify each of the following items as either cash (C), cash equivalents (CE), or neither (N):   **LO3**

a. Money market funds
b. Euros
c. A postdated check
d. A savings account
e. Traveler's checks

E7-8B. External versus Internal Audit Compare the purpose of an external audit to that of an internal audit.   **LO7**
(Appendix 7A)

E7-9B. The External Audit and Fraud Explain why the external audit is not considered a fraud audit.   **LO7**
(Appendix 7A)

PROBLEMS—SET A

P7-1A. Internal Control Regent Company encountered the following situations: **LO2, 4**

a. The person who opens the mail for Regent, Bill Stevens, stole a check from a customer and cashed it. To cover up the theft, he debited Sales Returns and Allowances and credited Accounts Receivable in the general ledger. He also posted the amount to the customer's account in the accounts receivable subsidiary ledger.

b. The purchasing agent, Susan Martin, used a company purchase order to order building materials from Builders Mart. Later, she telephoned Builders Mart and changed the delivery address to her home address. She told Builders Mart to charge the material to the company. At month-end, she approved the invoice from Builders Mart for payment.

c. Nashville Supply Company sent two invoices for the same order: the first on June 10 and the second on July 20. The accountant authorized payment of both invoices and both were paid.

d. On January 1, Jack Monty, a junior accountant for Regent, was given the responsibility of recording all general journal entries. At the end of the year, the auditors discovered that Monty had made 150 serious errors in recording transactions. The chief accountant was unaware that Monty had been making mistakes.

Required
For each situation, describe any violations of good internal control procedures and identify the steps that you would take to prevent each situation.

LO2, 4 **P7-2A.** **Internal Control** Each of the following lettered paragraphs briefly describes an independent situation involving some aspect of internal control.

Required

Answer the questions at the end of each paragraph or numbered section.

a. Robert Flynn is the office manager of Oswald Company, a small wholesaling company. Flynn opens all incoming mail, makes bank deposits, and maintains both the general ledger and the accounts receivable subsidiary ledger. An assistant records transactions in the credit sales journal and the cash receipts journal. The assistant also prepares a monthly statement for each customer and mails the statements to the customers. These statements list the beginning balance, credit sales, cash receipts, adjustments, and ending balance for the month.

1. If Flynn stole Customer A's $200 check (payment in full) and made no effort to conceal his embezzlement in the ledgers, how would the misappropriation be discovered?
2. What routine accounting procedure would disclose Flynn's $200 embezzlement in part (1), even if Flynn destroyed Customer A's subsidiary ledger account?
3. What circumstances might disclose Flynn's theft if he posted a payment to Customer A's account in the accounts receivable subsidiary ledger and set up a $200 account for a fictitious customer?
4. In part (3), why might Flynn be anxious to open the mail himself each morning?
5. In part (3), why might Flynn want to have the authority to write off accounts considered uncollectible?

b. A doughnut shop uses a cash register that produces a printed receipt for each sale. The register also prints each transaction on a paper tape that is locked inside the cash register. Only the supervisor has access to the cash-register tape. A prominently displayed sign promises a free doughnut to any customer who is not given a cash-register receipt with his or her purchase. How is this procedure an internal control device for the doughnut shop?

c. Jason Miller, a swindler, sent several businesses invoices requesting payment for office supplies that had never been ordered or delivered to the businesses. A five percent discount was offered for prompt payment. What internal control procedures should prevent this swindle from being successful?

d. The cashier for Uptown Cafeteria is located at the end of the food line. After customers have selected their food items, the cashier rings up the prices of the food and the customer pays the bill. The customer line frequently stalls while the person paying searches for the correct amount of cash. To speed things up, the cashier often collects money from the next customer or two who have the correct change without ringing up their food on the register. After the first customer finally pays, the cashier rings up the amounts for the customers who have already paid. What is the internal control weakness in this procedure? How might the internal control over the collection of cash from the cafeteria customers be strengthened?

LO4 **P7-3A.** **Internal Controls for Cash Received on Account** Schoff Company sells plumbing supplies to plumbing contractors on account. The procedures that Schoff uses to handle checks received from customers via the mail are described below:

a. Schoff instructs its customers to send payment checks to its street address, 619 Main Street, Scottsdale, Arizona.
b. Schoff does not provide a remittance advice to its customers for return with payment checks.
c. Checks are endorsed by the treasurer's office just prior to sending the checks to the bank for deposit.
d. The mailroom prepares a remittance list of all the checks received and files the only copy of the remittance list in a mailroom file cabinet.
e. The checks are sent to the controller's office. The controller's office uses the checks to post the accounts receivable subsidiary ledger and prepare the journal entry to record cash receipts. The checks are then sent to the treasurer's office.
f. The treasurer's office prepares the deposit slip (two copies) and sends one copy and the checks to the bank. The other copy of the deposit slip is filed in the treasurer's file cabinet.
g. The bank statement is sent to the controller, who prepares the bank reconciliation.

Required

Indicate how Schoff could improve each of these procedures. (Refer to **Exhibit 7-1** in the chapter to help you generate ideas.)

P7-4A. **Bank Reconciliation** On July 31, Sullivan Company's Cash in Bank account had a balance of $8,112.62. On that date, the bank statement indicated a balance of $9,098.55. A comparison of returned checks and bank advices revealed the following:

LO5

1. Deposits in transit July 31 amounted to $3,358.19.
2. Outstanding checks July 31 totaled $1,251.12.
3. The bank erroneously charged a $215 check of Solomon Company against the Sullivan bank account.
4. A $15 bank service charge has not yet been recorded by Sullivan Company.
5. Sullivan neglected to record $3,000 borrowed from the bank on a ten percent six-month note. The bank statement shows the $3,000 as a deposit.
6. Included with the returned checks is a memo indicating that J. Martin's check for $640 had been returned NSF. Martin, a customer, had sent the check to pay an account of $660 less a $20 discount.
7. Sullivan Company recorded a $107 payment for repairs as $1,070.

Required

a. Prepare a bank reconciliation for Sullivan Company at July 31.
b. Prepare the journal entry (or entries) necessary to bring the Cash in Bank account into agreement with the reconciled cash balance on the bank reconciliation.

P7-5A. **Bank Reconciliation** The bank reconciliation made by Winton, Inc., on August 31 showed a deposit in transit of $1,170 and two outstanding checks, No. 597 for $650 and No. 603 for $710. The reconciled cash balance on August 31 was $14,110.

LO5

The following bank statement is available for September:

Bank Statement							
TO Winton, Inc. St. Louis, MO						September 30 STATE BANK	
Date	Deposits	No.	Date	Charges	Date		Balance
					Aug.	31	$14,300
Sept. 1	$1,170	597	Sept. 1	$ 650	Sept.	1	14,820
2	1,120	607	5	1,850		2	15,940
5	850	608	5	1,100		5	13,840
9	744	609	9	552		8	13,200
15	585	610	8	640		9	13,392
17	1,540	611	17	488		15	13,162
25	1,028	612	15	815		17	14,214
30	680	614	25	920		25	14,322
		NSF	29	973		29	13,349
		SC	30	36		30	13,993

Item Codes:	EC: Error Correction	DM: Debit Memo	CM: Credit Memo
	SC: Service Charge	OD: Overdraft	RT: Returned Item
	IN: Interest Earned	NSF: Non-sufficient Funds	

A list of deposits made and checks written during September is shown below:

Deposits Made		Checks Written	
Sept. 1	$1,120	No. 607	$1,850
4	850	608	1,100
8	744	609	552
12	585	610	640
16	1,540	611	488
24	1,028	612	851
29	680	613	310
30	1,266	614	920
	$7,813	615	386
		616	420
			$7,517

The Cash in Bank account balance on September 30 was $14,406. In reviewing checks returned by the bank, the accountant discovered that check No. 612, written for $815 for advertising expense, was recorded in the cash disbursements journal as $851. The NSF check for $973, which Winton deposited on September 24, was a payment on account from customer D. Walker.

Required
a. Prepare a bank reconciliation for Winton, Inc., at September 30.
b. Prepare the necessary journal entries to bring the Cash in Bank account into agreement with the reconciled cash balance on the bank reconciliation.

LO3   P7-6A.   Reporting Cash Fey Company has the following items at year-end.

Currency and coin in safe	$ 4,100
Funds in savings account (requires $2,300 compensating balance)	26,540
Funds in checking account	6,750
Traveler's checks	625
Postdated check	1,250
Not-sufficient-funds check	880
Money market fund	32,400

Required
Identify the amount of the above items that should be reported as cash and cash equivalents on Fey Company's balance sheet.

LO2   P7-7A.   Internal Control Bart Simons has worked for Dr. Homer Spring for many years. Bart has been a model employee. He has not taken a vacation in over four years, always stating that work was too important. One of Bart's primary jobs at the clinic is to open mail and list the checks received. He also collects cash from patients at the cashier's window as patients leave. There are times that things are so hectic that Bart does not bother to give the patient a receipt; however, he assures them that he will make sure their account is properly credited. When things slow down at the clinic Bart often offers to help Lisa post payments to the patients' accounts receivable ledger. Lisa is always happy to receive help since she is also quite busy and because Bart is such a careful worker.

Required
Identify any internal control principles that may be violated in Dr. Spring's clinic.

LO2, 4   P7-8A.   Internal Control Listed below are (a) four potential errors or problems that could occur in the processing of cash transactions and (b) internal control principles. Review each error or problem and identify an internal control principle that could reduce the chance of the error or problem occurring. You may also cite more than one principle if more than one applies, or write none if none of the principles will correct the error or problem.

1. An employee steals cash collected from a customer's accounts receivable and hides the theft by issuing a credit memorandum indicating the customer returned the merchandise.

2. An official with authority to sign checks is able to steal blank checks and issue them without detection.

3. Due to a labor shortage many employees are hired without sufficient skills with the thought they can "learn on the job."

4. A salesperson often rings up a sale for less than the actual amount and then pockets the additional cash collected from the customer.

Internal control principles:

a.   Establish clear lines of authority and responsibility.
b.   Segregation of duties.
c.   Hire competent personnel.
d.   Use control numbers on all business documents.
e.   Develop plans and budgets.
f.   Maintain adequate accounting records.
g   Provide physical and electronic controls.
h.   Conduct internal audits.

P7-9A.   **Bank Reconciliation**   The Seattle Boat Company's bank statement for the month of September in-   **LO5**
dicated a balance of $13,375. The company's cash account in the general ledger showed a balance of
$9,778 on September 30. Other relevant information includes the following:

1. Deposits in transit on September 30 total $9,700.
2. The bank statement shows a debit memorandum for a $95 check printing charge.
3. Check number 238 payable to Simon Company was recorded in the accounting records for $496 and cleared the bank for this same amount. A review of the records indicated that the Simon account now has a $72 credit balance and the check to them should have been $568.
4. Outstanding checks as of September 30 totaled $11,600.
5. Check No. 276 was correctly written and paid by the bank for $818. The check was recorded in the accounting records as a debit to accounts payable and a credit to cash for $980.
6. The bank returned a NSF check in the amount of $990.
7. The bank included a credit memorandum for $2,620 representing a collection of a customer's note. The principle portion was $2,400 and the interest portion was $220. The interest had not been accrued.

Required
a.   Prepare the September bank reconciliation for Seattle Boat Company.
b.   Prepare any necessary adjusting entries.

P7-10A.   **Effective Cash Management**   Longo LLP is a new law firm struggling to manage its cash flow. Like   **LO6**
many new businesses, the firm has not yet developed a sufficient client base to cover its operating
costs. Additionally, the firm faced a number of large initial, but nonrecurring, start-up costs at the beginning of the year. Ongoing monthly costs include office rent and salary for a paralegal staff member.
Another problem that the firm faces is that several of its major clients have failed to pay their current,
but overdue, bills. Mick Longo, one of the two founding partners, has not taken any salary since the
firm began operations over eight months ago, and has decided to maintain a part-time job bartending
on weekends at a local resort to ensure that he has some cash to cover day-to-day expenses like travel.

Required
What suggestions would you make to Mick Longo to improve his firm's cash management practices?

PROBLEMS—SET B

P7-1B.   **Internal Control**   Wheeler Company encountered the following situations: **LO2, 4**

a.   Jenny Farrell, head of the receiving department, created a fictitious company named Quick Forms and used it to send invoices to Wheeler Company for business documents that Wheeler never or-dered or received. Farrell prepared receiving reports that stated that the business documents had been received. Wheeler's controller compared the receiving reports to the invoices and paid each one.

b. Wheeler Company lost one day's cash receipts. An employee took the receipts to the bank after the bank's closing hours to deposit them in the night depository slot. A creative thief had placed a sign on the slot saying it was out of order and all deposits should be placed in a metal canister placed next to the building. Wheeler's employee placed the deposit in the canister and left. Employees from two other companies did the same thing. Later that night, the thief returned and stole the deposits from the canister. (This is an actual case.)

c. Wheeler Company does not prenumber the sales invoices used for over-the-counter sales. A cashier pocketed cash receipts and destroyed all copies of the related sales invoices.

Required

For each situation, describe any violations of good internal control procedures and identify the steps that you would take to prevent each situation.

LO2, 4 **P7-2B.** **Internal Control** The Mountain Twister amusement ride has the following system of internal control over cash receipts. All persons pay the same price for a ride. A person taking the ride pays cash to the cashier and receives a prenumbered ticket. The tickets are issued in strict number sequence. The individual then walks to the ride site, hands the ticket to a ticket-taker (who controls the number of people getting on each ride), and passes through a turnstile. At the end of each day, the beginning ticket number is subtracted from the ending ticket number to determine the number of tickets sold. The cash is counted and compared with the number of tickets sold. The turnstile records how many people pass through it. At the end of each day, the beginning turnstile count is subtracted from the ending count to determine the number of riders that day. The number of riders is compared with the number of tickets sold.

Required

Which internal control feature would reveal each of the following irregularities?

a. The ticket-taker lets her friends on the ride without tickets.

b. The cashier gives his friends tickets without receiving cash from them.

c. The cashier gives too much change.

d. The ticket-taker returns the tickets she has collected to the cashier. The cashier then resells these tickets and splits the proceeds with the ticket-taker.

e. A person sneaks into the ride line without paying the cashier.

LO4 **P7-3B.** **Internal Controls for Cash Received from Retail Sales** Midland Stores is a retailer of men's clothing. Most customers pay cash for their purchases. The procedures that Midland uses for handling cash are described below:

a. Each department begins the day with whatever amount of cash remains in the cash register from the prior day. This is not a predetermined amount.

b. All sales associates share one cash drawer.

c. Each sales associate can handle all transactions, including returns and unusual transactions, without approval from a supervisor.

d. At the end of each day, one of the sales associates takes the cash drawer and the cash register totals to a private area where no one can observe what is being done, counts the cash in the drawer, and prepares a written report of sales and cash received. The cash, the register tape, and a copy of the report are sent to the controller's department.

e. The controller prepares the deposit slip and sends the deposit to the bank. The controller then prepares the journal entry to record the cash sales.

f. The controller does not keep any copies of the written report or the deposit slip.

g. The bank statement is sent to the controller, who prepares the bank reconciliation.

Required

Indicate how Midland could improve each of these procedures. (Refer to **Exhibit 7-2** in the chapter to help you generate ideas.)

LO5 **P7-4B.** **Bank Reconciliation** On May 31, the Cash in Bank account of Wallace Company, a sole proprietorship, had a balance of $6,000.50. On that date, the bank statement indicated a balance of $7,868.50. A comparison of returned checks and bank advices revealed the following:

1. Deposits in transit May 31 totaled $2,603.05.
2. Outstanding checks May 31 totaled $3,077.25.

3. The bank added to the account $19.80 of interest income earned by Wallace during May.
4. The bank collected a $2,400 note receivable for Wallace and charged a $30 collection fee. Both items appear on the bank statement.
5. Bank service charges in addition to the collection fee, not yet recorded, were $40.
6. Included with the returned checks is a memo indicating that L. Ryder's check for $686 had been returned NSF. Ryder, a customer, had sent the check to pay an account of $700 less a 2% discount.
7. Wallace Company incorrectly recorded the payment of an account payable as $360; the check was for $630.

Required
a. Prepare a bank reconciliation for Wallace Company at May 31.
b. Prepare the journal entry (or entries) necessary to bring the Cash in Bank account into agreement with the reconciled cash balance on the bank reconciliation.

P7-5B. **Bank Reconciliation** The bank reconciliation made by Sandler Company, a sole proprietorship, on March 31 showed a deposit in transit of $1,300 and two outstanding checks, No. 797 for $550 and No. 804 for $690. The reconciled cash balance on March 31 was $12,020.   LO5
The following bank statement is available for April 2015:

			Bank Statement				
TO	Sandler Company						April 30
	Fairbanks, AK					FAIRBANKS NATIONAL BANK	
Date	Deposits	No.	Date	Charges		Date	Balance
					Mar.	31	$11,960
Apr. 1......	$1,300	804	Apr. 2	$ 690	Apr.	1	13,260
3......	1,680	807	3	730		2	12,570
7......	1,250	808	7	1,240		3	13,520
13......	1,020	809	7	838		7	12,692
18......	840	810	16	1,040		13	13,386
23......	990	811	13	326		16	12,346
27......	1,340	813	27	640		18	12,686
30......	1,160	814	23	600		23	13,076
30......	75IN	NSF	18	500		27	13,776
		SC	30	40		30	14,971

Item Codes: EC: Error Correction   DM: Debit Memo   CM: Credit Memo
SC: Service Charge   OD: Overdraft   RT: Returned Item
IN: Interest Earned   NSF: Non-sufficient Funds

A list of deposits made and checks written during April is shown below:

Deposits Made		**Checks Written**	
Apr. 2	$1,680	No. 807	$ 730
6	1,250	808	1,240
10	1,020	809	838
17	840	810	1,040
22	990	811	236
24	1,340	812	948
29	1,160	813	640
30	1,425	814	600
	$0,705	815	372
		816	875
			$7,519

The Cash in Bank account balance on April 30 was $14,206. In reviewing checks returned by the bank, the accountant discovered that check No. 811, written for $326 for delivery expense, was recorded in the cash disbursements journal as $236. The NSF check for $500 was that of customer R. Koppa, deposited in April. Interest for April added to the account by the bank was $75.

Required

a.   Prepare a bank reconciliation for Sandler Company at April 30.

b.   Prepare the necessary journal entries to bring the Cash in Bank account into agreement with the reconciled cash balance on the bank reconciliation.

LO3   P7-6B.   Reporting Cash   Jenkins Company has the following items at year-end:

Currency and coin in safe.	$ 4,500
Funds in savings account (requires $2,500 compensating balance)	17,300
Funds in checking account	1,750
Traveler's checks	1,600
Postdated check	2,250
Not-sufficient-funds check.	550
Money market fund	12,600

Required

Identify the amount of the above items that should be reported as cash and cash equivalents on Jenkins Company's balance sheet.

LO2   P7-7B.   Internal Control   Jerry Finch has worked for Jones Hardware for many years. Jerry has been a model employee. He has not taken a vacation in over three years, always stating that work was too important. One of Jerry's primary jobs at the store is to open mail and list the checks received. He also collects cash from customers at the store's outdoor nursery area. There are times that things are so hectic that Jerry does not bother to use the register, simply making change from cash he carries with him. When things slow down at the store Jerry often offers to help Cindy post payments to the customer's accounts receivable ledger. Cindy is always happy to receive help since she is also quite busy and because Jerry is such a careful worker.

Required

Identify any internal control principles that may be violated in Jones Hardware store.

LO2, 4   P7-8B.   Internal Control   Listed below are (a) four potential errors or problems that could occur in the processing of cash transactions and (b) internal control principles. For each error or problem, identify an internal control principle that could reduce the chance of the error or problem occurring. You may also cite more than one principle if more than one applies, or write none if none of the principles will correct the error or problem.

1.   Three cashiers use one cash register and the cash in the drawer is often short of the recorded balance.

2.   The same employee is responsible for opening the mail, listing any checks received, preparing the deposit receipt, and recording to the accounts receivable journal. Several customers have complained that their balances are incorrect.

3.   In an effort to save printing costs, generic receipts without numbers are used for customer sales.

4.   Because things have been hectic, no budgets were prepared this year. One department seems to be doing less volume in revenue, but cost of goods sold appear to be high relative to sales.

Internal control principles:

a.   Establish clear lines of authority and responsibility.

b.   Segregation of duties.

c.   Hire competent personnel.

d.   Use control numbers on all business documents.

e.   Develop plans and budgets.

f.   Maintain adequate accounting records.

g.   Provide physical and electronic controls.

h.   Conduct internal audits.

LO5   P7-9B.   Bank Reconciliation   The Chicago Scooter Company's bank statement for the month of June indicated a balance of $3,350. The company's cash account in the general ledger showed a balance of $2,464 on June 30. Other relevant information includes the following:

1. Deposits in transit on June 30 total $2,550.
2. The bank statement shows a debit memorandum for a $10 check printing charge.
3. Check No. 160 payable to Simon Company was recorded in the accounting records for $124 and cleared the bank for this same amount. A review of the records indicated that the Simon account now has an $18 credit balance and the check to them should have been $142.
4. Outstanding checks as of June 30 totaled $3,100.
5. Check No. 176 was correctly written and paid by the bank for $203. The check was recorded in the accounting records as a debit to accounts payable and a credit to cash for $230.
6. The bank returned a NSF check in the amount of $311.
7. The bank included a credit memorandum for $630 representing a collection of a customer's note. The principal portion was $610 and the interest portion was $20. The interest had not been accrued.

Required
a. Prepare the June bank reconciliation for the Chicago Scooter Company.
b. Prepare any necessary adjusting entries.

SERIAL PROBLEM: KATE'S CARDS

(Note: This is a continuation of the Serial Problem: Kate's Cards from Chapters 1 through 6.)

SP7.  On February 15, 2016, Kate Collins, owner of Kate's Cards, asks you to investigate the cash handling activities in her business. She believes that a new employee might be stealing funds. "I have no proof," she says, "but I'm fairly certain that the January 31, 2016, undeposited receipts amounted to more than $12,000, although the January 31 bank reconciliation prepared by the cashier (who works in the treasurer's department) shows only $7,238.40. Also, the January bank reconciliation doesn't show several checks that have been outstanding for a long time. The cashier told me that these checks needn't appear on the reconciliation because he had notified the bank to stop payment on them and he had made the necessary adjustment on the books. Does that sound reasonable to you?"

At your request, Kate shows you the following (unaudited) January 31, 2016, bank reconciliation prepared by the cashier:

KATE'S CARDS Bank Reconciliation January 31, 2016					
Ending balance from bank statement		$ 4,843.69	Balance from general ledger		$10,893.89
Add: Deposits in transit		7,238.40			
		$12,082.09			
Less:			Less:		
Outstanding checks:			Bank service charge	$ 60.00	
No. 2351	$1,100.20		Unrecorded credit	1,200.00	(1,260.00)
No. 2353	378.32				
No. 2354	969.68	(2,448.20)			
Reconciled cash balance		$ 9,633.89	Reconciled cash balance		$ 9,633.89

You discover that the $1,200 unrecorded bank credit represents a note collected by the bank on Kate's behalf; it appears in the deposits column of the January bank statement. Your investigation also reveals that the December 31, 2015, bank reconciliation showed three checks that had been outstanding longer than 10 months: No. 1432 for $600, No. 1458 for $466.90, and No. 1512 for $253.10. You also discover that these items were never added back into the Cash account in Kate's books. In confirming that the checks shown on the cashier's January 31 bank reconciliation were outstanding on that date, you discover that check No. 2353 was actually a payment of $1,658.32 and had been recorded on the books for that amount.

To confirm the amount of undeposited receipts at January 31, you request a bank statement for February 1–12 (called a cutoff bank statement). This indeed shows a January 1 deposit of $7,238.40.

Required

a. Calculate the amount of funds stolen by the employee.
b. Describe how the employee concealed the theft.
c. What suggestions would you make to Kate about cash control procedures?

EXTENDING YOUR KNOWLEDGE

REPORTING AND ANALYSIS

COLUMBIA
SPORTSWEAR
COMPANY

EYK7-1. **Financial Reporting Problem: Columbia Sportswear Company** The financial statements for the **Columbia Sportswear Company** can be found in Appendix A at the end of this book.

Required

Use the financial statements and the accompanying notes to the financial statements to answer the following questions about Columbia Sportswear:

a. What title is used on Columbia's consolidated balance sheet for cash?
b. According to the information given in Note 2, what is the makeup of the cash and cash equivalents account?
c. According to information in Item 9A. Controls and Procedures, who is responsible for establishing and maintaining adequate internal control over financial reporting?
d. Deloitte and Touche, the independent auditor of Columbia Sportswear, issued a report on their audit of Columbia's internal control. What did they conclude?

COLUMBIA
SPORTSWEAR
COMPANY

UNDER ARMOUR,
INC.

EYK7-2. **Comparative Analysis Problem: Columbia Sportswear Company vs. Under Armour, Inc.** The financial statements for **Columbia Sportswear Company** can be found in Appendix A and **Under Armour, Inc.**'s financial statements can be found in Appendix B at the end of this book.

Required

Use the information in the companies' financial statements to answer the following questions:

a. What is the balance in cash and cash equivalents as of December 31, 2014?
b. What percentage of each company's total assets is made up of cash and cash equivalents as of December 31, 2014?
c. How much did cash and cash equivalents change during 2014 for each firm?
d. For each company, how did the change in cash for 2014 compare to its cash provided by operating activities?

EYK7-3. **Business Decision Problem** Qualitec Electronics Company is a distributor of microcomputers and related electronic equipment. The company has grown very rapidly. It is located in a large building near Chicago, Illinois. Jack Flanigan, the president of Qualitec, has hired you to perform an internal control review of the company. You conduct interviews of key employees, tour the operations, and observe various company functions. You discover the following:

1. Qualitec has not changed its ordering procedures since it was formed eight years ago. Anyone in the company can prepare a purchase order and send it to the vendor without getting any managerial approval. When the invoice arrives from the vendor, it is compared only to the purchase order before authorizing payment.

2. Qualitec does not have an organization chart. In fact, employees are encouraged to work on their own, without supervision. Flanigan believes that this approach increases creativity.

3. Business documents have been carefully designed by the controller. When the printer prints the documents, no control numbers are printed on them. Instead, employees using a form write the next sequential number on the form. The controller believes that this approach ensures that a proper sequencing of numbers will be maintained.

4. No budgets are prepared for the company.

5. All doors to the building remain unlocked from 7:00 a.m. to 11:00 p.m. Employees normally work from 7:30 a.m. to 5:00 p.m. A private security firm drives to the building to unlock it each morning and lock it each night. The security firm's employee leaves immediately after unlocking or locking. The company does not use time clocks or employee badges.

6. Flanigan believes that audits (either external or internal) are a waste of time. He has resisted the bank president's urging to hire a CPA firm to conduct an audit.

Required

Analyze the findings listed above. Then list all the internal control weaknesses that you can identify. For each weakness, describe one or more internal controls that Qualitec should install to overcome the weakness.

EYK7-4. **Financial Analysis Problem** The **Public Company Accounting Oversight Board (PCAOB)** was created as part of the Sarbanes-Oxley legislation to provide oversight to U.S. accounting firms. The PCAOB's address is http://www.pcaobus.org.

Required

Answer the following questions:

a. What is the mission of the PCAOB?
b. What is the title of the first auditing standard issued by the PCAOB?
c. According to the rules section of the site, what is required for a PCAOB rule to take effect?

CRITICAL THINKING

EYK7-5. **Accounting Research Problem** Refer to the consolidated balance sheets in the fiscal year 2014 annual report of **General Mills, Inc.** available on this book's website.

GENERAL MILLS, INC.

Required

a. What was the amount of cash and cash equivalents as of May 25, 2014?
b. By what amount did cash and cash equivalents increase or decrease during the year?
c. What statement elsewhere in the annual report contains an explanation of the increase or decrease in the cash and cash equivalents amount? In that statement, what amount of cash was provided or used by (1) operating activities, (2) investment activities, and (3) financing activities?
d. What members of the company signed off as to the assessment of the company's internal control (see Reports of management and Independent Registered Public Accounting Firm)?
e. What firm conducted the audit of General Mills?
f. What opinion did the accounting firm express about General Mills' financial statements?
g. In addition to their audit of the financial statements, what else did the auditing firm audit?

EYK7-6. **Accounting Communication Activity** You were recently hired as the head of a company's ethics division. As one of your first acts, you decide to prepare a letter to the company's Chairman of the Board explaining the importance of ethics within the company. What are some of the items that should be included in your letter?

EYK7-7. **Accounting Ethics Case** Gina Pullen is the petty cash cashier for a large family-owned restaurant. She has been presented on numerous occasions with properly approved receipts for reimbursement from petty cash that she believes are personal expenses of one of the five owners of the restaurant. She reports to the controller of the company. The controller is also a family member and is the person who approves the receipts for payment out of petty cash.

Required

What are the accounting implications if Pullen is correct? What alternatives should she consider?

EYK7-8. **Corporate Social Responsibility Problem** Corporate social responsibility and fraud prevention are often related. One way that the two are connected is in the creation of a culture of honesty and the ethical treatment of employees. This is often the result of the tone from the top, where the company leaders not only talk about these concepts, but also practice them.

Required

Discuss how a culture of honesty and the ethical treatment of employees can reduce the risk of fraud.

EYK7-9. **Forensic Accounting Problem** Internal control follows the concept of reasonable assurance. Pete Simmons, the chief compliance officer of Salem Company, stated that he does not want simply reasonable assurance. He wants absolute assurance in all aspects that apply to the financial statements of the company. Specifically, Pete stated, "As long as I am working here, we will run a perfectly tight system that ensures absolutely no fraud in our financial statements." Betty Flint, the

controller, disagreed with Pete and argued that anything more than reasonable assurance is both financially and practically impossible.

Required

Do you agree with Pete or Betty, and why?

EYK7-10. **Forensic Accounting Problem** Wayne James Nelson, a manager in the office of the Arizona State Treasurer, was found guilty of trying to defraud the state of nearly $2 million. Nelson's scheme involved issuing checks to bogus vendors. The amounts of the 23 checks issued are shown below:

The table lists the checks that a manager in the office of the Arizona State Treasurer wrote to divert funds for his own use. The vendors to whom the checks were issued were fictitious.

Date of Check	Amount
October 9, 1992	$ 1,927.48
	27,902.31
October 14, 1992	86,241.90
	72,117.46
	81,321.75
	97,473.96
October 19, 1992	93,249.11
	89,658.17
	87,776.89
	92,105.83
	79,949.16
	87,602.93
	96,879.27
	91,806.47
	84,991.67
	90,831.83
	93,766.67
	88,338.72
	94,639.49
	83,709.28
	96,412.21
	88,432.86
	71,552.16
TOTAL	**$1,878,687.58**

Required

Refer to the chart shown below that reports the occurrences of various digits in a number. Compare the first digit of the fraudulent checks to the table of Benford's Law. How do the two compare? Are there any other unusual patterns you detect in the check amounts?

Position of digit in number				
Digit	First	Second	Third	Fourth
0	.	.11968	.10178	.10018
1	.30103	.11389	.10138	.10014
2	.17609	.10882	.10097	.10010
3	.12494	.10433	.10057	.10006
4	.09691	.10031	.10018	.10002
5	.07918	.09668	.09979	.09998
6	.06695	.09337	.09940	.09994
7	.05799	.09035	.09902	.09990
8	.05115	.08757	.09864	.09986
9	.04576	.08500	.09827	.09982

Example: The number 147 has three digits, with 1 as the first digit, 4 as the second digit and 7 as the third digit. The table shows that under Benford's Law the expected proportion of numbers with a first digit 1 is 30.103% and the expected proportion of numbers with a third digit 7 is 9.902%.

Source: "A Taxpayer Compliance Application of Benford's Law," by M. J. Nigrini. *The Journal of American Taxation Association* 18, 1996.

EYK7-11. Analyzing IFRS Financial Statements The 2014 financial statements of LVMH Moet Hennessey-Louis Vuitton S.A. are presented in Appendix C at the end of this book. LVMH is a Paris-based holding company and one of the world's largest and best-known luxury goods companies. As a member of the European Union, French companies are required to prepare their consolidated (group) financial statements using International Financial Reporting Standards (IFRS). After reviewing LVMH's consolidated financial statements, consider the following questions:

Required
a. What was the amount of cash and cash equivalents as of December 31, 2014?
b. By what amount did cash and cash equivalents increase or decrease during the year?
c. What statement elsewhere in the annual report contains an explanation of the increase or decrease in the cash and cash equivalents amount? In that statement, what amount of cash was provided or used by (1) operating activities, and (2) financing activities?

EYK7-12. Working with the Takeaways The following conditions of material weaknesses were reported in a prior year independent auditors' report on internal control of the U.S. Department of Transportation Highway Trust Fund (HTF):

1. Weaknesses with respect to journal entry preparation:
   a. Lack of indication of preparer
   b. Lack of supporting documentation
   c. Lack of proper review and approval
2. Weaknesses with respect to the consolidated financial statement preparation and analysis process:
   a. Inadequate analysis of abnormal balances
   b. Inadequate analysis of account relationships
   c. Inadequate controls over journal entry processing
   d. Lack of oversight related to allocation transfers

Required
a. What is the possible negative effect of these material weaknesses?
b. If you were the reporting auditor, what would you recommend be done?

ANSWERS TO SELF-STUDY QUESTIONS:

1. c, (pp. 332–333)   2. c, (pp. 334–336)   3. d, (p. 336)   4. a, (p. 336)   5. c, (p. 357)   6. b, (p. 340)
7. c, (pp. 342, 345)   8. d, (p. 347)   9. a, (p. 349)   10. c, (pp. 346–347)

YOUR TURN! SOLUTIONS

Solution 7.1

1. This is a personnel policy control violation. The supervisor may be committing a fraud and covering up his acts. If the supervisor were forced to take a vacation, the employee filling in might observe some suspicious activity and uncover the fraud.
2. This is a physical control violation. The unattended inventory could be stolen through the open door.
3. This is a segregation of duties violation. The supervisor is in a position to order an improper purchase, receive the goods for his own purposes, record the goods as received by the company, and then have the company pay for the purchase.

Solution 7.2

1. (c) Treasurer's department
2. (a) Retail sales supervisor
3. (b) Mailroom
4. (e) Internal audit department
5. (d) Controller's department

Solution 7.3

1. (a) Add to bank statement balance
2. (b) Subtract from bank statement balance
3. (d) Subtract from cash general ledger account
4. (c) Add to cash general ledger account

Solution 7A.1

1. (a) Internal audit
2. (b) Financial statement audit
3. (c) Operational audit
4. (b) Financial statement audit
5. (c) Operational audit

8

Accounting for Receivables

PAST

In Chapter 7 we studied how companies can prevent errors and fraud with the use of internal controls.

PRESENT

In this chapter we turn our attention to the accounting for two important assets—accounts and notes receivable.

FUTURE

In Chapter 9 we will continue our study of a company's assets by looking at long-lived assets.

LEARNING OBJECTIVES

1. **Define** accounts receivable, explain losses from uncollectible accounts, and **describe** the allowance method of accounting for doubtful accounts. *(p. 382)*

2. **Describe** and **illustrate** the percentage of net sales method and the accounts receivable aging method for estimating a business's bad debts expense. *(p. 387)*

3. **Discuss** the accounting treatment of credit card sales. *(p. 392)*

4. **Illustrate** a promissory note receivable, **discuss** the calculation of interest on notes receivable, and **present** journal entries to record notes receivable and interest. *(p. 393)*

5. **Define** accounts receivable turnover and average collection period and **explain** their use in the analysis and management of accounts and notes receivable. *(p. 396)*

6. Appendix 8A: **Illustrate** the direct write-off method and **contrast** it with the allowance method for accounting for doubtful accounts. *(p. 400)*

MGM RESORTS INTERNATIONAL— MANAGING CREDIT FOR BIGGER PROFITS

MGM Resorts International is among the largest gaming companies in the world. The company owns 15 casino resorts, including Bellagio, MGM Grand Las Vegas, Mandalay Bay, Luxor, Excalibur, Monte Carlo, New York-New York, Circus Circus, and The Mirage. These establishments provide gaming, hotel accommodations, dining, and other entertainment for their clientele. Gaming, however, is the primary revenue-producing activity for these businesses.

Casino credit is an important marketing tool for gaming companies like MGM Resorts International. When used intelligently, it can result in significant increases in revenue since high-end casinos like Bellagio and The Mirage rely heavily on clientele that gamble on credit. Granting credit to gamblers also increases player loyalty because gamblers are inclined to play at casinos where they have a line of credit. Once credit is established, the gambler is allowed to write a marker and withdraw money to use to gamble. The credit, however, is only granted to clientele who utilize it. While there is no requirement that a gambler lose in order to maintain a line of credit, the credit is lost if it is not used. In other words, a casino grants credit to its clientele with the expectation that the more a gambler uses the line of credit, the more likely the casino is to win.

While credit lines clearly provide a boost to a casino's revenue, it is critical that the casino carefully manage these receivables. MGM Resorts International, for example, maintains strict controls over the issuance of markers and "aggressively pursues collection from those customers who fail to repay their markers on a timely basis." GAAP requires MGM Resorts International to recognize the likelihood that a casino may be unable to collect all of its outstanding markers on its financial statements. At year-end 2014, despite aggressive collection efforts, MGM Resorts International reported nearly $85 million in casino doubtful accounts, representing 27% of casino accounts receivable.

Accounts Receivable	Credit Card Sales	Notes Receivable	Analyzing and Managing Receivables
• Recording accounts receivable • Allowance methods: percentage of net sales and aging of receivables • Direct write-off method (Appendix 8A)	• Processing credit card sales • Recording receivables from credit card sales	• Promissory note • Interest on note • Maturity date • Recording entries • Disclosure of notes	• Accounts receivable turnover • Average collection period • Factoring and discounting

RECEIVABLES

Receivables are assets representing a company's right to receive cash or other assets at some point in the future. Receivables may be classified as either a current asset or a non-current asset, depending upon the date of the expected receipt of cash or other assets. The most common types of receivables are accounts and notes receivable, which arise when a company sells its products or services to its customers on credit. Other types of receivables include loans to employees, loans to other companies, and any interest receivable on such outstanding loans.

ACCOUNTING IN PRACTICE

Accounts Receivable

Accounts receivable can amount to a large percentage of total assets for a company. Below are representative accounts receivable as a percentage of total assets appearing on recent balance sheets of four well known companies in different industries.

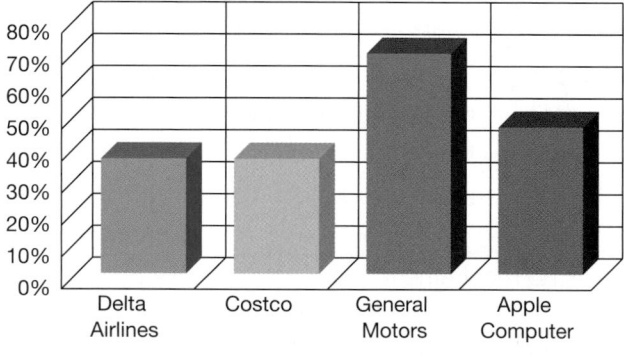

ACCOUNTS RECEIVABLE

LO1 **Define** accounts receivable, explain losses from uncollectible accounts, and **describe** the allowance method of accounting for doubtful accounts.

Many businesses sell goods and services to their customers on a credit basis, allowing customers to pay for their purchases over a period of time called the credit period. **Accounts receivable** is the asset, usually classified as current, that is created when a sale or service transaction is executed on a credit basis.

When a company executes a credit sale, it debits the Accounts Receivable account and credits the Sales Revenue account. This transaction is posted to the general ledger, increasing both the Accounts Receivable and Sales Revenue balances. To illustrate, assume that on December 1, 2016, the Claremont Company sells $20,000 of merchandise on account. The company will make the following journal entry on its books for the credit sale transaction:

2016			
Dec. 1	Accounts receivable	20,000	
	Sales revenue		20,000
	To record credit sales to customers.		

A   = L +   SE
+20,000   +20,000
                     Rev

When the credit sale is collected on December 20, the following entry is made:

Dec. 20	Cash	20,000	
	Accounts receivable		20,000
	To record cash collection.		

A   = L +   SE
+20,000
−20,000

Accounts receivable includes only those amounts relating to credit sales of goods or services. Other amounts due, such as from advances to employees or loans to affiliated companies, should be included with the Other Receivables account on the balance sheet. Other Receivables may be either a current asset or a noncurrent asset.

A.K.A. Accounts receivable are also sometimes referred to as *trade receivables*.

Balance Sheet Title for Accounts Receivable

ACCOUNTING IN PRACTICE

Regardless of what it is called, accounts receivable are not cash until they are collected. So, what should we call these receivables? Uncollected cash may seem like an appropriate account title, but this title is not commonly used by businesses. Instead, companies use several other titles, as can be seen from a survey of 600 large U.S. companies:

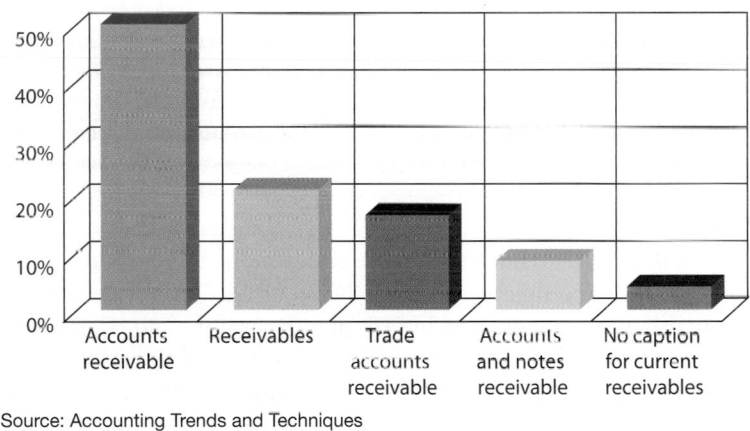

Source: Accounting Trends and Techniques

ACCOUNTING FOR BAD DEBTS

Businesses that extend credit to their customers anticipate some amount of credit losses—that is, losses from customers who fail to pay for their credit purchases. The magnitude of these losses is usually closely related to a firm's credit-granting policy. A **credit-granting policy** is a policy that a company follows to decide which customers should be allowed to buy goods and services on credit and how much credit those customers should be granted. Companies often base their credit-granting policy on a computerized credit score. (See Accounting in Practice: Credit Scoring Systems on the next page.) A company may deliberately relax its credit-granting policy to increase its sales, fully anticipating a parallel increase in its credit losses.

Businesses must also establish a **credit-collection policy**; that is, a policy establishing the amount of time that its customers may take before they are required to pay their outstanding accounts receivable. In Chapter 5, we discussed the credit period, or the allowed time period that a customer may take to pay for their credit purchases, and sales discounts, or the dollar amount that a customer may deduct from the purchase price of goods if they pay within an allowed discount period. Together, any sales discount, the discount period, and the credit period constitute a company's credit-collection policy. Maintaining an effective credit-collection policy is important for those businesses that allow their customers to buy goods and services on credit, since companies can have millions of dollars of their cash tied up in uncollected accounts receivable.

Most large companies have credit departments that administer the company's credit-granting and credit-collection policies. Credit personnel conduct credit investigations, establish credit limits, and follow up on any unpaid accounts. They also decide, following written collection procedures, when an account receivable is uncollectible, and consequently, when an account receivable should be written off a company's balance sheet as uncollectible.

A.K.A. The Bad Debts Expense is also sometimes referred to as the *Provision for Bad Debts.*

Credit losses are considered to be an operating expense of a business, and consequently, they are debited to an account called **Bad Debts Expense**. Normally, the Bad Debts Expense account is classified as a selling expense on the income statement, although some companies include it as part of their administrative expenses.

ACCOUNTING IN PRACTICE	**Credit Scoring Systems**

Most companies use a computerized credit scoring system to decide whether to extend credit to their customers. The credit scoring system is based on a set of formulas with multiple variables. Data from a customer's credit application and from credit reporting agencies are used by the system to calculate a credit score. The system then compares the score to predetermined limits and recommends whether or not credit be extended.

If credit is extended, the scoring system often recommends an upper limit on the amount of credit to be extended. Scoring systems focus on a customer's ability to generate net income and cash flow, the customer's current level of debt and required repayment schedule, and current assets. Many of the financial statement ratios discussed throughout this text are incorporated into credit scoring systems.

Allowance Method

Credit losses are an unfortunate but predictable consequence of extending credit to a business's customers. At the time that a credit sale is made, the seller does not know whether the account receivable will be collected in full, in part, or not at all. Further, any loss from an uncollectible account may not be known for several months, or even a year or more, following the credit sale. To achieve a proper matching of sales revenues and expenses, however, a company's accountants must estimate the amount of the bad debts expense to report on the income statement. This estimate is recorded in an end-of-period adjusting entry. The process of estimating and recording the bad debts expense for a business is most often executed using the **allowance method**.

PRINCIPLE ALERT	**Matching Concept**

The *matching concept* states that expenses should be linked with, or matched with, the revenues that they help to generate. A company sells its goods and services on credit because this business practice attracts more customers and, therefore, more sales revenue than if the company only permitted cash transactions. One of the costs associated with extending credit to customers is the bad debts expense. The matching concept requires that this expense be reported in the same accounting period as the related sales revenue. To accomplish the appropriate matching of sales revenue and expenses, accountants must estimate the bad debts expense because the specific accounts that will be uncollectible may not be known until a later accounting period.

Recording Estimated Bad Debts Expense Under the Allowance Method

The allowance method receives its name because the end-of-period adjusting entry credits a contra-asset account called the *Allowance for Doubtful Accounts*. The allowance method not only matches credit losses with the related credit sales in the same time period in which the sale occurs, but it also reports accounts receivable at their estimated realizable value in the end-of-period balance sheet. To illustrate, assume that the Claremont Corporation estimates its bad debts expense for 2016 to be $1,600 and makes the following adjusting entry in its general journal:

2016			
Dec. 31	Bad debts expense	1,600	
	Allowance for doubtful accounts		1,600
	To record the bad debts expense for the year.		

A = L + SE
−1,600   −1,600
             Exp

Notice that the credit entry is made to the **Allowance for Doubtful Accounts** rather than directly against the Accounts Receivable account. The reason for this is because when a firm records its estimate of the amount of its uncollectible accounts, it does not know precisely which of its customer accounts will be uncollectible.

> **A.K.A.** The Allowance for Doubtful Accounts is also often referred to as the *Allowance for Uncollectible Accounts*.

The Allowance for Doubtful Accounts is a contra-asset account with a normal credit balance. To report the expected collectible amount of accounts receivable on the balance sheet, the Allowance for Doubtful Accounts is subtracted from the Accounts Receivable account. Assuming that the Claremont Corporation had $100,000 of accounts receivable (and a zero balance in the Allowance for Doubtful Accounts prior to the December 31, 2016, adjusting entry), the year-end balance sheet presentation would appear as follows:

Current Assets		
Cash		$ 52,000
Accounts receivable	$100,000	
Less: Allowance for doubtful accounts	1,600	
Accounts receivable, net		98,400
Inventory		125,000
Other current assets		31,000
Total Current Assets		$306,400

The Allowance for Doubtful Accounts of $1,600 is subtracted from the $100,000 of Accounts Receivable to obtain the net realizable value of $98,400. In other words, customers owe Claremont Corporation $100,000 but Claremont does not expect to collect $1,600 of this amount. Instead, Claremont only expects to collect $98,400, referred to as the net balance of Accounts Receivable.

Going Concern Concept

PRINCIPLE ALERT

Accounts receivable are reported on the balance sheet at the amount that a company expects to collect in the future from its credit customers. This presentation assumes that the company will be in existence long enough to collect its accounts receivable, and therefore, it is an example of the *going concern concept*. As a principle of accounting, the going concern concept assumes that a business entity will continue to operate indefinitely in the future.

Writing Off Specific Accounts Receivable under the Allowance Method

A company's credit department manager is usually the employee with the authority to determine when an account receivable is uncollectible, and hence, when a specific account receivable should be written off and removed from a company's balance sheet. This might occur, for example, if the customer has not made any payments on its account for a specified period of time, say four months, or if the customer has declared bankruptcy. Assume, for example, that the credit manager of the Claremont Corporation authorizes a $300 write off of the Monroe Company's account receivable. When the accounting department is notified of the credit department manager's decision, it will make the following journal entry:

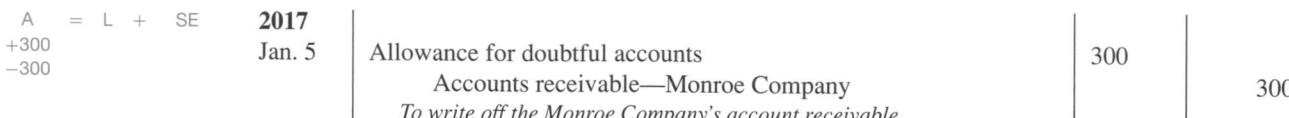

A	=	L	+	SE			
+300					**2017**		
−300					Jan. 5	Allowance for doubtful accounts	300
						Accounts receivable—Monroe Company		300
						To write off the Monroe Company's account receivable.	

The journal entry to write off an account receivable does not affect a company's net income or total assets. By means of the year-end adjusting entry, the bad debts expense is reported in the period when the related sales revenue is recorded. Because the Allowance for Doubtful Accounts is deducted from the Accounts Receivable account on the balance sheet, the *net* realizable value of accounts receivable is unchanged by the account write off. After the Monroe Company's account receivable has been written off, the Accounts Receivable and the Allowance for Doubtful Accounts T-accounts of Claremont Corporation appear as follows:

Accounts Receivable			
Beg.	100,000	300	Jan. 5
Bal.	99,700		

Allowance for Doubtful Accounts			
Jan. 5	300	1,600	Beg.
		1,300	Bal.

As can be seen in the above T-accounts, the net realizable value of Claremont's accounts receivable as of January 1, 2017, is $98,400 ($100,000 less $1,600 allowance for doubtful accounts). Following the January 5, 2017, account write-off, the net realizable value of the Claremont Corporation's accounts receivable remains $98,400 ($99,700 less $1,300 allowance for doubtful accounts) since both the Accounts Receivable account and the Allowance for Doubtful Accounts are reduced by the same amount ($300). The following table summarizes the allowance method.

Action	Journal Entry	Balance Sheet Effect (Increase/Decrease)	Income Statement Effect (Increase/Decrease)
Recording Estimated Bad Debts Expense (In period when sale occurred)	**DEBIT** Bad debts expense **CREDIT** Allowance for doubtful accounts	⬆ Allowance for doubtful accounts ⬇ Accounts receivable, net	⬆ Bad debts expense ⬇ Net income
Writing-Off Bad Debt (When receivable is determined uncollectible)	**DEBIT** Allowance for doubtful accounts **CREDIT** Accounts receivable	⬇ Accounts receivable ⬇ Allowance for doubtful accounts No Change Accounts receivable, net	**No Change**

| Balance Sheet Title for Uncollectible Accounts | ACCOUNTING IN PRACTICE |

No doubt about it, not all receivables will be collected! So how should a company title the amount that they likely will be unable to collect? Allowance for Doubtful Accounts is the most common account title, although several other titles are also used, as can be seen from a survey of 600 large U.S. companies:

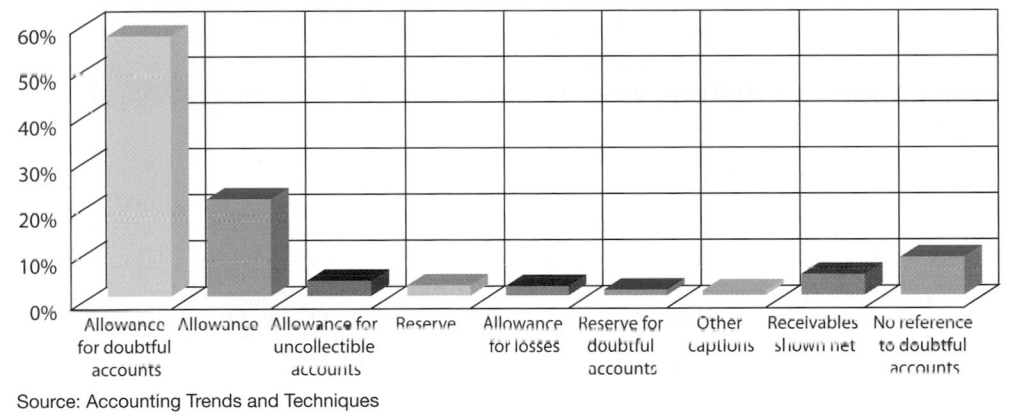

Source: Accounting Trends and Techniques

YOUR TURN! 8.1

The solution is on page 423.

Provide journal entries for the following transactions for the Turner Company:

May   2   Sold $40,000 of merchandise on account
May 17   Collected $35,000 of the May 2nd sale
May 31   Estimated $500 of the remaining accounts receivable may not be collected
June 15   Wrote off $200 of the existing accounts receivable

ESTIMATING CREDIT LOSSES

LO2 Describe and **illustrate** the percentage of net sales method and the accounts receivable aging method for estimating a business's bad debts expense.

When the allowance method is used, estimates of a company's expected credit losses are generally based on past business experience, with additional consideration given to forecasts of future sales activity, economic conditions, and any planned changes to a company's credit-granting policy. The most commonly used estimates of expected credit losses are related either to a company's credit sales for the period, or to the amount of accounts receivable outstanding at the end of a fiscal period. Companies may estimate credit losses using one or both methods, and a variety of different assumptions, before deciding on the best estimate that will be recorded in the financial statements.

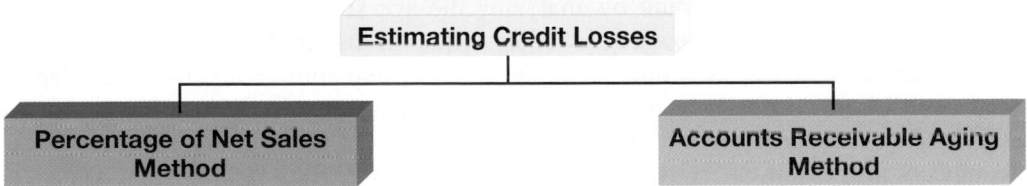

Percentage of Net Sales Method

Some companies estimate their expected credit losses as a percentage of their credit sales for a given period. Under this approach, the amount of the end-of-period adjusting entry for a business's expected bad debts expense is determined by multiplying the company's total credit sales for the period by a historical percentage that reflects past credit losses. For example, suppose that credit sales for 2016 for the Claremont Corporation are $80,000 and that past experience indicates that the company is likely to sustain a two percent loss on its credit sales. The adjusting entry for Claremont's expected credit losses of $1,600 for 2016 (2 percent × $80,000) would be recorded as follows in the general journal:

A	=	L	+	SE				
−1,600				−1,600 Exp				

2016			
Dec. 31	Bad debts expense	1,600	
	Allowance for doubtful accounts		1,600
	To record the bad debts expense for the year.		

Because the periodic estimate for doubtful accounts under this procedure is related to credit sales, a firm should review its allowance account regularly to ensure that the account maintains a reasonable balance. If the allowance account balance is too large or too small, and does not reflect the amount the company thinks will prove uncollectible, the percentage used to estimate the periodic credit losses should be revised accordingly.

A company that uses the **percentage of net sales method** usually applies the estimated uncollectible percentage only to its credit sales, excluding cash sales, since only credit sales are subject to credit losses. Further, any sales discounts and sales returns and allowances should be deducted from total credit sales before applying the historical uncollectible percentage.

YOUR TURN! 8.2

The solution is on page 423.

Taylor Company estimates three percent of its $600,000 credit sales will prove uncollectible. What journal entry will Taylor Company use to record this estimate?

Accounts Receivable Aging Method

A second approach to estimating a company's bad debts expense is to determine the appropriate balance for the Allowance for Doubtful Accounts account at year-end, and then determine the appropriate estimate of the bad debts expense necessary to achieve this balance. The year-end balance in the Allowance for Doubtful Accounts represents a firm's estimate of the year-end accounts receivable that will prove uncollectible. By comparing this year-end estimate to the balance in the Allowance account just prior to making the adjustment for bad debts, it is possible to indirectly determine the appropriate current period estimate of the company's bad debts expense. This approach is called the **accounts receivable aging method**.

When using the accounts receivable aging method, a company determines the amount needed in the allowance account by analyzing the age structure of its outstanding accounts receivable balances. An aging schedule similar to the one in **Exhibit 8-1** would be used. An **aging schedule** is simply an analysis that reveals how much time has elapsed since a credit sale originally occurred, and consequently, how long a customer's account receivable has remained unpaid. Assume, for example, that the firm whose aging schedule appears in **Exhibit 8-1** sells its goods on credit with a credit period of 30 days. The exhibit reveals that the Alton account is current, which means that the $320 billing was made within the last 30 days; however, the Bailey account is 0–30 days *past due,* which means that the account receivable is from 31 to 60 days old. The aging schedule also reveals that the Wall balance consists of a $50 billing made from 91 to 150 days ago and a $100 billing made from 151 days to seven months ago, and so on.

| Exhibit 8-1 | Aging Schedule of Customer Balances, December 31, 2016 | | | | | | |

| | | | Past Due | | | | |
Customer	Account Balance	Current	0–30 Days	31–60 Days	61–120 Days	121 Days to 6 Mos.	Over 6 Mos.
Alton, J.	320	$ 320					
Bailey, C.	400		$ 400				
many more accts . . .	...	...	...	...	...	...	...
Wall, M..	150					50	100
Zorn, W.	210			210			
	$50,000	$42,000	$4,000	$2,000	$1,000	$800	$200

Companies that analyze their uncollectible accounts experience using aged account balances develop probability-of-collection percentages to correspond with each age category. The probability of collection is subtracted from 100 percent to arrive at the probability of noncollection. At the end of each period, the probability-of-noncollection percentages are applied to the totals of each age category to determine the appropriate allowance account balance for a given category. For our example, these percentages are shown in the table below. As one might expect, the estimated probability of noncollection increases as the number of days past due increases. Applying the percentages to the totals in our aging schedule, we can calculate the required balance for the Allowance for Doubtful Accounts—that is, $1,560:

	Amount	Probability of Noncollection	Allowance Required
Current	$42,000	2%	$ 840
0–30 days past due	4,000	3%	120
31–60 days past due	2,000	5%	100
61–120 days past due	1,000	20%	200
121-180 days past due	800	25%	200
Over 180 days past due.	200	50%	100
Total allowance required.			$1,560

Since the aging method is just an estimation process, estimation errors are likely to occur, causing the allowance account to sometimes be over or underestimated. If, for example, the Allowance for Doubtful Accounts has an existing $400 credit balance (implying an overestimation error in the prior period), the year-end adjusting entry is:

2016			
Dec. 31	Bad debts expense	1,160	
	Allowance for doubtful accounts		1,160
	To record the bad debts expense for the period.		

A = L + SE
−1,160   −1,160
                  Exp

This entry brings the credit balance in the Allowance for Doubtful Accounts account to the required amount—$1,560, as shown below:

Allowance for Doubtful Accounts

	400	Beg.
	1,160	Dec. 31
	1,560	Bal.

Hint: In contrast to the percentage of net sales method, the accounts receivable aging method takes into account the beginning balance of the Allowance for Doubtful Accounts.

It is also possible to have a debit balance in the allowance account before the year-end adjustment, implying an underestimation error in the prior period. This would occur whenever the write-off of specific accounts receivable during the year exceeded the credit balance in the account as of the beginning of the year. Assume, for example, that the Allowance for Doubtful Accounts had a $350 debit balance prior to the recording of the December 31, 2016, adjusting entry, and that the aging schedule showed that the allowance account should have a $1,560 credit balance. The year-end adjusting entry would then be as follows:

A	=	L	+	SE			
−1,910				−1,910 Exp			

2016
Dec. 31	Bad debts expense	1,910	
	Allowance for doubtful accounts		1,910
	To record the bad debts expense for the period.		

The following Allowance for Doubtful Accounts T-account shows that this entry creates the desired year-end credit balance in the allowance account of $1,560:

Allowance for Doubtful Accounts			
Beg.	350	1,910	Dec. 31
		1,560	Bal.

THINKING GLOBALLY

Just when an account receivable is judged to be uncollectible is very much a cultural issue. In some Central and South American countries, buying goods and services on credit is almost unheard of! In these countries, it is considered in bad taste to owe someone money, and consequently, to preserve a company's good reputation and standing in the business community, companies pay cash for their purchases and avoid buying goods and services on credit. Therefore, in these countries it is extremely rare to see accounts receivable on the financial statements of businesses. In the United States, on the other hand, buying goods and services on credit is considered to be a normal business activity. In fact, a business manager would be chastised for failing to take advantage of any offered trade credit by paying cash for purchased goods or services. In the United States, most large businesses consider an account receivable to be uncollectible when it becomes 120 days old. Buying goods and services on credit in China is, likewise, quite common; however, buyers often take several years to pay for purchased goods, and consequently, accounts receivable are not considered to be uncollectible until 2 to 3 years have elapsed since the original credit sales transaction.

TAKEAWAY 8.1

Concept	➝ Method	➝ Assessment
Are the accounts receivable being collected in a timely manner?	List of accounts receivable along with how long they have been outstanding. Prepare an aging schedule.	Accounts in the older categories require additional collection attention.

Recoveries of Accounts Written Off under the Allowance Method Occasionally, an account written off against the allowance for doubtful accounts as uncollectible will later prove to be wholly or partially collectible. In such situations, a firm must first reinstate the customer's account receivable for the amount recovered before recording the collection of cash. Then the cash payment can be recorded in the customer's account. The journal entry made for the original account write-off is reversed to the extent of the recovery amount and the receipt of cash is recorded in the usual manner. For example, assume that the Claremont Corporation is using the allowance method and wrote off the Monroe Company's $300 account on January 5, 2017, but subsequently received a $200 payment on April 20, 2017. The following journal entries (including write-off) illustrate the recovery procedure:

To write off the account

2017				A = L + SE
Jan. 5	Allowance for doubtful accounts	300		+300
	Accounts receivable—Monroe Company		300	−300
	To write off the Monroe Company's account.			

To reinstate the account

Apr. 20	Accounts receivable—Monroe Company	200		A = L + SE
	Allowance for doubtful accounts		200	+200
	To reinstate the Monroe Company's account to the extent of the recovery.			−200

To record receipt of cash

Apr. 20	Cash	200		A = L + SE
	Accounts receivable—Monroe Company		200	+200
	To record collection of cash on account.			−200

These last two journal entries are prepared the same way even if the recovery occurs more than a year following the period in which the account was originally written off.

Lapping

FORENSIC ACCOUNTING

One type of fraud that forensic accountants are trained to detect is "lapping." Lapping is not actually a fraud, but rather is a technique that a fraudster uses to cover up a fraud, typically involving the theft of funds. Under lapping, an employee who has access to incoming payments from the collection of accounts receivables will steal some of the cash received from credit customers. The employee then applies another customer's payment to the outstanding balance from the individual's account whose payment was stolen to cover up the theft. The process is repeated in an effort to cover up the original misappropriation. In other words, after the initial theft, the fraudster must continually "rob Peter to pay Paul." One audit procedure that may detect a lapping scheme involves the confirmation of accounts receivable. As part of the year-end independent audit, or as part of a regular internal audit, a company's accountant will send out confirmation letters to a sample of customers from the list of outstanding accounts receivable and pay particular attention to replies from customers disputing the timing of their payments.

Phisher, Inc., analyzed its accounts receivable at the end of 2015, and arrived at the aged balances listed below, along with the percentage that is estimated to be uncollectible:

Age Group	Balance	Estimated Loss Percentage
0–30 days past due	$100,000	1
31–60 days past due	15,000	3
61–120 days past due	10,000	5
Over 120 days past due	20,000	10
	$145,000	

The company handles credit losses with the allowance method. The company has an existing credit balance in the Allowance account of $750.

a. Prepare the adjusting entry for estimated credit losses on December 31, 2015.
b. Prepare the journal entry to write off Phorest Company's account on May 12, 2016, in the amount of $480.

YOUR TURN! 8.3

The solution is on page 423.

CREDIT CARD SALES

LO3 Discuss the accounting treatment of credit card sales.

Many businesses, especially retailers, allow their customers to use credit cards for their purchase transactions. Popular credit cards include VISA, MasterCard, Discover, and American Express. When a customer uses a credit card to make a purchase, the seller collects cash from the credit card company, and the customer pays cash to the credit card company when billed at a later date. To facilitate this process, the seller prepares a sales slip using the credit card.

The issuer of a credit card, frequently a financial institution like **Chase Bank** or **Citibank**, will charge the seller a fee each time a card is used. The **credit card fee** usually ranges from one percent to five percent of the amount of the credit card purchase. Businesses are willing to incur this fee because credit cards provide considerable benefits to a seller. For example, the seller does not have to evaluate the creditworthiness of the customer using a credit card, and the business avoids any risk of noncollection of the account since this risk remains with the credit card issuer. Finally, the seller typically receives the cash from the credit card issuer faster than if the customer were granted trade credit by the seller.

Depending upon the type of credit card, there are two ways that a seller may collect from the credit card issuer: (1) immediately upon deposit of the credit card sales slip or (2) on a delayed basis after the credit card slips have been processed by the credit card issuer. For cards issued by a financial institution, cash is received immediately upon deposit of the sales slip at the financial institution. The journal entry to record a $1,000 credit card sale of this type on March 15, with a three percent credit card fee, is as follows:

A = L + SE				
+970 −30 Exp	Mar. 15	Cash	970	
+1,000		Credit card fee expense	30	
Rev		Sales revenue		1,000
		To record credit card sales and collection, less a three percent fee.		

If sales slips are instead sent to a credit card company for subsequent cash settlement, the journal entries to record the $1,000 credit card sale with subsequent collection on March 23 are as follows:

A = L + SE				
+970 −30 Exp	Mar. 15	Accounts receivable—Credit Card Company	970	
+1,000		Credit card fee expense	30	
Rev		Sales revenue		1,000
		To record credit card sales.		

A = L + SE				
+970	Mar. 23	Cash	970	
−970		Accounts receivable—Credit Card Company		970
		To record collection from credit card company.		

YOUR TURN! 8.4

The solution is on page 423.

Nafooz Company pays a two percent credit card fee on all credit sales, and receives a cash deposit immediately following each credit card transaction. If credit sales for the company total $50,000, what journal entry should be recorded to recognize the receipt of cash and the credit card fee expense?

NOTES RECEIVABLE

Promissory notes receivable are often used in sale transactions when the credit period is longer than the 30 to 60 day credit period that is typical for accounts receivable. Promissory notes are also used frequently in sales involving equipment and property because the dollar amount of these transactions can be quite large. Occasionally, a note will be substituted for an account receivable when an extension of the usual credit period is granted. Also, promissory notes are normally prepared when financial institutions make a loan to a business or an individual.

LO4 Illustrate a promissory note receivable, **discuss** the calculation of interest on notes receivable, and **present** journal entries to record notes receivable and interest.

A **promissory note** is a written promise to pay a certain sum of money on demand or at a fixed (or determinable) future date. The note is signed by the **maker** and made payable to the order of either a specific **payee** or to the **bearer**. The interest rate specified on the note is typically an annual rate. **Exhibit 8-2** illustrates a promissory note.

Exhibit 8-2	A Promissory Note

$2,000.00   Los Angeles, CA   May 3, 2016

Sixty days _____   after date   I promise to pay to

the order of _____   Susan Robinson

Two thousand and no/100 · dollars

for value received with interest at _____ 9% _____

payable at   First Bank of Los Angeles, CA

_____ James Stone ·

A note from a debtor is called a **note receivable** by the noteholder. A note is usually regarded as a stronger claim against a debtor than an account receivable because the terms of payment are specified in writing.

Interest on Notes Receivable

Interest is a charge for the use of money over time. Interest incurred on a promissory note receivable is interest income to the noteholder or payee of the note and interest expense to the maker of the note. Businesses are required to distinguish between operating and nonoperating items in their income statements; consequently, they place any interest expense or interest income on outstanding notes under the other income and expense heading in the income statement so that financial statement users will readily identify interest income or expense as being nonoperating in nature.

Interest on a short-term promissory note is paid at the maturity date of the note. The formula for determining the amount of interest expense to the maker and interest income to the noteholder is as follows:

$$\textbf{Interest} = \textbf{Principal} \times \textbf{Interest rate} \times \textbf{Interest time}$$

The principal is the face amount of a note; and, the interest rate is the annual rate of interest specified in the note agreement. Interest time is the fraction of a year that a note receivable is outstanding.

When a note is written for a certain number of months, interest time is expressed in twelfths of a year. For example, interest on a six-month note for $2,000 with a nine percent annual interest rate is calculated as:

$$\textbf{Interest} = \textbf{\$2,000} \times \textbf{0.09} \times \textbf{6/12} = \textbf{\$90}$$

When a note's duration, or time to maturity, is given in days, interest time is expressed as a fraction of a year; the numerator is the number of days that the note receivable will be outstanding and the denominator is 360 days. (Some lenders use 360 days, while others use 365 days; we use 360 days in our examples, exercises, and problems.) For example, interest on a 60 day note for $2,000 with a nine percent annual interest rate is:

$$\textbf{Interest} = \textbf{\$2,000} \times \textbf{0.09} \times \textbf{60/360} = \textbf{\$30}$$

Determining Maturity Date

When a note's duration is expressed in days, it is customary to count the exact number of days in each calendar month to determine the note's **maturity date**. For example, a 90 day note dated July 21 has an October 19 maturity date, which is determined as follows:

10	days in July (remainder of month—31 days minus 21 days)
31	days in August
30	days in September
19	days in October (number of days required to total 90)
90	

If the duration of a note is expressed in months, the maturity date is calculated simply by counting the number of months from the date of issue. For example, a two-month note dated January 31 would mature on March 31, a three-month note of the same date would mature on April 30 (the last day of the month), and a four-month note would mature on May 31.

Recording Notes Receivable and Interest

When a note is exchanged to settle an account receivable, a journal entry is made to reflect the note receivable and to reduce the balance of the related account receivable. For example, suppose that Jordon Company sold $12,000 of merchandise on account to Bowman Company. On October 1, after the regular credit period had elapsed, the Bowman Company gave the Jordon Company a 60 day, nine percent note receivable for $12,000. Jordon Company makes the following journal entry to record receiving the note:

A = L + SE
+12,000
−12,000

Oct. 1	Notes receivable—Bowman Company	12,000	
	Accounts receivable—Bowman Company		12,000
	Received 60 day, nine percent note in payment of account.		

If the Bowman Company pays its note receivable on the November 30 maturity date, the Jordon Company makes the following journal entry:

A = L + SE
+12,180   +180
                Rev
−12,000

Nov. 30	Cash	12,180	
	Interest income		180
	Notes receivable—Bowman Company		12,000
	Collected Bowman Company note. ($12,000 × 0.09 × 60/360 = $180).		

Recording Dishonored Notes

In the prior example, interest for 60 days at nine percent is recorded on the maturity date of the note even if the maker of the note (Bowman Company) defaults on or dishonors the note. When a note is dishonored at maturity, the amount of the combined principal plus interest is converted to an account receivable. This procedure leaves only the current, unmatured notes in the noteholder's Notes Receivable account. If the Bowman Company, for example, failed to pay its note on November 30 as expected, the Jordon Company would make the following journal entry:

Nov. 30	Accounts receivable—Bowman Company	12,180	
	Interest income		180
	Notes receivable—Bowman Company		12,000
	To record the dishonoring of a note by Bowman Company.		

A = L + SE
+180 Rev
+12,180
−12,000

Adjusting Entry for Interest

When the term of a promissory note extends beyond the end of an accounting period, a year-end adjusting entry is necessary to reflect the interest earned. To illustrate, assume that Jordon Company has a note receivable outstanding at December 31, 2016. The note receivable from the Garcia Company is dated December 21, 2016, has a principal amount of $6,000, an interest rate of 12 percent, and a maturity date of February 19, 2017. The adjusting entry that Jordon Company makes at December 31, 2016, to record the earned, but uncollected, interest income is as follows:

Dec. 31 Ⓐ	Interest receivable	20	
	Interest income		20
	To accrue interest income on the note from Garcia Company		
	($6,000 × 0.12 × 10/360 = $20).		

A = L + SE
+20   +20 Rev

When the note is subsequently paid on February 19, 2017, Jordon Company makes the following journal entry:

Feb. 19 Ⓑ	Cash	6,120	
	Interest income		100
	Interest receivable		20
	Notes receivable—Garcia Company		6,000
	Received payment of principal and interest from Garcia Company		
	($6,000 × 0.12 × 50/360 − $100).		

A = L + SE
+6,120   +100 Rev
−20
−6,000

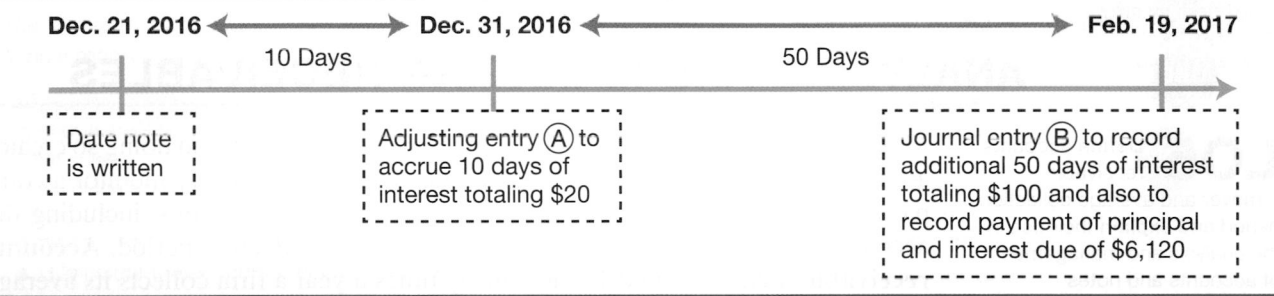

Dec. 21, 2016 ← 10 Days → **Dec. 31, 2016** ← 50 Days → **Feb. 19, 2017**

Date note is written

Adjusting entry Ⓐ to accrue 10 days of interest totaling $20

Journal entry Ⓑ to record additional 50 days of interest totaling $100 and also to record payment of principal and interest due of $6,120

PRINCIPLE ALERT

Revenue Recognition Principle

The adjusting entry to accrue interest income on an outstanding promissory note receivable at year-end illustrates the *revenue recognition principle*. This principle states that revenue should be recognized when services are performed or goods are sold. The holder of a promissory note provides the maker of the note with a service—the use of money for a specified time period. This service is provided each day that a note is outstanding and interest is the payment for this service. Interest income is not recorded each day. Normally, interest income for a note's full term is recorded when it is collected at the note's maturity. If the accounting period ends before a note's maturity date, an adjusting entry is made to record the accrued interest income for the services provided in the current period.

Dec. 31	Bad debts expense	4,700
	Allowance for doubtful accounts	4,700
	To provide for bad debts expense	
	($4,500 desired balance + $200 existing debit balance = $4,700).	

Allowance for Doubtful Accounts	
Beginning balance	($1,200)
Bad Debts Expense, 12/31/2015	(3,750)
Write-offs ($2,850 + $1,450 + $1,300) . . .	5,600
Recovery	(450)
Bad Debts Expense, 12/31/2015	(4,700)
Ending Balance	($4,500)

APPENDIX 8A: Direct Write-Off Method

LO6 **Illustrate** the direct write-off method and **contrast** it with the allowance method for accounting for doubtful accounts.

The direct write-off method of accounting for credit losses is an alternative to the allowance method. Under the **direct write-off method**, doubtful accounts are charged to the bad debts expense on the income statement in the period in which the accounts are determined to be uncollectible. Under this approach, there is no attempt to estimate the bad debts expense, nor is there any attempt to match this expense with sales revenues in the period in which the credit sales transaction originally occurred. As a consequence, U.S. GAAP does not permit the use of the direct write-off method unless the amount of the credit losses is immaterial. The reason for this is because the direct write-off method does not properly match credit losses with credit sales in the appropriate time period, violating the matching concept.

For example, an account receivable may not be determined to be uncollectible, and therefore written off, until several periods after the actual credit sales revenue is recorded. By way of contrast, the allowance method, through the use of an estimate of the bad debts expense, properly matches this expense with the associated sales revenue in the same period. The use of the direct write-off method also causes a consistent overstatement of accounts receivable on the balance sheet. Although not generally accepted for accounting purposes for most businesses, the direct write-off method is used by all companies for U.S. federal income tax purposes.

The journal entries made when the direct write-off method is used are illustrated below using data from the Claremont Corporation illustration appearing on pages 390-391:

To write off the account

A = L + SE
−300   −300 Exp

2017			
Jan. 5	Bad debts expense	300	
	Accounts receivable—Monroe Company		300
	To write off the Monroe Company's account.		

To reinstate the account

A = L + SE
+200   +200 Exp

Apr. 20	Accounts receivable—Monroe Company	200	
	Bad debts expense		200
	To reinstate the Monroe Company's account to the extent of the recovery.		

To record receipt of cash

A = L + SE
+200
−200

Apr. 20	Cash	200	
	Accounts receivable—Monroe Company		200
	To record collection of cash on account.		

If an account receivable written off in a prior year is reinstated during the current year and the Bad Debts Expense account has no existing balance from other write-offs (and no more write-offs are expected), then the account credited in the reinstatement entry is the Doubtful Accounts Recovery, a revenue account.

YOUR TURN! 8A.1

The solution is on page 423.

Harley Company has determined an account receivable in the amount of $750 from Rhea Inc. will be uncollectible and has decided to write the account off. Harley Company uses the direct write-off method because write-offs are considered immaterial. Provide the journal entry to write off the Rhea account.

SUMMARY OF LEARNING OBJECTIVES

Define accounts receivable, explain losses from uncollectible accounts, and describe the allowance method of accounting for doubtful accounts. (p. 382) **LO1**

- Accounts receivable is a current asset created when a sales transaction is executed on a credit basis.
- Accounts receivable does not include such receivables as loans to affiliate companies or advances to employees.
- The credit department of a company is responsible for conducting credit investigations of customers, establishing credit limits, and following up on overdue accounts.
- The allowance method is designed to record the bad debts expense in the same accounting period as the related credit sale.
- When the allowance method is used, specific accounts are written off by debiting the Allowance for Doubtful Accounts and crediting the Accounts Receivable account.

Describe and illustrate the percentage of net sales method and the accounts receivable aging method for estimating a business's bad debts expense. (p. 387) **LO2**

- The percentage of net sales method is used to determine estimated credit losses directly. Estimated credit losses are determined by multiplying credit sales (net of any sales discounts and sales returns and allowances) times the estimated percentage of uncollectible credit sales.
- The accounts receivable aging method determines the estimated credit loss indirectly. The balance in the Accounts Receivable account is segmented into age categories. Then the balance of each category is multiplied by the estimated uncollectible percentage for that age category. The results are added to obtain the desired balance in the Allowance for Doubtful Accounts. The desired balance is then compared to the existing balance in the Allowance for Doubtful Accounts to determine the estimated credit losses and bad debts expense for the period.
- Occasionally, accounts written off against the Allowance for Doubtful Accounts later prove to be wholly or partially collectible. When this happens, the Accounts Receivable account is first reinstated to the extent of the recovery, and then the cash collection is recorded.

Discuss the accounting treatment of credit card sales. (p. 392) **LO3**

- The credit card issuer can reimburse the merchant accepting the credit card immediately upon deposit of any sales slips or subsequently after processing the sales slips.
- In both situations, the credit card fee expense is recognized when the credit card sales slips are remitted to the credit card issuer.

Illustrate a promissory note receivable, discuss the calculation of interest on notes receivable, and present journal entries to record notes receivable and interest. (p. 393) **LO4**

- Interest on a short-term promissory note is determined using the following formula:

$$\text{Interest} = \text{Principal} \times \text{Interest rate} \times \text{Interest time}$$

- When a note is received in payment of an account receivable balance, the Notes Receivable account is debited and the Accounts Receivable account is credited.
- The noteholder recognizes interest income at the maturity date or in an end-of-period adjusting entry if the financial statements are prepared before the note matures.

Define *accounts receivable turnover* and *average collection period* and explain their use in the analysis and management of accounts and notes receivable. (p. 396) **LO5**

- Accounts receivable turnover = Net sales/Average accounts receivable
- Average collection period = 365/Accounts receivable turnover
- *Accounts receivable turnover* indicates how many times a year, on average, that a firm collects its accounts receivable. *Average collection period* indicates how many days it takes, on average, to collect an account receivable.

Appendix 8A: Illustrate the direct write-off method and contrast it with the allowance method for accounting for doubtful accounts. (p. 400) **LO6**

- Under the direct write-off method, uncollectible accounts are charged to the bad debts expense in the period in which they are determined to be uncollectible.

- For most companies, the direct write-off method is not a generally accepted method of accounting for credit losses; however, most companies use the direct write-off method for income tax purposes.
- U.S. GAAP does not permit the use of the direct write-off method unless the amount of the credit losses is immaterial.

SUMMARY	Concept ⟶	Method ⟶	Assessment
TAKEAWAY 8.1	Are the accounts receivable being collected in a timely manner?	List of accounts receivable along with how long they have been outstanding. Prepare an aging schedule.	Accounts in the older categories require additional collection attention.
TAKEAWAY 8.2	Are any of the existing accounts receivable in need of further attention?	Net sales and average accounts receivable $\text{Accounts receivable turnover} = \dfrac{\text{Net sales}}{\text{Average accounts receivable}}$ $\text{Average collection period} = \dfrac{365}{\text{Accounts receivable turnover}}$	Compare the average collection period to the company credit policy. Longer collection periods suggest the need for management attention.

KEY TERMS

Accounts receivable (trade receivable) (p. 382)

Accounts receivable aging method (p. 388)

Accounts receivable turnover (p. 396)

Aging schedule (p. 388)

Allowance for Doubtful Accounts (Allowance for Uncollectible Accounts) (p. 385)

Allowance method (p. 384)

Average collection period (p. 397)

Bad Debts Expense (Provision for Bad Debts) (p. 384)

Bearer (p. 393)

Corporate Social Responsibility (p. 396)

Credit card fee (p. 392)

Credit-collection policy (p. 383)

Credit-granting policy (p. 383)

Direct write-off method (p. 400)

Discounting (p. 397)

Factoring (p. 397)

Factors (p. 397)

Maker (p. 393)

Maturity date (p. 394)

Note receivable (p. 393)

Payee (p. 393)

Percentage of net sales method (p. 388)

Promissory note (p. 393)

Assignments with the ⬤ logo in the margin are available in BusinessCourse.
See the Preface of the book for details.

SELF-STUDY QUESTIONS

(Answers to the Self-Study Questions are available at the end of this chapter.)

LO1, 2   1. A firm, using the allowance method of recording credit losses, wrote off a customer's account in the amount of $500. Later, the customer paid the account. The firm reinstated the account by means of a journal entry and then recorded the collection. What is the result of these procedures?
   a. Increases total assets by $500
   b. Decreases total assets by $500
   c. Decreases total assets by $1,000
   d. Has no effect on total assets

LO2   2. A firm has accounts receivable of $90,000 and a debit balance of $900 in the Allowance for Doubtful Accounts. Two-thirds of the accounts receivable are current and one-third is past due. The firm estimates that two percent of the current accounts and five percent of the past due accounts will prove to be uncollectible. The adjusting entry to provide for the bad debts expense under the aging method should be for what amount?
   a. $2,700   c. $1,800
   b. $3,600   d. $4,500

3. A firm receives a six-month note from a customer. The note has a face amount of $4,000 and an interest rate of nine percent. What is the total amount of interest to be received?   **LO4**
   a. $1,080
   b. $30
   c. $360
   d. $180

4. A business has net sales of $60,000, a beginning balance in Accounts Receivable of $5,000, and an ending balance in Accounts Receivable of $7,000. What is the company's accounts receivable turnover?   **LO5**
   a. 10.0
   b. 12.0
   c. 8.6
   d. 9.2

5. A business has an accounts receivable turnover of ten. What is the company's average collection period?   **LO5**
   a. 36.0
   b. 30.8
   c. 34.6
   d. 36.5

6. Miller Company received a 90 day, six percent note receivable for $10,000 on December 1. How much interest should be accrued on December 31?   **LO4**
   a. $150
   b. $90
   c. $50
   d. $25

7. Smith Company uses the allowance method to record its expected credit losses. It estimates its losses at one percent of credit sales, which were $750,000 during the year. The Accounts Receivable balance was $220,000 and the Allowance for Doubtful Accounts had a credit balance of $1,000 at year-end. What amount is the debit to the Bad Debts Expense?   **LO1, 2**
   a. $7,500
   b. $8,500
   c. $6,500
   d. $3,200

8. Rankine & Company pays a three percent credit card fee on all credit sales, and receives a cash deposit immediately following each credit card transaction. If credit sales for the company total $15,000 on December 13, what journal entry should be recorded to recognize the receipt of cash and the credit card fee expense?   **LO3**
   a. Debit Cash $14,550; debit Credit Card Fee Expense $450.
   b. Debit Cash $15,000; credit Credit Card Fee Expense $450.
   c. Debit Cash $15,450; debit Credit Card Fee Expense $450.
   d. Debit Cash $15,450; credit Credit Card Fee Expense $450.

9. Which of the following statements is true?   **LO1, 2, 6**
   a. The direct write-off method is generally accepted.
   b. The percentage of net sales method estimates the bad debts expense indirectly.
   c. The accounts receivable aging method estimates the bad debts expense indirectly.
   d. None of the above is true.

10. On September 1, the Pavoreal Company accepted a $24,000, 60 day, nine percent, promissory note in exchange for overdue accounts receivable balance for the same amount from the Wagner Company. On November 30, the Wagner Company dishonored the note. What journal entry should be recorded on November 30?   **LO4**
    a. Debit Dishonored Note Receivable Expense; credit Notes Receivable.
    b. Debit Allowance for Doubtful Accounts; credit Notes Receivable.
    c. Debit Accounts Receivable; credit Interest Income; credit Notes Receivable.
    d. None of the above entries is correct.

QUESTIONS

1. In dealing with receivables, what do the terms *factoring* and *discounting* mean?

2. How does a credit scoring system work?

3. How do the allowance method and the direct write-off method of handling credit losses differ with respect to the timing of bad debts expense recognition?

4. When a firm provides for credit losses under the allowance method, why is the Allowance for Doubtful Accounts credited rather than Accounts Receivable?

5. What are the two most commonly used methods of estimating the bad debts expense when the allowance method is employed? Describe them.

6. Murphy Company estimates its bad debts expense by aging its accounts receivable and applying percentages to various age groups of the accounts. Murphy calculated a total of $2,100 in possible credit losses as of December 31. Accounts Receivable has a balance of $98,000, and the Allowance for Doubtful Accounts has a credit balance of $500 before adjustment at December 31. What is the December 31 adjusting entry to provide for credit losses? What is the net amount of accounts receivable that should be included in current assets?

7. On June 15, 2015, Rollins, Inc. sold $750 worth of merchandise to Dell Company. On November 20, 2015, Rollins, Inc., wrote off Dell's account. On March 10, 2016, Dell Company paid the account in full. What are the journal entries that Rollins, Inc. should make for the write-off and the recovery assuming that Rollins, Inc., uses (a) the allowance method of handling credit losses and (b) the direct write-off method?

8. Wood Company sold a $675 refrigerator to a customer who charged the sale using a VISA credit card. Wood Company deposits credit card sales slips daily; cash is deposited in Wood Company's checking account at the same time. Wood Company's bank charges a credit card fee of four percent of sales revenue. What journal entry should Wood Company make to record the sale?

9. Volter Inc. received a 60 day, nine percent note for $15,000 on March 5 from a customer. What is the maturity date of the note?

10. Stanley Company received a 150 day, eight percent note for $15,000 on December 1. What adjusting entry is needed to accrue the interest due on December 31?

11. Define *accounts receivable turnover* and explain its use. How is the *average collection period* determined?

12. At a recent board of directors meeting of Ascot, Inc., one of the directors expressed concern over the Allowance for Doubtful Accounts appearing on the company's balance sheet. "I don't understand this account," he said. "Why don't we just show accounts receivable at the amount we would receive if we sold them to a financial institution and get rid of that allowance account?"

    Prepare a written response to the director. Include in your response (1) an explanation of why the company has an allowance account, (2) what the balance sheet presentation of accounts receivable is supposed to show, and (3) how the basic principles of accounting relate to the analysis and presentation of accounts receivable.

13. What generally accepted accounting principle is being implemented when a company estimates its potential credit losses from its outstanding accounts receivable?

14. Why is the direct write-off method of accounting for credit losses not generally accepted?

15. When a previously written-off account receivable is collected, it must first be reinstated by debiting the Accounts Receivable account and crediting the Allowance for Doubtful Accounts. Explain the credit portion of the reinstatement journal entry.

SHORT EXERCISES

SE8-1. Accounting for Doubtful Accounts Rankine Company estimates its bad debts expense by aging its accounts receivable and applying percentages to various age groups of the accounts. Rankine calculated a total of $4,000 in possible credit losses as of December 31. Accounts Receivable has a balance of $128,000, and the Allowance for Doubtful Accounts has a credit balance of $500 before adjustment at December 31. What is the December 31 adjusting entry to provide for credit losses? What is the net amount of accounts receivable that should be included in current assets?

SE8-2. Reinstating Written-Off Accounts The Watergate Company uses the allowance method of recording credit losses and wrote off a customer's account in the amount of $800. Later, the customer paid the account. The company reinstated the account by means of a journal entry and then recorded the collection. What is the result of these procedures?

a. Increases total assets by $800
b. Decreases total assets by $800
c. Decreases total assets by $1,600
d. Has no effect on total assets

SE8-3. **Estimating the Bad Debts Expense** Winstead & Company has accounts receivable of $120,000 and   **LO2**
a debit balance of $1,000 in the Allowance for Doubtful Accounts. Two thirds of the accounts receivable are current and one third is past due. The firm estimates that two percent of the current accounts and five percent of the past due accounts will prove to be uncollectible. The adjusting entry to provide for the bad debts expense under the aging method should be for what amount?

a. $3,600
b. $4,600
c. $2,600
d. $1,600

SE8-4. **Average Collection Period** Smith & Sons has an accounts receivable turnover of 20. What is the   **LO5**
company's average collection period?

a. 18.25 days
b. 20.0 days
c. 22.25 days
d. 24.25 days

SE8-5. **Recording Dishonored Promissory Notes Receivable** On September 30, the Camelback Company   **LO4**
accepted a $50,000, 60 day, nine percent, promissory note in exchange for an overdue accounts receivable balance for the same amount from the Schwartz Company. On November 30, the Schwartz Company dishonored the note. What journal entry should be recorded on November 30?

a. Debit Dishonored Note Receivable Expense; credit Notes Receivable.
b. Debit Allowance for Doubtful Accounts; credit Notes Receivable.
c. Debit Accounts Receivable; credit Interest Income; credit Notes Receivable.
d. None of the above entries is correct.

SE8-6. **Accounting for Credit Card Sales** Chassoul & Company pays a three percent credit card fee on all   **LO3**
credit sales, and receives a cash deposit immediately following each credit card transaction. If credit sales for the company total $30,000 on January 15, what journal entry should be recorded to recognize the receipt of cash and the credit card fee expense?

a. Debit Cash $29,100; debit Credit Card Fee Expense $900.
b. Debit Cash $29,100; credit Credit Card Fee Expense $900.
c. Debit Cash $30,900; debit Credit Card Fee Expense $900.
d. Debit Cash $30,900; credit Credit Card Fee Expense $900.

SE8-7. **Calculating Accrued Interest Income on Promissory Notes Receivable** Likert Company received   **LO4**
a 90 day, six percent note receivable for $20,000 on November 1. How much interest income should be accrued on December 31?

a. $100
b. $200
c. $300
d. $400

SE8-8. **Calculating Interest on Promissory Notes Receivable** Dallas Company receives a six-month note   **LO4**
from a customer. The note has a face amount of $8,000 and an interest rate of nine percent. What is the total amount of interest income to be received?

a. $720
b. $540
c. $360
d. $180

LO5 **SE8-9. Accounts Receivable Turnover** Tarrant Company has net sales of $120,000, a beginning balance in Accounts Receivable of $10,000, and an ending balance in Accounts Receivable of $14,000. What is the company's accounts receivable turnover?

a.   10.0
b.   12.0
c.   8.6
d.   9.2

LO6
(Appendix 8A)

SE8-10. Direct Write-Off Method The direct write-off method is not generally accepted because:

a.   The method overstates the bad debts expense.
b.   It is too complex.
c.   The method fails to match sales revenue with expenses in the appropriate time period.
d.   The method causes liabilities to be overstated.

EXERCISES—SET A

LO2 **E8-1A. Credit Losses Based on Credit Sales** Lewis Company uses the allowance method for recording its expected credit losses. It estimates credit losses at 2 percent of credit sales, which were $900,000 during the year. On December 31, the Accounts Receivable balance was $150,000, and the Allowance for Doubtful Accounts had a credit balance of $12,200 before adjustment.

a.   Prepare the adjusting entry to record the credit losses for the year.
b.   Show how Accounts Receivable and the Allowance for Doubtful Accounts would appear in the December 31 balance sheet.

LO1, 2 **E8-2A. Credit Losses Based on Accounts Receivable** Hunter, Inc., analyzed its accounts receivable balances at December 31, and arrived at the aged balances listed below, along with the percentage that is estimated to be uncollectible:

Age Group	Balance	Probability of Noncollection
0–30 days past due	$ 90,000	1
31–60 days past due	20,000	2
61–120 days past due	11,000	6
121–180 days past due	6,000	10
Over 180 days past due	5,000	25
	$132,000	

The company handles credit losses using the allowance method. The credit balance of the Allowance for Doubtful Accounts is $820 on December 31, before any adjustments.

a.   Prepare the adjusting entry for estimated credit losses on December 31.
b.   Prepare the journal entry to write off the Rose Company's account on April 10 of the following year in the amount of $625.

LO1 **E8-3A. Recognizing Accounts Receivable** On June 7, Bixby Co. sells $1,000 of merchandise to Jasmine Co. on account. Jasmine Co. pays for this merchandise on June 21.

a.   Prepare the entry on Bixby's books to record the sale.
b.   Prepare the entry on Bixby's books to record the receipt of payment.

LO3 **E8-4A. Credit Card Sales** Ruth Anne's Fabrics accepts cash, personal checks, and two credit cards when customers buy merchandise. With the Great American Bank Card, Ruth Anne's Fabrics receives an immediate deposit in its checking account when credit card sales slips are deposited at the bank. The bank charges a three percent fee. With the United Merchants Card, Ruth Anne's Fabrics mails the credit card sales slips to United Merchants' regional processing center each day. United Merchants accumulates these slips for three days and then mails a check to Ruth Anne's Fabrics, after deducting a three percent fee. Prepare journal entries to record the following:

a.   Sales for March 15 were as follows:

Cash and checks	$ 950
Great American Bank Card (Deposited at the end of the day)	1,200
United Merchants Card (Mailed at the end of the day)	800
	$2,950

b.   Received a check for $1,950 from United Merchants on March 20.

E8-5A.   **Maturity Dates of Notes Receivable** Determine the maturity date and compute the interest for each   **LO4**
of the following notes:

	Date of Note	Principal	Interest Rate (%)	Term
a.	August 5	$ 6,000	9	120 days
b.	May 10	16,800	7	90 days
c.	October 20	24,000	9	45 days
d.	July 6	4,500	11	60 days
e.	September 15	9,000	8	75 days

E8-6A.   **Computing Accrued Interest** Compute the interest accrued on each of the following notes receiv-   **LO4**
able held by Northland, Inc., on December 31: (Round your answer to the nearest dollar.)

Maker	Date of Note	Principal	Interest Rate (%)	Term
Maple	11/21	$20,000	10	120 days
Wyman	12/13	14,000	9	90 days
Nahn	12/24	21,000	6	60 days

E8-7A.   **Accounts Receivable Turnover and Average Collection Period** The Forrester Corporation dis-   **LO5**
closed the following financial information (in millions) in its recent annual report:

	2015	2016
Net sales	$71,050	$81,662
Beginning accounts receivable (net)	3,896	4,100
Ending accounts receivable (net)	4,100	3,596

a.   Calculate the accounts receivable turnover ratio for both years.
b.   Calculate the average collection period for both years.
c.   Is the company's accounts receivable management improving or deteriorating?

E8-8A.   **Credit Losses Based on Credit Sales** Smith & Sons uses the allowance method of handling its credit   **LO2**
losses. It estimates credit losses at two percent of credit sales, which were $1,900,000 during the year.
On December 31, the Accounts Receivable balance was $300,000, and the Allowance for Doubtful
Accounts had a credit balance of $21,400 before adjustment.

a.   Prepare the adjusting entry to record the credit losses for the year.
b.   Show how Accounts Receivable and the Allowance for Doubtful Accounts would appear in the
December 31 balance sheet.

E8-9A.   **Credit Losses Based on Accounts Receivable** Miller, Inc., analyzed its accounts receivable bal-   **LO1, 2**
ances at December 31 and arrived at the aged balances listed below, along with the percentage that is
estimated to be uncollectible:

Age Group	Balance	Probability of Noncollection
0–30 days past due	$180,000	1
31–60 days past due	40,000	3
61–120 days past due	22,000	5
121–180 days past due	14,000	10
Over 180 days past due.	8,000	25
	$264,000	

The company handles credit losses using the allowance method. The credit balance of the Allowance for Doubtful Accounts is $1,150 on December 31, before any adjustments.

a. Prepare the adjusting entry for estimated credit losses on December 31.

b. Prepare the journal entry to write off the Lyons Company's account on April 10 of the following year in the amount of $525.

LO5 **E8-10A. Accounts Receivable Turnover and Average Collection Period** VanPoole Corporation disclosed the following financial information (in millions) in its recent annual report:

	2015	2016
Net sales.	$167,096	$181,662
Beginning accounts receivable (net)	13,896	14,105
Ending accounts receivable (net).	14,105	13,598

a. Calculate the accounts receivable turnover ratio for both years.

b. Calculate the average collection period for both years.

c. Is the company's accounts receivable management improving or deteriorating?

LO3 **E8-11A. Credit Card Sales** The Tin Roof accepts cash, personal checks, and two credit cards when customers buy merchandise. With the Great American Bank Card, The Tin Roof receives an immediate deposit in its checking account when credit card sales slips are deposited at the bank. The bank charges a two percent fee. With the United Merchants Card, The Tin Roof mails the credit card sales slips to United Merchants' regional processing center each day. United Merchants accumulates these slips for three days and then mails a check to The Tin Roof, after deducting a two percent fee. Prepare journal entries to record the following:

a. Sales for March 15 were as follows:

Cash and checks	$1,700
Great American Bank Card (Deposited at the end of the day).	2,500
United Merchants Card (Mailed at the end of the day)	1,400
	$5,600

b. Received a check for $3,906 from United Merchants on March 20.

LO4 **E8-12A. Maturity Dates of Notes Receivable** Determine the maturity date and compute the interest for each of the following notes:

	Date of Note	Principal	Interest Rate (%)	Term
a.	August 5.	$12,000	8	120 days
b.	May 10	33,600	7	90 days
c.	October 20	48,000	11	45 days
d.	July 16	9,000	10	60 days
e.	September 15.	19,000	8	75 days

LO4 **E8-13A. Computing Accrued Interest** Compute the interest accrued on each of the following notes receivable held by Kierland, Inc., on December 31:

Maker	Date of Note	Principal	Interest Rate (%)	Term
Abel	11/21	$36,000	12	120 days
Baker	12/13	32,000	9	90 days
Charlie	12/19	42,000	6	60 days

E8-14A. Allowance Method versus Direct Write-Off Method On March 10, Mize, Inc., declared a $2,200 account receivable from Anders Company as uncollectible and wrote off the account. On November 18, Mize received a $900 payment on the account from Anders.

 a. Assume that Mize uses the allowance method of handling credit losses. Prepare the journal entries to record the write-off and the subsequent recovery of Anders's account.

 b. Assume that Mize uses the direct write-off method of handling credit losses. Prepare the journal entries to record the write-off and the subsequent recovery of Anders's account.

 c. Assume that the payment from Anders arrives on the following February 5, rather than on November 18 of the current year. (1) Prepare the journal entries to record the write-off and subsequent recovery of Anders's account under the allowance method. (2) Prepare the journal entries to record the write-off and subsequent recovery of Anders's account under the direct write-off method.

LO6
(Appendix 8A)

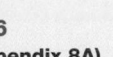

E8-15A. Allowance Method versus Direct Write-Off Method On March 10, Gardner, Inc., declared a $700 account receivable from the Gates Company as uncollectible and wrote off the account. On November 18, Gardner received a $200 payment on the account from Gates.

 a. Assume that Gardner uses the allowance method of handling credit losses. Prepare the journal entries to record the write-off and the subsequent recovery of Gates's account.

 b. Assume that Gardner uses the direct write-off method of handling credit losses. Prepare the journal entries to record the write-off and the subsequent recovery of Gates's account.

 c. Assume that the payment from Gates arrives on February 5 of the following year rather than on November 18 of the current year. (1) Prepare the journal entries to record the write-off and subsequent recovery of Gates's account under the allowance method. (2) Prepare the journal entries to record the write-off and subsequent recovery of Gates's account under the direct write-off method.

LO6
(Appendix 8A)

EXERCISES—SET B

E8-1B. Credit Losses Based on Credit Sales Highland Company uses the allowance method of handling credit losses. It estimates losses at three percent of credit sales, which were $1,400,000 during the year. On December 31, the Accounts Receivable balance was $280,000, and the Allowance for Doubtful Accounts had a credit balance of $1,800 before adjustment.

 a. Prepare the adjusting entry to record credit losses for the year.

 b. Show how the Accounts Receivable account and the Allowance for Doubtful Accounts would appear on the December 31 balance sheet.

LO2

E8-2B. Credit Losses Based on Accounts Receivable Maxwell, Inc. analyzed its accounts receivable balances at December 31 and arrived at the aged balances listed below, along with the percentage that is estimated to be uncollectible:

LO1, 2

Age Group	Balance	Probability of Noncollection
0–30 days past due	$100,000	1
31–60 days past due	18,000	2
61–120 days past due	20,000	6
121–180 days past due	7,000	11
Over 180 days past due	2,000	20
	$147,000	

The company handles credit losses with the allowance method. The credit balance of the Allowance for Doubtful Accounts is $840 on December 31, before any adjustments.

 a. Prepare the adjusting entry for estimated credit losses on December 31.

b.   Prepare the journal entry to write off Porter Company's account on the following May 12, in the amount of $680.

LO1   E8-3B.   Recognizing Accounts Receivable On August 9, Gunner Co. sells $450 of merchandise to Taylor Co. on account. Taylor Co. pays for this merchandise on September 1.

a.   Prepare the entry on Gunner's books to record the sale.
b.   Prepare the entry on Gunner's books to record the receipt of payment.

LO3   E8-4B.   Credit Card Sales Historically, 60 percent of the customer bills at the Andrews' Supper Club have been paid with cash or check, and 40 percent have been paid using either the Great American Bank Card or the United Merchants Card. Andrews pays a five percent fee with both cards. Great American Bank deposits cash in Andrews' checking account when the credit card sales slips are deposited. United Merchants makes an electronic funds transfer three days after the sales slips are mailed. Prepare journal entries to record the following:

a.   Sales for September 10 were as follows:

Cash and checks	$1,340
Great American Bank Card (Deposited at the end of the day).	500
United Merchants Card (Mailed at the end of the day)	300
	$2,140

b.   On September 13, Andrews received an electronic funds transfer from United Merchants for the September 10 sales.

LO4   E8-5B.   Maturity Dates of Notes Receivable Determine the maturity date and compute the interest for each of the following notes:

	Date of Note	Principal	Interest Rate (%)	Term
a.	July 10	$ 7,200	9	90 days
b.	April 25	12,000	8	120 days
c.	May 19	11,200	7	120 days
d.	June 10.	5,400	8	45 days
e.	October 29	30,000	6	75 days

LO4   E8-6B.   Computing Accrued Interest Compute the interest accrued on each of the following notes receivable held by Galloway, Inc., on December 31: (Round your answer to the nearest dollar.)

Maker	Date of Note	Principal	Interest Rate (%)	Term
Barton.	12/14	$10,000	8	120 days
Lawson.	12/13	25,000	9	90 days
Riley	12/19	9,000	11	60 days

LO5   E8-7B.   Accounts Receivable Turnover and Average Collection Period The Andrew Miller Corporation disclosed the following financial information (in millions) in its recent annual report:

	2015	2016
Net sales.	$97,096	$111,662
Beginning accounts receivable (net)	6,450	6,845
Ending accounts receivable (net)	6,845	6,598

a.   Calculate the accounts receivable turnover ratio for both years.
b.   Calculate the average collection period for both years.
c.   Is the company's accounts receivable management improving or deteriorating?

LO2   E8-8B.   Credit Losses Based on Credit Sales Harris Company uses the allowance method of handling its credit losses. It estimates credit losses at 1.5 percent of credit sales, which were $2,700,000 during the year. On December 31, the Accounts Receivable balance was $475,000, and the Allowance for Doubtful Accounts had a credit balance of $30,600 before adjustment.

a. Prepare the adjusting entry to record the credit losses for the year.
b. Show how Accounts Receivable and the Allowance for Doubtful Accounts would appear in the December 31 balance sheet.

E8-9B. Credit Losses Based on Accounts Receivable Graham, Inc., analyzed its accounts receivable balances at December 31 and arrived at the aged balances listed below, along with the percentage that is estimated to be uncollectible: **LO1, 2**

Age Group	Balance	Probability of Noncollection
0–30 days past due	$270,000	1
31–60 days past due	60,000	3
61–120 days past due	33,000	6
121–180 days past due	18,000	10
Over 180 days past due	12,000	25
	$393,000	

The company handles credit losses using the allowance method. The credit balance of the Allowance for Doubtful Accounts is $1,560 on December 31, before any adjustments.

a. Prepare the adjusting entry for estimated credit losses on December 31.
b. Prepare the journal entry to write off the Matthews Company's account on the following April 10, in the amount of $440.

E8-10B. Accounts Receivable Turnover and Average Collection Period The Longo Corporation disclosed the following financial information (in millions) in its recent annual report: **LO5**

	2015	2016
Net sales	$127,096	$112,550
Beginning accounts receivable (net)	8,896	7,740
Ending accounts receivable (net)	7,740	6,598

a. Calculate the accounts receivable turnover ratio for both years.
b. Calculate the average collection period for both years.
c. Is the company's accounts receivable management improving or deteriorating?

E8-11B. Credit Card Sales The Bedroom Store accepts cash, personal checks, and two credit cards when customers buy merchandise. With the Great American Bank Card, The Bedroom Store receives an immediate deposit in its checking account when credit card sales slips are deposited at the bank. The bank charges a five percent fee. With the United Merchants Card, The Bedroom Store mails the credit card sales slips to United Merchants' regional processing center each day. United Merchants accumulates these slips for three days and then mails a check to The Bedroom Store, after deducting a two percent fee. Prepare journal entries to record the following: **LO3**

a. Sales for March 15 were as follows:

Cash and checks	$2,550
Great American Bank Card (Deposited at the end of the day)	3,300
United Merchants Card (Mailed at the end of the day)	2,100
	$7,950

b. Received a check for $8,745 from United Merchants on March 20.

E8-12B. Maturity Dates of Notes Receivable Determine the maturity date and compute the interest for each of the following notes: **LO4**

		Date of Note	Principal	Interest Rate (%)	Term
a.		August 5	$18,000	8	120 days
b.		May 10	50,400	7	90 days
c.		October 30	72,000	9	45 days
d.		July 6	13,500	11	60 days
e.		September 15.	27,000	8	60 days

LO4

E8-13B. Computing Accrued Interest Compute the interest accrued on each of the following notes receivable held by Northland, Inc., on December 31:

	Maker	Date of Note	Principal	Interest Rate (%)	Term
a.	Delta	11/21	$54,000	7	120 days
b.	Echo	12/13	42,000	9	90 days
c.	Foxtrot	12/17	63,000	8	60 days

LO6
(Appendix 8A)

E8-14B. Allowance Method versus Direct Write-Off Method On March 10, Barrett, Inc., declared a $3,700 account receivable from Lamas Company as uncollectible and wrote off the account. On November 18, Barrett received a $1,600 payment on the account from Lamas.

a. Assume that Barrett uses the allowance method of handling credit losses. Prepare the journal entries to record the write-off and the subsequent recovery of Lamas's account.
b. Assume that Barrett uses the direct write-off method of handling credit losses. Prepare the journal entries to record the write-off and the subsequent recovery of Lamas's account.
c. Assume that the payment from Lamas arrives on the following February 5, rather than on November 18 of the current year. (1) Prepare the journal entries to record the write-off and subsequent recovery of Lamas's account under the allowance method. (2) Prepare the journal entries to record the write-off and subsequent recovery of Lamas's account under the direct write-off method.

LO6
(Appendix 8A)

E8-15B. Allowance Method versus Direct Write-Off Method On April 12, Maddox Company declared a $2,000 account receivable from the Ward Company as uncollectible and wrote off the account. On December 5, Maddox received a $600 payment on the account from Ward.

a. Assume that Maddox uses the allowance method of handling credit losses. Prepare the journal entries to record the write-off and the subsequent recovery of Ward's account.
b. Assume that Maddox uses the direct write-off method of handling credit losses. Prepare the journal entries to record the write-off and the subsequent recovery of Ward's account.
c. Assume that the payment from Ward arrives on the following January 18, rather than on December 5 of the current year. (1) Prepare the journal entries to record the write-off and subsequent recovery of Ward's account under the allowance method. (2) Prepare the journal entries to record the write-off and subsequent recovery of Ward's account under the direct write-off method.

PROBLEMS—SET A

LO2

P8-1A. Allowance Method Fullerton Company, which has been in business for three years, makes all of its sales on account and does not offer cash discounts. The firm's credit sales, collections from customers, and write-offs of uncollectible accounts for the three-year period are summarized below:

Year	Sales	Collections	Accounts Written Off
2015	$300,000	$287,000	$2,200
2016	385,000	390,000	3,350
2017	430,000	407,000	3,650

Required

a. If Fullerton Company had used the allowance method of recognizing credit losses and had provided for such losses at the rate of 1.2 percent of credit sales, what amounts in accounts receivable and the allowance for doubtful accounts would appear on the firm's balance sheet at the end of 2017? What total amount of bad debts expense would have appeared on the firm's income statement during the three year period?

b.   Comment on the use of the 1.2 percent rate to provide for credit losses in part *a*.

P8-2A.   Journal Entries for Credit Losses At the beginning of the year, Whitney Company had the following accounts on its books: **LO1, 2**

Accounts receivable.	$130,000 (debit)
Allowance for doubtful accounts	8,000 (credit)

During the year, credit sales were $1,173,000 and collections on account were $1,175,000. The following transactions, among others, occurred during the year:

Feb.   17   Wrote off R. Lowell's account, $4,000.
May   28   Wrote off G. Boyd's account, $2,400.
Oct.   13   Received $600 from G. Boyd, who is in bankruptcy proceedings, in final settlement of the account written off on May 28. This amount is not included in the $1,175,000 collections.
Dec.   15   Wrote off K. Marshall's account, $1,600.
         31   In an adjusting entry, recorded the allowance for doubtful accounts at 0.9 percent of credit sales for the year.

Required
a.   Prepare journal entries to record the credit sales, the collections on account, and the preceding transactions and adjustment.
b.   Show how Accounts Receivable and the Allowance for Doubtful Accounts would appear on the December 31 balance sheet.

P8-3A.   Credit Losses Based on Accounts Receivable At December 31, Schuler Company had a balance   **LO2** of $369,000 in its Accounts Receivable account and a credit balance of $4,200 in the Allowance for Doubtful Accounts account. The accounts receivable T-account consisted of $374,000 in debit balances and $5,000 in credit balances. The company aged its accounts as follows:

Current	$304,000
0–60 days past due	44,000
61–180 days past due	18,000
Over 180 days past due.	8,000
	$374,000

In the past, the company has experienced credit losses as follows: one percent of current balances, five percent of balances 0–60 days past due, 18 percent of balances 61–180 days past due, and 40 percent of balances over six months past due. The company bases its allowance for doubtful accounts on an aging analysis of accounts receivable.

Required
a.   Prepare the adjusting entry to record the allowance for doubtful accounts for the year.
b.   Show how Accounts Receivable (including the credit balances) and the Allowance for Doubtful Accounts would appear on the December 31 balance sheet.

P8-4A.   Credit Card Sales Valderi's Gallery sells quality art work, with prices for individual pieces ranging   **LO3** from $400 to $25,000. Sales are infrequent, typically only three to five pieces per week. The following transactions occurred during the first week of June 2015. Perpetual inventory is used.

June   1   Sold an $800 framed print ($500 cost) to Kerwin Antiques on account, with 2/10, n/30 credit terms.
         2   Sold three framed etchings totaling $2,400 ($1,500 cost) to Maria Alvado, who used the United Merchants Card to charge the cost of the etchings. Valderi mailed the credit card sales slip to United Merchants the same day. United Merchants will send a check within seven days after deducting a one percent fee.

June   4   Sold a $1,900 oil painting ($1,000 cost) to Shaun Chandler, who paid with a personal check.
         5   Sold a $2,000 watercolor ($1,500 cost) to Julie and John Malbie, who used their Great
              American Bank Card to charge the purchase of the painting. Valderi deposited the credit
              card sales slip the same day and received immediate credit in the company's checking
              account. The bank charged a one percent fee.
         6   Received payment from Kerwin Antiques for its June 1 purchase.
         7   Received a check from United Merchants for the June 2 sale.

Required
Prepare journal entries to record the Valderi Gallery transactions.

LO2, 4   P8-5A.   Journal Entries for Accounts and Notes Receivable Lancaster Inc. began business on January 1.

Certain transactions for the year follow:

June   8   Received a $20,000, 60 day, six percent note on account from R. Elliot.
Aug.   7   Received payment from R. Elliot on her note (principal plus interest).
Sept.   1   Received an $18,000, 120 day, seven percent note from B. Shore Company on account.
Dec.   16   Received a $14,400, 45 day, ten percent note from C. Judd on account.
       30   B. Shore Company failed to pay its note.
       31   Wrote off B. Shore's account as uncollectible. Lancaster, Inc. uses the allowance method
             of providing for credit losses.
       31   Recorded expected credit losses for the year by an adjusting entry. Accounts written off
             during this first year have created a debit balance in the Allowance for Doubtful Accounts
             of $24,500. An analysis of aged receivables indicates that the desired balance of the
             allowance account should be $21,300.
       31   Made the appropriate adjusting entries for interest.

Required
Record the foregoing transactions and adjustments in general journal form.

LO2   P8-6A.   Allowance Method The Huntington Company, which has been in business for three years, makes
all of its sales on account and does not offer cash discounts. The firm's credit sales, collections from
customers, and write-offs of uncollectible accounts for the three-year period are summarized below:

Year	Sales	Collections	Accounts Written Off
2015	$600,000	$574,000	$4,200
2016	770,000	760,000	6,900
2017	850,000	814,000	7,300

Required
a.   If the Huntington Company had used the allowance method of recognizing credit losses and
      had provided for such losses at the rate of 1.3 percent of credit sales, what amounts in Accounts
      Receivable and the Allowance for Doubtful Accounts would appear on the firm's balance sheet
      at the end of 2017? What total amount of bad debts expense would have appeared on the firm's
      income statement during the three year period?
b.   Comment on the use of the 1.3 percent rate to provide for credit losses in part *a*.

LO1, 2   P8-7A.   Journal Entries for Credit Losses At the beginning of the year, the Houston Company had the following accounts on its books:

Accounts receivable.	$264,000 (debit)
Allowance for doubtful accounts	15,800 (credit)

During the year, credit sales were $2,346,000 and collections on account were $2,350,000. The following transactions, among others, occurred during the year:

Feb.   17   Wrote off R. St. John's account, $7,500.
May   28   Wrote off G. Herberger's account, $4,800.
Oct.   13   Received $1,200 from G. Herberger, who is in bankruptcy proceedings, in final
             settlement of the account written off on May 28. This amount is not included in the
             $2,350,000 collections.

Dec. 15 Wrote off R. Clancy's account, $4,500.
      31 In an adjusting entry, recorded the allowance for doubtful accounts at 0.7 percent of credit sales for the year.

Required

a. Prepare journal entries to record the credit sales, the collections on account, and the preceding transactions and adjustment.
b. Show how Accounts Receivable and the Allowance for Doubtful Accounts would appear on the December 31 balance sheet.

P8-8A. Credit Losses Based on Accounts Receivable At December 31, the Selling Company had a balance of $754,000 in its Accounts Receivable account and a credit balance of $9,000 in the Allowance for Doubtful Accounts account. The company aged its accounts as follows:

LO2

Current	$608,000
0–60 days past due	88,000
61–180 days past due	40,000
Over 180 days past due	18,000
	$754,000

In the past, the company has experienced credit losses as follows: two percent of current balances, five percent of balances 0–60 days past due, 15 percent of balances 61–180 days past due, and 40 percent of balances over six months past due. The company bases its allowance for doubtful accounts on an aging analysis of accounts receivable.

Required

a. Prepare the adjusting entry to record the allowance for doubtful accounts for the year.
b. Show how Accounts Receivable and the Allowance for Doubtful Accounts would appear on the December 31 balance sheet.

P8-9A. Credit Card Sales Le Kai Gallery sells quality art work, with prices for individual pieces ranging from $1,000 to $50,000. Sales are infrequent, typically only six to ten pieces per week. The following transactions occurred during the first week of June. Perpetual inventory is used.

LO3

June 1 Sold an $1,800 framed print ($1,200 cost) to Likert Antiques on account, with 2/10, n/30 credit terms.
      2 Sold three framed etchings totaling $4,800 ($3,000 cost) to Annabelle Herrera, who used the United Merchants Card to charge the cost of the etchings. Le Kai mailed the credit card sales slip to United Merchants the same day. United Merchants will send a check within seven days after deducting a two percent fee.
      4 Sold a $3,600 oil painting ($2,000 cost) to Ryan LaLander, who paid with a personal check.
      5 Sold a $5,000 watercolor ($3,100 cost) to Julie and Bobby Herman, who used their Great American Bank Card to charge the purchase of the painting. Le Kai deposited the credit card sales slip the same day and received immediate credit in the company's checking account. The bank charged a one percent fee.
      6 Received payment from Likert Antiques for its June 1 purchase.
      7 Received a check from United Merchants for the June 2 sale.

Required

Prepare journal entries to record the Le Kai Gallery transactions.

P8-10A. Journal Entries for Accounts and Notes Receivable Pittsburgh, Inc., began business on January 1. Certain transactions for the year follow:

LO2, 4

June 8 Received a $15,000, 60 day, eight percent note on account from J. Albert.
Aug. 7 Received payment from J. Albert on his note (principal plus interest).
Sept. 1 Received a $36,000, 120 day, seven percent note from R.T. Matthews Company on account.
Dec. 16 Received a $28,800, 45 day, ten percent note from D. LeRoy on account.
      30 R.T. Matthews Company failed to pay its note.

Dec. 31 Wrote off R.T. Matthews' account as uncollectible. Pittsburgh, Inc., uses the allowance
method of providing for credit losses.
31 Recorded expected credit losses for the year by an adjusting entry. Accounts written off
during this first year have created a debit balance in the allowance for doubtful accounts
of $45,200. An analysis of aged receivables indicates that the desired balance of the
allowance account should be $41,000.
31 Made the appropriate adjusting entries for interest.

Required

Record the foregoing transactions and adjustments in general journal form.

PROBLEMS—SET B

LO2   P8-1B.   Allowance Method Steinbrook Company, which has been in business for three years, makes all of its
sales on account and does not offer cash discounts. The firm's credit sales, collections from customers, and write-offs of uncollectible accounts for the three-year period are summarized as follows:

Year	Sales	Collections	Accounts Written Off
2015	$751,000	$733,000	$5,300
2016	876,000	864,000	6,200
2017	975,000	938,000	6,500

Required

a. If Steinbrook Company used an allowance method of recognizing credit losses and provided for
such losses at the rate of one percent of credit sales, what amounts of accounts receivable and the
allowance for doubtful accounts should appear on the firm's balance sheet at the end of 2017?
What total amount of bad debts expense should appear on the firm's income statement during the
three-year period?

b. Comment on the use of the one percent rate to provide for credit losses in part *a*.

LO1, 2   P8-2B.   Journal Entries for Credit Losses At January 1, the Griffin Company had the following accounts
on its books:

Accounts receivable.	$130,000 (debit)
Allowance for doubtful accounts	7,000 (credit)

During the year, credit sales were $810,000 and collections on account were $794,000. The following
transactions, among others, occurred during the year:

Jan. 11 Wrote off J. Wolf's account, $3,000.
Apr. 29 Wrote off B. Avery's account, $1,000.
Nov. 15 Received $1,000 from B. Avery to pay a debt that had been written off April 29. This
amount is not included in the $794,000 collections.
Dec.   5 Wrote off D. Wright's account, $2,250.
31 In an adjusting entry, recorded the allowance for doubtful accounts at one percent of
credit sales for the year.

Required

a. Prepare journal entries to record the credit sales, the collections on account, the transactions, and
the adjustment.

b. Show how Accounts Receivable and the Allowance for Doubtful Accounts appear on the December 31 balance sheet.

LO2   P8-3B.   Credit Losses Based on Accounts Receivable At December 31, Rinehart Company had a balance
of $307,000 in its Accounts Receivable account and a credit balance of $2,800 in the Allowance for
Doubtful Accounts account. The accounts receivable T-account consisted of $310,600 in debit bal-
ances and $3,600 in credit balances. The company has aged its accounts as follows:

Current	$262,000
0–60 days past due	28,000
61–180 days past due	11,200
Over 180 days past due	9,400
	$310,600

In the past, the company has experienced credit losses as follows: one percent of current balances, six percent of balances 0–60 days past due, 15 percent of balances 61–180 days past due, and 30 percent of balances more than six months past due. The company bases its allowance for doubtful accounts on an aging analysis of accounts receivable.

Required
a.   Prepare the adjusting journal entry to record the provision for credit losses for the year.
b.   Show how Accounts Receivable (including the credit balances) and the Allowance for Doubtful Accounts appear on the December 31 balance sheet.

P8-4B.   **Credit Card Sales**   Captain Paul's Marina sells boats and other water recreational vehicles (approxi- **LO3** mately three vehicles are sold each week). The following transactions occurred during the third week of May:

May   15   Sold a $750 boat trailer ($500 cost) to Sam and Myrna Marston, who paid using a personal check.
16   Sold a $10,000 boat ($6,500 cost) to the Calumet Lake Patrol on account, with 2/10, n/30 terms.
18   Sold a $1,200 water scooter ($700 cost) to Kyle Bronson, who used the United Merchants Card to charge the cost of the water scooter. Captain Paul's mailed the credit card sales slip to United Merchants the same day. United Merchants will send a check within seven days, net of a two percent fee.
19   Sold a $6,000 fishing boat ($3,500 cost) to Michael Ferguson, who used the Great American Bank Card to pay for the boat. Captain Paul's deposited the credit card sales slip the same day and received an immediate credit in the company's checking account, net of a two percent fee.
20   Received payment from Calumet Lake Patrol for the boat purchased on May 16.
21   Received payment from United Merchants for the May 18 transaction.

Required
Prepare journal entries to record these transactions. Captain Paul's Marina uses the perpetual inventory system.

P8-5B.   **Journal Entries for Accounts and Notes Receivable**   Armstrong, Inc., began business on January 1. **LO2, 4** Several transactions for the year follow:

May   2   Received a $16,500, 60 day, ten percent note on account from the Holt Company.
July   1   Received payment from Holt for its note plus interest.
1   Received a $27,000, 120 day, ten percent note from B. Rich Company on account.
Oct.   29   B. Rich failed to pay its note.
Dec.   9   Wrote off B. Rich's account as uncollectible. Armstrong, Inc., uses the allowance method of providing for credit losses.
11   Received a $25,000, 90 day, nine percent note from W. Maling on account.
31   Recorded expected credit losses for the year by an adjusting entry. The allowance for doubtful accounts has a debit balance of $28,300 as a result of accounts written off during this first year. An analysis of aged accounts receivables indicates that the desired balance of the allowance account is $5,800.
31   Made the appropriate adjusting entries for interest.

Required
Record the foregoing transactions and adjustments in general journal form.

LO2 **P8-6B.** **Allowance Method** The Wallbrook Company, which has been in business for three years, makes all of its sales on account and does not offer cash discounts. The firm's credit sales, collections from customers, and write-offs of uncollectible accounts for the three-year period are summarized below:

Year	Sales	Collections	Accounts Written Off
2015	$1,502,000	$1,466,000	$10,600
2016	1,752,000	1,728,000	12,500
2017	2,050,000	1,876,000	13,000

Required

a. If the Wallbrook Company used an allowance method of recognizing credit losses and provided for such losses at the rate of one percent of credit sales, what amounts of accounts receivable and the allowance for doubtful accounts should appear on the firm's balance sheet at the end of 2017? What total amount of bad debts expense should appear on the firm's income statement during the three year period?

b. Comment on the use of the one percent rate to provide for credit losses in part *a*.

LO1, 2 **P8-7B.** **Journal Entries for Credit Losses** At January 1, the Chesley Company had the following accounts on its books:

Accounts receivable.	$255,000 (debit)
Allowance for doubtful accounts	13,600 (credit)

During the year, credit sales were $1,650,000 and collections on account were $1,588,000. The following transactions, among others, occurred during the year:

Jan. 11 Wrote off J. Smith's account, $5,800.
Apr. 29 Wrote off B. Bird's account, $1,500.
Nov. 15 Received $1,500 from B. Bird to pay a debt that had been written off April 29. This amount is not included in the $1,588,000 collections.
Dec.   5 Wrote off D. Finger's account, $4,300.
      31 In an adjusting entry, recorded the allowance for doubtful accounts at two percent of credit sales for the year.

Required

a. Prepare journal entries to record the credit sales, the collections on account, the transactions, and the adjustment.

b. Show how Accounts Receivable and the Allowance for Doubtful Accounts appear on the December 31 balance sheet.

LO2 **P8-8B.** **Credit Losses Based on Accounts Receivable** At December 31, the Hope Company had a balance of $622,000 in its accounts receivable account and a credit balance of $7,500 in the allowance for doubtful accounts account. The company has aged its accounts as follows:

Current	$524,000
0–60 days past due	56,000
61–180 days past due	25,200
Over 180 days past due.	16,800
	$622,000

In the past, the company has experienced credit losses as follows: one percent of current balances, six percent of balances 0–60 days past due, 18 percent of balances 61–180 days past due, and 30 percent of balances more than six months past due. The company bases its allowance for doubtful accounts on an aging analysis of accounts receivable.

Required

a. Prepare the adjusting journal entry to record the provision for credit losses for the year.

b. Show how Accounts Receivable and the Allowance for Doubtful Accounts appear on the December 31 balance sheet.

P8-9B. Credit Card Sales Lake Pleasant Marina sells boats and other water recreational vehicles (approxi- **LO3** mately three vehicles are sold each week). The following transactions occurred during the third week of May:

May 15 Sold a $1,350 boat trailer ($760 cost) to Ed and Jane Peeler, who paid using a personal check.

16 Sold a $20,000 boat ($13,000 cost) to the Lake Pleasant Lake Patrol on account, with 2/10, n/30 terms.

18 Sold a $2,600 water scooter ($1,500 cost) to Bryan Wagner, who used the United Merchants Card to charge the cost of the water scooter. Lake Pleasant Marina mailed the credit card sales slip to United Merchants the same day. United Merchants will send a check within seven days, net of a three percent fee.

19 Sold a $9,000 fishing boat ($4,500 cost) to Michael Moffett, who used the Great American Bank Card to pay for the boat. Lake Pleasant Marina deposited the credit card sales slip the same day and received an immediate credit in the company's checking account, net of a two percent fee.

20 Received payment from the Lake Pleasant Lake Patrol for the boat purchased on May 16.

21 Received payment from United Merchants for the May 18 transaction.

Required

Prepare journal entries to record these transactions. The Lake Pleasant Marina uses a perpetual inventory system.

P8-10B. Journal Entries for Accounts and Notes Receivable Dallmus, Inc., began business on January 1. **LO2, 4** Several transactions for the year follow:

May 2 Received a $28,800, 60 day, ten percent note on account from the Haskins Company.

July 1 Received payment from Haskins for its note plus interest.

1 Received a $61,000, 120 day, nine percent note from R. Longo Company on account.

Oct. 29 R. Longo failed to pay its note.

Dec. 9 Wrote off R. Longo's account as uncollectible. Dallmus, Inc., uses the allowance method of providing for credit losses.

11 Received a $42,000, 90 day, nine percent note from R. Canal on account.

31 Recorded expected credit losses for the year by an adjusting entry. Accounts written off during this first year have created a debit balance in the Allowance for Doubtful Accounts of $61,000. An analysis of aged accounts receivables indicates that the desired balance of the allowance account should be $12,500.

31 Made the appropriate adjusting entries for interest.

Required

Record the foregoing transactions and adjustments in general journal form.

SERIAL PROBLEM: KATE'S CARDS

(Note: This is a continuation of the Serial Problem: Kate's Cards from Chapters 1 through 7.)

SP8. Kate has put a lot of time and effort into streamlining the process to design and produce a greeting card. She has documented the entire process in a QuickTime video she produced on her iMac. The video takes the viewer through the step-by-step process of selecting hardware and software, and shows how to design and produce the card. Kate has met many people who would like to get into the production of greeting cards, but are overwhelmed by the process. Kate has decided to sell the entire package (hardware, software, and video tutorial) to aspiring card producers. The cost of the entire package to Kate is $4,500 and she plans to mark it up by $500 and sell it for $5,000.

John Stevens, an individual Kate met recently at a greeting card conference, would like to buy the package from Kate. Unfortunately, John does not have this much cash and would like for Kate to extend credit.

Kate believes that many of her customers will not be able to pay cash and, therefore, she will need to find some way to provide financing. One option she is exploring is to accept credit cards. She learned that the credit card provider charges a 2.5 percent fee and provides immediate cash upon receiving the sales receipts.

Kate would like you to answer the following questions:

1. What are the advantages and disadvantages of offering credit?
2. What precautions should she take before offering credit to people like John?
3. If Kate grants credit to John, the terms will be 2/10, n/30. Assuming the payment is made during the 10-day discount period, what would be the journal entry to record the sale and then the subsequent payment?
4. If instead of paying early, John pays in 25 days, what would be the journal entry to record the payment?
5. Rather than providing the financing directly, assume that Kate decides to allow the use of credit cards. Further, assume that during the month there is $15,000 worth of credit card sales. Provide the journal entry to record the sales, along with the associated credit card fee. The cost of the goods sold total $13,500.

EXTENDING YOUR KNOWLEDGE

REPORTING AND ANALYSIS

COLUMBIA
SPORTSWEAR
COMPANY

EYK8-1. **Financial Reporting Problem: Columbia Sportswear Company** The annual report of the **Columbia Sportswear Company** is presented in Appendix A at the end of this book.

  a. What was the amount of Accounts Receivables and the Allowance for Doubtful Accounts at the end of 2013 and 2014?

  b. What percent of total accounts receivables was the allowance for doubtful accounts at the end of 2013 and 2014?

COLUMBIA
SPORTSWEAR
COMPANY

UNDER ARMOUR,
INC.

EYK8-2. **Comparative Analysis Problem: Columbia Sportswear Company vs. Under Armour, Inc.** The annual report of the **Columbia Sportswear Company** is presented in Appendix A at the end of this book and the complete annual report of **Under Armour, Inc.** is on this book's Website.

Required

  a. Calculate the accounts receivable turnover and the average collection period for Columbia Sportswear and Under Armour, Inc. for 2014 and 2013. (To calculate the accounts receivable turnover, use the ending net accounts receivable balance as the denominator rather than average net accounts receivable.)

  b. Compare the average collection periods for the two companies and comment on possible reasons for the difference in the average collection periods for the two companies.

EYK8-3. **Business Decision Problem** Sally Smith owned a dance studio in San Francisco, California. Students could buy access to the dance classes by paying a monthly fee. Unfortunately, many of Sally's students were struggling actors and actresses who lacked the ability to pay their bills in a timely manner. Although the students were expected to pay for classes in advance, Sally had begun offering credit to many of her students in order to grow her business. This, however, created a serious liquidity problem for Sally.

Age Classification	Trade Receivables Outstanding Balance	Historical Estimate of Noncollection
0–30 days	$44,000	4%
31–60 days	31,000	8%
61–90 days	22,000	12%
91–120 days	13,000	14%
121–150 days	9,000	20%
> 150 days	5,000	50%

Sally's accountant, Matt Thomas, had tried to help her get a handle on the problem, but to little avail. One trick he had successfully used in the past to make Sally realize the seriousness of the problem was to overestimate the extent of Sally's debts; consequently, there currently existed a balance in the Allowance for Uncollectible Accounts totaling $2,700.

Required

1. The first step to help get Sally's business back on track is to write-off all receivables having a very low probability of collection (i.e., those accounts over 150 days). Which accounts are affected and by what amount?

2. Prepare an aging of Sally's remaining accounts receivable. What should be the balance in the Allowance for Uncollectible Accounts?

3. Sally is in need of an immediate cash infusion and Matt has advised her to sell some of her receivables. A local bank has offered her two alternatives:

   a. Factor $40,000 of "current" receivables (i.e., 0–30 days old) on a nonrecourse basis at a flat fee of eleven percent of the receivables sold.

   b. Factor $40,000 of "current" receivables on a recourse basis at a flat fee of six percent of the receivables sold.

   Which option should Sally choose? Why?

EYK8-4. **Financial Analysis Problem** **Abbott Laboratories** is a diversified health care company devoted to the discovery, development, manufacture, and marketing of innovative products that improve diagnostic, therapeutic, and nutritional practices. Abbott markets products in more than 130 countries and employs 50,000 people. **Pfizer Inc.** is a research-based, global health care company. Its mission is to discover and develop innovative, value-added products that improve the quality of life of people around the world. Pfizer manufactures products in 31 countries and markets these products worldwide. These two companies reported the following information in their financial reports:

ABBOTT LABORATORIES

PFIZER INC.

(in millions)	2014
Abbott Laboratories	
Net sales	$20,247
Beginning accounts receivable (net)	3,986
Ending accounts receivable (net)	3,586
Pfizer Inc.	
Net sales	$49,605
Beginning accounts receivable (net)	9,357
Ending accounts receivable (net)	8,669

Required

a. Calculate the accounts receivable turnover and the average collection period for Abbott Laboratories and Pfizer Inc. for 2014.

b. Compare the average collection periods for the two companies and comment on possible reasons for the difference in average collection periods for the two companies.

CRITICAL THINKING

EYK8-5. **Accounting Research Problem** Access the fiscal year 2014 annual report of **General Mills, Inc.**, available on this book's Website.

GENERAL MILLS, INC.

Required

a. What was the amount of total Accounts Receivables and the Allowance for Doubtful Accounts at the end of fiscal-year 2014 and 2013? (Note: This information can be found in note 17.)

b. What percent of total accounts receivables was the allowance for doubtful accounts at the end of 2014 and 2013?

c. Calculate the accounts receivable turnover and the average collection period for General Mills for 2014 and 2013. (For purposes of calculating the accounts receivable turnover, use the ending total accounts receivable balance as the denominator rather than the average total accounts receivable.)

d. Comment on whether General Mills' management of accounts receivable improved (or not) over the two year period.

EYK8-6. **Accounting Communications Activity** You have been hired as the accounting manager of Taylor, Inc., a provider of custom furniture. The company recently switched its method of paying its salespeople from a straight salary to a commission basis in order to encourage them to increase sales. The salespeople receive ten percent of the sales price at the time of the sale. You have noticed that the company's accounts receivable balance is growing because the salespeople are granting more credit to their customers.

Required

Draft a memorandum explaining why it is important to closely monitor the company's accounts receivable balance and why a large balance could lead to cash flow problems.

EYK8-7. **Accounting Ethics Case** Tractor Motors' best salesperson is Marie Glazer. Glazer's largest sales have been to Farmers Cooperative, a customer she brought to the company. Another salesperson, Bryan Blanchard, has been told in confidence by his cousin (an employee of Farmers Cooperative) that Farmers Cooperative is experiencing financial difficulties and may not be able to pay Tractor Motors what is owed.

Both Glazer and Blanchard are being considered for promotion to a new sales manager position.

Required

What are the ethical considerations that face Bryan Blanchard? What alternatives does he have?

EYK8-8. **Corporate Social Responsibility Problem** **MGM Resorts International** is committed to responsible gaming and strictly adheres to the Code of Conduct established by the American Gaming Association. The company's efforts include employee training, public awareness, and support for research initiatives through the National Center for Responsible Gaming.

Since MGM Resorts International makes money when people gamble, and the more people gamble, the more money the company makes, why would MGM Resorts International work to curtail gambling by some of the people they could make a lot of money from? Does this form of good citizenship run counter to the company's responsibilities to its stockholders?

EYK8-9. **Forensic Accounting Problem** The chapter highlight on forensic accounting discussed the technique of covering up receivables theft by lapping (see Forensic Accounting: Lapping on page 391), where one account is credited with the receipt from another account. The highlight stated that lapping may be detected by an auditor through the confirmation of accounts receivables. While detection is important, it is far better to prevent lapping from occurring in the first place. Can you think of any controls that can be put in place to help prevent lapping?

EYK8-10. **Analyzing IFRS Financial Statements** The 2014 financial statements of LVMH Moet Hennessey-Louis Vuitton S.A. are presented in Appendix C at the end of this book. LVMH is a Paris-based holding company and one of the world's largest and best-known luxury goods companies. As a member of the European Union, French companies are required to prepare their consolidated (group) financial statements using International Financial Reporting Standards (IFRS). At year-end 2014 (2013), LVMH's allowance account was 272 (242) million euros. After reviewing LVMH's consolidated financial statements, consider the following questions. (Additional information can be found in LVMH's complete annual report provided on this book's Website.)

Required

a. What was the gross amount of Trade and Other Receivables at fiscal year-end 2013 and 2014?
b. What percent of total trade and other receivables were the provision for impairment and the provision for product returns combined as of the end of 2013 and 2014?
c. Calculate the accounts receivable turnover and the average collection period for the company for 2013 and 2014.
d. Comment on whether LVMH's management of its trade receivables improved (or not) over the two-year period.

EYK8-11. **Working with the Takeaways** Below are selected data from a recent **MGM Resorts International** financial statement. Amounts are in thousands.

Net sales:	$9,809,663
Beginning of year accounts receivable:	623,108
End of year accounts receivable:	569,206

Required

Calculate the MGM Resorts International (a) accounts receivable turnover, and (b) average collection period.

ANSWERS TO SELF-STUDY QUESTIONS:

1. d, (pp. 390–391) 2. b, (pp. 388–390) 3. d, (pp. 393–394) 4. a, (pp. 396–397) 5. d, (p. 397)
6. c, (pp. 393–394) 7. a, (p. 385) 8. a, (p. 392) 9. c, (p. 388) 10. c, (pp. 394–395)

YOUR TURN! SOLUTIONS

Solution 8.1

May 2	Accounts receivable	40,000	
	Sales revenue		40,000
	To record credit sales.		

May 17	Cash	35,000	
	Accounts receivable		35,000
	To record cash collections.		

May 31	Bad debts expense	500	
	Allowance for doubtful accounts		500
	To record bad debts expense.		

June 15	Allowance for doubtful accounts	200	
	Accounts receivable		200
	To write off accounts receivable.		

Solution 8.2

Bad debts expense	18,000	
Allowance for doubtful accounts		18,000
To record the bad debts expense for the period.		

Solution 8.3

a.	Bad debts expense	3,200	
	Allowance for doubtful accounts		3,200
	To record the bad debts expense for the period.		

Bad debt expense = ($100,000 × 1%) + ($15,000 × 3%) + ($10,000 × 5%) + ($20,000 × 10%) − $750
= $3,200.

b.	Allowance for doubtful accounts	480	
	Accounts receivable		480
	To write off the Phorest Company uncollectible account.		

Solution 8.4

Cash	49,000	
Credit card fee expense	1,000	
Sales revenue		50,000
To record credit sales and collection, less a two percent fee.		

Solution 8.5

$40,000 × .05 × 3/12 = $500

Solution 8.6

a. Accounts receivable turnover = $30,000/[($2,800 + $3,200)/2] = 10
b. Average collection period = 365/10 = 36.5 days

Solution 8A.1

Bad debts expense	750	
Accounts receivable		750
To write off the Rhea Inc. uncollectible account.		

9

Accounting for Long-Lived and Intangible Assets

PAST

In Chapter 8 we studied how to account for accounts and notes receivable.

PRESENT

This chapter focuses on another important set of assets—long-lived plant assets and intangible assets.

FUTURE

Chapter 10 begins our study of the accounting for liabilities.

LEARNING OBJECTIVES

1. **Discuss** the nature of long-lived assets and **identify** the accounting guidelines relating to their initial measurement. *(p. 427)*

2. **Discuss** the nature of depreciation, **illustrate** three depreciation methods, and **explain** impairment losses. *(p. 430)*

3. **Discuss** the distinction between revenue expenditures and capital expenditures. *(p. 439)*

4. **Explain** and **illustrate** the accounting for disposals of plant assets. *(p. 441)*

5. **Discuss** the nature of, and the accounting for, intangible assets. *(p. 442)*

6. **Illustrate** the balance sheet presentation of plant assets and intangible assets. *(p. 446)*

7. **Define** the return on assets ratio and the asset turnover ratio and **explain** their use. *(p. 446)*

TESLA MOTORS INC.

Tesla Motors, Inc. is a manufacturer of electric cars. While Tesla is currently known for its high-end vehicles like the Model S, its CEO Elon Musk envisions the company as one day offering a mass-produced electric car at a price that will be affordable to the average car buyer.

Tesla cars are certainly known for their cutting-edge technology; its motor is descended directly from the design of Nikola Tesla, a Serbian-American physicist and electrical engineer for whom the company is named. Unlike other automobile manufacturers that predominantely build vehicles with internal combustion engines, and only build electric vehicles as a niche product, Tesla produces only electric vehicles. Tesla aims to increase the number and choices in electric vehicles by shaking up the automobile industry in both the types of vehicles sold and the way they are sold. Whereas electric vehicles offered by other manufacturers typically have very limited range and lack sports car performance, Tesla vehicles offer driving ranges in excess of 200 miles with breathtaking performance. Tesla also avoids the use of dealerships, instead choosing to sell their vehicles in company-owned showrooms and online.

One thing Tesla has in common with other automobile manufacturers like General Motors and Bavarian Motor Works is the need for large investments in plant assets such as land, buildings, and equipment to produce the products they sell. Companies like Tesla also typically maintain large investments in such intangible assets as trademarks and patents. Because of its large investment in these long-lived, revenue-producing assets, Tesla is referred to as a capital-intensive company. Wall Street analysts evaluate the capital intensity of companies by calculating a capital-intensity ratio, equal to the value of plant assets plus the value of intangible assets divided by the value of a company's total assets. Tesla's capital-intensity ratio is about 30 percent.

Plant Assets	Intangible Assets	Analyzing Long-Lived Assets
• Measuring acquisition cost of plant assets • Recording plant assets • Computing depreciation • Revenue and capital expenditures • Disposing of plant assets	• Measuring intangible asset costs • Recording intangible assets • Computing amortization • Examples of intangible assets • Balance sheet presentation of intangible assets	• Return on assets • Asset turnover

OVERVIEW OF LONG-LIVED ASSETS

A.K.A. Plant assets are often referred to as *fixed assets*.

A.K.A. Property, plant and equipment is often referred to simply as *PP&E*.

Consider for a moment the asset structure of Tesla Motors, Inc. Approximately 30 percent of the assets used to fulfill the company's mission of manufacturing and distributing power products are in the long-term asset category—plant assets. **Plant assets** refer to a firm's *long-lived property, plant and equipment*. Tesla reports plant assets of over $1,829 million. Intangible assets, on the other hand, refer to those economic resources that benefit a company's operations but which lack the physical substance that characterizes plant assets. Examples of intangible assets include copyrights, franchises, and patents. Tesla's reported intangible assets are comprised of emission permits related to their Tesla Factory. The benefits provided to a firm by its plant assets and its intangible assets extend over many accounting periods. In this chapter, we discuss the accounting for these long-lived assets.

The carrying value of long-lived assets is initially based on the asset's historical cost—that is, the cost incurred to acquire and place the asset into a revenue-producing state. The costs related to the use of long-lived assets must be matched with the revenues that they help to generate to insure that a business's net income is correctly determined. The portion of an asset's cost that is consumed or used up in any given period is called *depreciation expense when referring to plant assets*, and *amortization expense when referring to intangible assets*. Depreciation and amortization both refer to the process of allocating a portion of an asset's acquisition cost to expense on the income statement to reflect the consumption of the asset as it produces revenue for a business.

Exhibit 9-1 provides several examples of both categories of assets. The exhibit also identifies the appropriate term for the periodic consumption of the asset and its write-off to expense. Note that site land—that is, the land on which a business is operated—has an indefinite useful life, and therefore does not require any periodic write-off to expense.

Exhibit 9-1	Long-Lived Assets That Require Periodic Write-Off	
Asset Category	**Examples**	**Term for the Periodic Write-Off to Expense**
Plant Assets	*Buildings, equipment, tools, furniture, fixtures, vehicles*	Depreciation
Intangible Assets	*Patents, copyrights, leaseholds, franchises, trademarks, brand names*	Amortization

426

ACCOUNTING FOR LONG-LIVED ASSETS (COST DETERMINATION)

Exhibit 9-2 is a graphic presentation of the accounting issues associated with long-lived assets during an asset's useful life. The accounting issues include: ❶ Identifying the type, and amount, of expenditures that make up the acquisition cost of the asset. ❷ Determining the appropriate amount of an asset's cost to periodically charge against revenue to reflect the asset's consumption. This involves estimating the asset's useful life and its probable salvage value at disposal. ❸ Differentiating those expenditures related to the maintenance of an asset from those expenditures that increase an asset's productive capacity or extend its useful life. ❹ Determining any gain or loss to be recognized when a long-lived asset is disposed of.

LO1 Discuss the nature of long-lived assets and **identify** the accounting guidelines relating to their initial measurement.

Exhibit 9-2	Issues Associated with the Accounting for Long-lived Assets

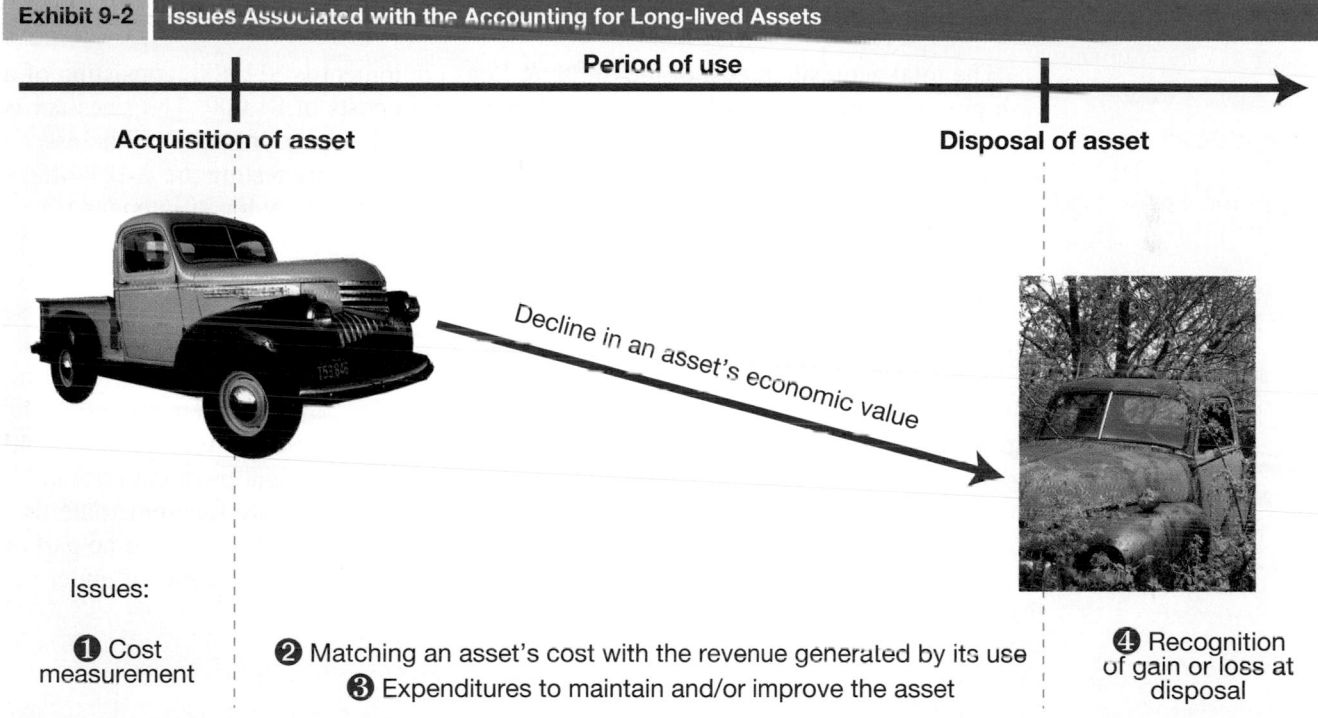

Acquisition Cost of Long-Lived Assets

Long-lived assets are initially recorded on the balance sheet at their acquisition cost. This measure is also called the asset's *historical cost* because it represents the amount expended when the asset was originally acquired. In general, the acquisition cost of a long-lived asset equals the cash and/or cash equivalent given up to acquire the asset *and* to prepare it for its intended use.

	Cost Principle	PRINCIPLE ALERT

The initial valuation of long-lived assets follows directly from the *cost principle* discussed in Chapter 1. To measure an asset's acquisition cost, accountants must not only identify the asset's cash-equivalent purchase price, but also identify whether any additional costs were incurred to get the asset to a company's place of business and in a condition for use by the business. Both costs are added to the asset's balance sheet value and are considered part of the asset's acquisition cost.

Cash Purchases

An asset's acquisition cost is often simply the amount of cash paid when the asset is acquired and readied for use by a business. Consider, for example, the following expenditures for a piece of equipment by Smith & Sons:

Purchase price components:		
Gross invoice price.	$10,000	
Less: Cash discount (1/10, n/30)	(100)	
Sales tax	500	$10,400
Related expenditures:		
Freight charges.	200	
Installation costs.	500	
Testing of installed machine.	300	1,000
Acquisition cost of equipment.		**$11,400**

The total acquisition cost of the Smith & Sons equipment is $11,400, consisting of a cash purchase price of $10,400 and related preparation costs of $1,000. The sales tax is a necessary component of the purchase price and should also be included in the asset's acquisition cost. Similarly, the costs of freight, installation, and testing are expenditures necessary to get the asset to the desired business location and ready for its intended use.

Deferred Payment Purchases

If an asset's purchase price is not immediately paid in cash, the cash-equivalent purchase price at the date of acquisition is determined and recorded in the asset account. Suppose, for example, that Smith & Sons purchased its equipment under a financing plan requiring a $400 cash down payment and a nine percent, $10,000 note payable due in one year. The implied cash price remains $10,400 even though more than $10,400 is eventually paid under the financing plan ($400 down payment + $10,000 principal payment on note + $900 interest payment = $11,300). Because the equipment is ready for immediate use, the extra $900 paid as interest is charged to interest expense and does not become part of its acquisition cost. The journal entry to record the purchase of the equipment under the financing plan is as follows:

A = L + SE	
+10,400	
−400 +10,000	

Equipment	10,400	
Cash		400
Notes payable		10,000
To record purchase of equipment.		

As in the case of a cash purchase, the expenditures for freight, installation, and testing are debited to the Equipment account when incurred.

Package Purchases

Sometimes several long-lived assets are purchased as a package. For example, assume that Smith & Sons purchased a freight terminal that included land, a building, and some loading equipment for an aggregate price of $190,000. For accounting purposes, the total purchase price should be divided among the three assets because (1) they should be reported in different asset accounts on the balance sheet to properly reflect the company's asset structure, (2) only the building and equipment are subject to depreciation, and (3) the equipment is likely to have an estimated useful life different from that of the building.

The total package price is allocated among the acquired assets on the basis of their relative market or appraisal values. For example, if the estimated market value of the land, building, and equipment is $60,000, $120,000, and $20,000, respectively, the allocation of the $190,000 acquisition price would be as follows:

Asset	Estimated Market Value	Percent of Total	Allocation of Purchase Price	Estimated Useful Life
Land	$ 60,000	30	$ 57,000 (30% × $190,000)	Indefinite
Building	120,000	60	114,000 (60% × $190,000)	30 years
Equipment	20,000	10	19,000 (10% × $190,000)	8 years
Totals	$200,000	100	$190,000	

Expenditures Related to Land

The purchase of land often raises a number of accounting issues. Suppose, for example, that Smith & Sons retains a local real estate broker at a fee of $2,000 to locate an appropriate site for the company's new office building. Assume, also, that the property selected for purchase has an existing building on it which will need to be razed. The terms of the sale include a down payment of $40,000 to the seller, with the buyer paying off an existing mortgage of $10,000 and $300 of accrued interest. In addition, Smith & Sons agrees to pay accrued real estate taxes of $800 owed by the seller. Other related expenditures include legal fees of $400 and a title insurance premium of $500. A local salvage company will be hired to raze the old building, paying Smith & Sons $200 for reclaimed materials. Applying the cost principle, the acquisition cost of the land is calculated as follows:

Payment to the seller	$40,000
Commission to real estate agent	2,000
Payment of mortgage and accrued interest due at time of sale	10,300
Payment of property taxes owed by seller.	800
Legal fees.	400
Title insurance premium.	500
	$54,000
Less: Net recovery from material reclamation	**200**
Cost of land	$53,800

Again, any expenditure for the property taxes, insurance, and legal fees should be capitalized, or added to, the acquisition cost of the land because they are necessary to complete the purchase transaction. Similarly, removing the old building also prepares the land for its intended use. The $200 net recovery from razing the existing structure, therefore, *reduces* the land's cost. A net payment to remove the old building would have *increased* the land's cost.

When a land site is acquired in an undeveloped area, a firm may pay a special assessment to the local government for such property improvements as streets, sidewalks, and sewers. These improvements are considered to be permanent improvements; and consequently, the special assessment is capitalized to (added to) the acquisition cost of the land.

A firm may also make property improvements that have limited lives. Classified as **land improvements**, they include such improvements as paved parking lots, driveways, private sidewalks, and fences. Expenditures for these assets are charged to a separate Land Improvement account on the balance sheet and depreciated over the estimated useful life of the improvements.

Leasehold Improvements

Expenditures made by a business to alter or improve leased property are called **leasehold improvements**. For example, a merchandising firm may make improvements, with the permission of the owner, to a leased building. **The Home Depot, Inc.,** a home improvement retail chain, leases a significant portion of its more than 2,000 U.S. stores and reports nearly $1.4 billion of leasehold improvements on its balance sheet. The improvements, or alterations, become part of the leased property and revert to the owner of the property at the end of the lease. The cost of the leasehold improvements is capitalized to the Leasehold Improvements account on the balance sheet and is depreciated over the life of the lease or the life of the improvements, whichever is shorter.

YOUR TURN! 9.1

The solution is on page 467.

Kelly Company purchased manufacturing equipment for $20,000 cash. In addition to the $20,000 purchase price, Kelly paid sales tax of $1,600, freight costs of $400, installation costs of $600, testing costs of $100, and $300 for unrelated supplies from the same company. Explain the accounting treatment for each of the expenditures.

CORPORATE SOCIAL RESPONSIBILITY

It is unlikely that the first company that you think of when asked to name the top companies in an annual ranking of socially-responsible businesses is a manufacturer of diesel engines. Perhaps you may need to revise your thinking. **Cummins Inc.** is a perennial top 10 finisher among Business Ethics 100 Best Corporate Citizens, a prestigious annual ranking by *Business Ethics* magazine. In fact, Cummins placed number one in the ranking in 2005!

Cummins is one of the best manufacturing companies in the world when it comes to air-emissions reduction research. The company's research efforts have paid off with a 90 percent reduction in diesel-engine emissions. Cummins' ten-year goal is to achieve zero, or close to zero, engine emissions.

NATURE OF DEPRECIATION

LO2 **Discuss** the nature of depreciation, **illustrate** three depreciation methods, and **explain** impairment losses.

With the exception of site land, the use of plant assets to generate revenue consumes the economic benefit provided by the assets. At some point—usually before they are totally worthless—these assets are disposed of, and often replaced. A diagram of a typical pattern of plant asset utilization is illustrated below:

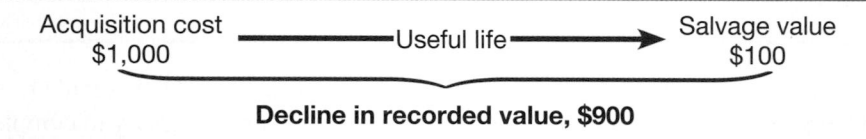

In this example, a plant asset is acquired for $1,000, used for several accounting periods, and then sold for $100. The $900 decline in recorded value is called **depreciation** and is an expense of generating the revenues recognized during the periods that the asset was in use. Thus, if a company's net income is to be a meaningful representation of the business's operating performance, $900 of expense must be allocated to the periods of asset use and matched with sales revenue. Failure to do so would overstate the company's net income for these periods.

As part of this allocation process, it is first necessary to estimate the asset's useful life and its expected future salvage value. **Useful life** is the expected period of economic usefulness to a business—that is, the period from the date of acquisition to the expected date of disposal. **Salvage value** (or *residual value*) is the expected net recovery (sales proceeds less disposal costs) when the asset is sold or removed from service. When the salvage value is insignificant, it may be ignored in the depreciation process under the materiality concept.

A.K.A. The salvage value of a plant asset is also often referred to as its *residual value* or *scrap value*.

Allocation versus Valuation: Depreciation Accounting

Although the idea is theoretically appealing, accountants do not base an asset's periodic depreciation expense on changes in the asset's market value or on the measured wear of the asset, primarily because a reliable, objective, and practical source for such data rarely exists. Rather, **depreciation accounting** is simply an attempt to allocate, in a *systematic* and *rational* manner, the difference between an asset's acquisition cost and its estimated salvage value over the *estimated* useful life of the asset. Consequently, depreciation accounting techniques are just convenient expedients for estimating asset utilization and should not be considered precise. Although imprecise, depreciation estimates facilitate a better assessment of a business's net income than would result from expensing the asset at either its date of acquisition or its date of disposal.

Expense Recognition (Matching) Concept	**PRINCIPLE ALERT**

Depreciation accounting represents an application of the expense recognition (*matching*) concept. Depreciable plant assets are used in a business's operating activities to help generate revenues. Each period that benefits from the use of a plant asset is assigned part of the asset's cost as depreciation expense. In so doing, the depreciation expense is matched with the sales revenue that the asset helps to generate. The matching that occurs through this allocation process extends throughout the asset's useful life.

Several factors are related to the periodic allocation of depreciation. Depreciation can be caused by wear from use, from natural deterioration, and from technical obsolescence. Each factor reduces the economic value of an asset. To some extent, maintenance (lubrication, adjustments, parts replacements, and cleaning) may partially arrest or offset wear and deterioration. Thus, when an asset's useful life and salvage value are estimated, a given level of maintenance is assumed.

Calculating Depreciation Expense

Estimating the periodic depreciation of a long-lived asset can be achieved in many ways. In this section, three widely used methods for calculating depreciation are illustrated.

1. Straight-line
2. Declining-balance
3. Units-of-production

For each method, we assume that equipment is purchased for $1,000. The equipment is assumed to have an estimated useful life of five years and has an estimated salvage value of $100.

Straight-Line Method

The **straight-line method** is the easiest depreciation method to understand and calculate. Consequently, this method is the most widely used depreciation method by U.S. businesses. Under the straight-line method, an equal amount of depreciation expense is allocated to each period of an asset's useful life. Straight-line depreciation is calculated as follows:

$$\text{Annual depreciation} = \frac{(\text{Acquisition cost} - \text{Salvage value})}{\text{Estimated useful life (in months or years)}}$$

For the purchased equipment, the annual straight-line depreciation expense is:

$$\frac{(\$1,000 - \$100)}{5 \text{ years}} = \$180 \text{ per year}$$

The journal entry to record the annual depreciation expense is:

A	=	L	+	SE
−180				−180 Exp

Depreciation expense—Equipment	180	
Accumulated depreciation—Equipment		180
To record depreciation expense for the year.		

A.K.A. The book value of an asset (acquisition cost less accumulated depreciation) is also referred to as the *net book value.*

Like other expense accounts, Depreciation Expense is deducted from sales revenue on the income statement and is closed at year-end to the Income Summary account. The offsetting credit entry is posted to a contra-asset account, Accumulated Depreciation, which is deducted from the Equipment account on the balance sheet to calculate the asset's book value. In this manner, the original acquisition cost of the asset is maintained in the asset account, and the cumulative balance of depreciation taken to date is carried in the contra-asset account, as long as the asset is in service. When an asset is disposed of, the asset's acquisition cost and accumulated depreciation are both removed from the accounts.

The following table shows the depreciation schedule for the equipment's five-year life under the straight-line method:

			End-of-Period Balance	
Year of Useful Life	**Balance of Equipment Account**	**Annual Depreciation Expense**	**Accumulated Depreciation Account**	**Asset's Book Value**
1	$1,000	**$180**	$180	$820
2	1,000	**180**	360	640
3	1,000	**180**	540	460
4	1,000	**180**	720	280
5	1,000	**180**	900	100
Total		**$900**		

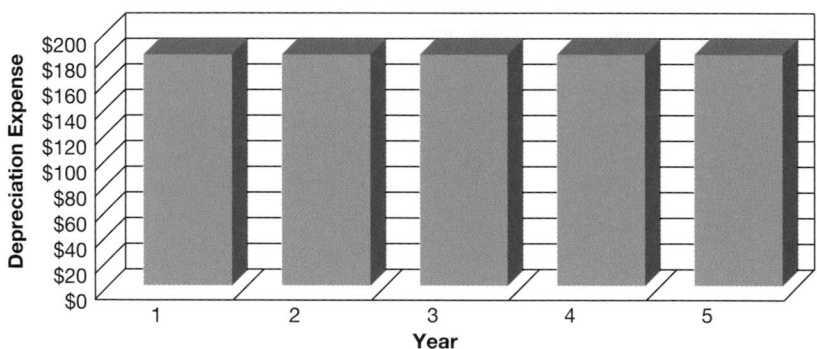

Notice that (1) the Equipment account always shows the original acquisition cost ($1,000) of the asset; (2) each period reflects $180 of depreciation expense; (3) the Accumulated Depreciation account balance is cumulative and shows the portion of the acquisition cost taken as depreciation to date; (4) the asset's book value is the original acquisition cost of the asset less the accumulated depreciation taken to date; and (5) the asset's book value at the end of the five-year period is equal to the asset's estimated salvage value. Thus, an asset's book value declines to its estimated salvage value as the asset is depreciated over its useful life.

For periods of less than one year, straight-line depreciation amounts are simply proportions of the annual depreciation charge. For example, if an asset is acquired on April 1, depreciation for the period ended December 31 would be $135, or 9/12 × $180. Assets acquired or disposed of during the first half of any month are usually treated as if the acquisition or disposal occurred on the first day of the month. When either event occurs during the last half of any month, it is assumed that the event occurred on the first day of the following month.

Note the role of the *going concern concept* in depreciation accounting. Absent evidence to the contrary, the going concern concept assumes that a business has an indefinite life. Depreciation accounting allocates an asset's acquisition cost to expense over the asset's useful life. Any depreciation method that allocates an asset's acquisition cost over many years—whether the useful life is five years or 25 years (or more)—implicitly assumes that a business will be in existence for at least that number of years.

Declining-Balance Method

The **declining-balance method** is an **accelerated depreciation method**. It calculates a company's depreciation expense as a constant percentage of an asset's book value as of the beginning of each period. The method takes its name from the fact that, over time, an asset's book value (acquisition cost − accumulated depreciation) declines as the asset is used up, yielding a decreasing depreciation expense. An asset's salvage value is not considered in the calculation of declining-balance depreciation, except that the depreciation of an asset stops when the asset's book value equals its estimated salvage value.

The declining-balance method is considered to be an "accelerated" method because the constant depreciation percentage it uses is a multiple of the straight-line depreciation rate (the straight-line depreciation rate = 100 percent/expected useful life in years). There are many versions of the declining-balance method because different multiples of the straight-line rate may be used. *Double-declining balance depreciation* uses a depreciation rate that is twice the straight-line rate; similarly, *150 percent-declining balance depreciation* uses a depreciation rate that is one and one-half times the straight-line rate.

For example, the straight-line depreciation rate for an asset with a five-year useful life is 20 percent per year (100 percent/5 years). Thus, to depreciate a five-year asset on an accelerated basis, the double-declining balance method uses a 40 percent depreciation rate (2 × 20 percent), while the 150 percent declining-balance method uses a 30 percent depreciation rate (1.5 × 20 percent).

Under the double-declining balance method, the annual depreciation expense is calculated as follows:

Annual depreciation = Book value at beginning of year × Double-declining balance rate

Referring to our example of the equipment purchased for $1,000, with a useful life of five years and an expected salvage value of $100, the periodic double-declining balance depreciation would be calculated as follows (amounts rounded to the nearest dollar):

Year of Useful Life	Acquisition Cost	Beginning Accumulated Depreciation	Beginning Book Value	Twice Straight-line Percentage		Annual Depreciation Expense
1	$1,000	$ 0	$1,000	× 40 percent	=	$400
2	1,000	400	600	× 40 percent	=	240
3	1,000	640	360	× 40 percent	=	144
4	1,000	784	216	× 40 percent	=	86
5	1,000	870	130	[exceeds limit]		30
Total						$900

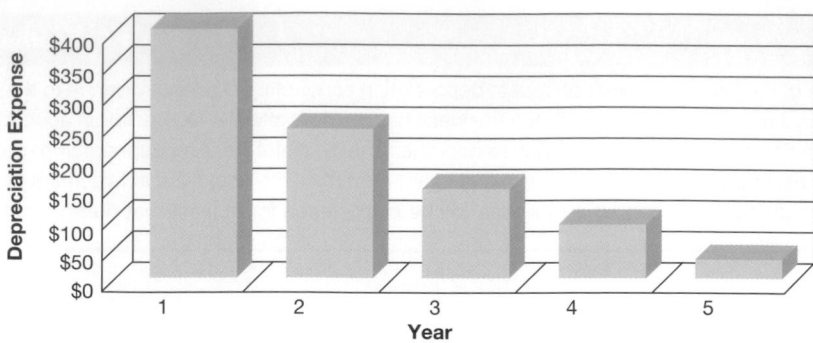

Notice in the fifth year that the depreciation expense is only $30, the amount needed to reduce the asset's book value to its estimated salvage value of $100. Assets are not depreciated below their estimated salvage value.

If an asset is purchased during a fiscal period, a pro-rata allocation of the first year's depreciation is calculated. If, for example, an asset is acquired on April 1, depreciation for the period ended December 31 would be $300, or [9/12 × (40 percent × $1,000)]. In subsequent periods, the usual procedure is followed; that is, the asset's book value at the beginning of the period is multiplied by the constant depreciation rate. For example, in the second year, depreciation on the asset would be $280, or [40 percent × ($1,000 − $300)].

Units-of-Production Method

The **units-of-production method** allocates depreciation in proportion to an asset's use in operations. Under this method, the depreciation per unit of production is first calculated by dividing the total depreciable cost of the asset (in our example, $1000 − $100 = $900) by the asset's projected units-of-production capacity:

$$\text{Depreciation per unit} = \frac{(\text{Acquisition cost} - \text{Salvage value})}{\text{Total estimated units of production}}$$

The total estimated units of production may represent the total expected miles that an asset will be driven, the total tons expected to be hauled, the total hours expected to be used, or the total number of expected cuttings, drillings, or stampings of parts by a piece of equipment. To illustrate, assume that a drilling tool will drill an estimated 45,000 parts during its expected useful life. The tool is purchased for $1,000 and has an expected salvage value of $100. Consequently, the depreciation per unit of production is:

$$\frac{(\$1,000 - \$100)}{45,000 \text{ parts}} = \$0.02 \text{ per part}$$

To find the asset's annual depreciation expense, the depreciation per unit of production is multiplied by the number of units actually produced during a given year:

Annual depreciation = Depreciation per unit × Units of production for the period

Assuming that the number of parts drilled over the five years were 8,000, 14,000, 10,000, 4,000, and 9,000, respectively, in Year 1 through Year 5, the units-of-production depreciation expense is calculated as follows:

Year of Useful Life	Depreciation per Unit		Annual Units of Production		Annual Depreciation Expense
1	$0.02	×	8,000	=	$160
2	0.02	×	14,000	=	280
3	0.02	×	10,000	=	200
4	0.02	×	4,000	=	80
5	0.02	×	9,000	=	180
Total					$900

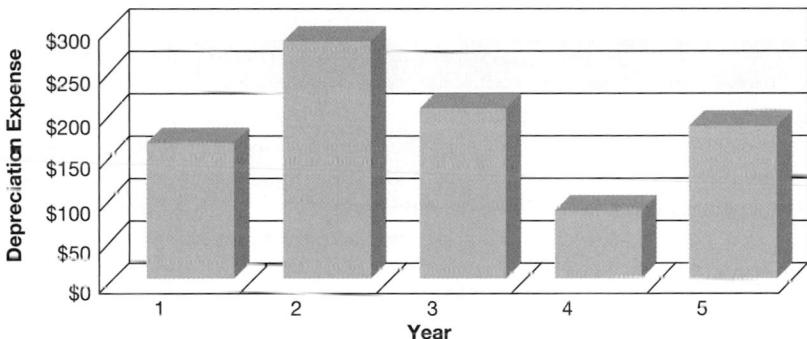

A Comparison of Alternative Depreciation Methods

The following chart compares the periodic depreciation expense from our equipment illustration. The chart shows the accelerated nature of the double-declining balance method relative to the straight-line method. Notice, for example, that the depreciation expense in Year 1 under the double-declining balance method is $400 but is only $180 under the straight-line method. In Year 2, the double-declining balance depreciation is $240 but again is only $180 for the straight-line method. It is not until Year 3 that the straight-line method produces a depreciation charge that exceeds the double-declining balance charge. Depreciation expense for the units-of-production method reflects the assumptions presented previously in the chapter. There is no general pattern for the annual depreciation expense under this method. The annual depreciation for the units-of-production method depends on the yearly productive activity of an asset, and this activity will vary from asset to asset. Finally, note that the total accumulated depreciation over the life of the asset is the same under all three methods, and is equal to the acquisition cost less salvage value, or $900.

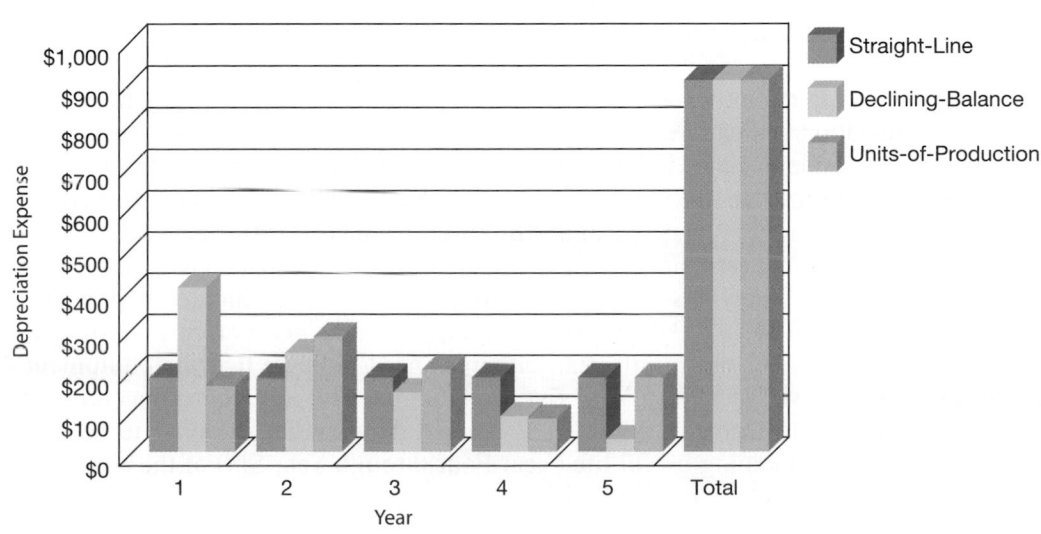

Annual Depreciation Expense			
Year	Straight-Line	Declining-Balance	Units-of-Production
1	$180	$400	$160
2	180	240	280
3	180	144	200
4	180	86	80
5	180	30	180
Total	$900	$900	$900

ACCOUNTING IN PRACTICE

Depreciation Methods

So many assets, so little time. Some accountants may feel that way when it comes to calculating the periodic depreciation expense for a business. They may also feel that variety is the spice of life. At least it appears that way given the various methods that companies choose to calculate the depreciation expense that appears in their income statements. Below are the depreciation methods used by 600 large U.S. companies. As can be seen, the straight-line method is by far the most popular depreciation method used:

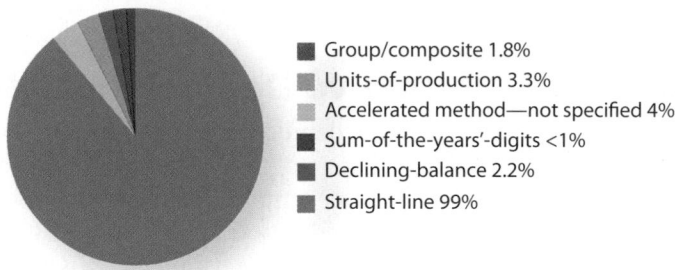

- Group/composite 1.8%
- Units-of-production 3.3%
- Accelerated method—not specified 4%
- Sum-of-the-years'-digits <1%
- Declining-balance 2.2%
- Straight-line 99%

*The totals exceed 100 percent because some firms use more than one method.
Source: Accounting Trends and Techniques

Depreciation Method Estimate Changes

It is important to remember that a business's periodic depreciation expense is based on estimates of both an asset's useful life and its salvage value. Circumstances change, however, and original estimates of both an asset's useful life and its salvage value may subsequently be found to be too high or too low. Once it is determined that the original estimates of either an asset's useful life or salvage value were incorrect, the calculation of the periodic depreciation expense for an asset's remaining useful life may be revised. When a depreciation estimate revision is found to be warranted, the revision is executed by allocating the undepreciated balance of the asset's book value over the revised remaining useful life. To illustrate this process, refer again to our example of equipment costing $1,000, with a five year life, and an estimated salvage value of $100.

If, based on original estimates, straight-line depreciation of $180 has been recorded for each of the first three years of the asset's useful life, the accumulated depreciation to date would total $540, or 3 × $180. Now, suppose that just before recording the depreciation expense for the fourth year, circumstances indicate that the equipment's useful life will total six years instead of five, and that its salvage value at the end of the sixth year will be $40 instead of $100. The revised depreciation expense to be taken during the revised remaining useful life (Year Four through Year Six) of the equipment is calculated as follows:

Original acquisition cost.	$1,000
Depreciation previously recorded (3 years @ $180)	**(540)**
Book value at start of fourth year.	$ 460
Revised salvage value	**(40)**
Revised remaining depreciable cost.	$ 420
Revised remaining useful life	3 years
Revised depreciation for fourth, fifth, and sixth years	$420/3 = $140 per year

Impairment Losses

Sometimes a change in the circumstances relating to a depreciable asset is so severe that the future cash flows from the asset's use and disposal are estimated to be *less* than its current book value. If an asset's remaining book value cannot be recovered through the future cash flows expected to be generated from the asset's use, the asset's value is said to be *impaired*. Under these circumstances, an impairment loss is recorded on the income statement, and the asset's book value on the balance sheet is reduced. The **impairment loss** is calculated as the difference between the asset's current book value and its current fair value.

To illustrate, assume that two years ago Cummins purchased equipment costing $500,000, with an estimated useful life of six years and a salvage value of $20,000. The equipment's book value is currently $340,000 ($500,000 cost less $160,000 accumulated depreciation). Unanticipated technological advances in equipment used by competitors, however, now severely limits the use of Cummins' equipment. An analysis by the company's CFO indicates that Cummins now expects that the net future cash flows to be generated from the use and disposal of the equipment over the next four years is $300,000. The limited uses for the equipment cause its current fair value to be only $200,000.

Cummins' equipment is impaired because its book value is not recoverable through its expected future cash flows—the $300,000 of expected future cash flows is less than the equipment's $340,000 current book value. Thus, an impairment loss is computed by comparing the equipment's book value with its current fair value, as follows:

Equipment book value	$340,000
Equipment current fair value	**(200,000)**
Impairment loss	$140,000

The journal entry to record the impairment loss is as follows:

Impairment loss on equipment	140,000		A = L + SE
Accumulated depreciation—Equipment		140,000	−140,000 −140,000
To record impairment loss on equipment.			Loss

Conservatism Concept   **PRINCIPLE ALERT**

The accounting for impaired plant assets illustrates the *conservatism concept*. In selecting between alternative accounting measures, the conservatism concept states that the least optimistic measure should be used. When a plant asset is impaired, it is reported on the balance sheet at its current fair value, an amount lower than its book value before any impairment loss is recorded. Unimpaired plant assets remain on the balance sheet at their book value, however, even though current fair values may be higher. U.S. GAAP mandates that asset values be written down when impaired, but prohibits the write-up of assets when their value appreciates.

While U.S. GAAP requires that long-lived assets be written down in value when they are judged to be impaired, they may not be written up in value if there is a subsequent recovery in their fair market value. Under International Financial Reporting Standards (IFRS), however, the accounting treatment of long-lived asset value recoveries is substantially different. Under IFRS, if an asset's value increases above its current book value, the asset's balance sheet value may be written up to the higher value by debiting the asset account for the amount of the increase. The balancing credit entry is to a stockholders' equity account called the asset revaluation reserve.

To illustrate, assume that Peabody International PLC, based in the United Kingdom, owns land in London that was originally purchased for 20 million British pounds. Current real estate appraisals, however, indicate that the fair market value of the land is now worth 50 million pounds. To recognize the increase in the land's fair market value, Peabody International would record the following journal entry:

Land	30 million pounds	
Asset revaluation reserve—Land		30 million pounds
To record the revaluation of land.		

Depreciation for Income Tax Purposes

Depreciation expense may be deducted by a business on its federal income tax return as a normal business expense. As a consequence, some refer to the tax deductibility of depreciation as a "tax shield" since depreciation expense lowers a business's taxable income, and hence, lowers the actual income taxes that must be paid. The depreciation expense deducted on a business's income tax return, however, may differ substantially from the depreciation expense reported on a company's income statement because the calculation of tax depreciation follows income tax regulations referred to as the **modified accelerated cost recovery system (MACRS)**.

MACRS establishes eight asset classes with prescribed useful lives ranging from three years to 31.5 years. Most machinery and equipment, for example, are in the seven-year asset class. When acquired, an asset is placed in the appropriate asset class (per MACRS guidelines) and depreciated over the prescribed useful life specified for that class.[1]

MACRS was introduced into U.S. tax law to encourage companies to invest in plant assets. Because the useful life specified under MACRS is usually shorter than an asset's accounting useful life, this method provides larger depreciation deductions during an asset's early years than was previously possible, much like the declining-balance method used for financial statement reporting. In a sense, the accelerated deductions under MACRS provide an interest-free loan to a business because they allow the firm to pay less income tax in the early years of an asset's life and more in the later years. During the intervening time period, the firm can use the postponed income tax payments to support the business's operations, without incurring any interest charges.

Change and modification characterize U.S. tax law. Tax depreciation guidelines will likely be modified again in the future. Keep in mind, however, that depreciation changes in the tax law do not affect the depreciation method and estimates that a firm may use in preparing its financial statements using U.S. GAAP for its shareholders and lenders.

---

[1] Depreciation in most asset classes must follow a half-year convention whereby one-half of the first year's depreciation expense is taken in the first year, regardless of when the asset was acquired, and one-half of the asset's last year's depreciation is taken in the year of disposal, regardless of when during the year the asset is disposed. The half-year convention means that assets in the three-year asset class are effectively depreciated over four different accounting periods, assets in the five-year property class are depreciated over six different accounting periods, and so on.

YOUR TURN! 9.2

The solution is on page 467.

The Salsbury Company purchased equipment costing $10,000 at the start of the year. The equipment has an estimated useful life of five years and a salvage value of $2,000. The CEO is unsure if the company should use the straight-line method or the double-declining balance method to depreciate the new equipment.

Required:
Prepare the journal entry for depreciation for the second year under each of the alternative depreciation accounting methods.

REVENUE VERSUS CAPITAL EXPENDITURES

LO3 Discuss the distinction between revenue expenditures and capital expenditures.

Revenue Expenditures

Revenue expenditures are expenditures relating to plant assets that are expensed when incurred. The following list identifies two common types of revenue expenditures:

1. Expenditures for ordinary maintenance and repairs of existing plant assets.
2. Expenditures to acquire low-cost items that benefit the firm for several periods.

Maintenance and Repairs

Some level of maintenance and repairs must be assumed when estimating the useful lives and salvage values of property, plant, and equipment. For example, a plant asset that is not maintained or repaired will have a shorter useful life than a similar asset that is properly maintained. Periodic upkeep—such as lubrication, cleaning, and replacement of minor parts—is necessary to maintain an asset's expected level and length of usefulness. These periodic upkeep costs—referred to as maintenance costs—are charged to expense as they are incurred.

Low-Cost Items

Most businesses purchase items that provide years of service at a relatively small cost, such as paperweights, staplers, and wastebaskets. Because of the small dollar amounts involved, establishing these items as assets on the balance sheet and depreciating them over their expected useful lives serves no useful purpose. The effect on the financial statements is insignificant and consequently, expensing these expenditures at the time of purchase is more efficient. The accounting for such low-cost items is thus completed in the period in which they are acquired.

Materiality Concept	PRINCIPLE ALERT

The practice of accounting for small dollar transactions in the most expedient fashion follows the *materiality concept*. Under this accounting concept, generally accepted accounting principles apply only to items of significance to the users of financial statements. Because the judgment of users will be unaffected by the accounting for immaterial dollar amounts, their immediate expensing does not diminish the usefulness of financial statements.

Capital Expenditures

Capital expenditures increase the book value of long-lived assets. To *capitalize* an amount means to increase an asset's book value by that amount. The following list identifies two typical capital expenditures related to property, plant, and equipment:

1. Initial acquisitions and additions.
2. Betterments.

Initial Acquisitions and Additions

At the beginning of this chapter, the accounting guidelines governing the initial measurement of long-lived assets were discussed. We noted that expenditures equal to an asset's implied cash purchase price, plus any costs necessary to prepare the asset for use, were debited to the asset account. These amounts are commonly referred to as capital expenditures.

These same accounting guidelines apply for additions to existing plant assets. Adding a new wing to a building or expanding the size of an asphalt parking lot are examples of additions. These capital expenditures should also be debited to an asset account. A separate account (and depreciation schedule) should be used for an addition when its estimated useful life differs from the remaining useful life of the existing plant asset.

Betterments

Betterments are expenditures that (1) extend the useful life of an asset, (2) improve the quality and/or quantity of the asset's output, or (3) reduce the asset's operating expenses. Examples include overhauling the engine or adding a power winch to a highway service truck, improving the precision of a machining device to reduce defects, or converting a building to solar power. Expenditures for betterments are generally debited to the appropriate asset account, and the subsequent periodic depreciation expense is increased to allocate the additional cost over the asset's remaining useful life.

YOUR TURN! 9.3

The solution is on page 467.

Hastings Company recorded the following expenditures during the year with regard to its delivery van:

1. Changed the engine oil
2. Repainted the van
3. Overhauled the engine that is expected to increase the useful life of the van
4. Repaired a dent in a fender
5. Converted the van to run on a biofuel with an estimated annual fuel cost savings of 30 percent.

Required:
Determine whether each of the above expenditures is a revenue expenditure or a capital expenditure.

WorldCom's Bad Accounting

 On the surface, the decision to capitalize or expense an expenditure related to a long-lived asset does not seem like the subject matter for one of the most infamous accounting scandals of all time. Unfortunately, to the many investors in **WorldCom** who saw the value of their investment disappear, this accounting decision had profound consequences.

Beginning in 2001, and continuing through mid-2002, WorldCom, under the direction of its CEO, CFO, Controller, and Director of General Accounting, used fraudulent accounting methods to portray a false picture of the company's financial health. The principal accounting gimmickry used by the company was to misclassify "line costs," a cost that should have been expensed each year, as a capital expenditure, thus adding to WorldCom's assets rather than adding to its expenses.

The fraud was discovered and brought to the attention of WorldCom's Board of Directors by a small team of internal auditors who had been conducting their investigation in secret, mostly at night. The Securities and Exchange Commission followed with its own investigation. The final conclusion—WorldCom's assets and pre-tax net income had been inflated by nearly $11 billion! Following a conviction for filing false financial reports with the SEC, WorldCom's CEO Bernard Ebbers was sentenced to 25 years in prison.

DISPOSALS OF PLANT ASSETS

LO4 Explain and illustrate the accounting for disposals of plant assets.

A business may dispose of its plant assets in a variety of ways. An asset may be sold, retired, or exchanged as partial payment for a new asset. The asset's usefulness to a firm may also be ended by an unfavorable or unanticipated event—the asset may be stolen or destroyed by a natural disaster.

Depreciation must extend through an asset's total useful life to a business. Consequently, depreciation must be recorded up to the disposal date, regardless of the manner of the asset's disposal. Should the disposal date not coincide with the end of an accounting period, a journal entry must record depreciation for the partial period—that is, the period from the date that depreciation was last recorded to the asset's disposal date.

The following data is used to illustrate the disposal of plant assets:

Equipment's acquisition cost.	$1,000
Estimated salvage value after five years	100
Annual straight-line depreciation	180

(Assume that depreciation to the date of disposal has been recorded.)

Sale of Plant Assets

Most sales of plant assets involve the following factors:

1. The sale transaction involves an exchange of a used plant asset for cash. Because the plant asset sold is no longer on hand, a journal entry must remove the asset account and the accumulated depreciation account from the books. These amounts together reflect the asset's book value.

2. Because plant assets are often sold for an amount higher or lower than their book value, a gain or loss will result. Sale proceeds in excess of book value create a gain, whereas book values in excess of sales proceeds create a loss.

Asset Sales for More Than Book Value

Assume that the equipment is sold for $230 midway through its fifth year of use. Depreciation was last recorded at the end of the fourth year. The journal entries to record the sale are:

			A = L + SE
Depreciation expense—Equipment	90		-90 -90 Exp
Accumulated depreciation—Equipment		90	
To record depreciation expense for six months ($180/2).			
			A = L + SE
Cash	230		+230 +40 Gain
Accumulated depreciation—Equipment	810		+810
Equipment		1,000	-1,000
Gain on sale of plant assets		40	
To record the sale of equipment for $230.			

Note that recording depreciation to the date of sale adds $90 to the Accumulated Depreciation account, which totals $810, calculated as [(4 × $180) + $90]. To reflect the sale properly, it is necessary to remove the entire amount of accumulated depreciation ($810) from the books. The gain of $40 is calculated as the sale proceeds of $230 minus the asset's book value of $190 ($1,000 − $810).

Asset Sales for Less Than Book Value

Assume that the equipment is sold for $30 at the end of the fifth year. The journal entry to record this sale is:

A	=	L	+	SE				
+30				−70 Loss	Cash		30	
+900					Loss on sale of plant assets		70	
−1,000					Accumulated depreciation—Equipment		900	
					Equipment			1,000
					To record the sale of equipment for $30.			

The loss on the asset sale equals the book value of $100 minus the sales proceeds of $30. The cash received is recorded, and the balances from both the Equipment account and the Accumulated Depreciation account are removed from the books.

If the equipment is sold for an amount exactly equal to its book value, no gain or loss results. Should the equipment be abandoned, stolen, or destroyed (with no insurance coverage) before the end of its expected useful life, a loss equal to its book value is recorded. Similarly, if the equipment is retired at the end of its useful life and has no salvage value, a loss equal to its book value is recorded.

Exchange of Plant Assets

A plant asset may be exchanged for another plant asset. The accounting for long-lived asset exchanges can be complex depending upon the relationship between the new asset and the asset being traded in. Consequently, the accounting for asset exchanges is covered in intermediate accounting textbooks.

YOUR TURN! 9.4

The solution is on page 467.

The Jones Company is self-insured, and consequently the company does not receive any insurance payments if it is involved in an accident. One of the Jones Company trucks was involved in a major accident and the company decided to sell the truck for scrap. At the time of the accident, the truck had a cost basis of $22,500 and accumulated depreciation of $15,000. The proceeds from the sale totaled $750.

Required:
Record the journal entry for the disposal of the truck.

ACCOUNTING IN PRACTICE

Career Opportunities at Tesla

When one thinks of a career at Tesla, one probably first thinks of somebody with an engineering or science background. While Tesla certainly hires people with these skills, they are also constantly looking for people with accounting skills to support its manufacturing. A recent search of career opportunities on Tesla's Website highlighted many accounting positions, including a Senior Corporate Accountant (Fixed Asset). Among the requirements is a bachelor's degree in accounting or finance with a preference for a CPA certification.

INTANGIBLE ASSETS

LO5 Discuss the nature of, and the accounting for, intangible assets.

Intangible assets are the various resources that benefit a business's operations, but which lack physical characteristics or substance. Intangible assets include, for example, the exclusive rights or privileges obtained from a governmental unit or by legal contract, such as patents, copyrights, franchises, trademarks, and leaseholds. Another intangible asset is goodwill, which reflects the beneficial attributes acquired in the acquisition of another company that cannot be attributed to any other recorded asset.

The term *intangible asset* is not used with precision in accounting. By convention, only certain assets are included in the intangible asset category. Some resources that lack physical substance, such as prepaid insurance, accounts receivable, and investments, are not classified as intangible assets. Because intangible assets lack physical characteristics, the related accounting procedures are more subjective than for such tangible assets as property, plant, and equipment.

Measurement of Intangible Assets (Cost Determination)

A firm should record intangible assets acquired from outside entities at their acquisition cost. Similarly, some intangible assets created internally by a firm are measured at their cost. For example, the costs to secure a trademark—such as attorney's fees, registration fees, and design costs—are charged to a Trademarks account.

The accounting for other expenditures related to intangible assets varies depending upon the type of expenditure and the nature of the intangible asset. **Research and development costs** are not capitalized to the balance sheet as an intangible asset because GAAP guidelines require that these expenditures be expensed when incurred. As a consequence, many significant costs incurred by a firm associated with developing a patentable product or process are not capitalized to the balance sheet. Legal costs associated with patent work may be capitalized, however, if they are material. The costs of developing, maintaining, or restoring an intangible asset are also expensed when incurred, provided that the asset is not specifically identifiable or has an indeterminate life. As a result of these accounting procedures, some companies may have important intangible assets that are carried at a nominal amount, or may even fail to appear at all on the firm's balance sheet.

It is noteworthy that one U.S. industry is exempted from the conservative accounting treatment of research and development costs. Under U.S. GAAP, software development companies may capitalize some costs associated with the development of software.

IFRS ALERT

The accounting for some intangible assets under IFRS differs significantly from the accounting under U.S. GAAP. For instance, under U.S. GAAP, all research and development costs must be expensed when incurred; however, under IFRS, development costs may be capitalized if a commercially viable product results from the original research effort. A significant consequence of this alternative accounting treatment is that IFRS-accounted companies enjoy a more fairly presented balance sheet, since most intangible assets are fully disclosed. On the balance sheets of many U.S. GAAP-accounted companies, there are many unreported intangible assets.

To illustrate, assume that British Laboratories PLC, a biotechnology company, spends five million British pounds on research for a cure for diabetes. The research leads to a promising compound that is shown in tests to effectively control the disease. Further testing is needed, however; and consequently, the company spends an additional three million British pounds to develop and test the drug compound before receiving a patent from the British Patent Office. Under these circumstances, the company would record an expense for its initial research effort, and an asset for the subsequent expenditure to develop the drug, as follows:

Research expense	5 million pounds	
Cash		5 million pounds
To record research expense.		
Development costs	3 million pounds	
Cash		3 million pounds
To capitalize development costs.		

In short, under IFRS, all research costs must be expensed when incurred. However, development costs may be capitalized to the balance sheet when a commercially viable product is evident.

Amortization of Intangibles

The **amortization** of an intangible asset carried on the balance sheet involves the periodic expensing of the asset's cost over the term of its expected useful life. Because salvage values are ordinarily not involved, the amortization of intangible assets typically entails (1) determining the asset's cost, (2) estimating the period over which it will benefit a company, and (3) allocating the cost in equal amounts to each accounting period involved. Straight-line amortization is typically used for intangible assets unless another method is shown to be more appropriate.

The amortization entry debits the Amortization Expense account and credits the Intangible Asset account. An Accumulated Amortization account could be used for the credit entry, but generally there is no particular benefit to financial statement users from accumulating amortization in a separate contra-asset account.

Not all intangible assets are amortized. Some intangible assets have a limited life because of legal or regulatory restrictions. Intangible assets classified as having a limited life are amortized over their expected useful life. Other intangible assets are considered to have an indefinite life because they are expected to generate cash flows for the company for the foreseeable future. Intangible assets with an indefinite life are not amortized.

EXAMPLES OF INTANGIBLE ASSETS

Patents

A **patent** is an exclusive privilege granted to an inventor by the U.S. Patent Office for a period of 20 years from the date the patent application is filed. A patent gives the patent holder the right to exclude others from making, using, or selling the invention. Patent laws were originated to encourage inventors by protecting them from imitators who might usurp the invention for commercial gain. Just what qualifies as a patentable idea, however, has become quite complex in the modern realm of technical knowledge. Consequently, long periods of patent "searching," and frequently, successful defense of infringement suits may precede the validation of a patent. Even though patents have a legal life of 20 years from application date, changes in technology or consumer tastes may shorten their economic life. Because of their uncertain value, patents are accounted for conservatively by most businesses. For example, most businesses amortize patents over a shorter period than 20 years. When patents are purchased, the buyer enjoys patent protection for the patent's remaining legal life.

CORPORATE SOCIAL RESPONSIBILITY

Intangible assets include items such as patents that provide protection from competitors using the patented device or process for up to 20 years. It is not uncommon for firms to vigorously defend their patents through aggressive lawsuits. Tesla believes so strongly in what electric vehicles can do for the planet that they have chosen to freely share its patents. This allows Tesla's competitors, along with any engineers who wish to use these patents, to work with the technology with the aim, according to Tesla, of strengthening the development of sustainable technology.

Copyright

A **copyright** protects its owner against the unauthorized reproduction of a specific written work, recorded work, or artwork. A copyright lasts for the life of the author plus 70 years. The purchase price of valuable copyrights can be substantial, and proper measurement and amortization are necessary for valid business income determination.

Franchises

Franchises most often involve exclusive rights to operate or sell a specific brand of products in a given geographic area. Franchises may be for definite or indefinite periods. Although many franchises are agreements between two private firms, various governmental units award franchises for public utility operations within their legal jurisdictions. The right to operate a **Kentucky Fried Chicken (KFC)** restaurant or to sell **Midas Mufflers** in a specific area illustrates franchise agreements in the private sector.

Types of Intangible Assets

Intangible assets are perhaps the most difficult asset category to fully comprehend. Intangible assets appearing on a company's balance sheet represent a varied collection of assets as can be seen from a sample of 600 large U.S. firms:

Type of Intangible Asset	Number	%
Goodwill	542	90%
Trademarks, brand names, copyrights	330	55%
Customer lists/relationships	320	53%
Technology	162	27%
Patents	161	27%
Licenses, franchises, memberships	114	19%
Non-compete covenants	112	18.7%
Contracts, agreements	104	17.3%
Other—described	65	10.8%

Source: Accounting Trends and Techniques.

Trademarks

Trademarks and **trade names** represent the exclusive and continuing right to use certain terms, names, or symbols, usually to identify a brand or family of products. An original trademark or trade name can be registered with the U.S. federal government for a nominal cost. A company may spend considerable time and money to determine an appropriate name or symbol for a product. Also, the purchase of well-known, and thus valuable, trademarks or trade names may involve substantial amounts of money. When the cost of a trademark or trade name is material, the amount is debited to an appropriate intangible asset account— Trademarks—and amortized over the period of expected benefit to a business.

Goodwill

Goodwill is an often misunderstood concept. In common usage, goodwill may represent the favorable reputation a firm has earned based on its prior operations, quality of service, or positive product characteristics. The term goodwill, however, has a much different meaning when used in accounting and finance. Goodwill represents the amount paid by one company in the acquisition of another company, above the amount that can be attributed to the identifiable net assets of the acquired company, including the other intangibles like those discussed above. The measurement of goodwill is complex because it can stem from many factors. Examples of such factors include exceptional customer relations, advantageous business location, operating efficiency, superior personnel, favorable financial sources, or perceived synergies between the acquiring company and the acquired company. Unlike most intangible assets, goodwill is not subject to periodic amortization. Instead, goodwill is evaluated annually for any impairment in value. If a company's goodwill is found to be impaired, the Goodwill account is written down to its fair value and an Impairment Loss is recorded on the income statement.

Goodwill Can Be a Significant Asset

Although accountants only record goodwill when another business entity is purchased (to the extent that the purchase price exceeds the fair value of the identifiable net assets acquired), the balance sheets of many major corporations contain significant amounts of goodwill. Recent balance sheets, for example, show the following amounts of goodwill: **Bank of America Corporation**, $69.2 billion; **General Electric Company**, $77.6 billion; **AT&T Inc.**, $69.2 billion; and **Procter & Gamble Company**, $53.7 billion. These amounts are evidence of the active acquisition efforts of these major corporations, and also of the large amounts that may be paid for goodwill in acquisition transactions.

YOUR TURN! 9.5

The solution is on page 467.

Match the descriptive explanation below with the correct term:

Amortization   Patent   Copyright
Franchise   Trademark

1. An exclusive right that protects an owner against the unauthorized reproduction of a specific written work.
2. The periodic write-off of an intangible asset to expense on the income statement.
3. An exclusive and continuing right to use a certain symbol to identify a brand or family of products.
4. An exclusive right to operate or sell a specific brand of products in a given geographic area.
5. An exclusive privilege granted to an inventor that gives the asset holder the right to exclude others from making, using, or selling the invention.

BALANCE SHEET PRESENTATION

LO6 Illustrate the balance sheet presentation of plant assets and intangible assets.

Plant assets and intangible assets are presented on the balance sheet below the Current Assets category. (Recall that the assets are listed on a classified balance sheet in descending order of liquidity.) For example, **Exhibit 9-3** reveals how these assets appear on the balance sheet of **Tesla Motors, Inc.** Tesla does not separately report its intangible assets because they are not considered material in amount.

Exhibit 9-3	Tesla Motors, Inc.	
TESLA MOTORS, INC. **Balance Sheet (asset section only)** **December 31, 2014 and 2013**		
Current Assets		
Cash and cash equivalents.	$1,905,713	$ 845,889
Short-term investments	17,947	3,012
Accounts receivable	226,604	49,109
Inventory	953,675	340,355
Other current assets	94,718	27,574
Total current assets.	3,198,657	1,265,939
Property, plant, and equipment, net	1,829,267	738,494
Other noncurrent assets.	821,327	412,497
Total assets.	$5,849,251	$2,416,930

RETURN ON ASSETS AND ASSET TURNOVER

LO7 Define the return on assets ratio and the asset turnover ratio, and explain their use.

The ability of a firm to use its assets effectively and efficiently is a sign of a healthy, well-managed company. The rate of return generated on a company's assets, referred to as the *return on assets ratio,* is a widely used indicator that focuses on this dimension of a firm's financial health. In practice, there is some variation in the calculation of this ratio, but one commonly used definition of the **return on assets** is:

$$\text{Return on assets} = \frac{\text{Net income}}{\text{Average total assets}}$$

This ratio relates data from two financial statements—the income statement and the balance sheet. The numerator consists of the net income for the year from the income statement.[2] The denominator in the ratio is the average balance of total assets for the year (add the total assets at the beginning of the year to the total assets at the end of the year and divide the sum by two) obtained from the balance sheet.

To illustrate the calculation of the return on assets ratio, we use data from General Motors, a competitor of Tesla in the automobile industry. The company reported 2014 net income of $3,949 million, total assets at the beginning of the year of $166,344 million, and year-end total assets of $177,677 million. General Motors' return on assets for the year is only 2.3 percent; calculated as $3,949/[($166,344 + $177,677)/2].

To evaluate a firm's return on assets, it is useful to consider the trend in the ratio, the return for other firms in the same industry, the industry's average return on assets, and the company's economic environment. For example, in the same year that General Motors generated a 2.3 percent return on its assets, Ford Motor Co., a competitor of General Motors, generated only a 1.6 percent return on assets. These results suggest that, for 2014, while General Motors reported a seemingly low ROA, the company utilized its assets more efficiently and profitably than did Ford.

Concept ⟶	Method ⟶	Assessment	TAKEAWAY 9.1
How effective is a company in using its assets to produce net income?	Net income and average total assets Return on assets ratio $= \dfrac{\text{Net income}}{\text{Average total assets}}$	A higher ratio value implies a higher, more effective level of asset utilization.	

The **asset turnover** ratio is another ratio that evaluates a company's effective use of its assets. This ratio measures how effectively a firm uses its assets to generate sales revenue. The asset turnover ratio is calculated as follows:

$$\text{Asset turnover} = \frac{\text{Net sales}}{\text{Average total assets}}$$

Referring again to the 2014 General Motors' data, the company reported net operating revenues (which is equivalent to net sales), of $155,929 million. Consequently, General Motors' asset turnover for the year is 0.91, or $155,929/[($166,344 + $177,677)/2], indicating that the company was able to generate $0.91 of sales revenue for every dollar invested in assets. A high asset turnover ratio indicates that a company is very effective in using its assets to generate sales revenue. For the preceding year, General Motors' asset turnover was 0.98. Thus, General Motors generated $0.98 in net sales in 2013 for each dollar invested in total assets. The decrease in General Motors' asset turnover from 0.98 to 0.91 indicates that the firm used its assets less effectively in 2014 than in 2013 to generate sales revenue.

---

[2] An alternative calculation of the return on assets ratio adds interest expense to net income in the ratio's numerator. This calculation keeps the method of financing a company's assets from influencing the calculation of the ratio.

Rollins Co. reported the following information in its 2015 financial statements:

Net sales.	$150,000
Net income.	25,000
Beginning of year total assets	130,000
End of year total assets	120,000

Compute the return on assets and asset turnover for Rollins Co. in 2015.

TAKEAWAY 9.2	Concept	Method	Assessment
	How effective is a company in generating sales revenue using its assets?	Average total assets and net sales $\text{Asset turnover ratio} = \dfrac{\text{Net sales}}{\text{Average total assets}}$	A higher ratio value implies a higher level of sales revenue generated for each dollar invested in assets.

COMPREHENSIVE PROBLEM

MBC

Segman Company purchased a machine on January 2 for $24,300. The machine has an expected useful life of three years and an expected salvage value of $900. The company expects to use the machine for 1,400 hours in the first year, 2,000 hours in the second year, and 1,600 hours in the third year.

Required
a. Calculate the depreciation expense for each year using each of the following depreciation methods: (1) straight-line, (2) units-of-production (assume that actual usage equals expected usage), (3) double-declining balance.

b. Assume that the machine was purchased June 1. Calculate the depreciation expense for each year using the following depreciation methods: (1) straight-line, (2) double-declining balance.

Solution
a. 1. Straight-line:
   Year 1: ($24,300 − $900)/3 = $7,800
   Year 2: ($24,300 − $900)/3 = $7,800
   Year 3: ($24,300 − $900)/3 = $7,800

2. Units-of-production:
   Depreciation per hour = ($24,300 − $900)/5,000 hours = $4.68 per hour
   Year 1: 1,400 hours × $4.68 = $6,552
   Year 2: 2,000 hours × $4.68 = $9,360
   Year 3: 1,600 hours × $4.68 = $7,488

3. Double-declining balance:
   Depreciation rate = (100/3) × 2 = 66 2/3 percent
   Year 1: $24,300 × 66 2/3 percent = $16,200
   Year 2: ($24,300 − $16,200) × 66 2/3 percent = $5,400
   Year 3: ($24,300 − $21,600) × 66 2/3 percent = $1,800

b. 1. Straight-line: Refer to calculations in (a)1.
   Year 1: $7,800 × 7/12 = $4,550
   Year 2: $7,800 (full year's depreciation)
   Year 3: $7,800 (full year's depreciation)
   Year 4: $7,800 × 5/12 = $3,250

2. Double-declining balance Refer to calculations in (a)3.
   Year 1: $16,200 \times 7/12 = \$9,450$
   Year 2: ($24,300 − $9,450) × 66 2/3 percent = $9,900
   Year 3: ($24,300 − $19,350) × 66 2/3 percent= $3,300
   Year 4: $750 [This amount reduces the machine's book value to its salvage value of $900 and is the maximum depreciation expense for the year. ($24,300 − $22,650) × 66 2/3 percent = $1,100 gives an amount in excess of the maximum $750 depreciation.]

SUMMARY OF LEARNING OBJECTIVES

Discuss the nature of long-lived assets and identify the accounting guidelines relating to their initial measurement. (p. 427) **LO1**
- The accounting for long-lived assets involves the determination of an asset's acquisition cost, periodic depreciation expense, subsequent capital expenditures, and disposal.
- The initial cost of a plant asset is its implied cash price plus any expenditure necessary to prepare the asset for its intended use.

Discuss the nature of depreciation, illustrate three depreciation methods, and explain impairment losses. (p. 430) **LO2**
- Depreciation is a cost allocation process; it allocates a long-lived asset's depreciable cost (acquisition cost less salvage value) in a systematic manner over the asset's estimated useful life.
- The most commonly used depreciation methods are straight-line, units-of-production, and declining-balance.
- Revisions of depreciation estimates are accomplished by recalculating depreciation charges for current and subsequent periods.
- When a plant asset is impaired, a loss is recognized equal to the difference between the asset's book value and its current fair value.

Discuss the distinction between revenue expenditures and capital expenditures. (p. 439) **LO3**
- Revenue expenditures are expensed as incurred and include the cost of ordinary repairs and maintenance and the purchase of low-cost items.
- Capital expenditures, which increase a plant asset's book value, include initial acquisitions, additions, and betterments.

Explain and illustrate the accounting for disposals of plant assets. (p. 441) **LO4**
- When a firm disposes of a plant asset, depreciation must be recorded on the asset up to the disposal date.
- Gains and losses on plant asset dispositions are determined by comparing an asset's book value to the proceeds received.

Discuss the nature of, and the accounting for, intangible assets. (p. 442) **LO5**
- Intangible assets acquired from other entities are initially valued at their acquisition cost. Some internally created intangible assets are also measured at their cost, but most expenditures related to internally developed intangible assets are expensed rather than capitalized.
- Research and development costs related to a firm's products and its production processes are expensed as incurred.
- Amortization is the periodic write-off to expense of an intangible asset's cost over the asset's useful life.
- Goodwill may be shown in the accounts only when it has been purchased as part of the acquisition of another business.

Illustrate the balance sheet presentation of plant assets and intangible assets. (p. 446) **LO6**
- Plant assets and intangible assets are shown on the balance sheet after long-term investments. Although technically an intangible asset, goodwill is reported separately on the balance sheet since it is not subject to amortization.

Define the return on assets ratio and the asset turnover ratio, and explain their use. (p. 446) **LO7**
- The return on assets ratio is calculated by dividing net income by average total assets; it represents an overall measure of a firm's profitability and how efficiently a company is using its assets to generate net income.

■   The asset turnover ratio is calculated by dividing net sales by average total assets; it provides an indication of the effective utilization of business assets to generate sales revenues.

SUMMARY	Concept ⟶	Method ⟶	Assessment
TAKEAWAY 9.1	How effective is a company in using its assets to produce net income?	Net income and average total assets $\text{Return on assets ratio} = \dfrac{\text{Net income}}{\text{Average total assets}}$	A higher ratio value implies a higher, more effective level of asset utilization.
TAKEAWAY 9.2	How effective is a company at generating sales using its assets?	Average total assets and net sales $\text{Asset turnover ratio} = \dfrac{\text{Net sales}}{\text{Average total assets}}$	A higher ratio value implies a higher level of sales revenue generated for each dollar invested in assets.

KEY TERMS

Accelerated depreciation method (p. 433)

Amortization (p. 443)

Asset turnover (p. 447)

Betterments (p. 440)

Capital expenditures (p. 439)

Copyright (p. 444)

Declining-balance method (p. 433)

Depreciation (p. 430)

Depreciation accounting (p. 431)

Franchises (p. 444)

Goodwill (p. 445)

Impairment loss (p. 437)

Intangible assets (p. 442)

Land improvements (p. 429)

Leasehold improvements (p. 429)

Modified accelerated cost recovery system (MACRS) (p. 438)

Net book value (p. 432)

Patent (p. 444)

Plant assets (fixed assets) (p. 426)

PP&E (p. 426)

Research and development costs (p. 443)

Return on assets (p. 446)

Revenue expenditures (p. 439)

Salvage value (residual value) (p. 430)

Straight-line method (p. 431)

Trademarks (p. 445)

Trade names (p. 445)

Units-of-production method (p. 434)

Useful life (p. 430)

Assignments with the ⓂⒷⒸ logo in the margin are available in ᵐʸBusinessCourse.
See the Preface of the book for details.

SELF-STUDY QUESTIONS

(Answers for the Self-Study Questions are available at the end of this chapter.)

LO1   1. **The acquisition cost of a plant asset is equal to the asset's implied cash price and:**
   a.   The interest paid on any debt incurred to finance the asset's purchase.
   b.   The market value of any noncash assets given up to acquire the plant asset.
   c.   The reasonable and necessary costs incurred to prepare the asset for its intended use.
   d.   The asset's estimated salvage value.

LO2   2. **On January 1, Rio Company purchased a delivery truck for $10,000. The company estimates the truck will be driven 80,000 miles over its eight-year useful life. The estimated salvage value is $2,000. The truck was driven 12,000 miles in its first year. Which method results in the largest depreciation expense for the first year?**
   a.   Units-of-production
   b.   Straight-line
   c.   Double-declining balance

LO4   3. **On the first day of the current year, Blakely Company sold equipment for less than its book value. Which of the following is part of the journal entry to record the sale?**
   a.   A debit to Equipment
   b.   A credit to Accumulated Depreciation—Equipment
   c.   A credit to Gain on Sale of Plant Assets
   d.   A debit to Loss on Sale of Plant Assets

4. Accounting for the periodic amortization of intangible assets is similar to which depreciation method?   LO5
   a. Straight-line
   b. Units-of-production
   c. Double-declining balance

5. An exclusive right to operate or sell a specific brand of products in a given geographic area is called: LO5
   a. A franchise.   c. A patent.
   b. Goodwill.   d. A copyright.

6. Which of the following statements is true?   LO5
   a. Goodwill is subject to amortization.
   b. Research and development costs may be capitalized to the balance sheet.
   c. Intangible assets are amortized to expense on the income statement.
   d. Goodwill arises because of a company's positive corporate image among its customers.

7. Which of the following statements is false?   LO3
   a. Expenditures for ordinary repairs are a capital expenditure.
   b. Betterment expenditures are a capital expenditure.
   c. Expenditures to acquire low cost assets are revenue expenditures.
   d. Material additions to a plant asset are capital expenditures.

8. Which of the following statements is true?   LO6
   a. Intangible assets are shown on the balance sheet net of the Accumulated Amortization account.
   b. Goodwill is shown on the balance sheet net of the Accumulated Amortization account.
   c. The Accumulated Depreciation account need not be used for plant assets.
   d. Plant assets are shown on the balance sheet net of the Accumulated Depreciation account.

9. A company reports net income of $6,000, net sales of $15,000, and average total assets of $24,000. What is the company's return on assets?   LO7
   a. 62.5 percent
   b. 25.0 percent
   c. 40.0 percent
   d. None of the above

10. A company reports net income of $6,000, net sales of $15,000, and average total assets of $24,000. What is the company's asset turnover?   LO7
    a. 0.625
    b. 0.250
    c. 0.400
    d. None of the above

11. Harley Company sold one of its worn out delivery trucks on December 31, 2016. The truck was purchased on January 1, 2013, for $50,000 and was depreciated on a straight-line basis over a 5-year life. There was no salvage value associated with the truck. If the truck was sold for $14,000, what was the amount of gain or loss recorded at the time of the sale?   LO4
    a. $4,000 loss   c. $4,000 gain
    b. $14,000 gain   d. $6,000 loss

QUESTIONS

1. What are the two major types of long-term assets that require a periodic write-off? Present examples of each, and indicate for each type of asset the term that denotes the periodic write-off to expense.

2. In what way is land different from other plant assets?

3. In general, what amounts constitute the acquisition cost of plant assets?

4. Foss Company bought land with a vacant building for $400,000. Foss will use the building in its operations. Must Foss allocate the purchase price between the land and building? Why or why not? Would your answer be different if Foss intends to raze the building and build a new one? Why or why not?

5. Why is the recognition of depreciation expense necessary to match revenue and expense properly?

6. What is the pattern of plant asset utilization (or benefit) that corresponds to each of the following depreciation methods: (a) straight-line, (b) units-of-production, (c) double-declining balance?

7. How should a revision of depreciation charges due to a change in an asset's estimated useful life or salvage value be handled? Which periods—past, present, or future—are affected by the revision?

8. When is a plant asset considered to be impaired? How is an impairment loss calculated?

9. What is the benefit of accelerating depreciation for income tax purposes when the total depreciation taken is no more than if straight-line depreciation were used?

10. Identify two types of revenue expenditures. What is the proper accounting for revenue expenditures?

11. Identify two types of capital expenditures. What is the proper accounting for capital expenditures?

12. What factors determine the gain or loss on the sale of a plant asset?

13. Folger Company installed a conveyor system that cost $192,000. The system can be used only in the excavation of gravel at a particular site. Folger expects to excavate gravel at the site for 10 years. Over how many years should the conveyor be depreciated if its physical life is estimated at (a) 8 years and (b) 12 years?

14. What are five different types of intangible assets? Briefly explain the nature of each type.

15. How should a firm account for research and development costs?

16. Under what circumstances is goodwill recorded?

17. How is the *return on assets* ratio calculated? What does this ratio reveal about a business?

18. How is the *asset turnover ratio* calculated? What does this ratio reveal about a business?

SHORT EXERCISES

LO1 **SE9-1. Calculate Amount to Capitalize** The Miller Company paid $10,000 to acquire a 100 ton press. Freight charges to deliver the equipment amounted to $1,500 and were paid by Miller. Installation costs amounted to $570, and machine testing charges amounted to $250. Calculate the amount that should be capitalized to the Equipment account.

LO2 **SE9-2. Depreciation Expense Using the Straight-Line Method** The Pack Company purchased an office building for $4,500,000. The building had an estimated useful life of 40 years and an expected salvage value of $500,000. Calculate the depreciation expense for the second year using the straight-line method.

LO2 **SE9-3. Depreciation Expense Using the Double-Declining Balance Method** The Pack Company purchased an office building for $4,500,000. The building had an estimated useful life of 40 years and an expected salvage value of $500,000. Calculate the depreciation expense for the second year using the double-declining balance method.

LO2 **SE9-4. Depreciation Expense Using the Units-of-Production Method** The Likert Company is a coal company based in West Virginia. The company recently purchased a new coal truck for $60,000. The truck had an expected useful life of 200,000 miles and an expected salvage value of $2,000. Calculate the depreciation expense using the units-of-production method assuming the truck travelled 40,000 miles on company business during the year.

LO4 **SE9-5. Sale of a Building** The Miller Company sold a building for $400,000 that had a book value of $450,000. The building had originally cost the company $12,000,000 and had accumulated depreciation to date of $11,550,000. Prepare a journal entry to record the sale of the building.

LO5 **SE9-6. Goodwill Impairment** Bruceton Farms Equipment Company had goodwill valued at $80 million on its balance sheet at year-end. A review of the goodwill by the company's CFO indicated that the goodwill was impaired and was now only worth $50 million. Prepare a journal entry to record the goodwill impairment on the books of the company.

LO5 **SE9-7. Amortization Expense** Smith & Sons obtained a patent for a new optical scanning device. The fees incurred to file for the patent and to defend the patent in court against several companies which challenged the patent amounted to $45,000. Smith & Sons concluded that the expected economic life of the patent was 12 years. Calculate the amortization expense that should be recorded in the second year, and record the journal entry for the amortization expense on the books of Smith & Sons.

LO7 **SE9-8. Return on Assets** The Kingwood Company reported net income of $50,000 and average total assets of $450,000. Calculate the company's return on assets.

SE9-9. Asset Turnover The Kingwood Company reported sales revenue of $520,000 and average total assets of $450,000. Calculate the company's asset turnover. **LO7**

SE9-10. Return on Assets and Asset Turnover Last year, the Miller Company reported a return on assets of 15 percent and an asset turnover of 1.6. In the current year, the company reported a return on assets of 19 percent but an asset turnover of only 1.2. If sales revenue remained unchanged from last year to the current year, what would explain the two ratio results? **LO7**

SE9-11. Sale of Equipment Prepare the journal entry for the following transactions: (1) Geysler Company sold some old equipment that initially cost $30,000 and had $25,000 of accumulated depreciation and received cash in the amount of $3,000. (2) Assume the same facts except Geysler received $9,000. **LO4**

SE9-12. Financial Statement Placement Name the financial statement where each of the following will appear: (IS) Income Statement; (BS) Balance Sheet; (SCF) Statement of Cash Flows; (N) None. **LO6**

  a. Book value of equipment purchased five years ago
  b. Market value of equipment purchased five years ago
  c. Cash proceeds from the sale of land
  d. Gain on the sale of buildings
  e. Accumulated depreciation on equipment
  f. Impairment loss on land

EXERCISES—SET A

E9-1A. Acquisition Cost of Long-Lived Asset The following data relate to a firm's purchase of a machine used in the manufacture of its product: **LO1**

Invoice price.	$30,000
Applicable sales tax	2,000
Cash discount taken for prompt payment	400
Freight paid	260
Cost of insurance coverage on machine while in transit	125
Installation costs	3,000
Testing and adjusting costs	475
Repair of damages to machine caused by the firm's employees	750
Prepaid maintenance contract for first year of machine's use.	000

Determine the acquisition cost of the machine.

E9-2A. Allocation of Package Purchase Price Tamock Company purchased a plant from one of its suppliers. The $950,000 purchase price included the land, a building, and factory machinery. Tamock also paid $6,000 in legal fees to negotiate the purchase of the plant. An appraisal showed the following values for the items purchased: **LO1**

Property	Assessed Value
Land.	$126,000
Building	456,000
Machinery.	318,000
Total	$900,000

Using the assessed value as a guide, allocate the total purchase price of the plant to the land, building, and machinery accounts in Tamock Company's records.

E9-3A. Depreciation Methods A delivery truck costing $20,000 is expected to have a $2,000 salvage value at the end of its useful life of four years or 100,000 miles. Assume that the truck was purchased on January 2. Calculate the depreciation expense for the second year using each of the following depreciation methods: (a) straight-line, (b) double-declining balance, and (c) units-of-production. (Assume that the truck was driven 30,000 miles in the second year.) **LO2**

LO2 **E9-4A.** **Revision of Depreciation** On January 2, 2012, Mosler, Inc., purchased equipment for $85,000. The equipment was expected to have a $10,000 salvage value at the end of its estimated six-year useful life. Straight-line depreciation has been recorded. Before adjusting the accounts for 2016, Mosler decided that the useful life of the equipment should be extended by three years and the salvage value decreased to $8,000.

    a. Prepare a journal entry to record depreciation expense on the equipment for 2016.

    b. What is the book value of the equipment at the end of 2016 (after recording the depreciation expense for 2016)?

LO2 **E9-5A.** **Impairment Loss** On July 1, 2012, Okin Company purchased equipment for $325,000; the estimated useful life was 10 years and the expected salvage value was $25,000. Straight-line depreciation is used. On July 1, 2016, economic factors cause the market value of the equipment to decrease to $90,000. On this date, Okin evaluates if the equipment is impaired and estimates future cash flows relating to the use and disposal of the equipment to be $195,000.

    a. Is the equipment impaired at July 1, 2016? Explain.

    b. If the equipment is impaired at July 1, 2016, calculate the amount of the impairment loss.

    c. If the equipment is impaired at July 1, 2016, prepare the journal entry to record the impairment loss.

LO3 **E9-6A.** **Revenue and Capital Expenditures** Shively Company built an addition to its chemical plant. Indicate whether each of the following expenditures related to the addition is a revenue expenditure or a capital expenditure:

    a. Shively's initial application for a building permit was denied by the city as not conforming to environmental standards. Shively disagreed with the decision and spent $6,000 in attorney's fees to convince the city to reverse its position and issue the permit.

    b. Due to unanticipated sandy soil conditions, and on the advice of construction engineers, Shively spent $58,000 to extend the footings for the addition to a greater depth than originally planned.

    c. Shively spent $3,000 to send each of the addition's subcontractors a side of beef as a thank-you gift for completing the project on schedule.

    d. Shively invited the mayor to a ribbon-cutting ceremony to open the plant addition. It spent $25 to purchase the ribbon and scissors.

    e. Shively spent $4,100 to have the company logo sandblasted into the concrete above the entrance to the addition.

LO4 **E9-7A.** **Sale of Plant Asset** Raine Company has a machine that originally cost $58,000. Depreciation has been recorded for four years using the straight-line method, with a $5,000 estimated salvage value at the end of an expected ten-year life. After recording depreciation at the end of four years, Raine sells the machine. Prepare the journal entry to record the machine's sale for:

    a. $37,000 cash.

    b. $36,800 cash.

    c. $28,000 cash.

LO5 **E9-8A.** **Amortization Expense** For each of the following unrelated situations, calculate the annual amortization expense and prepare a journal entry to record the expense:

    a. A patent with a 10-year remaining legal life was purchased for $300,000. The patent will be commercially exploitable for another eight years.

    b. A patent was acquired on a device designed by a production worker. Although the cost of the patent to date consisted of $52,300 in legal fees for handling the patent application, the patent should be commercially valuable during its entire remaining legal life of 10 years and is currently worth $378,000.

    c. A franchise granting exclusive distribution rights for a new solar water heater within a three-state area for five years was obtained at a cost of $70,000. Satisfactory sales performance over the five years permits renewal of the franchise for another four years (at an additional cost determined at renewal).

LO7 **E9-9A.** **Return on Assets Ratio and Asset Turnover Ratio** Campo Systems reported the following financial data (in millions) in its annual report:

	2015	2016
Net income.	$ 8,052	$ 7,250
Net sales.	52,350	36,117
Total assets	58,734	68,128

If the company's total assets are $55,676 in 2014, calculate the company's (a) return on assets and (b) asset turnover for 2015 and 2016.

E9-10A. Financial Statement Presentation Vera Corp. reported the following amounts for the year just ended: **LO6**

Land	$135,000
Patents	25,000
Equipment	40,000
Buildings.	150,000
Goodwill	35,000
Accumulated amortization	13,000
Accumulated depreciation	80,000

Prepare a partial balance sheet for these amounts.

EXERCISES—SET B

E9-1B. Acquisition Cost of Long-Lived Asset Fischer Construction purchased a used front-end loader for $32,000, terms 1/10, n/30, F.O.B. shipping point, freight collect. Fischer paid the freight charges of $330 and sent the seller a check for $31,680 one week after the machine was delivered. The loader required a new battery, which cost Fischer $180. Fischer also spent $240 to have the company name printed on the loader and $375 for one year's insurance coverage on it. Fischer hired a new employee to operate it at a wage of $20 per hour; the employee spent one morning (six hours) practicing with the machine and went to work at a construction site that afternoon. Calculate the amount at which the front-end loader should be reported on the company's balance sheet. **LO1**

E9-2B. Allocation of Package Purchase Price Andrew Lupino went into business by purchasing a car lubrication station, consisting of land, a building, and equipment. The seller's original asking price was $240,000. Lupino hired an appraiser for $3,000 to appraise the assets. The appraised valuations were land, $43,000; building, $95,000; and equipment, $62,000. After receiving the appraisal, Lupino offered $183,000 for the business. The seller refused this offer. Lupino then offered $187,000 for the business, which the seller accepted. Using the appraisal values as a guide, allocate the total purchase price of the car lubrication station to the Land, Building, and Equipment accounts. **LO1**

E9-3B. Depreciation Methods A machine costing $153,000 was purchased May 1. The machine should be obsolete after four years and, therefore, no longer useful to the company. The estimated salvage value is $15,000. Calculate the depreciation expense for each year of its expected useful life using each of the following depreciation methods: (a) straight-line, (b) double-declining balance. **LO2**

E9-4B. Revision of Depreciation Associated Clinic purchased a special machine for use in its laboratory on January 2, 2013. The machine cost $98,000 and was expected to last 10 years. Its salvage value was estimated to be $6,000. By early 2015, it was evident that the machine will be useful for a total of only seven years. The salvage value after seven years was estimated to be $7,500. Associated Clinic uses straight-line depreciation. Compute the proper depreciation expense on the machine for 2015. **LO2**

E9-5B. Impairment Loss On May 1, 2013, Silky, Inc., purchased machinery for $345,000; the estimated useful life was eight years and the expected salvage value was $15,000. Straight-line depreciation is used. On May 1, 2015, economic factors cause the market value of the machinery to decrease to $190,000. On this date, Silky evaluates whether the machinery is impaired. **LO2**

a. Assume that on May 1, 2015, Silky estimates future cash flows relating to the use and disposal of the machinery to be $270,000. Is the machinery impaired at May 1, 2015? Explain. If it is impaired, what is the amount of the impairment loss?

    b. Assume that on May 1, 2015, Silky estimates future cash flows relating to the use and disposal of the machinery to be $230,000. Is the machinery impaired at May 1, 2015? Explain. If it is impaired, what is the amount of the impairment loss?

LO3   **E9-6B.** **Revenue and Capital Expenditures** Indicate whether each of the following expenditures is a revenue expenditure or a capital expenditure for Blare Company:

    a. Paid $280 to replace a truck windshield that was cracked by a stone thrown up by another vehicle while the truck was being used to make a delivery.

    b. Paid $10 for a "No Smoking" sign for the conference room.

    c. Paid $900 to add a hard disk to an employee's computer.

    d. Paid $15 for a dust cover for a computer printer.

    e. Paid $280 to replace a cracked windshield on a used truck that was just purchased for company use. The company bought the truck knowing the windshield was cracked.

    f. Paid $500 for a building permit from the city for a storage shed the company is going to have built.

LO4   **E9-7B.** **Sale of Plant Asset** Noble Company has equipment that originally cost $68,000. Depreciation has been recorded for six years using the straight-line method, with a $9,000 estimated salvage value at the end of an expected eight-year life. After recording depreciation at the end of six years, Noble sells the equipment. Prepare the journal entry to record the equipment's sale for:

    a. $27,000 cash.

    b. $23,750 cash.

    c. $18,000 cash.

LO5   **E9-8B.** **Amortization Expense** For each of the following unrelated situations, calculate the annual amortization expense and prepare a journal entry to record the expense:

    a. A patent with a 15-year remaining legal life was purchased for $756,000. The patent will be commercially exploitable for another seven years.

    b. A patent was acquired on a device designed by a production worker. Although the cost of the patent to date consisted of $88,200 in legal fees for handling the patent application, the patent should be commercially valuable during its entire remaining legal life of 18 years and is currently worth $720,000.

    c. A franchise granting exclusive distribution rights for a new wind turbine within a three-state area for four years was obtained at a cost of $68,800. Satisfactory sales performance over the four years permits renewal of the franchise for another four years (at an additional cost determined at renewal).

LO7   **E9-9B.** **Return on Assets Ratio and Asset Turnover Ratio** Allied Systems reported the following financial data (in millions) in its annual report:

	2015	2016
Net income.	$19,300	$16,134
Net sales.	49,540	47,152
Total assets	68,734	78,128

If the company's total assets are $65,676 in 2014, calculate the company's (a) return on assets and (b) asset turnover for 2015 and 2016.

LO6   **E9-10B.** **Financial Statement Presentation** Evae Corp. reported the following amounts for the year just ended:

Land	$ 60
Trademarks	16
Equipment	83
Buildings.	110
Goodwill	30
Accumulated amortization	8
Accumulated depreciation	55

Prepare a partial balance sheet for these amounts.

PROBLEMS—SET A

P9-1A. Acquisition Cost of Long-Lived Assets The following items represent expenditures (or receipts) **LO1**
related to the construction of a new home office for Lowrey Company.

Cost of land site, which included an old apartment building appraised at $75,000	$ 173,000
Legal fees, including fee for title search.	2,100
Payment of apartment building mortgage and related interest due at time of sale.	9,300
Payment for delinquent property taxes assumed by the purchaser	6,000
Cost of razing the apartment building	17,000
Proceeds from sale of salvaged materials	(3,800)
Grading to establish proper drainage flow on land site	2,100
Architect's fees on new building	300,000
Proceeds from sales of excess dirt (from basement excavation) to owner of adjoining	
property (dirt was used to fill in a low area on property)	(2,000)
Payment to building contractor	5,000,000
Payment of medical bills of employee accidentally injured while inspecting building	
construction	1,600
Special assessment for paving city sidewalks (paid to city)	18,000
Cost of paving driveway and parking lot	25,000
Cost of installing lights in parking lot	9,500
Premium for insurance on building during construction	7,800
Cost of open house party to celebrate opening of new building.	8,000

Required
From the given data, calculate the proper balances for the Land, Building, and Land Improvements
accounts of Lowrey Company.

P9-2A. Allocation of Package Purchase Price and Depreciation Methods To expand its business, Small **LO1, 2**
Company paid $760,000 for most of the property, plant, and equipment of a small trucking company
that was going out of business. Before agreeing to the price, Small hired a consultant for $5,000 to
appraise the assets. The appraised values were as follows:

Land	$120,000
Building	440,000
Trucks.	144,000
Equipment	96,000
Total	$800,000

Small issued two checks totaling $765,000 to acquire the assets and pay the consultant on July 1. Small
depreciated the assets using the straight-line method on the building and on the equipment, and the double-
declining balance method on the trucks. Estimated useful lives and salvage values were as follows:

	Useful Life	Salvage Value
Building	20 years	$42,000
Trucks.	4 years	15,000
Equipment	8 years	10,000

Required
a. Calculate the amounts allocated to the various types of plant assets acquired on July 1.
b. Prepare the July 1 journal entries to record the purchase of the assets and the payment to the
consultant.
c. Prepare the December 31 journal entries to record depreciation expense for the year on the building, trucks, and equipment.

P9-3A. Depreciation Methods On January 2, 2015, Roth, Inc. purchased a laser cutting machine to be used **LO2**
in the fabrication of a part for one of its key products. The machine cost $90,000, and its estimated
useful life was four years or 850,000 cuttings, after which it could be sold for $5,000.

Required

a. Calculate each year's depreciation expense for the machine's useful life under each of the following depreciation methods:
    1. Straight-line.
    2. Double-declining balance.
    3. Units-of-production. Assume annual production in cuttings of 200,000; 350,000; 260,000; and 40,000.

b. Assume that the machine was purchased on July 1, 2015. Calculate each year's depreciation expense for the machine's useful life under each of the following depreciation methods:
    1. Straight-line.
    2. Double-declining balance.

LO1, 2, 3   **P9-4A.**   **Accounting for Plant Assets** Basin Corporation had the following transactions related to its delivery truck:

Year 1

Jan.	5	Purchased for $16,300 cash a new truck with an estimated useful life of four years and a salvage value of $4,300.
Feb.	20	Installed a new set of side-view mirrors at a cost of $68 cash.
June	9	Paid $325 for an engine tune-up, wheel balancing, and a periodic chassis lubrication.
Aug.	2	Paid a $410 repair bill for the uninsured portion of damages to the truck caused by Basin's own driver.
Dec.	31	Recorded depreciation on the truck for the year.

Year 2

May	1	Installed a set of parts bins in the truck at a cost of $800 cash. This expenditure was not expected to increase the salvage value of the truck.
Dec.	31	Recorded depreciation on the truck for the year.

Year 3

Dec.	31	Recorded depreciation on the truck for the year.

Basin's depreciation policies include (1) using straight-line depreciation, (2) recording depreciation to the nearest whole month, and (3) expensing all truck expenditures of $100 or less.

Required

Prepare journal entries to record these transactions and adjustments.

LO4   **P9-5A.**   **Disposal of Plant Asset** Citano Company has a used executive charter plane that originally cost $850,000. Straight-line depreciation on the plane has been recorded for six years, with a $70,000 expected salvage value at the end of its estimated eight-year useful life. The last depreciation entry was made at the end of the sixth year. Eight months into the seventh year, Citano disposes of the plane.

Required

Prepare journal entries to record:

a. Depreciation expense to the date of disposal.
b. Sale of the plane for cash at its book value.
c. Sale of the plane for $215,000 cash.
d. Sale of the plane for $195,000 cash.
e. Destruction of the plane in a fire. Citano expects a $190,000 insurance settlement.

LO1, 2, 5   **P9-6A.**   **Accounting for Intangible Assets and Leasehold Improvements** Berdahl Company owns several retail outlets. During the year, it expanded operations and entered into the following transactions:

Jan.	2	Signed an eight-year lease for additional retail space for an annual rent of $25,250. Paid the first year's rent on this date. (*Hint:* Debit the first year's rent to Prepaid Rent.)
	3	Paid $23,600 to a contractor for installation of a new oak floor in the leased facility. The oak floor's life is an estimated 50 years with no salvage value.
Mar.	1	Paid $45,000 to obtain an exclusive area franchise for five years to distribute a new line of gourmet chocolates.

July 1 Paid $46,000 to LogoLab, Inc., for designing a trademark for a new line of gourmet chocolates that Berdahl will distribute nationally. Berdahl will use the trademark for as long as the firm remains in business. Berdahl expects to be in business for at least another 50 years.

  1 Paid $36,000 for advertisement in a national magazine (June issue) introducing the new line of gourmet chocolates and the trademark.

Required

a. Prepare journal entries to record these transactions.

b. Prepare the necessary adjusting entries on December 31 for these transactions. Berdahl makes adjusting entries once a year. Berdahl uses straight-line depreciation and amortization.

P9-7A. Preparation of Balance Sheet Dooley Company's December 31 post-closing trial balance contains the following normal balances: **LO6**

Cash.	$ 11,000
Accounts payable.	20,000
Building	439,500
Long-term notes payable.	785,000
Common stock.	900,000
Retained earnings	75,000
Accumulated depreciation—Equipment	180,000
Land.	834,500
Accounts receivable.	22,500
Accumulated depreciation—Building.	135,000
Wages payable.	6,000
Patent (net of amortization)	120,000
Notes payable (short term).	131,000
Inventory.	206,000
Equipment	600,000
Allowance for doubtful accounts	1,500

Required

Prepare a December 31 classified balance sheet for Dooley Company.

P9-8A. Journal Entries for Plant Assets During the first few days of the year, Coast Company entered into the following transactions: **LO1, 2, 3**

1. Purchased a parcel of land with a building on it for $900,000 cash. The building, which will be used in operations, has an estimated useful life of 25 years and a salvage value of $60,000. The assessed valuations for property tax purposes show the land at $80,000 and the building at $720,000.

2. Paid $31,200 for the construction of an asphalt parking lot for customers. The parking lot is expected to last 12 years and has no salvage value.

3. Paid $25,000 for the construction of a new entrance to the building.

4. Purchased store equipment, paying the invoice price (including seven percent sales tax) of $78,760 in cash. The estimated useful life of the equipment is eight years, and the salvage value is $6,000.

5. Paid $240 freight on the new equipment.

6. Paid $1,650 to repair damages to floor caused when the store equipment was accidentally dropped as it was moved into place.

7. Paid $55 for an umbrella holder to place inside front door (customers may place wet umbrellas in the holder). The holder is expected to last 20 years.

Required

a. Prepare journal entries to record these transactions.

b. Prepare the December 31 journal entries to record depreciation expense for the year. Double-declining balance depreciation is used for the equipment, and straight-line depreciation is used for the building and parking lot.

LO2, 3 **P9-9A.** **Revision of Depreciation and Capital Expenditure** Porter Company uses straight-line depreciation for its equipment. On January 1, 2010, Porter purchased a new piece of equipment for $168,000 cash. The equipment's estimated useful life was ten years with $15,000 salvage value. In 2015, the company decided its original useful life estimate should be increased by five years. Beginning in 2015, depreciation was based on a 15-year total useful life and no change was made in the salvage value estimate. On January 3, 2016, Porter added a modification to the equipment that increased its productivity at a cost of $21,100 cash. These modifications did not change the equipment's useful life but did increase the estimated salvage value by $4,000.

Required

a. Prepare journal entries to record (1) the purchase of the equipment, (2) 2010 depreciation expense, (3) 2015 depreciation expense, (4) the 2016 modification, and (5) 2016 depreciation expense.

b. Calculate the book value of the equipment at the end of 2016 (that is, after recording the depreciation expense for 2016).

PROBLEMS—SET B

LO1 **P9-1B.** **Acquisition Cost of Long-Lived Assets** The following items represent expenditures (or receipts) related to the construction of a new home office for Secrest Investment Company.

Cost of land site, which included an abandoned railroad spur	$ 185,000
Legal fees, including title search, relating to land purchase	4,300
Cost of surveying land to confirm boundaries	1,100
Cost of removing railroad tracks	7,000
Payment of delinquent property taxes assumed by the purchaser	6,000
Proceeds from sale of timber from walnut trees cut down to prepare site for construction	(18,000)
Proceeds from sale of salvaged railroad track	(4,700)
Grading to prepare land site for construction	4,000
Cost of basement excavation (contracted separately)	3,700
Architect's fees on new building	129,000
Payment to building contractor—original contract price	3,200,000
Cost of changes during construction to make building more energy efficient	91,000
Cost of replacing windows broken by vandals	3,400
Cost of paving driveway and parking lot	17,000
Out-of-court settlement for mud slide onto adjacent property	12,500
Special assessment for paving city sidewalks (paid to city)	22,000
Cost of brick and wrought iron fence installed across front of property	16,500

Required

From the given data, compute the proper balances for the Land, Building, and Land Improvements accounts of Secrest Investment Company.

LO1, 2 **P9-2B.** **Allocation of Package Purchase Price and Depreciation Methods** In an expansion move, Beam Company paid $2,190,000 for most of the property, plant, and equipment of a small manufacturing firm that was going out of business. Before agreeing to the price, Beam hired a consultant for $25,000 to appraise the assets. The appraised values were as follows:

Land	$ 384,000
Building	912,000
Equipment	960,000
Trucks	144,000
Total	$2,400,000

Beam issued two checks totaling $2,215,000 to acquire the assets and pay the consultant on April 1. Beam depreciated the assets using the straight-line method for the building and equipment, and the double-declining balance method for the trucks. Estimated useful lives and salvage values were as follows:

	Useful Life	Salvage Value
Building	15 years	$86,000
Equipment	9 years	70,000
Trucks.	5 years	13,000

Required
a. Calculate the amounts allocated to the various types of plant assets acquired on April 1.
b. Prepare the April 1 journal entries to record the purchase of the assets and the payment of the consultant.
c. Prepare the December 31 journal entries to record the depreciation expense on the building, equipment, and trucks for the year.

P9-3B. Depreciation Methods On January 2, 2015, Alvarez Company purchased an electroplating machine **LO2** to help manufacture a part for one of its key products. The machine cost $218,700 and was estimated to have a useful life of six years or 781,200 platings, after which it could be sold for $23,400.

Required
a. Calculate each year's depreciation expense for the period 2015–2020 under each of the following depreciation methods:
   1. Straight-line.
   2. Double-declining balance.
   3. Units-of-production. (Assume annual production in platings of 140,000; 180,000; 150,000; 125,000; 105,000; and 81,200.)
b. Assume that the machine was purchased on September 1, 2015. Calculate each year's depreciation expense for the period 2015–2021 under each of the following depreciation methods:
   1. Straight-line.
   2. Double-declining balance.

P9-4B. Journal Entries for Plant Assets Stellar Delivery Service had the following transactions related to **LO1, 2, 3** its delivery truck:

Year 1
Mar. 1 Purchased for $32,500 cash a new delivery truck with an estimated useful life of five years and a $6,850 salvage value.
      2 Paid $600 for painting the company name and logo on the truck.
Dec. 31 Recorded depreciation on the truck for the year.

Year 2
July 1 Installed air conditioning in the truck at a cost of $1,808 cash. Although the truck's estimated useful life was unaffected, its estimated salvage value was increased by $400.
Sept. 7 Paid $450 for truck tune-up and safety inspection.
Dec. 31 Recorded depreciation on the truck for the year.

Year 3
Sept. 3 Installed a set of front and rear bumper guards at a cost of $145 cash.
Dec. 31 Recorded depreciation on the truck for the year.

Year 4
Dec. 31 Recorded depreciation on the truck for the year.

Stellar's depreciation policies include (1) using straight-line depreciation, (2) recording depreciation to the nearest whole month, and (3) expensing all truck expenditures of $150 or less.

Required
Prepare journal entries to record these transactions and adjustments.

P9-5B. Disposal of Plant Asset Canyon Company has a used delivery truck that originally cost $24,200. **LO4** Straight-line depreciation on the truck has been recorded for three years, with a $3,500 expected salvage value at the end of its estimated six-year useful life. The last depreciation entry was made at the end of the third year. Four months into the fourth year, Canyon disposes of the truck.

Required
Prepare journal entries to record:

a.   Depreciation expense to the date of disposal.
b.   Sale of the truck for cash at its book value.
c.   Sale of the truck for $15,000 cash.
d.   Sale of the truck for $12,000 cash.
e.   Theft of the truck. Canyon carries no insurance for theft.

LO1, 2, 5   **P9-6B.**   **Accounting for Plant and Intangible Assets** Selected transactions of Continental Publishers, Inc., for 2016 are given below:

Jan.   2 Paid $85,000 to purchase copyrights to a series of romantic novels. The copyrights expire in 40 years, although sales of the novels are expected to stop after 10 years.

Mar.   1 Discovered a satellite dish antenna has been destroyed by lightning. The loss is covered by insurance and a claim is filed today. The antenna cost $9,180 when installed on July 1, 2015, and was being depreciated over 12 years with a $900 salvage value. Straight-line depreciation was last recorded on December 31, 2015. Continental expects to receive an insurance settlement of $8,100.

April   1 Paid $140,000 to remodel space to create an employee exercise area on the lower level in a leased building. The building's remaining useful life is 40 years; the lease on the building expires in 12 years.

July   1 Paid $270,000 to acquire a patent on a new publishing process. The patent has a remaining legal life of 15 years. Continental estimates the new process will be utilized for 6 years before it becomes obsolete.

Nov.   1 Paid $90,000 to obtain a four-year franchise to sell a new series of computerized do-it-yourself manuals.

Required
a.   Prepare journal entries to record these transactions.
b.   Prepare the December 31 journal entries to record depreciation and amortization expense for assets acquired during the year. Continental uses straight-line depreciation and amortization.

LO6   **P9-7B.**   **Preparation of Balance Sheet** Conlon Corporation's December 31 post-closing trial balance contains the following normal account balances:

Cash	$ 1,000
Accounts payable	13,000
Building	260,000
Long-term notes payable	940,000
Common stock	400,000
Retained earnings	342,000
Accumulated depreciation—Equipment	130,000
Land	1,128,000
Accounts receivable	21,000
Accumulated depreciation—Building	70,000
Interst payable	24,000
Patent (net of amortization)	50,000
Notes payable (short term)	80,000
Inventory	137,000
Equipment	266,000
Allowance for doubtful accounts	1,000
Accumulated depreciation - Leasehold improvements	22,000
Leasehold improvements	140,000
Trademark (net of amortization)	19,000

Required
Prepare a December 31 classified balance sheet for Conlon Corporation.

LO1, 2, 3   **P9-8B.**   **Journal Entries for Plant Assets** During the first few days of the year, Inland Company entered into the following transactions:

1.   Purchased a parcel of land with a building on it for $1,750,000 cash. The building, which will be used in operations, has an estimated useful life of 30 years and a salvage value of $100,000.

The assessed valuations for property tax purposes show the land at $140,000 and the building at $1,260,000.

2. Paid $90,000 for the construction of an asphalt parking lot for customers. The parking lot is expected to last 15 years and has no salvage value.
3. Paid $250,000 for the construction of a new entrance to the building.
4. Purchased store equipment, paying the invoice price (including seven percent sales tax) of $89,660 in cash. The estimated useful life of the equipment is five years, and the salvage value is $4,000.
5. Paid $640 freight on the new equipment.
6. Paid $1,200 to repair damages to floor caused when the store equipment was accidentally dropped as it was moved into place.
7. Paid $25 for an umbrella holder to place inside front door (customers may place wet umbrellas in the holder). The holder is expected to last 30 years.

Required

a. Prepare journal entries to record these transactions.
b. Prepare the December 31 journal entries to record depreciation expense for the year. Double declining balance depreciation is used for the equipment, and straight-line depreciation is used for the building and parking lot.

P9-9B. Revision of Depreciation and Capital Expenditure Richter Company uses straight-line depreciation in accounting for its machines. On January 2, 2010, Richter purchased a new machine for $129,000 cash. The machine's estimated useful life was seven years with a $10,000 salvage value. In 2015, the company decided its original useful life estimate should be increased by three years. Beginning in 2015, depreciation was based on a 10-year total useful life, and no change was made in the salvage value estimate. On January 3, 2016, Richter added an automatic cut-off switch and a self-sharpening blade mechanism to the machine at a cost of $9,200 cash. These improvements did not change the machine's useful life but did increase the estimated salvage value to $11,200.

LO2, 3

Required

a. Prepare journal entries to record (1) the purchase of the machine, (2) 2010 depreciation expense, (3) 2015 depreciation expense, (4) the 2016 improvements, and (5) 2016 depreciation expense.
b. Calculate the book value of the machine at the end of 2016 (that is, after recording the depreciation expense for 2016).

SERIAL PROBLEM: KATE'S CARDS

(Note: This is a continuation of the Serial Problem: Kate's Cards from Chapters 1 through 8.)

SP9. Kate's business is growing faster than she had predicted. In order to keep up, she will need to purchase improved computer hardware. Kate has learned that the software that she uses runs much faster if her computer has a lot of memory. In addition, her files are very large and she is running out of free space on her existing hard drive. Finally, Kate has heard horror stories about hard disk drive crashes and the possibility that all of her work will be destroyed. In order to protect against this possibility, she has decided to invest in a large commercial grade backup system.

The cost of the memory and hard disk drive upgrade to Kate's computer will total $420. The cost of the backup system is $3,000. The memory and hard disk upgrade will increase the productivity of Kate's current computer; however, it will not extend its useful life. The backup system is expected to have a 5-year useful life.

Kate would like to know the following items:

1. How should the expenditure for the memory and hard disk drive upgrade be recorded? Provide the journal entry.
2. Kate's current computer has 42 months remaining for depreciation purpose (under the straight-line method). The original cost of the computer was $4,800 and had a four-year useful life. The current monthly depreciation is $100. How will this current expenditure affect the monthly depreciation?
3. Kate would like to know how depreciation on the backup system under both the straight-line method and the double-declining method differ. She is assigning a $500 salvage value to the equipment. Construct a table showing yearly depreciation under both methods.

EXTENDING YOUR KNOWLEDGE

REPORTING AND ANALYSIS

COLUMBIA
SPORTSWEAR
COMPANY

EYK9-1.   **Financial Reporting Problem: Columbia Sportswear Company** The financial statements for the **Columbia Sportswear Company** can be found in Appendix A at the end of this book.

Required
Answer the following questions.
- *a.* What was the total cost of Columbia's property, plant, and equipment at December 31, 2014?
- *b.* What was the total accumulated depreciation at December 31, 2014?
- *c.* What percentage of the total cost of property, plant, and equipment at December 31, 2014, was from building and improvements?
- *d.* How much depreciation and amortization expense was taken in 2014?
- *e.* What amount of property, plant, and equipment purchases (capital expenditures) occurred in 2014?

COLUMBIA
SPORTSWEAR
COMPANY

UNDER ARMOUR,
INC.

EYK9-2.   **Comparative Analysis Problem: Columbia Sportswear Company vs. Under Armour, Inc.** The financial statements for the **Columbia Sportswear Company** can be found in Appendix A at the end of this book, and the financial statements of **Under Armour, Inc.** can be found in Appendix B (the complete annual report is available on this book's Website).

Required
- *a.* Calculate the following ratios for Columbia Sportswear and for Under Armour, Inc. for 2014:
    1. Return on assets
    2. Asset turnover
- *b.* Comment on your findings.

EYK9-3.   **Business Decision Problem** Lyle Fleming, president of Fleming, Inc., wants you to resolve his dispute with Mia Gooden over the amount of a finder's fee due Gooden. Fleming hired Gooden to locate a new plant site to expand the business. By agreement, Gooden's fee was to be 15 percent of the "cost of the property (excluding the finder's fee), measured according to generally accepted accounting principles."

Gooden located Site 1 and Site 2 for Fleming to consider. Each site had a selling price of $150,000, and the geographic locations of both sites were equally acceptable to Fleming. Fleming employed an engineering firm to conduct the geological tests necessary to determine the relative quality of the two sites for construction. The tests, which cost $10,000 for each site, showed that Site 1 was superior to Site 2.

The owner of Site 1 initially gave Fleming 30 days—a reasonable period—to decide whether or not to buy the property. However, Fleming procrastinated in contracting the geological tests, and the results were not available by the end of the 30-day period. Fleming requested a two-week extension. The Site 1 owner granted Fleming the additional two weeks but charged him $6,000 for the extension (which Fleming paid). Fleming eventually bought Site 1.

Fleming sent Gooden a fee of $24,000, which was 15 percent of a cost computed as follows:

Sales price, Site 1.	$150,000
Geological tests, Site 1	10,000
Total	$160,000

Gooden believes that she is entitled to $26,400, based on a cost computed as follows:

Sales price, Site 1.	$150,000
Geological tests, Site 1	10,000
Geological tests, Site 2	10,000
Fee for time extension	6,000
Total	$176,000

Required

What fee is Gooden entitled to under the agreement? Explain.

EYK9-4.   **Financial Analysis Problem** Best Buy Co., Inc., is headquartered in Minneapolis, Minnesota.   BEST BUY CO.,
The company sells brand name consumer electronics, personal computers, home office products,   INC.
major appliances, entertainment software, and photographic equipment. Selected financial data for
Best Buy Co. follow (amounts in millions):

	2014	2013	2012
Total assets, beginning of year	$14,013	$16,787	$16,005
Total assets, end of year	$15,256	$14,013	$16,787
Revenues for the year	$40,339	$40,611	$38,252
Net income for the year	$ 1,233	$ 532	$ (441)

Required

a.   Calculate the return on assets for 2012–2014.

b.   In 2013, Best Buy's revenues grew by 6.2 percent, but in 2014 they declined by 1%. How did
this revenue growth correspond to Best Buy's ROA for 2014 and 2013?

CRITICAL THINKING

EYK9-5.   **Accounting Research Problem** The 2014 annual report of General Mills, Inc., for fiscal year   GENERAL MILLS,
2014 is available on this book's Website. Review the consolidated statements of earnings, the con-   INC.
solidated balance sheets, and Notes 2 and 17.

Required

a.   What is General Mills' gross cost of land, buildings, and equipment at May 25, 2014?

b.   What depreciation method is used in the financial statements?

c.   How much depreciation and amortization were expensed in fiscal 2014?

d.   How much depreciation has accumulated by May 25, 2014?

e.   How much research and development cost was expensed in fiscal 2014?

f.   What is General Mills' return on assets for fiscal 2014?

EYK9-6.   **Accounting Communication Activity** Peggy Zimmer, a friend of yours taking her first accounting class, is confused as to why there is a separate accumulated depreciation account. She argues
that it would be much simpler to just credit the asset that is being depreciated directly instead of
crediting accumulated depreciation.

Required

Explain to your friend in an informal memo a possible advantage that keeping the cost and accumulated depreciation separate can have for an analyst.

EYK9-7.   **Accounting Ethics Case** Linda Tristan, assistant controller for Ag-Growth, Inc., a biotechnology
firm, has concerns about the accounting analysis for the firm's purchase of a land site and building
from Hylite Corporation. The price for this package purchase was $1,800,000 cash. A memoran-
dum from the controller, Greg Fister, stated that the journal entry for this purchase should debit
Land for $1,350,000, debit Building for $450,000, and credit Cash for $1,800,000. The building, a
used laboratory facility, is to be depreciated over 10 years with a zero salvage value.

   The source documents supporting the transaction include two appraisals of the property, one
done for Ag-Growth and one done for Hylite Corporation. The appraisal for Ag-Growth valued
the land at $1,000,000 and the building at $500,000. The appraisal for Hylite Corporation (done
by a different appraiser) valued the land at $1,500,000 and the building at $750,000. Negotiations
between the two firms finally settled on an overall price of $1,800,000 for the land and the building.

   Tristan asked Fister how he arrived at the amounts to be recorded for the land and building since
each appraisal valued the land at only twice the building's value. "Well," replied Fister, "I used the
$1,500,000 land value from Hylite's appraiser and the $500,000 building value from our appraiser.
That relationship shows the land to be worth three times the building's value. Using that relationship, I assigned 75 percent of our actual purchase price of $1,800,000 to the land and 25 percent of
the purchase price to the building."

   "But why do it that way?" asked Tristan.

"Because it will improve our profits, before income taxes, by $150,000 over the next decade," replied Fister.

"But it just doesn't seem right," commented Tristan.

Required

a. How does the accounting analysis by Fister improve profits before income taxes by $150,000 over the next decade?
b. Is the goal of improving profits a sufficient rationale to defend the accounting analysis by Fister?
c. Do you agree with Fister's analysis? Briefly explain.
d. What actions are available to Tristan to resolve her concerns with Fister's analysis?

CUMMINS INC.

EYK9-8. Corporate Social Responsibility Problem Unlike Tesla Motors' emphasis on electric engines, Cummins, Inc. is best known for its design and manufacturing of diesel engines. Go to the **Cummins'** Website at http://cummins.com and navigate to the section on sustainability.

Required

1. Articulate Cummins' approach to corporate responsibility.
2. Cummins states that "corporate responsibility contributes directly to the long-term health, growth and profitability of our company." Explain how being a good corporate citizen may lead to increased growth and profitability.

WASTE MANAGEMENT, INC.

EYK9-9. Forensic Accounting Problem **Waste Management** is a leading provider of comprehensive trash and waste removal, recycling, and waste management services. In 2002, the Securities and Exchange Commission sued several members and former members of Waste Management's management team for fraud. Go to the S.E.C. press release at: http://www.sec.gov/news/headlines/wastemgmt6.htm to answer the following questions:

1. What does the complaint claim about Dean L. Buntrock, the company's founder, chairman of the board, and chief executive officer?
2. What accounting methods does the complaint claim were used by Waste Management in order to perpetuate the fraud?

EYK9-10. Analyzing IFRS Financial Statements The 2014 financial statements of LVMH Moet Hennessey-Louis Vuitton S.A. are presented in Appendix C at the end of this book. LVMH is a Paris-based holding company and one of the world's largest and best-known luxury goods companies. As a member of the European Union, French companies are required to prepare their consolidated (group) financial statements using International Financial Reporting Standards (IFRS). After reviewing LVMH's consolidated financial statements, consider the following questions. (Additional information can be found in LVMH's complete annual report provided on this book's Website.)

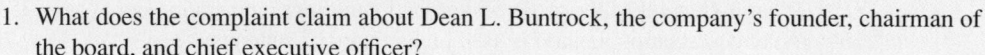

Required

a. What is LVMH's net cost of property, plant, and equipment at December 31, 2014?
b. What depreciation method is used in the company?
c. What is LVMH's net cost of goodwill and other intangible assets at December 31, 2014?
d. How does LVMH account for its research costs? Development costs?
e. What is LVMH's return on assets for the year ended December 31, 2014?

GOOGLE INC.

EYK9-11. Working with the Takeaways The following data (in millions) are taken from **Google**'s 2014 financial statements:

(in millions)	2014	2013
Net sales	$ 66,001	$ 55,519
Net income	14,444	12,920
Total assets	131,133	110,920

Calculate Google's 2014 asset turnover and return on assets.

ANSWERS TO SELF-STUDY QUESTIONS:

1. c, (p. 425)   2. c, (pp. 435-436)   3. d, (pp. 441–442)   4. a, (p. 443–444)   5. a, (pp. 442–444)
6. c, (pp. 442–444)   7. a, (pp. 439–440)   8. d, (p. 446)   9. b, (pp. 446–447)   10. a, (p. 447)   11. c, (p. 441)

YOUR TURN! SOLUTIONS

Solution 9.1

All of the costs, with the exception of the unrelated supplies, are considered to be part of the equipment's acquisition cost, and therefore should be capitalized to the equipment account. This includes the $20,000 purchase price, along with the $1,600 sales tax, $400 freight cost, $600 installation cost, and $100 testing cost, for a total acquisition cost of $22,700. The cost of the $300 of supplies should be accounted for as a supplies inventory (an asset) and allocated to expense on the income statement as it is used.

Solution 9.2

(a) Under the straight-line method, the annual depreciation expense is calculated as ($10,000 − $2,000)/5 years − $1,600 for each year. Thus, depreciation for the second year will require the following journal entry:

Depreciation expense	1,600	
Accumulated depreciation		1,600
To record depreciation expense.		

(b) The depreciation rate for a five-year asset under the double-declining balance method is 40 percent, or [(100 percent/5 years) × 2]. Depreciation expense is calculated as 40 percent times the book value of the asset as of the beginning of the year. Thus, the first year depreciation is $4,000 (40 percent × $10,000) and the second year depreciation is $2,400 [40 percent × ($10,000 − $4,000)]. Thus, the required journal entry is:

Depreciation expense	2,400	
Accumulated depreciation		2,400
To record depreciation expense.		

Solution 9.3

Items (1), (2), and (4) are revenue expenditures. Item (3) increases the van's useful life and item (5) reduces the van's operating costs, and thus these items are capital expenditures.

Solution 9.4

Cash	750	
Accumulated depreciation	15,000	
Loss on sale of truck	6,750	
Truck		22,500
To record the sale of truck.		

Solution 9.5

1. Copyright
2. Amortization
3. Trademark
4. Franchise
5. Patent

Solution 9.6

Return on assets = $25,000 / [($130,000 + $120,000)/2] = 20 percent
Asset turnover = $150,000 / [($130,000 + $120,000)/2] = 1.20

10

Accounting for Liabilities

PAST

Chapter 9 concluded our investigation of the accounting for assets.

PRESENT

In this chapter we turn our attention to the accounting for liabilities.

FUTURE

Chapter 11 examines the accounting for stockholders' equity.

LEARNING OBJECTIVES

1. **Describe** the nature of liabilities and **define** *current liabilities*. *(p. 470)*

2. **Illustrate** the accounting for long-term liabilities. *(p. 476)*

3. **Define** *contingent liabilities* and **explain** the rules for their accounting and disclosure in the financial statements. *(p. 486)*

4. **Define** the *current ratio, quick ratio*, and *times-interest-earned ratio* and **explain** their use. *(p. 490)*

5. Appendix 10A: **Explain** bond pricing and **illustrate** the straight-line and effective interest methods of amortizing bond discounts/premiums. *(p. 493)*

6. Appendix 10B: **Define** *capital leases* and *operating leases* and **distinguish** between them. *(p. 502)*

MICROSOFT CORPORATION

Microsoft Corporation is one of the world's most well-recognized companies. Founded in 1975 by Bill Gates and Paul Allen in Albuquerque, New Mexico, the company moved its headquarters in 1979 to Bellevue, Washington. That same year, Steve Ballmer joined the company and years later succeeded Gates as Microsoft's CEO. By 2012, Microsoft had global annual revenue of over $70 billion, employing over 90,000 employees in over 100 countries.

Until 2009, Microsoft remained largely debt free. The company's business model was so successful that it was unnecessary for the company to utilize debt financing. The high profit margins on the company's products enabled Microsoft to generate a significant free cash flow year in and year out and to finance its growth using internally generated operating cash flow. In 2009, however, the company issued its first bonds to the capital market. Wall Street analysts speculated that Microsoft really didn't need the cash provided by the debt issuance but rather sold the bonds to take advantage of the extremely low interest rates available at that time. Investment professionals speculated that CEO, Steve Ballmer, may have decided to "bulk up" the company's cash position in anticipation of a major corporate acquisition.

In this chapter, we examine how companies, like Microsoft, value and disclose liabilities on their balance sheets. We consider such current liabilities as accounts payable and accrued expenses payable, such noncurrent liabilities as bonds payable and term loans payable, and such contingent liabilities as pending lawsuits and environmental cleanup obligations.

ACCOUNTING FOR LIABILITIES				
Current Liabilities	**Long-Term Liabilities**	**Contingent Liabilities**	**Bond Pricing (Appendix 10A)**	**Leases (Appendix 10B)**
• Accounts payable • Notes payable and interest • Current portion of long-term debt • Sales and excise taxes • Payroll related liabilities • Income tax • Advance payments	• Notes payable • Bonds and bond pricing • Recording both discount and premium bonds • Retiring bonds • Accounting for notes and interest	• Defining contingent liabilities • Accounting for contingent liabilities • Examples of contingent liabilities	• Straight-line method • Effective interest method	• Financing with leases • Capital leases • Operating leases

CURRENT LIABILITIES

LO1 Describe the nature of liabilities and **define** *current liabilities*.

Liabilities are obligations resulting from past transactions or events that require a business to pay money, provide goods, or perform services in the future. **Current liabilities** are obligations that will require (1) the use of existing current assets or (2) the creation of other current liabilities. Most current liabilities are settled by using current assets, but sometimes a current liability is settled by the issuance of another current liability. A past due account payable, for example, may be settled by issuing a short-term note payable. Liabilities are classified as current using the same time frame used to classify current assets—the longer of one year or a firm's normal operating cycle. We discuss some typical current liabilities in this section.

Accounts Payable

In a balance sheet listing of current liabilities, amounts due to short-term creditors on accounts payable and notes payable are commonly shown first. Short-term creditors send invoices specifying the amount owed for goods or services that they have provided. As a result, the amount of any account or note payable is easily determined because it is based on the invoices received from a creditor.

At the end of an accounting period, accountants need to know whether any goods are in transit and what the shipping terms are for such goods. If the goods are shipped F.O.B. shipping point, ownership of the goods has transferred to the buyer and an account payable should be recorded at year-end (as well as an increase in inventory) even though the goods and an invoice have not yet arrived.

Notes Payable and Interest

Promissory notes are often issued in transactions when the credit period is longer than the 30 or 60 days typical for accounts payable. Although promissory notes are commonly used in credit sales transactions involving equipment and real property, a note may sometimes be exchanged for merchandise. A note payable may also be substituted for an account payable when an extension of the usual credit period is granted. And, a promissory note is prepared when a loan is obtained from a bank.

Interest is a charge for the use of money. Consequently, interest incurred on a promissory note is an expense to the maker of a note. Since businesses are required under GAAP to distinguish between operating and nonoperating expenses in their income statements, interest expense is reported under the Other Income and Expense category to highlight the fact that this expense is not considered to be an operating expense, and instead, is a financing expense of the business.

Interest on promissory notes can be structured in either of two ways: (1) as an amount paid in addition to the face amount of the note, called the *add-on interest method*, or (2) as an amount included in the face amount of the note, called the *discount method*. The add-on interest method is most commonly used, and consequently, we focus on that approach.

Add-On Interest Method

Interest on a short-term note payable using the *add-on interest method* is paid at the maturity date of the note. The formula for determining the amount of interest to be paid is as follows:

$$\textbf{Interest} = \textbf{Principal} \times \textbf{Interest rate} \times \textbf{Time}$$

The principal, or face amount, of a note is the amount borrowed. The interest rate is the annual rate of interest. Time is the fraction of a year that a note is outstanding.

When a note is written for a certain number of months, time is expressed in twelfths of a year. For example, interest on a three-month note for $4,000, with a nine percent annual interest rate is:

$$\textbf{Interest} = \textbf{\$4,000} \times \textbf{0.09} \times \textbf{3/12} = \textbf{\$90}$$

When a note's duration—that is, the length of the borrowing period—is given in days, time is expressed as a fraction of a year; the numerator is the number of days that the note will be outstanding and the denominator is 360 days. (Some lenders use 360 days, while others use 365 days; we will use 360 days in our examples.) For example, interest on a 60-day note for $3,000, with a nine percent annual interest rate is:

$$\textbf{Interest} = \textbf{\$3,000} \times \textbf{0.09} \times \textbf{60/360} = \textbf{\$45}$$

Determining the Maturity Date of a Note

When a note's duration is expressed in days, the exact number of days in each calendar month is counted to determine the note's **maturity date**. For example, a 90-day note dated July 21 has an October 19 maturity date, determined as follows:

10 days in July	(**remainder of month, 31 days minus 21 days**)
31 days in August	
30 days in September	
19 days in October	(**number of days required to total 90**)
90	

If the duration of a note is expressed in months, the maturity date is determined by counting the number of months from the date of issue. For example, a two-month note dated January 31 matures on March 31, a three-month note of the same date matures on April 30 (the last day of the month), and a four-month note matures on May 31.

Recording Notes Payable and Interest Expense

When a note payable is exchanged to settle an account payable, a journal entry is made to reflect the note payable and to reduce the balance of the related account payable. For example, suppose that the Jordon Company sold $12,000 of merchandise on account to

Bowman Company. On October 1, after the regular credit period had expired, Bowman Company gave the Jordon Company a 60-day, nine percent note for $12,000. As a consequence, the Bowman Company makes the following journal entry on October 1:

A = L + SE
−12,000
+12,000

Oct. 1	Accounts payable—Jordon Company	12,000	
	Notes payable—Jordon Company		12,000
	Gave 60-day, 9 percent note in payment of account.		

If the Bowman Company pays the note on the November 30 maturity date, the company makes the following journal entry:

A = L + SE
−12,180 −12,000 −180
          Exp

Nov. 30	Notes payable—Jordon Company	12,000	
	Interest expense	180	
	Cash		12,180
	Paid note to Jordon Company ($12,000 × 0.09 × 60/360 = $180).		

Interest Payable

At the end of the fiscal year, adjusting entries must be made to reflect any accrued, but unpaid, interest expense. For example, assume that the Bowman Company has one note payable outstanding at December 31, 2015, to Garcia Company. The note is dated December 21, 2015, has a principal amount of $6,000, an interest rate of 12 percent, and a maturity date of February 19, 2016. The adjusting entry that Bowman Company makes at December 31, 2015, is as follows:

A = L + SE
    −20
+20   Exp

2015			
Dec. 31	Interest expense	20	
	Interest payable		20
	To accrue interest expense on the note to Garcia Company		
	($6,000 × 0.12 × 10/360 = $20).		

When the note payable to Garcia Company is subsequently paid on February 19, 2016, the Bowman Company makes the following entry:

A = L + SE
−6,120 −6,000 −100
     −20   Exp

2016			
Feb. 19	Notes payable—Garcia Company	6,000	
	Interest payable	20	
	Interest expense	100	
	Cash		6,120
	Paid principal and interest to Garcia Company		
	($6,000 × 0.12 × 50/360 = $100).		

Current Portion of Long-Term Debt

The repayment of many long-term obligations involves a series of principal payment installments over several years. To report liabilities involving installments properly, any principal due within one year (or the operating cycle, if longer) is reported as a current liability on the balance sheet. Failure to reclassify the currently maturing portion of any long-term debt due within the next year as a current liability can mislead readers regarding the total current obligations of a business.

Sales and Excise Taxes Payable

Many products and services are subject to sales and excise taxes. The laws governing these taxes usually require the selling firm to collect the tax at the time of sale and to send the collections periodically to the appropriate tax collection agency. For example, assume that a particular product selling for $1,000 is subject to a six percent state sales tax and a ten percent federal excise tax. Each tax should be figured on the basic sale price only. The sale is recorded as follows:

Accounts receivable (*or* Cash)	1,160			A	= L	+ SE
Sales revenue		1,000		+1,160	+60	+1,000
Sales tax payable		60				Rev
Excise tax payable		100			+100	
To record sales and related taxes.						

The selling firm will periodically complete a tax reporting form and send the period's tax collections to the appropriate collection agency. The tax liability accounts are then debited and the Cash account is credited.

Payroll-Related Liabilities

Salaries and wages represent a major outlay in the cost structure of many businesses. For service firms, the largest expense category is usually the compensation paid to employees and the related payroll taxes and fringe benefits paid by the employer. Three types of current liabilities arise from a company's payroll: (1) accrued salaries and wages payable (discussed in Chapter 4), (2) amounts withheld from employees' paychecks by the employer, and (3) payroll taxes and fringe benefits paid by the employer.

Amounts Withheld from Employee Paychecks

When a business hires an employee, the firm establishes the employee's rate of pay. At the end of each pay period, the employer uses the employee's salary to determine the employee's **gross pay**, the amount earned before any withholdings. The employer then subtracts any withheld amounts to determine the employee's **net pay**, the amount of the paycheck. **Exhibit 10-1** demonstrates these relations.

Amounts Withheld by Legal Mandate   Some amounts withheld from an employee's gross pay are mandated by law. These amounts include federal income tax, state income tax, Social Security taxes, and Medicare taxes.

The amount of federal income tax withheld from an employee's paycheck is determined by referencing a table that uses the amount of the employee's gross pay, the employee's marital status, and the number of withholding allowances to which the employee is entitled. Most states require employers to use similar information in calculating state income tax withholding.

The Federal Insurance Contributions Act (FICA) dictates the percentages to be used in calculating the withholding amounts for Social Security and Medicare. The rates for employee withholding for 2015 were 6.2 percent of the first $118,500 of gross pay for Social Security and 1.45 percent of all gross pay for Medicare.

Amounts Withheld by Employee Request   Other amounts are withheld from an employee's gross pay by employee request. These amounts include premiums for life or health insurance, union dues, and payments into a self funded retirement plan.

Recording Gross Pay and Net Pay

To illustrate the recording of employee gross and net pay, assume that the payroll for the week ended August 15 for Centerline Company totaled $6,000. Amounts withheld were $1,200 for federal income tax, $405 for state income tax, $372 for Social Security, and $87 for Medicare. In addition, Centerline withheld $100 for union dues and $320 for health insurance premiums. Centerline makes the following entry to record the payroll:

A = L + SE
+1,200 −6,000
Exp
+405
+339
+100
+320
+3,636

Aug. 15	Salaries and wage expense	6,000	
	Federal income tax withholding payable		1,200
	State income tax withholding payable		405
	FICA taxes payable		459
	Union dues payable		100
	Health insurance premiums payable		320
	Payroll payable		3,516
	To record the payroll for the week ended August 15.		

At the appropriate time, the employer will remit the amounts withheld from employees to the proper recipients. To the extent that any of the payable amounts are not paid at the end of an accounting period, they are reported as current liabilities.

Exhibit 10-1	Determination of Net Pay

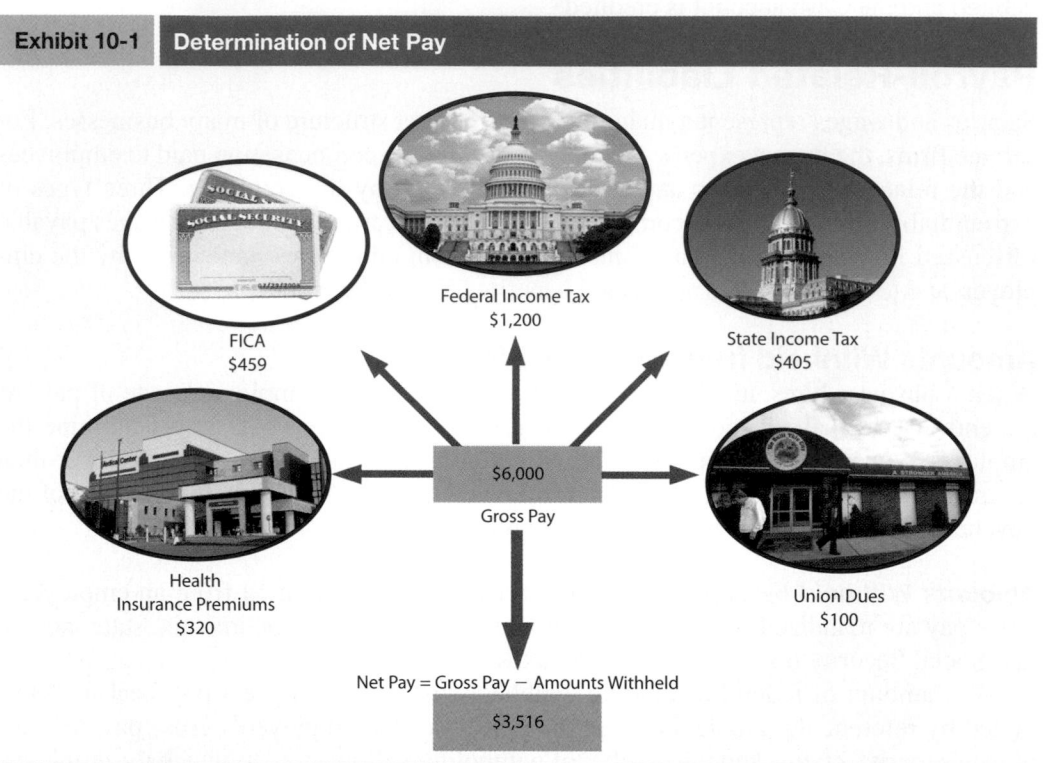

Payroll Taxes Paid by the Employer

An employer pays three types of taxes on the gross payroll amount: FICA taxes (Social Security and Medicare), federal unemployment tax, and state unemployment tax.

Each employer is required to pay an amount equal to the FICA taxes withheld from the employees' gross pay (2015 rates were 6.2 percent of the first $118,500 of gross pay for Social Security and 1.45 percent of gross pay for Medicare). As a result, the total Social Security collected in 2015 for each employee was 12.4 percent of the first $118,500 of gross pay, and the total Medicare collected was 2.9 percent of all gross pay.

Federal and state unemployment taxes are levied only on employers as a percentage of the gross payroll, subject to various limits. The current federal unemployment tax rate is 6.0 percent of the first $7,000 of an employee's gross pay. However, an employer is entitled to a credit against this tax for unemployment taxes paid to the state. The maximum credit allowed is 5.4 percent of the first $7,000 of gross pay. Many states set their basic unemployment tax rate at this maximum credit. In these states, the effective federal unemployment tax rate is 0.6 percent (6.0 percent − 5.4 percent), and the effective state unemployment tax rate is 5.4 percent.

Recording Payroll Taxes Paid by the Employer   Assume that the payroll for the week ended August 15 for Centerline Company totaled $6,000. Amounts withheld included $372 for Social Security and $87 for Medicare. Federal unemployment tax payable for the week was $36 (0.6 percent) and state unemployment tax payable was $324 (5.4 percent). Centerline makes the following entry to record its payroll taxes:

Aug. 15	Payroll tax expense	819		A = L + SE
	FICA taxes payable		459	−819
	Federal unemployment tax payable		36	+459 Exp
	State unemployment tax payable		324	+36
	To record the payroll taxes for the week ended August 15.			+324

If payroll taxes have not been remitted to the proper government agency by the end of the accounting period, they are classified as current liabilities in the balance sheet.

Archer Corporation had the following payroll data for April:

Office salaries.	$ 40,000
Sales salaries	86,000
Federal income taxes withheld.	25,600
Health insurance premiums withheld.	1,850
Union dues withheld.	950
Salaries (included above):	
Subject to both FICA taxes.	126,000
Subject to federal unemployment taxes.	76,000
Subject to state unemployment taxes	88,000

The combined FICA tax rate (for both employee withholding and employer) is 7.65 percent (6.2 percent plus 1.45 percent), the federal unemployment compensation tax rate is 0.6 percent, and the state unemployment compensation tax rate is 5.4 percent. The amounts subject to these taxes are given above.

Required

Prepare journal entries to record the following on April 30:

a. Accrual of the payroll.

b. Payment of the net payroll.

c. Accrual of the employer's payroll taxes.

d. Payment of all liabilities related to the payroll. (Assume that all liabilities are paid at the same time.)

Income Taxes Payable

The U.S. Federal Government, most states, and some municipalities levy income taxes against corporations, individuals, estates, and trusts. Sole proprietorships and partnerships are not taxable entities—their owners include any business income on the owner's personal income tax return.

The tax due is determined in accordance with tax law, rulings by taxing agencies, and court decisions. Because the administration of tax law is quite complex and many honest differences exist in their interpretation, the tax obligation reported on a tax return is only an estimate until the government reviews and accepts a firm's (or individual's) calculations.

Because corporations are separate taxable entities, they incur a legal obligation for income taxes whenever income is earned. Therefore, corporate financial statements routinely include income tax liabilities. For example, business income taxes of $8,000 are recorded as follows:

	Income tax expense	8,000		A = L + SE
	Income tax payable		8,000	+8,000 −8,000
	To record estimated income tax.			Exp

Corporations usually pay their estimated income taxes quarterly, with an annual tax return and final payment due within a few months following the end of a calendar year. Thus, any liability for income taxes in the financial statements is classified as a current liability since payment is expected in the short-term.

Advance Payments—Unearned Revenue

Airline tickets, gift cards, cruise-line tickets, season football tickets, and cellular phone connection charges are examples of advance payments for services. A customer pays cash in advance for these services and the service provider agrees to provide future services. As an example, assume that **Southwest Airlines Co.** sells a ticket for $400 on March 20 for travel on May 25. Southwest makes the following entry when the ticket is sold:

A = L + SE
+400 +400

Mar. 20	Cash	400	
	Unearned ticket revenue		400
	To record the sale of an airline ticket.		

When the passenger takes the scheduled flight, the airline makes the following entry:

A = L + SE
−400 +400 Rev

May 25	Unearned ticket revenue	400	
	Ticket revenue		400
	To record ticket revenue earned.		

LONG-TERM LIABILITIES

LO2 **Illustrate** the accounting for long-term liabilities.

At various times during a business's operating life, it will need to secure long-term funds to finance operations or the acquisition of various operating assets. When a business elects to finance its growth with long-term borrowing, it may do so by borrowing money with long-term notes or issuing bonds. An obligation in the form of a written note due after the current period is referred to as a **term loan** or long-term note payable. The borrower typically signs a note payable and the debt is referred to as a term loan. Whereas long-term notes are usually arranged with a single lender, bonds are usually issued to the general public with a large number of buyers. A **bond** is a long-term debt instrument that promises to pay interest periodically as well as a principal amount at maturity, to the bond investor. In the United States, bond interest is usually paid semiannually. The principal amount is referred to as the bond's face value (because it is printed on the face of the bond certificate), par value, or maturity value.

Long-Term Notes (Term Loans)

Term loans are often repaid in equal periodic installments. The agreement may require installment payments to be made monthly, quarterly, or semiannually. Each payment contains an interest amount and a partial repayment of principal. Because the installment payments are equal, each installment payment contains different amounts of interest and principal repayment. These component amounts change with each installment because the interest is computed on the unpaid principal, and the unpaid principal is reduced with each payment.

To illustrate, assume that on December 31, 2015, Reid, Inc., borrows $100,000 from a bank on a 12 percent, ten-year mortgage note payable. The note is to be repaid with equal quarterly installments of $4,326 (please see Appendix E for explanation on how to do this calculation). Thus, there will be 40 quarterly payments; and, the quarterly interest rate is three percent (12 percent/4 quarters). **Exhibit 10-2** presents the first eight quarterly payments (of the complete 40 quarterly payment schedule) and their division between interest expense and principal repayment. As the book value of the note declines over time (column D), the amount of interest expense also declines (column B). As a result, the amount of the fixed quarterly cash payment (column A) that is applied to repayment of the principal increases over time (column C). The entry to record the first quarterly payment follows:

2015			
Dec. 31	Cash	100,000	
	Mortgage note payable		100,000
	To record mortgage loan.		

A = L + SE
100,000 100,000

2016			
Mar. 31	Interest expense	3,000	
	Mortgage note payable	1,326	
	Cash		4,326
	To record quarterly mortgage loan payment.		

A − L + SE
−4,326 −1,326 3,000
                Exp

Exhibit 10-2	**Partial Mortgage Note Payment Schedule**

$100,000 mortgage note payable with quarterly payments of $4,326 and quarterly interest rate of three percent

Payment Date	A Cash Payment	B Interest Expense (3% × D)*	C Principal Repaid (A − B)	D Book Value of Note (Unpaid Principal)
2015				
December 31 (issue date)....				$100,000
2016				
March 31.................	$4,326	$3,000	$1,326	98,674
June 30.................	4,326	2,960	1,366	97,308
September 30............	4,326	2,919	1,407	95,901
December 31	4,326	2,877	1,449	94,452
2017				
March 31.................	4,326	2,834	1,492	92,960
June 30.................	4,326	2,789	1,537	91,423
September 30............	4,326	2,743	1,583	89,840
December 31	4,326	2,695	1,631	88,209

* 3 percent × Unpaid principal after previous payment (rounded to nearest dollar).

Types of Bonds

Companies issue different types of bonds to capitalize on certain lending situations, appeal to special investor groups, or provide special repayment patterns.

Secured bonds, for example, pledge specific property as security for meeting the terms of the bond agreement. The specific title of the bonds may indicate the type of property pledged—for example, real estate mortgage bonds (land or buildings), chattel mortgage bonds (machinery or equipment), and collateral trust bonds (negotiable securities).

Bonds that have no specific property pledged as security for their repayment are called **debenture bonds**. Buyers of debenture bonds rely on a borrower's general credit reputation. Because a lender's risk is usually greater than with secured bonds, the sale of unsecured bonds may require offering a higher rate of interest to attract bond buyers.

The maturity dates of **serial bonds** are staggered over a series of years. For example, a serial bond issue of $15 million may provide for $1 million of the bonds to mature each year for 15 years. An advantage of serial bonds is that bond investors can choose bonds with maturity dates that correspond with their desired length of investment.

Sinking fund bonds require that a borrower make payments each year to a trustee who is responsible for managing the funds needed to retire the bonds at maturity. The orderly retirement of bonds, or the accumulation of funds needed at maturity, as required by a sinking fund provision is generally viewed as making any bond safer (less risky) for the bondholders.

Convertible bonds grant the bondholder the right to convert the bonds into a company's common stock at some specific exchange (or conversion) ratio. This provision gives an investor the security of being a creditor during a certain stage of a firm's life, with the option of becoming a stockholder if the firm becomes sufficiently profitable. Because the conversion feature is attractive to potential investors, a company may issue convertible bonds at a lower interest rate than it would pay without the conversion feature.

Callable bonds allow the bond issuer to call in the bonds for redemption. Usually, an extra amount or premium must be paid to the holders of a called bond. A call provision offers borrowers additional financing flexibility that may be significant if funds become available at interest rates substantially lower than those currently being paid on the bonds. Borrowers can, in effect, also "call" any of their bonds by buying them in the open market.

ACCOUNTING IN PRACTICE

Bond Risk Ratings

The relative riskiness of different bonds may vary considerably. Bond investors who want to know the relative quality of a particular bond issue can consult a bond-rating service. Two major firms that rate the riskiness of bonds are **Standard & Poor's Corporation** (S&P) and **Moody's Investors Service** (Moody's). The rating categories used by these firms are similar. The schedule below shows the relationship between the ratings and the degree of risk using Standard & Poor's rating system:

Low Risk							High Risk
AAA	AA	A	BBB	BB	B	CCC	D

|- - - - - - - - Investment Grade Bonds - - - - - - - - -|- - - - - - - Junk Bonds - - - - - - - - -|

Investment grade bonds are highly-rated bonds with little risk that the issuing company will fail to pay interest as scheduled or fail to repay the principal at a bond's maturity. Junk bonds, on the other hand, are low-quality, high-yield bonds. In the S&P rating system, junk bonds are any bond rated BB and lower. Generally, bonds with poor credit ratings must offer higher interest rates than highly-rated bonds to attract potential buyers.

A.K.A. Junk bonds are often referred to as *high-yield bonds* because of the higher yield rates that typically accompany this type of debt investment.

Bond Prices

Bonds are typically sold in units (denominations) of $1,000 face (maturity) value, and the market price is expressed as a percentage of face value. Thus, a $1,000 face value bond that is quoted at 98 will sell for $980. For example, in the bond certificate illustrated in **Exhibit 10-3**, General Electric issued a total of $5 billion of unsecured bonds in denominations of $1,000. The bonds were priced (issued) at 99.626. Generally, bond prices fluctuate in response to changes in market interest rates, which are determined by government monetary policies (managing the demand and supply of money) and economic expectations. Bond prices are also affected by the financial outlook for the issuing firm.

A.K.A. A bond's face value is also referred to as its *maturity value*, *stated value*, or *settlement value*.

Exhibit 10-3	Bond Certificate

General Electric Company ← Bond Issuer

$5,000,000,000 ← Face value

5% Notes due 2013 ← Coupon rate

Issue price: 99.626%

We will pay interest on the notes semiannually on February 1 and August 1 of each year, beginning August 1, 2003. The notes will mature on February 1, 2013. We may not redeem the notes prior to maturity. ← Maturity date

The notes will be unsecured obligations and rank equally with our other unsecured debt securities that are not subordinated obligations. The notes will be issued in registered form in denominations of $1,000.

Neither the Securities and Exchange Commission nor any state securities commission has approved or disapproved of the notes or determined if this prospectus supplement or the accompanying prospectus is truthful or complete. Any representation to the contrary is a criminal offense.

	Per Note	Total
Public Offering Price(1)	99.626%	$4,981,300,000
Underwriting Discounts	.425%	$ 21,250,000
Proceeds to General Electric Company (before expenses)	99.201%	$4,960,050,000

(1) Plus accrued interest from January 28, 2003, if settlement occurs after that date.

The underwriters expect to deliver the notes in book-entry form only through the facilities of The Depository Trust Company, Clearstream, Luxembourg or the Euroclear System, as the case may be, on or about January 28, 2003.

Joint Bookrunners

Morgan Stanley   **Salomon Smith Barney**

Senior Co-Managers

Banc of America Securities LLC	Credit Suisse First Boston	Deutsche Bank Securities
Goldman. Sachs & Co.	JPMorgan	Merrill Lynch & Co.
	UBS Warburg	

Co-Managers

Banc One Capital Markets, Inc.	Barclays Capital	Blaylock & Partners, L.P.
BNP PARIBAN	Dresdner Kleinwort Wasserstein	Guzman & Company
HSBC	Loop Capital Markets	Ormes Capital Markets, Inc.
Utendahl Capital Partners, L.P.	The Williams Capital Group, L.P.	

A bond specifies a pattern of future cash flows, usually a series of interest payments and a single payment at maturity equal to the bond's face value. The amount of the periodic interest payment is determined by the **coupon rate** stated on the bond certificate. The General Electric bonds have a coupon rate of 5 percent. Interest rates are usually quoted as annual rates, so the coupon rate will need to be converted to a per period interest rate when interest is paid more than once a year. For example, in the U.S., bond interest is usually paid semiannually, with the payments six months apart. Thus, the amount of interest paid semiannually is calculated by multiplying one-half the coupon rate of interest times the bond's face value.

A.K.A. A bond's coupon rate of interest is also referred to as its *nominal rate* or *stated rate* of interest.

A bond's market price is determined by discounting the bond's future cash flows (both its principal and interest payments) to the present using the current **market rate of interest** for the bond as the discount rate, a process known as *computing the bond's present value*. The market rate is the rate of return investors expect on their investment.

IFRS ALERT

U.S. GAAP and IFRS are substantially aligned when it comes to the reporting of liabilities. Under both accounting systems, for example, current liabilities (Accounts Payable) are reported at their settlement or future value, or the amount of money required to satisfy the obligation when it becomes due. Similarly, both systems require that long-term liabilities, like Bonds Payable, be reported at their present value, or the amount of money necessary to currently satisfy the obligation. Where the two systems diverge is in regards to the reporting of some contingent liabilities (to be discussed shortly).

The **effective interest rate** is the market rate of interest used to price the bonds when they are originally issued. A bond's price may be equal to, less than, or greater than its face value. Bonds sell at *face value* when the market rate of interest equals the bond's coupon rate. Bonds sell at a *discount* (less than face value) when the market interest rate exceeds the bond's coupon rate; and, bonds sell at a *premium* (more than face value) when the market interest rate is less than the bond's coupon rate.

Since bonds are usually printed on one date and sold at a later date, the market rate and coupon rate will often differ due to a change in market interest rates after the bonds are printed. Market rates and coupon rates are frequently stated in percentage terms, although increasingly, these rates are stated as "basis points." One percentage point is equal to one hundred basis points. Thus, a bond with a coupon rate of three percent is said to have a coupon rate of 300 basis points.

Exhibit 10-4 shows the calculation of a bond's selling price using different market rates of interest. (See Appendix 10A for a discussion of the calculation of a bond's present value.) The bond is a $1,000, eight percent annual coupon rate, four-year bond with interest payable semiannually. The periodic interest payment is $40 ($1,000 × 0.08 × 1/2).

Exhibit 10-4	Calculation of Bond Selling Price at Different Market Rates		
Four-year $1,000 bond, eight percent annual coupon rate, interest payable semiannually. Eight semiannual interest payments of $40 ($1,000 × 0.08 × 1/2)			
	Yield Rate, Compounded Semiannually		
	10%	**8%**	**6%**
Present value of $1,000 at maturity			
$1,000 × 0.67684 present value factor*..... =	$677		
$1,000 × 0.73069 present value factor ..... =		$ 731	
$1,000 × 0.78941 present value factor ..... =			$ 789
Present value of eight $40 interest payments (rounded to nearest dollar)			
$40 × 6.46321 present value factor* .... =	259		
$40 × 6.73274 present value factor .... =		269	
$40 × 7.01969 present value factor........ =			281
Bond selling price......................	$936	$1,000	$1,070
Bond priced at	**Discount**	**Face value**	**Premium**

*See Appendix 10A for a discussion of present value factors.

As shown in the exhibit, the bond will:

1. Sell at a *discount* ($936 bond price) when the market rate (ten percent) exceeds the coupon rate (eight percent).

2. Sell at *face value* ($1,000 bond price) when the market rate (eight percent) equals the coupon rate (eight percent).

3. Sell at a *premium* ($1,070 bond price) when the market rate (six percent) is less than the coupon rate (eight percent).

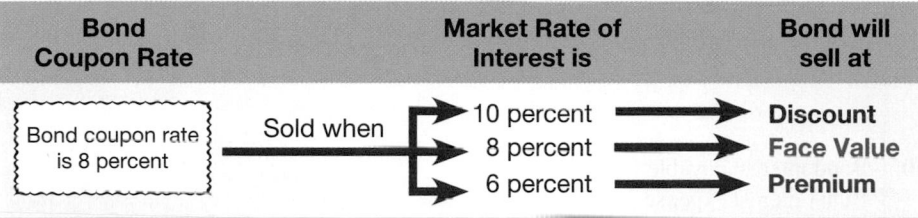

Recording Bonds

Bonds Issued at Face Value

To provide a simple illustration, we use a bond with a short period to maturity. Assume that on December 31, 2015, Reid, Inc., issues at face value $100,000 of eight percent bonds that mature in four years with interest paid on June 30 and December 31. The following entry records the bond, which is sold at its face value:

2015					A = L + SE
Dec. 31	Cash		100,000		+100,000 +100,000
	Bonds payable			100,000	
	To record the issuance of bonds.				

Interest of $4,000 ($100,000 × 0.08 × 6/12) will be paid on each of the eight payment dates (four years, semiannual payments). For example, the entry on June 30, 2016, the first interest payment date, is:

2016					A = L + SE
June 30	Bond interest expense		4,000		−4,000 −4,000
	Cash			4,000	Exp
	To record the payment of semiannual interest on bonds.				

When the bonds mature, Reid, Inc., records their retirement as follows (this assumes the December 31 interest payment is separately recorded):

2019					A = L + SE
Dec. 31	Bonds payable		100,000		−100,000 −100,000
	Cash			100,000	
	To record the retirement of bonds.				

Issuance Between Interest Dates

Not all bonds are sold on the exact day on which their interest payment period begins. Investors who buy bonds after the interest period begins are expected to "buy" any interest that has accrued on the bonds. Such bonds are said to be sold at a given price "plus accrued interest." The accrued interest is returned to the investor at the next interest payment date. This procedure simplifies the bond issuer's administrative work. Regardless of when bonds are issued, a full six months' interest is paid to all bondholders on each interest payment date.

To illustrate, assume that Reid, Inc. sold its $100,000, eight percent, four-year bonds at 100 plus accrued interest on February 28, 2016, instead of on December 31, 2015. The following journal entry is made:

A   =   L   + SE
+101,333 +100,000
           +1,333

2016			
Feb. 28	Cash	101,333	
	Bonds payable		100,000
	Bond interest payable		1,333
	To record bond issuance at 100 plus two months' accrued interest.		

The interest accrued on the bonds on February 28 is $1,333 ($100,000 × 0.08 × 2/12, rounded). On the first interest payment date, June 30, 2016, Reid, Inc., makes the following entry:

A   =   L   +   SE
−4,000 −1,333 −2,667
                 Exp

2016			
June 30	Bond interest payable	1,333	
	Bond interest expense	2,667	
	Cash		4,000
	To record the payment of semiannual interest on bonds payable.		

Bond interest expense recorded by Reid relates only to the four months since the bonds were issued.

Bonds Issued at a Discount

If the coupon rate of interest on the bonds issued is less than the current market rate, the bonds will be sold at a price less than their face value. In such cases, investors "discount" the price of the bonds to enable the buyer to earn the current market rate of interest. For example, assume that Reid, Inc.'s $100,000 issue of eight percent, four-year bonds is sold on December 31, 2015, for $93,552. This price permits investors to earn an effective interest rate of ten percent even though the bonds are only paying a cash coupon rate of eight percent. (For calculations, please see Appendix 10A.) The following entry records the issuance of the bonds at a discount:

A   =   L   + SE
+93,552 −6,448
        +100,000

2015			
Dec. 31	Cash	93,552	
	Discount on bonds payable	**6,448**	
	Bonds payable		100,000
	To record the issuance of bonds.		

The $6,448 discount is not a loss or an expense to Reid, Inc. It represents an adjustment to interest expense that will be made over the life of the bonds. This can be illustrated by comparing the funds that Reid, Inc., receives with the funds it must pay to the bondholders. Regardless of their selling price, the bonds represent an agreement to pay $132,000 to the bondholders ($100,000 principal at maturity plus eight semiannual interest payments of $4,000 each).

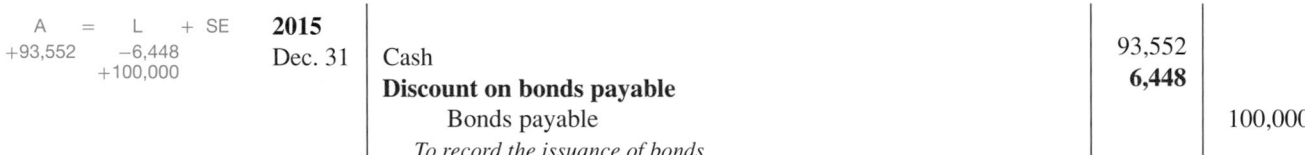

Total funds paid to bondholders	$132,000
Total funds received from bond sale	(93,552)
Difference equals total interest expense	38,448
Total semiannual interest payments ([$100,000 × 8% = $8,000] × 4 years) . .	(32,000)
Increase in interest expense beyond semiannual interest payments	
(aka *bond discount*)	**$ 6,448**

The total interest expense for this four-year bond issue is $38,448, the difference between the total cash paid to the bondholders and the proceeds from the sale of the bonds. The semiannual interest payments to bondholders total $32,000, so an additional $6,448 must be recognized as interest expense over the life of the bonds. The $6,448 is the amount of the bond discount. To reflect the larger periodic interest expense, the bond discount is *amortized over the eight interest payment periods*. Amortization of a bond discount means that, periodically, an amount is transferred from the Discount on Bonds Payable account to the Bond Interest Expense account.

There are two methods of bond amortization: the straight-line method and the effective interest method. Under the **straight-line interest method**, equal amounts are transferred from bond discount to interest expense for each interest payment period. The **effective interest method**, on the other hand, reflects a constant rate of interest over the life of the bonds. Appendix 10A illustrates both methods, but the effective interest method is the more commonly used accounting method for bond amortization.

Zero-coupon bonds are a special type of discount bond. As the name implies, these bonds pay no periodic interest payments, which causes them to be issued at a substantial discount from their face value. The face value is paid to the bondholder at maturity. The total interest implicit in the bond contract is the difference between the bond's original issue price and its face value at maturity. For example, a five-year, $1,000 zero-coupon bond issued for $713 will pay the lender $1,000 at the end of the five years. The total interest associated with this bond is $287 ($1,000 − $713). Zero-coupon bonds are particularly helpful to a borrower when the project being financed with the bond proceeds provides no cash inflows until the bond maturity date.

Bonds Issued at a Premium

If the market rate of interest had been below the eight percent offered by Reid, Inc., investors would have been willing to pay a premium to buy the bonds. Suppose that the effective interest rate was six percent. Reid Inc.'s $100,000, eight percent, four-year bonds would sell for $106,980 (for calculations, please see Appendix 10A). The issuance of the bonds on December 31, 2015, is recorded as follows:

2015				
Dec. 31	Cash		106,980	
	Bonds payable			100,000
	Premium on bonds payable			**6,980**
	To record issuance of bonds.			

$$A = L + SE$$
$$+106{,}980 \quad +100{,}000$$
$$+6{,}980$$

When bonds are issued at a premium, the book value of the bond liability is determined by adding the Premium on Bonds Payable account balance to the Bonds Payable account balance.

Like a bond discount, a bond premium is considered an adjustment of interest expense over the life of the bonds. We saw that a bond discount represents the excess of total interest expense over the total semiannual interest payments. A similar analysis shows that a bond premium represents the amount by which the total semiannual interest payments exceed the total interest expense. The analysis begins by comparing the total funds that will be paid to the bondholders over the four years (again, it is $132,000) with the proceeds received when the bonds are issued:

Total funds paid to bondholders	$132,000
Total funds received from bond sale	(106,980)
Difference equals total interest expense	25,020
Total semiannual interest payments ([$100,000 × 8% = $8,000] × 4 years)	(32,000)
Decrease in interest expense below semiannual interest payments (aka *bond premium*)	**$ 6,980**

The total interest expense for this four-year bond issue is $25,020, an amount that is $6,980 less than the total semiannual interest payments to be made to bondholders. The $6,980 is the amount of the bond premium. The bond premium is amortized to cause the periodic interest expense to be less than the semiannual interest payment.

Year-End Adjustments

When a periodic interest payment does not correspond with the fiscal year-end, an adjusting entry should be recorded reflecting the amount of interest expense incurred but not yet recorded. The adjusting entry includes a pro rata amortization of bond discount or bond premium for the portion of the year involved.

PRINCIPLE ALERT

Matching Concept

The adjusting entry to record interest expense incurred but not yet recorded is an application of the *expense recognition (matching) concept*. This accounting concept states that all expenses incurred to generate sales revenue must be recorded, regardless of when the expense is paid in cash. Interest is a charge for the use of money, and this charge is incurred every day that a borrower has use of, and benefits from, borrowed funds.

Bonds Payable Disclosed on the Balance Sheet

Bonds payable that mature more than one year in the future are classified as long-term liabilities on the balance sheet. Bonds payable maturing within the next year, on the other hand, are classified as current liabilities. Discount on Bonds Payable and Premium on Bonds Payable are contra accounts that adjust the value of Bonds Payable on the balance sheet. Discount on Bonds Payable is a deduction from and Premium on Bonds Payable is an addition to the face value of the bonds reported in the balance sheet. Many companies do not separately disclose the Discount on Bonds Payable account or the Premium on Bonds Payable account on their publicly disseminated balance sheet, but rather net these amounts against the Bonds Payable account.

At December 31, 2016, the Reid, Inc., bonds issued at a discount (see **Exhibit 10A-4**) appear on Reid's balance sheet as follows:

Bonds payable	$100,000
Less: Discount on bonds payable	5,058
Bonds payable, net	$94,942

On the same date, the Reid Inc. bonds issued at a premium (see **Exhibit 10A-5**) appear as follows:

Bonds payable	$100,000
Add: Premium on bonds payable.	5,375
Bonds payable, net	$105,375

Retirement of Bonds Before Maturity

Bonds are usually retired at their maturity dates with a journal entry debiting the Bonds Payable account and crediting the Cash account for the face value of the bonds. However, bonds can be retired before maturity—for example, to take advantage of more attractive financing terms. In accounting for the retirement of bonds before maturity, the following steps are used:

1. Remove the book value of the bonds being retired from the accounts (that is, remove the Bonds Payable amount and any related bond premium or discount).

2. Record the cash paid to retire the bonds.

3. Recognize any difference between the bonds' book value and the cash paid as a gain or loss on bond retirement.

To illustrate, assume that the Reid, Inc., bonds issued at a premium for $106,980 in our previous example were called for retirement at 105 at the end of 2018, after paying the semiannual interest on December 31, 2018. According to **Exhibit 10A-5**, the bonds' book value at the end of 2018 is $101,865. The following entry records the bond retirement:

2018			
Dec. 31	Bonds payable	100,000	
	Premium on bonds payable	1,865	
	Loss on bond retirement	3,135	
	Cash		105,000
	To retire bonds at 105 and record loss on retirement.		

A	=	L	+	SE
−105,000		−100,000		−3,135
		−1,865		Loss

Koby Company issued $300,000 of bonds for $325,000. (a) Prepare the journal entry to record the issuance of the bonds, and (b) illustrate how the bonds will be shown on the Koby Company's balance sheet at the issuance date.

YOUR TURN! 10.2

The solution is on page 526.

Advantages and Disadvantages of Long-Term Bonds and Notes

Issuing bonds and notes versus issuing common stock is an alternative way for a corporation to obtain needed long-term funds. The advantages of obtaining long-term funds by issuing bonds and notes instead of common stock include:

1. **No dilution of ownership interest.** Bondholders and noteholders are creditors, not shareholders, of a corporation. Issuing bonds and notes rather than common stock maintains the number of outstanding shares of stock at their current level.

2. **Tax deductibility of interest expense.** Interest expense is deductible as an expense on a corporation's income tax return. Dividend payments to shareholders are not tax deductible.

3. **Income to common shareholders can increase.** **Leverage** refers to the use of borrowed funds, particularly long-term debt, to finance a business's growth. When a firm is able to earn a return on its borrowed funds that exceeds the cost of borrowing the funds, then leverage is said to build shareholder value.

For example, assume that a firm can earn 15 percent on $5,000,000 obtained by issuing bonds and notes that have a ten percent interest rate. If the firm pays income taxes at a 40 percent rate, its net income will increase $150,000 each year, as follows:

Earnings on funds borrowed: 15 percent × $5,000,000	$750,000
Interest cost on funds borrowed: 10 percent × $5,000,000	**(500,000)**
Increase in income before income tax expense.	$250,000
Income tax expense on increase: 40 percent × $250,000	**(100,000)**
Increase in net income	$150,000

The $150,000 increase in net income accrues exclusively to the company's common stockholders.

Not all aspects of issuing bonds and notes, however, are necessarily desirable for the borrowing company. Among the disadvantages of issuing bonds and notes are the following:

1. **Interest expense is a contractual obligation.** In contrast with dividends on common stock, interest represents a fixed periodic expenditure that the firm is contractually obligated to pay.

2. **Funds borrowed have a specific repayment date.** Because bonds and notes normally have a defined maturity date, the borrower has a specific obligation to repay the borrowings at maturity.

3. **Borrowing agreement can restrict company actions.** The legal document setting forth the terms of a debt issue is called an *indenture*. Some of the provisions in an indenture may involve restrictions on dividend payments, restrictions on additional financing, and specification of minimum financial ratios that must be maintained. These provisions, called *debt covenants*, are intended to provide protection for debtholders by limiting a company's flexibility to act.

ACCOUNTING IN PRACTICE	**Microsoft Bond Issuance and Company Value**

As noted in the opening feature story, **Microsoft** was essentially debt free until 2009. Following the $3.75 billion in bonds that Microsoft issued in late 2009, part of a larger $6 billion debt issue that the board of directors approved, analysts weighed in on why they thought this occurred. Noting that Microsoft also authorized a plan to buy back $40 billion of its own stock over the following five years, Sid Parakh, an analyst at McAdams Wright Ragen stated, "They said a few months ago they would like to leverage the balance sheets; that's what they're doing. Lowering the cost of capital will probably benefit shareholder value in the long term."

CONTINGENT LIABILITIES

LO3 Define *contingent liabilities* and **explain** the rules for their accounting and disclosure in the financial statements.

Previously, we defined a liability as an obligation resulting from past transactions or events that require a firm to pay money, provide goods, or perform services in the future. Even though a past transaction or event has taken place, the existence of some liabilities still depends on the occurrence of a future event. These types of liability are called **contingent liabilities**. Whether or not a contingent liability is recorded in the accounts depends on the likelihood of the future event occurring and the measurability of the obligation.

If the future event will *probably occur* and the amount of the liability can be *reasonably estimated,* an estimated liability should be recorded in the accounts. The estimated liability for product warranties is a good example of this situation. Many firms guarantee their products for a period of time following their sale. Customers are likely to make claims under a warranty for goods that they had purchased, and a reasonable estimate of the amount of the warranty obligation can usually be made.

Some contingent liabilities are not recorded in the accounts but must be disclosed in a note to the financial statements. Contingent liabilities disclosed in this manner are (1) those for which the likelihood of the future event occurring is probable but no reasonable estimate of the future obligation is determinable or (2) those for which the likelihood of the future event occurring is *reasonably possible* (but not probable), regardless of the ability to measure the future amount. When the future amount is not determinable, the note should state that the amount cannot be estimated.

PRINCIPLE ALERT

Measuring Unit Concept and Full Disclosure Principle

The accounting guidelines for contingent liabilities illustrate the application of two principles of accounting: the *measuring unit concept* and the *full disclosure principle*. The measuring unit concept requires that information reported in the body of the financial statements be expressed in money terms. If a reasonable estimate of a contingent liability's dollar amount cannot be made, the measuring unit concept prevents the item from appearing in the balance sheet, even if its future occurrence is probable. However, the full disclosure principle requires that firms disclose all significant financial facts and circumstances to financial statement users. This principle leads to the reporting of likely, but unmeasurable contingent liabilities in the notes to the financial statements.

If the likelihood of the future event occurring is *remote,* the contingent liability is neither recorded in the accounts nor disclosed in the notes to the financial statements, regardless of the ability to measure the future amount. One exception to this guideline, however, is when a company guarantees the credit of others (discussed in the following section). Even remote contingent liabilities associated with credit guarantees must be disclosed in the notes to the financial statements.

ACCOUNTING IN PRACTICE

Estimated Liabilities Resulting from Lawsuits

Walmart Stores, Inc., is the world's largest retailer with over 10,000 stores around the globe. Each week, 200 million customers visit a Walmart store to take advantage of the company's notorious low prices. But while Walmart may be cheered by consumers for its low prices, others are more critical of the company. Walmart, for example, has been criticized and sued by community groups, trade unions, and environmental groups for, among other things, its extensive foreign product sourcing, treatment of employees and product suppliers, environmental policies, and store impact on local communities. One such lawsuit alleges that female employees were discriminated against in pay and promotions. The following description of the lawsuit appeared in the company's 2009 annual report:

> . . . The Company is a defendant in Dukes v. Walmart Stores, Inc., a class-action law-suit . . . The complaint alleges that the Company engaged in a pattern and practice of discriminating against women in promotions, pay, training, and job assignments . . . If the company is not successful in its appeal . . . the resulting liability could be material to the company . . . However, because of the uncertainty of the outcome of the appeal . . . the Company cannot reasonably estimate the possible loss or range of loss which may arise from the litigation.

Examples of Contingent Liabilities

Situations that may create contingent liabilities are discussed in the following sections. In each of these situations, accountants must assess the likelihood of the future event occurring and the measurability of the future amount because these factors determine the proper accounting treatment of the contingent liability.

Product Warranties

A proper matching of sales revenue and expenses requires that the estimated cost of honoring and servicing **product warranties** be recognized as an expense in the period of sale rather than in a later period when the warranty costs may actually be incurred and paid.

To illustrate, assume that a firm sells a product for $300 per unit, which includes a 30-day warranty against defects. Past experience indicates that three percent of the units will prove defective and that the average repair cost will be $40 per defective unit. Furthermore, during a particular month, product sales were $240,000, and 13 of the units sold during the month were defective and were repaired. Using this information, the accrued liability for product warranties at the end of the month can be calculated as follows:

Number of units sold ($240,000/$300).....................................	800
Rate of projected defective units.......................................	× 0.03
Total units expected to fail...	24
Less: Units that failed in the month of sale...........................	13
Units expected to fail in the remainder of the warranty period..............	11
Average repair cost per unit...	× $40
Estimated liability for product warranty at end of month....................	$440

This accrued liability is recorded at the end of the month of sale as follows:

A = L + SE	Product warranty expense	440
+440 −440	Estimated liability for product warranty	440
Exp	*To record estimated warranty expense.*	

When a unit fails in a future period, the repair costs will be recorded by debiting the Estimated Liability for Product Warranty account and crediting Cash, Supplies, and so forth.

PRINCIPLE ALERT   **Matching Concept**

The accounting for product warranties follows the *expense recognition (matching) concept*. This accounting concept states that expenses must be recorded in the same accounting period as the revenues they help generate. Product warranties make a company's products more attractive to buyers; consequently, product warranties help generate incremental sales revenues. Hence, one of the expenses that must be matched with sales revenues is the cost of honoring and servicing a product warranty. Because most warranty costs are incurred in periods following the period of sale, it is necessary to estimate these costs and record them in the same period when the sale of the product occurs to achieve a proper matching of revenues and expenses.

Lawsuits

In the course of its operations, a firm may pursue a claim in a court of law by filing a lawsuit. At any point, a firm may also be a defendant in one or more lawsuits involving potentially material financial settlements. Examples of litigation issues include product liability, patent infringement, unfair labor practices (see the Walmart Accounting in Practice on p. 487), and environmental matters. The resolution of a lawsuit may take many years. During the time a lawsuit is pending, the defendant has a contingent liability for any future financial settlement although it is impossible in most cases to arrive at a reasonable estimate of a company's possible losses. For this reason, lawsuit liabilities are most commonly disclosed in the notes to the financial statements and not on the face of the income statement or the balance sheet.

Environmental Cleanup Costs

Past actions by many companies in disposing of various types of industrial waste have caused subsequent environmental damage. Some estimates of the total cleanup costs for the United States run as high as $100 billion. Firms owning sites that require environmental remediation or that may require clean-up face a contingent liability for the remediation costs. Cleanup costs for a particular site may be very difficult to estimate. The party responsible for bearing the cost—the company or its insurance company—may also be at issue.

Credit Guarantees

To accommodate important, but less financially secure suppliers or customers, a firm may create a **credit guarantee** by cosigning a note payable. Until the original debtor satisfies the obligation, the cosigning firm is contingently liable for the debt. Even when the likelihood of default by a debtor is considered remote, the contingent liability associated with credit guarantees must be disclosed in the notes to the financial statements.

IFRS ALERT

The accounting for some contingent liabilities under U.S. GAAP and IFRS differs significantly. For example, under U.S. GAAP, purchase commitments—that is, an agreement by one company to buy merchandise from another company at a future date—are not reported on the balance sheet but, if material in amount, are disclosed in the notes to the financial statements. Under IFRS, however, purchase commitments are reported on the balance sheet when a company has a clear and demonstrable commitment to a second company to buy its goods. In essence, IFRS adopts a broader definition of what constitutes an accounting liability than does U.S. GAAP. Under U.S. GAAP, while purchase commitments are acknowledged to be economic liabilities of a business, they do not constitute an accounting liability until an exchange of assets occurs between the two companies.

Summary of Accounting Treatment for Liabilities

Exhibit 10-5 summarizes the accounting for different types of liabilities according to their unique characteristics.

Exhibit 10-5	Liabilities: Criteria and Financial Statement Treatment					
Different Characteristics that Determine the Type of Liability and How it is Recorded	**Recorded in Accounts and Reported on Balance Sheet**			**Disclosed in Footnote to Financial Statements**		**No Disclosure Required**
	Noncontingent	Contingent	Contingent	Contingent	Contingent	Contingent
Dependent on future event. . .	No	No	Yes	Yes	Yes	Yes
Likelihood of future event.	Already Occurred	Already Occurred	**Probable**	**Probable**	**Reasonably possible**	**Remote**
Amount of future obligation	Known	Reasonably estimable	Reasonably estimable	Not reasonably estimable	Known, or Reasonably estimable, or Not reasonably estimable	Known, or Reasonably estimable, or Not reasonably estimable
Common examples	Notes payable, Accounts payable, Dividends payable	Income tax payable, Estimated liability for frequent use awards	Estimated liability for product warranty	Lawsuits, Environmental cleanup, Guarantee of others' credit	Lawsuits, Environmental cleanup, Guarantee of others' credit	Lawsuits, Environmental cleanup

YOUR TURN! 10.3

The solution is on page 526.

For each of the following scenarios determine if the firm should (a) record as a liability; (b) disclose as a contingent liability; or (c) neither:

1. The Seco Co. has been sued by a group of individuals claiming the products they purchased from the company were defective and caused injuries. Seco's lawyers have determined that the product in question could not possibly have caused the types of damages claimed and further that the same group of individuals has unsuccessfully sued several other companies claiming their products caused the same injuries. The likelihood of losing this lawsuit is deemed remote.
2. The Everett Co. has guaranteed the loan of a subsidiary that is suffering minor financial distress. The chance that the loan will not be repaid is deemed remote.
3. Hiller Inc. has acquired a defunct mining company and assumed all its liabilities. Toxic waste from the defunct company was recently discovered to have leaked into some nearby wells. The evidence that the waste came from the mining company is very strong and the cost of cleanup is estimated to be $4 million.

TAKEAWAY 10.1	Concept ➡	Method ➡	Assessment
	Does the company have any contingent or off-balance sheet liabilities?	Notes to the financial statements Read the notes to the financial statements to identify contingent liabilities and operating leases	Consider the likely outcome and size of contingent liabilities and the amount of operating leases. If significant, consider these items in the analysis of the firm's liabilities.

FORENSIC ACCOUNTING

Accounting Software

 One definition of forensic accounting is "the use of accounting records and documents to determine the legality of past activities." Possible uses of forensic accounting include financial statements, government investigations, contract disputes, or even culling through a shoebox of receipts in preparation for an IRS audit. As a business owner, would you rather defend yourself in an investigation with a shoebox full of documents or with a detailed set of accounting records? While some small business owners feel that entry-level accounting systems such as **Intuit**'s Quickbooks are fine for their needs, they may want to consider the benefits of a more robust accounting package, such as **Microsoft** Dynamics GP accounting system. In today's technology driven society, a security breach is only a few keystrokes away. A hacker will have a much easier time penetrating the single layer of security in most entry-level packages than the eight levels of security in Microsoft Dynamics GP. In addition, the more robust accounting systems provide a richer data repository from which a forensic accountant can mine data in an effort to identify inconsistencies, a major weapon in the detection of fraud.

ANALYZING LIABILITIES

LO4 Define the *current ratio*, *quick ratio*, and *times-interest-earned ratio* and **explain** their use.

Current Ratio and Quick Ratio

The **working capital** of a firm is the difference between the value of its current assets and the value of its current liabilities. In general, having a higher working capital position is preferred to having a lower working capital position. In analyzing the adequacy of a firm's working capital, the current ratio is a widely used financial metric. The **current ratio** is calculated as follows:

$$\text{Current ratio} = \frac{\text{Current assets}}{\text{Current liabilities}}$$

Historically, a current ratio of 2.00 has been considered an acceptable current ratio; however, this is a general guide only. Many businesses operate successfully with a current ratio below 2.00, particularly service firms, because they do not need to maintain large amounts of inventory among their current assets. Similarly, many fast-food franchises operate successfully with a negative working capital position. These businesses produce large amounts of operating cash flow, have no accounts receivable, and extensively utilize the trade credit (accounts payable) provided by their suppliers.

The **quick ratio** is another ratio used to evaluate a company's working capital position. The quick ratio is calculated as follows:

$$\text{Quick ratio} = \frac{\left[\text{Cash and cash equivalents} + \text{Short-term investments} + \text{Accounts receivable}\right]}{\text{Current liabilities}}$$

Cash and cash equivalents, short-term investments, and accounts receivable are also known as quick assets. Quick assets are converted to cash more quickly than inventory or prepaid assets.

Comparing the quick ratio to the current ratio, the main current assets omitted from the numerator when calculating the quick ratio are inventory and prepaid assets. Consequently, the quick ratio is often preferred by investment professionals because it gives a more accurate picture of a company's ability to pay current liabilities.

The following are examples of the current and quick ratios for companies in different industries:

	Current Ratio	Quick Ratio
Verizon Communications (telecommunications)	1.01	0.84
Johnson & Johnson (health care products)	2.38	1.88
Duke Energy (utility)	1.24	0.56
Google (technology).	5.92	5.62

As can be seen from the above data, the current and quick ratios vary dramatically between industries.

Forensic Accounting	THINKING GLOBALLY

One of the key measures indicating the amount of liabilities, or leverage, used by a company is its net debt. Net debt is calculated as a firm's total liabilities minus its liquid (or quick) assets. The higher a firm's net debt, the higher the firm's leverage, or use of debt financing. Because of the widespread use of net debt as an indicator of a firm's use of leverage by investment professionals, some firms have attempted to manage the level of their reported net debt. To illustrate, consider the case of **Parmalat SpA**, an Italian dairy company. In late 2003, the company filed for bankruptcy after revealing that it had massively underreported its outstanding net debt. According to the company's forensic investigative auditor, **PricewaterhouseCoopers LLP**, Parmalat underreported its net debt position by overstating the amount of cash on hand and retaining worthless accounts receivable on the company's balance sheet.

Concept	→ Method	→ Assessment	TAKEAWAY 10.2
Can a firm pay its current liabilities?	Current assets, Quick assets, Current liabilities $\text{Current ratio} = \dfrac{\text{Current assets}}{\text{Current liabilities}}$ $\text{Quick ratio} = \dfrac{\text{Quick assets}}{\text{Current liabilities}}$	A higher current ratio and quick ratio indicates that a firm can readily pay its current liabilities.	

Times-Interest-Earned Ratio

A financial ratio of particular interest to current and potential long-term creditors is the times-interest-earned ratio. The **times-interest-earned ratio** is computed as follows:

$$\text{Times-interest-earned ratio} = \frac{\text{Income before interest expense and income taxes}}{\text{Interest expense}}$$

A.K.A. The times-interest-earned ratio is also referred to as the *interest coverage ratio*.

The principal on long-term debt, such as bonds payable, is not due until maturity, which may be many years into the future. Interest payments, however, are due every six months, and possibly monthly on term loans. Thus, creditors examine the times-interest-earned ratio to help assess the ability of a company to meet its periodic interest commitments. The ratio indicates the number of times that the fixed interest charges were earned during the year. Many investment professionals believe that the times-interest-earned ratio should be at least in the range of 3.0–4.0 for the extension of long-term credit to be considered a safe investment. The trend of the ratio in recent years and the nature of the industry (volatile or stable, for example) also influence the interpretation of this ratio.

Both the numerator and denominator in the times-interest-earned ratio are obtained from the income statement. The numerator uses income before interest expense and income taxes because that is the amount available to cover a business's current interest charges. The denominator is the business's total interest expense for the period. To illustrate, Reid, Inc., issued $100,000 of eight percent bonds at face value. The annual interest expense was $8,000. If this was Reid's only interest expense and Reid's income before interest expense and income taxes the first year were $28,000, Reid's times-interest-earned ratio for the year would be 3.5, or $28,000/$8,000.

The times-interest-earned ratio may differ substantially among industries and firms, depending upon a company's decision to use leverage to finance its assets and operations. The following are examples of times-interest-earned ratios for several companies in different industries:

Kellogg Company (grocery products)	8.4
MeadWestvaco Corporation (paper and paper products)	3.3
Amazon.com Inc. (online retailing)	15.4
Cisco Systems, Inc. (computer communications equip.)	18.0

TAKEAWAY 10.3	Concept	➡ Method ➡	Assessment
	Can a firm pay its current periodic interest payments?	Income before income taxes and interest expense, Interest expense Times-interest-earned ratio $= \dfrac{\text{Income before income taxes and interest expense}}{\text{Interest expense}}$	A higher times-interest-earned ratio indicates that a firm will have less difficulty paying its current interest expense.

YOUR TURN! 10.4

The solution is on page 527.

Magee Company reports the following in its current year financial statements:

Current assets	$120,000
Current liabilities	80,000
Cash and cash equivalents	10,000
Short-term investments	25,000
Accounts receivable	30,000
Income before interest expense and income taxes	20,000
Interest expense	4,000

Compute the following ratios for Magee Company:
a. Current ratio
b. Quick ratio
c. Times-interest-earned ratio

COMPREHENSIVE PROBLEM

The following are selected transactions for Tyler, Inc., for 2014 and 2015. The firm closes its books on December 31.

2014

Dec. 31 Issued $500,000 of 12 percent, ten-year bonds for $562,360, yielding an effective rate of ten percent. Interest is payable June 30 and December 31.

2015

June 30 Paid semiannual interest and recorded semiannual premium amortization on bonds.
Dec. 31 Paid semiannual interest and recorded semiannual premium amortization on bonds.
    31 Called one-half of the bonds in for retirement at 104.

Required

Record the transactions using (a) straight-line amortization and (b) effective interest amortization. Round amounts to the nearest dollar. You should read Appendix 10A prior to attempting this comprehensive problem.

Solution:

		(a) Straight-line Amortization		(b) Effective Interest Amortization	
2014					
Dec. 31	Cash	562,300		562,300	
	Bonds payable		500,000		500,000
	Premium on bonds payable		62,360		62,360
	Issued $500,000 of 12 percent, ten-year bonds for $562,360.				
2015					
June 30	Bond interest expense	26,882		28,118	
	Premium on bonds payable	3,118		1,882	
	Cash		30,000		30,000
	To record semiannual interest payment and premium amortization.	*[$62,360 ÷ 20 = $3,118].*		*[$562,360 × 0.05 = $28,118].*	
Dec. 31	Bond interest expense	26,882		28,024	
	Premium on bonds payable	3,118		1,976	
	Cash		30,000		30,000
	To record semiannual interest payment and premium amortization.	*[$62,360 ÷ 20 = $3,118].*		*[($562,360 − $1,882) × 0.05 = $28,024, rounded].*	
31	Bonds payable	250,000		250,000	
	Premium on bonds payable	28,062		29,251	
	Cash		260,000		260,000
	Gain on bond retirement		18,062		19,251
	To record retirement of $250,000 of bonds; Retirement payment: $250,000 × 1.04 = $260,000.	*[$56,124 × 50% = $28,062].*		*[$58,502 × 50% = $29,251].*	

APPENDIX 10A: Bond Pricing

We explained that (1) a bond agreement specifies a pattern of future cash flows—usually a series of interest payments and a single payment at maturity equal to the face value—and that (2) bonds are often sold at premiums or discounts to adjust their stated or coupon interest rates to the prevailing market rate of interest when they are issued.

Because of the role played by interest, the selling price of a bond that is necessary to yield a specific rate can be determined as follows:

L05 **Explain** bond pricing and **illustrate** the straight-line and effective interest methods of amortizing bond discounts/premiums.

❶ Use Appendix E's Table III to calculate the present value of the future principal repayment at the bond's effective rate of interest.

❷ Use Appendix E's Table IV to calculate the present value of the future series of interest payments at the bond's effective rate of interest.

❸ Add the two present value calculations obtained in steps one and two.

Exhibit 10A-1 illustrates the pricing of a $100,000 issue of eight percent, four-year bonds paying interest semiannually and sold on the date of issue to yield (1) eight percent, (2) ten percent, or (3) six percent. The price of the eight-percent bonds sold to yield eight percent equals the face (or par) value of the bonds. However, the bonds must sell for $93,552 to provide a yield of ten percent, whereas the bonds must sell for $106,980 to provide a yield of six percent.

Exhibit 10A-1	Calculating Bond Issue Price Using Present Value Tables

❶ $100,000 of eight percent, four-year bonds with interest payable semiannually sold to yield eight percent:

Future Cash Flows	Multiplier (Table III)	Multiplier (Table IV)	Present Values at 4% Semiannually
Principal repayment, $100,000 (a single amount received eight semiannual periods hence)	0.73069		$ 73,100
Interest payments, $4,000 at end of each of eight semiannual interest periods.		6.73274	26,900 (rounded)
Total present value (or issue price) of bonds			$100,000

❷ $100,000 of eight percent, four-year bonds with interest payable semiannually sold to yield ten percent:

Future Cash Flows	Multiplier (Table III)	Multiplier (Table IV)	Present Values at 5% Semiannually
Principal repayment, $100,000 (a single amount received eight semiannual periods hence)	0.67684		$ 67,700
Interest payments, $4,000 at end of each of eight semiannual interest periods.		6.46321	25,852
Total present value (or issue price) of bonds			$ 93,552

❸ $100,000 of eight percent, four-year bonds with interest payable semiannually sold to yield six percent:

Future Cash Flows	Multiplier (Table III)	Multiplier (Table IV)	Present Values at 3% Semiannually
Principal repayment, $100,000 (a single amount received eight semiannual periods hence)	0.78941		$ 78,900
Interest payments, $4,000 at end of each of eight semiannual interest periods.		7.01969	28,080
Total present value (or issue price) of bonds			$106,980

Straight-line Interest Method of Discount Amortization

When bonds are sold at either a discount or a premium the amount of interest that the company pays to bond-holders will differ from the amount of interest expense that is reported on the income statement. To see why this is the case, we will first consider the bond in **Exhibit 10A-1** that sells for $93,552; a discount of $6,448 from the face value of $100,000. This $6,448 discount represents an additional interest cost that the issuing company, Reid Inc., must pay because it borrowed $93,552 but will have to pay back $100,000 in addition to the semiannual $4,000 interest payments. To properly apply the matching principle, Reid, Inc. will recognize a portion of the $6,448 discount as additional interest expense each time it makes an interest payment, thus spreading the additional interest of $6,448 over the life of the bond.

Under the **straight-line interest method** an equal amount of the discount is amortized to expense at each payment date. **Exhibit 10A-2** presents an amortization table illustrating the straight-line method. The interest rates shown in columns A and B are one-half the annual rates. Column A lists the constant amount of interest paid each six months—that is, the coupon interest rate times the face value (4 percent × $100,000). The amounts in column B are obtained by dividing the $6,448 discount by the eight interest payments, or $806 per semiannual period. The total interest expense appearing in column C is the interest payment in column A plus the discount amortization in column B. The original $6,448 discount is reduced by $806 each period as shown in column D. The reported value of the bonds, shown in column E changes each period. For discounted bonds, the reported value increases each period until it reaches the face value on the maturity date because the discount is being reduced each period until it becomes zero.

Exhibit 10A-2	Bonds Sold at a Discount: Straight-line Interest Method				
	$100,000 of 8% four-year bonds with interest payable semiannually Issued on December 31, 2015, at $93,552 to yield 10%				
	A	B	C	D	E
Interest Period	Interest Paid (4% of face value)	Additional Interest ($6,448 discount divided by 8 periods)	Total Interest Expense (A + B)	Balance of Unamortized Discount (D − B)	Book Value of Bonds, End of Period ($100,000 − D)
At issue				$6,448	$ 93,552
2016 1	$4,000	$806	$4,806	5,642	94,358
2	4,000	806	4,806	4,836	95,164
2017 3	4,000	806	4,806	4,030	95,970
4	4,000	806	4,806	3,224	96,776
2018 5	4,000	806	4,806	2,418	97,582
6	4,000	800	4,806	1,612	98,388
2019 7	4,000	806	4,806	806	99,194
8	4,000	806	4,806	0	100,000

The following journal entry records the interest expense and discount amortization each period:

					A	=	L	+	SE
					4,000		+806		−4,806

2016			
June 30	Bond interest expense	4,806	
	Discount on bonds payable		806
	Cash		4,000
	To record semiannual interest payments and amortization.		

Amortizing the bond discount over the four-year life of the bonds leaves a zero balance in the Discount on Bonds Payable account on the maturity date of the bonds. The retirement of the bonds at maturity is then recorded by debiting Bonds Payable and crediting Cash for $100,000, the amount of their face value.

Straight-line Interest Method of Premium Amortization

When bonds are issued at a premium the interest expense each period will be less than the amount of cash paid. We can see this by again considering the Reid, Inc. bond from **Exhibit 10A-1**, this time considering the bond issued for $106,980, a premium of $6,980 over the face value of $100,000. The $6,980 premium represents a reduction of interest cost to Reid, Inc., because Reid borrowed $106,980 but will have to pay back only $100,000 in addition to the semiannual $4,000 interest payments. As with the discount discussed above, to properly apply the matching principle Reid, Inc. will recognize a portion of the $6,980 premium as a reduction of interest expense each time it makes an interest payment, thus spreading the $6,980 premium over the life of the bond.

Exhibit 10A-3 presents an amortization table illustrating the straight-line method. The interest rates shown in columns A and B are one-half the annual rates. Column A lists the constant amount of interest paid each six months—that is, the coupon interest rate times the face value (4 percent × $100,000). The amounts in column B are obtained by dividing the $6,980 premium by the eight interest payments, or $872.50 per semiannual period. The total interest expense appearing in column C is the interest payment in column A minus the premium amortization in column B. The original $6,980 premium is reduced by $872.50 each period as shown in column D. The reported value of the bonds, shown in column E, changes each period. For bonds issued at a premium, the value decreases each period until it reaches the face value on the maturity date because the premium is being reduced each period until it becomes zero.

Exhibit 10A-3	Bonds Sold at a Premium: Straight-line Interest Method

$100,000 of 8% four-year bonds with interest payable semiannually
Issued on December 31, 2015, at $106,980 to yield 6%

	Interest Period	A Interest Paid (4% of face value)	B Additional Interest ($6,980 premium divided by 8 periods)	C Total Interest Expense (A + B)	D Balance of Unamortized Premium (D – B)	E Book Value of Bonds, End of Period ($100,000 + D)
At issue					$6,980.00	$106,980.00
2016	1	$4,000	$872.50	$3,127.50	6,107.50	106,107.50
	2	4,000	872.50	3,127.50	5,235.00	105,235.00
2017	3	4,000	872.50	3,127.50	4,362.50	104,362.50
	4	4,000	872.50	3,127.50	3,490.00	103,490.00
2018	5	4,000	872.50	3,127.50	2,617.50	102,617.50
	6	4,000	872.50	3,127.50	1,745.00	101,745.00
2019	7	4,000	872.50	3,127.50	872.50	100,872.50
	8	4,000	872.50	3,127.50	0.00	100,000.00

The following journal entry records the interest expense and premium amortization each period:

A	=	L	+	SE
−4,000.00		−872.50		−3,127.50

2016			
June 30	Bond interest expense	3,127.50	
	Premium on bonds payable	872.50	
	Cash		4,000
	To record semiannual interest payments and amortization.		

Amortizing the bond premium over the four-year life of the bonds leaves a zero balance in the Premium on Bonds Payable account on the maturity date of the bonds. The retirement of the bonds at maturity is then recorded by debiting Bonds Payable and crediting Cash for $100,000, the amount of their face value.

Effective Interest Method of Discount Amortization

A bond premium or discount can be amortized to interest expense using the straight-line method or the effective interest method. GAAP requires the effective interest method, except in cases where the differences between the two methods is not material. The **effective interest method** of amortization recognizes a constant percentage of the book value of a bond as interest expense for each interest payment period. For bonds issued at a discount, the book value of a bond is the balance in the Bonds Payable account less the balance in the Discount on Bonds Payable account. To obtain a period's interest expense under the effective interest method, we multiply the bond's book value at the beginning of each period by the effective interest rate. The **effective interest rate** is the market rate of interest used to price the bonds when they are originally issued. The difference between this amount and the amount of interest paid (coupon interest rate × face value of bonds) is the amount of discount amortized.

When using the effective interest method of amortization, accountants often prepare an amortization schedule similar to the one in **Exhibit 10A-4**. This schedule covers the four-year life of the Reid, Inc., bonds issued at a discount. The interest rates shown in columns A and B are one-half the annual rates. Column A lists the constant amounts of interest paid each six months—that is, the coupon interest rate times the face value (4 percent × $100,000). The amounts in Column B are obtained by multiplying the book value as of the beginning of each period (column E) by the 5 percent effective interest rate. For example, the $4,678 interest expense for the first period is 5 percent times $93,552; for the second period, it is 5 percent times $94,230, or $4,712, and so on. The reported value of the bonds changes each period. For discounted bonds, the value increases each period because the book value increases over the life of the bonds until it reaches the face value on the maturity date. The amount of discount amortization for each period, given in column C, is the difference between the corresponding amounts in columns A and B. Column D lists the amount of unamortized discount at the end of each period.

Exhibit 10A-4	Bonds Sold at a Discount: Effective Interest Method

**$100,000 of 8%, four-year bonds with interest payable semiannually
issued on December 31, 2015, at $93,552 to yield 10%**

		A	B	C	D	E
Year	Interest Period	Interest Paid (4% of face value)	Interest Expense (5% of bond book value)	Periodic Amortization (B − A)	Balance of Unamortized Discount (D − C)	Book Value of Bonds, End of Period ($100,000 − D)
At issue. . . .					$6,448	$ 93,552
2016.	1	$4,000	$4,678	$678	5,770	94,230
	2	4,000	4,712	712	5,058	94,942
2017.	3	4,000	4,747	747	4,311	95,689
	4	4,000	4,784	784	3,527	96,473
2018.	5	4,000	4,824	824	2,703	97,297
	6	4,000	4,865	865	1,838	98,162
2019.	7	4,000	4,908	908	930	99,070
	8	4,000	4,930*	930	0	100,000

*Adjusted for cumulative rounding error of $24

The amounts recorded for each interest payment can be read directly from the amortization schedule. The following journal entries record the interest expense and discount amortization at the time of the first two interest payments:

2016					
June 30	Bond interest expense	4,678			
	Discount on bonds payable		678		
	Cash		4,000		
	To record semiannual interest payment and amortization.				

A = L + SE
−4,000 +678 −4,678 Exp

Dec. 31	Bond interest expense	4,712			
	Discount on bonds payable		712		
	Cash		4,000		
	To record semiannual interest payment and amortization.				

A = L + SE
−4,000 +712 −4,712 Exp

Amortizing the bond discount over the four-year life of the bonds leaves a zero balance in the Discount on Bonds Payable account on the maturity date of the bonds. The retirement of the bonds at maturity is then recorded by debiting Bonds Payable and crediting Cash for $100,000, the amount of their face value.

Materiality Concept	PRINCIPLE ALERT

Under U.S. GAAP, the effective interest method is the preferred method of bond amortization. It is generally accepted because it uses the actual market rate of interest when the bonds were originally issued to determine the amount of the periodic amortization. The effective interest method, however, is somewhat more complex than the straight-line method. Accounting standards permit the straight-line method of amortization to be used when the results are not materially different from those achieved under the effective interest method. This exception represents an application of the *materiality concept*. As previously discussed, the materiality concept permits insignificant accounting transactions to be recorded most expediently. Here, the materiality concept permits a simpler (and, thus, more expedient) straight-line method to be used when it results in insignificant differences from the theoretically superior effective interest method.

Effective Interest Method of Premium Amortization

The **effective interest method** of amortizing a bond premium is handled the same way as a bond discount amortization. Each interest period, a constant percentage of the bonds' book value as of the beginning of the period is recognized as interest expense; the difference between the interest expense and the semiannual interest payment is the amount of the premium amortization.

Exhibit 10A-5 shows the amortization schedule for the four-year life of the Reid, Inc., bonds that were issued at a premium. The coupon rate of 4 percent in column A and the effective interest rate of 3 percent in column B are one-half the annual rates because the calculations are for six-month periods.

Exhibit 10A-5	Bonds Sold at a Premium: Effective Interest Method				
$100,000 of 8%, four-year bonds with interest payable semiannually issued on December 31, 2015, at $106,980 to yield 6%					
		A	B	C	D	E
Year	Interest Period	Interest Paid (4% of face value)	Interest Expense (3% of bond book value)	Periodic Amortization (A − B)	Balance of Unamortized Premium (D − C)	Book Value of Bonds, End of Period ($100,000 + D)
At issue. . . .					$6,980	$106,980
2016.	1	$4,000	$3,209	$791	6,189	106,189
	2	4,000	3,186	814	5,375	105,375
2017.	3	4,000	3,161	839	4,536	104,536
	4	4,000	3,136	864	3,672	103,672
2018.	5	4,000	3,110	890	2,782	102,782
	6	4,000	3,083	917	1,865	101,865
2019.	7	4,000	3,056	944	921	100,921
	8	4,000	3,079*	921	0	100,000

*Adjusted for cumulative rounding error of $51

The journal entries for each interest payment are taken directly from the amortization schedule. The entries for the first two interest payments (June 30 and December 31) follow. Note that the periodic interest expense is less than the semiannual interest payment.

A = L + SE	**2016**			
−4,000 −791 −3,209 Exp	June 30	Bond interest expense	3,209	
		Premium on bonds payable	791	
		Cash		4,000
		To record semiannual interest payment and amortization.		

A = L + SE	Dec. 31			
−4,000 −814 −3,186 Exp		Bond interest expense	3,186	
		Premium on bonds payable	814	
		Cash		4,000
		To record semiannual interest payment and amortization.		

After amortizing the bond premium over the four-year life of the bonds, the balance in the Premium on Bonds Payable account is zero. When the bonds are retired at the end of four years, the journal entry to record the retirement debits Bonds Payable and credits Cash for the $100,000 face value of the bonds.

Exhibit 10A-6 shows the book value of the Reid, Inc. bonds from issuance to maturity. The bond issued at face value has a reported book value of $100,000 over its entire life. The book value of the bond sold at a premium is greater than the face value at issuance. As the premium is amortized over the life of the bond, the book value declines until it is equal to the face value. The book value of the bond sold at a discount behaves in the opposite fashion; it is less than the face value at issuance, and increases over time as the discount is amortized. At maturity, the book value of all three bonds is equal to the $100,000 face value.

Exhibit 10A-6	Book Value of Bonds, End of Period

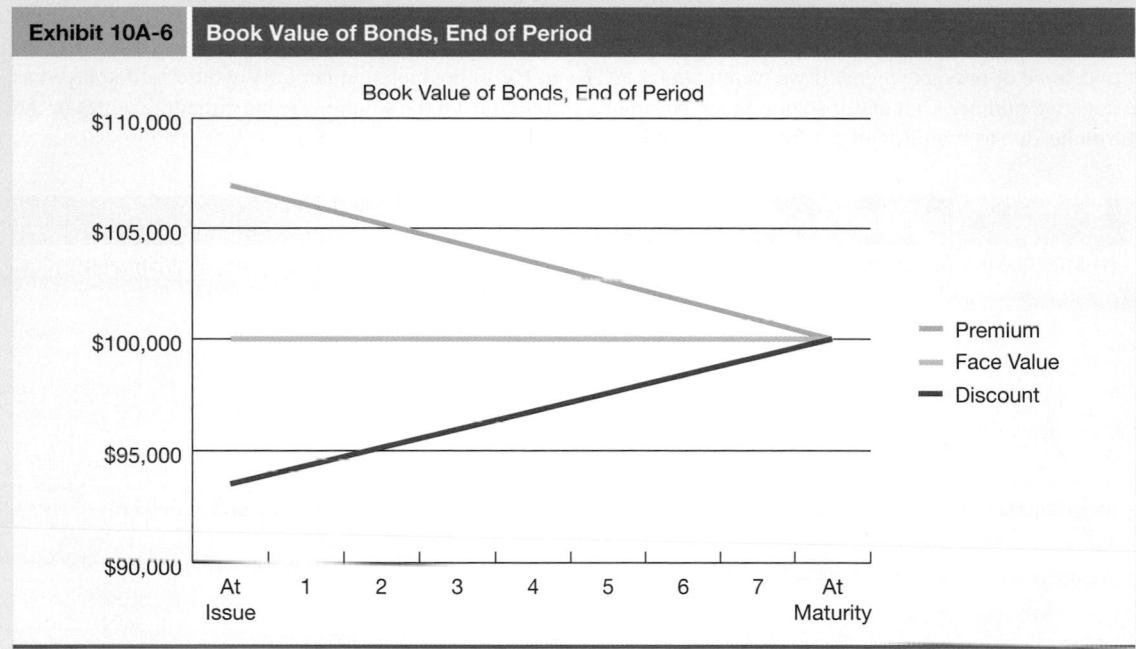

Using a Financial Calculator

While present value tables can provide a handy method to solve some time value of money problems, they are not suitable for many real-world situations. For example, many real-world interest rates are not "even integers" like those appearing in Table I through Table IV of Appendix E, nor are many problems limited to the number of time periods appearing in the tables. While it is still possible to solve these problems with the provided formulas, a financial calculator provides a quicker solution. Financial calculators can be distinguished from other calculators by the presence of dedicated keys for present and future values, along with keys for the number of periods, interest rates, and annuity payments. There exists many brands of financial calculators; however, all of them work in much the same way. We will illustrate the calculation of bond issuance prices from **Exhibit 10A-1** using a Hewlett-Packard 10BII financial calculator, as illustrated in **Exhibit 10A-7**. (It is usually necessary to do some preliminary setup on a financial calculator before performing time value of money calculations. For example, the HP 10BII calculator has a default setting of monthly compounding; this may need to be changed if the problem calls for a different number of compounding periods, such as annual. In addition, the calculator assumes interest payments occur at the end of each period; this will need to be changed if the problem requires beginning of period payments. See your calculator manual to determine how to make these setting changes.)

Exhibit 10A-7	Hewlett-Packard 10BII Financial Calculator

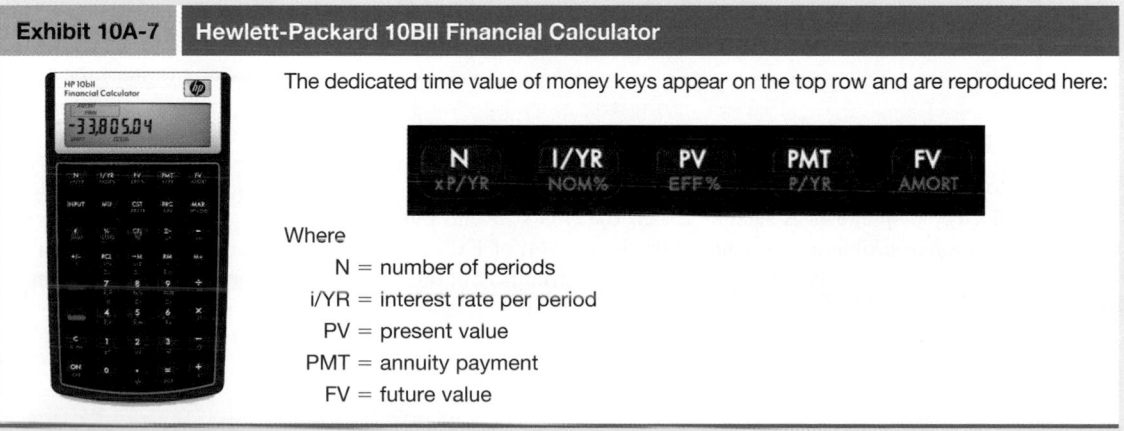

To solve a time value of money problem using a financial calculator, input the known values and then press the key of the unknown value. **Exhibit 10A-8** illustrates the bond value calculations from **Exhibit 10A-1**. The interest payment (PMT = $4,000) and principle at maturity (FV = $100,000) are shown as negative numbers, indicating cash outflows. Solving for the present value (PV) of these cash flows yields the price of the bond which is equal to the amount of cash received at issuance. Financial calculators require cash outflows and inflows to be of opposite signs. If we were to enter PMT and FV as positive numbers, PV would be displayed as a negative number. Calculator solutions can be slightly different from the solutions using either the tables or the formulas due to rounding of the future value and present value multipliers.

Exhibit 10A-8	Calculating Bond Issue Prices Using a Financial Calculator

(1) $100,000 of eight percent, four-year bonds with interest payable semiannually sold to yield eight percent:

Enter		Display		
8	N	N	=	8
4	I/YR	I/YR	=	4
−4,000	PMT	PMT	=	−4,000
−100,000	FV	FV	=	−100,000
Press	PV	PV	=	100,000

(2) $100,000 of eight percent, four-year bonds with interest payable semiannually sold to yield ten percent:

Enter		Display		
8	N	N	=	8
5	I/YR	I/YR	=	5
−4,000	PMT	PMT	=	−4,000
−100,000	FV	FV	=	−100,000
Press	PV	PV	=	93,537

(3) $100,000 of eight percent, four-year bonds with interest payable semiannually sold to yield six percent:

Enter		Display		
8	N	N	=	8
3	I/YR	I/YR	=	3
−4,000	PMT	PMT	=	−4,000
−100,000	FV	FV	=	−100,000
Press	PV	PV	=	107,020

ACCOUNTING IN PRACTICE	Getting a Car Loan

The expression "knowledge is power" certainly applies to the situation many of us face when shopping for a new car that we plan to finance. Sitting in the room with the car dealership's finance manager can be much more pleasant if one is armed with a financial calculator and the knowledge of how to calculate car payments. You no longer need to trust that the interest rate you are being quoted is the "real" interest rate you are being charged; you can simply do the calculation yourself and verify the number.

Using an Electronic Spreadsheet

In addition to present value tables and financial calculators, another way to solve time value of money problems is with an electronic spreadsheet such as Excel. Excel has several built-in functions that allow calculation of time value of money problems. Depending on the version of Excel, these functions are accessed differently. Within Excel 2010, go to the Insert function f_x in the Formulas ribbon. The required functions are located under the FINANCIAL option. Below are examples of how to use Excel to solve the same problems we previously solved using a financial calculator.

Example 1

Find the selling price (present value) of $100,000 of eight percent, four-year bonds with interest payable semi-annually sold to yield eight percent. Use the PV function and enter the values as follows:

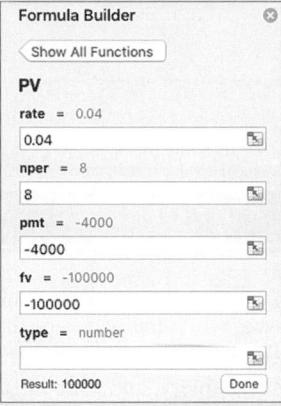

Example 2

Find the selling price (present value) of $100,000 of eight percent, four-year bonds with interest payable semi-annually sold to yield ten percent. Use the PV function and enter the values as follows:

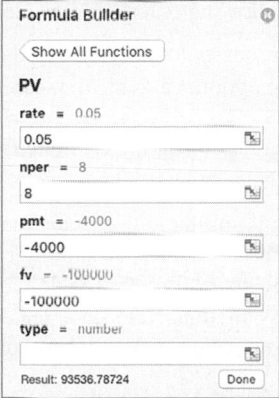

Example 3

Find the selling price (present value) of $100,000 of eight percent, four-year bonds with interest payable semi-annually sold to yield six percent. Use the PV function and enter the values as follows:

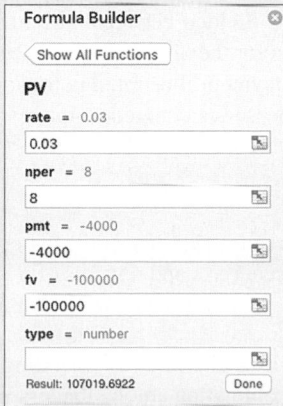

YOUR TURN! 10A.1

The solution is on page 527.

MBC

Use an Excel spreadsheet to find the selling price (present value) of a three-year $100,000 face value bond with coupon semiannual payments at four percent that is issued when bonds of similar risk are yielding six percent.

APPENDIX 10B: Leases

eLectures

MBC

LO6 Define *capital leases* and *operating leases* and **distinguish** between them.

A firm may rent property for a specified period of time under a contract called a **lease**. The company acquiring the right to use the property is the **lessee**, while the owner of the property is the **lessor**. The rights transferred to the lessee are called a **leasehold**. Examples of leased assets include land, buildings, factory machinery, and office equipment. A lessee's accounting treatment of a leased asset and lease liability depends upon whether a lease is a capital lease or an operating lease.

Capital Leases

A **capital lease** transfers to the lessee substantially all of the benefits and risks related to ownership of a leased asset. A lease meeting at least one of the following criteria is considered to be a capital lease:

1. The lease transfers ownership of the property to the lessee by the end of the lease term.
2. The lease contains a bargain purchase option, enabling the lessee to acquire the leased asset at a price below its fair market value.
3. The lease term is at least 75 percent of the remaining estimated economic life of the leased asset.
4. The present value of the lease payments is at least 90 percent of the fair value of the leased asset.

The economic effect of a capital lease is similar to that of an installment purchase. The lessee accounts for a capital lease by recording the leased property as an asset and establishing a liability for the lease obligation. The present value of the future lease payments determines the dollar amount of the capitalized lease asset and capitalized lease liability. For example, assume that Reid, Inc., leases equipment under a capital lease for ten years at $40,000 per year, and that the present value of the ten lease payments is $226,000.[1] Consequently, Reid records the capital lease as follows:

A	=	L	+ SE			
+226,000		+226,000		Leased equipment	226,000	
				Lease obligation		226,000
				To record 10-year capital lease.		

The leased equipment is depreciated over the life of the lease and appears among the firm's plant assets in the balance sheet. The total lease obligation is divided between current liabilities and long-term liabilities in the balance sheet based on the settlement dates for the obligation. The accounting for each lease payment is similar to the accounting for an installment note payment illustrated in the long-term liabilities section of this chapter. Part of each lease payment made by the lessee is charged to interest expense, and the remainder reduces the lease obligation.

Operating Leases

The typical rental agreement illustrates an **operating lease**: the lessee pays for the use of an asset for a limited period of time, and the lessor retains the usual risks and rewards of owning the asset. The lessee usually charges each lease payment to rent expense on the income statement. No leased asset or lease obligation is recorded on the lessee's balance sheet.

Lessees usually prefer to have any leases classified as operating leases rather than capital leases because this classification avoids reporting a lease obligation among the lessee's balance sheet liabilities. Having fewer balance sheet liabilities may make it easier for a lessee to borrow money from other lenders. Structuring a lease so that no liability is recorded (that is, having it qualify as an operating lease) is an example of a practice known as **off-balance-sheet financing**.

---

[1] Annual lease payments of $40,000 times present value of an ordinary annuity with a factor of 5.650 (12%) equals $226,000 (See Appendix E).

PRINCIPLE
ALERT

Leases and the Balance Sheet

What would balance sheets look like if lessees were required to capitalize all of their leases? Analysts and bond rating firms have long adjusted reported balance sheet numbers to take into account off-balance sheet operating leases, but soon they will no longer need to make these adjustments. In late 2015, the Financial Accounting Standards Board voted to require most leases to be treated as capital leases and included on the balance sheet as a liability. By some estimates, the total possible impact for all companies may be as high as $2 trillion of additional recorded debt. The new rule won't go into effect until 2019 however, and in the meantime the International Accounting Standards Board is working on a similar revamp of its lease accounting rules. For both standard-setting bodies, the new standards have been a long time in process, leading the former Chairman of the IASB, Sir David Tweedie, to quip that before he dies, he wants to fly on an airplane that is carried on its airline's balance sheet.

Source: Rapoport, Michael. "Coming to a Balance Sheet Near You: $2 Trillion in Leases." *Wall Street Journal*, 11 Nov. 18, 2015.

**YOUR TURN!
10B.1**

The solution is on
page 527.

Huff Company leased a new forklift for four years. Huff Co. will return the forklift at the end of the four years. The estimated economic life of the forklift is five years. At the time of the lease, the fair value of the forklift is $45,000. The monthly lease payments are $1,000 and the lease has an implied interest rate of six percent, for a present value of $42,580.

Provide a journal entry at the onset of the lease.

ACCOUNTING IN
PRACTICE

Leasing in the Airline Industry

Companies in the airline industry use leases to finance most of their flight equipment. The following are the (undiscounted) dollar amounts of capital and operating leases reported by several airlines:

Airline	Capital Lease Obligation	Operating Lease Obligation	Total Lease Obligation
American	$1,118,000	$10,613,000	$11,731,000
United Continental	1,852,000	9,421,000	11,273,000
Delta.................	1,127,000	14,268,000	15,395,000

These data reveal several important points. First, observe that the dominant form of airline equipment leasing, by a wide margin, is operating leasing. For example, over 90 percent ($14,268/$15,395) of Delta Air Lines' total lease obligation is in the form of operating leases. Second, since operating leases are carried off-balance sheet, the data suggest that most of the airline industry's total debt is not reported on the balance sheets of the respective airline carriers.

SUMMARY OF LEARNING OBJECTIVES

Describe the nature of liabilities and define *current liabilities*. (p. 470)

LO1

- Liabilities are obligations resulting from past transactions or events that require a business to pay money, provide goods, or perform services in the future.
- Current liabilities are obligations that will require, within the coming year or the normal operating cycle, whichever is longer, (1) the use of existing current assets or (2) the creation of other current liabilities.

Illustrate the accounting for long-term liabilities. (p. 476)

LO2

- A bond is a long-term debt instrument used by many businesses to provide financing for operations or asset purchases.
- Discounts and premiums may be recorded when the bonds are issued.

- Bonds payable are shown in the long-term liabilities section of the balance sheet, with any unamortized premium added or unamortized discount deducted.
- The entry for the retirement of bonds removes both the bonds payable and any related bond premium or bond discount from the accounts at the date of retirement and recognizes any gain or loss on retirement.

LO3 Define *contingent liabilities* and explain the rules for their accounting and disclosure in the financial statements. (p. 486)

- Even though a past transaction or event has taken place, the existence of some liabilities, called contingent liabilities, depends on the occurrence of a future event. Whether or not a contingent liability is recorded in the accounts depends on the likelihood of the future event occurring and the measurability of the obligation:
  1. If the future event will probably occur and the amount of the liability can be reasonably estimated, the contingent liability should be recorded in the accounts.
  2. If the likelihood of the future event occurring is probable, but no reasonable estimate of the future obligation is determinable, or the likelihood of the future event occurring is reasonably possible (but not probable), regardless of the ability to measure the future amount, the contingent liability should be disclosed in a note to the financial statements, but not recorded in the accounts.
  3. If the likelihood of the future event occurring is remote, the contingent liability is not recorded in the accounts or disclosed in a note to the financial statements. The only exception is a credit guarantee, which must be disclosed in a note to the financial statements.

LO4 Define the *current ratio, quick ratio,* and *times-interest-earned ratio* and explain their use. (p. 490)

- The current ratio is calculated as follows:

$$\text{Current ratio} = \frac{\text{Current assets}}{\text{Current liabilities}}$$

- The quick ratio is calculated as follows:

$$\text{Quick ratio} = \frac{[\text{Cash and cash equivalents} + \text{Short-term investments} + \text{Accounts receivable}]}{\text{Current liabilities}}$$

- Both the current and quick ratios measure a firm's ability to pay its current liabilities, as well as the strength of its working capital position.
- The times-interest-earned ratio measures the ability of a firm to meet its periodic interest commitments, and is calculated as:

$$\text{Times-interest-earned ratio} = \frac{\text{Income before interest expense and income taxes}}{\text{Interest expense}}$$

LO5 Appendix 10A: Explain bond pricing and illustrate the straight-line and effective interest methods of amortizing bond discounts/premiums. (p. 493)

- Because of the role played by interest, the selling price of the bond often differs from the face amount of the bond.
- We account for this difference by utilizing bond premium (when the market rate of interest is less than the coupon rate) and bond discount (when the market rate of interest is more than the coupon rate) accounts, which affect the book value of the liability.
- While the straight-line method may be simpler, the preferred method according to GAAP for amortizing bond premiums and discounts is the effective interest method.

LO6 Appendix 10B: Define *capital leases* and *operating leases* and distinguish between them. (p. 502)

- A capital lease transfers most of the usual risks and rewards of property ownership to the lessee. At the inception of the lease, the lessee records an asset (a leased asset) and a liability (a lease obligation). The asset is depreciated over its expected useful life, and the liability is reduced as the periodic lease payments are made.
- Under an operating lease, the lessor retains the usual risks and rewards of owning the property. The lessee records no lease asset or lease liability at the start of the lease. Each lease payment made by the lessee is charged to rent expense.

Concept ⟶	Method ⟶	Assessment	SUMMARY
Does the company have any contingent or off-balance sheet liabilities?	Notes to the financial statements Read the notes to the financial statements to identify contingent liabilities and operating leases	Consider the likely outcome and size of contingent liabilities and the amount of operating leases. If significant, consider these items in the analysis of the firm's liabilities.	TAKEAWAY 10.1
Can a firm pay its current liabilities?	Current assets, Quick assets, Current liabilities $\text{Current ratio} = \dfrac{\text{Current assets}}{\text{Current liabilities}}$ $\text{Quick ratio} = \dfrac{\text{Quick assets}}{\text{Current liabilities}}$	A higher current ratio and quick ratio indicates that a firm can readily pay its current liabilities.	TAKEAWAY 10.2
Can a firm pay its current periodic interest payments?	Income before income taxes and interest expense, Interest expense Times-interest-earned ratio $= \dfrac{\text{Income before income taxes and interest expense}}{\text{Interest expense}}$	A higher times-interest-earned ratio indicates that a firm will have less difficulty paying its current interest expense.	TAKEAWAY 10.3

KEY TERMS

Bond (p. 476)
Callable bonds (p. 478)
Capital lease (p. 502)
Contingent liabilities (p. 486)
Convertible bonds (p. 478)
Coupon rate (p. 479)
Credit guarantee (p. 489)
Current liabilities (p. 470)
Current ratio (p. 490)
Debenture bonds (p. 478)
Effective interest method (p. 483, 496, 497)
Effective interest rate (p. 480, 496)
Gross pay (p. 473)

High-yield bonds (p. 478)
Lease (p. 502)
Leasehold (p. 502)
Lessee (p. 502)
Lessor (p. 502)
Leverage (p. 485)
Liabilities (p. 470)
Market rate of interest (Real rate of interest; effective yield rate) (p. 480)
Maturity date (p. 471)
Maturity value (State value) (p. 479)
Net pay (p. 473)
Off-balance-sheet financing (p. 502)

Operating lease (p. 502)
Product warranties (p. 487)
Quick ratio (p. 491)
Secured bonds (p. 478)
Serial bonds (p. 478)
Sinking fund bonds (p. 478)
Straight-line interest method (p. 483, 494)
Term loan (p. 476)
Times-interest-earned ratio (Interest coverage ratio) (p. 491)
Working capital (p. 490)
Zero-coupon bonds (p. 483)

Assignments with the 🅼 logo in the margin are available in BusinessCourse.
See the Preface of the book for details.

SELF-STUDY QUESTIONS

(Answers to the Self-Study Questions are available at the end of this chapter.)

1. **Goldsteen Corporation obtained a $5,000 loan from a bank on April 1. If the bank charges eight percent interest annually, how much interest will be accrued at December 31?**   LO1
   a. $400
   b. $300
   c. $275
   d. $250

2. **Wong, Inc., sold merchandise on account for $1,840, which is subject to a ten percent excise tax and a five percent sales tax. What would the entry to record this sale include?**   LO1
   a. A debit of $1,600 to Accounts Receivable
   b. A debit of $2,116 to Accounts Receivable
   c. A credit of $1,600 to Sales
   d. A dedit of $1,840 to Sales

LO1

3. Jansen Company sells a product for $400 per unit, which includes a 30-day warranty against product defects. Experience indicates that four percent of the units sold will prove defective, requiring an average repair cost of $50 per unit. During the first month of business, product sales were $320,000, and 20 of the units sold were found to be defective and repaired during the month. What is the accrued liability for product warranties at month-end?

    a. $1,000
    b. $600
    c. $1,600
    d. $2,000

LO1

4. Which of the following payroll related taxes are not withheld from an employee's earnings?

    a. Medicare taxes
    b. Income taxes
    c. Federal unemployment taxes
    d. Social Security taxes

LO3

5. Which of the following is *not* considered to be a contingent liability?

    a. Environmental cleanup costs
    b. Notes payable
    c. Credit guarantees
    d. Lawsuit

LO5
(Appendix 10A)

6. On May 1, 2013, a firm issued $400,000 of 12-year, nine percent bonds payable at 96 1/2 plus accrued interest. The bonds are dated January 1, and interest is payable on January 1 and July 1 of each year. The amount the firm receives on May 1 from the sale of the bonds (see Appendix 10A) is:

    a. $386,000.
    b. $422,000.
    c. $392,000.
    d. $398,000.

LO5

7. A firm issued $250,000 of ten-year, 12 percent bonds payable on January 1, for $281,180, yielding an effective rate of ten percent. Interest is payable on January 1 and July 1 each year. The firm records amortization on each interest date. Bond interest expense for the first six months using effective interest amortization (see Appendix 10A) is:

    a. $15,000.
    b. $16,871.
    c. $14,059.
    d. $14,331.

LO2

8. In financial statement presentations, the Discount on Bonds Payable account is:

    a. Added to Bond Interest Expense.
    b. Deducted from Bonds Payable.
    c. Added to Bonds Payable.
    d. Deducted from Bond Interest Expense.

LO6
(Appendix 10B)

9. An example of off-balance-sheet financing is a(n):

    a. Term loan.
    b. Operating lease.
    c. Zero-coupon bond.
    d. Capital lease.

LO4

10. Apolo Company reported year-end current assets of $75,000 and current liabilities of $25,000. The company's current ratio is:

    a. 1/3
    b. 3
    c. 4
    d. $50,000

LO4

11. Cristo Company reported net income of $50,000 after subtracting $10,000 for interest expense and $20,000 for taxes. Compute the company's times-interest-earned ratio:

    a. 2.5
    b. 5
    c. 8
    d. 3

QUESTIONS

1. For accounting purposes, how are liabilities defined?

2. At what amount are current liabilities presented on the balance sheet?

3. What does the term *current liabilities* mean?

4. What formula should Hardy Company use to calculate the total amount of interest on a note payable that uses add-on interest?

5. Gordon Company signed a note payable on November 20. Gordon has a December 31 year-end. It paid the note, including interest, on the maturity date, February 20. What accounts did Gordon debit and what account did it credit on February 20?

6. Jack Swanson gave a creditor a 90-day, eight percent note payable for $7,200 on December 16. What adjusting entry should Swanson make on December 31?

7. What are two examples of voluntary deductions from an employee's gross pay?

8. On whom is the FICA tax levied? What does the FICA tax finance?

9. What is the difference between accounting for product warranties on (a) failed units repaired in the month of sale and (b) failed units repaired in a subsequent month but that are still covered by warranty?

10. **American Paging, Inc.,** is the seventh largest paging company in the United States. In a recent balance sheet, it reported a current liability of $8,452,379 that was labeled Unearned Revenues and Deposits. A note to the financial statements explained:

   > AMERICAN PAGING, INC.

   > Unearned revenues and deposits primarily represent monthly charges to customers for radio paging rental and dispatch billed in advance. Such revenues and deposits are recognized in the following month when service is provided or are applied against the customer's final bill or last month's rent.

   What basic principle of accounting guides American Paging's handling of its unearned revenues and deposits?

11. What do the following terms mean? (a) term loan, (b) bonds payable, (c) trustee, (d) secured bonds, (e) serial bonds, (f) call provision, (g) convertible bonds, (h) face value, (i) coupon rate, (j) bond discount, (k) bond premium, and (l) amortization of bond premium or discount.

12. What are the advantages and disadvantages of issuing bonds rather than common stock?

13. A $3,000,000 issue of ten-year, nine percent bonds was sold at 98 plus accrued interest three months after the bonds were dated. What net amount of cash is received when the bonds are sold?

14. If the effective interest amortization method is used for bonds payable, how does the periodic interest expense change over the life of the bonds when they are issued (a) at a discount and (b) at a premium?

15. On April 30, one year before maturity, Eastern Company retired $200,000 of nine percent bonds payable at 101. The book value of the bonds on April 30 was $197,600. Bond interest was last paid on April 30. What is the gain or loss on the retirement of the bonds?

16. What are *contingent liabilities*? List three examples of contingent liabilities. When should contingent liabilities be recorded in the accounts?

17. What is the difference between an operating lease and a capital lease?

18. Define the terms *current ratio* and *quick ratio*. What does each ratio tell us?

19. Define the times-interest-earned ratio and explain how it is used.

SHORT EXERCISES

SE10-1. **Contingent Liabilities** The CEO of Smith & Sons, Inc., negotiated with its principal supplier of raw materials to purchase 10,000 units for a total price of $100,000. The units are to be delivered in 90 days. The CEO is uncertain whether she should record the purchase commitment on the company's balance sheet as a liability or not. She asks for your advice. What would you advise her? **LO3**

SE10-2. **Determining Bond Premium or Discount** Smith & Sons, Inc., decides to sell $1,000,000 in bonds to finance the construction of a new warehouse. The bonds will carry an annual coupon rate of **LO2**

interest of four percent, to be paid semiannually, and will mature in five years. (a) If the market rate of interest at the time of issuance is five percent, will the bonds sell at their face value, a discount, or a premium? (b) If the market rate of interest at the time of issuance is four percent, will the bonds sell at their face value, a discount, or a premium? (c) If the market rate of interest at the time of issuance is three percent, will the bonds sell at their face value, a discount, or a premium?

LO3   **SE10-3.**   **Contingent Liabilities** Smith & Sons, Inc., received notification from a local attorney that the company was being sued for $5,000,000 for patent infringement. A review of the situation by the company's CEO led to the conclusion that Smith & Sons had indeed infringed upon the other company's patented product. Nonetheless, the CEO thought the amount of $5,000,000 was excessive and intended to litigate the issue. How should the lawsuit be reported in Smith & Sons' annual report?

LO6   **SE10-4.**   **Operating and Capital Leases** The CEO of Smith & Sons, Inc., was considering a lease for a new administrative headquarters building. The building was old, but was very well located near the company's principal customers. The leasing agent estimated that the building's remaining useful life was ten years, and at the end of its useful life, the building would probably be worth $100,000. The proposed lease term was eight years, and as an inducement to Smith & Sons' CEO to sign the lease, the leasing agent indicated a willingness to include a statement in the lease agreement that would allow Smith & Sons to buy the building at the end of the lease for only $75,000. As the CEO considered whether or not to sign the lease, she wondered whether the lease could be accounted for as an off-balance-sheet operating lease. What would you advise her?

The following information relates to SE10-5 through SE10-7:

SMITH & SONS, INC. Income Statement For Years Ended December 31, 2016 and 2015		
(in millions)	2016	2015
Net sales.	$10,000	$ 9,500
Cost of goods sold.	(5,500)	(5,200)
Gross profit.	4,500	4,300
Selling and administrative expenses	(2,800)	(2,700)
Income from operations.	1,700	1,600
Interest expense.	(300)	(250)
Income before income taxes	1,400	1,350
Income tax expense.	(420)	(400)
Net income.	$ 980	$ 950

SMITH & SONS, INC. Balance Sheet December 31, 2016 and 2015		
(in millions)	2016	2015
Assets		
Current assets		
Cash and cash equivalents	$ 200	$ 400
Accounts receivable.	900	800
Inventory.	500	650
Other current assets.	400	250
Total current assets	2,000	2,100
Property, plant, & equipment (net)	2,600	2,500
Other assets.	5,700	5,900
Total Assets	$10,300	$10,500

continued

SMITH & SONS, INC. Balance Sheet December 31, 2016 and 2015		
(in millions)	2016	2015
Liabilities and Stockholders' Equity		
Current liabilities. . . .	$ 3,000	$ 2,900
Long-term liabilities . . .	5,000	5,400
Total liabilities. . . .	8,000	8,300
Stockholders' equity – common. . . .	2,300	2,200
Total Liabilities and Stockholders' Equity . . .	$10,300	$10,500

SE10-5. **Current Ratio** Calculate the current ratio for Smith & Sons, Inc., for 2015 and 2016, and comment on the company's working capital position. Did the company's ability to pay its current liabilities improve over the two years? **LO4**

SE10-6. **Quick Ratio** Calculate the quick ratio for Smith & Sons, Inc., for 2015 and 2016, and comment on the company's working capital position. Did the company's ability to pay its current liabilities improve over the two years? **LO4**

SE10-7. **Times-Interest-Earned Ratio** Calculate the times-interest-earned ratio for Smith & Sons, Inc., for 2015 and 2016, and comment on the company's ability to pay its current interest payments. Did the company's ability to pay its current interest charges improve? **LO4**

SE10-8. **Premium and Discount of a Bond or Debenture** The Johnson & Johnson Company reported the following borrowings in a prior annual report: **LO2**

Borrowing ($ in millions)	Amount	Effective Interest Rate (%)
a. 3.00 percent, zero-coupon bond, due 2020 . . .	$202	3.00
b. 4.95 percent debentures, due 2033. . .	500	5.00
c. 3.80 percent debentures, due 2017. . .	500	3.82
d. 6.95 percent bonds, due 2025. . .	293	6.90

For each borrowing, indicate whether the bond or debenture was originally sold at its face value, a discount, or a premium.

SE10-9. **Bond Interest Expense** Smith & Sons, Inc., sold $100,000 face value, six percent coupon rate, four-year bonds, for an aggregate issue price of $96,000. Calculate the total interest expense to be recorded by the company over the four-year life of the bonds. **LO2**

SE10-10. **Bond Interest Expense** During 2013, Smith & Sons, Inc., issued $400 million of zero-coupon bonds, due in 2023. The proceeds from the bond issuance were $186.6 million. Calculate the total interest expense that the company will incur over the life of the bonds. **LO2**

EXERCISES—SET A

E10-1A. **Liabilities on the Balance Sheet** For each of the following situations, indicate the amount shown as a liability on the balance sheet of Kane, Inc., at December 31: **LO1**

a. Kane has accounts payable of $110,000 for merchandise included in the year-end inventory.
b. Kane agreed to purchase a $28,000 drill press in the following January.
c. During November and December of the current year, Kane sold products to a firm and guaranteed them against product failure for 90 days. Estimated costs of honoring this provision next year are $2,200.
d. On December 15, Kane declared a $70,000 cash dividend payable on January 15 of the following year to shareholders of record on December 31.

  e. Kane provides a profit-sharing bonus for its executives equal to five percent of the reported before-tax income for the current year. The estimated before-tax income for the current year is $600,000.

LO1 **E10-2A.** **Maturity Dates of Notes Payable** Determine the maturity date and compute the interest for each of the following notes payable with add-on interest:

	Date of Note	Principal	Interest Rate (%)	Term
a.	August 5	$15,000	9	120 days
b.	May 10	8,400	7	90 days
c.	October 5	12,000	9	45 days
d.	July 6	4,500	10	60 days
e.	September 15	12,000	8	75 days

LO1 **E10-3A.** **Accrued Interest Payable** Compute the interest accrued on each of the following notes payable owed by Northland, Inc., on December 31:

Lender	Date of Note	Principal	Interest Rate (%)	Term
Maple	11/21	$18,000	11	120 days
Wyman	12/13	14,000	8	90 days
Nahn	12/10	16,000	12	60 days

LO1 **E10-4A.** **Adjusting Entries for Interest** The following note transactions occurred during the year for Towell Company:

Nov. 25 Towell issued a 60-day, nine percent note payable for $8,000 to Hyatt Company for merchandise.

Dec. 7 Towell signed a 120-day, $15,000 note at the bank at ten percent.

   22 Towell gave Barr, Inc., a $12,000, eight percent, 60-day note in payment of account.

Prepare the general journal entries necessary to adjust the interest accounts at December 31.

LO1 **E10-5A.** **Excise and Sales Tax Calculations** Barnes Company has just billed a customer for $1,010, an amount that includes an eleven percent excise tax and a four percent state sales tax.

  a. What amount of revenue is recorded?

  b. Prepare a general journal entry to record the transaction on the books of Barnes Company.

LO1 **E10-6A.** **Advance Payments for Goods** The Chicago Daily Times Corporation (CDT) publishes a daily newspaper. A 52-week subscription sells for $221. Assume that CDT sells 100 subscriptions on January 1. None of the subscriptions are cancelled as of March 31.

  a. Prepare a journal entry to record the receipt of the subscriptions on January 1.

  b. Prepare a journal entry to record one week of earned revenue on March 25.

LO1 **E10-7A.** **Warranty Costs** Milford Company sells a motor that carries a 3-month unconditional warranty against product failure. Based on a reliable statistical analysis, Milford knows that between the sale and the end of the product warranty period, three percent of the units sold will require repair at an average cost of $60 per unit. The following data reflect Milford's recent experience:

	October	November	December	Dec. 31 Total
Units sold	23,000	22,000	25,000	70,000
Known product failures from sales in:				
October	120	180	160	460
November		130	220	350
December			210	210

Calculate, and prepare a journal entry to record, the estimated liability for product warranties at December 31. Assume that warranty costs of known failures have already been reflected in the records.

E10-8A. Financial Statement Presentation of Bond Accounts Indicate the proper financial statement classification for each of the following accounts: **LO2**

> Gain on Bond Retirement (material amount)
> Discount on Long-term Bonds Payable
> Mortgage Notes Payable
> Long-term Bonds Payable
> Bond Interest Expense
> Bond Interest Payable
> Premium on Long-term Bonds Payable

E10-9A. Early Retirement of Bonds Elston Company issued $500,000 of eight percent, 20-year bonds at 106 on January 1, 2010. Interest is payable semiannually on July 1 and January 1. Through January 1, 2016, Elston amortized $5,000 of the bond premium. On January 1, 2016, Elston retired the bonds at 103 (after making the interest payment on that date). Prepare the journal entry to record the bond retirement on January 1, 2016. **LO2**

E10-10A. Installment Term Loan On December 31, 2014, Thomas, Inc. borrowed $850,000 on an eight percent, 15-year mortgage note payable. The note is to be repaid in equal semiannual installments of $49,156 (payable on June 30 and December 31). Prepare journal entries to reflect (a) the issuance of the mortgage note payable, (b) the payment of the first installment on June 30, 2015, and (c) the payment of the second installment on December 31, 2015. Round amounts to the nearest dollar. **LO2**

E10-11A. Installment Term Loan On December 31, 2012, Kelly, Inc. borrowed $850,000 on a seven percent, 10-year mortgage note payable. The note is to be repaid in equal annual installments of $121,021 (payable on December 31). Prepare journal entries to reflect (a) the issuance of the mortgage note payable, (b) the payment of the first installment on December 31, 2013, and (c) the payment of the second installment on December 31, 2014. Round amounts to the nearest dollar. **LO2**

E10-12A. Contingent Liabilities Determine which of the following transactions represent contingent liabilities for Hermani Rental and indicate the proper accounting treatment at the company's fiscal year-end, by placing the letter of the correct accounting treatment in the space provided. **LO3**

A. Accrue a liability and disclose in the financial statement notes
B. Disclose in the financial statement footnotes only
C. No disclosure

1. Hermani Rental cosigned a loan for $75,000 due in one year for Wyler Company. Wyler is a very profitable company and is very liquid, making it a remote chance Hermani will have to pay the loan.	
2. One of Hermani's rental tents collapsed at a wedding and injured the bride and groom. Hermani's legal counsel believes it is probable that Hermani will have to pay damages of $400,000.	
3. Hermani Rental is being audited by the Internal Revenue Service. Its tax returns for the past two years are being examined. At the company's year-end, the audit is still in process. Hermani's CPA believes that payment of significant taxes is possible.	

E10-13A. Ratio Analysis Presented below are summary financial data from Pompeo's annual report: **LO4**

Amounts in millions	
Balance sheet	
Cash and cash equivalents	$ 1,865
Marketable securities	19,100
Accounts receivable (net)	9,367
Total current assets	39,088
Total assets	123,078

continued

continued from previous page

Amounts in millions	
Current liabilities.	39,255
Long-term debt	7,279
Shareholders' equity	68,278
Income Statement	
Interest expense	375
Net income before taxes	14,007

Calculate the following ratios:
a. Times-interest-earned ratio
b. Quick ratio
c. Current ratio

LO2, 5
(Appendix 10A)

E10-14A. Issue Price of a Bond Conner Enterprises issued $150,000 of 10%, five-year bonds with interest payable semiannually. Determine the issue price if the bonds are priced to yield (a) 10%, (b) 6%, and (c) 12%.

LO2, 5
(Appendix 10A)

E10-15A. Issue Price of a Bond Lunar, Inc., plans to issue $700,000 of 10% bonds that will pay interest semiannually and mature in five years. Assume that the effective interest rate is 12 percent per year compounded semiannually. Calculate the selling price of the bonds.

LO2, 5
(Appendix 10A)

E10-16A. Bonds Payable Journal Entries; Straight-Line Interest Amortization On December 31, 2014, White Company issued $800,000 of 20-year, eight percent bonds payable for $662,727, yielding an effective interest rate of ten percent. Interest is payable semiannually on June 30 and December 31. Prepare journal entries to reflect (a) the issuance of the bonds, (b) the semiannual interest payment and discount amortization (straight-line interest method) on June 30, 2015, and (c) the semiannual interest payment and discount amortization on December 31, 2015. Round amounts to the nearest dollar.

LO2, 5
(Appendix 10A)

E10-17A. Bonds Payable Journal Entries; Straight-Line Interest Amortization On December 31, 2014, Grey Company issued $200,000 of 20-year, eight percent bonds payable for $221,355, yielding an effective interest rate of seven percent. Interest is payable semiannually on June 30 and December 31. Prepare journal entries to reflect (a) the issuance of the bonds, (b) the semiannual interest payment and premium amortization (straight-line interest method) on June 30, 2015, and (c) the semiannual interest payment and premium amortization on December 31, 2015. Round amounts to the nearest dollar.

LO2, 5
(Appendix 10A)

E10-18A. Bonds Payable Journal Entries; Effective Interest Amortization On December 31, 2014, Daggett Company issued $800,000 of ten-year, nine percent bonds payable for $662,361, yielding an effective interest rate of twelve percent. Interest is payable semiannually on June 30 and December 31. Prepare journal entries to reflect (a) the issuance of the bonds, (b) the semiannual interest payment and discount amortization (effective interest method) on June 30, 2015, and (c) the semiannual interest payment and discount amortization on December 31, 2015. Round amounts to the nearest dollar.

E10-19A. Bonds Payable Journal Entries; Effective Interest Amortization On December 31, 2014, Coffey Company issued $300,000 of 10-year, ten percent bonds payable for $340,771, yielding an effective interest rate of eight percent. Interest is payable semiannually on June 30 and December 31. Prepare journal entries to reflect (a) the issuance of the bonds, (b) the semiannual interest payment and premium amortization (effective interest method) on June 30, 2015, and (c) the semiannual interest payment and premium amortization on December 31, 2015. Round amounts to the nearest dollar.

LO6
(Appendix 10B)

E10-20A. Leases On January 1, Spider, Inc., entered into two lease contracts. The first lease contract was an eight-year lease for a computer with $15,000 annual lease payments due at the end of each year. Spider took possession of the computer on January 1. The second lease contract was a six-month lease, beginning January 1 for warehouse storage space with $1,500 monthly lease payments due the first of each month. Spider made the first month's payment on January 1. The present value of the lease payments under the first contract is $93,096. The present value of the lease payments under the second contract is $8,178.

a. The first lease contract is a capital lease. Prepare the journal entry for this lease on January 1.
b. The second lease contract is an operating lease. Prepare the journal entry for this lease on January 1.

EXERCISES—SET B

E10-1B. **Liabilities on the Balance Sheet** For each of the following situations, indicate the amount shown as a liability on the balance sheet of Anchor, Inc., at December 31:   **LO1**

    a. Anchor's general ledger shows a credit balance of $125,000 in Long-Term Notes Payable. Of this amount, a $25,000 installment becomes due on June 30 of the following year.

    b. Anchor estimates its unpaid income tax liability for the current year is $34,000; it plans to pay this amount in March of the following year.

    c. On December 31, Anchor received a $15,000 invoice for merchandise shipped on December 28. The merchandise has not yet been received. The merchandise was shipped F.O.B. shipping point.

    d. During the year, Anchor collected $10,500 of state sales tax. At year-end, it has not yet remitted $1,400 of these taxes to the state department of revenue.

    e. On December 31, Anchor's bank approved a $5,000, 90-day loan. Anchor plans to sign the note and receive the money on January 2 of the following year.

E10-2B. **Maturity Dates of Notes Payable** Determine the maturity date and compute the interest for each of the following notes payable: **LO1**

	Date of Note	Principal	Interest Rate (%)	Term
a.	July 10	$7,200	9	90 days
b.	April 4	6,000	8	120 days
c.	May 19	5,600	7 ½	120 days
d.	June 10	6,500	8	45 days
e.	October 29	10,000	6	60 days

E10-3B. **Accrued Interest Payable** Compute the interest accrued on each of the following notes payable owed by Galloway, Inc., on December 31:   **LO1**

Lender	Date of Note	Principal	Interest Rate (%)	Term
Barton	12/4	$10,000	12	150 days
Lawson	12/13	14,000	9	90 days
Riley	12/19	15,000	11	60 days

E10-4B. **Adjusting Entries for Interest** The following note transactions occurred during the year for Zuber Company: **LO1**

Nov.   25 Zuber issued a 120-day, 12 percent note payable for $8,000 to Porter Company for merchandise.

Dec.   10 Zuber signed a 120-day, $7,200 note at the bank at ten percent.

       23 Zuber gave Dale, Inc., a $9,000, eight percent, 60-day note in payment of account.

Prepare the journal entries necessary to adjust the interest accounts at December 31.

E10-5B. **Excise and Sales Tax Calculations** Allied Company has just billed a customer for $1,160, an amount that includes a ten percent excise tax and a six percent state sales tax.   **LO1**

    a. What amount of revenue is recorded?

    b. Prepare a journal entry to record the transaction on the books of Allied Company.

E10-6B. **Advance Payment for Services** The Columbus Bluebirds football team sells a 15-game season ticket for $180. Assume that the team sells 1,000 season tickets on August 10. The tickets are all used for admission.   **LO1**

    a. Prepare a journal entry to record the sale of the season tickets on August 10.

    b. Prepare a journal entry to record one game of earned revenue on September 12.

E10-7B. **Warranty Costs** Brigham Company sells an electric timer that carries a 3-month unconditional warranty against product failure. Based on a reliable statistical analysis, Brigham knows that between   **LO1**

the sale and the end of the product warranty period, four percent of the units sold will require repair at an average cost of $40 per unit. The following data reflect Brigham's recent experience:

	October	November	December	Dec. 31 Total
Units sold	36,000	34,000	45,000	115,000
Known product failures from sales in:				
October.	320	550	210	1,080
November.		230	360	590
December.			410	410

Calculate, and prepare a journal entry to record, the estimated liability for product warranties at December 31. Assume that warranty costs of known failures have already been reflected in the records.

LO2 **E10-8B.** **Bonds Payable on the Balance Sheet** The adjusted trial balance for the Lancer Corporation at the end of 2015 contains the following accounts:

Bond interest payable	$ 25,000
9% Bonds payable due 2017.	600,000
10% Bonds payable due 2019.	500,000
Discount on 9% bonds payable.	19,000
Premium on 10% bonds payable.	15,000
Zero coupon bonds payable due 2021	170,500
8% Bonds payable due 2023.	100,000

Prepare the long-term liabilities section of the balance sheet. Indicate the balance sheet classification for any accounts listed above that do not belong in the long-term liabilities section.

LO2 **E10-9B.** **Early Retirement of Bonds** Norwich, Inc., issued $250,000 of 8 percent, 20-year bonds at 98 on June 30, 2009. Interest is payable semiannually on December 31 and June 30. Through June 30, 2015, Norwich amortized $3,000 of the bond discount. On June 30, 2015, Norwich retired the bonds at 101 (after making the interest payment on that date). Prepare the journal entry to record the bond retirement on June 30, 2015.

LO2 **E10-10B.** **Installment Term Loan** On December 31, 2014, Beam, Inc., borrowed $500,000 on a six percent, ten-year mortgage note payable. The note is to be repaid in equal quarterly installments of $16,714 (beginning March 31, 2015). Prepare journal entries to reflect (a) the issuance of the mortgage note payable, (b) the payment of the first installment on March 31, 2015, and (c) the payment of the second installment on June 30, 2015. Round amounts to the nearest dollar.

LO2 **E10-11B.** **Installment Term Loan** On December 31, 2014, James, Inc., borrowed $300,000 on a six percent, ten-year mortgage note payable. The note is to be repaid in equal semiannual installments of $20,165 (beginning July 1, 2015). Prepare journal entries to reflect (a) the issuance of the mortgage note payable, (b) the payment of the first installment on July 1, 2015, and (c) the payment of the second installment on December 31, 2015. Round amounts to the nearest dollar.

LO3 **E10-12B.** **Contingent Liabilities** Determine which of the following transactions represent contingent liabilities for Koby Leasing and indicate the proper accounting treatment at the company's fiscal year-end, by placing the letter of the correct accounting treatment in the space provided.

A. Accrue a liability and disclose in the financial statement notes
B. Disclose in the financial statement footnotes only
C. No disclosure

1. Koby Leasing was sued by a customer who claimed the equipment they leased was not up to the standards described by Koby. Koby stands by its claims and can support all the item's specifications. Koby plans to vigorously defend itself and believes the chances of losing the lawsuit are remote.	
2. A government audit of Koby found that the company is in violation of several work safety regulations. Koby has been notified that it will be assessed a fine of $25,000. Koby has agreed to make the safety changes so that it will be in compliance with the regulations.	
3. Koby Leasing has been served a lawsuit by a customer that claims he was injured from one of the products leased from Koby. Koby plans to defend itself in court, but its lawyers believe there is a 50/50 chance that they will lose and be forced to pay $50,000.	

E10-13B. Ratio Analysis Presented below are summary financial data from the Jackson Co. annual report: **LO4**

Amounts in millions	
Balance sheet	
Cash and cash equivalents	$ 2,200
Marketable securities	16,200
Accounts receivable (net)	10,000
Total current assets	42,000
Total assets	155,000
Current liabilities	30,000
Long-term debt	47,500
Shareholders' equity	79,500
Income Statement	
Interest expense	6,400
Net income before taxes	36,800

Calculate the following ratios:

a. Times-interest-earned ratio
b. Quick ratio
c. Current ratio

E10-14B. Issue Price of a Bond Maggie Enterprises issued $100,000 of 6%, five year bonds with interest payable semiannually. Determine the issue price if the bonds are priced to yield (a) 6%, (b) 10%, and (c) 2%.
LO2, 5
(Appendix 10A)

E10-15B. Issue Price of a Bond Tide, Inc., plans to issue $600,000 of 9% bonds that will pay interest semiannually and mature in ten years. Assume that the effective interest is 8 percent per year compounded semiannually. Calculate the selling price of the bonds.
LO2, 5
(Appendix 10A)

E10-16B. Bonds Payable Journal Entries; Straight-Line Interest Amortization On December 31, 2014, Black Company issued $600,000 of 15-year, 11 percent bonds payable for $558,706, yielding an effective interest rate of 12 percent. Interest is payable semiannually on June 30 and December 31. Prepare journal entries to reflect (a) the issuance of the bonds, (b) the semiannual interest payment and discount amortization (straight-line interest method) on June 30, 2015, and (c) the semiannual interest payment and discount amortization on December 31, 2015. Round amounts to the nearest dollar.
LO2, 5
(Appendix 10A)

E10-17B. Bonds Payable Journal Entries; Straight-Line Interest Amortization On December 31, 2014, Brown Company issued $400,000 of five-year, 12 percent bonds payable for $430,887, yielding an effective interest rate of ten percent. Interest is payable semiannually on June 30 and December 31. Prepare journal entries to reflect (a) the issuance of the bonds, (b) the semiannual interest payment and premium amortization (straight-line interest method) on June 30, 2015, and (c) the semiannual interest payment and premium amortization on December 31, 2015. Round amounts to the nearest dollar.
LO2, 5
(Appendix 10A)

E10-18B. Bonds Payable Journal Entries; Effective Interest Amortization On December 31, 2014, Blair Company issued $600,000 of 20-year, 11 percent bonds payable for $480,015, yielding an effective interest rate of 14 percent. Interest is payable semiannually on June 30 and December 31. Prepare journal entries to reflect (a) the issuance of the bonds, (b) the semiannual interest payment and
LO2, 5
(Appendix 10A)

discount amortization (effective interest method) on June 30, 2015, and (c) the semiannual interest payment and discount amortization on December 31, 2015. Round amounts to the nearest dollar.

LO2, 5
(Appendix 10A)

MBC

E10-19B. **Bonds Payable Journal Entries; Effective Interest Amortization** On December 31, 2014, Kay Company issued $400,000 of five-year, 12 percent bonds payable for $430,887, yielding an effective interest rate of ten percent. Interest is payable semiannually on June 30 and December 31. Prepare journal entries to reflect (a) the issuance of the bonds, (b) the semiannual interest payment and premium amortization (effective interest method) on June 30, 2015, and (c) the semiannual interest payment and premium amortization on December 31, 2015. Round amounts to the nearest dollar.

LO6
(Appendix 10B)

MBC

E10-20B. **Leases** On January 1, Cooper, Inc., entered into two lease contracts. The first lease contract was an eight-year lease for a sound system with $25,000 annual lease payments due at the end of each year. Spider took possession of the sound system on January 1. The second lease contract was a nine-month lease, beginning January 1 for warehouse storage space with $1,750 monthly lease payments due the first of each month. Cooper made the first month's payment on January 1. The present value of the lease payments under the first contract is $155,159. The present value of the lease payments under the second contract is $15,238.

a. The first lease contract is a capital lease. Prepare the journal entry for this lease on January 1.
b. The second lease contract is an operating lease. Prepare the journal entry for this lease on January 1.

PROBLEMS—SET A

LO1

MBC

P10-1A. **Journal Entries for Accounts and Notes Payable** Logan Company had the following transactions:

Apr.	8	Issued a $5,000, 60-day, six percent note payable in payment of an account with Bennett Company.
May	15	Borrowed $40,000 from Lincoln Bank, signing a 60-day note at nine percent.
June	7	Paid Bennett Company the principal and interest due on the April 8 note payable.
July	6	Purchased $12,000 of merchandise from Bolton Company; signed a 90-day note with ten percent interest.
July	14	Paid the May 15 note due Lincoln Bank.
Oct.	2	Borrowed $30,000 from Lincoln Bank, signing a 120-day note at 12 percent.
	4	Defaulted on the note payable to Bolton Company.

Required
a. Record these transactions in general journal form.
b. Record any adjusting entries for interest in general journal form. Logan Company has a December 31 year-end.

LO1

MBC

P10-2A. **Adjusting Entries for Interest** At December 31, 2014, Hoffman Corporation had two notes payable outstanding (notes 1 and 2). At December 31, 2015, Hoffman also had two notes payable outstanding (notes 3 and 4). These notes are described below:

	Date of Note	Principal Amount	Interest Rate	Number of Days
December 31, 2014				
Note 1................	11/16/2014	$15,000	8%	120
Note 2................	12/4/2014	16,000	9	60
December 31, 2015				
Note 3................	12/7/2015	9,000	9	60
Note 4................	12/21/2015	18,000	12	30

Required
a. Prepare the adjusting entries for interest at December 31, 2014.
b. Assume that the adjusting entries were made at December 31, 2014. Prepare the 2015 journal entries to record payment of the notes that were outstanding at December 31, 2014.
c. Prepare the adjusting entries for interest at December 31, 2015.

P10-3A. **Recording Payroll and Payroll Taxes** Beamon Corporation had the following payroll for April: **LO1**

Officers' salaries	$34,000
Sales salaries	67,000
Federal income taxes withheld	19,000
FICA taxes withheld	7,500
Health insurance premiums withheld	1,800
Union dues withheld	1,200
Salaries (included above) subject to federal unemployment taxes	55,000
Salaries (included above) subject to state unemployment taxes	58,000

Required
Prepare journal entries on April 30 to record:

a. Accrual of the monthly payroll.
b. Payment of the net payroll.
c. Accrual of employer's payroll taxes. (Assume that the FICA tax matches the amount withheld, the federal unemployment tax is 0.6 percent, and the state unemployment tax is 5.4 percent.)
d. Payment of all liabilities related to this payroll. (Assume that all are settled at the same time.)

P10-4A. **Recording Payroll and Payroll Taxes** The following data are taken from Fremont Wholesale **LO1**
Company's May payroll:

Administrative salaries	$42,000
Sales salaries	51,000
Custodial salaries	7,000
Total payroll	$100,000
Salaries subject to 1.45 percent Medicare tax	$100,000
Salaries subject to 6.2 percent Social Security tax	75,000
Salaries subject to federal unemployment taxes	14,000
Salaries subject to state unemployment taxes	21,000
Federal income taxes withheld from all salaries	17,800

Assume that the company is subject to a two percent state unemployment tax (due to a favorable experience rating) and a 0.6 percent federal unemployment tax.

Required
Record the following in general journal form on May 31:

a. Accrual of the monthly payroll.
b. Payment of the net payroll.
c. Accrual of the employer's payroll taxes. (Assume that the FICA tax matches the amount withheld).
d. Payment of these payroll-related liabilities. (Assume that all are settled at the same time.)

P10-5A. **Excise and Sales Tax Calculations** Fulton Corporation initially records its sales at amounts that **LO1**
exclude any related excise and sales taxes. During June, Fulton recorded total sales of $650,000. An
analysis of June sales indicated the following:

1. Thirty percent of sales were subject to both a ten percent excise tax and a six percent sales tax.
2. Fifty percent of sales were subject only to the sales tax.
3. The balance of sales was for labor charges not subject to either excise or sales tax.

Required
a. Calculate the related liabilities for excise and sales taxes for June.
b. Prepare the necessary journal entry at June 30 to record the monthly payment of excise tax and sales tax to the government.

P10-6A. **Noncontingent and Contingent Liabilities** The following independent situations represent various **LO1, 3**
types of liabilities:

1. One of the employees of Martin Company was severely injured when hit by one of Martin's trucks in the parking lot. The 35-year-old employee will never be able to work again. Insurance coverage is minimal. The employee has sued Martin Company and a jury trial is scheduled.

2. A shareholder has filed a lawsuit against Sweitzer Corporation. Sweitzer's attorneys have reviewed the facts of the case. Their review revealed that similar lawsuits have never resulted in a cash award and it is highly unlikely that this lawsuit will either.

3. Armstrong Company signed a 60-day, ten percent note when it purchased merchandise from Fischer Company.

4. Richmond Company has been notified by the Department of Environment Protection (DEP) that a state where it has a plant is filing a lawsuit for groundwater pollution against Richmond and another company that has a plant adjacent to Richmond's plant. Test results have not identified the exact source of the pollution. Richmond's manufacturing process can produce by-products that pollute ground water.

5. Fredonia Company has cosigned a note payable to a bank for one of its customers. The customer received all of the proceeds of the note. Fredonia will have to repay the loan if the customer fails to do so. Fredonia Company believes that it is unlikely that it will have to pay the note.

6. Holt Company manufactured and sold products to Z-Mart, a retailer that sold the products to consumers. The manufacturer's warranty offers replacement of the product if it is found to be defective within 90 days of the sale to the consumer. Historically, 1.2 percent of the products are returned for replacement.

Required

Prepare a multicolumn analysis that presents the following information for each of these situations:

a. Number of the situation.

b. Type of liability: (1) noncontingent or (2) contingent.

c. Accounting treatment: (1) record in accounts, (2) disclose in a note to the financial statements, or (3) neither record nor disclose.

LO2 P10-7A. Bonds Payable Journal Entries; Issued at Par Plus Accrued Interest Askew, Inc., which closes its books on December 31, is authorized to issue $600,000 of nine percent, 20-year bonds dated May 1, with interest payments on November 1 and May 1.

Required

Prepare journal entries to record the following events, assuming that the bonds were sold at 100 plus accrued interest on October 1:

a. The bond issuance.

b. Payment of the first semiannual period's interest on November 1.

c. Accrual of bond interest expense at December 31.

d. Payment of the semiannual interest on May 1 of the following year.

e. Retirement of $300,000 of the bonds at 101 on May 1, Year 2 (immediately after the interest payment on that date).

LO4 P10-8A. Current Ratio, Quick Ratio, and Times-Interest-Earned Ratio The following data is from the current accounting records of Florence Company:

Cash.	$120
Accounts receivable (net of allowance of 40).	200
Inventory.	150
Other current assets.	80
Accounts payable.	110
Other current liabilities.	170

The president of the company is concerned that the company is in violation of a debt covenant that requires the company to maintain a minimum current ratio of 2.0. He believes the best way to rectify this is to reverse a bad debt write-off in the amount of $10 that the company just recorded. He argues that the write-off was done too early, and that the collections department should be given more time to collect the outstanding receivables. The CFO argues that this will have no effect on the current ratio, so a better idea is to use $10 of cash to pay accounts payable early.

Required

    a. Which idea, the president's or the CFO's, is better for attaining a minimum 2.0 current ratio?

    b. Will either the quick ratio or the times-interest-earned ratios be affected by either of these ideas?

P10-9A. **Effective Interest Amortization** On December 31, Caper, Inc., issued $250,000 of eight percent, ten-year bonds for $218,844, yielding an effective interest rate of ten percent. Semiannual interest is payable on June 30 and December 31 each year. The firm uses the effective interest method to amortize the discount.

LO5
(Appendix 10A)

Required

    a. Prepare an amortization schedule showing the necessary information for the first two interest periods. Round amounts to the nearest dollar.

    b. Prepare the journal entry for the bond issuance on December 31.

    c. Prepare the journal entry to record the bond interest payment and discount amortization at June 30 of the following year.

    d. Prepare the journal entry to record the bond interest payment and discount amortization at December 31 of the following year.

P10-10A. **Effective Interest Amortization** On January 1, Eagle, Inc., issued $800,000 of ten percent, 20-year bonds for $958,342, yielding an effective interest rate of eight percent. Semiannual interest is payable on June 30 and December 31 each year. The firm uses the effective interest method to amortize the premium.

LO5
(Appendix 10A)

Required

    a. Prepare an amortization schedule showing the necessary information for the first two interest periods. Round amounts to the nearest dollar.

    b. Prepare the journal entry for the bond issuance on January 1.

    c. Prepare the journal entry to record the bond interest payment and premium amortization at June 30.

    d. Prepare the journal entry to record the bond interest payment and premium amortization at December 31.

PROBLEMS—SET B

P10-1B. **Journal Entries for Accounts Payable and Notes Payable** Simon Company had the following transactions:

LO1

Apr.	15	Issued a $6,000, 60-day, eight percent note payable in payment of an account with Marion Company.
May	22	Borrowed $45,000 from Sinclair Bank, signing a 60-day note at nine percent.
June	14	Paid Marion Company the principal and interest due on the April 15 note payable.
July	13	Purchased $15,000 of merchandise from Sharp Company; signed a 90-day note with ten percent interest.
	21	Paid the May 22 note due Sinclair Bank.
Oct.	2	Borrowed $38,000 from Sinclair Bank, signing a 120-day note at 12 percent.
	11	Defaulted on the note payable to Sharp Company.

Required

    a. Record these transactions in general journal form.

    b. Record any adjusting entries for interest in general journal form. Simon Company has a December 31 year-end.

P10-2B. **Adjusting Entries for Interest** At December 31, 2014, Portland Corporation had two notes payable outstanding (notes 1 and 2). At December 31, 2015, Portland also had two notes payable outstanding (notes 3 and 4). These notes are described below.

LO1

	Date of Note	Principal Amount	Interest Rate	Number of Days
December 31, 2014				
Note 1.	11/25/2014	$35,000	8%	90
Note 2.	12/16/2014	16,800	9	60
December 31, 2015				
Note 3.	12/11/2015	15,400	9	120
Note 4.	12/7/2015	18,000	12	90

Required

a. Prepare the adjusting entries for interest at December 31, 2014.

b. Assume that the adjusting entries were made at December 31, 2014, and that no adjusting entries were made during 2015. Prepare the 2015 journal entries to record payment of the notes that were outstanding at December 31, 2014.

c. Prepare the adjusting entries for interest at December 31, 2015.

LO1   P10-3B.   Recording Payroll and Payroll Taxes Manchester, Inc., had the following payroll for March:

Officers' salaries.	$39,000
Sales salaries	70,000
Federal income taxes withheld.	21,000
FICA taxes withheld	7,900
Health insurance premiums withheld.	2,500
Salaries (included above) subject to federal unemployment taxes	65,000
Salaries (included above) subject to state unemployment taxes.	75,000

Required

Prepare journal entries on March 31 to record:

a. Accrual of the monthly payroll.

b. Payment of the net payroll.

c. Accrual of employer's payroll taxes. (Assume that the FICA tax matches the amount withheld, the federal unemployment tax is 0.6 percent, and the state unemployment tax is 5.4 percent.)

d. Payment of all liabilities related to this payroll. (Assume that all are settled at the same time.)

LO1   P10-4B.   Recording Payroll and Payroll Taxes The following data are taken from Jefferson Distribution Company's March payroll:

Administrative salaries	$34,000
Sales salaries	54,000
Custodial salaries.	8,000
Total payroll	$96,000
Salaries subject to 1.45 percent Medicare tax.	$96,000
Salaries subject to 6.2 percent Social Security tax	$96,000
Salaries subject to federal unemployment taxes.	66,000
Salaries subject to state unemployment taxes	76,000
Federal income taxes withheld from all salaries	18,600

Assume that the company is subject to a 5.2 percent state unemployment tax and an 0.6 percent federal unemployment tax.

Required

Record the following in general journal form on March 31:

a. Accrual of the monthly payroll.

b. Payment of the net payroll.

c. Accrual of the employer's payroll taxes. (Assume that the FICA tax matches the amount withheld).

d. Payment of these payroll-related liabilities. (Assume that all are settled at the same time.)

P10-5B. **Excise and Sales Tax Calculations** Madison Corporation initially records its sales at amounts that exclude any related excise and sales taxes. During May, Madison recorded total sales of $750,000. An analysis of May sales indicated the following: **LO1**

1. Twenty percent of sales were subject to both a ten percent excise tax and a five percent sales tax.
2. Sixty percent of sales were subject only to the sales tax.
3. The balance of sales was for labor charges not subject to either excise or sales tax.

Required
a. Calculate the related liabilities for excise and sales taxes for May.
b. Prepare the necessary journal entry at May 31, to record the monthly payment of excise tax and sales tax to the government.

P10-6B. **Noncontingent and Contingent Liabilities** The following independent situations represent various types of liabilities: **LO1, 3**

1. Marshall Company has a manufacturing plant located in a small, rural community. The only other major employer in the area is Baker Company, which is experiencing financial problems. Marshall agrees to guarantee a loan for Baker, so Baker will remain in the community. Baker will receive all the proceeds of the loan. However, Marshall will have to repay the loan if Baker fails to do so. Marshall believes that Baker will repay the loan.
2. The village of High Creek and the town of Middlebury have been jointly using a rural dump site for 25 years. The state Department of Natural Resources has notified the two municipalities that wells on the nearby farms are polluted and that the dump site will be closed while further testing is done. Cleanup could cost as much as $25 million.
3. Two people walking on the sidewalk in front of the building owned by First United Bank were injured when part of the building collapsed on them. They are 25 years old and both are totally disabled. The building had been in poor condition for a long time. Insurance coverage is minimal. Both are suing First United Bank, and a jury trial is scheduled.
4. Winters Company sells garden tractors through 120 dealers located throughout the United States. Winters provides a two-year warranty for all parts and labor on these tractors. Each year, the average warranty cost per tractor sold is approximately $40.
5. Cronnin Company signed a 90-day note when it bought a new delivery truck for $25,000.
6. The CPA firm of Boyd and Lampe is being sued by one of the owners of an audit client that went bankrupt three years after Boyd and Lampe conducted an audit. The CPA firm has no insurance for this type of lawsuit. The attorneys for the CPA firm have stated that similar cases have never been successful, and they expect the same result here.

Required
Prepare a multicolumn analysis that presents the following information for each of these situations:

a. Number of the situation.
b. Type of liability: (1) noncontingent or (2) contingent.
c. Accounting treatment: (1) record in accounts, (2) disclose in a note to the financial statements, or (3) neither record nor disclose.

P10-7B. **Bonds Payable Journal Entries; Issued at Par Plus Accrued Interest** Cheney, Inc., which closes its books on December 31, is authorized to issue $800,000 of six percent, 20-year bonds dated March 1, with interest payments on September 1 and March 1. **LO2**

Required
Prepare journal entries to record the following events, assuming that the bonds were sold at 100 plus accrued interest on July 1.

a. The bond issuance.
b. Payment of the semiannual interest on September 1.
c. Accrual of bond interest expense at December 31.
d. Payment of the semiannual interest on March 1 of the following year.
e. Retirement of $200,000 of the bonds at 102 on March 1, Year 3 (immediately after the interest payment on that date).

LO4 **P10-8B.** **Current Ratio, Quick Ratio, and Times-Interest-Earned Ratio** The following data is from the current accounting records of Sierra Company:

Cash.	$240
Accounts receivable (net of allowance of 80).	400
Inventory.	300
Other current assets.	160
Accounts payable.	220
Other current liabilities.	340

The president of the company is concerned that the company may be in violation of a debt covenant that requires the company to maintain a minimum current ratio of 2.0. He believes the best way to rectify the problem is to reverse a bad debt write-off in the amount of $20 that the company just recorded. He argues that the write-off was done too early and that the collections department should be given more time to collect the outstanding amounts. The CFO argues that this will have no effect on the current ratio, so a better idea is to use $20 of cash to pay accounts payable early.

Required
a. Which idea, the president's or the CFO's, is better for attaining a minimum 2.0 current ratio?
b. Will either the quick ratio or the times-interest-earned ratios be affected by either of these ideas?

LO5
(Appendix 10A)

P10-9B. **Effective Interest Amortization** On December 31, 2015, Echo, Inc., issued $720,000 of 11 percent, five-year bonds for $693,504, yielding an effective interest rate of 12 percent. Semiannual interest is payable on June 30 and December 31 each year. The firm uses the effective interest method to amortize the discount.

Required
a. Prepare an amortization schedule showing the necessary information for the first two interest periods. Round amounts to the nearest dollar.
b. Prepare the journal entry for the bond issuance on December 31.
c. Prepare the journal entry to record bond interest expense and discount amortization at June 30 of the following year.
d. Prepare the journal entry to record bond interest expense and discount amortization at December 31 of the following year.

LO5
(Appendix 10A)

P10-10B. **Effective Interest Amortization** On January 1, 2015, Raines, Inc., issued $250,000 of ten percent, 15-year bonds for $293,230, yielding an effective interest rate of eight percent. Semiannual interest is payable on June 30 and December 31 each year. The firm uses the effective interest method to amortize the premium.

Required
a. Prepare an amortization schedule showing the necessary information for the first two interest periods. Round amounts to the nearest dollar.
b. Prepare the journal entry for the bond issuance on January 1, 2015.
c. Prepare the journal entry to record the bond interest payment and premium amortization at June 30.
d. Prepare the journal entry to record the bond interest payment and premium amortization at December 31.

SERIAL PROBLEM: KATE'S CARDS

(Note: This is a continuation of the Serial Problem: Kate's Cards from Chapters 1 through 9.)

SP10. Recall that Kate previously obtained a $15,000 bank loan, signing a note payable, on November 30. The note required semiannual interest payments at the rate of six percent. The entire principal balance was due two years from the origination date of the note. Kate has been accruing interest on a monthly basis in the amount of $75. Kate would like to know how she should record the interest in May, the month she makes the first interest payment. She is unsure how much expense will need to be recorded in May.

The upcoming interest payment is really not Kate's main concern right now. She was just notified by a lawyer that she is being sued for copyright infringement. Mega Cards Incorporated, one of the largest greeting card companies, believes that one of Kate's designs is too similar to one of Mega's designs for it to be coincidence, and has, therefore, decided to sue Kate's Cards. Mega has a prior reputation for suing small companies and settling out of court for lesser damages. Kate, however, knows that her design is original and that she had never previously seen the Mega design that is the subject of the lawsuit. She has determined to fight the lawsuit, regardless of the cost. She doesn't know, however, how this will affect her financial statements.

1. Record the May journal entry for Kate's first interest payment. How much interest expense is reported in May?
2. How should Kate report the copyright infringement lawsuit in her financial statements?

EXTENDING YOUR KNOWLEDGE

REPORTING AND ANALYSIS

EYK10-1. Financial Reporting Problem: Columbia Sportswear Company The financial statements for the **Columbia Sportswear Company** can be found in Appendix A at the end of this book.

COLUMBIA
SPORTSWEAR
COMPANY

Required
Answer the following questions:

a. How much were Columbia's current liabilities as of December 31, 2014?
b. What two items made up the largest percentage of Columbia's December 31, 2014, current liabilities?
c. What was the largest component of Columbia's December 31, 2014, accrued liabilities?
d. What was the largest component of Columbia's December 31, 2014, other long-term liabilities?

EYK10-2. Comparative Analysis Problem: Columbia Sportswear Company vs Under Armour Inc. The financial statements for the **Columbia Sportswear Company** can be found in Appendix A at the end of this book, and the financial statements of **Under Armour, Inc.** can be found in Appendix B (the complete annual report is available on this book's Website).

COLUMBIA
SPORTSWEAR
COMPANY

UNDER ARMOUR,
INC.

Required
Answer the following questions:

a. Compute the current ratio for Columbia Sportswear and Under Armour, Inc. as of December 31, 2014, and comment on what this ratio implies about each company's liquidity and working capital position.
b. Compute the debt-to-total assets ratio for Columbia Sportswear and Under Armour, Inc. as of December 31, 2014, and comment on what this ratio implies about each company's solvency.

EYK10-3. Business Decision Problem Kingston Corporation has total assets of $5,200,000 and has been earning an average of $800,000 before income taxes the past several years. The firm is planning to expand plant facilities to manufacture a new product and needs an additional $2,000,000 in funds, on which it expects to earn 18 percent before income tax. The income tax rate is expected to be 40 percent for the next several years. The firm has no long-term debt outstanding and presently has 75,000 shares of common stock outstanding. The firm is considering three alternatives:

1. Obtain the $2,000,000 by issuing 25,000 shares of common stock at $80 per share.
2. Obtain the $2,000,000 by issuing $1,000,000 of ten percent, 20-year bonds at face value and 12,500 shares of common stock at $80 per share.
3. Obtain the $2,000,000 by issuing $2,000,000 of ten percent, 20-year bonds at face value.

Required
As a shareholder of Kingston Corporation, which of the three alternatives would you prefer if your main concern is enhancing the firm's earnings per share? (Hint: Divide net income by the number of outstanding common shares to determine the company's earnings per share.)

EYK10-4. Financial Analysis Problem **Abbott Laboratories** is a diversified health care company devoted to the discovery, development, manufacture, and marketing of innovative products that improve

ABBOTT
LABORATORIES

diagnostic, therapeutic, and nutritional practices. The company's balance sheet for three recent years contains the following data:

	Year 3	Year 2	Year 1
Cash and cash equivalents	$ 6,812,820	$ 3,648,371	$ 8,809,339
Investment securities	1,284,539	1,803,079	1,122,709
Trade receivables (net of allowance)	7,683,920	7,184,034	6,541,941
Inventories	3,284,249	3,188,734	3,264,877
Other current assets.	4,703,246	6,493,311	3,575,025
Total current assets	$23,768,774	$22,317,529	$23,313,891
Total current liabilities	$15,480,228	$17,262,434	$13,049,489

Required

a. Compute the current ratio for Years 1–3.
b. Compute the quick ratio for Years 1–3.
c. Comment on the three-year trend in these ratios.

CRITICAL THINKING

GENERAL MILLS, INC.

EYK10-5. **Financial Analysis on the Web: General Mills, Inc.** The fiscal year 2014 annual report of **General Mills, Inc.** is available on this book's Website. Refer to the consolidated statement of earnings, the consolidated balance sheets, and Notes 8 and 15.

Required

a. What was the total dollar amount of current liabilities as of May 25, 2014?
b. What percent of long-term debt was considered current as of May 25, 2014?
c. What were the current ratio and quick ratio as of May 25, 2014?
d. What is the total amount of long-term liabilities reported by General Mills as of May 25, 2014?
e. How much principal payments on the long-term debt is General Mills anticipating paying in fiscal year 2015?
f. Are General Mills' leases capital leases or operating leases? Explain.

EYK10-6. **Accounting Communication Activity** Cedric Salos is considering different ways to raise money for the expansion of his company's operations. Cedric is not sure about the advantages of issuing bonds versus issuing common stock. In addition, he is not sure which features he should consider including with the bonds if he selects that form of financing. He asks you to explain, in simple terms, the answers to his questions.

Required

Write a short memorandum to Cedric explaining the advantages of issuing bonds over issuing common stock and the features that should be considered for inclusion with the bonds.

EYK10-7. **Accounting Ethics Case** Sunrise Pools, Inc., is being sued by the Crescent Club for negligence when installing a new pool on Crescent Club's property. Crescent Club alleges that the employees of Sunrise Pools damaged the foundation of the clubhouse and part of the golf course while operating heavy machinery to install the pool.

The lawsuit is for $1.5 million. At the time of the alleged incident, Sunrise Pools carried only $600,000 of liability insurance.

While reviewing the draft of Sunrise Pools' annual report, its president deletes all references to this lawsuit. She is concerned that disclosure of this lawsuit in the annual report will be viewed by Crescent Club as admission of Sunrise's wrongdoing, even though she privately admits that Sunrise employees were careless and believes that Sunrise Pools will be found liable for an amount in excess of $1 million. The president sends the amended draft of the annual report to the vice president of finance with a note stating that the lawsuit will not be disclosed in the annual report and that the lawsuit will not be disclosed to the board of directors.

Required

Is the president's concern valid? What ethical problems will the vice president of finance face if he follows the president's instructions?

EYK10-8. Corporate Social Responsibility Problem The chapter highlight on **Microsoft**'s corporate social responsibility efforts (see page 476) discussed the company's Unlimited Potential partnerships. Go to Microsoft's Website and navigate to the section "About Microsoft;" then navigate to the section on corporate citizenship. Download the Corporate Citizenship Report. In addition to Unlimited Potential, what are some other ways that Microsoft demonstrates its commitment to being a good corporate citizen?

MICROSOFT

EYK10-9. Forensic Accounting Problem Billing schemes are frauds in which an employee causes the victim organization to issue fraudulent payments by submitting invoices for nonexistent goods or services, inflated invoices, or invoices for personal items. One type of billing scheme uses a shell company that is set up for the purpose of committing the fraud. The shell company is often nothing more than a fake corporate name and a post-office mailbox.

What are some of the ways that shell company invoices can be detected?

EYK10-10. Working with the Takeaways Below are selected data from **Microsoft**'s recent financial statements:

	Year 2	Year 1
Net income.	$16,978	$23,150
Tax expense.	5,289	4,921
Interest expense.	0	0
Cash and cash equivalents	6,938	9,610
Short-term investments	56,102	43,162
Accounts receivable.	17,815	17,454
Other current assets.	4,229	4,692
Current liabilities.	32,688	28,774

Required

Calculate the following ratios for Year 1 and Year 2 and comment on the trend:

a.   Current ratio

b.   Quick ratio

EYK10-11. Analyzing IFRS Financial Statements The 2014 financial statements of LVMH Moet Hennessey-Louis Vuitton S.A. are presented in Appendix C at the end of this book. LVMH is a Paris-based holding company and one of the world's largest and best-known luxury goods companies. As a member of the European Union, French companies are required to prepare their consolidated (group) financial statements using International Financial Reporting Standards (IFRS). Using LVMH's financial data for 2013 and 2014, calculate the company's (a) current ratio, (b) quick ratio, and (c) times-interest-earned ratio. Is LVMH's working capital position improving or declining over the two-year period? Can LVMH readily service its interest payments from its income before interest expense and income taxes? (*Hint:* LVMH's interest expense is labeled "cost of net financial debt" on its consolidated income statement.)

IFRS

ANSWERS TO SELF-STUDY QUESTIONS:

YOUR TURN! SOLUTIONS

Solution 10.1

a.	Apr. 30	Office salaries expense	40,000	
		Sales salaries expense	86,000	
		Federal income tax withholding payable		25,600
		FICA tax payable		9,639
		Health insurance premiums payable		1,850
		Union dues payable		950
		Payroll payable		87,961
		To accrue payroll for April		
		(FICA taxes = 0.0765 × $126,000 = $9,639).		
b.	30	Payroll payable	87,961	
		Cash		87,961
		To pay April payroll.		
c.	30	Payroll tax expense	14,847	
		FICA tax payable		9,639
		Federal unemployment tax payable		456
		State unemployment tax payable		4,752
		To record employer's payroll taxes (FICA Tax = 0.0765 ×		
		$126,000 = $9,639; Federal Unemployment Tax = 0.006 ×		
		$76,000 = $456; State Unemployment Tax = 0.054 × $88,000		
		= $4,752).		
d.	30	Federal income tax withholding payable	25,600	
		FICA tax payable	19,278	
		Health insurance premiums payable	1,850	
		Union dues payable	950	
		Federal unemployment tax payable	456	
		State unemployment tax payable	4,752	
		Cash		52,886
		To record the payment of payroll-related liabilities.		

Solution 10.2

(a)	Cash	325,000	
	Bonds payable		300,000
	Premium on bonds payable		25,000
	To record the issuance of bonds payable		

(b)

Long-term liabilities		
Bonds payable	$300,000	
Add: Premium on bonds payable.	25,000	$325,000

Solution 10.3

1. Because the likelihood of losing the lawsuit is deemed remote it does not need to be recognized or disclosed by Seco Co.
2. Even though the contingency is deemed remote, credit guarantees must be disclosed in the notes to the financial statements.
3. The liability should be recorded on the balance sheet because the likelihood of payment is both high and can be estimated.

Solution 10.4
a. Current ratio = $120,000 / $80,000 = 1.50
b. Quick ratio = ($10,000 + $25,000 + $30,000) / $80,000 = 0.8125
c. Times-interest-earned ratio = $20,000 / $4,000 = 5.0

Solution 10A.1
The selling price will be $94,582.81

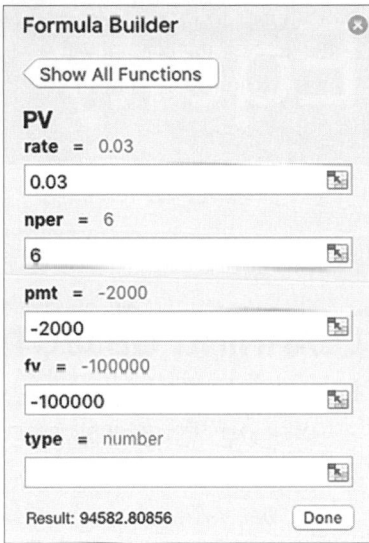

Solution 10B.1
The present value of the lease payments is $42,580, which is over 90 percent of the asset's fair value of $45,000. In addition, the four-year lease is for over 75% of the asset's five-year economic life. Therefore the lease needs to be recorded as a capital lease as follows:

Leased equipment	42,580	
Lease obligation		42,580

11

Stockholders' Equity

PAST

Chapter 10 examined the accounting for liabilities.

PRESENT

In this chapter, we turn our attention to the accounting for stockholders' equity.

FUTURE

In Chapter 12, we shift our focus to the statement of cash flows.

LEARNING OBJECTIVES

1. **Define** the corporate form of organization and **discuss** its principal characteristics. *(p. 530)*

2. **Explain** the difference between par value stock and no-par value stock. *(p. 533)*

3. **Identify** and **discuss** the two types of capital stock and their respective stockholder rights. *(p. 534)*

4. **Describe** the accounting for issuances of capital stock. *(p. 538)*

5. **Define** and **discuss** the accounting for stock splits. *(p. 540)*

6. **Explain** the accounting for treasury stock. *(p. 540)*

7. **Identify** and **distinguish** between cash dividends and stock dividends. *(p. 542)*

8. **Illustrate** the statement of retained earnings and the statement of stockholders' equity. *(p. 546)*

9. **Define** the *return on common stockholders' equity, dividend yield,* and *dividend payout ratio* and **explain** their use. *(p. 548)*

STARBUCKS

Starbucks is the largest coffeehouse company in the world, with over 21,000 stores in 65 countries and territories. The first Starbucks coffeehouse was opened in Seattle, Washington, in 1971 to sell high quality coffee beans and equipment.

An important event in Starbucks' history occurred in 1982 when Howard Schultz joined the company. Schultz had a different strategic vision for Starbucks. He believed that the company should not only sell coffee beans, but coffee and espresso drinks as well. Starbucks' owners, however, rejected the idea. Schultz was so committed to his vision that he decided to leave the company and start the Il Giornale coffee bar chain in 1985.

In 1987, the Starbucks chain was sold to Schultz's Il Giornale, which was re-branded as Starbucks. Soon after, the company began to rapidly expand at an explosive rate. During the 1990s, Starbucks opened a new store almost every workday!

Where do firms get the necessary capital for expansion? While not every large firm is a corporation, many are, and one of the most important characteristics of the corporate form of organization is the ability to raise new capital by selling ownership shares in the company. Starbucks had its initial public offering of its common shares in 1992.

Without a doubt, the modern corporation dominates the national and international economic landscape. In the United States, corporations generate well over three-fourths of the combined sales revenue of all forms of business organization, even though less than one of every five businesses is organized as a corporation. The corporate form of organization is used in a variety of business settings—from large multinational corporations with more than a million stockholders operating in countries all over the world, to small, family-owned businesses operating only in their local community.

Why do fast growing firms like Starbucks choose the corporate form of organization? There are several reasons, but certainly one of the primary reasons is the relative ease of attracting large amounts of capital as compared to other organizational forms of business.

lacks a par value. Thus, if the preferred stock has a $100 par value and a six percent dividend rate, the preferred stockholders receive $6 per share in dividends. However, the dividend is owed to the stockholders only if, and when, declared by the board of directors.

Preferred dividends are usually **cumulative**—that is, regular dividends to preferred stockholders omitted in the past must be paid in addition to the current year's dividend before any dividend distribution can be made to the common stockholders. If a preferred stock is **noncumulative**, omitted dividends do not carry forward.

To illustrate the difference between cumulative and noncumulative preferred stock, assume that a company ending its second year of operations has 1,000 shares of $100 par value, six percent preferred stock and 100,000 shares of $1 par value common stock outstanding. The company declared no dividends last year. This year a dividend of $27,000 is declared. The distribution of the $27,000 between the two stockholder classes depends on whether the preferred stock is cumulative or noncumulative. If the preferred stock is cumulative, preferred stockholders receive $12 per share before common stockholders receive anything, as illustrated below:

	Preferred	Common	Total
Total par value of outstanding shares	$100,000	$100,000	$200,000
Preferred stock is cumulative			
Preferred dividends in arrears (6 percent)	$ 6,000		$ 6,000
Regular preferred dividend (6 percent).	6,000		6,000
Remainder to common.		$ 15,000	15,000
Total distribution	$ 12,000	$ 15,000	$ 27,000
Preferred stock is noncumulative			
Regular preferred dividend (6 percent).	$ 6,000		$ 6,000
Remainder to common.		$ 21,000	21,000
Total distribution	$ 6,000	$ 21,000	$ 27,000

Dividends in arrears (that is, dividends omitted in past years) on cumulative preferred stock are not an accounting liability and do not appear in the liability section of the balance sheet. They do not become an obligation of the corporation until the board of directors formally declares such dividends. Any dividends in arrears are disclosed to investors in the notes to the financial statements.

Asset Distribution Preference

Preferred stockholders normally have a preference over common stockholders with respect to the receipt of assets in the event of a corporate liquidation. When a corporation liquidates, any creditor claims are settled first. Preferred stockholders then have the right to receive assets equal to the par value of their shares, or a larger stated liquidation value per share, before any assets are distributed to common stockholders. The preferred stockholders' preference to assets in liquidation also includes any dividends in arrears.

Other Preferred Stock Features

Although preferred stockholders do not ordinarily have the right to vote in the election of the board of directors, this right can be accorded by contract. Some state laws require that all capital stock issued by a corporation be given voting rights. Further, preferred stock may contain features that cause the shares to resemble common stock. Preferred stock may, for example, be **convertible** into common stock at a specified conversion rate. When this feature is present, the market price of the preferred shares often moves in a fashion consistent with the related common shares. When the price of the common stock rises, the value of the conversion feature is enhanced, and consequently, the value of the preferred shares should also rise.

Preferred stock may be **participating**. A *participating preferred stock* shares any special dividend distributions with common stock beyond the regular preferred stock dividend rate. (Special dividends are discussed on p. 541.) After receiving its regular dividend preference, preferred stock normally does not participate in any special dividend distribution until the common stock is allowed a dividend amount corresponding to the regular preferred stock dividend rate At this point, the two classes of stock begin to share the special dividend distribution at the same rate. The preferred stock participation feature may be partial (which limits the participation to a certain amount) or full (which places no limit on the rate of participation).

Preferred stock may be **callable**, which means that a corporation can redeem the shares after a length of time and at a price specified in the stock contract. The call feature makes the preferred stock similar to a bond, since many bonds are callable or have a limited life. Most preferred stocks are callable, with the call or redemption price set slightly above the original preferred stock issuance price.

FORENSIC ACCOUNTING

Using Forensic Accounting to Pick Stocks

A new investment product has been introduced for those who want to use the techniques of forensic accounting to help in their investing. The Forensic Accounting ETF is a fund that attempts to track the Del Vecchio Earnings Quality Index. This index looks at all 500 stocks in the S&P 500 and grades them from A through F based on the quality of their reported earnings. Earnings quality is defined based on judging the sustainability of the reported earnings. While the methodology that uses forensic accounting techniques is proprietary, some of the things that are known to be looked at are reserve concerns, cost of goods for inventory issues, and aggressive revenue recognition.

ACCOUNTING IN PRACTICE

Preferred Shares and the Capital Market

Although legally, and from an accounting standpoint, preferred shares are considered to be part of a company's stockholders' equity, the capital market takes a different point of view. Most investment professionals consider a company's preferred stock to be part of the company's debt structure. Thus, from a capital market perspective, the only true stockholders of a business are its common stockholders. This point of view is apparent in the calculation of such ratios as the return on common stockholders' equity, discussed shortly, which excludes a company's preferred stockholders' equity.

Match the description in the right column with the appropriate term in the left column:

1. Authorized
2. Outstanding
3. Common stock
4. Preemptive right
5. Preferred stock
6. Cumulative preference

a. The right to receive dividends omitted in prior years.
b. The most basic class of stock ownership.
c. Stock with one or more preferences over common stock.
d. The maximum number of shares of each class of stock that may be issued.
e. Shares actually held by stockholders.
f. The right to maintain a proportionate ownership interest in a corporation.

YOUR TURN! 11.2

The solution is on page 574.

STOCK ISSUANCES FOR CASH

LO4 Describe the accounting for issuances of capital stock.

When issuing capital stock to investors, a corporation may use the services of an investment bank, a specialist in marketing securities to the capital market. The investment bank may *underwrite* a stock issue by agreeing to sell the shares on a firm commitment basis— that is, buying the shares from the corporation and then reselling them to investors. Under a firm commitment agreement, a corporation does not risk being unable to sell its stock. The underwriter bears this risk in return for the fees and profits generated by selling the shares to investors at a price higher than it paid to the corporation. An investment bank that is unwilling to underwrite a stock issue may handle the issuance of the shares on a *best efforts* basis. In this case, the investment bank agrees to sell as many shares as possible at a set price, but the corporation bears the risk of any unsold shares.

When capital stock is issued to investors, the appropriate capital stock account is credited for the par value of the stock issued, or if the stock is no-par value stock, with its stated value, if any. The asset received in exchange for the stock (usually cash) is debited, and any difference is credited to the Paid-in Capital in Excess of Par Value account.

To illustrate the journal entries to record various stock issuances in exchange for cash, assume that Smith & Sons issued two different types of capital stock during its first year of operations:

Issuing Stock At A Premium

1. Issued 1,000 shares of $100 par value, 9% preferred stock at $107 cash per share:

A = L + SE
+107,000 +100,000 PS
+7,000 PS

Cash	107,000	
Preferred stock		100,000
Paid-in capital in excess of par value—Preferred stock		7,000

In this transaction, the preferred stock is issued at a price greater than its par value—that is, the shares were sold at a premium. The par value of the preferred stock issued is credited to the Preferred Stock account and the $7,000 premium is credited to the Paid-in Capital in Excess of Par Value account. If there is more than one class of par value stock, the account title may indicate the class of stock to which the premium relates, in this case Paid-in Capital in Excess of Par Value—Preferred Stock.

Issuing No-Par Stock

2. Issued 30,000 shares of no-par value common stock, stated value $5, at $8 cash per share:

A = L + SE
+240,000 +150,000 CS
+90,000 CS

Cash	240,000	
Common stock		150,000
Paid-in capital in excess of stated value—Common stock		90,000

When no-par value stock has a stated value, as in Entry 2, the stated value of the total shares issued is credited to the proper capital stock account, and any additional amount received is credited to the account Paid-in Capital in Excess of Stated Value. If there is no stated value for the no-par value stock, the entire proceeds are credited to the appropriate capital stock account. In the second journal entry, if the common stock had no stated value, the entire $240,000 amount would have been credited to the Common Stock account.

These two stock issuances are reflected in **Exhibit 11-2**, which presents the stockholders' equity section from Smith & Sons' year-end balance sheet. (Retained earnings are assumed to be $25,000.) The stockholders' equity section is divided into two major categories: ❶ Paid-in Capital and ❷ Retained Earnings. **Paid-in capital** is the amount of capital contributed to the corporation from various capital stock transactions such as the issuance of preferred stock and common stock. The capital contributed by stockholders through the issuance of stock is divided between the legal capital (the par value or stated value of the stock) and the amounts received in excess of the legal capital. Later in this chapter we discuss treasury stock transactions that may affect a corporation's paid-in capital. **Retained earnings** represent the cumulative net income and losses of the company that have not been distributed to stockholders as a dividend.

EXHIBIT 11-2	Stockholders' Equity Section of the Balance Sheet		

Paid-in Capital		
9% Preferred stock, $100 par value, 1,000 shares authorized, issued, and outstanding.	$100,000	
No-par common stock, stated value $5, 40,000 shares authorized; 30,000 shares issued and outstanding	150,000	$250,000
Additional paid-in capital		
In excess of par value—Preferred stock.	7,000	
In excess of stated value—Common stock	90,000	97,000
Total Paid-in Capital		347,000
Retained earnings		25,000
Total Stockholders' Equity		$372,000

(❶ brackets Paid-in Capital section; ❷ brackets Retained earnings)

Noncash Stock Issuances

Sometimes a corporation will exchange its common stock for services, operating assets, or for its own convertible debt or convertible preferred stock. For example, some start-up companies lacking cash will exchange their common stock for professional services provided by attorneys and accountants. When this occurs, a journal entry is made to debit the Professional Services Expense account and a credit is made to Common Stock—Par Value and to the Paid-in Capital in Excess of Par Value—Common Stock account for the fair value of the services received.

When common stock is exchanged for operating assets, a similar journal entry is made, although the debit in this case is to the Land or Equipment account. When common stock is exchanged for convertible bonds (discussed in Chapter 10), the value of the newly issued stock is assumed to be equal to the book value of the bonds. An exchange of convertible bonds for common stock is executed by debiting the Bonds Payable account and the Premium on Bonds Payable account (or crediting the Discount on Bonds Payable account) and crediting the Common Stock account and the Paid-in Capital in Excess of Par Value—Common Stock for any excess of the bonds' book value over the stock's par value. When preferred stock is converted into a company's common stock, the newly issued common stock assumes the book value of the preferred stock. That is, the Preferred Stock—Par Value and the Paid-in Capital in Excess of Par Value—Preferred Stock are debited while the Common Stock—Par Value and Paid-in Capital in Excess of Par Value—Common Stock are credited.

Wyatt Industries began operations on June 1 by issuing 10,000 shares of $1 par value common stock for cash at $9 per share. How much Additional Paid-in Capital will be reported by Wyatt Industries?

YOUR TURN! 11.3

The solution is on page 574.

STOCK SPLITS

LO5 Define and discuss the accounting for stock splits.

Occasionally, a corporation may issue additional shares of common stock to its stockholders through a **forward stock split**. The principal reason that companies execute a forward stock split is to reduce the market price of their shares. A forward stock split increases the number of shares outstanding and is accounted for by reducing the par value or stated value of the stock affected. A forward stock split does not change the balances of any of the stockholders' equity accounts; however, a memorandum entry is made in the general journal to show the altered par value or stated value of the stock and to note the increase in the number of shares issued and outstanding. For example, if Smith & Sons has 10,000 shares of $10 par value common stock outstanding and announces a 2-for-1 forward stock split, it would simply reduce the par value of its common stock to $5 per share and issue to its stockholders 10,000 new common shares. Thus, after the forward stock split, each stockholder would have twice the number of shares held prior to the split, and the value of the Common Stock account would remain unchanged at $100,000 (10,000 shares × $2 = 20,000 shares × $5 = $100,000). If you owned one share of Smith & Sons $10 par value stock before the 2-for-1 forward stock split you would own two shares of Smith & Sons $5 par value stock after the stock split.

Before 2-for-1 forward stock split   After 2-for-1 forward stock split

Occasionally, a company may execute a **reverse stock split** by increasing the par value of the stock and reducing the number of shares outstanding. Reverse stock splits are designed to increase a company's stock price. Most major stock exchanges have a minimum trading price that a company must meet or exceed in order to be traded on the exchange. When a company's stock price falls below the minimum trading price, the shares may be delisted, making it difficult for stockholders to find buyers for their shares. Meeting and exceeding an exchange's minimum listing price is one of the principal reasons for reverse stock splits.

YOUR TURN! 11.4

The solution is on page 574.

Aston Enterprises currently has 500,000 common shares outstanding with a par value of $3.00. Joe Smith owns 500 of those shares. If Aston were to execute a 3-for-1 split, what would be the resulting share information for both Aston and Smith?

TREASURY STOCK

LO6 Explain the accounting for treasury stock.

When a corporation acquires its own outstanding shares for a purpose other than retiring (cancelling) them, the acquired shares are called **treasury stock**. Treasury stock may be purchased for a variety of reasons, including reissuing them to officers and employees in profit sharing programs or employee stock option plans. Whatever the purpose, treasury stock purchases reduce a company's stockholders' equity. Treasury shares do not carry voting privileges or preemptive rights, are not paid dividends, and do not receive assets in the event of a corporation's liquidation.

		ACCOUNTING IN
	Greenmail	**PRACTICE**

Corporations usually purchase their own shares by buying them through a brokerage firm on the open market or by making a tender offer to stockholders. Under a tender offer, the company offers to buy back its shares of stock at a specified price per share. Another way to acquire treasury stock is to negotiate a purchase of shares from a single large stockholder. In some cases, this latter technique may involve greenmail. *Greenmail* is a ploy in which an investor purchases a large number of a company's shares, threatens to take control of the company, and then sells the shares back to the company at a premium. Management pays the premium to entice the investor to "be quiet and go away." Although it is not illegal, payment of an unjustified greenmail premium is likely to upset other stockholders and may lead to legal action against a company.

Accounting for Treasury Stock

Accountants record treasury stock at its acquisition cost, debiting the Treasury Stock account and crediting the Cash account. The Treasury Stock account is a contra-stockholders' equity account, and its balance is deducted when deriving total stockholders' equity on the balance sheet. To illustrate the accounting for the purchase of treasury stock, assume that Smith & Sons had 20,000 shares of $10 par value common stock outstanding and then purchased 1,000 shares at $12 per share. The journal entry to record the purchase is:

Treasury stock	12,000	
Cash		12,000
To record purchase of 1,000 shares of treasury stock at $12 per share.		

$$A = L + SE$$
$$-12,000 \qquad -12,000$$
$$TS$$

If a balance sheet is prepared following this transaction, the stockholders' equity section would appear as follows (the values for Paid-in Capital in Excess of Par Value and Retained Earnings are assumed):

SMITH & SONS, INC. Stockholders' Equity	
Paid-in Capital	
Common stock, $10 par value, authorized and issued 20,000 shares; 1,000 shares in treasury, 19,000 shares outstanding	$200,000
Paid-in capital in excess of par value	20,000
Total Paid-in Capital	220,000
Retained earnings	40,000
	260,000
Less: Treasury stock (1,000 shares) at cost	**12,000**
Total Stockholders' Equity	$248,000

Note that the $200,000 par value of all *issued* stock is disclosed, although the 1,000 treasury shares are no longer outstanding. The total cost of the 1,000 shares, however, is later deducted as the last component in the presentation of total stockholders' equity.

If Smith & Sons subsequently resells 500 shares of its treasury stock at $14 per share, the following journal entry is made:

					Cash	7,000	
A	=	L	+	SE	Treasury stock		6,000
+7,000				+6,000 TS	Paid-in capital—Treasury stock		1,000
				+1,000 TS			

Note that the $1,000 "gain" on the resale of the treasury stock is accounted for as an increase in shareholders' equity and not as net income.

IFRS ALERT

Under IFRS and U.S. GAAP, treasury stock is reported on the balance sheet as a contra stockholders' equity account. That is, the repurchase cost of any treasury stock is subtracted from total stockholders' equity. In addition, both IFRS and U.S. GAAP preclude the recognition of any gain or loss by a company from stock transactions involving its own shares—that is, any "gain" or "loss" from trading in a company's own shares is recorded as part of Paid-in Capital in Excess of Par Value. By way of contrast, some countries permit treasury stock to be reported on the asset side of the balance sheet as an investment in marketable securities. Under IFRS and U.S. GAAP, treasury stock does not satisfy the definition of an asset, and therefore, cannot be reported on the balance sheet as marketable securities. It is also noteworthy that in some countries, treasury stock purchases are illegal because they are viewed as a form of stock price manipulation.

YOUR TURN! 11.5

The solution is on page 574.

The Fullerton Corporation purchased 5,000 shares of its outstanding $2 par value common stock for $75,000 cash on November 1. Management anticipates holding the stock in the treasury until it resells the stock. By how much would the Fullerton Corporation debit Treasury Stock for this purchase?

CASH DIVIDENDS AND STOCK DIVIDENDS

LO7 Identify and distinguish between cash dividends and stock dividends.

Dividends are a distribution of assets or shares of stock from a corporation to its stockholders. A corporation can distribute dividends to stockholders only after its board of directors has formally voted to declare a distribution. Dividends are usually paid in cash but may also be paid as property or additional shares of stock in the firm. Legally, declared dividends are an obligation of the firm, and an entry to record the dividend obligation is made on the *dividend declaration date*. Cash and property dividends payable are carried as liabilities, and stock dividends to be issued are shown in the stockholders' equity section of the balance sheet. At the date of declaration, a *record date* and *payment date* are also established. For example, assume that on April 25 (the declaration date), the board of directors of Smith & Sons declares a cash dividend payable on June 1 (the payment date) to those investors who own shares of stock on May 15 (the record date). Stockholders owning stock on the record date receive the dividend even if they dispose of their shares before the payment date. Therefore, shares sold between the record date and the payment date are sold *ex dividend*—that is, they are sold without the right to receive the dividend.

Most dividend declarations are accounted for by reducing retained earnings. Dividends are distributions of earnings and are not shown as expenses on the income statement. Also, dividends cannot be deducted as expenses for income tax purposes. Under certain conditions, however, state laws may permit distributions from additional paid-in capital. Stockholders should be informed of the source of such dividends, because, in a sense, any dividend paid from a company's paid-in capital is a nontaxable return of capital rather than a taxable distribution of earnings.

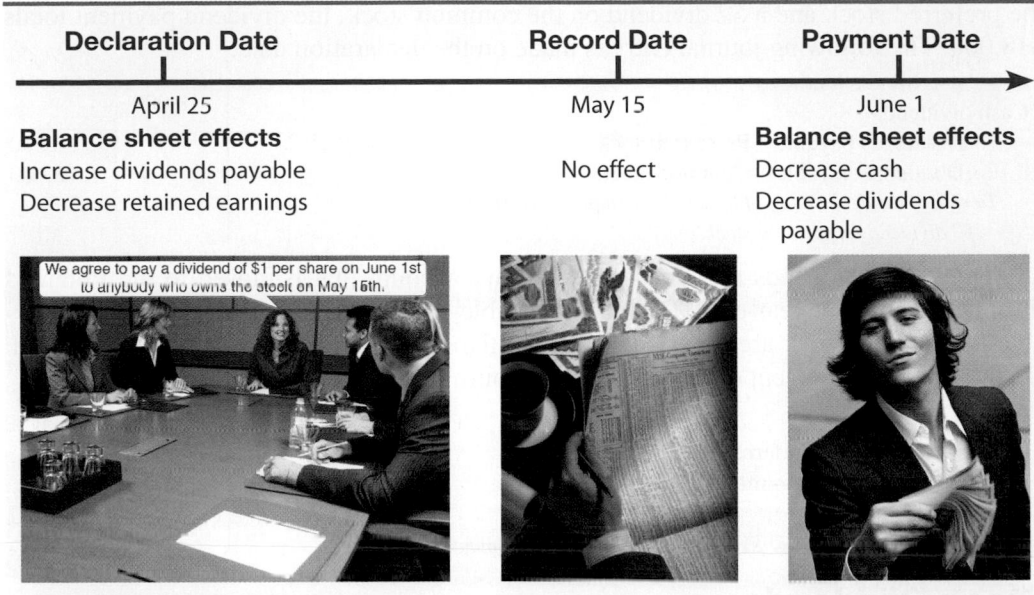

Declaration Date	Record Date	Payment Date
April 25	May 15	June 1
Balance sheet effects		**Balance sheet effects**
Increase dividends payable	No effect	Decrease cash
Decrease retained earnings		Decrease dividends payable

We agree to pay a dividend of $1 per share on June 1st to anybody who owns the stock on May 15th.

While U.S. corporations principally distribute cash and/or stock dividends, property dividend distributions are common among Japanese corporations. For example, **McDonald's Holding Company of Japan** annually distributes to its stockholders coupons for a free Big Mac as a property dividend. And, **DyDo Drinco, Inc.**, distributes to its stockholders samples of its beverage products as a property dividend. Companies that distribute their products or coupons for their products to stockholders as a property dividend believe that by making stockholders more familiar with the company's products, they will retain the investment commitment of their stockholders on a longer term basis than would otherwise be the case.

Cash Dividends

The majority of dividends distributed by corporations are paid in cash. Although companies may pay such dividends annually, many firms pay quarterly dividends. Dividends that are paid routinely are called regular dividends. The **Johnson & Johnson Company** and **PepsiCo, Inc.**, for example, pay regular quarterly dividends. Some companies occasionally pay a special dividend. Special dividends occur infrequently and represent the distribution of excess cash that has been accumulated by a business and for which the business has no immediate operational need.

When a company declares a **cash dividend**, the company must have both an appropriate amount of retained earnings and the necessary amount of cash on hand. Uninformed investors often believe that a large retained earnings balance automatically permits generous dividend distributions. A company, however, may successfully accumulate earnings and at the same time not be sufficiently liquid to pay large cash dividends. Many companies, especially new firms in growth industries, finance their expansion from assets generated through earnings and pay out small cash dividends or none at all.

Cash dividends are based on the number of shares outstanding. When a company's directors declare a cash dividend, an entry is made by debiting the Cash Dividends account and crediting the Dividends Payable account. To illustrate, assume that Smith & Sons has 1,000 shares of $100 par value, six percent preferred stock and 6,000 shares of $10 par value common stock outstanding. If the company declares the regular $6 dividend on the preferred stock and a $2 dividend on the common stock, the dividend payment totals $18,000. The following journal entry is made on the declaration date:

A = L + SE
+6,000 −18,000
Div
+12,000

Cash dividends	18,000	
Dividends payable—Preferred stock		6,000
Dividends payable—Common stock		12,000
To record the declaration of $6 dividend on preferred stock and		
$2 dividend on common stock.		

The Cash Dividends account is a temporary account that is closed to the Retained Earnings account at year-end.[1] Dividends Payable—Preferred Stock and Dividends Payable—Common Stock are reported as current liabilities on the balance sheet until paid. On the dividend payment date, the following journal entry is made:

A = L + SE
−18,000 −6,000
−12,000

Dividends payable—Preferred stock	6,000	
Dividends payable—Common stock	12,000	
Cash		18,000
To record the payment of dividends on preferred and common shares.		

Stock Dividends

Companies may also distribute shares of their own stock as dividends to stockholders in lieu of, or in addition to, cash dividends. A company may issue **stock dividends** when it does not wish to deplete its working capital by paying a cash dividend. Young and growing companies often issue stock dividends because cash is usually needed to acquire new facilities and to expand.

The accounting for a stock dividend results in a transfer of a portion of retained earnings to the paid-in capital accounts. Thus, the distribution of a stock dividend signals to investors management's desire to "plow back" earnings into the company. Although stock dividends may take a number of forms, usually common shares are distributed to common stockholders. We limit our discussion to this type of stock dividend distribution.

Small Stock Dividends

Small stock dividends are share distributions that involve less than 25 percent of the total number of shares previously outstanding. Small stock dividends are *recorded at the market value* of the shares issued, causing retained earnings to decrease and paid-in capital to increase by this amount. To illustrate the journal entries for a declaration of a small stock dividend, assume that the stockholders' equity of Smith & Sons is as follows prior to the declaration of a ten percent stock dividend:

Common stock, $5 par value, 20,000 shares issued and outstanding	$100,000
Paid-in capital in excess of par value.	**20,000**
Total Paid-in Capital.	120,000
Retained earnings	**65,000**
Total Stockholders' Equity	$185,000

With 20,000 shares outstanding, the declaration of a ten percent stock dividend requires the issuance of an additional 2,000 shares (10 percent × 20,000 shares). If the current market price per share is $11, the total market value of the shares to be distributed is $22,000 (2,000 shares × $11), resulting in the following journal entry:

---

[1] Some companies, especially those paying regular dividends, debit the Retained Earnings account directly on the dividend declaration date.

Stock dividends	22,000	
Stock dividend distributable		10,000
Paid-in capital in excess of par value		12,000
To record declaration of 10 percent stock dividend on common shares.		

A = L + SE
−22,000
Div
+10,000
CS
+12,000
CS

The amount of the credit to the Stock Dividend Distributable account is the par value of the shares to be distributed (2,000 shares × $5). If a balance sheet is prepared between the declaration date and the distribution date of a stock dividend, the Stock Dividend Distributable account is shown in stockholders' equity immediately after the Common Stock account. When the shares are distributed, the following journal entry is made:

Stock dividend distributable	10,000	
Common stock		10,000
To record issuance of stock dividend on common shares.		

A = L + SE
−10,000
CS
+10,000
CS

The Stock Dividends account is a temporary account that is closed to the Retained Earnings account at year-end, as shown by the following journal entry:

Retained earnings	22,000	
Stock dividends		22,000
To close the Stock Dividends account.		

A = L + SE
−22,000
RE
+22,000
Div

A comparison of the stockholders' equity and outstanding shares, before and after the stock dividend, appears below. Note that retained earnings decreased by $22,000 and paid-in capital increased by $22,000, but total stockholders' equity remains unchanged:

	Before Stock Dividend	After Stock Dividend
Common stock, $5 par value	$100,000	$110,000
Paid-in capital in excess of par value.	20,000	32,000
Total Paid-in Capital	120,000	142,000
Retained earnings	65,000	43,000
Total Stockholders' Equity	$185,000	$185,000
Common shares issued and outstanding	20,000	22,000

The relative ownership interest of a common stockholder is unaltered by the receipt of a common stock dividend. If a ten percent stock dividend is distributed, all stockholders increase their proportionate holdings by ten percent, and the total shares outstanding are increased in the same proportion. Small stock dividends rarely affect the market value of the underlying stock.

Large Stock Dividends

When the number of shares issued as a stock dividend is large enough to impact the stock's market value per share, stockholders may not perceive the same benefits as they do for a small stock dividend. This is because issuing a large number of shares is likely to reduce the market price of the shares, much the same way that a stock split, discussed earlier in the chapter, reduces the market price per share. To see this, note that a 100 percent large stock dividend is the same as a 2-for-1 forward stock split. Accordingly, the accounting for large stock dividends (those over 25 percent) differs from the accounting for small stock dividends. The journal entry to record the declaration of a large stock dividend debits the Stock Dividends account and credits the Stock Dividend Distributable account for the par or stated value of the shares issued. Once the stock is issued, the increase in paid-in capital is reflected in the Common Stock account.[2]

YOUR TURN! 11.6

The solution is on page 574.

Fango Company's president would like to know the financial impact that a cash dividend and a stock dividend will have on the company's retained earnings account. The current balance in retained earnings is $500,000. The company has 10,000 shares of $1 par value common stock outstanding with a current market value of $20 per share. The potential cash dividend will be $3 per share and the potential stock dividend will be ten percent.

Required
Compute the Fango Company retained earnings balance after

a. A $3 per share cash dividend
b. A ten percent stock dividend

RETAINED EARNINGS AND THE STATEMENT OF STOCKHOLDER'S EQUITY

LO8 **Illustrate** the statement of retained earnings and the statement of stockholders' equity.

A **statement of retained earnings** presents an analysis of the Retained Earnings account for a given accounting period. An example of a statement of retained earnings is presented in **Exhibit 11-3**. The statement begins with the retained earnings balance as of the beginning of the period ❶, then reports the items that caused retained earnings to change during the period ❷, and ends with the end-of-period balance in retained earnings ❸.

EXHIBIT 11-3	Statement of Retained Earnings
	GEYSER CORPORATION **Statement of Retained Earnings** **For Year Ended December 31, 2016**

❶	Retained earnings, January 1, 2016..........................	$48,000
❷	Add: Net income	32,000
		80,000
	Less: Cash dividends declared	19,000
❸	Retained earnings, December 31, 2016......................	$61,000

---

[2] A stock's par value or stated value per share is not changed by a stock dividend. However, a stock split reduces the par value or stated value in proportion to the increase in the number of shares issued. This difference leads to a difference in accounting treatment—only a memorandum entry is made for a stock split, whereas a large stock dividend requires a journal entry to transfer the legal capital of the shares to be issued from retained earnings to common stock.

Statement of Stockholders' Equity

Rather than reporting a statement of retained earnings, most corporations integrate the information regarding retained earnings into a more comprehensive statement called a **statement of stockholders' equity**. This statement shows an analysis of all of the stockholders' equity accounts for the period. **Exhibit 11-4** presents an example of a statement of stockholders' equity. The statement begins with the beginning balances of the various stockholders' equity accounts ❶, reports the items causing changes in these accounts ❷, and ends with the end-of-period balances ❸.

The statement of stockholders' equity in **Exhibit 11-4** reveals all of the events affecting the Geyser Corporation's stockholders' equity during 2016. These events are the earning of net income, the issuance of common stock, the issuance of treasury stock, the declaration of a cash dividend, and the acquisition of treasury stock. Note that the information in the retained earnings column (highlighted using a dotted red box) contains the same information as a statement of retained earnings.

EXHIBIT 11-4	Statement of Stockholders' Equity

GEYSER CORPORATION
Statement of Stockholders' Equity
For Year Ended December 31, 2016

		Common Stock	Paid-in Capital in Excess of Par Value	Paid-in Capital from Treasury Stock	Retained Earnings	Treasury Stock	Total
❶	Balance, January 1, 2016.......	$200,000	$120,000	$18,000	$48,000	$(14,000)	$372,000
	Net income..................				32,000		32,000
	6,000 Common shares issued ...	30,000	24,000				54,000
❷	500 Treasury shares issued			2,000		3,500	5,500
	Cash dividends declared				(19,000)		(19,000)
	200 Treasury shares acquired ...					(2,000)	(2,000)
❸	Balance, December 31, 2016....	$230,000	$144,000	$20,000	$61,000	$(12,500)	$442,500

IFRS ALERT

There are a number of significant terminology differences between U.S. GAAP and IFRS with respect to the reporting of stockholders' equity:

U.S. GAAP	IFRS
Common stock	Share capital
Paid-in capital in excess of par value	Share premium
Retained earnings	Retained profits
Accumulated other comprehensive income	Other reserve accounts

---

Dior Company had beginning balances at January 1, 2016, of $100,000 Common Stock, $900,000 Paid-in Capital in Excess of Par Value, $50,000 Retained Earnings, and $(10,000) Treasury Stock. Net income for the year was $30,000. Dior paid a cash dividend of $8,000. Dior also issued 1,000 new $1 par value common shares for $15 each.

Required

Prepare a statement of stockholders' equity for the Dior Company for 2016.

YOUR TURN! 11.7

The solution is on page 575.

ANALYZING STOCKHOLDERS' EQUITY

LO9 Define the *return on common stockholders' equity, dividend yield,* and *dividend payout ratio* and **explain** their use.

Return on Common Stockholders' Equity

A financial ratio of particular interest to common stockholders is the return on common stockholders' equity. This ratio measures the overall profitability of the common stockholders' investment in a company. The **return on common stockholders' equity** is calculated as follows:

$$\text{Return on common stockholders' equity} = \frac{(\text{Net income} - \text{Preferred stock dividends})}{\text{Average common stockholders' equity}}$$

By subtracting the preferred stock dividends from net income, the numerator represents the net income available exclusively to the common stockholders. The denominator averages the common stockholders' equity for the year (sum the beginning and ending common stockholders' equity and then divide by 2). If a company has preferred stock outstanding, the common stockholders' equity is calculated by subtracting the preferred stockholders' equity (the sum of the preferred stock par value and the preferred stock paid-in capital in excess of par value) from total stockholders' equity.

To illustrate the calculation of the return on common stockholders' equity, financial data from **Johnson Controls, Inc.,** is used. Johnson Controls manufactures automotive heating systems, environmental control systems, automotive batteries, and plastic packaging. The company's 2014 financial data are as follows (in millions of dollars):

Net income.	$ 1,215
Preferred stock dividends	0
Preferred stockholders' equity, beginning of year	0
Preferred stockholders' equity, end of year.	0
Common stockholders' equity, beginning of year	12,314
Common stockholders' equity, end of year	11,311

Johnson Controls' return on common stockholders' equity for the year is 10.3 percent, calculated as ($1,215 − $0)/[($12,314 + $11,311)/2].

TAKEAWAY 11.1	Concept ⟶	Method ⟶	Assessment
	How profitable is the stockholders' investment in a company?	Statement of stockholders' equity and the income statement. Calculate the return on common stockholders' equity.	The higher the return on common stockholders' equity, the higher the profitability of the stockholders' investment in a business.

Dividend Yield and Dividend Payout Ratio

Investors differ in their expectations regarding their investments—some investors are primarily interested in appreciation in the market value of their shares, while other investors focus on receiving current income in the form of dividends. Dividend yield and dividend payout ratio are ratios that are helpful to this latter group of investors.

Dividend Yield
Dividend yield measures the current rate of return in cash dividends from an investment in a company's shares. The ratio may be calculated for either common or preferred shares,

and is calculated by dividing the latest annual dividend per share by the current market price of the stock:

$$\text{Dividend yield} = \frac{\text{Annual dividend per share}}{\text{Market price per share}}$$

To illustrate, **Worthington Industries**, a manufacturer of steel and plastic products, declared cash dividends per common share of $0.61. At its fiscal year-end, Worthington's common stock had a market price of $13.99 per share. Consequently, at year-end, the company's dividend yield was 4.4 percent, or $0.61/$13.99.

Dividend yields are included in the stock tables published in *The Wall Street Journal* and *Barrons,* as well as online resources such as Yahoo! Finance, so it is easy for investors to compare current dividend yields for different stocks. The following are dividend yields for several well-known companies:

The Coca-Cola Company	2.9 percent
AT&T	5.4 percent
IBM Corporation	2.7 percent
J.C. Penney Company	0 percent
Chevron Corp.	3.8 percent
Wal-Mart Stores, Inc.	2.2 percent

Concept	Method	Assessment	TAKEAWAY 11.2
What is a company's current rate of return to stockholders in the form of dividends?	Statement of stockholders' equity and a company's current market price per share. Calculate the company's dividend yield by dividing the annual dividend per share by the company's market price per share.	The higher a company's dividend yield, the greater the rate of return to stockholders in the form of dividends.	

Dividend Payout Ratio

The **dividend payout ratio** measures the percentage of net income available to common stockholders that is paid out as dividends. The ratio is calculated as follows:

$$\text{Dividend payout ratio} = \frac{\text{Annual dividend per share}}{\text{Earnings per share}}$$

Dividend payout ratios vary considerably among corporations. Companies that are considered "growth" companies often have low payout ratios because they use the net income generated by operations to help finance their growth. By way of contrast, "mature" companies that lack significant growth opportunities often distribute a high percentage of their net income as dividends. A good example of a mature company is the local utility company whose growth is limited by the net increase of new homes and businesses in the community and the approved rate increases by the local public utility commission.

Some corporations try to maintain a reasonably stable dividend payout ratio, so their payout ratios do not vary much from one year to the next. Other corporations try to keep their dividend per share either constant or increasing each year at a constant rate. If net income fluctuates quite a bit from year to year, these latter corporations will show dividend payout ratios that are quite variable over time. However, no company likes to cut their dividend per share because of the negative signal it sends to stockholders.

The following are the dividend payout ratios for some well-known corporations:

Best Buy Co. Inc. (retail)	24 percent
Microsoft Corporation (technology).	46 percent
Procter & Gamble Co. (consumer goods)	77 percent

YOUR TURN! 11.8

The solution is on page 575.

Century Co. reports the following information for the current year:

Net income.	$150,000
Preferred stock dividends	15,000
Beginning of year common stockholders' equity.	650,000
End of year common stockholders' equity.	700,000
Annual common dividend per share	0.75
Market price of common shares	33.00
Earnings per common share	3.00

Calculate Century's (a) return on common stockholders' equity; (b) dividend yield; and (c) dividend payout ratio.

TAKEAWAY 11.3	Concept	→ Method	→ Assessment
	What percentage of a company's net income is paid out to stockholders as a dividend?	Statement of stockholders' equity and the income statement. Calculate the dividend payout ratio by dividing the annual dividend per share by a company's earnings per share.	The higher the dividend payout ratio, the higher the percentage of net income paid to stockholders as a dividend.

COMPREHENSIVE PROBLEM

Following is the stockholders' equity section of Bayside Corporation's December 31 balance sheet:

Paid-in Capital		
7 Percent preferred stock, $50 par value, 5,000 shares authorized, issued, and outstanding	$ 250,000	
Common stock, $6 par value, 700,000 shares authorized; 200,000 issued, of which 10,000 shares are in the treasury	1,200,000	$1,450,000
Additional Paid-in Capital		
In excess of par value—Preferred stock.	80,000	
In excess of par value—Common stock.	1,000,000	
From treasury stock	22,000	1,102,000
Total Paid-in Capital		2,552,000
Retained earnings.		2,223,000
		4,775,000
Less: Treasury stock (10,000 common shares) at cost		140,000
Total Stockholders' Equity		$4,635,000

Required

a. What is Bayside's legal capital at December 31?

b. What is the number of common shares outstanding at December 31?

c. What is the average amount per share received from the original issuance of common stock?

d. Assuming that the preferred stock is cumulative with no dividends in arrears, what total dollar amount of preferred dividends needs to be declared at December 31, before the common stockholders may receive a dividend?

e. Has Bayside ever sold treasury stock for more than the treasury stock cost when it was acquired? Briefly explain.

f. Assume that Bayside splits its common stock 3-for-1 on the following January 1. What is the total amount of paid-in capital immediately after the split?

Solution

a. $1,450,000 (the par value of the issued preferred stock and common stock).

b. 190,000 shares (200,000 issued common shares less 10,000 shares in the treasury).

c. $11 [($1,200,000 par value of issued shares + $1,000,000 paid-in capital in excess of par value)/200,000 issued shares].

d. $17,500 (7 percent × $250,000).

e. Yes, the stockholders' equity section shows additional paid-in capital of $22,000 from treasury stock. This type of paid-in capital represents the excess of proceeds from the sale of treasury stock over that treasury stock's cost.

f. $2,552,000 (splitting the common stock does not change any of the account balances composing paid in capital; the common stock's par value will decrease to $2 per share, and the common shares issued will increase to 600,000).

SUMMARY OF LEARNING OBJECTIVES

Define the corporate form of organization and discuss its principal characteristics. (p. 530)   **LO1**

- A corporation is a separate legal entity chartered by the state in which it is formed.

- The liability of corporate stockholders for the debts of a business is limited to the value of their ownership interest in a corporation, whereas claims against partners and sole proprietors may extend to their personal resources.

- Unlike sole proprietorships and partnerships, corporations must report paid-in capital separately from the accumulated balance of retained earnings. Distributions to stockholders are limited by the amount of retained earnings and other capital as specified by state law.

Explain the difference between par value stock and no-par value stock. (p. 533)   **LO2**

- Par value is the face value printed on a stock certificate. It has no economic significance but may have legal significance.

- No-par value stock has no face value printed on the stock certificate, although generally the board of directors sets a stated value for a corporation's capital stock.

Identify and discuss the two types of capital stock and their respective stockholder rights. (p. 534)   **LO3**

- Common stock represents a corporation's basic ownership class of stock; common shares carry the right to vote and may or may not pay a dividend.

- Preferred stock may differ from common stock in several ways. Typically, preferred stock has, at a minimum, some type of dividend preference and a prior claim to assets in the event of a corporate liquidation, relative to common stock.

Describe the accounting for issuances of capital stock. (p. 538)   **LO4**

- When capital stock is issued, the appropriate capital stock account is credited with the par value or stated value of the shares issued. The asset exchanged for the stock (usually cash) is debited for its fair value. Any difference is placed in the Paid-in Capital in Excess of Par Value account.

Define and discuss the accounting for stock splits. (p. 540)   **LO5**

- Stock splits change the par or stated value of capital stock and affect the number of shares outstanding. Only a memorandum notation records stock splits in the general journal. Forward stock splits increase the number of shares outstanding and lower its par or stated value, while reverse stock splits do the opposite.

LO6 **Explain the accounting for treasury stock. (p. 540)**

- Treasury stock represents reacquired shares of a firm's capital stock. It is commonly recorded at its acquisition cost and is deducted from total stockholders' equity on the balance sheet.

LO7 **Identify and distinguish between cash dividends and stock dividends. (p. 542)**

- Cash dividends reduce retained earnings and are a current liability when declared.
- Stock dividends are accounted for by a transfer of retained earnings to the appropriate capital stock and paid-in capital accounts at the fair market value of the shares distributed for small stock dividends and at par value for large stock dividends.

LO8 **Illustrate the statement of retained earnings and the statement of stockholders' equity. (p. 546)**

- A statement of retained earnings presents the financial effect of events causing retained earnings to change during an accounting period.
- A statement of stockholders' equity presents the financial effect of events causing each component of stockholders' equity (including retained earnings) to change during an accounting period.

LO9 **Define the *return on common stockholders' equity, dividend yield,* and *dividend payout ratio* and explain their use. (p. 548)**

- The return on common stockholders' equity is computed as (net income − preferred stock dividends)/ average common stockholders' equity. It indicates the profitability of the common stockholders' investment in a company.
- Dividend yield is computed by dividing a stock's annual dividend per share by its current market price per share. For investors, this ratio identifies the annual rate of return in dividends from an investment in a company's shares.
- The dividend payout ratio is computed by dividing the annual dividend per share by a company's earnings per share.

SUMMARY	Concept ⟶	Method ⟶	Assessment
TAKEAWAY 11.1	How profitable is the stockholders' investment in a company?	Statement of stockholders' equity and the income statement. Calculate the return on common stockholders' equity.	The higher the return on common stockholders' equity, the higher the profitability of the stockholders' investment in a business.
TAKEAWAY 11.2	What is a company's current rate of return to stockholders in the form of dividends?	Statement of stockholders' equity and a company's current market price per share. Calculate the company's dividend yield by dividing the annual dividend per share by the company's market price per share.	The higher a company's dividend yield, the greater the rate of return to stockholders in the form of dividends.
TAKEAWAY 11.3	What percentage of a company's net income is paid out to stockholders as a dividend?	Statement of stockholders' equity and the income statement. Calculate the dividend payout ratio by dividing the annual dividend per share by a company's earnings per share.	The higher the dividend payout ratio, the higher the percentage of net income paid to stockholders as a dividend.

KEY TERMS

Articles of
  incorporation (p. 530)
Authorized shares (p. 534)
Callable (p. 537)
Cash dividend (p. 543)
Common stock (p. 534)
Convertible (p. 536)
Corporation (p. 530)
Cumulative (p. 536)
Dividend payout ratio (p. 549)
Dividends (p. 542)

Dividend yield (p. 548)
Forward stock split (p. 540)
Issued shares (p. 534)
Noncumulative (p. 536)
No-par value stock (p. 534)
Outstanding shares (p. 534)
Paid-in capital (p. 539)
Participating (p. 537)
Par value (p. 533)
Preemptive right (p. 535)
Preferred stock (p. 535)

Retained earnings (p. 539)
Return on common
  stockholders' equity (p. 548)
Reverse stock split (p. 540)
Stated value (p. 534)
Statement of retained
  earnings (p. 546)
Statement of stockholders'
  equity (p. 547)
Stock dividends (p. 544)
Treasury stock (p. 534, 540)

Assignments with the ⓂⒷⒸ logo in the margin are available in Ⓜⓨ BusinessCourse.
See the Preface of the book for details.

SELF-STUDY QUESTIONS

(Answers to the Self-Study Questions are available at the end of this chapter.)

1. **What is the usual liability of stockholders for corporation actions?**   **LO1**
   a. Unlimited
   b. Limited to the par value or stated value of the shares of stock they hold
   c. Limited to the amount of their investment in the corporation
   d. Limited to the amount of a corporation's retained earnings

2. **Which type of stock may have dividends in arrears?**   **LO3**
   a. Cumulative preferred stock
   b. Common stock
   c. Noncumulative preferred stock
   d. Treasury stock

3. **Wyler Company issued 20,000 shares of $10 par value common stock in exchange for a building**   **LO4**
   with a current fair value of $1,000,000. In recording this transaction, what amount should be
   credited to the Paid-in Capital in Excess of Par Value account?
   a. $1,000,000   c. $800,000
   b. $200,000   d. $980,000

4. **Which of the following accounts has a normal debit balance?**   **LO6**
   a. Common Stock
   b. Paid-in Capital in Excess of Stated Value
   c. Preferred Stock
   d. Treasury Stock

5. **Which of the following events decreases a corporation's stockholders' equity?**   **LO7**
   a. A payment of a previously declared cash dividend
   b. A declaration of a six percent stock dividend
   c. A 2-for-1 forward stock split
   d. A declaration of a $1 cash dividend per share on preferred stock

6. **When a company wants to reduce the market price per share of its stock, what action should it**   **LO5**
   take?
   a. Issue a cash dividend
   b. Issue a stock dividend
   c. Do a reverse stock split
   d. Do a forward stock split

7. **What type of company is typically characterized by a high dividend payout ratio?**   **LO9**
   a. Technology company
   b. High-growth company
   c. Mature, low-growth company
   d. All of the above

LO3

8. Preferred stock that may be converted into common stock has which of the following characteristics?
- *a.* Call feature
- *b.* Cumulative feature
- *c.* Participation feature
- *d.* Convertible feature

LO7

9. A dividend that is paid every quarter or every year is called?
- *a.* Regular dividend
- *b.* Special dividend
- *c.* Property dividend
- *d.* Stock dividend

LO8

10. The statement of stockholders' equity includes each of the following except:
- *a.* Retained Earning
- *b.* Treasury Stock
- *c.* Paid-in Capital in Excess of Par Value
- *d.* Accounts Receivable

QUESTIONS

1. What is the meaning of each of the following terms: *corporation, articles of incorporation, corporate charter, board of directors, corporate officers,* and *organization costs*?

2. What is meant by the limited liability of a stockholder? Does this characteristic enhance or reduce a corporation's ability to raise capital?

3. Contrast the federal income taxation of a corporation with that of a sole proprietorship and a partnership. Which of the three types of organizations must file a federal income tax return?

4. Define *par value stock*. What is the significance of a stock's par value?

5. What is the preemptive right of a stockholder?

6. What are the basic differences between preferred stock and common stock? What are the typical features of preferred stock?

7. What features make preferred stock similar to debt? What features make it similar to common stock?

8. What is meant by dividends in arrears? If dividends are two years in arrears on $500,000 of six percent preferred stock and dividends are declared this year, what amount of total dividends must preferred stockholders receive before any distributions can be made to common stockholders?

9. Distinguish between authorized shares and issued shares. Why might the number of shares issued be more than the number of shares outstanding?

10. What are the different sources of paid-in capital?

11. Define a *forward stock split*. What is the major reason for a forward stock split?

12. Define *treasury stock*. Why might a corporation acquire treasury stock? How is treasury stock shown on the balance sheet?

13. If a corporation purchases 600 shares of its own common stock at $10 per share and resells the shares at $14 per share, where would the $2,400 [($14 − $10) × 600 shares] increase in capital appear in the financial statements? Why is no gain reported?

14. Assume that a corporation has preferred shares outstanding. How is the return on common stockholders' equity computed?

15. What is a stock dividend? How does a common stock dividend paid to common stockholders affect their respective ownership interests?

16. What is the difference between the accounting for a small stock dividend and the accounting for a large stock dividend?

17. What information is presented in a statement of retained earnings? What information is presented in a statement of stockholders' equity?

18. Where do the following accounts (and their balances) appear in the balance sheet?
   - *a.* Dividends Payable—Common Stock
   - *b.* Stock Dividend Distributable

19. How is a corporation's dividend yield calculated?

20. Bleaker Company declares and pays its annual dividend near the end of its fiscal year. For the current year, Bleaker's dividend payout ratio was 40 percent, its earnings per common share were $5.80, and it had 50,000 shares of common stock outstanding all year. What total amount of dividends did Bleaker declare and pay in the current year?

SHORT EXERCISES

SE11-1. **Issuance of Common Stock** Smith & Sons, Inc., is authorized to issue one million shares of $1 par value common stock. In the company's initial public offering, 500,000 shares are sold to the investing public at a price of $5 per share. One month following Smith & Sons' initial public offering, 1,000 of its common shares were sold by one investor to another at a price of $10 per share. How should this transaction be recorded in the accounts of Smith & Sons? Why?   **LO1**

SE11-2. **Issuance of No-Par Common Stock** Jackson & Company issued 100,000 shares of $1 par value common stock at a price of $5 per share and issued 10,000 shares of no-par value common stock at a price of $10 per share. Prepare the journal entry to record the issuance of the no-par value common stock. How does this entry differ from the entry to record the $1 par value common stock?   **LO2**

SE11-3. **Allocating Liquidation Between Common Stockholders and Preferred Stockholders** The Arcadia Company is liquidating. After paying off all of its creditors, the company has $1 million to distribute between its preferred stockholders and its common stockholders. The aggregate par value of the preferred stock is $900,000 and the aggregate par value of its common stock is $2 million. How much of the remaining $1 million in assets should be distributed to the preferred stockholders and how much should be distributed to the common stockholders?   **LO3**

SE11-4. **Issuance of Common Stock** Smith & Sons, Inc., is authorized to issue one million shares of $1 par value common stock. The company actually sells 500,000 shares at $10 per share. Prepare the journal entry to record the issuance of the 500,000 shares.   **LO4**

SE11-5. **Outstanding Shares** Pearce & Company has 10 million shares of $2 par value common stock outstanding. The company believes that its current market price of $100 per share is too high and decides to execute a 4-for-1 forward stock split to lower the price. How many shares will be outstanding following the stock split, and what will be the new par value per share?   **LO5**

SE11-6. **Treasury Stock Purchase** Jackson & Company has no-par value common stock outstanding that is selling at $20 per share. The company's CEO believes that the stock price is undervalued and decides to buy back 10,000 shares. Prepare the journal entry to record the purchase of the treasury stock.   **LO6**

SE11-7. **Dividends Paid and Dividends in Arrears** The Arcadia Company has 100,000 shares of cumulative, six percent, $100 par value preferred stock outstanding. Last year the company failed to pay its regular dividend, but the board of directors would like to resume paying its regular dividend this year. Calculate the dividends in arrears and the total dividend that must be paid this year.   **LO7**

The following information relates to SE11-8 through SE11-10:

Smith & Sons, Inc., disclosed the following information in a recent annual report:

	2015	2016
Net income.	$ 35,000	$ 55,000
Preferred stock dividends	3,000	3,000
Average common stockholders' equity	1,200,000	1,500,000
Dividend per common share	1.20	1.20
Earnings per share	1.90	2.05
Market price per common share, year-end	19.50	21.00

SE11-8. **Return on Common Stockholders' Equity** Calculate the return on common stockholders' equity for Smith & Sons for 2015 and 2016. Did the return improve from 2015 to 2016?   **LO9**

LO9   **SE11-9.**   **Dividend Yield** Calculate the dividend yield for Smith & Sons for 2015 and 2016. Did the dividend yield improve from 2015 to 2016?

LO9   **SE11-10.**   **Dividend Payout Ratio** Calculate the dividend payout for Smith & Sons for 2015 and 2016. Did the dividend payout increase from 2015 to 2016?

LO8   **SE11-11.**   **Change in Stockholders' Equity** Nikron Corporation issued 10,000 shares of $0.50 par value common stock during the year for $20 each. Nikron also repurchased treasury stock for $15,000. Net income for the year was $120,000. The company also paid cash dividends of $25,000. What was the total change in Nikron's stockholders' equity for the year?

EXERCISES—SET A

LO7   **E11-1A.**   **Dividend Distribution** Lakeside Company has the following shares outstanding: 20,000 shares of $50 par value, six percent cumulative preferred stock and 80,000 shares of $10 par value common stock. The company declared cash dividends amounting to $160,000.

  a.   If no dividends in arrears on the preferred stock exist, how much in total dividends, and in dividends per share, is paid to each class of stock?

  b.   If one year of dividends in arrears exist on the preferred stock, how much in total dividends, and in dividends per share, is paid to each class of stock?

LO4   **E11-2A.**   **Share Issuances for Cash** Finlay, Inc., issued 9,000 shares of $50 par value preferred stock at $68 per share and 12,000 shares of no-par value common stock at $12 per share. The common stock has no stated value. All issuances were for cash.

  a.   Prepare the journal entries to record the share issuances.

  b.   Prepare the journal entry for the issuance of the common stock assuming that it had a stated value of $5 per share.

  c.   Prepare the journal entry for the issuance of the common stock assuming that it had a par value of $1 per share.

LO5   **E11-3A.**   **Forward Stock Split** On March 1 of the current year, Sentry Corporation has 500,000 shares of $20 par value common stock that are issued and outstanding. The general ledger shows the following account balances relating to the common stock:

Common stock.	$10,000,000
Paid-in capital in excess of par value.	3,400,000

On March 2, Sentry Corporation splits its stock 2-for-1 and reduces the par value to $10 per share.

  a.   How many shares of common stock are issued and outstanding immediately following the stock split?

  b.   What is the balance in the Common Stock account immediately following the stock split?

  c.   What is the balance in the Paid-in Capital in Excess of Par Value account immediately following the stock split?

  d.   Is a journal entry required to record the forward stock split? If yes, prepare the entry.

LO4, 6   **E11-4A.**   **Treasury Stock** Coastal Corporation issued 25,000 shares of $5 par value common stock at $15 per share and 6,000 shares of $50 par value, eight percent preferred stock at $85 per share. Later, the company purchased 3,000 shares of its own common stock at $20 per share.

  a.   Prepare the journal entries to record the share issuances and the purchase of the common shares.

  b.   Assume that Coastal sold 2,000 shares of the treasury stock at $25 per share. Prepare the general journal entry to record the sale of this treasury stock.

  c.   Assume that Coastal sold the remaining 1,000 shares of treasury stock at $18 per share. Prepare the journal entry to record the sale of this treasury stock.

LO7   **E11-5A.**   **Cash Dividends** Sanders Corporation has the following shares outstanding: 7,000 shares of $50 par value, six percent preferred stock and 45,000 shares of $1 par value common stock. The company has $328,000 of retained earnings. At year-end, the company declares its regular $3 per share cash dividend on the preferred stock and a $2.20 per share cash dividend on the common stock. Three weeks later, the company pays the dividends.

a. Prepare the journal entry for the declaration of the cash dividends.

b. Prepare the journal entry for the payment of the cash dividends.

E11-6A. Stock Dividends Witt Corporation has 70,000 shares of $5 par value common stock outstanding. At year-end, the company declares a five percent stock dividend. The market price of the stock on the declaration date is $21 per share. Four weeks later, the company issues the shares of stock to stockholders.

LO7

a. Prepare the journal entry for the declaration of the stock dividend.

b. Prepare the journal entry for the issuance of the stock dividend.

c. Assume that the company declared a 30 percent stock dividend rather than a five percent stock dividend. Prepare the journal entries for (1) the declaration of the stock dividend and (2) the issuance of the stock dividend.

E11-7A. Statement of Retained Earnings Use the following data to prepare a statement of retained earnings for Shepler Corporation.

LO8

Total retained earnings originally reported at January 1	$350,000
Cash dividends declared during the year	75,000
Net income for the year	193,000
Stock dividend declared during the year	40,000

E11-8A. Conversion of Preferred Stock into Common Stock Smith & Sons, Inc., has 15,000 shares of $100 par value, six percent preferred stock and 80,000 shares of $1.00 par value common stock outstanding. The preferred stock is convertible into the company's common stock at a conversion rate of 1-to-20; that is, each share of preferred stock is convertible into 20 shares of common stock. The preferred stock had been sold for its par value when issued. Prepare the journal entry to record the conversion of all of the company's preferred stock into common stock.

LO3

E11-9A. Reverse Stock Split Titanium Metals Company had 20,000,000 shares of $0.01 par value common stock outstanding which had been sold for an aggregate amount of $300,000,000. The company's shares are traded on the New York Stock Exchange, which has a minimum listing price of $1 per share. Recently, the company's common stock has been trading on the exchange below $1 per share, and the exchange has notified the company that its common stock would be delisted in 30 days if the stock price did not rebound above its minimum listing price. In response to this notification, Titanium Metals authorized a 1-for-20 reverse stock split. Following the reverse stock split:

LO5

a. How many common shares will be outstanding?

b. What will be the new par value per share?

c. How will the reverse stock split be recorded in the company's accounts?

E11-10A. Return on Common Stockholders' Equity, Dividend Yield, and Dividend Payout The following information relates to Waterloo Components, Inc.:

LO9

	2015	2016
Net income	$ 65,000	$ 80,000
Preferred stock dividends	5,000	5,000
Average common stockholders' equity	2,000,000	2,100,000
Dividend per common share	1.40	1.50
Earnings per share	2.90	2.95
Market price per common share, year-end	27.50	30.00

a. Calculate the company's return on common stockholders' equity for 2015 and 2016.

b. Calculate the company's dividend yield for 2015 and 2016.

c. Calculate the company's dividend payout for 2015 and 2016.

E11-11A. Characteristics of a Corporation Label each of the following characteristics of a corporation as either an (A) advantage, or a (D) disadvantage:

LO1

a. Limited liability

    b.   Taxation

    c.   Regulations

    d.   Transferability of ownership

LO4   **E11-12A. Cash and Noncash Share Issuances** Guild Corporation was organized on June 1. The company's charter authorizes 500,000 shares of $5 par value common stock. On July 1, the attorney who helped organize the corporation accepted 600 shares of Guild common stock in settlement for the services provided (the services were valued at $7,600). On July 15, Guild issued 5,000 common shares for $65,000 cash. On September 15, Guild issued 2,000 common shares to acquire a vacant land site appraised at $28,000. Prepare the journal entries to record the stock issuances on July 1, July 15, and September 15.

LO4, 6   **E11-13A. Stock Issuance and Treasury Stock** Century, Inc., recorded certain capital stock transactions shown in the following journal entries: (1) issued common stock for $20 cash per share, (2) purchased treasury shares at $25 per share, and (3) sold some of the treasury shares:

1.	Cash	500,000	
	Common stock		75,000
	Paid-in capital in excess of par value		425,000
2.	Treasury stock	100,000	
	Cash		100,000
3.	Cash	81,000	
	Treasury stock		75,000
	Paid-in capital from treasury stock		6,000

    a.   How many shares were originally issued?

    b.   What was the par value of the shares issued?

    c.   How many shares of treasury stock were acquired?

    d.   How many shares of treasury stock were sold?

    e.   At what price per share was the treasury stock sold?

LO7   **E11-14A. Cash and Stock Dividends** Debra Corporation has 30,000 shares of $1 par value common stock outstanding. The company has $250,000 of retained earnings. At year-end, the company declares a cash dividend of $2.00 per share and a five percent stock dividend. The market price of the stock at the declaration date is $30 per share. Three weeks later, the company pays the dividends.

    a.   Prepare the journal entry for the declaration of the cash dividend.

    b.   Prepare the journal entry for the declaration of the stock dividend.

    c.   Prepare the journal entry for the payment of the cash dividend.

    d.   Prepare the journal entry for the payment of the stock dividend.

LO5, 7   **E11-15A. Large Stock Dividend and Forward Stock Split** Low Corporation has 50,000 shares of $20 par value common stock outstanding and retained earnings of $750,000. The company declares a 100 percent stock dividend. The market price at the declaration date is $20 per share.

    a.   Prepare the journal entries for (1) the declaration of the dividend and (2) the issuance of the dividend.

    b.   Assume that the company splits its stock 2-for-1 and reduces the par value from $20 to $10 rather than declaring a 100 percent stock dividend. How does the accounting for the forward stock split differ from the accounting for the 100 percent stock dividend?

EXERCISES—SET B

LO7   **E11-1B. Dividend Distribution** Bower Corporation has the following shares outstanding: 15,000 shares of $50 par value, eight percent preferred stock and 50,000 shares of $5 par value common stock. During its first three years in business, the firm declared no dividends in the first year, $280,000 of dividends in the second year, and $60,000 of dividends in the third year.

    a.   If the preferred stock is cumulative, determine the total amount of dividends paid to each class of stock in each of the three years.

    b.   If the preferred stock is noncumulative, determine the total amount of dividends paid to each class of stock in each of the three years.

E11-2B.   Share Issuances for Cash Henlay, Inc., issued 10,000 shares of $20 par value preferred stock at   **LO4**
$48 per share and 8,000 shares of no-par value common stock at $15 per share. The common stock
has no stated value. All issuances were for cash.

   a.   Prepare the journal entries to record the share issuances.
   b.   Prepare the journal entry for the issuance of the common stock assuming that it had a stated
value of $10 per share.
   c.   Prepare the journal entry for the issuance of the common stock assuming that it had a par value
of $2 per share.

E11-3B.   Forward Stock Split On September 1, Oxford Company has 400,000 shares of $15 par value com-   **LO5**
mon stock that are issued and outstanding. The general ledger shows the following account balances
relating to the common stock:

Common stock.	$6,000,000
Paid-in capital in excess of par value.	$2,250,000

On September 2, Oxford splits its stock 3-for-2 and reduces the par value to $10 per share.

   a.   How many shares of common stock are issued and outstanding immediately following the stock
split?
   b.   What is the balance in the Common Stock account immediately following the stock split?
   c.   What is the likely reason that Oxford Company split its stock?

E11-4B.   Treasury Stock Inland Corporation issued 50,000 shares of $3 par value common stock at $21   **LO4, 6**
per share and 9,000 shares of $30 par value, ten percent preferred stock at $85 per share. Later, the
company purchased 2,000 shares of its own common stock at $23 per share.

   a.   Prepare the journal entries to record the share issuances and the purchase of the common shares.
   b.   Assume that Inland sold 1,500 shares of the treasury stock at $28 per share. Prepare the general
journal entry to record the sale of this treasury stock.
   c.   Assume that Inland sold the remaining 500 shares of treasury stock at $20 per share. Prepare the
journal entry to record the sale of this treasury stock.

E11-5B.   Cash Dividends Rock Corporation has the following shares outstanding: 8,000 shares of $40 par   **LO7**
value, ten percent preferred stock and 50,000 shares of $2 par value common stock. The company
has $428,000 of retained earnings. At year-end, the company declares its regular $4 per share cash
dividend on the preferred stock and a $3.20 per share cash dividend on the common stock. Two
weeks later, the company pays the dividends.

   a.   Prepare the journal entry for the declaration of the cash dividends.
   b.   Prepare the journal entry for the payment of the cash dividends.

E11-6B.   Stock Dividends Litt Corporation has 90,000 shares of $10 par value common stock outstanding. At   **LO7**
year-end, the company declares a five percent stock dividend. The market price of the stock on the declaration date is $25 per share. Three weeks later, the company issues the shares of stock to stockholders.

   a.   Prepare the journal entry for the declaration of the stock dividend.
   b.   Prepare the journal entry for the issuance of the stock dividend.
   c.   Assume that the company declared a 50 percent stock dividend rather than a five percent stock
dividend. Prepare the journal entries for (1) the declaration of the stock dividend and (2) the
issuance of the stock dividend.

E11-7B.   Statement of Retained Earnings Use the following data to prepare a statement of retained earn-   **LO8**
ings for Schauer Corporation.

Total retained earnings originally reported as of January 1.	$347,000
Stock dividends declared during the year	15,000
Cash dividends declared during the year.	40,000
Net income for the year	65,000

E11-8B.   Conversion of Preferred Stock into Common Stock Groff & Sons, Inc., has 20,000 shares of   **LO3**
$50 par value, nine percent preferred stock and 100,000 shares of $0.50 par value common stock

outstanding. The preferred stock is convertible into the company's common stock at a conversion rate of 1-to-50; that is, each share of preferred stock is convertible into 50 shares of common stock. The preferred stock had been sold for its par value when issued. Prepare the journal entry to record the conversion of all of the company's preferred stock into common stock.

LO5   **E11-9B.**   **Reverse Stock Split**   The Waterford Company had 50,000,000 shares of $0.10 par value common stock outstanding which had been sold for an aggregate amount of $500,000,000. The company's shares are traded on the New York Stock Exchange, which has a minimum listing price of $1 per share. Recently, the company's common stock has been trading on the exchange below $1 per share, and the exchange has notified the company that its common stock would be delisted in 30 days if the stock price did not rebound above its minimum listing price. In response to this notification, Waterford authorized a 1-for-40 reverse stock split. Following the reverse stock split:

    a.   How many common shares will be outstanding?
    b.   What will be the new par value per share?
    c.   How will the reverse stock split be recorded in the company's accounts?

LO9   **E11-10B.**   **Return on Common Stockholders' Equity, Dividend Yield, and Dividend Payout**   The following information relates to Litchfield, Inc.:

	2015	2016
Net income.	$ 125,000	$ 150,000
Preferred stock dividends	15,000	18,000
Average common stockholders' equity	4,000,000	4,200,000
Dividend per common share	2.80	3.20
Earnings per share	5.80	6.00
Market price per common share, year-end	58.00	59.50

    a.   Calculate the company's return on common stockholders' equity for 2015 and 2016.
    b.   Calculate the company's dividend yield for 2015 and 2016.
    c.   Calculate the company's dividend payout for 2015 and 2016.

LO1   **E11-11B.**   **Characteristics of a Corporation**   Label each of the following characteristics of a corporation as either an (A) advantage, or a (D) disadvantage:

    a.   Organizational costs
    b.   Continuity of existence
    c.   Capital raising capability
    d.   Separate legal entity

LO4   **E11-12B.**   **Cash and Noncash Share Issuances**   Chavoy Corporation was organized on July 1. The company's charter authorizes 100,000 shares of $1 par value common stock. On August 1, the attorney who helped organize the corporation accepted 950 shares of Chavoy common stock in settlement for the services provided (the services were valued at $9,800). On August 15, Chavoy issued 6,000 common shares for $75,000 cash. On October 15, Chavoy issued 3,000 common shares to acquire a vacant land site appraised at $50,000. Prepare the journal entries to record the stock issuances on August 1, August 15, and October 15.

LO4, 6   **E11-13B.**   **Stock Issuance and Treasury Stock**   Diva, Inc., recorded certain capital stock transactions shown in the following journal entries: (1) issued common stock for $20 cash per share, (2) purchased treasury shares at $25 per share, and (3) sold some of the treasury shares:

1.	Cash	437,000	
	Common stock		43,700
	Paid-in capital in excess of par value		393,300
2.	Treasury stock	77,000	
	Cash		77,000
3.	Cash	63,360	
	Treasury stock		52,800
	Paid-in capital from treasury stock		10,560

a. How many shares were originally issued?
b. What was the par value of the shares issued?
c. How many shares of treasury stock were acquired?
d. How many shares of treasury stock were sold?
e. At what price per share was the treasury stock sold?

E11-14B. Cash and Stock Dividends Mandrich Corporation has 25,000 shares of $10 par value common stock outstanding. The company has $450,000 of retained earnings. At year-end, the company declares a cash dividend of $2.10 per share and a five percent stock dividend. The market price of the stock at the declaration date is $35 per share. Four weeks later, the company pays the dividends.   **LO7**

a. Prepare the journal entry for the declaration of the cash dividend.
b. Prepare the journal entry for the declaration of the stock dividend.
c. Prepare the journal entry for the payment of the cash dividend.
d. Prepare the journal entry for the payment of the stock dividend.

E11-15B. Large Stock Dividend and Forward Stock Split Key Corporation has 50,000 shares of $10 par value common stock outstanding and retained earnings of $820,000. The company declares a 100 percent stock dividend. The market price at the declaration date is $17 per share.   **LO5, 7**

a. Prepare the journal entries for (1) the declaration of the dividend and (2) the issuance of the dividend.
b. Assume that the company splits its stock 5-for-1 and reduces the par value from $10 to $2 rather than declaring a 100 percent stock dividend. How does the accounting for the forward stock split differ from the accounting for the 100 percent stock dividend?

PROBLEMS—SET A

P11-1A. Dividend Distribution Rydon Corporation began business on March 1, 2013. At that time, it issued 20,000 shares of $60 par value, seven percent cumulative preferred stock and 100,000 shares of $5 par value common stock. Through the end of 2015, there had been no change in the number of preferred and common shares outstanding.   **LO7**

Required
a. Assume that Rydon declared dividends of $0 in 2013, $185,000 in 2014, and $200,000 in 2015. Calculate the total dividends and the dividends per share paid to each class of stock in 2013, 2014, and 2015.
b. Assume that Rydon declared dividends of $0 in 2013, $90,000 in 2014, and $150,000 in 2015. Calculate the total dividends and the dividends per share paid to each class of stock in 2013, 2014, and 2015.

P11-2A. Stockholders' Equity: Transactions and Balance Sheet Presentation Tunic Corporation was organized on April 1, with an authorization of 25,000 shares of six percent, $50 par value preferred stock and 200,000 shares of $5 par value common stock. During April, the following transactions affecting stockholders' equity occurred: **LO4, 8**

Apr. 1 Issued 80,000 shares of common stock at $20 cash per share.
      3 Issued 2,000 shares of common stock to attorneys and promoters in exchange for their services in organizing the corporation. The services were valued at $31,000.
      8 Issued 3,000 shares of common stock in exchange for equipment with a fair market value of $55,000.
     20 Issued 6,000 shares of preferred stock for cash at $60 per share.

Required
a. Prepare journal entries to record the above transactions.
b. Prepare the stockholders' equity section of the balance sheet at April 30. Assume that the net income for April is $51,000.

P11-3A. Stockholders' Equity: Transactions and Balance Sheet Presentation The stockholders' equity accounts of Windham Corporation at January 1 appear below: **LO4, 6**

8 Percent preferred stock, $25 par value, 50,000 shares authorized; 6,800 shares issued and outstanding.	$170,000
Common stock, $10 par value, 200,000 shares authorized; 50,000 shares issued and outstanding.	500,000
Paid-in capital in excess of par value—Preferred stock	68,000
Paid-in capital in excess of par value—Common stock	200,000
Retained earnings	270,000

During the year, the following transactions occurred:

Jan.	10	Issued 35,000 shares of common stock for $17 cash per share.
	23	Purchased 10,000 shares of common stock as treasury stock at $19 per share.
Mar.	14	Sold one-half of the treasury shares acquired January 23 for $21 per share.
July	15	Issued 3,500 shares of preferred stock in exchange for equipment with a fair market value of $128,000.
Nov.	15	Sold 2,000 of the treasury shares acquired January 23 for $24 per share.
Dec.	31	Closed the net income of $59,000 to the Retained Earnings account.

Required

a. Set up T-accounts for the stockholders' equity accounts as of the beginning of the year and enter the January 1 balances.

b. Prepare journal entries to record the foregoing transactions and post to T-accounts (set up any additional T-accounts needed). Do not prepare the journal entry for the Dec. 31 transaction, but post the appropriate amount to the Retained Earnings T-account. Determine the ending balances for the stockholders' equity accounts.

c. Prepare the December 31 stockholders' equity section of the balance sheet.

LO4, 5, 6   **P11-4A.**   **Stockholders' Equity: Transactions and Balance Sheet Presentation** The stockholders' equity of Summit Corporation at January 1 follows:

7 Percent preferred stock, $100 par value, 20,000 shares authorized; 5,000 shares issued and outstanding.	$ 500,000
Common stock, $15 par value, 100,000 shares authorized; 40,000 shares issued and outstanding.	600,000
Paid-in capital in excess of par value—Preferred stock	24,000
Paid-in capital in excess of par value—Common stock	360,000
Retained earnings	325,000
Total Stockholders' Equity	$1,809,000

The following transactions, among others, occurred during the year:

Jan.	12	Announced a 4-for-1 common stock split, reducing the par value of the common stock to $3.75 per share. The authorization was increased to 400,000 shares.
Mar.	31	Converted $40,000 face value of convertible bonds payable (the book value of the bonds was $43,000) to common stock. Each $1,000 bond converted to 125 shares of common stock.
June	1	Acquired equipment with a fair market value of $70,000 in exchange for 500 shares of preferred stock.
Sept.	1	Acquired 10,000 shares of common stock for cash at $10 per share.
Oct.	12	Sold 1,500 treasury shares at $12 per share.
Nov.	21	Issued 5,000 shares of common stock at $11 cash per share.
Dec.	28	Sold 1,200 treasury shares at $9 per share.
	31	Closed net income of $95,000 to the Retained Earnings account.

Required

a. Set up T-accounts for the stockholders' equity accounts as of the beginning of the year and enter the January 1 balances.

b. Prepare journal entries for the given transactions and post them to the T-accounts (set up any additional T-accounts needed). Do not prepare the journal entry for the Dec. 31 transaction, but post the appropriate amount to the Retained Earnings T-account. Determine the ending balances for the stockholders' equity accounts.

c. Prepare the stockholders' equity section of the balance sheet at December 31.

P11-5A. **Stockholders' Equity: Information and Entries from Comparative Data** Comparative stock-holders' equity sections from two successive years of balance sheets from Smiley, Inc., are as follows:

LO4, 6

	Dec. 31, 2015	Dec. 31, 2014
Paid-in Capital		
8 Percent preferred stock, $40 par value, authorized 20,000 shares; issued and outstanding, 2014: 8,000 shares; 2015: 12,000 shares . . .	$ 480,000	$ 320,000
Common stock, no-par value, $10 stated value, authorized 80,000 shares; issued, 2014: 32,000 shares; 2015: 40,000 shares	400,000	320,000
Additional Paid-in Capital		
In excess of par value—Preferred stock.	224,000	144,000
In excess of stated value—Common stock	232,000	160,000
From treasury stock	21,000	
Retained earnings	300,000	229,000
		$1,173,000
Less: Treasury stock (8,000 shares common) at cost	0	179,000
Total Stockholders' Equity	$1,657,000	$ 994,000

No dividends were declared or paid during 2015.

Required

Prepare the journal entries for the transactions affecting stockholders' equity that occurred during 2015. Do not prepare the journal entry for closing net income to retained earnings. Assume that any share transactions were for cash.

P11-6A. **Retained Earnings: Transactions and Statement** The stockholders' equity accounts of Rayburn Corporation as of January 1 appear below:

LO7, 8

Common stock, $10 par value, 400,000 shares authorized; 160,000 shares issued and outstanding.	$800,000
Paid-in capital in excess of par value.	920,000
Retained earnings	513,000

During the year, the following transactions occurred:

June   7 Declared a 20 percent stock dividend; market value of the common stock was $15 per share.

       28 Issued the stock dividend declared on June 7.

Dec.   5 Declared a cash dividend of $1.50 per share.

       26 Paid the cash dividend declared on December 5.

Required

a. Prepare journal entries to record the foregoing transactions.

b. Prepare a statement of retained earnings. The net income for the year is $425,000.

P11-7A. **Retained Earnings: Transactions and Statement** The stockholders' equity of Cyclone Corpora-tion at January 1 follows:

LO7, 8

6 Percent preferred stock, $10 par value, 40,000 shares authorized; 25,000 shares issued and outstanding.	$ 250,000
Common stock, $1 par value, 300,000 shares authorized; 80,000 shares issued and outstanding	80,000
Paid-in capital in excess of par value—Common stock	560,000
Retained earnings	830,000
Total Stockholders' Equity	$1,720,000

The following transactions, among others, occurred during the year:

June 18 Declared a 60 percent stock dividend on all outstanding shares of common stock. The market value of the stock was $14 per share.

July 1 Issued the stock dividend declared on June 18.

Dec. 20 Declared the annual cash dividend on the preferred stock and a cash dividend of $1.60 per share on the common stock, payable on January 20 to stockholders of record on December 28.

Required

a. Prepare journal entries to record the foregoing transactions.

b. Prepare a statement of retained earnings. The net income for the year is $410,000.

LO4, 5, 6 **P11-8A.** **Stockholders' Equity Transactions, Journal Entries, and T-Accounts** The stockholders' equity of Fremantle Corporation at January 1 follows:

8 Percent preferred stock, $100 par value, 20,000 shares authorized; 5,000 shares issued and outstanding	$ 500,000
Common stock, $1 par value, 100,000 shares authorized; 40,000 shares issued and outstanding	40,000
Paid-in capital in excess of par value—Preferred stock	200,000
Paid-in capital in excess of par value—Common stock	800,000
Retained earnings	625,000
Total Stockholders' Equity	$2,165,000

The following transactions, among others, occurred during the year:

Jan. 1 Announced a 2-for-1 common stock split, reducing the par value of the common stock to $0.50 per share.

Mar. 31 Converted $75,000 face value of convertible bonds payable (the book value of the bonds was $83,000) to common stock. Each $1,000 bond converted to 110 shares of common stock.

June 1 Acquired equipment with a fair market value of $45,000 in exchange for 300 shares of preferred stock.

Sept. 1 Acquired 15,000 shares of common stock for cash at $20 per share.

Nov. 21 Issued 5,000 shares of common stock at $22 cash per share.

Dec. 28 Sold 1,000 treasury shares at $23 per share.

31 Closed net income of $125,000, to the Retained Earnings account.

Required

a. Set up T-accounts for the stockholders' equity accounts as of the beginning of the year and enter the January 1 balances.

b. Prepare journal entries for the given transactions and post them to the T-accounts (set up any additional T-accounts needed). Do not prepare the journal entry for the Dec. 31 transaction, but post the appropriate amount to the Retained Earnings T-account. Determine the ending balances for the stockholders' equity accounts.

LO4, 5, 6 **P11-9A.** **Stockholders' Equity Section of the Balance Sheet** Using your analysis from P11-8A, prepare the stockholders' equity section of the Fremantle Corporation's balance sheet.

P11-10A. Stockholders' Equity: Transactions and Statement The stockholders' equity section of Night Corporation's balance sheet at January 1 follows: **LO4, 6, 7, 8**

Common stock, $5 par value, 300,000 shares authorized, 60,000 shares Issued, 6,000 shares in treasury..................................		$300,000
Additional paid-in capital		
In excess of par value...	$480,000	
From treasury stock	30,000	510,000
Retained earnings		348,000
		1,150,000
Less: Treasury stock (6,000 shares) at cost........................		138,000
		$1,020,000

The following transactions affecting stockholders' equity occurred during the year:

Jan.	8	Issued 15,000 shares of previously unissued common stock for $21 cash per share.
Mar	12	Sold all of the treasury shares for $28 cash per share.
June	30	Declared a five percent stock dividend on all outstanding shares of common stock. The market value of the stock was $25 per share.
July	10	Issued the stock dividend declared on June 30.
Oct.	7	Acquired 2,500 shares of common stock as treasury stock at $26 cash per share.
Dec.	18	Declared a cash dividend of $1.00 per outstanding common share, payable on January 9 to stockholders of record on December 31.

Required

a. Prepare journal entries to record the foregoing transactions.
b. Prepare a statement of stockholders' equity. Net income for the year is $341,000.

P11-11A. Stockholders' Equity: Transaction Descriptions from Account Data The following T-accounts contain keyed entries representing five transactions involving the stockholders' equity of Riverview, Inc.: **LO4, 6**

Cash

(1)	75,000	15,600	(4)
(2)	100,000		
(5)	8,400		

Land

(3)	95,000	

Preferred Stock, $10 Par

	15,000	(1)

Paid-in Capital in Excess of Par Value—Preferred Stock

	60,000	(1)

Common Stock, $20 Par

	100,000	(2)
	80,000	(3)

Paid-in Capital in Excess of Par Value—Common Stock

	15,000	(3)

Paid-in Capital from Treasury Stock

	600	(5)

Treasury Stock

(4)	(600 shares	7,800	(5)
	of common)	15,600	

Required

Using this information, give detailed descriptions, including number of shares and price per share when applicable, for each of the five transactions.

PROBLEMS—SET B

P11-1B. Dividend Distribution Gardner Corporation began business on June 30, 2013. At that time, it issued 20,000 shares of $50 par value, six percent, cumulative preferred stock and 90,000 shares of **LO7**

$10 par value common stock. Through the end of 2015, there had been no change in the number of preferred and common shares outstanding.

Required

a. Assume that Gardner declared dividends of $62,700 in 2013, $0 in 2014, and $345,000 in 2015. Calculate the total dividends and the dividends per share paid to each class of stock in 2013, 2014, and 2015.

b. Assume that Gardner declared dividends of $0 in 2013, $120,000 in 2014, and $177,000 in 2015. Calculate the total dividends and the dividends per share paid to each class of stock in 2013, 2014, and 2015.

LO4, 6 **P11-2B.** **Stockholders' Equity: Transactions and Balance Sheet Presentation** Beaker Corporation was organized on July 1, with an authorization of 50,000 shares of $5 no-par value preferred stock ($5 is the annual dividend) and 100,000 shares of $10 par value common stock. During July, the following transactions affecting stockholders' equity occurred:

July 1 Issued 31,000 shares of common stock at $21 cash per share.
     12 Issued 3,500 shares of common stock in exchange for equipment with a fair market value of $71,000.
     15 Issued 5,000 shares of preferred stock for cash at $40 per share.

Required

a. Prepare journal entries to record the foregoing transactions.

b. Prepare the stockholders' equity section of the balance sheet at July 31. The net income for July is $52,000.

LO4, 6 **P11-3B.** **Stockholders' Equity: Transactions and Balance Sheet Presentation** The stockholders' equity accounts of Scott Corporation at January 1 follow:

Common stock, $1 par value, 350,000 shares authorized;	
150,000 shares issued and outstanding.	$150,000
Paid-in capital in excess of par value.	600,000
Retained earnings	346,000

During the year, the following transactions occurred:

Jan.   5 Issued 10,000 shares of common stock for $15 cash per share.
      18 Purchased 4,000 shares of common stock as treasury stock at $14 cash per share.
Mar. 12 Sold one-fourth of the treasury shares acquired January 18 for $17 per share.
July 17 Sold 600 shares of the remaining treasury stock for $13 per share.
Oct.   1 Issued 5,000 shares of eight percent, $25 par value preferred stock for $35 cash per share. These are the first preferred shares issued out of 50,000 authorized shares.
Dec. 31 Closed the net income of $85,000 to the Retained Earnings account.

Required

a. Set up T-accounts for the stockholders' equity accounts as of the beginning of the year and enter the January 1 balances.

b. Prepare journal entries to record the foregoing transactions and post to T-accounts (set up any additional T-accounts needed). Do not prepare the journal entry for the Dec. 31 transaction, but post the appropriate amount to the Retained Earnings T-account. Determine the ending balances for the stockholders' equity accounts.

c. Prepare the December 31 stockholders' equity section of the balance sheet.

LO4, 5, 6 **P11-4B.** **Stockholders' Equity: Transactions and Balance Sheet Presentation** The following is the stockholders' equity of Clipper Corporation at January 1:

8 Percent preferred stock, $40 par value, 10,000 shares authorized;	
7,000 shares issued and outstanding.	$ 280,000
Common stock, $20 par value, 50,000 shares authorized;	
25,000 shares issued and outstanding.	500,000
Paid-in capital in excess of par value—Preferred stock	70,000
Paid-in capital in excess of par value—Common stock	385,000
Retained earnings	238,000
Total Stockholders' Equity	$1,473,000

The following transactions, among others, occurred during the year:

Jan.   15   Issued 2,000 shares of preferred stock for $62 cash per share.
20   Issued 4,000 shares of common stock at $36 cash per share.
31   Converted $20,000 face value of convertible bonds payable (the book value of the bonds is $18,500) to common stock. Each $1,000 bond converted to 25 shares of common stock.

May   18   Announced a 2-for-1 common stock split, reducing the par value of the common stock to $10 per share. The authorization was increased to 100,000 shares.

June   1   Acquired equipment with a fair market value of $40,000 in exchange for 2,000 shares of common stock.

Sept.   1   Purchased 3,500 shares of common stock as treasury stock at $18 cash per share.
Oct.   12   Sold 900 treasury shares at $21 per share.
Dec.   22   Issued 600 shares of preferred stock for $59 cash per share.
28   Sold 1,100 of the remaining treasury shares at $16 per share.
31   Closed net income of $135,000 to the Retained Earnings account.

Required

a.   Set up T-accounts for the stockholders' equity accounts as of the beginning of the year and enter the January 1 balances.

b.   Prepare journal entries for the given transactions and post them to the T-accounts (set up any additional T-accounts needed). Do not prepare the journal entry for the Dec. 31 transaction, but post the appropriate amount to the Retained Earnings T-account. Determine the ending balances for the stockholders' equity accounts.

c.   Prepare the stockholders' equity section of the balance sheet at December 31.

P11-5B.   Stockholders' Equity: Information and Entries from Comparative Data   Comparative stockholders' equity sections from two successive years of balance sheets from Mammoth, Inc., are as follows:

LO4, 6

	Dec. 31, 2015	Dec. 31, 2014
Paid-in Capital		
10 percent preferred stock, $20 par value, authorized 50,000 shares;	$ 500,000	$ 400,000
issued and outstanding, 2014: 20,000 shares; 2015: 25,000 shares		
Common stock, no-par value, $10 stated value, authorized 120,000 shares;	600,000	480,000
issued, 2014: 48,000 shares; 2015: 60,000 shares.		
Additional Paid-in Capital		
In excess of par value—Preferred stock.	225,000	160,000
In excess of stated value—Common stock	540,000	336,000
From treasury stock	20,000	
Retained earnings	390,000	335,000
	2,275,000	1,711,000
Less: Treasury stock (10,000 shares common) at cost	0	136,000
Total stockholders' equity.	$2,275,000	$1,575,000

No dividends were declared or paid during 2015.

Required

Prepare the journal entries for the transactions affecting stockholders' equity that occurred during 2015. Do not prepare the journal entry for closing net income to retained earnings. Assume that any share transactions were for cash.

LO7, 8 **P11-6B.** **Retained Earnings: Transactions and Statement** The stockholders' equity of Striker Corporation at January 1 appears below:

Common stock, $10 par value, 200,000 shares authorized;	
80,000 shares issued and outstanding..	$800,000
Paid-in capital in excess of par value...	480,000
Retained earnings	305,000

During the year, the following transactions occurred:

May	12	Declared a nine percent stock dividend; market value of the common stock was $22 per share.
June	6	Issued the stock dividend declared on May 12.
Dec.	5	Declared a cash dividend of $1.25 per share.
	30	Paid the cash dividend declared on December 5.

Required

a. Prepare journal entries to record the foregoing transactions.
b. Prepare a statement of retained earnings. Net income for the year is $275,000.

LO7, 8 **P11-7B.** **Retained Earnings: Transactions and Statement** The stockholders' equity of Elson Corporation at January 1 is shown below:

5 Percent preferred stock, $100 par value, 10,000 shares authorized;	
4,000 shares issued and outstanding..	$ 400,000
Common stock, $5 par value, 200,000 shares	
authorized; 50,000 shares issued and outstanding	250,000
Paid-in capital in excess of par value—Preferred stock	40,000
Paid-in capital in excess of par value—Common stock	300,000
Retained earnings	656,000
Total Stockholders' Equity	$1,646,000

The following transactions, among others, occurred during the year:

Apr.	1	Declared a 100 percent stock dividend on all outstanding shares of common stock. The market value of the stock was $14 per share.
	15	Issued the stock dividend declared on April 1.
Dec.	7	Declared a two percent stock dividend on all outstanding shares of common stock. The market value of the stock was $15 per share.
	17	Issued the stock dividend declared on December 7.
	20	Declared the annual cash dividend on the preferred stock and a cash dividend of 90 cents per common share, payable on January 15 to common stockholders of record on December 31.

Required

a. Prepare journal entries to record the foregoing transactions.
b. Prepare a statement of retained earnings. Net income for the year is $265,000.

LO4, 5, 6 **P11-8B.** **Stockholders' Equity Transactions, Journal Entries, and T-Accounts** The stockholders' equity of Xeltron Corporation at January 1 follows:

10 percent Preferred stock, $100 par value, 20,000 shares authorized; 4,000 shares issued and outstanding		$ 400,000
Common stock, $4 par value, 100,000 shares authorized; 40,000 shares issued and outstanding.		160,000
Paid-in capital in excess of par value—Preferred stock		400,000
Paid-in capital in excess of par value—Common stock		800,000
Retained earnings		850,000
Total Stockholders' Equity		$2,610,000

The following transactions, among others, occurred during the year:

Jan.	1	Announced a 2-for-1 common stock split, reducing the par value of the common stock to $2.00 per share.
Mar.	31	Converted $100,000 face value of convertible bonds payable (the book value of the bonds was $103,000) to common stock. Each $1,000 bond converted to 120 shares of common stock.
June	1	Acquired equipment with a fair market value of $40,000 in exchange for 200 shares of preferred stock.
Sept.	1	Acquired 10,000 shares of common stock for cash at $20 per share.
Nov.	21	Issued 5,000 shares of common stock at $22 cash per share.
Dec.	28	Sold 500 treasury shares at $23 per share.
	31	Closed net income of $125,000 to the Retained Earnings account.

Required

a. Set up T-accounts for the stockholders' equity accounts as of the beginning of the year and enter the January 1 balances.

b. Prepare journal entries for the given transactions and post them to the T-accounts (set up any additional T-accounts needed). Do not prepare the journal entry for the Dec. 31 transaction, but post the appropriate amount to the Retained Earnings T-account. Determine the ending balances for the stockholders' equity accounts.

P11-9B. **The Stockholders' Equity Section of the Balance Sheet** Using your analysis from P11-8B, prepare the Stockholders' Equity section of the Xeltron Corporation's balance sheet.   **LO4, 5, 6**

P11-10B. **Stockholders' Equity: Transactions and Statement** The stockholders' equity section of Day Corporation's balance sheet at January 1 follows: **LO4, 6, 7, 8**

Common stock, $10 par value, 200,000 shares authorized, 35,000 shares issued, 4,000 shares are in the treasury...............................		$350,000
Additional paid-in capital		
In excess of par value...	$315,000	
From treasury stock	18,000	333,000
Retained earnings		298,000
		981,000
Less: Treasury stock (4,000 shares) at cost............................		84,000
Total Stockholders' Equity..		$897,000

The following transactions affecting stockholders' equity occurred during the year:

Jan.	8	Issued 15,000 shares of previously unissued common stock for $23 cash per share.
Mar.	12	Sold all of the treasury shares for $29 cash per share.
June	30	Declared a six percent stock dividend on all outstanding shares of common stock. The market value of the stock was $35 per share.
July	10	Issued the stock dividend declared on June 30.
Oct.	7	Acquired 1,500 shares of common stock as treasury stock at $28 cash per share.
Dec.	18	Declared a cash dividend of 80 cents per outstanding common share, payable on January 9 to stockholders of record on December 31.

Required

a. Prepare journal entries to record the foregoing transactions.

b. Prepare a statement of stockholders' equity. Net income for the year is $192,000.

LO4, 6 **P11-11B.** **Stockholders' Equity: Transaction Descriptions from Account Data** The following T-accounts contain keyed entries representing five transactions involving the stockholders' equity of Riverview, Inc.:

Cash			
(1)	90,000	12,800	(4)
(2)	40,000		
(5)	6,480		

Land		
(3)	85,000	

Preferred Stock, $50 Par		
	75,000	(1)

Paid-in Capital in Excess of Par Value—Preferred Stock		
	15,000	(1)

Common Stock, $10 Par		
	40,000	(2)
	50,000	(3)

Paid-in Capital in Excess of Par Value—Common Stock		
	35,000	(3)

Paid-in Capital from Treasury Stock		
	1,360	(5)

Treasury Stock			
(4)	(900 shares of common)	5,120	(5)
	12,800		

Required

Using this information, give detailed descriptions, including number of shares and price per share when applicable, for each of the five transactions.

SERIAL PROBLEM: KATE'S CARDS

(Note: This is a continuation of the Serial Problem: Kate's Cards from Chapters 1 through 10.)

SP11. Kate's business continues to flourish. It hardly seems that just eleven months ago, in September of 2015, that Kate started the business. She is especially pleased that she was able to successfully defend herself against what turned out to be a mistaken attempt to sue her for copyright infringement. She was able to clearly demonstrate that her card designs were unique and significantly different from the designs sold by Mega Cards.

Kate has decided to take on an investor. Taylor Kasey believes that Kate's Cards represents a good investment and wishes to invest money to help Kate expand the business. Kate, however, is somewhat unsure how to structure Taylor's investment. Taylor wishes to be an equity investor rather than simply providing a loan to Kate. Kate wants to know whether she should issue Taylor common stock or preferred stock for her investment.

1. Discuss the difference between the two classes of stock and suggest which type is more appropriate for Kate to issue.

2. Kate has decided that she does not want to give up voting control of Kate's Cards. Since Taylor prefers to be a passive investor, but does wish to have a steady income from dividends, the decision is made to issue 50 shares of $100 par value, 6 percent cumulative preferred stock.

   Provide the journal entry to record the issuance of the preferred stock for cash.

3. Kate also wishes to pay dividends on both her common shares and the preferred stock. She is a little confused between cash and stock dividends.

   Explain the difference between a cash dividend and a stock dividend. Since Kate is the only stockholder of the common stock, what would be the effect of issuing a 10 percent stock dividend?

4. Kate decides to issue cash dividends on both the common stock and the preferred stock. Currently there are 50 outstanding preferred shares and 500 common shares outstanding. The dividends that Kate paid were $6 per share on the preferred shares and $2 per share on the common shares.

   Provide the journal entry for the payment of the cash dividends.

5. Kate's Cards has a net income of $1,500 for the current month of August 2016. Kate had decided that the business will have a fiscal year-end of August 31, so this is the completion of the company's first year. Kate will be preparing her annual financial statements; however, she would also like to see a monthly statement of retained earnings for August 2016. In addition, she would like to see how the stockholders' equity section of the balance sheet will look after the addition of the preferred stock. The stockholders' equity section from July 2016 is shown below:

Stockholders' Equity	
Common stock (5,000 shares authorized, 500 shares issued and outstanding)	$ 500
Paid-in capital in excess of par value—common stock	9,500
Retained earnings	15,000
Total stockholders' equity	$25,000

Prepare a statement of retained earnings for the month of August 2016 and the stockholders' equity section of the balance sheet as of August 31, 2016.

EXTENDING YOUR KNOWLEDGE

REPORTING AND ANALYSIS

EYK11-1. Financial Reporting Problem: Columbia Sportswear Company The financial statements for the **Columbia Sportswear Company** can be found in Appendix A at the end of this book.

COLUMBIA
SPORTSWEAR
COMPANY

Required
Answer the following questions:

a. How many shares of common stock are authorized at the end of 2014?
b. What percentage of the common shares authorized are outstanding at the end of 2014?
c. Does Columbia Sportswear have any preferred shares outstanding at the end of 2014?
d. How many shares of common stock did Columbia Sportswear repurchase in 2014? What was the dollar amount of this repurchase?
e. What amount of dividends per share did Columbia Sportswear report for 2014? 2013? 2012?

EYK11-2. Comparative Analysis Problem: Columbia Sportswear Company vs Under Armour, Inc. The financial statements for the **Columbia Sportswear Company** can be found in Appendix A at the end of this book, and the financial statements of **Under Armour, Inc.** can be found in Appendix B (the complete annual report is available on this book's Website).

COLUMBIA
SPORTSWEAR
COMPANY
UNDER ARMOUR,
INC.

Required
Answer the following questions:

a. Calculate the return on common stockholders' equity for each company for 2014.
b. Calculate the dividend payout ratio for each company for 2014.
c. Based on these ratios, which company performed better for its shareholders during 2014?

EYK11-3. Business Decision Problem Egghead, Inc., was a software chain that had over 100 stores across the U.S. Initially its founders and employees owned the company privately. The company eventually went public with an initial public offering (IPO) of 3.6 million shares (the company had 12 million shares prior to the IPO). The new shares were priced at $15 each. The company did not hold any treasury shares.

Required
a. Assume that the common shares had a $1 par value. Provide the journal entry to record the issuance of new shares.
b. Discuss whether you think Egghead's board of directors and existing shareholders had to approve the public issuance before it occurred.
c. Provide some reasons why Egghead wished to raise $54 million with equity rather than debt.

EYK11-4. Financial Analysis Problem The following data was obtained prior to the acquisition of **Gillette Company** by **Procter & Gamble**. Gillette Company, the Procter & Gamble Company, and

GILLETTE
COMPANY
PROCTER &
GAMBLE

Colgate-Palmolive Company are three firms in the personal care consumer products industry. During the prior year, the average return on common stockholders' equity for the personal care consumer products industry was 28.1 percent. In the same year, the relevant financial data for Gillette, Procter & Gamble, and Colgate-Palmolive were as follows (in millions):

	Gillette	Procter & Gamble	Colgate-Palmolive
Preferred stockholders' equity, beginning	$ 99.2	$1,969.0	$ 418.3
Preferred stockholders' equity, ending	99.0	1,942.0	414.3
Preferred dividends	4.7	102.0	21.6
Common stockholders' equity, beginning	1,397.2	5,472.0	2,201.5
Common stockholders' equity, ending	1,380.0	6,890.0	1,460.7
Net income	426.9	2,211.0	548.1

Required

a. Calculate Gillette Company's return on common stockholders' equity.

b. Evaluate Gillette Company's return on common stockholders' equity by comparing it with the following:

1. The average for the personal care consumer products industry.
2. The return earned by the Procter & Gamble Company.
3. The return earned by Colgate-Palmolive Company.
4. The return earned by Gillette Company in the previous year (in the previous year, Gillette's net income was $513.4 million, preferred stock dividends were $4.8 million, and average common stockholders' equity was $1,227.3 million).

CRITICAL THINKING

EYK11-5. Financial Analysis on the Web: General Mills, Inc. The fiscal year 2014 annual report of **General Mills, Inc.** is available on this book's Website.

Required

a. How many shares of common stock is General Mills authorized to issue? How many common shares are issued as of May 25, 2014?

b. What is the par value of General Mills' common stock?

c. Does General Mills have any preferred shares? If so, how many shares of preferred stock are outstanding on May 25, 2014?

d. How many treasury shares did General Mills purchase on the open market during the 2014 fiscal year? What did General Mills pay to purchase these shares? How many common shares are in the treasury as of May 25, 2014?

e. What is General Mills' return on common stockholders' equity for the 2014 fiscal year?

f. What is the cash dividend per share declared by General Mills in fiscal year 2014? 2013? 2012?

g. What are General Mills' basic earnings per share in fiscal year 2014? 2013? 2012?

h. What is General Mills' dividend payout ratio for fiscal year 2014? 2013? 2012?

EYK11-6. Accounting Communication Activity Your neighbor, Norman Vetter, has always been tinkering in his garage with his inventions. He believes he has finally come up with one that could really sell well. He is a little concerned about some potential safety issues, but he believes those issues will be worked out. He wants to form a business to manufacture and sell his invention and has come to you for advice. In particular, he would like to know the advantages and disadvantages of forming a corporation, rather than simply organizing as a sole proprietor.

Required

Write a brief memorandum to your neighbor explaining the advantages and disadvantages of the corporate form of organization.

EYK11-7. Accounting Ethics Case Colin Agee, chairperson of the board of directors and chief executive officer of Image, Inc., is pondering a recommendation to make to the firm's board of directors in response to actions taken by Sam Mecon. Mecon recently informed Agee and other board mem-

bers that he (Mecon) had purchased 15 percent of the voting stock of Image at $12 per share and is considering an attempt to take control of the company. His effort to take control would include offering $16 per share to stockholders to induce them to sell shares to him. Mecon also indicated that he would abandon his takeover plans if the company would buy back his stock at a price 50 percent over its current market price of $13 per share.

Agee views the proposed takeover by Mecon as a hostile maneuver. Mecon has a reputation of identifying companies that are undervalued (that is, their underlying net assets are worth more than the price of the outstanding shares), buying enough shares to take control of the company, replacing top management, and, on occasion, breaking up the company (that is, selling off the various divisions to the highest bidder). The process has proven profitable to Mecon and his financial backers. Stockholders of the companies taken over have also benefited because Mecon paid them attractive prices to buy their shares.

Agee recognizes that Image is currently undervalued by the stock market but believes that eventually the company will significantly improve its financial performance to the long-run benefit of its stockholders.

Required
What are the ethical issues that Agee should consider in arriving at a recommendation to make to the board of directors regarding Mecon's offer to be "bought out" of his takeover plans?

EYK11-8. **Corporate Social Responsibility Problem** In the corporate social responsibility highlight regarding Starbucks on page 532 in this chapter, it was stated that Starbucks believes in measuring and monitoring the company's CSR progress. One of Starbucks' commitments is to ethical coffee sourcing. Two of the metrics that the company uses in this regard are the pounds of coffee purchased from C.A.F.E. and the pounds of green coffee purchased from Fair Trade Certified cooperatives. Go to the Starbucks Website and navigate to the section on global responsibility to download the report on Ethical Coffee Sourcing. Identify how the company is doing with respect to these two metrics.

EYK11-9. **Forensic Accounting Problem** The Forensic Accounting Box on page 535 of this chapter noted that forensic accounting techniques are being used to help pick stocks for investing. How might identifying accounting concerns be useful for investors?

EYK11-10. **Working With The Takeaways** The following data is from a recent **General Electric Company** annual report. All amounts, except per share data, are in $ millions).

GENERAL
ELECTRIC
COMPANY

Net income	$ 17,410
Preferred stock dividends	75
Average common stockholders' equity	110,112
Dividends per share	1.24
Earnings per share	1.72
Per share market price of common stock at year-end	16.20

Required
Compute the following ratios for the General Electric Company:
a. Return on common stockholders' equity
b. Dividend yield
c. Dividend payout

EYK11-11. **IFRS Financial Statements** The 2014 financial statements of LVMH Moet Hennessey-Louis Vuitton S.A. are presented in Appendix C at the end of this book. LVMH is a Paris-based holding company and one of the world's largest and best-known luxury goods companies. As a member of the European Union, French companies are required to prepare their consolidated (group) financial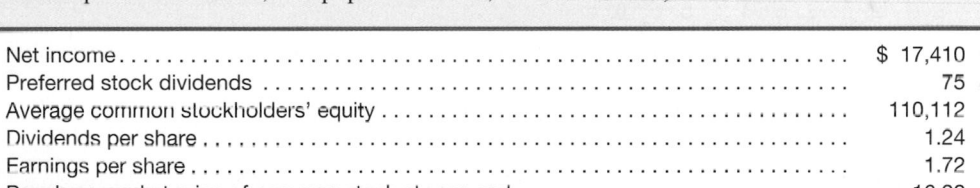

statements using International Financial Reporting Standards (IFRS). Calculate LVMH's (a) return on common stockholders' equity, (b) dividend yield, and (c) dividend payout for 2014 and 2013. Additional information that you will need is below:

	2014	2013
Earnings per share (in euros)	11.27	6.87
Dividend per share (in euros)	3.20	3.10
Market price per share (in euros)	131.90	132.35

ANSWERS TO SELF-STUDY QUESTIONS:

1. c, (p. 531)　2. a, (p. 536)　3. c, (pp. 538–539)　4. d, (pp. 540–541)　5. d, (pp. 542–543)　6. d, (p. 540)
7. c, (p. 549)　8. d, (p. 536)　9. a, (p. 543)　10. d, (p. 547)

YOUR TURN! SOLUTIONS

Solution 11.1

1. Disadvantage
2. Advantage
3. Advantage
4. Disadvantage
5. Disadvantage
6. Advantage

Solution 11.2
1. d　**2.** e　**3.** b　**4.** f　**5.** c　**6.** a

Solution 11.3
Paid-in capital in excess of par value = ($9 − $1) × 10,000 shares = $80,000

Solution 11.4
After the split Aston Enterprises would report 1,500,000 shares outstanding with a par value of $1.00. Joe Smith would own 1,500 shares of Aston.

Solution 11.5
$75,000

Solution 11.6
a. A cash dividend will lower retained earnings by $30,000 ($3 × 10,000 shares) to $470,000.
b. A ten percent stock dividend will lower retained earnings by $20,000 (.10 × 10,000 × $20) to $480,000.

Solution 11.7

DIOR COMPANY Statement of Stockholders' Equity For Year Ended December 31, 2016					
	Common Stock	Paid-in Capital in Excess of Par Value	Retained Earnings	Treasury Stock	Total
Balance, January 1, 2016.......	$100,000	$900,000	$50,000	$(10,000)	$1,040,000
Net income.................			30,000		30,000
1,000 common shares issued ...	1,000	14,000			15,000
Cash dividend			(8,000)		(8,000)
Balance, December 31, 2016....	$101,000	$914,000	$72,000	$(10,000)	$1,077,000

Solution 11.8

a. Return on common stockholders' equity = ($150,000 − $15,000)/[($650,000 + $700,000)/2] = 20 percent

b. Dividend yield = $0.75/$33.00 = 2.3 percent

c. Dividend payout ratio = $0.75/$3.00 = 25 percent

12

Statement of Cash Flows

PAST

Chapter 11 examined the accounting for stockholders' equity.

PRESENT

In this chapter we turn our attention to the statement of cash flows.

FUTURE

Chapter 13 completes our study of financial accounting by looking at the analysis and interpretation of financial statements.

LEARNING OBJECTIVES

1. **Discuss** the content and format of the statement of cash flows. *(p. 578)*

2. **Explain** the preparation of a statement of cash flows using the indirect method. *(p. 584)*

3. **Define** several ratios used to analyze the statement of cash flows and **explain** their use. *(p. 592)*

4. Appendix 12A: **Explain** the preparation of a statement of cash flows using the direct method. *(p. 597)*.

HOME DEPOT: A Company with a Vision

Home Depot is the largest home improvement retailer in the United States. Founded in 1978 in Atlanta, Georgia, the company now operates over 2,200 stores in the United States, Canada, and Mexico. The company's founders had a vision that led to the company's tremendous growth:

"We founded [The Home Depot] with a special vision—to create a company that would keep alive the values that were important to us. Values like respect among all people, excellent customer service and giving back to communities and society."

—Arthur Blank, co-founder, Home Depot

It takes a lot of cash to build and operate over 2,200 stores, especially when the average Home Depot store is over 105,000 square feet. In fiscal year 2014 Home Depot spent over $1.4 billion on capital expenditures. This represents the fifth year in a row that the company expended over $1 billion dollars in capital expenditures.

How can a financial statement user determine where a company obtained the cash to fund such growth? In this chapter we examine the statement of cash flows and learn how a company discloses both the sources and uses of its cash. Understanding the content, format, and construction of the statement of cash flows enables a financial statement user to assess just how a company like Home Depot was able to finance its capital expenditures for new store growth.

```
                    ┌─────────────────────────────────────────┐
                    │      STATEMENT OF CASH FLOWS             │
                    └─────────────────────────────────────────┘
          ┌──────────────────────┬──────────────────────┬──────────────────────┐
  ┌───────────────────┐  ┌───────────────────┐  ┌───────────────────┐
  │  Classification   │  │ Preparing the Statement of │  │    Analyzing      │
  │  of Cash Flows    │  │    Cash Flows     │  │   Cash Flows      │
  ├───────────────────┤  ├───────────────────┤  ├───────────────────┤
  │ • Cash and cash   │  │ • Indirect method │  │ • Free cash flow  │
  │   equivalents     │  │ • Direct method   │  │ • Operating-cash-flow-to- │
  │ • Operating       │  │   (Appendix       │  │   current-liabilities │
  │   activities      │  │   12A)            │  │ • Operating-cash-flow-to- │
  │ • Investing       │  │                   │  │   capital-expenditures ratio │
  │   activities      │  │                   │  │                   │
  │ • Financing       │  │                   │  │                   │
  │   activities      │  │                   │  │                   │
  └───────────────────┘  └───────────────────┘  └───────────────────┘
```

CASH AND CASH EQUIVALENTS

LO1 Discuss the content and format of the statement of cash flows.

Do you maintain a checkbook in which you record the checks you write and the bank deposits you make? If so, you are keeping a record of your cash flows—the checks you write are your cash outflows and the bank deposits you make are your cash inflows. Businesses also experience cash inflows and outflows; but, they do more than just record their cash flows because GAAP requires that businesses prepare an entirely separate financial statement explaining where their cash flow came from and how it was used.

The statement of cash flows complements the balance sheet and the income statement. While a balance sheet reports a company's financial position as of a point in time, usually the end of a fiscal period, the statement of cash flows explains the change in one component of a company's financial position—its cash—from one balance sheet date to the next. The income statement, on the other hand, reveals the results of a company's operating activities for the period, and these operating activities are a major source and use of the cash reported in a company's statement of cash flows.

In the eyes of most creditors, investors, and managers, cash is a business's most important asset. Without cash, a business would be unable to pay its employees, its lenders, its suppliers, its service providers, or its shareholders. In short, cash is the only asset that a business can't operate without.

The dilemma for most managers, however, is knowing exactly how much cash to keep on hand. Although managers know that they need to keep some cash on hand in a checking account and/or petty cash fund to pay their immediate bills, they also know that cash is the lowest return generating asset that a business has. Keeping too much cash on hand means that a business is not maximizing the value of its assets. For this reason, most managers spend considerable time assessing their cash needs—an activity called **cash management**. Because the science of cash management is inexact, managers have derived ways to help them minimize the amount of cash that they need to keep on hand while also maximizing the return on a business's assets. One such method is to invest any excess cash in alternative investments that are readily convertible back into cash and earn a higher rate of return than cash, but which do not place the invested cash at risk of loss. These alternative investments are known as cash equivalents.

Cash equivalents are short-term, highly liquid investments that are (1) easily convertible into cash and (2) close enough to maturity so that their market value is relatively insensitive to interest rate changes (generally, investments with maturities of three months or less). U.S. Treasury bills, certificates of deposit (CDs), commercial paper (short-term notes issued by corporations), and money market funds are examples of cash equivalents. Because firms may differ as to exactly which investments they consider to be cash equivalents, GAAP requires that each firm disclose in the notes to the financial statements the company's policy regarding which investments are treated as cash equivalents.

When preparing a statement of cash flows, the cash and cash equivalents are added together and treated as a single amount. This is done because the purchase and sale of investments in cash equivalents are considered to be part of a firm's overall cash management strategy rather than a source or use of cash. As financial statement users evaluate a firm's cash flows, it should not matter whether the cash is on hand, deposited in a bank account, or invested in cash equivalents. Transfers back and forth between a firm's Cash account and its investments in cash equivalents, consequently, are not treated as cash inflows or outflows in the statement of cash flows.

When discussing the statement of cash flows, accountants often just use the word *cash* rather than the term *cash and cash equivalents*. We follow that practice in this chapter.

Definition of Cash Equivalents	ACCOUNTING IN PRACTICE

There are some differences between firms regarding which investments of cash are considered to be cash equivalents. For example, **PepsiCo, Inc.**, the beverage and snack food company, states in the notes to its financial statements that "Cash equivalents are investments with original maturities of three months or less." **International Game Technology**, a manufacturer of gaming machines and proprietary gaming software systems, on the other hand, notes that "In addition to cash deposits at major banks, cash and equivalents include other marketable securities with original maturities of 90 days or less, primarily in U.S. Treasury-backed money market funds." The commonality among all firms, however, is that cash equivalents represent a temporary investment of excess cash in risk-free investments until such time as the cash is needed to support a business's operations.

ACTIVITY CLASSIFICATIONS IN THE STATEMENT OF CASH FLOWS

A statement of cash flows classifies a company's cash receipts and cash payments into three major business activity categories: operating activities, investing activities, and financing activities. Grouping cash flows into these categories identifies the effect on cash of each of the major business activities of a firm (see Chapter 1). The combined effects on cash from all three categories explain the net change in cash for the period. The net change in cash is then reconciled with the beginning and ending balances of cash from the balance sheet. **Exhibit 12-1** illustrates the basic format for a statement of cash flows.

Exhibit 12-1	Format for the Statement of Cash Flows

SAMPLE COMPANY
Statement of Cash Flows
For Year Ended December 31, 2016

Cash Flow from Operating Activities		
(Details of cash flow from operating activities).	$###	
Cash provided (used) by operating activities		$###
Cash Flow from Investing Activities		
(Details of investing cash inflows and outflows).	###	
Cash provided (used) by investing activities		###
Cash Flow from Financing Activities		
(Details of financing cash inflows and outflows)	###	
Cash provided (used) by financing activities		###
Net increase (decrease) in cash		###
Cash at beginning of year		###
Cash at end of year		$###

Operating Activities

A company's income statement reflects the transactions and events that constitute its operating activities. The focus of a firm's operating activities involves selling goods or rendering services. The cash flow from **operating activities** is defined broadly enough, however, to include any cash receipts or payments that are not classified as investing activities or financing activities. For example, cash received from a lawsuit settlement and cash payments to charity are treated as cash flow from operating activities. The following are examples of cash inflows and outflows relating to a firm's operating activities:

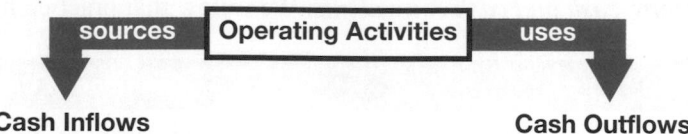

Cash Inflows	Cash Outflows
1. Receipts from customers for sales of goods or services.	1. Payments to suppliers.
2. Receipts of interest and dividends.	2. Payments to employees.
3. Other receipts that are not related to investing or financing activities, such as lawsuit settlements and refunds received from suppliers.	3. Payments of interest to creditors.
	4. Payments of taxes to governmental agencies.
	5. Other payments that are not related to investing or financing activities, such as contributions to charity.

Investing Activities

A firm's **investing activities** include those transactions involving (1) the acquisition or disposal of plant assets and intangible assets, (2) the purchase or sale of stocks, bonds, and other securities (that are not cash equivalents), and (3) the lending and subsequent collection of money.[1] The related cash receipts and cash payments appear in the investing activities section of the statement of cash flows. Examples of these cash flows include:

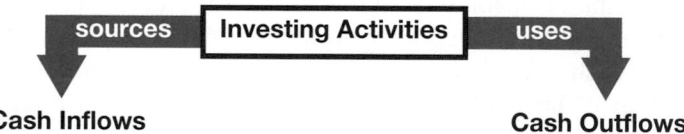

Cash Inflows	Cash Outflows
1. Receipts from the sale of plant assets and intangible assets.	1. Payments to purchase plant assets and intangible assets.
2. Receipts from sales of investments in stocks, bonds, and other securities (other than cash equivalents).	2. Payments to purchase stocks, bonds, and other securities (other than cash equivalents).
3. Receipts from repayments of loans by borrowers.	3. Payments made to lend money to borrowers.

Financing Activities

A firm engages in **financing activities** when it obtains cash from shareholders, returns cash to shareholders, borrows from creditors, and repays amounts borrowed from creditors. Cash flows related to these events are reported in the financing activities section of the statement of cash flows. Examples of these cash flows include:

---

[1] There are exceptions to the classification of these events as investing activities. For example, the purchase or sale of mortgage loans by a mortgage banker, like Bank of America, and the purchase or sale of securities in the trading account of a broker/dealer in financial securities, like Merrill Lynch, represent operating activities for these businesses.

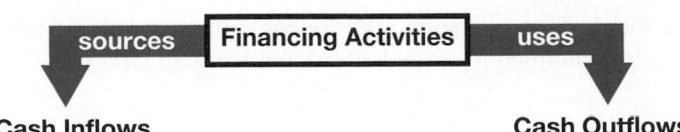

Cash Inflows

1. Receipts from the issuance of common stock and preferred stock and from sales of treasury stock.
2. Receipts from the issuance of bonds payable, mortgage notes payable, and other notes payable.

Cash Outflows

1. Payments to acquire treasury stock.
2. Payments of dividends.
3. Payments to settle outstanding bonds payable, mortgage notes payable, and other notes payable.

Observe that paying cash to settle such obligations as accounts payable, wages payable, interest payable, and income tax payable is an operating activity, not a financing activity. Also observe that cash received as interest and dividends and cash paid as interest are classified as cash flows from operating activities, although cash paid as dividends to a company's stockholders is classified as a financing activity.

An Illustration of Activity Classification Usefulness

The classification of cash flows into the three business activity categories helps financial statement users analyze and interpret a company's cash flow data. To illustrate, assume that companies D, E, and F operate in the same industry, and that each company reported a $100,000 increase in cash during the period. Information from each company's statement of cash flows is summarized below:

	Company		
	D	**E**	**F**
Cash flow from operating activities	$100,000	$ 0	$ 0
Cash flow from investing activities:			
Sale of plant assets	0	100,000	0
Cash flow from financing activities:			
Issuance of notes payable	0	0	100,000
Net increase in cash.	$100,000	$100,000	$100,000

Although each company's increase in cash was exactly $100,000, the source of the cash increase varied by company. This variation affects the analysis of the cash flow data, particularly for potential creditors who must evaluate the likelihood of the repayment of funds loaned to a company. Based only on this cash flow data, a potential creditor would feel more comfortable lending money to Company D than to either Company E or F. D's cash increase came from its operating activities, whereas E's cash increase came from the sale of plant assets, a source that is unlikely to recur, and F's cash increase came from borrowed funds. Company F faces additional future uncertainty when the interest and principal payments on the existing notes become due, and for this reason, a potential creditor would be less inclined to extend additional loans to Company F.

NONCASH INVESTING AND FINANCING ACTIVITIES

Although many investing and financing activities affect cash and therefore are included in the investing and financing sections of the statement of cash flows, some significant investing and financing events do not affect current cash flow. Examples of **noncash investing and financing activities** are the issuance of stock or bonds in exchange for plant assets or intangible assets, the exchange of long-term assets for other long-term assets, and the conversion of long-term debt into common stock. A common feature among each of these transactions is that no cash is exchanged between the parties involved in the transaction.

Noncash investing and financing transactions generally do, however, affect future cash flows. Issuing bonds in exchange for equipment, for example, requires future cash payments for interest and principal on the bonds. On the other hand, converting bonds into common stock eliminates the future cash payments related to the bonds' interest and principal. Knowledge of these types of events, therefore, should be helpful to financial statement users who wish to evaluate a firm's future cash flows.

Information regarding noncash investing and financing transactions is disclosed in a separate accounting schedule. The separate schedule may be placed immediately below the statement of cash flows or it may be placed among the notes to the financial statements.

PRINCIPLE ALERT   **Objectivity Principle**

The *objectivity principle* asserts that the usefulness of financial statements is enhanced when the underlying data are objective and verifiable. Measuring cash and the changes in cash are among the most objective measurements that accountants make. The statement of cash flows, therefore, is the most objective financial statement required under generally accepted accounting principles. This characteristic of the statement of cash flows is welcomed by investors and creditors interested in evaluating the quality of a firm's net income and assets. Financial statement users often feel more confident about the quality of a company's net income and assets when there is a high correlation between, or relationship with, a company's cash flow from operating activities and its net income.

USING THE STATEMENT OF CASH FLOWS

The Financial Accounting Standards Board believes that one of the principal objectives of financial reporting is to help financial statement users assess the amount, timing, and uncertainty of a business's future cash flows. These assessments, in turn, help users evaluate prospective future cash receipts from their investments in, or loans to, a business. Although the statement of cash flows describes a company's past cash flows, the statement is also useful for assessing future cash flows since the recent past is often a very good predictor of the future.

The statement of cash flows shows the cash effects of a firm's operating, investing, and financing activities. Distinguishing among these different categories of cash flow helps financial statement users compare, evaluate, and predict a business's future cash flows. With cash flow information, creditors and investors are better able to assess a company's ability to repay its liabilities and pay dividends. A firm's need for outside financing can also be evaluated using the statement of cash flows. Further, the statement enables users to observe and analyze management's investing and financing policies, plans, and strategies.

The statement of cash flows also provides information useful in evaluating a firm's financial flexibility. **Financial flexibility** is a company's ability to generate sufficient amounts of cash to respond to unanticipated needs and opportunities. Information about past cash flows, particularly cash flow from operations, helps in assessing financial flexibility. An evaluation of a firm's ability to survive an unexpected drop in demand for its goods and services, for example, may include a review of its past cash flow from operations. The larger these past cash flows, the greater will be a firm's ability to withstand adverse changes in future economic conditions.

Some investors and creditors find the statement of cash flows useful in evaluating the "quality" of a firm's net income. As we saw in Chapter 4, determining net income under the accrual basis of accounting requires many accruals, deferrals, allocations, and valuations. These adjustment and measurement procedures introduce greater subjectivity into a company's income determination than some financial statement users are comfortable with. Consequently, these users can relate a more objective performance measure—a firm's cash flow from operations—to net income. To these users, the higher the relationship between a company's net income and the cash flow from operations, the higher is the quality of the firm's net income.

CASH FLOW FROM OPERATING ACTIVITIES

The first section of the statement of cash flows presents a firm's cash flow from operating activities. Two alternative formats are available to present the cash flow from operating activities: the indirect method and the direct method. Both methods report the same amount of cash flow from operating activities and differ only in how the cash flow from operating activities is presented.

The **indirect method** starts with net income using the accrual basis of accounting and applies a series of adjustments to convert it to net income under the cash basis of accounting, which is equivalent to the cash flow from operating activities. The adjustments to net income do not represent specific cash flows; consequently, the indirect method does not report any detail concerning individual operating cash inflows and outflows.

The **direct method** shows individual amounts of cash inflows and cash outflows for the major operating activities. The net difference between these inflows and outflows is the cash flow from operating activities.

The Financial Accounting Standards Board encourages companies to use the direct method but permits the use of the indirect method. Despite the FASB's preference for the direct method, more than 95 percent of companies preparing the statement of cash flows use the indirect method. The indirect method is popular because (1) it is easier and less expensive to prepare than the direct method and (2) the direct method requires a supplemental disclosure showing cash flow from operating activities prepared under the indirect method.

Popularity of Method for Reporting the Cash Flow From Operations

Do you think a direct approach in communicating with financial statement users is best, or should your approach be more indirect? When it comes to reporting the cash flow from operations, companies appear to favor the indirect approach by a wide margin as evidenced by the responses to a survey of 600 large U.S. companies.

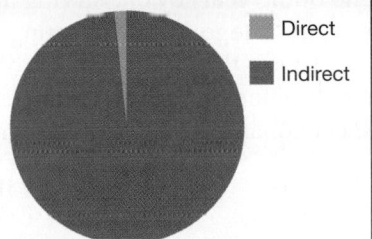

Source: Accounting Trends and Techniques

A Comparison of Accrual-Basis and Cash-Basis Amounts

Accountants calculate net income on the income statement using the accrual basis of accounting. The cash flow from operating activities, presented on the statement of cash flows, represents a company's net income using the cash basis of accounting. There is no necessary relationship between the two numbers. Compared with net income, the cash flow from operating activities may be larger, smaller, or about the same amount. Financial data from past annual reports of three well-known companies—**Chiquita Brands**, **Levi Strauss**, and **Harley-Davidson**—bear this out.

	Net Income or (Loss)	Cash Flow Provided (Used) by Operating Activities
Chiquita Brands Intl. Inc.	$(323,725,000)	$ 8,204,000
Levi Strauss & Co.	$ 229,285,000	$ 224,809,000
Harley-Davidson Inc.	$ 654,718,000	$(684,649,000)

Classify each of the cash flow events listed below as either an (1) operating activity, (2) investing activity, or (3) financing activity:

1. Cash received from customers
2. Cash sale of land
3. Cash paid to suppliers
4. Cash purchase of equipment
5. Payment on note payable

6. Cash dividend payment
7. Cash wages paid
8. Purchase of treasury stock
9. Cash sale of investments

The following section on preparing the statement of cash flows uses the indirect method. Appendix 12A uses the direct method. Your instructor can choose to cover either one or both methods. If the indirect method is skipped, then read Appendix 12A and return to the section (8 pages ahead) titled "Analyzing Cash Flows."

PREPARING THE STATEMENT OF CASH FLOWS USING THE INDIRECT METHOD

LO2 Explain the preparation of a statement of cash flows using the indirect method.

To prepare a statement of cash flows using the indirect method, the following information is needed: a company's income statement, comparative balance sheets for the current and prior year, and possibly additional data taken from the company's financial statements. **Exhibit 12-2** presents this information for the Bennett Company. We will use this data to prepare Bennett's 2016 statement of cash flows using the indirect method. As will be seen shortly, Bennett's statement of cash flows will explain the $25,000 increase in the company's cash account that occurred during 2016 (from $10,000 at the beginning of the year to $35,000 at the end of the year) by classifying the firm's cash inflows and outflows into the three business activity categories of operating, investing, and financing.

To see that the statement of cash flows can be prepared using only a company's income statement and the changes in its balance sheet accounts, consider again the balance sheet equation that was first introduced in Chapter 1:

$$\text{Assets (A)} = \text{Libilities (L)} + \text{Stockholders' equity (SE)} \qquad (1)$$

Separating a firm's assets into its cash (CA) and noncash assets (NCA) gives:

$$CA + NCA = L + SE \qquad (2)$$

And, rewriting the balance sheet equation in changes form yields:

$$\Delta CA + \Delta NCA = \Delta L + \Delta SE \qquad (3)$$

Finally, rearranging the components of the equation shows that the change in cash (which is the end result of the statement of cash flows) can be computed from the change in all of the other balance sheet accounts:

$$\Delta CA = \Delta L - \Delta NCA + \Delta SE \qquad (4)$$

Exhibit 12-2	Financial Data of Bennett Company

BENNETT COMPANY
Income Statement
For Year Ended December 31, 2016

Sales revenue.		$250,000
Cost of goods sold.	$148,000	
Wages expense	52,000	
Insurance expense	5,000	
Depreciation expense.	10,000	
Income tax expense.	11,000	
Gain on sale of plant assets	(8,000)	218,000
Net income		$ 32,000

Additional Data for 2016

1. Sold plant assets costing $20,000 for $28,000 cash.
2. Declared and paid cash dividends of $13,000.

BENNETT COMPANY
Balance Sheets

As of December 31	2016	2015
Assets		
Cash.	$ 35,000	$ 10,000
Accounts receivable.	39,000	34,000
Inventory.	54,000	60,000
Prepaid insurance	17,000	4,000
Long-term investments	15,000	—
Plant assets	180,000	200,000
Accumulated depreciation	(50,000)	(40,000)
Patent.	60,000	—
Total assets	$350,000	$268,000
Liabilities and Equity		
Accounts payable.	$ 10,000	$ 19,000
Income tax payable	5,000	3,000
Common stock.	260,000	190,000
Retained earnings	75,000	56,000
Total liabilities and equity.	$350,000	$268,000

IFRS ALERT

Currently, both U.S. GAAP and IFRS permit a company to present its statement of cash flows using either the direct method or the indirect method. A topic being considered by the FASB/IASB convergence project would limit the preparation of the statement of cash flows to just the direct method. The direct method is currently preferred by both the FASB and the IASB, although most U.S. firms present their statement of cash flows using the indirect method.

Five Steps to Preparing a Statement of Cash Flows

The process to prepare a statement of cash flows using the indirect method involves five steps. The approach begins by focusing initially only on the balance sheet and then proceeds to integrate a business's income statement through a series of systematic adjustments to a preliminary statement of cash flows derived solely from balance sheet data.

Step One Using just the beginning and ending balance sheets (see Columns 1 and 2 in **Exhibit 12-3**), calculate the change in each balance sheet account by subtracting the beginning balance sheet amount from the ending amount. The results of this step for the Bennett Company are presented in Column 3 of **Exhibit 12-3**. To simplify this step, the change in the Plant Assets account is combined with the Accumulated Depreciation account—that is, the change in the Plant Assets account is calculated on a net of accumulated depreciation basis.

To verify the accuracy of the Step One calculations, simply compare the sum of the changes in the asset accounts ($82,000) with the sum of the changes in the liability and stockholders' equity accounts ($82,000). These totals must be equal. If the totals are not equal, it indicates the presence of a subtraction error that must be identified and corrected before proceeding to Step Two.

Exhibit 12-3	Preparing a Statement of Cash Flows: The Indirect Method			
	BENNETT COMPANY Balance Sheet December 31, 2016			
	(1) Beginning of Year	**(2)** End of Year	**(3)** Change for Year	**(4)** Cash Flow Classification
Assets				
Cash.....................	$ 10,000	$ 35,000	**$25,000**	**Cash flow increase**
Accounts receivable........	34,000	39,000	5,000	Operating
Inventory.................	60,000	54,000	(6,000)	Operating
Prepaid insurance	4,000	17,000	13,000	Operating
Long-term investments	0	15,000	15,000	Investing
Plant assets (net)	160,000	130,000	(30,000)	Investing/Operating
Patent....................	0	60,000	60,000	Investing/Operating
Total assets	$268,000	$350,000	$82,000	
Liabilities and Equity				
Accounts payable..........	$ 19,000	$ 10,000	$ (9,000)	Operating
Income tax payable	3,000	5,000	2,000	Operating
Common stock............	190,000	260,000	70,000	Financing
Retained earnings	56,000	75,000	19,000	Operating/Financing
Total liabilities and equity....	$268,000	$350,000	$82,000	

An important figure identified during Step One is the "bottom line" of the statement of cash flows, namely the change in the cash account. **Exhibit 12-3** reveals that the cash account of the Bennett Company increased by $25,000 from the beginning of the year to the end of the year. Hence, all of the various cash inflows and outflows for the company must aggregate to this figure.

Step Two Identify the appropriate business activity category—operating, investing, or financing—for each balance sheet account. The cash flow activity classifications are presented in Column 4 of **Exhibit 12-3**.

Although measuring the change in the balance sheet accounts in Step 1 is a straightforward arithmetic activity, there can be some confusion over the correct activity classification for some of the balance sheet accounts in Step 2. The change in accounts receivable, inventory, prepaid insurance, accounts payable, and income tax payable are all easily identified as operating activities because they are associated with the day-to-day operations of a business. The change in common stock, on the other hand, is clearly a financing activity because it is associated with raising capital to finance a business. The change in net plant assets, however, can be both an investing activity and an operating activity. Purchases and sales of plant assets are associated with the capital investment needed to run a business, and thus are an investing activity. However, the depreciation expense associated with plant assets is an operating activity since the depreciation of plant assets is deducted as an expense in the calculation of a company's net income. Similarly, the change in intangible assets such as patents can be both an investing activity and an operating activity because the acquisition or sale of intangibles is an investing activity, whereas the amortization of intangibles is an expense deducted in the calculation of net income, and hence, an operating activity. Finally, the change in retained earnings can be both an operating activity and a financing activity because retained earnings is increased by net income, an operating activity, but decreased by the payment of dividends, a financing activity.

As a general rule, the following cash flow activity classifications apply, although exceptions exist:

Balance Sheet Account	Cash Flow Activity Category
Current assets	Operating
Noncurrent assets	Investing/Operating
Current liabilities.	Operating
Noncurrent liabilities.	Financing
Capital stock	Financing
Retained earnings	Operating/Financing

Examples of exceptions to the above cash flow activity classifications include the following:

- Marketable securities, a current asset, are an investing activity item.
- Current maturities of long-term debt, a current liability, are a financing activity item.
- Employee pension obligations, a noncurrent liability, are an operating activity item.

Step Three Having completed Steps One and Two, you are now ready to build a preliminary statement of cash flows using the calculated increases or decreases in the various balance sheet accounts from Step One and the identified activity classifications from Step Two. The preliminary statement of cash flows for the Bennett Company using the change values from Column 3 of **Exhibit 12-3** and the cash flow activity classifications from Column 4 is presented in **Exhibit 12-4**.

Because a statement of cash flows measures the inflows and outflows of cash for a business, it is important to note that the sign of the asset account changes calculated in Step One must be reversed for purposes of preparing the preliminary statement of cash flows in **Exhibit 12-4**. This can be seen in equation (4) above in which the change in noncash assets has a negative sign. For instance, **Exhibit 12-4** shows that the change in accounts receivable was an increase of $5,000, whereas the change in inventory was a decrease of $6,000. When preparing the indirect method statement of cash flows, a $5,000 increase in accounts receivable represents a subtraction from net income (a cash outflow), and a decline in inventory of $6,000 represents an addition to net income (a cash inflow), to arrive at the cash flow from operations. To illustrate why an increase in accounts receivable must be subtracted from net income to arrive at operating cash flow, consider how sales revenue is initially recorded. Assume that a $2,000 sale of goods is paid for with $1,200 in cash and the remaining amount recorded as an increase in accounts receivable. In this example, net income increases by $2,000, but cash is increased by only $1,200. Therefore, net income must be reduced by the $800 increase in accounts receivable in order to yield the correct cash flow from operations. Hence, when preparing the preliminary statement of cash flows in Step Three, it is important to remember to reverse the sign of the change values for the asset accounts. This is unnecessary for the liability and stockholders' equity accounts as can also be seen from equation (4) above.

Exhibit 12-4	An Illustration of a Preliminary Statement of Cash Flows: The Indirect Method

BENNETT COMPANY
Preliminary Statement of Cash Flows
For Year Ended December 31, 2016

Operating Activities

Retained earnings	$19,000
Accounts receivable	(5,000)
Inventory	6,000
Prepaid insurance	(13,000)
Accounts payable	(9,000)
Income tax payable	2,000
Cash flow from operating activities	0

Investing Activities

Long-term investments	(15,000)
Plant assets (net)	30,000
Patent	(60,000)
Cash flow for investing activities	(45,000)

Financing Activities

Common stock	70,000
Cash flow from financing activities	70,000
Change in cash (from the balance sheet)	$25,000

Exhibit 12-4 presents the preliminary statement of cash flows for the Bennett Company. This preliminary statement suggests that the firm's cash flow from operating activities was $0, the cash flow from investing activities was negative $45,000, and the cash flow from financing activities was $70,000. As required, the cash inflows and outflows aggregate to the change in cash from the balance sheet, an increase of $25,000.

Step Four   To this point we have used the balance sheet exclusively to provide the needed inputs to our statement of cash flows. For most businesses, however, cash flow will also be generated by a firm's ongoing operations. Hence, it is now appropriate to introduce the operations related data found on the company's income statement (see **Exhibit 12-2**).

In this step, we accomplish two important actions involving the preliminary statement of cash flows in **Exhibit 12-4**. First, the change in retained earnings from the balance sheet will be replaced by net income from the income statement. For the Bennett Company, the change in retained earnings of $19,000 does not equal net income of $32,000. The difference of $13,000 ($32,000 − $19,000) represents a cash dividend paid to Bennett's shareholders. Thus, when we replace retained earnings of $19,000 with net income of $32,000, it is also necessary to report the $13,000 cash dividend payment as a cash outflow under the financing activities section in **Exhibit 12-5**. Increasing the cash flow from operations and decreasing the cash flow from financing activities by an equivalent amount ($13,000) allows the statement of cash flows to remain in balance with the net change in cash of $25,000.

Second, we adjust the Bennett Company's net income for any **noncash expenses** such as the depreciation of plant assets and the amortization of intangibles that were deducted in the process of calculating the firm's accrual basis net income.[2] These noncash

---

[2] Depreciation expense and amortization expense are called noncash expenses because these expenses do not involve any current period cash outflow. Depreciation expense, for example, represents the allocation of the purchase price of plant assets over the many periods that these assets produce sales revenue for a business. The matching principle requires that the cost of plant assets be matched with the sales revenue produced by these assets, and this is accomplished on the income statement by the deduction of the periodic depreciation charge.

expenses must be added back to net income in the operating activities section to correctly measure the firm's operating cash flow. However, to keep the preliminary statement of cash flows in balance with an increase in cash of $25,000, it is also necessary to subtract equivalent amounts in the investing activities section.

To summarize, the adjustments to the Bennett Company's preliminary statement of cash flows in **Exhibit 12-4** are:

1. Net income of $32,000 replaces the change in retained earnings of $19,000 in the operating activities section. This action adds $13,000 to the cash flow from operating activities. To keep the statement of cash flows in balance with the change in cash of $25,000, it is necessary to subtract $13,000 elsewhere on the statement. Since retained earnings is calculated as follows:

    > Retained earnings (beginning)
    > + Net income for the period
    > − Dividends declared
    > − Retained earnings (ending)

    the outflow of $13,000 is also reflected as a cash dividend to shareholders under the financing activities section.

2. Depreciation expense of $10,000, a noncash deduction from net income, is added back to net income to avoid understating the cash flow from operations. However, to keep the statement of cash flows in balance with the change in cash of $25,000, a similar amount is subtracted from plant assets under the investing activities section.

Step Five   To provide the most useful cash flow data, a final step is required: Make any appropriate adjustments to the operating activities section to calculate a company's operating cash flow. As noted above, a firm's operating cash flow should include only the cash flows from operating activities. Consequently, to calculate the cash flow from operating activities of a business, it is necessary to review a company's income statement to identify and remove the financial effects of any nonoperating transactions included in net income.[3]

To illustrate this point, note that the Bennett Company sold plant assets during the year at a gain of $8,000 ($28,000 sales price less $20,000 cost). This event is an investing activity and therefore properly belongs in the investing activities section. However, the gain of $8,000 is included in net income in the operating activities section. Thus, to correctly assess Bennett's cash flows, it is necessary to subtract the gain from the operating activities section and add it to the change in plant assets in the investing activities section. When combined with the adjustment for depreciation expense from Step Four, the cash flow from plant assets is $28,000 ($30,000 change in plant assets − $10,000 adjustment for depreciation expense + $8,000 adjustment for gain). The adjusted amount of $28,000 is equal to the cash received on the sale of plant assets

Exhibit 12-5 presents the final statement of cash flows for Bennett Company and includes not only the adjustments from Step Four, but also the adjustment to remove any nonoperating gains and losses from the cash flow from operating activities (Step Five). Note that the company's statement of cash flows remains in balance with the change in cash of $25,000 after the adjustments in both of these steps. This result is possible because whatever amount was added to (or subtracted from) net income under the cash flow from operating activities, an equivalent amount was subtracted from (or added to) the investing activities or the financing activities.

---

[3] An exception is interest expense, which most investment professionals view as a financing activity. Regardless, interest payments are required to be included in the cash flow from operating activities.

Exhibit 12-5	Statement of Cash Flows—The Indirect Method

BENNETT COMPANY
Statement of Cash Flows
For Year Ended December 31, 2016

Cash Flow from Operating Activities

Net income	$32,000	
Add (deduct) items to convert net income to cash basis		
Depreciation	10,000	
Gain on sale of plant assets	(8,000)	
Accounts receivable increase	(5,000)	
Inventory decrease	6,000	
Prepaid insurance increase	(13,000)	
Accounts payable decrease	(9,000)	
Income tax payable increase	2,000	
Cash provided by operating activities		$15,000
Cash Flow from Investing Activities		
Purchase of long-term investments	(15,000)	
Sale of plant assets	28,000	
Purchase of patent	(60,000)	
Cash used by investing activities		(47,000)
Cash Flow from Financing Activities		
Issuance of common stock	70,000	
Payment of dividends	(13,000)	
Cash provided by financing activities		57,000
Net increase in cash		25,000
Cash at beginning of year		10,000
Cash at end of year		$35,000

Bennett's statement of cash flows reveals that the cash flow provided by operating activities is $15,000, the cash flow used by investing activities is negative $47,000, and the cash flow provided by financing activities is $57,000. The resulting total cash flow of $25,000 exactly equals the increase in cash on the balance sheet of $25,000, as required.

The following illustration summarizes the five-step process to prepare an indirect method statement of cash flows:

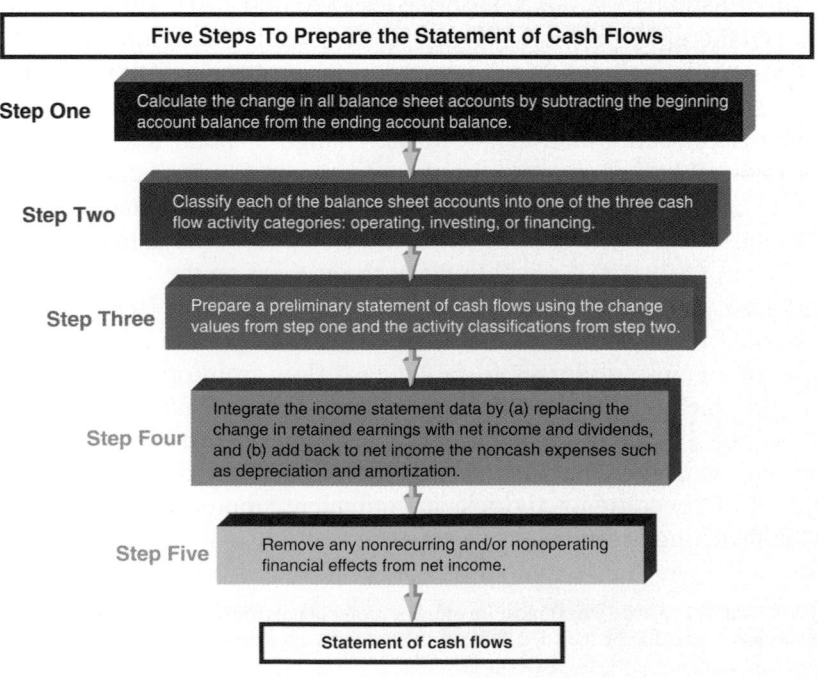

Five Steps To Prepare the Statement of Cash Flows

Step One — Calculate the change in all balance sheet accounts by subtracting the beginning account balance from the ending account balance.

Step Two — Classify each of the balance sheet accounts into one of the three cash flow activity categories: operating, investing, or financing.

Step Three — Prepare a preliminary statement of cash flows using the change values from step one and the activity classifications from step two.

Step Four — Integrate the income statement data by (a) replacing the change in retained earnings with net income and dividends, and (b) add back to net income the noncash expenses such as depreciation and amortization.

Step Five — Remove any nonrecurring and/or nonoperating financial effects from net income.

Statement of cash flows

According to **Home Depot**, "Our values are our beliefs, principles and standards that do not change over time. Values are the resources we draw on when asked to make decisions. They form the groundwork for our ethical behavior. All that we do at The Home Depot must be consistent with the values of the Company. We believe in *Doing the Right Thing*, having *Respect for all People*, building *Strong Relationships*, *Taking Care of Our People*, *Giving Back*, providing *Excellent Customer Service*, *Encouraging Entrepreneurial Spirit* and providing strong *Shareholder Returns*."

Home Depot believes that "Doing the Right Thing" leads to doing well for all its stakeholders, including its shareholders. As Home Depot states, "We will conduct our business and ourselves in a way that enhances and preserves the reputation of the Company while providing our shareholders with a fair return on their investment." There seems to be a lot of truth in this as Home Depot has managed to stay profitable even as the poor U.S. economy has battered the construction industry. In fiscal years 2008 and 2007, during the height of the construction downturn, the company still managed to produce cash flows from operating activities each year in excess of $5 billion.

YOUR TURN! 12.2

The solution is on page 625.

Husky Company's 2016 income statement and comparative balance sheets as of December 31 of 2016 and 2015 are shown below:

HUSKY COMPANY Income Statement For Year Ended December 31, 2016		
Sales revenue.		$1,270,000
Cost of goods sold.	$860,000	
Wages expense	172,000	
Insurance expense.	16,000	
Depreciation expense.	34,000	
Interest expense.	18,000	
Income tax expense.	58,000	1,158,000
Net income.		$ 112,000

HUSKY COMPANY Balance Sheets	Dec. 31, 2016	Dec. 31, 2015
Assets		
Cash.	$ 22,000	$ 10,000
Accounts receivable.	82,000	64,000
Inventory.	180,000	120,000
Prepaid insurance	10,000	14,000
Plant assets	500,000	390,000
Accumulated depreciation	(136,000)	(102,000)
Total assets	$658,000	$496,000
Liabilities and Stockholders' Equity		
Accounts payable.	$ 14,000	$ 20,000
Wages payable.	18,000	12,000
Income tax payable	14,000	16,000
Bonds payable	260,000	150,000
Common stock.	180,000	180,000
Retained earnings	172,000	118,000
Total liabilities and stockholders' equity	$658,000	$496,000

Cash dividends of $58,000 were declared and paid during 2016. Plant assets were purchased for cash, and bonds payable were issued for cash. Accounts payable relate to merchandise purchases.

Required
Prepare a 2016 statement of cash flows for the Husky Company using the indirect method.

For readers skipping the indirect method, please resume reading here.

ANALYZING CASH FLOWS

LO3 **Define** several ratios used to analyze the statement of cash flows and **explain** their use.

Data from the statement of cash flows are often used to calculate financial measures to evaluate a company's cash flow health. Three such measures include a company's free cash flow, the operating cash flow to current liabilities ratio, and the operating cash flow to capital expenditures ratio.

Free Cash Flow

Free cash flow (FCF) is often used by investment professionals and investors to evaluate a company's cash-flow strength. FCF is an important performance reference point for investment professionals because it is less subject to the accounting trickery that may characterize accrual basis net income of some firms. Free cash flow is calculated as follows:

> **FCF = Cash flow from operating activities − Capital expenditures**

As discussed in Chapter 9, capital expenditures refer to the required reinvestment in a business's plant and intangible assets necessary to enable a firm to remain a going concern. A firm with strong free cash flow will carry a higher stock value than one with weak (or no) free cash flow.

TAKEAWAY 12.1	Concept →	Method →	Assessment
	Does a company generate cash flows in excess of its capital expenditure needs?	Statement of cash flows. FCF = Cash flow from operating activities − Capital expenditures	The higher the free cash flow, the greater is a company's ability to generate cash for needs other than capital expenditures.

Operating-Cash-Flow-to-Current-Liabilities Ratio

Two measures previously introduced—the current ratio and the quick ratio—emphasize the relationship of a company's current or quick assets to its current liabilities in an attempt to measure the ability of a firm to pay its current liabilities. The **operating-cash-flow-to-current-liabilities ratio** is another measure of a company's ability to pay its current liabilities. While the current and quick ratios focus on a firm's ability to pay liabilities using existing current or quick assets, the operating cash flow to current liabilities highlights a firm's ability to pay its current liabilities using its operating cash flow. The ratio is calculated as follows:

$$\text{Operating-cash-flow-to-current-liabilities ratio} = \frac{\text{Cash flow from operating activities}}{\text{Average current liabilities}}$$

The cash flow from operating activities is obtained from the statement of cash flows. The denominator is the average of the beginning and ending current liabilities for the year.

The following amounts (in millions of dollars) were taken from the financial statements of the **Gannett Co., Inc.**, a diversified news and information company that publishes *USA Today*:

Cash flow from operating activities	$1,017,186
Current liabilities at beginning of the year	962,163
Current liabilities at end of the year	1,153,141

The operating cash flow to current liabilities ratio for the Gannett Co. is calculated as follows:

$$\frac{\$1,017,186}{\left[\dfrac{(\$962,163 + \$1,153,141)}{2}\right]} = 0.96$$

The higher this ratio, the greater is a firm's ability to pay current liabilities using its operating cash flow. A ratio of 0.5 is considered a strong ratio; consequently, Gannett's ratio of 0.96 would be interpreted as very strong. A ratio of 0.96 indicates that Gannett generates $0.96 of operating cash flow for every dollar of current liabilities.

Concept	⟶	Method	⟶	Assessment	TAKEAWAY 12.2
Will a company have sufficient cash to pay its current liabilities as they become due?		Statement of cash flows and balance sheet. Operating-cash-flow-to-current-liabilities ratio $=$ $\dfrac{\text{Cash flow from operating activities}}{\text{Average current liabilities}}$		The higher the ratio, the higher the probability that a company will have sufficient operating cash flow to pay its current liabilities as they become due.	

Operating-Cash-Flow-to-Capital-Expenditures Ratio

To remain competitive, a business must be able to replace, and expand when appropriate, its property, plant, and equipment. A ratio that evaluates a firm's ability to finance its capital investments from operating cash flow is the **operating-cash-flow-to-capital-expenditures ratio**. This ratio is calculated as follows:

$$\text{Operating-cash-flow-to-capital expenditures ratio} = \frac{\textbf{Cash flow from operating activities}}{\textbf{Annual net capital expenditures}}$$

The numerator in this ratio comes from the statement of cash flows. Information for the denominator may be found in one or more places in the financial statements. Data regarding a company's capital expenditures are presented in the investing activities section of the statement of cash flows. (When capital expenditures are reported in the statement of cash flows, the amount is often broken into two figures—(1) Proceeds from the sale of property, plant and equipment and (2) Purchases of property, plant and equipment. The appropriate "capital expenditures" figure for purpose of calculating this ratio is the net of the two amounts.) Data on capital expenditures are also part of the required industry segment disclosures in the notes to the financial statements. Finally, management's discussion and analysis of the financial statements may identify a company's annual capital expenditures.

A ratio in excess of 1.0 indicates that a firm's current operating activities are providing cash in excess of the amount needed to fund its desired investment in plant assets and would normally be considered a sign of financial strength. The interpretation of this ratio is influenced by the trend in recent years, the ratio being achieved by other firms in the same industry, and the stage of a firm's life cycle. A firm in the early stages of its life cycle—when periods of rapid expansion may occur—may be expected to experience a lower ratio than a firm in the later stage of its life cycle—when maintenance of plant capacity may be more likely than an expansion of plant capacity.

To illustrate the ratio's calculation, **Abbott Laboratories**, a manufacturer of pharmaceutical and health care products, reported capital expenditures (in thousands of dollars) of $1,287,724. Abbott's cash flow from operating activities was $6,994,620. Thus, Abbott's operating-cash-flow-to-capital-expenditures ratio for the year was 5.43, or ($6,994,620/$1,287,724). The following are operating-cash-flow-to-capital-expenditures ratios for other well-known companies:

PepsiCo Inc. (Consumer foods and beverages)	2.98
Lockheed Martin Corporation (Aerospace).	4.77
Norfolk Southern Corporation (Freight transportation services).	1.87
Federal Mogul Corporation (Precision parts)	2.04

ACCOUNTING IN PRACTICE

Know Your Cash Flow

The expression "Cash is King" certainly holds true for any small business. It is critical for entrepreneurs to understand the difference between net income and cash flow. Cash is what is needed to pay the bills. While earning a positive net income is nice, it is cash and not net income that runs the business. Many small businesses have failed because of a lack of managing cash flows.

TAKEAWAY 12.3	Concept	→ Method →	Assessment
	Does a company generate sufficient operating cash flows to finance its capital expenditure needs?	Statement of cash flows. $$\text{Operating-cash-flow-to-capital-expenditures ratio} = \frac{\text{Cash flow from operating activities}}{\text{Annual net capital expenditures}}$$	The higher the ratio, the higher the probability that a company will generate sufficient operating cash flow to finance its capital expenditure needs.

YOUR TURN! 12.3

The solution is on page 625.

MBC

The following selected data were obtained from the financial statements of Blake Enterprises:

Cash flow from operating activities	$40,000
Annual net capital expenditures.	12,500
Average current liabilities	30,000

Calculate the following financial measures for Blake Enterprises:

1. Free cash flow
2. Operating-cash-flow-to-current-liabilities ratio
3. Operating-cash-flow-to-capital-expenditures ratio

COMPREHENSIVE PROBLEM

Terry Company's income statement and comparative balance sheets at December 31, 2016 and 2015, are as follows:

TERRY COMPANY Income Statement For Year Ended December 31, 2016		
Sales revenue.		$385,000
Dividend income.		5,000
		390,000
Cost of goods sold.	$233,000	
Wages expense	82,000	
Advertising expense.	10,000	
Depreciation expense.	11,000	
Income tax expense.	17,000	
Loss on sale of investments.	2,000	355,000
Net income.		$ 35,000

TERRY COMPANY Balance Sheets		
	Dec. 31, 2016	**Dec. 31, 2015**
Assets		
Cash.	$ 8,000	$ 12,000
Accounts receivable.	22,000	28,000
Inventory.	94,000	66,000
Prepaid advertising.	12,000	9,000
Long-term investments	30,000	40,000
Plant assets	178,000	130,000
Accumulated depreciation	(72,000)	(61,000)
Total assets	$272,000	$224,000
Liabilities and Stockholders' Equity		
Accounts payable.	$ 27,000	$ 14,000
Wages payable.	6,000	2,500
Income tax payable	3,000	4,500
Common stock.	139,000	125,000
Retained earnings	97,000	79,000
Unrealized loss on investments	—	(1,000)
Total liabilities and stockholders' equity	$272,000	$224,000

Cash dividends of $17,000 were declared and paid during 2016. Plant assets were purchased for cash, and, later in the year, additional common stock was issued for cash. Investments costing $10,000 were sold for cash at a $1,000 loss.

Required

a. Calculate the change in cash that occurred during 2016.

b. Prepare a 2016 statement of cash flows using the indirect method.

Solution

a. $8,000 ending balance − $12,000 beginning balance = $4,000 decrease in cash

b. 1. Use the indirect method to determine the cash flow from operating activities.

- The adjustments to convert Terry Company's net income of $35,000 to the cash provided by operating activities of $38,000 are shown in the following statement of cash flows.

2. Analyze changes in remaining noncash asset (and contra asset) accounts to determine cash flows from investing activities.
   - Long-term investments: $10,000 decrease resulted from sale of investments for cash at a $1,000 loss. Cash received from sale of investments = $9,000 ($10,000 cost − $1,000 loss).
   - Plant assets: $48,000 increase resulted from purchase of plant assets for cash. Cash paid to purchase plant assets = $48,000.
   - Accumulated depreciation: $11,000 increase resulted from the recording of 2016 depreciation. No cash flow effect.
3. Analyze changes in remaining liability and stockholders' equity accounts to determine cash flows from financing activities.
   - Common stock: $14,000 increase resulted from the issuance of stock for cash. Cash received from issuance of common stock = $14,000.
   - Retained earnings: $18,000 increase resulted from net income of $35,000 and dividend declaration of $17,000. Cash paid as dividends = $17,000.

   The statement of cash flows (indirect method) is as follows:

TERRY COMPANY Statement of Cash Flows For the Year Ended December 31, 2016		
Cash Flow from Operating Activities		
Net income	$35,000	
Add (deduct) items to convert net income to cash basis		
Depreciation	11,000	
Loss on sale of investments	2,000	
Accounts receivable decrease	6,000	
Inventory increase.	(28,000)	
Prepaid advertising increase.	(3,000)	
Accounts payable increase.	13,000	
Wages payable increase.	3,500	
Income tax payable decrease	(1,500)	
Cash provided by operating activities.		$38,000
Cash Flow from Investing Activities		
Sale of investments	9,000	
Purchase of plant assets	(48,000)	
Cash used by investing activities		(39,000)
Cash Flow from Financing Activities		
Issuance of common stock.	14,000	
Payment of dividends.	(17,000)	
Cash used by financing activities		(3,000)
Net decrease in cash		(4,000)
Cash at beginning of year		12,000
Cash at end of year		$ 8,000

APPENDIX 12A: Preparing the Statement of Cash Flows Under the Direct Method

Although it is quite straightforward to create a direct method statement of cash flows given access to a company's internal accounting records, such access is rarely available to anyone except a company's management team. All that is necessary is to pull the numbers directly off the Cash general ledger account and place them in the appropriate section of the statement of cash flows. This is why the direct method is referred to as "direct." The cash flow from operations is taken directly from the company's general ledger, rather than being indirectly computed from net income. Unfortunately, investment professionals, lenders, and stockholders rarely have access to such proprietary internal data. Thus, it is necessary to be able to create direct method cash flow information using only such publicly available data as the indirect method statement of cash flows.

LO4 Explain the preparation of a statement of cash flows using the direct method.

The process to convert an indirect method statement of cash flows to the direct method requires two steps. First, replace net income (the first line item under the operating activities section of the indirect method statement format) with the line items appearing on a firm's income statement. For instance, Bennett Company's income statement in **Exhibit 12-2** contains the following line items:

Sales revenue.	$250,000
Cost of goods sold.	(148,000)
Wages expense	(52,000)
Insurance expense.	(5,000)
Depreciation expense.	(10,000)
Income tax expense.	(11,000)
Gain on sale of plant assets.	8,000
Net income.	$ 32,000

Thus, for the Bennett Company, we begin by replacing the net income of $32,000 under the operating activities section in **Exhibit 12-5** with the seven income statement line items shown above, which aggregate to $32,000.

The second step involves adjusting the income statement line items identified in Step One with the remaining line items from the operating activities section of the indirect method statement of cash flows. **Exhibit 12A-1** summarizes the procedures for converting individual income statement items to the corresponding cash flows from operating activities.

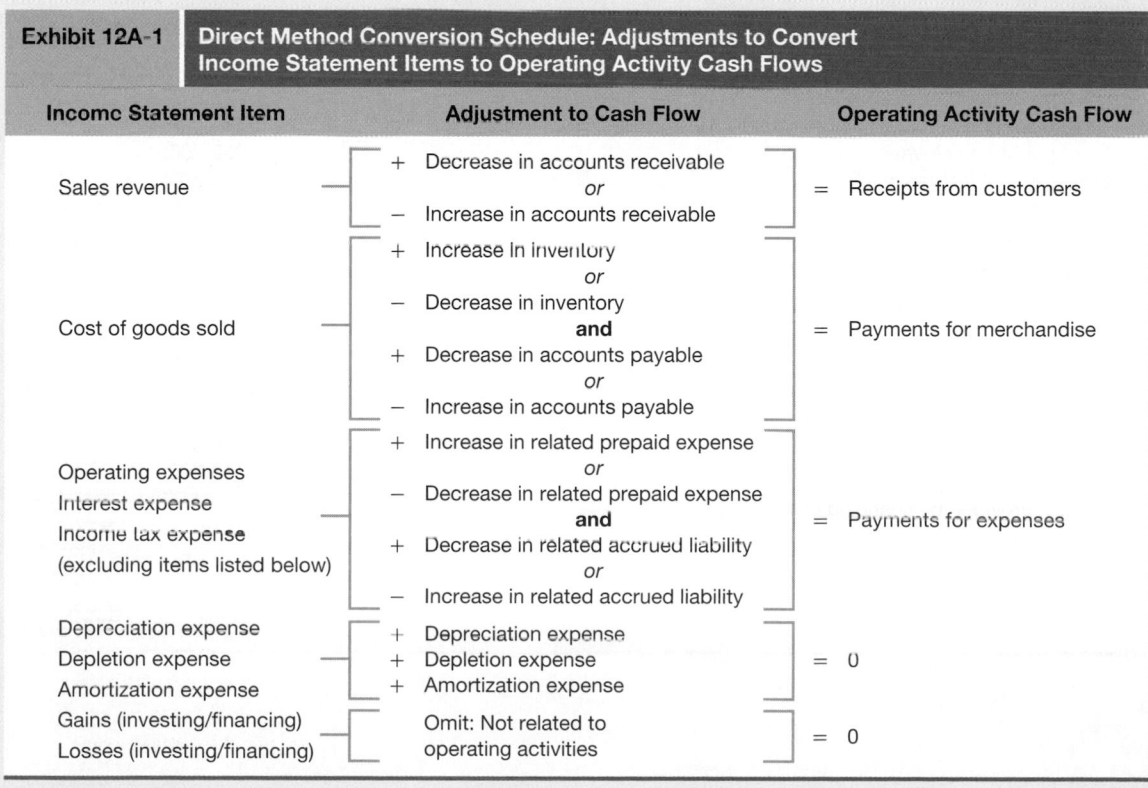

Exhibit 12A-1 — **Direct Method Conversion Schedule: Adjustments to Convert Income Statement Items to Operating Activity Cash Flows**

Income Statement Item	Adjustment to Cash Flow	Operating Activity Cash Flow
Sales revenue	+ Decrease in accounts receivable *or* − Increase in accounts receivable	= Receipts from customers
Cost of goods sold	+ Increase in inventory *or* − Decrease in inventory **and** + Decrease in accounts payable *or* − Increase in accounts payable	= Payments for merchandise
Operating expenses / Interest expense / Income tax expense (excluding items listed below)	+ Increase in related prepaid expense *or* − Decrease in related prepaid expense **and** + Decrease in related accrued liability *or* − Increase in related accrued liability	= Payments for expenses
Depreciation expense / Depletion expense / Amortization expense	+ Depreciation expense + Depletion expense + Amortization expense	= 0
Gains (investing/financing) / Losses (investing/financing)	Omit: Not related to operating activities	= 0

Using Bennett Company's data in **Exhibit 12-5**, those adjustments would appear as follows:

Income Statement Line Items		Operating Activities Line Items	Direct Method Cash Flow	
Sales revenue............	$250,000	**Less** $5,000 accounts receivable	Cash received from customers	$245,000
Cost of goods sold........	(148,000)	**Add** $6,000 inventory	Cash paid for merchandise	(151,000)
		Less $9,000 accounts payable		
Wage expense	(52,000)	**No adjustment**	Cash paid to employees..........	(52,000)
Insurance expense........	(5,000)	**Less** $13,000 prepaid insurance	Cash paid for insurance..........	(18,000)
Depreciation expense......	(10,000)	**Add** $10,000 depreciation		
Income tax expense.......	(11,000)	**Add** $2,000 income tax payable	Cash paid for income taxes	(9,000)
Gain on sale of plant		**Less** $8,000 gain on sale of		
assets	8,000	plant assets		
Net income.............	$ 32,000		Cash flow from operations.......	$ 15,000

Exhibit 12A-2 presents the Bennett Company's direct method statement of cash flows after undertaking the above two steps. As expected, the direct method cash flow from operating activities of $15,000 is exactly equivalent to the indirect method result of $15,000 as reported in **Exhibit 12-5**. Note that the cash flow from investing activities and the cash flow from financing activities are exactly the same in both **Exhibit 12-5** and **Exhibit 12A-2**. The only difference between the two exhibits is the manner in which the cash flow from operating activities is calculated. In **Exhibit 12-5**, the cash flow from operating activities is calculated by beginning with net income and then adjusting for various noncash expenses (depreciation expense) and nonoperating transactions (gain on sale of plant assets), as well as adjusting for the changes in the various working capital accounts (accounts receivable, inventory, prepaid insurance, accounts payable, and taxes payable). In **Exhibit 12A-2**, net income is replaced with the income statement line items and the noncash expenses and working capital adjustments are disaggregated to the individual line items. But in each case, the operating cash flow is $15,000. A company using the direct method must also separately disclose the reconciliation of net income to cash flow from operating activities prepared using the indirect method.

Exhibit 12A-2	Statement of Cash Flows Under the Direct Method

BENNETT COMPANY
Statement of Cash Flows
For Year Ended December 31, 2016

Cash Flow from Operating Activities		
Cash received from customers		$245,000
Cash paid for merchandise purchased	$(151,000)	
Cash paid to employees..	(52,000)	
Cash paid for insurance	(18,000)	
Cash paid for income taxes	(9,000)	(230,000)
Cash provided by operating activities		15,000
Cash Flow from Investing Activities		
Purchase of long-term investments......................................	(15,000)	
Sale of plant assets	28,000	
Purchase of patent..	(60,000)	
Cash used by investing activities		(47,000)
Cash Flow from Financing Activities		
Issuance of common stock	70,000	
Payment of dividends..	(13,000)	
Cash provided by financing activities...................................		57,000
Net increase in cash...		25,000
Cash at beginning of year		10,000
Cash at end of year		$ 35,000

Husky Company's 2016 income statement and comparative balance sheets as of December 31 of 2016 and 2015 are shown below:

YOUR TURN! 12A.1

The solution is on pages 625-626.

HUSKY COMPANY Income Statement For the Year Ended December 31, 2016		
Sales revenue.		$1,270,000
Cost of goods sold.	$860,000	
Wages expense	172,000	
Insurance expense	16,000	
Depreciation expense.	34,000	
Interest expense.	18,000	
Income tax expense.	58,000	1,158,000
Net income.		$ 112,000

HUSKY COMPANY Balance Sheets		
	Dec. 31, 2016	**Dec. 31, 2015**
Assets		
Cash.	$ 22,000	$ 10,000
Accounts receivable.	82,000	64,000
Inventory.	180,000	120,000
Prepaid insurance	10,000	14,000
Plant assets	500,000	390,000
Accumulated depreciation	(136,000)	(102,000)
Total assets	$658,000	$496,000
Liabilities and Stockholders' Equity		
Accounts payable.	$ 14,000	$ 20,000
Wages payable.	18,000	12,000
Income tax payable	14,000	16,000
Bonds payable	260,000	150,000
Common stock.	180,000	180,000
Retained earnings	172,000	118,000
Total liabilities and stockholders' equity	$658,000	$496,000

Cash dividends of $58,000 were declared and paid during 2016. Plant assets were purchased for cash, and bonds payable were issued for cash. Bond interest is paid semiannually on June 30 and December 31. Accounts payable relate to merchandise purchases.

Required

Prepare a 2016 statement of cash flows using the direct method.

SUMMARY OF LEARNING OBJECTIVES

Discuss the content and format of the statement of cash flows. (p. 578)

LO1

- The statement of cash flows explains the net increase or decrease in cash and cash equivalents during the period.
- The statement of cash flows separates cash flows into operating, investing, and financing activity categories.
- The statement of cash flows also provides a required supplemental disclosure reporting noncash investing and financing activities.
- The statement of cash flows should help users compare, evaluate, and predict a firm's cash flows and also help evaluate its financial flexibility.

LO2   **Explain the preparation of a statement of cash flows using the indirect method. (p. 584)**
- The indirect method of preparing the cash flow from operating activities section reconciles net income to cash flow from operating activities.

LO3   **Define several ratios used to analyze the statement of cash flows and explain their use. (p. 592)**
- Free cash flow is defined as a company's cash flow from operations less its capital expenditures; the metric provides a measure of a firm's cash flow that can be used to fund business activities beyond the replacement of property, plant, and equipment.
- The operating-cash-flow-to-current-liabilities ratio is calculated by dividing a company's cash flow from operating activities by its average current liabilities for the year; the ratio reveals a firm's ability to repay current liabilities from operating cash flow.
- The operating-cash-flow-to-capital-expenditures ratio is calculated by dividing a firm's cash flow from operating activities by its annual net capital expenditures; the ratio evaluates a firm's ability to fund its capital investment using operating cash flow.

LO4   **Appendix 12A: Explain the preparation of a statement of cash flows using the direct method. (p. 597)**
- The direct method of preparing the cash flow from operating activities section shows the major categories of operating cash receipts and payments.
- The FASB encourages use of the direct method but permits use of either the direct or the indirect method.
- A firm using the direct method must separately disclose the reconciliation of net income to cash flow from operating activities.

SUMMARY	Concept	→ Method	→ Assessment
TAKEAWAY 12.1	Does a company generate cash flows in excess of its capital expenditure needs?	Statement of cash flows. FCF = Cash flow from operating activities − Capital expenditures	The higher the free cash flow, the greater is a company's ability to generate cash for needs other than capital expenditures.
TAKEAWAY 12.2	Will a company have sufficient cash to pay its current liabilities as they become due?	Statement of cash flows and balance sheet. Operating-cash-flow-to-current-liabilities ratio = Cash flow from operating activities / Average current liabilities	The higher the ratio, the higher the probability that a company will have sufficient operating cash flow to pay its current liabilities as they become due.
TAKEAWAY 12.3	Does a company generate sufficient operating cash flows to finance its capital expenditure needs?	Statement of cash flows. Operating-cash-flow-to-capital-expenditures ratio = Cash flow from operating activities / Annual net capital expenditures	The higher the ratio, the higher the probability that a company will generate sufficient operating cash flow to finance its capital expenditure needs.

KEY TERMS

Cash equivalents (p. 578)
Cash management (p. 578)
Direct method (p. 583)
Financial flexibility (p. 583)
Financing activities (p. 580)

Free cash flow (FCF) (p. 592)
Indirect method (p. 583)
Investing activities (p. 580)
Noncash expenses (p. 588)
Noncash investing and financing activities (p. 582)

Operating activities (p. 580)
Operating-cash-flow-to-capital-expenditures ratio (p. 593)
Operating-cash-flow-to-current-liabilities ratio (p. 592)

Assignments with the ⬤ logo in the margin are available in BusinessCourse.
See the Preface of the book for details.

SELF-STUDY QUESTIONS

(Answers to the Self-Study Questions are at the end of the chapter.)

1. Which of the following is not disclosed in a statement of cash flows?   LO1
   a. A transfer of cash to a cash equivalent investment
   b. The amount of cash at year-end
   c. Cash outflows from investing activities during the period
   d. Cash inflows from financing activities during the period

2. Which of the following events will appear in the cash flows from investing activities section of the   LO1
statement of cash flows?
   a. Cash received as interest
   b. Cash received from issuance of common stock
   c. Cash purchase of truck
   d. Cash payment of dividends

3. Which of the following events will appear in the cash flows from financing activities section of the   LO1
statement of cash flows?
   a. Cash purchase of equipment
   b. Cash purchase of bonds issued by another company
   c. Cash received as repayment for funds loaned
   d. Cash purchase of treasury stock

4. Tyler Company has net income of $49,000 and the following related items: LO2

Depreciation expense	$ 5,000
Accounts receivable Increase	2,000
Inventory decrease	10,000
Accounts payable decrease	4,000

Using the indirect method, what is Tyler's cash flow from operations?
   a. $42,000   *c.* $58,000
   b. $46,000   *d.* $38,000

5. Free cash flow is a measure of a firm's   LO3
   a. interest free debt.
   b. ability to generate net income.
   c. ability to generate cash and invest in new capital expenditures.
   d. ability to collect accounts receivable in a timely manner.

6. Which of the following events will not appear in the cash flows from financing activities section of   LO1
the statement of cash flow?
   a. Borrowing cash from a bank
   b. Issuance of stock in exchange for plant assets
   c. Sales of common stock
   d. Payment of dividends on preferred stock

7. Taylor Company reports free cash flow of $15,000, total cash of $18,000, net income of $50,000,   LO3
current assets of $90,000, average current liabilities of $60,000, and cash flow from operating activities
of $48,000. Compute the operating-cash-flow-to-current-liabilities ratio for Taylor Company.
   a. 0.83
   b. 0.80
   c. 0.30
   d. 1.25

8. Which of the following is not a cash equivalent?   LO1
   a. Short-term U.S. Treasury bill
   b. Short-term certificate of deposit
   c. Money-market account
   d. IBM common stock

LO2

9. **Which of the following expenses are not added back to net income when using the indirect method to prepare a statement of cash flows?**
   a. Amortization expense
   b. Depletion expense
   c. Interest expense
   d. Depreciation expense

LO4
(Appendix 12A)

10. **Smith & Sons reports interest expense of $90,000 on its income statement. The beginning and ending balances for interest payable reported on its balance sheet are $10,000 and $15,000, respectively. How much cash did Smith & Sons pay for interest expense this period?**
    a. $85,000
    b. $95,000
    c. $100,000
    d. $105,000

LO4
(Appendix 12A)

11. **Which of the following methods will disclose the cash received from customers in the statement of cash flows?**
    a. Indirect method
    b. Reconciliation method
    c. Direct method
    d. Both direct and indirect methods

LO4
(Appendix 12A)

12. **Smith & Sons reports sales revenue of $1,000,000 on its income statement. Its balance sheet reveals beginning and ending accounts receivable of $60,000 and $92,000, respectively. What is the amount of cash collected from customers of the company?**
    a. $1,032,000
    b. $968,000
    c. $1,060,000
    d. $1,092,000

QUESTIONS

1. What is the definition of *cash equivalents?* Give three examples of cash equivalents.

2. Why are cash equivalents included with cash in a statement of cash flows?

3. What are the three major types of activities classified on a statement of cash flows? Give an example of a cash inflow and a cash outflow in each classification.

4. In which of the three activity categories of a statement of cash flows would each of the following items appear? Indicate for each item whether it represents a cash inflow or a cash outflow:
   a. Cash purchase of equipment
   b. Cash collection on loans
   c. Cash dividends paid
   d. Cash dividends received
   e. Cash proceeds from issuing stock
   f. Cash receipts from customers
   g. Cash interest paid
   h. Cash interest received

5. Why is a statement of cash flows a useful financial statement?

6. What is the difference between the direct method and the indirect method of presenting the cash flow from operating activities?

7. In determining the cash flow from operating activities using the indirect method, why is it necessary to add depreciation back to net income? Give an example of another item that is added back to net income under the indirect method.

8. Vista Company sold land for $98,000 cash that had originally cost $70,000. The company recorded a gain on the sale of $28,000. How is this event reported in a statement of cash flows using the indirect method?

9. A firm uses the indirect method. Using the following information, what is its cash flow from operating activities?

Net income.	$88,000
Accounts receivable decrease.	13,000
Inventory increase	9,000
Accounts payable decrease.	3,500
Income tax payable increase	1,500
Depreciation expense.	6,000

10. If a business had a net loss for the year, under what circumstances would the statement of cash flows show a positive cash flow from operating activities?

11. A firm is converting its accrual revenues to corresponding cash amounts using the direct method. Sales revenue on the income statement are $925,000. Beginning and ending accounts receivable on the balance sheet are $58,000 and $44,000, respectively. What is the amount of cash received from customers?

12. A firm reports $86,000 wages expense in its income statement. If beginning and ending wages payable are $3,900 and $2,800, respectively, what is the amount of cash paid to employees?

13. A firm reports $43,000 advertising expense in its income statement. If beginning and ending prepaid advertising are $6,000 and $7,600, respectively, what is the amount of cash paid for advertising?

14. Rusk Company sold equipment for $5,100 cash that had cost $35,000 and had $29,000 of accumulated depreciation. How is this event reported in a statement of cash flows using the direct method?

15. What separate disclosures are required for a company that reports a statement of cash flows using the direct method?

16. How is the *operating-cash-flow-to-current-liabilities ratio* calculated? Explain its use.

17. How is the *operating-cash-flow-to-capital-expenditures ratio* calculated? Explain its use.

18. The statement of cash flows provides information that may be useful in predicting future cash flows, evaluating financial flexibility, assessing liquidity, and identifying a company's financing needs. It is not, however, the best financial statement for learning about a firm's financial performance during a period. Information about a company's financial performance is provided by the income statement. Two basic principles—the revenue recognition principle and the matching concept—work to distinguish the income statement from the statement of cash flows. (a) Define the revenue recognition principle and the matching concept. (b) Briefly explain how these two principles work to make the income statement a better report regarding a firm's periodic financial performance than the statement of cash flows.

SHORT EXERCISES

Use the following information regarding the Seville Corporation to answer Short Exercises 12-1 through 12-3.

Accounts payable increase	$ 9,000
Accounts receivable increase	4,000
Accrued liabilities decrease	3,000
Amortization expense.	6,000
Cash balance, January 1	22,000
Cash balance, December 31	15,000
Cash paid as dividends	29,000
Cash paid to purchase land	90,000
Cash paid to retire bonds payable at par.	60,000
Cash received from issuance of common stock	35,000
Cash received from sale of equipment	17,000
Depreciation expense.	20,000
Gain on sale of equipment	1,000
Inventory decrease.	13,000
Net income.	76,000
Prepaid expenses increase	2,000

LO1, 2   **SE12-1.**   **Cash Flow from Operating Activities**   Using the information for the Seville Corporation above, calculate the cash flow from operating activities.

LO1, 2   **SE12-2.**   **Cash Flow from Investing Activities**   Using the information for the Seville Corporation above, calculate the cash flow from investing activities.

LO1, 2   **SE12-3.**   **Cash Flow from Financing Activities**   Using the information for the Seville Corporation above, calculate the cash flow from financing activities.

The following information for Smith & Sons relates to Short Exercises 12-4 through 12-6:

Cash flow from operating activities	$1,500,000
Capital expenditures	850,000
Current liabilities, beginning of year	300,000
Current liabilities, end of year	360,000

LO3   **SE12-4.**   **Free Cash Flow**   Using the above data, calculate the free cash flow for Smith & Sons.

LO3   **SE12-5.**   **Operating-Cash-Flow-to-Current-Liabilities Ratio**   Using the above data, calculate the operating-cash-flow-to-current-liabilities ratio for Smith & Sons.

LO3   **SE12-6.**   **Operating-Cash-Flow-to-Capital-Expenditures Ratio**   Using the above data, calculate the operating-cash-flow-to-capital-expenditures ratio for Smith & Sons.

LO4
(Appendix 12A)   **SE12-7.**   **Converting Sales Revenue to Cash**   Smith & Sons is converting its sales revenues to corresponding cash amounts using the direct method. Sales revenue on the income statement are $1,025,000. Beginning and ending accounts receivable on the balance sheet are $58,000 and $34,000, respectively. Calculate the amount of cash received from customers.

LO4
(Appendix 12A)   **SE12-8.**   **Direct Method**   Using the following data for Smith & Sons, calculate the cash paid for rent:

Rent expense	$80,000
Prepaid rent, January 1	10,000
Prepaid rent, December 31	8,000

LO4
(Appendix 12A)   **SE12-9.**   **Direct Method**   Using the following data for Smith & Sons, calculate the cash received as interest:

Interest income	$26,000
Interest receivable, January 1	3,000
Interest receivable, December 31	3,700

LO4
(Appendix 12A)   **SE12-10.**   **Direct Method**   Using the following data for Smith & Sons, calculate the cash paid for merchandise purchased:

Cost of goods sold	$108,000
Inventory, January 1	19,000
Inventory, December 31	22,000
Accounts payable, January 1	11,000
Accounts payable, December 31	7,000

EXERCISES—SET A

LO1   **E12-1A.**   **Classification of Cash Flows**   For each of the items below, indicate whether the cash flow item relates to an operating activity, an investing activity, or a financing activity:

a.   Cash receipts from customers for services rendered
b.   Sale of long-term investments for cash
c.   Acquisition of plant assets for cash
d.   Payment of income taxes

    e.   Bonds payable issued for cash

    f.   Payment of cash dividends declared in previous year

    g.   Purchase of short-term investments (not cash equivalents) for cash

E12-2A. **Classification of Cash Flows** For each of the items below, indicate whether it is (1) a cash flow from an operating activity, (2) a cash flow from an investing activity, (3) a cash flow from a financing activity, (4) a noncash investing and financing activity, or (5) none of the above: **LO1**

    a.   Paid cash to retire bonds payable at a loss

    b.   Received cash as settlement of a lawsuit

    c.   Acquired a patent in exchange for common stock

    d.   Received advance payments from customers on orders for custom-made goods

    e.   Gave large cash contribution to local university

    f.   Invested cash in 60-day commercial paper (a cash equivalent)

E12-3A. **Cash Flow from Operating Activities (Indirect Method)** The Lincoln Company owns no plant assets and had the following income statement for the year: **LO2**

Sales revenue.		$800,000
Cost of goods sold.	$470,000	
Wages expense	120,000	
Rent expense.	42,000	
Insurance expense	15,000	647,000
Net income.		$153,000

Additional information about the company includes:

	End of Year	Beginning of Year
Accounts receivable.	$54,000	$49,000
Inventory.	60,000	76,000
Prepaid insurance	8,000	7,000
Accounts payable.	24,000	18,000
Wages payable.	9,000	11,000

Use the preceding information to calculate the cash flow from operating activities using the indirect method.

E12-4A. **Statement of Cash Flows (Indirect Method)** Use the following information regarding the Lund Corporation to (a) prepare a statement of cash flows using the indirect method and (b) compute Lund's operating-cash-flow-to-current-liabilities ratio.   **LO2, 3**

Accounts payable increase	$ 11,000
Accounts receivable increase	4,000
Accrued liabilities decrease	3,000
Amortization expense.	7,000
Cash balance, January 1	22,000
Cash balance, December 31	16,000
Cash paid as dividends	31,000
Cash paid to purchase land	90,000
Cash paid to retire bonds payable at par.	60,000
Cash received from issuance of common stock	35,000
Cash received from sale of equipment	17,000
Depreciation expense.	29,000
Gain on sale of equipment	5,000
Inventory decrease.	13,000
Net income.	78,000
Prepaid expenses increase	3,000
Average current liabilities	120,000

LO2   E12-5A.   Cash Flow from Operating Activities (Indirect Method) The Arcadia Company owns no plant assets and had the following income statement for the year:

Sales revenue.		$930,000
Cost of goods sold.	$640,000	
Wages expense	210,000	
Rent expense	42,000	
Utilities expense.	11,000	903,000
Net income.		$ 27,000

Additional information about the company includes:

	End of Year	Beginning of Year
Accounts receivable.	$67,000	$59,000
Inventory.	62,000	86,000
Prepaid rent	8,000	7,000
Accounts payable.	22,000	28,000
Wages payable.	9,000	7,000

Use the preceding information to calculate the cash flow from operating activities using the indirect method.

LO2   E12-6A.   Statement of Cash Flows (Indirect Method) Use the following information regarding the Newcastle Corporation to prepare a statement of cash flows using the indirect method:

Accounts payable decrease.	$ 3,000
Accounts receivable increase	7,000
Wages payable decrease.	9,000
Amortization expense.	16,000
Cash balance, January 1	31,000
Cash balance, December 31	9,000
Cash paid as dividends	6,000
Cash paid to purchase land	100,000
Cash paid to retire bonds payable at par.	69,000
Cash received from issuance of common stock	45,000
Cash received from sale of equipment	11,000
Depreciation expense.	39,000
Gain on sale of equipment	14,000
Inventory increase	11,000
Net income.	94,000
Prepaid expenses increase	8,000

LO3   E12-7A.   Cash Flow Ratios Spencer Company reports the following amounts in its annual financial statements:

Cash flow from operating activities	$45,000	Capital expenditures	$ 31,000*
Cash flow from investing activities.	(35,000)	Average current assets.	80,000
Cash flow from financing activities.	(5,000)	Average current liabilities	60,000
Net income.	22,000	Total assets	180,000

* This amount is a cash outflow

  a.   Compute Spencer's free cash flow.
  b.   Compute Spencer's operating-cash-flow-to-current-liabilities ratio.
  c.   Compute Spencer's operating-cash-flow-to-capital-expenditures ratio.

E12-8A. **Operating Cash Flows (Direct Method)** Calculate the cash flow in each of the following cases:

LO4
(Appendix 12A)

a. Cash paid for advertising:

Advertising expense.	$62,000
Prepaid advertising, January 1.	12,000
Prepaid advertising, December 31.	15,000

b. Cash paid for income taxes:

Income tax expense.	$29,000
Income tax payable, January 1	7,100
Income tax payable, December 31	5,900

c. Cash paid for merchandise purchased:

Cost of goods sold.	$180,000
Inventory, January 1.	30,000
Inventory, December 31.	24,000
Accounts payable, January 1.	10,000
Accounts payable, December 31.	12,000

E12-9A. **Statement of Cash Flows (Direct Method)** Use the following information regarding the cash flows of Mason Corporation to prepare a statement of cash flows using the direct method:

LO4
(Appendix 12A)

Cash balance, December 31	$ 6,000
Cash paid to employees and suppliers	158,000
Cash received from sale of land.	40,000
Cash paid to acquire treasury stock	10,000
Cash balance, January 1	18,000
Cash received as interest.	6,000
Cash paid as Income taxes	9,000
Cash paid to purchase equipment.	89,000
Cash received from customers	197,000
Cash received from issuing bonds payable.	30,000
Cash paid as dividends	19,000

E12-10A. **Operating Cash Flows (Direct Method)** Refer to the information in Exercise E12-3A. Calculate the cash flow from operating activities using the direct method. Show a related cash flow for each revenue and expense.

LO4
(Appendix 12A)

E12-11A. **Investing and Financing Cash Flows** During the year, Paxon Corporation's Long-Term Investments account (at cost) increased $25,000, the net result of purchasing stocks costing $90,000 and selling stocks costing $65,000 at a $7,000 loss. Also, the Bonds Payable account decreased by $35,000, the net result of issuing $100,000 of bonds at 104 and retiring bonds with a face value (and book value) of $135,000 at a $9,000 gain. What items and amounts will appear in the (a) cash flows from investing activities and the (b) cash flows from financing activities sections of Paxon's statement of cash flows?

LO2, 4
(Appendix 12A)

EXERCISES—SET B

E12-1B. **Classification of Cash Flows** For each of the items below, indicate whether the cash flow item relates to an operating activity, an investing activity, or a financing activity:

LO1

a. Cash loaned to borrowers
b. Cash paid as interest on bonds payable

    c. Cash received from issuance of preferred stock
    d. Cash paid as state income taxes
    e. Cash received as dividends on stock investments
    f. Cash paid to acquire treasury stock
    g. Cash paid to acquire a franchise to distribute a product line

LO1 **E12-2B. Classification of Cash Flows** For each of the items below, indicate whether it is (1) a cash flow from an operating activity, (2) a cash flow from an investing activity, (3) a cash flow from a financing activity, (4) a noncash investing and financing activity, or (5) none of the above:

    a. Received cash as interest earned on bond investment
    b. Received cash as refund from supplier
    c. Borrowed cash from bank on six-month note payable
    d. Exchanged, at a gain, stock held as an investment for a parcel of land
    e. Invested cash in a money market fund (cash may be easily withdrawn from the fund)
    f. Loaned cash to help finance the start of a new biotechnology firm

LO2, 3 **E12-3B. Cash Flow from Operating Activities (Indirect Method)** The following information was obtained from Galena Company's comparative balance sheets:

	End of Year	Beginning of Year
Cash	$ 19,000	$ 9,000
Accounts receivable.	44,000	35,000
Inventory.	55,000	49,000
Prepaid rent	6,000	8,000
Long-term investments	21,000	34,000
Plant assets	150,000	106,000
Accumulated depreciation	(42,000)	(32,000)
Accounts payable.	24,000	20,000
Income tax payable	4,000	6,000
Common stock.	121,000	92,000
Retained earnings	106,000	91,000
Capital expenditures	13,200	

Assume that Galena Company's income statement showed depreciation expense of $10,000, a gain on sale of investments of $7,000, and a net income of $51,000. (a) Calculate the cash flow from operating activities using the indirect method and (b) compute Galena's operating-cash-flow-to-capital-expenditures ratio.

LO2 **E12-4B. Cash Flow from Operating Activities (Indirect Method)** Cairo Company had a $24,000 net loss from operations. Depreciation expense for the year was $9,600, and a dividend of $5,000 was declared and paid. The balances of the current asset and current liability accounts at the beginning and end of the year are as follows:

	End	Beginning
Cash	$ 3,500	$ 7,000
Accounts receivable.	16,000	29,000
Inventory.	50,000	53,000
Prepaid expenses.	6,000	9,000
Accounts payable.	12,000	8,000
Accrued liabilities	6,000	7,600

Did Cairo Company's operating activities provide or use cash? Use the indirect method to determine your answer.

LO2 **E12-5B. Cash Flow From Operating Activities (Indirect Method)** The Smithfield Company owns no plant assets and had the following income statement for the year:

Sales revenue.		$1,120,000
Cost of goods sold.	$770,000	
Wages expense	210,000	
Rent expense	65,000	
Insurance expense.	45,000	1,090,000
Net income.		$ 30,000

Additional information about the company includes:

	End of Year	Beginning of Year
Accounts receivable.	$74,000	$49,000
Inventory.	70,000	74,000
Prepaid insurance	5,000	7,000
Accounts payable.	26,000	28,000
Wages payable	11,000	13,000

Use the preceding information to calculate the cash flow from operating activities using the indirect method.

E12-6B. Statement of Cash Flows (Indirect Method) Use the following information regarding the Fremantle Corporation to prepare a statement of cash flows using the indirect method: **LO2**

Accounts payable increase	$ 14,000
Accounts receivable increase	4,000
Accrued liabilities decrease	5,000
Amortization expense.	26,000
Cash balance, January 1	21,000
Cash balance, December 31	108,000
Cash paid as dividends	49,000
Cash paid to purchase land.	103,000
Cash paid to retire bonds payable at par.	70,000
Cash received from issuance of common stock	75,000
Cash received from sale of equipment	17,000
Depreciation expense.	65,000
Gain on sale of equipment	14,000
Inventory decrease.	11,000
Net income.	126,000
Prepaid expenses increase	2,000

E12-7B. Cash Flow Ratios Morgan Company reports the following amounts in its annual financial statements: **LO3**

Cash flow from operating activities	$65,000	Capital expenditures	$ 52,500*
Cash flow from investing activities.	(60,000)	Average current assets.	130,000
Cash flow from financing activities.	(8,500)	Average current liabilities	90,000
Net income.	37,500	Total assets	225,000

* This amount is a cash outflow

a.   Compute Morgan's free cash flow.
b.   Compute Morgan's operating-cash-flow-to-current-liabilities ratio.
c.   Compute Morgan's operating-cash-flow-to-capital-expenditures ratio.

LO4
(Appendix 12A)

E12-8B.   Operating Cash Flows (Direct Method) Calculate the cash flow in each of the following cases:

a.   Cash paid for rent:

Rent expense	$62,000
Prepaid rent, January 1	10,000
Prepaid rent, December 31	8,000

b.   Cash received as interest:

Interest income.	$16,000
Interest receivable, January 1	5,000
Interest receivable, December 31	3,700

c.   Cash paid for merchandise purchased:

Cost of goods sold.	$98,000
Inventory, January 1.	19,000
Inventory, December 31.	22,000
Accounts payable, January 1.	11,000
Accounts payable, December 31.	9,000

LO4
(Appendix 12A)

E12-9B.   Statement of Cash Flows (Direct Method) Use the following information regarding the cash flows of Gilbert Corporation to prepare a statement of cash flows using the direct method:

Cash balance, December 31	$ 12,000
Cash paid to employees and suppliers	151,000
Cash received from sale of equipment	88,000
Cash paid to retire bonds payable.	70,000
Cash balance, January 1	20,000
Cash paid as interest	7,000
Cash paid as income taxes	24,000
Cash paid to purchase patent	76,000
Cash received from customers	216,000
Cash received from issuing common stock.	35,000
Cash paid as dividends	19,000

LO4
(Appendix 12A)

E12-10B. Operating Cash Flows (Direct Method) The Howell Company's current year income statement contains the following data:

Sales revenue.	$775,000
Cost of goods sold.	550,000
Gross profit.	$225,000

Howell's comparative balance sheets show the following data (accounts payable relate to merchandise purchases):

	End of Year	Beginning of Year
Accounts receivable.	$ 71,000	$60,000
Inventory.	115,000	96,000
Prepaid expenses.	3,000	8,000
Accounts payable.	31,000	35,000

Compute Howell's current-year cash received from customers and cash paid for merchandise purchased.

E12-11B. Investing and Financing Cash Flows Refer to the information in Exercise 12-3B. During the year, Galena Company purchased plant assets for cash, sold investments for cash (the entire $7,000 gain developed during the year), and issued common stock for cash. The firm also declared and paid cash dividends. What items and amounts will appear in (a) the cash flow from investing activities and (b) the cash flow from financing activities sections of a statement of cash flows?

LO2, 4
(Appendix 12A)

PROBLEMS—SET A

P12-1A. Statement of Cash Flows (Indirect Method) The Wolff Company's income statement and comparative balance sheets at December 31 of 2016 and 2015 are shown below:

LO2, 3

WOLFF COMPANY Income Statement For the Year Ended December 31, 2016		
Sales revenue....		$645,000
Cost of goods sold....	$430,000	
Wages expense	86,000	
Insurance expense....	12,000	
Depreciation expense....	13,000	
Interest expense....	12,000	
Income tax expense....	29,000	582,000
Net income....		$ 63,000

WOLFF COMPANY Balance Sheets	Dec. 31, 2016	Dec. 31, 2015
Assets		
Cash....	$ 52,000	$ 8,000
Accounts receivable....	41,000	32,000
Inventory....	90,000	60,000
Prepaid insurance	5,000	7,000
Plant assets	219,000	195,000
Accumulated depreciation....	(68,000)	(55,000)
Total assets	$339,000	$247,000
Liabilities and Stockholders' Equity		
Accounts payable....	$ 7,000	$ 10,000
Wages payable....	9,000	6,000
Income tax payable	6,000	7,000
Bonds payable....	141,000	75,000
Common stock....	90,000	90,000
Retained earnings	86,000	59,000
Total liabilities and stockholders' equity	$339,000	$247,000

Cash dividends of $36,000 were declared and paid during 2016. Plant assets were purchased for cash and bonds payable were issued for cash. Bond interest is paid semi-annually on June 30 and December 31. Accounts payable relate to merchandise purchases.

Required
a. Calculate the change in cash that occurred during 2016.
b. Prepare a statement of cash flows using the indirect method.
c. Compute free cash flow.
d. Compute the operating-cash-flow-to-current-liabilities ratio.
e. Compute the operating-cash-flow-to-capital-expenditures ratio.

LO2   P12-2A.   Statement of Cash Flows (Indirect Method) Arctic Company's income statement and comparative balance sheets as of December 31 of 2016 and 2015 follow:

ARCTIC COMPANY Income Statement For the Year Ended December 31, 2016		
Sales revenue.		$740,000
Cost of goods sold.	$534,000	
Wages expense	190,000	
Advertising expense.	31,000	
Depreciation expense.	24,000	
Interest expense.	18,000	
Gain on sale of land	(25,000)	772,000
Net loss		$ (32,000)

ARCTIC COMPANY Balance Sheets	Dec. 31, 2016	Dec. 31, 2015
Assets		
Cash	$ 71,000	$ 28,000
Accounts receivable.	42,000	49,000
Inventory.	107,000	113,000
Prepaid advertising.	10,000	14,000
Plant assets	360,000	222,000
Accumulated depreciation	(80,000)	(56,000)
Total assets	$510,000	$370,000
Liabilities and Stockholders' Equity		
Accounts payable.	$ 17,000	$ 31,000
Interest payable	6,000	—
Bonds payable	210,000	—
Common stock.	245,000	245,000
Retained earnings	62,000	94,000
Treasury stock	(30,000)	—
Total liabilities and stockholders' equity	$510,000	$370,000

During 2016, Arctic sold land for $70,000 cash that had originally cost $45,000. Arctic also purchased equipment for cash, acquired treasury stock for cash, and issued bonds payable for cash. Accounts payable relate to merchandise purchases.

Required
a.   Calculate the change in cash that occurred during 2016.
b.   Prepare a statement of cash flows using the indirect method.

LO2   P12-3A.   Statement of Cash Flows (Indirect Method) The Dairy Company's income statement and comparative balance sheets as of December 31 of 2016 and 2015 follow:

DAIRY COMPANY Income Statement For the Year Ended December 31, 2016		
Sales revenue.		$700,000
Cost of goods sold.	$460,000	
Wages and other operating expenses	95,000	
Depreciation expense.	22,000	
Goodwill amortization expense	7,000	
Interest expense.	10,000	
Income tax expense.	36,000	
Loss on bond retirement	5,000	635,000
Net income.		$ 65,000

DAIRY COMPANY Balance Sheets	Dec. 31, 2016	Dec. 31, 2015
Assets		
Cash.	$ 22,000	$ 18,000
Accounts receivable.	43,000	28,000
Inventory.	103,000	129,000
Prepaid expenses.	12,000	10,000
Plant assets	360,000	336,000
Accumulated depreciation	(87,000)	(84,000)
Goodwill	43,000	50,000
Total assets	$496,000	$487,000
Liabilities and Stockholders' Equity		
Accounts payable.	$ 32,000	$ 26,000
Interest payable	4,000	7,000
Income tax payable	6,000	8,000
Bonds payable	60,000	100,000
Common stock.	252,000	248,000
Retained earnings	142,000	98,000
Total liabilities and stockholders' equity	$496,000	$487,000

During the year, the company sold for $17,000 cash old equipment that had cost $36,000 and had $19,000 accumulated depreciation. New equipment worth $60,000 was acquired in exchange for $60,000 of bonds payable. Bonds payable of $100,000 were retired for cash at a loss. A $21,000 cash dividend was declared and paid. All stock issuances were for cash.

Required
a. Compute the change in cash that occurred in 2016.
b. Prepare a statement of cash flows using the indirect method.

P12-4A. Statement of Cash Flows (Indirect Method) The Rainbow Company's income statement and comparative balance sheets as of December 31 of 2016 and 2015 follow: **LO2**

RAINBOW COMPANY Income Statement For Year Ended December 31, 2016		
Sales revenue.		$750,000
Dividend income.		19,000
		769,000
Cost of goods sold.	$440,000	
Wages and other operating expenses	130,000	
Depreciation expense.	39,000	
Patent amortization expense	7,000	
Interest expense.	13,000	
Income tax expense.	44,000	
Loss on sale of equipment.	5,000	
Gain on sale of investments.	(10,000)	668,000
Net income.		$101,000

RAINBOW COMPANY Balance Sheets	Dec. 31, 2016	Dec. 31, 2015
Assets		
Cash and cash equivalents	$ 25,000	$ 29,000
Accounts receivable	45,000	30,000
Inventory	103,000	77,000
Prepaid expenses	10,000	6,000
Long-term investments—available for sale	—	50,000
Fair value adjustment to investments	—	7,000
Land	190,000	100,000
Buildings	445,000	350,000
Accumulated depreciation—Buildings	(91,000)	(75,000)
Equipment	179,000	225,000
Accumulated depreciation—Equipment	(42,000)	(46,000)
Patents	50,000	32,000
Total assets	$914,000	$785,000
Liabilities and Stockholders' Equity		
Accounts payable	$ 22,000	$ 18,000
Interest payable	6,000	5,000
Income tax payable	8,000	12,000
Bonds payable	165,000	125,000
Preferred stock ($100 par value)	100,000	75,000
Common stock ($5 par value)	379,000	364,000
Paid-in-capital in excess of par value—Common	133,000	124,000
Retained earnings	101,000	55,000
Unrealized gain on investments	—	7,000
Total liabilities and stockholders' equity	$914,000	$785,000

During the year, the following transactions occurred:

1. Sold long-term investments costing $50,000 for $60,000 cash. Unrealized gains totaling $7,000 related to these investments had been recorded in earlier years. At year-end, the fair value adjustment and unrealized gain account balances were eliminated.
2. Purchased land for cash.
3. Capitalized an expenditure made to improve the building.
4. Sold equipment for $14,000 cash that originally cost $46,000 and had $27,000 accumulated depreciation.
5. Issued bonds payable at face value for cash.
6. Acquired a patent with a fair value of $25,000 by issuing 250 shares of preferred stock at par value.
7. Declared and paid a $55,000 cash dividend.
8. Issued 3,000 shares of common stock for cash at $8 per share.
9. Recorded depreciation of $16,000 on buildings and $23,000 on equipment.

Required
a. Calculate the change in cash and cash equivalents that occurred during 2016.
b. Prepare a statement of cash flows using the indirect method.

LO3   P12-5A.   **Analyzing Cash Flow Ratios** Molly Enterprises reported the following information for the past year of operations:

Transaction	Free Cash Flow $250,000	Operating-Cash-Flow-to-Current-Liabilities Ratio 1.0 times	Operating-Cash-Flow-to-Capital-Expenditures Ratio 3.0 times
a. Recorded credit sales of $7,000			
b. Collected $4,000 owed from customers			
c. Purchased $18,000 of equipment on long-term credit			
d. Purchased $16,000 of equipment for cash			
e. Paid $5,000 of wages with cash			
f. Recorded utility bill of $1,750 that has not been paid			

For each transaction, indicate whether the ratio will (I) increase, (D) decrease, or (N) have no effect.

P12-6A. **Statement of Cash Flows (Direct Method)** Refer to the data given for the Wolff Company in Problem P12-1A.

LO3, 4
(Appendix 12A)

Required
a. Calculate the change in cash that occurred during 2016.
b. Prepare a statement of cash flows using the direct method.
c. Compute free cash flow.
d. Compute the operating-cash-flow-to-current-liabilities ratio.
e. Compute the operating-cash-flow-to-capital-expenditures ratio.

P12-7A. **Statement of Cash Flows (Direct Method)** Refer to the data given for the Arctic Company in Problem P12-2A.

LO4
(Appendix 12A)

Required
a Calculate the change in cash that occurred during 2016.
b. Prepare a statement of cash flows using the direct method.

P12-8A. **Statement of Cash Flows (Direct Method)** Refer to the data given for the Dairy Company in Problem P12-3A.

LO4
(Appendix 12A)

Required
a. Compute the change in cash that occurred in 2016.
b. Prepare a statement of cash flows using the direct method. Use one cash outflow for "cash paid for wages and other operating expenses." Accounts payable relate to inventory purchases only.

P12-9A. **Statement of Cash Flows (Direct Method)** Refer to the data given for the Rainbow Company in Problem P12-4A.

LO4
(Appendix 12A)

Required
a. Calculate the change in cash that occurred in 2016.
b. Prepare a statement of cash flows using the direct method. Use one cash outflow for "cash paid for wages and other operating expenses." Accounts payable relate to inventory purchases only.

PROBLEMS—SET B

P12-1B. **Statement of Cash Flows (Indirect Method)** The Rural Company's income statement and comparative balance sheets as of December 31 of 2016 and 2015 are shown below:

LO2, 3

RURAL COMPANY
Income Statement
For the Year Ended December 31, 2016

Sales revenue.		$645,000
Cost of goods sold.	$376,000	
Wages expense	107,000	
Depreciation expense.	22,000	
Rent expense.	28,000	
Income tax expense.	31,000	564,000
Net income.		$ 81,000

RURAL COMPANY
Balance Sheets

	Dec. 31, 2016	Dec. 31, 2015
Assets		
Cash.	$ 41,000	$ 33,000
Accounts receivable.	52,000	60,000
Inventory.	142,000	116,000
Prepaid rent	14,000	10,000
Plant assets	420,000	300,000
Accumulated depreciation.	(127,000)	(105,000)
Total assets	$542,000	$414,000
Liabilities and Stockholders' Equity		
Accounts payable.	$ 29,000	$ 17,000
Wages payable.	14,000	7,000
Income tax payable	7,000	8,000
Common stock.	295,000	252,000
Paid-in-capital in excess of par value	72,000	58,000
Retained earnings	125,000	72,000
Total liabilities and stockholders' equity	$542,000	$414,000

Cash dividends of $28,000 were declared and paid during 2016. Plant assets were purchased for cash and additional common stock was issued for cash. Accounts payable relate to merchandise purchases.

Required
a. Calculate the change in cash that occurred during 2016.
b. Prepare a statement of cash flows using the indirect method.
c. Compute free cash flow.
d. Compute the operating-cash-flow-to-current-liabilities ratio.
e. Compute the operating-cash-flows-to-capital-expenditures ratio.

LO2 **P12-2B.** **Statement of Cash Flows (Indirect Method)** The Sweet Company's income statement and comparative balance sheets as of December 31 of 2016 and 2015 are presented below:

SWEET COMPANY
Income Statement
For the Year Ended December 31, 2016

Sales revenue.		$950,000
Cost of goods sold.	$507,000	
Wages expense	207,000	
Depreciation expense.	62,000	
Insurance expense.	13,000	
Interest expense.	12,000	
Income tax expense.	57,000	
Gain on sale of equipment	(16,000)	842,000
Net income.		$108,000

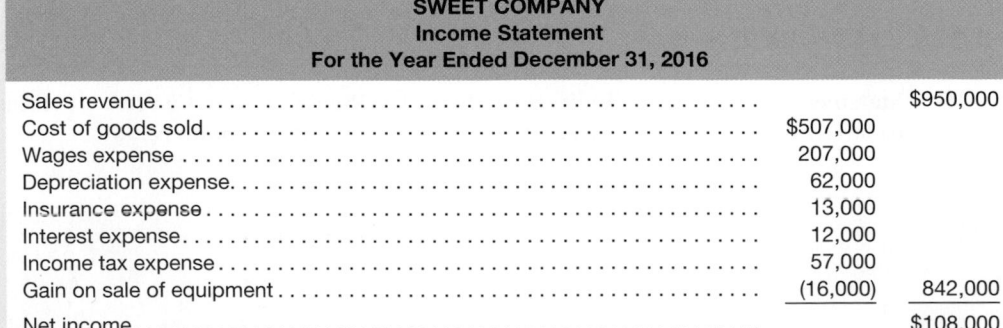

SWEET COMPANY Balance Sheets		
	Dec. 31, 2016	Dec. 31, 2015
Assets		
Cash	$ 32,000	$ 33,000
Accounts receivable	68,000	43,000
Inventory	177,000	126,000
Prepaid insurance	9,000	11,000
Plant assets	887,000	770,000
Accumulated depreciation	(191,000)	(175,000)
Total assets	$982,000	$808,000
Liabilities and Stockholders' Equity		
Accounts payable	$ 37,000	$ 27,000
Interest payable	5,000	—
Income tax payable	11,000	18,000
Bonds payable	145,000	80,000
Common stock	660,000	585,000
Retained earnings	176,000	98,000
Treasury stock	(52,000)	—
Total liabilities and stockholders' equity	$982,000	$808,000

During the year, Sweet Company sold equipment for $27,000 cash that originally cost $57,000 and had $46,000 accumulated depreciation. New equipment was purchased for cash. Bonds payable and common stock were issued for cash. Cash dividends of $30,000 were declared and paid. At the end of the year, shares of treasury stock were purchased for cash. Accounts payable relate to merchandise purchases.

Required
a.   Compute the change in cash that occurred during 2016.
b.   Prepare a statement of cash flows using the indirect method.

P12-3B.   **Statement of Cash Flows (Indirect Method)** The Huber Company's income statement and com-   **LO2**
parative balance sheets as of December 31 of 2016 and 2015 follow:

HUBER COMPANY Income Statement For the Year Ended December 31, 2016		
Sales revenue		$810,000
Cost of goods sold	$530,000	
Wages and other operating expenses	172,000	
Depreciation expense	29,000	
Patent amortization expense	6,000	
Interest expense	18,000	
Income tax expense	25,000	
Gain on exchange of land for patent	(37,000)	743,000
Net income		$ 67,000

HUBER COMPANY Balance Sheets		
	Dec. 31, 2016	Dec. 31, 2015
Assets		
Cash.	$ 49,000	$ 16,000
Accounts receivable.	64,000	49,000
Inventory.	85,000	64,000
Land	117,000	160,000
Building and equipment	441,000	361,000
Accumulated depreciation	(122,000)	(100,000)
Patent.	74,000	—
Total assets	$708,000	$550,000
Liabilities and Stockholders' Equity		
Accounts payable.	$ 36,000	$ 26,000
Interest payable	13,000	5,000
Income tax payable	7,000	12,000
Bonds payable	180,000	75,000
Common stock.	350,000	350,000
Retained earnings	122,000	82,000
Total liabilities and stockholders' equity	$708,000	$550,000

During 2016, $27,000 of cash dividends were declared and paid. A patent valued at $80,000 was obtained in exchange for land. Equipment that originally cost $20,000 and had $7,000 accumulated depreciation was sold for $13,000 cash. Bonds payable were sold for cash and cash was used to pay for structural improvements to the building.

Required

a. Compute the change in cash that occurred during 2016.

b. Prepare a statement of cash flows using the indirect method.

LO2   P12-4B.   **Statement of Cash Flows (Indirect Method)** The Towne Company's income statement and comparative balance sheets as of December 31 of 2016 and 2015 follow:

TOWNE COMPANY Income Statement For the Year Ended December 31, 2016		
Service fees earned		$317,000
Dividend and interest income.		14,000
		$331,000
Wages and other operating expenses	$285,000	
Depreciation expense.	55,000	
Franchise amortization expense	10,000	
Loss on sale of equipment.	7,000	
Gain on sale of investments.	(17,000)	340,000
Net loss		$ (9,000)

TOWNE COMPANY		
Balance Sheets		
	Dec. 31, 2016	**Dec. 31, 2015**
Assets		
Cash.	$ 43,000	$ 33,000
Accounts receivable.	13,000	18,000
Interest receivable	—	4,000
Prepaid expenses.	16,000	10,000
Long-term investments—available for sale	—	70,000
Fair value adjustment to investments.	—	10,000
Plant assets	696,000	655,000
Accumulated depreciation	(237,000)	(185,000)
Franchise	91,000	29,000
Total assets	$622,000	$644,000
Liabilities and Stockholders' Equity		
Accrued liabilities	$ 12,000	$ 14,000
Notes payable		26,000
Common stock ($10 par value)	595,000	535,000
Retained earnings	35,000	59,000
Unrealized gain on investments	—	10,000
Treasury stock	(20,000)	—
Total liabilities and stockholders' equity	$622,000	$644,000

During the year, the following transactions occurred:

1. Sold equipment for $9,000 cash that originally cost $19,000 and had $3,000 accumulated depreciation.
2. Sold long-term investments that had cost $70,000 for $87,000 cash. Unrealized gains totaling $10,000 related to these investments had been recorded in earlier years. At year-end, the fair value adjustment and unrealized gain account balances were eliminated.
3. Paid cash to extend the company's exclusive franchise for another three years.
4. Paid off a note payable at the bank on January 1.
5. Declared and paid a $15,000 dividend.
6. Purchased treasury stock for cash.
7. Acquired land valued at $60,000 by issuing 6,000 shares of common stock.

Required
a. Compute the change in cash that occurred in 2016.
b. Prepare a statement of cash flows using the indirect method.

P12-5B. Analyzing Cash Flow Ratios Molly Enterprises reported the following information for the past year of operations: **LO3**

Transaction	Free Cash Flow $300,000	Operating-Cash-Flow-to-Current-Liabilities Ratio 1.2 times	Operating-Cash-Flow-to-Capital-Expenditures Ratio 4.0 times
a. Recorded credit sales of $15,000			
b. Collected $6,000 owed from customers			
c. Purchased $45,000 of equipment on long-term credit			
d. Purchased $70,000 of equipment for cash			
e. Paid $17,000 of wages with cash			
f. Recorded utility bill of $14,750 that has not been paid			

For each transaction, indicate whether the ratio will (I) increase, (D) decrease, or (N) have no effect.

LO3, 4
(Appendix 12A)

P12-6B. **Statement of Cash Flows (Direct Method)** Refer to the data given for the Rural Company in Problem P12-1B.

Required
a.   Compute the change in cash that occurred during 2016.
b.   Prepare a statement of cash flows using the direct method.
c.   Compute free cash flow.
d.   Compute the operating-cash-flow-to-current-liabilities ratio.
e.   Compute the operating-cash-flow-to-capital-expenditures ratio.

LO4
(Appendix 12A)

P12-7B. **Statement of Cash Flows (Direct Method)** Refer to the data given for the Sweet Company in Problem P12-2B.

Required
a.   Compute the change in cash that occurred during 2016.
b.   Prepare a statement of cash flows using the direct method.

LO4
(Appendix 12A)

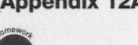

P12-8B. **Statement of Cash Flows (Direct Method)** Refer to the data given for the Huber Company in Problem P12-3B.

Required
a.   Compute the change in cash that occurred during 2016.
b.   Prepare a statement of cash flows using the direct method. Use one cash outflow for "cash paid for wages and other operating expenses." Accounts payable relate to inventory purchases only.

LO4
(Appendix 12A)

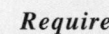

P12-9B. **Statement of Cash Flows (Direct Method)** Refer to the data given for the Towne Company in Problem P12-4B.

Required
a.   Compute the change in cash that occurred during 2016.
b.   Prepare a statement of cash flows using the direct method. Use one cash outflow for "cash paid for wages and other operating expenses."

SERIAL PROBLEM: KATE'S CARDS

(Note: This is a continuation of the Serial Problem: Kate's Cards from Chapter 1 through Chapter 11.)

SP12. Kate has just completed her first year running Kate's Cards. She has been preparing monthly income statements and balance sheets, so she knows that her company has been profitable and that there is cash in the bank. She has not, however, prepared a statement of cash flows. Kate provides you with the year-end income statement and balance sheet and asks that you prepare a statement of cash flows for Kate's Cards.

Additional information:

1.   There was no disposals of equipment during the year.
2.   Dividends in the amount of $1,300 were paid in cash during the year.
3.   Prepaid expenses relate to operating expenses.

Required
a.   Prepare a statement of cash flows for Kate's Cards for the year ended August 31, 2016, using the indirect method. Hint: Since this was Kate's first year of operations, the beginning balance sheet account balances were zero.
b.   Prepare a statement of cash flows for Kate's Cards for the year ended August 31, 2016, using the direct method. (Appendix 12A)

KATE'S CARDS	
Income Statement	
Year Ended August 31, 2016	
Sales revenue	$135,000
Cost of goods sold	72,000
Gross profit	63,000
Operating expenses	
Wages	18,000
Consulting	11,850
Insurance	1,200
Utilities	2,400
Depreciation	3,250
Total operating expenses	36,700
Income from operations	26,300
Interest expense	900
Income before income tax	25,400
Income tax expense	8,900
Net income	$ 16,500

KATE'S CARDS	
Balance Sheet	
As of August 31, 2016	
Assets	
Current assets	
Cash	$12,300
Accounts receivable	11,000
Inventory	16,000
Prepaid insurance	1,000
Total current assets	40,300
Equipment	17,500
Accumulated depreciation	(3,250)
Total assets	$54,550
Liabilities	
Current liabilities	
Accounts payable	$ 6,200
Unearned revenue	1,250
Other current liabilities	1,900
Total current liabilities	9,350
Note payable	15,000
Total liabilities	24,350
Stockholders' equity	
Common stock	500
Additional paid-in-capital	9,500
Preferred stock	5,000
Retained earnings	15,200
Total stockholders' equity	30,200
Total liabilities and stockholders' equity	$54,550

EXTENDING YOUR KNOWLEDGE

REPORTING AND ANALYSIS

COLUMBIA
SPORTSWEAR
COMPANY

EYK12-1. Financial Reporting Problem: Columbia Sportswear Company The financial statements for the **Columbia Sportswear Company** can be found in Appendix A at the end of this book.

Required
Answer the following questions:
a. How much did Columbia Sportswear's cash and cash equivalents decrease in 2014?
b. What was the largest source of cash and cash equivalents in 2014?
c. What was the single largest use of cash and cash equivalents in 2014?
d. How much dividends were paid in 2014?
e. Why do depreciation and amortization, both noncash items, appear on Columbia's statement of cash flows?

COLUMBIA
SPORTSWEAR
COMPANY

UNDER ARMOUR,
INC.

EYK12-2. Comparative Analysis Problem: Columbia Sportswear Company vs Under Armour, Inc. The financial statements for the Columbia Sportswear Company can be found in Appendix A at the end of this book, and the financial statements of Under Armour, Inc. can be found in Appendix B (the complete annual report is available on this book's Website).

Required
Answer the following questions:
a. Compute the free cash flow in 2014 for both Columbia Sportswear and Under Armour, Inc.
b. Compute the operating cash flows to capital expenditures for both Columbia Sportswear and Under Armour, Inc.
c. Comment on the ability of each company to finance its capital expenditures.

EYK12-3. Business Decision Problem Recently hired as assistant controller for Finite, Inc., you are sitting next to the controller as she responds to questions at the annual stockholders' meeting. The firm's financial statements contain a statement of cash flows prepared using the indirect method. A stockholder raises his hand.

Stockholder: "I notice that depreciation expense is shown as an addition in the calculation of the cash flow from operating activities."

Controller: "That's correct."

Stockholder: "What depreciation method do you use?"

Controller: "We use the straight-line method for all plant assets."

Stockholder: "Well, why don't you switch to an accelerated depreciation method, such as double-declining balance, increase the annual depreciation amount, and thus increase the cash flow from operating activities?"

The controller pauses, turns to you, and replies, "My assistant will answer your question."

Required
Prepare an answer to the stockholder's question.

PARKER HANNIFIN
CORPORATION

EYK12-4. Financial Analysis Problem Parker Hannifin Corporation, headquartered in Cleveland, Ohio, manufactures motion control and fluid system components for a variety of industrial users. The firm's financial statements contain the following data (Year 3 is the most recent year; dollar amounts are in thousands):

	Year 3	Year 2	Year 1
Current assets at year-end.........................	$1,018,354	$1,056,443	$1,055,776
Current liabilities at year-end	504,444	468,254	358,729
Current liabilities at beginning of year	468,254	358,729	345,594
Cash provided by operating activities	259,204	229,382	235,186
Capital expenditures	99,914	91,484	84,955

a. Calculate Parker Hannifin's current ratio (current assets/current liabilities) for Years 1, 2, and 3.
b. Calculate Parker Hannifin's operating-cash-flow-to-current-liabilities ratio for Years 1, 2, and 3.
c. Comment on the three-year trend in Parker Hannifin's current ratio and operating-cash-flow-to-current-liabilities ratio. Do the trends in these two ratios reinforce each other or contradict each other as indicators of Parker Hannifin's ability to pay its current liabilities?
d. Calculate Parker Hannifin's operating-cash-flow-to-capital-expenditures ratio for Years 1, 2, and 3. Comment on the strength of this ratio over the three-year period.

CRITICAL THINKING

EYK12-5. Accounting Research Problem: General Mills, Inc. The fiscal year 2014 annual report of General Mills, Inc. is available on this book's Website.

GENERAL MILLS, INC.

Required

a. Refer to Note 2. How does General Mills define its cash equivalents?
b. What method does General Mills use to report its cash provided by operating activities?
c. What is the change in cash and cash equivalents experienced by General Mills during fiscal 2014? What is the amount of cash and cash equivalents as of May 25, 2014?
d. What is General Mills' operating-cash-flow-to-capital-expenditures ratio for fiscal year 2014?
e. Calculate General Mills' 2014 operating-cash-flow-to-current-liabilities ratio.

EYK12-6. Accounting Communication Activity Susan Henderson, the vice president of marketing, was told by the CEO that she needs to understand the numbers because the company's existence depends on making money. It has been a long time since Susan took a class in accounting. She recalls that companies report net income and cash flows in two separate statements. She feels pretty comfortable with the income statement, but is somewhat lost looking at the statement of cash flows. She asks you to help explain this statement.

Required

Write a brief memo to Susan explaining the form and content of the statement of cash flows, along with a short discussion of how to analyze the statement.

EYK12-7. Accounting Ethics Case Due to an economic recession, Anton Corporation faces severe cash flow problems. Management forecasts that payments to some suppliers will have to be delayed for several months. Jay Newton, controller, has asked his staff for suggestions on selecting the suppliers for which payments will be delayed.

"That's a fairly easy decision," observes Tim Haslem. "Some suppliers charge interest if our payment is late, but others do not. We should pay those suppliers that charge interest and delay payments to the ones that do not charge interest. If we do this, the savings in interest charges will be quite substantial."

"I disagree," states Tara Wirth. "That position is too 'bottom line' oriented. It's not fair to delay payments only to suppliers who don't charge interest for late payments. Most suppliers in that category are ones we have dealt with for years; selecting these suppliers would be taking advantage of the excellent relationships we have developed over the years. The fair thing to do is to make pro-rata payments to each supplier."

"Well, making pro-rata payments to each supplier means that *all* our suppliers will be upset because no one receives full payment," comments Sue Myling. "I believe it is most important to maintain good relations with our long-term suppliers; we should pay them currently and delay payments to our newer suppliers. The interest costs we end up paying these newer suppliers is the price we must pay to keep our long-term relationships solid."

Required

Which suppliers should Jay Newton select for delayed payments? Discuss.

EYK12-8. Corporate Social Responsibility Problem The corporate social responsibility highlighted in this chapter (see page 591) mentions that **Home Depot** believes in giving back. One of the ways the company has done this is through its Team Depot program of employee volunteerism. Under this program, Home Depot employees volunteer their own time to work together on projects that

THE HOME DEPOT, INC.

benefit communities in which the company does business. Each year the program provides millions of hours of employee volunteerism.

One of the many programs that benefits from Team Depot is Habitat for Humanity. Do a computer search and report how Team Depot has helped Habitat for Humanity.

EYK12-9. Forensic Accounting Problem Cash larceny involves the fraudulent stealing of an employer's cash. These schemes often target the company's bank deposits. The fraudster steals the money after the deposit has been prepared, but before the deposit is taken to the bank. Most often these schemes involve a deficiency in the internal control system where segregation of duties is not present. The perpetrator is often in charge of recording receipts, preparing the deposit, delivering the deposit to the bank, and verifying the receipted deposit slip. Without proper segregation of duties, the fraudster is able cover up the theft.

In addition to segregation of duties, what internal control procedures might help deter and detect cash larceny?

EYK12-10. Working with the Takeaways For the fiscal year ended February 2, 2014, Home Depot reports (in millions) cash provided by operating activities of $7,628. For the same period, average current liabilities were reported to be $10,749, annual capital expenditures were $1,389, and proceeds from sales of property and equipment were $89. Calculate the free cash flow, operating-cash-flow-to-current-liabities ratio, and the operating-cash-flow-to-capital-expenditures ratio for Home Depot and comment on the results.

EYK12-11. Analyzing IFRS Financial Statements The 2014 financial statements of LVMH Moet Hennessey-Louis Vuitton S.A. are presented in Appendix C at the end of this book. LVMH is a Paris-based holding company and one of the world's largest and best-known luxury goods companies. As a member of the European Union, French companies are required to prepare their consolidated (group) financial statements using International Financial Reporting Standards (IFRS). After reviewing LVMH's consolidated financial statements calculate LVMH's (a) free cash flow, (b) operating-cash-flow-to-current-liabilities ratio (use the year-end current liabilities instead of the average current liabilities), and (c) operating-cash-flow-to-capital-expenditures ratio for 2013 and 2014. What do the ratio results reveal about LVMH? *Hint:* Capital expenditures are classified as "Operating investments" on LVMH Consolidated cash flow statement.

ANSWERS TO SELF-STUDY QUESTIONS:

YOUR TURN! SOLUTIONS

Solution 12.1

1. Operating
2. Investing
3. Operating
4. Investing
5. Financing
6. Financing
7. Operating
8. Financing
9. Investing

Solution 12.2

HUSKY COMPANY Statement of Cash Flows For the Year Ended December 31, 2016		
Cash Flow from Operating Activities		
Net income	$112,000	
Add (deduct) items to convert net income to cash basis		
Depreciation	34,000	
Accounts receivable increase	(18,000)	
Inventory increase	(60,000)	
Prepaid insurance decrease	4,000	
Accounts payable decrease	(6,000)	
Wages payable increase	6,000	
Income tax payable decrease	(2,000)	
Cash provided by operating activities		$ 70,000
Cash Flow from Investing Activities		
Purchase of plant assets		(110,000)
Cash Flow from Financing Activities		
Issuance of bonds payable	110,000	
Payment of dividends	(58,000)	
Cash provided by financing activities		52,000
Net increase in cash		12,000
Cash at beginning of year		10,000
Cash at end of year		$ 22,000

Solution 12.3

Free cash flow: $40,000 − $12,500 = $27,500
Operating-cash-flow-to-current-liabilities-ratio: $40,000/$30,000 = 1.33
Operating-cash-flow-to-capital-expenditures-ratio: $40,000/$12,500 = 3.20

Solution 12A.1

Supporting Calculations:

Cash received from customers:
$1,270,000 Sales revenue − $18,000 Accounts receivable increase = $1,252,000

Cash paid for merchandise purchased:
$860,000 Cost of goods sold + $60,000 Inventory increase + $6,000 Accounts payable decrease = $926,000

Cash paid to employees:
$172,000 Wages expense − $6,000 Wages payable increase = $166,000

Cash paid for insurance:
$16,000 Insurance expense − $4,000 Prepaid insurance decrease = $12,000

Cash paid for interest:
Equal to the $18,000 balance in interest expense

Cash paid for income taxes:
$58,000 Income tax expense + $2,000 Income tax payable decrease = $60,000

Purchase of plant assets:
$500,000 Ending plant assets − $390,000 Beginning plant assets = $110,000

Issuance of bonds payable:
$260,000 Ending bonds payable − $150,000 Beginning bonds payable = $110,000

Payment of dividends
$58,000 given in problem data

Other Analysis

Accumulated depreciation increased by $34,000, which is the amount of depreciation expense.

Common stock account balance did not change.

Retained earnings increased by $54,000, which is the difference between the net income of $112,000 and the dividends declared of $58,000.

HUSKY COMPANY
Statement of Cash Flows (Direct Method)
For the Year Ended December 31, 2016

Cash Flow from Operating Activities

Cash received from customers.		$1,252,000
Cash paid for merchandise purchased.	$(926,000)	
Cash paid to employees.	(166,000)	
Cash paid for insurance	(12,000)	
Cash paid for interest	(18,000)	
Cash paid for income taxes	(60,000)	(1,182,000)
Cash provided by operating activities.		70,000
Cash Flow from Investing Activities		
Purchase of plant assets		(110,000)
Cash Flow from Financing Activities		
Issuance of bonds payable.	110,000	
Payment of dividends.	(58,000)	
Cash provided by financing activities.		52,000
Net increase in cash.		12,000
Cash at beginning of year		10,000
Cash at end of year		$ 22,000

PAST

In Chapter 12, we examined the statement of cash flows.

PRESENT

In this chapter we complete our study of financial accounting by looking at the analysis and interpretation of financial statements.

FUTURE

In Chapter 14, we will introduce managerial accounting and examine how accounting information is used within organizations to make business decisions.

13

Analysis and Interpretation of Financial Statements

LEARNING OBJECTIVES

1. **Identify** persistent earnings and **discuss** the content and format of the income statement. *(p. 630)*

2. **Identify** the sources of financial information used by investment professionals and **explain** horizontal financial statement analysis. *(p. 634)*

3. **Explain** vertical financial statement analysis. *(p. 639)*

4. **Define** and **discuss** financial ratios for analyzing a firm. *(p. 641)*

5. **Discuss** the limitations of financial statement analysis. *(p. 656)*

6. Appendix 13A: **Describe** financial statement disclosures. *(p. 658)*

PROCTER & GAMBLE

The **Procter & Gamble Company (P&G)** is one of America's oldest companies, dating back to 1837 when candle maker William Procter and soap maker James Gamble combined their small businesses. Over the next few decades the company introduced such well-known products as Ivory soap and Crisco shortening that are still sold today.

P&G has continued to grow, with annual sales of over $80 billion. Not all of the company's growth, however, is the result of internally developed products like Crest toothpaste, Head & Shoulders shampoo, and Pampers diapers. A significant part of P&G's growth has come from mergers and acquisitions. P&G's largest acquisition occurred in 2005 when it acquired Gillette for $57 billion.

Acquisitions, such as the one involving Gillette, are complex transactions. Perhaps the hardest part of any merger or acquisition is to determine the appropriate price to pay—in this case $57 billion. How did P&G determine how much to pay for Gillette? Many factors go into such an analysis, but it often comes down to how much a company like Gillette will be able to add to P&G's future persistent earnings.

In this chapter we explore some of the ways that investment professionals determine how much a company is worth. The process involves analyzing a company's persistent earnings potential as well as the various risks associated with a company's day-to-day operations.

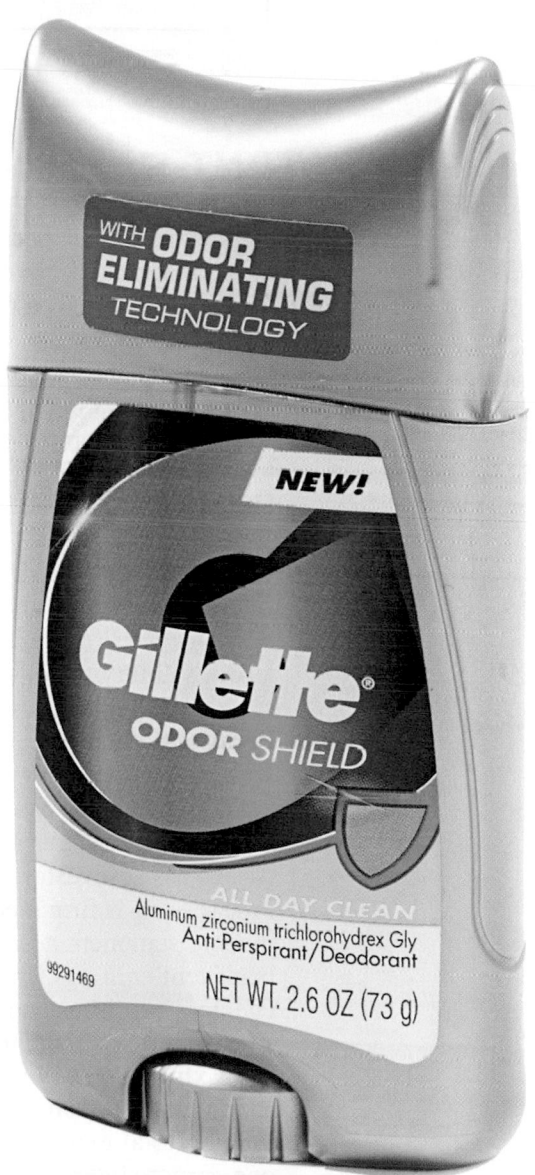

ANALYSIS AND INTERPRETATION OF FINANCIAL STATEMENTS

Persistent Earnings	Analytical Techniques
• Persistent earnings • Discontinued operations • Changes in accounting principles • Comprehensive income	• Sources of information • Horizontal analysis • Trend analysis • Vertical analysis • Ratio analysis • Limitations of financial analysis • Financial statement disclosures (Appendix 13A)

PERSISTENT EARNINGS AND THE INCOME STATEMENT

LO1 **Identify** persistent earnings and **discuss** the content and format of the income statement.

Net income is the "bottom line" measure of firm performance. It is a measure that depends on such accrual accounting procedures as the revenue recognition and expense matching policies selected by a firm's management. Generally accepted accounting principles have historically emphasized the importance of accounting earnings because past accounting earnings have been found to be a good predictor of a firm's future operating cash flow. Modern valuation theory tells us that the economic value of a company is the present value of the company's future operating cash flows. Thus, an important role for accounting numbers is their use by investment professionals when assessing the economic value of a company (like Gillette in the feature story).

One of the determinants of the ability of historical accounting earnings to predict future cash flow is the extent to which earnings recur over time, or what is known as *earnings persistence*. Since the value of a share of common stock today is a function of a firm's ability to consistently generate earnings year in and year out, the persistence (or sustainability) of a company's operating earnings is closely linked to its economic value. **Persistent earnings** are also sometimes referred to as *sustainable earnings* or *permanent earnings*, whereas non-persistent earnings are often referred to as **transitory earnings**. In general, transitory earnings include such single-period events as special items, restructuring charges, changes in accounting principle, and discontinued operations.

To assist investors in their assessment of a company's persistent earnings, and hence in assessing a firm's economic value, companies are required under GAAP to classify income statement accounts in a manner that aids a financial statement user in assessing persistent earnings. In Chapter 4, we discussed the classified income statement. In this chapter, we discuss a refinement of the classified income statement called the multiple-step or multi-step income statement.

Exhibit 13-1 illustrates the basic format of the multi-step income statement. While a **single-step income statement** derives the net income of a business in one step by subtracting total expenses from total revenues, a **multiple-step income statement** derives one or more intermediate performance measures before net income is reported. Examples of such intermediate performance measures are gross profit, net operating income, and net income from continuing operations before taxes.

Exhibit 13-1	The Multi-Step Income Statement

KALI COMPANY
Income Statement
For Year Ended December 31, 2016

Sales revenue.		$ 500	Usual and frequent
Cost of goods sold.		200	Usual and frequent
Gross profit.		300	
Operating expenses.		250	Usual and frequent
Net operating income.		50	
Other income and expense			
Interest income.	25		**Unusual**
Interest expense.	(35)		**Unusual**
Gain on sale of equipment	15	5	**Unusual**
Net income from continuing operations before tax		55	
Income tax		20	Usual and frequent
Net income from continuing operations.		35	
Gain from operations of discontinued division (net of tax).	15		**Infrequent**
Loss on disposal of discontinued division (net of tax)	(5)	10	
Net income		$ 45	
Earning per share (100 shares outstanding).		$0.45	

The income statement is organized in such a way that items with greater persistence are reported higher up in the income statement, whereas items considered more transitory are reported further down in the statement. Thus, accounts representing financial events that are both usual and frequent are reported first. Usual refers to whether an item is central to a firm's core operations, whereas **unusual items** display a high degree of abnormality and/or are unrelated, or only incidentally related, to the normal activities of a business. Frequent refers to how often an item is expected to occur, with infrequent items not reasonably expected to recur in the foreseeable future. Usual and frequent items typically consist of such income statement accounts as sales revenue, cost of goods sold, and other operating expenses. Just below these usual and frequent items are items that are either unusual or infrequent, but not both. Income statement accounts such as interest expense, interest income, and gains on sales of equipment are often frequently recurring items; however, they are not considered part of a firm's central operations and therefore are considered unusual. Examples of infrequent items include such financial events as asset write-downs and restructuring charges. These items are not expected to occur regularly, but are not considered unusual in nature.

Each of the above items is reported as part of a company's continuing operations and is shown before any income tax expense. GAAP, however, requires certain single-period items, or one-time events, to be reported on an after-tax basis. For example, income from discontinued operations, or the part of a business which is being shuttered or sold, are shown net of the financial effect of any applicable income taxes. Reporting discontinued operations on a net-of-tax basis allows the income tax expense reported on the income statement to reflect only the income taxes associated with a firm's continuing operations.

Most believe that the income statement is more useful when certain types of transactions and events are reported in separate sections. For this reason, information about discontinued operations is disclosed separately in the income statement. Segregating these categories of information from the results of continuing operations makes it easier for financial statement users to identify a company's persistent earnings.

The creation of sections within the income statement, however, complicates the reporting of a company's income tax expense. Items affecting the overall amount of income tax expense may appear in more than one section. If this is the case, accountants allocate a company's total income tax expense among those sections of the income statement in which the items affecting the tax expense appear.

Regardless of the format used for the income statement, companies are required to report net income on a per common share basis, called **earnings per share (EPS)**, on the income statement immediately following net income.

IFRS ALERT

Like U.S. GAAP, IFRS encourages companies to use a multi-step income statement when presenting a company's periodic performance. Tesco, the world's third largest retailer, presents its IFRS accounted income statement in Appendix C at the end of this book. Examining Tesco's income statement reveals that the retailer presents four measures of firm performance: gross profit, operating profit, profit before tax, and profit for the year. These indicators correspond to the four performance measures reported by the Kali Company in Exhibit 13.1: gross profit, net operating income, net income from continuing operations before tax, and net income. The income statements under U.S. GAAP and IFRS are very similar, with only minor labeling differences—like using "profit" instead of "income."

Discontinued Operations

Discontinued Operations

When a company sells, abandons, or otherwise disposes of a segment of its operations, a **discontinued operations** section of the income statement reports information about the discontinued business segment. The discontinued operations section presents two categories of information:

1. The income or loss from the segment's operations for the portion of the year before its discontinuance.

2. Any gain or loss from the disposal of the segment.

This section is reported on the income statement immediately after information regarding a firm's continuing operations.

To illustrate the reporting of discontinued operations, assume that on July 1, 2016, Kali Company, a diversified manufacturing company, sold its pet food division. **Exhibit 13-1** illustrates the income statement for Kali Company, including information regarding its pet food division in the discontinued operations section. From January 1 through June 30, Kali's pet food division operated at a profit, net of income taxes, of $15. The loss, net of income taxes, from the sale of the division's assets and liabilities was $5. Note that when there is a discontinued operations section, the difference between a firm's continuing sales revenues and expenses is labeled net income from continuing operations.

Changes in Accounting Principles

Occasionally a company may implement a **change in accounting principle**—that is, a switch from one generally accepted method to another. Examples include a change in inventory costing method, such as from FIFO to weighted-average cost, or a change in depreciation method, such as from declining balance to straight-line. These changes are permitted when a business can demonstrate that the reported financial results under the new accounting method are superior to the results reported under the replaced method.

Changing accounting principles can present a problem for financial statement users analyzing a company's performance over time because different accounting principles are likely to produce different financial statement results. Consequently, financial statements of prior years, issued in comparative form with current year financial statements, must also be presented using the new accounting principles as if the new method had been used all along.

Consistency Principle	PRINCIPLE ALERT

The *consistency principle* states that, unless otherwise disclosed, financial statements use the same accounting methods from one period to the next. A consistent use of accounting methods enhances the comparability of financial data across time. The consistency principle impacts the accounting for a change in accounting principles in several ways. First, to change an accounting principle, a company must be able to justify that the reported results under the new principle are preferable. Second, a company must present its prior year financial statements as though the new principle had been in use all along. In actual practice, only the prior year financial statements presented with the current year financial statements must be presented using the new accounting method. For all financial statements prior to those presented with the current statements, a lump sum adjustment is made to retained earnings on the statement of retained earnings and the statement of stockholders' equity.

Comprehensive Income

Most items that generate wealth changes in a business are required to be shown on the income statement. There are, however, a few items that do not appear as part of the regular content of the income statement and instead are classified under a category labeled **comprehensive income**. A business's comprehensive income includes its net income, any changes in the market value of certain marketable securities (see Appendix D at the end of this book), and any unrealized gains and losses from translating foreign currency denominated financial statements into U.S. dollars. This latter topic is covered in more advanced accounting textbooks.

Companies are given some flexibility as to how they report their comprehensive income. They are allowed to utilize two alternative formats under GAAP: (1) appending comprehensive income to the bottom of the income statement; or (2) creating a separate statement of comprehensive income. In addition to comprehensive income for the current period, GAAP requires a company to report accumulated other comprehensive income as part of stockholders' equity on the balance sheet. Accumulated other comprehensive income serves the same role for comprehensive income as retained earnings serves for regular net income—it reports the cumulative amount of comprehensive income as of the balance sheet date.

Pampers and UNICEF	CORPORATE SOCIAL RESPONSIBILITY

Maternal and neonatal tetanus is a disease that kills 59,000 people annually. **P&G**, through its Pampers product, has teamed up with UNICEF to fight this completely preventable disease. For every purchase of a pack of Pampers, P&G donates one dose of the tetanus vaccine. Pampers' funding has helped protect 100 million women and their babies against maternal and neonatal tetanus (MNT) and has helped eliminate this disease in Myanmar and Uganda. P&G and UNICEF are committed to the elimination of MNT from the face of the earth.

P&G and UNICEF have gone even further in their teamwork. P&G offers its employees in Europe, the Middle East, and Africa, a three-month paid sabbatical to work with UNICEF. The program is aimed at employees who have always wanted to perform humanitarian work but have lacked the financial resources to do so.

YOUR TURN! 13.1

The solution is on
page 692.

Conner Company, a retail company, entered into the following transactions during the year:

1. Sold merchandise to customers
2. Settled a major lawsuit
3. Wrote down the book value of a closed warehouse
4. Paid employee wages
5. Disposed of a line of discount stores
6. Paid income taxes

Required
Classify each of the above items as either persistent earnings or transitory earnings.

SOURCES OF INFORMATION

LO2 Identify the
sources of financial
information used by investment
professionals and **explain** horizontal
financial statement analysis

Except for closely held companies, businesses publish their financial statements at least annually. Most large companies also issue quarterly financial
data. Normally, annual financial statements are attested to by a certified public accountant, and investment professionals carefully review the independent
accountant's opinion to assess the reliability of the published financial data.

Companies listed on stock exchanges must also submit financial statements,
called a 10-K for the annual report and 10-Q for the quarterly report, to the U.S. Securities
and Exchange Commission (SEC). These statements are available to any interested party
and are generally more useful than annual reports because they contain greater detail.

Investment professionals may also want to compare the performance of a particular
firm with that of the other firms in the same industry. Data on industry norms, median
financial ratios by industry, and other relationships are available from such data collection
services as Dun & Bradstreet, Moody's, and Standard and Poor's. In addition, some brokerage firms compile industry norms and financial ratios from their own computer databases.

**ACCOUNTING IN
PRACTICE**

SEC EDGAR Database

An example of a financial database is **EDGAR**, the Electronic Data Gathering, Analysis, and Retrieval
system, maintained by the U.S. SEC (www.sec.gov/edgar.shtml). This computer database aids financial statement analysis by performing automated data collection, validation, indexing, acceptance,
and forwarding of submissions by companies and others who are required by law to file forms with
the U.S. Securities and Exchange Commission. The primary intent of the SEC in creating EDGAR was
to increase the efficiency of the securities market for the benefit of investors, corporations, and the
economy, by accelerating the receipt, acceptance, dissemination, and analysis of corporate information filed with the agency. An "efficient" securities market means that investors are able to make the
best possible decisions regarding where and when to invest their funds.

Analytical Techniques

The absolute dollar amounts of net income, sales revenue, total assets, and other key data
are usually not meaningful when analyzed in isolation. For example, knowing that a company's annual net income is $1 million is of little informational value unless the amount
of the income can be related to other factors. A $1 million profit might represent excellent
performance for a company with less than $10 million in invested capital. On the other
hand, $1 million in net income would be considered meager for a firm that had several
hundred million dollars in invested capital. Thus, significant information can be derived
by examining the relationship between two or more accounting variables, such as net
income and total assets, net income and sales revenue, or net income and stockholders'
equity. To describe these relationships clearly and to make comparisons easy, the relationships are often expressed in terms of ratios or percentages.

For example, we might express the relationship of $15,000 in net income to $150,000 in sales revenue as a ten percent ($15,000/$150,000) rate of return on sales. To describe the relationship between sales revenue of $150,000 and inventory of $20,000, we might use a ratio or a percentage; ($150,000/$20,000) may be expressed as 7.5, 7.5:1, or 750 percent.

Changes in selected financial statement items compared in successive financial statements are often expressed as percentages. For example, if a firm's net income increased from $40,000 last year to $48,000 this year, the $8,000 increase related to last year (the base year) is expressed as a 20 percent increase ($8,000/$40,000) in net income. To express a dollar increase or decrease as a percentage, however, the analyst must make the base year amount a positive figure. If, for example, a firm had a net loss of $4,000 in one year and net income of $20,000 in the next, the $24,000 increase cannot be meaningfully expressed as a percentage. Similarly, if a firm reported no marketable securities in last year's balance sheet but showed $15,000 of such securities in this year's statement, the $15,000 increase cannot be expressed as a meaningful percentage.

When evaluating a firm's financial statements for two or more years, analysts often use **horizontal analysis**. Horizontal analysis is a technique that can be useful for detecting an improvement or deterioration in a firm's performance and for spotting trends regarding a firm's financial well-being. The term **vertical analysis** is used to describe the analysis of a single year of financial data.

HORIZONTAL ANALYSIS

The type of horizontal analysis most often used by investment professionals is **comparative financial statement analysis** for two or more years, showing dollar and/or percentage changes for important financial statement items and totals. Dollar increases and decreases are divided by data from the base year to obtain percentage changes. To illustrate, the 2014 and 2013 financial statements of Procter & Gamble (P&G) are presented in **Exhibits 13-2**, **13-3**, and **13-4**. We will use the data in these statements throughout this chapter to illustrate various analytical techniques.

When analyzing financial statements, the investment professional is likely to focus his or her immediate attention on those financial statement items or percentages that are significant in amount. Although percentage changes are helpful in identifying significant items, they can sometimes be misleading. An unusually large percentage change may occur simply because the dollar amount of the base year is small. For example, P&G had a decrease in other non-operating income of $775, from $939 in 2013 to $164 in 2014. This represents a decrease of 82.5 percent, yet the dollar amount of this line item is quite small and insignificant relative to the other reported dollar amounts on P&G's income statement. The financial statement user's attention should be directed first to changes in key financial statement totals: sales revenue, operating income, net income, total assets, total liabilities, and so on. Next, the changes in significant individual items, such as accounts receivable, inventory, and property, plant and equipment should be examined.

P&G's total assets increased 3.6 percent from 2013 to 2014 (see **Exhibit 13-3**), and net sales increased 0.6 percent over the same time period (see **Exhibit 13-2**). (Recall from Chapter 5 that net sales equals gross sales revenue less any sales returns and allowances and sales discounts.) A small percentage increase in net sales coincided with a larger increase in total assets, reflecting a continued recovery of the economy in 2014, and indicating that P&G undertook certain business strategies to increase capacity to meet increasing demand. One potential note of concern is the relationship between cost of goods sold and net sales. While net sales increased by 0.6 percent, cost of goods sold increased by 2.6 percent, leading to a deterioration in P&G's gross profit margin percentage. P&G was able, however, to reduce selling, general, and administrative expense by 5.8 percent which ultimately helped contribute to an overall increase in net earnings of 2.9 percent in 2014.

Exhibit 13-2	Procter & Gamble Income Statement

THE PROCTER & GAMBLE COMPANY
Consolidated Income Statements

(in millions)	Year Ended 2014	Common-Size	Year Ended 2013	Common-Size	$ Change	% Change
Net sales.	$83,062	100.0%	$82,581	100.0%	$ 481	0.6 %
Cost of goods sold.	42,460	51.1%	41,391	50.1%	1,069	2.6 %
Gross profit.	40,602	48.9%	41,190	49.9%	(588)	(1.4)%
Selling, general, and administrative expense.	25,314	30.5%	26,860	32.5%	(1,546)	(5.8)%
Operating income.	15,288	18.4%	14,330	17.4%	958	6.7 %
Interest expense.	709	0.9%	667	0.8%	42	6.3 %
Other non-operating income	164	0.2%	939	1.1%	(775)	(82.5)%
Earnings from continuing operations before taxes	14,743	17.7%	14,602	17.7%	141	1.0 %
Income taxes on continuing operations	3,178	3.8%	3,391	4.1%	(213)	(6.3)%
Net earnings from continuing operations	11,565	13.9%	11,211	13.6%	354	3.2 %
Net earnings from discontinued operations, net of taxes	78	0.1%	101	0.1%	(23)	(22.8)%
Net earnings.	11,643	14.0%	11,312	13.7%	331	2.9 %
Earnings per share	4.19		4.04		0.15	3.7 %
Dividends per share	2.45		2.29		0.16	7.0 %

We can see from P&G's statement of cash flows (**Exhibit 13-4**) that even though cash flow from operations declined from 2013 to 2014, P&G decreased its cash outflow used by investing activities to a greater extent. As a result, they were able to increase end-of-year cash from 2013 to 2014. Finally, **Exhibit 13-4** reveals that P&G repurchased its common stock (treasury stock) in both 2013 and 2014, and increased its dividend payments, both of which increased the amount of the cash it returned to shareholders during this period of slow growth.

From this limited analysis of comparative financial statements, an investment professional might conclude that P&G's operating performance for 2014 was slightly better when compared with that of 2013, mostly the result of cost controls in 2014. Further analysis using some of the techniques summarized later in the chapter, however, may cause that opinion to be either affirmed or modified. The foregoing analysis did reveal some concerns, in particular, a deteriorating gross profit margin and a shrinking cash flow provided by operating activities.

PRINCIPLE ALERT	**Consistency Principle**

Horizontal analysis is a process of analyzing a firm's financial data across two or more years by examining dollar changes, percentage changes, and/or trend percentages. The utility of horizontal analysis, however, is dependent upon the effective implementation of the *consistency principle*. This accounting principle requires that a firm use the same accounting methods from one period to the next or, if a firm finds it necessary (or required) to change an accounting method, that the financial effects of any change be fully disclosed in the financial statements. The consistency principle assures financial analysts that, unless otherwise noted, changes in the accounts over time represent underlying economic changes in a business, and not the result of an accounting method change.

Exhibit 13-3	Procter & Gamble Balance Sheet

THE PROCTER & GAMBLE COMPANY
Consolidated Balance Sheets

(in millions)	2014	Common-Size	2013	Common-Size	$ Change	% Change
Assets						
Current assets						
Cash and cash equivalents..............	$8,558	5.9 %	$5,947	4.3 %	$2,611	43.9 %
Short-term investments	2,128	1.5 %			2,128	
Accounts receivable....................	6,386	4.4 %	6,508	4.7 %	(122)	(1.9)%
Inventories	6,759	4.7 %	6,909	5.0 %	(150)	(2.2)%
Other current assets...................	7,786	5.4 %	4,626	3.3 %	3,160	68.3 %
Total current assets...................	31,617	21.9 %	23,990	17.2 %	7,627	31.8 %
Property, plant, and equipment, net	22,304	15.5 %	21,666	15.6 %	638	2.9 %
Intangible assets	84,547	58.6 %	86,760	62.3 %	(2,213)	(2.6)%
Other noncurrent assets.................	5,798	4.0 %	6,847	4.9 %	(1,049)	(15.3)%
Total assets.........................	$144,266	100.0 %	$139,203	100.0 %	$5,003	3.6 %
Liabilities and Stockholders' Equity						
Current liabilities						
Accounts payable.....................	$8,461	5.9 %	$8,777	6.3 %	$(316)	(3.6)%
Other current liabilities	25,265	17.5 %	21,260	15.3 %	4,005	18.8 %
Total current liabilities................	33,726	23.4 %	30,037	21.6 %	3,689	12.3 %
Long-term debt	19,811	13.7 %	19,111	13.7 %	700	3.7 %
Other noncurrent liabilities	20,753	14.4 %	21,406	15.4 %	(653)	(3.1)%
Total liabilities	74,290	51.5 %	70,554	50.7 %	3,736	5.3 %
Preferred stock........................	1,111	0.8 %	1,137	0.8 %	(26)	(2.3)%
Common stock.........................	4,009	2.8 %	4,009	2.9 %		0.0 %
Additional paid-in capital	63,911	44.3 %	63,538	45.6 %	373	0.6 %
Treasury stock	(75,805)	(52.5)%	(71,966)	(51.7)%	(3,839)	5.3 %
Retained earnings	84,990	58.9 %	80,197	57.6 %	4,793	6.0 %
Other Stockholders' equity	(8,240)	(5.7)%	(8,206)	(5.9)%	(34)	0.4 %
Total stockholders' equity..............	69,976	48.5 %	68,709	49.3 %	1,267	1.8 %
Total liabilities and stockholders' equity...	$144,266	100.0 %	$139,263	100.0 %	$5,003	3.6 %

TREND ANALYSIS

To observe percentage changes over time in selected financial data, investment professionals often calculate **trend percentages**. Most companies provide summaries of their key financial data for the past five or ten years in their annual reports. With such information, the financial statement user can examine changes over periods longer than just the past two years. For example, suppose an analyst is interested in the trend in sales and net income for P&G for the past five years. The following are P&G's sales revenue and net income figures for 2010 through 2014:

PROCTER & GAMBLE COMPANY
Annual Performance

	2010		2011		2012		2013		2014	
	Millions of Dollars	Percentage of Base Year	Millions of Dollars	Percentage of Base Year	Millions of Dollars	Percentage of Base Year	Millions of Dollars	Percentage of Base Year	Millions of Dollars	Percentage of Base Year
Net sales..............	$75,785	100	$79,385	105	$82,006	108	$82,581	109	$83,062	110
Net income............	12,736	100	11,797	93	10,756	84	11,312	89	11,643	91

Exhibit 13-4	Procter & Gamble Statement of Cash Flows

THE PROCTER & GAMBLE COMPANY
Consolidated Statements of Cash Flows

(in millions)	Year Ended 2014	Year Ended 2013	$ Change	% Change
Operating activities				
Net earnings.	$11,643	$11,312		
Depreciation and amortization	3,141	2,982		
Other adjustments to net income.	304	(479)		
Changes in accounts receivable	87	(415)		
Changes in inventories.	8	(225)		
Change liabilities	1	1,253		
Change in other operating activities.	(1,226)	445		
Net cash flow provided by operating activities.	13,958	14,873	(915)	(6.2)%
Investing activities				
Capital expenditures	(3,848)	(4,008)		
Investments	(544)	(1,605)		
Other cash flows from investing activities	285	(682)		
Net cash flow used by investing activities	(4,107)	(6,295)	2,188	(34.8)%
Financing activities				
Dividends	(6,911)	(6,519)		
Net stock purchases	(6,005)	(5,986)		
Net borrowings.	3,543	1,985		
Other cash flows from financing activities	2,094	3,449		
Net cash used by financing activities	(7,279)	(7,071)	(208)	2.9%
Effect of exchange rate changes	39	4		
Change in cash and cash equivalents	2,611	1,511		
Beginning cash and cash equivalents	5,947	4,436		
Ending cash and cash equivalents.	$ 8,558	$ 5,947		

These data suggest an inconsistent growth pattern for the company, but the pattern of changes from year to year can be determined more precisely by calculating trend percentages. To do this, we select a base year and then divide the data for each of the remaining years by the base-year data. The result is an index of the changes occurring throughout the period. If, for example, 2010 is selected as the base year, all data for 2011 through 2014 will be related to 2010, which is represented as 100 percent.

To create the table of data displayed above, we divide each year's net sales—from 2011 through 2014—by $75,785, P&G's 2010 net sales (in millions of dollars). Similarly, P&G's net income for 2011 through 2014 is divided by $12,736, the company's 2010 net income (in millions of dollars).

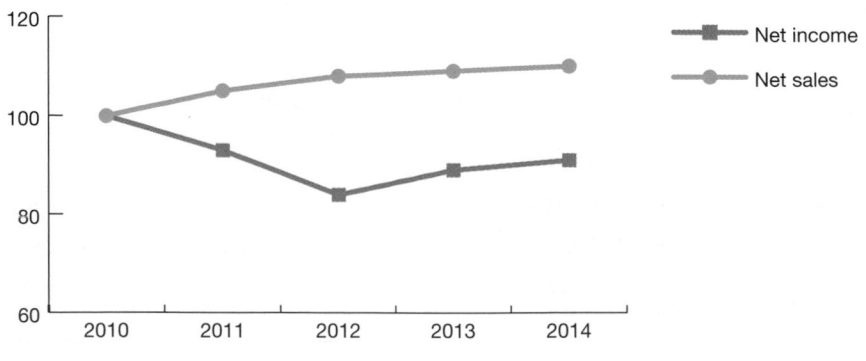

P&G's trend percentages above reveal that the company's growth in net sales out-stripped its growth in net income for the entire five-year period. The horizontal analysis of P&G's financial data also reveals that, while sales continued to grow modestly each year, P&G's net income initially declined for two years before recovering the final three years. P&G appeared to have taken steps to counter the adverse impact on its profitability.

It is important to exercise care when interpreting trend percentages. Since all index percentages are related to a base year, it is important to select a good representative base year. For example, if 2010 was an unusual period for the firm, perhaps because of some large transitory items, its use in the trend analysis would be of limited value.

Other data items that an investment professional may relate to sales revenue and net income over multiple years include total assets, a company's investment in plant assets, and its cash flow from operations, among others.

The following data pertain to the Farrow Company:

	2016	2015
Sales revenue.	$800,000	$750,000
Net income.	120,000	100,000
Total assets	300,000	290,000

Calculate both the amount in dollars and the percentage change in 2016 using horizontal analysis and 2015 as the base year.

YOUR TURN! 13.2

The solution is on page 692.

Concept	Method	Assessment	TAKEAWAY 13.1
How does a company's current performance compare with the prior year?	Income statement and balance sheet for current and prior year. The income statement and balance sheet should be compared using the prior year as the base. Percentage changes in financial statement amounts can be computed as the change between years divided by the base year amount.	Significant changes should be analyzed to determine the reason for any change.	

VERTICAL ANALYSIS

The relative importance of various accounts in a company's financial statements for a single year can be highlighted by showing them as a percentage of a key financial statement figure. A financial statement that presents the various account balances as a percentage of a key figure is called a **common-size financial statement**. Sales revenue (or net sales) is the key figure used to construct a common-size income statement, whereas total assets is the key figure used to construct a common-size balance sheet.

LO3 Explain vertical financial statement analysis.

A financial statement may present both the dollar amounts and common-size percentages. For example, **Exhibit 13-2** presents P&G's 2014 income statement in dollars and common-size percentages. The common-size percentages show each item in the income statement as a percentage of the company's net sales.

The common-size income statement allows financial statement users to readily compare P&G's ability to manage and control its various expenses while the level of its sales revenue changes over time. For example, P&G's net earnings increased from 13.7 percent of sales in 2013 to 14.0 percent of sales in 2014. We can also observe that there are only small changes in almost all of the line items as a percentage of net sales. Common-size income statements are also useful when comparing across firms, especially when the firms are significantly different in size. We would expect firms of different sizes to report different levels of sales revenues and expenses on a dollar basis. But, we would expect far more similarities when the comparison is done on a common-size basis.

Common-size percentages can also be used to analyze balance sheet data. For example, by examining a firm's current assets and long-term assets as a percentage of total assets, we can determine whether a company is becoming more or less liquid over time. Another use of common-size percentages with balance sheet data is to evaluate the changing sources of financing used by a business. For example, the proportion of total assets supplied by short-term creditors, long-term creditors, preferred stockholders, and common stockholders of P&G are shown in **Exhibit 13-3**.

P&G's common-size balance sheets reveal that P&G is relying slightly more on debt financing than equity financing in 2014 compared to 2013. The primary means that P&G used to make this shift in financing appears to be through an increase in other current liabilities, from 15.3 percent of total assets in 2013 to 17.5 percent in 2014, and an increase in the repurchase of its common shares as treasury stock, from 51.7 percent of total assets in 2013 to 52.5 percent of total assets in 2014. We also see that although P&G experienced an increase in the dollar amount of total assets, the relative composition of those assets remained quite stable between 2013 and 2014.

YOUR TURN! 13.3

The solution is on page 693.

Hint: When preparing common-size income statements, expenses are expressed as a positive percentage of net sales even though they are subtractions on the income statement.

The Sanford Company reported the following income statement in 2015:

SANFORD COMPANY Income Statement For the Year Ended December 31, 2015	
Sales revenue.	$13,500
Cost of goods sold.	5,400
Gross profit.	8,100
Selling and administrative expenses	1,350
Income from operations.	6,750
Interest expense.	675
Other expense	135
Income before income taxes	5,940
Income tax expense.	2,295
Net income.	$ 3,645

Required

Prepare a 2015 common-size income statement for Sanford Company.

TAKEAWAY 13.2	Concept ➡	Method ➡	Assessment
	How do the relationships within a company's income statement and balance sheet compare to those of prior years?	Income statement and balance sheet for current and prior year. Each income statement item should be presented as a percentage of sales revenue and each balance sheet item should be presented as a percentage of total assets. Financial statements in this form are called common-size statements.	The percentages should be analyzed for differences between years and significant changes should be analyzed to determine the reason for any change.

Financial statement analysis is executed, worldwide, in exactly the same way. Common-size financial statements and the financial ratios discussed below are currency neutral and can be effectively used anywhere in the world. Not all ratios are relevant, however, in all countries. For example, in emerging countries that lack the financial infrastructure to support a credit system, ratios involving accounts receivable and accounts payable are likely to be irrelevant since sales transactions in those countries are only executed on a cash basis. Similarly, solvency ratios like the times-interest-earned ratio (discussed shortly) are irrelevant since bank financing in lesser-developed countries is rare (although it is becoming more prevalent with the advent of micro-finance in these countries).

RATIO ANALYSIS

In prior chapters, a number of financial ratios were introduced. At this juncture, we classify those ratios by their analytical objective and review their analysis and interpretation by calculating them for a single company. P&G's financial statements in **Exhibit 13-2** , **Exhibit 13-3** and **Exhibit 13-4** provide the data for these calculations (all amounts are in millions). Also, representative industry averages are presented for comparison purposes where available. Some of the financial ratios that are commonly calculated by investment professionals, lenders, and managers are presented and explained in **Exhibit 13-5**.

LO4 **Define** and **discuss** financial ratios for analyzing a firm.

Analyzing Firm Profitability

Several ratios assist in evaluating how efficiently a firm has performed in its quest for profits, or what is referred to as firm profitability. These ratios include (1) the gross profit percentage, (2) the return on sales, (3) asset turnover, (4) the return on assets, and (5) the return on common stockholders' equity.

Gross Profit Percentage

The **gross profit percentage** is a closely watched ratio for both retailers and manufacturers, among other industries. The ratio is calculated as:

$$\text{Gross profit percentage} = \frac{\text{Gross profit on sales}}{\text{Net sales}}$$

A.K.A Gross profit is often referred to as *gross margin*.

This ratio shows the effect on firm profitability of changes in a firm's product pricing structure, sales mix, and merchandise costs. **Gross profit**, or **gross profit on sales**, is defined as the difference between net sales and cost of goods sold and reveals the amount of sales revenue remaining after subtracting the cost of products sold.

P&G's common-size income statements (see **Exhibit 13-2**) reveal that its gross profit percentage decreased from 49.9 percent in 2013 to 48.9 percent in 2014. These percentages are derived using the following figures:

	2014	2013
Gross profit.	$40,602	$41,190
Net sales.	83,062	82,581
Gross profit percentage.	**48.9%**	**49.9%**
Industry average.	52.1%	

In addition to the negative trend in P&G's gross profit percentage, we also note that P&G's ratio is below the industry average of 52.1 percent.

Exhibit 13-5	Key Financial Ratios	
Ratio	**Definition**	**Explanation**

Analyzing Firm Profitability

• Gross profit percentage	$\dfrac{\text{Gross profit on sales}}{\text{Net sales}}$	Percentage of income generated from sales after deducting the cost of goods sold.
• Return on sales	$\dfrac{\text{Net income}}{\text{Net sales}}$	Percentage of net income remaining from a dollar of sales after subtracting all expenses.
• Asset turnover	$\dfrac{\text{Net sales}}{\text{Average total assets}}$	Amount of sales generated from each dollar invested in assets.
• Return on assets	$\dfrac{\text{Net income}}{\text{Average total assets}}$	Rate of return generated on a company's investment in assets from all sources.
• Return on common stockholders' equity	$\dfrac{(\text{Net income} - \text{Preferred stock dividends})}{\text{Average common stockholders' equity}}$	Rate of return generated by a business for its common shareholders.

Analyzing Short-Term Firm Liquidity

• Working capital	Current assets − Current liabilities	The difference between a firm's current assets and its current liabilities.
• Current ratio	$\dfrac{\text{Current assets}}{\text{Current liabilities}}$	Amount of current assets available to service current liabilities
• Quick ratio	$\dfrac{(\text{Cash and cash equivalents} + \text{Short-term investments} + \text{Accounts receivable})}{\text{Current liabilities}}$	Amount of liquid assets available to service current liabilities
• Operating-cash-flow-to-current-liabilities ratio	$\dfrac{\text{Cash flow from operating activities}}{\text{Average current liabilities}}$	Amount of cash flow from operating activities available to service current liabilities.
• Accounts receivable turnover	$\dfrac{\text{Net sales}}{\text{Average accounts receivable (net)}}$	Number of sales/collection cycles experienced by a firm.
• Average collection period	$\dfrac{365}{\text{Accounts receivable turnover (net)}}$	Number of days required, on average, to collect an outstanding accounts receivable.
• Inventory turnover	$\dfrac{\text{Cost of goods sold}}{\text{Average inventory}}$	Number of production/sales cycles experienced by a firm.
• Days' sales in inventory	$\dfrac{365}{\text{Inventory turnover}}$	Number of days, on average, required to sell the inventory currently on hand.

Analyzing Long-Term Firm Solvency

• Debt-to-equity ratio	$\dfrac{\text{Total liabilities}}{\text{Total stockholders' equity}}$	Percentage of total assets provided by creditors.
• Times-interest-earned ratio	$\dfrac{\text{Income before interest expense and income taxes}}{\text{Interest expense}}$	Extent to which current operating income covers current debt service charges.
• Operating-cash-flow-to-capital-expenditures ratio	$\dfrac{\text{Cash flow from operating activities}}{\text{Annual net capital expenditures}}$	The ability of a firm's operations to provide sufficient cash to replace and expand its property, plant, and equipment.

Financial Ratios for Common Stockholders

• Earnings per share	$\dfrac{(\text{Net income} - \text{Preferred stock dividends})}{\text{Weighted-average number of common shares outstanding}}$	The net income available to common shareholders calculated on a per share basis.
• Price-earnings ratio	$\dfrac{\text{Market price per share}}{\text{Earnings per share}}$	A measure of the price of a share of common stock relative to the share's annual earnings.
• Dividend yield	$\dfrac{\text{Annual dividend per share}}{\text{Market price per share}}$	The earnings on an investment in stock coming from dividends.
• Dividend payout ratio	$\dfrac{\text{Annual dividend per share}}{\text{Earnings per share}}$	The percentage of net income paid out to shareholders as dividends.

Return on Sales (Profit Margin)

Another important measure of firm profitability is the **return on sales**. This ratio reveals the percentage of each dollar of net sales that remains as profit after subtracting all operating and nonoperating expenses. The return on sales is calculated as follows:

A.K.A Return on sales is often referred to as *profit margin*.

$$\text{Return on sales} = \frac{\text{Net income}}{\text{Net sales}}$$

When common-size income statements are available, the return on sales equals the net income percentage. P&G's common-size income statements in **Exhibit 13-2** reveal that its return on sales increased from 13.7 percent in 2013 to 14.0 percent in 2014. These percentages are calculated using the following figures:

	2014	2013
Net income. . . .	$11,643	$11,312
Net sales.	83,062	82,581
Return on sales.	**14.0%**	**13.7%**
Industry average.	11.6%	

The increase in the return on sales for P&G is encouraging, and as noted above, P&G's increase in its return on sales is mostly attributable to the company's cost control. Additionally, P&G's 2014 return on sales exceeds the industry average.

The return on sales and gross profit percentages should be used only when analyzing companies from the same industry or when comparing a firm's performance across multiple time periods (as we did above) since the ratio may vary widely across industries. Retail jewelers, for example, have much larger gross profit percentages (an industry average of 45.0 percent) than do retail grocers (an industry average of 23.0 percent). Industry averages for the asset turnover ratio, discussed next, would also be expected to vary significantly from one industry to another.

Asset Turnover

The **asset turnover ratio** measures how efficiently a firm uses its assets to generate sales revenue by calculating the amount of sales dollars generated annually for each dollar of assets invested in the company. This ratio is calculated as follows:

$$\text{Asset turnover} = \frac{\text{Net sales}}{\text{Average total assets}}$$

P&G's asset turnover is calculated as (total assets were $132,244 at year-end 2012):

		2014	2013
Net sales.		$ 83,062	$ 82,581
Total assets			
Beginning of year	(a)	139,263	132,244
End of year	(b)	144,266	139,263
Average [(a + b)/2]		141,765	135,754
Asset turnover		**0.59**	**0.61**
Industry average.		0.73	

P&G's asset turnover decreased slightly from 2013 to 2014, indicating that the company is less effective in using its assets to generate sales revenue. Specifically, the company generated $0.59 in net sales for every dollar invested in total assets in 2014, compared to $0.61 in 2013. This ratio result is also below the industry average of $0.73.

Industries that are characterized by low gross profit percentages generally have relatively high asset turnover ratios. Retail grocery chains, for example, typically turnover their assets five to six times per year. By way of contrast, retail jewelers average only one to two asset turnovers per year. These industry differences largely reflect the high cost of products sold by jewelers versus the low cost of products sold by retail grocers.

Return on Assets

The rate of return on total assets, called the **return on assets**, is an overall measure of a firm's profitability. It reveals the rate of profit earned per dollar of assets under a firm's control. The return on assets is calculated as follows:

$$\text{Return on assets} = \frac{\text{Net income}}{\text{Average total assets}}$$

P&G's return on assets is calculated as:

	2014	2013
Net income.	$ 11,643	$ 11,312
Average total assets	141,765	135,754
Return on assets	**8.2%**	**8.3%**
Industry average.	8.6%	

P&G's return on assets declined from 8.3 percent in 2013 to 8.2 percent in 2014; however the percentage is consistent with the industry average.

The return on asset ratio summarizes the financial impact of two component ratios: the return on sales and asset turnover; that is, the return on assets is the multiplicative product of these latter two ratios, as follows:

Ratio:	Return on sales	×	Asset turnover	=	Return on assets
Ratio calculation:	$\dfrac{\text{Net income}}{\text{Net sales}}$	×	$\dfrac{\text{Net sales}}{\text{Average total asset}}$	=	$\dfrac{\text{Net income}}{\text{Average total assets}}$
P&G:	**14.0 percent**	×	**0.59**	=	**8.3 percent**

Return on Common Stockholders' Equity

The **return on common stockholders' equity** measures the profitability of the ownership interest held by a company's common stockholders. The ratio shows the percentage of income available to common stockholders—that is, net income less any preferred stock dividends—for each dollar of common stockholder equity invested in a business, as follows:

$$\frac{\text{Return on common}}{\text{stockholders' equity}} = \frac{(\text{Net income} - \text{Preferred stock dividends})}{\text{Average common stockholders' equity}}$$

The return on common stockholders' equity for P&G is calculated as (common stockholders' equity was $62,840 at year-end 2012):

	2014	2013
Net income.	$11,643	$11,312
Less: Preferred stock dividends.	253	244
Common stock earnings	11,390	11,068
Common stockholders' equity:		
Beginning of year . . . . (a)	67,572	62,840
End of year . . . . (b)	68,865	67,572
Average [(a + b)/2].	68,219	65,206
Return on common stockholders' equity.	**16.7%**	**17.0%**
Industry average.	20.1%	

P&G's return on common stockholders' equity declined by 0.3 percent, from 17.0 percent in 2013 to 16.7 percent in 2014. Unlike the return on assets, P&G's return on common stockholders' equity is well below the industry average.

YOUR TURN! 13.4

The solution is on page 693.

The following data was obtained from the current financial statements for Kelly Corporation:

Net sales.	$30,000
Cost of goods sold.	10,500
Net income.	4,500
Average total assets.	50,000
Average common stockholders' equity	35,000
Preferred dividends	500

Required

Calculate the following ratios for Kelly Corporation:

a. Gross profit percentage

b. Return on sales

c. Asset turnover

d. Return on assets

e. Return on common stockholders' equity

Concept ⟶	Method ⟶	Assessment	TAKEAWAY 13.3
How much profit is a company generating relative to the amount of assets invested in the company?	Income statement and balance sheet. Calculate the return on assets by dividing net income by the average total assets for the year.	The higher the return on assets, the better a company is doing in terms of generating profits utilizing the assets under its control.	

Analyzing Short-Term Firm Liquidity

A firm's **working capital** is the difference between its current assets and current liabilities. Maintaining an adequate working capital enables a firm to repay its current obligations on a timely basis and to take advantage of any available purchase discounts associated with the timely payment of accounts payable. Shortages of working capital, on the other hand, can force a company into borrowing at inopportune times and unfavorable interest rates. As a consequence, many long-term debt contracts contain provisions that require the borrowing firm to maintain an adequate working capital position. A firm's working capital is calculated as follows:

$$\text{Working capital} = \text{Current assets} - \text{Current liabilities}$$

Analysis of a firm's short-term liquidity utilizes several financial ratios that relate to various aspects of a company's working capital. These ratios are (1) the current ratio, (2) the quick ratio, (3) operating-cash-flow-to-current-liabilities ratio, (4) accounts receivable turnover and average collection period, and (5) inventory turnover and days' sales in inventory.

Current Ratio

The **current ratio** is calculated as a firm's current assets divided by its current liabilities:

$$\text{Current ratio} = \frac{\text{Current assets}}{\text{Current liabilities}}$$

This ratio is a widely used measure of a firm's ability to meet its current obligations and to have funds available for use in daily operations. The following calculations reveal that P&G's current ratio improved from 0.80 in 2013 to 0.94 (or 0.94:1) in 2014:

	2014	2013
Current assets	$31,617	$23,990
Current liabilities.	33,726	30,037
Current ratio	**0.94**	**0.80**
Industry average.	1.6	

In essence, P&G had $0.94 in current assets for every $1 in current liabilities at the end of 2014.

In the past, a generally accepted rule of thumb was that a firm's current ratio should be approximately 2:1, indicating that a company should maintain twice the dollar amount of current assets as was needed to satisfy its current liabilities. Improved cash flow management techniques and alternate forms of short-term financing (such as bank lines of credit) have reduced the need for businesses to maintain such a high current ratio. Still, many creditors prefer to see a higher current ratio and consider a low ratio as a potential warning sign of short-term liquidity problems.

Evaluating the adequacy of a firm's current ratio may involve comparing it with the recent past (P&G's current ratio improved slightly from 2013 to 2014) or with an industry average (P&G's ratio is below the industry average of 1.6). What is considered an appropriate current ratio varies by industry. A service firm with little or no inventory, such as a car wash service, would be expected to have a smaller current ratio than would a firm carrying a large inventory, such as a hardware retailer. The composition (or mix) of a firm's current assets significantly influences any evaluation of a firm's short-term liquidity. The quick ratio, discussed next, explicitly considers the composition of a firm's current assets when evaluating short-term liquidity.

Quick Ratio

A.K.A. The quick ratio is also referred to as the *acid-test ratio.*

The **quick ratio** reveals the relationship between a firm's liquid, or quick, assets and its current liabilities. Quick assets include cash and cash equivalents, short-term investments, and accounts receivable. The quick ratio omits a company's inventory and prepaid assets, which may not be particularly liquid. Consequently, the quick ratio may give a more accurate picture of a company's ability to meet its current obligations since the ratio ignores a firm's potentially illiquid inventory and prepaid expenses.

Comparing the quick ratio and the current ratio indicates the financial impact of a company's inventory on its working capital. For example, a company might have an acceptable current ratio, but if its quick ratio falls to an unacceptable level, a financial analyst is likely to be concerned about the amount of inventory on hand, and consequently, analyze the company's inventory position more thoroughly.

The quick ratio is calculated as follows:

$$\text{Quick ratio} = \frac{(\text{Cash and cash equivalents} + \text{Short-term investments} + \text{Accounts receivable})}{\text{Current liabilities}}$$

The quick ratio for P&G is calculated as:

	2014	2013
Cash and cash equivalents, short-term investments, and accounts receivable..................................	$17,072	$12,455
Current liabilities......................................	33,726	30,037
Quick ratio..	**0.51**	**0.41**
Industry average.......................................	0.28	

P&G's quick ratio increased from 0.41 in 2013 to 0.51 in 2014, and its 2014 quick ratio is well above the industry average of 0.28. P&G's increased quick ratio is mainly due to a large increase in cash and cash equivalents and short-term investments in 2014.

Operating-Cash-Flow-to-Current-Liabilities Ratio

Ultimately, cash will be needed to settle a business's current liabilities. Another ratio indicating a firm's ability to pay its current liabilities as they come due focuses on a company's operating cash flow. The **operating-cash-flow-to-current-liabilities ratio** is calculated as follows:

$$\text{Operating-cash-flow-to-current-liabilities ratio} = \frac{\text{Cash flow from operating activities}}{\text{Average current liabilities}}$$

The operating-cash-flow-to-current-liabilities ratio relates the net cash available as a result of operating activities to the average current liabilities outstanding during the period. A higher ratio indicates that a firm has a greater ability to settle its current liabilities using its operating cash flow.

P&G's operating-cash-flow-to-current-liabilities ratio is calculated as (current liabilities at the end of 2012 was $24,907; no industry average is available):

		2014	2013
Cash flow from operating activities		$13,958	$14,873
Current liabilities			
Beginning of year	(a)	30,037	24,907
End of year	(b)	33,726	30,037
Average [(a+b)/2]		31,882	27,472
Operating-cash-flow-to-current-liabilities ratio		**0.44**	**0.54**

P&G's operating-cash-flow-to-current-liabilities ratio declined from 2013 to 2014, a result of a decline in cash provided by operating activities and an increase in average current liabilities.

Accounts Receivable Turnover

The speed with which accounts receivable are collected is of considerable interest to investment professionals when evaluating a firm's short-term liquidity. **Accounts receivable turnover** indicates how many times a year a firm collects its average outstanding accounts receivable, and thus, measures how fast a firm converts its accounts receivable into cash. The quicker a firm is able to convert its accounts receivables into cash, the less cash the company needs to keep on hand to satisfy its current liabilities. Accounts receivable turnover is calculated as follows:

$$\text{Accounts receivable turnover} = \frac{\text{Net sales}}{\text{Average accounts receivable (net)}}$$

Recall from Chapter 8 that accounts receivable less the allowance for doubtful accounts—that is, the net balance of accounts receivable—is the amount of receivables that the company expects to collect from customers. The accounts receivable turnover for P&G is calculated as (accounts receivable at the end of 2012 were $6,068):

		2014	2013
Net sales.		$83,062	$82,581
Average accounts receivable (net)			
Beginning of year	(a)	6,508	6,068
End of year	(b)	6,386	6,508
Average [(a + b)/2]		6,447	6,288
Accounts receivable turnover		**12.88**	**13.13**
Industry average.		10.12	

The higher the accounts receivable turnover, the faster a company is able to convert its accounts receivable into cash. P&G's accounts receivable turnover decreased slightly from 13.13 in 2013 to 12.88 in 2014. However, P&G's 2014 accounts receivable turnover is well above the industry average of 10.12 for the year.

Average Collection Period

A.K.A. The average collection period is also referred to as the *days' sales outstanding, or DSO.*

An extension of the accounts receivable turnover is the **average collection period**. The average collection period reveals how many days it takes, on average, for a company to collect an account receivable. The ratio is calculated as follows:

$$\text{Average collection period} = \frac{365}{\text{Accounts receivable turnover (net)}}$$

P&G's average collection period is calculated as:

	2014	2013
Average collection period		
2014: 365/12.88; 2013: 365/13.13.	**28.3 days**	**27.8 days**
Industry average.	36.1 days	

P&G's average collection period increased slightly in 2014. This may have resulted from such actions as P&G relaxing the credit standards they apply to their customers or by extending the allowed credit period. Alternatively, it may reflect that P&G's customers have experienced deteriorating cash flows, and thus they are not able to pay their accounts as promptly. Knowledge of P&G's credit terms would permit a more complete analysis of these results. If, for example, P&G's credit terms are n/20, then an average collection period of 28.3 days indicates that the company has a problem with slow-paying customers. If, on the other hand, P&G's credit terms are n/30, then the 2014 average collection period shows no particular problem with the company's speed of receivable collection.

Inventory Turnover

An analyst concerned about a company's inventory position is likely to evaluate the company's **inventory turnover**. This ratio indicates whether the inventory on hand is disproportionate to the amount of sales revenue. Excessive inventories not only tie up company funds and increase storage costs but may also lead to subsequent losses if the goods become outdated or unsalable. In general, a higher turnover is preferred to a lower turnover. The calculation of inventory turnover is as follows:

$$\text{Inventory turnover} = \frac{\text{Cost of goods sold}}{\text{Average inventory}}$$

P&G's inventory turnover is calculated as (inventory at the end of 2012 was $6,721):

		2014	2013
Cost of goods sold.		$42,460	$41,391
Inventory			
Beginning of year	(a)	6,909	6,721
End of year	(b)	6,759	6,909
Average [(a + b)/2].		6,834	6,815
Inventory turnover		**6.21**	**6.07**
Industry average.		5.23	

P&G's inventory turnover increased from 6.07 in 2013 to 6.21 in 2014. In addition, the company's 2014 inventory turnover of 6.21 is above the industry average of 5.23.

The cost of goods sold is used in the calculation of inventory turnover because the inventory measure in the denominator is a *cost* figure; consequently, it is appropriate to also use a cost figure in the numerator. By way of contrast, accounts receivable turnover uses net sales in the calculation because accounts receivable is based on sales revenue, which includes a markup for the company's expected profit.

A low inventory turnover can result from an overextended inventory position or from inadequate sales volume. For this reason, an appraisal of a firm's inventory turnover should be accompanied by a review of the quick ratio and an analysis of trends in both inventory and sales revenue.

Days' Sales in Inventory

The **days' sales in inventory** ratio is derived from a firm's inventory turnover ratio and reveals how many days it takes, on average, for a firm to sell its inventory on hand. The ratio is calculated as follows:

$$\text{Days' sales in inventory} = \frac{365}{\text{Inventory turnover}}$$

P&G's days' sales in inventory is calculated as:

	2014	2013
2014: 365/6.21; 2013: 365/6.07.	**58.8 days**	**60.1 days**
Industry average.	69.8 days	

P&G's days' sales in inventory reveals that the average amount of time required to sell its inventory decreased by 1.3 days from 60.1 days in 2013 to 58.8 days in 2014. Also, P&G's average length of time to sell its inventory is lower than the industry average by eleven days. The improvement in P&G's days' sales in inventory will positively impact the company's profitability due to the related decrease in inventory storage costs and a decrease in its inventory financing costs.

By combining the days' sales in inventory with the average collection period, it is possible to estimate the average time period from the acquisition of inventory, to the sale of inventory, to the eventual collection of cash. The sum of the days' sales in inventory plus the average collection period measures the length of the company's **operating cycle**. Although operating cycles will naturally vary across different industries, a shorter operating cycle is preferred as it is an indicator of the operating efficiency and working capital management of the company. In 2014, for example, it took P&G 87.1 days (58.8 days' sales in inventory + 28.3 days average collection period) to sell its average inventory and collect the related cash from its customers. This operating cycle is significantly better than the industry average of 105.9 days by nearly nineteen days and slightly better than P&G's 2013 period of 87.9 days (60.1 days + 27.8 days).

YOUR TURN! 13.5

The solution is on page 693.

The following selected data was obtained from the financial statements of Justin Corporation:

Current assets	$ 60,000
Current liabilities for both current and prior year	40,000
Cash flow from operating activities	55,000
Net sales.	100,000
Average accounts receivable.	15,000
Cost of goods sold.	70,000
Average inventory.	9,000

Required

Calculate the following financial measures and ratios for Justin Corporation:

a. Working capital

b. Current ratio

c. Operating-cash-flow-to-current-liabilities ratio

d. Accounts receivable turnover

e. Days' sales in inventory

TAKEAWAY 13.4	Concept	➡	Method	➡	Assessment
	How financially capable is a company to pay its current liabilities as they come due?		Income statement, balance sheet, and statement of cash flows. Calculate the current ratio, the quick ratio, and the operating-cash-flow-to-current-liabilities ratio.		The higher the ratios, the higher the probability that a company will have the ability to pay its current liabilities as they become due.

Analyzing Long-Term Firm Solvency

The preceding set of ratios examined a firm's short-term liquidity. A separate set of ratios analyzes a firm's long-term solvency, or its long-term debt repayment capability. Ratios in this latter group include (1) the debt-to-equity ratio, (2) the times-interest-earned ratio, and (3) the operating-cash-flow-to-capital-expenditures ratio.

Debt-to-Equity Ratio

The **debt-to-equity ratio** evaluates the financial structure of a firm by relating a company's total liabilities to its total stockholders' equity. This ratio considers the extent to which a company relies on creditors versus stockholders to provide financing. The debt-to-equity ratio is calculated as follows:

$$\text{Debt-to-equity ratio} = \frac{\text{Total liabilities}}{\text{Total stockholders' equity}}$$

This ratio uses year-end balances for the ratio's components, rather than averages, since we are interested in the firm's capital structure as of a particular point in time. The total stockholders' equity for a business is its total assets minus its total liabilities.

The debt-to-equity ratio gives creditors an indication of the margin of protection available to them (creditors' claims to assets have priority over stockholders' claims). The lower the ratio, the greater the protection being provided to creditors. A firm with a low ratio also has greater flexibility when seeking additional borrowed funds at a low rate of interest than does a firm with a high ratio.

P&G's debt-to-equity ratio is calculated as:

	2014	2013
Total liabilities (year-end)	$74,290	$70,554
Total stockholders' equity (year-end)	69,976	68,709
Debt-to-equity ratio	**1.06**	**1.03**
Industry average	0.66	

P&G's debt-to-equity ratio increased from 1.03 in 2013 to 1.06 in 2014, indicating a small increase in reliance on debt to finance its operations. In addition, the company's 2014 ratio is above the industry average, suggesting an increased risk of insolvency. Still, this ratio is far from a point where it would represent a major concern.

Times-Interest-Earned Ratio

To evaluate the ability of a company to pay its current interest charges from its operating income, an analyst may investigate the relationship between the company's current interest charges and its net income. For example, an extremely high debt-to-equity ratio for a company may indicate extensive borrowing by the company; however, if its operating earnings are sufficient to meet the interest charges on the debt several times over, an analyst may regard the situation quite favorably.

A.K.A. The times-interest-earned ratio is also referred to as the *interest coverage ratio*.

Analysts, particularly long-term credit analysts, almost always consider the **times-interest-earned ratio** of a company with interest-bearing debt. This ratio is calculated by dividing the income before interest expense and income taxes by the annual interest expense:

$$\text{Times-interest-earned ratio} = \frac{\text{Income before interest expense and income taxes}}{\text{Interest expense}}$$

P&G's times-interest-earned ratio is calculated as:

	2014	2013
Income before interest expense and income taxes	$15,452	$15,269
Interest expense	709	667
Times-interest-earned ratio	**21.8**	**22.9**
Industry average	24.7	

P&G's operating income available to meet its interest charges decreased slightly from 22.9 times in 2013 to 21.8 times in 2014. This ratio is below the industry average of 24.7, but still indicates that P&G exhibits an exceptionally good margin of safety for creditors. Generally speaking, a company that earns its interest charges several times over is regarded as a satisfactory risk by long-term creditors.

Operating-Cash-Flow-to-Capital-Expenditures Ratio

The ability of a firm's operations to provide sufficient cash to replace and expand its property, plant, and equipment is revealed by the **operating-cash-flow-to-capital-expenditures ratio**. To the extent that acquisitions of plant assets can be financed using cash provided by operating activities, a firm does not have to use other financing sources, such as long-term debt. This ratio is calculated as follows:

$$\text{Operating-cash-flow-to-capital-expenditures ratio} = \frac{\text{Cash flow from operating activities}}{\text{Annual net capital expenditures}}$$

A ratio of 1.0 indicates that a firm's current operating activities provide sufficient cash to fully fund any investment in plant capacity. A ratio in excess of 1.0 indicates that a company has more than sufficient operating cash flow to fund any needed expansion in plant capacity.

The operating-cash-flow-to-capital-expenditures ratio for P&G is:

	2014	2013
Cash flow from operating activities	$13,958	$14,873
Annual net capital expenditures.	3,848	4,008
Operating-cash-flow-to-capital-expenditures ratio	**3.6**	**3.7**

In 2014, P&G's operating-cash-flow-to capital-expenditures ratio was 3.6, a slight decrease from 3.7 in 2013. It appears that P&G is generating plenty of operating cash flow to cover its net capital expenditures in each year.

YOUR TURN! 13.6

The solution is on page 693.

GuidedExamples
MBC

The following selected data was obtained from the financial statements for the Hartford Corporation:

Total liabilities.	$180,000
Total stockholders' equity	600,000
Cash flow from operating activities	100,000
Annual capital expenditures.	30,000
Net income.	55,000
Interest expense.	5,000
Income tax expense.	25,000

Required

Calculate the following ratios for Hartford Corporation:

a. Debt-to-equity ratio

b. Times-interest-earned ratio

c. Operating-cash-flow-to-capital-expenditures ratio

Concept	⟶	Method	⟶	Assessment	TAKEAWAY 13.5
How solvent is a company?		Income statement, balance sheet, and statement of cash flows. Calculate the debt-to-equity ratio, the times-interest-earned ratio, and the operating-cash-flow-to-capital-expenditures ratio.		The higher the times-interest-earned and the operating-cash-flow-to-capital-expenditures ratios, and the lower the debt-to-equity ratio, the greater is a company's solvency.	

Financial Ratios for Common Stockholders

Present and potential common stockholders share an interest with a business's creditors in analyzing the profitability, short-term liquidity, and long-term solvency of a company. There are also other financial ratios that are primarily of interest to common stockholders. These ratios include (1) earnings per share, (2) the price-earnings ratio, (3) dividend yield, and (4) the dividend payout ratio.

Earnings per Share

Because stock market prices are quoted on a per-share basis, the reporting of earnings per share of common stock is useful to investors. **Earnings per share (EPS)** is calculated by dividing the net income available to common stockholders by the weighted average number of common shares outstanding during a year. The net income available to common stockholders is a company's net income less any preferred stock dividends. Preferred stock dividends are subtracted from net income to arrive at the net income available exclusively to a company's common stock stockholders. Thus, earnings per share is calculated as follows:

$$\text{Earnings per share} = \frac{(\text{Net income} - \text{Preferred stock dividends})}{\text{Weighted-average number of common shares outstanding}}$$

Since earnings per share are a required disclosure on a company's income statement, investment professionals do not have to calculate this financial metric. P&G's income statements reveal the following earnings per share (see **Exhibit 13-2**):

	2014	2013
Earnings per share	$4.19	$4.04

P&G's earnings per share increased from $4.04 in 2013 to $4.19 in 2014, an increase of 3.7 percent. This is slightly higher than the 2.9 percent increase in P&G's net income over the same period. The result is due to the small increase in P&G's treasury stock, which reduces the number of common shares outstanding.

Price-Earnings Ratio

The **price-earnings ratio** is calculated by dividing the market price per share of common stock by a company's earnings per share:

A.K.A. The price earnings ratio is also referred to as the *P/E multiple*.

$$\text{Price-earnings ratio} = \frac{\text{Market price per share}}{\text{Earnings per share}}$$

For many analysts and investors, this ratio is an important tool for assessing a stock's valuation. For example, after evaluating the financial strengths of several comparable companies, an analyst may decide which company to invest in by comparing the price-earnings ratio of each company. Assuming that the companies have equivalent persistent earnings and financial risk profiles, the company with the lowest price-earnings ratio may represent the best investment opportunity.

When calculating the price-earnings ratio, it is customary to use the latest market price per share and the earnings per share for the last four quarters of a company's operations. P&G's price-earnings ratios as of the end of fiscal years 2013 and 2014 are:

	2014	2013
Market price per share (at year-end)	$78.59	$76.99
Earnings per share	4.19	4.04
Price-earnings ratio	**18.8**	**19.1**
Industry average.	22.3	

The market price of a share of P&G's common stock at year-end 2014 was 18.8 times the company's 2014 earnings per share. Since P&G's price-earnings ratio at the end of 2014 is below industry average, this may indicate that the company's shares are undervalued, and thus, that its stock may represent a good investment.

Dividend Yield

Investor expectations vary greatly with personal economic circumstances and with the overall economic outlook. Some investors are more interested in the potential share price appreciation of a stock than in any dividends that a company may pay on its outstanding shares. When shares are disposed of in the future, the capital gains provision of U.S. income tax law generally taxes capital gains at a rate that is lower than the tax rate applied to dividend income. Some investors, on the other hand, are more concerned with dividends than with stock price appreciation. These investors desire a high **dividend yield** on their investments. Dividend yield is calculated by dividing a company's current annual dividend per share by the current market price per share:

$$\text{Dividend yield} = \frac{\textbf{Annual dividend per share}}{\textbf{Market price per share}}$$

P&G's dividend yield per common share is calculated as (the dividend per share is disclosed in **Exhibit 13-2**):

	2014	2013
Annual dividend per share	$2.45	$2.29
Market price per share (at year-end)	78.59	76.99
Dividend yield	**3.1%**	**3.0%**
Industry average.	2.8%	

P&G's dividend yield increased from 3.0 percent in 2013 to 3.1 percent in 2014, and is slightly above the industry average of 2.8 percent.

Dividend Payout Ratio

Investors who emphasize the yield on their investments may also be interested in a firm's **dividend payout ratio**—that is, the percentage of net income paid out as dividends to stockholders. The payout ratio indicates whether a firm has a conservative or a liberal dividend policy, and may also indicate whether a firm is conserving funds for internal financing of its growth. The dividend payout ratio is calculated as follows:

$$\text{Dividend payout ratio} = \frac{\text{Annual dividend per share}}{\text{Earnings per share}}$$

P&G's dividend payout ratio is calculated as:

	2014	2013
Annual dividends per share	$2.45	$2.29
Earnings per share	4.19	4.04
Dividend payout ratio.	**58.5%**	**56.7%**
Industry average.	50.0%	

P&G's dividend payout ratio increased from 56.7 percent in 2013 to 58.5 percent in 2014. This payout ratio is consistent with the payout ratio for most comparable mature U.S. industrial corporations, but is slightly higher than the industry average for P&G.

Payout ratios for mature industrial corporations vary between 40 percent and 60 percent of net income. Many corporations, however, need funds for internal financing of growth and pay out little (if any) of their net income as dividends. At the other extreme, some companies—principally utility companies—may pay out as much as 70 percent of their net income as dividends.

The following selected data was obtained from financial statements for Baylor Corporation:

Earnings per share	$ 4.50
Market price per share of common stock	54.00
Dividends per share of common stock	1.50

Required
Calculate the following ratios for Baylor Corporation:

a. Dividend yield
b. Dividend payout ratio

YOUR TURN! 13.7

The solution is on page 693.

Concept →	Method →	Assessment	TAKEAWAY 13.6
How much dividends are common stockholders likely to receive?	Earnings per share, dividends per share, and market price of common stock. Calculate the dividend yield and dividend payout ratio.	The higher the dividend yield and the dividend payout ratio, the greater the company's dividend distribution policy.	

Accounting as an Aid to Investing

ACCOUNTING IN PRACTICE

The days of corporations offering traditional pension plans where the employee is guaranteed certain benefits at retirement are numbered. More and more employers are switching to plans such as a 401(k) where the employee is responsible for deciding what the plan invests in. Having a knowledge of the accounting techniques demonstrated in this chapter can certainly provide a better understanding of the risks and rewards of investing.

LIMITATIONS OF FINANCIAL STATEMENT ANALYSIS

LO5 Discuss the limitations of financial statement analysis.

The ratios, percentages, and other relationships described in this chapter reflect the analytical techniques used by investment professionals and experienced investors. Nonetheless, they must be interpreted with due consideration of the general economic conditions, the conditions of the industry in which a company operates, and the relative position of individual companies within an industry.

Financial statement users must also be aware of the inherent limitations of financial statement data. Problems of comparability are frequently encountered. Companies within the same industry may use different accounting methods that can cause problems in comparing certain key relationships. For instance, inventory turnover is likely to be quite different for a company using LIFO than for one using FIFO. Inflation may also distort certain financial data and ratios, especially those resulting from horizontal analysis. For example, trend percentages calculated from data unadjusted for inflation may be deceptive.

Financial statement users must also be careful when comparing companies within a particular industry. Factors such as firm size, diversity of product line, and mode of operations can make firms within the same industry dissimilar in their reported results. Moreover, some firms, particularly conglomerates, are difficult to classify by industry. If segment information is available, the financial statement user may compare the statistics for several industries. Often, trade associations prepare industry statistics that are stratified by size of firm or type of product, facilitating financial statement analysis.

FORENSIC ACCOUNTING

It is generally considered more difficult to deter financial statement fraud than it is to deter other types of fraud such as embezzlement. The best approach to fraud deterrence is to put into place a strong set of internal controls. Unfortunately, senior management, such as a firm's CEO and CFO, are the most likely employees to commit financial statement fraud. These individuals are able to use their position of authority to override most internal controls. Thus, it is important to consider alternative approaches to fraud deterrence. Potential alternative approaches are based on the fraud triangle concept, in which fraud is related to the interaction of three factors: (1) pressure, (2) opportunity, and (3) rationalization.

The fraud element of pressure can be reduced by avoiding the practice of setting unachievable financial goals and utilizing compensation systems that are considered fair but which do not create excessive incentives to commit fraud. Although internal controls may be circumvented by senior management, it is still important to maintain a strong system of internal controls and to establish clear and uniform accounting procedures with no exception clauses. In addition, a strong internal control department reporting to the board of directors provides further deterrence. Finally, the creation and promotion of a culture of honesty and integrity throughout an organization makes the rationalization of financial statement fraud much more difficult.

Knox Instruments, Inc., is a manufacturer of various medical and dental instruments. Financial statement data for the firm follow:

(thousands of dollars, except per-share amount)	2016
Sales revenue.	$200,000
Cost of goods sold.	98,000
Net income.	10,750
Dividends	4,200
Cash provided by operating activities	7,800
Earnings per share.	3.07

KNOX INSTRUMENTS, INC. Balance Sheets		
(thousands of dollars)	Dec. 31, 2016	Dec. 31, 2015
Assets		
Cash.	$ 3,000	$ 2,900
Accounts receivable (net).	28,000	28,800
Inventory.	64,000	44,000
Total current assets	95,000	75,700
Plant assets (net)	76,000	67,300
Total Assets	$171,000	$143,000
Liabilities and Stockholders' Equity		
Current liabilities.	$ 45,200	$ 39,750
10% Bonds payable.	20,000	14,000
Total Liabilities	65,200	53,750
Common stock, $10 par value.	40,000	30,000
Retained earnings	65,800	59,250
Total Stockholders' Equity.	105,800	89,250
Total Liabilities and Stockholders' Equity	$171,000	$143,000

Required

a. Using the given data, calculate the nine financial ratios below for 2016. Compare the ratio results for Knox Instruments, Inc., with the following industry averages and comment on its operations.

Median Ratios for the Industry

1.	Current ratio	2.7
2.	Quick ratio	1.6
3.	Average collection period	73 days
4.	Inventory turnover	2.3
5.	Operating-cash-flow-to-current-liabilities ratio	0.22
6.	Debt-to-equity ratio	0.50
7.	Return on assets	4.9 percent
8.	Return on common stockholders' equity	10.2 percent
9.	Return on sales	4.1 percent

b. Calculate the dividends paid per share of common stock. (Use the average number of shares outstanding during the year.) What was the dividend payout ratio?

c. If the 2016 year-end market price per share of Knox's common stock is $25, what is the company's (1) price-earnings ratio and (2) dividend yield?

Solution

a.

1. Current ratio = $95,000/$45,200 = 2.10
2. Quick ratio = $31,000/$45,200 = 0.69
3. Average collection period:
   Accounts receivable turnover = $200,000/($28,800 + $28,000)/2 = 7.04
   Average collection period = 365/7.04 = 51.8 days
4. Inventory turnover = $98,000/($44,000 + $64,000)/2 = 1.81
5. Operating-cash-flow-to-current-liabilities ratio = $7,800/($39,750 + $45,200)/2 = 0.18
6. Debt-to-equity ratio = $65,200/$105,800 = 0.62
7. Return on assets = $10,750/($143,000 + $171,000)/2 = 6.8 percent
8. Return on common stockholders' equity = $10,750/($89,250 + $105,800)/2 = 11.0 percent
9. Return on sales = $10,750/$200,000 = 5.4 percent

Although the firm's current ratio of 2.10 is below the industry median, it is still acceptable; however, the quick ratio of 0.69 is well below the industry median. This indicates that Knox's inventory (which is omitted from this calculation) is excessive. This is also borne out by the firm's inventory turnover of 1.81 times, which compares with the industry median of 2.3 times. The firm's average collection period of 51.8 days is significantly better than the industry median of 73 days, while the operating-cash-flow-to-current-liabilities ratio is close to the industry median. Knox's debt-to-equity ratio of 0.62 indicates that the firm has proportionately more debt in its capital structure than the median industry firm, which has a debt-to-equity ratio of 0.50. Knox's operations appear efficient as its return on assets, return on common stockholders' equity, and return on sales all exceed the industry medians.

b. Average number of shares outstanding = (4,000,000 + 3,000,000)/2 = 3,500,000 shares.
$4,200,000 dividends/3,500,000 shares = $1.20 dividend per share.
Dividend payout ratio = $1.20/$3.07 = 39.1 percent.

c. Price-earnings ratio = $25/$3.07 = 8.1.
Dividend yield = $1.20/$25 = 4.8 percent.

APPENDIX 13A: Financial Statement Disclosures

LO6 Describe financial statement disclosures.

Disclosures related to a company's financial statements fall into one of three categories: (1) parenthetical disclosures on the face of the financial statements, (2) notes to the financial statements, and (3) supplementary information. Most disclosures amplify or explain aggregated information contained in the financial statements. Some disclosures, however, provide additional information.

Parenthetical Disclosures

Parenthetical disclosures are placed next to an account title or other descriptive label in the financial statements. Their purpose is to provide additional detail regarding the item or account. An example of parenthetical disclosures indicating the amount of the allowance for doubtful accounts follows:

	2016	2015
Accounts receivable, less allowances for doubtful accounts (2011—$7,545; 2010—$7,098)...	$351,538	$300,181

Instead of using a parenthetical disclosure, companies may choose to present the additional detail in the notes to the financial statements.

Notes to the Financial Statements

Although much information is gathered, summarized, and reported in a company's financial statements, the financial statements alone are limited in their ability to convey a complete picture of a company's financial status. *Notes* are added to the financial statements to help fill in these gaps. In fact, over time, accountants have given so much attention to the financial statement notes that the notes now consume more page space in the annual report than the financial statements themselves. Notes may cover a wide variety of topics. Typically, they deal with significant accounting policies, explanations of complex or special transactions, details of reported amounts, commitments, contingencies, business segments, quarterly data, and subsequent material events.

Significant Accounting Policies

GAAP contains a number of instances for which alternative accounting procedures are equally acceptable. For example, there are several generally accepted depreciation and inventory valuation methods. The particular accounting policies selected by a company affect the financial data presented. Knowledge of a firm's specific accounting principles and methods of applying these principles helps users more fully understand a company's financial statements. Accordingly, these principles and methods are disclosed in a **summary of significant accounting policies**, which is typically the first note to the financial statements.

For example, the annual report of the **Columbia Sportswear Company** contains the following description of its inventory policy:

> Inventories are carried at the lower of cost or market. Cost is determined using the first-in, first-out method. The Company periodically reviews its inventories for excess, close-out or slow moving items and makes provisions as necessary to properly reflect inventory value.

Explanations of Complex or Special Transactions

The complexity of certain transactions means that not all important aspects are likely to be reflected in the accounts. Financial statement notes, therefore, report additional relevant details about such transactions. Typical examples include notes discussing the financial aspects of pension plans, profit-sharing plans, acquisitions of other companies, borrowing agreements, stock option and other incentive plans, and income taxes.

Transactions with related parties are special transactions requiring disclosure in the financial statement notes. Related party transactions include transactions between a firm and its (1) principal owners, (2) members of management, (3) subsidiary companies, or (4) affiliate companies.

Details of Reported Amounts

Financial statements often summarize several groups of accounts into a single aggregate dollar amount. For example, a balance sheet may show one asset account labeled *Property, Plant, and Equipment,* or it may list *Long-Term Debt* as a single amount among the liabilities. Notes report more detail, presenting schedules that list the types and amounts of property, plant, and equipment and long-term debt. Other items that may be summarized in the financial statements and detailed in the notes include inventories, other current assets, notes payable, accrued liabilities, stockholders' equity, and a company's income tax expense.

The notes to Columbia Sportswear Company's 2014 annual report contain several examples of financial statement items that are detailed, including accounts receivable (**Note 6**), property, plant, and equipment (**Note 7**), short-term borrowing and credit lines (**Note 9**), accrued liabilities (**Note 10**), other long-term liabilities (**Note 12**), and income taxes (**Note 11**).

Commitments

A firm may have contractual arrangements existing as of a balance sheet date in which both parties to the contract still have acts yet to be completed. If performance under these **commitments** will have a significant financial impact on a firm, the existence and nature of the commitments should be disclosed in the notes to the financial statements. Examples of commitments reported in the notes include contracts to purchase materials or equipment, contracts to construct facilities, salary commitments to executives, commitments to retire or redeem stock, and commitments to deliver goods.

Columbia Sportswear Company reports the following commitments in its annual report:

> During its normal course of business, the Company has made certain indemnities, commitments and guarantees under which it may be required to make payments in relation to certain transactions. These include (i) intellectual property indemnities to the Company's customers and licensees in connection with the use, sale and/or license of Company products, (ii) indemnities to various lessors in connection with facility leases for certain claims arising from such facility or lease, (iii) indemnities to customers, vendors and service providers pertaining to claims based on the negligence or willful misconduct of the Company, (iv) executive severance arrangements and (v) indemnities involving the accuracy of representations and warranties in certain contracts. The duration of these indemnities, commitments and guarantees varies, and in certain cases, may be indefinite. The majority of these indemnities, commitments and guarantees do not provide for any limitation of the maximum potential for future payments the Company could be obligated to make. The Company has not recorded any liability for these indemnities, commitments and guarantees in the accompanying Consolidated Balance Sheets.

Contingencies

Contingent liabilities were discussed in Chapter 10. As noted there, if the future event that would turn a contingency into an obligation is not likely to occur, or if the liability cannot be reasonably estimated, the **contingency** is disclosed in a note to the financial statements. Typical contingencies disclosed in the notes include pending lawsuits, environmental cleanup costs, possible income tax assessments, credit guarantees, and discounted notes receivable.

Under Armour, Inc. reports the following regarding contingencies in its annual report:

The company is, from time to time, involved in routine legal matters incidental to its business. The company believes that the ultimate resolution of any such current proceedings and claims will not have a material adverse effect on its consolidated financial position, results of operations or cash flows.

Segments

Many firms diversify their business activities and operate in several different industries. A firm's financial statements often combine information from all of a company's operations into aggregate amounts. This complicates the financial statement user's ability to analyze the statements because the interpretation of financial data is influenced by the industry in which a firm operates. Different industries face different types of risk and have different rates of profitability. In making investment and lending decisions, financial statement users evaluate risk and required rates of return. Having financial data available by industry segment is helpful to such evaluations.

The FASB recognizes the usefulness of industry data to investors and lenders. Public companies with significant operations in more than one industry must report certain financial information by industry **segment**. Typically, these disclosures are in the financial statement notes. The major disclosures by industry segment are sales revenue, operating profit or loss, identifiable assets (the assets used by the segment), capital expenditures, and depreciation.

Other types of segment data may also be disclosed. Business operations in different parts of the world are subject to different risks and opportunities for growth. Thus, public companies with significant operations in foreign countries must report selected financial data by foreign geographic area. The required data disclosures include sales revenue, operating profit or loss (or other profitability measure), and identifiable assets. Also, if a firm has export sales or sales revenue to a single customer that are ten percent or more of total sales revenue, the amount of such sales revenue must be separately disclosed.

Note 19 to **Columbia Sportswear's** financial statements in its annual report illustrates segment disclosures by foreign versus domestic segments.

Quarterly Data

Interim financial reports cover periods shorter than one year. Companies that issue interim reports generally do so quarterly. These reports provide financial statement users with timely information on a firm's progress and are useful in predicting a company's annual financial results. The SEC requires that certain companies disclose selected quarterly financial data in their annual reports to stockholders. Included among the notes, the data reported for each quarter include sales revenue, gross profit, net income, and earnings per share. **Quarterly data** permit financial statement users to analyze such things as the seasonal nature of operations, the impact of diversification on quarterly activity, and whether the firm's activities lead or lag general economic trends.

The Columbia Sportswear Company provides quarterly financial information as supplemental data in its annual report.

Subsequent Events

If a company issues a large amount of securities or suffers a casualty loss after the balance sheet date, this information should be reported in a note, even though the situation arose subsequent to the balance sheet date. Firms are responsible for disclosing any significant events that occur between the balance sheet date and the date the financial statements are issued. This guideline recognizes that it takes several weeks for financial statements to be prepared and audited before they are issued. Events occurring during this period may have a material effect on a firm's operations and should be disclosed. Other examples of **subsequent events** requiring disclosure are sales of assets, significant changes in long-term debt, and acquisitions of other companies.

For example, **Under Armour, Inc.** reported the following subsequent event in its annual report:

In February 2012, 150.0 thousand shares of Class B Convertible Common Stock were converted into shares of Class A Common Stock on a one-for-one basis in connection with a stock sale.

Supplementary Information

Supplementing the financial statements are several additional disclosures—management's discussion and analysis of the financial statements and selected financial data covering a five- to ten-year period along with possible other supplementary disclosures that are either required of certain companies by the SEC or recommended (but not required) by the FASB.

Management Discussion and Analysis

Management may increase the usefulness of financial statements by sharing some of their knowledge about a company's financial condition and operations. This is the purpose of the disclosure devoted to the management discussion and analysis. In this supplement to the financial statements, management identifies and comments on events and trends influencing a company's liquidity, operating results, and financial resources. Management's position within a company not only provides it with insights unavailable to outsiders, but also may introduce certain biases into the analysis. Nonetheless, management's comments, interpretations, and explanations should contribute to a better understanding of a company's financial statements.

A.K.A. The management discussion and analysis is also referred to simply as the *MD&A*.

Comparative Selected Financial Data

The analysis of a company's financial performance is enhanced when financial data for several years are available. By analyzing trends over time, it is possible for a financial statement user to learn much more about a company than would be possible by analyzing only a single year of data. Year-to-year changes may give clues as to a firm's future growth or may highlight areas for concern. Corporate annual reports to stockholders present complete financial statements in comparative form, showing the current year and one or two preceding years. Beyond this, however, the financial statements are supplemented by a summary of selected key financial statistics for a five- or ten-year period. The financial data presented in this historical summary usually include sales revenue, net income, dividends, earnings per share, working capital, and total assets.

SUMMARY OF LEARNING OBJECTIVES

Identify persistent earnings and discuss the content and format of the income statement. (p. 630) **LO1**

- Persistent earnings are earnings that are likely to recur, while transitory earnings are unlikely to recur.
- The continuing income of a business may be reported in a single-step format or in a multiple-step format.
- Gains and losses from discontinued operations are reported in a special income statement section following income from continuing operations.
- The effect of most changes in accounting principle requires restatement of prior financial statements as if the new method had been applied all along.
- Companies are required to report other comprehensive income in addition to regular income in their financial statements.

Identify the sources of financial information used by investment professionals and explain horizontal financial statements analysis. (p. 634) **LO2**

- Data sources for investment professionals include published financial statements, filings with the U.S. Securities and Exchange Commission, and statistics available from financial data services.
- A common form of horizontal analysis involves analyzing dollar and percentage changes in comparative financial statements for two or more years.
- Analyzing trend percentages of key figures, such as sales revenue, net income, and total assets for a number of years, related to a base year, is often useful.

Explain vertical financial statement analysis. (p. 639) **LO3**

- Vertical analysis deals with the relationship of financial statement data for a single year.
- Common-size statements express financial statement items as a percentage of another key item, such as expressing income statement items as a percentage of sales revenue and balance sheet items as a percentage of total assets.

LO4 **Define and discuss financial ratios for analyzing a firm. (p. 641)**

- Ratios for analyzing firm profitability include the gross profit percentage, the return on sales, asset turnover, the return on assets, and the return on common stockholders' equity.
- Ratios for analyzing short-term firm liquidity include the current ratio, quick ratio, operating-cash-flow-to-current-liabilities ratio, accounts receivable turnover, average collection period, inventory turnover, and days' sales in inventory.
- Ratios for analyzing long-term firm solvency include the debt-to-equity ratio, the times-interest-earned ratio, and the operating-cash-flow-to-capital-expenditures ratio.
- Ratios of particular interest to common stockholders include a company's earnings per share, the price-earnings ratio, dividend yield, and the dividend payout ratio.

LO5 **Discuss the limitations of financial statement analysis. (p. 656)**

- When analyzing financial statements, financial statement users must be aware of a firm's accounting methods, the effects of inflation, and the difficulty of currently identifying a firm's industry classification.

LO6 **Appendix 13A: Describe financial statement disclosures. (p. 658)**

- Parenthetical disclosures on the face of the financial statements provide additional detail regarding the item or account.
- Notes to the financial statements provide information on significant accounting policies, explanations of complex or special transactions, details of reported amounts, commitments, contingencies, segments, quarterly data, and subsequent events.
- Supplemental information includes the management discussion and analysis, and comparable selected financial information.

SUMMARY OF FINANCIAL STATEMENT RATIOS

Analyzing Firm Profitability

$$\text{Gross profit percentage} = \frac{\text{Gross profit on sales}}{\text{Net sales}}$$

$$\text{Return on sales} = \frac{\text{Net income}}{\text{Net sales}}$$

$$\text{Asset turnover} = \frac{\text{Net sales}}{\text{Average total assets}}$$

$$\text{Return on assets} = \frac{\text{Net income}}{\text{Average total assets}}$$

$$\text{Return on common stockholders' equity} = \frac{\left(\text{Net income} - \text{Preferred stock dividends}\right)}{\text{Average common stockholders' equity}}$$

Analyzing Short-Term Firm Liquidity

$$\text{Current ratio} = \frac{\text{Current assets}}{\text{Current liabilities}}$$

$$\text{Quick ratio} = \frac{(\text{Cash and cash equivalents} + \text{Short-term investments} + \text{Accounts receivable})}{\text{Current liabilities}}$$

$$\text{Operating-cash-flow-to-current-liabilities ratio} = \frac{\text{Cash flow from operating activities}}{\text{Average current liabilities}}$$

$$\text{Accounts receivable turnover} = \frac{\text{Net sales}}{\text{Average accounts receivable (net)}}$$

$$\text{Average collection period} = \frac{365}{\text{Accounts receivable turnover (net)}}$$

$$\text{Inventory turnover} = \frac{\text{Cost of goods sold}}{\text{Average inventory}}$$

$$\text{Days' sales in inventory} = \frac{365}{\text{Inventory turnover}}$$

Analyzing Long-Term Firm Solvency

$$\text{Debt-to-equity ratio} = \frac{\text{Total liabilities}}{\text{Total stockholders' equity}}$$

$$\text{Times-interest-earned ratio} = \frac{\text{Income before interest expense and income taxes}}{\text{Interest expense}}$$

$$\text{Operating-cash-flow-to-capital-expenditures ratio} = \frac{\text{Cash flow from operating activities}}{\text{Annual net capital expenditures}}$$

Financial Ratios for Common Stockholders

$$\text{Earnings per share} = \frac{(\text{Net income} - \text{Preferred stock dividends})}{\text{Weighted average common shares outstanding}}$$

$$\text{Price-earnings ratio} = \frac{\text{Market price per share}}{\text{Earnings per share}}$$

$$\text{Dividend yield} = \frac{\text{Annual dividend per share}}{\text{Market price per share}}$$

$$\text{Dividend payout ratio} = \frac{\text{Annual dividend per share}}{\text{Earnings per share}}$$

SUMMARY	Concept ⟶	Method ⟶	Assessment
TAKEAWAY 13.1	How does a company's current performance compare with the prior year?	Income statement and balance sheet for current and prior year. The income statement and balance sheet should be compared using the prior year as the base. Percentage changes in financial statement amounts can be computed as the change between years divided by the base year amount.	Significant changes should be analyzed to determine the reason for any change.
TAKEAWAY 13.2	How do the relationships within a company's income statement and balance sheet compare to those of prior years?	Income statement and balance sheet for current and prior year. Each income statement item should be presented as a percentage of sales revenue and each balance sheet item should be presented as a percentage of total assets. Financial statements in this form are called common-size statements.	The percentages should be analyzed for differences between years and significant changes should be analyzed to determine the reason for any change.
TAKEAWAY 13.3	How much profit is a company generating relative to the amount of assets invested in the company?	Income statement and balance sheet. Calculate the return on assets by dividing net income by the average total assets for the year.	The higher the return on assets, the better a company is doing with respect to generating profits utilizing the assets under its control.
TAKEAWAY 13.4	How financially capable is a company to pay its current liabilities as they come due?	Income statement, balance sheet, and statement of cash flows. Calculate the current ratio, the quick ratio, and the operating-cash-flow-to-current-liabilities ratio.	The higher the ratios, the higher the probability that a company will have the ability to pay its current liabilities as they come due.
TAKEAWAY 13.5	How solvent is a company?	Income statement, balance sheet, and statement of cash flows. Calculate the debt-to-equity ratio, the times-interest-earned ratio, and the operating-cash-flow-to-capital-expenditures ratio.	The higher the times-interest-earned and the operating-cash-flow-to-capital-expenditures ratios, and the lower the debt-to-equity ratio, the greater is a company's solvency.
TAKEAWAY 13.6	How much dividends are common stockholders likely to receive?	Earnings per share, dividends per share, and market price of common stock. Calculate the dividend yield and dividend payout ratio.	The higher the dividend yield and the dividend payout ratio, the greater the company's dividend distribution policy.

KEY TERMS

Accounts receivable turnover (p. 648)

Asset turnover ratio (p. 643)

Average collection period (days' sales outstanding, or DSO) (p. 648)

Change in accounting principle (p. 632)

Commitments (p. 659)

Common-size financial statement (p. 639)

Comparative financial statement analysis (p. 635)

Comprehensive income (p. 633)

Contingency (p. 660)

Current ratio (p. 646)

Days' sales in inventory (p. 649)

Debt-to-equity ratio (p. 651)

Discontinued operations (p. 632)

Dividend payout ratio (p. 654)

Dividend yield (p. 654)

Earnings per share (EPS) (p. 632, 653)

Gross profit (Gross margin) (p. 641)

Gross profit on sales (p. 641)

Gross profit percentage (p. 641)

Horizontal analysis (p. 635)

Inventory turnover (p. 649)

MD&A (p. 661)

Multiple-step income statement (p. 630)

Operating-cash-flow-to-capital-expenditures ratio (p. 652)

Operating-cash-flow-to-current-liabilities ratio (p. 647)

Operating cycle (p. 650)

Persistent earnings (p. 630)

Price-earnings ratio (P/E multiple) (p. 653)

Quarterly data (p. 660)

Quick ratio (profit margin) (p. 646)

Return on assets (p. 644)

Return on common stockholders' equity (p. 644)

Return on sales (p. 643)

Segment (p. 660)

Single-step income statement (p. 630)

Subsequent events (p. 660)

Summary of significant accounting policies (p. 659)

Times-interest-earned ratio (interest coverage ratio) (p. 651)

Transitory earnings (p. 630)

Trend percentages (p. 637)

Unusual items (p. 631)

Vertical analysis (p. 635)

Working capital (p. 645)

Assignments with the ⓜ logo in the margin are available in 🅑usinessCourse.
See the Preface of the book for details.

SELF-STUDY QUESTIONS

(Answers to the Self-Study Questions are at the end of this chapter.)

1. Assume that an income statement contains each of the three sections listed below. Which will be the last section presented in the income statement?   **LO1**
    a. Gross profit
    b. Income from continuing operations
    c. Discontinued operations

2. When constructing a common-sized income statement, all amounts are expressed as a percentage of: **LO3**
    a. net income.
    b. gross profit.
    c. net sales.
    d. income from operations.

Questions 3–9 of the Self-Study Questions are based on the following data:

HYDRO COMPANY Balance Sheet December 31, 2015			
Cash............................	$ 40,000	Current liabilities.........................	$ 80,000
Accounts receivable (net)............	80,000	10% Bonds payable.....................	120,000
Inventory........................	130,000	Common stock.......................	200,000
Plant and equipment (net)	250,000	Retained earnings	100,000
Total Assets	$500,000	Total Liabilities and Stockholders' Equity	$500,000

Sales revenues for 2015 were $800,000, gross profit was $320,000, and net income was $36,000. The income tax rate was 40 percent. One year ago, accounts receivable (net) were $76,000, inventory was $110,000, total assets were $460,000, and stockholders' equity was $260,000. The bonds payable were outstanding all year and the 2015 interest expense was $12,000.

3. The current ratio of Hydro Company at 12/31/2015, calculated using the above data, was 3.13 and the company's working capital was $170,000. Which of the following would happen if the firm paid off $20,000 of its current liabilities on January 1, 2016?   **LO4**
    a. Both the current ratio and working capital would decrease.
    b. Both the current ratio and working capital would increase.
    c. The current ratio would increase, but working capital would remain the same.
    d. The current ratio would increase, but working capital would decrease.

4. What was the firm's inventory turnover for 2015?   **LO4**
    a. 6.67
    b. 4
    c. 6
    d. 3.69

LO4 5. **What was the firm's return on common stockholders' equity for 2015?**
   a. 25.7 percent
   b. 12.9 percent
   c. 17.1 percent
   d. 21.4 percent

LO4 6. **What was the firm's average collection period for 2015?**
   a. 36.5 days
   b. 37.4 days
   c. 35.6 days
   d. 18.3 days

LO4 7. **What was the firm's times-interest-earned ratio for 2015?**
   a. 4
   b. 3
   c. 5
   d. 6

LO4 8. **What was the firm's return on sales for 2015?**
   a. 4.0 percent
   b. 4.5 percent
   c. 5.0 percent
   d. 5.5 percent

LO4 9. **What was the firm's return on assets for 2015?**
   a. 6.0 percent
   b. 7.0 percent
   c. 7.5 percent
   d. 8.0 percent

LO2 10. **When performing trend analysis, each line item is expressed as a percentage of:**
   a. net income.
   b. the base year amount.
   c. the prior year amount.
   d. total assets.

LO5 11. **Recognized limitations of financial statement analysis include each of the following except:**
   a. companies in the same industry using different accounting methods.
   b. inflation.
   c. different levels of profitability between companies.
   d. difficulty of classifying by industry conglomerates.

LO6
(Appendix 13A) 12. **Financial statement disclosures include each of the following except:**
   a. notes to the financial statements.
   b. parenthetical disclosures.
   c. supplementary information.
   d. promotional giveaways.

QUESTIONS

1. What is the difference between a single-step income statement and a multiple-step income statement?

2. Which of the following amounts would appear only in a multiple-step income statement?
   a. Income from continuing operations.
   b. Income from discontinued operations.
   c. Gross profit on sales.
   d. Net income.

3. What is a business segment? Why are gains and losses from a discontinued segment reported in a separate section of the income statement?

4. How do horizontal analysis and vertical analysis of financial statements differ?

5. "Financial statement users should focus attention on each item showing a large percentage change from one year to the next." Is this statement correct? Why?

6. What are trend percentages and how are they calculated? What pitfalls must financial statement users avoid when preparing trend percentages?

7. What are common-size financial statements and how are they used?

8. What item is the key figure (that is, 100 percent) in a common-size income statement? A common-size balance sheet?

9. During the past year, Lite Company had net income of $5 million, and Scanlon Company had net income of $8 million. Both companies manufacture electrical components for the construction industry. What additional information would you need to compare the profitability of the two companies?

10. Under what circumstances can the return on sales be used to assess the profitability of a company? Can this ratio be used to compare the profitability of companies from different industries? Explain.

11. What is the relationship between asset turnover, return on assets, and return on sales?

12. Blare Company had a return on sales of 6.5 percent and an asset turnover of 2.40. What is Blare's return on assets?

13. What does the return on common stockholders' equity measure?

14. How does the quick ratio differ from the current ratio?

15. For each of the following ratios, is a high ratio or low ratio considered, in general, a positive sign?
    a. Current ratio
    b. Quick ratio
    c. Operating-cash-flow-to-current-liabilities ratio
    d. Accounts receivable turnover
    e. Average collection period
    f. Inventory turnover
    g. Days' sales in inventory

16. What is the significance of the debt-to-equity ratio and how is it computed?

17. What does the times-interest-earned ratio indicate and how is it calculated?

18. What does the operating-cash-flow-to-capital-expenditures ratio measure?

19. Clair, Inc., earned $4.50 per share of common stock in the current year and paid dividends of $2.34 per share. The most recent market price per share of the common stock is $46.80. What is the company's (a) price-earnings ratio, (b) dividend yield, and (c) dividend payout ratio?

20. What are two inherent limitations of financial statement data?

SHORT EXERCISES

Use the following financial data for Hi-Tech Instruments to answer Short Exercises 13-1 through 13-10:

2016 (Thousands of Dollars, except Earnings per Share)	
Sales revenue	$210,000
Cost of goods sold	125,000
Net income	8,300
Dividends	2,600
Earnings per share	4.15

HI-TECH INSTRUMENTS, INC.
Balance Sheets

(Thousands of Dollars)	Dec. 31, 2016	Dec. 31, 2015
Assets		
Cash	$ 18,300	$ 18,000
Accounts receivable (net)	46,000	41,000
Inventory	39,500	43,700
Total Current Assets	103,800	102,700
Plant assets (net)	52,600	50,500
Other assets	15,600	13,800
Total Assets	$172,000	$167,000
Liabilities and Stockholders' Equity		
Notes payable—banks	$ 6,000	$ 6,000
Accounts payable	22,500	18,700
Accrued liabilities	16,500	21,000
Total Current Liabilities	45,000	45,700
9% Bonds payable	40,000	40,000
Total Liabilities	85,000	85,700
Common stock, $25 par value (2,000,000 shares)	50,000	50,000
Retained earnings	37,000	31,300
Total Stockholders' Equity	87,000	81,300
Total Liabilities and Stockholders' Equity	$172,000	$167,000

Industry Average Ratios for Competitors	
Quick ratio	1.3
Current ratio	2.4
Accounts receivable turnover	5.9 times
Inventory turnover	3.5 times
Debt-to-equity ratio	0.73
Gross profit percentage	42.8 percent
Return on sales	4.5 percent
Return on assets	7.6 percent

LO4 **SE13-1.** **Quick Ratio** Calculate the company's quick ratio for 2016 and compare the result to the industry average.

LO4 **SE13-2.** **Current Ratio** Calculate the company's current ratio for 2016 and compare the result to the industry average.

LO4 **SE13-3.** **Accounts Receivable Turnover** Calculate the company's accounts receivable turnover for 2016 and compare the result to the industry average.

LO4 **SE13-4.** **Inventory Turnover** Calculate the company's inventory turnover for 2016 and compare the result to the industry average.

LO4 **SE13-5.** **Debit-to-Equity Ratio** Calculate the company's 2016 debt-to-equity ratio and compare the result to the industry average.

LO4 **SE13-6.** **Gross Profit Percentage** Calculate the company's 2016 gross profit percentage and compare the result to the industry average.

LO4 **SE13-7.** **Return on Sales** Calculate the company's return on sales for 2016 and compare the result to the industry average.

LO4 **SE13-8.** **Return on Assets** Calculate the company's return on assets for 2016 and compare the result to the industry average.

LO4 **SE13-9.** **Dividends per Share** Calculate the company's dividend paid per share of common stock. What was the dividend payout ratio?

LO4 **SE13-10.** **Earnings per Share** If the company's most recent price per share of common stock is $62.25, what is the company's price-earnings ratio and dividend yield?

LO1 **SE13-11.** **Persistent Earnings** Identify each of the following items as either (P) persistent, or (T) transitory.

　　a.　Sale of merchandise.
　　b.　Settlement of a lawsuit.
　　c.　Interest income.
　　d.　Payment to vendors.
　　e.　Loss from expropriations of property by a foreign government.

LO2 **SE13-12.** **Horizontal Analysis** Total assets were $1,000,000 in 2016, $900,000 in 2015, and $950,000 in 2014. What was the percentage change from 2014 to 2015 and from 2015 to 2016? Was the change an increase or a decrease?

LO3 **SE13-13.** **Common-Size Income Statement** A partial common-size income statement for Prag Company for three years is shown below.

Item	2016	2015	2014
Net sales	100.0	100.0	100.0
Cost of goods sold	60.5	63.0	62.5
Other expenses	21.0	19.0	20.5

Did Prag's net income as a percentage of net sales increase, remain the same, or decrease over the three-year period?

SE13-14. **Financial Statement Analysis Limitations** Which of the following is not considered a limitation of financial statement analysis?

LO5

   a. Firms may use different accounting methods.

   b. Firms may be audited by different auditing firms.

   c. Inflation may distort trend analysis.

   d. It may be difficult to classify large conglomerate firms by industry.

SE13-15. **Financial Statement Disclosures** Which of the following is not a common form of financial statement disclosure?

LO6
(Appendix 13A)

   a. Notes to financial statements.

   b. Supplemental information.

   c. Parenthetical disclosure.

   d. Bullet points.

EXERCISES—SET A

E13-1A. **Income Statement Sections** During the current year, Dale Corporation sold a segment of its business at a gain of $210,000. Until it was sold, the segment had a current period operating loss of $75,000. The company had $850,000 income from continuing operations for the current year. Prepare the lower part of the income statement, beginning with the $850,000 income from continuing operations. Follow tax allocation procedures, assuming that all changes in income are subject to a 35 percent income tax rate. Disregard earnings per share disclosures.

LO1

E13-2A. **Earnings per Share** Lucky Corporation began the year with a simple capital structure consisting of 240,000 shares of outstanding common stock. On April 1, 5,000 additional common shares were issued, and another 30,000 common shares were issued on August 1. The company had net income for the year of $589,375. Calculate the earnings per share of common stock.

LO4

E13-3A. **Comparative Income Statements** Consider the following income statement data from the Ross Company:

LO2

	2016	2015
Sales revenue	$550,000	$450,000
Cost of goods sold	336,000	279,000
Selling expenses	105,000	99,000
Administrative expenses	60,000	50,000
Income tax expense	7,800	5,400

   a. Prepare a comparative income statement, showing increases and decreases in dollars and in percentages.

   b. Comment briefly on the changes between the two years.

E13-4A. **Common-Size Income Statements** Refer to the income statement data given in Exercise E13-3A.

LO3

   a. Prepare common-size income statements for each year.

   b. Compare the common-size income statements and comment briefly.

E13-5A. **Ratios Analyzing Firm Profitability** The following information is available for Buhler Company:

LO4

Annual Data	2016	2015
Net sales	$8,600,000	$8,200,000
Gross profit on sales	3,050,000	2,736,000
Net income	567,600	488,000

Year-End Data	Dec. 31, 2016	Dec. 31, 2015
Total assets	$6,500,000	$6,000,000
Stockholders' equity	4,000,000	3,200,000

Calculate the following ratios for 2016:

a.   Gross profit percentage

b.   Return on sales

c.   Asset turnover

d.   Return on assets

e.   Return on common stockholders' equity (Buhler Company has no preferred stock.)

LO4   **E13-6A.**   **Working Capital and Short-Term Liquidity Ratios**   Bell Company has a current ratio of 3.00 on December 31. On that date the company's current assets are as follows:

Cash...	$ 29,000
Short-term investments	49,400
Accounts receivable (net)...	170,000
Inventory..	200,000
Prepaid expenses..	11,600
Current assets	$460,000

Bell Company's current liabilities at the beginning of the year were $140,000 and during the year its operating activities provided a cash flow of $60,000.

a.   What are the firm's current liabilities on December 31?

b.   What is the firm's working capital on December 31?

c.   What is the quick ratio on December 31?

d.   What is Bell's operating-cash-flow-to-current-liabilities ratio?

LO4   **E13-7A.**   **Accounts Receivable and Inventory Ratios**   Bell Company, whose current assets at December 31 are shown in Exercise E13-6A, had net sales for the year of $900,000 and cost of goods sold of $550,000. At the beginning of the year, Bell's accounts receivable (net) were $160,000 and its inventory was $195,000.

a.   What is the company's accounts receivable turnover for the year?

b.   What is the company's average collection period for the year?

c.   What is the company's inventory turnover for the year?

d.   What is the company's days' sales in inventory for the year?

LO4   **E13-8A.**   **Ratios Analyzing Long-Term Firm Solvency**   The following information is available for Antler Company:

Annual Data	2016	2015
Interest expense...	$ 90,000	$ 82,000
Income tax expense...	203,500	185,000
Net income..	496,500	400,000
Capital expenditures	320,000	380,000
Cash provided by operating activities	425,000	390,000

Year-End Data	Dec. 31, 2016	Dec. 31, 2015
Total liabilities..	$2,400,000	$1,900,000
Total stockholders' equity	4,000,000	3,800,000

Calculate the following:

a.   2016 debt-to-equity ratio.

b.   2016 times-interest-earned ratio.

c.   2016 operating-cash-flow-to-capital-expenditures ratio.

E13-9A. Financial Ratios for Common Stockholders Kluster Corporation has only common stock out-standing. The firm reported earnings per share of $5.25 for the year. During the year, Kluster paid dividends of $2.10 per share. At year end the current market price of the stock was $63 per share. Calculate the following:

    a.   Year-end price-earnings ratio

    b.   Dividend yield

    c.   Dividend payout ratio

LO4

E13-10A. Financial Statement Limitations You have been asked to perform financial statement analysis on the Patton Company. The Patton Company is a large chain of retail outlets that sells a wide range of household items. Last year the company introduced its own credit card and is pleased that profit from this financing activity now accounts for over twenty percent of the company's total profit. As part of your analysis you have chosen to compare the Patton Company to Johnson Stores, a much larger chain of stores. Johnson Stores sells household items and groceries, but it does not have its own credit card. Your analysis includes both horizontal trend analysis and vertical analysis. Identify some of the limitations from the description above.

LO5

E13-11A. Financial Statement Notes The notes to financial statements present information on significant ac-counting policies, complex or special transactions, details of reported amounts, commitments, con tingencies, segments, quarterly data, and subsequent events. Indicate which type of note disclosure is illustrated by each of the following notes:

LO6
(Appendix 13A)

    a.   The company has agreed to purchase seven EMB-120 aircraft and related spare parts. The ag-gregate cost of these aircraft is approximately $41,250,000, subject to a cost escalation provi-sion. The aircraft are scheduled to be delivered over the next two fiscal years.

    b.   The company has deferred certain costs related to major accounting and information systems enhancements that are anticipated to benefit future years. Upon completion, the related cost is amortized over a period not exceeding five years.

    c.   The company has guaranteed loans and leases of independent distributors approximating $27,500,000 as of December 31 of the current year.

    d.   An officer of the company is also a director of a major raw material supplier of the company. The amount of raw material purchases from this supplier approximated $410,000 in the current year.

EXERCISES—SET B

E13-1B. Income Statement Sections During the current year, Newtech Corporation sold a segment of its business at a loss of $225,000. Until it was sold, the segment had a current period operating loss of $200,000. The company has $750,000 income from continuing operations for the current year. Pre-pare the lower part of the income statement, beginning with the $750,000 income from continuing operations. Follow tax allocation procedures, assuming that all changes in income are subject to a 40 percent income tax rate. Disregard earnings per share disclosures.

LO1

E13-2B. Earnings per Share Ewing Corporation began the year with a simple capital structure consisting of 35,000 shares of common stock outstanding. On May 1, 10,000 additional common shares were issued, and another 10,000 common shares were issued on September 1. The company had a net income for the year of $468,000. Calculate the earnings per share of common stock.

LO4

E13-3B. Comparative Balance Sheets Consider the following balance sheet data for Great Buy Co., Inc., an electronics and major appliance retailer, at February 26, 2016 and February 27, 2015 (amounts in thousands):

LO2

	Feb. 26, 2016	Feb. 27, 2015
Cash and cash equivalents	$ 59,872	$ 7,138
Accounts receivables	52,944	37,968
Merchandise inventories	637,950	249,991
Other current assets	13,844	9,829
Current Assets	764,610	304,926
Property and equipment (net)	172,724	126,442
Other assets	15,160	7,774
Total Assets	$952,494	$439,142
Current Liabilities	$402,028	$186,005
Long-term liabilities	239,022	70,854
Total Liabilities	641,050	256,859
Common stock	2,087	1,149
Additional paid-in-capital	224,089	137,151
Retained earnings	85,268	43,983
Total Stockholders' Equity	311,444	182,283
Total Liabilities and Stockholders' Equity	$952,494	$439,142

a. Prepare a comparative balance sheet, showing increases in dollars and percentages.

b. Comment briefly on the changes between the two years.

LO3 **E13-4B.** **Common-Size Balance Sheets** Refer to the balance sheet data given in Exercise E13-3B.

a. Prepare common-size balance sheets for each year (use total assets as the base amount for computing percentages).

b. Compare the common-size balance sheets and comment briefly.

LO4 **E13-5B.** **Ratios Analyzing Firm Profitability** The following information is available for Crest Company:

Annual Data	2016	2015
Sales revenue	$6,600,000	$6,000,000
Cost of goods sold	4,006,400	3,800,000
Net income	310,000	264,000

Year-End Data	Dec. 31, 2016	Dec. 31, 2015
Total assets	$2,850,000	$2,500,000
Common stockholders' equity	1,900,000	1,800,000

Calculate the following ratios for 2016:

a. Gross profit percentage

b. Return on sales

c. Asset turnover

d. Return on assets

e. Return on common stockholders' equity (Crest Company declared and paid preferred stock dividends of $25,000 in 2016.)

LO4 **E13-6B.** **Working Capital and Short-Term Firm Liquidity Ratios** Favor Company has a current ratio of 2.15 on December 31. On that date its current assets are as follows:

Cash and cash equivalents	$ 28,000
Short-term investments	87,000
Accounts receivable (net)	125,000
Inventory	178,500
Prepaid expenses	11,500
Current assets	$430,000

Favor Company's current liabilities at the beginning of the year were $195,000 and during the year its operating activities provided a cash flow of $33,830.

   a.   What are the firm's current liabilities at December 31?
   b.   What is the firm's working capital on December 31?
   c.   What is the quick ratio on December 31?
   d.   What is the firm's operating-cash-flow-to-current-liabilities ratio?

E13-7B. Accounts Receivable and Inventory Ratios Favor Company, whose current assets at December 31 are shown in Exercise E13-6B, had net sales for the year of $580,000 and cost of goods sold of $345,900. At the beginning of the year, accounts receivable (net) were $121,000 and inventory was $154,650.   **LO4**

   a.   What is the company's accounts receivable turnover?
   b.   What is the company's average collection period?
   c.   What is the company's inventory turnover?
   d.   What is the company's days' sales in inventory?

E13-8B. Ratios Analyzing Long-Term Firm Solvency The following information is available for Percy Company: **LO4**

Annual Data	2016	2015
Interest expense.	$170,000	$166,000
Income tax expense.	126,000	117,000
Net income.	294,000	275,000
Capital expenditures	435,000	350,000
Cash provided by operating activities	247,000	223,000

Year-End Data	Dec. 31, 2016	Dec. 31, 2015
Total liabilities.	$3,500,000	$2,900,000
Total stockholders' equity	2,200,000	1,900,000

Calculate the following:

   a.   2016 debt-to-equity ratio
   b.   2016 times-interest-earned ratio
   c.   2016 operating-cash-flow-to-capital-expenditures ratio

E13-9B. Financial Ratios for Common Stockholders Henshue Corporation has only common stock outstanding. The firm reported earnings per share of $2.00 for the year. During the year, Henshue paid dividends of $0.85 per share. At year end, the current market price of the stock was $35.15 per share.   **LO4**
    Calculate the following:

   a.   Year-end price-earnings ratio
   b.   Dividend yield
   c.   Dividend payout ratio

E13-10B. Financial Statement Limitations You have been asked to perform financial statement analysis on the Anderson Company. The Anderson Company is a large manufacturer of construction machinery and vehicles. Last year the company closed down a segment of the business that produced mining equipment because it was not providing an adequate return on assets. This segment represented fifteen percent of the company's total assets. As part of your analysis you have chosen to compare the Anderson Company to Bertran, Inc., a much smaller manufacturer of equipment, although Bertran, Inc. also performs contract repairs for many other brands of equipment. Your analysis includes both horizontal trend analysis and vertical analysis. Identify some of the limitations from the description above.   **LO5**

E13-11B. Financial Statement Notes Notes to the financial statements present information on significant accounting policies, complex or special transactions, details of reported amounts, commitments, contingencies, segments, quarterly data, and subsequent events. Indicate the type of note disclosure that is illustrated by each of the following notes: **LO6**
    (Appendix 13A)

a. Sales by the Farm and Equipment segment to independent dealers are recorded at the time of shipment to those dealers. Sales through company-owned retail stores are recorded at the time of sale to retail customers.

b. Members of the board of directors, the advisory board, and employees are not charged the vendor's commission on property sold at auction for their benefit. (From the notes of an auctioneer company.)

c. Sales to an airline company accounted for approximately 45 percent of the company's net sales in the current year.

d. The company's product liability insurance coverage with respect to insured events occurring after January 1 of the current year is substantially less than the amount of that insurance available in the recent past. The company is now predominantly self-insured in this area. The reduction in insurance coverage reflects trends in the liability insurance field generally and is not unique to the company.

PROBLEMS—SET A

LO1 **P13-1A.** **Income Statement Format** The following information from Belvidere Company's current operations is available:

Administrative expenses	$ 73,000
Cost of goods sold	464,000
Sales revenue	772,000
Selling expenses	87,000
Interest expense	10,000
Loss from operations of discontinued segment	60,000
Gain on disposal of discontinued segment	40,000
Income taxes:	
Amount applicable to ordinary operations	60,000
Reduction applicable to loss from operations of discontinued segment	24,000
Amount applicable to gain on disposal of discontinued segment	16,000

Required
a. Prepare a multiple-step income statement. (Disregard earnings per share.)
b. Prepare a single-step income statement. (Disregard earnings per share.)

LO4 **P13-2A.** **Earnings per Share** Leland Corporation began the year with 150,000 shares of common stock outstanding. On March 1 an additional 10,000 shares of common stock were issued. On August 1, another 16,000 shares of common stock were issued. On November 1, 6,000 shares of common stock were acquired as Treasury Stock. Leland Corporation's net income for the calendar year is $516,000.

Required
Calculate the company's earnings per share.

LO1, 4 **P13-3A.** **Earnings per Share and Multiple-Step Income Statement** The following summarized data relate to Bowden Corporation's current operations:

Sales revenue	$760,000
Cost of goods sold	450,000
Selling expenses	65,000
Administrative expenses	72,000
Loss on sale of equipment	5,000
Income tax expense	42,000
Shares of common stock	
Outstanding at January 1	20,000 shares
Additional issued at May 1	7,000 shares
Additional issued at November 1	2,000 shares

Required

Prepare a multiple-step income statement for Bowden Corporation for the year. Include earnings per share disclosure at the bottom of the income statement.

P13-4A. **Trend Percentages** Net sales, net income, and total asset figures for Vibrant Controls, Inc., for five consecutive years are given below (Vibrant manufactures pollution controls): LO2

	Annual Amounts (Thousands of Dollars)				
	Year 1	Year 2	Year 3	Year 4	Year 5
Net sales.	$71,500	$79,800	$85,275	$88,400	$94,700
Net income.	3,200	3,650	3,900	4,250	4,790
Total assets	42,500	46,200	48,700	51,000	54,900

Required

a. Calculate trend percentages, using Year 1 as the base year.
b. Calculate the return on sales for each year. (Rates above 2.8 percent are considered good for manufacturers of pollution controls; rates above 6.4 percent are considered very good.)
c. Comment on the results of your analysis.

P13-5A. **Changes in Various Ratios** Presented below is selected information for Brimmer Company: LO4

	2016	2015
Sales revenue.	$920,000	$840,000
Cost of goods sold.	575,000	545,000
Interest expense.	20,000	20,000
Income tax expense.	27,000	30,000
Net income.	61,000	52,000
Cash flow from operating activities	65,000	55,000
Capital expenditures	45,000	45,000
Accounts receivable (net), December 31	126,000	120,000
Inventory, December 31.	196,000	160,000
Stockholders' equity, December 31.	450,000	400,000
Total assets, December 31.	750,000	675,000

Required

a. Calculate the following ratios for 2016. The 2015 results are given for comparative purposes.

		2015
1.	Gross profit percentage	33.5 percent
2.	Return on assets	8.3 percent
3.	Return on sales	6.2 percent
4.	Return on common stockholders' equity (no preferred stock was outstanding).	13.9 percent
5.	Accounts receivable turnover.	7.50
6.	Average collection period.	48.7 days
7.	Inventory turnover	3.61
8.	Times-interest-earned ratio	4.80
9.	Operating-cash-flow-to-capital-expenditures ratio	1.22

b. Comment on the changes between the two years.

P13-6A. **Ratios from Comparative and Common-Size Data** Consider the following financial statements for Waverly Company. LO2, 3, 4

During 2016, management obtained additional bond financing to enlarge its production facilities. The company faced higher production costs during the year for such things as fuel, materials, and freight. Because of temporary government price controls, a planned price increase on products was delayed several months.

As a holder of both common and preferred stock, you decide to analyze the financial statements:

WAVERLY COMPANY Balance Sheets (Thousands of Dollars)	Dec. 31, 2016	Dec. 31, 2015
Assets		
Cash and cash equivalents	$ 19,000	$ 12,000
Accounts receivable (net)	55,000	43,000
Inventory	120,000	105,000
Prepaid expenses	20,000	14,000
Plant and other assets (net)	471,000	411,000
Total Assets	$685,000	$585,000
Liabilities and Stockholders' Equity		
Current liabilities	$ 91,000	$ 82,000
10% Bonds payable	225,000	160,000
9% Preferred stock, $50 Par Value	75,000	75,000
Common stock, $10 Par Value	200,000	200,000
Retained earnings	94,000	68,000
Total Liabilities and Stockholders' Equity	$685,000	$585,000

WAVERLY COMPANY Income Statements (Thousands of Dollars)	2016	2015
Sales revenue	$820,000	$678,000
Cost of goods sold	545,000	433,920
Gross profit on sales	275,000	244,080
Selling and administrative expenses	175,000	149,200
Income before interest expense and income taxes	100,000	94,880
Interest expense	22,500	16,000
Income before income taxes	77,500	78,880
Income tax expense	22,900	21,300
Net income	$ 54,600	$ 57,580
Other financial data (thousands of dollars)		
Cash provided by operating activities	$ 65,200	$ 60,500
Preferred stock dividends	6,750	6,750

Required

a. Calculate the following for each year: current ratio, quick ratio, operating-cash-flow-to-current-liabilities ratio (current liabilities were $77,000,000 at January 1, 2015), inventory turnover (inventory was $87,000,000 at January 1, 2015), debt-to-equity ratio, times-interest-earned ratio, return on assets (total assets were $490,000,000 at January 1, 2015), and return on common stockholders' equity (common stockholders' equity was $235,000,000 at January 1, 2015).

b. Calculate common-size percentages for each year's income statement.

c. Comment on the results of your analysis.

LO4 **P13-7A.** **Constructing Statements from Ratio Data** The following are the 2015 financial statements for Omicron Company, with almost all dollar amounts missing:

OMICRON COMPANY Balance Sheet December 31, 2015				
Cash	$?	Current liabilities	$	?
Accounts receivable (net)	?	8% Bonds payable		?
Inventory	?	Common stock		?
Equipment (net)	?	Retained earnings		950,000
		Total Liabilities and		
Total Assets	$6,000,000	Stockholders' Equity		$6,000,000

OMICRON COMPANY Income Statement For the Year Ended December 31, 2015		
Sales revenue.	$	?
Cost of goods sold.		?
Gross profit.		?
Selling and administrative expenses		?
Income before interest expense and income taxes		?
Interest expense.		80,000
Income before income taxes		?
Income tax expense (30%).		?
Net income.		$580,000

The following information is available about Omicron Company's financial statements:

1. Quick ratio, 0.95.
2. Inventory turnover (inventory at January 1 was $924,000), 5 times.
3. Return on sales, 8.0 percent.
4. Accounts receivable turnover (accounts receivable (net) at January 1 were $860,000), 8 times.
5. Gross profit percentage, 32 percent.
6. Return on common stockholders' equity (common stockholders' equity at January 1 was $3,300,000), 16 percent.
7. The interest expense relates to the bonds payable that were outstanding all year.

Required

Compute the missing amounts, and complete the financial statements of Omicron Company. *Hint:* Complete the income statement first.

P13-8A. **Ratios Compared with Industry Averages** Because you own the common stock of Phantom Corporation, a paper manufacturer, you decide to analyze the firm's performance for the most recent year. The following data are taken from the firm's latest annual report: **LO4**

	Dec. 31, 2016	Dec. 31, 2015
Quick assets.	$ 700,000	$ 552,000
Inventory and prepaid expenses	372,000	312,000
Other assets.	4,788,000	4,200,000
Total Assets	$5,860,000	$5,064,000
Current liabilities.	$ 724,000	$ 564,000
10% Bonds payable.	1,440,000	1,440,000
8% Preferred stock, $100 par value.	480,000	480,000
Common stock, $10 par value.	2,700,000	2,160,000
Retained earnings	516,000	420,000
Total Liabilities and Stockholders' Equity	$5,860,000	$5,064,000

For 2016, net sales amount to $11,280,000, net income is $575,000, and preferred stock dividends paid are $42,000.

Required

a.   Calculate the following ratios for 2016.
   1. Return on sales
   2. Return on assets
   3. Return on common stockholders' equity
   4. Quick ratio
   5. Current ratio
   6. Debt-to-equity ratio

b. Trade association statistics and information provided by credit agencies reveal the following data on industry norms:

	Median	Upper Quartile
Return on sales	4.9 percent	8.6 percent
Return on assets	6.5 percent	11.2 percent
Return on common stockholders' equity	10.6 percent	17.3 percent
Quick ratio	1.0	1.8
Current ratio	1.8	3.0
Debt-to-equity-ratio	1.08	0.66

Compare Phantom Corporation's performance with industry performance.

LO4   P13-9A.   Ratios Compared with Industry Averages Packard Plastics, Inc., manufactures various plastic and synthetic products. Financial statement data for the firm follow:

	2016 (Thousands of Dollars, except Earnings per Share)
Sales revenue	$825,000
Cost of goods sold	540,000
Net income	50,500
Dividends	15,000
Earnings per share	4.25

Packard Plastics, Inc. Balance Sheets (Thousands of Dollars)	Dec. 31, 2016	Dec. 31, 2015
Assets		
Cash	$ 4,100	$ 2,700
Accounts receivable (net)	66,900	60,900
Inventory	148,000	140,000
Total Current Assets	219,000	203,600
Plant assets (net)	215,000	194,000
Other assets	13,900	3,900
Total Assets	$447,900	$401,500
Liabilities and Stockholders' Equity		
Notes payable—banks	$ 31,000	$ 25,000
Accounts payable	27,600	23,000
Accrued liabilities	25,100	24,800
Total Current Liabilities	83,700	72,800
10% Bonds payable	150,000	150,000
Total Liabilities	233,700	222,800
Common stock, $10 par value (12,500,000 shares)	125,000	125,000
Retained earnings	89,200	53,700
Total Stockholders' Equity	214,200	178,700
Total Liabilities and Stockholders' Equity	$447,900	$401,500

Required

a. Using the given data, calculate items 1 through 8 below for 2016. Compare the performance of Packard Plastics, Inc., with the following industry averages and comment on its operations.

		Median Ratios for Manufacturers of Plastic and Synthetic Products
1.	Quick ratio	1.2
2.	Current ratio	1.9
3.	Accounts receivable turnover.	7.9 times
4.	Inventory turnover	7.8 times
5.	Debt-to-equity ratio	0.95
6.	Gross profit percentage	32.7 percent
7.	Return on sales	3.5 percent
8.	Return on assets	6.3 percent

b. Calculate the dividends paid per share of common stock. What was the dividend payout ratio?

c. If the most recent price per share of common stock is $50.25, what is the price-earnings ratio? The dividend yield?

P13-10A. Financial Statement Notes: Quarterly Data Quarterly data are presented below for Company A and Company B. One of these companies is Gibson Greetings, Inc., which manufactures and sells greeting cards. The other company is Hon Industries, Inc., which manufactures and sells office furniture. Both companies are on a calendar year basis. **LO2, 4**

	(Amounts in Thousands)				
	First Quarter	Second Quarter	Third Quarter	Fourth Quarter	Year
Company A					
Net sales.	$186,111	$177,537	$203,070	$213,608	$780,326
Gross profit	55,457	53,643	64,024	69,374	242,498
Company B					
Net sales.	$ 84,896	$ 83,796	$142,137	$235,336	$546,165
Gross profit.	53,900	52,983	66,018	104,961	277,862

Required

a. Compute the percent of annual net sales generated each quarter by Company A. Round to the nearest percent.

b. Compute the percent of annual net sales generated each quarter by Company B. Round to the nearest percent.

c. Which company has the most seasonal business? Briefly explain.

d. Which company is Gibson Greetings, Inc.? Hon Industries, Inc.? Briefly explain.

e. Which company's interim quarterly data are probably most useful for predicting annual results? Briefly explain.

PROBLEMS—SET B

P13-1B. Income Statement Format The following information from Tricon Company's operations is available: **LO1**

Administrative expenses	$ 145,000
Cost of goods sold	928,000
Sales revenue	1,650,000
Selling expenses	174,000
Interest expense	14,000
Loss from operations of discontinued segment	120,000
Gain on disposal of discontinued segment	90,000
Income taxes	
Amount applicable to ordinary operations	115,000
Reduction applicable to loss from operations of discontinued segment	68,000
Amount applicable to gain on disposal of discontinued segment	30,000

Required

a. Prepare a multiple-step income statement. (Disregard earnings per share amounts.)

b. Prepare a single-step income statement. (Disregard earnings per share amounts.)

LO4 P13-2B. **Earnings per Share** Island Corporation began the year with 50,000 shares of common stock outstanding. On May 1, an additional 12,000 shares of common stock were issued. On July 1, 20,000 shares of common stock were acquired as treasury stock. On September 1, the 6,000 treasury shares of common stock were reissued. Island Corporation's net income for the calendar year is $230,000.

Required

Compute earnings per share.

LO1, 4 P13-3B. **Earnings per Share and Multiple-Step Income Statement** The following summarized data are related to Garner Corporation's operations:

Sales revenue	$2,216,000
Cost of goods sold	1,290,000
Selling expenses	180,000
Administrative expenses	142,800
Loss from plant strike	95,000
Income tax expense	204,000
Shares of common stock	
Outstanding at January 1	65,000 shares
Additional issued at April 1	17,000 shares
Additional issued at August 1	3,000 shares

Required

Prepare a multiple-step income statement for Garner Corporation. Include earnings per share disclosure at the bottom of the income statement. Garner Corporation has no preferred stock.

LO2 P13-4B. **Trend Percentages** Sales of automotive products for Ford Motor Company and General Motors Corporation for a five-year period are:

	Net Sales of Automotive Products (Millions of Dollars)				
	Year 1	**Year 2**	**Year 3**	**Year 4**	**Year 5**
Ford Motor Company	$82,879	$81,844	$72,051	$ 84,407	$ 91,568
General Motors Corporation	99,106	97,312	94,828	103,005	108,027

Net sales for Pfizer Inc. and Abbott Laboratories for the same five years follow:

	Net Sales (Millions of Dollars)				
	Year 1	Year 2	Year 3	Year 4	Year 5
Pfizer Inc.	$5,672	$6,406	$6,950	$7,230	$7,478
Abbott Laboratories	5,380	6,159	6,877	7,852	8,408

Required

a. Calculate trend percentages for all four companies, using Year 1 as the base year.

b. Comment on the trend percentage of Ford Motor Company and General Motors Corporation.

c. Comment on the trend percentages of Pfizer Inc. and Abbott Laboratories.

P13-5B. Changes in Various Ratios Selected information follow for Cycle Company:

LO2, 4

	2016	2015
Sales revenue.	$680,000	$520,000
Cost of goods sold.	407,700	310,000
Interest expense.	20,000	14,000
Income tax expense.	6,200	5,100
Net income.	26,000	20,300
Cash flow from operating activities	29,500	26,500
Capital expenditures	42,000	25,000
Accounts receivable (net), December 31	182,000	128,000
Inventory, December 31.	225,000	180,000
Stockholders' equity, December 31.	205,000	165,000
Total assets, December 31.	460,000	350,000

Required

a. Calculate the following ratios for 2016. The 2015 results are given for comparative purposes.

		2015
1.	Gross profit percentage.	40.4 percent
2.	Return on assets	6.5 percent
3.	Return on sales	3.9 percent
4.	Return on common stockholders' equity (no preferred stock was outstanding).	14.2 percent
5.	Accounts receivable turnover.	4.77
6.	Average collection period.	76.5 days
7.	Inventory turnover	2.07
8.	Times-interest-earned ratio	2.81
9.	Operating-cash-flow-to-capital-expenditures ratio	1.06

b. Comment on the changes between the two years.

P13-6B. Ratios from Comparative and Common-Size Data Consider the following financial statements for Vega Company.

LO2, 3, 4

During the year, management obtained additional bond financing to enlarge its production facilities. The plant addition produced a new high-margin product, which is supposed to improve the average rate of gross profit and return on sales.

As a potential investor, you decide to analyze the financial statements:

VEGA COMPANY Balance Sheets (Thousands of Dollars)	Dec. 31, 2016	Dec. 31, 2015
Assets		
Cash.	$ 22,000	$ 16,100
Accounts receivable (net).	39,000	21,400
Inventory.	105,000	72,000
Prepaid expenses.	1,500	4,000
Plant and other assets (net)	463,500	427,500
Total Assets	$631,000	$541,000
Liabilities and Stockholders' Equity		
Current liabilities.	$ 77,000	$ 46,000
9% Bonds payable.	187,500	150,000
8% Preferred stock, $50 par value.	60,000	60,000
Common stock, $10 par value.	225,000	225,000
Retained earnings	81,500	60,000
Total Liabilities and Stockholders' Equity	$631,000	$541,000

VEGA COMPANY Income Statements (Thousands of Dollars)	2016	2015
Sales revenue.	$850,000	$697,500
Cost of goods sold.	552,000	465,000
Gross profit on sales.	298,000	232,500
Selling and administrative expenses	231,000	174,000
Income before interest expense and income taxes	67,000	58,500
Interest expense.	17,000	13,500
Income before income taxes	50,000	45,000
Income tax expense.	14,100	12,500
Net income.	$ 35,900	$ 32,500
Other financial data (thousands of dollars):		
Cash provided by operating activities	$ 30,000	$ 25,000
Preferred stock dividends.	5,000	4,800

Required

a. Calculate the following for each year: current ratio, quick ratio, operating-cash-flow-to-current-liabilities ratio (current liabilities were $40,000,000 at January 1, 2015), inventory turnover (inventory was $68,000,000 at January 1, 2015), debt-to-equity ratio, times-interest-earned ratio, return on assets (total assets were $490,000,000 at January 1, 2015), and return on common stockholders' equity (common stockholders' equity was $265,000,000 at January 1, 2015).

b. Calculate common-size percentage for each year's income statement.

c. Comment on the results of your analysis.

LO4 **P13-7B.** **Constructing Statements from Ratio Data** The following are the financial statements for Timber Company, with almost all dollar amounts missing:

TIMBER COMPANY Balance Sheet December 31			
Cash..........................	$?	Current liabilities..................	$?
Accounts receivable (net)...........	?	10% Bonds payable..............	144,000
Inventory.......................	?	Common stock...................	?
Equipment (net)	?	Retained earnings	50,000
		Total Liabilities and	
Total Assets	$576,000	Stockholders' Equity...........	$576,000

TIMBER COMPANY Income Statement For the Year Ended December 31	
Sales revenue...	$?
Cost of goods sold..	?
Gross profit on sales	?
Selling and administrative expenses	?
Income before interest expense and income taxes..................	?
Interest expense...	?
Income before income taxes	?
Income tax expense (30%)...	?
Net income...	$70,200

The following information is available about Timber Company's financial statements:

1. Quick ratio, 1.75.
2. Current ratio, 3.0.
3. Return on sales, 8.0 percent.
4. Return on common stockholders' equity (common stockholders' equity at January 1 was $340,000), 20 percent.
5. Gross profit percentage, 30 percent.
6. Accounts receivable turnover (accounts receivable (net) at January 1 were $97,200), 12 times.
7. The interest expense relates to the bonds payable that were outstanding all year.

Required
Compute the missing amounts, and complete the financial statements of Timber Company. (*Hint:* Complete the income statement first.)

P13-8B. **Ratios Compared with Industry Averages** You are analyzing the performance of Lumite Corporation, a manufacturer of personal care products, for the most recent year. The following data are taken from the firm's latest annual report: **LO4**

	Dec. 31, 2016	Dec. 31, 2015
Quick assets..	$ 385,000	$ 350,000
Inventory and prepaid expenses	950,000	820,000
Other assets..	4,165,000	3,700,000
Total Assets	$5,500,000	$4,870,000
Current liabilities	$ 600,000	$ 500,000
10% Bonds payable.......................................	1,300,000	1,300,000
7% Preferred stock	900,000	900,000
Common stock, $5 par value..............................	1,900,000	1,800,000
Retained earnings	800,000	370,000
Total Liabilities and Stockholders' Equity	$5,500,000	$4,870,000

In 2016, net sales amount to $8,800,000, net income is $680,000, and preferred stock dividends paid are $65,000.

Required

a. Calculate the following for 2016:
   1. Return on sales
   2. Return on assets
   3. Return on common stockholders' equity
   4. Quick ratio
   5. Current ratio
   6. Debt-to-equity ratio

b. Trade association statistics and information provided by credit agencies reveal the following data on industry norms:

	Median	Upper Quartile
Return on sales	3.7 percent	10.6 percent
Return on assets	5.8 percent	14.2 percent
Return on common stockholders' equity	18.5 percent	34.2 percent
Quick ratio	1.0	1.8
Current ratio	2.2	3.7
Debt-to-equity ratio	1.07	0.37

Compare Lumite Corporation's performance with industry performance.

LO4 P13-9B. **Ratios Compared with Industry Averages** Avery Instrument, Inc., is a manufacturer of various measuring and controlling instruments. Financial statement data for the firm are as follows:

	2016 (Thousands of Dollars, except Earnings per Share)
Sales revenue	$220,000
Cost of goods sold	125,000
Net income	8,000
Dividends	2,600
Earnings per share	4.25

AVERY INSTRUMENTS, INC. Balance Sheets (Thousands of Dollars)	Dec. 31, 2016	Dec. 31, 2015
Assets		
Cash	$ 18,500	$ 18,000
Accounts receivable (net)	46,000	43,000
Inventory	39,500	43,700
Total Current Assets	104,000	104,700
Plant assets (net)	52,600	51,500
Other assets	15,600	13,800
Total Assets	$172,200	$170,000
Liabilities and Stockholders' Equity		
Notes payable—banks	$ 6,000	$ 6,000
Accounts payable	22,700	18,700
Accrued liabilities	16,500	24,000
Total Current Liabilities	45,200	48,700
9% Bonds payable	40,000	40,000
Total Liabilities	85,200	88,700
Common stock, $25 par value (2,000,000 shares)	50,000	50,000
Retained earnings	37,000	31,300
Total Stockholders' Equity	87,000	81,300
Total Liabilities and Stockholders' Equity	$172,200	$170,000

Required

a. Using the given data, calculate ratios 1 through 8 for 2016. Compare the performance of Avery Instruments, Inc., with the following industry averages and comment on its operations.

		Median Ratios for Manufacturers of Measuring and Controlling Instruments
1.	Quick ratio	1.3
2.	Current ratio	2.4
3.	Accounts receivable turnover...............	5.9 times
4.	Inventory turnover	3.5 times
5.	Debt-to-equity ratio	0.73
6.	Gross profit percentage	44.3 percent
7.	Return on sales	4.5 percent
8.	Return on assets	7.6 percent

b. Calculate the dividends paid per share of common stock. What was the dividend payout ratio?
c. If the most recent price per share of common stock is $63, what is the price-earnings ratio? The dividend yield?

P13-10B. Financial Statement Notes: Quarterly Data Quarterly data are presented below for Company C and Company D. One of these companies is Toys "R" Us, a children's specialty retail chain. The company's fiscal year ends on the Saturday nearest to January 31. The other company is the Gillette Company prior to its acquisition by Procter & Gamble. Gillette manufactures and sells blades, razors, and toiletries. Gillette was on a calendar year basis.

LO2, 4

	(Amounts in Thousands)				
	First Quarter	Second Quarter	Third Quarter	Fourth Quarter	Year
Company C					
Net Sales	$1,216.6	$1,237.3	$1,339.7	$1,617.2	$5,410.8
Gross profit..................	753.1	773.6	839.0	1,000.8	3,366.5
Company D					
Net Sales	$1,172.5	$1,249.1	$1,345.8	$3,401.8	$7,169.2
Gross profit..................	362.5	384.6	423.2	1,030.3	2,200.6

Required

a. Compute the percentage of annual net sales generated each quarter by Company C. Round to the nearest percent.
b. Compute the percentage of annual net sales generated each quarter by Company D. Round to the nearest percent.
c. Which company has the most seasonal business? Briefly explain.
d. Which company is Toys "R" Us? The Gillette Company? Briefly explain.

SERIAL PROBLEM: KATE'S CARDS

(Note: This is a continuation of the Serial Problem: Kate's Cards from Chapter 1 through Chapter 12.)

SP13. Kate is very pleased with the results of the first year of operations for Kate's Cards. She ended the year on a high note, with the company's reputation for producing quality cards leading to more business than she can currently manage. Kate is considering expanding and bringing in several employees. In order to do this, she will need to find a larger location and also purchase more equipment. All this means additional financing. Kate has asked you to look at her year-end financial statements as if you were a banker considering giving Kate a loan. Comment on your findings and provide calculations to support your comments.

KATE'S CARDS
Income Statement
Year Ended August 31, 2016

Sales revenue	$135,000
Cost of goods sold	72,000
Gross profit	63,000
Operating expenses	
Wages	18,000
Consulting	11,850
Insurance	1,200
Utilities	2,400
Depreciation	3,250
Total operating expenses	36,700
Income from operations	26,300
Interest expense	900
Income before income tax	25,400
Income tax expense	8,900
Net income	$ 16,500

KATE'S CARDS
Balance Sheet
August 31, 2016

Assets	
Current assets	
Cash	$12,300
Accounts receivable	11,000
Inventory	16,000
Prepaid insurance	1,000
Total current assets	40,300
Equipment	17,500
Accumulated depreciation	3,250
Total assets	$54,550
Liabilities	
Current liabilities	
Accounts payable	$ 6,200
Unearned revenue	1,250
Other current liabilities	1,900
Total current liabilities	9,350
Note payable	15,000
Total liabilities	24,350
Stockholders' equity	
Common stock	500
Additional paid-in-capital	9,500
Preferred stock	5,000
Retained earnings	15,200
Total stockholders' equity	30,200
Total liabilities and stockholders' equity	$54,550

KATE'S CARDS Statement of Cash Flows Year Ended August 31, 2016	
Cash flow from operating activities	
Net income	$16,500
Add depreciation	3,250
Increase in accounts receivable	(11,000)
Increase in inventory.	(16,000)
Increase in prepaid expenses.	(1,000)
Increase in accounts payable.	6,200
Increase in unearned revenue.	1,250
Increase in other current liabilities	1,900
Cash provided by operating activities	1,100
Cash flow from investing activities	
Purchase of equipment.	(17,500)
Cash used by investing activities.	(17,500)
Cash flow from financing activities	
Proceeds from bank note	15,000
Issuance of common stock.	10,000
Issuance of preferred stock	5,000
Cash dividends.	(1,300)*
Cash provided by financing activities	28,700
Net increase in cash.	12,300
Cash at beginning of year	0
Cash at end of year	$12,300

*Kate issued cash dividends on both the common stock and the preferred stock. There are 50 preferred shares outstanding and 500 common shares outstanding. The dividends that Kate paid were $6 per share on the preferred shares and $2 per share on the common shares.

EXTENDING YOUR KNOWLEDGE

REPORTING AND ANALYSIS

EYK13-1. **Financial Reporting Problem: Columbia Sportswear Company** The financial statements for the Columbia Sportswear Company can be found in Appendix A at the end of this book.

> COLUMBIA
> SPORTSWEAR
> COMPANY

You are considering an investment in Columbia Sportswear after a recent outdoor trip in which you really liked some of the clothes you purchased from the company. You decide to do an analysis of the company's financial statements in order to help you make an informed decision.

Required

a. Using the five-year selected financial data reported in the annual report, produce a five-year trend analysis, using 2010 as a base year, of (1) net sales, (2) net income, and (3) total assets. Comment on your findings.

b. Calculate the (1) gross profit percentage, (2) return on sales, and (3) return on assets for 2013 and 2014. Comment on Columbia Sportswear's profitability. (2012 total assets = $1,458,842,000)

c. Calculate the (1) current ratio, (2) quick ratio, and (3) operating-cash-flow-to-current liabilities ratio for 2013 and 2014. (2012 current liabilities = $252,059,000) Comment on Columbia Sportswear's liquidity.

d. Calculate the debt-to-equity ratio for 2013 and 2014. Comment on Columbia Sportswear's solvency.

EYK13-2. **Comparative Analysis Problem: Columbia Sportswear Company vs Under Armour, Inc.** The financial statements for the Columbia Sportswear Company can be found in Appendix A at the end of this book, and the financial statements of Under Armour, Inc. can be found in Appendix B (the complete annual report is available on this book's Website).

> COLUMBIA
> SPORTSWEAR
> COMPANY
>
> UNDER ARMOUR,
> INC.

Required

Based on the information from the financial statements of each company, do the following.

a.   Calculate the percentage change in (1) net sales, (2) net income, (3) cash flow from operating activities, and (4) total assets from 2013 to 2014.

b.   What conclusions can you draw from this analysis?

EYK13-3. **Business Decision Problem**   Crescent Paints, Inc., a paint manufacturer, has been in business for five years. The company has had modest profits and has experienced few operating difficulties until this year, 2016, when president Alice Becknell discussed her company's working capital problems with you, a loan officer at Granite Bank. Becknell explained that expanding her firm has created difficulties in meeting obligations when they come due and in taking advantage of cash discounts offered by manufacturers for the timely payment of the company's accounts payable. She would like to borrow $50,000 from Granite Bank. At your request, Becknell submits the following financial data for the past two years:

	2016	2015
Sales revenue.	$2,000,000	$1,750,000
Cost of goods sold.	1,320,000	1,170,000
Net income.	42,000	33,600
Dividends.	22,000	18,000
December 31, 2014, data.		
Total assets	1,100,000	
Accounts receivable (net).	205,000	
Inventory.	350,000	

CRESCENT PAINTS, INC. Balance Sheets	Dec. 31, 2016	Dec. 31, 2015
Assets		
Cash.	$ 31,000	$ 50,000
Accounts receivable (net).	345,000	250,000
Inventory.	525,000	425,000
Prepaid expenses.	11,000	6,000
Total Current Assets.	912,000	731,000
Plant assets (net)	483,000	444,000
Total Assets	$1,395,000	$ 1,175,000
Liabilities and Stockholders' Equity		
Notes payable—banks.	$ 100,000	$ 35,000
Accounts payable.	244,000	190,000
Accrued liabilities.	96,000	85,000
Total Current Liabilities.	440,000	310,000
10% Mortgage payable	190,000	250,000
Total Liabilities	630,000	560,000
Common stock.	665,000	535,000
Retained earnings	100,000	80,000
Total Stockholders' Equity	765,000	615,000
Total Liabilities and Stockholders' Equity	$1,395,000	$1,175,000

Calculate the following items for both years from the given data and then compare them with the median ratios for paint manufacturers provided by a commercial credit firm:

		Median Ratios for Paint Manufacturers
1.	Current ratio	2.5
2.	Quick ratio	1.3
3.	Accounts receivable turnover.	8.1
4.	Average collection period.	44.9 days
5.	Inventory turnover	4.9
6.	Debt-to-equity ratio	0.78
7.	Return on assets	4.8%
8.	Return on sales	2.4%

Required

Based on your analysis, decide whether and under what circumstances you would grant Becknell's request for a loan. Explain the reasons for your decision.

EYK13-4. Financial Analysis Problem Listed below are selected financial data for three corporations: **Honeywell International, Inc.** (environmental controls), **The Dow Chemical Company** (chemicals and plastic products), and **Abbott Laboratories** (health care products). These data cover five years (Year 5 is the most recent year; net income in thousands):

(margin note) HONEYWELL INTERNATIONAL, INC.

THE DOW CHEMICAL COMPANY

ABBOTT LABORATORIES

	Year 5	Year 4	Year 3	Year 2	Year 1
Honeywell International, Inc.					
Net income.	$278,900	$322,200	$246,800	$331,100	$381,900
Earnings per common share	$2.15	$2.40	$1.78	$2.35	$2.52
Dividend per common share	$1.00	$0.91	$0.84	$0.77	$0.70
The Dow Chemical Company					
Net income.	$938,000	$644,000	$276,000	$942,000	$1,384,000
Earnings per common share	$3.88	$2.33	$0.99	$3.46	$5.10
Dividend per common share	$2.60	$2.60	$2.60	$2.60	$2.60
Abbott Laboratories					
Net income*	$1,399,100	$1,239,100	$1,088,700	$965,800	$859,800
Earnings per common share*	$1.69	$1.47	$1.27	$1.11	$0.96
Dividend per common share	$0.68	$0.60	$0.50	$0.42	$0.35

*Before accounting change

Required

a.   Calculate the dividend payout ratio for each company for each of the five years.

b.   Companies may differ in their dividend policy; that is, they may differ in whether they emphasize a constant dividend amount per share, a steady growth in dividend amount per share, a target or constant dividend payout ratio, or some other criterion. Based on the data available, identify what appears to be each of the above firm's dividend policy over the five-year period.

CRITICAL THINKING

EYK13-5. Accounting Research Problem: General Mills, Inc. The fiscal year 2014 annual report of General Mills, Inc. is available on this book's Website.

(margin note) GENERAL MILLS, INC.

Required

a.   Calculate (or identify) the following financial ratios for 2013 and 2014:
1.   Gross profit percentage
2.   Return on sales
3.   Asset turnover (2012, total assets = $21,096.8 million)
4.   Return on assets (2012, total assets = $21,096.8 million)
5.   Return on common stockholders' equity (2012, total stockholders' equity = $6,882.7 million)
6.   Current ratio
7.   Quick ratio

8. Operating-cash-flow-to-current-liabilities ratio (2012, current liabilities = $3,843.2 million)
9. Accounts receivable turnover (2012, accounts receivable = $1,323.6 million)
10. Average collection period
11. Inventory turnover (2012, inventory = $1,478.8 million)
12. Days' sales in inventory
13. Debt-to-equity ratio
14. Times-interest-earned ratio
15. Operating-cash-flow-to-capital-expenditures ratio
16. Earnings per share
17. Price-earnings ratio (Use year-end adjusted closing stock price of $53.81 for 2014 and $48.98 for 2013.)
18. Dividend yield
19. Dividend payout ratio

b. Comment briefly on the changes from fiscal 2013 to fiscal 2014 in the ratios computed above.

EYK13-6. **Accounting Communication Activity** Pete Hollingsworth is currently taking an accounting course and is confused about what his professor told the class about analyzing financial statements. Pete would like you to lead a study session on the topic. In order to help everyone out, you decide to write a short memo describing some of the key points.

Required
Include the following items in your memo:
a. What is meant by trend analysis and how is it helpful?
b. How are common-size statements constructed and what are their uses?
c. What are a few common profitability, liquidity, and solvency ratios and how are they interpreted?
d. What are some limitations of financial statement analysis?

EYK13-7. **Accounting Ethics Case** Chris Nelson, the new assistant controller for Grand Company, is preparing for the firm's year-end closing procedures. On December 30, 2016, a memorandum from the controller directed Nelson to make a journal entry debiting Cash and crediting Long-Term Advances to Officers for $1,000,000. Not finding the $1,000,000 in the cash deposit prepared for the bank that day, Nelson went to the controller for a further explanation. In response, the controller took from her desk drawer a check for $1,000,000 payable to Grand Company from Jason Grand, chief executive officer of the firm. Attached to the check was a note from Jason Grand saying that if this check were not needed to return it to him next week.

"This check is paying off a $1,000,000 advance the firm made to Jason Grand six years ago," stated the controller. "Mr. Grand has done this every year since the advance; each time we have returned the check to him in January of the following year. We plan to do so again this time. In fact, when Mr. Grand retires in four years, I expect the board of directors will forgive this advance. However, if the firm really needed the cash, we would deposit the check."

"Then why go through this charade each year?" inquired Nelson.

"It dresses up our year-end balance sheet," replied the controller. "Certain financial statement ratios are improved significantly. Further, the notes to the financial statements don't have to reveal a related-party loan. Lots of firms engage in year-end transactions designed to dress up their financial statements."

Required
a. What financial statement ratios are improved by making the journal entry contained in the controller's memorandum?
b. Is the year-end handling of Jason Grand's advance an ethical practice? Discuss.

EYK13-8. **Corporate Social Responsibility Problem** The chapter highlighted one way in which the **Procter & Gamble Company** demonstrates its commitment to being a good corporate citizen (see Page 633). Go to Procter & Gamble's Website and navigate to the section on sustainability. From there you can download their annual sustainability report. The report contains a section on social responsibility. In addition to the joint effort with UNICEF, what are some other ways that P&G demonstrates its commitment to being a good corporate citizen?

EYK13-9. **Forensic Accounting Problem** Accrual accounting is based on the principle that revenue should be reported when earned and that expenses associated with that revenue should be matched against the revenue in the same period. Some financial statement frauds violate this fundamental concept in order to overstate net income in the current year. Provide an example of how this may be accomplished.

EYK13-10. **Working with the Takeaways** Below are income statements and balance sheets for the Fango Company for 2016 and 2015:

FANGO COMPANY Income Statement For the Years Ended December 31, 2016 and 2015		
(in millions)	**2016**	**2015**
Sales revenue.	$10,000	$9,500
Cost of goods sold.	5,500	5,200
Gross profit.	4,500	4,300
Selling and administrative expenses	2,800	2,700
Income from operations	1,700	1,600
Interest expense.	300	250
Income before income taxes	1,400	1,350
Income tax expense.	420	400
Net income.	$ 980	$ 950

FANGO COMPANY Balance Sheet December 31, 2016 and 2015		
(in millions)	**2016**	**2015**
Assets		
Current assets		
Cash and cash equivalents	$ 200	$ 400
Accounts receivable.	900	800
Inventory.	700	650
Other current assets.	400	250
Total current assets	2,200	2,100
Property, plant, & equipment (net)	2,600	2,500
Other assets.	5,700	5,900
Total assets	$10,500	$10,500
Liabilities and Stockholders' Equity		
Current liabilities.	$ 3,000	$ 2,900
Long-term liabilities	5,000	5,400
Total liabilities.	8,000	8,300
Stockholders' equity—common.	2,500	2,200
Total liabilities and stockholders' equity	$10,500	$10,500

Required

Calculate the following ratios for the Fango Company for 2016 and 2015 and discuss your findings:

1. Profitability
   a. Return on sales
   b. Return on common stockholders' equity (common stockholders' equity was $2,000 on December 31, 2014)

2. Liquidity
   a. Current ratio
   b. Accounts receivable turnover (accounts receivable was $780 on December 31, 2014)
   c. Inventory turnover (inventory was $620 on December 31, 2014)
3. Solvency
   a. Debt-to-equity ratio
   b. Times-interest-earned ratio

EYK13-11. Analyzing IFRS Financial Statements The 2014 financial statements of **LVMH Moet Hennessey-Louis Vuitton S.A.** are presented in Appendix C at the end of this book. LVMH is a Paris-based holding company and one of the world's largest and best-known luxury goods companies. As a member of the European Union, French companies are required to prepare their consolidated (group) financial statements using International Financial Reporting Standards (IFRS). fter reviewing LVMH's consolidated financial statements, calculate the following for 2014 and 013:

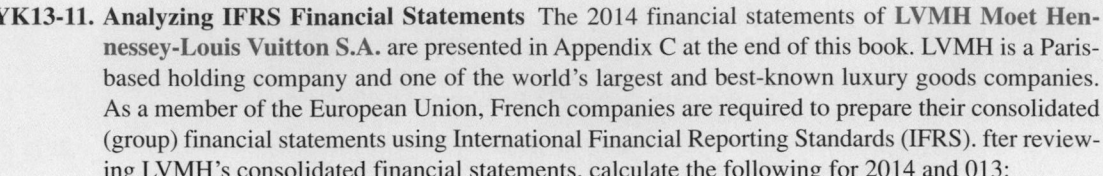

a. Current ratio
b. Quick ratio
c. Accounts receivable turnover
d. Inventory turnover
e. Debt-to-equity ratio
f. Times-interest-earned ratio *(Hint: interest expense is called "Cost of net financial debt.")*
g. Return on sales
h. Return on assets
i. Return on common stockholders' equity

ANSWERS TO SELF-STUDY QUESTIONS:

1. c, (p. 632)   2. c, (p. 640)   3. c, (p. 646)   4. b, (p. 649)   5. b, (p. 645)   6. c, (p. 649)
7. d, (p. 652)   8. b, (p. 643)   9. c, (p. 644)   10. b, (p. 638)   11. c, (p. 656)   12. d, (p. 658–661)

YOUR TURN! SOLUTIONS

Solution 13.1

1. Persistent
2. Transitory
3. Transitory
4. Persistent
5. Transitory
6. Persistent

Solution 13.2

	Increase in 2016	
	Amount	Percent
Sales revenue	$50,000	6.7 percent [($800,000 − $750,000)/$750,000]
Net income	20,000	20.0 percent [($120,000 − $100,000)/$100,000]
Total assets	10,000	3.4 percent [($300,000 − $290,000)/$290,000]

Solution 13.3

	Amount	Percent
SANFORD COMPANY		
Income Statement		
For the Year Ended December 31, 2015		
Sales revenue.	$13,500	100.0
Cost of goods sold.	5,400	40.0
Gross profit.	8,100	60.0
Selling and administrative expenses	1,350	10.0
Income from operations.	6,750	50.0
Interest expense.	675	5.0
Other expense	135	1.0
Income before income taxes	5,940	44.0
Income tax expense.	2,295	17.0
Net income.	$ 3,645	27.0

Solution 13.4

a. Gross profit percentage = ($30,000 − $10,500)/$30,000 = 65.0 percent
b. Return on sales = $4,500/$30,000 = 15.0 percent
c. Asset turnover = $30,000/$50,000 = 0.60
d. Return on assets = $4,500/$50,000 = 9.0 percent
e. Return on common stockholders' equity = ($4,500 − $500)/$35,000 = 11.4 percent

Solution 13.5

a. Working capital = $60,000 − $40,000 = $20,000
b. Current ratio = $60,000/$40,000 = 1.5
c. Operating-cash-flow-to-current-liabilities ratio = $55,000/$40,000 = 1.375
d. Accounts receivable turnover = $100,000/$15,000 = 6.67 times
e. Days' sales in inventory = 365/($70,000/$9,000) = 46.9 days

Solution 13.6

a. Debt-to-equity ratio = $180,000/$600,000 = 0.30
b. Times-interest-earned ratio = ($55,000 + $5,000 + $25,000)/$5,000 = 17.0 times
c. Operating-cash-flow-to-capital-expenditures ratio = $100,000/$30,000 = 3.33 times

Solution 13.7

a. Dividend yield = $1.50/$54.00 = 2.8 percent
b. Dividend payout ratio = $1.50/$4.50 = 33.3 percent

14

Overview of Managerial Accounting

PAST

The second half of this book builds upon many of the concepts introduced in the preceding financial accounting chapters.

PRESENT

Chapter 14 introduces managerial accounting. Moreover, it presents an overview of two companies used throughout the remainder of the book to illustrate various concepts and procedures common to managerial accounting and decision making.

FUTURE

Chapter 15 defines basic costing terminology and introduces different types of manufacturing inventories. It illustrates how costs flow through the inventories and explains the schedule of cost of goods manufactured.

LEARNING OBJECTIVES

1. **Define** managerial accounting and **describe** its objectives. *(p. 696)*

2. **Describe** the three types of business entities. *(p. 697)*

3. **Discuss** major trends in business and managerial accounting. *(p. 698)*

4. **Describe** important characteristics of two companies used throughout the remainder of the book to illustrate key concepts and processes. *(p. 701)*

5. **Describe** career options in managerial accounting. *(p. 703)*

6. **Understand** differences between various professional certifications available to managerial accountants. *(p. 705)*

amazon.com®

AMAZON.COM: THREE COMPANIES UNDER ONE ROOF

Amazon.com (Amazon) is the world's largest online retailer. Amazon claims to offer "Earth's Biggest Selection," offering millions of unique products through its website. If you have ever purchased something online, you have most likely visited Amazon's retail website.

What you may not know is that Amazon offers much more than retail consumer products. For example, it is a major provider of cloud computing services, known as "Amazon Web Services." Companies (including the U.S. Department of Health and Human Services) may "rent" online computing resources to develop business applications, host corporate data, and run data analyses. The market for these public cloud services was $45.7 billion in 2014, with Amazon leading two of the three major product groups in the public cloud services market. Within the third group, Amazon competes with **Microsoft Corp.** and **Google, Inc.** for the bulk of the market.

In addition to being a retailer and a service provider, Amazon is also a manufacturer. It produces an e-book reader, the Amazon Kindle; a tablet computer, the Kindle Fire HD; and, a smartphone, the Fire Phone.

Despite these manufactured products, Amazon is very focused on making profits on its digital content, not its hardware. Chief Executive Jeff Bezos says: "We want to make money when people use our devices, not when they buy our devices."

So, although most people think of Amazon as an online retailer, you now know better—Amazon is a retailer, a service firm, and a manufacturer all in one!

OVERVIEW OF MANAGERIAL ACCOUNTING				
Introduction to Managerial Accounting	**Types of Business Entities**	**Major Trends in Business and Managerial Accounting**	**Introducing Two New Companies**	**Careers in Managerial Accounting**
• Managerial accounting versus financial accounting • Objectives of managerial accounting	• Manufacturing firms • Merchandising firms • Service firms	• Outsourcing • Factory automation • Just-in-time inventory systems • Lean manufacturing • Customer profitability • Big data and predictive analytics	• Fezzari • Environmental Business Consultants	• Alternative career paths • Work/life balance • Professional certifications

INTRODUCTION TO MANAGERIAL ACCOUNTING

LO1 **Define** managerial accounting and **describe** its objectives.

Businesses make decisions every day that impact their competitiveness in the market. What is our target market? What products or services should we offer? How should we price our goods or services to compete effectively with our competitors? How much should we pay our employees to attract and retain great talent? Where should we locate our office or fulfillment center to minimize delivery time and cost? How do we build awareness of our firm and products or services within our target market? How do we achieve our objectives with limited resources? How many employees do we need to hire in the coming year to meet anticipated demand for our products or services? Which employees should we assign to work on this project?

These questions, and many others, require an understanding of broad business disciplines, including finance, marketing, organizational behavior, supply chain management, operations management, and strategy. However, a common element to all of these questions is the need to have a clear understanding of the financial implications of each alternative course of action. For example, in setting the price of a good or service, management needs to not only understand the customers' needs and expectations, competitors' positions in the marketplace, and the anticipated demand for the product or service, but also the business's costs of providing them.

Managerial Accounting versus Financial Accounting

The second half of this text focuses on **managerial accounting**, which plays a vital role in *internal* decision making. The first half of this text discussed **financial accounting**, which focuses on reporting a company's financial performance to *external* parties. Whereas financial accountants are typically engaged in measuring and reporting the financial results of a business's *past* actions and activities, management accountants utilize data from many different sources, such as financial, operational, sales, and human resources, to help top management make decisions regarding *future* performance. Financial accountants report the results of past transactions in accordance with a set of standards known as generally accepted accounting principles (GAAP). Management accountants provide information to management in a form that is timely, relevant, decision-useful, and in a format that is easily accessible to management but not determined by any external organization. Thus, whereas financial accountants prepare financial reports to assist external stakeholders, such as investors, creditors, and regulators, management accountants provide information to managers (internal users) so that they can plan, manage, and make strategic decisions regarding the growth and profitability of the business.

Objectives of Managerial Accounting

Management accountants are professionals who work in business, across all areas of an organization, in decision support, planning, and control functions. They partner with personnel from their firm's executive management to its line employees to make strategic business decisions. Management accountants must capture, analyze, and report critical data in a timely manner. To address important strategic questions like those mentioned previously, management accountants will identify data needed to answer those questions. Such data will usually include financial information, but often include non-financial information from both inside and outside the company. If the necessary data aren't readily available, management accountants may help design systems to capture the data. Sometimes, the data are available, but must be summarized in a form that is useful to management. Management accountants can help develop reports that allow management to make sense of the data. They are also proactive in identifying relevant information to help recommend needed improvements in all aspects of their firm's business.

Hint: Because the information management accountants provide managers is so important, they must ensure that it is both accurate and relevant.

TYPES OF BUSINESS ENTITIES

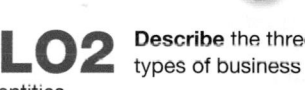

Manufacturing firms are companies that convert materials such as sheets of steel and coils of wire and components such as electric motors and microprocessors into finished products. The manufacturer utilizes human labor; utilities such as electricity, natural gas, and water; and factory assets such as buildings, machinery, and computers to convert the materials and components into sellable products.

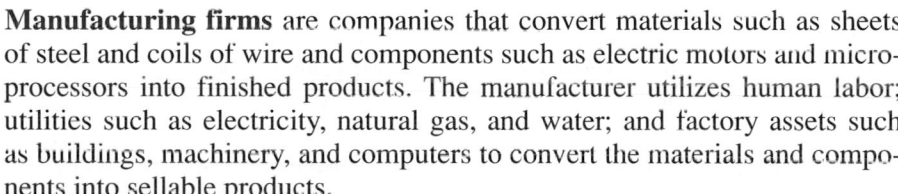

LO2 **Describe** the three types of business entities.

Merchandising firms are companies that purchase finished products from manufacturers for warehousing, display, and sale to consumers. Wholesalers typically buy finished products in large quantities and store them in large warehouses until they can be sold and shipped in smaller quantities to local retailers. The retailer utilizes human labor or electronic advertising to sell products from a "brick-and-mortar" store or through an online store available through a website.

Service firms are companies that provide services to customers. Examples include companies in health care, legal, and accounting services. The types of costs incurred by these firms are generally similar to those of other types of firms except they don't sell a product. Hence, they normally do not carry inventory.

Accounting for manufacturing operations is usually more complex because more activities are involved in producing a product than in purchasing and selling merchandise or providing a service.

Each year, *Forbes* magazine ranks the worlds "most reputable" companies. The 2013 ranking[1] indicates that roughly 77% of the world's most reputable, and presumably best known, companies are manufacturing firms. You probably recognize most of them and are likely familiar with their products. For example, BMW, Rolex, Daimler (Mercedes-Benz), Sony, Microsoft, Canon, Nestlé, Lego Group, Intel, Apple, and Adidas are among the most reputable manufacturing firms in the world. Interestingly, only 9% of the most reputable firms are retailers. You're familiar with retailers like Amazon.com, Giorgio Armani, eBay, and Starbucks. Notably missing from this list are some of the world's largest retailers, such as Walmart, Target, Costco, Home Depot, and

---

[1] Jacquelyn Smith, "The World's Most Reputable Companies," *Forbes*, April 9, 2013.

Lowe's. A slightly higher percentage of the world's most reputable firms, about 14%, are service companies. This list contains well-known companies like Google, Marriott International, FedEx, the BBC, UPS, and several airlines (Deutsche Lufthansa, Qantas Airways, Air France-KLM, SAS [Scandinavian Airlines], Singapore Airlines, and British Airways), whereas the U.S.-based airlines are all noticeably absent.

YOUR TURN! 14.1

The solution is on page 709.

For each of the following companies, identify whether they are a manufacturing, merchandising, or service firm.

Exxon Mobil Co.	Walmart
Southwest Airlines	Hershey Co.
Costco	Boston Consulting Group

CORPORATE SOCIAL RESPONSIBILITY

More Than the Bottom Line

Being a good corporate citizen means more than just providing large returns to a company's shareholders; it means considering all the company's stakeholders. In addition to shareholders, other stakeholders include employees, customers, suppliers, the environment, and the community—essentially, all of society. But does a company have to sacrifice shareholder returns in order to provide for these other stakeholders? Enlightened companies are learning that the answer is no. In fact, providing for all stakeholders can enhance shareholder returns.

Amazon.com, the top retailer on Forbes' list of the world's 100 most reputable companies, has learned that being a good corporate citizen is good for business. One example of this is Amazon's Frustration-Free Packaging program that eliminates hard plastic clamshell cases that prove so difficult to open and replaces the plastic cases with 100 percent recyclable packaging that is not only less frustrating but also better for the planet and less costly to the manufacturer.

As Amazon explains on its website:

> At Amazon, if we do our job right, our greatest contribution to the good of society will come from our core business activities: lowering prices, expanding selection, driving convenience, driving frustration-free packaging, creating Kindle, innovating in web services, and other initiatives we'll work hard on in the future.
>
> We also contribute to the communities where our employees and customers live. Our contributions can be seen in many ways—through our donations to dozens of non-profits across the United States, through the disaster relief campaigns that we host on our homepage, through our employees' volunteer efforts, through the grants that we make to the writing community, and through the Amazon Web Services credits that we provide to educators.

MAJOR TRENDS IN BUSINESS AND MANAGERIAL ACCOUNTING

Outsourcing

LO3 Discuss major trends in business and managerial accounting.

Many companies have ceased trying to maintain a general focus. Instead, they have increasingly tried to identify their strengths and focus on these activities. **Outsourcing** occurs when a business hires or contracts with another business to provide a product or service that had previously been provided within the business. Examples might include the hiring of a third party to handle a company's customer service call center, hiring a landscaping service, and hiring an expert to develop and maintain the company website. One advantage is that it allows the company to focus on its core competency (e.g., the manufacturing of a product or provision of a service). Also, it may allow the company to pay for only the level of service that it needs, without having to worry about hiring and training staff, paying for excess capacity, or staffing to meet seasonal demand.

The growth and development of the Internet has allowed companies to provide specialized business services virtually from anywhere in the world. For example, many firms outsourced their customer service centers to India and other countries around the world. A call to your Internet service provider for technical support may be answered by someone in India, who is able to test your Internet connection and even reprogram your modem remotely over the Internet.

The anticipated cost savings that result from outsourcing do not always materialize as expected, however. Deloitte Consulting found in a 2005 survey that one-quarter of the companies that had outsourced tasks had reversed their strategy and brought the task back inside the company. There are many reasons for this, including miscommunication, lower quality of intermediate products or services, and unexpected delays in the production process.

Factory Automation

Factory automation is a widely recognized trend in modern manufacturing facilities. Factory automation exists in many forms. **Stand-alone automation** incorporates a robot or computer-controlled machine into an existing manufacturing process to perform a single function, such as welding. Stand-alone automation is usually undertaken to reduce both labor and material costs.

Flexible-manufacturing-system automation involves multiple cells of two or more automated machines. All of the machines in each cell are controlled by a computer. The machines in each cell are interconnected to allow an automated flow of product through the **manufacturing cell**. This type of automated system produces the product from start to finish. The functions performed within the cell can be changed quickly by changing the program in the computer that controls the process.

When deciding whether to automate all or part of a manufacturing process, a manufacturer must compare the costs associated with the automation with the benefits to be derived from the automation. The costs may include the cost of the automated equipment, the costs of eliminating direct labor workers, and the costs of reorganizing the manufacturing operation. The benefits may include lower direct labor costs, better product quality, and fewer defective units. In general, automation should reduce direct labor costs and increase factory overhead costs. However, the increase in factory overhead should be less than the decrease in direct labor costs.

Just-in-Time Inventory Systems

Manufacturing firms typically maintain inventories (materials, work in process, and finished goods) as buffers against unforeseen delays. For example, a manufacturer would keep a supply of various materials on hand to protect against a supplier's being late in the delivery of materials needed to produce a particular product. This approach is sometimes referred to as maintaining **just-in-case inventories** (just-in-case the supplier does not deliver when scheduled), or **safety stocks**. Safety stocks create carrying costs for the manufacturer, including casualty insurance, warehousing costs, and the cost of capital on the investment in the inventory. Higher levels of inventory create higher levels of carrying costs.

Just-in-time (JIT) inventory systems seek to eliminate the safety stock balances. A company operating under a complete just-in-time philosophy would have no inventories at the end of each day of operations, that is, zero balances of materials, work in process, and finished goods. Materials would be ordered so that only the materials needed for production each day would be received each morning. Production would be scheduled so that all products started during the day would be completed by the end of the day (resulting in no work in process inventory) and shipped to customers by the end of the day (resulting in no finished goods inventory). Just-in-time means that materials are received just in time to be placed into production and that products are completed just in time to be shipped to customers.

Most manufacturing companies have been unable to reach the ideal zero balance level of all three manufacturing inventories. To guard against delayed shipments due to inclement weather or other problems, manufacturers may order materials so they arrive one or two days before they are actually needed. Even with this approach, the true just-in-case quantities are still minimized. In addition, manufacturers may be subject to seasonal demand for their products, so that they may be required to build finished goods inventory during low-demand periods of the year so they can meet customer demand during high-demand periods of the year.

Lean Manufacturing

Henry Ford is credited with integrating an entire production process by combining interchangeable parts with a moving conveyance system to produce the Model T Ford. His approach allowed the Ford Company to significantly reduce the production time and cost of producing an automobile. However, initially he was only able to provide one model in one color—black. Even when additional body styles became available, they were drop-on features from outside suppliers that were added at the very end of the production line. All models used the same chassis.

As demand for more variety increased, U.S. car manufacturers responded, but production times increased. Attempts to reduce the time to deliver an automobile meant larger and faster fabrication machines, larger parts inventories, and more complex operational and accounting information systems.

Mr. Kiichiro Toyoda studied the U.S. car manufacturing process and identified innovations that would improve the process flow and the variety of model offerings. He called this approach the Toyota Production System. By focusing on the flow of product through the entire manufacturing process, Toyota reduced the number of fabrication machines, lined up the machines in process sequence, reduced setup times, and introduced a system whereby a product was "pulled" through the process by demand from the subsequent step in the process.[2] This is the basis of **lean manufacturing**.

Lean manufacturing concepts have been adopted by manufacturers all over the world and have begun to be applied to other disciplines, including logistics and distribution, services, retail, health care, and construction. Lean manufacturing has also impacted companies' business information systems, performance measures, reports, and decisions.

Customer Profitability

In the past, companies focused their efforts on the development and standardization of products and services. As discussed previously, management attention was given to wringing all reasonable cost savings from the production process through the automation of manufacturing processes, the modification of product flow to improve efficiencies, the improvement of product quality, and the streamlining of production and delivery systems to minimize inventory on hand.

As markets have become more competitive and available products more homogeneous, companies have shifted to trying to differentiate themselves from their competitors through service. Customers have access to a tremendous amount of information about product features, prices, and quality via the Internet and have become more demanding of quality customer service.

Likewise, companies have a tremendous amount of information about their customers, including the frequency and volume of product purchases by type, their history of

---

[2] http://www.sae.org/manufacturing/lean/

change orders, special handling and delivery requests, product returns, and customer service calls. Companies have begun to distinguish among their high-demand and low-demand customers relative to the cost of service to the customer and to focus on ways to increase customer profitability, not just product margin.

Big Data and Predictive Analytics

Bernard Marr, CEO and Director of Research at Advanced Performance Institute, posted an article in the blog "The Big Data Guru"[3] on Amazon.com's use of customer data to predict who will order what and when. In the article, he notes that Amazon has obtained a patent for what it calls "Anticipatory Shipping." The concept is that Amazon believes that its customer data will allow it to predict what you want and ship it to your door even before you order it. Already, Amazon customizes your online shopping experience by remembering what you bought previously, what you have on your wish list, what you have previously rated and reviewed, and what other customers who searched for similar items bought.

Amazon is not the only company trying to read your mind. The development of new and faster ways of analyzing the data trail that you leave behind following every online search, purchase, and social media interaction is allowing companies of all sizes to anticipate your desires and customize their products and services to better meet those needs.

INTRODUCING TWO NEW COMPANIES

Throughout the managerial accounting chapters of the textbook we will highlight two companies to explain key concepts and illustrate how real companies implement different managerial accounting practices. To provide a real-world view of manufacturing and retail sales, we frequently highlight Fezzari Performance Bicycles. Although it is important for students to understand the manufacture and sale of inventory, the U.S. economy has evolved into a much more service-oriented network of businesses. Hence, we will focus significant attention on how managerial accounting practices are used in the service sector and provide illustrations based on a consulting business, Environmental Business Consultants, LLC. Both of these companies will become very familiar to you throughout the various managerial accounting chapters of the book.

LO4 **Describe** important characteristics of two companies used throughout the remainder of the book to illustrate key concepts and processes.

Fezzari—A U.S. Bicycle Manufacturer and Distributor

Fezzari is a manufacturer and distributor located in Lindon, Utah, that designs, engineers, manufactures, and builds both mountain and road bikes. Fezzari's business model uses primarily a consumer-direct approach, with the vast majority of its sales completed through web-based, direct orders. This direct-order approach allows Fezzari to cut out the middleman (the local bike shop) and provide its customers with a higher-quality product at a lower cost than the brand-name bike manufacturers. Fezzari provides a 23-point custom setup with each bike sold, allowing the company to provide customers with a custom fit.

Fezzari's business model is not without risk. Most cyclists, particularly those who want to purchase a higher-end bike for

---

[3] http://smartdatacollective.com/bernardmarr/182796/amazon-using-big-data-analytics-read-your-mind.

several thousand dollars, want to be able to see, touch, and even ride the bike before purchase. Almost three-quarters of all bikes are sold in the United States through mass merchandisers (department, discount, and chain toy stores), and local bike shops account for an additional 15% of bike sales. However, according to the National Bicycle Dealers Association, the local bike shops' 14% unit sales are equivalent to 50% of the dollar value of bikes sold in 2013. Fezzari competes primarily with the local bike dealers for sales. By using a consumer-direct, web-based sales model, most Fezzari customers are unable to "kick the tires" before purchase like they can in a mass merchandiser or local bike shop.

Nevertheless, Fezzari's growth has been impressive. Fezzari sold its first bike in 2006 and now sells thousands of bikes each year. The company achieved a 20% year-over-year annual growth rate and is looking to expand its current facility to better service its growing customer base.

Although transactions are typically begun through the company's website, virtually all transactions involve one or more phone calls to gather information from the customer that is needed in the custom-build process. Not only does Fezzari gather body measurements (e.g., height, weight, inseam length, torso length, arm length, etc.), it also asks about the customer's age, the type of riding that the customer plans to do, and injuries that the customer may have experienced that might impact range of motion or flexibility.

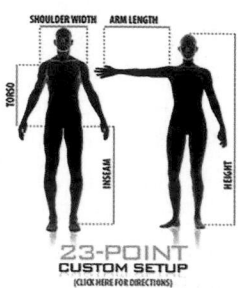

Once the specific bike model and components are selected, Fezzari orders the required parts from its suppliers. A minimal quantity of parts is kept in inventory so that the bike assembly can be started without waiting for the parts to arrive. A technician assembles the bike to the customer's specifications, tunes it up, and then test rides it to ensure that it works properly. A second technician then checks the assembly, testing every screw

and component, then checks the tune, and performs a second test ride. The bike is then sent to packing to be prepared for shipment by a packer. A second packer checks the pack for completeness. The bike is then sent to the shipping bay, where a final check is performed. The assembly and packaging process can take up to 8 to 12 hours for one of Fezzari's high-end bikes, depending on the degree of customization.

The bicycle manufacturing business is seasonal, with sales picking up in the early spring and not slowing down until the early fall. As a result, Fezzari's employee headcount varies from winter to summer, almost doubling from its low point to its high point.[4]

Environmental Business Consultants, LLC—A U.S. Service Firm

Environmental Business Consultants, LLC (EBC) is a fictitious management consulting firm headquartered in Los Angeles, California, based on an actual company. It was formed in 1984 by three individuals who had worked together at one of the large international accounting firms. EBC provides consulting services to the local government market, including cities, counties, and special districts, in the areas of recycling and solid waste and water/wastewater management services.

---

[4] We are grateful to Fezzari Performance Bicycles for providing significant access to its business model and management philosophy. Moreover, the company has given us access to management and many company resources.

In the western United States, most local governments contract with private companies for garbage, recycling, and water services. Wastewater, or sewer, services are often provided by a regional sewer district created by the local governments utilizing the service. In many cases, the local governments do not have the necessary personnel resources or expertise to manage these services effectively. They frequently turn to outside consultants to assist them. These outside consultants include engineering firms, large international and regional accounting firms, and local consulting firms. Competition is fierce and success is largely based on relationships and reputation.

EBC has performed thousands of consulting projects for hundreds of municipal agencies, assisting them with the procurement, management, and delivery of solid waste, water, and wastewater services. With a focus on west coast agencies, EBC offers its clients a breadth of experience coupled with responsiveness, accountability, and personal commitment. EBC has an excellent reputation within its chosen market.

EBC has grown from the three founders and a secretary in 1984 to six owners located in offices in both northern and southern California with a staff of over 30 accountants, economists, engineers, and management consultants.

EBC obtains its client work primarily through requests from clients for whom the firm has worked for many years and also by responding to competitive requests for proposals issued by other municipal agencies. In most instances, EBC will meet with the client to discuss the project and gain an understanding of the client's needs. EBC will then prepare a written proposal outlining a scope of work to be performed for a specified fee. Competitive proposals typically require a presentation of the proposal to the client, where the client has the opportunity to ask questions and discuss the details of the proposed approach.

CAREERS IN MANAGERIAL ACCOUNTING

Alternative Career Paths

LO5
accounting.

Describe career options in managerial

Some college students believe that graduating with a degree in accounting leads to one thing: a career in public accounting, often with one of the "Big 4" accounting firms. This may be particularly true at one of the top 5 or 10 college accounting programs in the United States, because the Big 4 spend considerable time and money recruiting students from these schools. A 2013 study published by the American Institute of Certified Public Accountants reported that just over 61,000 bachelor's and almost 21,000 master's students graduated from accounting degree programs in the United States. Approximately 40,000, or 49%, of these students began their careers in public accounting. Regardless of where they begin their careers, it is clear that most accountants will eventually work as management accountants in industry. The U.S. Bureau of Labor Statistics reports that approximately 75% of all U.S. accountants and auditors work in management accounting and academic roles.[5]

A start in public accounting can be advantageous for some students because of the ongoing training and experience that can be obtained as these graduates are exposed to different companies and business functions. Audit or tax attestation experience is often required to be licensed as a certified public accountant (CPA), as discussed further in the next section. Many students want to be certified as CPAs because they believe this professional designation can open doors for future job opportunities. However, upwards of 90% of those who begin their careers in public accounting will leave public accounting and

---

[5] American Institute of Certified Public Accountants, Inc., 2013 Trends in the Supply of Accounting Graduates and the Demand for Public Accounting Recruits," 2013, http://www.aicpa.org/InterestAreas/AccountingEducation/NewsAndPublications/DownloadableDocuments/2013_TrendsReport.pdf.

join a company in business or industry within a few years of graduation. Thus, the study of managerial accounting is critical for the success of virtually all accountants.

One of the reasons for this migration from public accounting to private industry is the myriad of opportunities for accountants. Accounting careers may be forged in government, public accounting, private business, and academia. Every business, from the small "mom-and-pop" store to the multinational conglomerate, needs the skills and expertise of an accountant. Accountants fill many roles, with titles such as accounting manager, controller, chief financial officer, treasurer, budget analyst, finance director, internal auditor, forensic accountant, environmental accountant, trustee in bankruptcy, Internal Revenue Service (IRS) criminal investigation special agent, tax consultant, small business owner, and management accountant. A management accountant might:

- be involved in evaluating the relative costs and benefits of outsourcing certain elements of a business;

- be involved in evaluating whether to "insource" services that have previously been outsourced;

- conduct an analysis and help management decide whether or not to automate a manufacturing process;

- be part of the team that determines the appropriate level of safety stock and seasonal inventory required to ensure that the company can meet customer demand;

- be part of the team that helps to implement lean manufacturing at the company;

- be charged with analyzing customer profitability by determining which customers should be offered special incentives to increase the size and reduce the frequency of their orders and which customers are unprofitable and should either be dropped or receive a reduced level of customer service, or

- help to develop a program that implements anticipatory shipping, similar to that which is under development by Amazon.

Work/Life Balance

Beginning a career in accounting entails a commitment to client service—although the "clients" may be either internal management or external entities. Because accounting typically involves the reporting of results of operations, accountants are regularly working under a deadline—reports are due by a certain date or within a certain number of days of the end of a period. To make the deadline often requires accountants to work whatever hours are needed, resulting in periods of late nights and weekends from time to time. Certain positions or career choices tend to require more overtime than others, although all accountants should expect to work more than a 40-hour work week on a regular basis. Employees of large accounting firms that audit publicly traded companies typically work an average of 55–60 hours per week. Management-level finance professionals, including management accountants, work an average of 47 hours per week, and non-management finance professionals work an average of 42 hours per week.[6] Government accountants probably have the most reliable work schedules, typically working 40 hours per week.

TAKEAWAY 14.1

Although your college diploma may say "Accounting," your services are not limited to working for accounting firms. An accounting degree is extremely flexible, and will continue to provide value as you progress through the world of business.

---

[6] Thomas Thompson Jr., Financial Executives Research Foundation, Paul McDonald, and Robert Half, *Benchmarking the Finance Function: 2013* (Morristown, NJ: Financial Executives Research Foundation, 2014).

PROFESSIONAL CERTIFICATIONS

Chapter 1 of this text briefly introduced a few of the certifications relevant to the accounting profession. Here we discuss in further detail some of their requirements and benefits.

LO6 Understand differences between various professional certifications available to managerial accountants.

Certified Public Accountant (CPA)

The CPA is the most widely recognized and respected professional accounting certification in the United States. The CPA professional certification has been administered by the American Institute of CPAs (AICPA) or its predecessors since 1887. The AICPA is the largest member association representing the accounting profession. It has more than 412,000 members worldwide. The AICPA administers the CPA exam, a four-part exam that covers Auditing and Attestation, Business Environment and Concepts, Financial Accounting and Reporting, and Regulation.

Passing the CPA exam is only the first step to obtaining a CPA license. Licensure is handled by each of the 55 State/Territory Boards of Accountancy. Licensure requirements vary slightly from state to state; however, most states require 150 hours of college credit plus a year or more of real-world work experience. Once licensed, CPAs are required to follow a strict Professional Code of Conduct and to complete a certain number of hours of continuing professional education.

Certified Management Accountant (CMA)

The CMA is a professional certification administered by the Institute of Management Accountants (IMA) intended to indicate a level of knowledge and proficiency with accounting and financial management skills, including financial planning, analysis, control, decision support, and professional ethics. CMA candidates are required to hold a bachelor's degree from an accredited college or university, hold membership in the IMA, pass a two-part exam, and have at least two continuous years of professional experience in management accounting or financial management. The exam consists of two four-hour parts, with Part 1 covering Financial Reporting, Planning, Performance, and Control and Part 2 covering Financial Decision Making.

The IMA reports that in 2013 more than 40,000 professionals held the CMA certificate. According to a 2013 IMA salary survey, professionals who have earned the CMA earn almost $36,000 more in average annual compensation than noncertified peers.

Other Professional Certifications

There are numerous other professional certifications that indicate specialized skill or experience. These include certified fraud examiner, certified financial planner, certified internal auditor, and enrolled agent.

Exhibit 14-1 shows the URL where you can find additional information regarding each of these professional certifications.

Exhibit 14-1	Information Regarding Professional Certifications
Certified Public Accountant	www.aicpa.org
Certified Management Accountant	www.imanet.org
Certified Fraud Examiner	www.acfe.com
Certified Financial Planner	www.cfp.net
Certified Internal Auditor	https://na.theiia.org
Enrolled Agent	www.irs.gov/Tax-Professionals/Enrolled-Agent/Enrolled-Agent-Information

SUMMARY OF LEARNING OBJECTIVES

LO1   Define managerial accounting and describe its objectives. (p. 696)

- Managerial accounting focuses on internal decision making.
- Managerial accounting utilizes both financial and operational information.
- Managerial accounting provides information that is timely, relevant, decision-useful, and in a format that is easily accessible to management.
- Management accountants partner with personnel to plan, manage, and make strategic business decisions.

LO2   Describe the three types of business entities. (p. 697)

- Manufacturing firms convert materials into finished products.
- Merchandising firms purchase finished products from manufacturers for warehousing, display, and sale to consumers.
- Service firms are companies that perform services for customers.

LO3   Discuss major trends in business and managerial accounting. (p. 698)

- Outsourcing occurs when a business hires or contracts with another business to provide a product or service that had previously been provided within the business with the objective of reducing cost and allowing the business to focus on its core competencies.
- Stand-alone automation of a factory incorporates a robot or computer-controlled machine into an existing manufacturing process. Flexible-manufacturing-system automation of a factory operation involves the use of multiple cells of two or more automated machines. Each cell produces a product from start to finish.
- Traditional manufacturing inventories are used as buffers against unforeseen delays.
- Just-in-time inventory systems (rather than just-in-case inventory systems) minimize the amount of inventory that is on hand.
- Lean manufacturing focuses on the flow of the entire production process and uses customer demand to "pull" the product through production, thereby reducing setup times and inventory costs.
- Managerial accounting can help companies distinguish between high-demand and low-demand customers relative to their cost of service. This allows them to focus on ways to increase customer profitability.
- The development of new and faster ways of analyzing the data trail that customers leave behind following every online search, purchase, and social media interaction is allowing companies of all sizes to anticipate customers' desires and customize company products and services to better meet those needs.

LO4   Describe the important characteristics of two companies used throughout the remainder of the book to illustrate key concepts and processes. (p. 701)

- Fezzari is a manufacturer and distributor of bikes.
- Fezzari primarily sells direct to the customer through web-based transactions.
- Environmental Business Consultants (EBC) is a fictitious management consulting firm.
- EBC provides services to local government clients in California.

LO5   Describe career options in managerial accounting. (p. 703)

- Careers in managerial accounting might lead to or include titles such as management accountant, accounting manager, controller, chief financial officer, treasurer, budget analyst, finance director, internal auditor, forensic accountant, environmental accountant, trustee in bankruptcy, IRS criminal investigation special agent, tax consultant, and small business owner.
- Almost 90% of those accountants who begin their careers in public accounting will leave for a position in business or industry.

LO6   Understand differences between various professional certifications available to managerial accountants. (p. 705)

- The CPA is the most widely recognized and respected professional accounting certification in the United States.
- The CPA is administered by the American Institute of Certified Public Accountants (AICPA).
- The CMA is a professional certification intended to indicate a level of knowledge and proficiency with accounting and financial management skills, including financial planning, analysis, control, decision support, and professional ethics.
- The CMA is administered by the Institute of Management Accountants (IMA).
- There are numerous other professional certifications that indicate specialized skill or experience.

KEY TERMS

Financial accounting (p. 696)

Flexible-manufacturing-system
  automation (p. 699)

Just-in-case inventories (p. 699)

Just-in-time (JIT) inventory systems (p. 699)

Lean manufacturing (p. 700)

Managerial accounting (p. 696)

Manufacturing cell (p. 699)

Manufacturing firms (p. 697)

Merchandising firms (p. 697)

Outsourcing (p. 698)

Safety stocks (p. 699)

Service firms (p. 697)

Stand-alone automation (p. 699)

Assignments with the ⓜ logo in the margin are available in BusinessCourse.
See the Preface of the book for details.

SELF-STUDY QUESTIONS

(Answers to Self-Study Questions are at the end of this chapter.)

1. **Which of the following group of terms best describes the role of managerial accounting?** LO1
    a. Internal decision-making, future-focused
    b. Internal decision-making, past-focused
    c. External reporting, future-focused
    d. External reporting, past-focused

2. **A company that sells finished products that it has acquired from a manufacturer to consumers is a** LO2
    a. Manufacturer
    b. Merchandiser
    c. Service firm

3. **What business model does Fezzari follow to sell its products to its customers?** LO4
    a. Sales through local bike shops.
    b. Sales through large mass merchandisers.
    c. Sales direct to customers through web-based orders.
    d. Sales of bike components to other bike manufacturers.

4. **Approximately what percentage of accountants who begin their careers in public accounting will
    leave for positions in businesses and corporations?** LO5
    a. 50%
    b. 75%
    c. 90%
    d. 95%

5. **Which of the following is the professional certification intended to indicate a level of knowledge
    and proficiency with accounting and financial management skills, including financial planning,
    analysis, control, decision support, and professional ethics?** LO6
    a. CPA
    b. CMA
    c. CFE
    d. CIA

QUESTIONS

1. How does managerial accounting differ from financial accounting? LO1
2. Which type of accounting would produce reports relevant to stockholders? LO1
3. Name the three types of business entities and briefly describe the nature of each. LO2
4. In what way do manufacturing firms and merchandising firms work together to provide end consumers
    with products? LO2
5. Pick any large company and identify which type of business entity it is. LO2
6. Describe a manufacturing cell and contrast a cell to the equipment arrangement in a traditional manufac- LO3
    turing operation.

15

Managerial Accounting Concepts and Cost Flows

PAST

Chapter 14 introduced managerial accounting. It explored career opportunities in managerial accounting, its objectives, and professional certifications for managerial accountants.

PRESENT

Chapter 15 defines basic costing terminology and introduces different types of manufacturing inventories. It illustrates how costs flow through the inventories and explains the schedule of cost of goods manufactured.

FUTURE

Chapter 16 introduces and explains job costing in more detail for both manufacturing and service industries. It also explains overhead allocation.

LEARNING OBJECTIVES

1. **Identify** the key objectives of a managerial accounting system and **define** product costs and period costs; variable, fixed, and mixed costs; direct and indirect costs; and cost control. *(p. 712)*

2. **Describe** the three manufacturing inventories—materials, work in process, and finished goods—and **discuss** the categories of manufacturing costs and how these costs flow among the inventories and cost of goods sold. *(p. 716)*

3. **Define** total manufacturing costs, cost of goods manufactured, and cost of goods sold, and **illustrate** the schedule of cost of goods manufactured and sold and the income statement. *(p. 723)*

4. **Illustrate** the journal entries to record product cost flows using a perpetual inventory system. *(p. 727)*

APPLE INC.: INNOVATIVE CONSUMER ELECTRONICS

In Chapter 4, we reviewed the classified financial statements and key ratios for **Apple Inc.** In this chapter, we will revisit Apple from the perspective of a manager and think about basic costing terminology and cost flows throughout the company.

At 37 years old, Apple Inc. is the world's second largest information technology company by sales revenue ($264 billion in 2015)[1] and the largest publicly traded corporation by market capitalization ($608 billion in 2015).[2] Although it started as a seller of personal computers (PCs), it has expanded its products to include consumer electronics, consumer software, and commercial servers. Apple's PC line includes the Mac computer and the iPad tablet. It added a consumer electronics line, which includes the iPod music player and the iPhone smartphone. Its consumer software line includes the OS X and iOS operating systems, the iTunes media browser, the Safari web browser, and iLife and iWork creativity and production software.

How did Apple grow from a garage-based start-up to overtake companies like Commodore, Tandy, IBM, Microsoft, Sun Microsystems and Xerox? There is no single answer to that question, and many books have been written describing Apple's growth and success. Talented, creative leaders and employees provided the vision. Certainly, innovative products designed with the consumer experience in mind were critical. So too were strategic alliances with Intel for processors and EMI for digital music titles, not to mention the purchase of numerous companies to acquire their technology and software.

Perhaps equally important to Apple's success was the development of management processes and approaches, such as assigning a "directly responsible individual" for each project, an efficient and effective supply chain, and the strategic creation of international subsidiaries to minimize the amount of taxes paid. Each of these management processes and approaches has one element in common—the need for detailed financial and other business information. Without this information, Apple would not be able to compensate its employees fairly, price its products competitively, or determine an appropriate price to pay for new technology companies. The development and maintenance of this information is largely the responsibility of management accountants, who use managerial accounting systems to capture, summarize, and report critical data to be used in making strategic business decisions.

---

[1] 2015 Apple Form 10-K.

[2] https://ycharts.com/companies/AAPL/market_cap

| MANAGERIAL ACCOUNTING CONCEPTS AND COST FLOWS |

Objectives of a Managerial Accounting System	**Inventories and Cost Categories**	**Product Cost Flows**	**Illustration of Product Cost Accumulation**
• Product costing in a manufacturing environment • Product costing in a service and merchandising environment • Cost control	• Inventories • Manufacturing product cost categories	• Raw materials • Labor • Manufacturing overhead • Cost of goods manufactured • Cost of goods sold	• Introduction of T-accounts • Schedule of cost of goods manufactured • Calculating cost of goods sold • Income statement for a manufacturing firm • Illustration of product cost journal entries

KEY OBJECTIVES OF A MANAGERIAL ACCOUNTING SYSTEM

Business operations vary widely in complexity. However, all managerial accounting systems have the objective of providing management with financial and other business information that is useful in analyzing and making business decisions.

LO1 **Identify** the key objectives of a managerial accounting system and **define** product costs and period costs; variable, fixed, and mixed costs; direct and indirect costs; and cost control.

Hint: A cost object is anything to which costs may be traced. Examples for Apple include everything from an mp3 file to a tablet PC to a service department.

Product Costing in a Manufacturing Environment

Business managers need information about the cost of their products and services in order to control costs and set prices that will result in a profit to the owners and provide the ability to grow the business. For example, Apple is clearly interested in knowing its costs and market share for its manufactured products (such as the iPhone and the iPad) for determining merchandise prices.

Product costing involves accumulating and allocating the costs of all inputs in the manufacturing or acquisition process to individual products. The individual products represent a type of **cost object**, which may be anything for which business managers must determine a cost. The manufacturer must know its product costs in order to measure inventory values and calculate the profitability of its products for reporting on its financial statements. Using product costing information, management can also determine which products to continue producing and which products to drop. This chapter introduces product costing.

Product versus Period Costs

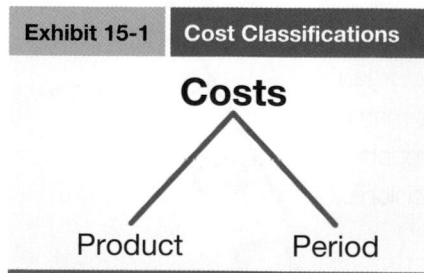

| Exhibit 15-1 | Cost Classifications |

Exhibit 15-1 indicates that costs can be classified into two broad categories for companies that sell products. **Product costs** include all costs necessary to bring a product to completion, regardless of the period in which they are incurred. For a manufacturer, product costs include material and components, human labor, utilities, and the use of factory assets. These costs are all recorded initially in inventory accounts.

Period costs are expensed in the period incurred and not assigned to products. The benefits associated with these costs are assumed to expire in the period incurred rather than in the period in which the product is sold. For manufacturers, selling expenses and non-factory administrative expenses are considered period costs. These are reported on the income statement. Some departments in a manufacturing firm, such as personnel, may benefit both factory and non-factory activities. The costs of these departments are therefore partly product cost and partly period cost.

Exhibit 15-2 presents Apple's partial income statement for its 2014 fiscal year, illustrating its product and period costs:

Exhibit 15-2	Apple's Partial Income Statement		
APPLE INC. **Income Statement** **For the Year Ended September 27, 2014** **(in $millions)**			
Sales.			$182,795
Cost of goods sold *(Product costs)*			112,258
Gross profit on sales.			$ 70,537
Operating expenses *(Period costs)*			
Selling, general and administrative expenses		$11,993	
Research and development		6,041	18,034
Income from operations			$ 52,503

Variable, Fixed, and Mixed Costs

Another way to classify costs that can be helpful to decision makers is to classify them based on their behavior (see **Exhibit 15-3**). A **variable cost** is a cost that *varies in total but is fixed per unit* for a certain period of time and range of activity. In total, variable costs change proportionately with changes in the volume of activity. The cost of a microprocessor chip used in an iPad and the hourly wage paid to the iPad assembly employees are variable costs. To illustrate, assume the cost of the microprocessor chip used in producing one Apple iPad is approximately $30. If Apple produces 100,000 iPads during a period, the total cost of the chips used would be $3,000,000. Alternatively, if Apple produces 1,000,000 iPads, the total cost of the chips would be $30,000,000, still $30 per iPad. In **Exhibit 15-4**, total variable costs increase by $30 for each additional iPad produced. Yet, the cost per iPad is a constant $30 per unit.

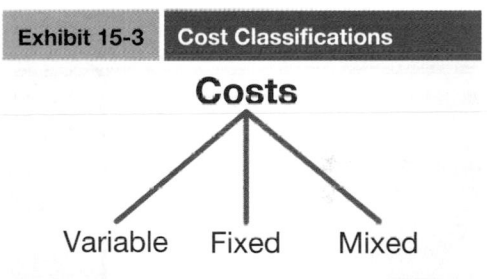

Exhibit 15-3	Cost Classifications

Costs

Variable   Fixed   Mixed

A **fixed cost** is *fixed in total but variable on a per-unit basis* for a particular period of time and range of activity. Fixed costs do not change when the volume of activity changes. Examples are depreciation on buildings and property taxes. Assume that the depreciation on the iPad manufacturing facility is $5 million per month, as shown in **Exhibit 15-4**. If only 100,000 iPads are produced in a month, the depreciation per unit is $50. If 1,000,000 iPads are produced, the depreciation per unit is $5. As we will discuss later, making decisions based on fixed costs per unit can be problematic.

Mixed costs—sometimes called **semi-variable costs**—have both fixed and variable components. A mixed cost changes linearly with changes in activity, but there is still a positive cost when the activity level is zero, as shown in **Exhibit 15-4**. As an example of a mixed cost, consider Apple's utility expense at the factory that produces the iPad. Assume that even if Apple shuts down production for one month, it still incurs a minimum amount for utilities, say $200,000. When production resumes, the costs of heating, air conditioning, lighting, and water increase with usage as production increases. We discuss

A.K.A. Mixed costs are sometimes called semi-variable costs as they have both fixed and variable components.

Hint: The classification of costs into these three distinct groups can often be more difficult than it may appear at first glance.

how to determine the variable and fixed portions of a mixed cost in Chapter 19. **Exhibit 15-4** presents a graphic illustration of these three different types of costs.

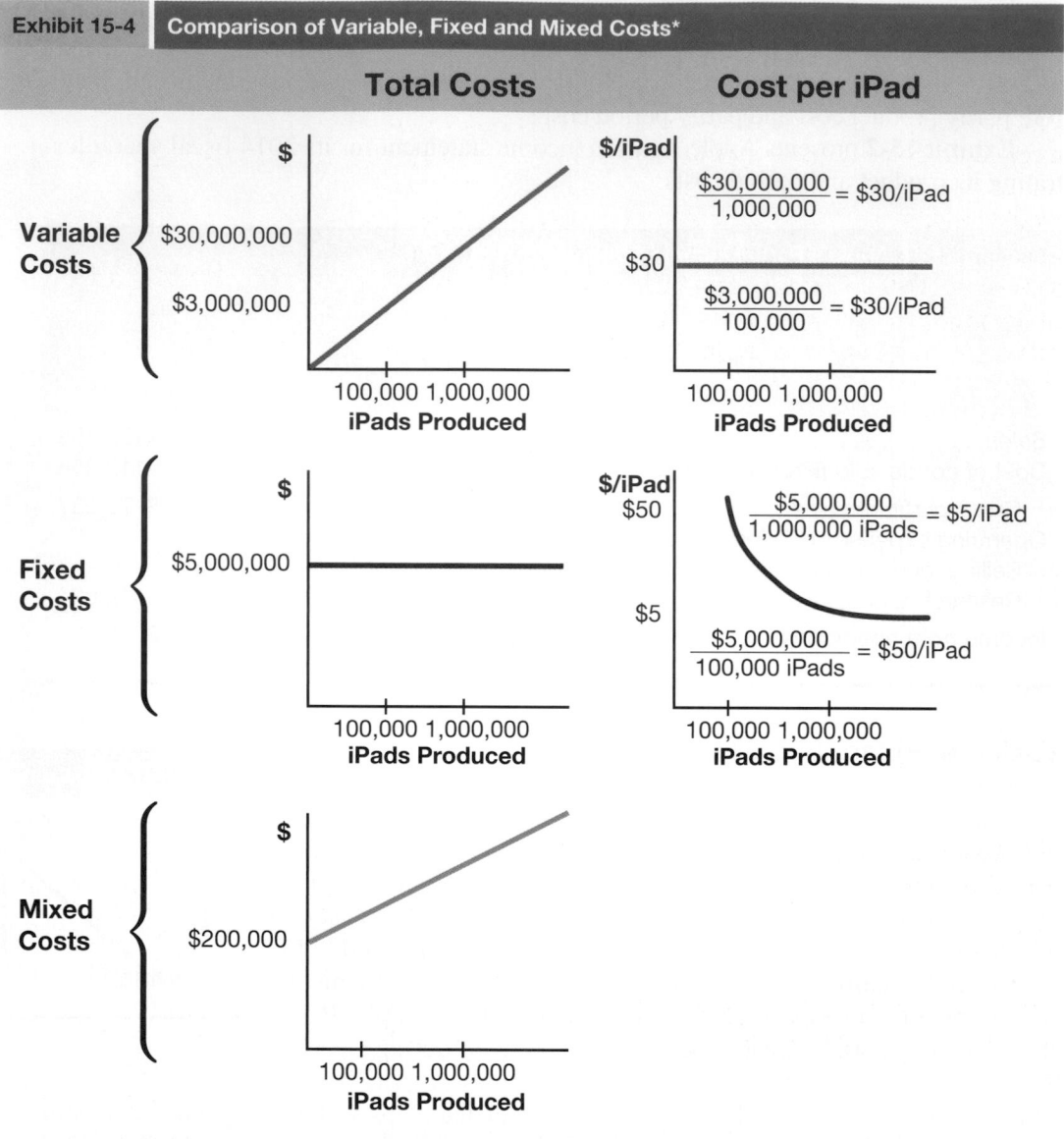

Exhibit 15-4	Comparison of Variable, Fixed and Mixed Costs*

*Assumes all costs are linear

Product costs may be variable (direct material and direct labor), fixed (some overhead costs such as depreciation on assets employed in producing the good or service), or mixed (some overhead costs such as utilities).

Direct and Indirect Costs

Finally, costs can also be classified as *direct* or *indirect* costs (see **Exhibit 15-5**). A **direct cost** is a cost that can be easily and cost-effectively traced to a specific cost object, such as a unit of product. In a manufacturing company, two obvious direct costs are the main materials and labor used to produce a unit of product. However, other costs may be directly traced as well. For example, in determining the cost of an iPad, Apple would attempt to trace as many costs as possible directly to each iPad unit.

Clearly, the main materials such as the liquid crystal display (LCD) screen and the microprocessor and the labor involved in assembly would be traced directly to each iPad. However, in a highly automated process, it is possible that Apple could also trace some robotic assembly costs directly to each iPad.

An **indirect cost**, therefore, is a cost that cannot be easily and cost-effectively traced to a specific cost object. If Apple were interested in the cost of one of the thousands of products shipped from one of its warehouses, the depreciation expense for that warehouse would be an indirect cost, because it is not easily traced to any one unit of product that passes through the warehouse. It would be considered a common cost for all products of the warehouse. As noted in the previous examples, a particular cost may be considered direct or indirect, depending on the cost object.

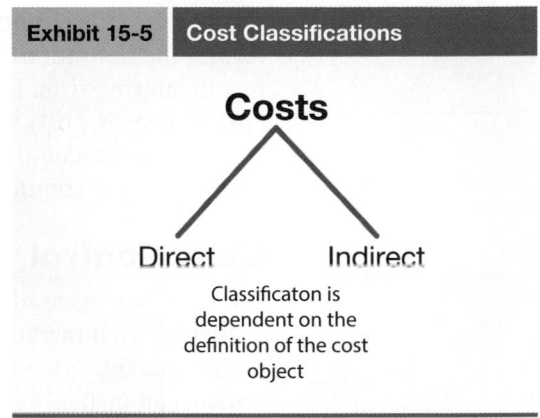

| Exhibit 15-5 | Cost Classifications |

Costs

Direct   Indirect

Classificaton is dependent on the definition of the cost object

---

YOUR TURN! 15.1

The solution is on page 748.

Which of the following would be considered a direct cost of an iPad? (Choose all that apply.)

Assembly labor
iPad case
CEO salary
Microprocessor
Depreciation on Apple corporate headquarters
Health insurance for factory workers
Touch-screen
Adhesive on the serial number label

Product Costing in a Service and Merchandising Environment

SERVICE AND MERCHANDISING

Product versus Period Costs

Like manufacturers, service firms need to understand the cost of providing their services to customers. Although these firms do not produce a tangible product, they must know the cost of their services to determine the proper fee for those services and ensure a return to their owners. Service firms may include labor and other directly traceable costs in determining the **cost of jobs or projects**. Merchandising companies record the cost of acquired inventory as a product cost, whereas items such as salaries and wages, utilities, and depreciation are recorded immediately as operating expenses.

Service firms expense **period costs** in the period the costs are incurred. The benefits associated with these costs are assumed to expire in the period incurred rather than in the period in which the product is sold. Like manufacturers, selling expenses and non-factory administrative expenses are considered period costs.

Variable, Fixed, and Mixed Costs

The definitions of variable, fixed, and mixed costs are the same for service and merchandise firms as those given previously for manufacturers. An example of a variable cost in a consulting firm would be office supplies expense, which would increase with the number of consulting projects performed. The consulting firm's office lease expense would be considered a fixed cost because it would not vary with the number of projects performed. The firm's contribution to the employee 401(k) profit-sharing retirement plan would be a mixed cost assuming that the plan required a minimum contribution of 3%, and that additional contributions would be made based on the level of profit earned in a year.

Direct and Indirect Costs

Again, the definitions of direct and indirect costs are the same as given previously for a manufacturing firm. In a service company, wages or salaries are the most common direct cost. However, costs such as photocopying, postage, and travel can be traced to a particular job. Service companies would typically consider marketing costs and costs associated with employee continuing education classes as indirect costs.

Cost Control

Business managers also need information that will assist them in competing effectively in their chosen market. As information becomes more easily available to customers in a global market, price competition can become more intense. For example, because customers can instantly compare prices for products and services on their smartphones, tablets, and computers, businesses might have little or no control over the prices that they can charge. Therefore, business managers must control their costs to ensure a reasonable profit. **Cost control** involves the accumulation of information to measure management performance and evaluate operational efficiency. Subsequent chapters present cost control approaches and techniques that are used by businesses of all types. For example, Chapter 22 illustrates how business managers use budgets to evaluate actual versus expected performance. Chapter 23 introduces the use of standard costs as a way of identifying where and why operations deviate from management's expectations.

INVENTORIES AND COST CATEGORIES

Inventories

LO2 **Describe** the three manufacturing inventories—materials, work in process, and finished goods—and **discuss** the categories of manufacturing costs and how these costs flow among the inventories and cost of goods sold.

Manufacturing Firms

At any point in time, manufacturing operations typically have units of product at various stages of completion. Three inventories are usually maintained on a perpetual basis to reflect these stages—materials, work in process, and finished goods.

The **materials inventory** includes factory materials and components that have been purchased but not yet placed into production. Some of the items in the materials inventory, such as sheets of steel or microprocessors, were finished products to the supplying company but are materials and components to the purchasing company. All items in the materials inventory account are recorded at their net delivered cost (i.e., product cost plus in-bound shipping).

The **work in process inventory** of a manufacturing firm includes units of product that have been placed in production but have not yet been completed. All the costs of material and components, direct human labor, utilities, and use of factory assets (overhead costs) are included in the work in process inventory. All items in the work in process inventory account are recorded at cost.

The **finished goods inventory** of a manufacturing firm includes all units of product that have been completed but have not been sold. All items in the finished goods inventory account were recorded at cost in the work in process inventory account and transferred to the finished goods inventory account.

Many manufacturing firms also maintain an inventory of factory and office supplies for the manufacturing operation. **Factory supplies** are consumable items, such as cleaning supplies and machinery lubricants, used in the factory but not incorporated into the product; **office supplies** include copy paper, toner, and paper clips, items used in the office but not charged to a particular job. The inventory of factory and office supplies is usually maintained on a periodic basis, so the cost of factory and office supplies used during a period is determined at period-end after the supplies on hand are counted.

Merchandising and Service Firms

Merchandising firms have only one inventory account—merchandise inventory. This is similar to the finished goods inventory account at a manufacturer because it contains finished products that are available for immediate sale. As discussed previously, manufacturing firms usually have three primary inventory accounts: materials, work in process, and finished goods.

Service firms typically have only one inventory account—work in process inventory. This account represents the service firm's partially completed projects. Service firms would include the cost of direct labor and overhead in work in process inventory. Although service firms may utilize office supplies on their projects, these costs are usually immaterial and not considered a materials inventory. Because completed projects are billed to the customer immediately upon completion, there is no need for a finished goods inventory. These inventories are reported in the current assets section of the balance sheet, as illustrated in **Exhibit 15-6**.

Exhibit 15-6	Comparison of Merchandising, Service, and Manufacturing Inventories				
Merchandising Firm		**Service Firm**		**Manufacturing Firm**	
Cash	$ 10,000	Cash	$ 10,000	Cash	$ 10,000
Short-term investments . .	20,000	Short-term investments . .	20,000	Short-term investments . .	20,000
Receivables	45,000	Receivables	45,000	Receivables	45,000
Merchandise inventory . . .	80,000	Work in process inventory	80,000	Inventories:	
Prepaid expenses.	15,000	Prepaid expenses.	15,000	Materials	35,000
Total current assets	$170,000	Office supplies	5,000	Work in process	55,000
		Total current assets	$175,000	Finished goods	25,000
				Prepaid expenses.	15,000
				Factory supplies	5,000
				Total current assets	$210,000

Factory Supplies versus Indirect Materials

Factory supplies are different from indirect materials. Factory supplies are used in the factory but are not part of the product itself. Lubricant used on the machine that stamps the sheet metal used in a laptop computer would be a factory supply. Indirect materials are part of the product, but are difficult to trace to each individual product. Solder used to attach computer chips to a motherboard would be an indirect material. Both factory supplies and indirect materials can become part of manufacturing overhead.

Manufacturing Product Cost Categories

Product costs in a manufacturing setting can be classified into three subcategories (see **Exhibit 15-7**):

1. **Direct materials** include all of the important materials and components that physically make up the product (such as sheets of steel and electric motors). Incidental material items, such as glue and fasteners, are considered **indirect materials** and are included in manufacturing overhead. Both direct material items and indirect material items are included in the materials inventory. Therefore, all items in the materials inventory will be used as either direct material or indirect material.

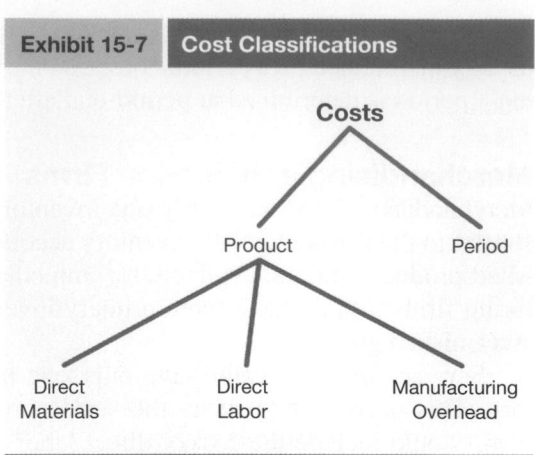

Exhibit 15-7 | **Cost Classifications**

Hint: "Manufacturing product costs" include all direct materials, direct labor, and manufacturing overhead for a period of time and represent the additions to work in process inventory. "Manufacturing costs" should not be confused with "manufacturing overhead costs," although both terms have the word "manufacturing" in them.

2. **Direct labor** includes the salary and wage cost of factory employees who work directly on the product (such as machine operators, assemblers, and painters). The salary and wage cost of factory employees who do not work directly on the product (such as supervisors, inspectors, and material handlers) is considered **indirect labor**, which is included in manufacturing overhead. The total amount of factory labor (direct and indirect) is identified on a manufacturing firm's factory payroll.

Apple Inc. Corporate Headquarters

iPad Factory

A.K.A. Manufacturing overhead has several other names that are commonly used in practice, such as **factory overhead**, factory burden, or indirect manufacturing costs.

3. **Manufacturing overhead** consists of all manufacturing costs not included in direct material and direct labor. Manufacturing overhead includes indirect material, indirect labor, factory supplies used, factory payroll tax and fringe benefits costs, factory utilities, and factory building and machinery costs (such as depreciation, insurance, property taxes, and repairs and maintenance). Manufacturing overhead specifically *excludes* selling and non-factory administrative expenses because these expenses are not incurred in the manufacturing process.

YOUR TURN! 15.2

The solution is on page 748.

Which of the following would be considered a manufacturing cost of an iPad? (Choose all that apply.)

    Assembly labor
    Sales-force salary
    Factory supervisor salary
    Depreciation on the iPad factory
    Depreciation on Apple corporate headquarters
    Health insurance for corporate finance employees
    Touch-screen

Combined Costs

Manufacturing Firms

Manufacturing cost categories are frequently combined for convenience. As illustrated in **Exhibit 15-8**, the sum of direct material and direct labor for a particular product is known as prime cost. **Prime cost** is made up of the elements of product cost that are easily and directly traceable to individual products. **Conversion cost** is the sum of direct labor and manufacturing overhead. Conversion cost represents the elements of product cost necessary to convert the materials and components to the final finished products.

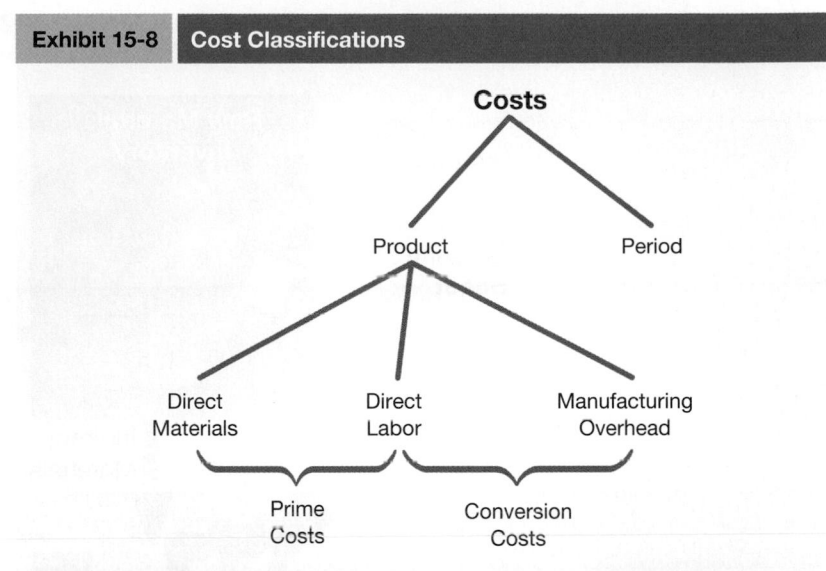

| Exhibit 15-8 | Cost Classifications |

Service Firms

Prime cost and conversion cost can also apply to a service firm. A service firm's prime cost is limited to direct labor cost (because no direct materials are typically used). A service firm's conversion cost is the sum of direct labor and applied general overhead.

Although Apple is not primarily a service firm, it has a technical support department that assists customers with hardware and software questions that arise in the normal operation of Apple products. Prime costs for the technical support department would simply include the wages and salaries of support personnel because the service department would have no direct materials. Conversion costs for the technical support department would include both the wages and salaries of support personnel in addition to overhead costs such as depreciation on office equipment, employee health insurance premiums, the costs associated with janitorial services, and utilities.

SERVICE AND MERCHANDISING

PRODUCT COST FLOWS

Raw Materials

The materials inventory frequently contains both direct and indirect materials. As direct materials are used in production, they are traced directly to specific units of product. Thus, the cost of direct materials flows from raw materials inventory directly into work in process inventory. On the other hand, indirect materials cannot be traced to particular units of product. As a result, as they are used in the production process, their cost is transferred from raw materials inventory to manufacturing overhead. For example, it may not be cost effective for Apple to trace the cost of screws to each iPad. As a result, screws are likely classified as indirect materials and their cost would be transferred from raw materials inventory to manufacturing overhead as they are used in production. Overhead costs are then allocated (applied) to particular jobs. **Exhibit 15-9a** illustrates the flow of both direct and indirect materials from raw materials inventory to the work in process and manufacturing overhead, respectively.

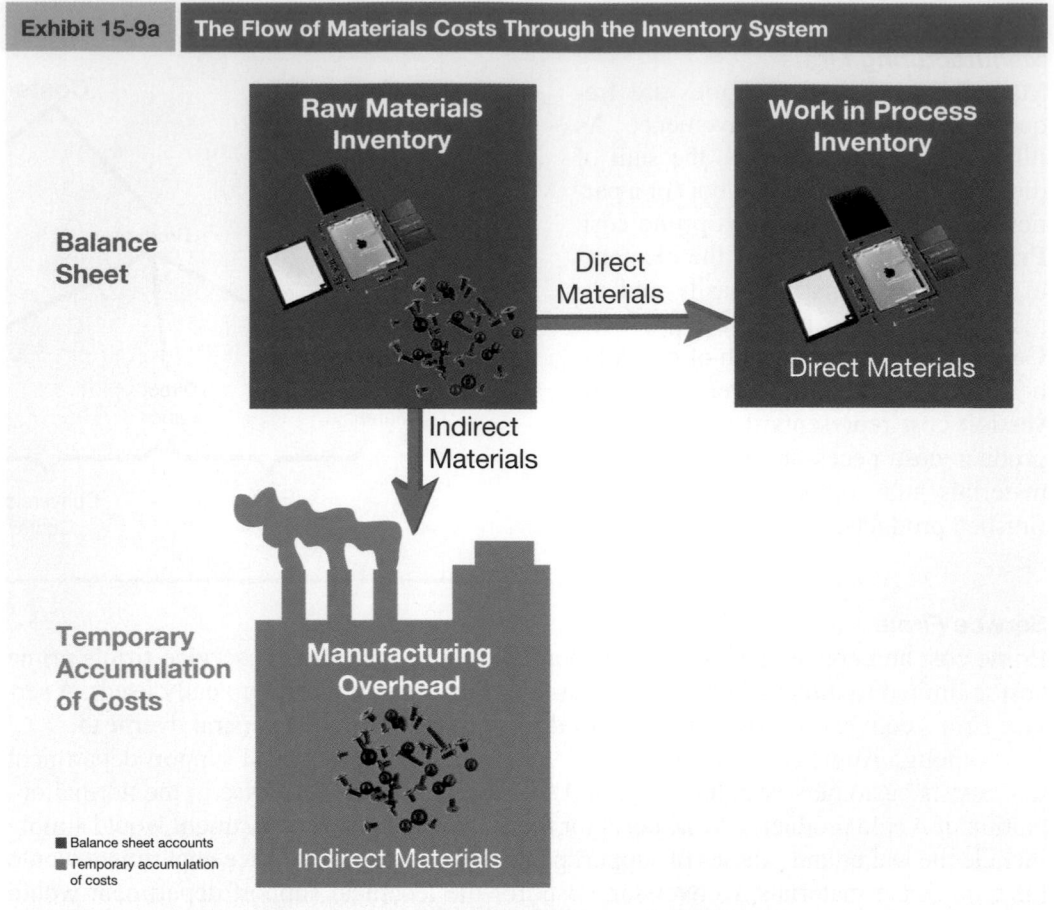

Exhibit 15-9a The Flow of Materials Costs Through the Inventory System

Labor

Both direct and indirect labor costs are incurred in the manufacturing process. The wages of employees who work directly on units of product are traced directly to specific units. Therefore, when these labor costs are incurred, they are recorded in work in process inventory. On the other hand, the wages of factory employees not working directly on the product cannot be traced directly to particular units. They are recorded as manufacturing overhead and allocated to jobs based on a predetermined overhead application rate. In the iPad manufacturing facility, the costs of employees directly involved in the assembly of iPads are recorded directly in work in process inventory. On the other hand, the salaries and wages of supervisors, maintenance personnel, and quality inspectors in the iPad factory would be classified as indirect labor and recorded as manufacturing overhead. **Exhibit 15-9b** illustrates how both direct and indirect labor flow into work in process and manufacturing overhead, respectively.

| Exhibit 15-9b | The Flow of Labor Costs Through the Inventory System |

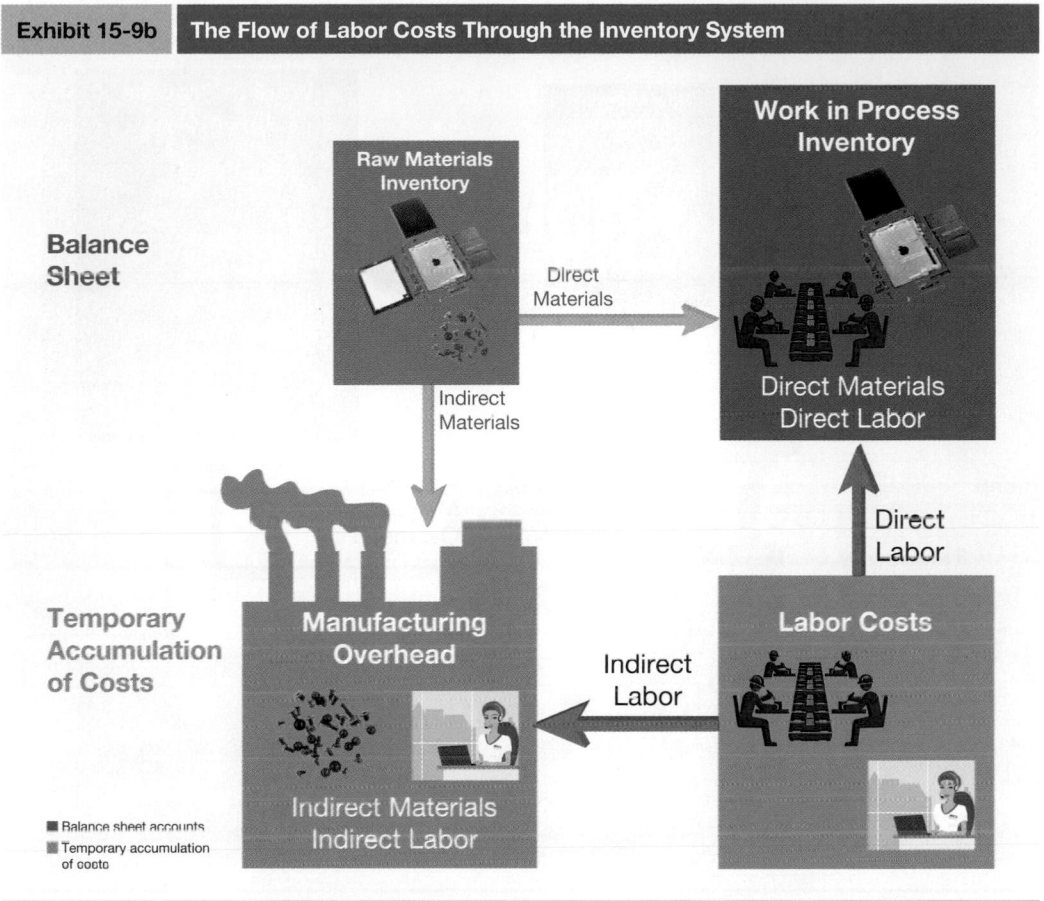

Manufacturing Overhead

Because overhead costs are, by definition, indirect costs that can not be traced to a particular unit of product, they are accumulated in manufacturing overhead during the accounting period. Indirect materials and indirect labor are just two examples of indirect costs accumulated in manufacturing overhead. Other examples include costs that cannot be traced to a particular unit of product, such as depreciation on the factory and factory equipment, factory utilities, insurance on production facilities, property taxes related to the factory, and so forth. The problem accountants face is that it is impossible to know with certainty how much manufacturing overhead will accumulate during a particular period. Rather than waiting until the end of the period to divide the actual manufacturing overhead costs by the number of units actually produced to allocate the costs to jobs passing through the production process, accountants use their knowledge from past periods to calculate an estimated overhead rate at the beginning of the period to allocate overhead to jobs as they pass through the production process. We discuss the process for estimating and allocating manufacturing overhead in more detail in Chapter 16. However, **Exhibit 15-9c** illustrates the flow of overhead costs from manufacturing overhead to the work in process inventory.

Hint: Actual indirect costs are recorded on the debit side of the manufacturing overhead account, whereas overhead applied to units produced is recorded on the credit side because overhead is allocated to jobs (in the work in process inventory account).

| Exhibit 15-9c | The Flow of Manufacturing Overhead Costs Through the Inventory System |

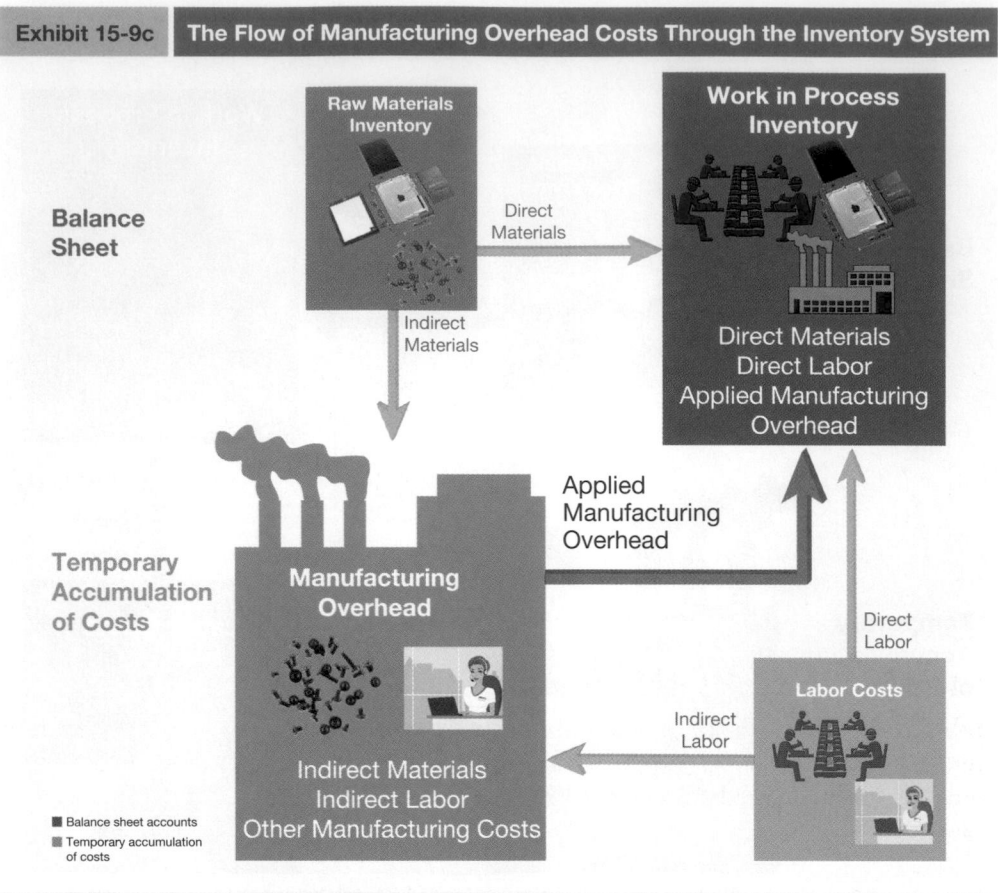

Cost of Goods Manufactured

Total manufacturing costs consist of direct materials, direct labor, and manufacturing overhead. **Exhibit 15-9d** summarizes how all of these costs flow into work in process inventory.

The product costs that flow from work in process to the finished goods during an accounting period are known as **cost of goods manufactured (COGM)**. The schedule of cost of goods manufactured (which we demonstrate in the next section) summarizes all of the different costs incurred in the production of inventory: (1) direct materials, (2) labor costs, and (3) manufacturing overhead. All of these costs flow into work in process inventory. The total cost of goods manufactured is transferred to finished goods inventory, as illustrated in **Exhibit 15-9e**.

| Exhibit 15-9d | The Flow of Total Manufacturing Costs Through the Inventory System |

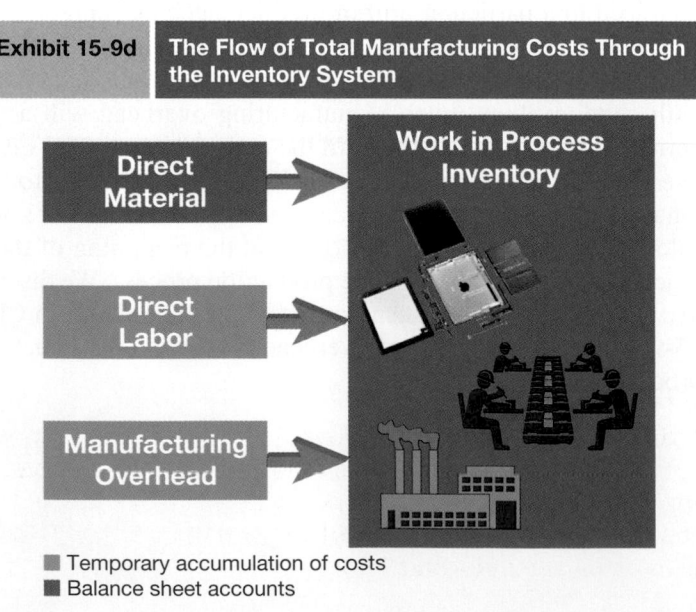

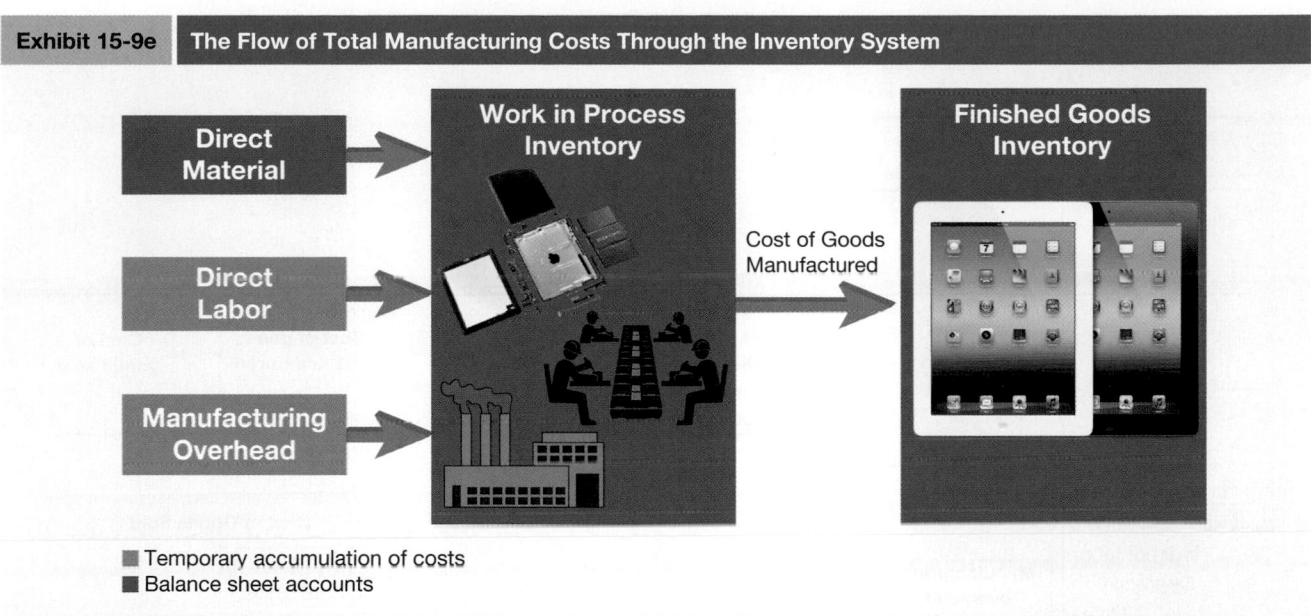

Exhibit 15-9e | The Flow of Total Manufacturing Costs Through the Inventory System

■ Temporary accumulation of costs
■ Balance sheet accounts

Cost of Goods Sold

Exhibit 15-9f illustrates the flow of all product costs through the inventory system of a manufacturing firm. All costs that are accumulated in work in process eventually flow to finished goods and, when the products are sold, are recognized as **cost of goods sold (COGS)**.

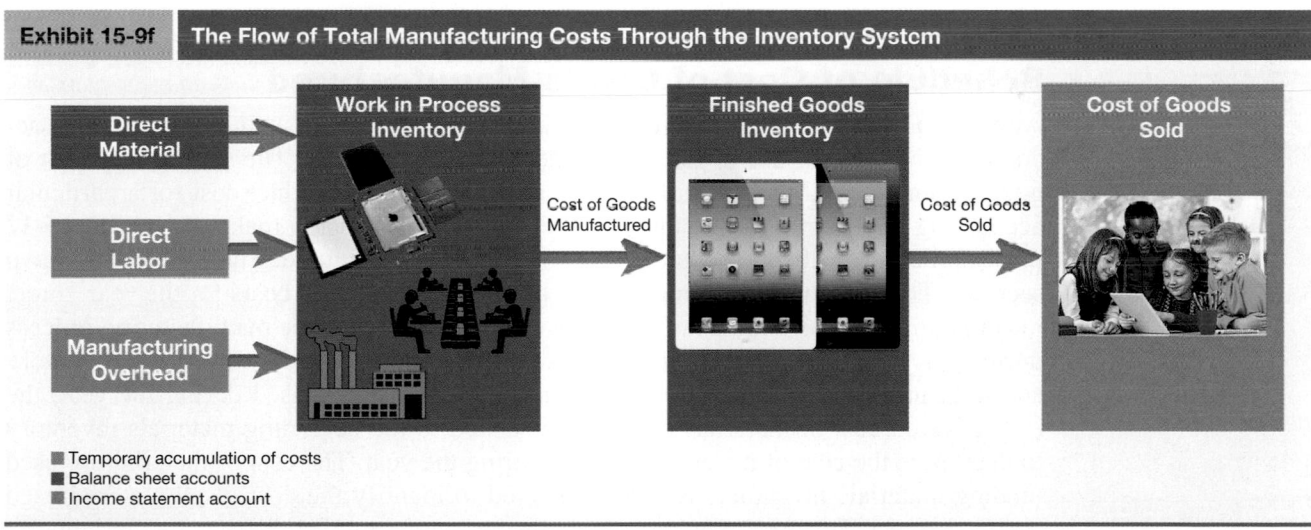

Exhibit 15-9f | The Flow of Total Manufacturing Costs Through the Inventory System

■ Temporary accumulation of costs
■ Balance sheet accounts
■ Income statement account

ILLUSTRATION OF PRODUCT COST ACCUMULATION

Introduction of T-Accounts

Exhibit 15-9f illustrates the flow of all product costs through the inventory accounts. As you learn in financial accounting, each account can be represented by a T-account, which is a visual illustration of the flow of dollars into and out of the account. **Exhibit 15-10** illustrates the T-accounts associated with each item in **Exhibit 15-9f**.

LO3 Define total manufacturing costs, cost of goods manufactured, and cost of goods sold, and **illustrate** the schedule of cost of goods manufactured and sold and the income statement.

Exhibit 15-10	The Flow of Total Manufacturing Costs Through the Inventory Accounts

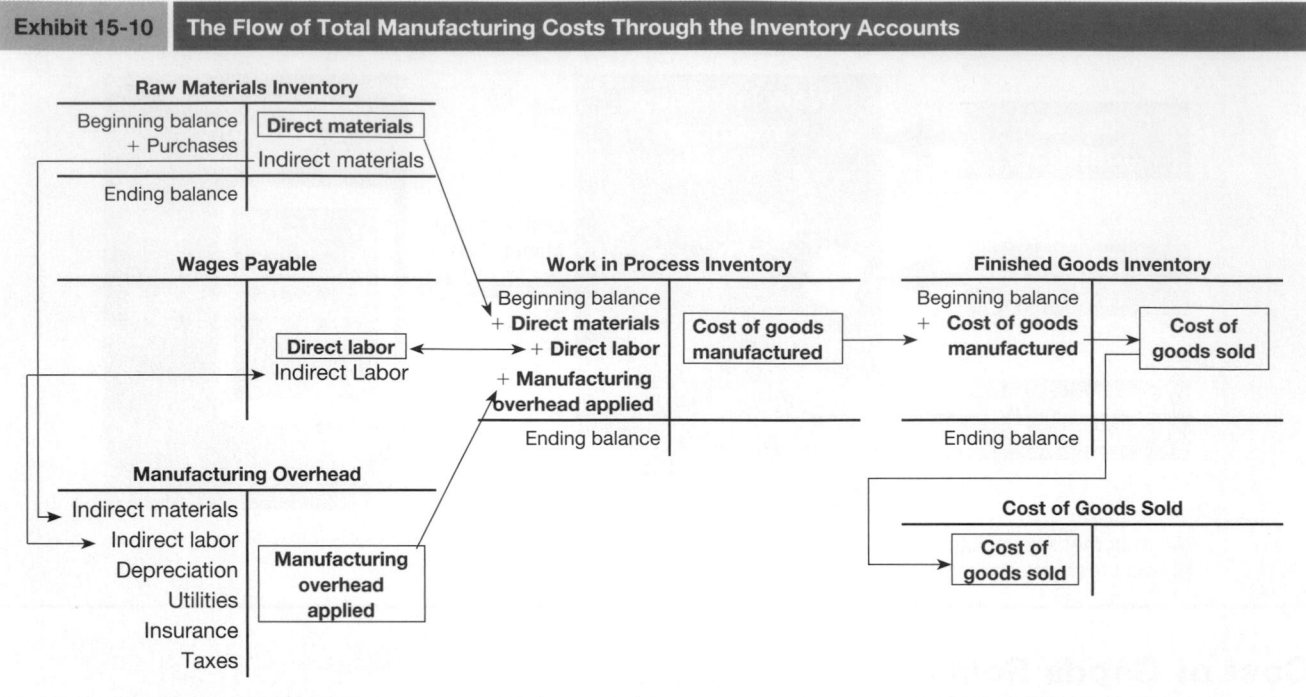

Real-World Manufacturing Example

We introduced Fezzari Performance Bicycles in Chapter 14. Fezzari is a manufacturer of road and mountain bikes. Using estimates of sales and manufacturing costs at Fezzari, **Exhibit 15-11** shows how the costs of manufacturing bikes flow through the inventory accounts.

Schedule of Cost of Goods Manufactured

Although **Exhibit 15-11** is helpful in visualizing the flow of costs through Fezzari's accounts, it is not very useful for management decision making. The schedule of cost of goods manufactured presents information about an entity's product cost for a particular accounting period in a format that is more suitable for decision making. **Exhibit 15-12** presents Fezzari's 2016 schedule of cost of goods manufactured. The schedule has two sections. The first section summarizes the **total manufacturing costs** for the year: direct material, direct labor, and manufacturing overhead incurred in the manufacturing process during the year. These are all of the costs that flow into the work in process inventory account during the year. In the calculation of direct material used during the year, the net delivered cost of materials purchased is added to the beginning materials inventory to determine the cost of material available during the year. The cost of material not used (ending materials inventory) is then subtracted to identify the cost of all material used during the year. This total represents both direct material used and indirect material used. We subtract indirect material used to determine the direct material used. Direct labor is presented on a single line. The detail of manufacturing overhead is calculated by summing all of the individual components of manufacturing overhead.

Exhibit 15-11	The Flow of Fezzari's Costs Through the Inventory Accounts

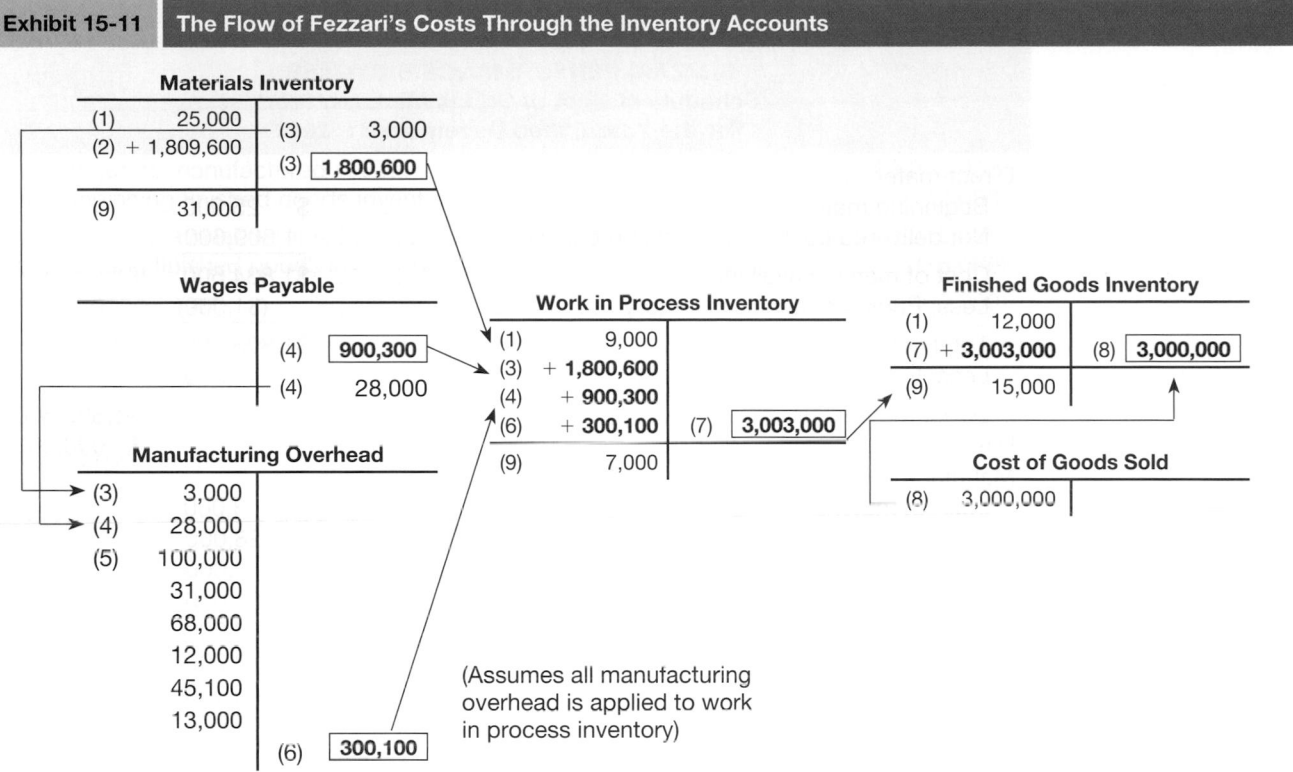

(1) Beginning inventory balances.

(2) $1,809,600 of materials inventory is purchased and received.

(3) Materials inventory is used in the production process. $1,800,600 of direct materials is used and transferred to work in process inventory. $3,000 of indirect materials is used and transferred to and accumulated in the manufacturing overhead account.

(4) Factory wages are incurred in the production process. $900,300 of direct labor is incurred and recorded in both the work in process inventory and wages payable accounts. $28,000 of indirect labor is incurred and recorded in both the manufacturing overhead and wages payable accounts.

(5) Additional indirect manufacturing costs are incurred during the production process and accumulated in the

manufacturing overhead account. These costs include the lease on the factory of $100,000, factory utilities of $31,000, factory insurance of $68,000, property taxes on the factory of $12,000, depreciation on factory machinery of $45,100 and other factory overhead of $13,000.

(6) At the end of the period, the $300,100 of costs accumulated in manufacturing overhead are applied to work in process inventory.

(7) As bikes are completed, their total manufacturing costs of $3,003,000 are transferred from the work in process inventory to the finished goods inventory.

(8) When bikes are sold, their total manufacturing costs of $3,000,000 are transferred out of finished goods inventory and recognized as a cost of goods sold expense. This entry is recorded along with the related sales entry.

(9) Ending inventory balances.

The second section of the schedule of cost of goods manufactured determines the cost of goods manufactured—the cost of goods completed during the year and transferred to finished goods. In this section, total manufacturing costs for the year are added to the amount representing the work in process at the beginning of the year to determine the total cost of work in process during the year. The cost of incomplete units (ending work in process inventory) is then subtracted to determine the cost associated with the completed units (cost of goods manufactured). These are all of the numbers that appear in the work in process inventory account.

Materials inventory	$ 3
Work in process inventory	680
Finished goods inventory	1,081

When a manufacturing firm uses the perpetual inventory system for Materials Inventory, Work in Process Inventory, and Finished Goods Inventory, cost of goods sold can be determined directly by reference to the Cost of Goods Sold account in the general ledger. Total manufacturing costs and cost of goods manufactured, however, are not directly available in a general ledger account. Assume Apple's subsidiary records for 2014 contain the following data:

1. Net delivered cost of materials purchased was $45,228.
2. Direct labor totaled $10,270.
3. The cost of direct materials used in production was $41,223.
4. Manufacturing overhead consists of the following:

Indirect material	$ 4,000
Indirect labor	3,000
Various costs	50,107
Year-end adjustments	4,000*
	$61,107

*This is composed of $1,000 for manufacturing supplies and $3000 for depreciation on factory machinery.

Based on this information, assume Apple records the following entries for 2014:

1. Acquisition of materials

Materials inventory	45,228	
Accounts payable		45,228
To record the delivered cost of materials purchased.		

2. Use of direct material and indirect material

Work in process inventory	41,223	
Manufacturing overhead	4,000	
Materials inventory		45,223
To record the transfer of direct material ($41,223) to the work in		
process inventory and the transfer of indirect material ($4,000) to		
manufacturing overhead.		

3. Incurrence of factory payroll

Work in process inventory	10,270	
Manufacturing overhead	3,000	
Wages payable		13,270
To record the factory payroll as direct labor ($10,270) to the work		
in process inventory and as indirect labor ($3,000) to manufacturing		
overhead.		

4. Incurrence of manufacturing overhead costs during year

Manufacturing overhead	50,107	
Accounts payable or cash		50,107
To record various factory costs incurred during the year as		
manufacturing overhead.		

5. Recognition of certain manufacturing overhead costs with year-end adjustments

Manufacturing overhead	4,000	
Manufacturing supplies		1,000
Accumulated depreciation—factory machinery		3,000

To record cost of supplies used for and depreciation on factory machinery.

6. Application of manufacturing overhead

Work in process inventory	61,107	
Manufacturing overhead		61,107

To record the application of manufacturing overhead to the work in process inventory. (The procedures for determining this application will be described in a subsequent chapter.)

Cost Flows

Exhibit 15-15 presents T-accounts to which these summary entries have been posted. The arrows in **Exhibit 15-15** indicate the flows of product cost. Direct material flows from Materials Inventory to Work in Process Inventory, whereas indirect material flows from Materials Inventory to Manufacturing Overhead. Direct labor flows from Wages Expense to Work in Process Inventory, whereas indirect labor flows from Wages Payable to Manufacturing Overhead. Actual manufacturing overhead comes from several sources, and manufacturing overhead applied flows to Work in Process Inventory.

Hint: In practice, applied manufacturing overhead rarely equals the actual manufacturing overhead incurred during a period, as illustrated in this example. Chapter 16 explains how to deal with over- or underapplied overhead.

Exhibit 15-15	Apple Inc. Flow of Manufacturing Costs

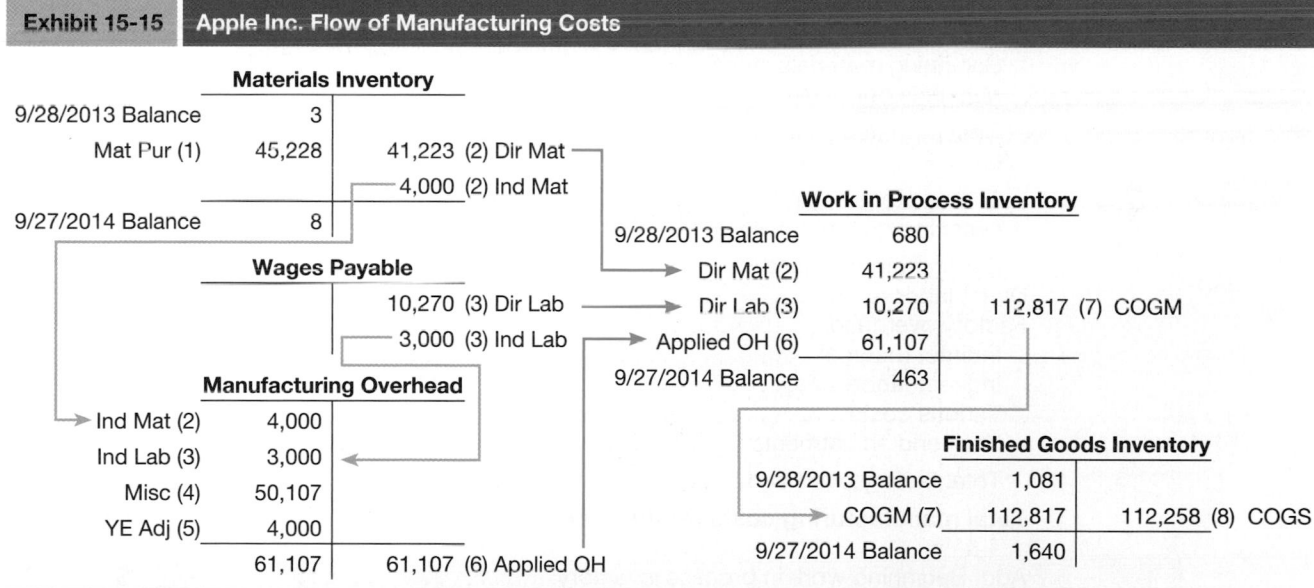

Cost of goods manufactured (the product cost of goods completed during the accounting period) flows from Work in Process Inventory to Finished Goods Inventory. The cost of goods sold flows from Finished Goods Inventory to the Cost of Goods Sold account. These cost flows are represented by the following journal entries:

7. Recognition of cost of goods manufactured

Finished goods inventory	112,817	
Work in process inventory		112,817

To record the transfer of the cost associated with goods completed from the work in process inventory to the finished goods inventory.

8. Recognition of cost of goods sold

Cost of goods sold		112,258	
Finished goods inventory			112,258
To record the transfer of the cost associated with goods sold to customers from the finished goods inventory to cost of goods sold— recorded with the related sales entry.			

TAKEAWAY 15.2

The three manufacturing inventory accounts (direct materials, work in process, and finished goods) comprise the inventory balance reported on a company's balance sheet. The expense associated with producing the inventory (cost of goods sold) is reported on the income statement when the product is sold, which may be in a period after the product was manufactured. The purpose of journal entries 1–8 in **Exhibit 15-15** is to determine these amounts as accurately as possible.

Based on the information in these journal entries and as summarized in the T-accounts in **Exhibit 15-15**, **Exhibit 15-16** presents Apple Inc.'s schedule of cost of goods manufactured for 2014.

Exhibit 15-16	Schedule of Costs of Goods Manufactured

APPLE INC.
Schedule of Cost of Goods Manufactured
For the Year Ended September 27, 2014
(in $millions)

Direct material:		
Beginning materials inventory.	$ 3	
Materials purchased	45,228	
Cost of materials available	$45,231	
Less: Ending materials inventory	8	
Total materials used	$45,223	
Less: Indirect materials used	4,000	
Direct materials used		$ 41,223
Direct labor.		$ 10,270
Factory overhead:		
Indirect material	$ 4,000	
Indirect labor.	3,000	
Various costs	50,107	
Year-end adjustments	4,000	
Total factory overhead		$ 61,107
Total manufacturing costs for the year		**$112,600**
Add: Beginning work in process inventory.		$ 680
Total cost of work in process during the year		113,280
Less: Ending work in process inventory.		(463)
Cost of goods manufactured		**$112,817**

Financial Statements

Exhibit 15-17 presents Apple Inc.'s 2014 income statement.

Exhibit 15-17	Income Statement

APPLE INC.
Income Statement
For the Year Ended September 27, 2014
(in $millions)

Sales.		$182,795
Cost of goods sold.		112,258
Gross profit on sales.		$ 70,537
Operating expenses:		
Selling, general, and administrative expenses	$11,993	
Research and development	6,041	18,034
Income from operations.		$ 52,503
Other income/(expense).		980
Income before income tax		$ 53,483
Income tax expense.		13,073
Net income.		$ 39,510
Basic earnings per share of common stock.		
(6,085.572 weighted average shares).		$ 6.49

Exhibit 15-18 shows the retained earnings statement for Apple Inc., given that it declared cash dividends of $11,215 during 2014.

Exhibit 15-18	Statement of Retained Earnings

APPLE INC.
Statement of Retained Earnings
For the Year Ended September 27, 2014
(in $millions)

Retained earnings, September 28, 2013	$104,256
Add: Net income for 2014	39,510
Less: Dividends declared.	(11,215)
Less: Repurchase of common stock	(45,399)
Retained earnings, September 27, 2014	$ 87,152

Exhibit 15-19 presents the September 27, 2014, balance sheet for Apple Inc. Note that the multiple inventory accounts are combined into a single line in the current assets section for presentation purposes.

Exhibit 15-19	Report Form of a Classified Balance Sheet

APPLE INC.
Balance Sheet
As of September 27, 2014
(in $ millions)

Assets

Current assets

Cash	$ 13,844
Short-term investments	11,233
Accounts receivable	27,219
Inventory	2,111
Other current assets	14,124
Total current assets.	68,531

Long-term assets

Property, plant and equipment	20,624
Intangible assets	8,758
Other long-term assets.	133,926
Total long-term assets	163,308
Total assets	$231,839

Liabilities

Current liabilities

Accounts payable	$ 30,196
Other current liabilities	33,252
Total current liabilities	63,448
Long-term liabilities	56,844
Total liabilities	120,292

Stockholders' Equity

Common stock	23,313
Retained earnings	87,152
Other equity	1,082
Total stockholders' equity	111,547
Total liabilities and stockholders' equity	$231,839

CORPORATE SOCIAL RESPONSIBILITY	**Environmental Performance Reporting at Apple**

There are probably few companies as secretive as Apple. The company is very careful to control any leaks on its upcoming products. Apple uses this strategy of keeping things secret in order to increase the anticipation before new product announcements. The strategy seems to be working well, based on the excitement surrounding these new product events.

One area that Apple is not secretive about is its environmental responsibility. Apple uses its detailed managerial accounting system to measure the environmental impact of how every product is manufactured. Unlike the secrecy surrounding what the next new product will be, Apple believes in full transparency regarding its environmental performance and reports on this performance in its comprehensive Product Environmental Reports. Every Apple product is measured and rated in four categories: climate change, restricted substances, energy efficiency, and material efficiency.

As stated on Apple's website, "We strive to create products that are the best they can be in every way. . . . the same passion for innovation goes into how we think about environmental responsibility. It's why we work tirelessly to reduce our impact on climate change, find ways to use greener materials, and conserve the resources we all need to thrive."

A famous expression in business is that you can't manage what you can't measure. For Apple to be a leader in both product development and environmental responsibility, the company depends on its managerial accounting systems to provide the information needed to properly manage everything the company does.

SERVICE INDUSTRY IN FOCUS

Environmental Business Consultants, LLC (EBC), is a consulting firm that specializes in the areas of recycling and solid waste and water/wastewater management services. The firm has offices located in northern and southern California. EBC has serviced hundreds of municipal agencies since 1984. Both the firm's executives and consultants work on client projects. EBC's 2016 adjusted trial balance is shown below.

SERVICE AND MERCHANDISING

Description	Trial Balance Debit	Trial Balance Credit
Cash.	390,000	
Accounts receivable.	474,000	
Allowance for uncollectible accounts.		—
Work in process inventory	247,000	
Other current assets.	32,000	
Furniture and fixtures	150,000	
Accumulated depreciation—furniture		150,000
Office equipment	277,000	
Accumulated depreciation—equipment.		198,000
Accounts payable.		—
Other current liabilities		37,500
Non-current liabilities		3,000
Owners' capital		90,000
Retained earnings		573,000
Sales.		4,146,000
Reimbursable costs	431,000	
Executive salaries.	844,500	
Clerical salaries	217,500	
Consultant salaries.	1,050,000	
Employee benefits	145,500	
Payroll taxes.	123,000	
Employee bonuses.	126,000	
Marketing expenses.	48,000	
Employee continuing education expenses.	27,000	
Office lease expense	202,500	
Office supplies expense.	64,500	
Other general administrative expense	355,500	
Other income/(expense).		7,500
	5,205,000	5,205,000

Required

1. Classify each of the expense line items in the trial balance as:
   a. Direct or indirect. Assume that the cost object is a consulting project.
   b. Fixed or variable. Assume that the cost object is one of EBC's two offices.
   c. Product or period. Assume that the cost object is a consulting project.

2. Prepare a schedule of cost of services for EBC for the year ended December 31, 2016. Assume that the beginning Work in Process Inventory balance was $223,000. Regardless of your classification in Requirement 1, assume that all executive and consultant salaries, benefits, and taxes are product costs and that EBC treats all bonuses and continuing education expenses as period costs.

3. Prepare an income statement for EBC for the year ended December 31, 2016.

Solution

1*a.*

Line Item	Direct Cost	Indirect Cost
Reimbursable costs	X	
Executive salaries.	X	X
Clerical salaries		X
Consultant salaries.	X	
Employee benefits	X	X
Payroll taxes.	X	X
Employee bonuses.	X	X
Marketing expenses.		X
Employee continuing education expenses.		X
Office lease expense		X
Office supplies expense.		X
Other general administrative expenses		X

1*b.*

Line Item	Fixed Cost	Variable Cost
Reimbursable costs		X
Executive salaries.	X	
Clerical salaries	X	
Consultant salaries.	X	
Employee benefits	X	
Payroll taxes.	X	
Employee bonuses.		X
Marketing expenses.		X
Employee continuing education expenses.		X
Office lease expense	X	
Office supplies expense.		X
Other general administrative expenses	X	X

1*c.*

Line Item	Product Cost	Period Cost
Reimbursable costs	X	
Executive salaries.	X	
Clerical salaries		X
Consultant salaries.	X	
Employee benefits	X	X
Payroll taxes.	X	X
Employee bonuses.		X
Marketing expenses.		X
Employee continuing education expenses.		X
Office lease expense	X	
Office supplies expense.	X	X
Other general administrative expenses	X	X

2.

Environmental Business Consultants, LLC Statement of Cost Services As of December 31, 2016		
Direct Labor		$2,380,500
General Overhead:		
Office lease expense	$202,500	
Office supplies expense.	64,500	
Total General Overhead		267,000
Total Manufacturing Costs for the Year		2,647,500
Add: Beginning Work in Process Inventory		223,000
Total Cost of Work in Process during the Year		2,870,500
Less: Ending Work in Process Inventory		(247,000)
Cost of Services.		$2,623,500

3.

Environmental Business Consultants, LLC Income Statement For the Year Ended December 31, 2016		
Gross Sales		$4,146,000
Less Reimbursable Costs		$ (431,000)
Net Sales		$3,715,000
Cost of Services.		2,623,500
Gross Profit on Sales		1,091,500
Operating Expenses:		
Employee bonuses	126,000	
Marketing expenses	48,000	
Employee continuing education expenses.	27,000	
Other general administrative expenses	355,500	
Total Operating Expenses		556,500
Income from Operations		535,000
Other Income/(Expense).		7,500
Net Income.		$ 542,500

COMPREHENSIVE PROBLEM

MBC

At December 31, 2016, the end of its fiscal year, Perez Manufacturing Corporation collected the following data for 2016:

Materials inventory, January 1	$ 80,000
Materials inventory, December 31	60,000
Work in process inventory, January 1	100,000
Work in process inventory, December 31	140,000
Finished goods inventory, January 1	120,000
Finished goods inventory, December 31	110,000
Net delivered cost of materials purchased	180,000
Direct labor	280,000
Indirect material	15,000
Indirect labor	75,000
Factory supplies used	16,000
Factory depreciation	30,000
Factory repairs and maintenance	22,000
Selling expenses	64,000
Non-factory administrative expenses	58,000

Required

Prepare a schedule of cost of goods manufactured and sold for Perez Manufacturing Corporation for the year ended December 31, 2016, assuming that there were no other manufacturing overhead items than those listed above.

Solution

PEREZ MANUFACTURING CORPORATION
Schedule of Cost of Goods Manufactured
For the Year Ended December 31, 2016

Direct material:		
Beginning materials inventory	$ 80,000	
Net delivered cost of materials purchased	180,000	
Cost of materials available	$260,000	
Less: Ending materials inventory	60,000	
Total material used	$200,000	
Less: Indirect material used	15,000	
Direct material used		$185,000
Direct labor		280,000
Manufacturing overhead:		
Indirect material	$ 15,000	
Indirect labor	75,000	
Manufacturing supplies used	16,000	
Manufacturing depreciation	30,000	
Manufacturing repairs and maintenance	22,000	
Total manufacturing overhead		158,000
Total manufacturing costs for the year		**$623,000**
Add: Beginning work in process inventory		100,000
Total Cost of work in process during the year		$723,000
Less: Ending work in process inventory		140,000
Cost of goods manufactured		**$583,000**
Add: Beginning finished goods inventory		120,000
Cost of goods available for sale		$703,000
Less: Ending finished goods inventory		110,000
Cost of goods sold		**$593,000**

SUMMARY OF LEARNING OBJECTIVES

Identify the key objectives of a managerial accounting system and define product costs and period costs; variable, fixed, and mixed costs; and direct and indirect costs; and cost control. (p. 712)   **LO1**

■ The primary objectives of managerial accounting systems are to provide management with financial and other business information that is useful in analyzing and making business decisions.

■ Product costs include all costs necessary to bring a product to completion.

■ Period costs are expensed in the period incurred and not assigned to products.

■ A variable cost varies in total but is fixed per unit for a certain range of activity. A fixed cost is fixed in total but varies per unit for a certain range of activity. Mixed costs have both fixed and variable cost components.

■ A direct cost can easily be traced to a cost object. An indirect cost cannot be easily traced to a cost object.

Describe the three manufacturing inventories—materials, work in process, and finished goods—and discuss the categories of manufacturing costs and how these costs flow among the inventories and cost of goods sold. (p. 716)   **LO2**

■ Materials inventory includes all factory materials and components that have been purchased but not yet placed into production.

■ Work in process inventory includes all units of product that have been placed into production but not yet completed.

■ Finished goods inventory includes all units of product that have been completed but not yet sold.

■ Total product costs consist of direct material, direct labor, and manufacturing overhead (which includes indirect material and indirect labor).

■ Prime cost is direct material plus direct labor. Product costs are easily and directly traceable to individual products. Conversion cost is direct labor plus manufacturing overhead. Conversion cost represents the elements of product cost necessary to convert the materials and components to the final finished products.

■ Product cost flows from the Materials Inventory account to the Work in Process Inventory account to the Finished Goods Inventory account and finally to the Cost of Goods Sold account.

Define total manufacturing costs, cost of goods manufactured, and cost of goods sold, and illustrate the schedule of cost of goods manufactured and sold and the income statement. (p. 723)   **LO3**

■ Total manufacturing costs is the sum of direct material, direct labor, and manufacturing overhead incurred during the accounting period.

■ Cost of goods manufactured (cost of product transferred to finished goods inventory during the accounting period) is total manufacturing costs plus beginning work in process inventory minus ending work in process inventory.

■ Cost of goods sold is cost of goods manufactured plus beginning finished goods inventory minus ending finished goods inventory.

■ The schedule of cost of goods manufactured and sold has subtotals that reveal total manufacturing costs, cost of goods manufactured, and cost of goods sold.

Illustrate the journal entries to record product cost flows using a perpetual inventory system. (p. 727)   **LO4**

■ Direct material, direct labor, and manufacturing overhead costs are accumulated in the Work in Process Inventory account.

■ When manufacturing is completed, product costs are transferred from the Work in Process Inventory account to the Finished Goods Inventory account.

■ When goods are sold, product costs are transferred from the Finished Goods Inventory account to Cost of Goods Sold.

KEY TERMS

Conversion cost (p. 719)

Cost control (p. 716)

Cost object (p. 712)

Cost of goods manufactured (COGM) (p. 722)

Cost of goods sold (COGS) (p. 723)

Cost of jobs or projects (p. 715)

Direct costs (p. 714)

Direct labor (p. 718)

Direct materials (p. 718)

Factory overhead (p. 718)

Factory supplies (p. 716)

Finished goods inventory (p. 716)

Fixed cost (p. 713)

Indirect cost (p. 715)

Indirect labor (p. 718)

Indirect materials (p. 718)

Manufacturing
   overhead (p. 718)

Materials inventory (p. 716)

Mixed costs (p. 713)

Office supplies (p. 716)

Period costs (p. 713, 715)

Prime cost (p. 719)

Product costing (p. 712)

Product costs (p. 712, 717)

Semi-variable costs (p. 713)

Total manufacturing
   costs (p. 722, 724)

Variable cost (p. 713)

Work in process
   inventory (p. 716)

Assignments with the ⊛ logo in the margin are available in **my BusinessCourse**.
See the Preface of the book for details.

SELF-STUDY QUESTIONS

(Answers to Self-Study Questions are at the end of this chapter.)

LO1   1. **Which of the following is never an element of product cost?**
    a. Insurance
    b. Utilities
    c. Advertising
    d. Supplies

LO2   2. **Which of the following is not an element of manufacturing overhead?**
    a. Factory office salaries
    b. Plant manager's salary
    c. Product inspector's salary
    d. Company president's salary

LO3   3. **The sum of direct materials, direct labor, and manufacturing overhead plus beginning work in process inventory minus ending work in process inventory computes**
    a. total manufacturing costs.
    b. cost of goods manufactured.
    c. cost of goods sold.
    d. total cost of work in process.

LO4   4. **The journal entry to record the distribution of the factory payroll requires**
    a. a debit to Work in Process Inventory for direct labor.
    b. a debit to Work in Process Inventory for indirect labor.
    c. a debit to Manufacturing Overhead for direct labor.
    d. a credit to Manufacturing Overhead for direct labor.

LO3   5. **A manufacturer incurred $20,000 of direct material, $10,000 of direct labor, and $15,000 of manufacturing overhead during 2016. Beginning work in process inventory was $8,000. If cost of goods manufactured was $47,000, what was the amount of the ending work in process inventory?**
    a. $55,000
    b. $6,000
    c. $10,000
    d. $53,000

QUESTIONS

LO1   1. How are product costs accounted for differently from period costs? Give examples of each.

LO3   2. What is the basic format of the income statement of a manufacturing firm?

LO2   3. Name the three inventory accounts maintained by manufacturing firms and briefly describe the nature of each.

LO2   4. Name and briefly describe the three major categories used to account for manufacturing costs.

LO2   5. Define prime cost and conversion cost.

LO2   6. List six examples of manufacturing overhead costs.

LO3   7. In what way is total manufacturing cost different from cost of goods manufactured?

LO3   8. If the cost of work in process during the year is $480,000 and ending work in process inventory is $50,000, what is the amount of cost of goods manufactured?

LO3   9. If beginning and ending finished goods inventories are $55,000 and $45,000, respectively, and the cost of goods sold is $420,000, what is the cost of goods manufactured?

LO4   10. What journal entry would be made to record the transfer of $12,000 of direct material and $2,500 of indirect material from the material inventory?

LO4   11. What journal entry would be made to record the distribution of a factory payroll consisting of $11,000 of direct labor and $4,000 of indirect labor?

LO4   12. What journal entry would be made to record the payment of $1,500 cash for factory utilities?

LO4   13. What journal entry would be required to record the transfer of completed products costing $15,000?

EXERCISES—SET A

E15-1A. Schedule of Cost of Goods Manufactured and Sold At December 31, 2016, the end of its fiscal **LO3**
year, Lederman Manufacturing Corporation collected the following data for 2016:

Materials inventory, January 1	$ 25,000
Materials inventory, December 31	15,000
Work in process inventory, January 1	30,000
Work in process inventory, December 31	41,000
Finished goods inventory, January 1	51,000
Finished goods inventory, December 31	36,000
Net delivered cost of materials purchased.	125,000
Direct labor.	148,000
Indirect material	12,000
Indirect labor	37,000
Factory supplies used	10,000
Factory depreciation	65,000
Factory repairs and maintenance.	21,000
Selling expenses (total).	62,000
Non-factory administrative expenses (total).	58,000

Prepare a schedule of cost of goods manufactured and sold for Lederman Manufacturing Corporation
for the year ended December 31, 2016, assuming that there were no other manufacturing overhead
items than those listed above.

E15-2A. Income Statement Lederman Manufacturing Corporation (see E15-1A) sold 15,000 units of product **LO3**
for $40 each during 2016. During the year, 5,000 shares of common stock were outstanding. Prepare
an income statement for the year (ignore income taxes).

E15-3A. Cost of Goods Manufactured and Cost of Goods Sold For each of the following unrelated compa- **LO3**
nies, compute the cost of goods manufactured and the cost of goods sold.

	A	B	C
Selling expenses	$ 500	$ 800	$ 600
Factory insurance.	260	245	140
Ending finished goods inventory	810	750	515
Non-factory administrative expenses.	250	450	350
Direct labor.	2,560	2,760	2,120
Beginning materials inventory	520	670	350
Beginning work in process inventory	1,120	840	1,070
Indirect material used.	390	420	230
Factory utilities	240	275	150
Factory depreciation	730	760	380
Ending work in process inventory	1,360	790	950
Ending materials inventory.	440	710	410
Indirect labor	425	280	160
Beginning finished goods inventory.	850	725	480
Factory repairs and maintenance.	215	230	175
Net delivered cost of materials purchased.	3,140	4,410	2,870
Factory supplies used	330	310	210

E15-4A. Prime Cost and Conversion Cost Piper Consulting Company incurred the following during 2016: **LO2**

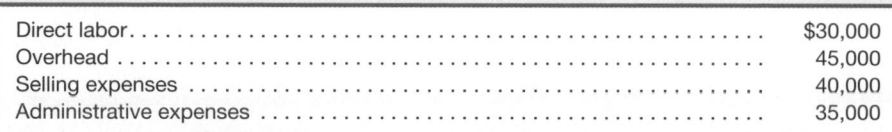

Direct labor.	$30,000
Overhead	45,000
Selling expenses	40,000
Administrative expenses	35,000

Calculate prime cost and conversion cost for Piper Consulting Company during 2016.

LO4   **E15-5A. Entries for Product Cost Flow** The following transactions occurred during January 2016 for Richards Manufacturing Company:

Jan.   5   Acquired $3,000 of material on account that will be used to produce product for resale.

11   Requisitioned $2,500 of material for use as direct material in the factory.

16   Completed the manufacturing of products with a total product cost of $11,000 and transferred them to the warehouse.

Record these transactions in general journal form. Assume that Richards Manufacturing Company uses the perpetual inventory system.

LO4   **E15-6A. Entries for Product Cost Flow** Record the following transactions that occurred during March 2016 for Harris Manufacturing Company, which uses the perpetual inventory system:

Mar.   12   Transferred $10,000 of completed goods from the factory to the warehouse.

15   Requisitioned $6,000 of material for use in the factory as direct material and $1,000 for indirect material.

18   Sold goods costing $8,000 for $12,000 on account.

EXERCISES—SET B

LO3   **E15-1B. Schedule of Cost of Goods Manufactured and Sold** At December 31, 2016, the end of its fiscal year, Kelly Metal Products Corporation collected the following data for 2016:

Materials inventory, January 1	$ 32,000
Materials inventory, December 31	22,000
Work in process inventory, January 1	34,000
Work in process inventory, December 31	45,000
Finished goods inventory, January 1	21,000
Finished goods inventory, December 31	18,000
Net delivered cost of materials purchased	210,000
Direct labor	135,000
Indirect material	13,000
Indirect labor	25,000
Factory supplies used	12,000
Factory depreciation	78,000
Factory repairs and maintenance	28,000
Selling expenses (total)	63,000
Non-factory administrative expenses (total)	57,000

Required
Prepare a schedule of cost of goods manufactured and sold for Kelly Metal Products Corporation for the year ended December 31, 2016, assuming that there were no other manufacturing overhead items than those listed above.

LO3   **E15-2B. Income Statement** Kelly Metal Products Corporation (see E15-1B) sold 20,000 units of product for $35 each during 2016. During the year, 10,000 shares of common stock were outstanding. Prepare an income statement for the year (ignore income taxes).

LO3   **E15-3B. Cost of Goods Manufactured and Cost of Goods Sold** For each of the following unrelated columns of data for the year, compute the cost of goods manufactured and the cost of goods sold.

	A	B	C
Selling expenses	$ 600	$ 700	$ 900
Factory insurance	180	270	300
Ending finished goods inventory	620	660	930
Non-factory administrative expenses	300	400	800
Direct labor	2,130	2,850	3,160
Beginning materials inventory	425	575	850
Beginning work in process inventory	840	920	1,290
Indirect material used	270	325	520
Factory utilities	350	360	500
Factory depreciation	820	740	965
Ending work in process inventory	790	985	1,425
Ending materials inventory	385	610	820
Indirect labor	225	410	365
Beginning finished goods inventory	565	680	950
Factory repairs and maintenance	330	250	415
Net delivered cost of materials purchased	2,780	3,620	8,170
Factory supplies used	210	230	260

E15-4B. Prime Cost and Conversion Cost Benton Engineering Services Company incurred the following during 2016:

LO2

Direct labor	$47,000
Overhead	63,000
Selling expenses	56,000
Administrative expenses	51,000

Calculate prime cost and conversion cost for Benton Engineering Services Company during 2016.

E15-5B. Entries for Product Cost Flow The following transactions occurred during February 2016 for Thompson Manufacturing Company:

LO4

Feb. 10   Acquired $5,000 of material on account that will be used to produce product for resale.

11   Requisitioned $4,000 of material for use as direct material in the factory.

16   Completed the manufacturing of products with a total product cost of $24,000 and transferred them to the warehouse.

Record these transactions in general journal form. Assume that Thompson Manufacturing Company uses the perpetual inventory system.

E15-6B. Entries for Product Cost Flow Record the following transactions that occurred during April 2016 for Boyd Manufacturing Corporation, which uses the perpetual inventory system:

LO4

Apr. 21   Transferred $16,000 of completed goods from the factory to the warehouse.

25   Requisitioned $9,000 of material for use in the factory as direct material and $2,000 for indirect material.

28   Sold goods costing $6,000 for $10,000 on account.

PROBLEMS—SET A

P15-1A. Schedule of Cost of Goods Manufactured and Sold The following amounts are available for 2016 for Bourne Manufacturing Company:

LO3

Administrative salaries (non-factory)	$ 70,000
Administrative rent (non-factory)	35,000
Advertising and promotion expense	41,000
Depreciation—administrative	22,000
Depreciation—factory	30,000
Depreciation—selling	17,000
Direct labor	175,000
Factory rent	18,000
Factory supplies used	12,000
Finished goods inventory (January 1)	57,000
Finished goods inventory (December 31)	52,000
Indirect material used	14,000
Indirect labor	19,000
Materials inventory (January 1)	13,000
Materials inventory (December 31)	20,000
Net delivered cost of materials purchased	138,000
Other factory overhead	26,000
Sales	845,000
Sales salaries expense	72,000
Work in process inventory (January 1)	18,000
Work in process inventory (December 31)	31,000

Required

Using the above data, prepare a schedule of cost of goods manufactured and sold.

LO3   **P15-2A. Cost of Goods Manufactured and Sold** The following data relate to three independent production periods of Riverside Manufacturing Company. Missing data are indicated by question marks.

	A	B	C
Materials:			
Beginning inventory	$ 52	$ 164	$110
Purchases	?	700	500
Ending inventory	74	100	?
Total material used	330	?	440
Direct labor	580	960	800
Manufacturing overhead:			
Indirect material	96	?	120
Indirect labor	160	150	350
Other	?	200	340
Total manufacturing overhead	520	480	?
Work in process inventories:			
Beginning	?	90	260
Ending	70	?	100
Finished goods inventories:			
Beginning	?	400	80
Ending	335	120	330
Cost of goods manufactured	1,384	?	?
Cost of goods sold	1,339	2,324	?

Required

Using the above data, determine the missing amounts. (You should set up a schedule of cost of goods manufactured and sold, fill in the known data, and calculate the missing amounts.)

LO4   **P15-3A. Journal Entries** Taylor Manufacturing Company uses the perpetual inventory system to record transactions related to its manufacturing inventories. The following transactions occurred during March 2016:

Mar. 6 Recorded the payroll: $10,000 of direct labor and $2,000 of indirect labor.
       8 Received $14,000 of materials and components that had been ordered on account.

Mar. 10 Completed product costing $22,000 and transferred it to the warehouse. Requisitioned $5,000 of material for use in the factory; $4,000 was used as direct material and the remainder was used as indirect material.

12 Sold on account product costing $3,000 for $4,500.

15 Applied $6,000 of manufacturing overhead cost to the product currently being worked on.

21 Paid $500 cash for a special material component that was shipped via overnight delivery.

27 Sold product costing $2,900 for $5,000 cash.

Required

Prepare general journal entries to record these transactions.

P15-4A. Journal Entries Paulson Manufacturing Company uses the perpetual inventory system to account for its manufacturing inventories. The following are Paulson's transactions during July 2016:   **LO4**

July 5 Received material costing $2,000 from a supplier. The material was purchased on account.

9 Requisitioned $6,000 of material for use in the factory, consisting of $5,000 of direct material and $1,000 of indirect material.

11 Recorded the factory payroll: $13,500 of direct labor and $1,500 of indirect labor.

17 Incurred various overhead costs totaling $14,000. (Credit Accounts Payable.)

20 Applied $20,000 of manufacturing overhead to the products being manufactured.

23 Completed product costing $16,000 and moved it to the warehouse.

26 Sold goods with a product cost of $3,000 on account for $5,000.

Required

a. Set up T-accounts for the following four accounts and post the July 1, 2016 balances: Materials Inventory, $7,000; Work in Process Inventory, 25,000; Finished Goods Inventory, $10,000; and Cost of Goods Sold, $30,000.

b. Record the transactions listed above in general journal form, post relevant portions to the four T-accounts, and balance the four accounts.

P15-5A. Total Manufacturing Cost, Income Statement, Unit Cost, and Selling Price Two inventors, recently organized as Innovation, Inc., consult you regarding a planned new product. They have estimates of the costs of materials, labor, overhead, and other expenses for 2016 but need to know how much to charge for each unit to earn a profit in 2016 equal to 15% of their estimated total long-term investment of $400,000 (ignore income taxes). Their plans indicate that each unit of the new product requires the following: **LO3**

Direct material	4 lb. of a material costing $5/lb.
Direct labor	2 hrs. of a metal former's time at $11/hr.
	0.6 hr. of an assembler's time at $8/hr.

Major items of production overhead would be annual rent of $46,460 for a factory building, $28,660 rent for machinery, and $21,700 of indirect material. Other production overhead is estimated to be $233,280. Selling expenses are an estimated 30% of total sales, and non-factory administrative expenses are 20% of total sales.

The consensus at Innovation is that during 2016 10,000 units of product should be produced for selling and another 2,000 units should be produced for the next year's beginning inventory. Also, an extra 3,000 pounds of material will be purchased as beginning inventory for the next year. Because of the nature of the manufacturing process, all units started must be completed, so work in process inventories are negligible.

Required

a. Incorporate the above data into a schedule of estimated total manufacturing costs and compute the unit production cost for 2016.

b. Prepare an estimated income statement that would provide the target amount of profit for 2016.

c. What unit sales price should Innovation charge for the new product?

PROBLEMS—SET B

LO3 **P15-1B. Schedule of Cost of Goods Manufactured and Sold** The following amounts are available for 2016 for Bishop Manufacturing Company:

Administrative salaries (non-factory)	$ 85,000
Administrative rent (non-factory)	47,000
Advertising and promotion expense	93,000
Depreciation—administrative	77,000
Depreciation—factory	95,000
Depreciation—selling	36,000
Direct labor	325,000
Factory rent	68,000
Factory supplies used	23,000
Finished goods inventory (January 1)	61,000
Finished goods inventory (December 31)	63,000
Indirect material used	27,000
Indirect labor	44,000
Materials inventory (January 1)	22,000
Materials inventory (December 31)	30,000
Net delivered cost of materials purchased	210,000
Other factory overhead	55,000
Sales	938,000
Sales salaries expense	71,000
Work in process inventory (January 1)	33,000
Work in process inventory (December 31)	29,000

Required
Using the above data, prepare a schedule of cost of goods manufactured and sold.

LO3 **P15-2B. Cost of Goods Manufactured and Sold** The following data relate to three independent production periods of Randolph Manufacturing Company. Missing data are indicated by question marks.

	A	B	C
Materials:			
Beginning inventory	$ 78	$ 410	$ 220
Purchases	?	1,750	1,000
Ending inventory	111	250	?
Total material used	495	?	880
Direct labor	870	2,400	1,600
Manufacturing overhead:			
Indirect material	144	?	110
Indirect labor	240	375	700
Other	?	500	680
Total manufacturing overhead	780	1,100	?
Work in process inventories:			
Beginning	?	225	520
Ending	105	?	200
Finished goods inventories:			
Beginning	?	1,000	160
Ending	495	300	660
Cost of goods manufactured	2,076	?	?
Cost of goods sold	2,016	5,275	?

Required
Using the above data, determine the missing amounts. (You should set up a schedule of cost of goods manufactured and sold, fill in the known data, and calculate the missing amounts.)

P15-3B. Journal Entries Travis Manufacturing Company uses the perpetual inventory system to record trans-   **LO4**
actions related to its manufacturing inventories. The following transactions occurred during August 2016:

Aug.   5   Received $9,000 of materials and components that had been ordered on account.

   7   Recorded the payroll: $6,500 of direct labor and $1,500 of indirect labor.

   11   Sold on account product costing $3,500 for $5,200.

   16   Completed product costing $16,000 and transferred it to the warehouse.

   20   Requisitioned $7,000 of material for use in the factory; $5,900 was used as direct material
and the remainder was used as indirect material.

   25   Applied $10,000 of manufacturing overhead cost to the product currently being worked
on.

   29   Paid $400 cash for a special material component that was shipped via overnight delivery.

   31   Sold product costing $1,000 for $1,700 cash.

Required
Prepare general journal entries to record these transactions.

P15-4B. Journal Entries Porter Manufacturing Company uses the perpetual inventory system to account for   **LO4**
its manufacturing inventories. The following are Porter's transactions during September 2016:

Sept.   5   Received material costing $3,000 from a supplier. The material was purchased on account.

   9   Requisitioned $7,000 of material for use in the factory, consisting of $5,600 of direct
material and $1,400 of indirect material.

   11   Recorded the factory payroll: $14,000 of direct labor and $2,000 of indirect labor

   17   Incurred various overhead costs totaling $15,000. (Credit Accounts Payable.)

   20   Applied $21,000 of manufacturing overhead to the products being manufactured.

   23   Completed product costing $17,000 and moved it to the warehouse.

   26   Sold goods with a product cost of $4,000 on account for $6,000.

Required

a.   Set up a T-account for the following four accounts and post the September 1, 2016, balance
listed after the account title: Materials Inventory, $8,000; Work in Process Inventory, $26,000;
Finished Goods Inventory, $11,000; and Cost of Goods Sold, $32,000.

b.   Record the transactions listed above in general journal form, post relevant portions to the four
T-accounts, and balance the four accounts.

P15-5B. Total Manufacturing Costs, Income Statement, Unit Cost, and Selling Price You are consulted by   **LO3**
Investors, Inc., a group of investors planning a new product. They have estimates of the costs of materials, labor, overhead, and other expenses for 2016 but need to know how much to charge for each unit to
earn a profit in 2016 equal to 10% of their estimated investment of $500,000 (ignore income taxes).

   Their plans indicate that each unit of the new product requires the following:

Direct Material	4 lb. of a material costing $6 per lb.
Direct Labor	3 hrs. of a die cutter's time at $9 per hr.
	2 hrs. of an assembler's time at $8 per hr.

Major items of production overhead would be annual rent of $40,000 on the factory building and
$25,000 on machinery as well as indirect material of $21,000. Other production overhead is an estimated
60% of total direct labor costs. Selling expenses are an estimated 20% of total sales, and non-factory
administrative expenses are 10% of total sales.

   The consensus at Investors is that during 2016 4,000 units of product should be produced for selling
and another 1,000 units should be produced for the next year's beginning inventory. Also, an extra 6,000
pounds of material will be purchased as beginning inventory for the next year. Because of the nature of the
manufacturing process, all units started must be completed, so work in process inventories are negligible.

Required

a.   Incorporate the above data into a schedule of estimated total manufacturing costs and compute
the unit production cost for 2016.

b.   Prepare an estimated income statement that would provide the target amount of profit for 2016.

c.   What unit sales price should Investors charge for the new product?

CERTIFIED MANAGEMENT ACCOUNTANT (CMA®) EXAM SAMPLE QUESTIONS

CMA15-1. All of the following would appear on a schedule of cost of goods manufactured except for

    a. ending work-in-process inventory.

    b. beginning finished goods inventory.

    c. the cost of raw materials used.

    d. applied manufacturing overhead.

CMA15-2. Given the following data for Scurry Company, what is the cost of goods sold?

Beginning inventory of finished goods	$100,000
Cost of goods manufactured	700,000
Ending inventory of finished goods	200,000
Beginning work-in-process inventory	300,000
Ending work-in-process inventory	50,000

    a. $500,000

    b. $600,000

    c. $800,000

    d. $950,000

CMA15-3. Which one of the following items would not be considered a manufacturing cost?

    a. Cream for an ice cream maker

    b. Sales commissions for a car manufacturer

    c. Plant property taxes for an ice cream maker

    d. Tires for an automobile manufacturer

CMA15-4. Which one of the following refers to a cost that remains the same as the volume of activity decreases within the relevant range?

    a. Average cost per unit

    b. Variable cost per unit

    c. Unit fixed cost

    d. Total variable cost

CMA15-5. Taylor Corporation is determining the cost behavior of several items in order to budget for the upcoming year. Past trends have indicated the following dollars were spent at three different levels of output.

	Unit Levels		
	10,000	12,000	15,000
Cost A	$25,000	$29,000	$35,000
Cost B	10,000	15,000	15,000
Cost C	15,000	18,000	22,500

In establishing a budget for 14,000 units, Taylor should treat Costs A, B, and C, respectively, as

    a. mixed, fixed, and variable.

    b. variable, fixed, and variable.

    c. mixed, mixed, and mixed.

    d. variable, mixed, and mixed.

EXTENDING YOUR KNOWLEDGE

EYK15-1. **Business Decision Case** James Alvarez, an engineer, needs some accounting advice. In their spare time during the past year, Alvarez and his college-aged son, Robert, have manufactured a small weed-trimming sickle in a rented building near their home. Robert, who has had one accounting course in college, keeps the books.

Alvarez is pleased about the results of their first year's operations. He asks you to look over the following income report prepared by Robert before they leave on a well-deserved vacation to Hawaii, after which they plan to expand their business significantly.

Sales (34,000 units at $10 each)		$340,000
Costs of producing 35,000 units:		
Materials:		
Precast blades at $1.50 each.	$ 57,000	
Preturned handles at $1 each.	40,000	
Labor costs of hired assemblers	26,600	
Labor costs of hired painters	33,000	
Rent on building	14,900	
Rent on machinery	7,100	
Utilities for production	8,000	
Other production costs	11,900	
Advertising expense.	26,200	
Sales commissions.	35,700	
Delivery of products to customers	14,350	
Total costs	$274,750	
Less: Ending inventory of 1,000 units at average production		
costs of $7.85 (or $274,750/35,000 units)	7,850	
Cost of goods sold.		266,900
Net income.		$ 73,100

After you examine the income report, Alvarez responds to your questions and assures you that (1) no theft or spoilage of materials has occurred, (2) no partially completed units are involved, and (3) he and son Robert have averaged 30 hours each per week in the business for 50 weeks. Ignore income taxes in this situation.

Required

a.   Identify any apparent discrepancy in the income report in the cost of materials used.

b.   Recalculate the cost of goods manufactured, the average cost per unit produced, and the net income for the year.

c.   What factors should James consider regarding the profitability of his venture before deciding to expand it significantly?

EYK15-2.   **Apple's 2014 Environmental Responsibility Report can be found at the following link:** http://images.apple.com/environment/reports/docs/apple_environmental_responsibility_report_0714.pdf

Skim this report. Why do you think Apple is so transparent with regard to its environmental activity but so secretive regarding its product development?

EYK15-3.   **Ethics Case** Great Cakes is a large bakery known for its quality "boxed cake" products. Its motto is "We Use Only the Best Ingredients." Ralph Sands, the purchasing supervisor, is responsible for ordering the ingredients for all the bakery products. He is being considered for a promotion based on his proven ability to purchase ingredients at the best price available.

The cost of all the ingredients has risen substantially over the past few months. Sands decides to purchase 25% of the ingredients at a lower quality than Great Cakes normally uses because the cost is significantly less. Without relying on the company's test kitchens, he believes this substitution will not be noticed by the customers and the lower cost will counterbalance the increased costs of the other ingredients.

Sands explains this decision to his friend, Lynn Pall, the company's accountant, one day at lunch. He also tells her that he does not intend to inform management of the inclusion of the lower-quality ingredients in the bakery's products.

Required

What ethical considerations arise from Ralph Sands' decisions? What problems face Lynn Pall because of his actions?

ANSWERS TO SELF-STUDY QUESTIONS:

1. c, (p. 712)   2. d, (p. 718)   3. b, (p. 725)   4. a, (p. 728)   5. b, (p. 725)

YOUR TURN! SOLUTIONS

Solution 15.1
Assembly labor
iPad case
Microprocessor
Touch screen

Solution 15.2
Assembly labor
Factory supervisor salary
Depreciation on the iPad factory
Touch-screen

DECISION TIME SOLUTION

Solution 15.1
d. All of the above.
Negotiating lower costs for the bike components with Fezzari's suppliers would likely be the most productive choice, since materials comprise approximately 60% of the total product cost. However, increasing the training of assembly technicians could result in increased productivity and reduced direct labor costs. Relocating the manufacturing facility might allow Fezzari to reduce the facility lease cost, thereby reducing overhead costs.

16

Cost Accounting Systems: Job Order Costing

PAST

Chapter 15 defined basic costing terminology and introduced different types of manufacturing inventories. It illustrated how costs flow through the inventories and explained the schedule of cost of goods manufactured.

PRESENT

Chapter 16 introduces and explains job costing in more detail for both manufacturing and service industries. It also explains overhead allocation.

FUTURE

Chapter 17 introduces process costing and how it differs from job order costing. It illustrates equivalent units and the flow of costs through the inventory accounts, as well as introduces the production cost report.

LEARNING OBJECTIVES

1. **Describe** the two basic types of cost accounting systems, **discuss** how they may be used in both manufacturing and nonmanufacturing environments, and **explain** the need for the timely determination of product costs. *(p. 752)*

2. **Explain** the need for a predetermined overhead rate, **demonstrate** its calculation, and **compare** annual and monthly rates. *(p. 755)*

3. **Describe** and **explain** a job order costing system, **identify** types of records used in job order costing, and **demonstrate** the journal entries that accompany the flow of product costs. *(p. 757)*

4. **Discuss** the procedures and journal entries used to account for finished goods and the sale of finished goods. *(p. 763)*

5. **Describe** the procedures for cost allocation for service departments. *(p. 768)*

6. **Contrast** plant-wide overhead rates and departmental overhead rates. *(p. 771)*

CH2M HILL: GLOBAL SERVICE PROVIDER

CH2M Hill is a U.S.-based consulting, design, construction, operation, and program management service firm that provides services to clients worldwide. In 2013, it ranked 415th on the Fortune 500 list of the largest U.S. companies. CH2M Hill has performed thousands of projects on six continents and in more than 180 countries.

CH2M Hill's projects are typically very large and complex. For example, CH2M Hill was hired for the Panama Canal Expansion Program. This project is intended to double the canal's capacity and allow it to accommodate the larger ships now used to transport goods around the world. CH2M Hill has responsibility to assist the Panama Canal Authority with construction management oversight, risk management, quality, and safety; to advise on design/engineering oversight; and to interface with the designer/builder of the new locks on both the Atlantic and Pacific sides of the canal.

Another massive project is CH2M Hill's task to replace the entire sanitary sewer system for the country of Singapore. CH2M Hill's role includes managing the installation of 90 kilometers of large conveyance tunnels under the entire island nation that will collect wastewater from multiple sewers for treatment at one of two treatment plants. The company is also responsible for the design and construction management of the first (and larger) of the two treatment plants.

Some of CH2M Hill's projects involve not just construction of massive facilities, but deconstruction as well. The Maine Yankee Atomic Power Company hired CH2M Hill to assist with the decommissioning of its nuclear power facility in Wiscasset, Maine. The decommissioning of a nuclear power facility involves complex challenges due to a variety of contaminants, including numerous radioactive isotopes. The decommissioning includes the demolition and removal of most structures on the site as well as the construction of a dry cask storage facility for used nuclear fuel.

CH2M Hill's client contracts typically take one of three forms: fixed-price contracts, where clients pay an agreed amount negotiated in advance for a specific scope of work; cost-plus contracts, where clients pay CH2M Hill's actual costs (direct and indirect) plus a fixed fee (profit); and time and materials contracts, where clients pay a negotiated hourly billing rate for the actual time spent on the project plus CH2M Hill's actual out-of-pocket costs.

As you think about the massive scale of these projects, you might wonder how CH2M Hill keeps track of all of the costs (materials, labor, and overhead) incurred over weeks, months, and even years. To properly track the costs and customer billings associated with each of its projects, CH2M Hill must use some very sophisticated job order costing systems!

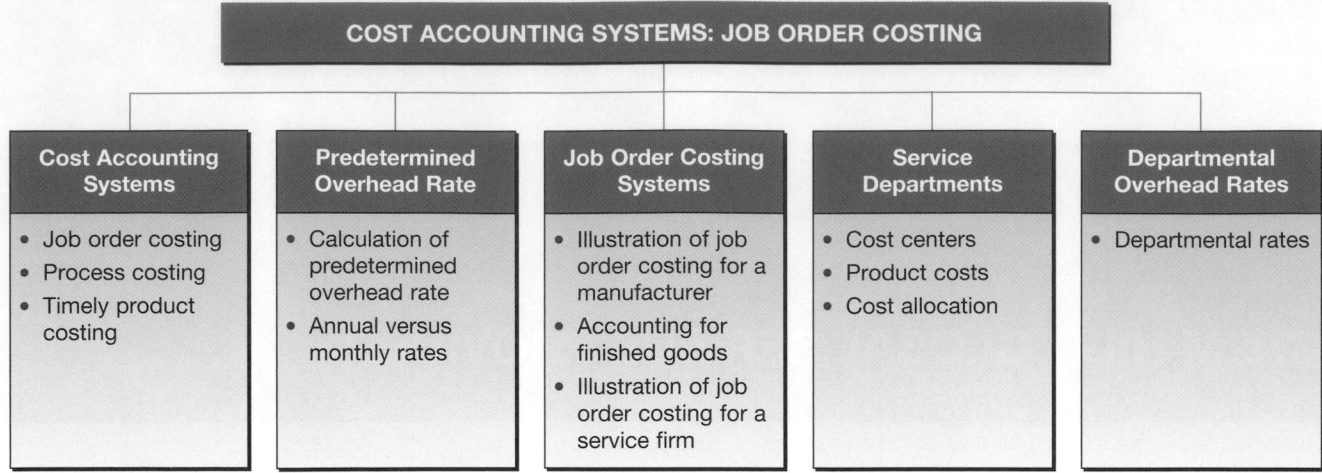

COST ACCOUNTING SYSTEMS: JOB ORDER COSTING

Cost Accounting Systems	Predetermined Overhead Rate	Job Order Costing Systems	Service Departments	Departmental Overhead Rates
• Job order costing • Process costing • Timely product costing	• Calculation of predetermined overhead rate • Annual versus monthly rates	• Illustration of job order costing for a manufacturer • Accounting for finished goods • Illustration of job order costing for a service firm	• Cost centers • Product costs • Cost allocation	• Departmental rates

COST ACCOUNTING SYSTEMS

LO1 **Describe** the two basic types of cost accounting systems, **discuss** how they may be used in both manufacturing and nonmanufacturing environments, and **explain** the need for the timely determination of product costs.

Virtually all manufacturing and service firms have a cost accounting system consisting of forms, procedures, and records used to develop and report timely information about product and service costs. Any orderly method of developing product or service cost information constitutes a cost accounting system. Typically, some amount of cost is accumulated and related to some unit of activity or accomplishment. Examples include accumulating the cost of cutting and forming materials, assembling parts, and painting the final product that results in a completed unit of product such as a lawnmower, a computer, or a custom-designed executive jet aircraft, or the costs associated with CH2M Hill's overseeing the widening of the Panama Canal. Although a cost accounting system could be maintained independently of a firm's formal accounting system, most comprehensive cost accounting systems are integrated into the formal accounting system.

Cost accounting systems are usually illustrated for manufacturing situations involving product costs per unit. Note, however, that reliable cost-per-unit-of-production information is vital to managerial decision making in all types of entities, including service firms and governmental units. For example, a hospital may need to know the cost per patient of providing a specific surgical procedure, an insurance company may want to know the cost of providing health care insurance to a particular group, and a city may need to know the cost per ton of trash removal. Many of the cost accounting concepts and techniques that we discuss in this and subsequent chapters therefore apply to nonmanufacturing as well as manufacturing entities.

Two Basic Types Of Cost Accounting Systems

Job order costing systems and process costing systems are designed to develop timely information about product and job costs, manufacturing inventories, and per-unit costs.

A **job order costing system** is used for *customized* products and services. Therefore, job order costing is characterized by a series of *unique products* or *jobs* undertaken either to fill specific orders from customers or to produce a general stock of products from which future customer orders are filled. In a job order costing system, the costs of direct material, direct labor, and manufacturing overhead are accumulated separately for each job or product, as illustrated in **Exhibit 16-1**.

Job order costing is used by construction companies (to accumulate the cost of each construction project), printing companies

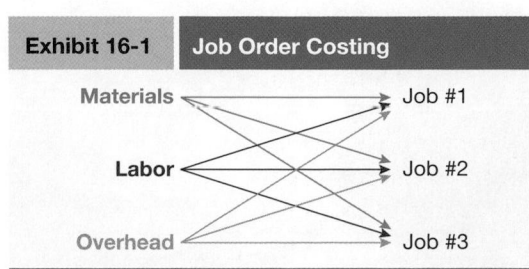

Exhibit 16-1 **Job Order Costing**

(to track the cost of each printing job), manufacturers of consumer products (to determine the cost per unit of each product manufactured), and hospitals (to determine the cost per patient). For example, CH2M Hill keeps track of the costs associated with its Singapore project separately from those associated with its Panama project.

A **process costing system** (**Exhibit 16-2**) lends itself to the production of a *large volume* of *homogenous products* manufactured in a continual flow operation, such as the distillation of fuels or manufacture of paint or wire. In these manufacturing contexts, the materials and operations are involved repetitively during each manufacturing period. Direct material, direct labor, and manufacturing overhead are accumulated by a production department or process for a period and then divided by the units produced during that period to calculate a per-unit cost. Assembly-line operations of entities such as breweries or flour mills and mass-production operations such as power plants and chemical companies would use process costing.

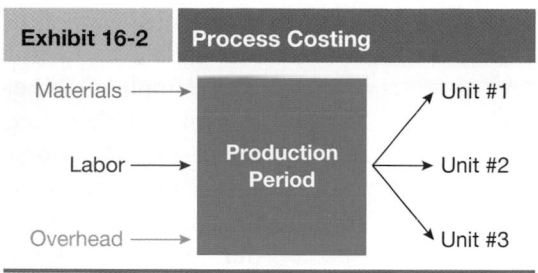

Job order costing and process costing are two extremes along the spectrum of costing systems. A company will design its own accounting system to fit its particular needs. Many companies blend ideas from both job order costing and process costing systems.

Choosing a Cost Accounting System | **ACCOUNTING IN PRACTICE**

Both job order and process costing systems allocate materials, labor, and overhead costs to determine unit costs. In a job order system, costs are identified with specific jobs or products, but a process costing system identifies costs with production processes and averages them over all jobs completed or products made during the period. The type of cost accounting system used by a particular company depends on the nature of the company's operations. One company may, in fact, use job order costing to account for one part of its operation and use process costing to account for another part of its operation. For example, Fezzari Performance Bicycles (introduced in Chapter 14) uses job costing for each unique bike order received. Yet, the manufacture of bicycle frames is accounted for using process costing because each frame of a particular size and model is identical.

Which costing system (job order or process) would most likely be used by the following industries?

Chemicals	Paints
Printing	Glass
Aircraft	Furniture
Oil refining	Machinery

YOUR TURN! 16.1

The solution is on page 795.

Timely Product Costing

Manufacturing Firms

A cost accounting system—either job order costing or process costing—must provide for the timely determination of product costs. Companies need to calculate product costs to determine work in process and finished goods inventory balances, which they report in periodic financial statements. In order to accurately calculate income, companies must develop a way to identify product costs for products sold and for products that remain on hand, either finished or unfinished.

Managers use engineering studies and cost analyses to establish budgets. They then compare actual product costs to budgets so that problems can be identified and remedial action can be taken when necessary. Managers also use product costs as one of the considerations in setting product prices.

To identify costs with a product or group of products, a manufacturer must trace production costs—direct material, direct labor, and manufacturing overhead—to products. To account for materials used, a company may keep track of the costs of materials requisitioned for production by job, product, or department. Labor costs can similarly be accounted for based on timekeeping records or by identifying a particular product or job with total payroll costs of personnel in the factory production departments. A manufacturing firm cannot, however, directly determine the amount of manufacturing overhead that should be identified with particular products or a group of products. The reason is quite simple: Overhead costs are accumulated during a particular accounting period, but it is impossible to know exactly how much overhead cost will accumulate until the *end* of the period. The problem is that companies need to assign product costs *during* the period *before* total overhead costs can be determined for the period. It isn't feasible to wait until the end of the period to determine total product costs to bill customers for jobs completed during the period. Consequently, firms typically assign manufacturing overhead costs to products during the period based on estimates by using predetermined overhead rates.

SERVICE AND MERCHANDISING

Service Firms

The same principles apply to a service company like CH2M Hill. CH2M Hill is also interested in the timely determination of the costs of its projects (or jobs) in order to prepare periodic financial reports and determine income or loss on each project.

Because CH2M Hill's projects typically extend more than a year in length, it is likely that it will have many projects that are in process at the end of each reporting period. Project managers may help to establish budgets, compare budgets to actual results, and take action to control project costs.

For example, the Panama Canal Expansion Program required CH2M Hill to trace labor costs for assigned project managers, engineers, and other consultants to this project over the course of several years. These individuals' salaries and benefits were assigned directly to the project for the period of their involvement on the project team. In addition, CH2M Hill traced other direct project costs to the project as well, such as team member travel, lodging, and meals incurred while working on the project. Corporate overhead was assigned to the project on a monthly basis to allow management to determine project profitability at any point in time.

© istockphoto.com

YOUR TURN! 16.2

The solution is on page 795.

Why is manufacturing overhead assigned to products by using a predetermined overhead rate?

CORPORATE SOCIAL RESPONSIBILITY

Shortage of Highly Trained Engineers

As was noted in the opening vignette, CH2M Hill manages some massive engineering projects. Projects of this size and complexity involve many highly trained engineers. A problem that companies like CH2M Hill face is the acute shortage of engineering talent, especially among women, Hispanics, and African Americans, groups that will comprise a large percentage of the future workforce. As part of its corporate responsibility initiative, CH2M Hill is doing something about this pressing problem.

CH2M believes that "today's children are tomorrow's leaders" is a core tenet of sustainability. The company also understands how important it is to invest in future generations and to mentor them toward careers in engineering and science. CH2M Hill offers summer programs at no cost to the families that introduce their children to these important fields of study. As John Madia, CH2M Hill's chief human resources officer, states, "For most kids, particularly children of color and girls, STEM [Science, Technology, Engineering, and Mathematics] learning opens minds and doors where they have few role models. In helping to grow a diverse pool of future talent, our firm benefits by putting into practice our values of creating partnerships to help sustain and build better communities."

Source: CH2MHILL 2014 Sustainability and Corporate Citizenship Report

PREDETERMINED OVERHEAD RATES

Predetermined manufacturing overhead rates are so named because (1) they are calculated prior to the beginning of each accounting period; (2) they deal with production overhead, that is, all production costs other than direct material and direct labor; and (3) they are usually stated in terms of a rate, such as $20 per direct labor hour. Before the beginning of each year, management normally prepares budgets. Included in the total budget is a production budget, which estimates utilization of the firm's productive capacity in terms of a common measure of activity. Traditionally, firms have used volume measures that are already being recorded for other purposes, such as direct labor hours (recorded for payroll) and machine hours (recorded for depreciation). More recently, more sophisticated and detailed measures have been implemented by some firms, as discussed briefly later in this chapter and in more detail in Chapter 18. Also included in the total budget is an estimate of overhead costs for the year.

LO2 **Explain** the need for a predetermined overhead rate, **demonstrate** its calculation, and **compare** annual and monthly rates.

TAKEAWAY 16.1

If a company's predetermined manufacturing overhead rate is $20 per direct labor hour, this means that every time an actual direct labor hour is incurred, $20 in overhead is added or applied to work in process inventory and removed from the overhead account.

| Multiple Predetermined Overhead Rates | ACCOUNTING IN PRACTICE |

Often, companies calculate more than one predetermined manufacturing overhead rate for a given period. For example, some firms will calculate a predetermined variable overhead rate and a predetermined fixed overhead rate. Why? Doing so allows management to evaluate a production department's control of costs that are expected to vary with the level of production (often within the control of local management) separately from those costs that are related to the capacity to do work (often fixed in nature and largely out of local management's hands).

Calculation of Predetermined Overhead Rate

A **predetermined manufacturing overhead rate** is computed by dividing the budgeted or estimated total overhead cost for the year by the budgeted or estimated level of the application base. The application base is simply the activity used to assign overhead. This application base is generally the **cost driver** most closely related to the accumulation of overhead costs. This cost driver is typically the utilization of the facility's productive capacity for the year (such as total estimated direct labor hours or total estimated machine hours). Calculations of predetermined rates are typically based on one-year production periods, but they could be calculated based on shorter horizons, such as quarterly or monthly production periods. Companies should choose the application base that corresponds to the period over which activity decisions are typically made.

Assume that the most appropriate measure of activity for applying overhead at CH2M Hill is direct labor hours. If CH2M's management estimates 50 million direct labor hours for 2016 and the estimated total manufacturing overhead cost for 2016 is $2,200 million, the overhead rate for 2016 may be calculated as follows:

$$2016 \text{ Predetermined manufacturing overhead rate} = \frac{\text{Estimated overhead cost for 2016}}{\text{Estimated direct labor hours for 2016}}$$

$$= \frac{\$2,200 \text{ million}}{50 \text{ million hours}}$$

$$= \$44 \text{ per direct labor hour}$$

Hint: *Applied overhead is a product of the predetermined overhead rate and actual hours for that job, not budgeted hours.*

If, during March 2016, a particular project requires 1,000 direct labor hours, $44,000 of manufacturing overhead (1,000 × $44) would be assigned to this project.

Before selecting the allocation base for applying overhead to products or projects, a firm should carefully analyze the relationship between overhead incurred and various alternative measures of activity. Direct labor hours or direct labor costs would be used as the measure of activity in a service company that has labor-intensive projects. However, in a factory in which automation has replaced many of the production workers, machine hours may be a more appropriate measure.

Using a predetermined overhead rate, management can estimate the overhead costs of any job at any stage of production, computing "costs to date" both for control purposes and for inventory costing. This method also eliminates wide fluctuations in unit costs that might result if actual recorded overhead costs were assigned to products during short interim periods when production departed markedly from normal levels.

TAKEAWAY 16.2

The total estimated overhead divided by the total estimated activity level of the application base (such as machine hours or direct labor hours) equals the predetermined overhead rate. Management tries to select an activity base that is common to all of the jobs that the company produces.

YOUR TURN! 16.3

The solution is on page 795.

Assume you own a manufacturing company that budgets an estimated $250,000 in overhead for the coming year and 10,000 direct labor hours. Also assume your manufacturing overhead application base is direct labor hours. Actual overhead during the year amounts to $216,000 and employees work 9,000 actual direct labor hours. Compute the predetermined overhead rate and the amount of overhead that is applied to work in process inventory.

Annual versus Monthly Rates

Assume, for example, that normal production is 100,000 direct labor hours per year and that production fluctuates seasonally throughout the year. Suppose also that a large share of actual manufacturing overhead cost is spread fairly evenly over the year. (Such costs as depreciation, maintenance, utilities, and supervisory costs remain fairly constant from month to month.) **Exhibit 16-3** illustrates the possible differences between assigned

Exhibit 16-3	Comparison of Actual Monthly and Predetermined Annual Overhead Rates			
	Manufacturing Overhead Costs Incurred Each Month*	**Direct Labor Hours Worked Each Month**	**Actual Monthly Overhead Rates**	**Predetermined Annual Overhead Rate**
January.......	$ 9,900	4,000	$2.48	$1.50
February......	$ 9,300	3,000	$3.10	$1.50
March........	$ 10,500	5,000	$2.10	$1.50
April	$ 12,300	8,000	$1.54	$1.50
May..........	$ 14,100	11,000	$1.28	$1.50
June	$ 14,700	12,000	$1.23	$1.50
July..........	$ 16,500	15,000	$1.10	$1.50
August	$ 15,300	13,000	$1.18	$1.50
September	$ 13,500	10,000	$1.35	$1.50
October	$ 12,300	8,000	$1.54	$1.50
November.....	$ 11,100	6,000	$1.85	$1.50
December.....	$ 10,500	5,000	$2.10	$1.50
	$150,000	100,000		

*Assumed to be $7,500 each month plus 60 cents per direct labor hour.

overhead costs based on actual monthly overhead rates and those based on an annual overhead rate. The predetermined annual rate in this example is $1.50 per direct labor hour ($150,000/100,000 direct labor hours). The actual monthly rates vary from $3.10 in February to $1.10 in July, with only the months of April and October close to the annual average of $1.50 per direct labor hour. Using actual monthly rates and assuming that a particular unit of product requires 3 direct labor hours, a unit produced in July when production activity was highest would be assigned overhead costs of $3.30 (3 × $1.10). In contrast, a unit produced in February when production activity was lowest would be assigned overhead costs of $9.30 (3 × $3.10). The $6 difference is hardly defensible, especially when the two units of product may be virtually identical. The use of a predetermined overhead rate employing a yearly average produces more meaningful unit-cost figures.

JOB ORDER COSTING SYSTEMS

Job order costing systems are designed to accumulate product costs—direct material, direct labor, and manufacturing overhead—by job and in total. **Exhibit 16-4** illustrates the flow of the documents in a job order costing system that might be used by Fezzari for an order of a high-end triathlon/time-trial bike.

When the customer places the order for the bike, Fezzari would create a **sales order** specifying the bike model and customer-specified options. Based on this sales order, the assembly department would create a **production order** directing the assembly employees to build the bike in accordance with the customer's specifications. Before assembly can begin, the assembly technician must gather the correct parts together. This is done based on a **bill of materials**, or list of each required part for the particular bike model. The technician creates a **materials requisition,**

LO3 Describe and explain a job order costing system, **identify** types of records used in job order costing, and **demonstrate** the journal entries that accompany the flow of product costs.

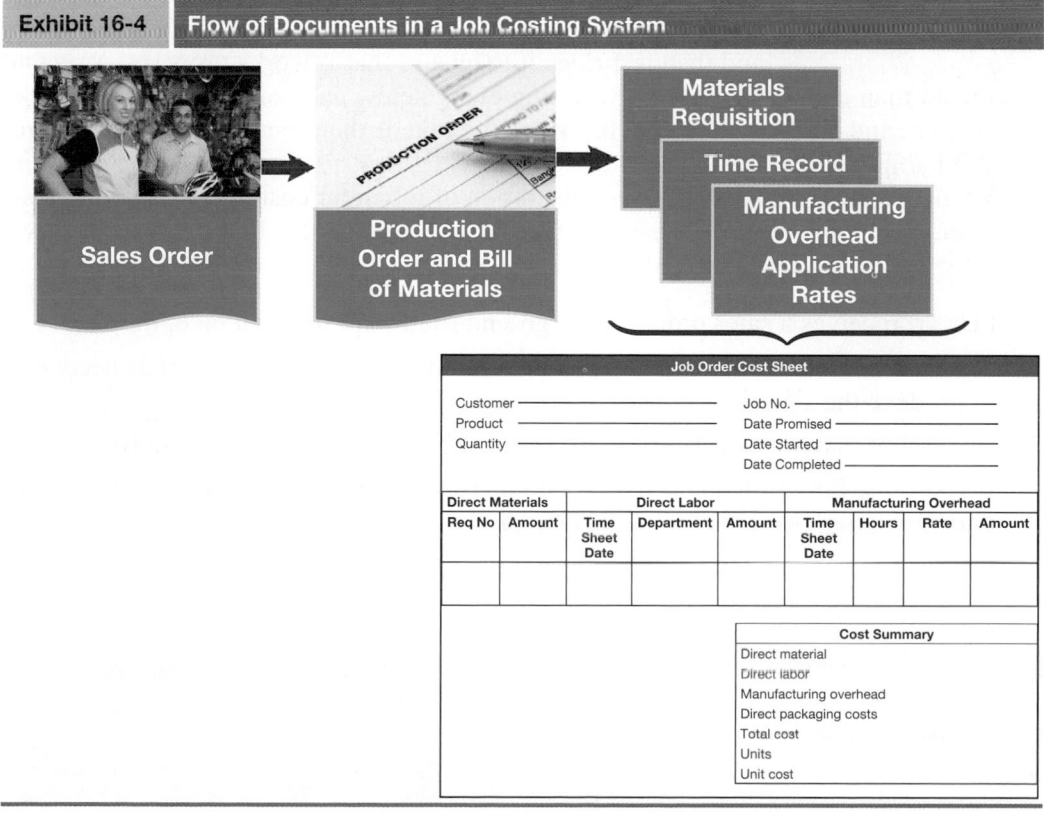

| Exhibit 16-4 | Flow of Documents in a Job Costing System |

requesting that the bike components on the bill of materials be pulled from inventory and brought to the assembly station. As the technician assembles the bike, she would keep track of her time on a **time record**, either in written form on a timesheet or electronically through a time clock. As the job progresses, the materials used, labor expended, and overhead applied would be accumulated on a **job order cost sheet**. A job order cost sheet is a record of the materials, labor, and overhead for each job and serves as a subsidiary record or subset of the work in process account. When the bike is finished, the job order cost sheet would be closed.

Illustration of Job Order Costing for a Manufacturer

Almost 40 million Americans age seven and older ride a bike six times or more in a given year. The U.S. bicycle industry has been remarkably stable at $6 billion in sales since 2003, with a slight dip in 2013 due to the U.S. recession. Approximately 11.3 million bicycles of wheel sizes over 20" were imported or produced domestically in 2013. It is estimated that 99% of these bikes were imported from China and Taiwan. Domestic bike manufacturers, over 100 in all, produce approximately 56,000 units per year. Department, discount, and chain toy stores sell approximately 74% of the bikes sold, followed by specialty local bike shops (LBSs) at 15%, chain sporting goods stores at 6.5%, outdoor specialty retailers at 2.5%, and "other" at 2%.[1]

Fezzari Performance Bicycles is a U.S. bike manufacturer that builds both mountain bikes and road bikes. Located in Lindon, Utah, it sells a few thousand bikes per year, from a $500 entry-level mountain and hybrid bike to a high-end full-suspension mountain bike and triathlon bike that sells for over $10,000. As described in Chapter 14, once a customer selects a specific bike model and components, Fezzari orders the required parts from its suppliers. Fezzari maintains a minimal quantity of parts in inventory so that the bike assembly can be started without waiting for ordered parts to arrive. A technician assembles the bike to the customer's specifications, tunes it up, and then test rides it to ensure that it works properly. A second technician then checks the assembly, testing every screw and component, then checks the tune-up, and performs a second test ride. The bike is then sent to packing to be prepared for shipment.

We now turn to a comprehensive illustration of job order costing, which provides a conjectural example of how Fezzari's job costing system works. In this illustration, we make the following assumptions:

Hint: A bill of materials is a list of all parts or components needed for the manufacture of the finished product.

1. Fezzari receives a sales order for a high-end triathlon/time-trial bike, the T5.

2. A production order is then issued, along with the related bill of materials necessary to produce the T5.

3. The bill of materials, or list of parts, for the T5 is as shown in **Exhibit 16-5**.

4. It takes one Fezzari technician eight hours to assemble and test the bike and a second technician two hours to perform a quality check.

5. Fezzari uses a predetermined overhead rate of $17 per hour based on annual direct labor hours to assign overhead to products.

---

[1] http://nbda.com/articles/industry-overview-2013-pg34.htm

Exhibit 16-5	Bill of Materials - T5			
Item	**Description**	**Quantity**	**Cost**	**Extension**
Frame	Fezzari Racing Design FA1 3K Monocoque Carbon Aero TT Frame. . .	1	$4,000	$4,000
Fork	Fezzari Racing XrA 3K Aero Fork, Carbon Steerer Tube	1	integrated	
Headset	Cane Creek Orbit IS-2 7075/T6 Crown Race, 1⅛" Steerer Tube.	1	integrated	
Shifters	Shimano Dura-Ace 9000, 22 Speed.	2	$ 350	$ 700
Shift cables		2	$ 15	$ 30
Front Derailleur	Shimano Dura-Ace 9000, Brazed On	1	$ 70	$ 70
Rear Derailleur	Shimano Dura-Ace 9000, short cage (22 speed)	1	$ 140	$ 140
Cassette	Shimano Dura-Ace 9000	1	$ 175	$ 175
Crank	Vision Trimax Carbon	1	$ 350	$ 350
Chainrings	FSA BB30 Trimax 54/39t	1	$ 60	$ 60
Bottom Bracket	FSA BB30 Ceramic	1	$ 30	$ 30
Chain	Shimano Dura-Ace 9000	1	$ 35	$ 35
Handlebars	Vision Trimax Carbon	1	$ 190	$ 190
Stem	Fezzari Ultra Light	1	$ 90	$ 90
Tape/Grips	Fizik	1	$ 18	$ 18
Saddle	Fizik Arione Tri 2.	1	$ 100	$ 100
Seatpost	Fezzari Racing Design XrTT Aero 3K Carbon	1	integrated	
Rims	Reynolds 90 Areo, Carbon Clinchers.	2	$1,200	$2,400
Hubs	Reynolds 90 Areo, Carbon Clinchers.	2	included	
Spokes	Reynolds 90 Areo, Carbon Clinchers.	36	included	
Tires	Maxxis Xenith Hors Categorie M-201, 700 x 23c, race tire	2	$ 90	$ 180
Tubes	Fezzari Performance Road Tubes	2	$ 7	$ 14
Brakes	Shimano Dura-Ace 9000	2	$ 15	$ 30
Brake Levers	Vision Metro Cargon.	2	$ 50	$ 100
Brake Cables		2	$ 13	$ 26
				$8,738

Accounting for Materials

For a high-end bike like the T5, Fezzari orders the frame from its Taiwanese supplier and the tires and other components from other local suppliers upon receipt of the order. Thus, the first transaction to record is the *purchase* of materials. Fezzari purchased parts listed on the bill of materials for a total cost of $8,738. Following is the entry to record this purchase:

1	Materials inventory	8,738	
	Accounts payable		8,738
	To record the purchase of materials.		

The next transaction is the *requisition* of the following materials from the materials inventory for use in the production of the T5: $4,000 for the frame, $700 for the shifters, $30 for the shift cables, and so forth. **Exhibit 16-6** shows a sample requisition for a Fezzari T5.

Assume that in addition to the direct materials listed on the bill of materials, the assembly of the T5 requires $30 of indirect materials (lubricants, bar end plugs, etc.). The entry to record the requisitioning and use of both direct and indirect materials is as follows:

2	Work in process inventory	8,738	
	Manufacturing overhead	30	
	Materials inventory		8,768
	To record the requisitioning of materials—both direct and indirect.		

Hint: A materials requisition form is a list of items to be pulled from inventory for use in manufacturing a product.

Exhibit 16-6	Materials Requisition Form				
Date 8/5		Job. No. 372		Requisition No. 567	
		Quantity			
Item		**Authorized**	**Issued**	**Unit Price**	**Amount**
Frame		1	1	$4,000	$4,000
Fork		1	1	integrated	
Headset		1	1	integrated	
Shifters		2	2	$ 350	$ 700
Shift cables.		2	2	$ 15	$ 30
Front Derailleur.		1	1	$ 70	$ 70
Rear Derailleur		1	1	$ 140	$ 140
Cassette		1	1	$ 175	$ 175
Crank		1	1	$ 350	$ 350
Chainrings		1	1	$ 60	$ 60
Bottom Bracket		1	1	$ 30	$ 30
Chain		1	1	$ 35	$ 35
Handlebars.		1	1	$ 190	$ 190
Stem.		1	1	$ 90	$ 90
Tape/Grips		1	1	$ 18	$ 18
Saddle		1	1	$ 100	$ 100
Seatpost.		1	1	integrated	
Rims		2	2	$1,200	$2,400
Hubs.		2	2	included	
Spokes		36	36	included	
Tires		2	2	$ 90	$ 180
Tubes		2	2	$ 7	$ 14
Brakes		2	2	$ 15	$ 30
Brake Levers		2	2	$ 50	$ 100
Brake Cables		2	2	$ 13	$ 26
Total					$8,738

Authorized by: TC   Issued by: GAP   Received by: CB

The effect of the various postings of these transactions is shown in **Exhibit 16-7**. The amount of direct materials used would also be recorded on the job order cost sheet for Job 372 (see **Exhibit 16-11**).

Exhibit 16-7	Entries for Recording the Acquisition and Use of Materials

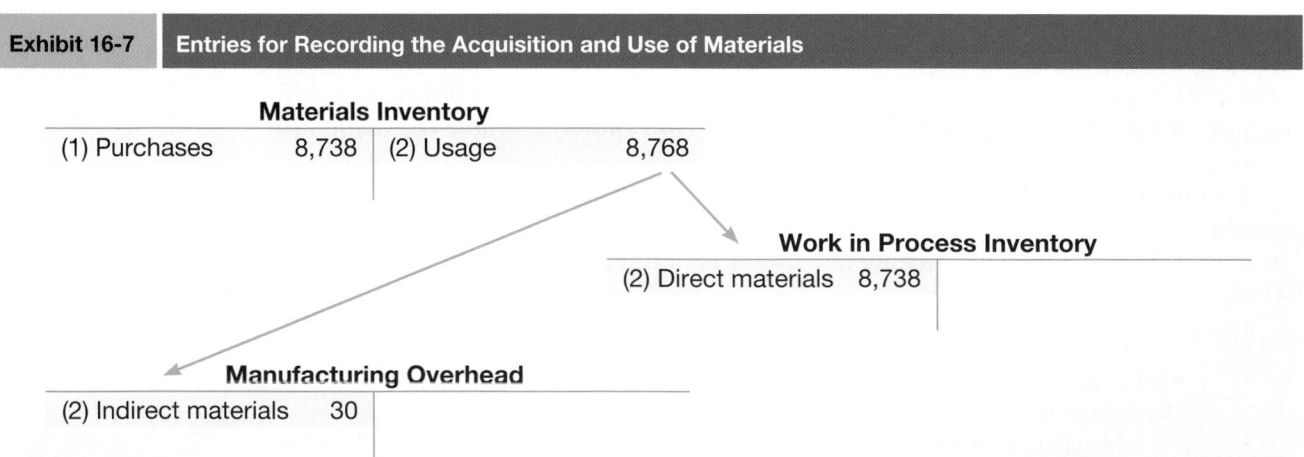

Accounting for Labor

Manufacturing firms (including Fezzari) typically use **time clocks** or time records to collect the total amount of time that each employee worked during a particular pay period. **Exhibit 16-8** shows a sample time record for a Fezzari employee.

Exhibit 16-8	Time Record						
Employee Name: Robert							Employee No. 42
Skill Specification:		Technician			Date:		8/5
Time Started	Time Stopped	Total Time	Hourly Labor Rate	Department		Job No.	Total Cost
8:00	12:00	4	$25	Assembly		372	$100
1:00	5:00	4	$25	Assembly		372	$100
Total		8					$200
Approved by *LSH*							

Hint: A time record is a method of recording and organizing time spent on a product or job.

Time clocks collect only total time worked; time records collect hours worked on particular jobs. Time clocks and computer time records are used to prepare the payroll recorded in Wages Payable.

Tracking Time   **ACCOUNTING IN PRACTICE**

In practice, companies use various methods to track employees' time. Where employees are paid on an hourly-rate basis for hours worked, time clocks are used. In some firms, employees place a small paper card in the time clock at the beginning and end of their work shift, and the card is imprinted (or "punched") with the date and time. More commonly, employees slide or wave an employee ID card through or in front of a card reader that records the date and time information. The most recent innovation in tracking employees' time involves a device that recognizes an employee's fingerprint, iris, or face, eliminating the need for a physical card of any kind. Where employees are salaried, but there is a need to attribute hours worked to a particular job or product for costing purposes, time records are used. Employees record the amount of time that they spend each day working on a particular job or jobs so that customers can be billed the appropriate amount for labor.

Assume that Fezzari uses time records to identify labor costs with specific jobs. Hourly wage rates are used to compute the labor costs for the various products assembled. The sum of the amounts calculated using the time records should equal the total wages payable for the period. In fact, the amounts calculated from the time records are used to distribute the wages payable to the individual jobs. To assemble the T5, $200 (8 hours × $25 per hour) of direct labor was incurred. The entry to record the distribution of the wages payable is as follows:

3	Work in process inventory	200	
	Wages payable		200
	To distribute the wages payable.		

The effect of the posting of this transaction is shown in **Exhibit 16-9**. The amount of direct labor incurred would also be recorded on the job order cost sheet for Job 372 (see **Exhibit 16-11**).

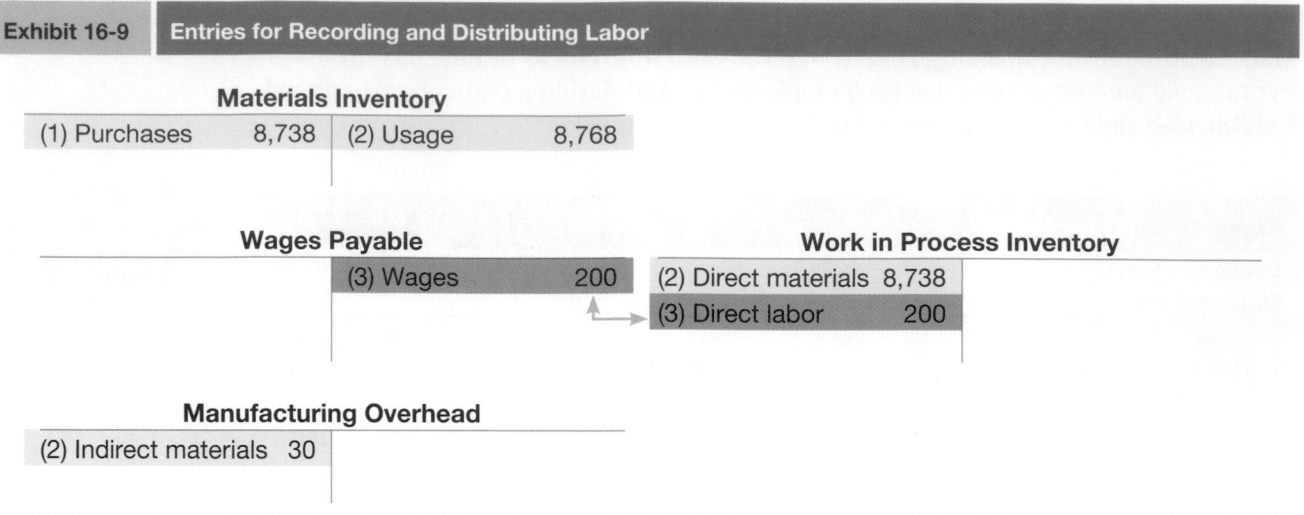

Exhibit 16-9 | **Entries for Recording and Distributing Labor**

Accounting for Manufacturing Overhead

Factory costs are routinely charged to manufacturing overhead as incurred or through adjusting entries at the end of the accounting period. One of the elements of manufacturing overhead—indirect materials—has already been recorded through the transactions related to materials. Other general manufacturing overhead costs incurred by Fezzari during the period are recorded as they are incurred: indirect labor, $28,000; factory utilities, $31,000; factory lease, $100,000; factory insurance, $68,000; factory property taxes, $12,000; and other manufacturing overhead, $13,000. Manufacturing overhead to be recorded as a year-end adjustment is depreciation on the factory equipment of $45,100. The following are the journal entries to record these items:

4	Manufacturing overhead	252,000	
	Cash, Accounts payable, or Wages payable		252,000
	To record elements of manufacturing overhead as incurred.		

5	Manufacturing overhead	45,100	
	Accumulated depreciation—factory equipment		45,100
	To record depreciation on factory equipment.		

As explained previously, actual manufacturing overhead costs are not assigned directly to individual jobs. Instead, through the use of a predetermined overhead rate, the work in process inventory account is charged with manufacturing overhead applied. During the budgeting process, Fezzari determined its predetermined overhead rate to be $17 per direct labor hour. The T5 order accumulated 8 hours of direct labor. As a result, $136 of manufacturing overhead is applied to the job.

The journal entry to record the application of manufacturing overhead to Job 372 is as follows:

6	Work in process inventory	136	
	Manufacturing overhead		136
	To record the application of manufacturing overhead to the work in process inventory using the predetermined overhead rate.		

The effect of the various postings of these transactions is shown in **Exhibit 16-10**. The amount of overhead applied would also be recorded on the job order cost sheet for Job 372 (see **Exhibit 16-11**).

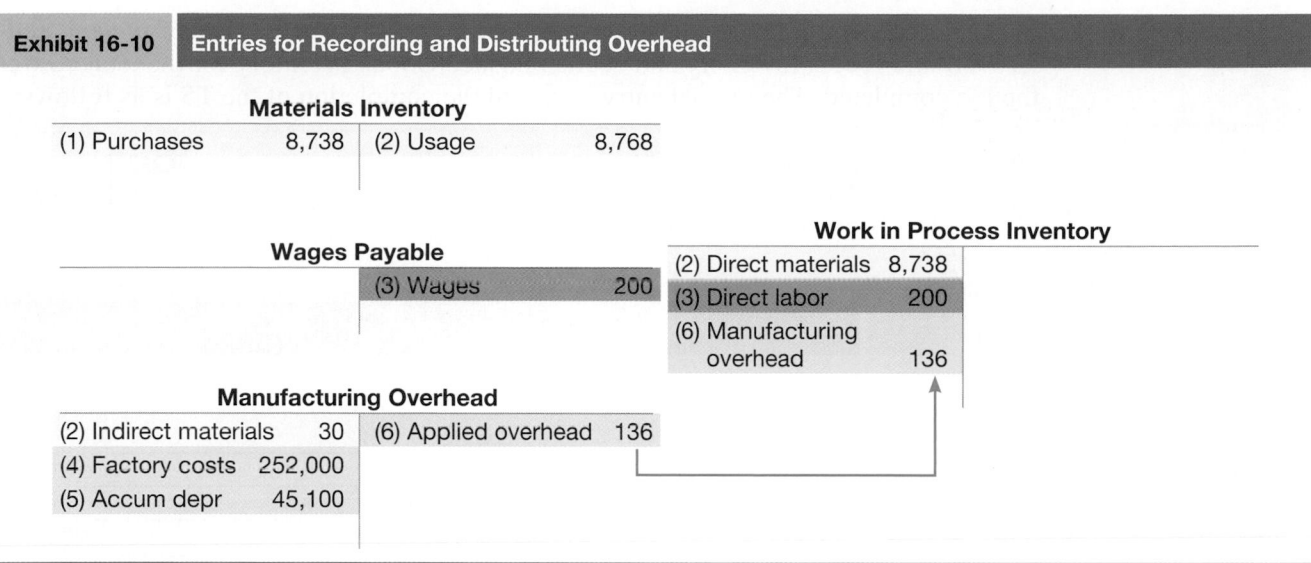

Exhibit 16-10	Entries for Recording and Distributing Overhead

Materials Inventory

| (1) Purchases | 8,738 | (2) Usage | 8,768 |

Wages Payable

| | | (3) Wages | 200 |

Work in Process Inventory

(2) Direct materials	8,738
(3) Direct labor	200
(6) Manufacturing overhead	136

Manufacturing Overhead

(2) Indirect materials	30	(6) Applied overhead	136
(4) Factory costs	252,000		
(5) Accum depr	45,100		

Accounting For Packaging and Finished Goods

When products are finished, they are transferred from Work in Process Inventory to Finished Goods Inventory. The costs transferred from Work in Process to Finished Goods Inventory include all manufacturing costs. However, these costs also include packaging costs.

LO4 Discuss the procedures and journal entries used to account for finished goods and the sale of finished goods.

Treatment of Packaging Costs	ACCOUNTING IN PRACTICE

A product is not complete or finished until it is packaged in the container in which it will be sold. Packaging costs are part of the product cost transferred to the Finished Goods Inventory account.

Fezzari spends two hours to inspect, partially dissemble, and package the T5 for shipment to the customer. The two hours of inspecting are recorded in a time record at a pay rate of $25 per hour. Approximately $75 is required for the shipment container and packing materials. The packing materials are purchased on account and immediately placed into Work in Process. Remember that Fezzari applies overhead based on direct labor hours. Thus, Fezzari would also record $34 (2 hours × $17 per hour) to Work in Process Inventory. The total packaging costs applied to Work in Process is $125.

7	Work in process inventory	50	
	Cash and wages payable		50
	To record the packaging labor for Job 372.		
8	Work in process inventory	75	
	Accounts payable		75
	To record the cost of packing material for Job 372.		
9	Work in process inventory	34	
	Manufacturing overhead		34
	To record the application of manufacturing overhead to the work in process inventory using the predetermined overhead rate.		

When the T5 bike order is completed, the unit cost of the T5 is obtained by summing the costs charged to the job. **Exhibit 16-11** shows the completed job cost sheet for Fezarri's Job 372. The job cost sheet accumulates all product costs for the job including; direct material, direct labor, manufacturing overhead and packaging. The report also identifies the total unit cost of $9,233. Notice that this amount also matches the total of the debits to the work in process inventory account in **Exhibit 16-12**. The accountant credits Work in Process Inventory and debits Finished Goods Inventory for the total cost of the job completed. The journal entry to record the completion of the T5 is as follows:

10	Finished goods inventory	9,233	
	Work in process inventory		9,233
	To record the completion of Job 372.		

Exhibit 16-11	Fezzari's Job Cost Sheet for Job No. 372

Fezzari Job Cost Sheet

Customer   Ryan Hobson   Job No.   372

Product   T5   Date Promised   5/15

Quantity   1   Date Started   8/1

                                       Date Completed   8/6

Direct Materials		Direct Labor			Manufacturing Overhead			
Req No	Amount	Time Sheet Date	Department	Amount	Time Sheet Date	Hours	Rate	Amount
567	$8,738	8/5	Assembly	$200	8/5	8	$17/DLH	$136

Cost Summary	
Direct material	$8,738
Direct labor	$200
Manufacturing overhead	$136
Total packaging costs	$159*
Total cost	**$9,233**
Units	1
Unit cost	$9,233

*Total packaging costs include materials of $75, labor of $50, and overhead of $34.

When the T5 is delivered to the customer, the cost of the bike is removed from the finished goods subaccount. Two journal entries are recorded. The first entry is a debit to Accounts Receivable and a credit to Sales for the selling price of the bike. The second entry is a debit to Cost of Goods Sold and a credit to Finished Goods Inventory for the cost of the bike. The entries to record the sale of the T5 are as follows:

11	Accounts receivable	10,500	
	Sales		10,500
	To record the sale of Job 372.		

12	Cost of goods sold	9,233	
	Finished goods inventory		9,233
	To record the cost of Job 372.		

The effect of the various postings of these transactions is shown in **Exhibit 16-12**. Note that entry 11 is not shown in this exhibit because it involves the revenue associated with the sale, not the cost of the job. The job order cost sheet for Job 372 would also be closed.

| Exhibit 16-12 | Entries for Completing the Job and Recording the Sale |

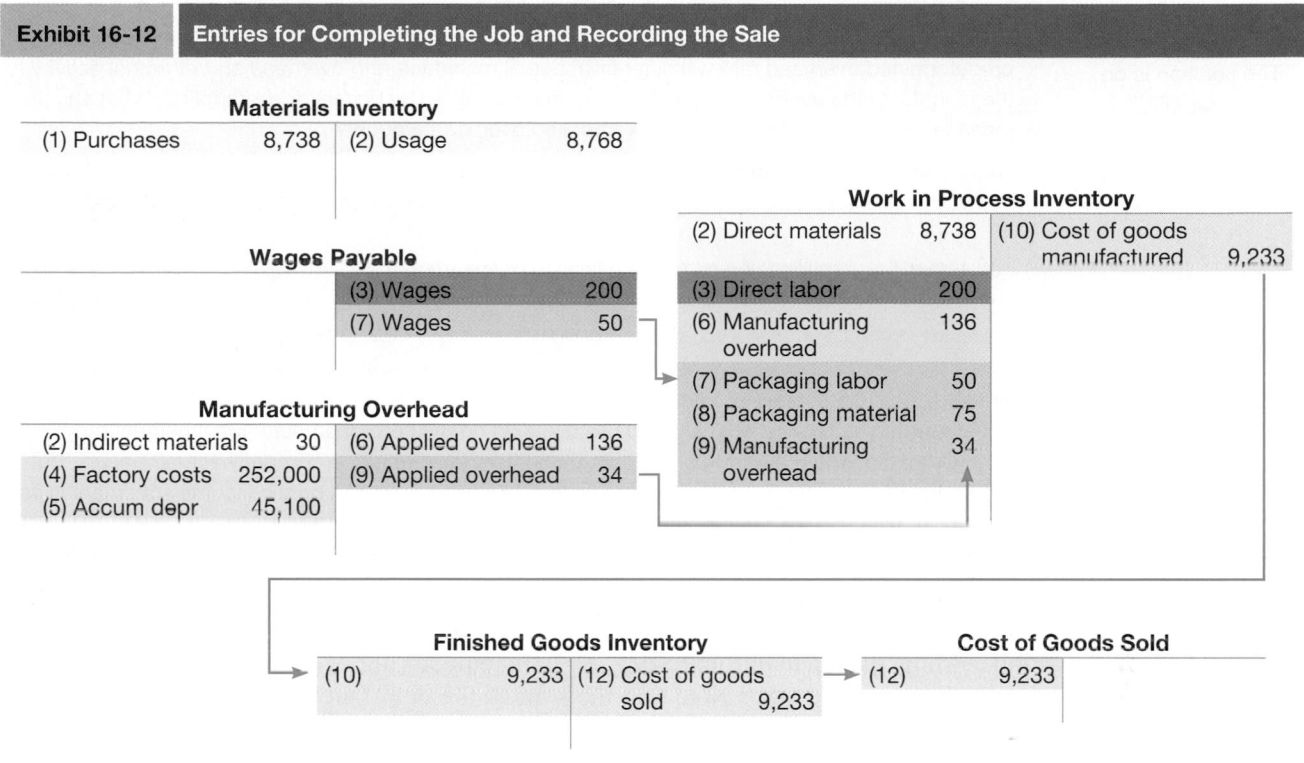

Disposition of Under- and Overapplied Overhead

As introduced in Chapter 15 and described earlier in this chapter, overhead costs are accumulated in the manufacturing overhead account during an accounting period (usually a year). During the same period, overhead costs are being applied to products or jobs based on a predetermined overhead rate. It is not until the end of the period, after all actual overhead costs have been recorded and all overhead has been applied to products and jobs, that management determines whether the amount of overhead applied to products and jobs is greater or less than the amount of actual overhead costs recorded. If more has been applied than recorded, overhead is said to be **overapplied**. If less has been applied than recorded, overhead is said to be **underapplied**.

At year-end, a journal entry is made to dispose of the underapplied or overapplied amount of manufacturing overhead. If the amount of underapplied or overapplied overhead is insignificant, an entry is made to transfer the amount to the cost of goods sold account. The under- or overapplied overhead is almost always immaterial in practice. An overapplied amount is transferred by debiting Manufacturing Overhead and crediting Cost of Goods Sold. An underapplied amount is transferred by debiting Cost of Goods Sold and crediting Manufacturing Overhead.

When the under- or overapplied amount is significant, it should be allocated to all of the jobs that were worked on during the year. This is accomplished by a journal entry that transfers the amount to Work in Process Inventory, Finished Goods Inventory, and Cost of Goods Sold. An overapplied amount is transferred by debiting Manufacturing Overhead and crediting Work in Process Inventory, Finished Goods Inventory, and Cost of Goods Sold. An underapplied amount is transferred by debiting Work in Process Inventory, Finished Goods Inventory, and Cost of Goods Sold sold and crediting Manufacturing Overhead. The amount transferred is allocated proportionately among Work in Process Inventory, Finished Goods Inventory, and Cost of Goods Sold based on the amount of Applied Overhead that is in each of the three accounts at the end of the year.

Hint: After the disposition of over- or underapplied overhead, the balance in the overhead account should be $0.

Because the estimated manufacturing overhead and/or the estimated activity level used in the predetermined overhead rate will differ from actual manufacturing overhead and/or actual activity, the manufacturing overhead applied to work in process will be under- or overapplied. What should management do with this under- or overapplied overhead amount?

a. Add/subtract from cost of goods sold.

b. Allocate among work in process inventory, finished goods inventory, and cost of goods sold.

c. Either a or b, depending on the significance of the amount.

TAKEAWAY 16.3

After the disposition of over- or underapplied overhead to cost of goods sold or cost of goods sold and the inventory accounts, cost of goods sold should be the correct amount. Management may apply overhead during the year in an amount that differs from what the company actually incurs, but at the end of the year, the cost of the company's products as reported on the income statement is as accurate as management can make it.

Exhibit 16-13 reflects the various postings of the journal entries related to manufacturing overhead. Items from entries 4, 5, 6, and 9 are highlighted in bold type. In addition, assume that an additional $292,280 in manufacturing overhead was applied to other jobs throughout the year. Note that the sum of the debits in manufacturing overhead is $297,130 but that the sum of the credits is $292,450. In other words, actual factory costs were $297,130, but only $292,450 of manufacturing overhead was applied to the work in process inventory account. Therefore, overhead was underapplied by $4,680. Assume that this amount is insignificant.

The journal entry to record the transfer of the underapplied overhead is as follows:

13	Cost of goods sold	4,680	
	Manufacturing overhead		4,680
	To record the disposition of underapplied overhead.		

When perpetual inventory procedures are used in cost accounting systems, the ending balances in Materials Inventory, Work in Process Inventory, and Finished Goods Inventory reflect all the transactions of the accounting period that increase and decrease inventories. These ending balances are adjusted only if a discrepancy is discovered when the year-end physical counts of inventory are taken.

| **Exhibit 16-13** | **Entries for Closing Underapplied Overhead** |

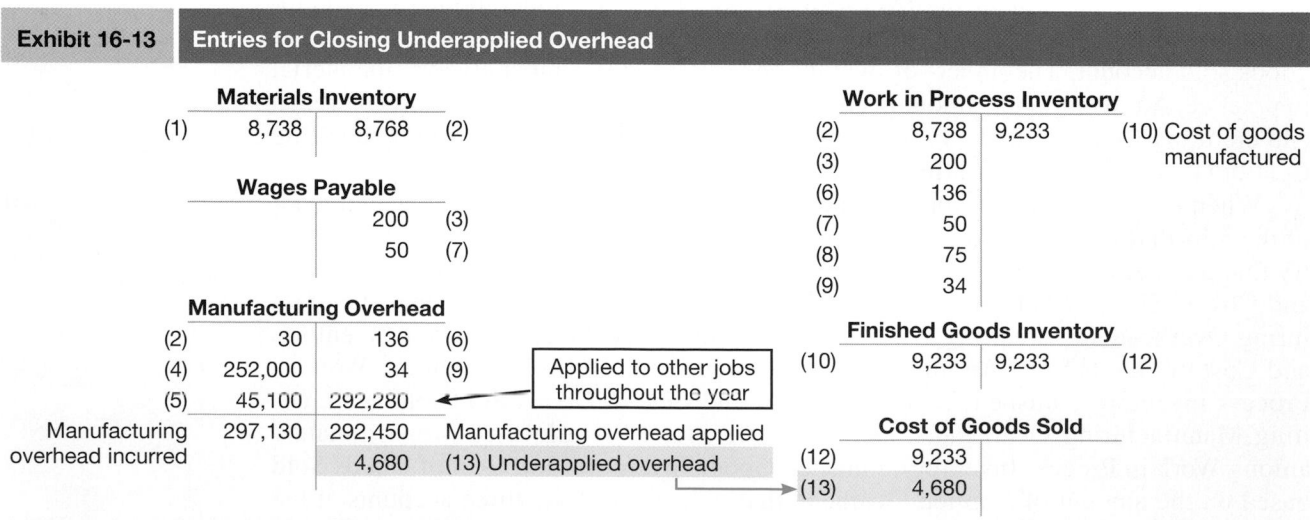

Materials Inventory

| (1) | 8,738 | 8,768 | (2) |

Wages Payable

| | | 200 | (3) |
| | | 50 | (7) |

Manufacturing Overhead

(2)	30	136	(6)
(4)	252,000	34	(9)
(5)	45,100	292,280	
Manufacturing overhead incurred	297,130	292,450	Manufacturing overhead applied
		4,680	(13) Underapplied overhead

Applied to other jobs throughout the year

Work in Process Inventory

(2)	8,738	9,233	(10) Cost of goods manufactured
(3)	200		
(6)	136		
(7)	50		
(8)	75		
(9)	34		

Finished Goods Inventory

| (10) | 9,233 | 9,233 | (12) |

Cost of Goods Sold

| (12) | 9,233 | | |
| (13) | 4,680 | | |

As illustrated in the Fezzari example in **Exhibits 15-12, 13**, and **14** of Chapter 15, the entries shown in the accounts in **Exhibit 16-13** could be used to create a Schedule of Cost of Goods Manufactured and a Schedule of Cost of Goods Sold for the T5. Together with other information about sales and costs of Fezzari's other products and selling and administrative expenses, Fezzari management could then prepare an Income Statement for the period.

Illustration of Job Order Costing for a Service Firm

Job order costing is also used by service companies. An abbreviated illustration using a CH2M Hill project will demonstrate the use of job order costing in a service environment.

One of the services that CH2M Hill provides to clients is assistance with implementation of lean enterprise solutions. Essentially, CH2M Hill utilizes proven approaches and methods to streamline client manufacturing and office processes. One such client was the Perrier Group of America. The objective of the CH2M Hill project was to determine the optimal location for a new bottling facility needed for projected five-year sales growth in the company's Northeast Region. CH2M Hill evaluated Perrier's entire supply chain, from the spring to the customer. The result of the project was the determination of new raw materials requirements to support projected growth, the optimal location of the bottling facility, and the amount and location of additional warehouse facilities to support increased sales during peak periods of the year.

Accounting for Materials

Because this project was for services, no materials were used. This is typical of service projects.

Accounting for Labor

CH2M Hill's project manager, engineers, and consultants recorded their time working on the Perrier project on a time record or timesheet. These employees also worked on other projects during the same period and recorded the time worked on those projects separately. Assume that during one period, the assigned employees worked a total of 40 hours on the Perrier project and that the portion of their salaries associated with the time spent on the Perrier project was $5,000. This would have been recorded as follows:

Work in process—Perrier	5,000	
Salaries payable		5,000
To record salaries on the Perrier project.		

Accounting for Overhead

Assume that CH2M Hill uses a predetermined overhead rate for consulting engagements of $150 per hour. Because 40 hours of labor was charged to the Perrier project for the period, a total of $6,000 ($150 × 40 hours) of overhead would have been applied to the project. The entry to record the application of overhead is the same as shown earlier for Fezzari:

Work in process—Perrier	6,000	
Overhead		6,000
To record the application of overhead to the Perrier project using the		
predetermined overhead rate.		

Recording the Sale

Recall that with the completion of a product, the accumulated cost of the product is moved from work in process inventory to finished goods inventory. However, service companies do not have a finished goods inventory. Instead, when a project is completed, the accumulated cost of the service is removed from work in process inventory as the final project invoice is prepared. In our illustration, assume that when CH2M Hill completed the project, the Work in Process—Perrier account had a total balance of $245,000 and that the contract between CH2M Hill and Perrier was for $300,000. CH2M Hill would have recorded the following journal entries in its financial records:

Accounts receivable	300,000	
Sales		300,000
To record the final billing for the Perrier project.		
Cost of goods sold	245,000	
Work in process—Perrier		245,000
To record the cost of the Perrier project.		

ACCOUNTING FOR SERVICE DEPARTMENTS

LO5 Describe the procedures for cost allocation for service departments.

Most factories are so large and so complex that a high degree of organizational specialization naturally exists in their operations. Production usually involves a series of specialized departments, such as cutting, reshaping, grinding, subassembly, final assembly, painting, and packaging. In addition to these production departments, a typical factory also has highly specialized service departments, which may be involved with purchasing, materials handling, personnel, warehousing, inspection, maintenance, and even food service (cafeterias). Whereas production departments work directly on products, service departments provide production departments with support services that contribute indirectly to the completion of products.

Service Departments as Cost Centers

Service departments are often viewed by management as cost centers. That is, the costs of each service department are accumulated separately so management can identify the total cost of such services. Also, unit costs for each service—such as maintenance cost per square foot of floor space—can be derived for comparison with other operating periods and/or other sources of the service such as outside contractors. Most accounting systems account for service departments as cost centers.

Service Department Costs as Product Costs

Although service departments do not perform actual work on specific products, they do provide essential services to the production departments. Thus, service department costs are appropriately considered among the related production department costs and are included in final product costs as part of manufacturing overhead.

TAKEAWAY 16.4

Departments can be divided into two broad classes:

1. Operating or production departments where the main purpose of the organization is carried out, such as the machining department
2. Service departments that assist the activities of operating or production departments, such as maintenance or emergency medical services

By their nature, service departments do not use direct materials or direct labor. Their costs are part of manufacturing overhead. These departments do not work directly on a product, so overhead rates, in the strict sense, are not computed for them. Instead, service department costs become part of product costs by being allocated among several production departments, according to the approximate benefits received by each production department. Service department costs become part of each production department's overhead to be applied to Work in Process.

The T-account diagram (with typical titles and amounts) in **Exhibit 16-14** illustrates how service department costs (1) are accumulated on a cost center basis, (2) are allocated to one or more production departments, and (3) become part of the product costs when manufacturing overhead is applied to work in process for each production department. To simplify this illustration, we assume that these amounts result in no over- or underapplied overhead.

Exhibit 16-14	Allocation of Service Department Costs to Production Departments' Overhead Accounts

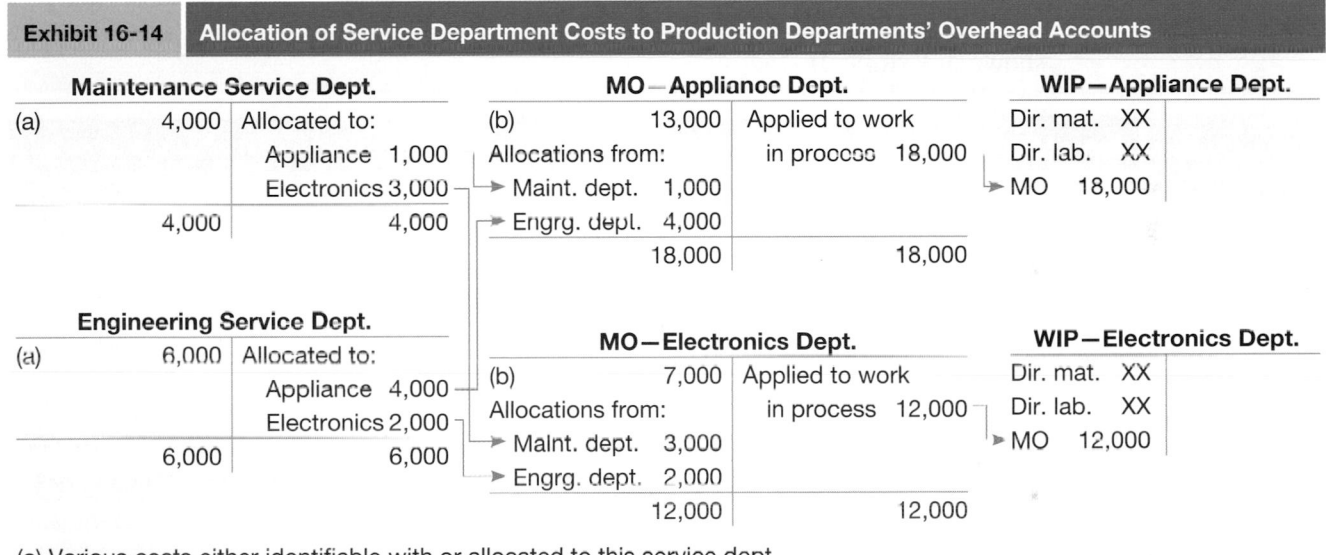

(a) Various costs either identifiable with or allocated to this service dept.
(b) Various overhead costs either identifiable with or allocated to this production dept.

Note that $4,000 is accumulated as the total cost for the Maintenance Department; then $1,000 and $3,000 are allocated to the Appliance and Electronics Departments (manufacturing departments), respectively. The allocated service department costs are in turn included in the totals of $18,000 and $12,000 of overhead costs applied from the respective production departments. Similar observations can be made for the Engineering Department.

Method of Cost Allocation

Costs are allocated among various departments on a basis that reflects the proportion of the service or activity that benefits each department. Some examples of allocated costs and their possible allocation bases are as follows:

Service Cost	Possible Allocation Basis
Personnel salaries	Number of employees in each department
Building depreciation	Square feet of floor space used
Utilities	Machine hours used
Building maintenance	Square feet of floor space used
Machine maintenance	Machine hours used
Heat and light	Cubic feet of building space used

Choosing an Allocation Basis

Once an allocation basis is chosen, it could remain unchanged for a long period of time. The selection of an allocation basis represents a policy decision that is typically reviewed only when major inequities exist.

The concern for cost control may justify the use of elaborate devices and schemes to measure service benefits. Some examples are departmental electric meters, timekeeping systems reflecting actual hours of service requested and used, and weighting techniques in which requests for rush or peak-hour services are assigned higher costs than requests honored at the convenience of the service department.

To allocate a particular cost, we simply divide the total cost among a series of departments in proportion to departmental shares of the appropriate base activity. For example, suppose that $8,000 of personnel department cost is allocated between the Appliance Department (manufacturing department) with 15 employees and the Electronics Department (manufacturing department) with 25 employees. The number of production employees is the allocation basis. The two distinct steps involved and illustrative calculations are shown in **Exhibit 16-15**.

Exhibit 16-15	Service Department Allocation	
Step		

1	$\dfrac{\text{Total cost to be allocated}}{\text{Total allocation base}}$	= Allocation rate
	$\dfrac{\$8,000}{40 \text{ employees}}$	= $200 per employee

2	Allocation rate × $\dfrac{\text{Actual amount of allocation}}{\text{basis for the department}}$	= Specific amount allocated
	$200 × 15 employees	= $3,000 (for Appliance Department)
	$200 × 25 employees	= $5,000 (for Electronics Department)
	Total amount allocated	$8,000

ACCOUNTING IN PRACTICE | **Service Department Allocation**

The allocation procedure should be simple and easily understood by all involved. If the allocation computations become too complex, their cost may exceed any benefits.

As a final step, we should check allocations and verify that the sum of allocated amounts equals the total amount allocated.

Exhibit 16-16 illustrates a worksheet that could be used to accumulate and allocate manufacturing overhead in a multidepartment manufacturing operation that includes service departments. Note the following:

1. Three categories of costs are involved:
   a. Those directly identifiable with departments
   b. Those requiring allocations to production and service departments
   c. Service department costs allocated to production departments

2. A total overhead amount is first accumulated for each service department and each production department.

3. After service department costs are allocated, the total overhead is assigned to the production departments only.

4. The final amounts assigned to each production department are used to calculate departmental overhead rates for each production department. (See the footnotes to **Exhibit 16-16**.)

The amounts, proportions, and variety of costs shown in **Exhibit 16-16** have been chosen for simplicity of presentation to stress the basic concepts.

We might ask why service department costs are not allocated to other service departments. More sophisticated allocation techniques may involve allocations of some service department costs to other service departments and even mutual assignment of all of one or more service department costs to all other service departments. Discussions of these techniques are for a more advanced text.

Exhibit 16-16	Overhead Distribution Worksheet for the Year Ended December 31, 2016					
		Service Depts.		Production Depts.		
		Maint.	Engin.	Appl.	Elect.	Allocation Basis
(a) Directly identifiable with depts.						
Indirect labor		$ 8,000	$20,000	$38,500	$18,500	Wages payable analysis
Factory supplies used		3,000	2,000	9,000	10,000	Requisition forms
(b) Allocated to production and service depts.						
Building depreciation		600	1,200	3,000	1,200	Square feet of floor space
Personal property taxes		400	800	1,500	1,300	Assessed value of equip. used
Total overhead cost to be allocated		$12,000	$24,000	$52,000	$31,000	
(c) Allocation of service depts.						
Maint. (assumed as 2/3 for Appl. and 1/3 for Elect.)		(12,000)		8,000	4,000	Sq. ft. of factory area used
Engin. (assumed as 1/6 for Appl. and 5/6 for Elect.)			(24,000)	4,000	20,000	Machine hours
Totals		–0–	–0–	$64,000*	$55,000†	

* Assuming an overhead allocation basis of 20,000 machine hours, the overhead rate for the Appl. Dept. is $3.20 per machine hr ($64,000/20,000 machine hrs).

† Assuming an overhead allocation basis of $110,000 direct labor (DL), the overhead rate for the Elect. Dept. is 50 cents per DL dollar ($55,000/$110,000 DL).

DEPARTMENTAL OVERHEAD RATES

LO6 Contrast plant-wide overhead rates and departmental overhead rates.

Manufacturing companies that use traditional overhead rates typically use either a plant-wide (or company-wide) overhead rate or departmental overhead rates. A **plant-wide (or company-wide) overhead rate** is determined by dividing estimated total plant (or company) overhead for the year by estimated utilization of the total plant (or company) productive capacity for the year. The discussions and illustration in this chapter have incorporated a plant-wide overhead rate. When a plant-wide overhead rate is adopted, the cost accounting system uses a single predetermined rate for applying overhead to work done in all the producing departments, such as bending, drilling, welding, assembling, and painting.

Departmental Overhead Rates

Some manufacturing companies have adopted a cost accounting system that uses **departmental overhead rates**. When departmental overhead rates are used, a separate overhead rate is predetermined for each producing department in the factory by dividing the estimated overhead associated with each department by the estimated utilization of the capacity of that department.

A manufacturer would use departmental overhead rates for two primary reasons. First, the predetermined overhead rate in one department may be significantly different from the rate in another department. For instance, in department 1, the overhead rate might be $5 per direct labor hour, whereas the overhead rate in department 2 might be $20 per direct labor hour. Second, the capacity measure in one department may be different from the capacity measure in another department. For example, if department 1 is highly automated, then machine hours would be an appropriate measure of capacity for department 1. However, if department 2 is direct-labor intensive, then direct labor hours would be an appropriate measure of capacity for department 2.

When departmental overhead rates are used, the manufacturer accumulates the appropriate measure of capacity for each department for each job so that the appropriate overhead rates can be applied. Assume that a particular manufacturer has three producing departments: machining, painting, and assembling.

The capacity measure for machining and painting is machine hours, whereas the capacity measure for assembly is direct labor hours. For Job 368, the factory accumulated 30 machine hours of machining, 20 machine hours of painting, and 40 direct labor hours of assembling. Machining has a predetermined overhead rate of $4 per machine hour, painting has a predetermined overhead rate of $3 per machine hour, and assembling has a predetermined overhead rate of $2 per direct labor hour. Manufacturing overhead would be applied to Job 368 as follows:

Machining (30 machine hours × $4)	$120
Painting (20 machine hours × $3)	60
Assembling (40 direct labor hours × $2)	80
Total manufacturing overhead applied to Job 368	$260

Departmental overhead rates usually provide a more equitable application of manufacturing overhead to individual jobs than do plant-wide rates. However, when there are significant variations in volume or complexity among the individual jobs, neither plant-wide nor departmental overhead rates may provide an equitable application of manufacturing overhead among the individual jobs. Instead, **activity-based costing** may be more appropriate. Activity-based costing is discussed in detail in Chapter 18.

YOUR TURN! 16.4

The solution is on page 795.

Why would a company use a departmental overhead rate rather than a plant-wide overhead rate?

SERVICE INDUSTRY IN FOCUS

SERVICE AND MERCHANDISING

Environmental Business Consultants, LLC (EBC) worked on and completed two projects during June 2016: a review of appropriate rates for solid waste and recycling collection within Klamath County, and a competitive procurement of landfill disposal services for the City of Redding. The following information relates to these two projects:

	Rate Review Project—Klamath	Procurement Project—Redding
WIP Inventory balance at June 1, 2016	$46,320	$85,318
Hours worked during June.	100	74
Payroll cost per hour:		
Partner	$ 60	$ 60
Manager	$ 38	$ 38
Staff	$ 24	$ 24
Overhead rate per labor hour.	$ 25	$ 25

During June, the partner charged 10 hours to the rate review project and 20 hours to the procurement project; the manager charged 30 hours to the rate review project and 24 hours to the procurement project; and the staff charged 60 hours to the rate review project and 30 hours to the procurement project.

On June 30, EBC billed its clients for the completed projects. The invoice for the rate review project was for $60,000 and for the procurement project was $105,000.

Required

1. Prepare the journal entry to distribute the payroll to the projects during June. (Assume that the correct entry was made when the payroll was paid.)

2. Prepare the journal entry to apply the overhead to the projects during June.

3. Prepare the journal entry(ies) to record the completion of the projects as of the end of June. (Hint: Don't forget the work that was performed on the jobs prior to June, which is reflected in the beginning WIP balance. Also, don't forget that there is no finished goods inventory in a service firm—once the project is complete, it is billed to the client.)

4. Determine the amount of profit or loss that EBC earned on each of the two projects.

Solution

1.

WIP—Klamath	3,180	
WIP—Redding	2,832	
Payroll expense		6,012

Klamath: ($60 × 10 hours) + ($38 × 30 hours) + ($24 × 60 hours) = $3,180
Redding: ($60 × 20 hours) + ($38 × 24 hours) + ($24 × 30 hours) = $2,832

2.

WIP—Klamath	2,500	
WIP—Redding	1,850	
Overhead		4,350

Klamath: (10 + 30 + 60) × $25 = 2,500
Redding: (20 + 24 + 30) × $25 = 1,850

3.

Accounts receivable—Klamath	60,000	
Sales revenue		60,000
Cost of sales	52,000	
WIP—Klamath		52,000

(46,320 + 3,180 + 2,500)

Accounts receivable—Redding	105,000	
Sales revenue		105,000
Cost of sales	90,000	
WIP—Klamath		90,000

(85,318 + 2,832 + 1,850)

4.

Klamath:	Sales revenue	$ 60,000
	Cost of goods sold	52,000
	Gross profit	$ 8,000

Redding:	Sales revenue	$105,000
	Cost of goods sold	90,000
	Gross profit	$ 15,000

COMPREHENSIVE PROBLEM

The annual budget for Diamond Corporation for 2016 included the following costs and expenses:

Direct material	$ 30,000
Direct labor ($8 per hour)	120,000
Sales commissions.......................	28,000
Factory supervision	16,000
Indirect labor	27,000
Factory depreciation	25,000
Factory taxes	7,000
Factory insurance........................	6,000
Factory utilities..........................	9,000

Required

a. Compute the plant-wide predetermined manufacturing overhead rate for 2016 using direct labor hours as the activity measure.

b. Determine the amount of manufacturing overhead that would be applied to jobs during March 2016 when 1,100 direct labor hours were actually incurred.

Solution

a. Budgeted manufacturing overhead:

Factory supervision	$16,000
Indirect labor	27,000
Factory depreciation	25,000
Factory taxes	7,000
Factory insurance........................	6,000
Factory utilities..........................	9,000
Budgeted manufacturing overhead	$90,000

Budgeted direct labor hours:

$$\frac{\$120,000}{\$8/hour} = 15,000 \text{ budgeted direct labor hours}$$

Predetermined overhead rate

$$\frac{\text{Budgeted manufacturing overhead}}{\text{Budgeted direct labor hours}} = \frac{\$90,000}{15,000} = \$6 \text{ per direct labor hour}$$

b. 1,100 hours × $6 = $6,600 applied manufacturing overhead

SUMMARY OF LEARNING OBJECTIVES

LO1 **Describe the two basic types of cost accounting systems, discuss how they may be used in both manufacturing and nonmanufacturing environments, and explain the need for the timely determination of product costs. (p. 752)**

- A costing system is an orderly process for tracking product or service cost information.
- In a manufacturing environment, materials, labor, and overhead costs are accumulated and assigned to specific jobs and products.
- In a nonmanufacturing (service) setting, labor and overhead costs are accumulated and assigned to specific customers.
- A job order costing system is used when production is characterized by a series of unique products or jobs undertaken either to fill specific orders from customers or to produce a general stock from which future orders will be filled.

- A process costing system lends itself to the production of a large volume of homogeneous products manufactured in a continual flow operation.
- A cost accounting system must trace, on a timely basis, direct materials, direct labor, and manufacturing overhead to products or jobs.

Explain the need for a predetermined overhead rate, demonstrate its calculation, and compare annual and monthly rates. (p. 755)   LO2

- The predetermined overhead rate is calculated by dividing the estimated total manufacturing overhead cost for the year by the estimated utilization of the factory productive capacity during the upcoming year.
- The overhead rate should be calculated on an annual basis. Monthly overhead rates may fluctuate significantly from month to month.
- Companies should choose the application base that corresponds to the period over which activity decisions are typically made.

Describe and explain a job order costing system, identify types of records used in job order costing, and demonstrate the journal entries that accompany the flow of product costs. (p. 757)   LO3

- Materials requisitions authorize issuance from the materials inventory.
- Time records document the labor time by job.
- The *job order cost sheet* summarizes the product costs—direct materials, direct labor, and manufacturing overhead applied—for one job; the predetermined overhead rate is used to apply manufacturing overhead.
- When material is requisitioned from the materials inventory, the Work in Process Inventory account is debited for the cost of direct material and the Manufacturing Overhead account is debited for the cost of indirect material.
- When the wages payable is distributed, the Work in Process Inventory account is debited for the cost of direct labor and the Manufacturing Overhead account is debited for the cost of indirect labor.
- Actual manufacturing overhead costs are recorded by debiting the Manufacturing Overhead account.
- Manufacturing overhead is applied to jobs by debiting the Work in Process Inventory account and crediting the Manufacturing Overhead account.

Discuss the procedures and journal entries used to account for finished goods and the sale of finished goods. (p. 763)   LO4

- A product is not complete or finished until it is packaged in the container in which it will be sold. Packaging costs are part of the product cost transferred to the Finished Goods Inventory account.
- The cost of finished goods is recorded by debiting the Finished Goods Inventory account and crediting the Work in Process Inventory account.
- The sale of finished goods is recorded by debiting the Cost of Goods Sold account and crediting the Finished Goods Inventory account for the cost of the goods sold and by debiting the Accounts Receivable account and crediting the Sales account for the selling price.
- At year end, a journal entry is made to dispose of the **underapplied** or **overapplied** amount of manufacturing overhead. If the amount of **underapplied** or **overapplied** overhead is significant, an entry is made to transfer the amount to the Cost of Goods Sold Account.

Describe the procedures for cost allocation for service departments. (p. 768)   LO5

- Service department costs are overhead costs that are allocated to production departments and eventually assigned to products as part of the production department's overhead.
- Each different service cost may be allocated using a different allocation basis.
- Departments can be divided into two broad classes, operating or production departments where the main purpose of the organization is carried out, and service departments that assist the activities of operating or production departments.

Contrast plant-wide overhead rates and departmental overhead rates. (p. 771)   LO6

- When departmental overhead rates are used, a separate rate is calculated for each producing department in the factory.
- A plant-wide (or company-wide) overhead rate is determined by dividing estimated total plant (or company) overhead for the year by estimated utilization of the total plant (or company) productive capacity for the year.

KEY TERMS

Activity-based costing (p. 772)

Bill of materials (p. 757)

Cost driver (p. 755)

Departmental overhead rates (p. 771)

Job order costing system (p. 752)

Job order cost sheet (p. 758)

Materials requisition (p. 757)

Overapplied (p. 765)

Plant-wide (or company-wide) overhead rate (p. 771)

Predetermined manufacturing overhead rate (p. 755)

Process costing system (p. 753)

Production order (p. 757)

Sales order (p. 757)

Time clocks (p. 761)

Time record (p. 758)

Underapplied (p. 765)

Assignments with the 🔵 logo in the margin are available in ᵐʸBusinessCourse.
See the Preface of the book for details.

SELF-STUDY QUESTIONS

(Answers to Self-Study Questions are at the end of this chapter.)

LO2 1. Predetermined manufacturing overhead rates should be
     a. higher than actual manufacturing overhead rates.
     b. lower than actual manufacturing overhead rates.
     c. based on monthly budgets.
     d. based on annual budgets.

LO3 2. Which account is debited to record the issuance of material to production for incorporation into the product?
     a. Direct Materials
     b. Materials Inventory
     c. Work in Process Inventory
     d. Factory Supplies

LO4 3. Which of the following is usually *not* found on a job order cost sheet?
     a. Manufacturing overhead
     b. Finished units currently on hand
     c. Direct materials
     d. Unit cost

LO4 4. When should the balance of the manufacturing overhead account be zero?
     a. At the end of each month
     b. After year-end closing
     c. Never
     d. Each time a job is completed

LO5 5. Which of the following is *not* one of the categories of cost involved in the allocation of service department costs?
     a. Service department costs allocated to production departments
     b. Costs directly identifiable with departments
     c. Costs requiring allocation to departments
     d. Selling department costs

QUESTIONS

LO1 1. Briefly describe a cost accounting system.

LO1 2. What types of entities, other than manufacturers, use cost accounting systems?

LO1 3. Contrast a job order costing system and a process costing system.

LO1 4. Give three examples of types of companies that would use job order costing.

LO2 5. Why do we name it a *predetermined* manufacturing overhead rate?

LO2 6. How is a predetermined manufacturing overhead rate determined?

LO2 7. Briefly justify the use of an annual predetermined manufacturing overhead rate as opposed to actual monthly manufacturing overhead.

LO2 8. Wesley Manufacturing Company uses a predetermined plant-wide manufacturing overhead rate of $25 per direct labor hour. During April, Job 541 had $3,000 of direct materials assigned to it; 60 hours of direct labor at $10 per hour were incurred for the job. What is the total product cost accumulated on Job 541 during April?

LO2 9. Parker Manufacturing, Inc., employs an overhead rate of 140% of direct labor cost. The Job 783 cost sheet shows that $5,000 in direct materials has been used and that $8,000 in direct labor has been incurred. If 1,000 units of product have been produced on Job 783, what is the unit cost of the product?

10. Briefly explain the sequential flow of product costs through a cost accounting system. **LO3**

11. What type of records would be used or maintained for the following manufacturing activities? **LO3**

    a. Determining the amount of a specific material on hand
    b. Issuing direct material for production
    c. Assigning the direct labor costs for a particular worker
    d. Accumulating the cost of a particular product or batch of products

12. Explain the general format and give examples of the data that would appear on (a) a sales order, (b) a bill **LO3** of materials, and (c) a job order cost sheet.

13. Why can we say that the sale of a manufactured product is recorded at two different amounts? **LO4**

14. Slaton Company records both actual overhead and applied overhead in one account, Manufacturing Over- **LO4** head. On January 31, the account has a credit balance. Has overhead been under- or overapplied during January?

15. Lyle Manufacturing Company applies manufacturing overhead at the rate of 150% of direct labor cost. **LO4** During October 2016, Lyle incurred $82,000 of direct labor costs and $120,000 of manufacturing overhead costs. What is the amount of over- or underapplied manufacturing overhead for October 2016?

16. Contrast service departments with production departments. Give three examples of a service department. **LO5**

17. Why might service departments be treated as cost centers? **LO5**

18. Explain what each of the following statements means: **LO5**

    a. Service departments do not work directly on products.
    b. Service department costs are manufacturing overhead costs.
    c. Overhead rates are not used for service departments.
    d. In spite of part (c), service department costs become part of product costs.

19. How do we choose a basis for allocating a cost to several departments? **LO5**

20. How is an allocation rate calculated? How is the specific amount allocated to a department calculated? **LO5**

21. Briefly describe the general format, data, and calculations that would appear on an overhead distribution **LO5** worksheet for a company with a number of production and service departments.

EXERCISES—SET A

E16-1A. Calculate and Use Overhead Rate Selected data for the consulting department of Austin Consulting, **LO3, 5** Inc., follow:

Estimated consulting overhead cost for the year.	$270,000
Estimated direct labor cost for the year (@ $9/hr.).	180,000
Actual manufacturing overhead cost for January	16,000
Actual direct labor cost for January (1,200 hours).	11,000

Assuming that direct labor cost is the basis for applying consulting overhead,

    a. Calculate the predetermined overhead rate.
    b. Prepare a journal entry that applies consulting overhead for January.
    c. By what amount is consulting overhead over- or underapplied in January?

E16-2A. Calculate and Use Overhead Rate Using the data in Exercise E16-1A, but assuming that the basis **LO3, 5** for applying consulting overhead is direct labor hours, complete requirements (a) through (c).

E16-3A. Calculate and Use Overhead Rate During the coming accounting year, Baker Manufacturing, Inc., **LO3** anticipates the following costs, expenses, and operating data:

Direct material (16,000 lb.)	$ 80,000
Direct labor (@ $10/hr.).	140,000
Indirect material	12,000
Indirect labor	22,000
Sales commissions.	34,000
Factory administration	16,000
Non factory administrative expenses.	20,000
Other manufacturing overhead*	48,000

*Provides for operating 35,000 machine hours.

a. Calculate the predetermined manufacturing overhead rate for the coming year for each of the following application bases: (1) direct labor hours, (2) direct labor costs, and (3) machine hours.

b. For each item in requirement *a*, determine the proper application of manufacturing overhead to Job 63, to which 16 direct labor hours, $150 of direct labor cost, and 40 machine hours have been charged.

LO4 **E16-4A. Applied vs. Actual Manufacturing Overhead** Davis Manufacturing Corporation applies manufacturing overhead on the basis of 150% of direct labor cost. An analysis of the related accounts and job order cost sheet indicates that during the year total manufacturing overhead incurred was $315,000 and that at year-end Work in Process Inventory, Finished Goods Inventory, and Cost of Goods Sold included $40,000, $20,000, and $140,000, respectively, of direct labor incurred during the current year.

a. Determine the underapplied manufacturing overhead at year-end (assume it is significant).

b. Prepare a journal entry to record the disposition of the underapplied manufacturing overhead.

LO3 **E16-5A. Flow of Product Costs through Accounts** Assuming a routine manufacturing activity, present journal entries (account titles only) for each of the following transactions:

a. Purchased material on account.

b. Recorded wages payable earned but not paid.

c. Requisitioned both direct material and indirect material.

d. Assigned direct and indirect labor costs.

e. Recorded factory depreciation and accrued factory property tax.

f. Applied manufacturing overhead to production.

g. Completed work on products.

h. Sold finished goods on account.

LO3 **E16-6A. Job Order Cost Sheets** For each of the manufacturing transactions or activities indicated in Exercise E16-5A, briefly identify the detailed forms, records, or documents (if any) that would probably underlie each journal entry.

LO4 **E16-7A. Perpetual Inventories** The following summary data are from the job order cost sheets of Hampton Company:

| Job | Dates | | | Total Costs Assigned at April 30 | Total Production Costs Added in May |
	Started	Finished	Shipped		
1	4/10	4/20	5/9	$7,300	
2	4/18	4/30	5/20	5,400	
3	4/24	5/10	5/25	2,900	$5,700
4	4/28	5/20	6/3	3,600	4,800
5	5/15	6/10	6/20		2,600
6	5/22	6/18	6/28		3,800

Using the above data, compute (a) the finished goods inventory at May 1 and May 31, (b) the work in process inventory at May 1 and May 31, and (c) the cost of goods sold for May. Hampton began operations with Job 1.

LO4 **E16-8A. Finished Goods and Cost of Goods Sold** Before the completed production for June is recorded, the work in process inventory account for James Company appears as follows:

Work in Process Inventory	
Balance June 1	16,000
Direct material	45,000
Direct labor	32,000
Manufacturing overhead applied	34,000

Assume that completed production for June includes Jobs 107, 108, and 109 with total costs of $28,000, $59,000, and $25,000, respectively.

a. Determine the cost of unfinished jobs at June 30 and prepare a journal entry to record completed production.

b. Using general journal entries, record the sale of Job 107 for $40,000 on account.

E16-9A. Preparing a Job Order Cost Sheet Riverwood Accounting Company has the following account in its cost records:

Work in Process—Jones Audit			
Direct labor............	20,000	Services completed	44,000
Project overhead	28,000		

Riverwood applies overhead to projects at a predetermined rate based on direct labor costs. Assume that Riverwood uses a job order costing system and that Jones Audit is the only job in process at the end of the period. Complete the following cost sheet for services still in process for Jones Audit.

Job Order Cost Sheet—Jones Audit (Services in Process)	
Direct labor............................	_____
Project overhead	_____
Total cost	_____

E16-10A. Service Department Cost Allocation Presented below are certain operating data for the four departments of Tally Manufacturing Company.

	Service		Production	
	1	**2**	**1**	**2**
Total manufacturing overhead costs either identifiable with or allocated to each department................................	$60,000	$72,000	$90,000	$98,000
Square feet of factory floor space			40,000	80,000
Number of factory workers....................			50	10
Planned direct labor hours for the year			20,000	30,000

Allocate, to the two production departments, the costs of service departments 1 and 2, using factory floor space and number of workers, respectively, as bases.

What is the apparent overhead rate for each production department if planned direct labor hours are the overhead application base?

EXERCISES—SET B

E16-1B. Calculate and Use Overhead Rate Selected data for the consulting department of Kingman Consulting, Inc., follow:

Estimated consulting overhead cost for the year................	$405,000
Estimated direct labor cost for the year (@ $9/hr.)..............	324,000
Actual consulting overhead cost for May.....................	26,000
Actual direct labor cost for May (2,400 hrs.)	22,000

Assuming that direct labor cost is the basis for applying consulting overhead,

a.   Calculate the predetermined overhead rate.
b.   Prepare a journal entry that applies consulting overhead for May.
c.   By what amount is consulting overhead over- or underapplied in May?

E16-2B. Calculate and Use Overhead Rate Using the data in Exercise E16-1B, but assuming that the basis for applying consulting overhead is direct labor hours, complete requirements (a) through (c).

LO3 **E16-3B. Calculate and Use Manufacturing Overhead Rate** During the coming accounting year, Ester Manufacturing, Inc., anticipates the following costs, expenses, and operating data:

Direct material (15,000 lb.)............	$45,000
Direct labor (@ $12/hr.)..............	96,000
Indirect material....................	7,000
Indirect labor	12,000
Sales commissions.................	18,000
Factory administration..............	13,000
Nonfactory administrative expenses ...	14,000
Other manufacturing overhead*.......	28,000

*Machine hours are 30,000 hours.

   a. Calculate the predetermined manufacturing overhead rate for the coming year for each of the following application bases: (1) direct labor hours, (2) direct labor costs, and (3) machine hours.

   b. For each item in requirement (a), determine the proper application of manufacturing overhead to Job 128, to which 9 direct labor hours, $100 of direct labor cost, and 32 machine hours have been charged.

LO4 **E16-4B. Applied vs. Actual Manufacturing Overhead** Sloan Manufacturing Corporation applies manufacturing overhead on the basis of 120% of direct labor cost. An analysis of the related accounts and job order cost sheets indicates that during the year total manufacturing overhead incurred was $210,000 and that at year-end Work in Process Inventory, Finished Goods Inventory, and Cost of Goods Sold included $30,000, $20,000, and $150,000, respectively, of direct labor incurred during the current year.

   a. Determine the manufacturing overapplied overhead at year-end (assume it is significant).

   b. Prepare a journal entry to record the disposition of the overapplied overhead.

LO3 **E16-5B. Flow of Product Costs Through Accounts** The following T accounts present a cost flow in which all or part of typical manufacturing transactions are indicated by parenthetical letters on the debit or credit side of each account.

Material Inventory		Wages Payable		Manufacturing Overhead	
(a)	(c)	(i)	(b)	(c)	(f)
	(e)		(d)	(d)	
				(e)	

Work in Process Inventory		Finished Goods Inventory		Cost of Goods Sold	
(c)	(g)				
(d)		(g)	(h)	(h)	
(f)					

For each parenthetical letter, present a general journal entry with explanation indicating the apparent transaction or procedure that has occurred (disregard amounts).

LO3 **E16-6B. Job Order Cost Sheets** For each of the manufacturing transactions or activities indicated by the parenthetical letters in Exercise E16-5B, briefly identify the detailed forms or documents (if any) that would probably underlie each journal entry.

LO4 **E16-7B. Perpetual Inventories** The following summary data are from the job order cost sheets of Castle Company:

	Dates			Total Assigned Costs at September 30	Total Production Costs Added in October
Job	Started	Finished	Shipped		
1.........	9/10	9/20	10/11	$9,000	
2.........	9/17	9/29	10/22	6,600	
3.........	9/25	10/11	10/27	3,500	$7,100
4.........	9/27	10/19	11/4	4,400	5,700
5.........	10/14	11/10	11/18		3,200
6.........	10/23	11/17	11/29		4,900

Using the data provided, compute (a) the finished goods inventory at October 1 and October 31, (b) the work in process inventory at October 1 and October 31, and (c) the cost of goods sold for October. Castle began operations with Job 1.

E16-8B. Finished Goods and Cost of Goods Sold Before the completed production for August is recorded, the work in process inventory account for Bayfield Company appears as follows: **LO4**

Work in Process Inventory	
Balance, August 1	15,000
Direct material	33,000
Direct labor	20,000
Manufacturing overhead applied	20,000

Assume that completed production for August includes Jobs 317, 318, and 319 with total costs of $31,000, $18,000, and $22,000, respectively.

a. Determine the cost of unfinished jobs at August 31 and prepare a journal entry to record completed production.

b. Using general journal entries, record the sale of Job 317 for $45,000 on account.

E16-9B. Job Order Cost Sheet Everglade Accounting Company has the following account in its cost records: **LO4**

Work in Process—Davis Audit			
Direct labor	48,000	Services completed	95,000
Project overhead	57,600		

Everglade applies overhead to projects at a predetermined rate based on direct labor costs. Assume that Everglade uses a job order costing system and that Davis Audit is the only job in process at the end of the period. Complete the following cost sheet for services still in process for Davis Audit.

Job Order Cost Sheet—Davis Audit (Services in Process)	
Direct labor	_____
Project overhead	_____
Total cost	_____

E16-10B. Service Department Cost Allocation Presented below are certain operating data for the four departments of Modern Manufacturing Company. **LO5**

	Service		Production	
	1	**2**	**1**	**2**
Total overhead cost either identifiable with or to each department	$45,000	$60,000	$55,000	$116,000
Square feet of factory floor space			90,000	45,000
Number of factory workers			20	60
Planned direct labor hours for the year			25,000	32,000

Allocate, to the two production departments, the costs of service departments 1 and 2, using factory floor space and number of workers, respectively, as bases.

What is the apparent manufacturing overhead rate for each production department if planned direct labor hours are the overhead application base?

PROBLEMS—SET A

Note: In both problem sets, assume perpetual inventory procedures, a single Manufacturing Overhead account, first-in, first-out (FIFO) costing of inventories, and that the Materials Inventory account is the control account for both direct material and indirect material.

LO3, 5

SERVICE AND MERCHANDISING

P16-1A. Determine and Use Overhead Rate Cortez Consulting, Inc., expects the following costs and expenses during the coming year:

Direct labor (@ $9/hr.)	$162,000
Sales commissions	37,000
Overhead	144,000

Required

a. Compute a predetermined overhead rate applied on the basis of direct labor hours.

b. Prepare a general journal entry to apply overhead during an interim period when 1,500 direct labor hours were worked.

c. What amount of overhead would be assigned to Job 466, to which $180 in direct labor had been charged?

LO3

P16-2A. Determine and Use Overhead Rate The following selected ledger accounts of Cameron Company are for February (the second month of its accounting year):

MATERIALS INVENTORY

Feb. 1 balance	31,500	February credits	113,000
February debits	104,000		

MANUFACTURING OVERHEAD

February debits	137,200	Feb. 1 balance	11,600
		February credits	136,350

WORK IN PROCESS INVENTORY

Feb. 1 balance	22,400	February credits	345,000
February debits:			
Direct material	95,000		
Direct labor	151,500		
Manufacturing overhead	136,350		

WAGES PAYABLE

February debits	193,500	Feb. 1 balance	45,000
		February credits	177,000

FINISHED GOODS INVENTORY

Feb. 1 balance	76,500	February credits	383,700
February debits	345,000		

Required

a. Determine the amount of indirect material requisitioned for production during February.

b. How much indirect labor cost was apparently incurred during February?

c. Calculate the manufacturing overhead rate based on direct labor cost.

d. Was manufacturing overhead for February under- or overapplied, and by what amount?

e. Was manufacturing overhead for the first two months of the year under- or overapplied, and by what amount?

f. What is the cost of production completed in February?

g. What is the cost of goods sold in February?

P16-3A. Job Cost Journal Entries Holiday Manufacturing had the following inventories at December 31,   **LO3**
2015, the end of its fiscal year:

Materials inventory	$19,000
Work in process inventory	20,000
Finished goods inventory	13,000

During January 2016, the following transactions occurred:

1. Purchased materials on account, $126,000.
2. Requisitioned direct material of $110,000 and indirect material of $20,000.
3. Incurred wages payable, $61,000.
4. Assigned total wages payable, of which $11,000 was considered indirect labor.
5. Incurred other manufacturing overhead, $32,800. (Credit Accounts Payable.)
6. Applied manufacturing overhead on the basis of 110% of direct labor costs.
7. Determined completed production, $206,000. Use this information to determine the amount of
    WIP transferred to finished goods inventory.
8. Determined cost of goods sold, $203,000. Use this information to determine the reduction to fin-
    ished goods inventory.

Required
a.   Prepare general journal entries to record these transactions.
b.   If the above transactions covered a full year's operations, prepare a journal entry to dispose of the
       overhead account balance. Assume that the balance is significant. Also assume that the following
       accounts contained the indicated amounts of manufacturing overhead applied during 2016:

Work in process inventory	$ 6,000
Finished goods.	4,000
Cost of goods sold.	45,000

P16-4A. Job Cost Journal Entries Prior to the beginning of 2016, Lowe Company estimated that it would in-   **LO3, 4**
cur $176,000 of manufacturing overhead cost during 2016, using 16,000 direct labor hours to produce
the desired volume of goods. On January 1, 2016, beginning balances of Materials Inventory, Work in
Process Inventory, and Finished Goods Inventory were $28,000, $-0-, and $43,000, respectively.

Required
Prepare general journal entries to record the following for 2016:

a.   Purchased materials on account, $39,000.
b.   Of the total dollar value of materials used, $31,000 represented direct material and $11,000 indi-
       rect material.
c.   Determined total factory labor, $135,000 (15,000 hrs. @ $9/hr.).
d.   Of the factory labor, 80% was direct and 20% indirect.
e.   Applied manufacturing overhead based on direct labor hours to work in process.
f.   Determined actual manufacturing overhead other than those items already recorded, $92,000.
       (Credit Accounts Payable.)
g.   Ending inventories of work in process and finished goods were $32,000 and $57,000, respec-
       tively. Determine the cost of finished goods (credit WIP) and the cost of goods sold (credit FG
       inventory). Make separate entries.
h.   Transferred the balance in Manufacturing Overhead to Cost of Goods Sold.

P16-5A. Job Cost Journal Entries and T Accounts Following are certain operating data for Durango   **LO3, 4**
Manufacturing Company for January 2016:

	Materials Inventory	Work in Process Inventory	Finished Goods Inventory
Beginning inventory	$57,000	$24,000	$75,000
Ending inventory.	33,000	40,500	48,000

Total sales were $1,800,000, on which the company earned a 40% gross profit. Durango uses a predetermined manufacturing overhead rate of 120% of direct labor costs. Manufacturing overhead applied was $360,000. Exclusive of indirect material used, total manufacturing overhead incurred was $243,000; it was overapplied by $22,500.

Required

Compute the following items. (Set up T accounts for Materials Inventory, Work in Process Inventory, Finished Goods Inventory, and Manufacturing Overhead; fill in the known amounts; and then use the normal relationships among the various accounts to compute the unknown amounts.)

a. Cost of goods sold.

b. Cost of goods manufactured.

c. Direct labor incurred.

d. Direct material used.

e. Indirect material used.

f. Total materials purchased.

LO3, 4 **P16-6A. Job Cost Journal Entries and T Accounts** Summarized data for the first month's operations of Dobson Welding Foundry during 2016 are presented below. A job order costing system is used.

1. Materials purchased on account, $58,000.
2. Amounts of materials requisitioned and foundry labor used:

Job	Materials	Foundry Labor
1	$ 4,400	$2,600
2	7,000	5,000
3	3,200	2,400
4	12,000	4,600
5	4,800	2,800
6	1,400	1,200
Indirect material	6,200	
Indirect labor		3,400

3. Foundry overhead is applied at the rate of 200% of direct labor costs.
4. Miscellaneous foundry overhead incurred:

Prepaid foundry insurance written off	$ 1,480
Property taxes on foundry building accrued	2,360
Foundry utilities payable accrued	5,280
Depreciation on foundry equipment.	7,440
Other costs incurred on account	10,320

5. Ending work in process consisted of Jobs 4 and 6.
6. Jobs 1 and 3 and one-half of Job 2 were sold on account for $20,000, $17,400, and $14,400, respectively.

Required

a. Open general ledger T accounts for Materials Inventory, Wages Payable, Foundry Overhead, Work in Process Inventory, Finished Goods Inventory, and Cost of Goods Sold. Also set up subsidiary T accounts as job order cost sheets for each job.

b. Prepare general journal entries to record the summarized transactions for the month, and post appropriate entries to any accounts listed in requirement (a). Key each entry parenthetically to the related number in the problem data.

c. Determine the balances of any accounts necessary and prepare schedules of jobs in ending work in process and jobs in ending finished goods to confirm that they agree with the related control accounts.

LO3, 4 **P16-7A. Complex Job Cost Journal Entries and Analysis** During June 2016, its first month of operations, Weston Manufacturing Company completed the transactions listed below. Weston uses a job order costing system. Materials requisitions and the wages payable summary are analyzed on the 15th and the last day of each month, and charges for direct material and direct labor are entered directly on specific job order cost sheets. Manufacturing overhead at the rate of 140% of direct labor costs is recorded on individual job order cost sheets when a job is completed and at month-end for any job then in process. At month-end, entries to the general ledger accounts summarize materials requisitions, distribution of wages, payable costs, and the application of manufacturing overhead for the month. All other entries to general ledger accounts are made as they occur.

1. Purchased materials on account, $130,000.
2. Paid miscellaneous manufacturing overhead costs, $32,600.
3. An analysis of materials requisitions and the wages payable summary for June 1–15 indicates the following cost distribution:

Job	Materials	Factory Labor
1	$21,600	$36,800
2	10,400	16,000
3	4,400	10,800
Indirect material	7,600	
Indirect labor		35,400
	$44,000	$99,000

4. Jobs 1 and 2 were completed on June 15 and transferred to finished goods inventory on the next day. (Enter the appropriate manufacturing overhead amounts on the job order cost sheets, mark them completed, and make a general journal entry transferring the appropriate amount of cost to the Finished Goods Inventory account.)
5. Paid miscellaneous manufacturing overhead costs, $23,400.
6. Sold Job 1 on account, $185,600 (recognized its cost of sales in the general journal).
7. An analysis of materials requisitions and wages payable summary for June 16–30 indicates the following cost distribution:

Job	Materials	Factory Labor
3	$22,800	$16,800
4	18,000	32,400
5	7,800	13,000
6	3,000	4,600
Indirect material	6,800	
Indirect labor		29,400
	$58,400	$96,200

8. Jobs 3 and 4 were completed on June 30 and transferred to finished goods inventory on the same day. (See transaction 4.)
9. Sold Job 3 on account, $155,600 (recognized its cost of sales in the general journal).
10. Recorded the following additional manufacturing overhead:

Depreciation on factory building	$26,000
Depreciation on factory equipment	15,200
Expiration of prepaid factory insurance	4,200
Accrual of factory property taxes payable	7,000
	$52,400

11. Recorded monthly general journal entry for the costs of all materials used.
12. Recorded monthly general journal entry for the distribution of wages payable costs.
13. Recorded manufacturing overhead on the job order cost sheets for jobs in ending work in process and in the general journal for all manufacturing overhead applied during the month.

Required

a. Set up the following general ledger T accounts: Materials Inventory, Wages Payable, Manufacturing Overhead, Work in Process Inventory, Finished Goods Inventory, Cost of Goods Sold, and Sales.

b. Set up T accounts for each of Jobs 1–6 as job order cost sheets.

c. Noting the accounting procedures described in the first paragraph of the problem, do the following:

    i. Record general journal entries for all transactions. Note that general journal entries are not required in transactions 3 and 7. Post only those portions of these entries affecting the general ledger accounts set up in requirement (a).

    ii. Enter the applicable amounts directly on the appropriate job order cost sheets for transactions 3, 4, 7, 8, and 13. Note parenthetically the nature of each amount entered.

d. Present a brief analysis showing that the general ledger accounts for Work in Process Inventory and for Finished Goods Inventory agree with the related job order cost sheets.

e. Explain in one sentence each what the balance of each general ledger account established in requirement (a) represents.

LO5, 6   **P16-8A. Manufacturing Overhead Distribution Worksheet** The following are selected operating data for the production and service departments of Bluestone Company for 2016.

	Departments			
	Service		Production	
	1	2	1	2
Overhead costs (identified by department)				
Indirect material	$48,400	$ 82,200	$ 25,440	$ 516,000
Indirect labor.	$97,200	$144,000	$ 32,584	$1,439,000
Square feet of building floor space used	4,800	7,200	12,000	24,000
Assessed value of equipment used	$21,000	$ 63,000	$126,000	$ 210,000
Cubic yards of factory space used			88,000	132,000
Machine hours			51,200	204,800
Direct labor.			$ 20,000	$ 400,000

Building depreciation of $96,000 is allocated on the basis of square feet of floor space. Personal property taxes of $36,000 are allocated on the basis of assessed values of equipment used. Costs for service departments 1 and 2 are allocated to production departments on the basis of cubic yards of factory space and machine hours, respectively.

Required

a. Prepare a 2016 overhead distribution worksheet for Bluestone Company similar to the one prepared for **Exhibit 16-16**.

b. Compute the manufacturing overhead rates for production departments 1 and 2 using machine hours and direct labor costs, respectively, for allocation bases.

PROBLEMS—SET B

LO3, 5   **P16-1B. Determine and Use Consulting Rate** Oxford Consulting, Inc., expects the following costs and expenses during the coming year:

Direct labor (@ $8/hr.).	$336,000
Sales commissions.	72,000
Overhead	378,000

Required

a. Compute a predetermined overhead rate applied on the basis of direct labor hours.

b. Prepare a general journal entry to apply overhead during an interim period when 3,500 direct labor hours were worked.

c. What amount of overhead would be assigned to Job 325, to which $304 in direct labor had been charged?

P16-2B. Determine and Use Manufacturing Overhead Rate The following selected ledger accounts of the   **LO3** Lakewood Manufacturing Company are for May (the fifth month of its accounting year):

Materials Inventory			
May 1 balance	40,000	May credits.	150,000
May debits	125,000		

Factory Overhead			
May debits	160,000	May 1 balance	14,000
		May credits.	144,000

Work In Process Inventory			
May 1 balance	28,000	May credits.	440,000
May debits:			
Direct material.	129,000		
Direct labor	180,000		
Manufacturing overhead. . .	144,000		

Factory Payroll Payable			
May debits	228,000	May 1 balance	50,000
		May credits.	196,000

Finished Goods Inventory			
May 1 balance	102,000	May credits.	510,000
May debits	440,000		

Required

a. Determine the amount of indirect material requisitioned for production during May.

b. How much indirect labor cost was apparently incurred during May?

c. Calculate the manufacturing overhead rate based on direct labor cost.

d. Was manufacturing overhead for May under- or overapplied, and by what amount?

e. Was manufacturing overhead for the first five months of the year under- or overapplied, and by what amount?

f. What is the cost of production completed in May?

g. What is the cost of goods sold in May?

P16-3B. Job Cost Journal Entries Dillon Manufacturing had the following inventories at December 31,   **LO3** 2015, the end of its fiscal year:

Materials inventory	$15,000
Work in process inventory	17,000
Finished goods inventory	30,000

During January 2016, the following transactions occurred:

1. Purchased materials on account, $125,000.
2. Requisitioned total materials of $130,000, of which $8,000 was considered indirect material.
3. Incurred wages payable, $105,000.
4. Assigned total wages payable, of which $15,000 was considered indirect labor.
5. Incurred other manufacturing overhead, $57,000. (Credit Accounts Payable.)
6. Applied manufacturing overhead on the basis of 80% of direct labor costs.

7. Determined ending work in process, $14,000. Use this information to calculate the amount of WIP transferred to finished goods inventory (credit WIP).
8. Determined ending finished goods, $26,000. Use this information to calculate the cost of goods sold (credit FG inventory).

Required
a. Prepare general journal entries to record these transactions.
b. If the above transactions covered a full year's operations, prepare a journal entry to dispose of the overhead account balance. Assume that the balance is significant. Also assume that the following accounts contained the indicated amounts of manufacturing overhead applied during 2016:

Work in process inventory	$ 3,000
Finished goods inventory	6,000
Cost of goods sold	63,000

LO3, 4   **P16-4B. Job Cost Journal Entries** Prior to the beginning of 2016, Stapleton Company estimated that it would incur $153,000 of manufacturing overhead cost during 2016, using 17,000 direct labor hours to produce the desired volume of goods. On January 1, 2016, beginning balances of Materials Inventory, Work in Process Inventory, and Finished Goods Inventory were $48,000, $-0-, and $87,000, respectively.

Required
Prepare general journal entries to record the following for 2016:
a. Purchased materials on account, $316,000.
b. Of the total dollar value of materials used, $284,000 represented direct material and $35,000 indirect material.
c. Determined total factory labor, $189,000 (18,000 hrs. @ $10.50/hr.).
d. Of the factory labor, 15,800 were direct labor hours.
e. Applied manufacturing overhead based on direct labor hours to work in process.
f. Determined actual manufacturing overhead other than those items already recorded, $83,000. (Credit Accounts Payable.)
g. Ending inventories of work in process and finished goods were $57,000 and $71,800, respectively. Determine the cost of finished goods (credit WIP) and the cost of goods sold (credit FG inventory). Make separate entries.
h. Transferred the balance in Manufacturing Overhead to Cost of Goods Sold.

LO3, 4   **P16-5B. Job Cost Journal Entries and T Accounts** Following are certain operating data for Redwood Manufacturing Company for January 2016:

	Materials Inventory	Work in Process Inventory	Finished Goods Inventory
Beginning inventory	$40,000	$50,000	$80,000
Ending inventory.	70,000	60,000	56,000

Total sales were $2,000,000, on which the company earned a 40% gross profit. Redwood uses a predetermined manufacturing overhead rate of 110% of direct labor costs. Manufacturing overhead applied was $396,000. Exclusive of indirect material used, total manufacturing overhead incurred was $300,000; it was underapplied by $24,000.

Required
Compute the following items. (Set up T accounts for Materials Inventory, Work in Process Inventory, Finished Goods Inventory, and Manufacturing Overhead; fill in the known amounts; and then use the normal relationships among the various accounts to compute the unknown amounts.)
a. Cost of goods sold.
b. Cost of goods manufactured.
c. Direct labor incurred.
d. Direct material used.
e. Indirect material used.
f. Total materials purchased.

P16-6B. Job Cost Journal Entries and T Accounts Summarized data for the first month's operations of   **LO3, 4**
Slater Foundry during 2016 are presented below. A job order costing system is used.

1. Materials purchased on account, $88,000.
2. Amounts of materials requisitioned and foundry labor used:

Job	Materials	Foundry Labor
1....................................	$ 4,600	$ 3,600
2....................................	5,200	6,000
3....................................	3,800	8,800
4....................................	13,400	12,000
5....................................	6,400	7,200
6....................................	4,000	2,000
Indirect material......................	11,000	
Indirect labor.........................		18,000

3. Foundry overhead is applied at the rate of 150% of direct labor costs.
4. Miscellaneous foundry overhead incurred:

Prepaid foundry insurance written off.........................	$ 1,880
Property taxes on foundry building accrued...................	3,760
Foundry utilities payable accrued............................	4,400
Depreciation on foundry equipment..........................	8,400
Other costs incurred on account............................	14,640

5. Ending work in process consisted of Jobs 4 and 6. 6. Jobs 1 and 3 and one-half of Job 2 were sold
on account for $25,200, $31,600, and $18,920, respectively.

Required
a.   Open general ledger T accounts for Materials Inventory, Wages Payable, Foundry Overhead,
Work in Process Inventory, Finished Goods Inventory, and Cost of Goods Sold. Also set up subsidiary T accounts as job order cost sheets for each job.
b.   Prepare general journal entries to record the summarized transactions for the month, and post appropriate entries to any accounts listed in requirement (a). Key each entry parenthetically to the
related number in the problem data.
c.   Determine the balances of any accounts necessary and prepare schedules of jobs in ending work
in process and jobs in ending finished goods to confirm that they agree with the related control
accounts.

P16-7B. Complex Job Cost Journal Entries and Analysis During June 2016, its first month of operations,   **LO3, 4**
Logan Manufacturing Company completed the transactions listed below. Logan uses a job order costing system. Materials requisitions and the wages payable summary are analyzed on the 15th and the
last day of each month, and charges for direct material and direct labor are entered directly on specific
job order cost sheets. Manufacturing overhead at the rate of 160% of direct labor costs is recorded on
individual job order cost sheets when a job is completed and at month-end for any job then in process.
At month-end, entries to the general ledger accounts summarize materials requisitions, distribution of
wages payable costs, and the application of manufacturing overhead for the month. All other entries
to general ledger accounts are made as they occur.

1. Purchased materials on account, $210,000.
2. Paid miscellaneous manufacturing overhead costs, $52,000.
3. An analysis of materials requisitions and the wages payable summary for June 1–15 indicates the
following cost distribution:

Job	Materials	Factory Labor
1	$34,000	$60,000
2	16,000	26,000
3	8,000	18,000
Indirect material	14,000	
Indirect labor		56,000
Total	$72,000	$160,000

4. Jobs 1 and 2 were completed on June 15 and transferred to finished goods inventory on the next day. (Enter the appropriate manufacturing overhead amounts on the job order cost sheets, mark them completed, and make a general journal entry transferring the appropriate amount of cost to the Finished Goods Inventory account.)

5. Paid miscellaneous manufacturing overhead costs, $38,000.

6. Sold Job 1 on account, $300,000 (recognized its cost of sales in the general journal).

7. An analysis of materials requisitions and wages payable summary for June 16–30 indicates the following cost distribution:

Job	Materials	Factory Labor
3	$36,000	$28,000
4	30,000	54,000
5	12,000	20,000
6	6,000	8,000
Indirect material	10,000	
Indirect labor		46,000
Total	$94,000	$156,000

8. Jobs 3 and 4 were completed on June 30 and transferred to finished goods inventory on the same day. (See transaction 5.)

9. Sold Job 3 on account, $250,000 (recognized its cost of sales in the general journal).

10. Recorded the following additional manufacturing overhead:

Depreciation on factory building	$42,000
Depreciation on factory equipment	24,000
Expiration of prepaid factory insurance	7,000
Payable.	13,000
	$86,000

11. Recorded monthly general journal entry for the costs of all materials used.

12. Recorded monthly general journal entry for the distribution of wages payable costs.

13. Recorded manufacturing overhead on the job order cost sheets for jobs in ending work in process and in the general journal for all manufacturing overhead applied during the month.

    a. Set up the following general ledger T accounts: Materials Inventory, Wages Payable, Manufacturing Overhead, Work in Process Inventory, Finished Goods Inventory, Cost of Goods Sold, and Sales.

    b. Set up T accounts for each of Jobs 1–6 as job order cost sheets.

    c. Noting the accounting procedures described in the first paragraph of the problem, do the following:

       1. Record general journal entries for all transactions. Note that general journal entries are not required in transactions 3 and 7. Post only those portions of these entries affecting the general ledger accounts set up in requirement (a).

       2. Enter the applicable amounts directly on the appropriate job order cost sheets for transactions 3, 4, 7, 8, and 13. Note parenthetically the nature of each amount entered.

    d. Present a brief analysis showing that the general ledger accounts for work in process inventory and for finished goods inventory agree with the related job order cost sheets.

e. Explain in one sentence each what the balance of each general ledger account established in requirement (a) represents.

P16-8B. Manufacturing Overhead Distribution Worksheet The following are selected operating data for the production and service departments of Danville Company for 2016.   **LO5, 6**

| | Departments | | | |
| | Service | | Production | |
	1	2	1	2
Manufacturing overhead costs (identified by department)				
Factory supplies used	$12,800	$21,440	$ 67,840	$137,600
Indirect labor	$25,920	$38,400	$ 86,400	$384,000
Square feet of building floor space used	7,200	10,800	18,000	36,000
Assessed value of equipment used	$28,000	$84,000	$168,000	$280,000
Cubic yards of factory space used			132,000	198,000
Machine hours			51,200	204,800
Direct labor ($10 per hour)			$250,000	$500,000

Building depreciation of $51,200 is allocated on the basis of square feet of floor space. Personal property taxes of $19,200 are allocated on the basis of assessed values of equipment used. Costs for service departments 1 and 2 are allocated to production departments on the basis of cubic yards of factory space and machine hours, respectively.

Required

a. Prepare a 2016 manufacturing overhead distribution worksheet for Danville Company similar to the one prepared for **Exhibit 16-16.**

b. Compute the manufacturing overhead rates for production departments 1 and 2 using machine hours and direct labor hours, respectively, for allocation bases.

CERTIFIED MANAGEMENT ACCOUNTANT (CMA®) EXAM SAMPLE QUESTIONS

CMA16-1. Henry Manufacturing, which uses direct labor hours to apply overhead to its product line, undertook an extensive renovation and modernization program two years ago. Manufacturing processes were reengineered, considerable automated equipment was acquired, and 60% of the company's nonunion factory workers were terminated.

Which of the following statements would apply to the situation at Henry?

I. The company's factory overhead rate has likely increased.
II. The use of direct labor hours seems to be appropriate.
III. Henry will lack the ability to properly determine labor variances.
IV. Henry has likely reduced its ability to quickly cut costs in order to respond to economic downturns.

a. I, II, III, and IV.
b. I and IV only.
c. II and IV only.
d. I and III only.

CMA16-2. Using the following budget data for Valley Corporation, which produces only one product, calculate the company's predetermined manufacturing overhead application rate for variable overhead. *Hint:* The factory supervisor's salary is direct labor, since it is incurred regardless of production. SG&A expenses relate to the entire operations of Valley Corporation and not just related to manufacturing.

Units to be produced	11,000
Units to be sold	10,000
Indirect materials, varying with production	$ 1,000
Indirect labor, varying with production.	10,000
Factory supervisor's salary, incurred regardless of production.	20,000
Depreciation on factory building and equipment.	30,000
Utilities to operate factory machines	12,000
Security lighting for factory	2,000
Selling, general and administrative (SG&A) expenses	5,000

a. $2.09
b. $2.30
c. $4.73
d. $5.00

CMA16-3. Baldwin Printing Company uses a job order costing system and applies overhead based on machine hours. A total of 150,000 machine hours have been budgeted for the year. During the year, an order for 1,000 units was completed and incurred the following.

Direct material costs.	$1,000
Direct labor costs	1,500
Actual overhead	1,980
Machine hours	450

The accountant calculated the inventory cost of this order to be $4.30 per unit. The annual budgeted overhead in dollars was

a. $577,500.
b. $600,000.
c. $645,000.
d. $660,000.

CMA16-4. Boston Furniture Company manufactures several steel products. It has three production departments, Fabricating, Assembly, and Finishing. The service departments include Maintenance, Material Handling, and Designing. Currently, the company does not allocate service department costs to the production departments. John Baker, who has recently joined the company as the new cost accountant, believes that service department rates should be developed and charged to the production departments for services requested. If the company adopts this new policy, the production department managers would be **least** likely to

a. request an excessive amount of service.
b. replace outdated and inefficient systems.
c. refrain from using necessary services.
d. be encouraged to control costs.

CMA16-5. John Sheng, cost accountant at Starlet Company, is developing departmental manufacturing overhead application rates for the company's tooling and fabricating departments. The budgeted overhead for each department and the data for one job are shown below.

	Departments	
	Tooling	**Fabricating**
Supplies	$ 850	$ 200
Supervisors' salaries	1,500	2,000
Indirect labor	1,200	4,880
Depreciation.	1,000	5,500
Repairs	4,075	3,540
Total budgeted manufacturing overhead.	$8,625	$16,120
Total direct labor hours	460	620
Direct labor hours on Job #231	12	3

Using the departmental overhead application rates, total overhead applied to Job #231 in the Tooling and Fabricating Departments will be

a. $225.
b. $303.
c. $537.
d. $671.

EXTENDING YOUR KNOWLEDGE

EYK16-1. Business Decision Case   Elizabeth Flanigan and Associates is an engineering and design firm that specializes in developing plans for recycling plants for municipalities. The firm uses a job costing system to accumulate the cost associated with each design project. Flanigan employs three levels of employee: senior engineers, associate engineers, and clerical staff. The salary cost of the senior engineers and the associate engineers is assigned to each project as direct labor. The salary cost of the clerical staff is included in overhead, along with the cost of engineering supplies, automobile travel, and equipment depreciation. The cost of airline travel, motels, building permits, and fees from other consultants is charged to each project as direct material. Overhead is applied to projects using a predetermined overhead rate based on total engineering hours. The rate for 2014 is $5 per hour.

The six different salary levels for 2015 for the employees of Elizabeth Flanigan and Associates are listed below. The hourly rate is determined by dividing the yearly salary by 2,000 hours per year.

> **Senior engineer**
> Level 1: $44,000 per year ($22 per hour)
> Level 2: $36,000 per year ($18 per hour)
> **Associate engineer**
> Level 3: $30,000 per year ($15 per hour)
> Level 4: $24,000 per year ($12 per hour)
> **Clerical staff**
> Level 5: $16,000 per year ($8 per hour)
> Level 6: $12,000 per year ($6 per hour)

The billings that are sent to the municipalities for engineering services utilize cost-plus billing. Typically, the total costs accumulated for a project (direct material, direct labor, and overhead) are multiplied by 140% to determine the amount of the billing. The difference between the billed amount and the accumulated cost is the "plus" in cost plus.

During March 2015, Flanigan accumulated the following information related to Job 295 for Johnson Creek City:

Senior engineer hours	
Level 1	52
Level 2	84
Associate engineer hours	
Level 3	106
Level 4	44
Clerical hours	
Level 5	20
Level 6	66
Building permits	$1,500
Airline travel and motel	$865

Required

a. What amount should be billed to Johnson Creek City for March 2015?

b. How much profit was earned on Job 295 during March 2015?

EYK16-2. Corporate Social Responsibility Problem The CSR box in this chapter discusses CH2M Hill's efforts to offer summer programs at no cost introducing underrepresented groups to STEM education. The company's stated goal is twofold: to increase the pool of future engineering talent and to build better communities.

Some would look at these efforts as costly programs with no tangible financial benefit. There is certainly no guarantee that these children will work for CH2M Hill in the future, or even that they will choose careers in engineering. In fact, these efforts may end up supplying talent for CH2M Hill's competitors and driving up future engineering wages.

What do you think?

EYK16-3. Ethics Case Metal Creations, Inc., is a custom manufacturer that uses a job order costing system. Currently, Metal Creations has 35% excess capacity in its factory. Charlie Rollins, the president, has instituted a campaign to obtain new customers. Rollins has offered the salespeople a bonus equal to 25% of the gross profit on work for new customers. The average gross profit rate has been 30% of the contract price.

Steve Starling, the sales manager for Metal Creations, wants to submit a proposal to a new customer that undercuts the usual pricing structure by 30%. As a result, this job would have no gross profit using the regular job order costing system. Instead, Starling suggests that the overhead rate applied to this job should be only 40% of the normal overhead rate, resulting in a gross profit of 28%. Starling suggests that the controller should handle this contract herself, and that no one else in the organization should know about it, especially the other salespeople, because the creative approach to overhead application might create problems.

Required

Does taking an order at a significantly reduced price create an ethical problem? Does altering the accounting for a particular order create an ethical problem? Does asking the controller to handle the contract and keep the accounting confidential create an ethical problem?

ANSWERS TO SELF-STUDY QUESTIONS:

1. d, (p. 755)   2. c, (p. 759)   3. b, (p. 764)   4. b, (p. 765)   5. d, (pp. 770–771)

YOUR TURN! SOLUTIONS

Solution 16.1

Industry	Cost System
Chemicals	Process
Printing	Job order
Aircraft	Job order
Oil refining	Process
Paints	Process
Glass	Process
Furniture	Job order
Machinery	Job order

Solution 16.2

1. Manufacturing overhead cannot be traced directly to a particular product or job.
2. Manufacturing overhead consists of many unlike items.
3. Manufacturing actual overhead costs may not be known until after a period is over.

Solution 16.3

Estimated manufacturing overhead	$250,000
Divided by budgeted direct labor hours.	10,000
Predetermined overhead rate per direct labor hour.	$ 25
Actual direct labor hours	$ 9,000
Multiplied by predetermined overhead rate	× 25
Applied overhead	$225,000

Solution 16.4

1. Overhead cannot be traced directly to a particular product or job. Manufacturing overhead cost for one department might be significantly different from that of another department.
2. The activity basis in one department might be different from that of another. One department may be labor intensive and another department may be machine intensive.

DECISION TIME SOLUTION

Solution 16.1

c. Either *a* or *b*, depending on the significance of the amount.

17 Cost Accounting Systems: Process Costing

PAST

Chapter 16 introduced and explained job costing in more detail for both manufacturing and service industries. It also explained overhead allocation.

PRESENT

Chapter 17 introduces process costing and how it differs from job order costing. It illustrates equivalent units and the flow of costs through the inventory accounts, as well as introduces the product cost report.

FUTURE

Chapter 18 explores activity-based costing and its benefits relative to traditional plant-wide and departmental overhead allocation, and contrasts it with activity-based management.

LEARNING OBJECTIVES

1. **Compare** and **contrast** job order costing and process costing. *(p. 798)*

2. **Describe** the basic concepts of process costing. *(p. 800)*

3. **Explain** techniques for determining unit costs when process costing is used. *(p. 802)*

4. **Explain** the procedures used to prepare the product cost report using the weighted average method in a process costing system. *(p. 809)*

5. **Illustrate** the journal entries used with process costing. *(p. 811)*

6. Appendix 17A: **Explain** techniques for determining unit costs when the FIFO method for process costing is used. *(p. 816)*

7. Appendix 17A: **Explain** the procedures used to prepare the product cost report using the FIFO method in a process costing system. *(p. 822)*

8. Appendix 17A: **Illustrate** the journal entries used with FIFO process costing. *(p. 824)*

GENERAL MILLS INC.

General Mills Inc. is a Fortune 500 company based in Golden Valley, Minnesota. Consumers know General Mills best for its ready-to-eat cereal products, of which they consume 60 million servings per day. The quality of these cereal products can be traced back to Gold Medal flour in 1880, which today remains the number-one-selling brand of flour in the United States. General Mills' brand portfolio includes more than 100 leading U.S. brands and numerous category leaders around the world, with 2014 overall company sales reaching $17.9 billion. Some of the top-selling brands include Betty Crocker, Yoplait, Totinos, Pillsbury, Cheerios, Trix, and Lucky Charms. One unique manufacturing feature these brands share is that they are produced in mass quantities, with little to distinguish one cupful of cereal or yogurt from another.

Manufacturers like General Mills that produce massive quantities of inventory that are indistinguishable from one another rely on process costing to track inventory costs. The company had an inventory balance on May 31, 2015, of $1.5 billion, of which $486 million consisted of raw materials and work in process, and $1.3 billion consisted of finished goods. Rather than track the cost of each piece of cereal, General Mills tracks the total costs of inventory produced over a given period and divides these total costs by the pounds of inventory produced to obtain an average price per pound for each product. This costing system stands in stark contrast to industries such as custom cabinet manufacturing, in which costs are tallied on a job cost record for each unique custom cabinet rather than spreading them over multiple identical units of inventory.

This chapter examines how companies like General Mills utilize process costing in order to properly value their inventory. We focus on how the weighted average method of process costing provides useful information to managers and illustrates the journal entries required throughout the manufacturing process. We also introduce the concept of equivalent units and their application to process costing.

COST ACCOUNTING SYSTEMS: PROCESS COSTING

Introduction to Process Costing	Characteristics of Process Costing	Process Costing Steps	The Product Cost Report	Journal Entries Illustrated	Process Costing Using FIFO Method (Appendix 17A)
• Job order costing review • Processing costing	• Manufacturing departments • Basic processing patterns	• Visualize physical flow of units • Calculate equivalent units • Determine per-unit costs • Calculate cost of goods manufactured • Calculate ending work in process inventory	• Illustration of the product cost report • Multiple production processes	• Material • Labor • Manufacturing overhead	• Process costing steps • The product cost report • Journal entries illustrated

INTRODUCTION TO PROCESS COSTING

LO1 **Compare** and **contrast** job order costing and process costing.

The early sections of this chapter explain and illustrate the concepts and procedures that are typical in a process costing system that involves only one processing department using the weighted average cost flow assumption. Appendix 17A illustrates the procedures and differences under the first-in, first-out (FIFO) cost flow assumption.

Job Order Costing Review

Prior chapters have introduced and discussed the concepts used in job order costing. Recall that job order costing accumulates costs for each specific job in a separate work in process inventory account dedicated to that unique job. **Exhibit 17-1** presents the typical flow of product costs in a job order costing system for Job 372. Direct material and direct labor are traced to each specific job, whereas indirect overhead costs are allocated to each job.

Exhibit 17-1	Product Cost Flows in a Job Order Costing System

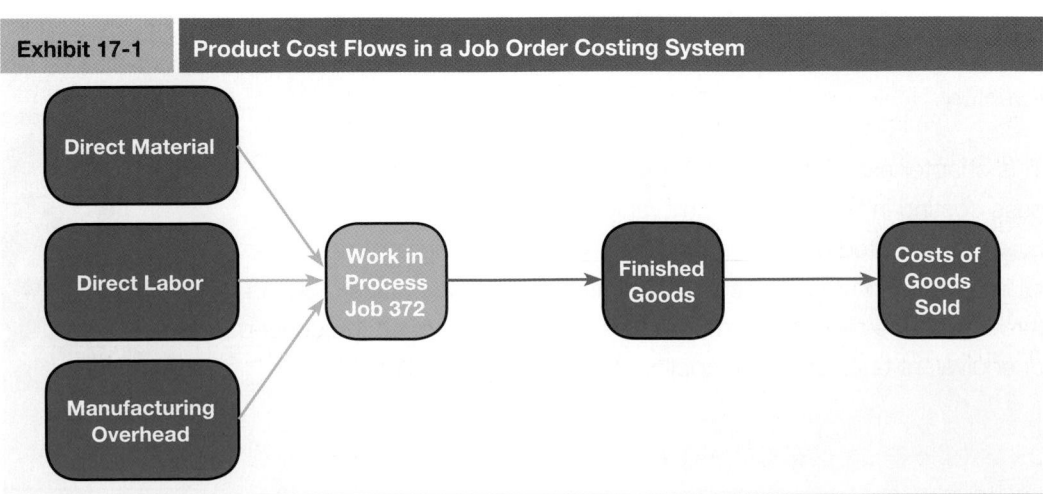

Although production costs are tracked separately for each job, companies also need to understand their total costs. Hence, costs for all of the individual jobs are accumulated in the work in process control account, which represents the overall cost summary of all jobs currently in production. For example, **Exhibit 17-2** lists four individual jobs that are currently in process. The work in process inventory control account represents the sum of all jobs that are currently in process. Overhead costs are accumulated and applied to the work in process inventory control account based on an annual predetermined overhead rate. Specifically, actual overhead costs, including indirect material and indirect labor, are accumulated in the manufacturing overhead account as debits, and the applied overhead is transferred to Work in Process Inventory with a credit. Perpetual inventory techniques are typically used to move product cost from Work in Process Inventory to Finished Goods Inventory and finally to Cost of Goods Sold, as illustrated in **Exhibit 17-2**.

Exhibit 17-2	Job Order Costing Summary (Accumulating Costs by Job)

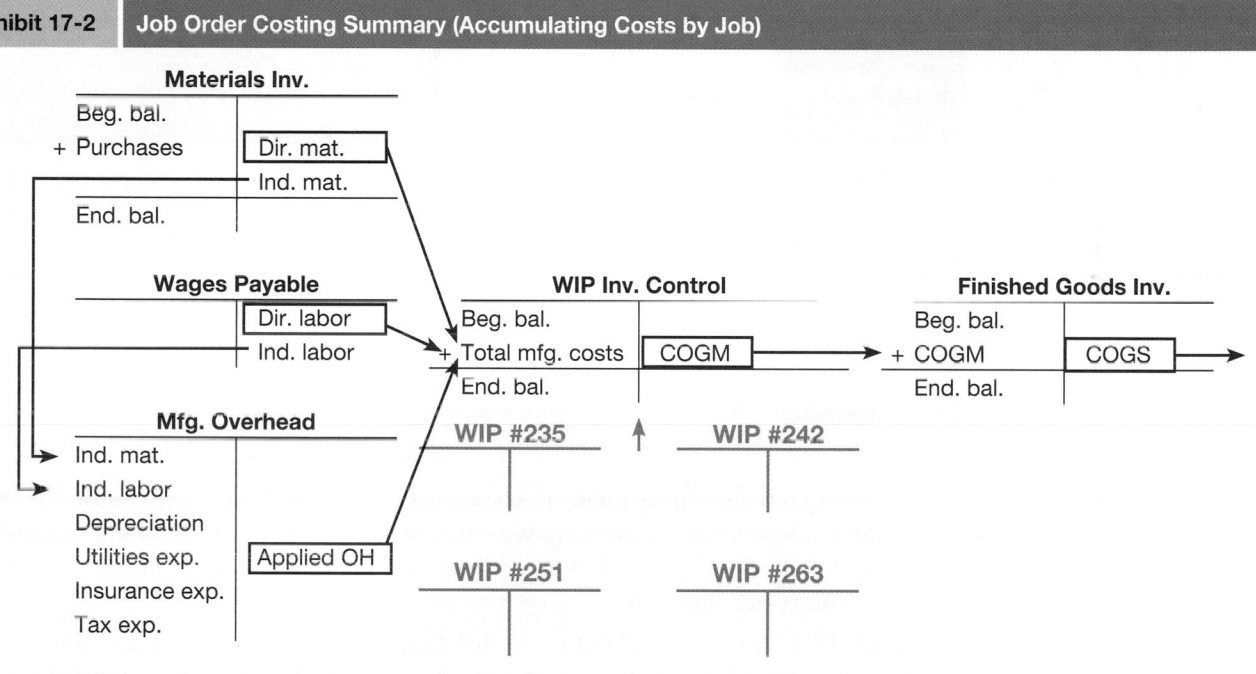

Job order costing is appropriate when products or services are characterized by customization to meet the customer's specifications. Job order costing can result when products are produced or jobs are undertaken to (1) fill specific customer orders or (2) produce a stock of products from which future orders can be filled.

Process Costing

Process costing, however, is used when large volumes of identical (homogeneous) products are manufactured in a continuous-flow operation, such as the production of fuels, chemicals, small appliances, building materials, and electricity. In process costing, product costs are accumulated by department, not by job or product. We note at the outset that although it is possible to use process costing in a service environment, it is not common. For example, a service agency that provides identical services to each customer could calculate an average cost per customer. However, most of the examples in this chapter focus on manufacturing companies because process costing is much more common in a manufacturing setting. We provide a detailed service example at the end of the chapter.

TAKEAWAY 17.1

Job order costing is used for unique products or orders, whereas process costing is used for uniform products.

CHARACTERISTICS OF PROCESS COSTING

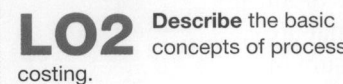

LO2 Describe the basic concepts of process costing.

Exhibit 17-3 presents the typical flow of product cost in a **process costing system**. The following process costing characteristics are evident in **Exhibit 17-3**:

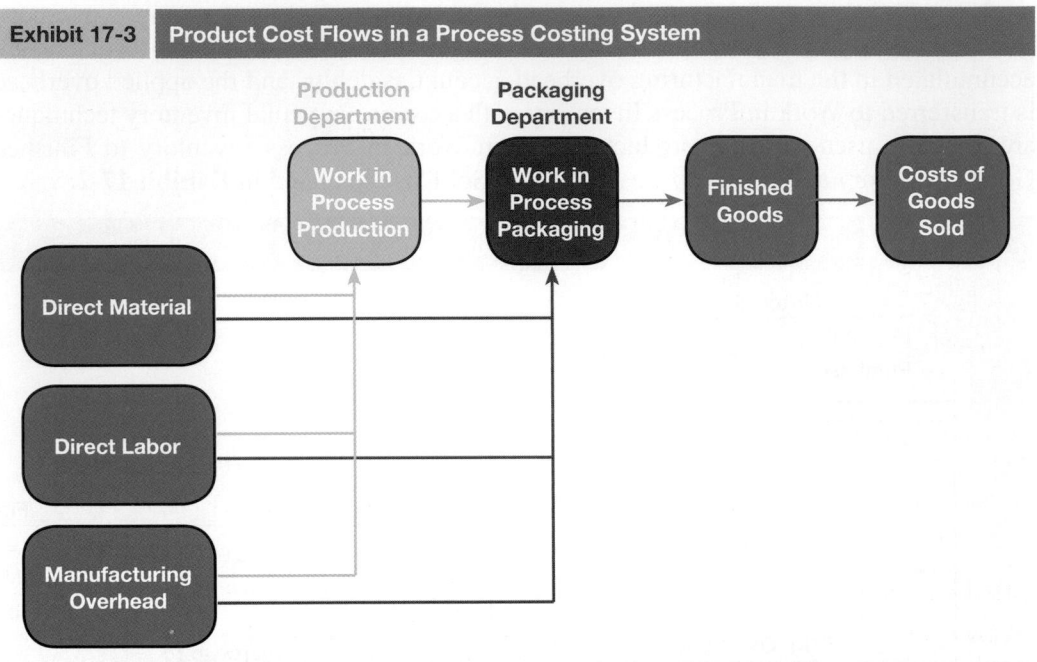

| Exhibit 17-3 | Product Cost Flows in a Process Costing System |

1. Each manufacturing department has a separate work in process inventory account. **Exhibit 17-3** assumes a company with two manufacturing departments: production and packaging. Costs are accumulated for each department in a separate work in process inventory account.

Hint: A process can be defined as a step in the manufacture of a product. In a process costing system, materials, labor, and overhead are charged to processing departments rather than to specific jobs.

2. **Exhibit 17-4** shows how the costs in this process flow through the accounts. Direct material, direct labor, and manufacturing overhead costs can be added to the work in process inventory account in each department. **Exhibit 17-4** shows all three elements of product cost being added to both work in process inventory accounts.

3. Products physically move through the process on a first-in, first-out (FIFO) basis. That is, the unfinished units in work in process are assumed to be completed first in the subsequent period before new units are started.

4. Under process costing, managers use a **product cost report** to accumulate costs by process or department. These costs are then allocated to specific units of product that pass through that process or department using either the weighted average or FIFO allocation method. In this chapter, we focus on the weighted average costing method, and Appendix 17A explains the FIFO costing method.

Exhibit 17-4	Process Costing Summary (Accumulating Costs by Process or Department)

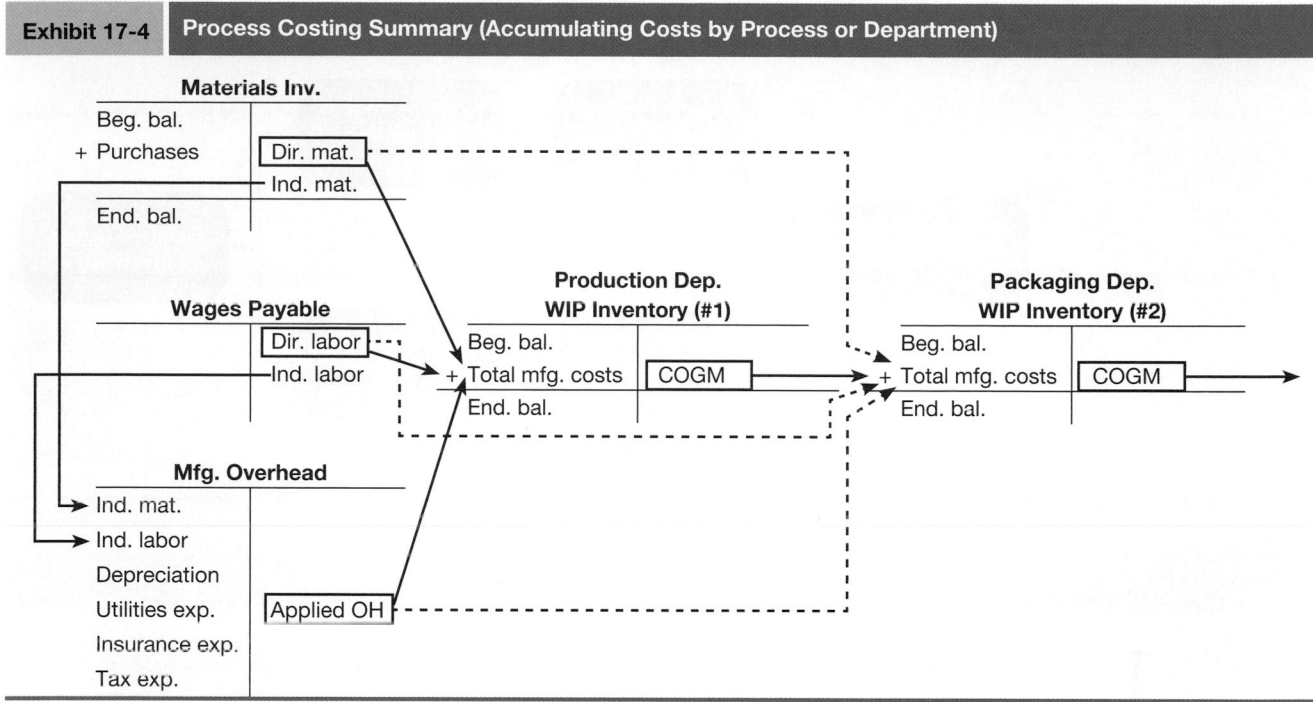

Manufacturing Departments

Typically, multiple manufacturing departments are identified when process costing is used. Products will flow through these departments at different stages of the manufacturing process. For example, a consumer product might be processed through three departments, machining, painting, and assembling. In any particular manufacturing plant, some products may go through many departments, and other products may go through only a few departments, depending on the nature of the work to be done. Regardless, the work in any department must be performed uniformly on all units, and the output of the department must be uniform in nature.

Basic Processing Patterns

There are two basic patterns for arranging the departments in a process costing setting: sequential and parallel processing. **Exhibit 17-5** presents a **sequential product processing** pattern, in which products follow a single path through the manufacturing process to finished goods inventory.

Exhibit 17-5	Sequential Product Processing

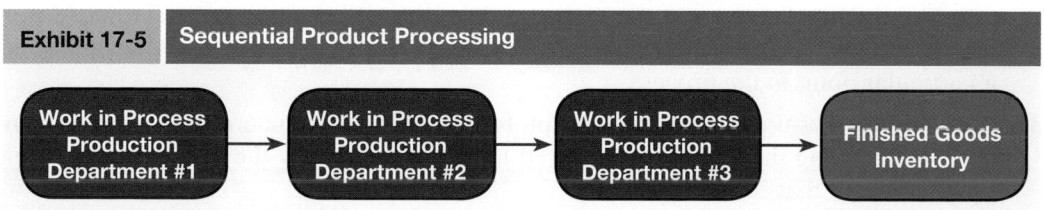

Exhibit 17-6 presents a simple example of **parallel product processing**. Numerous variations of parallel processing are possible, but similar products may begin with the same raw materials or processing in one department and then follow slightly different processes to arrive in finished goods inventory.

Exhibit 17-6	Parallel Product Processing

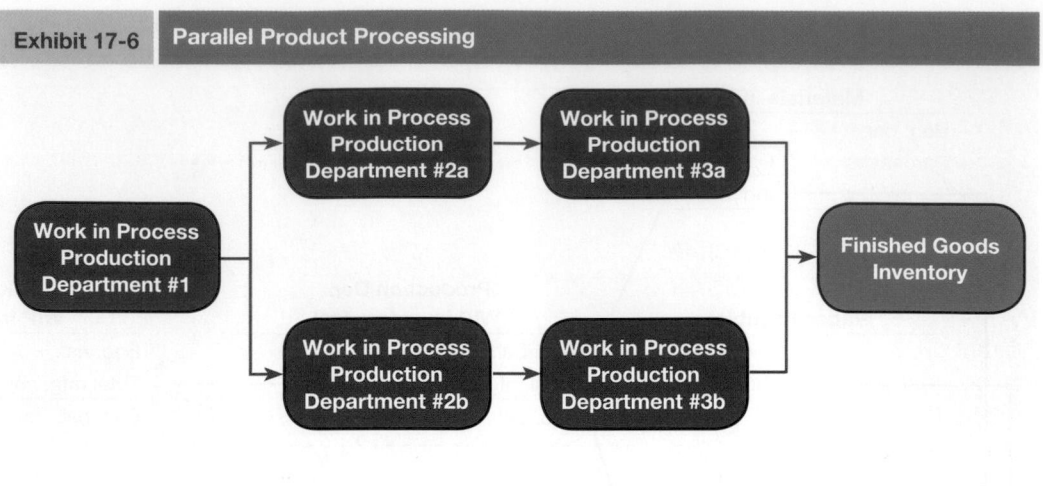

Each processing department has two essential features:
1. The activity performed in each department is performed uniformly on all products passing through it.
2. The output of each department is homogeneous.

PROCESS COSTING STEPS

LO3 Explain techniques for determining unit costs when process costing is used.

The techniques described in this chapter require the calculation of unit costs to facilitate the end-of-period transfer of product cost from one work in process inventory account to another, from the final work in process inventory account to the finished goods inventory account, and from the finished goods inventory account to the cost of goods sold account. In process costing, unit costs are usually calculated on a monthly basis. These unit costs can be compared to unit costs of prior accounting periods to determine when additional cost control measures are necessary.

Process costing requires five steps or calculations:

1. Visualize or chart the physical flow of the units through the system.

2. Determine the equivalent whole units of work completed (or **equivalent units** of production) during the period. This calculation is usually performed separately for materials and **conversion costs** (i.e., labor and overhead) because conversion costs are usually added uniformly throughout the process, whereas materials are often added at a particular point in the process.

3. Compute the per-unit cost of production for the period for materials and conversion costs by dividing the total costs incurred in each category by the equivalent units of production for that cost category.

4. Using the per-unit costs for material and conversion costs, compute the dollar value of the units completed and transferred (Cost of Goods Manufactured) to the next department.

5. Using the same per-unit costs, compute the dollar value of the unfinished units that remain in the department (these ending work in process units will usually be completed in the following period).

The objective of each step is the same for both the weighted average and FIFO methods of cost allocation. However, the execution of the steps is slightly different between the two methods. We discuss these steps in more detail for the weighted average method in the following sections. For illustration purposes, assume that the Big G division of General Mills uses process costing to account for its cereal production and that it has the results for January as illustrated in **Exhibit 17-7**.

Exhibit 17-7	Big G Process Costing Example	
Work in process, January 1:		
Direct materials	$	166,400
Direct labor		38,100
Manufacturing overhead		76,300
Total beginning work in process	$	280,800
Work done during January:		
Direct material (grain) added		$19,250,000
Direct labor incurred		3,210,000
Manufacturing overhead applied		9,540,000
Total costs incurred during January		$32,000,000
Units in process at January 1 (20% complete)		2,600 tons
Units started during January		58,500 tons
Units in process at January 31 (40% complete)		3,500 tons

Further, assume that all materials are added at the beginning of the process, whereas labor and manufacturing overhead costs are added evenly throughout the process. The T-account in **Exhibit 17-8** illustrates the purpose of process costing: to allocate actual costs incurred between units completed and transferred out, and partially completed units remaining in ending inventory.

Exhibit 17-8	The Objective: Allocate Costs between Ending Inventory and Those Transferred Out

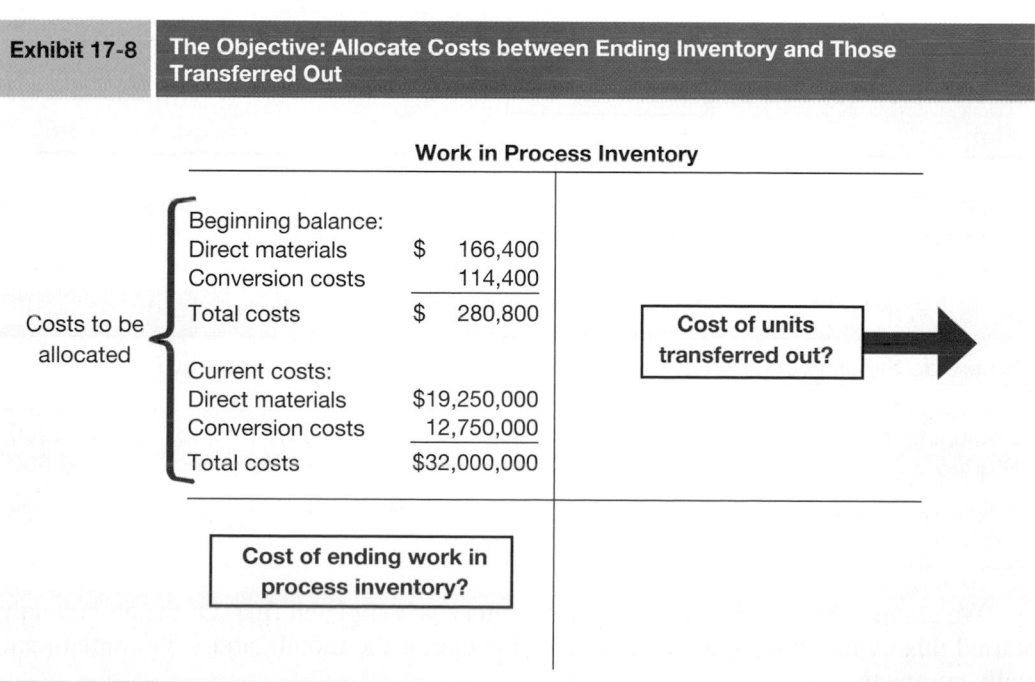

We know the costs associated with the beginning work in process inventory on January 1 ($280,800). We also know the costs incurred during the month of January for direct materials ($19,250,000), direct labor ($3,210,000), and manufacturing overhead ($9,540,000). For simplicity, because we assume both direct labor and manufacturing overhead costs are applied uniformly during the production process, we combine them and simply refer to them as "conversion costs." Because we started the period with partially completed inventory, during the period we will first finish the previously started units and then begin work on new units. We also end the period with partially completed units. We don't know how much of these costs should be applied to units transferred out at the end of the period and how much should remain with the partially complete ending inventory. Process costing helps us calculate an average cost per unit to apply to (1) the units completed and transferred out at the end of the period and (2) the units remaining in ending inventory.

Step 1: Visualize the Physical Flow of the Units

The starting point in process costing is to visualize how the units flow through the production process, as illustrated in **Exhibit 17-9**. In the General Mills Big G example, the quantity produced is measured in tons of cereal processed during the month of January. Sometimes it is useful to visualize how the units correspond to the dollars in the T-account in **Exhibit 17-8**.

Exhibit 17-9	T-account to Summarize the Physical Flow of Units

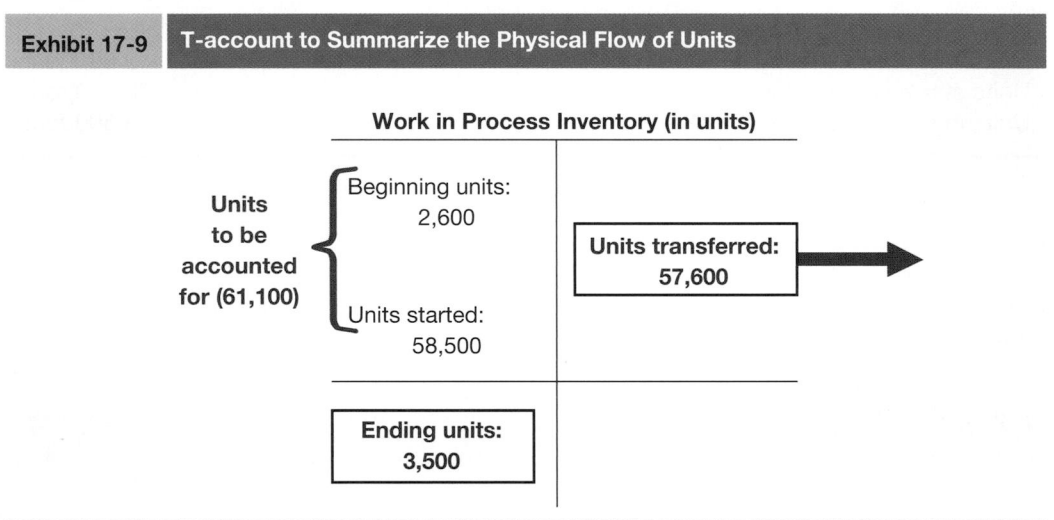

Another way to visualize the flow of the cereal produced during January is by asking where the units come from and where they end up, as shown in **Exhibit 17-10**.

Exhibit 17-10	Step 1: Visualize the Physical Flow of the Units

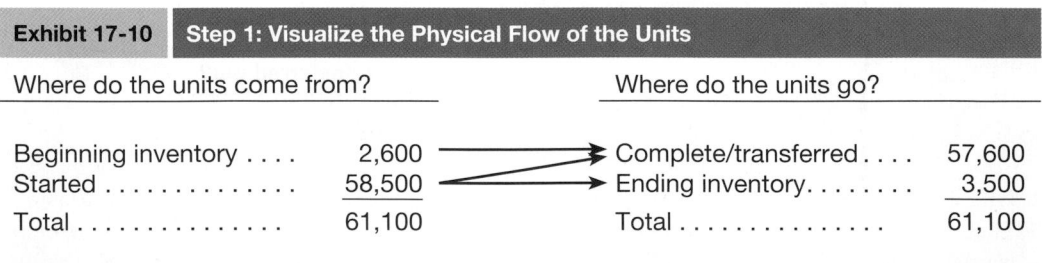

We assume that all of the beginning inventory is completed first. Of the 58,500 units started this month, 55,000 are complete by the end of the month, and 3,500 remain partially complete.

Step 2: Calculate the Equivalent Units

Introduction to Equivalent Units

The average cost per unit is calculated by dividing total costs by the total number of units produced. The work in process accounts described in **Exhibits 17-5** and **17-6** illustrate how total costs are accumulated and tracked through the system. Accountants are good at keeping track of costs. However, cost accountants face a major problem in allocating costs in continuous-flow manufacturing processes. At any given point in time, units of product are at various stages of completion. Hence, it is difficult to determine the number of units to use in the average cost per unit calculation:

Hint: Instead of tracking specific costs incurred to produce each unit of product as in job order costing, process costing accumulates costs by department and then calculates an average cost per unit to be assigned to all units of product produced during that period.

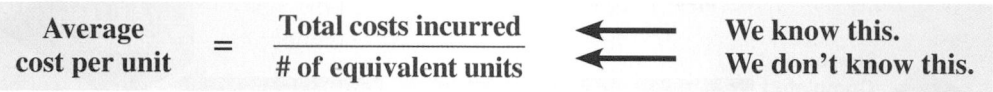

$$\text{Average cost per unit} = \frac{\text{Total costs incurred}}{\text{\# of equivalent units}}$$

We know this.
We don't know this.

The notion of equivalent units of production is a key concept in process costing. When units of product are produced in a continuous process, engineers and manufacturing supervisors must estimate the average percentage completion of units in a given department at the end of each period. Accountants use this information to estimate the number of equivalent *complete* units of product. For example, the following illustration shows eight glasses of water that are *half* full. How many *full* glasses of water is this equivalent to?

8 Glasses ½ Full = 4 Full Glasses

The eight half-full glasses are approximately equivalent to four full glasses. This example illustrates what accountants do each period in determining the average cost per unit in a given department.

To properly determine per-unit costs, we must first calculate equivalent units of production to be used in the denominator of the average cost per unit calculation. **Equivalent units** are the equivalent number of *whole units* completed during the period. In the previous illustration, the eight partially full glasses of water are equivalent to four full glasses (similar to four equivalent complete units of production). The calculation of equivalent units of production requires accountants to (1) track the *actual quantity* of products at each stage of production and (2) estimate the *average amount of work completed* on each unit of product in terms of conversion costs and direct material costs.

Engineers or production experts estimate the percentage of work completed in terms of conversion costs, on average. As illustrated in **Exhibit 17-11**, because the 2,600 tons of cereal on hand on January 1 is 20% complete (based on work completed during

December), Big G only has to complete the remaining 80% of the processing during the month of January. During January, Big G begins work on 55,000 tons of cereal that is both started and completed during the month of January. Finally, Big G begins work on an additional 3,500 tons of cereal that is not completed by the end of the month. Engineers determine that only 40% of the processing is complete on this batch of cereal by January 31.

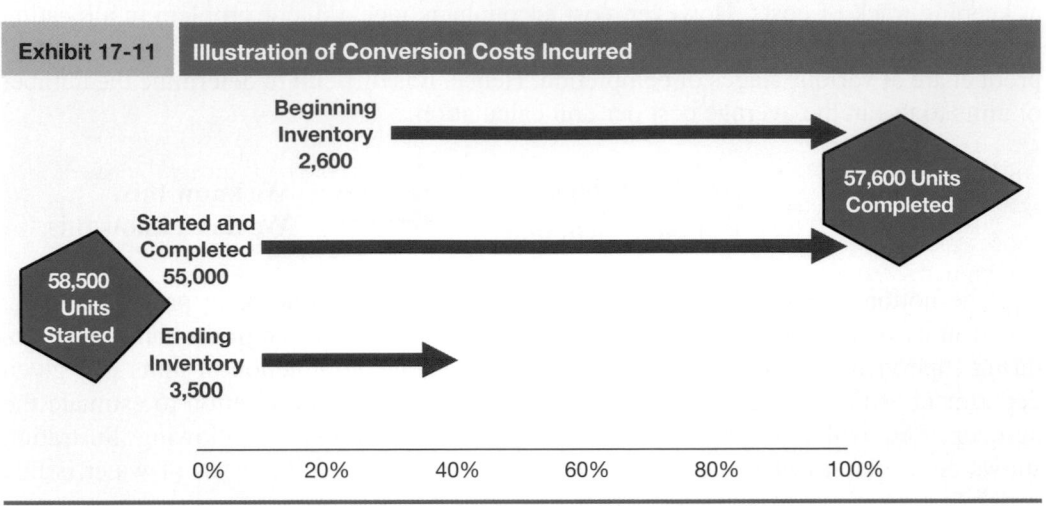

| Exhibit 17-11 | Illustration of Conversion Costs Incurred |

Hint: The weighted average method is called a "rollback" method because the average includes all work done in the current period plus work done on beginning inventory in the prior period.

We assume that all direct material is added at the beginning of the process; therefore, the average amount of work completed on each unit of product related to direct materials is 100%.

Calculating equivalent units can be performed using either the weighted average or the FIFO cost flow assumption. We illustrate the **weighted average method** here and the FIFO method in **Appendix 17A**. A key difference between the two methods is that the weighted average method mixes inventory layers, whereas the **FIFO method** keeps inventory layers separate. To keep these layers separate, the FIFO method tracks costs incurred during December separate from those incurred during January, the weighted average method averages all costs incurred in the production of a batch of units, regardless of when those costs were incurred. Thus, the FIFO method asks "What costs were incurred during THIS PERIOD?" whereas the weighted average method simply asks "How much work is complete (regardless of when the work was done)?"

Equivalent Unit Calculation for Direct Materials—Weighted Average

Because materials are added at the beginning of the process, all units that have been started (61,100) are 100% complete with respect to materials. **Exhibit 17-12** illustrates the calculation of equivalent units in terms of direct materials based on the weighted average cost flow assumption.

Exhibit 17-12	Step 2: Calculate the Equivalent Units—Direct Materials				
	Physical Units (tons)		**Proportion Completed**		**Equivalent Units (tons)**
Complete and transferred	57,600	×	100%	=	**57,600**
Ending inventory.	3,500	×	100%	=	**3,500**
Total	61,100				61,100

Equivalent Unit Calculation for Conversion Costs—Weighted Average

When considering conversion costs (direct labor and manufacturing overhead), it is often useful to visualize the amount of work done during the period on each unique set of inventory passing through the production process, as previously illustrated in **Exhibit 17-11**. Despite the fact that some of the units were started during December, the weighted average method simply asks what percentage of the work has been completed by the end of January, as illustrated in **Exhibit 17-13**.

Exhibit 17-13	Step 2: Calculate the Equivalent Units—Conversion Costs					
		Physical Units (tons)		Proportion Completed		Equivalent Units (tons)
Complete and transferred		57,600	×	100%	=	**57,600**
Ending inventory.		3,500	×	40%	=	**1,400**
Total		61,100				59,000

We can summarize the flow of the units worked on during the period and how the amount of work completed translates them into equivalent units, as illustrated in **Exhibit 17-14**.

Exhibit 17-14	Summary of Steps 1 and 2: Unit Flows and Equivalent Units Calculations							
					Step 2: Calculate the Equivalent Units			
Step 1: Visualize the Physical Flow of the Units						Equivalent Units		
Where do the units come from?		Where do the units go?			% Work Done?	Dir. Mat.	% Work Done?	Conv. Costs
Beg. Inv.	2,600	Compl./transf.		57,600	100%	**57,600**	100%	**57,600**
Started	58,500	End. Inv.		3,500	100%	**3,500**	40%	**1,400**
Total	61,100	Total		61,100		**61,100**		**59,000**

TAKEAWAY 17.3

An equivalent unit is the amount of work necessary to produce one complete physical unit of product. For example, doing 80% of the work on 200 units is equivalent to doing 100% of the work on 160 units.

YOUR TURN! 17.1

The solution is on page 843.

Assume all materials are added at the beginning of the production process, and conversion costs are added uniformly throughout the process. Beginning work in process is comprised of 100 units, which are 35% complete with respect to conversion costs. Also assume that 700 units are started and completed during the period, and ending work in process includes 90 units that are 75% complete with respect to conversion costs. Compute equivalent units of production for direct materials and conversion costs under the weighted average cost flow assumption. (*Hint:* For fractional units, round up.)

Step 3: Determine the Per-Unit Costs

The product cost report summarizes where the costs come from and where they go (i.e., where they are allocated). In order to calculate an average cost per unit of direct materials and conversion costs, we first need to summarize the total costs incurred for direct materials and conversion costs. These numbers were illustrated in the T-account in **Exhibit 17-8**. The top part of our product cost report simply asks where the costs come from and organizes them into categories: Direct Materials and Conversion Costs, as illustrated in **Exhibit 17-15**.

Exhibit 17-15	Product Cost Report: Where Do the Costs Come From?

Product Cost Report
General Mills Big G Division
January Production

Where do the costs come from?	Total	Direct Materials	Conversion Costs
Beginning inventory	$ 280,800	$ 166,400	$ 114,400
Current	32,000,000	19,250,000	12,750,000
Total costs to account for	$32,280,800	$19,416,400	$12,864,400

We then calculate the average cost per unit by dividing total costs in each category by total equivalent units in each category from Step 2. In other words, we divide total materials costs by total equivalent units of materials ($19,416,400/61,100 equivalent units) to get an average cost per unit of $317.78. Similarly, we divide total conversion costs by total equivalent units of conversion costs ($12,864,400/59,000 equivalent units) to get an average cost per unit of $218.04. **Exhibit 17-16** summarizes this calculation.

Exhibit 17-16	Step 3: Product Cost Report: Determine Per-Unit Costs

Product Cost Report
General Mills Big G Division
January Production

Where do the costs come from?	Total	Direct Materials	Conversion Costs
Beginning inventory	$ 280,800	$ 166,400	$ 114,400
Current	32,000,000	19,250,000	12,750,000
Total costs to account for	$32,280,800	$19,416,400	$12,864,400
÷ Total equivalent units		61,100	59,000
Average cost/unit		$ 317.7807	$ 218.0407

Note that the weighted average method includes *all* costs incurred on units worked on during the month, whereas the FIFO method only includes costs incurred during the *current* period. Hence, both the numerator (costs incurred) and the denominator (equivalent units) will differ between the weighted average and FIFO methods.

Step 4: Calculate the Cost of Goods Manufactured

At the end of each month and for each department, we calculate the cost of goods manufactured (illustrated in **Exhibit 17-17**), which is comprised of the cost of the goods that are completed and transferred to the finished goods inventory. Under the weighted average cost flow assumption, the Big G division's cost of goods manufactured during January consists of 57,600 equivalent units of materials and conversion costs (shown in **red** in **Exhibit 17-14**) multiplied by their respective per-unit costs computed in Step 2 (shown in **green** in **Exhibit 17-16**).

Exhibit 17-17	Step 4: Cost of Goods Manufactured Calculation		
Materials.	**[57,600** EU × **$317.7807]**	18,304,168	
Conversion costs	**[57,600** EU × **$218.0407]**	12,559,143*	
Total cost of goods manufactured.		$30,863,311	

*Difference due to rounding

Step 5: Calculate the Ending Work in Process Inventory

Exhibit 17-18 illustrates the final step, which is to calculate the **cost of goods remaining** in ending work in process. Assuming all materials are added at the beginning and conversion costs are added evenly throughout the process, we multiply the equivalent units of materials and conversion costs in ending inventory (denoted in **red** in **Exhibit 17-14**) by their respective unit costs (shown in **green** in **Exhibit 17-16**) computed in Step 2, as shown in **Exhibit 17-18**.

Exhibit 17-18	Step 5: Calculate Cost of Ending Inventory		
Materials.	**[3,600** EU × **$317.7807]**	1,112,232	
Conversion costs	**[1,400** EU × **$218.0407]**	305,257	
Total cost of ending inventory		$1,417,489	

	General Mills Tries to Make a Difference	CORPORATE SOCIAL RESPONSIBILITY

If you read the current popular media reports, you are likely to get the idea that the only stakeholders a corporation cares about are its shareholders. General Mills thinks differently. The goal of General Mills is to stand among the world's most socially responsible food companies. The company believes that being a good corporate citizen means considering all its stakeholders. To do this, General Mills seeks to create long-term economic, social, and environmental value.

General Mills recognizes that its customers depend on the company to provide healthy food choices. One example of what General Mills is doing in this area is an improvement in the health profile of 76% of its retail U.S. sales volume since 2005. To help the environment, General Mills has reduced its waste generation by 41% since 2005. General Mills' is also committed to sustainable sourcing, with a goal of 50% of its annual raw material purchases to be from sustainable sources by 2020. General Mills strives to create a culture of ethics with 95% of employees stating that General Mills leaders demonstrate a commitment to ethical business. Finally, General Mills commitment to community included over $151 million of donations to charitable causes in 2014 and over $1.5 billion since the General Mills Foundation was established in 1954.

Source: https://www.generalmills.com/en/Responsibility/Overview

THE PRODUCT COST REPORT

Using the Big G example, the product cost report illustrated in **Exhibit 17-19** summarizes all of the steps in the total cost allocation process from (1) visualizing the physical flow of the units, to (2) calculating equivalent units, to (3) calculating unit costs, to (4) calculating cost of goods manufactured, to (5) calculating ending inventory. Moreover, **Exhibit 17-19** also provides Big G's product cost report. Note that in this illustration, the equivalent units of production for materials and conversion costs (the numbers in **red**) are multiplied by the corresponding cost per unit figures for materials and conversion costs (the numbers in **green**) to calculate the cost allocation to cost of goods manufactured and ending inventory.

LO4 Explain the procedures used to prepare the product cost report using the weighted average method in a process costing system.

Exhibit 17-19	Summary of the Five Process Costing Steps

Flow of the Units and Equivalent Units Calculation

Step 2: Calculate the Equivalent Units

Step 1: Visualize the Physical Flow of the Units

Where do the units come from?		Where do the units go?		Equivalent Units			
				% Work Done?	Dir. Mat.	% Work Done?	Conv. Costs
Beg. inv............	2,600	Compl./transf.......	57,600	100%	57,600	100%	57,600
Started	58,500	End. inv...........	3,500	100%	3,500	40%	1,400
Total	61,100	Total	61,100		61,100		59,000

Product Cost Report
General Mills Big G Division
January Production

Step 3: Determine Per-Unit Costs

Where do the costs come from?	Total		Dir. Mat.	Conv. Costs
Beginning inventory	$ 280,800		$ 166,400	$ 114,400
Current..........................	32,000,000		19,250,000	12,750,000
Total costs to account for	$32,280,800		$19,416,400	$12,864,400
÷ Total equivalent units			61,100	59,000
Average cost/equivalent unit			$317.7807	$218.0407

Where do the costs go?

Step 4: Calculate the Cost of Goods Manufactured

Complete/transferred:			
Materials........................	$18,304,168		[57,600 × $317.7807]
Conversion costs	12,559,143*		[57,600 × $218.0407]
Cost of goods manuactured.........		$30,863,311	

Step 5: Calculate the Cost of the Ending Inventory

Ending inventory:			
Materials........................	$ 1,112,232		[3,500 × $317.7807]
Conversion costs	305,257		[1,400 × $218.0407]
Cost of ending inventory............		1,417,489	
Total costs allocated		$32,280,800	

*Difference due to rounding

Exhibit 17-20	Final Allocation of Costs to Ending Inventory and Cost of Goods Manufactured (and Transferred Out)

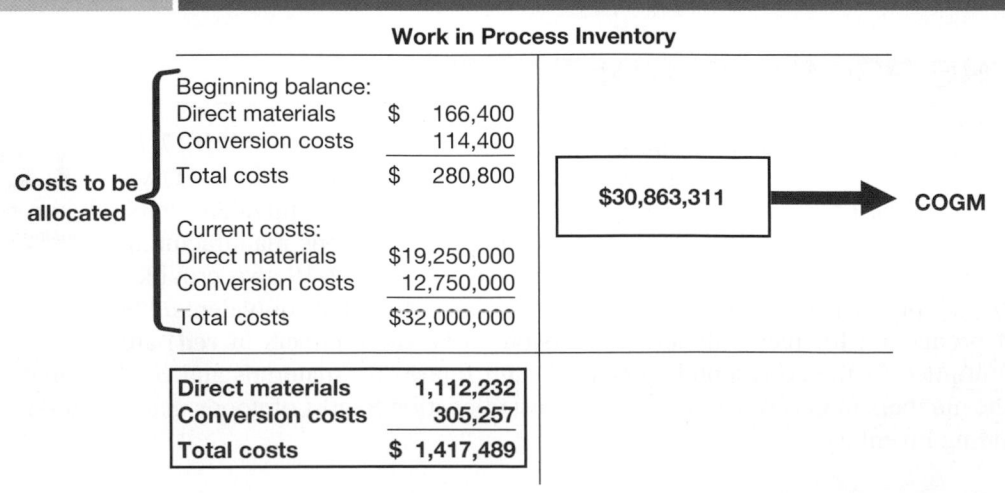

As a final check to see that we have performed all of the calculations correctly, the sum of the Cost of Goods Manufactured ($30,863,311) and the ending Working Process Inventory balance (1,417,489) should equal the total costs that we determined at the outset needed to be allocated (Beginning balance $280,800 + Current costs 32,000,000 = $32,280,800). Specifically, the T-account in **Exhibit 17-20** summarizes the process costing allocation of costs between costs transferred out and costs remaining in ending inventory.

Companies with Multiple Production Processes

At the outset of this chapter, we described situations in which a company produces its products through a long series of production processes. So far, we have illustrated process costing in a single department. When a company's production process involves a series of different departments, costs are accumulated by production process. The costs transferred out of one department are transferred into the next department. Hence, as units of product move from one department or process to the next, they carry the costs from all prior processes with them. From a practical perspective, the only thing that changes in the product costing process is that an extra column is added for transferred-in costs. For example, the $30,863,311 transferred out of the production process described in the previous section would become the transferred-in costs for the next department.

JOURNAL ENTRIES ILLUSTRATED

After computing these amounts, Big G would record the following journal entries related to January production. *These entries assume that materials are added at the beginning of the process, and that labor and overhead are added evenly over the month of January.*

LO5 **Illustrate** the journal entries used with process costing.

Material

During January, assume that Big G purchased $20,000,000 of grain on account. The following is a summary journal entry for the January purchases:

1	Materials inventory	20,000,000	
	Accounts payable		20,000,000
	To record January material purchases.		

The direct material requisitioned during January for the processing department is shown in the following entry:

2	Work in process	19,250,000	
	Materials inventory		19,250,000
	To record direct material used during January.		

Labor

During January, Big G accrued $3,210,000 of direct labor expense. The journal entry to record this payroll would be as follows:

3	Work in process	3,210,000	
	Wages payable		3,210,000
	To record the payroll for January.		

Manufacturing Overhead

Assume that Big G has recorded its manufacturing overhead costs (such as maintenance, depreciation, and utilities) in Manufacturing Overhead as incurred. Also assume that Big G applies manufacturing overhead costs to Work in Process using predetermined overhead rates. The following entry records the amount of applied manufacturing overhead for the processing department:

4	Work in process	9,540,000	
	Manufacturing overhead		9,540,000
	To apply manufacturing overhead to work in process		
	inventory.		

As a result of the journal entries recorded during the month, the Work in Process account contains the following balance as of the end of the month:

	Work in Process
Beginning balance	$ 280,800
Direct material	19,250,000
Direct labor.	3,210,000
Factory overhead	9,540,000
Balance before month-end adjustments	$32,280,800

At the end of the month, an additional journal entry is needed to transfer product costs from the processing department to Finished Goods (the amount of Cost of Goods Manufactured). The following entry records the Cost of Goods Manufactured:

5	Finished goods	30,863,311	
	Work in process		30,863,311
	To transfer the cost of completed product from work in		
	process inventory.		

YOUR TURN! 17.2

The solution is on
page 843.

Assume the following cost information related to May production, and only one manufacturing department. What journal entries would be made to capture May production?

Direct material	$24,000
Direct labor.	32,400
Manufacturing overhead applied	48,600

SERVICE INDUSTRY IN FOCUS

**SERVICE AND
MERCHANDISING**

Environmental Business Consultants, LLC (EBC) has a contract with Terrabean Coffee, a large retail coffee company with 5,000 shops across North America, to manage the company's waste disposal and recycling services. Under the contract with Terrabean, EBC is responsible for negotiating, monitoring, and servicing contracts with dozens of garbage and recycling collection companies in major cities throughout the United States and Canada. These contracts generally require the garbage and recycling collection companies to collect both garbage and recyclables on a daily basis from between 10 and 30 shops, 365 days per year. When collection is missed, invoices are questioned, service is changed, new shops are opened, or other issues arise, the shop managers call EBC for assistance.

EBC maintains a call center to receive these calls and coordinate the appropriate response. The call center employees record each call and refer the issue to the EBC manager responsible for that location for follow-up. Locations are assigned to one of five geographic regions: Northeast (includes major metropolitan areas in eastern Canada), Southeast, Midwest, Southwest, and Northwest (includes major metropolitan areas in western Canada). EBC uses process costing with a weighted average cost flow assumption to assign the call center cost to each geographic region on a per-call unit cost. Overhead is applied per labor hour worked. Thus, the percentage complete can be applied to both labor and overhead. Because some questions/complaints take more than a day or two to resolve, there are typically some "unfinished" calls at the end of each period.

For the fiscal year ended September 30, 2016, the EBC call center reported the following information regarding calls handled:

Work in process, October 1, 2015:	$350
Work done during fiscal year 2016:	
Direct labor incurred.	$262,500
Overhead applied.	245,000
Total costs incurred during fiscal year 2016	$507,500
Calls in process at October 1, 2015 (30% complete)	50 calls
Calls started and finished during fiscal year 2016	35,200 calls
Calls in process at September 30, 2016 (40% complete)	40 calls

Required

1. Determine the equivalent number of calls completed during fiscal year 2016.
2. Determine the per-unit cost of each call.
3. Determine the cost of the calls completed.
4. Determine the cost of ending work in process inventory at September 30, 2016.

Solution: **Exhibit 17-21** shows the solution.

Exhibit 17-21	Service Industry In Focus Solution

Flow of the Units and Equivalent Units Calculation

Where do the units come from?		Where do the units go?		% Work Done?	Conv. Costs
Calls in process (10/1/2015) .	50	Calls complete	35,210	100%	**35,210**
Calls started and finished. . .	35,200	Calls in process (9/30/2016) ..	40	40%	**16**
Total	35,250	Total	35,250		35,226

Product Cost Report
Environmental Business Consultants, LLC
Fiscal 2016 Service Calls

Where do the costs come from?		Conv. Costs
Beginning WIP	$ 350	$ 350
Current period costs	507,500	507,500
Total costs to account for ..	$507,850	$507,850
÷ Total equivalent units		35,226
Average cost/equivalent unit (rounded)		**$14.4169**

Where do the costs go?		
Cost of calls completed ..	507,619*	[35,210 × $14.4169]
Cost of ending inventory. .	231	[16 × $14.4169]
Total costs allocated	$507,850	

*Difference due to rounding.

COMPREHENSIVE PROBLEM (INCLUDING TRANSFERRED-IN COSTS)

Kensington Corp. makes gourmet brownies. Brownies are produced in a three-stage process. In the Baking Department, the raw materials for the brownies are mixed, poured into large trays, and baked. In the Finishing Department, frosting is applied to the brownies and they are sliced while still in the baking trays. Finally, in the Packing Department, the brownies are divided into smaller packages containing 12 brownies per package and prepared for shipping. Kensington has tracked the following information for the Baking and Finishing Departments during October 2016:

	Baking	Finishing
Trays in beginning inventory	200	100
Trays started / transferred in	5,100	?
Trays in ending inventory	100	300
Total cost of brownies transferred out in October	$18,200	?

The beginning inventory in the Finishing Department included $350 of transferred-in costs from the Baking Department incurred during September, $25 of materials, and $80 of conversion costs. During October, the Finishing Department incurred $1,075 for materials and $4,170 for conversion costs. The Finishing Department's beginning inventory was estimated to be 60% complete, and the ending inventory was estimated to be 20% complete. The frosting (the only new material added in the Finishing Department) is added when the brownies are 25% through the production process.

One purpose of this comprehensive example is to illustrate a more realistic example of how costs flow through a process with multiple departments or processes. Therefore, because this problem focuses on the second of three departments (the Finishing Department), we must consider transferred-in costs in addition to the direct material costs and conversion costs incurred in the current department. Transferred-in costs merely represent the costs transferred from one department to the next and are therefore considered 100% complete as they are carried forward to the next department. In this problem, the costs incurred in the Baking Department stay with the trays of baked brownies as they come into the Finishing Department. The 100 trays in the beginning inventory (transferred in during September) carried $350 of costs from the Baking department, whereas the units transferred in during October carried $18,200 of costs from the Baking Department.

Required

1. Assuming Kensington uses the weighted average cost flow assumption, prepare the October product cost report for the Finishing Department. Be sure to include your equivalent units calculations.

2. Give the journal entry to transfer completed brownies from the Finishing Department to the Packing Department.

Solution To Comprehensive Problem

Before preparing the solution for the Finishing Department, it is important to first determine the number of trays transferred out of the Baking Department. The 5,200 trays transferred OUT of the Baking Department are the trays transferred IN to the Finishing Department. Obviously, Kensington would need to prepare a product cost report to determine the cost of the brownie trays transferred out. Because this problem focuses on the second department in the production process, the costs incurred to bake these 5,200 trays is simply given ($18,200). This number is used in the Finishing Department as the cost of trays transferred in.

1. We first illustrate the percentage complete and T-accounts (in units and dollars) that are helpful in preparing the product cost report. Note that each arrow in the timeline represents the conversion costs incurred in the Finishing Department during October for each inventory group: (1) the beginning inventory balance (BB), (2) the trays transferred in and finished during the period (Transferred-in/Finished), and (3) the trays transferred in and remaining in ending inventory (EB).

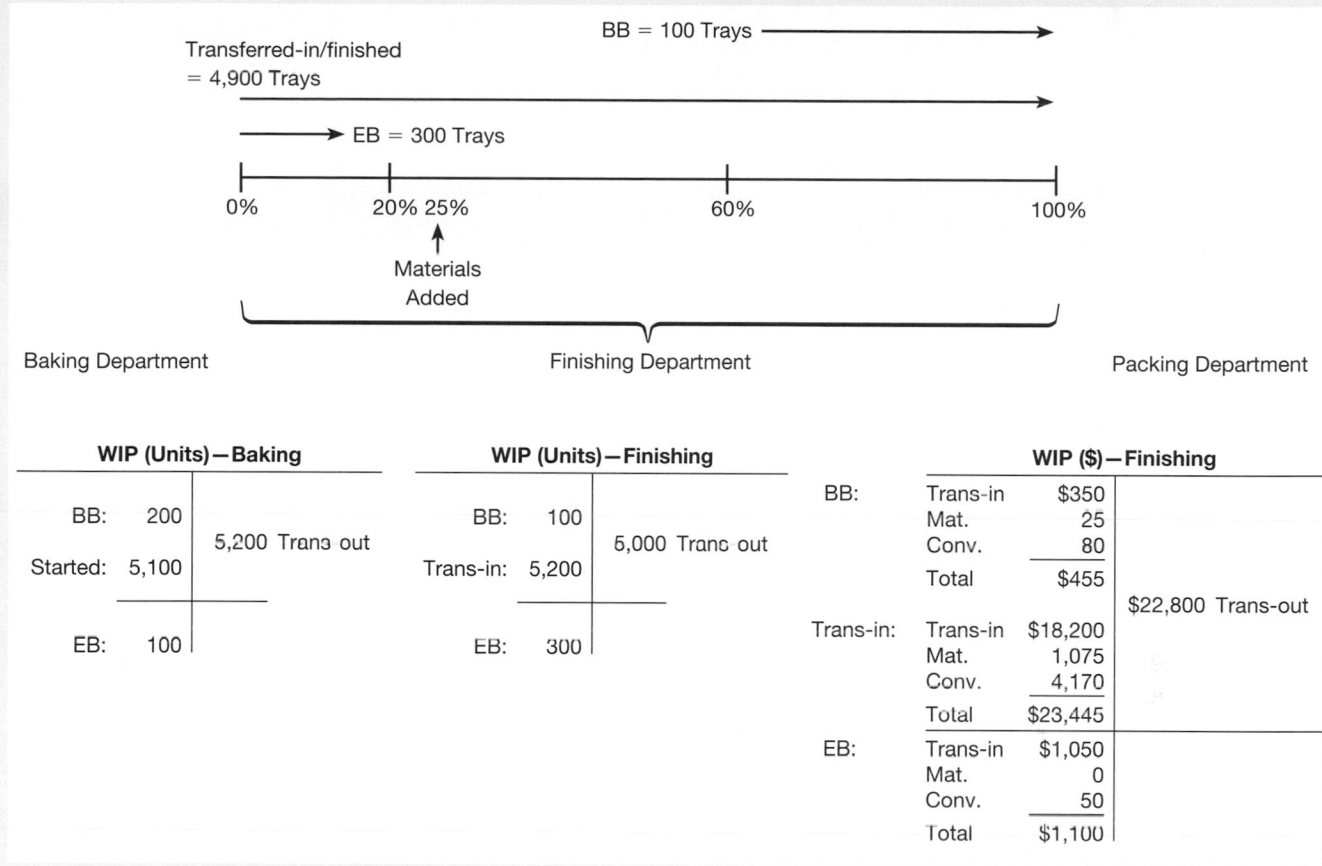

We then calculate equivalent units and prepare the product cost report.

		Finishing Department						
				%		% Work		% Work	
Where do the units come from?		**Where do the units go?**	**Trans-in**	**Trans-in**	**% Work Done?**	**Dir. Mat.**	**% Work Done?**	**Conv. Costs**
Beg. inv.	100	Compl./transf.... 5,000	100%	5,000	100%	5,000	100%	5,000
Started	5,200	End. inv........ 300	100%	300	0%	0	20%	60
Total	5,300	Total 5,300		5,300		5,000		5,060

Product Cost Report				
Where do the costs come from?		**Trans-in**	**Dir. Mat.**	**Conv. Costs**
Beg. inv.	$ 455	$ 350	$ 25	$ 80
Current	23,445	18,200	1,075	4,170
Total costs to account for	$23,900	$18,550	$ 1,100	$ 4,250
÷ Total equivalent units		5,300	5,000	5,060
Average cost/equiv. unit		$3.5000	$0.2200	$0.8399

Where do the costs go?				
Compl./transf.:				
Trans-in	$17,500	[5,000 × $3.500]		
Direct materials	1,100		[5,000 × $0.2200]	
Conversion costs	4,200*			[5,000 × $0.8399]
COGM	$22,800			
End. inv.:				
Trans-in	1,050	[300 × $3.500]		
Direct materials	—			
Conversion costs	50*			[60 × $0.8399]
Cost of ending inv.	1,100			
Total costs allocated	$23,900			

* Rounded to the nearest dollar.

2.

WIP—Packing Department		22,800	
WIP—Finishing Department			22,800

APPENDIX 17A: Process Costing Using FIFO Method

This appendix illustrates the use of process costing and the first-in, first-out method, or FIFO method, to assign product costs to the goods transferred out and to the ending work in process inventories. In this appendix, we will continue the Big G example introduced in the chapter.

PROCESS COSTING STEPS

LO6 Explain techniques for determining unit costs when the FIFO method for process costing is used.

In this chapter, we discussed process costing and the use of the weighted average cost allocation method to transfer product costs from one work in process inventory account to another, from the final work in process inventory account to the finished goods inventory account, and from the finished goods inventory account to the cost of goods sold account. In this appendix, we will accomplish the same task, but we will use the FIFO cost allocation method to assign and transfer product costs. The following steps are the same as those used for the weighted average method. However, the execution of these steps is slightly different. Recall, process costing requires five steps or calculations:

1. Visualize or chart the physical flow of the units through the system.
2. Determine the equivalent whole units of work completed (or equivalent units of production) during the period. This calculation is usually performed separately for materials and conversion costs (i.e., labor and overhead) because conversion costs are usually added uniformly throughout the process, whereas materials are often added at a particular point in the process.
3. Compute the per-unit cost of production for the period for materials and conversion costs by dividing the total costs incurred in each category by the equivalent units of production for that cost category.
4. Using the per-unit costs for material and conversion costs, compute the dollar value of the units completed and transferred (Cost of Goods Manufactured) to the next department.
5. Using the same per-unit costs, compute the dollar value of the unfinished units that remain in the department (these ending work in process units will usually be completed in the following period).

We discuss these steps in more detail with respect to the FIFO cost allocation method in the following sections. Recall that the Big G division of General Mills uses process costing to account for its cereal production and that it had the results for January as illustrated in **Exhibit 17-1A**.

Exhibit 17-1A	Big G Process Costing Example

Work in process, January 1:		
Direct materials	$	166,400
Direct labor		38,100
Manufacturing overhead		76,300
Total beginning work in process	$	280,800
Work done during January:		
Direct material (grain) added		$19,250,000
Direct labor incurred		3,210,000
Manufacturing overhead applied		9,540,000
Total costs incurred during January		$32,000,000
Units in process at January 1 (20% complete)		2,600 tons
Units started during January		58,500 tons
Units in process at January 31 (40% complete)		3,500 tons

Further, assume that all materials are added at the beginning of the process, whereas labor and manufacturing overhead costs are added evenly throughout the process. The T-account in **Exhibit 17-2A** illustrates the purpose of process costing, to allocate actual costs incurred between units completed and transferred out and partially completed units remaining in ending inventory:

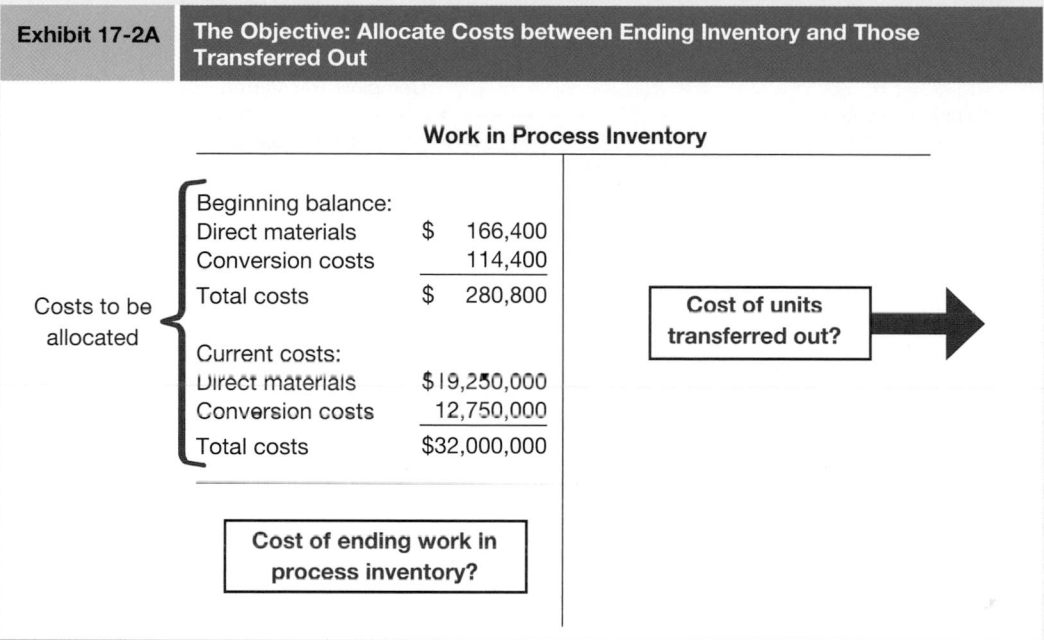

Exhibit 17-2A	The Objective: Allocate Costs between Ending Inventory and Those Transferred Out

We know the costs associated with the beginning work in process inventory on January 1 ($280,800). We also know the costs incurred during the month of January for direct materials ($19,250,000), direct labor ($3,210,000), and manufacturing overhead ($9,540,000). For simplicity, because we assume both direct labor and manufacturing overhead costs are applied uniformly during the production process, we combine them and simply refer to them as "conversion costs." Because we started the period with partially completed inventory, during the period we will finish the previously started units and also begin work on new units. We also end the period with partially completed units. We don't know how much of these costs should be applied to units transferred out at the end of the period and how much should remain with the partially complete ending inventory. Process costing helps us calculate an average cost per unit to apply to (1) the units completed and transferred out at the end of the period and (2) the units remaining in ending inventory.

Step 1: Visualize the Physical Flow of the Units

The starting point in process costing is to visualize how the units flow through the production process, as illustrated in **Exhibit 17-3A**. In the General Mills Big G example, the quantity produced is measured in tons of cereal processed during the month of January. Sometimes it is useful to visualize how the units correspond to the dollars in the T-account in **Exhibit 17-2A**.

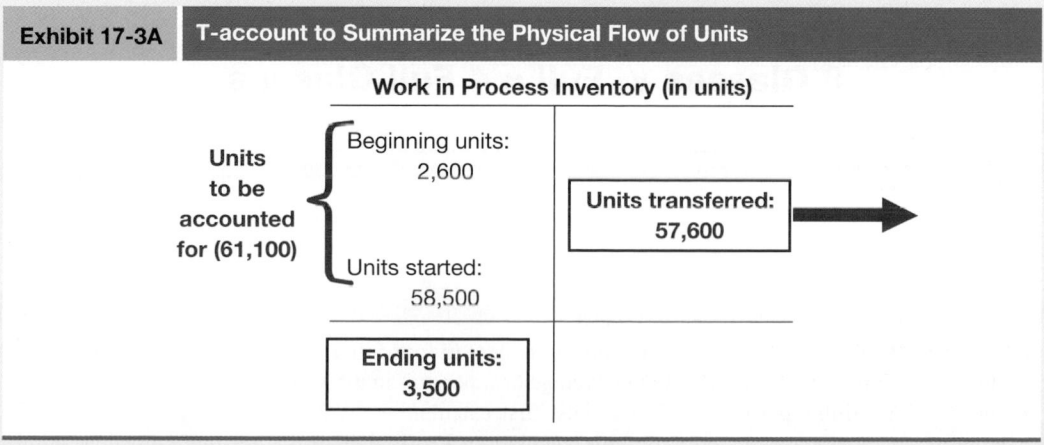

Exhibit 17-3A	T-account to Summarize the Physical Flow of Units

Another way to visualize the flow of the cereal produced during January is by asking where the units come from and where they end up, as shown in **Exhibit 17-4A**.

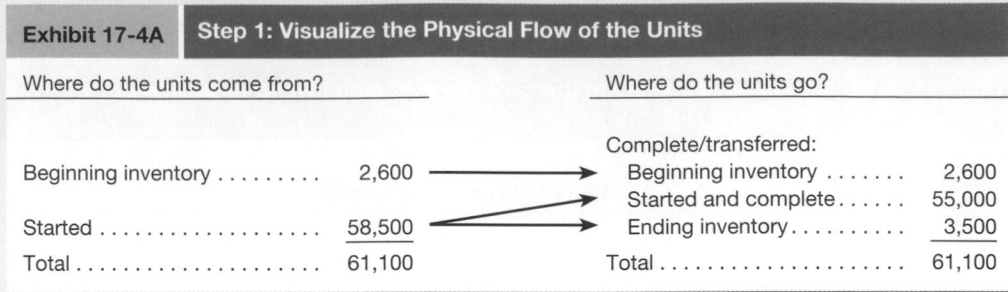

Exhibit 17-4A	Step 1: Visualize the Physical Flow of the Units		
Where do the units come from?		**Where do the units go?**	
		Complete/transferred:	
Beginning inventory	2,600	Beginning inventory	2,600
		Started and complete	55,000
Started	58,500	Ending inventory	3,500
Total	61,100	Total	61,100

We assume that all 2,600 units in beginning inventory are completed first. Then, of the 58,500 units started this month, 55,000 are complete by the end of the month, and 3,500 remain partially complete. Unlike the weighted average method, which mixes inventory layers (i.e., not distinguishing between work done in each period), the FIFO method keeps the beginning inventory separate from units started during the period and accounts for each inventory layer separately. Whereas the weighted average method does not distinguish between work done in different periods, the FIFO method does not mix costs incurred in different periods.

Step 2: Calculate the Equivalent Units

Introduction to Equivalent Units

Hint: Instead of tracking specific costs incurred to produce each unit of product as in job order costing, process costing accumulates costs by department and then calculates an average cost per unit to be assigned to all units of product produced during that period.

The average cost per unit is calculated by dividing total costs by the total number of units produced. The work in process accounts previously described in **Exhibits 17-5** and **17-6** illustrate how total costs are accumulated and tracked through the system. Accountants are good at keeping track of costs. However, cost accountants face a major problem in allocating costs in continuous-flow manufacturing processes. At any given point in time, units of product are at various stages of completion. Hence, it is difficult to determine the number of units to use in the average cost per unit calculation:

$$\text{Average cost per unit} = \frac{\text{Total costs incurred}}{\text{\# of equivalent units}} \quad \begin{matrix} \longleftarrow & \textbf{We know this.} \\ \longleftarrow & \textbf{We don't know this.} \end{matrix}$$

The notion of equivalent units of production is a key concept in process costing. When units of product are produced in a continuous process, engineers and manufacturing supervisors must estimate the average percentage completion of units in a given department at the end of each period. Accountants use this information to estimate the number of equivalent *complete* units of product. For example, the following illustration shows eight glasses of water that are *half* full. How many *full* glasses of water is this equivalent to?

8 Glasses ½ Full = 4 Full Glasses

The eight half-full glasses are approximately equivalent to four full glasses. This example illustrates what accountants do each period in determining the average cost per unit in a given department.

To properly determine per-unit costs, we must first calculate equivalent units of production to be used in the denominator of the average cost per unit calculation. **Equivalent units** are the equivalent number of *whole units* completed during the period. In the previous illustration, the eight partially full glasses of water are equivalent to four full glasses (similar to four equivalent complete units of production). The calculation of equivalent units of production requires accountants to (1) track the *actual quantity* of products at each stage of production and (2) estimate the *average amount of work completed* on each unit of product in terms of conversion costs and direct material costs.

Engineers or production experts estimate the percentage of work completed in terms of conversion costs, on average. As illustrated in **Exhibit 17-5A**, because the 2,600 tons of cereal on hand on January 1 is 20% complete (based on work completed during December), Big G only has to complete the remaining 80% of the processing during the month of January. During January, Big G begins work on 55,000 tons of cereal that is both started and completed during the month of January. Finally, Big G begins work on an additional 3,500 tons of cereal that is not completed by the end of the month. Engineers determine that only 40% of the processing is complete on this batch of cereal by January 31. We assume that all direct material is added at the beginning of the process; therefore, the average amount of work completed on each unit of product related to direct materials is 100%.

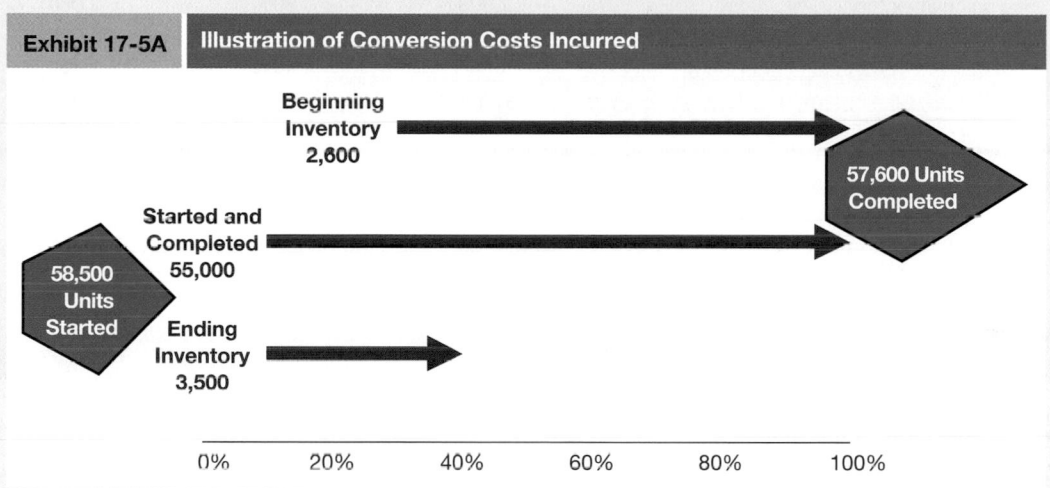

| Exhibit 17-5A | Illustration of Conversion Costs Incurred |

A key difference between the weighted average method and the FIFO method is that the weighted average mixes costs across inventory layers, whereas the FIFO method keeps costs incurred across inventory layers (i.e., incurred in different periods) separate. Whereas the weighted average method averages all costs incurred in the production of a batch of units, regardless of when those costs were incurred, the FIFO method keeps costs incurred during December separate from those incurred during January. Thus, the weighted average method asks "How much work is complete (regardless of when the work was done)?" whereas the FIFO method asks "What costs were incurred during THIS PERIOD?" A critical feature of the FIFO method is that because materials are added at the *beginning* of the process in this example, the beginning inventory units moved beyond the point of adding materials during the last period. Thus, NO materials are added THIS PERIOD. Because the beginning inventory was started last month, the materials for the beginning inventory were actually added during December. Thus, no new materials are added to these 2,600 units during January.

Hint: An item that is 20% complete at the beginning of the period means 80% of the work is done this period, not 20%.

Equivalent Unit Calculation for Direct Materials—FIFO

The materials for the units started and completed during the month and for the ending inventory are added during this period. **Exhibit 17-6A** illustrates the calculation of equivalent units based on the FIFO cost flow assumption. The units in each "layer" of inventory are multiplied by the percentage of materials added during the CURRENT period (January) to calculate the equivalent units of material added during THIS PERIOD, as shown in **Exhibit 17-6A**.

Exhibit 17-6A	Step 2: Calculate the Equivalent Units—Direct Materials					
		Physical Units (tons)		Proportion Completed		Equivalent Units (tons)
Beginning inventory........................		2,600	×	0%	=	0
Started and finished during January...........		55,000	×	100%	=	**55,000**
Ending inventory............................		3,500	×	100%	=	**3,500**
Total.....................................		61,100				58,500

Equivalent Unit Calculation for Conversion Costs—FIFO

When considering conversion costs (direct labor and manufacturing overhead), it is often useful to visualize the amount of work done during the period on each unique set of inventory passing through the production process, as previously illustrated in **Exhibit 17-5A**, which summarizes the work performed in the Big G division during the month of January. Because materials are added at the beginning of the period, the arrows only represent the amount of conversion costs applied to the process during the *current* period. We can then calculate the number of equivalent units with respect to conversion costs incurred during January, as illustrated in **Exhibit 17-7A**.

Exhibit 17-7A	**Step 2: Calculate the Equivalent Units—Conversion Costs**					
		Physical Units (tons)		Proportion Completed This Month		Equivalent Units (tons)
Beginning inventory		2,600	×	80%	=	2,080
Started and finished during January		55,000	×	100%	=	55,000
Ending inventory.		3,500	×	40%	=	1,400
Total		61,100				58,480

Again, we calculate equivalent units of production by multiplying the number of units in each "layer" of inventory by the percentage of conversion costs added during the current period.

We can then summarize the flow of the units worked on during the period and how the amount of work completed during the period translates them into equivalent units, as illustrated in **Exhibit 17-8A**.

Exhibit 17-8A	**Summary of Steps 1 and 2: Unit Flows and Equivalent Units Calculations**

Step 1: Visualize the Physical Flow of the Units

Step 2: Calculate the Equivalent Units

Where do the units come from?		Where do the units go?			Equivalent Units			
					% in Jan.?	Materials	% in Jan.?	Conv. Costs
		Complete/transferred:						
Beginning inventory . . .	2,600	Beginning inventory	2,600		0%	0	80%	2,080
		Started and completed	55,000		100%	55,000	100%	55,000
Started	58,500	Ending inventory.	3,500		100%	3,500	40%	1,400
Total	61,100	Total	61,100			58,500		58,480

TAKEAWAY 17.3

An equivalent unit is the amount of work necessary to produce one complete physical unit of product. For example, doing 80% of the work on 200 units is equivalent to doing 100% of the work on 160 units.

YOUR TURN! 17.3

The solution is on page 843.

MBC

Assume all materials are added at the beginning of the production process, and conversion costs are added uniformly throughout the process. Beginning work in process is comprised of 100 units, which are 35% complete with respect to conversion costs. Also assume that 700 units are started and completed during the period, and ending work in process includes 90 units that are 75% complete with respect to conversion costs. Compute equivalent units of production for direct materials and conversion costs under the FIFO cost flow assumption. (*Hint:* For fractional units, round up.)

Step 3: Determine the Per-Unit Costs

The product cost report summarizes where the costs come from and where they go (i.e., where they are allocated). The FIFO method differs from the weighted average method in an important way. The FIFO method does not mix "layers" of costs incurred during different periods. The $280,800 of costs in beginning inventory at the start of the month were incurred during December. When we calculate the average cost per unit, we calculate the average cost per unit of costs incurred during the CURRENT PERIOD. Hence, the costs incurred last month to help the inventory to reach the 20% point stay with those beginning inventory units and are NOT ALLOCATED across the units started during THIS PERIOD. In order to calculate an average cost per unit of materials and conversion costs incurred during THIS PERIOD, we first need to separate the current-period costs into their materials and conversion cost components. These numbers were illustrated in the T-account in **Exhibit 17-2A**. **Exhibit 17-9A** illustrates two important points. First, the beginning inventory costs incurred in the prior period are carried down and assigned to stay with the beginning inventory units. Second, only the costs incurred during the current period are allocated and used subsequently in the average cost per unit calculation.

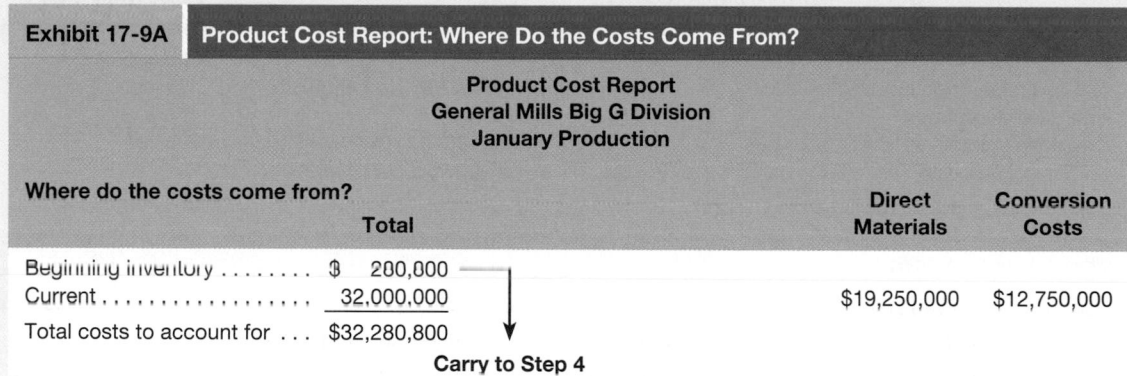

| **Exhibit 17-9A** | **Product Cost Report: Where Do the Costs Come From?** |

Product Cost Report
General Mills Big G Division
January Production

Where do the costs come from? Total		Direct Materials	Conversion Costs
Beginning inventory	$ 280,000		
Current	32,000,000	$19,250,000	$12,750,000
Total costs to account for . . .	$32,280,800		

Carry to Step 4

We then calculate the average cost per unit by dividing current-period costs in each category by total equivalent units in each category from Step 2. In other words, we divide current materials costs by total equivalent units of materials ($19,250,000 / 58,500 equivalent units) to get an average cost per unit of $329.06. Similarly, we divide current conversion costs by total equivalent units of conversion costs ($12,750,000 / 58,480 equivalent units) to get an average cost per unit of $218.02. **Exhibit 17-10A** summarizes this calculation.

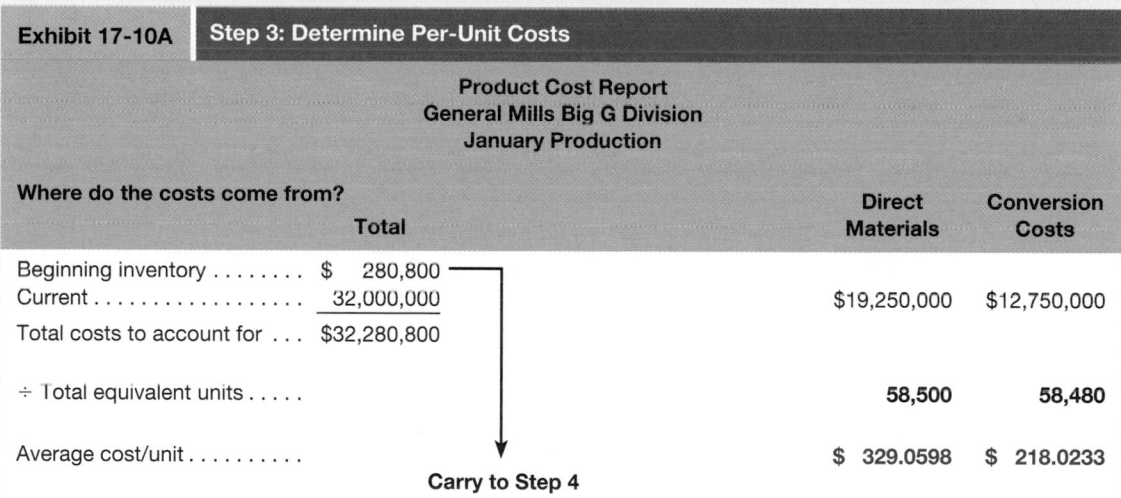

| **Exhibit 17-10A** | **Step 3: Determine Per-Unit Costs** |

Product Cost Report
General Mills Big G Division
January Production

Where do the costs come from? Total		Direct Materials	Conversion Costs
Beginning inventory	$ 280,800		
Current	32,000,000	$19,250,000	$12,750,000
Total costs to account for . . .	$32,280,800		
÷ Total equivalent units		58,500	58,480
Average cost/unit		$ 329.0598	$ 218.0233

Carry to Step 4

Note that under the FIFO cost flow assumption, the costs from the prior period associated with the beginning inventory stay with the beginning inventory and are not allocated to any other units. The costs incurred during the current period are allocated across all work incurred during the current period. Hence, under the FIFO cost flow assumption, the accountant keeps the "layers" of inventory separate. In the Big G example, note that the per-unit costs of materials and conversions costs only include costs incurred during January.

Step 4: Calculate the Cost of Goods Manufactured

At the end of each month and for each department, we calculate the cost of goods manufactured and transferred out (illustrated in **Exhibit 17-11A**). Under the FIFO cost flow assumption, the Big G division's product completed and transferred out during January consists of (1) the product in beginning work in process (2,080 equivalent tons) and (2) the product started and completed during the period (55,000 equivalent tons). Specifically, it is comprised of all costs to manufacture the beginning inventory (both this period and last period) and the cost of units started and finished this period. To determine the dollar cost value of the product transferred to finished goods (called Cost of Goods Manufactured), we multiply the equivalent units of materials and conversion costs transferred (shown in **red** in **Exhibit 17-8A**) by their respective per-unit costs computed in Step 2 (shown in **green** in **Exhibit 17-10A**) and add these costs to the cost value of the beginning work in process, as shown in **Exhibit 17-11A**.

Exhibit 17-11A	Step 4: Cost of Goods Manufactured Calculation	
		Carry from Step 3
Beginning inventory:		
Costs incurred in December..........................		$ 280,800
Conversion costs incurred in January	[**2,080** EU × **$218.0233**]	453,488
Started and finished:		
Materials...	[**55,000** EU × **$329.0598**]	18,098,291*
Conversion costs	[**55,000** EU × **$218.0233**]	11,991,279*
Total cost of goods manufactured		$30,823,858

* Difference due to rounding.

Step 5: Calculate the Ending Work in Process Inventory

Exhibit 17-12A illustrates the final step, which is to calculate the cost of goods remaining in ending work in process inventory. Assuming all materials are added at the beginning and conversion costs are added evenly through the process, we multiply the equivalent units of materials and conversion costs in ending inventory (denoted in **red** in **Exhibit 17-8A**) by their respective unit costs (shown in **green** in **Exhibit 17-10A**) computed in Step 2, as follows:

Exhibit 17-12A	Step 5: Calculate Cost of Ending Inventory	
Materials..	[**3,500** EU × **$329.0598**]	$ 1,151,709
Conversion costs	[**1,400** EU × **$218.0233**]	305,233
Total cost of goods remaining in ending inventory		$ 1,456,942

Cost of goods manufactured and transferred out (**Exhibit 17-11A**) ...	$30,823,858
Cost of ending inventory (**Exhibit 17-12A**)......................	1,456,942
Total cost to account for (**Exhibit 17-10A**).....................	$32,280,800

THE PRODUCT COST REPORT

LO7

Explain the procedures used to prepare the product cost report using the FIFO method in a process costing system.

The product cost report in **Exhibit 17-13A** summarizes the last three steps in the cost allocation process. The report calculates the cost of goods manufactured and transferred out of work in process and into finished goods. The report also calculates the cost of the remaining ending balance in work in process. Using the Big G example, **Exhibit 17-13A** also summarizes all of the steps in the total cost allocation process from (1) visualizing the physical flow of the units, to (2) calculating equivalent units, to (3) calculating per-unit costs, to (4) calculating cost of goods manufactured, to (5) calculating ending inventory. Finally, **Exhibit 17-13A** provides Big G's product cost report. Note that in this illustration, the equivalent units of production for materials and conversion costs (the numbers in **red**) are multiplied by the corresponding cost per unit figures for materials and conversion costs (the numbers in **green**) to calculate the cost allocation amounts used to assign costs to cost of goods manufactured and ending inventory.

Exhibit 17-13A	Summary of the Five Process Costing Steps

Flow of the Units and Equivalent Units Calculation

Step 1: Visualize the Physical Flow of the Units

Step 2: Calculate the Equivalent Units

Where do the units come from?		Where do the units go?		% in Jan.?	Materials	% in Jan.?	Conversion Costs
					Equivalent Units		
		Complete/transferred:					
Beginning inventory	2,600	Beginning inventory	2,600	0%	0	80%	**2,080**
		Started and completed. .	55,000	100%	**55,000**	100%	**55,000**
Started	58,500	Ending inventory.	3,500	100%	**3,500**	40%	**1,400**
Total	61,100	Total	61,100		58,500		58,480

Product Cost Report
General Mills Big G Division
January Production

Step 3: Determine Per-Unit Costs

Where do the costs come from?			Direct Materials	Conversion Costs
	Total			
Beginning inventory	$ 280,800			
Current	32,000,000		$19,250,000	$12,750,000
Total costs to account for	$32,280,800			
÷ Total equivalent units			58,500	58,480
Average cost/unit			**$329.0598**	**$218.0233**

Where do the costs go?

Step 4: Calculate the Cost of Goods Manufactured

Beginning inventory:				
Costs incurred in December.	$ 280,800			
Costs incurred in January.	453,488		[0 × $329.0598] +	[2,080 × $218.0233]
Started and finished	30,089,570*		[55,000 × $329.0598] +	[55,000 × $218.0233]
Cost of goods manufactured		$30,823,858		

Step 5: Calculate the Cost of the Ending Inventory

Ending inventory:				
Materials	$ 1,151,709		[3,500 × $329.0598]	
Conversion costs	305,233			[1,400 × $218.0233]
Cost of ending inventory.		1,456,942		
Total costs allocated		$32,280,800		

As a final check to see that we have performed all of the calculations correctly, the sum of Cost of Goods Manufactured ($30,823,858) and the ending work in process balance (1,456,942) should equal the total costs that we determined at the outset needed to be allocated (Beginning Balance $280,800 + Current Costs $32,000,000 = $32,280,800). Specifically, the T-account in **Exhibit 17-14A** summarizes the process costing allocation of costs between costs transferred out and costs remaining in ending inventory.

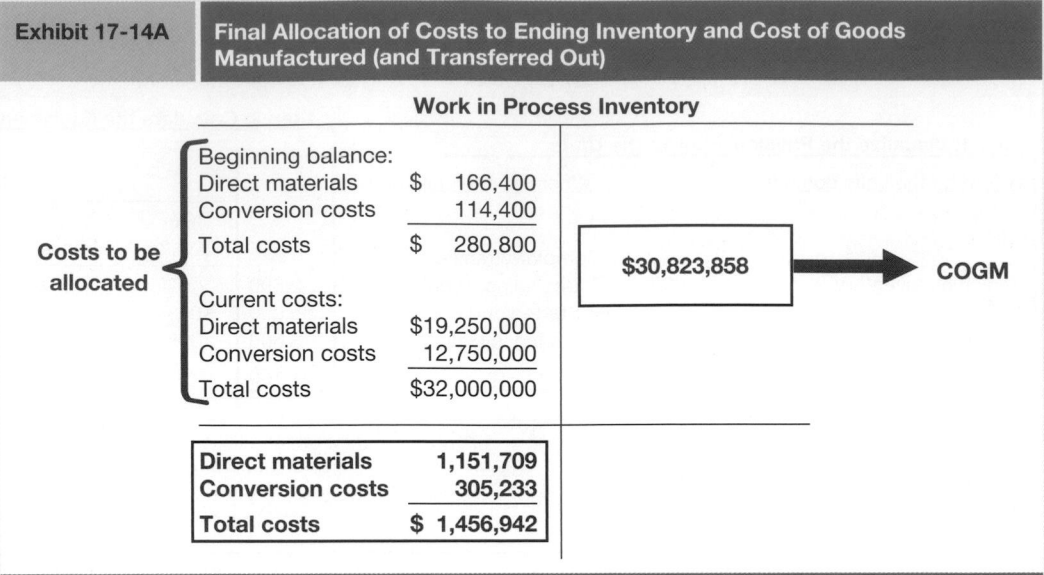

Exhibit 17-14A	Final Allocation of Costs to Ending Inventory and Cost of Goods Manufactured (and Transferred Out)

Work in Process Inventory

Costs to be allocated

Beginning balance:
Direct materials $ 166,400
Conversion costs   114,400
Total costs $ 280,800

Current costs:
Direct materials $19,250,000
Conversion costs   12,750,000
Total costs $32,000,000

$30,823,858 → COGM

Direct materials	1,151,709
Conversion costs	305,233
Total costs	$ 1,456,942

Companies with Multiple Production Processes

At the outset of this chapter, we described situations in which a company produces its products through a long series of production processes. So far, we have illustrated process costing in a single department. When a company's production process involves a series of different departments, costs are accumulated by production process. The costs transferred out of one department are transferred into the next department. Hence, as units of product move from one department or process to the next, they carry the costs from all prior processes with them. From a practical perspective, the only thing that changes in the product costing process is that an extra column is added for transferred-in costs. For example, the $30,823,858 transferred out of the production process described in the previous section would become the **transferred-in costs** for the next department.

JOURNAL ENTRIES ILLUSTRATED

LO8 **Illustrate** the journal entries used with FIFO process costing.

After computing these amounts, Big G would record the following journal entries related to January production. *These entries assume that materials are added at the beginning of the process, and that labor and overhead are added evenly over the month of January.*

Material

During January, assume that Big G purchased $20,000,000 of grain on account. The following is a summary journal entry for the January purchases:

1	Materials inventory	20,000,000	
	Accounts payable		20,000,000
	To record January material purchases.		

The direct material requisitioned during January for the processing department is shown in the following entry:

2	Work in process	19,250,000	
	Materials inventory		19,250,000
	To record direct material used during January.		

Labor

During January, Big G accrued $3,210,000 of direct labor expense. The journal entry to record this payroll would be as follows:

3	Work in process	3,210,000	
	Wages payable		3,210,000
	To record the payroll for January.		

Manufacturing Overhead

Assume that Big G has recorded its manufacturing overhead costs (such as maintenance, depreciation, and utilities) in Manufacturing Overhead as incurred. Also assume that Big G applies manufacturing overhead costs to Work in Process using predetermined overhead rates. The following entry records the amount of applied manufacturing overhead for the processing department:

4	Work in process	9,540,000	
	Manufacturing overhead		9,540,000
	To apply manufacturing overhead to work in process inventory.		

As a result of the journal entries recorded during the month, the Work in Process account contains the following balance as of the end of the month:

	Work in Process
Beginning balance	$ 280,800
Direct material	19,250,000
Direct labor.	3,210,000
Factory overhead	9,540,000
Balance before month-end adjustments	$32,280,800

At the end of the month, an additional journal entry is needed to transfer product costs from the processing department to Finished Goods (the amount of Cost of Goods Manufactured). The following entry records the Cost of Goods Manufactured:

5	Finished goods	30,823,858	
	Work in process		30,823,858
	To transfer the cost of completed product from work in process inventory.		

Assume the following cost information for May production and only one manufacturing department. What journal entries would be made to capture May production?

Direct material	$24,000
Direct labor.	32,400
Manufacturing overhead applied	48,600

YOUR TURN! 17.4

The solution is on page 843.

SUMMARY OF LEARNING OBJECTIVES

Compare and contrast job order costing and process costing. (p. 798)   **LO1**

- Job order costing is used when production consists of a variety of different products or unique customer orders.
- Process costing is used when production consists of a large volume of the same (homogeneous) product produced in a continual flow.

LO2   **Describe the basic concepts of process costing. (p. 800)**

- There is a separate work in process account for each department under a process costing system, whereas there is only one work in process control account in a job order costing system.
- In a process costing environment, products flow through multiple departments that are arranged in either a sequential pattern or a parallel pattern.

LO3   **Explain techniques for determining unit costs when process costing is used. (p. 802)**

- Visualize or chart the physical flow of the units through the system.
- Determine the equivalent whole units of work completed (or equivalent units of production) during the period. This calculation is usually performed separately for materials and conversion costs (i.e., labor and overhead) because conversion costs are usually added uniformly throughout the process, whereas materials are often added at a particular point in the process.
- Compute the per-unit cost of production for the period for materials and conversion costs by dividing the total costs incurred in each category by the equivalent units of production for that cost category.
- Using the per-unit costs for material and conversion costs, compute the dollar value of the units completed and transferred (cost of goods manufactured) to the next department.
- Using the same per-unit costs, compute the dollar value of the unfinished units that remain in the department (these ending work in process units will usually be completed in the following period).

LO4   **Explain the procedures used to prepare the product cost report using the weighted average method in a process costing system. (p. 809)**

- The product cost report and its supporting calculations include all of the five steps in the process costing procedure.
- The weighted average method mixes inventory layers and asks the question "how much work has been completed?" in calculating equivalent units of production.

LO5   **Illustrate the journal entries used with process costing. (p. 811)**

- At each stage of the manufacturing process, costs are added to the work in process account of the department where the work is completed. The journal entries are identical to those illustrated under a job order costing system.
- Direct materials are added to the materials inventory account when they are purchased.
- Materials used in the manufacturing process are transferred from the materials inventory account with a credit and debited to the appropriate work in process account.
- Labor and overhead are recorded as debits to the appropriate work in process account.

LO6   **Appendix 17A: Explain techniques for determining unit costs when the FIFO method for process costing is used. (p. 816)**

- The five process costing steps are the same under the FIFO method as under the weighted average method.
- In assigning manufacturing costs, one must consider three batches (or layers) of product: units from beginning work in process, units started and finished during this period, and units remaining in the ending work in process. Instead of mixing the layers (as in the weighted average method), the FIFO method keeps these three layers of inventory separate.
- The key difference between the weighted average and FIFO methods is that under the FIFO method, costs per equivalent unit are calculated by dividing current costs by current equivalent units; prior period costs and equivalent units are excluded from these calculations but are included in the total costs to be accounted for.

LO7   **Appendix 17A: Explain the procedures used to prepare the product cost report using the FIFO method in a process costing system. (p. 822)**

- When work in process inventories exist at the beginning and the end of the accounting period, the measurement of work accomplished requires that partially finished units be converted to equivalent units for accounting purposes.
- When materials are added at a different rate than conversion work is accomplished, equivalent units must be computed separately for material and conversion.
- The product cost report and its supporting calculations include all of the five steps in the process costing procedure.

■ The FIFO method keeps inventory layers separate and asks the question "how much work was completed during THIS PERIOD?" in calculating equivalent units of production.

Appendix 17A: Illustrate the journal entries used with FIFO process costing. (p. 824) **LO8**

■ At each stage of the manufacturing process, costs are added to the work in process account of the department where the work is completed. The journal entries are identical to those illustrated under a job order costing system.

■ Direct materials are added to the materials inventory account when they are purchased.

■ Materials used in the manufacturing process are transferred from the materials inventory account with a credit and debited to the appropriate work in process account.

■ Labor and overhead are recorded as debits to the appropriate work in process account.

KEY TERMS

Conversion costs (p. 802)

Cost of goods remaining (p. 809)

Equivalent units (p. 802, 805, 818)

FIFO method (p. 806)

Parallel product processing (p. 801)

Process costing (p. 799)

Process costing system (p. 800)

Product cost report (p. 800)

Sequential product processing (p. 801)

Transferred-in costs (p. 824)

Weighted average method (p. 806)

Assignments with the ⬤ logo in the margin are available in ᵐʸBusinessCourse.
See the Preface of the book for details.

SELF-STUDY QUESTIONS

(Answers to Self-Study Questions are at the end of this chapter.)

1. **Which of the following costs will not be part of product cost when using a process costing system?** **LO2**
   a. Prior department cost
   b. Conversion cost
   c. Byproduct cost
   d. Material cost

2. **For which of the following will there be multiple accounts in the general ledger when using process costing?** **LO2**
   a. Finished goods
   b. Work in process
   c. Materials
   d. Wages payable

3. **Which of the following will not influence the calculation of equivalent units when the FIFO cost flow assumption is used?** **LO6**
   a. Units processed in prior departments.
   b. Ending inventory units
   c. Beginning inventory units
   d. Units sold

QUESTIONS

1. What are the important differences between job order and process costing systems? **LO1**

2. How are all manufacturing costs for a series of processing departments accumulated into finished goods inventory? **LO1, 2**

3. Why do unit cost computations in a manufacturing process require equivalent unit computations? **LO2, 3**

4. Why do we say that process cost accounting is basically an averaging computation? **LO3**

5. What is meant by the term *equivalent unit*? **LO3**

6. What are conversion costs? **LO3**

7. Why must we sometimes compute equivalent units separately for materials and for conversion costs? **LO3**

8. Describe the three "layers" of inventory that are typically involved in a period's production under the FIFO accounting method. In what special situation are there only two layers? **LO6, 7, 8**

9. Why is it true that in each department's work in process inventory account all beginning inventory and current-period costs must end up either being transferred out or in ending work in process inventory? **LO3**

EXERCISES—SET A

LO3 **E17-1A. Equivalent Units Calculations—Weighted Average Method** Ferris Corporation makes a powdered rug shampoo in two sequential departments, Compounding and Drying. Materials are added at the beginning of the process in the Compounding Department. Conversion costs are added evenly throughout each process. Ferris uses the weighted average method of process costing. In the Compounding Department, beginning work in process was 4,000 pounds (70% processed), 37,000 pounds were started in process, 36,000 pounds transferred out, and ending work in process was 60% processed.

Calculate equivalent units for March 2016 for the Compounding Department.

LO3 **E17-2A. Equivalent Units Calculations—Weighted Average Method** The following are selected operating data for Jackson Company's Blending Department for April 2016. Tinting and packaging operations are carried out subsequently in other departments.

Beginning inventory	4,000 units, 60% complete
Started and completed.	70,000 units
Ending inventory.	6,000 units, 30% complete

Calculate the equivalent units completed using the weighted average method, assuming that the material is added at the beginning of the process and conversion costs are incurred evenly throughout.

LO3, 4 **E17-3A. Equivalent Units and Product Cost Report—Weighted Average Method** In its first month's operations (January 2016), Allred Company's Department 1 incurred charges of $120,000 for direct materials (10,000 units), $33,000 for direct labor, and $58,000 for manufacturing overhead. At month-end, 8,800 units had been finished and transferred out. The remaining units were finished with respect to material but only 25% complete with respect to conversion costs.

Assuming Allred uses the weighted average method and that materials are added at the beginning of the process and conversion costs occur evenly, compute the following:

a. The equivalent units of materials and conversion costs.
b. The cost per equivalent unit of materials and conversion costs.
c. The total cost assigned to the units transferred out.
d. The total cost assigned to the ending inventory.
e. Prove that your solutions to requirements (c) and (d) sum to the total costs to be accounted for.

LO3, 4 **E17-4A. Equivalent Units and Product Cost Report—Weighted Average Method** The following data (and annotations) are for the work in process account of the first of Crocker Company's four departments used in manufacturing its only product for October of 2016.

Work in Process—Department 1	
Beginning balance (2,000 units, 70% complete)	
Direct material.	$ 15,500
Conversion costs	9,600
Transferred to department 2: (20,000 units).	(a)
Direct material (21,000 units)	157,500
Direct labor.	145,200
Manufacturing overhead	48,300
Ending balance [____(b)____ units, 25% complete]	(c)

Assuming that Crocker uses the weighted average method and that materials are added at the beginning of the process and conversion costs are incurred evenly throughout, solve for the three missing numbers.

LO3, 4 **E17-5A. Equivalent Units and Product Cost Report—Weighted Average Method** The following data (and annotations) are for Sutter Company's processing department work in process account for the month of June 2016:

Beginning inventory (700 units, 40% complete)	
Direct naterial	$ 2,850
Conversion costs	7,930
Current period	
Direct material (5,000 units)	35,000
Direct labor	59,600
Manufacturing overhead applied	37,800

Sutter uses the weighted average method. Materials are added at the beginning of the process and conversion costs are incurred evenly throughout. Ending work in process is comprised of 900 units, 70% complete. Compute the following:

a.   Equivalent units for materials and conversion.
b.   Cost per equivalent unit for materials and conversion.
c.   Total cost assigned to the units transferred out.

E17-6A. Equivalent Units Calculations—FIFO Method Ferris Corporation makes a powdered rug shampoo in two sequential departments, Compounding and Drying. Materials are added at the beginning of the process in the Compounding Department. Conversion costs are added evenly throughout each process. Ferris uses the FIFO method of process costing. In the Compounding Department, beginning work in process was 4,000 pounds (70% processed), 37,000 pounds were started in process, 36,000 pounds transferred out, and ending work in process was 60% processed.   **LO6**

Calculate equivalent units for March 2016 for the Compounding Department.

E17-7A. Equivalent Units Calculations—FIFO Method The following selected operating data are for Jackson Company's Blending Department for the month of April 2016. Tinting and packaging operations are carried out subsequently in other departments.   **LO6**

Beginning inventory	4,000 units, 60% complete
Started and completed.	70,000 units
Ending inventory.	6,000 units, 30% complete

Calculate the equivalent units accomplished using the FIFO method, assuming that the material is added at the beginning of the process and conversion costs are incurred evenly throughout.

E17-8A. Equivalent Units and Product Cost Report—FIFO Method In its first month's operations (January 2016), Allred Company's Department 1 incurred charges of $120,000 for direct materials (10,000 units), $33,000 for direct labor, and $58,000 for manufacturing overhead. At month-end, 8,800 units had been finished and transferred out. The remaining units were finished with respect to material but only 25% complete with respect to conversion costs.   **LO6, 7**

Assuming Allred uses the FIFO method and that materials are added at the beginning of the process and conversion costs occur evenly, compute the following:

a.   The equivalent units for material and conversion.
b.   The cost per equivalent unit for material and conversion.
c.   The total cost assigned to the units transferred out.
d.   The total cost assigned to the ending inventory.
e.   Prove that your solutions to requirements (c) and (d) sum to the total costs to be accounted for.

E17-9A. Equivalent Units and Product Cost Report—FIFO Method The following data (and annotations) are for the work in process account of the first of Crocker Company's four departments used in manufacturing its only product October of 2016.   **LO6, 7**

Work in Process—Department 1	
Beginning balance (2,000 units, 70% complete)	$ 25,100
Transferred to department 2: (20,000 units).	(a)
Direct material (21,000 units)	157,500
Direct labor.	145,200
Manufacturing overhead	48,300
Ending balance [___(b)___ units, 25% complete]	(c)

Assuming that Crocker uses the FIFO method and that materials are added at the beginning of the process and conversion costs are incurred evenly throughout, solve for the three missing numbers.

LO6, 7   **E17-10A. Equivalent Units and Product Cost Assignment—FIFO Method** The following data (and annotations) are related to the June 2016 charges appearing in the work in process account for Sutter Company's first processing department:

Beginning inventory (700 units, 40% complete)	
Direct material.	$ 5,780
Conversion costs	5,000
Current period	
Direct materials (5,000 units)	50,000
Direct labor.	59,600
Manufacturing overhead applied	22,800

Sutter uses the FIFO method. Direct materials are added at the beginning of the process and conversion costs are incurred evenly throughout. Ending work in process totals 900 units, 70% complete. Compute the following:

a.   Equivalent units for direct materials and conversion costs.
b.   Cost per equivalent unit for direct materials and conversion costs.
c.   Total cost assigned to the units transferred out.

LO5   **E17-11A. Cost Flows Through Journal Entries** The Mixing Department performs a series of processes in which a fluid chemical is concentrated. Records indicate that the Mixing Department has been charged with $64,000 of direct labor costs. The manufacturing overhead rate is 150% of direct labor costs. Beginning work in process was $224,000, and ending work in process totaled $34,000. One-half of this period's completed products is sold on account at a price equal to 160% of its cost.

Prepare journal entries to record (1) various costs charged to the Mixing Department this period, (2) transfer of this period's completed product, and (3) sale of one-half of this period's production.

EXERCISES—SET B

LO3   **E17-1B. Equivalent Units Calculations—Weighted Average Method** Terrace Corporation makes an industrial cleaner in two sequential departments, Compounding and Drying. All material is added at the beginning of the process in the Compounding Department. Conversion costs are added evenly throughout each process. Terrace uses the weighted average method of process costing. In the Compounding Department, beginning work in process was 2,000 pounds (60% processed), 34,000 pounds were started, 32,000 pounds were transferred out, and ending work in process was 70% processed.

Calculate equivalent units for the Compounding Department for August 2016.

LO3   **E17-2B. Equivalent Units Calculations—Weighted Average Method** The following are selected operating data for Jackson Company's Blending Department for November 2016. Painting and packaging operations are carried out subsequently in other departments.

Beginning inventory	3,000 units, 70% complete
Started and completed.	60,000 units
Ending inventory.	5,000 units, 40% complete

Calculate the equivalent units finished for the month of November using the weighted average method, assuming that the material is added at the beginning of the process and conversion costs are incurred evenly throughout.

LO3, 4   **E17-3B. Equivalent Units and Product Cost Assignment—Weighted Average Method** In its first month of operations (May 2016), Allred Company's Department 1 incurred charges of $72,000 for direct materials (9,000 units), $38,700 for direct labor, and $13,500 for manufacturing overhead. At month-end, 8,500 units had been finished and transferred out. Those remaining were finished with respect to material but only 40% finished with respect to conversion.

Assuming Allred uses the weighted average method and that materials are added at the beginning of the process and conversion occurs evenly, compute the following:

a. The equivalent units for material and conversion.
b. The cost per equivalent unit for material and conversion.
c. The total cost assigned to the units transferred out.
d. The total cost assigned to the ending inventory.
e. Prove that your solutions to requirements (c) and (d) sum to the total costs to be accounted for.

E17-4B. Equivalent Units and Product Cost Report—Weighted Average Method The following data (and annotations) for March 2016 are for the work in process account of the first of Olympus Company's four departments used in manufacturing its only product.

LO3, 4

Work in Process—Department 1	
Beginning balance (3,000 units, 40% complete)	
Direct material.	$12,600
Conversion costs	5,600
Transferred to Department 2: (23,000 units)	(a)
Direct material (24,000 units)	96,000
Direct labor.	77,300
Manufacturing overhead	36,700
Ending balance [___(b)___ units, 25% complete]	(c)

Assuming that Olympus uses the weighted average method, that materials are added at the beginning of the process and that conversion costs are incurred evenly throughout, solve for the three missing numbers.

E17-5B. Equivalent Units and Product Cost Report—Weighted Average Method The following data (and annotations) are for Empire Company's processing department work in process account for the month of September 2016:

LO3, 4

Beginning inventory (1,500 units, 70% complete)	
Direct material.	$21,950
Conversion costs	10,000
Current period	
Direct material (6,000 units)	50,000
Direct labor.	41,000
Manufacturing overhead applied	65,700

Empire uses the weighted average method. Materials are added at the beginning of the process and conversion costs are incurred evenly throughout. Ending work in process is comprised of 1,000 units, 60% complete. Compute the following:

a. Equivalent units for direct materials and conversion.
b. Cost per equivalent unit for direct materials and conversion.
c. Total cost assigned to the units transferred out.

E17-6B. Equivalent Units Calculations—FIFO Method Terrace Corporation makes an industrial cleaner in two sequential departments, Compounding and Drying. All material is added at the beginning of the process in the Compounding Department. Conversion costs are added evenly throughout each process. Terrace uses the FIFO method of process costing. In the Compounding Department, beginning work in process was 2,000 pounds (60% processed), 34,000 pounds were started, 32,000 pounds were transferred out, and ending work in process was 70% processed.

LO6

Calculate equivalent units for the Compounding Department for August 2016.

E17-7B. Equivalent Units Calculations—FIFO Method The following are selected operating data for Jackson Company's Blending Department for November 2016. Painting and packaging operations are carried out subsequently in other departments.

LO6

Beginning inventory	3,000 units, 70% complete
Started and completed.	60,000 units
Ending inventory.	5,000 units, 40% complete

Calculate the equivalent units finished for the month of November using the FIFO method, assuming that the material is added at the beginning of the process and conversion costs are incurred evenly throughout.

LO6, 7   **E17-8B.   Equivalent Units and Product Cost Report—FIFO Method** In its first month of operations (May of 2016), Allred Company's Department 1 incurred charges of $72,000 for direct material (9,000 units), $38,700 for direct labor, and $13,500 for manufacturing overhead. At month-end, 8,500 units had been finished and transferred out. Those units remaining were finished with respect to material but only 40% finished with respect to conversion.

Assuming Allred uses the FIFO method and that materials are added at the beginning of the process and conversion costs are incurred evenly throughout the period, compute the following:

a.   The equivalent units for materials and conversion costs.
b.   The cost per equivalent unit for materials and conversion costs.
c.   The total cost assigned to the units transferred out.
d.   The total cost assigned to the ending inventory.
e.   Prove that your solutions to requirements (c) and (d) sum to the total costs to be accounted for.

LO6, 7   **E17-9B.   Equivalent Units and Product Cost Report—FIFO Method** The following data (and annotations) for March 2016 are for the work in process account of the first of Olympus Company's four departments used in manufacturing its only product.

Work in Process—Department 1	
Beginning balance (3,000 units, 40% complete)	$18,200
Transferred to Department 2: (23,000 units)	(a)
Direct material (24,000 units)	96,000
Direct labor.	77,300
Manufacturing overhead	36,700
Ending balance [____(b)____ units, 25% complete]	(c)

Assuming that Olympus uses the FIFO method, that materials are added at the beginning of the process and that conversion costs are incurred evenly throughout, solve for the three missing numbers.

LO6, 7   **E17-10B.   Equivalent Units and Product Cost Report—FIFO Method** Following are the September 2016 charges (and certain annotations) appearing in the work in process account for Empire Company's processing department:

Beginning inventory (1,500 units, 70% complete)	
Direct material.	$21,950
Conversion costs	10,000
Current period	
Direct materials (6,000 units)	72,000
Direct labor	32,500
Manufacturing overhead applied	52,200

Empire uses the FIFO method. Materials are added at the beginning of the process and conversion costs are incurred evenly throughout. Ending work in process is comprised of 1,000 units, 60% complete. Compute the following:

a.   Equivalent units for direct materials and conversion.
b.   Cost per equivalent unit or units transferred in and conversion.
c.   Total cost assigned to the units transferred out.

LO5   **E17-11B.   Cost Flows Through Journal Entries** The Mixing Department performs a series of processes in which a fluid chemical is concentrated. Records indicate that the Mixing Department has been charged with $50,000 of direct labor costs. The manufacturing overhead rate is 170% of direct labor costs. Beginning work in process was $170,000, and ending work in process totaled $36,000. One-half of this period's completed products is sold on account at a price equal to 150% of its cost.

Prepare journal entries to record (1) various costs charged to the Mixing Department this period, (2) transfer of this period's completed product, and (3) sale of one-half of this period's production.

PROBLEMS—SET A

P17-1A. Calculate Equivalent Units, Unit Costs, and Transferred Costs—Weighted Average Method   **LO3, 4**
Godfrey Manufacturing, Inc., operates a plant that produces its own regionally-marketed Spicy Steak
Sauce. The sauce is produced in two processes, blending and bottling. In the Blending Department,
all materials are added at the start of the process, and labor and overhead are incurred evenly through-
out the process. Godfrey uses the weighted average method. The following data from the Work in
Process—Blending Department account for January 2016 is missing a few items:

Work in Process—Blending Department	
January 1 inventory (5,000 gallons, 60% processed)	
Direct material.	$ 12,000
Conversion costs	5,900
Transferred to Bottling Department (60,000 gallons).	————
January charges:	
Direct material (61,000 gallons)	152,500
Direct labor.	73,600
Manufacturing overhead	48,800
January 31 Inventory (———— gallons, 70% processed)	————

Required
Assuming Godfrey uses the weighted average method in process costing, calculate the following
amounts for the Blending Department:

a. Number of units in the January 31 inventory.
b. Equivalent units for materials and conversion costs.
c. January cost per equivalent unit for materials and conversion costs.
d. Cost of the units transferred to the Bottling Department.
e. Cost of the incomplete units in the January 31 inventory.

P17-2A. Calculate Equivalent Units, Unit Costs, and Transferred Costs—Weighted Average   **LO3, 4**
Method Arrow Company processes a food seasoning powder through its Compounding and
Packaging departments. In the Compounding Department, direct materials are added at the beginning of the process, and direct labor and manufacturing overhead are incurred evenly throughout the
process. Arrow uses the weighted average method. Costs in the Compounding Department can be
summarized as follows:

Inventory, August 1, 2016 (2,000 units, 40% complete)	
Direct material.	$ 980
Conversion costs	4,100
Current period (31,000 units started)	
Direct material.	33,050
Direct labor.	62,560
Manufacturing overhead.	75,650
	$176,340

At August 31, 2016, 3,000 units were in process, 30% complete with respect to conversion costs.

Required
Calculate the following for the Compounding Department:

a. Equivalent units for materials and conversion costs during August.
b. Costs per equivalent unit for materials and conversion costs.
c. Total cost of units transferred to the Packaging Department.
d. Inventory cost at August 31, 2016.

P17-3A. Product Cost Report—Weighted Average Method Reston Manufacturing Corporation produces   **LO3, 4**
a cosmetic product in three consecutive processes. The costs of Department 1 for May 2016 were as
follows:

Cost of beginning inventory		
Direct material.		$ 9,800
Conversion costs		16,590
Costs added in Department 1:		
Direct material.	$295,400	
Direct labor	298,550	
Manufacturing overhead.	203,130	797,080

Department 1 handled the following units during May:

Units in process, May 1, 2016	2,000
Units started in Department 1	40,000
Units transferred to Department 2	39,000
Units in process, May 31, 2016	3,000

On average, the May 1 units were 30% complete. The May 31 units were 60% complete. Materials are added at the beginning of the process, and conversion costs occur evenly throughout the process in Department 1. Reston uses the weighted average method for process costing.

Required
Prepare the product cost report for Department 1 for May.

LO3, 4 **P17-4A. Product Cost Report—Weighted Average Method** Morrow Manufacturing Company uses the weighted average method for process costing. Morrow produces processed food products that pass through three sequential departments. The costs for Department 1 for September 2016 were as follows:

Cost of beginning inventory:	
Material	$ 11,850
Conversion	20,480
	$ 32,330
Costs added in Department 1 during September:	
Direct material.	$338,750
Direct labor	341,370
Manufacturing overhead.	245,990
	926,110

Department 2 handled the following units during September:	
Units in process, September 1	2,000
Units started in Department 1	48,000
Units transferred out to Department 2	46,000
Units in process, September 30	4,000

On average, the September 1 units were 30% complete, and the September 30 units were 60% complete. Materials are added at the beginning of the process and conversion costs occur evenly throughout the process in Department 1.

Required
Prepare the product cost report for September for Department 1.

LO3, 4, 5 **P17-5A. Two Departments, Journal Entries with Supporting Calculations—Weighted Average Method** (Note: This problem includes two departments. The second department may be beyond the scope of most classes. Instructors may choose to assign only the requirements related to Department 1.)

    Patterson Laboratories, Inc., produces one of its products in two successive departments. All materials are added at the beginning of the process in Department 1; no materials are used in Department 2. Conversion costs are incurred evenly in both departments. Patterson uses the weighted average method for process costing. January 1, 2016, inventory account balances are as follows:

Materials inventory.	$30,000
Work in process—Department 1 (3,000 units, 30% complete)	
Direct materials.	4,560
Conversion costs	10,640
Work in process—Department 2 (4,000 units, 40% complete)	48,100
Finished goods inventory (2,000 units @ $16)	32,000

During January, the following transactions occurred:

1. Purchased material on account, $90,000.
2. Placed $84,000 of material into process in Department 1. This $84,000 represents 24,000 units of materials.
3. Distributed total payroll costs: $108,000 of direct labor to Department 1, $62,700 of direct labor to Department 2, and $51,000 of indirect labor to Manufacturing Overhead.
4. Incurred other actual manufacturing overhead costs, $81,000. (Credit Other Accounts.)
5. Applied overhead to the two processing departments: $88,000 to Department 1 and $43,900 to Department 2.
6. Transferred 25,000 completed units from Department 1 to Department 2. The 2,000 units remaining in Department 1 were 20% completed with respect to conversion costs.
7. Transferred 26,000 completed units from Department 2 to finished goods inventory. The 3,000 units remaining in Department 2 were 75% completed with respect to conversion costs.
8. Sold 20,000 units on account at $27 per unit. Patterson uses FIFO inventory costing procedures for the finished goods inventory.

Required

a. Record the January transactions in general journal form for Department 1 and Department 2.
b. Prepare a product cost report (with its supporting calculations) for Department 1.
c. Prepare a product cost report (with its supporting calculations) for Department 2.
d. Determine the balances remaining in the Materials Inventory account, in each work in process account, and in the Finished Goods Inventory account.

P17-6A. Calculate Equivalent Units, Unit Costs, and Transferred Costs—FIFO Method Godfrey **LO6, 7**
Manufacturing, Inc., operates a plant that produces its own regionally marketed Spicy Steak Sauce.
The sauce is produced in two processes, blending and bottling. In the Blending Department, all materials are added at the start of the process, and labor and overhead are incurred evenly throughout the process. Godfrey uses the FIFO method. The following data from the Work in Process—Blending Department account for January 2016 is missing a few items:

Work in Process—Blending Department	
January 1 inventory (5,000 gallons, 60% processed)	$17,900
Transferred to Bottling Department (60,000 gallons).	———
January charges:	
Direct material (61,000 gallons)	152,500
Direct labor.	73,600
Manufacturing overhead	48,800
January 31 inventory (_____ gallons, 70% processed)	———

Required
Assuming Godfrey uses the FIFO method in process costing, calculate the following amounts for the Blending Department:

a. Number of units in the January 31 inventory.
b. Equivalent units for materials and conversion costs.
c. January cost per equivalent unit for materials and conversion costs.
d. Cost of the units transferred to the Bottling Department.
e. Cost of the incomplete units in the January 31 inventory

LO6, 7 **P17-7A.** **Calculate Equivalent Units, Unit Costs, and Transferred Costs—FIFO Method** Arrow Company processes a food seasoning powder through its Compounding and Packaging departments. In the Compounding Department, direct materials are added at the beginning of the process, and direct labor and manufacturing overhead are incurred evenly throughout the process. Arrow uses the FIFO method. August 2016 costs in the Compounding Department can be summarized as follows:

Inventory, August 1 (2,000 units, 40% complete)	$ 5,080
Direct material (31,000 units)	33,050
Direct labor.	62,560
Manufacturing overhead	75,650
	$176,340

At August 31, 3,000 units were in process, 30% complete with respect to conversion costs.

Required

Calculate the following for the Compounding Department:

a. Equivalent units during August.
b. Costs per equivalent unit.
c. Total cost of units transferred to finished goods inventory.
d. Inventory cost at August 31.

LO7 **P17-8A.** **Product Cost Report—FIFO Method** Reston Manufacturing Corporation produces a cosmetic product in three consecutive processes. The costs of Department 1 for May 2016 were as follows:

Cost of beginning inventory		$606,390
Costs added in Department 1:		
Direct material.	$80,400	
Direct labor	81,550	
Manufacturing overhead.	55,130	217,080

Department 1 handled the following units during May:

Units in process, May 1	2,000
Units started in Department 1	40,000
Units transferred to Department 2	39,000
Units in process, May 31	3,000

On average, the May 1 units were 30% complete; the May 31 units were 60% complete. Materials are added at the beginning of the process and conversion costs occur evenly throughout the process in Department 1. Reston uses the FIFO method for process costing.

Required

Prepare the product cost report for Department 1 for May.

PROBLEMS—SET B

LO3, 4 **P17-1B.** **Calculate Equivalent Units, Unit Costs, and Transferred Costs—Weighted Average Method** Kipling Manufacturing, Inc., operates a plant that produces its own regionally-marketed Super Salad Dressing. The dressing is produced in two processes, blending and bottling. In the Blending Department, all materials are added at the beginning of the process, and labor and overhead are incurred evenly throughout the process. Kipling uses the weighted average method. The Work in Process—Blending Department account for January 2016 follows:

Work in Process—Blending Department	
January 1 inventory (4,000 gallons, 75% finished)	
Direct material.	$ 31,200
Conversion costs	8,800
Transferred to Bottling Department (70,000 gallons).	
January charges:	
Direct material (71,000 gallons)	568,000
Direct labor.	164,000
Manufacturing overhead.	186,000
January 31 inventory (_____ gallons, 60% processed)	

Required

Calculate the following amounts for the Blending Department:

a. Number of units in the January 31 inventory.
b. Equivalent units for materials cost and conversion costs.
c. January cost per equivalent unit for materials and conversion costs.
d. Cost of the units transferred to the Bottling Department.
e. Cost of the incomplete units in the January 31 inventory.

P17-2B. Calculate Equivalent Units, Unit Costs, and Transferred Costs—Weighted Average   **LO3, 4**
Method Bradford Company processes a scouring powder through its Compounding Department and Packaging Department. In the Compounding Department, direct materials are added at the beginning of the process, and direct labor and manufacturing overhead are incurred evenly throughout the process. Bradford uses the weighted average method. Costs charged to the Compounding Department in October 2016 follow:

Inventory, October 1 (5,000 units, 25% complete)	
Direct material.	$ 2,400
Conversion costs	1,850
Current period (82,000 units started):	
Direct material.	171,550
Direct labor.	67,770
Manufacturing overhead.	71,470
	$315,040

At October 31, 7,000 units were in process, 40% completed.

Required

Calculate the following for the Compounding Department:

a. Equivalent units during October.
b. Costs per equivalent unit.
c. Total cost of units transferred to the Packaging Department.
d. Inventory cost at October 31.

P17-3B. Product Cost Report—Weighted Average Method Gomez Manufacturing Corporation produces a   **LO4**
dandruff shampoo in three consecutive processes. The costs of Department 1 for June 2016 were as follows:

Cost of beginning inventory		
Direct material.		$ 5,500
Conversion costs		12,740
Costs added in Department 1:		
Direct material.	$223,670	
Direct labor.	358,300	
Manufacturing overhead.	155,400	737,370

Department 1 handled the following units during June:

Units in process, June 1	2,000
Units started in Department 1	45,000
Units transferred to Department 2	46,000
Units in process, June 30	1,000

On average, the June 1 units were 40% complete; the June 30 units were 70% complete. Direct materials are added at the beginning of the process, and conversion costs occur evenly throughout the process in Department 1. Gomez uses the weighted average method for process costing.

Required

Prepare the product cost report for Department 1 for June.

LO3, 4 **P17-4B. Equivalent Units and Product Cost Report—Weighted Average Method** Summers Manufacturing Corporation produces chemical products using a continual process. Summers uses the weighted average method for process costing. All manufacturing is accomplished in one department. Materials are added at the beginning of the process while conversion costs are incurred evenly throughout the process.

The work in process inventory at the beginning of February 2016 consisted of 10,000 gallons that were 20% complete. The work in process at the end of February consisted of 15,000 gallons that were 40% complete. During February 195,000 gallons were transferred to finished goods.

The beginning inventory contained $90,000 of materials and $30,000 of conversion costs. Product costs incurred during February consisted of $2,010,000 of materials and $3,186,000 of conversion costs.

Required

Calculate equivalent units, cost per equivalent unit, and prepare the product cost report for Summers Manufacturing Corporation for the month of February.

LO3, 4, 5 **P17-5B. Two Departments, Journal Entries with Supporting Calculations—Weighted Average Method** (Note: This problem includes two departments. The second department may be beyond the scope of most classes. Instructors may choose to assign only the requirements related to Department 1.)

Parker Laboratories, Inc., produces one of its products in two successive departments. All materials are added at the beginning of the process in Department 1. No materials are used in Department 2. Conversion costs are incurred evenly in both departments. August 1, 2016, inventory account balances are as follows:

Materials inventory	$15,000
Work in process—Department 1 (6,000 units, 25% finished)	
Direct materials	11,500
Conversion costs	18,750
Work in process—Department 2 (4,000 units, 35% finished)	41,000
Finished goods inventory (4,000 units @ $12.50)	50,000

During August, the following transactions occurred:

1. Purchased material on account, $58,000.
2. Placed 16,000 units of material at $4 per unit into process in Department 1.
3. Distributed total payroll costs: $83,770 of direct labor to Department 1, $42,300 of direct labor to Department 2, and $19,100 of indirect labor to Manufacturing Overhead.
4. Incurred other actual manufacturing overhead costs, $21,200. (Credit Other Accounts.)
5. Applied overhead to the two processing departments: Department 1, $21,280, Department 2, $17,900.
6. Transferred 20,000 completed units from Department 1 to Department 2. The 2,000 units remaining in Department 1 were 30% completed with respect to conversion costs.
7. Transferred 15,000 completed units from Department 2 to Finished Goods Inventory. The 9,000 units remaining in Department 2 were 40% completed with respect to conversion costs.
8. Sold 13,000 units on account at $24 per unit. Parker uses weighted average inventory costing for finished goods inventory.

Required

a. Record the August transactions in general journal form for Department 1 and Department 2.

b. Prepare a product cost report (with its supporting calculations) for Department 1.
c. Prepare a product cost report (with its supporting calculations) for Department 2.
d. Determine the balances remaining in the Materials Inventory account, in each work in process account, and in the Finished Goods Inventory account.

P17-6B. Calculate Equivalent Units, Unit Costs, and Transferred Costs—FIFO Method Kipling Manufacturing, Inc., operates a plant that produces its own regionally-marketed Super Salad Dressing. The dressing is produced in two processes, blending and bottling. In the Blending Department, all materials are added at the beginning of the process, and labor and overhead are incurred evenly throughout the process. Kipling uses the FIFO method. The Work in Process—Blending Department account for January 2016 follows:

LO6, 7

Work in Process—Blending Department	
January 1 inventory (4,000 gallons, 75% finished)	$ 40,000
Transferred to Bottling Department (70,000 gallons)...........................	————
January charges:	
Direct material (71,000 gallons)	568,000
Direct labor...	164,000
Manufacturing overhead..	186,000
January 31 inventory (_____ gallons, 60% processed)	————

Required

Calculate the following amounts for the Blending Department:

a. Number of units in the January 31 inventory.
b. Equivalent units for materials cost and conversion costs.
c. January cost per equivalent unit for materials and conversion costs.
d. Cost of the units transferred to the Bottling Department.
e. Cost of the incomplete units in the January 31 inventory.

P17-7B. Calculate Equivalent Units, Unit Costs, and Transferred Costs—FIFO Method Bradford Company processes a scouring powder through its Compounding Department and Packaging Department. In the Compounding Department, direct materials are added at the beginning of the process, and direct labor and manufacturing overhead are incurred evenly throughout the process. Bradford uses the FIFO method. Costs charged to the Compounding Department in October 2016 follow:

LO6, 7

Inventory, October 1 (5,000 units, 25% complete)	$ 4,250
Direct material (82,000 units)	245,550
Direct labor...	31,770
Manufacturing overhead	33,470
	$315,040

At October 31, 7,000 units were in process, 40% completed.

Required

Calculate the following for the Compounding Department:

a. Equivalent units during October.
b. Costs per equivalent unit.
c. Total cost of units transferred to the Packaging Department.
d. Inventory cost at October 31.

P17-8B. Product Cost Report—FIFO Method Gomez Manufacturing Corporation produces a dandruff shampoo in three consecutive processes. The costs of Department 1 for June 2016 were as follows:

LO7

Cost of beginning inventory		$ 18,240
Costs added in Department 1:		
Direct material..	$219,670	
Direct labor...	361,300	
Manufacturing overhead..	156,400	737,370

Department 1 handled the following units during June:

Units in process, June 1.	2,000
Units started in Department 1	45,000
Units transferred to Department 2	46,000
Units in process, June 30.	1,000

On average, the June 1 units were 40% complete. The June 30 units were 70% complete. Materials are added at the beginning of the process and conversion costs occur evenly throughout the process in Department 1. Gomez uses the FIFO method for process costing.

Required
Prepare the product cost report for Department 1 for June.

CERTIFIED MANAGEMENT ACCOUNTANT (CMA®) EXAM SAMPLE QUESTIONS

CMA17-1. During December, Krause Chemical Company had the following selected data concerning the manufacture of Xyzine, an industrial cleaner.

Production Flow	Physical Units	
Completed and transferred to the next department	100	
Add: Ending work-in-process inventory	10	(40% complete as to conversion)
Total units to account for	110	
Less: Beginning work-in-process inventory	20	(60% complete as to conversion)
Units started during December	90	

All material is added at the beginning of processing in this department, and conversion costs are added uniformly during the process. The beginning work-in-process inventory had $120 of raw material and $180 of conversion costs incurred. Material added during December was $540 and conversion costs of $1,484 were incurred. Krause uses the weighted-average process-costing method. The total raw material costs in the ending work-in-process inventory for December is

a. $120.
b. $72.
c. $60.
d. $36.

CMA17-2. Mack Inc. uses a weighted-average process costing system. Direct materials and conversion costs are incurred evenly during the production process. During the month of October, the following costs were incurred.

Direct materials	$39,700
Conversion costs	70,000

The work-in-process inventory as of October 1 consisted of 5,000 units, valued at $4,300, that were 20% complete. During October, 27,000 units were transferred out. Inventory as of October 31 consisted of 3,000 units that were 50% complete. The weighted-average inventory cost per unit completed in October was

a. $3.51.
b. $3.88.
c. $3.99.
d. $4.00.

CMA17-3. Colt Company uses a weighted-average process cost system to account for the cost of producing a chemical compound. As part of production, Material B is added when the goods are 80% complete. Beginning work-in-process inventory for the current month was 20,000 units, 90% complete. During the month, 70,000 units were started in process, and 65,000 units were completed. There were

no lost or spoiled units. If the ending inventory was 60% complete, the total equivalent units for Material B for the month was

a. 65,000 units.

b. 70,000 units.

c. 85,000 units.

d. 90,000 units.

CMA17-4. San Jose Inc. uses a weighted-average process costing system. All materials are introduced at the start of manufacturing, and conversion costs are incurred evenly throughout production. The company started 70,000 units during May and had the following work-in-process inventories at the beginning and end of the month.

May 1	30,000 units, 40% complete
May 31	24,000 units, 25% complete

Assuming no spoilage or defective units, the total equivalent units used to assign costs for May are

	Materials	Conversion Cost
a.	70,000	70,000.
b.	82,000	82,000.
c.	100,000	70,000.
d.	100,000	82,000.

CMA17-5. During December, Krause Chemical Company had the following selected data concerning the manufacture of Xyzine, an industrial cleaner.

Production Flow	Physical Units	
Completed and transferred to the next department	100	
Add: Ending work-in-process inventory	10	(40% complete as to conversion)
Total units to account for	110	
Less: Beginning work-in-process inventory	20	(60% complete as to conversion)
Units started during December	90	

All material is added at the beginning of processing in this department, and conversion costs are added uniformly during the process. The beginning work-in-process inventory had $120 of raw material and $180 of conversion costs incurred. Material added during December was $540 and conversion costs of $1,484 were incurred. Krause uses the weighted-average process-costing method. The total conversion costs assigned to units transferred to the next department in December was

a. $1,664.

b. $1,600.

c. $1,513.

d. $1,484.

CMA17-6. During December, Krause Chemical Company had the following selected data concerning the manufacture of Xyzine, an industrial cleaner.

Production Flow	Physical Units	
Completed and transferred to the next department	100	
Add: Ending work-in-process inventory	10	(40% complete as to conversion)
Total units to account for	110	
Less: Beginning work-in-process inventory	20	(60% complete as to conversion)
Units started during December	90	

All material is added at the beginning of processing in this department, and conversion costs are added uniformly during the process. The beginning work-in-process inventory had $120 of raw material and $180 of conversion costs incurred. Material added during December was $540 and conversion costs of $1,484 were incurred. Krause uses the first-in, first-out (FIFO) process-costing method. The equivalent units of production used to calculate conversion costs for December was

a.   110 units.
b.   104 units.
c.   100 units.
d.   92 units.

CMA17-7. Jones Corporation uses a first-in, first-out (FIFO) process costing system. Jones has the following unit information for the month of August.

	Units
Beginning work-in-process inventory, 100% complete for materials, 75% complete for conversion cost.	10,000
Units completed and transferred out	90,000
Ending work-in-process inventory, 100% complete for materials, 60% complete for conversion costs.	8,000

The number of equivalent units of production for conversion costs for the month of August is

a.   87,300.
b.   88,000.
c.   92,300.
d.   92,700.

EXTENDING YOUR KNOWLEDGE

EYK17-1. Ethics Case Sweet Fragrances Company uses process costing to account for the manufacture of its perfume. The factory consists of three departments: blending, bottling, and packaging.

The production manager of the bottling department, Janine Post, has recommended that her department not be charged for new labels that are more elaborate and expensive than those used in previous years. The new labels were designed as a tie-in for the marketing and advertising campaigns. Post recommends that the costs of the labels be charged to advertising expense. This would result in slightly lower product costs charged to the bottling department than last year.

The company has instituted a bonus plan for all managers based on keeping costs within a range of previous years' costs.

Sam Block, the accounting manager, reviews all recommendations by all managers before they are presented to top management.

Required
What ethical considerations may arise from Janine Post's recommendation? What alternative recommendations might be made?

ANSWERS TO SELF-STUDY QUESTIONS:

1. c, (pp. 800–801)   2. b, (p. 801)   3. a, (p. 819)

YOUR TURN! SOLUTIONS

Solution 17.1

Remember that when using the weighted average method, the question is "what percentage of the work has been completed?"

Where do the units come from?		Where do the units go?		% Work Done?	Direct Materials	% Work Done?	Conversion Costs
					Equivalent Units		
Beginning inventory . . .	100	Complete/transferred . . .	800	100%	**800**	100%	**800**
Started	790	Ending inventory.	90	100%	**90**	75%	**68**
Total	890	Total	890		890		868

Solution 17.2

Work in process	24,000	
Materials inventory		24,000
Work in process	32,400	
Wages payable		32,400
Work in process	48,600	
Manufacturing overhead		48,600

Solution 17.3

Remember that when using the FIFO method, the question is "what percentage of the work was completed during THIS PERIOD?"

Where do the units come from?		Where do the units go?		% in Jan.?	Direct Materials	% in Jan.?	Conversion Costs
					Equivalent Units		
		Complete/transferred:					
Beginning inventory	100	Beginning inventory	100	0%	**0**	65%	**65**
		Started and completed . . .	700	100%	**700**	100%	**700**
Started	790	Ending inventory.	90	100%	**90**	75%	**68**
Total	890	Total	890		790		833

Solution 17.4

Work in process	24,000	
Materials inventory		24,000
Work in process	32,400	
Wages payable		32,400
Work in process	48,600	
Manufacturing overhead		48,600

18

Activity-Based Costing

PAST

Chapter 17 introduced process costing and how it differs from job order costing. It illustrated equivalent units and the flow of costs through the inventory accounts, as well as introduced the production cost report.

PRESENT

Chapter 18 explores activity-based costing, explains its benefits relative to traditional company-wide and departmental overhead allocation, and contrasts it with activity-based management.

FUTURE

Chapter 19 utilizes our understanding of cost behavior to determine break-even and make planning and budgeting decisions.

LEARNING OBJECTIVES

1. **Explain** the changes in the modern production environment that have affected cost structures. *(p. 847)*

2. **Understand** the concept of activity-based costing (ABC) and how it is applied. *(p. 848)*

3. **Explain** the difference between traditional company-wide and departmental overhead methods and ABC. *(p. 851)*

4. **Describe** the implementation of an ABC system. *(p. 855)*

5. **Explain** customer profitability analysis based on ABC. *(p. 857)*

6. **Explain** the difference between ABC and activity-based management. *(p. 859)*

CALIFORNIA STATE BAR ASSOCIATION

Among its several responsibilities, the **California State Bar Association** regulates the professional conduct of the state's lawyers. The State Bar's discipline system is designed to protect the public, the courts, and the legal profession from lawyers who violate the state's ethical code of professional conduct, the Rules of Professional Conduct.

When a complaint is received from a member of the public regarding the conduct of one of its member lawyers, a complaint analyst determines whether the alleged conduct is in fact a violation of the Rules of Professional Conduct. If so, the complaint is referred to the Office of Investigation for investigation of the allegations. If the investigation concludes that probable misconduct occurred, the Office of Trials files formal charges and prosecutes the alleged attorney in the State Bar Court. The State Bar Court hears the charges and may recommend to the State Supreme Court to either suspend or disbar an attorney who is found to have violated the Rules of Professional Conduct or been convicted of serious crimes. If an allegation proceeds through the process to a formal trial, it can involve hundreds of hours of State Bar analysts', investigators', trial lawyers', judges' and other personnel's time, as well as significant expense.

The state's Business and Professions Code section 6086.10 authorizes the State Bar to recover a portion of the costs of pursuing action against disciplined lawyers. These costs include "charges determined by the State Bar to be 'reasonable costs' of investigation, hearing, and review." What constitutes "reasonable costs"?

To answer this question, the State Bar engaged an independent consulting firm to assist in the analysis. Over a two-week period, State Bar employees were asked to keep detailed track of the time that they spent performing various tasks related to disciplinary procedures. These and other data were then used to compute average times spent on the tasks by each employee type (analyst, investigator, trial lawyer, etc.). Multiplying these average times by the number of tasks performed for a particular type of complaint and the total number of complaints received in the period gave a measure of the work performed in each office. The total cost incurred by each office could then be divided by the amount of work performed to calculate the reasonable cost of an investigation of various types

of complaints, hearings, and reviews. The result was a schedule of fees approved by the state legislature. For example, in 2013 a lawyer convicted of a violation of the Rules of Professional Conduct over the course of a multi-day trial would be assessed almost $16,000 in addition to other discipline.

The process used to determine the amount of "reasonable costs" is called activity-based costing (ABC). Each of the State Bar offices (Office of Investigation, Office of Trials, etc.) is a "cost pool" that is allocated to a "product" (a type of case) based on a "cost driver" (a task performed). Although ABC is traditionally used to determine the cost of products, it can have application in a service setting as well.

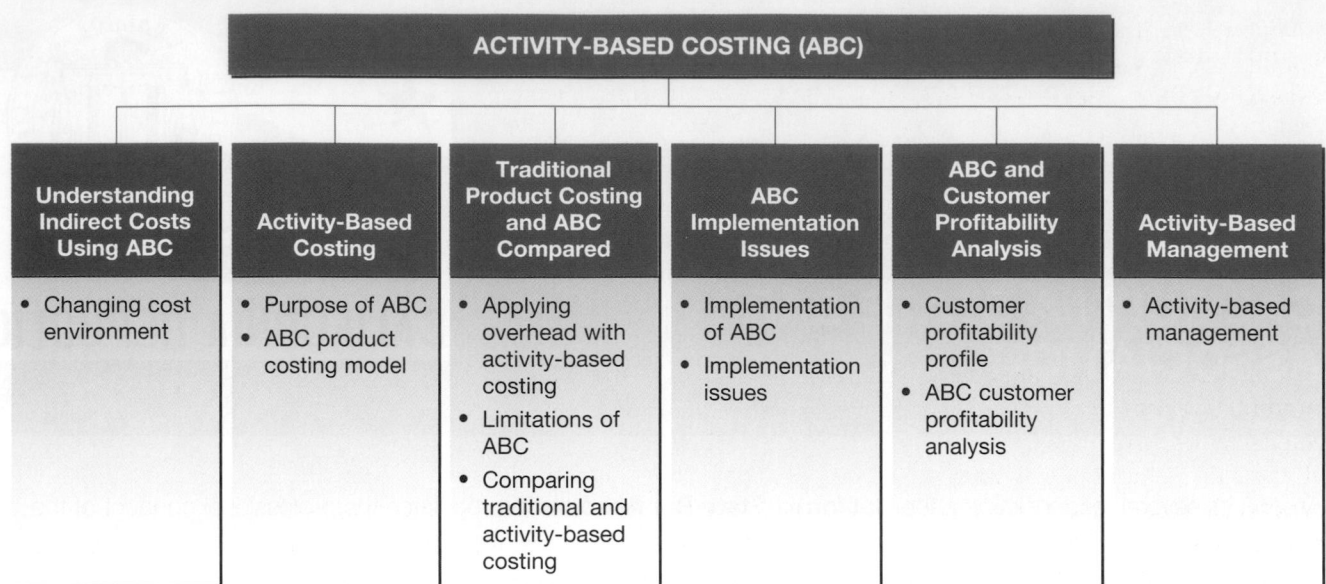

UNDERSTANDING INDIRECT COSTS USING ACTIVITY-BASED COSTING

Effective management of costs is a hallmark of sound financial management, and indirect costs (commonly referred to as overhead) are the most challenging costs to measure and manage. Direct costs, including direct materials and direct labor, can be readily traced to a job, product, or other unit of work. Indirect costs, which are typically incurred for the benefit of several different products or cost objects, are not as easily traced to specific units or projects. Managing indirect costs is a major concern of managers because this broad category of costs has become increasingly more common over time.

Many companies that once thrived have failed, arguably, because they did not manage effectively a growing pool of indirect costs. You might say they failed because they did not fully understand their business or their business model. If a business's actual cost of producing and selling products is more than the revenues generated by those products, the business will not succeed in the long term.

It is well documented that for many years the **U.S. Postal Service (USPS)**, a service entity, has struggled with mounting losses while its competitors, **UPS** and **FedEx**, have thrived in a highly competitive marketplace. At a meeting of the President's Commission on the United States Postal Service (created to examine the problems of the USPS), the discussion focused on differences in the cost systems at the USPS and UPS. It was reported that the USPS cost system attributes only 58% of its operating costs to it various products, whereas UPS attributes 100% of its costs to its products. The UPS representative on the panel stated that UPS does not price any product below its full cost. With only 58% of its costs attributed to products, the USPS cannot know whether any of its products, individually, is making a profit.[1]

As global competition puts increasing pressure on companies to price products more competitively, cost management is increasingly important. Organizations and entities such as UPS, **Coca-Cola, IBM**, the **City of Indianapolis**, and **Toronto's Hospital for Sick Children** have benefited greatly from a type of cost system referred to as **activity-based costing (ABC)**. In this chapter we will define and discuss ABC systems, compare ABC with

---

[1] James A. Johnson and Harry J. Pearce, Co-chairs, "Minutes of Meeting of the President's Commission on the U.S. Postal Service," May 28, 2003, p3, http://www.ustreas.gov/offices/domestic-finance/usps/pdf/may_28_minutes.pdf

traditional costing systems, and demonstrate how ABC can be used to analyze customer profitability. Finally, we will introduce the notion of **activity-based management (ABM)**, which uses ABC information to better manage processes and activities within an organization.

Changing Cost Environment

As technology has advanced over the last century, there has been a fundamental shift in manufacturing organizations from labor-intensive to automated assembly processes. These changes have had a profound influence on the activities performed to meet customer needs and, consequently, the costs of producing goods and services.

LO1 Explain the changes in the modern production environment that have affected cost structures.

At the beginning of the twentieth century, products had long life cycles, production procedures were relatively straightforward, production was labor intensive, and only limited numbers of related products were produced in a single plant. It was said of the Model T Ford that "you could have any color you wanted, as long as it was black." The largest cost elements of most manufactured goods were the cost of raw materials and the wages paid to production employees. Manufacturing overhead was a relatively small portion of the overall cost of manufacturing products.

The twentieth century saw an accelerating shift from traditional labor-based activities to production procedures requiring large investments in automated equipment. In the past, production employees used equipment to assist them in performing their jobs. Now employees spend considerable time scheduling, setting up, maintaining, and moving materials to and from equipment. They spend relatively little time on actual production. The equipment does the work, and the employees keep it running efficiently. Increased complexity of production procedures and an increase in the variety of products produced in a single facility have also caused a shift toward more support personnel and fewer production employees. The result is a significant increase in manufacturing overhead as a percentage of total product cost. This change in the typical production cost structure over the past century is illustrated in **Exhibit 18-1**.

Exhibit 18-1	Changing Cost Environment*

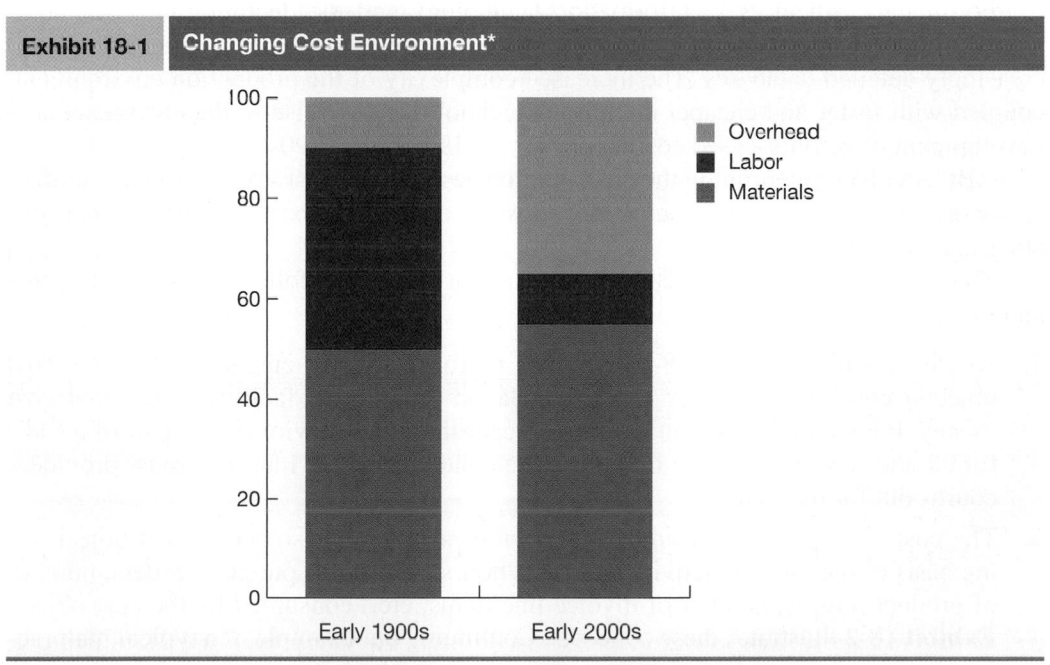

* "The Constraints Management Handbook," James F. Cox, III, Michael S. Spencer, CRC Press, 1997, p. 54.

In the "low-tech," labor-intensive manufacturing environment, factors related to direct labor were often the primary drivers of manufacturing overhead costs; however, in today's "high-tech" automated environment there are many other factors that drive manufacturing overhead costs, and the specific set of cost drivers differs from organization to organization.

Chapter 16 on product costing illustrates a simplified traditional system for allocating manufacturing overhead to products using a single, volume-based cost driver, such as direct labor hours. The following section introduces ABC, which recognizes the multiple activities that drive manufacturing overhead costs in today's production environment.

ACTIVITY-BASED COSTING

LO2 Understand the concept of activity-based costing (ABC) and how it is applied.

The manufacturing overhead cost pool has been referred to as a "bucket" of common costs. The constant growth of costs classified as overhead has forced us to search for increasingly detailed methods to analyze these costs. If overhead costs are low in comparison with material and labor costs and if factories produce few products in large production runs, the use of a single overhead rate based on direct labor hours or machine hours may be adequate. However, as the amount of overhead costs grows, as manufacturing facilities produce a wider variety of products, and as competition intensifies, the inadequacies of a single overhead rate based on a single cost driver such as direct labor hours become evident.

Fortunately, advances in information technology and the declining costs of computerized information systems have facilitated the development and maintenance of increasingly detailed databases. The increased complexity of the production environment, coupled with faster and cheaper computing technology, gave rise to the emergence and development of activity-based costing during the 1980s and 1990s.

ABC involves determining the cost of **activities** (discrete tasks or steps in a manufacturing or service process) and tracing those costs to cost objects based on their proportionate usage of the activities.

The concepts underlying ABC can be summarized in the following two statements and illustrations:

1. As illustrated in **Exhibit 18-2**, activities performed to fill customer needs (or cost objects) consume resources (materials, labor, equipment, facilities, etc.) that cost money. For example, a client complaint regarding misbehavior on the part of a California attorney may require that a trial be conducted. The State Bar must provide a courtroom for the trial.

2. The cost of resources consumed by activities should be assigned to cost objects on the basis of the units of activity (machine hours, number of purchase orders, number of product returns, number of invoice line items, etc.) consumed by the cost object. **Exhibit 18-2** illustrates these concepts. Continuing our example, if a typical malpractice trial complaint takes eight hours to complete, the hourly cost of the courtroom should be assigned to the complaint. In addition to the court cost pool, other examples of State Bar cost pools include the costs associated with receiving and documenting customer complaints (intake), the costs associated with investigating the complaints

(investigation), and the costs associated with preparing and prosecuting the complaints (Office of Trials).

The cost object is typically a product or service provided to a customer. In our example, the cost object is the client's complaint—that is, we want to know what it costs to follow up on each client complaint so that we can recover the appropriate cost from the wayward attorney. Depending on the information needs of decision makers, as we will discuss later in this chapter, the cost object could be the customer.

To summarize, ABC is a system of analysis that identifies and measures the cost of key activities, and then traces these activity costs to products or other cost objects based on the quantity of activity consumed by the cost objects. ABC is based on the premise that activities drive costs and that costs should be assigned to products (or other cost objects) in proportion to the volume of activities they consume. Although activity cost analysis is most often associated with product costing, it offers many benefits for controlling and managing costs, as we will see later in this chapter. As the Accounting in Practice box, (page 164), explains, ABC was actually used first to improve cost management before it was used for product costing.

Exhibit 18-2	Activity-Based Costing Illustration

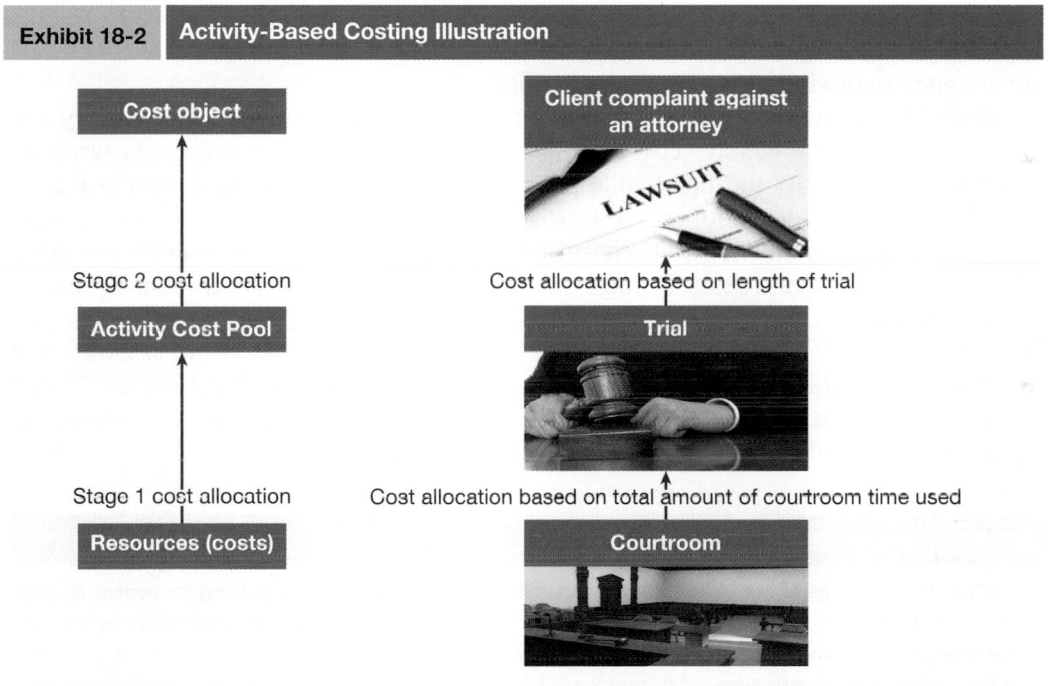

Standards of Professionalism

The opening vignette of this chapter discusses how the California State Bar Association determines the reasonable costs of pursuing action against disciplined lawyers. Because of the extraordinary responsibility society places upon the attorneys within our democracy, it is critical that groups such as the California State Bar Association maintain the highest ethical standards for its members. Just how does the Association see this responsibility? The following is quoted from the California Attorney Guidelines of Civility and Professionalism:

> "As officers of the court with responsibilities to the administration of justice, attorneys have an obligation to be professional with clients, other parties and counsel, the courts and the public. This obligation includes civility, professional integrity, personal dignity, candor, diligence, respect, courtesy, and cooperation, all of which are essential to the fair administration of justice and conflict resolution."

ABC Product Costing Model

Traditional costing considers the cost of a product to be its direct costs for materials and labor plus some allocated portion of manufacturing overhead, using overhead rates typically based on direct labor or machine hours. ABC is based on the notion that companies incur costs because of the activities they conduct in pursuit of their goals and objectives. For example, various activities take place to produce a particular product, such as setting up, maintaining, or monitoring the machines to make the product, physically moving raw materials and work in process, and so forth. Each of these activities has a cost; therefore, the total cost of producing a product using ABC is the sum of the direct materials and direct labor costs of that product, plus the cost of other activities conducted to produce that product.

The left side of **Exhibit 18-2** illustrates the general two-stage ABC product cost model. The first stage includes the assignment of overhead resource costs, such as indirect labor, depreciation, and utilities, to activity cost pools for the key activities identified. Typical activity cost pools in a manufacturing environment include pools for machine setup, material movement, and engineering. The second stage assigns those activity cost pools to cost objects.

Remember that **Exhibit 18-2** is focused solely on overhead costs—the direct product or service costs, such as direct materials and direct labor, are directly assigned to cost objects and are excluded from the activity cost pools. Only indirect product costs (overhead) are assigned to products via activity cost pools.

Hint: If an increase in an activity does not cause a measurable increase in a particular cost, there is not a logical causal relationship.

Probably the most critical step in ABC is identifying **cost drivers**. The activity cost driver for a particular cost (or cost pool) is the characteristic selected for measuring the quantity of the activity for a particular period of time. In the example shown in **Exhibit 18-2**, if an activity cost pool is established for a trial, it is necessary to select some basis for measuring the quantity of trial activity associated with the costs in the pool. The quantity of trial activity could be measured by the number of trials held, the amount of time the courtroom is in use, the number of staff working in the courtroom, or some other measure. It is critical that the activity measure used has a logical causal relationship to the costs in the pool and that the quantity of the activity is highly correlated with the amount of cost in the pool. Statistical methods, such as regression analysis and correlation analysis, can be very useful in selecting activity cost drivers.

ACCOUNTING IN PRACTICE **Development of ABC**

ABC came to the forefront in the 1980s and 1990s; however, it was beginning to evolve as early as the 1960s when finance and accounting staff at **General Electric** (GE) attempted to improve the usefulness of accounting information in controlling ever-increasing indirect costs. The GE staff noted that indirect costs were often the result of "upstream" decisions, such as engineering design and change orders, which were made long before the costs were actually incurred. Frequently, the engineering department was not informed of the consequences its actions had on the other parts of the organization.

The second phase of the development of ABC was accomplished by business consultants, professors, and manufacturing companies during the 1970s and early 1980s. By generating more accurate cost and profitability measures for the various products offered by companies, these consultants and professors hoped to improve product cost information used in pricing and product mix decisions. ABC has since been extended to assess customer profitability.

In the late 1980s and 1990s, ABC was being promoted by many of the leading consulting firms, and it almost became a fad, much as total quality management (TQM) and just-in-time (JIT) systems had before it. Consequently, many companies that jumped on the ABC bandwagon early in its life later determined that it was not for them. Most of the companies that abandoned ABC probably adopted it initially for the wrong reasons.

Knowledge of the historical development of ABC is important in order to clearly understand what ABC analysis was intended to accomplish, as well as what it was not intended to accomplish.

Once the budgeted cost in the activity pool and the budgeted activity cost driver have been determined, the cost per unit of activity is calculated as the total cost divided by the total amount of activity. This is the predetermined rate that will be used to apply costs to products or services during the period. For example, if total costs assigned to the trial activity pool in July were $100,000 and 100 hours of courtroom time were available in July, the cost per courtroom hour for the month would be $1,000. If during July a particular trial took eight hours of courtroom time, the total courtroom cost that would be assigned to the trial would be $8,000 ($1,000 × 8 hours).

TRADITIONAL PRODUCT COSTING AND ABC COMPARED

Recall that in Chapter 16, Fezzari Performance Bicycles applied overhead using a company-wide overhead rate of $17.00 per direct labor hour. This may seem to be a very low overhead rate until you remember that Fezzari is primarily assembling parts that have been manufactured by other suppliers. Fezzari's factory doesn't have large, expensive manufacturing equipment that you might associate with other types of manufacturers.

LO3 Explain the difference between traditional company-wide and departmental overhead methods and ABC.

We assumed that each hour of labor worked on a project caused $17.00 of overhead to be incurred. In that case, all overhead costs were associated with one factor, direct labor hours. As discussed at the beginning of this chapter, such an assumption is often not appropriate with modern methods of producing goods or services where manufacturing overhead is related to a diverse set of activities and cost drivers.

Where overhead costs or capacity measures vary significantly from one department to the next, a separate overhead rate may be calculated for each department. Chapter 16 introduced the concept of departmental overhead rates, where a separate overhead rate is predetermined for each producing department in a factory. In most multiproduct manufacturing environments, this approach represents a cost system improvement over using a single, company-wide overhead rate, and it reduces the likelihood of cost cross-subsidization, which occurs when one product is assigned too much cost as a result of another being assigned too little cost.

Assume that Fezzari has two production departments, Assembly and Packaging, and that these departments have overhead costs of $240,100 and $60,000, respectively. Assume, further, that Fezzari management determined that the Assembly Department overhead costs should be allocated to bicycles on the basis of direct labor hours and that the Packaging Department overhead costs should be allocated to bicycles on the basis of units produced. **Exhibit 18-3** shows that the resulting department predetermined overhead rates would be $10.00 per direct labor hour for the Assembly Department and $13.33 per unit for the Packaging Department.

Exhibit 18-3	Computing Department Overhead Rates		
Overhead costs per unit		**Assembly**	**Packaging**
Total department manufacturing overhead (direct department costs plus allocated costs)....		$240,100	$60,000
Quantity of overhead application base			
Direct Labor Hours........................		÷ 24,000	
Units Produced............................			÷ 4,500
Department manufacturing overhead rates........		$ 10.00	$13.33
		per direct labor hour	*per unit*

Department overhead rates may improve product costing results for many organizations, and in fact may be satisfactory. However, this method does not attempt to reflect the actual activities used in producing the different products.

Applying Overhead with Activity-Based Costing

An even more precise method of measuring the cost of products than company-wide or departmental rates is the ABC method. As stated earlier, ABC typically involves two stages of cost allocation. The first stage is identifying and measuring the cost of activities used to produce the various products. The second stage is summing the cost of those activities to determine the ultimate cost of the products.

ACCOUNTING IN PRACTICE | **Benefits of ABC**

A 2009 study by Stratton, Desroches, Lawson, and Hatch of 348 manufacturing and service companies worldwide indicated that activity-based costing continues to provide strategic and operational benefits. Although the study showed that there has been a decline in ABC users since the 1990s, when it was first widely adopted, the following graphic from the study report supports the conclusion that users of ABC have a higher level of confidence than non-ABC users that their cost system provides more accurate cost measurements.

Comparisons of ABC to Non-ABC Users on Three Key Benefits

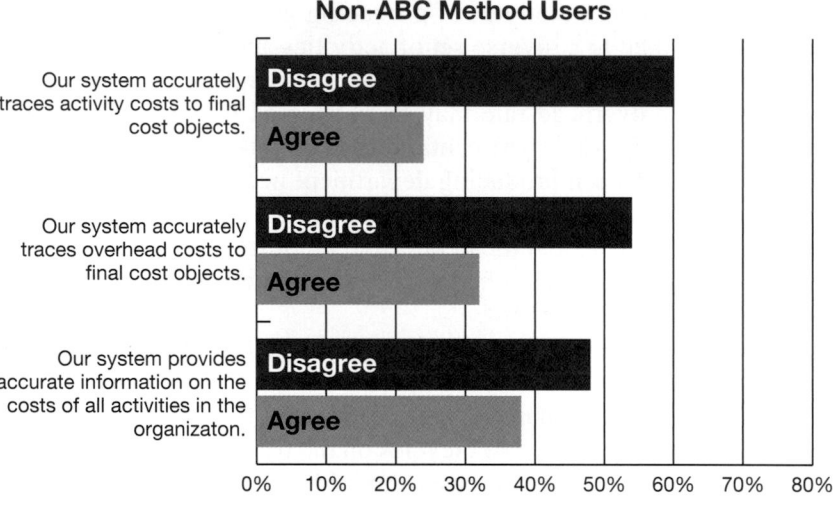

Non-ABC Method Users

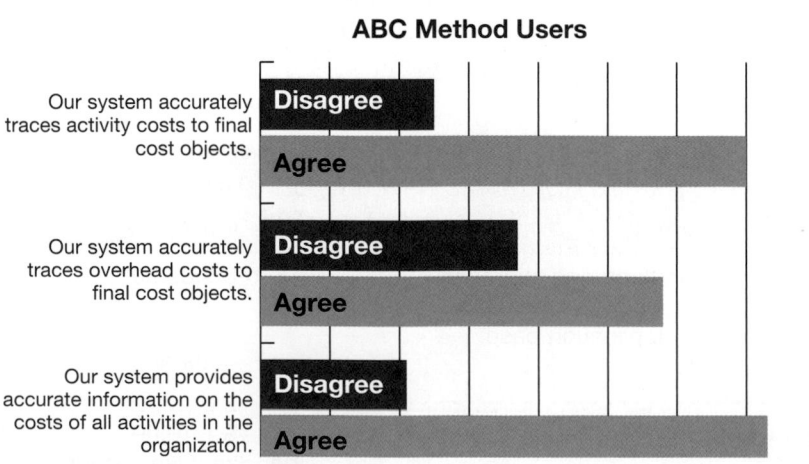

ABC Method Users

Source: W. O. Stratton, D. Desroches, R. A. Lawson, and T. Hatch. (2009). "Activity-Based Costing: Is It Still Relevant?" *Management Accounting Quarterly*, Vol.10, No. 3, pp. 31–40.

The overhead rates for each Fezzari department were determined in the last section as $10.00 and $13.33, respectively. The easiest way to assign these costs to products is by using one base and one rate for all products going through a given process (e.g., assembly). However, different products typically use different amounts of resources from a given process and using the same base and overhead rate for all may distort the cost for some or all products.

Overhead costs in the Assembly and Packaging Departments consisted of two types of costs: **production department costs** and support department costs. Production department overhead costs are costs that are incurred by the production department, such as indirect labor, indirect materials, depreciation on equipment, supervisory wages, and so forth. Support department costs are costs allocated from other departments (for the Fezzari example, the support departments include Design, Receiving/Inventory, and Building) that provide services to both Assembly and Packaging. Fezzari's accountant determined that the production department overhead costs in Assembly were driven primarily by labor hours, whereas support department overhead costs in Packaging were driven primarily by units produced. It was also determined that each component of design, receiving/inventory, and building represents a separate activity cost pool, and that these costs should be assigned to the products based on specific cost drivers rather than a single cost driver for the entire department.

Exhibit 18-4 presents a detailed analysis of overhead cost data for July's operations.

Exhibit 18-4	ABC Stage One: Assign Costs to Activities			
Overhead Activity	**Total Activity Cost**	**Activity Cost Driver (number of)**	**Quantity of Activity**	**Unit Activity Rates***
Production departmental overhead costs				
Assembly	$ 10,000	Direct labor hours.	24,000	$ 0.42
Packaging.	3,000	Units produced.	4,500	$ 0.67
Allocated support costs				
Receiving/Inventory	21,000	Units produced.	4,500	$ 4.67
Design.	20,000	Change orders	31,500	$ 0.63
Building.	246,100	Units produced.	4,500	$54.69
Total	$300,100			

* Rounded

Assume that Fezzari management wants to compare the use of a company-wide, departmental, and ABC overhead allocation method on the cost of two road bikes, the top-end T5 (from Chapter 16) and the entry-level Catania. The T5 is typically purchased by serious triathletes who are very particular about the setup and customization of their bikes, whereas the Catania is typically purchased by fitness newbies who know little about bike components and fit and are primarily driven by price in the selection of their bikes. For simplicity, assume that these are the only two bikes produced by Fezzari. The amounts of activity attributed to the T5 and Catania and the overhead cost per unit based on ABC costs are shown in **Exhibit 18-5**.

Exhibit 18-5	ABC Stage Two: Assign Activities to Cost Objects						
Bicycle Model				T5		Catania	
Activity	Cost Driver	Cost per Unit of Activity	Quantity of Activity	Cost of Activity*	Quantity of Activity	Cost of Activity*
Assembly	Direct labor hours...	$ 0.42	12,000	$ 5,000.00	12,000	$ 5,000.00
Packaging	Units produced.....	0.67	1,500	1,000.00	3,000	2,000.00
Receiving/Inventory	Units produced.....	4.67	1,500	7,000.00	3,000	14,000.00
Design	Change orders	0.63	22,500	14,285.71	9,000	5,714.29
Building	Units produced.....	54.69	1,500	82,033.33	3,000	164,066.67
Total overhead product cost				$109,319.04		$190,780.96
Units produced........................				1,500.00		3,000.00
Overhead per unit of product*				$ 72.88		$ 63.59

*Differences due to rounding.

Exhibit 18-6 summarizes the allocated overhead costs for Fezzari's two products using the three different overhead cost assignment methods.

Exhibit 18-6	Overhead Cost per Unit Using Various Overhead Methods		
		T5	Catania
Company-wide overhead rate*................................		$136.00	$68.00
Departmental overhead rates**		93.33	53.33
ABC		72.88	63.59

*Direct labor hours per unit × $17.00 = (12,000/1,500) × $17 = $136 (T5); = (12,000/3,000) × $17 = $68 (Catania)

**(Direct labor hours per unit × $10) + $13.33 per unit = ((12,000/1,500) × $10) + $13.33 = $93.33 (T5);
  = ((12,000/3,000) × $10) + $13.33 = $53.33 (Catania)

ABC product costing reveals a different cost picture. Using either a company-wide overhead rate or departmental rates, the T5 bike is bearing more than its share of total overhead costs.

Using either of these methods could lead the company into pricing the T5 too high in the market. With a more accurate overhead cost of $72.88, rather than $93.33 or $136.00, the company clearly has the ability to compete on price with other companies in this market. In Fezzari's case, overhead is a relatively minor cost relative to the cost of the direct materials, as shown in Chapter 16. This is due to the fact that Fezzari is mainly an assembler of parts, rather than a manufacturer of those parts. However, in other industries, the effect of adopting ABC may be much more significant.

However, regardless of the differences among the various cost methods, inaccurate costing can affect management's assessment of product profitability and its decisions regarding which products to continue to produce and which products to discontinue. Flawed product costing information can cause management mistakenly to decide to keep products that are losing money, while deciding to discontinue products that are profitable. Using a company-wide or departmental overhead allocation method could have led Fezzari management to shift its emphasis from the high-end bike to the low-end bike market, a decision that could have been damaging to the company.

YOUR TURN! 18.1

The solution is on page 881.

Assume you are a controller for a manufacturing company that uses a traditional product costing system, but is looking to transition to ABC. The CEO has asked you why this would be a useful transition. What would you tell him regarding the benefits of activity-based costing?

Limitations of ABC Illustration

Several limitations of the Fezzari illustration should be mentioned. For the sake of simplicity, the example was limited to manufacturing cost considerations. A complete analysis would also require considerations of nonmanufacturing costs, such as marketing, distribution, and customer service, before a final determination of product profitability could be made. Finally, in calculating the activity cost per unit of activity, it is necessary to decide how to measure the total quantity of activity. For example, for Fezzari, the receiving/inventory cost per unit was calculated as $4.67 based on the actual quantity of 4,500 bicycles produced for the period. Alternatively, the receiving cost could have been calculated based on **practical capacity**, which is the maximum possible volume of activity, while allowing for normal downtime for repairs and maintenance. If the plant has a practical capacity to produce 5,000 bicycles per period, the cost per bike based on the practical capacity is $4.20 per purchase order. Using this overhead rate in costing products, only $18,900 would have been assigned to the two products, which required only 4,500 bicycles, and the remaining $2,100 for the 500 bicycles of excess (or idle) capacity not used would be written off as an operating expense of the period as underapplied overhead. Practical capacity is generally regarded as better than actual capacity for calculating activity costs because it does not hide the cost of idle capacity within product costs, and it gives a truer cost of the activities used to produce the product.

Comparing Traditional and Activity-Based Costing

Procedurally, ABC is not a new method for assigning costs to cost objectives. Traditional costing systems have used a two-stage allocation model (similar to the ABC model) to assign costs to cost pools (such as departments) and subsequently assign those cost pools to products using an allocation base. In most traditional costing systems, overhead is assigned to one or more cost pools based on departments and functional characteristics (such as labor-related, machine-related, and space-related costs) and then reassigned to products using a general allocation base such as direct labor hours or machine hours. ABC is different in that it divides the overall manufacturing processes into activities. ABC accumulates costs in cost pools for the major activities and then assigns the costs of these activities to products or other cost objectives that benefit from these activities. *Conceptually,* ABC is different because of the way it views the operations of the company; *procedurally,* it uses a methodology that has been around for a long time.

The challenge in using ABC is specifying the model—that is, determining how many activity pools should be established for a given cost measurement purpose, which costs should be assigned to each activity pool, and the appropriate activity driver for each pool. Specifying the model also includes determining the resource cost drivers for assigning indirect resource costs to the various activity cost pools.

TAKEAWAY 18.2

It is important to note that although using traditional overhead costing or activity-based costing results in different per-unit overhead costs, the total amount of allocated overhead remains unchanged. Only the unit rates will change between the two methods.

ABC IMPLEMENTATION ISSUES

The distortion in product costs for Fezzari from using traditional cost systems based on company-wide or departmental rates, although hypothetical, is not uncommon. Studies have shown that distortions of this type occur regularly in traditional systems in which a significant variation exists in the volume and complexity of products and services produced. Traditional systems tend

LO4 ABC system.

Describe the implementation of an

to over-cost high-volume, low-complexity products, and they tend to under-cost low-volume, high-complexity products. These studies indicate that the typical amount of over-costing is up to 200% for high-volume products with low complexity and that the typical under-costing can be more than 1,000% for low-volume, highly complex products. In companies with a large number of different products, traditional costing can show that most products are profitable. After changing to ABC, however, these companies might find that 10 to 15% of the products are profitable while the remainder are unprofitable. Adopting ABC often leads to increased profits merely by changing the product mix to minimize the number of unprofitable products.[2]

Most companies initially do not abandon their traditional cost system and move to a system that uses ABC for management and financial reporting purposes because financial statements must withstand the scrutiny of auditors and tax authorities. This scrutiny typically implies more demands on the cost accounting system for consistency, objectivity, and uniformity than required when the system is used only for management purposes. In addition, ABC systems must be built facility by facility rather than being embedded in a software program that can be used by all facilities within the company.[3] Often, companies maintain traditional costing for external reporting purposes and ABC for pricing and other internal decision-making purposes.

Once an ABC system has been developed for a production facility, including an activities list (sometimes called an activities dictionary), identification of activity cost drivers, and calculation of cost per unit of driver activity, the activity costs of a current or proposed product can be readily determined. In ABC, as illustrated for Fezzari, manufacturing a product is viewed simply as the combination of activities selected to make it; therefore, the activity cost of a product or service is the sum of the costs of those activities. This approach to viewing a product enables management to evaluate the importance of each of the activities consumed in making a product. Possibly some activities can be eliminated or a lower-cost activity substituted for a more costly one without reducing the quality or performance of the product.

ACCOUNTING IN PRACTICE   **Results of ABC**

In the 1980s, the **Coca-Cola Company** used ABC to determine that it was less costly—and thus more profitable—to deliver soft drink concentrate to some fountain drink retailers (such as fast-food restaurants) in nonreturnable, disposable containers rather than in returnable stainless steel containers, which had been standard in the industry for many years.

Although an ABC system may be complex, it merely mirrors the complexity of an organization's design, manufacturing, and distribution systems. If a firm's products are diverse and its production and distribution procedures complex, the ABC system will also be complex; however, if its products are homogeneous and its production environment relatively simple, its ABC system should also be relatively simple. Even in highly complex manufacturing environments, ABC systems usually have no more than 10 to 20 cost pools. Many ABC experts in practice have observed that creating a large number of activity cost pools for a given costing application normally does not significantly improve cost accuracy above that of a smaller number of cost pools. As with any information system design, the costs of developing and maintaining the system must not exceed its benefits; hence, although adding more activity cost pools may result in some small amount of increased accuracy, it may be so small as not to be cost effective.

In addition to using ABC for product costing purposes, other important uses for ABC have also been found. One of the most useful applications for ABC discussed in the next

---

[2] Gary Cokins, Alan Stratton, and Jack Helbling, An ABC Manager's Primer (Montvale, NJ: Institute of Management Accountants, 1993).

[3] Robert S. Kaplan and Robin Cooper, *Cost and Effect* (Boston: Harvard Business School Press, 1998), p.105.

section is in evaluating customer costs and distribution channel costs. Other applications include costing administrative functions such as processing accounts receivable or accounts payable; costing the process of hiring and training employees; and costing such menial tasks as processing a letter or copying a document. As illustrated by the California State Bar illustration at the beginning of the chapter, any process, function, or activity performed in an organization, whether it is related to production, marketing and sales, finance and accounting, human resources, or even research and development, is a candidate for ABC analysis. In short, almost any cost objective that has more than an insignificant amount of indirect costs can be more effectively measured using ABC.

ABC AND CUSTOMER PROFITABILITY ANALYSIS

One of the most beneficial applications of activity-based costing is in the analysis of the profitability of customers. Companies that have a large number of diverse customers also usually have widely varied profits from serving those customers. Many companies never attempt to calculate the profit earned from individual customers. They merely assume that if they are selling products above their costs, and that overall the company is earning a profit, then each of the customers must be profitable. Unfortunately, the cost incurred to sell goods and services, and to provide services, to individual customers is not usually proportionate with the gross profits generated by those sales. Customers with high sales volume are not necessarily the most profitable. Profitability of individual customers depends on whether the gross profits from sales to those customers exceed the customer-specific costs of serving those customers. Some customers are simply more costly than others, and some may even be unprofitable, and the unprofitable customers are eating away at the total profits of the company. In an ideal world, only profitable customers would be retained, and unprofitable customers would be either converted to a profitable status or they would be dropped as customers.

LO5 | **Explain** customer profitability analysis based on ABC.

Customer Profitability Profile

If a company knows the amount of profits (or losses) generated by each of its customers, a customer profitability profile can be prepared, as illustrated in the following section.

ABC Customer Profitability Analysis Illustrated

Let's assume that Pure Water Company is a "green" company located in the West that manufactures and sells all-natural compounds for purifying water distributed through large public water systems. Let's also assume that Ron James, the CEO and founder of Pure Water, personally developed the compounds using natural materials obtained from remote regions of the world. He knows that he has a product that is far superior to the traditional processes based on synthetic chemicals that have been used for generations to purify water. After five years in business, Pure Water has built a solid and growing customer base, but it has to invest significant time and expense servicing customers, especially those that have recently embraced its approach to water purification. Some customers require a lot of "hand-holding," with frequent visits and telephone calls, and they tend to purchase frequently in small amounts, often requiring repackaging. Other customers require little attention and support, and many of them purchase in large amounts once a year.

Although the company is making money, there is concern that profits could be higher if sales and other customer-related costs could be decreased. Ron James decided to ask Environmental Business Consultants (EBC; introduced in Chapter 14) to conduct a customer profitability analysis using activity-based costing. As a first step, EBC determined that there were five primary activities related to serving customers: visits of customers by sales representatives, remote contacts (phone, email, fax), processing and shipping of customer orders, repackaging, and billing and collection. After extensive analysis, including numerous interviews and statistical analyses of activity and cost data, EBC determined the cost drivers and cost per unit of activity for the five customer-related activities, shown in **Exhibit 18-7**.

Exhibit 18-7	Pure Water's Customer Service Activity Per-Unit Costs	
Activity	**Activity Cost Driver**	**Cost per Unit of Driver Activity**
Visits to customers	Visits.	$800
Remote contacts	Number of contacts	75
Processing and Shipping	Customer orders	450
Repackaging	Number of requests	250
Billing and Collection	Invoices	90

After collecting activity driver data on each of these activities for Pure Water's major customers, EBC prepared the customer activity cost and profitability analysis presented in **Exhibit 18-8** for its five largest customers (in terms of sales dollars) in the order of greatest to least profit for the most recent year.

Exhibit 18-8	Pure Water Customer Activity Cost and Profitability Analysis					
	Consolidated Water, Inc.	**West Coast Utilities**	**Seattle Water District**	**Manhattan Water Authority**	**Great Lakes Utility**	**Total**
Customer Activity Cost Analysis:						
Activity Cost Driver Data						
Visits to customers	1	1	3	5	4	
Remote contacts	3	2	5	7	8	
Processing and shipping	1	4	3	3	5	
Repackaging.	0	0	0	2	3	
Billing and collection.	1	4	3	3	5	
Customer Activity Cost						
Visits to customers	800	800	2,400	4,000	3,200	
Remote contacts	225	150	375	525	600	
Processing and shipping	450	1,800	1,350	1,350	2,250	
Repackaging.	0	0	0	500	750	
Billing and collection.	90	360	270	270	450	
Total Activity Cost.	1,565	3,110	4,395	6,645	7,250	
Customer Profitability Analysis						
Customer sales.	16,250	15,000	17,500	20,000	12,000	80,750
Less cost of goods sold	9,750	9,000	10,500	12,000	7,200	48,450
Gross profit on sales.	6,500	6,000	7,000	8,000	4,800	32,300
Less activity costs	1,565	3,110	4,395	6,645	7,250	22,965
Customer profitability	4,935	2,890	2,605	1,355	(2,450)	9,335
Customer profitability ratio*	30.4%	19.3%	14.9%	6.8%	(20.4)%	11.6%

*Customer profitability ÷ Sales

Because Pure Water is selling only one product to all of its customers, and has the same pricing policy for all customers, there is a constant 40% gross profit ratio across all customers, and the combined net profitability of these customers is 11.6% of sales. However, all customers are not equally profitable. The high level of support required by

Manhattan and Great Lakes resulted in a net customer loss from sales to Great Lakes and only a 6.8% customer profitability ratio for Manhattan.

Armed with the information in the customer activity cost and profitability analysis, Pure Water can take proactive steps to increase its overall profitability ratio. An obvious option would be to try to terminate its relationship with Great Lakes because the company is clearly losing money on that customer. If Great Lakes were terminated as a customer, and assuming that all of the activity costs associated with Great Lakes could be avoided by the termination, Pure Water's total sales would drop to $68,750 (or $80,750 minus $12,000), but its total profit would increase to $11,785 (or $9,335 plus $2,450), resulting in a profitability ratio on the remaining four customers of 17.1%.

A more proactive approach would be to work with Great Lakes and Manhattan, which have high support requirements, such as repackaging, frequent visits, and phone contacts, to try to lower the level of high-cost support activities without reducing sales to those customers. This could result in maintaining the current level of gross profit, but generating a significantly higher level of total net customer profitability.

Once a company has profitability data on each of its customers (or categories of customers), only then can it proceed to try to convert them to profitability, or seek to terminate the relationships with those customers. Just as we saw that ABC provided a model for producing more accurate product cost data, ABC is also a valuable tool for generating customer profitability data.

Two caveats should be considered when using activity cost data to manage customer profitability. First, there may be justifiable reasons (such as having a new customer that requires a high level of early-stage support, trying to penetrate a new geographic market, or existing relationships with other more profitable customers) for keeping customers that have lower profitability, or even customers that are not profitable. If so, these customers should be managed intensely to attempt to reduce the activities devoted to their support. Second, eliminating a customer may not immediately translate into an immediate reduction of activity costs. Some activity costs may not have a variable cost behavior pattern, and eliminating customers may merely create excess capacity in the short term.

TAKEAWAY 18.3

Increasing the volume of customers may not always be desirable. Customer profitability analysis helps management assess whether it is worthwhile to pursue increasing the company's customer base.

ACTIVITY-BASED MANAGEMENT

Activity-based costing has been highly touted as a technique for improving the measurement of the cost and profitability of products, customers, and other cost objectives. In the early development of ABC, it was discovered that a by-product of accurately measuring costs using ABC is that management invariably gains a much better understanding of the processes and activities that are used to create cost objects, such as products. Although ABC could be justified on the basis of its value as a tool in helping produce more accurate cost measurements for various cost objectives, its greatest potential value may be in its by-products. The access to ABC data enables managers to engage in **activity-based management (ABM),** defined as the identification and selection of activities to maximize the value of the activities while minimizing their cost from the perspective of the final consumer. In other words, ABM is concerned with how to efficiently and effectively manage activities and processes to provide value to the final consumer.

LO6 Explain the difference between ABC and activity-based management.

Hint: It is often not feasible to perform a cost analysis on every activity, so management must exercise judgment in choosing activities to track costs for.

Defining processes and identifying key activities helps management better understand the business and evaluate whether activities being performed add value to the customer. ABM focuses managerial attention on what is most important among the activities performed to create value for customers.

A helpful analogy in understanding what ABC can do for a company is to compare a company's operations with a large retail store, such as a **Home Depot** store. In a Home Depot store there is a clearly marked price on each of the tens of thousands of individual items that customers may decide to purchase. Similarly, every activity that takes place in any organization has a cost that can be determined and that management can use to make a judgment about the activity's value. In an ideal world, a manager could walk through the business and evaluate the cost of every activity being performed—maybe thousands of different activities—and then decide which ones are worth the cost and which ones are not adding value. But because generating ABC data has a cost, management must decide which ABC data are likely to be useful and cost beneficial. Our discussion here is only an introduction to activity-based costing and some of its applications. As the following Accounting in Practice points out, over the past quarter of a century, ABC has matured well beyond merely accurately measuring costs of products and customers. More advanced ABC topics and methods are covered in advanced managerial accounting (or cost accounting) courses.

ACCOUNTING IN PRACTICE

Current Status of ABC

One of the leading thinkers and authors on the topic of activity-based costing over the past 25 years has been Peter B. B. Turney. He recently traced the evolution of ABC within the context of a product life cycle, showing how ABC functionality has expanded since it was first introduced in the 1980s. Turney asserts that ABC is now in its fourth generation, where it has become "an integral part of business performance management solutions, including profitability management, performance measurement, financial management, sustainability, and human capital management." In its current state of development, a single ABC model can support a number of needs, including historical cost measurement, resource planning, performance measurement, and other analyses.

SERVICES INDUSTRY IN FOCUS

SERVICE AND MERCHANDISING

Customer Profitability Analysis

Environmental Business Consultants (EBC) serves three different sizes of clients (large, medium, and small). EBC's solid waste rate review projects are fairly standardized and routine; hence, the pricing is also standardized for all clients. Although the company is profitable overall, the CFO thinks the net margins should be higher. She is concerned that customer support costs are eating up some of the margin and has decided to do a customer profitability analysis based on the three different sizes of clients to see if some of the client groups may actually be less profitable than others. The following data for the most recent period have been collected to support the analysis:

Support Activity	Driver	Cost per Driver Unit
A. Scope change requests	Number of requests	$150
B. Visits to client	Number of visits	$200
C. Communication	Number of calls	$ 50

Customer Group	Activity A	Activity B	Activity C	Profit Before Support Costs
Large	36	72	180	$390,000
Medium	75	150	205	100,500
Small.....................	21	42	80	52,000

Required

1. Calculate the customer profitability for each customer group, taking into account the support activity required for each customer group.

2. Comment on the usefulness of this type of analysis. What reasonable actions might the CEO take as a result of this analysis?

Solution

1. Activity A—Scope change requests

   Activity B—Visits to client

   Activity C—Communication

Activity	Large	Medium	Small
A (@ $150)	$ 5,400	$ 11,250	$ 3,150
B (@ $200)	14,400	30,000	8,400
C (@ $50)	9,000	10,250	4,000
Total support costs	$ 28,800	$ 51,500	$15,550
Profit before support costs	390,000	100,500	52,000
Customer profits..............................	$361,200	$ 49,000	$36,450
Ratio of support costs to profit before support costs:	7.4%	51.2%	29.9%

2. This analysis is beneficial to EBC because it shows that large clients consume the lowest amount in terms of support services required. Medium clients are a significantly larger consumer of activities for all three of the support activities. Calculating the ratio of total support costs to profit before support costs provides additional insight into the relative profitability of the client groups. All three client groups are profitable; however, this analysis provides useful information for improving profits by working with the medium and small client groups to control support activities and related costs and attempt to bring their support costs in line with the large client group.

SUMMARY OF LEARNING OBJECTIVES

Explain the changes in the modern production environment that have affected cost structures. (p. 847) LO1

- Manufacturing organizations have shifted from labor-intensive to automated assembly processes.
- Activity-based costing recognizes that multiple activities drive manufacturing overhead costs in today's production environment.

Understand the concept of activity-based costing (ABC) and how it is applied. (p. 848) LO2

- ABC involves determining the cost of activities and tracing those costs to cost objects based on their proportionate usage of the activities.
- ABC is based on the premise that activities drive costs and that costs should be assigned to products in proportion to the volume of activities they consume.

LO3   **Explain the difference between traditional company-wide and departmental overhead methods and ABC. (p. 851)**

- Company-wide and departmental overhead methods base overhead costs on one cost driver, whereas ABC allocates overhead based on a diverse set of activities and cost drivers.

- ABC divides the overall manufacturing processes into activities, accumulates costs in cost pools for the major activities, and then assigns the costs of these activities to products or other cost objectives that benefit from these activities.

- The challenge in using ABC is determining how many activity pools should be established for a given cost measurement purpose, which costs should be assigned to each activity pool, and the appropriate activity driver for each pool.

- A complete ABC analysis would require considerations of nonmanufacturing costs, such as marketing, distribution, and customer service, before a final determination of product profitability could be made.

- Practical capacity, the maximum possible volume of activity, is generally regarded as better than actual capacity for calculating activity costs because it does not hide the cost of idle capacity within product costs, and it gives a truer cost of the activities used to produce the product.

- Procedurally, ABC is not a new method for assigning costs to objects. Traditional costing systems have used a two-stage allocation model similar to ABC to assign costs to cost pools and subsequently assign those cost pools to products using an allocation base.

LO4   **Describe the implementation of an ABC system. (p. 855)**

- Most companies initially do not abandon their traditional cost system and move to a system that uses ABC for management and financial reporting purposes because financial statements must withstand the scrutiny of auditors and tax authorities.

- Often, companies maintain traditional costing for external reporting purposes and ABC for pricing and other internal decision-making purposes.

- Although an ABC system may be complex, it merely mirrors the complexity of an organization's design, manufacturing, and distribution systems. If a firm's products are diverse and its production and distribution procedures complex, the ABC system will also be complex; however, if its products are homogeneous and its production environment relatively simple, its ABC system should also be relatively simple.

- One of the most useful applications for ABC is evaluating customer costs and distribution channel costs.

LO5   **Explain customer profitability analysis based on ABC. (p. 857)**

- A customer profitability profile can be prepared if a company knows the amount of profits (or losses) generated by each of its customers.

- Even if the company is making a profit overall, individual customers may be sold to at a loss.

- If customers have low profitability, there may be justifiable reasons for keeping them, but they should be managed intensely to attempt to reduce the activities devoted to their support.

LO6   **Explain the difference between ABC and activity-based management. (p. 859)**

- The access to ABC data enables managers to engage in activity-based management (ABM), which is the identification and selection of activities to maximize the value of the activities while minimizing their cost from the perspective of the final consumer.

- ABM focuses managerial attention on what is most important among the activities performed to create value for customers.

KEY TERMS

Activities (p. 848)	**Activity-based management**	**Practical capacity** (p. 855)
Activity-based costing	**(ABM)** (p. 847, 859)	**Production department**
(ABC) (p. 846)	**Cost drivers** (p. 850)	**costs** (p. 853)

Assignments with the ⬤ logo in the margin are available in BusinessCourse.
See the Preface of the book for details.

SELF-STUDY QUESTIONS

(Answers to Self-Study Questions are at the end of this chapter.)

1. **Which of the following is not an element of ABC?**   LO2
   a. Tracing costs to cost objects   c. Identifying the cost drivers
   b. Calculating a predetermined rate   d. All are elements of ABC.

2. **ABC differs from traditional product costing in which of the following ways?**   LO4
   a. Overhead is allocated to products in ABC.   c. Diverse cost drivers are used.
   b. Estimated costs are used.   d. It is completely accurate.

3. **Which of the following is not a benefit of customer profitability analysis?**   LO5
   a. Identifies unprofitable customers
   b. Helps track cost spent on customers
   c. Helps managers identify actions to improve specific customer profitability
   d. Speeds up production process

QUESTIONS

1. Summarize the concepts underlying activity-based costing in two sentences.   LO2
2. What steps are required to implement the two-stage activity-based costing model?   LO2
3. Define activity cost pool, activity cost driver, and cost per unit of activity.   LO2
4. Name two possible activity cost drivers for each of the following activities: maintenance, materials move-   LO2
   ment, machine setup, inspection, materials purchases, and customer service.
5. What is the premise of activity-based costing for product costing purposes?   LO2
6. In what ways does ABC product costing differ from traditional product cost methods?   LO3
7. Explain why ABC often reveals that low-volume products are over-costed and high-volume products are   LO4
   under-costed.
8. How can ABC be used to improve customer profitability analysis?   LO5
9. Explain activity-based management and how it differs from activity-based costing.   LO6

EXERCISES—SET A

E18-1A. Activities and Cost Drivers For each of the following activities, select the most appropriate cost   LO2
driver. Each cost driver may be used only once.

Activity	Cost Driver
1. Pay vendors	a. Number of different kinds of raw materials
2. Evaluate vendors	b. Number of classes offered
3. Inspect raw materials	c. Number of tables
4. Plan for purchases of raw materials	d. Number of employees
5. Packaging	e. Number of operating hours
6. Supervision	f. Number of units of raw materials received
7. Employee training	g. Number of moves
8. Clean tables	h. Number of vendors
9. Machine maintenance	i. Number of checks issued
10. Move in-process product from one work station to the next	j. Number of customer orders

E18-2A. Stage 1 ABC For Machine Shop: Assigning Costs to Activity As the chief engineer of a small   LO2
fabrication shop, Brenda Tolliver refers to herself as a "jack-of-all-trades." When an order for a new
product comes in, Brenda must do the following:

1. Design the product to meet customer requirements.
2. Prepare a bill of materials (a list of materials required to produce the product).
3. Prepare an operations list (a sequential list of the steps involved in manufacturing the product).

Each time the foundry manufactures a batch of the product, Brenda must perform these activities:

1. Schedule the job.
2. Supervise the setup of machines that will work on the job.
3. Inspect the first unit produced to verify that it meets specifications.

Brenda supervises the production employees who perform the actual work on individual units of product. She is also responsible for employee training, ensuring that production facilities are in proper operating condition, and attending professional meetings. Brenda's estimates (in percent) of time spent on each of these activities last year are as follows:

Designing product	12%
Preparing bills of materials.	5%
Preparing operations lists.	12%
Scheduling jobs	15%
Supervising setups.	5%
Inspecting first units	2%
Supervising production	20%
Training employees	18%
Maintaining facility	7%
Attending professional meetings	4%
	100%

Required
Assuming Brenda Tolliver's salary is $132,000 per year, determine the dollar amount of her salary assigned to unit-, batch-, product-, and facility-level activities. (You may need to review Chapter 15 before answering this question.)

LO2   **E18-3A. Two-Stage ABC for Manufacturing: Reassigning Costs to Cost Objectives** National Technology, LTD. has developed the following activity cost information for its manufacturing activities:

Activity	Activity Cost
Machine setup	$60.00 per batch
Movement	15.00 per batch
	0.10 per pound
Drilling.	3.00 per hole
Welding	4.00 per inch
Shaping	25.00 per hour
Assembly	18.00 per hour
Inspection.	2.00 per unit

Filling an order for a batch of 50 fireplace inserts that weighed 150 pounds each required the following:

- Three batch moves
- Two sets of inspections
- Drilling five holes in each unit
- Completing 80 inches of welds on each unit
- Thirty minutes of shaping for each unit
- One hour of assembly per unit

Required
Determine the activity cost of converting the raw materials into 50 fireplace inserts.

LO2   **E18-4A. Two-Stage ABC for Manufacturing** Assume **Sherwin-Williams Company**, a large paint manufacturer, has determined the following activity cost pools and cost driver levels for the latest period:

Activity Cost Pool	Activity Cost	Activity Cost Driver
Machine setup	$950,000	2,500 setup hours
Material handling	820,000	5,000 materials moves
Machine operation	200,000	20,000 machine hours

The following data are for the production of single batches of two products, Mirlite and Subdue:

	Mirlite	Subdue
Gallons produced...........	50,000	30,000
Direct labor hours...........	400	250
Machine hours	800	250
Direct labor cost............	$ 10,000	$ 7,500
Direct materials cost.........	$350,000	$150,000
Setup hours	15	12
Material moves.............	60	35

Required
Determine the batch and unit costs per gallon of Mirlite and Subdue using ABC.

E18-5A. Customer Profitability Analysis HyStandard Services, Inc. provides residential painting services for three home building companies, Alpine, Blue Ridge, and Pineola, and it uses a job costing system for determining the costs for completing each job. The job cost system does not capture any cost incurred by HyStandard for return touchups and refinishes after the homeowner occupies the home. HyStandard paints each house on a square footage contract price, which includes painting as well as all refinishes and touchups required after the homes are occupied. Each year, the company generates about one-third of its total revenues and gross profits from each of the three builders. The HyStandard owner has observed that the builders, however, require substantially different levels of support following the completion of jobs. The following data have been gathered:

LO5

SERVICE AND
MERCHANDISING

MBC

Support Activity	Driver	Cost per Driver Unit
Major refinishes	Hours on jobs	$60
Touchups	Number of visits	$100
Communication	Number of calls	$40

Builder	Major Refinishes	Touchups	Communication
Alpine	00	150	360
Blue Ridge	35	110	205
Pineola	42	115	190

Required
Assuming that each of the three customers produces gross profits of $100,000, calculate the profitability from each builder after taking into account the support activity required for each builder.

EXERCISES—SET B

E18-1B. Developing List of Activities for Baggage Handling at an Airport As part of a continuous improvement program, you have been asked to determine the activities involved in the baggage-handling process of a major airline at one of the airline's hubs. Prior to conducting observations and interviews, you decide that a list of possible activities would help you to better observe key activities and ask meaningful questions.

LO2

SERVICE AND
MERCHANDISING

Required
For incoming aircraft only, develop a sequential list of baggage-handling activities. Your list should contain between 8 and 10 activities.

E18-2B. Stage 1 ABC at a College: Assigning Costs to Activities An economics professor at Prince Town University devotes 50 percent of her time to teaching, 35 percent of her time to research and writing, and 15 percent of her time to service activities such as committee work and student advising. The professor teaches two semesters per year. During each semester, she teaches one section of an

LO2

SERVICE AND
MERCHANDISING

MBC

introductory economics course (with a maximum enrollment of 50 students) and one section of a graduate economics course (with a maximum enrollment of 30 students). Including course preparation, classroom instruction, and appointments with students, each course requires an equal amount of time. The economics professor is paid $135,000 per year.

Required
Determine the activity cost of instruction per student in both the introductory and the graduate economics courses.

LO2 **E18-3B. Stage 2 ABC for a Wholesale Company** Information is presented for the activity costs of Oxford Wholesale Company:

Activity Cost per Unit of Activity Driver	
Customer relations per month	$100.00 per customer
Selling	0.06 per sales dollar
Accounting	5.00 per order
Warehousing	0.50 per unit shipped
Packing	0.25 per unit shipped
Shipping	0.20 per pound shipped

The following information pertains to Oxford Wholesale Company's activities in Massachusetts for the month of March 2016:

Number of orders	235
Sales revenue	$122,200
Cost of goods sold	$68,940
Number of customers	25
Units shipped	4,700
Pounds shipped	70,500

Required
Determine the profitability of sales in Massachusetts for March 2016.

LO2 **E18-4B. Two-Stage ABC for Manufacturing** Detroit Foundry, a large manufacturer of heavy equipment components, has determined the following activity cost pools and cost driver levels for the year:

Activity Cost Pool	Activity Cost	Activity Cost Driver
Machine setup	$600,000	12,000 setup hours
Material handling	120,000	2,000 tons of materials
Machine operation	500,000	10,000 machine hours

The following data are for the production of single batches of two products, C23 Cams and U2 Shafts during the month of August:

	C23 Cams	U2 Shafts
Units produced	500	300
Machine hours	4	5
Direct labor hours	200	400
Direct labor cost	$ 5,000	$10,000
Direct materials cost	$30,000	$20,000
Tons of materials	13	8
Setup hours	3	7

Required
Determine the unit costs of C23 Cams and U2 Shafts using ABC.

LO2, 3 **E18-5B. Activity-Based Costing** Slack Corporation has the following predicted indirect costs and cost drivers for 2016 for the given activity cost pools:

	Fabrication Department	Finishing Department	Cost Driver
Maintenance.	$ 20,000	$10,000	Machine hours
Materials handling	30,000	15,000	Material moves
Machine setups	70,000	5,000	Machine setups
Inspections.	—	25,000	Inspection hours
	$120,000	$55,000	

The following activity predictions were also made for the year:

	Fabrication Department	Finishing Department
Machine hours	10,000	5,000
Materials moves.	3,000	1,500
Machine setups	700	50
Inspection hours.	—	1,000

It is assumed that the cost per unit of activity for a given activity does not vary between departments.

Slack's president, Charles Slack, is trying to evaluate the company's product mix strategy regarding two of its five product models, ZX300 and SL500. The company has been using a company-wide overhead rate based on machine hours but is considering switching to either department rates or activity-based rates. The production manager has provided the following data for the production of a batch of 100 units for each of these models:

	ZX300	SL500
Direct materials cost.	$12,000	$18,000
Direct labor cost.	$5,000	$4,000
Machine hours (Fabrication).	500	700
Machine hours (Finishing).	200	100
Materials moves.	30	50
Machine setups	5	9
Inspection hours.	30	60

Required

a. Determine the cost of one unit each of ZX300 and SL500, assuming a company-wide overhead rate is used based on total machine hours.

b. Determine the cost of one unit of ZX300 and SL500, assuming department overhead rates are used. Overhead is assigned based on machine hours in both departments.

c. Determine the cost of one unit of ZX300 and SL500, assuming activity-based overhead rates are used for maintenance, materials handling, machine setup, and inspection activities.

d. Comment on the results of these cost calculations.

PROBLEMS—SET A

P18-1A. Calculating Manufacturing Overhead Rates Glassman Company accumulated the following data for 2016:

LO3

Milling Department manufacturing overhead.	$344,000
Finishing Department manufacturing overhead.	$120,000
Machine hours used	
Milling Department	10,000 hours
Finishing Department	2,000 hours
Labor hours used	
Milling Department	1,000 hours
Finishing Department	1,000 hours

Required

a.   Calculate the company-wide manufacturing overhead rate using machine hours as the allocation base.
b.   Calculate the company-wide manufacturing overhead rate using direct labor hours as the allocation base.
c.   Calculate department overhead rates using machine hours in Milling and direct labor hours in Finishing as the allocation bases.
d.   Calculate department overhead rates using direct labor hours in Milling and machine hours in Finishing as the allocation bases.
e.   Which of these allocation systems seems to be more appropriate? Explain.

LO4   **P18-2A. Calculating Activity-Based Costing Overhead Rates** Assume that manufacturing overhead for Glassman Company in the previous exercise consisted of the following activities and costs:

Setup (1,000 setup hours)	$144,000
Production scheduling (400 batches).	60,000
Production engineering (60 change orders)	120,000
Supervision (2,000 direct labor hours)	56,000
Machine maintenance (12,000 machine hours)	84,000
Total activity costs	$464,000

The following additional data were provided for Job 845:

Direct materials costs	$7,000
Direct labor cost (5 Milling direct labor hours;	
35 Finishing direct labor hours)	$1,000
Setup hours	5 hours
Production scheduling	1 batch
Machine hours used (25 Milling machine hours;	
5 Finishing machine hours).	30 hours
Production engineering	3 change orders

Required

a.   Calculate the cost per unit of activity driver for each activity cost category.
b.   Calculate the cost of Job 845 using ABC to assign the overhead costs.
c.   Calculate the cost of Job 845 using the company-wide overhead rate based on machine hours calculated in the previous exercise.
d.   Calculate the cost of Job 845 using a machine hour departmental overhead rate for the Milling Department and a direct labor hour overhead rate for the Finishing Department (see P18-1A).

LO3, 4   **P18-3A. Traditional Product Costing Versus Activity-Based Costing** Assume that **Panasonic Company** has determined its estimated total manufacturing overhead cost for one of its plants to be $204,000, consisting of the following activity cost pools for the current month:

Activity Centers	Activity Costs	Cost Drivers	Activity Level
Assembly setups	$ 45,000	Setup hours	1,500
Materials handling	15,000	Number of moves.	300
Assembly	120,000	Assembly hours	12,000
Maintenance.	24,000	Maintenance hours.	1,200
Total	$204,000		

Total direct labor hours used during the month were 8,000. Panasonic produces many different electronic products, including the following two products produced during the current month:

	Model X301	Model Z205
Units produced....	1,000	1,000
Direct materials costs....	$15,000	$15,000
Direct labor costs....	$12,500	$12,500
Direct labor hours....	500	500
Setup hours....	50	100
Materials moves....	25	50
Assembly hours....	800	800
Maintenance hours....	10	40

Required

a.   Calculate the total per-unit cost of each model using direct labor hours to assign manufacturing overhead to products.

b.   Calculate the total per-unit cost of each model using activity-based costing to assign manufacturing overhead to products.

c.   Comment on the accuracy of the two methods for determining product costs.

d.   Discuss some of the strategic implications of your answers to the previous requirements.

P18-4A.   Customer Profitability Analysis   Gonalong, Inc., has 10 customers that account for all of its $4,500,000   **LO5**
of net income. Its activity-based costing system is able to assign all costs, except for $650,000 of general
administrative costs, to key activities incurred in connection with serving its customers. A customer
profitability analysis based on activity costing produced the following customer profits and losses:

Customer #1....	$ 346,000
#2....	624,000
#3....	(257,000)
#4....	969,000
#5....	1,040,000
#6....	872,000
#7....	628,000
#8....	322,000
#9....	(105,000)
#10....	711,000
Total....	$5,150,000

Required

Prepare a customer profitability profile graph. Sort the customers in order of profitability from most
profitable to least profitable, then plot the cumulative profit with total profits along the y-axis and customers along the x-axis. What is the maximum amount of profit that Gonalong could achieve if they
were to eliminate their unprofitable customers?

P18-5A.   Customer Profitability Analysis   Refer to the previous exercise P18-4A for Gonalong, Inc.   **LO5**

Required

a.   If Gonalong were to notify customers 3 and 9 that it will no longer be able to provide them services in the future, will that increase company profits by $362,000? Why or why not?

b.   What is the primary benefit of preparing a customer profitability analysis?

P18-6A.   ABC—A Service Application   Grand Haven is a senior living community that offers a full range of   **LO2**
services including independent living, assisted living, and skilled nursing care. The assisted living division provides residential space, meals, and medical services (MS) to its residents. The current cost-   **SERVICE AND**
ing system adds the cost of all of these services (space, meals, and MS) and divides by total resident   **MERCHANDISING**
days to get a cost per resident day for each month. Recognizing that MS tends to vary significantly
among the residents, Grand Haven's accountant recommended that an ABC system be designed to
calculate more accurately the cost of MS provided to residents. She decided that residents should
be classified into four categories (A, B, C, D) based on the level of services received, with group A
representing the lowest level of service and D representing the highest level of service. Two cost drivers being considered for measuring MS costs are number of assistance calls and number of assistant
contacts. A contact is registered each time an assistance professional provides medical services or aid
to a resident. The accountant has gathered the following data for the most recent annual period:

Resident Classification	Annual Resident Days	Annual Assistance Hours	Number of Assistance Contacts
A.................	8,760	15,000	60,000
B.................	6,570	20,000	52,000
C.................	4,380	22,500	52,000
D.................	2,190	32,500	52,000
	21,900	90,000	216,000

Other data:	
Total cost of medical services for the period	$2,500,000
Total cost of meals and residential space	$1,642,500

Required (Round Answers to the Nearest Dollar)

a. Determine the ABC cost of a resident day for each category of residents using assistance hours as the cost driver.

b. Determine the ABC cost of a resident day for each category of residents using assistance contacts as the cost driver.

c. Which cost driver do you think provides the more accurate measure of the cost per day for a Grand Haven resident?

LO2   **P18-7A. Two-Stage ABC for Manufacturing** Merlot Company has determined its activity cost pools and cost drivers to be the following:

Cost Pools	
Setup	$ 56,000
Material handling	12,800
Machine operation	240,000
Packing..	60,000
Total indirect manufacturing costs........................	$368,800

Cost drivers	
Setups...	350
Material moves	640
Machine hours	20,000
Packing orders	1,200

One product made by Merlot, metal casements, used the following activities during the period to produce 500 units:

Setups	20
Material moves..	80
Machine hours	1,900
Packing orders..	150

Required

a. Calculate the cost per unit of activity for each activity cost pool for Merlot Company.

b. Calculate the manufacturing overhead cost per metal casement manufactured during the period.

LO2   **P18-8A. Activity-Based Costing in a Service Organization** Red River Banking Company has ten automatic teller machines (ATMs) spread throughout the city maintained by the ATM Department. You have been assigned the task of determining the cost of operating each machine. Management will use the information you develop, along with other information pertaining to the volume and type of transactions at each machine, to evaluate the desirability of continuing to operate each machine and/or changing security arrangements for a particular machine.

SERVICE AND MERCHANDISING

The ATM Department consists of a total of six employees: a supervisor, a head cashier, two associate cashiers, and two maintenance personnel. The associate cashiers make between two and four daily trips to each machine to collect and replenish cash and to replenish supplies, deposit tickets, and so forth. Each machine contains a small computer that automatically summarizes and reports transactions to the head cashier. The head cashier reconciles the activities of the two associate cashiers to the computerized reports. The supervisor, who does not handle cash, reviews the reconciliation. When an automatic teller's computer, a customer, or a cashier reports a problem, the two maintenance employees and one cashier are dispatched immediately. The cashier removes all cash and transaction records, and the maintenance employees repair the machine.

Maintenance employees spend all of their time on maintenance-related activities. The associate cashiers spend approximately 50 percent of their time on maintenance-related activities and 50 percent on daily trips. The head cashier's time is divided, with 75 percent directly related to daily trips to each machine and 25 percent related to supervising cashiers on maintenance calls. The supervisor devotes 20 percent of the time to daily trips to each machine and 80 percent to the equal supervision of each employee. Cost information for a recent month follows:

Salaries	
Supervisor.	$4,000
Head cashier.	3,000
Other ($1,800 each)	7,200
Lease and operating costs	
Cashiers' service vehicle	1,200
Maintenance service vehicle.	1,400
Office rent and utilities	2,300
Machine lease, space rent, and utilities ($1,500 each).	15,000
Total	$34,100

Related monthly activity information for this month follows:

Machine	Routine Trips	Maintenance Hours
1	30	5
2	90	17
3	60	15
4	60	30
5	120	15
6	30	10
7	90	25
8	120	5
9	60	20
10	60	18
Total	720	160

Additional information follows:

- The office is centrally located with about equal travel time to each machine.
- Maintenance hours include travel time.
- The cashiers' service vehicle is used exclusively for routine visits.
- The office space is divided equally between the supervisor and the head cashier.

Required

a. Determine the monthly operating costs of machines 7 and 8 when cost assignments are based on the number of machines.

b. Determine the activity cost of a routine trip and a maintenance hour for the month given. Round answers to the nearest cent.

c. Determine the operating costs assigned and reassigned to machines 7 and 8 when activity-based costing is used.

d. How can ABC cost information be used by Red River Banking Company to improve the overall management of monthly operating costs?

P18-9A. Product Costing: Company-wide Overhead Versus ABC LaMesa produces machine parts as a contract provider for a large manufacturing company. LaMesa produces two particular parts, shafts and gears. The competition is keen among contract producers, and LaMesa's top management realizes   **LO3, 4**

how vulnerable its market is to cost-cutting competitors. Hence, having a very accurate understanding of costs is important to LaMesa's survival.

LaMesa's president, Jose Rodriguez, has observed that the company's current cost to produce shafts is $21.35, and the current cost to produce gears is $12.36. He indicated to the controller that he suspects some problems with the cost system because LaMesa is suddenly experiencing extraordinary competition on shafts, but it seems to have a virtual corner on the gears market. He is even considering dropping the shaft line and converting the company to a one-product manufacturer of gears. He asked the controller, Felix Bernhardt, to conduct a thorough cost study and to consider whether changes in the cost system are necessary. The controller collected the following data about the company's costs and various manufacturing activities for the most recent month:

	Shafts	Gears
Production units	50,000	10,500
Selling price	$31.86	$24
Overhead per unit (based on direct labor hours)	$12.82	$6.10
Materials and direct labor cost per unit	$8.53	$6.26
Number of production runs	10	20
Number of purchasing and receiving orders processed	40	100
Number of machine hours	12,750	6,000
Number of direct labor hours	25,000	2,500
Number of engineering hours	5,000	5,000
Number of material moves	50	40

The controller was able to summarize the company's total manufacturing overhead into the following pools:

Setup costs	$ 30,000
Machine cost	175,000
Purchasing and receiving costs	210,000
Engineering costs	200,000
Materials handling costs	90,000
Total	$705,000

Required

a. Calculate LaMesa's current company-wide overhead rate based on direct labor hours.
b. Verify LaMesa's calculation of overhead cost per unit of $12.82 for shafts and $6.10 for gears.
c. Calculate the manufacturing overhead cost per unit for shafts and gears using activity-based costing, assuming each of the five cost pools represents a separate activity pool. Use the most appropriate activity driver for assigning activity costs to the two products.
d. Comment on LaMesa's current cost system and the reason the company is facing fierce competition for shafts but little competition for gears.

PROBLEMS—SET B

LO2, 3   **P18-1B. Activity-Based Costing and Conventional Costs Compared** Hickory Grill Company manufactures two types of cooking grills: the Gas Cooker and the Charcoal Smoker. The Cooker is a premium product sold in upscale outdoor shops; the Smoker is sold in major discount stores. Following is information pertaining to the manufacturing costs for the current month.

	Gas Cooker	Charcoal Smoker
Units	1,000	5,000
Number of batches	50	10
Number of batch moves	80	20
Direct materials	$40,000	$100,000
Direct labor	$20,000	$ 25,000

Manufacturing overhead follows:

Activity	Cost	Cost Driver
Materials acquisition and inspection	$30,800	Amount of direct materials cost
Materials movement	16,200	Number of batch moves
Scheduling	36,000	Number of batches
	$83,000	

Required

a. Determine the total and per-unit costs of manufacturing the Gas Cooker and Charcoal Smoker for the month, assuming all manufacturing overhead is assigned on the basis of direct labor dollars.

b. Determine the total and per-unit costs of manufacturing the Gas Cooker and Charcoal Smoker for the month, assuming manufacturing overhead is assigned using activity-based costing.

P18-2B. Activity-Based Costing Versus Conventional Costing Refer to the previous exercise in P18-1B for Hickory Grill. **LO2, 3**

Required

a. Comment on the differences between the solutions to requirements (a) and (b). Which is more accurate? What errors might managers make if all manufacturing overhead costs are assigned on the basis of direct labor dollars?

b. Comment on the adequacy of the preceding data to meet management's needs.

P18-3B. Traditional Product Costing Versus Activity-Based Costing High Country Outfitters, Inc., makes **LO2, 3** backpacks for large sporting goods chains that are sold under the customers' store brand names. The accounting department has identified the following overhead costs and cost drivers for next year:

Overhead Item	Expected Costs	Cost Driver	Maximum Quantity
Setup costs	$936,000	Number of setups	7,200
Ordering costs	240,000	Number of orders	60,000
Maintenance	1,200,000	Number of machine hours	80,000
Power	120,000	Number of kilowatt hours	600,000

Total predicted direct labor hours for next year is 60,000. The following data are for two recently completed jobs:

	Job 201	Job 202
Cost of direct materials	$13,500	$15,000
Cost of direct labor	$19,125	$71,250
Number of units completed	1,125	915
Number of direct labor hours	270	330
Number of setups	18	22
Number of orders	24	45
Number of machine hours	540	450
Number of kilowatt hours	270	360

Required

a. Determine the unit cost for each job using a traditional company-wide overhead rate based on direct labor hours.

b. Determine the unit cost for each job using ABC. (Round answers to two decimal places.)

c. As the manager of High Country, is there additional information that you would want to help you evaluate the pricing and profitability of Jobs 201 and 202?

d. Assuming the company has been using the method required in part a, how should management react to the findings in part b?

LO5 P18-4B. Customer Profitability Analysis Rogers Aeronautics, LTD, is a British aeronautics subcontract company that designs and manufactures electronic control systems for commercial airlines. The vast majority of all commercial aircraft are manufactured by Boeing in the U.S. and Airbus in Europe; however, there is a relatively small group of companies that manufacture narrow-body commercial jets. Assume for this exercise that Rogers does contract work for the two major manufacturers plus three companies in the second tier.

Because competition is intense in the industry, Rogers has always operated on a fairly thin 20% gross profit margin; hence, it is crucial that it manage non-manufacturing overhead costs effectively in order to achieve an acceptable net profit margin. With declining profit margins in recent years, Rogers Aeronautics' CEO, Len Rogers, has become concerned that the cost of obtaining contracts and maintaining relations with its five major customers may be getting out of hand. You have been hired to conduct a customer profitability analysis.

Rogers Aeronautics' non-manufacturing overhead consists of $2.5 million of general and administrative (G&A) expense, (including, among other expenses, the CEO's salary and bonus and the cost of operating the company's corporate jet) and selling and customer support expenses of $3 million (including 5% sales commissions and $1,050,000 of additional costs).

The accounting staff determined that the $1,050,000 of additional selling and customer support expenses related to the following four activity cost pools:

Activity	Activity Cost Driver	Cost per Unit of Activity
1. Sales visits	Number of visit days	$1,200
2. Product adjustments	Number of adjustments	1,500
3. Phone and email contacts	Number of calls/contacts	150
4. Promotion and entertainment events	Number of events	1,500

Financial and activity data on the five customers follows (Sales and Gross Profit data in millions):

Customer	Sales	Gross Profit	Quantity of Sales and Support Activity			
			Activity 1	Activity 2	Activity 3	Activity 4
#1	$17	$3.40	106	23	220	82
#2	$12	2.4	130	36	354	66
#3	$3	0.6	52	10	180	74
#4	$4	0.8	34	6	138	18
#5	$3	0.6	16	5	104	10
	$39	$7.80	338	80	996	250

In addition to the above, the sales staff used the corporate jet at a cost of $800 per hour for trips to customers as follows:

Customer #1.	24 hours
Customer #2.	36 hours
Customer #3.	5 hours
Customer #4.	0 hours
Customer #5.	6 hours

The total cost of operating the airplane is included in general and administrative expense; none is included in selling and customer support costs.

Required

a. Prepare a customer profitability analysis for Rogers Aeronautics that shows the gross profits less all expenses that can reasonably be assigned to the five customers.
b. Now assuming that the remaining general and administrative costs are assigned to the five customers based on relative sales dollars, calculate net profit for each customer.
c. Discuss the merits of the analysis in part *a* versus part *b*.

P18-5B. Two-Stage ABC for Manufacturing with Variances Montreat Manufacturing has developed the **LO2** following activity cost pool information for its 2016 manufacturing activities:

	Budgeted Activity Cost	Activity Cost Driver at Practical Capacity
Purchasing and materials handling	$675,000	900,000 kilograms
Setup	700,000	1,120 setups
Machine operations	954,000	12,000 hours
First unit inspection	50,000	1,000 batches
Packaging...............................	250,000	312,500 units

Actual 2016 production information is as follows:

	Standard Product A	Standard Product B	Specialty Products
Units.....................................	150,000	100,000	50,000
Batches	100	80	600
Setups*..................................	300	160	900
Machine operations (hours)	6,000	3,000	2,000
Kilograms of raw materials................	400,000	300,000	200,000
Direct materials costs....................	$900,000	$600,000	$820,000

*Some products require setups on two or more machines.

Required

a. Determine the unit cost of each product for Montreat Manufacturing.

b. Explain why the unit cost of the specialty products is so much higher than the unit cost of Standard Product A or Standard Product B.

P18-6B. ABC Costing for a Service Organization Fairfield Mortgage Company is a full-service residential **LO2** mortgage company in the Atlanta area that operates in a very competitive market. The CEO, Richard Sissom, is concerned about operating costs associated with processing mortgage applications and has decided to install an ABC costing system to help him get a handle on costs. Although labor hours seem to be the primary driver of the cost of processing a new mortgage, the labor cost for the different activities involved in processing new loans varies widely. The Accounting Department has provided the following data for the company's five major cost pools for 2016:

Activity Cost Pools		Activity Drivers	
Taking customer applications ...	$ 300,000	Time—assistant managers........	12,000 hours
Conducting credit investigations .	450,000	Time—credit managers	16,500 hours
Underwriting.................	525,000	Time—Underwriting Department ...	10,000 hours
Preparing loan packages	200,000	Time—Processing Department	8,000 hours
Closing loans	600,000	Time—Legal Department hours	6,000 hours
	$2,075,000		52,500 hours

During 2016, the company processed and issued 5,000 new mortgages, two of which are summarized here with regard to activities used to process the mortgages:

	Loan 5066	Loan 5429
Application processing hours......................	1.50	2.75
Credit investigating hours	4.00	3.00
Underwriting hours...............................	2.50	4.75
Processing hours	3.50	3.00
Legal processing hours	1.50	1.50
Total hours	13.00	15.00

Required

a. Determine the cost per unit of activity for each activity cost pool.

b. Determine the cost of processing loans 5066 and 5429.

c. Determine the cost of preparing loans 5066 and 5429 assuming that an average cost per hour for all activities is used.

d. Compare and discuss your answers to requirements (*b*) and (*c*).

LO3   **P18-7B. Product Costing: Department Versus ABC for Overhead**   Advertising Technologies, Inc. (ATI) specializes in providing both published and online advertising services for the business marketplace. The company monitors its costs based on the cost per column inch of published space printed in print advertising media and based on the cost per minute of telephone advertising time delivered on "The AD Line," a computer-based, online advertising service. ATI has one new competitor, Tel-a-Ad, in its local teleadvertising market; and with increased competition, ATI has seen a decline in sales of online advertising in recent years. ATI's president, Robert Beard, believes that predatory pricing by Tel-a-Ad has caused the problem. The following is a recent conversation between Robert and Jane Minnear, director of marketing for ATI.

Jane: I just received a call from one of our major customers concerning our advertising rates on "The AD Line" who said that a sales rep from another firm (it had to be Tel-a-Ad) had offered the same service at $1 per minute, which is $1.50 per minute less than our price.

Robert: It's costing about $1.27 per minute to produce that product. I don't see how they can afford to sell it so cheaply. I'm not convinced that we should meet the price. Perhaps the better strategy is to emphasize producing and selling more published ads, which we're more experienced with and where our margins are high and we have virtually no competition.

Jane: You may be right. Based on a recent survey of our customers, I think we can raise the price significantly for published advertising and still not lose business.

Robert: That sounds promising; however, before we make a major recommitment to publishing, let's explore other possible explanations. I want to know how our costs compare with our competitors. Maybe we could be more efficient and find a way to earn a good return on teleadvertising.

After this meeting, Robert and Jane requested an investigation of production costs and comparative efficiency of producing published versus online advertising services. The controller, Tim Gentry, indicated that ATI's efficiency was comparable to that of its competitors and prepared the following cost data:

	Published Advertising	Online Advertising
Estimated number of production units.	200,000	10,000,000
Selling price	$200	$2.50
Direct product costs.	$21,000,000	$5,000,000
Overhead allocation*	$9,800,000	$7,700,000
Overhead per unit.	$49	$0.77
Direct costs per unit.	$105	$0.50
Number of customers.	180,000	25,000
Number of salesperson days	32,000	5,500
Number of art and design hours	35,000	5,000
Number of creative services subcontract hours	100,000	25,000
Number of customer service calls	72,000	8,000

*Based on direct labor costs

Upon examining the data, Robert decided that he wanted to know more about the overhead costs because they were such a high proportion of total production costs. He was provided the following list of overhead costs and told that they were currently being assigned to products in proportion to direct labor costs.

Selling costs	$7,500,000
Visual and audio design costs	3,000,000
Creative services costs	5,000,000
Customer service costs	2,000,000

Required

Using the data provided by the controller, prepare analyses to help Robert and Jane in making their decisions. (*Hint:* Prepare cost calculations for both product lines using ABC to see whether there is any significant difference in their unit costs). Should ATI switch from the fast-growing, online advertising market back into the well-established published advertising market? Does the charge of predatory pricing seem valid? Why are customers likely to be willing to pay a higher price to get published services? Do traditional costing and activity-based costing lead to the same conclusions?

P18-8B. **Unit-Level and Multiple-Level Cost Assignments** CarryAll Company produces briefcases from leather, fabric, and synthetic materials in a single production department. The basic product is a standard briefcase made from leather and lined with fabric. CarryAll has a good reputation in the market because the standard briefcase is a high-quality item that has been produced for many years.   **LO2**

Last year, the company decided to expand its product line and produce specialty briefcases for special orders. These briefcases differ from the standard in that they vary in size, contain both leather and synthetic materials, and are imprinted with the buyer's logo (the standard briefcase is simply imprinted with the CarryAll name in small letters). The decision to use some synthetic materials in the briefcase was made to hold down the materials cost. To reduce the labor costs per unit, most of the cutting and stitching on the specialty briefcases is done by automated machines, which are used to a much lesser degree in the production of the standard briefcases. Because of these changes in the design and production of the specialty briefcases, CarryAll management believed that they would cost less to produce than the standard briefcases. However, because they are specialty items, they were priced slightly higher; standards are priced at $30 and specialty briefcases at $32.

After reviewing last month's results of operations, CarryAll's president became concerned about the profitability of the two product lines because the standard briefcase showed a loss while the specialty briefcase showed a greater profit margin than expected. The president is wondering whether the company should drop the standard briefcase and focus entirely on specialty items. Units and cost data for last month's operations as reported to the president are as follows:

	Standard	Specialty
Units produced.	10,000	2,500
Direct materials		
Leather (1 sq. yd. × $15.00; ½ sq. yd. × $15.00)	$15.00	$ 7.50
Fabric (1 sq. yd. × $5.00; 1 sq. yd. × $5.00).	5.00	5.00
Synthetic.		5.00
Total Materials	20.00	17.50
Direct Labor (½ hr. × $12.00; ¼ hr. × $12.00).	6.00	3.00
Manufacturing Overhead (½ hr. × $8.98; ¼ hr. × $8.98).	4.49	2.25
Cost per unit.	$30.49	$22.75

Manufacturing overhead is applied on the basis of direct labor hours. The rate of $8.98 per direct labor hour was calculated by dividing the total overhead ($50,500) by the direct labor hours (5,625). As shown in the table, the cost of a standard briefcase is $0.49 higher than its $30 sales price; the specialty briefcase has a cost of only $22.75, for a gross profit per unit of $9.25. The problem with these costs is that they do not accurately reflect the activities involved in manufacturing each product. Determining the costs using ABC should provide better product costing data to help gauge the actual profitability of each product line.

The manufacturing overhead costs must be analyzed to determine the activities driving the costs. Assume that the following costs and cost drivers have been identified:

- The Purchasing Department's cost is $6,000. The major activity driving these costs is the number of purchase orders processed. During the month, the Purchasing Department prepared the following number of purchase orders for the materials indicated:

Leather	20
Fabric	30
Synthetic material.	50

- The cost of receiving and inspecting materials is $7,500. These costs are driven by the number of deliveries. During the month, the following number of deliveries were made:

Leather	30
Fabric	40
Synthetic material	80

- Production line setup cost is $10,000. Setup activities involve changing the machines to produce the different types of briefcases. Each setup for production of the standard briefcases requires one hour; each setup for specialty briefcases requires two hours. Standard briefcases are produced in batches of 200, and specialty briefcases are produced in batches of 25. During the last month, there were 50 setups for the standard item and 100 setups for the specialty item.
- The cost of inspecting finished goods is $8,000. All briefcases are inspected to ensure that quality standards are met. However, the final inspection of standard briefcases takes very little time because the employees identify and correct quality problems as they do the hand cutting and stitching. A survey of the personnel responsible for inspecting the final products showed that 150 hours were spent on standard briefcases and 250 hours on specialty briefcases during the month.
- Equipment-related costs are $6,000. Equipment-related costs include repairs, depreciation, and utilities. Management has determined that a logical basis for assigning these costs to products is machine hours. A standard briefcase requires 1/2 hour of machine time, and a specialty briefcase requires two hours. Thus, during the last month, 5,000 hours of machine time relate to the standard line and 5,000 hours relate to the specialty line.
- Plant-related costs are $13,000. These costs include property taxes, insurance, administration, and others. For the purpose of determining average unit costs, they are to be assigned to products using machine hours.

Required

a. Using activity-based costing concepts, what overhead costs should be assigned to the two products?
b. What is the unit cost of each product using activity-based costing concepts?
c. Reevaluate the president's concern about the profitability of the two product lines.
d. Discuss the merits of activity-based management as it relates to CarryAll's ABC cost system.

CERTIFIED MANAGEMENT ACCOUNTANT (CMA®) EXAM SAMPLE QUESTIONS

CMA18-1. A profitable company with five departments uses plantwide overhead rates for its highly diversified operation. The firm is studying a change to either allocating overhead by using departmental rates or using activity-based costing (ABC). Which one of these two methods will likely result in the use of a greater number of cost allocation bases and more accurate costing results?

	Greater Number of Allocation Bases	More Accurate Costing Results
a.	Departmental	Departmental
b.	Departmental	ABC
c.	ABC	Departmental
d.	ABC	ABC

CMA18-2. All of the following are likely to be used as a cost allocation base in activity-based costing **except** the

a. number of different materials used to manufacture the product.
b. units of materials used to manufacture the product.
c. number of vendors supplying the materials used to manufacture the product.
d. cost of materials used to manufacture the product.

CMA18-3. Pelder Products Company manufactures two types of engineering diagnostic equipment used in construction. The two products are based upon different technologies, x-ray and ultra-sound, but are manufactured in the same factory. Pelder has computed the manufacturing cost of the x-ray and ultra-sound products by adding together direct materials, direct labor, and overhead cost applied based on the number of direct labor hours. The factory has three overhead departments that support the single production line that makes both products. Budgeted overhead spending for the departments is as follows.

Department			
Engineering design	**Material handling**	**Setup**	**Total**
$6,000	$5,000	$3,000	$14,000

Pelder's budgeted manufacturing activities and costs for the period are as follows.

	Product	
Activity	**X-Ray**	**Ultra-Sound**
Units produced and sold	50	100
Direct materials used	$5,000	$ 8,000
Direct labor hours used	100	300
Direct labor cost.	$4,000	$12,000
Number of parts used	400	600
Number of engineering changes	2	1
Number of product setups.	8	7

The budgeted cost to manufacture one ultra-sound machine using the activity-based costing method is

    a. $225.
    b. $264.
    c. $293.
    d. $305.

CMA18-4. The Chocolate Baker specializes in chocolate baked goods. The firm has long assessed the profitability of a product line by comparing revenues to the cost of goods sold. However, Barry White, the firm's new accountant, wants to use an activity-based costing system that takes into consideration the cost of the delivery person. Listed below are activity and cost information relating to two of Chocolate Baker's major products.

	Muffins	**Cheesecake**
Revenue	$53,000	$46,000
Cost of goods sold.	26,000	21,000
Delivery Activity		
Number of deliveries	150	85
Average length of delivery	10 Minutes	15 Minutes
Cost per hour for delivery.	$20.00	$20.00

Using activity-based costing, which one of the following statements is correct?

    a.   The muffins are $2,000 more profitable.
    b.   The cheesecakes are $75 more profitable.
    c.   The muffins are $1,925 more profitable.
    d.   The muffins have a higher profitability as a percentage of sales and, therefore, are more advantageous.

CMA18-5. Atmel Inc. manufactures and sells two products. Data with regard to these products are given below.

	Product A	Product B
Units produced and sold	30,000	12,000
Machine hours required per unit	2	3
Receiving orders per product line	50	150
Production orders per product line	12	18
Production runs	8	12
Inspections	20	30

Total budgeted machine hours are 100,000. The budgeted overhead costs are shown below.

Receiving costs	$ 450,000
Engineering costs	300,000
Machine setup costs	25,000
Inspection costs	200,000
Total budgeted overhead costs	$ 975,000

Using activity-based costing, the per unit overhead cost allocation of receiving costs for product A is

a. $3.75.
b. $10.75.
c. $19.50.
d. $28.13.

EXTENDING YOUR KNOWLEDGE

LO4

EYK18-1. Business Decision Case The Reserve Club is a traditional private golf and country club that has three different categories of memberships: golf, tennis & swimming, and social. Golf members have access to all amenities and programs in the Club, Tennis & Swimming members have access to all amenities and programs except use of the golf course, and Social members have access to only the social activities of the club, excluding golf, tennis, and swimming. All members have clubhouse privileges, including use of the bar and restaurant, which is operated by an outside contractor. During the past year, the average membership in each category, along with the number of club visits during the year, was

	Members	Visits
Golf	260	9,360
Tennis & Swimming	50	1,500
Social	120	2,160

Some members of the Club have been complaining that heavy users of the Club are not bearing their share of the costs through their membership fees. Dess Rosmond, General Manager of the Reserve Club, agrees that monthly fees paid by the various member groups should be based on the annual average amount of cost-related activities provided by the club for the three groups, and he intends to set fees on that basis for the coming year. The annual direct costs of operating the golf course, tennis courts, and swimming pool have been calculated by the Club's controller as follows:

Golf course	$900,000
Swimming pool	50,000
Tennis courts	25,000

The operation of the bar and restaurant and all related costs, including depreciation on the bar and restaurant facilities, are excluded from this analysis. In addition to the above costs, the Club incurs general overhead costs in the following amounts for the most recent (and typical) year:

General Ledger Overhead Accounts	Amounts
Indirect labor for the Club management staff (the general manager, assistant general manager, membership manager, and club controller)....................	$250,000
Utilities (other than those directly related to golf, swimming and tennis)...............	24,000
Website maintenance..	2,000
Postage	5,000
Computers and information systems maintenance	7,500
Clubhouse maintenance and depreciation.....................................	30,000
Liability insurance...	4,000
Security contract	12,000
	$334,500

Dess believes that the best way to assign most of the overhead costs to the three membership categories is with an activity-based system that recognizes four key activities that occur regularly in the club:

    Recruiting and providing orientation for new members

    Maintaining the membership roster and communicating with members

    Planning, scheduling and managing Club events

    Maintaining the financial records and reporting for the Club

Required

a.   Identify and explain which overhead costs can reasonably be assigned to one or more of the four key activities, and suggest a basis for making the assignment.

b.   Identify a cost driver for each activity cost pool that would seem to be suitable for assigning the activity cost pool to the three membership categories.

c.   Suggest a method for assigning any overhead costs to the three membership categories that cannot reasonably be assigned to activity pools.

d.   Comment on the suitability of ABC to this cost assignment situation.

ANSWERS TO SELF-STUDY QUESTIONS:

1. d, (pp. 850–851)   2. c, (p. 855)   3. d, (pp. 857–859)

YOUR TURN! SOLUTION

Solution 18.1

Your response might include the following major points:

1. An ABC costing system would help the company to more completely identify all of the activities that cause the company to incur the overhead cost in the first place.
2. An ABC costing system would provide for more accurate tracing of overhead costs to products because the overhead costs are more closely associated with the related activity (or cost driver).
3. Having a better understanding of the costs of each product will help management set production priorities, sales targets, and prices to maximize company profits.

19

Cost-Volume-Profit Relationships

PAST

Chapter 18 explored activity-based costing and its benefits relative to traditional company-wide and departmental overhead allocation, and contrasted it with activity-based management.

PRESENT

Chapter 19 utilizes our understanding of cost behavior to determine break-even and make planning and budgeting decisions.

FUTURE

Chapter 20 discusses the preparation of a variable income statement and reporting for segments of a business.

LEARNING OBJECTIVES

1. **Develop** an understanding of how specific types of costs change in response to volume changes. *(p. 884)*

2. **Define** the concept of *relevant range. (p. 887)*

3. **Outline** the approach to developing cost formulas. *(p. 888)*

4. **Present** a discussion of and a formula for calculating the break-even point. *(p. 893)*

5. **Define** *contribution margin* and *contribution margin ratio* and **present** alternate break-even formulas and examples of their application. *(p. 895)*

6. **Discuss** approaches to planning net income using cost-volume-profit analyses. *(p. 897)*

iTUNES

When your great-grandmother was growing up, if she wanted to listen to her favorite musician sing her latest smash hit over and over, she would purchase a vinyl record and play it on a small turntable in her bedroom or her parents' hi-fi stereo turntable in the living room. The only way to listen to music in the car was on the radio, with the choice of radio station usually controlled by her mom and dad. Your grandparents probably listened to 8-track cartridges (which consist of a continuous-loop magnetic tape) or compact cassettes through the car's entertainment system. However, by the time your parents were rebelling against their parents' musical preferences, vinyl record and cassette sales were in decline. For your parents, the compact disc (CD) was the medium of choice, and by the late 1980s other forms of recorded music began to disappear from music stores. The CD became the dominant form of recorded music sales.

Once again, the way the new generation acquires and listens to its favorite artists has changed with the rise of the Internet and electronic music files. The late 1990s and early 2000s witnessed a decline in the sales of music CDs due to the availability of MP3 file sharing over the Internet. This generation's teenagers and young adults can easily purchase and share their favorite music with friends over the Internet and, sometimes, download copies from easily accessible websites for free. Because the Internet provides easy opportunities for pirating, the music industry has been in a state of crisis.

Given the industry's struggles with the electronic dissemination of music, iTunes was launched by Apple in 2003. An Internet-based music retailing business, it was originally conceived as a "break-even" business intended to drive sales of Apple hardware, principally the iPod, which had been introduced in 2001. Apple's business strategy was to provide individual songs at "cost" that could be downloaded to the iPod as part of the customer's music library to be played on demand. Apple would make its profit on the sale of the iPod.

Many industry experts predicted that iTunes was doomed to fail from the start. Why would consumers pay even $0.99 per song when they could access songs for free on the Internet? Instead, during its first week, it witnessed the sale of more than 1 million songs and became the largest online music company in the world.[1] What happened? Consumers were drawn in by iTunes' simplicity and ease of use, and by the higher-quality downloads than were available from other Internet sites.

Now, just over 10 years later, iTunes is selling over 25 billion songs a month to its 800 million customers. And, due to the addition of the Mac App Store and the sale of Apple software through iTunes, it is no longer a "break-even" business, but a highly profitable one, generating by one estimate $2 billion per year, or a 15% operating margin.[2]

This chapter explores how cost-volume-profit analysis can help a company such as Apple to determine the number of songs that it would need to sell to break even on its new business, or help Fezzari to predict the number of bikes it must sell to achieve a particular profit level.

---

[1] https://www.apple.com/pr/library/2003/05/05iTunes-Music-Store-Sells-Over-One-Million-Songs-in-First-Week.html
[2] http://www.valuewalk.com/2013/03/apple-inc-aapl-itunes-store-from-break-even-to-15-margins/

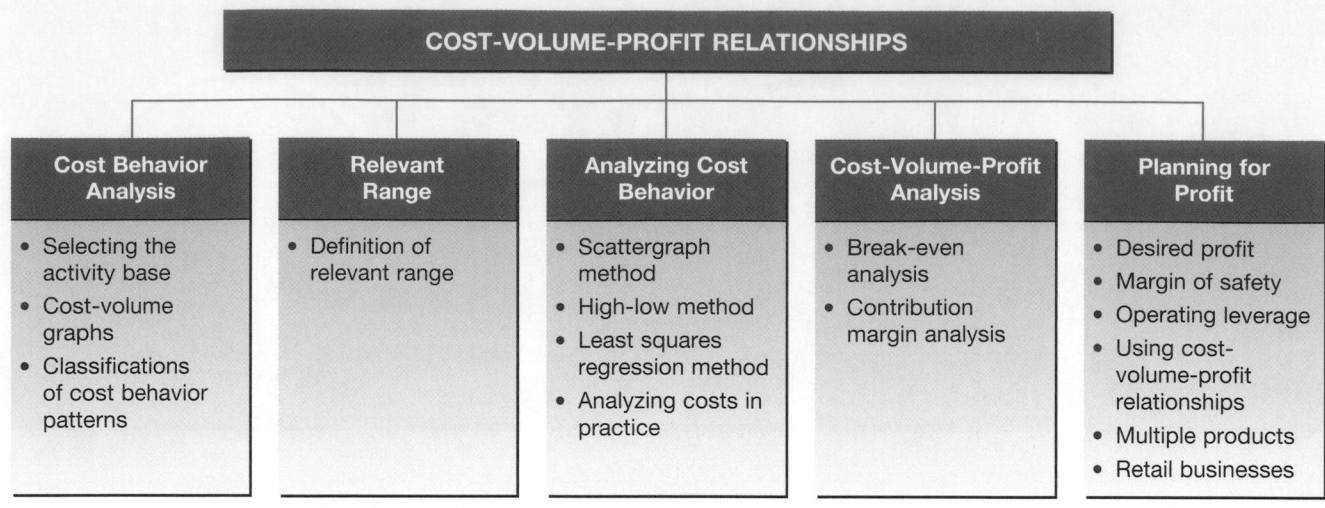

COST-VOLUME-PROFIT RELATIONSHIPS				
Cost Behavior Analysis	**Relevant Range**	**Analyzing Cost Behavior**	**Cost-Volume-Profit Analysis**	**Planning for Profit**
• Selecting the activity base • Cost-volume graphs • Classifications of cost behavior patterns	• Definition of relevant range	• Scattergraph method • High-low method • Least squares regression method • Analyzing costs in practice	• Break-even analysis • Contribution margin analysis	• Desired profit • Margin of safety • Operating leverage • Using cost-volume-profit relationships • Multiple products • Retail businesses

"We lose money on every sale—but make up the difference in volume."

ANONYMOUS

A.K.A. Cost-volume-profit analysis is often referred to in practice by its abbreviation, CVP, or break-even analysis.

Management must study a number of factors when planning the future course for an organization. One of the most important factors is the relationships among sales (revenue), costs (expenses), and profit (net income). **Cost-volume-profit (CVP) analysis** is used to study these relationships.

CVP analysis is appropriately used by for-profit organizations as well as not-for-profit (NFP) organizations. NFPs use the analysis with a target profit of zero. All of the relationships studied in the analysis are equally valid for both types of organizations.

COST BEHAVIOR ANALYSIS

LO1 **Develop** an understanding of how specific types of costs change in response to volume changes.

Cost behavior analysis is the study of how specific costs respond to changes in the volume of business activity. Each specific cost incurred by an organization may be affected differently by changes in the volume of business activity. Some costs will increase proportionately as volume increases, some costs will change disproportionately, and some costs will remain the same. Other factors besides volume can also cause changes in specific costs. For example, an increase in the assessment rate can increase property tax expense, whereas a decrease in electricity rates can lower total utility expense. These types of changes, however, are not typically caused by changes in business activity volume.

Selecting the Activity Basis

For meaningful managerial analysis, costs must be related to some measure of business activity. As we introduced in Chapter 16 and discussed further in Chapter 18, this measure of business activity is referred to as a cost driver. Cost drivers can include units of product, direct labor hours, machine hours, or percentage of capacity. A critical aspect is that the activity measure used must have a logical causal relation with costs, and the quantity of the activity must be highly correlated with the level of costs. Management must consider the objective of the analysis when selecting the most relevant and useful cost driver. For example, if iTunes managers want to analyze the cost of iTunes servers for budgeting purposes, they might choose the number of song downloads as the business activity or cost driver. CVP analysis can often use several bases, depending on the objectives of the analysis.

To help demonstrate various cost behaviors, we'll return to the Fezzari example. Fezzari produces a carbon water bottle cage that can be used on both road and mountain bikes. In the first part of this chapter, we explore several examples related to the various costs associated with producing Fezzari's water bottle cages. We discuss various types of cost behaviors and graph those behaviors in cost-volume graphs. Later in the chapter, we further analyze those costs and how they relate to profits.

Cost-Volume Graphs

One of the most useful tools for analyzing the relationship between changes in cost and volume is the **cost-volume graph**. A cost-volume graph illustrates the relationship between costs and volume. These graphs typically plot total costs on the vertical axis and either volume or activity level on the horizontal axis. Recall from Chapter 15 that companies typically have both variable and fixed costs. **Exhibits 19-1** and **19-2** are examples of cost-volume graphs, plotting total cost on the *y*-axis and the number of water bottle cages on the *x*-axis. Keep in mind that the total cost line in **Exhibits 19-1** and **19-2** is comprised of both fixed and variable costs. Point A in **Exhibit 19-1** indicates that at a volume level of 5,000 units the associated cost is $7,500. Similarly, point B in **Exhibit 19-1** represents a cost of $22,500 for a volume level of 35,000 units.

Cost-volume graphs are particularly valuable when available cost-volume data are plotted on the same graph and other cost-volume relationships are estimated by fitting a line to the known points. In **Exhibit 19-1**, for example, we use three known data points (an increased number of known data points should be used to develop a more reliable graph). The known data points, represented by solid points, are as follows:

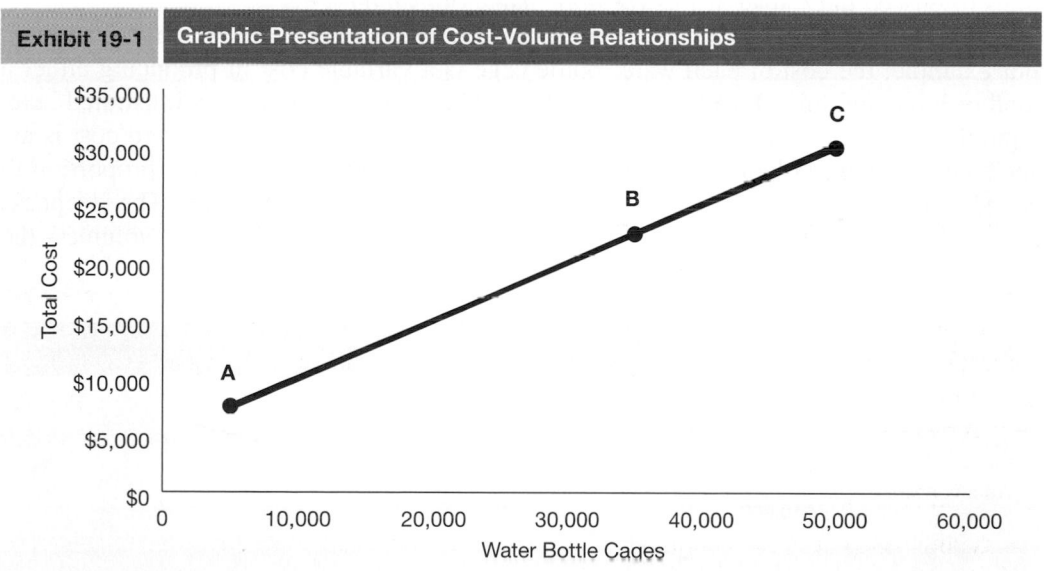

By connecting the known data points with a straight line, we can estimate the costs associated with other volume levels. For example, as illustrated in **Exhibit 19-2**, the open points indicate that for volumes of 22,500, 42,500, and 59,000 units, the related costs would be $16,250, $26,250, and $34,500, respectively. We discuss important limitations to using the cost-volume relationship to estimate costs later in the chapter.

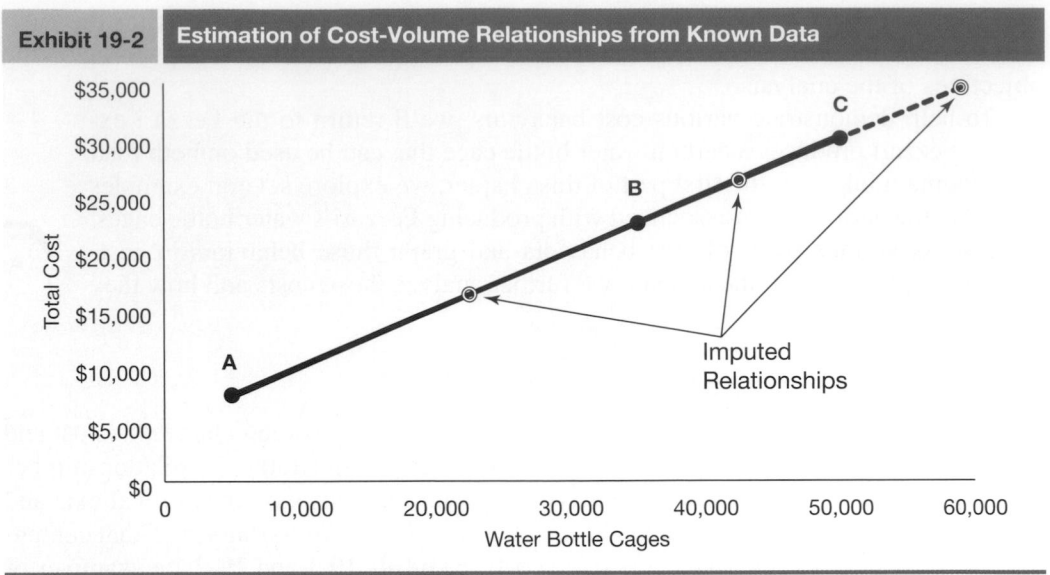

| Exhibit 19-2 | Estimation of Cost-Volume Relationships from Known Data |

Management often uses known data to estimate unknown data. More data typically will produce more reliable estimates. Having reliable estimates helps management predict profits or losses at various levels of activity.

Classifications of Cost Behavior Patterns

To better analyze cost behavior patterns, we typically classify costs (based on the definitions discussed in Chapter 15) as *variable, fixed,* or *mixed.*

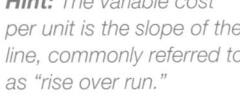

Hint: The variable cost per unit is the slope of the line, commonly referred to as "rise over run."

Total variable costs change proportionately with changes in the volume of activity. For example, the cost of each water bottle cage is a variable cost in producing either a road or mountain bike. **Exhibit 19-3** is a typical variable cost graph. As illustrated here, a purely variable cost pattern always passes through the origin, because zero cost is associated with zero volume. Also, because variable costs respond in direct proportion to changes in volume, a variable cost line always slopes upward to the right. The steepness of the slope depends on the amount of cost associated with each unit of volume—the greater the unit cost, the steeper the slope.

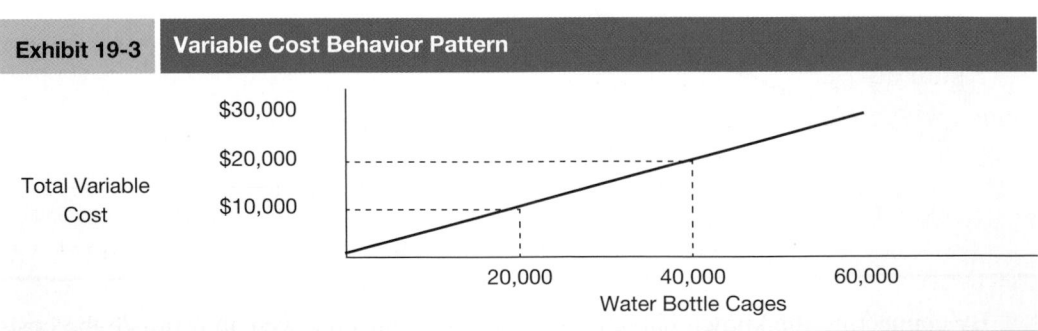

| Exhibit 19-3 | Variable Cost Behavior Pattern |

Fixed costs do not change when the volume of activity changes. Depreciation on manufacturing machinery is an example of a fixed cost.

Because fixed costs do not respond to changes in volume, they are represented by horizontal lines on a cost-volume graph. In **Exhibit 19-4**, fixed costs are $5,000 regardless of the volume level considered.

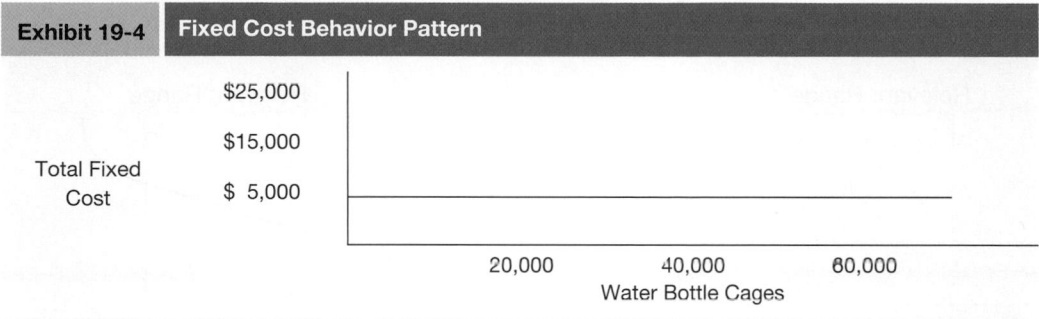

Exhibit 19-4 Fixed Cost Behavior Pattern

Mixed costs—sometimes called *semi-variable costs*—can be described as having both fixed and variable components. Mixed costs respond to volume changes but less than proportionately. For example, assume that Fezzari has several sales associates who receive a fixed salary every month, but they also earn a commission based on their sales volume each month. Because sales associates' compensation is comprised of both a variable and a fixed component, compensation of sales associates would be considered a mixed cost.

A mixed cost is a single cost containing both a fixed and variable component. For analysis and planning purposes, mixed costs are typically broken down into their fixed and variable components. Total costs are then the sum of all of a company's fixed and variable costs over a period of time. As shown in **Exhibit 19-5**, total costs are comprised of both fixed and variable costs.

Hint: The fixed portion of a mixed service cost represents the basic charge for a service. The variable portion represents the charge for the use of the service.

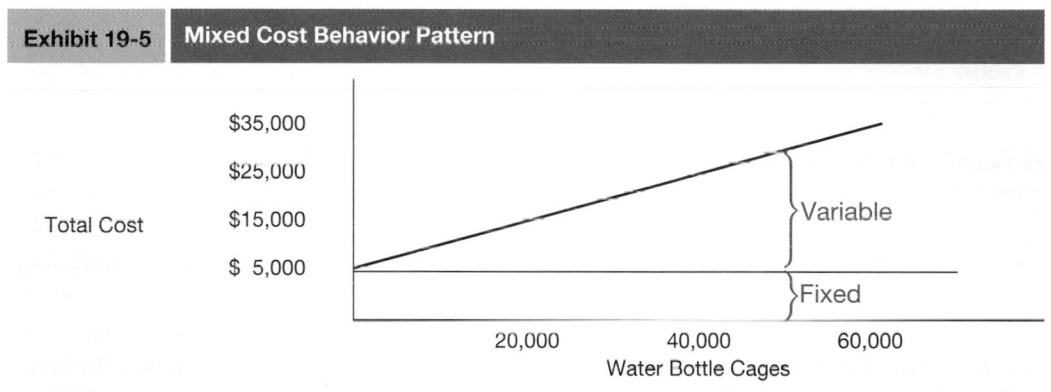

Exhibit 19-5 Mixed Cost Behavior Pattern

RELEVANT RANGE

The cost behavior illustrations provided thus far are oversimplified because they portray linear cost behavior over the entire range of possible activity. Actually, plotting costs against volume may not always produce a single straight line. For example, certain costs may increase abruptly at intervals in a "step" pattern. Others may exhibit a curvilinear pattern when plotted over a wide range of activity. We present examples graphically of these cost patterns in **Exhibit 19-6**.

LO2 Define the concept of *relevant range.*

The **relevant range** is the range of activity over which the behavior of a cost behaves consistently. Clearly, an assumption of linear costs over the entire scale on either axis in these two cases causes some degree of error. The significance of this error is often minimized by the fact that many of the firm's decisions involve relatively small changes in volume. The actual cost pattern at extremely low or high volume levels is not relevant to the firm's decisions. The cost pattern only needs to be reasonably linear within this relevant range of activity. For example, **Exhibit 19-6** illustrates that the cost function approximates a straight line within the relevant range indicated, even though costs are clearly not linear outside this range.

Exhibit 19-6	Illustrations of Relevent Ranges

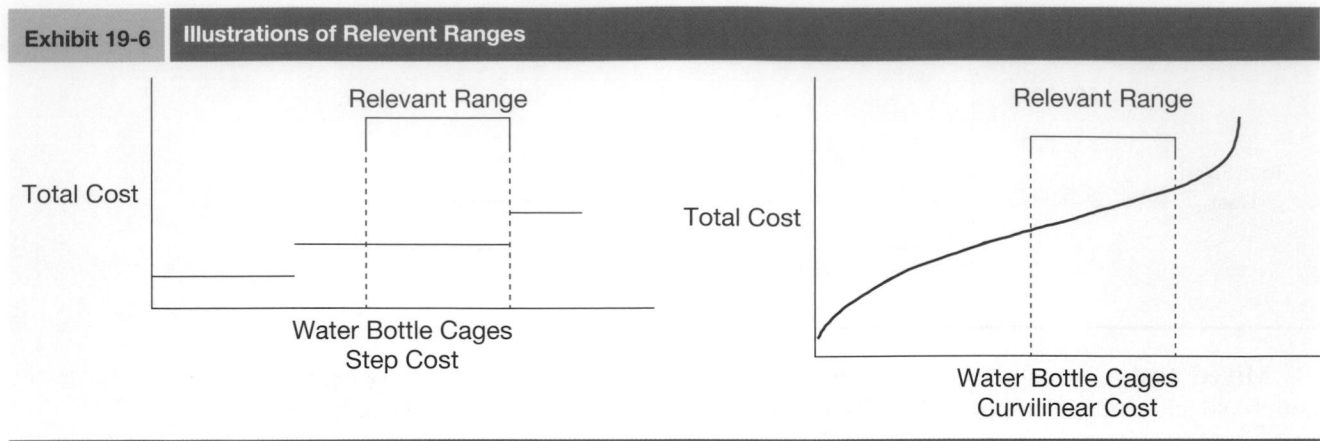

The cost-volume relationships for fixed cost, variable cost, and mixed cost typically remain the same for only one range of activity and for only one time period (frequently 1 year). Therefore fixed, variable, and mixed costs are assumed to have a consistent relationship in terms of volume within this relevant range during the given time period. The cost relationships, however, may change when moving to a different range of activity or a different time period. For example, a higher level of activity (above the current relevant range) could require a higher level of supervisory personnel, which would result in a higher level of fixed salary expense (as shown in the step cost graph in **Exhibit 19-6**). Alternatively, a higher direct material cost due to significantly higher demand for the direct material could lead to a different relationship (as shown in the curvilinear cost graph in **Exhibit 19-6**).

ANALYZING COST BEHAVIOR

LO3 **Outline** the approach to developing cost formulas.

Managers often have detailed information about costs. Nevertheless, in order to perform CVP analysis to make better decisions, they need to break total costs into fixed and variable components. Although some costs are easy to classify as variable or fixed costs, it isn't always easy to split mixed (semi-variable) costs into variable and fixed components. We illustrate three approaches for better understanding the nature of a company's costs: (1) the scattergraph method, (2) the high-low method, and (3) the least squares regression method. We note at the outset that these methods differ both in their ease of application and in their accuracy. For example, the scattergraph method is fast and easy, but it isn't very accurate. On the other extreme, the least squares regression method may take a little more effort, but it is much more accurate. Managers need to weigh costs and benefits in determining which approach is most useful.

Scattergraph Method

For purposes of cost analysis, a mixed cost is divided into its fixed and variable components. We accomplish this by any one of several approaches that vary in their degree of sophistication. One simple method entails plotting the observed cost at several levels of volume on a graph. If cost behavior in actual situations were perfectly correlated, the observations (points) would form a straight line (see **Exhibit 19-1** for an example). More realistically, however, we expect only a discernible pattern.

Assume that Fezzari purchases its carbon water bottle cages from a company in Taiwan that produces similar products for companies around the world. **Exhibit 19-7** reports the supplier's manufacturing costs for various levels of production over the past eight months (sorted by production volume):

Cost	Water Bottle Cages
$27,000	44,000
$29,500	48,000
$30,000	51,000
$31,500	52,000
$32,500	54,000
$32,000	55,000
$36,000	63,000
$38,000	66,000

Exhibit 19-7	Scattergraph Method

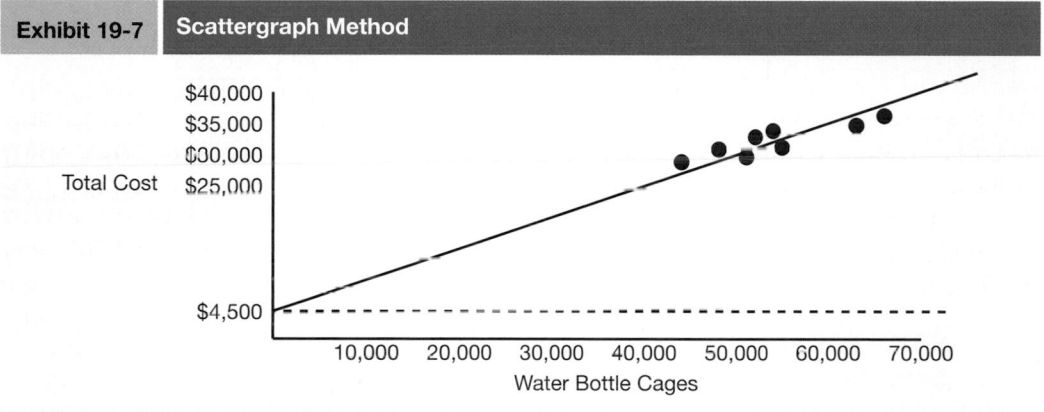

After plotting the actual costs relative to volume over the past eight months, the individual performing the analysis would simply draw a line that places approximately half of the dots above and half below the line. The line in **Exhibit 19-7** has been subjectively determined to approximate the pattern of data points on this scattergraph. Extending this line to the vertical axis indicates a $4,500 fixed portion of total costs. To determine the approximate formula for the total cost line, we subtract this $4,500 fixed cost from the total $27,000 cost at 44,000 water bottle cages to find a total variable portion of $22,500. Therefore, the rate of variations is $22,500/44,000 cages, or $0.51, per water bottle cage. Hence, we could describe this mixed cost as $4,500 fixed cost plus $0.51 per water bottle cage of variable cost. We summarize the equation as follows:

$$\text{Total cost} = \$4,500 + (\$0.51 \times \text{water bottle cages})$$

YOUR TURN! 19.1

The solution is on page 925.

Your manager asks you to interpret the semi-variable cost graph in **Exhibit 19-7** for your company. Briefly explain what is meant by each of the following points on the graph:

y-intercept	x-axis
Slope of the line	Any point along the line

High-Low Method

When too few cost observations are available to plot a graph, or when the analyst wishes to avoid visually fitting lines to data, the high-low method can be used to approximate the position and slope of the cost line. This relatively simple method compares costs at the highest and lowest levels of activity for which representative cost data are available. The line is drawn between the highest- and lowest-volume data points, as shown in **Exhibit 19-8**. The variable cost per activity unit (here, per water bottle cage) is determined by dividing the difference in costs at these two levels by the difference in activity. The fixed element of cost is then isolated by multiplying the variable cost per unit by either the top or bottom level of activity and then subtracting the resulting product from the total cost at the selected activity level.

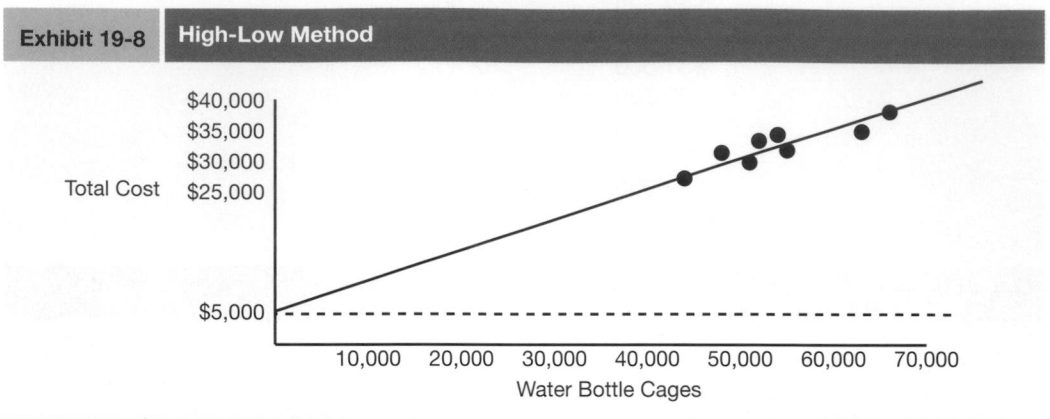

Exhibit 19-8	High-Low Method

Using the same data from our prior example, the lowest and highest levels of activity are 44,000 and 66,000 cages, respectively, and the following are the total costs for these two levels:

Level of Activity		Total Cost
High	66,000 Water bottle cages	$38,000
Low.	44,000 Water bottle cages	$27,000
Difference	22,000 (increase)	$11,000 (increase)

Because an increase of 22,000 cages is associated with an $11,000 increase in total cost (remember that by definition only the variable portion of the cost could increase), the variable portion of the total mixed cost must be $11,000/22,000 water bottle cages, or $0.50 per water bottle cage. Subtracting the total variable portion from the total mixed cost at the high- and low-activity levels gives us the fixed portion of total cost as follows:

	Volume Levels	
	Low	High
Total mixed cost.	$27,000	$38,000
Less variable portions:		
$0.50 × 44,000 Water bottle cages	22,000	
$0.50 × 66,000 Water bottle cages		33,000
Fixed portion of total cost	$ 5,000	$ 5,000

The high-low analysis tells us that any volume level has $5,000 of fixed cost plus a variable portion of $0.50 per water bottle cage, which can be formulated as follows:

$$\text{Total cost} = \$5,000 + (\$0.50 \times \text{water bottle cages})$$

In other words, we can now easily compute the total cost for varying levels of production. However, if either the high or low value used in this method is not representative of the actual cost behavior (that is, the value is an outlier), the resulting cost formula is inexact.

Given the following levels of volume and cost, calculate the variable cost per unit and fixed cost within this relevant range using the high-low method:

Cost	Volume	Cost	Volume
$15,000	5,000 units	$24,500	9,750 units
$13,000	4,000 units	$18,000	6,500 units
$19,300	7,150 units	$21,000	8,000 units

YOUR TURN! 19.2

The solution is on page 925.

Least Squares Regression Method

We can obtain an even better approximation by fitting the line to the cost data points by the least squares regression method. The least squares regression method is a statistical tool that uses all of the data points to separate a mixed cost into its variable and fixed components. A regression line is fitted to the data points so that the distance from each point to the line is minimized for all points. **Exhibit 19-9** illustrates this concept using all data points.

Exhibit 19-9	Least Squares Regression

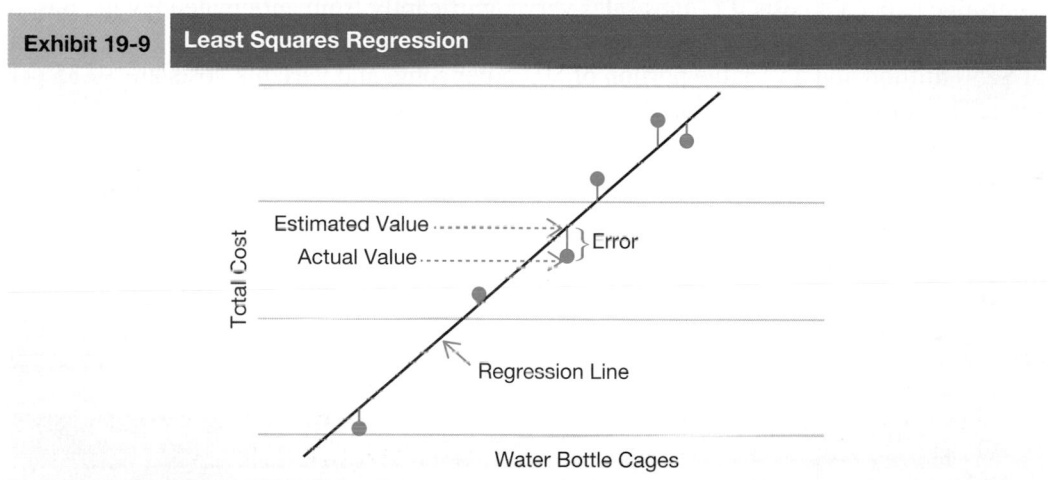

In **Exhibit 19-9**, the distances from the data points and the regression line are the regression errors—the amount by which the value estimated by the regression line differs from the actual data point.

The formulas that are used to compute the least squares regression are fairly complex and beyond the scope of this text. However, the computations can be easily made with a computer program. When the data points are entered into a Microsoft Excel spreadsheet and the least squares regression is executed, we get the following values for fixed cost and variable cost per unit:

Fixed cost:	$6,083
Variable cost per water bottle cage:	**$ 0.48**

The resulting linear equation would be written as:

Total cost = $6,083 + ($0.48 × water bottle cages)

Looking back, we can see how each method arrives at a somewhat different result:

Scattergraph equation:	Total cost = $4,500 + ($0.51 × water bottle cages)
High-low equation:	**Total cost = $5,000 + ($0.50 × water bottle cages)**
Least squares equation:	**Total cost = $6,083 + ($0.48 × water bottle cages)**

Although the scattergraph and high-low methods are the easiest to implement, they are also less accurate. They work well for quick estimates. However, with the availability of desktop computers and programs that can compute least squares regressions, and given the limitations of the scattergraph and high-low methods, managers generally prefer to use the least squares regression method to estimate the fixed and variable portions of a mixed cost.

Analyzing Costs in Practice

How might we use this understanding of cost behavior as business managers? The budget for a business, which is discussed in detail in **Chapter 22**, is a financial plan that reflects anticipated or planned amounts of such items as revenue, costs, cash balances, and net income. Underlying most aspects of budgeting is some assumed number of units or dollars of sales, as well as an analysis of the total cost incurred for that level of operation.

For an example, assume that iTunes management is preparing the budget for the next fiscal year. Because of uncertainty regarding the continued economic recovery from a recent recession, management wants to prepare a budget that will allow it to quickly determine expected costs if iTunes sales vary significantly from anticipated levels. Based on the previous year, total fixed costs are $2.0 billion, mixed costs have a fixed portion of $250 million and a variable portion of $0.05 per song, and variable costs are $0.35 per song. The formula for budgeting the total cost is as follows:

> **Total cost = Total fixed cost + (Variable cost per song × # of songs sold)**
>
> **Total cost = $2.25 billion fixed cost + ($0.40 Variable cost × # of songs sold)**

By using this formula, iTunes management can forecast costs at different levels of activity. **Exhibit 19-10** illustrates how each type of cost behavior pattern is considered in the formula.

Exhibit 19-10	**iTunes Cost Factors Example**							
Type of Cost	**Total Cost (in millions)**		**Total Fixed Cost (in millions)**		**Variable Cost per Song**		**Number of Songs (in millions)**
Variable costs.......	$10,500	=	$ 0	+	$0.35	×	30,000
Mixed costs:							
Variable portion....	1,500	=	$ 0	+	0.05	×	30,000
Fixed portion......	250	=	$ 250	+	0	×	30,000
Fixed costs.........	2,000	=	$2,000	+	0	×	30,000
Total cost	$14,250	=	$2,250	+	$0.40	×	30,000

Notice in **Exhibit 19-10** that by combining the various cost factors into the aggregate formula, iTunes management can determine expected costs not only at the 30-billion-song level but also at other levels simply by inserting the appropriate volume figure in the final formula. For example, total budgeted cost at 45 billion songs is $20.250 billion ($2.25 billion + [$0.40 × 45 billion songs]) and at 62 billion songs, total budgeted cost is $27.05 billion ($2.25 billion + [$0.40 × 62 billion songs]).

A word of caution is appropriate here. Because the cost formula relies so heavily on cost analysis, all of the limitations of cost analysis (assumed linearity, relevant ranges, and so on) apply. Also, categorizing many costs into fixed and variable components is often quite complex and inexact. All of these limitations to some degree affect the potential usefulness of managerial cost analysis. It is important to note that these models provide data that can be used to help managers make decisions. However, managers should not blindly follow the outputs from their models. Managers ultimately need to evaluate all relevant information to make sound decisions. In some cases, the simple analytical approach presented here is sufficient, but it cannot be followed blindly.

COST-VOLUME-PROFIT (CVP) ANALYSIS

Break-Even Analysis

Management frequently wants to know the sales level (in dollars) or the number of units that must be sold in order to cover its costs. The level at which total revenues equal total costs is called the **break-even point**. The break-even point can be expressed in dollars or in units sold. As an example, we illustrate several important calculations for one of Fezzari's medium-range road bikes, the Foré CR1, using the condensed income statement data shown in **Exhibit 19-11**.

LO4 Present a discussion of and a formula for calculating the break-even point.

Exhibit 19-11	Fezzari Foré CR1 Operating Income	
Sales (3,000 units @ $1,500)		$4,500,000
Costs:		
Variable cost (3,000 units @ $1,138).	$3,414,000	
Fixed cost	595,000	
Total cost		$4,009,000
Net operating income.		$ 491,000

This information assumes that all mixed costs have been accurately divided into their fixed and variable components and combined with other fixed and variable costs. We now examine some of the uses of this information.

The Cost-Volume-Profit Chart

To prepare a cost-volume-profit (CVP) chart for the Foré CR1, we use the same basic graph employed previously to explain and portray cost behavior patterns. In **Exhibit 19-12** the vertical axis measures both total revenues and total costs. As in previous exhibits, volume is measured along the horizontal axis. In this Fezzari product line, the activity basis is the number of Foré CR1s manufactured and sold. Total revenues and total costs are measured in thousands of dollars along the vertical axis.

With zero revenue for zero units sold, the graph of total revenues always passes through the origin. We draw the total revenue line by connecting the origin with any other point that represents total revenue for some volume amount. For Fezzari's CR1, total revenue for 3,000 units is $4,500,000, point **A** in **Exhibit 19-12**. To construct the total revenue line, we simply draw a straight line from the origin to **A** and extend it beyond **A**.

We now construct the total cost line in the same manner. With fixed costs of $595,000, the total cost line must intersect the vertical axis at the fixed costs level, $595,000. To produce 3,000 bicycles, Fezzari incurs total costs of $4,009,000. Given this information, we can plot point **B** and draw the total cost line connecting the intersection of the fixed cost line and the vertical axis with **B** as shown in **Exhibit 19-12**. After constructing the total cost line, its intersection with the total revenue line marks the break-even point.

Extending the dashed horizontal and vertical lines from the break-even point, we find that Fezzari's break-even point can be described as either (1) 1,644 units of production or (2) $2,466,000 of total sales revenue. (We explain the calculation of these numbers next.) Note that all levels of sales below the break-even point indicate a loss, and levels of sales above the break-even point result in a profit. In other words, Fezzari earns a profit from its CR1 product line when the total revenue line is above the total cost line, and it incurs a loss when the reverse is true. **Exhibit 19-12** indicates the profit and loss areas. The amount of profit or loss at any volume level is determined by measuring the vertical distance between the total cost and total revenue lines. For example, the difference between points **A** and **B** indicates the profit of $491,000 for selling 3,000 CR1 road bikes.

| **Exhibit 19-12** | **Fezzari Foré CR1 Cost-Volume-Profit Chart** |

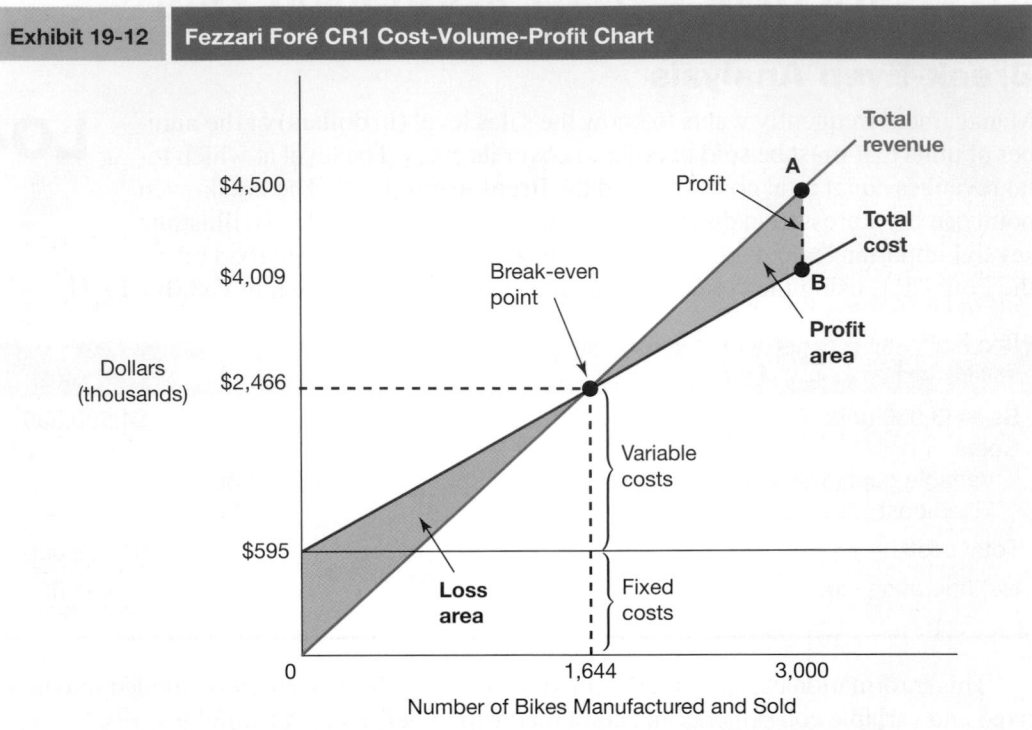

Tesla Breaks Even!

On December 2, 2012, Tesla, the start-up electric car manufacturer, finally broke even! CEO Elon Musk announced that the company has stopped burning cash and reached the break-even point, a major milestone for any start-up. "Am happy to report that Tesla was narrowly cash flow positive last week. Continued improvement expected through year end," Musk tweeted. According to the *Wall Street Journal*, in November of 2012, Tesla told the Securities and Exchange Commission that it was producing 200 cars per week, "which is at the critical threshold needed for Tesla to generate positive operating cash flow," and expected to increase that to 400 cars per week in December.

The Basic Assumptions of Break-Even Analysis

In our construction of a break-even chart, we assumed linear relationships over a wide range of activity. This approach implies the following:

1. Total fixed cost and total variable cost per unit are constant over the entire range of analysis.
2. Selling price per unit remains the same regardless of the volume of sales.
3. When more than one product is involved and sales volume varies, each product's percentage of total sales (i.e., the sales mix) does not change.

Even though these assumptions somewhat limit the usefulness of break-even analysis, it is still a convenient method of measuring the effect of changes in sales, costs, volumes, and profits.

Break-Even Formula

The following formula reflects the basic relationship between the break-even point and costs; the break-even point is that point at which total revenue equals total cost:

> **Break-even sales = Total variable costs + Total fixed costs**

Break-even sales and total variable costs can be expressed as follows:

> **(Selling price per unit × Number of units) = (Variable cost per unit × Number of units) + Total fixed costs**

Using the data for Fezzari's Foré CR1 with this formula, we can calculate Fezzari's break-even point in units and sales dollars. First, we solve for Y, which represents the number of units at the break-even level. We can then multiply the number of break-even units by the sales price to determine break-even sales.

Break-even sales	**= Total variable costs + Total fixed costs**
\$1,500 Y	= \$1,138 Y + \$595,000
\$1,500 Y − \$1,138 Y	= \$595,000
\$362 Y	= \$595,000
Y	= **1,644 units (rounded)**
\$1,500 × 1,644	= **\$2,466,000**

Exhibit 19-13 illustrates the break-even calculation based on Fezzari's flexible budget using 1,644 units as the break-even level of activity. Obviously, "break-even" literally means net profit of exactly zero. Because it isn't practical to sell partial units, the break-even calculation will normally indicate how many full units must be sold to produce enough contribution margin to cover fixed costs. In this example, 1,644 CR1 road bikes sold allows the company to "break-even," with \$128 left over, whereas selling 1,643 units would have resulted in a small loss. Hence, we round to the number of complete units that allows the company to just exceed the zero-profit threshold.

Exhibit 19-13	Fezzari Foré CR1 Fezzari Break-Even Calculation
Sales (1,644 units @ \$1,500)	\$2,466,000
Variable cost (1,644 units @ \$1,138)	1,870,872
Contribution margin	\$ 595,128
Fixed cost	595,000
Net operating income	\$ 128

Contribution Margin Analysis

Because total variable costs change proportionately with changes in total revenue, each time additional revenue is generated, additional variable costs are also generated. The difference between the revenue generated and the variable costs generated is called the **contribution margin**. The restructured **variable operating income statement** for Fezzari's CR1 shown in **Exhibit 19-14** illustrates the importance of contribution margin.

LO5 Define *contribution margin* and *contribution margin ratio* and **present** alternate break-even formulas and examples of their application.

Exhibit 19-14	Fezzari Foré CR1 Operating Income	
Sales (3,000 units @ $1,500)		$4,500,000
Variable cost (3,000 units @ $1,138)		3,414,000
Contribution margin.		**$1,086,000**
Fixed cost.		595,000
Net operating income.		$ 491,000

When using the variable format for the income statement, we first deduct all variable costs from sales to calculate the contribution margin. We then deduct fixed costs from the contribution margin to calculate operating income. Thus, contribution margin can be viewed as a measure of what is left over after covering variable costs to go toward covering fixed costs and generating profits. At 3,000 units, the total contribution margin is $1,086,000. The contribution margin per unit is calculated as the selling price per unit minus the variable cost per unit. In the Fezzari CR1 example, the contribution margin per unit of $362 would be calculated as the selling price per unit of $1,500 minus the $1,138 variable cost per unit. The contribution margin per unit means that for each additional CR1 sold beyond the break-even point, $362 of additional contribution margin is generated to help produce additional profit.

Contribution Margin Ratio

Hint: The contribution margin is defined as the amount of sales revenue after variable expenses are deducted that is used to cover fixed costs and provide a profit. At the break-even point, the contribution margin equals fixed costs (i.e., profit is zero).

A related concept often used in break-even analysis is the **contribution margin ratio**, which is the ratio of the contribution margin to sales. The formula to calculate the contribution margin ratio can use either *total* amounts:

$$\text{Contribution margin ratio} = \frac{\text{Contribution margin}}{\text{Sales}}$$

or *per-unit* amounts:

$$\text{Contribution margin ratio} = \frac{\text{Unit contribution margin}}{\text{Unit sales price}}$$

In the Fezzari CR1 example:

$$\text{Contribution margin ratio} = \frac{\$1,086,000}{\$4,500,000} = 0.24 \text{ (rounded)}$$

or

$$\text{Contribution margin ratio} = \frac{\$362}{\$1,500} = 0.24 \text{ (rounded)}$$

The contribution margin ratio is easier to work with than the unit contribution margin if a company has more than one product line. The contribution margin ratio allows comparisons among product lines, which we illustrate later in the chapter.

Alternative Break-Even Formulas

Two alternative break-even formulas[3] can be directly derived from our previous break-even formula. To calculate the break-even point either in *units:*

$$\text{Break-even units} = \frac{\text{Total fixed cost}}{\text{Unit contribution margin}}$$

or in *sales dollars:*

$$\text{Break-even sales dollars} = \frac{\text{Total fixed cost}}{\text{Contribution margin ratio}}$$

In the Fezzari CR1 example, we can calculate the break-even point using these two formulas. Using the first formula (expressed in units):

$$\text{Break-even units} = \frac{\$595,000}{\$362} = 1,644 \text{ units}$$

Using the second formula (expressed in sales dollars):

$$\text{Break-even sales} = \frac{\$595,000}{0.24} = \$2,479,167 \,^{4}$$

The results obtained from any of the break-even formulas can be verified by placing the amounts in an income statement format and verifying that net income equals zero.

TAKEAWAY 19.2

Break-even analysis is helpful to management because it helps determine the total sales volume or the selling price per unit that must be achieved in order to exactly cover total costs. If companies do not consider the break-even point, they may experience losses even though they were expecting profits.

PLANNING FOR PROFIT

Desired Profit

Target Profits without Taxes

With an understanding of the cost-volume-profit relationship, business managers can develop plans for desired levels of profit. Rather than making the

LO6 Discuss approaches to planning net income using cost-volume-profit analyses.

---

[3] These formulas can be derived from the general break-even formula provided previously:

Break-even sales = Total variable cost + Total fixed cost

(Selling price per unit × Number of units) = (Variable cost per unit × Number of units) + Total fixed costs

(Selling price per unit × Number of units) − (Variable cost per unit × Number of units) = Total fixed costs

(Selling price per unit − Variable cost per unit) × Number of units = Total fixed costs

(Contribution margin per unit) × Number of units = Total fixed costs

$$\text{Number of units} = \frac{\text{Total fixed costs}}{\text{Contribution margin per unit}}$$

The second formula can be derived simply by multiplying both sides of this equation by the selling price per unit.

[4] This solution differs from the sales revenue computed previously because the contribution margin used has been rounded to the nearest hundredth.

calculations for break-even, where profit is equal to zero, they use formulas that include a *desired profit*. These formulas are similar to the previous CVP break-even formula and take into consideration the additional desired net income (or profit):

Desired sales = Total variable costs + Total fixed costs + Desired net income [5]

A.K.A. The desired profit is also referred to as desired net income.

Recall that the definition of contribution margin is what is left over from sales, after covering variable costs, to cover fixed costs and generate profits. Using the contribution margin approach, we can then rearrange our CVP formula to solve for the level of units and sales to achieve our desired net income:

$$\text{Desired units} = \frac{\text{Total fixed costs} + \text{Desired net income}}{\text{Unit contribution margin}}$$

And

$$\text{Desired sales} = \frac{\text{Total fixed costs} + \text{Desired net income}}{\text{Contribution margin ratio}}$$

Assume that Fezzari wants to attain a net income of $1,000,000 before income tax on its CR1 line. Using these formulas, we can determine the level of output in sales dollars or units as follows:

Using the CVP equation:

$1,500 × Y	= $1,138Y + $595,000 + $1,000,000
$1,500Y − $1,138Y	= $1,595,000
$362Y	= $1,595,000
Y	= **4,406 units**
4,406 units × $1,500	= **$6,609,000**

Using the contribution margin approach:

$$\text{Desired units} = \frac{\$595,000 + \$1,000,000}{\$362}$$
$$= 4,406 \text{ units}$$
$$\text{Desired sales} = \frac{\$595,000 + \$1,000,000}{0.24}$$
$$= \$6,645,833 \,[6]$$

---

[5] Note that the desired net income in these formulas is pre-tax net income. When taxes are applicable, managers need to adjust the formulas to account for taxes in order to determine a desired after-tax net income.

[6] This calculation differs from the sales revenue computed using the first formula because the contribution margin used has been rounded to the nearest hundredth.

DECISION TIME

The solution is on
page 925.

A U.S. shoe retailer performed a CVP analysis and determined that at a level of $500,000 in sales, $350,000 in variable costs, and $200,000 in fixed costs would be incurred. Therefore, the company would have a loss of $50,000. If all else remains the same, what change or changes could the company make in order to break even or earn a profit?

   a. Increase selling price per unit
   b. Increase number of units sold
   c. Either or both of the above

Target Profits with Taxes

Fezzari's management might want to develop plans using net income (after tax) rather than net income before income taxes. In this case, net income (after tax) must be converted to net income before income tax so the formulas presented previously can be used:

$$\text{Net income before income tax} = \frac{\text{Net income}}{1 - \text{Income tax rate}}$$

Assume that Fezzari's management wants to attain an after-tax net income of $700,000 when the income tax rate is 30%. Net income before income tax can be calculated as follows:

$$\text{Net income before income tax} = \frac{\$700,000}{1 - 0.3} = \frac{\$700,000}{0.7} = \$1,000,000$$

A brief income statement verifies the calculations made in the preceding sections:

Sales (4,406 units × $1,500)	$6,609,000
Less: Variable cost (4,406 units × $1,138).	5,014,028
Contribution margin	$1,594,972
Less: Fixed cost	595,000
Net operating income.	$ 999,972
Income tax ($999,972 × 0.30)	299,992
Net income.	$ 699,980[7]

CVP Disclosure   ACCOUNTING IN PRACTICE

The Securities and Exchange Commission requires all publicly held companies to include a "management discussion and analysis (MD&A) of the results of operations" in quarterly and annual reports. This analysis may include cost-volume-profit data. For example, in its 2013 annual report, Yum! Brands, the parent company for restaurant chains such as Taco Bell, Kentucky Fried Chicken, and Pizza Hut, kicks off its MD&A section with a discussion of its focus on target profits, which is the result of careful CVP analysis on the part of management.

---

[7] Difference from target net income after tax of $700,000 due to rounding.

Margin of Safety

The **margin of safety** is the amount by which the actual sales level of a company exceeds the break-even sales level. It represents the company's "breathing room" in which it will remain profitable. If sales decrease by more than the margin of safety, then the company will incur an operating loss. The formula for calculating the margin of safety follows:

$$\text{Margin of safety} = \text{Actual sales} - \text{Break-even sales}$$

In the Fezzari CR1 example, **Exhibit 19-13** indicates that Fezzari needs sales of $2,466,000 (i.e., 1,644 CR1s) to break even. Assume Fezzari achieves sales of $3,000,000 in a given year. Its margin of safety for that year would be calculated as:

$$\text{Margin of safety} = \$3,000,000 - \$2,466,000 = \$534,000$$

In other words, Fezzari could decrease sales by up to $534,000 and still achieve a profit.

Another way of looking at the "breathing room" beyond break-even sales is on a ratio (or percentage) basis, referred to as the margin-of-safety ratio. It is calculated as follows:

$$\text{Margin-of-safety ratio} = \frac{\text{Margin of safety}}{\text{Actual sales}}$$

For example, continuing the previous Fezzari example (and assuming sales of $3,000,000), the margin-of-safety ratio would be calculated as:

$$\text{Margin-of-safety ratio} = \frac{\$534,000}{\$3,000,000} = 17.8\%$$

In other words, Fezzari could decrease CR1 sales by up to 17.8% and still achieve a profit.

Operating Leverage

Apple's iTunes division and Fezzari have relatively low fixed costs. On the other hand, other companies or industries are characterized by relatively high fixed costs, including utilities (e.g., Pacific Gas and Electric Co. and Florida Power & Light) and auto manufacturers (e.g., General Motors Company and Toyota Motor Corporation). One measure of a firm's relative level of fixed costs is **operating leverage**. Operating leverage is computed as follows:

$$\text{Operating leverage} = \frac{\text{Contribution margin}}{\text{Net operating income}}$$

Note that the difference between the numerator (contribution margin) and the denominator (net operating income) is the amount of fixed costs (look back at the variable income statement in **Exhibit 19-14** to confirm this). Thus, this ratio is really a measure of a company's operating cost structure, or its level of fixed costs (relative to variable costs). If two companies have the same level of sales and costs, but the cost structure (i.e., the mix between variable and fixed costs) is different, the company with relatively higher fixed costs will have the higher operating leverage. At one extreme, a company that has no fixed costs (i.e., all costs are variable) will have an operating leverage of 1.0 because its contribution margin and net operating income will be the same. **Exhibit 19-15** illustrates graphically a company with an operating leverage of 1.0. Note that because there are no fixed costs, as long as the per-unit sales price of the product is greater than the cost of the product, each sale generates an operating profit equal to the unit contribution margin.

Exhibit 19-15	Structure with All Variable Costs

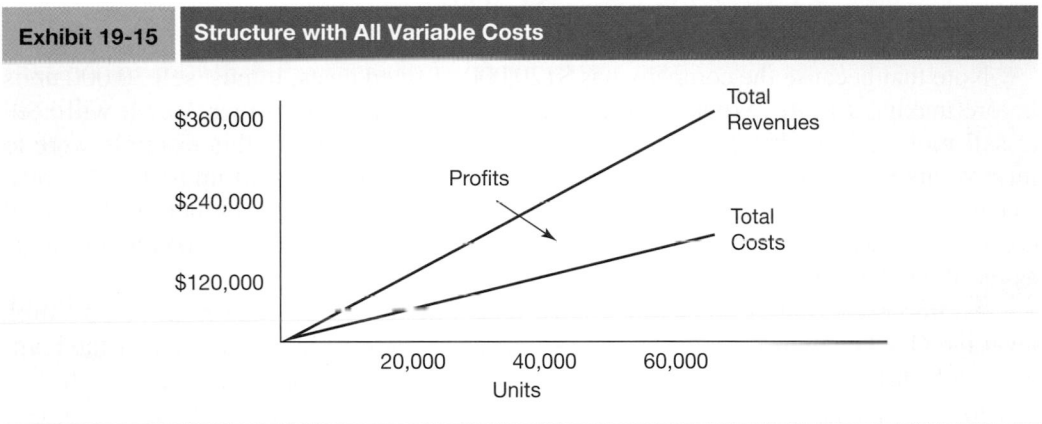

The company illustrated in **Exhibit 19-15** sells its products for $6 per unit, and the variable costs to produce a unit of product amount to $2 per unit. Thus, the contribution margin per unit is $4 ($6 − $2). Because the company has no fixed costs, when it sells its first unit of product to a customer, it will generate $4 of operating profit. Each additional unit of product sold will likewise result in additional operating profits of $4 per unit.

Because a world without fixed costs isn't reasonable, operating leverage is an important measure to help managers assess how their cost structure (their unique mix of variable and fixed costs) influences their break-even point. The higher a company's fixed costs, the more units it will need to sell in order to break even. Hence, a company struggling to break even would want to avoid fixed costs in order to lower its break-even point.

As a company's relative mix of costs shifts more toward fixed costs, its operating leverage increases, suggesting greater risk. **Exhibit 19-16** graphically illustrates a company with an operating leverage greater than 1.0 (i.e., with both fixed and variable costs). Assume the company has fixed costs of $120,000, variable costs of $2 per unit, and a selling price of $6 per unit.

Exhibit 19-16	Structure with Fixed and Variable Costs

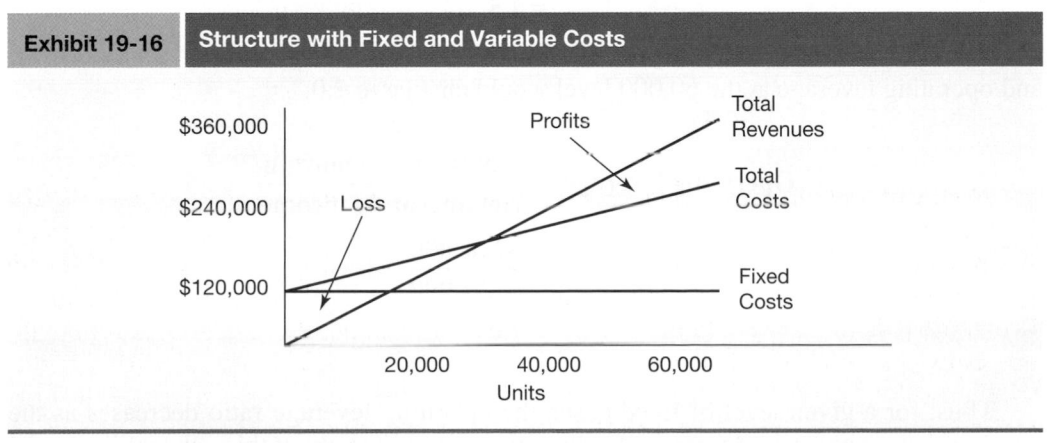

Break-even for this company would be computed as follows:

$$\textbf{Break-even units} = \frac{\textbf{Total fixed cost}}{\textbf{Unit contribution margin}}$$

$$\textbf{Break-even units} = \frac{\$120,000}{\$4 / \textbf{unit}} = \textbf{30,000 units}$$

Note that because the company has $120,000 of fixed costs, it must sell 30,000 units before making a profit. What happens as a company's fixed costs increase? It will need to sell more units to break even. For example, if the company in this example were to increase its fixed costs to $160,000, its break-even point would shift up to 40,000 units. Because it would be harder for the company to break even with this higher level of fixed costs, its risk would increase. Operating leverage can be a useful metric to help managers assess the risk associated with their fixed costs.

An important thing to remember about operating leverage is that a firm's operating leverage changes with its level of output and sales. For example, assume that the company in **Exhibit 19-16** is operating at a level of sales above break-even where it achieves a profit. Compare the company's performance if the company sells 50,000 units or 60,000 units; its operating income would be calculated as follows:

	Sales Volume	
	50,000	60,000
Sales ($6/unit)...................................	$300,000	$360,000
Less: Variable cost ($2/unit)........................	(100,000)	(120,000)
Contribution margin	200,000	240,000
Less: Fixed cost..................................	(120,000)	(120,000)
Net operating income.............................	$ 80,000	$120,000

Operating leverage at the 50,000 level of sales would be 2.5, computed as follows:

$$\textbf{Operating leverage} = \frac{\textbf{Contribution margin}}{\textbf{Net operating income}}$$

$$= \frac{\$200,000}{\$80,000}$$

$$= 2.5$$

and operating leverage at the 60,000 level would change to 2.0:

$$\textbf{Operating leverage} = \frac{\textbf{Contribution margin}}{\textbf{Net operating income}}$$

$$= \frac{\$240,000}{\$120,000}$$

$$= 2.0$$

Thus, for a given level of fixed costs, the operating leverage ratio decreases as the levels of output and sales increase. Another way of thinking about this concept is that for a given level of fixed costs, if the company can barely maintain a positive operating profit (i.e., it can barely cover its fixed costs), it is constantly operating under a high degree of uncertainty about whether or not it will be able to cover its fixed costs and turn a profit. Hence, its operating leverage would be high. To the extent that the company can comfortably sell more than the number of units required to break even (i.e., it has a high margin of safety), it has less risk of falling short and reporting a loss. Hence, for a given level of fixed costs, as output and sales increase, operating leverage (and the associated risk of reporting a loss) will decrease. The degree of operating leverage can be used to determine, at a given level of sales, how a percentage change in the level of sales will impact net operating profit:

% Increase in operating income = % Increase in sales × Operating leverage

Fezzari's CR1 example illustrates this concept. Assume that Fezzari's management anticipates a 20% increase in sales in the coming year. What should the resulting operating income be? From **Exhibit 19-17**, we can calculate Fezzari's operating leverage as follows:

$$\text{Operating leverage} = \frac{\text{Contribution margin}}{\text{Net operating income}}$$

$$\text{Operating leverage} = \frac{\$1,086,000}{\$491,000} = 2.2118 \text{ (rounded)}$$

If sales increase by 20%, operating income should be $708,200, calculated as follows:

% Increase in operating income = % Increase in sales × Operating leverage

$$44.236\% = 20\% \times 2.2118$$

$$\$708,200^* = \$491,000 \times (1 + 0.44236)$$

* Difference due to rounding.

Exhibit 19-17 proves this calculation.

Exhibit 19-17	**Fezzari Foré CR1 Operating Income Comparison**		
		Sales Increase	
Sales (3,000 units @ $1,500)	$4,500,000	20%	$5,400,000
Variable cost (3,000 units @ $1,138)	3,414,000	20%	$4,096,800
Contribution margin	$1,086,000		$1,303,200
Fixed cost	595,000		595,000
Net operating income	$ 491,000		$ 708,200

Note that operating leverage for the CR1 product line is not a constant, but is computed for each level of sales. For example, Fezzari's new operating leverage (following the 20% increase in sales) would be:

$$\text{Operating leverage} = \frac{\$1,303,200}{\$708,200} = 1.8402 \text{ (rounded)}$$

Your supervisor is concerned about your company's degree of operating leverage. She explains that other companies in your industry have operating leverage averaging over 3.0. Your sales for the current year are $2,500,000, variable costs are $1,400,000, and fixed costs are $600,000. Should you be concerned?

CORPORATE SOCIAL RESPONSIBILITY

True Innovation

Anyone who pays monthly water bills for a home, condo, business, or anything else knows that water is becomingly increasingly scarce. Apple recognizes this, and has constructed manufacturing processes that reuse as much water as possible. When it comes to Apple's relationship with suppliers, the company does not simply criticize inefficient suppliers but rather works "with suppliers that don't meet our standards for water reuse" and "help them improve until they do."

Water use is not the only environmental impact Apple considers in its manufacturing processes; as highlighted on Apple's environmental responsibility web page, "We believe true innovation must consider everything." This all-inclusive approach to environmental consideration includes a partnership with the Conservation Fund to "protect and create the type of forests we use in our packaging," develop "a renewable micro-hydro project to power our data center in Prineville, Oregon," and construct "a solar farm in China to offset energy used by our offices and retail stores." While environmental impact is a necessary aspect of Apple's operations, the company has implemented processes that reduce the environmental impact and improve the company's relationship with its various stakeholders and with the general public.

Using Cost-Volume-Profit Relationships

Cost-volume-profit relationships can be used in a number of ways during planning and budgeting sessions to test possible courses of action. The following three independent situations, based on Fezzari's operating income presented in **Exhibit 19-11**, reveal ways that Fezzari might use cost-volume-profit relationships to make business decisions.

Situation 1

Assume that Fezzari's managers are considering reducing the average price of the CR1 (on a per-unit basis) from $1,500 to $1,300. *How would this change affect the break-even point in units?*

$$\text{Break-even units} = \frac{\text{Total fixed cost}}{\text{Unit contribution margin}}$$

$$= \frac{\$595,000}{(\$1,300 - \$1,138)}$$

$$= 3,673 \text{ units}$$

The $200 price decrease would cause the break-even point to increase from 1,644 units (previously calculated) to 3,673 units.

Situation 2

Assume that Fezzari's managers are considering an advertising campaign that would increase the CR1's fixed costs by $50,000 to $645,000 and allow a price increase from $1,500 to $1,600 per unit. *How would this change affect the break-even point in units* for the CR1 product line?

$$\text{Break-even units} = \frac{\text{Total fixed cost}}{\text{Unit contribution margin}}$$

$$= \frac{\$645,000}{(\$1,600 - \$1,138)}$$

$$= 1,396 \text{ units}$$

The $50,000 advertising campaign and the related $100 price increase would cause the CR1 break-even point to decrease from 1,644 units to 1,369 units.

Situation 3

Assume that Fezzari's managers are considering eliminating the sales commission program and increasing the sales force base salaries. This change would decrease the CR1 unit variable cost from $1,138 to $1,088 and would increase fixed costs from $595,000 to $695,000. Average unit sales price would remain at $1,500. If the company wants to achieve an after-tax net income for the CR1 product line of $700,000 and if the income tax rate is 30%, *what would the impact be on desired units sold of eliminating the sales commission program?*

$$\text{Desired units} = \frac{\text{Total fixed cost} + \text{Desired net income before income tax}}{\text{Unit contribution margin}}$$

With the current sales commissions program:

$$\text{Desired units} = \frac{\$595,000 + \dfrac{\$700,000}{(1 - 0.30)}}{\$1,500 - \$1,138} = 4,406 \text{ units}$$

Without the current sales commissions program:

$$\text{Desired units} = \frac{\$695,000 + \dfrac{\$700,000}{(1 - 0.30)}}{\$1,500 - \$1,088} = 4,114 \text{ units}$$

The elimination of the sales commission program would decrease the desired CR1 volume from 4,406 units to 4,114 units. As a result, Fezzari would be able to sell 292 fewer CR1s at the same price and still attain the same desired after-tax net income.

Break-Even Analysis and Multiple Products

As indicated previously, we must assume in break-even analysis that only one product is involved or that the product mix (the ratio of units of each product sold to the total units sold) is constant. Break-even sales can be computed for a sales mix of two or more products by calculating the weighted average unit contribution margin.

Assume that a company sells three units of product A for every unit of B (note that this information indicates that the sales mix is 75% A and 25% B) and has fixed costs of $88,000. Also assume the following relationships between selling price and variable costs:

	Product A	Product B
Unit selling price.............	$14.00	$7.00
Less: Unit variable cost	8.00	3.00
Unit contribution margin........	$ 6.00	$4.00

The weighted average unit contribution margin can be calculated as follows:

Product A: $6.00 × 0.75 =	$4.50
Product B: $4.00 × 0.25 =	1.00
Weighted average unit contribution margin	$5.50

The break-even volume can then be calculated:

$$\text{Break-even units} = \frac{\text{Total fixed cost}}{\text{Unit contribution margin}}$$

$$= \frac{\$88,000}{\$5.50}$$

$$= 16,000 \text{ units}$$

The 16,000 units include units of A and units of B. The exact mix and related contribution margin are calculated as illustrated in **Exhibit 19-18**.

Exhibit 19-18	Multiple Product Break-Even Analysis			
Product	**Product Mix**	**Units Sold**	**Unit Contribution Margin**	**Total Contribution Margin**
A....................	0.75	12,000	$6.00	$72,000
B....................	0.25	4,000	$4.00	16,000
Total		16,000		$88,000

These concepts could be applied to any product mix or number of products.

A change in the product mix will usually change the break-even point, because each product typically has a unique contribution margin.

Cost-Volume-Profit Analysis for Retail Businesses

Most retailing industries have developed relationships between product costs and retail price that need to be maintained in order to be profitable. Each segment of each industry has its own ideal relationship. For example, a men's clothing store would typically have a lower ratio of retail price to product cost than a custom tailor, whereas a downhill ski shop would typically have a higher ratio than a general sports retail store.

Many restaurants strive to have the price of their meals set at 2.5 times the cost of the food used in the meal. Portion control is a key element in applying this ratio. For each food item or ingredient to be included in one portion or meal, a standard quantity (weight or volume) must be established. This standard recipe can be used to determine the food cost of a meal. For example, if a restaurant serves 8 ounces of ingredient A (costing 35 cents per ounce) plus 2 ounces of ingredient B (costing 25 cents per ounce), this would yield a food cost of $3.30 per portion and a target price of $8.25 (based on the 2.5 rule).

Retail establishments also have varying staffing needs. The number of employees on duty will change, for example, depending on the time of day. For instance, assume Joe's Food Shack, located on a southern California beach, has one cook and one cashier working from 11:00 AM to 2:00 PM, two cooks and three cashiers working from 2:00 PM to 5:00 PM, and two cooks and two cashiers working from 5:00 PM to 9:00 PM. The number and type of employees on duty must be predetermined. Therefore, the cost to employ these servers and cooks is fixed over a given shift. They are typically paid the same amount regardless of how many meals are served. Customer tips (which are not an expense of the company) would vary, depending in part on the number of meals served.

These concepts should be incorporated in cost-volume-profit analysis for a restaurant. Assume Joe's Food Shack serves only three food choices: hamburgers, hot dogs, and nachos, with food costs per item of $5.00, $4.00, and $3.00, respectively. Because Joe's is the only establishment on the entire beach, Joe's can charge monopoly prices for its food items. Using the 2.5 ratio, the related prices are $12.50, $10.00, and $7.50, respectively. If 20% of the items sold are hamburgers, 50% are hot dogs, and 30% are nachos, then the average revenue per food item sold would be $9.75 and the average food cost would be $3.90, as illustrated in **Exhibit 19-19**.

Exhibit 19-19	Cost and Pricing Analysis for Joe's Food Shack				
Food Type	**Proportion**	**Cost per Unit**	**Weighted Average Cost**	**Price per Unit**	**Weighted Average Price**
Hamburger	20%	$5.00	$1.00	$12.50	$2.50
Hot dog	50%	4.00	2.00	10.00	5.00
Nachos	30%	3.00	0.90	7.50	2.25
Total			$3.90		$9.75

The weighted average unit contribution margin, therefore, is $9.75 − $3.90 − $5.85.

If the total fixed costs, including personnel, are $64,350 for a typical 30-day month when the restaurant is open every day for the scheduled hours, the break-even volume would be calculated as follows:

$$\frac{\$64,350}{\$5.85} = 11,000 \text{ food items per month}$$

Thus, this sales mix is comprised of 2,200 hamburgers (11,000 × 0.20), 5,500 hot dogs (11,000 × 0.50), and 3,300 nachos (11,000 × 0.30),

| | Management Perspective on Cost Analysis | ACCOUNTING IN PRACTICE |

Managing costs is a prevailing concern for managers. The concepts introduced in this chapter underlie most efforts to analyze and project cost in a variety of decision situations. In practice, because projections of future costs are subject to many complicating factors, for most companies they are *estimates of probable costs* rather than precise determinations. Properly used—with full recognition of their limitations—cost behavior analyses can be highly useful to management.

SERVICE INDUSTRY IN FOCUS

Environmental Business Consultants (EBC) has two offices, one in northern California and one in southern California. EBC provides three basic services to its clients: rate reviews, contract procurement and negotiations, and operational studies. EBC management wants to determine how many projects of each service would need to be performed in 2015 to achieve a before-tax profit of $650,000. EBC managers have gathered the following information from 2013 for the analysis.

The proportion of projects done in each office was as follows:

	Northern California	Southern California
Rate reviews........................	30%	50%
Contract procurements	60%	30%
Operational studies	10%	20%

The average contribution margin for each project type was as follows:

	Northern California	Southern California
Rate reviews........................	$ 5,100	$24,124
Contract procurements	28,000	37,000
Operational studies	10,035	20,000

EBC has budgeted 2015 fixed expenses to be $2,251,159 and $644,341 in the northern and southern California offices, respectively.

Required

1. How many projects of each type must EBC perform in the northern California office if managers expect the office to generate $450,000 of the desired total income?

2. How many projects of each type must EBC perform in the southern California office if managers expect the office to generate $200,000 of the desired total income?

Solution

1. The weighted average contribution margin for the northern California office is:

$ 5,100 × 0.30 =	$ 1,530
$28,000 × 0.60 =	16,800
$10,035 × 0.10 =	1,004
Weighted average contribution margin	$19,334

The number of total projects needed is:

$$\text{Needed projects} = \frac{\$2,251,159 + \$450,000}{\$19,334}$$

$$= 140 \text{ projects (rounded)}$$

The number of projects by type is:

Rate reviews............	(140 × 0.30)	42
Contract procurements ...	(140 × 0.60)	84
Operational studies	(140 × 0.10)	14

2. The weighted average contribution margin for the southern California office is:

$24,124 × 0.50 =	$12,062
$37,000 × 0.30 =	11,100
$20,000 × 0.20 =	4,000
Weighted average contribution margin	$27,162

The number of total projects needed is:

$$\text{Needed projects} = \frac{\$644,341 + \$200,000}{\$27,162}$$

$$= 31 \text{ projects (rounded)}$$

The number of projects by type is:

Rate reviews............	(31 × 0.50)	16 (rounded)
Contract procurements ...	(31 × 0.30)	9 (rounded)
Operational studies	(31 × 0.20)	6 (rounded)

COMPREHENSIVE PROBLEM

Maricopa Corporation has developed the budget for its next year of operations. The budget included the following:

Sales of 100,000 units at $5
Units sold will equal units produced
Variable costs for 100,000 units:

Direct material....................	$125,000
Direct labor......................	100,000
Variable overhead.................	30,000
Selling and administrative expense ...	45,000
Total fixed cost....................	120,000

Income tax rate of 30%

Required
a. What is Maricopa's break-even point, in units and in dollars, for next year?
b. Demonstrate that the unit amount reconciles with the dollar amount.
c. What amount of sales revenue would Maricopa need to realize next year in order to generate a net income of $63,000 after tax?
d. Demonstrate the correctness of the calculations in requirement (c) by constructing an income statement.

Solution

a. Variable costs:

Direct material	$125,000
Direct labor.	100,000
Variable overhead.	30,000
Selling and administrative	45,000
Total variable cost at 100,000 units . . .	$300,000

$$\$300,000 / 100,000 \text{ units} = \$3 \text{ per unit}$$

$$\text{Unit contribution margin} = \$5 - \$3 = \$2$$

$$\text{Contribution margin ratio} = \frac{\$2}{\$5} = 0.4$$

$$\text{Break-even units} = \frac{\text{Total fixed cost}}{\text{Unit contribution margin}}$$
$$= \frac{\$120,000}{\$2}$$
$$= 60,000 \text{ units}$$

$$\text{Break-even sales} = \frac{\text{Total fixed cost}}{\text{Contribution margin ratio}}$$
$$= \frac{\$120,000}{0.4}$$
$$= \$300,000$$

b. 60,000 units $\times$ $5 unit selling price = $300,000

c.

$$\text{Desired sales} = \frac{\text{Total fixed cost} + \dfrac{\text{Net income}}{1 - \text{Income tax}}}{\text{Contribution margin ratio}}$$

$$= \frac{\$120,000 + \dfrac{\$63,000}{1 - 0.3}}{0.4}$$

$$= \$525,000$$

d.

Sales.	$525,000
Variable cost ([1 − 0.4] × $525,000) . . .	315,000
Contribution margin	$210,000
Fixed cost.	120,000
Net income before income tax.	$ 90,000
Income tax at 30%.	27,000
Net income.	$ 63,000

SUMMARY OF LEARNING OBJECTIVES

LO1 **Develop an understanding of how specific types of costs change in response to volume changes. (p. 884)**

- For meaningful managerial analysis, costs must be related to some measure of business activity or cost driver. A critical aspect is that the activity measure used must have a logical causal relation with costs, and the quantity of the activity must be highly correlated with the level of costs.

- One of the most useful tools for analyzing the relationship between changes in cost and volume is the *cost-volume graph*. Such graphs typically plot total costs on the vertical axis and either volume or activity level on the horizontal axis. Cost-volume graphs are particularly valuable when available cost-volume data are plotted on the same graph and other cost-volume relationships are estimated by fitting a line to the known points.
- The behavior of total cost in response to volume changes is divided into three basic categories within a relevant range:
  - Variable, which responds proportionately, with zero cost at zero volume
  - Fixed, which is constant
  - Mixed, which responds, but less than proportionately, due to the fixed component
- Total cost for most entities is best represented by the mixed cost pattern.

Define the concept of *relevant range*. (p. 887)   **LO2**

- We can assume linearity of cost because it is approximately true within the range of volume relevant to the analysis.
- The relevant range is the range of activity over which the behavior of a cost behaves consistently.
- Within the relevant range, *per-unit* costs behave as follows when volume is increased:
  - Variable costs remain constant.
  - Fixed costs decrease proportionately.
  - Variable plus fixed cost decreases, but not proportionately.

Outline the approach to developing cost formulas. (p. 888)   **LO3**

- In order to perform CVP analysis to make better decisions, total costs need to be broken into fixed and variable components. We illustrate three approaches for accomplishing this: (1) the scattergraph method, (2) the high-low method, and (3) the least squares regression method.
- The scattergraph method entails plotting the observed cost at several levels of volume on a graph, then drawing a line that places approximately half of the dots above and half below the line.
- The high-low method is relatively simple and compares costs at the highest and lowest levels of activity for which representative cost data are available. A line is then drawn between the highest- and lowest-volume data points.
- The least squares regression method is a statistical tool that uses all of the data points to separate a mixed cost into its variable and fixed components. A regression line is fitted to the data points so that the distance from each point to the line is minimized for all points.
- A general formula for planning total cost is as follows: Total cost = Total fixed cost + (Variable cost per unit × Number of units).

Present a discussion of and a formula for calculating the break-even point. (p. 893)   **LO4**

- The break-even point (where Revenues = Costs) can be derived by graph, formula, or contribution margin analysis.
- Assumptions underlying break-even analysis include the following:
  - Total fixed cost and per-unit variable cost are constant over the entire relevant range.
  - Selling price per unit remains the same regardless of the volume of sales.
  - When more than one product is involved and sales volume varies, each product's percentage of total sales (sales mix) does not change.

Define *contribution margin* and *contribution margin ratio* and present alternate break-even formulas   **LO5**
and examples of their application. (p. 895)

- Contribution margin = Revenue − Variable cost

- $$\text{Contribution margin ratio} = \frac{\text{Contribution margin}}{\text{Sales}}$$

  or

- $$\text{Contribution margin ratio} = \frac{\text{Unit contribution margin}}{\text{Unit selling price}}$$

■ Formulas used in break-even analysis include the following:

❏ $\text{Break-even units} = \dfrac{\text{Total fixed cost}}{\text{Unit contribution margin}}$

❏ $\text{Break-even sales} = \dfrac{\text{Total fixed cost}}{\text{Contribution margin ratio}}$

LO6   **Discuss approaches to planning net income using cost-volume-profit analyses. (p. 897)**

■ Formulas used in planning net income include the following:

❏ Desired sales = Total variable cost + Total fixed cost + Desired net income

❏ $\text{Desired units} = \dfrac{\text{Total fixed cost} + \text{Desired net income}}{\text{Unit contribution margin}}$

❏ $\text{Desired sales} = \dfrac{\text{Total fixed cost} + \text{Desired net income}}{\text{Contribution margin ratio}}$

■ Often management wants to develop plans using net income after tax instead of net income. The relationship between net income before income tax and net after-tax income is demonstrated by the following formula:

❏ $\text{Net income before income tax} = \dfrac{\text{Net after-tax income}}{1 - \text{Income tax rate}}$

■ Margin of safety = Actual sales − Break-even sales
■ One measure of a firm's relative level of fixed costs is operating leverage. Operating leverage is computed as follows:

❏ $\text{Operating leverage} = \dfrac{\text{Contribution margin}}{\text{Net operating income}}$

■ Break-even and net income planning computations involving multiple products incorporate the concept of weighted average unit contribution margin.

KEY TERMS

Break-even point (p. 893)	**Cost-volume-profit (CVP)** **analysis** (p. 884)	**Relevant range** (p. 887)
Contribution margin (p. 895)	**Fixed costs** (p. 886)	**Total variable costs** (p. 886)
Contribution margin **ratio** (p. 896)	**Margin of safety** (p. 900)	**Variable operating income** **statement** (p. 895)
Cost behavior analysis (p. 884)	**Mixed costs** (p. 887)	
Cost-volume graph (p. 885)	**Operating leverage** (p. 900)	

Assignments with the ⓂBC logo in the margin are available in my BusinessCourse.
See the Preface of the book for details.

SELF-STUDY QUESTIONS

(Answers to Self-Study Questions are at the end of this chapter.)

LO2   1. **When moving from the low end to the high end of a relevant range, straight-line depreciation expense per unit**
   a.   Increases.
   b.   Decreases.
   c.   Remains the same.
   d.   Changes unpredictably.

2. **In a typical cost formula**   **LO3**
   a. Fixed costs are per unit and variable costs are per unit.
   b. Fixed costs are per unit and variable costs are in total.
   c. Fixed costs are in total and variable costs are in total.
   d. Fixed costs are in total and variable costs are per unit.

3. **At the break-even point**   **LO4**
   a. Contribution margin = fixed costs.
   b. Variable costs = fixed costs.
   c. Sales − contribution margin.
   d. Contribution margin = 0.

4. **Contribution margin ratio is**   **LO5**
   a. Unit sales price/unit contribution margin.
   b. I/margin of safety.
   c. Total contribution margin/sales.
   d. Variable cost/fixed cost.

5. **Net income before income tax is**   **LO6**
   a. Net income/(1 − income tax rate).
   b. Income tax rate/net income.
   c. Net income + contribution margin.
   d. Net income/income tax rate.

QUESTIONS

1. Define the terms *cost behavior* and *relevant range*.   **LO1, 2**

2. Identify some common activity bases in terms of which the volume of a manufacturing operation might be stated. What general criterion might be used in choosing an activity base?   **LO1**

3. Name and define briefly the three most widely recognized cost behavior patterns.   **LO1**

4. Explain (a) how a mixed cost can be considered "partly fixed and partly variable," and (b) why a firm's total cost is best represented by the mixed cost pattern.   **LO1, 3**

5. Briefly describe the two most straightforward techniques for dividing a mixed cost into its fixed and variable components.   **LO3**

6. "Actual costs often behave in a nonlinear fashion. Therefore, assumptions of linearity invalidate most cost behavior analyses." Do you agree or disagree with this statement? Briefly defend your position.   **LO2**

7. Describe how fixed and variable costs per unit respond to volume increases.   **LO1, 3**

8. Present a formula based on units for planning total cost, and explain how mixed costs are incorporated into the formula.   **LO3**

9. Define and briefly explain three approaches to break-even analysis.   **LO4**

10. Patrick's Bakery Shop has fixed costs per month of $3,600, and variable costs are 55% of sales. What amount of monthly sales allows the shop to break even?   **LO4**

11. Quality Car Wash has fixed costs per month of $16,800, and variable costs are 20% of sales. The average amount collected per car washed during the past year has been $5. How many cars must be washed per month to break even?   **LO4**

12. You have graphed the cost-volume-profit relationships for a company on a break-even chart after being informed of certain assumptions. Explain how the lines on the chart would change if (a) fixed costs increased over the entire range of activity, (b) selling price per unit decreased, and (c) variable costs per unit increased.   **LO4**

13. Define *contribution margin*. Is it best expressed as a total amount or as a per-unit amount? In what way is the term descriptive of the concept it represents?   **LO5**

14. Explain the approach to break-even analysis that is used for a mix of two or more products.   **LO6**

15. Explain how break-even formulas can provide income-planning analyses.   **LO6**

16. In planning net income, how can (post tax) net income be incorporated into the planning formula?   **LO6**

EXERCISES—SET A

LO1

SERVICE AND
MERCHANDISING

E19-1A. Cost-Volume Graphs Set up a cost-volume graph. Volume should range from zero to 24,000 units (in 4,000-unit increments), and cost should range from zero to $24,000 (in $4,000 increments). Plot each of the following groups of cost data using different marks for each group. After completing the graph, indicate the type of cost behavior exhibited by each group.

Volume (applicable to each group)	Group A Costs	Group B Costs	Group C Costs
2,000	$ 6,600	$ 2,400	$8,000
6,000	9,800	7,000	8,000
10,000	13,000	12,000	8,000
20,000	21,000	24,000	8,000

LO3

SERVICE AND
MERCHANDISING

E19-2A. High-Low Method Apply the high-low method of cost analysis to the three cost data groups in E19-1A. What cost behavior patterns are apparent? Express each as a cost formula.

LO2, 3

MBC

E19-3A. Relevant Range and High-Low Method The following selected data relate to the major cost categories experienced by Shaw Company at varying levels of operating volumes. Assuming that all operating volumes are within the relevant range, calculate the appropriate costs in each column in which blanks appear.

	Total Cost (@ 3,000 units)	Total Cost (@ 4,000 units)	Variable Cost per Unit	Total Fixed Cost	Total Cost (@ 5,000 units)
Direct labor (variable)	$60,000	$80,000	_____	_____	_____
Factory supervision (semivariable). . .	50,000	65,000	_____	_____	_____
Factory depreciation (fixed)	30,000	30,000	_____	_____	_____

LO3

SERVICE AND
MERCHANDISING

MBC

E19-4A. Total Cost Formula Davis Company has analyzed its overhead costs and derived a general formula for their behavior: $60,000 + $14 per direct labor hour employed. The company expects to use 50,000 direct labor hours during the next accounting period. What overhead rate per direct labor hour should be applied to jobs worked during the period?

LO4

E19-5A. Break-Even Chart Set up a break-even chart similar to the one in **Exhibit 19-12** with proportional scales from zero to $72,000 (in $12,000 increments) on the vertical axis and from zero to 12,000 units of production (in 2,000-unit increments) on the horizontal axis. Prepare the break-even chart for Morton Company, assuming total fixed costs of $18,000 and unit selling price and unit variable cost for the company's one product of $6 and $4, respectively. Label the total revenue line and the total cost line. Indicate the break-even point in units and dollars.

LO6

MBC

E19-6A. Net Income Planning Nolden Company has charged a selling price of $20 per unit, incurred variable costs of $14 per unit, and total fixed costs of $90,000. What unit sales volume is necessary to earn the following related amounts of net income before income tax? (a) $18,000; (b) $27,000; or (c) equal to 20% of sales revenue.

LO4, 5, 6

MBC

E19-7A. Cost-Volume Profit Analysis Hailstorm Company sells a single product for $22 per unit. Variable costs are $14 per unit and fixed costs are $60,000 at an operating level of 7,000 to 12,000 units.
a. What is Hailstorm Company's break-even point in units?
b. How many units must be sold to earn $12,000 before income tax?
c. How many units must be sold to earn $13,000 after income tax, assuming a 35% tax rate?

LO6

MBC

E19-8A. Break-Even with Multiple Products Warner Company has $228,000 of total fixed costs and sells products A and B with a product mix of 40% A and 60% B. Selling prices and variable costs for A and B result in contribution margins per unit of $10 and $6, respectively. Compute the break-even point.

LO1

MBC

E19-9A. Cost Patterns The graphs below represent approximations of cost behavior patterns. The horizontal axis of each graph represents units and the vertical axis represents dollars of total cost.

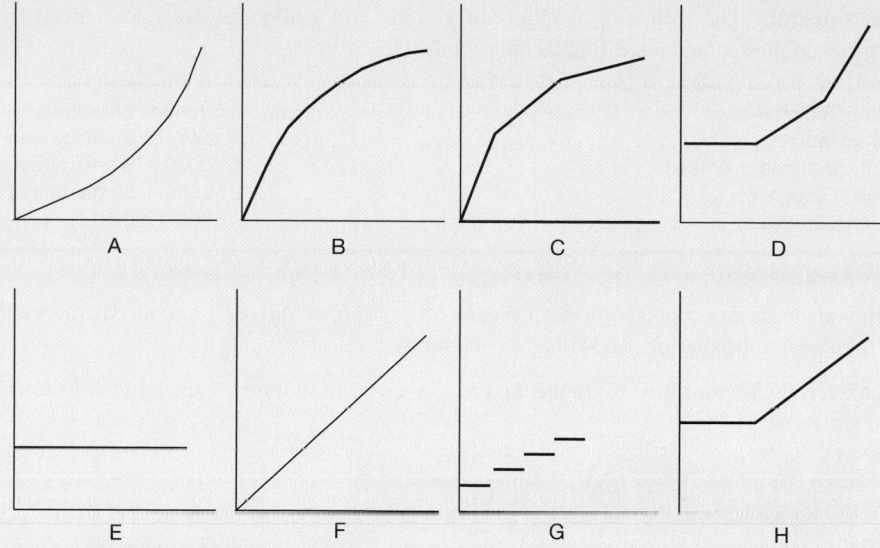

Select the graph that best matches each of the situations described below. Each graph may be selected more than once.

a. Straight-line depreciation of a factory building.

b. Utility bill for electricity that includes a fixed charge per month plus a constant usage rate per hour for hours in excess of 100.

c. Cost of microchip incorporated into a product.

d. Labor cost of machine operators who become more productive as they gain experience.

e. Water bill that includes a flat fee for the first 10,000 gallons used plus an increasing usage charge for each additional 10,000 gallons used.

f. Cost of factory supplies when increasing quantities bring cost discounts as each price break level is attained.

g. Salaries of quality inspectors when one additional inspector is hired for each 20,000 units produced.

h. Cost of an advertising campaign.

EXERCISES—SET B

E19-1B. High-Low Method The highest and lowest levels of activity for the Denton Company were 54,000 direct labor hours and 36,000 direct labor hours, respectively. If maintenance costs were $320,000 at the 54,000-hour level and $230,000 at the 36,000-hour level, what cost might we expect at an operating level of 40,000 direct labor hours?

LO3

SERVICE AND MERCHANDISING

E19-2B. High-Low Method During the past year, Cutler, Inc., operated within the relevant range of its fixed costs. Monthly production volume during the year ranged from 40,000 to 60,000 units of product and corresponding total manufacturing costs ranged from $4.00 to $3.80 per unit. Determine the total cost behavior pattern experienced by Cutler, Inc.

LO3

E19-3B. Relevant Range and High-Low Method The following selected data relate to the major cost categories experienced by Sterling Company at varying levels of operating volumes. Assuming that all operating volumes are within the relevant range, calculate the appropriate costs in each column in which blanks appear:

LO2, 3

	Total Cost (@ 5,000 units)	Total Cost (@ 6,000 units)	Variable Cost per Unit	Total Fixed Cost	Total Cost (@ 7,000 units)
Direct labor (variable)	$60,000	$72,000	—	—	—
Factory supervision (semivariable) . . .	20,000	22,000	—	—	—
Factory depreciation (fixed)	18,000	18,000	—	—	—

LO3   **E19-4B. Cost Formula** The following amounts of various cost categories are experienced by Columbia Factories in producing and selling its only product:

Direct material	$8 per unit of product
Direct labor...	$10 per direct labor hour*
Manufacturing overhead	$12,000 + $4 per direct labor hour
Selling expenses	$14,000 + $3 per unit of product
Administrative...	$7,000 + $0.50 per unit of product

*Each unit of product requires one-half direct labor hour.

Combine the various cost factors into a general total cost formula for Columbia Factories and determine the total cost of producing and selling 20,000 units.

LO4   **E19-5B. Break-Even Calculations** Compute the break-even point in units for each of the following independent situations:

	Unit Selling Price	Unit Variable Cost	Total Fixed Cost
a.	$10	$7	$ 90,000
b.	12	9	144,000
c.	5	3	54,000

Confirm each answer using contribution margin ratio analysis.

LO6   **E19-6B. Net Income Planning** Holland Corporation earned an after-tax net income of $120,000 last year. Fixed costs were $600,000. The selling price per unit of its product was $120, of which $50 was a contribution to fixed cost and net income. The income tax rate was 40%.

   a.   How many units of product were sold last year?

   b.   What was the break-even point in units last year?

   c.   The company wishes to increase its after-tax net income by 20% this year. If selling prices and the income tax rate remain unchanged, how many units must be sold?

LO6   **E19-7B. Cost-Volume-Profit Analysis** Gannon Company sells a single product for $15 per unit. Variable costs are $10 per unit and fixed costs are $90,000 at an operating level of 16,000 to 30,000 units.

   a.   What is Gannon Company's break-even point in units?

   b.   How many units must be sold to earn $20,000 before income tax?

   c.   How many units must be sold to earn $30,000 after income tax, assuming a 40% tax rate?

LO6   **E19-8B. Multiple Product Break-Even Analysis** Wynn Company has $142,000 total fixed cost and sells products A and B with a product mix of 70% A and 30% B. Selling prices and variable costs for A and B result in contribution margins per unit of $8 and $5, respectively. Compute the break-even point.

LO1   **E19-9B. Cost Patterns** The following graph depicts cost-volume relationships for Tallmadge Company:

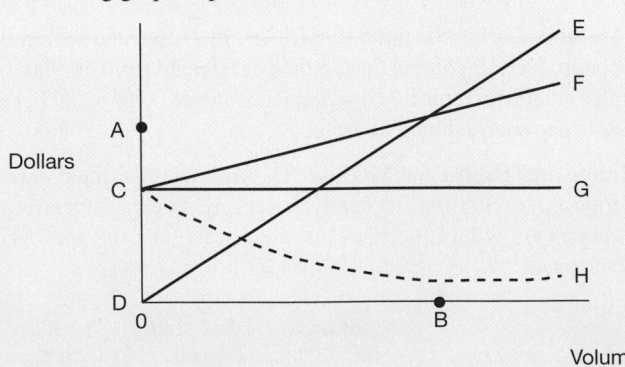

Choose a labeled point *or* line on the graph that *best* represents the behavior of each of the following items as operating volume is increased. Answers may be the same for more than one item. Answer each item independently.

a.   Total sales revenue.
b.   Total costs.
c.   Total variable costs.
d.   Total fixed costs.
e.   Total mixed cost.
f.   Break-even point.

PROBLEMS—SET A

P19-1A. Net Income Planning Selected operating data for Oakbrook Company in four independent situations are shown below.

LO4, 5

SERVICE AND
MERCHANDISING

MBC

	A	B	C	D
Sales.	$300,000	$ c.	$ e.	$260,000
Variable expense	$ a.	$91,000	$ f.	$ g.
Fixed expense	$ b.	$62,000	$43,200	$ 89,000
Net income before tax (loss).	$ 20,000	$15,000	$28,800	$ (11,000)
Units sold	30,000	d.		
Unit contribution margin.	$ 5.20	$ 7.00		
Contribution margin ratio			0.4	h.

Required
Fill in the blanks for each independent situation. Show your calculations.

P19-2A. Graphing Mixed Cost During a recent six-month period, Wade Corporation had the following monthly production volume and total monthly maintenance expense:

LO1, 2, 3

	Units Produced	Maintenance Expense
March	21,000	$140,000
April	15,000	112,000
May.	30,000	184,000
June	27,000	172,000
July.	35,000	208,000
August	25,000	160,000

Required
Assume that all volumes are in the relevant range.

a.   Explain why the data indicate that the maintenance expense is neither a fixed nor a variable expense.
b.   Construct a graph similar to the one in **Exhibit 19-7** and plot the maintenance expense data.
c.   Fit a line (by sight) to the cost observation points and estimate the cost formula.
d.   Confirm your answer in requirement (c) with high-low analysis.

P19-3A. Cost Formulas Shorewood Manufacturing produces a single product requiring the following direct material and direct labor:

LO2, 3, 6

MBC

Description	Cost per Unit of Input	Required Amount per Unit of Product
Material A	$ 8/pound	10 ounces
Material B	5/pound	8 ounces
Material C	20/gallon	0.3 gallon
Cutting labor.	9/hour	30 minutes
Shaping labor.	11/hour	15 minutes
Finishing labor	12/hour	45 minutes

Manufacturing overhead consists of indirect material, $0.60 per unit of product; indirect labor, $1,000 per month plus $0.70 per unit of product; factory maintenance, $14,000 per year plus $0.55 per unit of product; factory depreciation, $15,000 per year; and annual factory property taxes, $8,000. Selling and administrative expenses include the salaries of a sales manager, $30,000 per year; an office manager, $18,000 per year; and two salespersons, each of whom is paid a base salary of $11,000 per year and a commission of $3 per unit sold. Advertising and promotion of the product are done through a year-round media package program costing $1,000 per week.

Required

a. Analyze all cost and expense factors to determine a general formula (based on units of production) for total cost.

b. Assuming a relevant range of 10,000 to 20,000 units, what is the estimated unit cost for producing and selling 10,000 units? 20,000 units? Explain the variation in unit cost at the two levels of production.

c. If 15,000 units are produced and sold in a year, what selling price results in a net income before income tax of $60,000?

LO2, 3 **P19-4A. High-Low and Cost Formula** Harrison Company has accumulated the following total manufacturing overhead costs for two levels of activity (within the relevant range):

	Low	High
Activity (direct labor hours)...	80,000	120,000
Total manufacturing overhead	$468,000	$604,000

The total overhead cost includes variable, fixed, and mixed costs. At 120,000 direct labor hours, the total cost breakdown is as follows:

Variable cost..	$264,000
Fixed cost...	160,000
Semi-mixed cost	180,000

Required

a. Using the high-low method of cost analysis, determine the variable portion of the semi-variable cost per direct labor hour. Determine the total fixed cost component of the mixed cost.

b. What should the total planned overhead cost be at 100,000 direct labor hours?

LO1, 2, 3 **P19-5A. Cost Formula** Princeton Manufacturing Company summarizes the following total cost data for the month of March. Princeton has a normal capacity per month of 25,000 units of product that sell for $40 each. For the foreseeable future, sales volume should equal normal capacity of production.

Direct material	$295,000
Direct labor..	165,000
Variable overhead..	85,000
Fixed overhead (Note 1)...	140,000
Selling expense (Note 2)...	80,000
Administrative expense (fixed)	56,000
	$821,000

Notes:

1. Beyond normal capacity, fixed overhead cost increases $6,350 for each 1,000 units *or fraction thereof until* a maximum capacity of 30,000 units is reached.

2. Selling expenses are a 5% sales commission plus shipping costs of $1.20 per unit.

Required

a. Using the information available, prepare a formula to estimate Princeton's total cost at various production volumes up to normal capacity.

b. Prove your answer in requirement (a) relative to the total cost figure for 25,000 units.

c. Calculate the planned total cost at 20,000 units, and explain why total cost did not decrease in proportion to the reduced volume.

d. If Princeton were operating at normal capacity and accepted an order for 500 more units, what would it have to charge for the order to earn a net income before income tax of $8 per unit on the new sale?

P19-6A. Net Income Planning Superior Corporation sells a single product for $60 per unit, of which $36 is contribution margin. Fixed costs total $72,000 and net income before income tax is $28,800.

LO4, 5, 6

SERVICE AND MERCHANDISING

MBC

Required

Determine the following (show key computations):

a. The present sales volume in dollars.
b. The break-even point in units.
c. The sales volume in units necessary to attain a net income before income tax of $39,600.
d. The sales volume in units necessary to attain a net income before income tax equal to 20% of sales revenue.
e. The sales volume in units necessary to attain an after-tax net income of $43,200 if the tax rate is 40%.

P19-7A. Break-Even and Net Income Planning The controller of Grafton Company is preparing data for a conference call concerning certain *independent* aspects of its operations.

LO4, 5, 6

Required

Prepare answers to the following questions for the controller:

a. Total fixed cost is $1,440,000 and a unit of product is sold for $12 in excess of its unit variable cost. What is the break-even in units?
b. The company will sell 60,000 units of product—each having a unit variable cost of $22—at a price that will enable the product to absorb $600,000 of fixed cost. What minimum unit sales price must be charged to break even?
c. Net income before income tax of $320,000 is desired after covering $1,200,000 of fixed costs. What minimum contribution margin ratio must be maintained if total sales revenue is to be $3,800,000?
d. Net income before income tax is 10% of sales revenue, the contribution margin ratio is 30%, and the break-even dollar sales is $640,000. What is the amount of total revenue?
e. Fixed costs total $1,000,000, the variable cost per unit is $30, and selling price per unit is $80. What dollar sales volume will generate an after-tax net income of $84,000 when the income tax rate is 40%?

P19-8A. Break-Even and Net Income Planning Paulson Company has recently leased facilities for the manufacture of a new product. Based on studies made by its accounting personnel, the following data are available:

LO4, 5, 6

Estimated annual sales: 40,000 units.

Estimated Costs	Amount	Unit Cost
Direct material	$ 696,000	$17.40
Direct labor	584,000	14.60
Manufacturing overhead	376,000	9.40
Administrative expenses	187,200	4.68
	$1,843,200	$46.08

Selling expenses are expected to be 10% of sales, and the selling price is $64 per unit. Ignore income tax in this problem.

Required

a. Compute a break-even point in dollars and in units. Assume that manufacturing overhead and administrative expenses are fixed but that other costs are variable.
b. What would net income before income tax be if 30,000 units were sold?
c. How many units must be sold to earn a net income before income tax of 10% of sales?

LO4, 5, 6 **P19-9A. Multiple Product Break-Even and Net Income Planning** Grand Company manufactures and sells the following three products:

	Economy	Standard	Deluxe
Unit sales	10,000	6,000	4,000
Unit sales price.	$48	$56	$68
Unit variable cost	$30	$32	$36

Required
Assume that total fixed cost is $339,000.

a. Compute the net income before income tax based on the sales volumes shown above.
b. Compute the break-even point in total dollars of revenue and in units for each product.
c. Prove your break-even calculations by computing the total contribution margin related to your answer in requirement (b).

PROBLEMS—SET B

LO4, 5 **P19-1B. Net Income Planning** Selected operating data for Verona Company in four independent situations are shown below.

	A	B	C	D
Sales.	$320,000	$ c.	$ e.	$280,000
Variable expense	$ a.	$48,000	$ f.	$ g.
Fixed expense	$ b.	$56,000	$240,000	$120,000
Net income before tax	$ 40,000	$16,000	$ 96,000	$ (8,000)
Units sold	7,000	d.		
Unit contribution margin.	$ 20	$ 9		
Contribution margin ratio			0.70	h.

Required
Fill in the blanks for each independent situation. Show your calculations.

LO1, 2, 3 **P19-2B. Graphing Mixed Cost** During the past operating year, Davenport Corporation had the following monthly volume of production and total monthly maintenance expense:

	Units Produced	Maintenance Expense		Units Produced	Maintenance Expense
January.	120,000	$22,400	July.	124,000	$22,800
February	144,000	25,400	August	154,000	26,600
March	156,000	26,800	September	128,000	23,400
April	130,000	23,200	October	160,000	27,200
May.	140,000	25,000	November.	152,000	26,400
June	150,000	26,400	December.	156,000	26,800

Required
Assume that all volumes are in the relevant range.

a. Explain why the data indicate that the maintenance expense is neither a fixed nor a variable expense.
b. Construct a graph similar to the one in **Exhibit 19-7** and plot the maintenance expense data.
c. Fit a line (by sight) to the cost observation points, and estimate the cost formula.
d. Confirm your answer in requirement (c) with high-low analysis.

LO2, 3, 6 **P19-3B. Cost Formulas** Colonial Manufacturing produces a single product requiring the following direct material and direct labor:

Description	Cost per Unit of Input	Required Amount per Unit of Product
Material A	$ 9/pound	24 ounces
Material B	6/pound	12 ounces
Material C	12/gallon	0.5 gallon
Cutting labor	10/hour	45 minutes
Shaping labor	12/hour	15 minutes
Finishing labor	11/hour	30 minutes

Manufacturing overhead consists of indirect materials, $0.80 per unit of product; indirect labor, $10,000 per year plus $1.20 per unit of product; factory maintenance, $1,000 per month plus $0.60 per unit of product; factory depreciation, $22,000 per year; and annual factory property taxes, $20,000. Selling and administrative expenses include the salaries of a sales manager, $30,000 per year, an office manager, $18,000 per year, and two salespersons, each of whom is paid a base salary of $12,000 per year and a commission of $4 per unit sold. Advertising and promotion of the product are done through a year-round media package program costing $600 per week.

Required

a. Analyze all cost and expense factors to determine a general formula (based on units of production) for total cost.

b. Assuming a relevant range of 20,000 to 40,000 units, what is the estimated unit cost for producing and selling 20,000 units? 40,000 units? Explain the variation in unit cost at the two levels of production

c. If 35,000 units are produced and sold in a year, what selling price results in a net income before taxes of $56,800?

P19-4B. High-Low and Cost Formula Adams Company has accumulated the following total manufacturing overhead costs for two levels of activity (within the relevant range):

LO2, 3

	Low	High
Activity (direct labor hours)	30,000	50,000
Total manufacturing overhead	$270,000	$362,000

The total overhead cost includes variable, fixed, and mixed costs. At 50,000 direct labor hours, the total cost breakdown is as follows:

Variable cost	$200,000
Fixed cost	90,000
Semi-variable cost	72,000

Required

a. Using the high-low method of cost analysis, determine the variable portion of the mixed cost per direct labor hour. Determine the total fixed cost component of the mixed cost.

b. What should the total planned overhead cost be at 40,000 direct labor hours?

P19-5B. Cost Formula The following total cost data are for Phoenix Manufacturing Company, which has a normal capacity per period of 40,000 units of product that sell for $60 each. For the foreseeable future, sales volume should equal normal capacity of production.

LO1, 2, 3

Direct material	$ 640,000
Direct labor	400,000
Variable overhead	200,000
Fixed overhead (Note 1)	216,000
Selling expense (Note 2)	280,000
Administrative expense (fixed)	88,000
	$1,824,000

Notes:

1. Beyond normal capacity, fixed overhead cost increases $6,240 for each 2,000 units *or fraction thereof* until a maximum capacity of 50,000 units is reached.
2. Selling expenses are a 10% sales commission plus shipping costs of $1 per unit.

Required

a. Using the information available, prepare a formula to estimate Phoenix's total cost at various production volumes up to normal capacity.
b. Prove your answer in requirement (a) against the above total cost figure at 40,000 units.
c. Calculate the planned total cost at 30,000 units, and explain why total cost did not decrease in proportion to the reduced volume.
d. If Phoenix were operating at normal capacity and accepted an order for 600 more units, what would it have to charge for the order to earn a net income before tax of $8 per unit on the new sale?

LO4, 5, 6   **P19-6B.** **Net Income Planning** Midvale Corporation sells a single product for $100 per unit, of which $40 is contribution margin. Total fixed cost is $120,000, and net income before income tax is $48,000.

SERVICE AND
MERCHANDISING

Required

Determine the following (show key computations):

a. The present sales volume in dollars.
b. The break-even point in units.
c. The sales volume in units necessary to attain a net income before income tax of $60,000.
d. The sales volume in units necessary to attain a net income before income tax equal to 10% of sales revenue.
e. The sales volume in units necessary to attain a net income of $54,000 if the tax rate is 40%.

LO4, 5, 6   **P19-7B.** **Break-Even and Net Income Planning** The controller of Wright Company is preparing data for a conference concerning certain *independent* aspects of its operations.

Required

Prepare answers to the following questions for the controller:

a. Total fixed cost is $720,000, and a unit of product is sold for $10 in excess of its unit variable cost. What is the break-even unit volume?
b. The company will sell 30,000 units of product—each having a unit variable cost of $14—at a price that will enable the product to absorb $360,000 of fixed cost. What minimum unit sales price must be charged to break even?
c. Net income before income tax of $150,000 is desired after covering $410,000 of fixed cost. What minimum contribution margin ratio must be maintained if total sales revenue is to be $1,600,000?
d. Net income before income tax is 20% of sales revenue, the contribution margin ratio is 60%, and the break-even dollar sales is $200,000. What is the amount of total revenue?
e. Total fixed cost is $350,000, variable cost per unit is $26, and unit sales price is $50. What dollar sales volume will generate an after-tax net income of $60,000 when the income tax rate is 40%?

LO4, 5, 6   **P19-8B.** **Break-Even and Net Income Planning** Venice Company has recently leased facilities for the manufacture of a new product. Based on studies made by its accounting personnel, the following data are available:

Estimated annual sales		60,000 units

Estimated Costs	Amount	Unit Cost
Direct material	$ 666,000	$11.10
Direct labor	468,000	7.80
Manufacturing overhead	540,000	9.00
Administrative expenses	291,600	4.86
	$1,965,600	$32.76

Selling expenses are expected to be 10% of sales, and the selling price is $42 per unit. Ignore income tax in this problem.

Required

a. Compute a break-even point in dollars and in units. Assume that manufacturing overhead and administrative expenses are fixed but that other costs are variable.

b. What would net income before income tax be if 50,000 units were sold?

c. How many units must be sold to earn a net income before income tax of 10% of sales?

P19-9B. Multiple Product Break-Even and Net Income Planning Madison Company manufactures and sells the following three products:

LO4, 5, 6

SERVICE AND MERCHANDISING

	Red	Blue	Green
Unit sales	20,000	30,000	50,000
Unit sales price.	$30	$62	$18
Unit variable cost	$18	$38	$14

Required

Assume that total fixed cost is $324,800.

a. Compute the net income before income tax based on the sales volumes shown above.

b. Compute the break-even point in total dollars of revenue and in specific unit sales volume for each product.

c. Prove your break-even calculations by computing the total contribution margin related to your answer in requirement (b).

CERTIFIED MANAGEMENT ACCOUNTANT (CMA®) EXAM SAMPLE QUESTIONS

CMA19-1. Bolger and Co. manufactures large gaskets for the turbine industry. Bolger's per unit sales price and variable costs for the current year are as follows.

Sales price per unit $300
Variable costs per unit 210

Bolger's total fixed costs aggregate $360,000. As Bolger's labor agreement is expiring at the end of the year, management is concerned about the effect a new agreement will have on its unit break-even point. The controller performed a sensitivity analysis to ascertain the estimated effect of a $10 per unit direct labor increase and a $10,000 reduction in fixed costs. Based on these data, it was determined that the break-even point would

a. decrease by 1,000 units.
b. decrease by 125 units.
c. increase by 375 units.
d. increase by 500 units.

CMA19-2. All of the following are assumptions of cost-volume-profit analysis **except**

a. total fixed costs do not change with a change in volume.
b. revenues change proportionately with volume.
c. variable costs per unit change proportionately with volume.
d. sales mix for multi-product situations do not vary with volume changes.

CMA19-3. Carson Inc. manufactures only one product and is preparing its budget for next year based on the following information.

Selling price per unit.	$100
Variable costs per unit	75
Fixed costs.	250,000
Effective tax rate.	35%

If Carson wants to achieve a net income of $1.3 million next year, its sales must be

    a. 62,000 units.

    b. 70,200 units.

    c. 80,000 units.

    d. 90,000 units.

CMA19-4. Break-even quantity is defined as the volume of output at which revenues are equal to

    a. marginal costs.

    b. total costs.

    c. variable costs.

    d. fixed costs.

CMA19-5. Ticker Company sells two products. Product A provides a contribution margin of $3 per unit, and Product B provides a contribution margin of $4 per unit. If Ticker's sales mix shifts toward Product A, which one of the following statements is **correct**?

    a. The total number of units necessary to break even will decrease.

    b. The overall contribution margin ratio will increase.

    c. Operating income will decrease if the total number of units sold remains constant.

    d. The contribution margin ratios for Products A and B will change.

EXTENDING YOUR KNOWLEDGE

EYK19-1. Business Decision Case The following total cost data are for Ralston Manufacturing Company, which has a normal capacity per period of 400,000 units of product that sell for $18 each. For the foreseeable future, regular sales volume should continue at normal capacity of production.

Direct material	$1,720,000
Direct labor.	1,120,000
Variable overhead.	560,000
Fixed overhead (Note 1).	880,000
Selling expense (Note 2).	720,000
Administrative expense (fixed)	200,000
	$5,200,000

Notes:

1. Beyond normal capacity, fixed overhead cost increases $30,000 for each 20,000 units *or fraction thereof* until a maximum capacity of 640,000 units is reached.

2. Selling expenses are a 10% sales commission. Ralston pays only one-half of the regular sales commission rates on any sale of 20,000 or more units.

Ralston's sales manager has received a special order for 48,000 units from a large discount chain at a special price of $16 each, F.O.B. factory. The controller's office has furnished the following additional cost data related to the special order:

1. Changes in the product's construction will reduce direct material $1.80 per unit.

2. Special processing will add 25% to the per-unit direct labor costs.

3. Variable overhead will continue at the same proportion of direct labor costs.

4. Other costs should not be affected.

Required

    a. Present an analysis supporting a decision to accept or reject the special order. Assume Ralston's regular sales are not affected by this special order.

    b. What is the lowest unit sales price Ralston could receive and still make a before-tax profit of $39,600 on the special order?

EYK19-2. Ethics Case Gina DeMarc, a partner in a large CPA firm, has been approached by Bruce Jonas, a manager, with the following recommendation for incentive bonuses for staff members. Jonas recommends that the firm continue to pay each staff member a straight annual salary (which has been traditionally the only payment made) plus a bonus based on the staff member's ability to achieve a

10% reduction in time spent on each client's work. The firm would also pay a 5% finder's fee for any new client the staff member brings into the firm.

Jonas believes this will motivate the staff to work more efficiently, to sell the firm to new clients, and to service more clients in any given time period. This should also generate more revenue for the firm.

Required
How would you advise Gina DeMarc? What ethical issues should she consider?

ANSWERS TO SELF-STUDY QUESTIONS:

1. b, (p. 888) 2. d, (p. 889) 3. a, (p. 894) 4. c, (p. 896) 5. a, (p. 899)

YOUR TURN! SOLUTIONS

Solution 19.1
y-intercept = Total fixed costs ($4,500)
Slope = Variable cost per unit
x-axis = Level of activity (water bottle cages produced)
Points on the line = Total costs at that level of output

Solution 19.2
Mixed cost: $2 per unit plus $5,000

$$\frac{\$24,500 - \$13,000}{9,750 - 4,000} = \$2 \text{ per unit}$$

$24,500 − ($2 × 9,750) = $5,000 fixed cost
Or
$13,000 − ($2 × 4,000) = $5,000 fixed cost

Solution 19.3

Sales.	$2,500,000
− Variable costs	(1,400,000)
Contribution margin	1,100,000
− Fixed costs	(600,000)
Operating income.	$ 500,000

Operating leverage = $1,100,000/$500,000 = 2.2
Depending on the industry, this may indicate a need for concern because the industry average is significantly higher.

DECISION TIME SOLUTION

Solution 19.1
c. Either or both of the above.
If the retailer were to increase the average price of the shoes or quantity sold by 10% or more, it would break even or earn a profit.

20

Variable Costing: A Tool for Decision Making

PAST

Chapter 19 utilized our understanding of cost behavior to determine break-even and make planning and budgeting decisions.

PRESENT

Chapter 20 discusses the preparation of a variable income statement

FUTURE

Chapter 21 describes some of the tools and techniques that management can use in making strategic business decisions.

LEARNING OBJECTIVES

1. **Describe** the difference in the treatment of product costs between variable costing and absorption costing. *(p. 928)*

2. **Prepare** an income statement under both variable costing and absorption costing methods. *(p. 930)*

3. **Explain** why net income differs between absorption costing and variable costing. **Reconcile** the two different income amounts. *(p. 932)*

4. **Describe** the advantages and disadvantages of the variable costing method. *(p. 934)*

GENERAL MOTORS

General Motors (GM) designs, manufactures, and sells cars, trucks, and automobile parts worldwide. In North America, they are recognized by their Buick, Cadillac, Chevrolet, and GMC brands. Outside North America, in addition to these brands, they also manufacture and market vehicles under the Holden, Opel, and Vauxhall brands.

The global automotive industry is highly competitive and overall manufacturing capacity in the industry exceeds global demand. Many manufacturers have relatively high fixed labor costs as well as significant limitations on their ability to close facilities and reduce fixed costs. Automobile manufacturers typically respond to these relatively high fixed costs by attempting to sell more vehicles by adding vehicle enhancements, providing subsidized financing or leasing programs, offering marketing incentives, or reducing vehicle prices. In doing so, they are able to reduce the per-vehicle fixed manufacturing cost. However, manufacturers in lower-cost countries such as China and India have recently emerged as competitors in key emerging markets and announced their intention of exporting their products to the North American market as a bargain alternative to entry-level automobiles. These actions will limit GM's control over vehicle pricing, market share, and operating results, and present a significant risk to GM's ability to increase its per-vehicle prices.

In the year ending December 31, 2014, GM reported operating income of just over $1.5 billion.[1] This is a reduction of $3.6 billion from the prior fiscal year. GM reports the results of its operations in accordance with generally accepted accounting principles (GAAP). In accordance with GAAP, this means that the amount that GM reports for inventories on the balance sheet includes all production costs (materials, labor, and manufacturing overhead).

GM's reported inventories declined from $14.0 billion in 2013 to $13.6 billion in 2014, a decrease of approximately $400 million. As described more fully in this chapter, because a significant portion of GM's costs are fixed, this means that fixed manufacturing costs incurred in previous years (that had been recorded as part of inventories on the balance sheet) were expensed in 2014, reducing income from what it would have been had GM sold fewer vehicles! Say what? Read on…

---

[1] General Motors 10-K Report dated February 4, 2015.

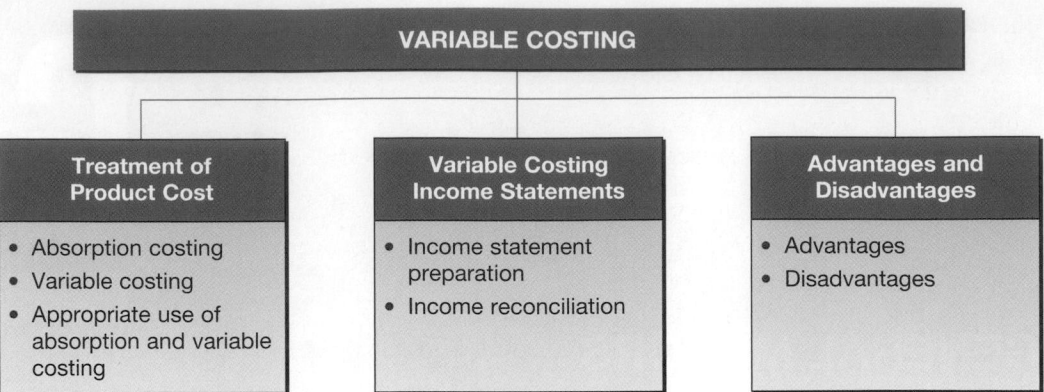

TREATMENT OF PRODUCT COSTS

LO1   **Describe** the difference in the treatment of product costs between variable costing and absorption costing.

A.K.A. Absorption costing is also referred to as *full costing* because it includes both variable and fixed components of product costs.

Absorption Costing

In **Chapter 15**, we define product costs as **all** manufacturing costs: direct material, direct labor, and variable and fixed manufacturing overhead. These costs are capitalized as inventory during the production period and recognized as expense (cost of goods sold) only when the related merchandise is sold. This method of attaching all manufacturing costs to the product is known as **absorption costing**. When using absorption costing, and production is greater than sales, a portion of the current period's fixed costs is attached to the inventory that is added to the balance sheet. As a result, a company can defer recognition of fixed costs as an expense by merely producing more inventory than it sells in a period. **Exhibit 20-1a** presents the absorption costing income statement for Fezzari.

Exhibit 20-1a	Absorption Costing Income Statement for Fezzari

FEZZARI PERFORMANCE BICYCLES
Absorption Costing Income Statement
For the Year Ended December 31, 2016

Sales..		$4,500,000
Cost of goods sold (including fixed manufacturing costs)....		3,001,600
Gross profit on sales..............................		$1,498,400
Operating expenses:		
Selling expenses.................................	$400,000	
Administrative expenses..........................	340,000	740,000
Income from operations..............................		$ 758,400
Other income and expense:		
Interest expense..................................		5,000
Income before income tax...........................		$ 753,400
Income tax expense.................................		263,690
Net income...		$ 489,710

A.K.A. Variable costing is also referred to as *direct costing*. The latter is a misnomer, however, because variable costs—not direct costs—are capitalized under direct costing.

Variable Costing

In contrast, for internal reporting purposes, some companies use **variable costing** to determine the cost of their manufactured products. Under variable costing, only *variable* manufacturing costs are capitalized as inventory. This includes direct material, direct labor, and the variable portion of manufacturing overhead. All fixed manufacturing overhead costs are expensed in the period incurred. These fixed manufacturing costs are treated as a period cost in the same manner as selling, general, and administrative expenses. As a result, under variable costing, costs of goods sold amounts do not include the fixed portion of manufacturing overhead. **Exhibit 20-1b** presents the variable costing income statement for Fezzari.

Exhibit 20-1b	Variable Costing Income Statement for Fezzari		

FEZZARI PERFORMANCE BICYCLES
Variable Costing Income Statement
For the Year Ended December 31, 2016

Sales.			$4,500,000
Variable cost of goods sold		$2,776,500	
Variable selling expenses		300,000	
Variable non-factory administrative expenses		50,000	3,126,500
Contribution margin			$1,373,500
Fixed expenses:			
Fixed manufacturing costs		$ 225,100	
Fixed selling expenses		100,000	
Fixed non-factory administrative expenses		290,000	615,100
Income from operations			$ 758,400
Other income and expense:			
Interest expense			5,000
Income before income tax			$ 753,400
Income tax expense.			263,690
Net income.			$ 489,710

The only difference between absorption and variable costing is that when production exceeds sales, a portion of fixed manufacturing overhead is capitalized under absorption costing, whereas it is fully expensed under variable costing. **Exhibit 20-2** illustrates this difference.

Exhibit 20-2	Illustration of Absorption vs. Variable Costing	

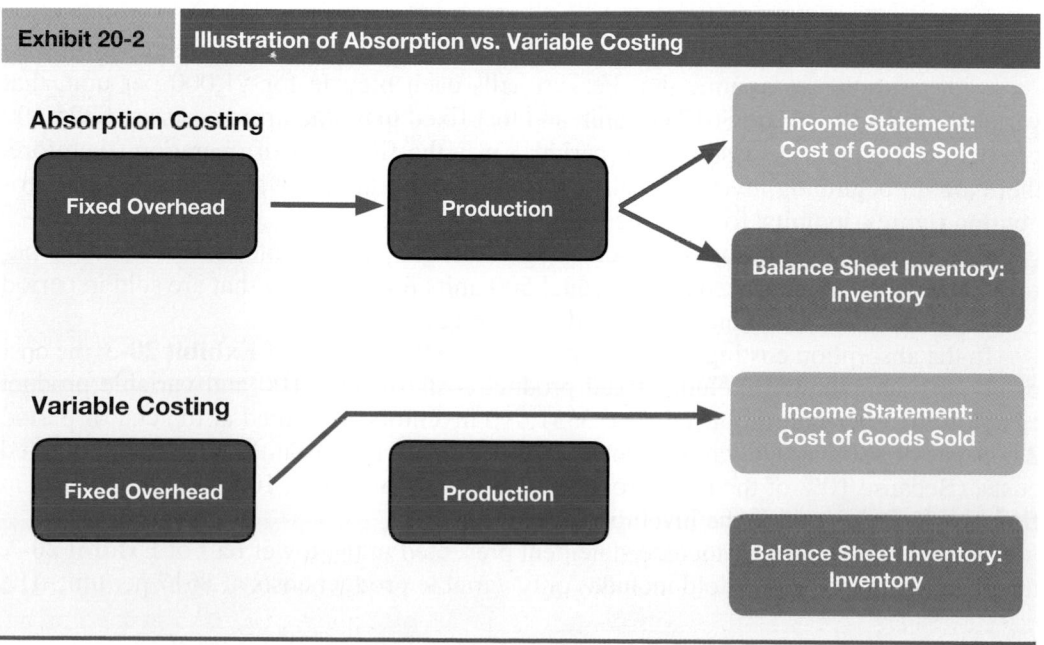

Appropriate Use of Absorption Costing and Variable Costing

In general, variable costing (carrying only variable costs in the inventory accounts) is considered a departure from generally accepted accounting standards. These standards require that published financial reports attested to by CPAs be prepared on an absorption costing basis. In these reports, all manufacturing costs should be attributed to products, and inventories of work in process and finished goods should contain their allocable shares of manufacturing costs, both fixed and variable. Likewise, the Internal Revenue Service has generally insisted on the use of absorption costing in determining net income for tax purposes, with some adjustments.

Although variable costing should not be used to prepare financial statements for external use, management may use variable costing statements for internal decision making. A principal benefit is that variable costing usually causes net income figures to move in the same direction as sales.

With absorption costing, net income may increase in periods when production volume exceeds sales (increasing inventory on the balance sheet) and decrease when sales volume exceeds production (decreasing inventory on the balance sheet). Why is this important to understand? This is important knowledge because it may be possible for managers to increase reported net income to meet analysts' expectations by increasing production of product during the last few weeks of a reporting period. Of course, this short-term "fix" could result in excess inventory levels that lead to obsolescence and inventory write-offs in subsequent periods.

TAKEAWAY 20.1

Variable costing cannot be used for external financial reporting.

VARIABLE COSTING INCOME STATEMENT

LO2 Prepare an income statement under both variable costing and absorption costing methods.

Income Statement Preparation

Exhibit 20-3 provides a comparison of partial income statements for Fezzari for three periods, using both absorption costing and variable costing. It clearly illustrates the effects just discussed. For this simple illustration, we assume that Fezzari sells each bicycle for $1,000 per unit, that variable product costs are $617 per unit, and that fixed manufacturing costs are $225,100 per period. Further, we assume that period 1 was the first year of operation (therefore, there are no beginning inventory balances). The exhibit also provides the sales and production figures, in units, for three periods.

Fezzari normally produces and sells 4,500 units per period. Note, however, that in period 2 the company produced an additional 500 units for inventory that are sold in period 3 together with the 4,000 units produced in period 3.

In the absorption costing statement presented in the top half of **Exhibit 20-3**, the cost of goods manufactured includes fixed product costs of $225,100 and variable product costs of $617 per unit produced. The $331,010 inventory presented at the end of period 2 consists of $308,500 in variable costs (500 units × $617 per unit) and $22,510 in fixed costs. (Because 10% of the units produced remains in inventory, 10% of the $225,100 in fixed costs is assigned to the inventory.)

In the variable costing income statement presented in the lower half of **Exhibit 20-3**, the variable cost of goods sold includes only variable product costs at $617 per unit. The

$308,500 inventory at the end of period 2 consists of only the $617 variable product cost times the 500 units in the inventory.

Exhibit 20-3	Absorption vs. Variable Costing Partial Income Statements

FEZZARI PERFORMANCE BICYCLES

	Period 1	Period 2	Period 3	Total
Beginning inventory (units)................	—	—	500	—
Production (units)........................	4,500	5,000	4,000	13,500
Sales (units)	4,500	4,500	4,500	13,500
Ending inventory (units)	—	500	—	—

Variable cost: 500 units × $617 = $308,500
Fixed cost: 500 units × $225,100/5,000 units =   22,510
Total cost: $331,010

Absorption Costing Income Statement

		Period 1	Period 2	Period 3	Total
(1)	Sales.....................	$4,500,000	$4,500,000	$4,500,000	$13,500,000
(2)	Beginning inventory	—	—	331,010	—
(3)	Cost of goods manufactured	3,001,600	3,310,100	2,693,100	9,004,800
(4)	Less ending inventory....................	—	331,010	—	—
(5)	Cost of goods sold [(2) + (3) − (4)]	$(3,001,600)	$(2,979,090)	$(3,024,110)	$ (9,004,800)
(6)	Gross profit on sales [(1) + (5)].............	$1,498,400	$1,520,910	$1,475,890	$ 4,495,200

Variable cost: 500 units × $617 = $308,500
Fixed cost: 0
Total cost: $308,500

Variable Costing Income Statement

		Period 1	Period 2	Period 3	Total
(1)	Sales.....................	$4,500,000	$4,500,000	$4,500,000	$13,500,000
(2)	Beginning inventory	—	—	308,500	—
(3)	Variable cost of goods manufactured.......	2,776,500	3,085,000	2,468,000	8,329,500
(4)	Less ending inventory....................	—	308,500	—	—
(5)	Variable cost of goods sold [(2) + (3) − (4)]	$(2,776,500)	$(2,776,500)	$(2,776,500)	$ (8,329,500)
(6)	Contribution margin [(1) + (5)]...........	$1,723,500	$1,723,500	$1,723,500	$ 5,170,500
(7)	Fixed manufacturing costs................	(225,100)	(225,100)	(225,100)	(675,300)
(8)	Income from operations [(6) + (7)]	$1,498,400	$1,498,400	$1,498,400	$ 4,495,200

TAKEAWAY 20.2

Absorption costing and variable costing differ on only one item. Fixed manufacturing overhead is included in the cost of products under absorption costing but excluded from the cost of products under variable costing.

A total of $4,495,200 gross profit/income from operations is reported for the three periods under both methods. However, the variable costing method indicates the same income from operations figures in each period ($1,498,400), which are correlated with the constant sales volume over the three periods. On the other hand, under the absorption costing method, income from operations moves up and down with production (from $1,498,400 to $1,520,910 to $1,475,890). The reason, of course, is that the fixed costs are added to the inventory (and therefore not included in cost of goods sold) when production exceeds sales in period 2 and are released (through cost of goods sold) when the company sells more than it produces in period 3.

CORPORATE SOCIAL RESPONSIBILITY	**Triple Bottom Line Reporting**

This chapter has introduced an internal reporting approach called variable costing, which allows management to more easily focus on the contribution of customers, products, product lines, business segments, and other business units to the overall profitability of the company. Another type of reporting has also gained in importance. That other type of reporting, called triple-bottom-line reporting, considers not just financial results, but also environmental and social results as well. GM is committed to acting in a socially responsible manner, behavior that earns high marks in a triple bottom line. As stated on GM's web site, "Through the lens of sustainability, we view industry challenges and change as new business opportunities that can drive additional value for our customers. We call this Customer-Driven Sustainability. From designing more fuel-efficient vehicles and deploying advanced-safety technologies to being the workplace of choice for employees and the neighbor of choice for communities, we make strategic decisions based on how the outcome of those decisions ultimately translates into value for our customers." An example of this behavior is illustrated by GM's greening of the General Motors Baltimore Operations complex. The LEED Silver building exceeds the voluntary U.S. Environmental Protection Agency's ENERGY STAR® Challenge for Industry, which requires a 10 percent reduction in energy intensity within 5 years. "We believe reducing our environmental footprint is good for the climate and good for our business," said Greg Martin, executive director of Global Public Policy. "Wherever we can, we are reducing our energy use, powering our plants with renewable energy and conserving resources."

Income Reconciliation

LO3 Explain why net income differs between absorption costing and variable costing. **Reconcile** the two different income amounts.

Once the relationship between variable costing and absorption costing is understood, it is possible to determine the differences between variable income and absorption income using a "short-cut" calculation without having to prepare separate financial statements. Remember that the only difference between variable income and absorption income is the treatment of the fixed costs of production—under absorption costing, some of these fixed production costs are included in inventory on the balance sheet, whereas they are all expensed under variable costing. So, if inventory increases by 500 units from one period to the next (as illustrated previously in **Exhibit 20-3**), each unit in inventory will have $45.02 ($22,510/500 units) of fixed manufacturing costs. Because all fixed manufacturing costs have been expensed under the variable costing approach, absorption income should be $22,510 more than variable income, as shown:

$45.02 fixed manufacturing cost per unit × 500 units added to inventory = $22,510

$1,520,910 (absorption income)	−	$22,510 (fixed manufacturing cost added to inventory)	=	$1,498,400 (variable income)

The impact of differences between production and sales under both absorption and variable costing is summarized in **Exhibit 20-4**.

Exhibit 20-4	Impact of Varying Levels of Production		
	Income Statement	**Balance Sheet**	**Explanation**
Production = Sales	No difference in reported income	No change in inventory values	Current period fixed costs expensed under both absorption and variable costing methods
Production > Sales	Absorption net income is greater than variable net income	Absorption balance sheet inventory increases by more than variable balance sheet inventory	Some current period fixed costs are added to inventory under absorption costing method, but all are expensed under variable costing method
Production < Sales	Absorption net income is less than variable net income	Absorption balance sheet inventory decreases by more than variable balance sheet inventory	Some prior period fixed costs that are in the beginning inventory balance under absorption costing method are expensed in the current period as cost of goods sold, but only current period fixed costs are expensed under variable costing method

Assume that Fezzari's reported absorption costing income was $1,600,000 in 2016. What would variable costing income be if Fezzari's inventory increased by 100 units during 2016 and fixed manufacturing cost was equal to $50 per unit?

YOUR TURN! 20.1

The solution is on page 946.

To highlight the effect of variable costing on inventories and income in the foregoing illustration, we consider only manufacturing costs. When detailed income statements are prepared under the variable costing method, fixed and variable costs of all types—including selling and administrative expenses—must be properly segregated. **Exhibit 20-5** presents an example of a detailed income statement prepared in accordance with the variable costing concept. As illustrated by the arrows in **Exhibit 20-5**, absorption net income changes with the level of production and variable net income changes with the level of sales. Because unit sales does not change over the three periods, reported variable net income does not change. The reason is that, as noted previously, fixed costs are not included in the inventory account on the balance sheet, but are expensed in the period that they are incurred under variable costing.

Contribution margin can be determined by deducting all variable expenses (cost of goods sold, selling, and administrative expenses) from sales. (This concept was previously introduced in Chapter 19.) All types of fixed expenses (manufacturing, selling, and administrative) are deducted to arrive at net income.

Exhibit 20-5	Absorption vs. Variable Costing Income Statements

FEZZARI PERFORMANCE BICYCLES

	Period 1	Period 2	Period 3	Total
Beginning inventory (units)...............	—	—	500	—
Production (units)...............	4,500	5,000	4,000	13,500
Sales (units)...............	4,500	4,500	4,500	13,500
Ending inventory (units)...............	—	500	—	—

Absorption Costing Income Statement

		Period 1	Period 2	Period 3	Total
(1)	Sales...............	$ 4,500,000	$ 4,500,000	$ 4,500,000	$13,500,000
(2)	Beginning inventory	—	—	331,010	—
(3)	Cost of goods manufactured	3,001,600	3,310,100	2,693,100	9,004,800
(4)	Less ending inventory...............	—	331,010	—	—
(5)	Cost of goods sold [(2) + (3) − (4)]	$(3,001,600)	$(2,979,090)	$(3,024,110)	$ (9,004,800)
(6)	Gross profit on sales [(1) + (5)]...........	$ 1,498,400	$ 1,520,910	$ 1,475,890	$ 4,495,200
	Operating expenses:				
(7)	Selling expenses...............	(400,000)	(400,000)	(400,000)	(1,200,000)
(8)	Administrative expenses...............	(340,000)	(340,000)	(340,000)	(1,020,000)
(9)	Income from operations [(6) + (7) + (8)].........	$ 758,400	$ 780,910	$ 735,890	$ 2,275,200

Variable Costing Income Statement

		Period 1	Period 2	Period 3	Total
(1)	Sales...............	$ 4,500,000	$ 4,500,000	$ 4,500,000	$13,500,000
(2)	Beginning inventory	—	—	308,500	—
(3)	Variable cost of goods manufactured.........	2,776,500	3,085,000	2,468,000	8,329,500
(4)	Less ending inventory...............	—	308,500	—	—
(5)	Variable cost of goods sold [(2) + (3) − (4)]	$(2,776,500)	$(2,776,500)	$(2,776,500)	$ (8,329,500)
(6)	Variable selling expenses...............	(300,000)	(300,000)	(300,000)	(900,000)
(7)	Variable administrative expenses...............	(50,000)	(50,000)	(50,000)	(150,000)
(8)	**Contribution margin** [(1) + (5) + (6) + (7)]....	$ 1,373,500	$ 1,373,500	$ 1,373,500	$ 4,120,500
	Fixed expenses:				
(9)	Fixed manufacturing costs...............	(225,100)	(225,100)	(225,100)	(675,300)
(10)	Fixed selling expenses...............	(100,000)	(100,000)	(100,000)	(300,000)
(11)	Fixed administrative expenses	(290,000)	(290,000)	(290,000)	(870,000)
(12)	Income from operations [(8) + (9) + (10) + (11)] ...	$ 758,400	$ 758,400	$ 758,400	$ 2,275,200

ADVANTAGES AND DISADVANTAGES OF VARIABLE COSTING

The following advantages and disadvantages of using variable costing result from the fact that under variable costing no fixed overhead costs are assigned to inventory carrying values.

LO4 **Describe** the advantages and disadvantages of the variable costing methods.

Advantages

1. Variable costing assigns only variable costs to inventory. Reporting inventory values in this manner helps managers avoid making "death spiral" decisions.

2. Under variable costing, because all fixed costs are reported separately, managers are able to see how much fixed cost must be covered before a profit will be generated.

3. Reported net income tends to follow sales volume, eliminating the incentive to temporarily boost income by producing more product than can be sold in the short term.

4. Cost-volume-profit (CVP) relationships are more easily discerned from variable costing income statements than from conventional absorption costing statements. The cost information needed for CVP analysis (which was discussed in **Chapter 19**) is readily available from variable cost financial statements.

5. Variable costing statements make it easier to determine the contribution of customers, products, product lines, business segments, and other business units to the overall profitability of the company. This is typically obscured by the allocation of fixed costs under absorption costing.

Disadvantages

1. Accounting measures derived under variable costing are not in conformity with generally accepted accounting principles, nor are they acceptable for reporting purposes under the Internal Revenue Code.

2. Inventories (and therefore working capital and owners' equity) tend to be understated.

3. Carrying inventories at only their variable costs may lead to long-run pricing decisions that provide for recovery of variable cost only rather than total cost, which will not produce net income in the long run.

4. Variable costing generally requires that a "second set" of accounting records be kept, increasing the cost of the required accounting systems and possible confusion among managers.

Hint: A "death spiral" decision is one in which management eliminates a product or division that has a positive contribution margin, but shows a loss when other non-controllable costs are allocated to it. By eliminating the product or division, the positive contribution margin is lost so that other products or divisions now have to cover all of the fixed costs. This may cause another product or division to appear unprofitable, leading to additional decisions to eliminate products or divisions that have positive contribution margins.

SERVICES INDUSTRY IN FOCUS

Environmental Business Consultants (EBC) compensates all of its employees as salaried workers. Thus, EBC considers its labor cost as fixed—that is, EBC consultants are paid their full salary and benefits regardless of the number of consulting projects that they perform during a year. The only other fixed cost is the office lease expense. A partial trial balance for 2016 is provided below.

SERVICE AND MERCHANDISING

Description	Trial Balance		Variable or Fixed	Direct Service or SGA
	Debit	Credit		
Sales.		4,146,000		
Reimbursable costs	431,000		V	D
Executive salaries.	844,500		F	D
Clerical salaries	217,500		F	D
Consultant salaries.	1,050,000		F	D
Employee benefits	145,500		F	D
Payroll taxes.	123,000		F	D
Employee bonuses.	126,000		V	SGA
Marketing expenses.	48,000		V	SGA
Employee continuing education expenses. . . .	27,000		V	SGA
Office lease expense	202,500		F	D
Office supplies expense.	64,500		V	D
Other general administrative expense	355,500		V	SGA

Assume that EBC's beginning absorption Work-in-Process Inventory is $223,000 and its ending absorption Work-in-Process (WIP) Inventory is $247,000. Further, assume that EBC's beginning variable WIP inventory is $5,400 and its ending variable WIP inventory is $6,000.

Required

a. Determine income from operations using
   1. Absorption costing.
   2. Variable costing.
b. Compare the income from operations derived under the two methods.

Solution

a. 1.

ENVIRONMENTAL BUSINESS CONSULTANTS, LLC		
Absorption Income Statement		
For the Year Ended December 31, 2016		
Gross sales.		$4,146,000
Less reimbursable costs		(431,000)
Net sales.		$3,715,000
Direct labor.		$2,380,500
General overhead:		
Office lease expense	$202,500	
Office supplies expense.	64,500	
Total general overhead.		267,000
Total service costs for the year		$2,647,500
Add: beginning work-in-process inventory		223,000
Total cost of work in process during the year		$2,870,500
Less: ending work-in-process inventory		(247,000)
Cost of services		2,623,500
Gross profit on sales.		$1,091,500
Operating expenses:		
Employee bonuses.	$126,000	
Marketing expenses	48,000	
Employee continuing education expenses.	27,000	
Other general administrative expenses	355,500	
Total operating expenses.		556,500
Income from operations.		$ 535,000

2.

ENVIRONMENTAL BUSINESS CONSULTANTS, LLC **Variable Income Statement** **For the Year Ended December 31, 2016**		
Gross sales.		$4,146,000
Less reimbursable costs		$ (431,000)
Net sales.		$3,715,000
Beginning variable WIP		$ 5,400
Variable costs		
Office supplies expense		64,500
Less ending variable WIP.		(6,000)
Variable cost of service		$ 63,900
Other variable expenses		
Employee bonuses	$ 126,000	
Marketing expenses	40,000	
Employee continuing education expenses. . . .	27,000	
Other general administrative expenses	355,500	
Total other variable cost		556,500
Total variable costs		$ 620,400
Contribution margin		$3,094,600
Fixed costs		
Direct labor	$2,380,500	
Office lease expense	202,500	
Total fixed costs.		2,583,000
Income from operations.		$ 511,600

b.

Absorption income from operations.		$535,000
Less:		
Increase in fixed costs in WIP inventory:		
Ending (247,000 − 6,000)	241,000	
Beginning (223,000 − 5,400)	217,600	
		(23,400)
Variable income from operations		$511,600

COMPREHENSIVE PROBLEM

Tuttle Manufacturing Company produces only one product, which sells for $50. Product costs at the normal level of manufacturing operations (10,000 units) are the following:

Direct material	$14 per unit
Direct labor..................................	$12 per unit
Variable overhead............................	$ 4 per unit
Fixed overhead..............................	$49,500

Selling expenses (100% variable) are $3 per unit; administrative expenses (100% fixed) are $30,000. During the year, Tuttle produced 11,000 units and sold 9,000 units. Tuttle had no beginning inventory of product.

Required

a. Determine net income (ignoring income taxes) using
   1. Absorption costing.
   2. Variable costing.
b. Compare the total net income derived under the two methods.

Solution

a.

Absorption Costing		
Sales (9,000 units × $50)...........................		$450,000
Cost of goods sold:		
Direct material (11,000 × $14)	$154,000	
Direct labor (11,000 × $12)	132,000	
Variable overhead (11,000 × $4)	44,000	
Fixed overhead...............................	49,500	
	379,500	
Less: Ending inventory [($379,500/11,000) × 2,000] ...	69,000	
Cost of goods sold.............................		310,500
Gross profit....................................		$139,500
Selling expense (9,000 units × $3)................	27,000	
Administrative expense	30,000	57,000
Net income....................................		$ 82,500

Variable Costing		
Sales (9,000 units × $50)...........................		$450,000
Variable expenses:		
Direct material (11,000 × $14)	$154,000	
Direct labor (11,000 × $12)	132,000	
Variable overhead (11,000 × $4)	44,000	
	330,000	
Less: Ending inventory [($330,000/11,000) × 2,000] ...	60,000	
Variable cost of goods sold		270,000
Variable selling expense (9,000 × $3)		27,000
Contribution margin		153,000
Fixed expenses:		
Fixed overhead...............................	49,500	
Administrative expense	30,000	79,500
Net income....................................		$ 73,500

b.

Comparison	
Absorption costing net income	$82,500
Variable costing net income.	73,500
Difference (explained below)	$ 9,000

The amount of fixed overhead contained in the absorption costing ending inventory is $9,000 [($49,500/11,000) × 2,000].

The amount of fixed overhead contained in the variable costing ending inventory is 0. The different treatment of fixed overhead fully explains the difference.

SUMMARY OF LEARNING OBJECTIVES

Describe the difference in the treatment of product costs between variable costing and absorption costing. (p. 928)

LO1

- Absorption costing capitalizes all manufacturing costs as inventory during the production period and recognizes them as expense (cost of goods sold) only when the related merchandise is sold.
- Variable costing does not assign fixed manufacturing overhead as a product cost but expenses it in the period incurred.
- Accounting measures derived under variable costing are not in accord with generally accepted accounting principles, nor are they acceptable for tax reporting.

Prepare an income statement under both variable costing and absorption costing methods. (p. 930)

LO2

- For absorption costing, include the fixed costs and variable costs of manufacturing in the computation of cost of goods sold.
- For variable costing, only include the variable costs of manufacturing in the computation of cost of goods sold. Expense all fixed costs, including fixed manufacturing costs, in the period.

Explain why net income differs between absorption costing and variable costing. Reconcile the two different income amounts. (p. 932)

LO3

- The difference between absorption income and variable income will be the amount of fixed manufacturing costs either added to or subtracted from work-in-process inventory during the period.
- When production volume exceeds sales volume, absorption income will be greater than variable income.
- When production volume is less than sales volume, absorption income will be less than variable income.

Describe the advantages and disadvantages of the variable costing methods. (p. 934)

LO4

- The primary advantage of variable costing is that reported income follows changes in production volume, reducing the risk of "death spiral" decisions.
- Variable costing provides all of the information required for CVP analysis.
- The primary disadvantage of variable costing is that it is not acceptable for financial statement reporting or tax reporting.
- Because variable costing requires the maintenance of a "second set" of books, it is more costly.

KEY TERMS

Absorption costing (p. 928)
Contribution margin (p. 933)

Variable costing (p. 928)

Assignments with the ⊕ logo in the margin are available in ᵐʸ BusinessCourse.
See the Preface of the book for details.

SELF-STUDY QUESTIONS

(Answers to Self-Study Questions are at the end of this chapter.)

LO1 1. In determining inventory costs, which of the following cost elements is included when using absorption costing but excluded when using variable costing?
   a. Selling costs
   b. Direct labor cost
   c. Non-factory administrative costs
   d. Fixed overhead

LO2 2. If unit production exceeds unit sales during the period, absorption income will be
   a. less than variable income.
   b. more than variable income.
   c. equal to variable income.

LO2 3. If unit production is less than unit sales during the period, absorption income will be
   a. less than variable income.
   b. more than variable income.
   c. equal to variable income.

LO2 4. If unit production is equal to unit sales during the period, absorption income will be
   a. less than variable income.
   b. more than variable income.
   c. equal to variable income.

LO1, 4 5. True or false: Variable costing may be used by management in preparing audited financial statements.
   a. True
   b. False

QUESTIONS

LO4 1. What is variable costing? List its advantages and disadvantages.

LO3 2. What generalizations can be made about the difference in income reported under variable and absorption costing?

LO3 3. When inventories are increasing, will absorption income be higher or lower than variable income?

LO1 4. Which method, absorption or variable costing, is used for internal management reporting purposes?

LO1 5. Which method, absorption or variable costing, is used for external reporting purposes in accordance with generally accepted accounting principles?

EXERCISES—SET A

LO2 **E20-1A. Variable and Absorption Costing** During its first year, Walnut, Inc., showed an $18 per-unit profit under absorption costing but would have reported a total profit $16,000 less under variable costing. If production exceeded sales by 500 units and an average contribution margin of 62.5% was maintained, what is the apparent:
   a. Fixed cost per unit?
   b. Sales price per unit?
   c. Variable cost per unit?
   d. Unit sales volume if total profit under absorption costing was $198,000?

LO2 **E20-2A. Variable and Absorption Costing** Chandler Company sells its product for $100 per unit. Variable manufacturing costs per unit are $40, and fixed manufacturing costs at the normal operating level of 12,000 units are $240,000. Variable selling expenses are $16 per unit sold. Fixed administrative expenses total $104,000. Chandler had no beginning inventory in 2016. During 2016, the company produced 12,000 units and sold 9,000. Would net income for Chandler Company in 2016 be higher if calculated using variable costing or using absorption costing? Calculate reported income using each method.

E20-3A. Variable and Absorption Costing—Service Company Lawn RX, Inc. prepares a variable costing income statement for internal management and an absorption costing income statement for its bank. Lawn RX provides a quarterly lawn care service that is sold for $150. The variable and fixed cost data are as follows:

Direct labor.	$ 100.00
Overhead:	
Variable cost per unit	$ 5.00
Fixed cost.	$100,000
Marketing, general, and administrative:	
Variable cost (per contract completed)	$ 6.00
Administrative expense (fixed) (per month)	$ 42,000

During 2016, 10,000 service contracts were signed and 9,500 service contracts were completed. Lawn RX had no service contracts at the beginning of the year.

Required
a.   Calculate reported income for management.
b.   Calculate reported income for the bank.
c.   Reconcile the two income amounts.

EXERCISES—SET B

E20-1B. Variable and Absorption Costing During its first year, Concord, Inc., showed a $21 per-unit profit under absorption costing but would have reported a total profit $16,800 less under variable costing. If production exceeded sales by 700 units and an average contribution margin of 60% was maintained, what is the apparent:

a.   Fixed cost per unit?
b.   Sales price per unit?
c.   Variable cost per unit?
d.   Unit sales volume if total profit under absorption costing was $189,000?

E20-2B. Variable and Absorption Costing Grant Company sells its product for $50 per unit. Variable manufacturing costs per unit are $30, and fixed manufacturing costs at the normal operating level of 18,000 units are $90,000. Variable selling expenses are $4 per unit sold. Fixed administrative expenses total $155,000. Grant had 7,000 units at a per-unit cost of $35 in beginning inventory in 2016. During 2016, the company produced 18,000 units and sold 20,000. Would net income for Grant Company in 2016 be higher if calculated using variable costing or using absorption costing? Calculate reported income using each method.

E20-3B. Variable and Absorption Costing—Service Company Tech Helpers Company prepares a variable costing income statement for internal management and an absorption costing income statement for its bank. Tech Helpers provides a personal computer maintenance service that is sold for $100. The variable and fixed cost data are as follows:

Direct labor.	$ 25.00
Overhead:	
Variable cost per unit	$ 5.00
Fixed cost.	$240,000
Marketing, general, and administrative:	
Variable cost (per service contract completed)	$ 5.00
Fixed cost (per month)	$ 20,000

During 2015, 4,000 service contracts were started and 5,000 service contracts were completed. At the beginning of 2016, Tech Helpers had 1,000 service contracts in process at a per-unit cost of $90 in beginning work-in-process inventory.

LO2, 3
SERVICE AND MERCHANDISING

LO2

LO2

LO2, 3
SERVICE AND MERCHANDISING

Required

a.   Calculate reported income for management.

b.   Calculate reported income for the bank.

c.   Reconcile the two income amounts.

PROBLEMS—SET A

LO2, 3   **P20-1A. Variable and Absorption Costing** Scott Manufacturing makes only one product with total unit manufacturing costs of $54, of which $36 is variable. No units were on hand at the beginning of 2015. During 2015 and 2016, the only product manufactured was sold for $84 per unit, and the cost structure did not change. Scott uses the first-in, first-out inventory method and has the following production and sales for 2015 and 2016:

	Units Manufactured	Units Sold
2015	120,000	90,000
2016	120,000	130,000

Required

a.   Prepare gross profit computations for 2015 and 2016 using absorption costing.

b.   Prepare gross profit computations for 2015 and 2016 using variable costing.

c.   Explain how your answers illustrate the impact of differences between production and sales volumes on the gross profits reported each year under absorption and variable costing.

LO2   **P20-2A. Variable and Absorption Costing** Summarized data for 2016 (the first year of operations) for Gorman Products, Inc., are as follows:

Sales (75,000 units)	$3,000,000
Production costs (80,000 units):	
Direct material.	880,000
Direct labor	720,000
Manufacturing overhead:	
Variable.	544,000
Fixed	320,000
Operating expenses:	
Variable.	168,000
Fixed	240,000
Depreciation on equipment	60,000
Real estate taxes	18,000
Personal property taxes (on inventory and equipment)	28,800
Personnel department expenses	30,000

Required

a.   Prepare an income statement based on full absorption costing.

b.   Prepare an income statement based on variable costing.

c.   Assume that you must decide quickly whether to accept a special one-time order for 1,000 units for $30 per unit. Which income statement presents the most relevant data? Determine the apparent profit or loss on the special order based solely on these data.

d.   If the ending inventory is destroyed by fire, which costing approach would you use as a basis for filing an insurance claim for the fire loss? Why?

LO2   **P20-3A. Variable and Absorption Costing—Service Company** Jensen's Tailoring provides custom tailoring services. After the company's first year of operations, its owner prepared the following summarized data report for 2016:

Sales (500 completed jobs)	$100,000
Tailoring costs (550 jobs):	
Direct labor.	47,000
Manufacturing overhead:	
Variable.	12,000
Fixed.	9,000
Operating expenses:	
Variable.	5,600
Fixed.	5,800

Required

a. Prepare an income statement based on full absorption costing.

b. Prepare an income statement based on variable costing.

c. Assume that you must decide quickly whether to accept a special one-time order to alter 50 band costumes for $150 per costume. Which income statement presents the most relevant data? Determine the apparent profit or loss on the special order based solely on these data.

PROBLEMS—SET B

P20-1B. Variable and Absorption Costing Frances Manufacturing makes a product with total unit manufacturing cost of $64, of which $36 is variable. No units were on hand at the beginning of 2015. During 2015 and 2016, the only product manufactured was sold for $96 per unit, and the cost structure did not change. Frances uses the first-in, first-out inventory method and has the following production and sales for 2015 and 2016:

LO2, 3

	Units Manufactured	Units Sold
2015	100,000	70,000
2016	100,000	120,000

Required

a. Prepare gross profit computations for 2015 and 2016 using absorption costing.

b. Prepare gross profit computations for 2015 and 2016 using variable costing.

c. Explain how your answers illustrate the impact of differences between production and sales volumes on the gross profits reported each year under absorption and variable costing.

P20-2B. Variable and Absorption Costing Summarized data for 2016 (the first year of operations) for Trenton Products, Inc., are as follows:

LO2

Sales (200,000 units)	$8,000,000
Production costs (210,000 units):	
Direct material.	2,100,000
Direct labor	1,680,000
Manufacturing overhead:	
Variable.	1,260,000
Fixed.	1,050,000
Operating expenses:	
Variable.	560,000
Fixed.	640,000

Required

a. Prepare an income statement based on full absorption costing.

b. Prepare an income statement based on variable costing.

c. Assume that you must decide quickly whether to accept a special one-time order for 1,000 units for $28 per unit. Which income statement presents the most relevant data? Determine the apparent profit or loss on the special order based solely on these data.

d. If the ending inventory is destroyed by fire, which costing approach would you use as a basis for filing an insurance claim for the fire loss? Why?

LO2

SERVICE AND
MERCHANDISING

P20-3B. Variable And Absorption Costing—Service Company Rocky's Automotive specializes in performing automobile safety checks. After the company's first year of operations, its accountant prepared the following summarized data report for the safety checks for 2016:

Sales (7,000 safety checks)	$700,000
Production costs (7,010 safety checks):	
Direct labor	490,700
Shop overhead:	
Variable	112,160
Fixed	70,100
Operating expenses:	
Variable	21,030
Fixed	16,000

Required

a. Prepare an income statement based on full absorption costing.

b. Prepare an income statement based on variable costing.

c. Assume that you must decide quickly whether to accept a special one-time order for 20 safety checks on local police cars for $80 per safety check. Determine the apparent profit or loss on the special order based solely on these data.

CERTIFIED MANAGEMENT ACCOUNTANT (CMA®) EXAM SAMPLE QUESTIONS

CMA20-1. When comparing absorption costing with variable costing, the difference in operating income can be explained by the difference between the

    a. units sold and the units produced, multiplied by the unit sales price.

    b. ending inventory in units and the beginning inventory in units, multiplied by the budgeted fixed manufacturing cost per unit.

    c. ending inventory in units and the beginning inventory in units, multiplied by the unit sales price.

    d. units sold and the units produced, multiplied by the budgeted variable manufacturing cost per unit.

CMA20-2. Mill Corporation had the following unit costs for the recently concluded calendar year:

	Variable	Fixed
Manufacturing	$8.00	$3.00
Nonmanufacturing	$2.00	$5.50

Inventory for Mill's sole product totaled 6,000 units on January 1 and 5,200 units on December 31. When compared to variable costing income, Mill's absorption costing income is

    a. $2,400 lower.

    b. $2,400 higher.

    c. $6,800 lower.

    d. $6,800 higher.

CMA20-3. If a manufacturing company uses variable costing to cost inventories, which of the following costs are considered inventoriable costs?

    a. Only raw material, direct labor, and variable manufacturing overhead costs.

    b. Only raw material, direct labor, and variable and fixed manufacturing overhead costs

c. Only raw material, direct labor, variable manufacturing overhead, and variable selling and administrative costs

d. Only raw material and direct labor costs

CMA20-4. During the month of May, Robinson Corporation sold 1,000 units. The cost per unit for May was as follows:

	Cost Per Unit
Direct materials	$ 5.50
Direct labor	3.00
Variable manufacturing overhead	1.00
Fixed manufacturing overhead	1.50
Variable administrative costs	.50
Fixed administrative costs	3.50
Total	$15.00

May's income using absorption costing was $9,500. The income for May, if variable costing had been used, would have been $9,125. The number of units Robinson produced during May was

a. 750 units.

b. 925 units.

c. 1,075 units.

d. 1,250 units.

CMA20-5. Which one of the following is the **best** reason for using variable costing?

a. Fixed factory overhead is more closely related to the capacity to produce than to the production of specific units.

b. All costs are variable in the long term.

c. Variable costing is acceptable for income tax reporting purposes.

d. Variable costing usually results in higher operating income than if a company uses absorption costing.

EXTENDING YOUR KNOWLEDGE

EYK20-1. Business Decision Case Ben and Chris have been lifelong friends. They are engineer-minded and have always dreamed of starting a manufacturing company. They want to manufacture tires, but realize that this industry is heavily regulated and that achieving profitable operations will require skillful management. Despite the odds, they form Smooth Ride, Inc., and resolve to only stay in business if they report a positive net income after the company's first year of operations. At the end of 2016, its first year of operations, Smooth Ride reported the following summarized data:

Sales (105,000 tires)	$13,125,000
Production costs (120,000 tires):	
Direct material	4,750,000
Direct labor	3,675,000
Manufacturing overhead:	
Variable	2,300,000
Fixed	950,000
Operating expenses:	
Variable	1,050,000
Fixed	800,000
Depreciation on machinery	455,000
Property taxes	330,000
Personnel department expenses	140,000

Required

a. Prepare income statements based on full absorption costing and based on variable costing. Based on the reported incomes using these methods, did Smooth Ride exceed the expectations of Ben and Chris?

b. Smooth Ride follows generally accepted accounting standards. Which method, full absorption or variable costing, will the company use to report its net income?

ANSWERS TO SELF-STUDY QUESTIONS:

1. d, (pp. 928–929)   2. b, (p. 933)   3. a, (p. 933)   4. c, (p. 933)   5. b, (p. 935)

YOUR TURN! SOLUTION

Solution 20.1
$1,600,000 − (100 × $50) = $1,595,000

PAST

Chapter 20 discussed the
preparation of a variable income
statement.

PRESENT

Chapter 21 describes some of
the tools and techniques that
management can use in making
short-term business decisions.

FUTURE

Chapter 22 discusses
the budgeting process,
the components of the
master budget, and the
interrelationships of the
individual budgets, and
presents an illustration of a
budget for a manufacturer
and a service company.

LEARNING OBJECTIVES

1. **Describe** management's use of accounting information in the decision-making process. **Define** relevant costs and **describe** the use of differential analysis. *(p. 950)*

2. **Demonstrate** when to accept a special order. *(p. 955)*

3. **Demonstrate** when to make or buy needed parts. *(p. 957)*

4. **Demonstrate** when to drop an unprofitable product or segment. *(p. 958)*

5. **Demonstrate** when to sell a product or process it further. *(p. 959)*

6. **Demonstrate** how to determine which product to produce. *(p. 963)*

JOHN DEERE

What did you have for dinner last night? If it included fresh produce, grains, dairy, or meat from U.S. farms, there is a six in ten chance that it was planted, fertilized, irrigated, harvested, or fed with a John Deere product. As the global leader in the manufacture of agricultural equipment, John Deere's strategy is to be the equipment supplier of choice to the farmers who will help meet the worldwide growth in the demand for food.

John Deere didn't start out with the intent of becoming the world's largest manufacturer of agriculture and construction equipment. In 1837, John Deere, a blacksmith in Illinois, was simply looking for a way to help the local farmers plow their fields without frequently stopping to clean sticky prairie soil off of their wooden or cast-iron plows. A broken steel sawmill blade gave him the chance. He knew that the soil would easily slide off of a polished-steel plow, which he crafted from the sawmill blade. Five years later, he built 100 of the plows; in 1849, 2,136 plows; and in 1875, 50,000 plows.

In 1863, the company built the first Hawkeye Riding Cultivator, a farm implement adapted for riding. Twelve years later, the company developed the Gilpin Sulky Plow, which put the farmer on a seat. That plow would defeat 50 other plows in a field trial at the Paris Universal Exposition, winning first place. Before the end of the 19th century, steam tractors began to appear on the American farm, although John Deere did not begin manufacturing tractors until 1918.

One hundred and twenty-six years after John Deere made his first polished steel plow, the company he founded surpassed International Harvester to become the world's largest producer and seller of farm and industrial tractors and equipment. Today, the company's products and services include everything from small-engine lawn mowers for the home market to monster 9R tractors with up to 560-horsepower. How did this world-leading company grow out of a simple blacksmith shop? Along the way, the company's management faced many challenges and questions, including:

- Whether to introduce new products and product lines;
- Whether to produce or purchase new technology (e.g., steam tractors);
- Whether to drop products and product lines (e.g., bicycles and snowmobiles);
- How to deal with restricted production capacity during World War II; and,
- How to handle global expansion of manufacturing facilities and product sales.

In this chapter, we examine some of the decision tools and techniques that managers may use in answering these strategic questions.

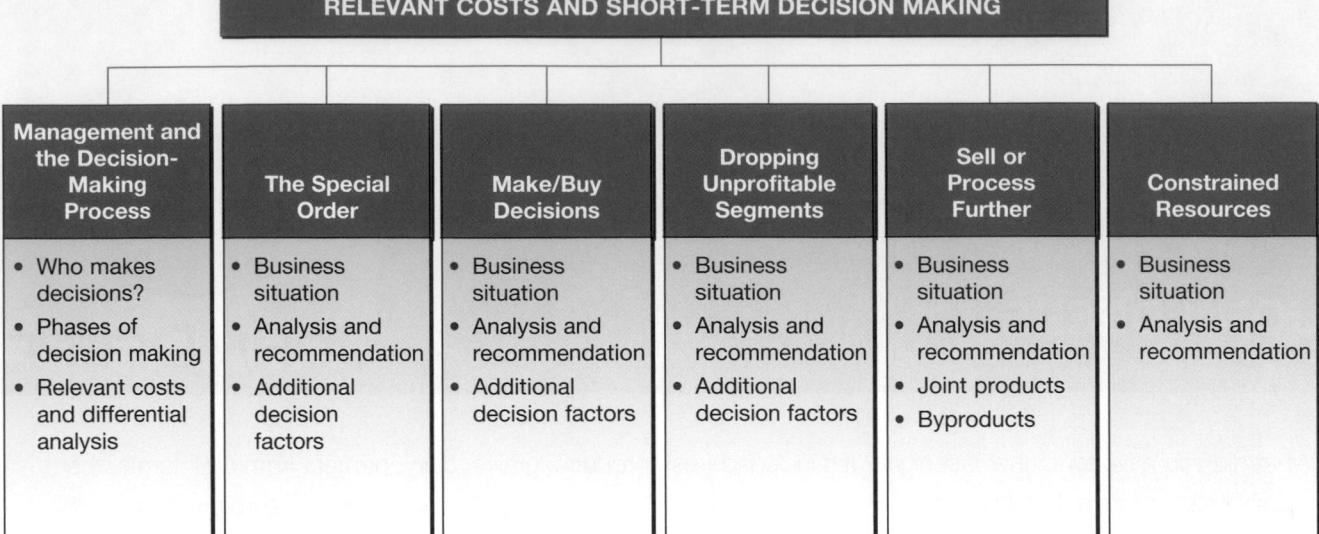

The traditional measurement is not the right measurement; if it were, there would be no need for decisions.

PETER DRUCKER

A well-developed accounting system is a continuing source of operational information for management. The quality of information available to management will influence the success of the operating decisions based on that information. In this chapter, we consider the management decision-making process and some cost concepts that are used in managerial analyses.

There are many definitions of **management**. In the broad sense, anyone who directs the activities of others is a manager. For a manufacturing firm like John Deere, this includes shop supervisors, department heads, plant supervisors, division managers, and the company president. A large, complex firm may have many management levels.

MANAGEMENT AND THE DECISION-MAKING PROCESS

Who Makes Decisions?

LO1 Describe management's use of accounting information in the decision-making process. **Define** relevant costs and **describe** the use of differential analysis.

As **Exhibit 21-1** illustrates, upper-level management is responsible for establishing long-range goals and policies, including major financing, expansion into new markets (foreign and domestic), and acquisitions of or mergers with other firms. Middle-level management may deal with the strategies and tactics related to the automation of a department, the establishment of new product lines, and the direction of the marketing plan. Such matters as daily production quotas, compliance with planned costs, and other detailed operating concerns are the responsibility of lower-level management. To varying degrees, therefore, all levels of management are involved in decision making.

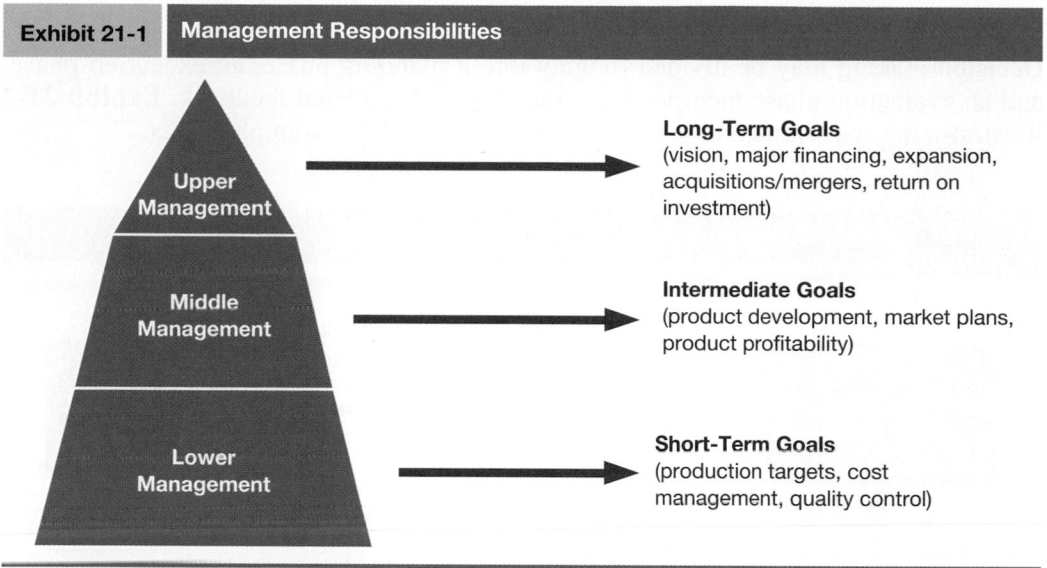

One of the responsibilities of top management is the development of a strategic plan.

Decision making requires that a choice be made among alternatives. The business decision process is analogous to the play of a well-organized football team. Virtually all elements of decision making are present in football: the establishment of the objectives and goals that lead to winning; the development of organization, strategy, and tactics in a competitive environment; the creation of plays with the hope of achieving particular results; the period of execution; and, finally, the informal evaluation of performance on the field followed by a formal evaluation when game films are analyzed.

CORPORATE SOCIAL RESPONSIBILITY

This chapter discusses the concept of decision making. One of the decisions a company like John Deere must make is how many resources it should invest in items benefiting non-shareholder stakeholders, and whether these investments will benefit shareholders in the long run. John Deere has been making these types of decisions for well over a century. Some of the early decisions, noted on its web site, include:

- 1901—Deere implements voluntary workers' compensation program. This is 10 years before the first U.S. workers' compensation statutes.
- 1920—Deere designs and builds its own cloth-screen filtering system to clean exhaust from plow-grinding operations.
- 1936—First foundry equipped with air-pollution-controlled molding equipment.
- 1938—Product safety committee formed; warning decals placed on corn pickers; shielding for power take-offs introduced.
- 1940—Power take-off shields installed on tractors and made available in retrofit programs for tractors produced after 1932.
- 1947—Corporate industrial safety department established.
- 1949—First boiler equipped with a device to control fly-ash emission at Waterloo Tractor Works. Planter Works, Moline, Illinois, installs a wetcap to control cupola emissions.

These investments in its employees' welfare and in the environment appear to have been wise ones, as John Deere is still around more than a hundred years later, delivering billions of dollars of annual net income to its shareholders.

Phases of Decision Making

Decision making may be divided roughly into a planning phase, an execution phase, and an evaluation phase incorporating some form of remedial feedback. **Exhibit 21-2** illustrates the sequential nature of the elements of most decision processes.

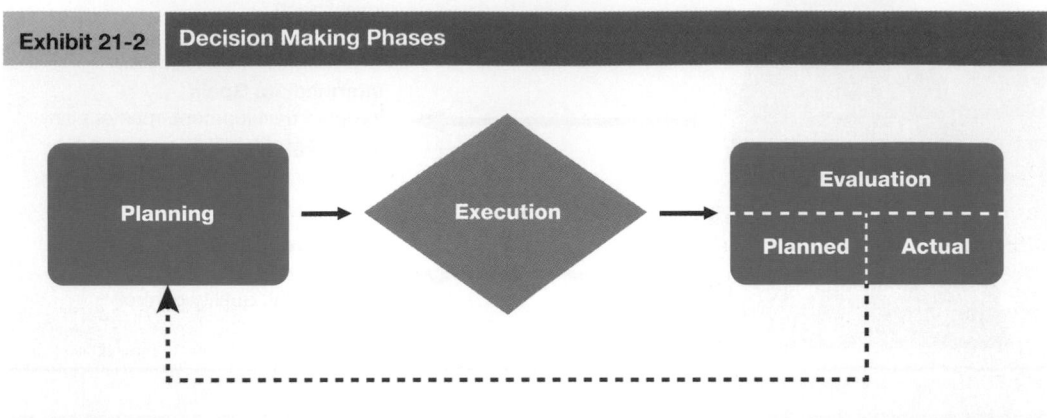

Exhibit 21-2   Decision Making Phases

The **planning phase** begins with *goal identification,* the specification of objectives to be sought or accomplished. One of the most common business goals is the long-run optimization of net income, often expressed in terms of return on assets. Other goals include target growth rates in sales revenue or total assets, target market shares in various markets, or leadership in product research, innovation, and quality.

The next steps in planning are identifying feasible alternative courses of action for achieving desired goals and estimating their qualitative and quantitative effects on the specified goals. Because planning involves the future, data related to the alternative courses of action must be estimated and projected in an environment of uncertainty.

The **execution phase** begins with the actual moment of decision: management commits to a specific plan of action. Because of the complexity of modern business, some elaborate plans may need lead times of several years. Poor planning, or the absence of planning, may lead to operating crises that carry significant penalties for the firm in terms of extra costs, lost opportunities, and—in extreme cases— bankruptcy.

Once a decision has been made, the plan is implemented, which usually involves the acquisition and commitment of materials, labor, and long-lived assets such as machinery and buildings. Management is kept informed through periodic accounting reports on the acquisition and use of these facilities during the execution phase.

In the **evaluation phase**, steps are taken to control the outcome of a specific plan of action. Virtually every important aspect of business—costs, product quality, inventory levels, and sales revenue—must be reasonably well controlled if a firm is to operate successfully. Measuring performance is an essential element of control. Performance measurement must compare actual operations with planned operations to allow management to take remedial action when significant unfavorable variations exist. Managerial accounting data and reports play a key role in informing management about performance in various areas during the evaluation phase of decision making.

Decision processes do not, however, fall into three neatly divided phases. Changes in competition, technology, and customer demand must be considered. Furthermore, most management teams are engaged in all three decision-making phases at any given time. They may be planning decisions in one area, executing them in a second, and evaluating them in a third.

TAKEAWAY 21.2

Feedback data are important for effective management. The generation of feedback data for management is one of the central purposes of managerial accounting.

RELEVANT COSTS AND DIFFERENTIAL ANALYSIS

Decision making involves choosing among different alternatives. In business, managers make decisions by evaluating the costs and benefits associated with each alternative. However, not all costs and benefits should be considered. Sound decision making is based on the widely accepted decision rule that only the aspects of a choice that differ among alternatives are relevant to a decision.

For example, imagine that you want to see an action movie in the theater. There are two theaters in your local community that are showing the movie. As a college student on a limited budget, you are careful with your money and want to choose the least-cost alternative, so you assemble the following information:

Cost/benefit	Theater #1	Theater #2
Ticket price.	$ 9.25	$ 9.25
Parking	$ 3.00	$ 4.00
Popcorn and drink	$10.00	$10.00
Concessions coupon	N/A	50% off
Gas for car	$0.10/mile	$0.10/mile
Car insurance (based on 10,000 miles per year)	$0.06/mile	$0.06/mile
Depreciation on car (based on 10,000 miles per year). . .	$0.30/mile	$0.30/mile
Distance to theater.	5 miles	10 miles

When you are deciding which theater to attend, the admission price is irrelevant if both theaters charge the same price. However, if the cost to park is $4 at one and $3 at the other, then the $1 differential parking cost is relevant to the choice. Likewise, if the popcorn and drink are $10 at both theaters, but you have a coupon for half off at one theater, the $5 savings is also relevant to the choice. If you plan to drive to the theater, the cost of the gas that would be consumed would be relevant if the theaters are different distances away, but the cost that you paid for your car (reflected in the annual depreciation cost) would not be because it was incurred in the past and is considered a **sunk cost**. Finally, the cost of insurance will be incurred regardless of which theater you choose, so it is not relevant to the decision. The decision process is simplified by concentrating only on the factors that are different between the alternatives the manager is evaluating. Thus, **relevant costs** in making a decision are defined as those that differ between alternatives.

In choosing between alternatives, managers must exercise care to avoid including irrelevant data that could lead to a poor decision. In the theater example, two categories of irrelevant costs were identified: costs that do not differ among the alternatives and sunk costs. Sunk costs are costs that have been incurred in the past and cannot be avoided regardless of the decision made.

Finally, managers should consider opportunity costs. Opportunity cost is the future benefit that is given up when a choice is made. In our theater example, assume that a third alternative is to stay home and study for an upcoming exam. A potential opportunity cost of choosing to go to the theater is the higher score that might result from the additional three hours of study.

Quantitative vs. Qualitative Factors in Decision Making

Differential analysis considers revenues and expenses that differ among alternatives. However, it does not include qualitative factors, such as impact on labor force or customer base. Thus, the results of differential analysis are only one input into the decision-making process—successful managers must also consider qualitative factors.

Suppose that by 1860 John Deere had determined that he could use his blacksmith shop to produce and sell either plows or hayforks. His decision would have been in favor of the product promising the higher net income based on the estimated operating data shown in **Exhibit 21-3**.

Exhibit 21-3	**John Deere Estimated Operating Data**		
		Alternatives	
		Plows	**Hayforks**
Units that can be produced and sold.		14,000	20,000
Unit selling price.		$ 12.00	$ 7.00
Manufacturing costs:			
Variable (per unit)		$ 4.00	$ 2.00
Fixed (total).		$44,400	$44,400
Selling and administrative expenses:			
Variable (per unit)		$ 1.00	$ 1.00
Fixed (total).		$ 3,000	$ 3,000

We may compare the alternatives by preparing comparative income statements, as shown in **Exhibit 21-4**, from these data.

Exhibit 21-4	**Product Choice Differential Analysis**		
		Alternatives	
	Plows	**Hayforks**	**Difference**
Revenue			
(14,000 units @ $12)	$168,000		
(20,000 units @ $7)		$140,000	$28,000
Cost of goods sold (manufacturing costs):			
Variable (14,000 @ $4 per unit).	56,000		
(20,000 @ $2 per unit).		40,000	16,000
Fixed (total)	44,400	44,400	—
Selling and administrative expenses:			
Variable (@ $1.00 per unit)	14,000	20,000	(6,000)
Fixed (total)	3,000	3,000	—
Total expenses.	$117,400	$107,400	$10,000
Net income.	$ 50,600	$ 32,600	$18,000

This analysis shows an $18,000 increase in net income associated with plows as a result of a $28,000 increase in total revenue that is partially offset by a $10,000 net increase in cost of goods sold and variable selling and administrative expenses.

A simple differential analysis of the same situation is as follows, where consideration is limited to the revenue and expense factors that differ if plows are produced rather than hayforks:

Differential revenue:	
Revenue forgone on last 6,000 units [$7 × 6,000].	$(42,000)
Additional revenue from increased sales price [($12 − $7) × 14,000].	70,000
Net additional revenue	$ 28,000
Differential costs:	
Additional cost of goods sold [($4 − $2) × 14,000].	$ 28,000
Savings on last 6,000 units [$2 × 6,000]	(12,000)
Savings on variable selling and administrative expenses ($1.00 × 6,000) . .	(6,000)
Net differential income in favor of plows	$ 18,000

Note that the cost of John Deere's blacksmith shop would be considered a sunk cost, and not relevant to the choice between producing plows or hayforks.

Clearly, the differential approach indicates the same net advantage for plows as the income statements but it does so more concisely. In reality, a company's income statement is much more complex than that presented in Exhibit 21-4. Therefore, management uses the more efficient differential analysis in decision making.

A.K.A. A *differential cost*, also called an *incremental cost*, is any cost present in one alternative but absent in whole or part in another alternative.

Are fixed costs always irrelevant in differential analysis?

DECISION TIME 21.1

The solution is on page 981.

ILLUSTRATIONS OF DIFFERENTIAL ANALYSIS

The Special Order

Businesses occasionally receive special orders from purchasers who request a price concession. The prospective buyer may suggest a price or ask for a bid. Sometimes the buyer may request that the firm produce a special version of a product to be identified with the buyer's private brand. As long as no overriding qualitative considerations exist, management should evaluate such propositions and accept the special order if incremental revenues exceed incremental costs.

LO2 **Demonstrate** when to accept a special order.

Business Situation

Assume that Fezzari Bicycles makes an entry-level mountain bike, the Lone Peak, which it sells to retail customers for $549. A bike share company has proposed that Fezzari supply 300 bikes for $400 per bike for a new bike share program in Salt Lake City, Utah. The bikes would carry the brand name of the bike share company. If Fezzari were to accept the order, a special machine attachment would be needed in production to differentiate the bike and affix the private brand logo. This attachment, which costs $1,500, would be discarded after the completion of this order. Also assume that Fezzari has unused production capacity, and thus anticipates no change in fixed capacity costs. The following unit cost data are available for the regular production of the Lone Peak bike:

Direct material	$233
Direct labor.	100
Variable manufacturing overhead.	20
Fixed manufacturing overhead (allocated)	47
Total cost per unit	$400

Analysis and Recommendation

At first glance, the proposal seems unprofitable because the unit cost figure is $400, which is exactly equal to the buyer's offered price, and an additional one-time cost of $1,500 must be incurred to process the order. However, the fixed overhead of $47 included in the $400 total unit cost is not relevant to the decision and should not be considered because Fezzari's total fixed costs will be incurred whether or not the special order is accepted. The differential cost and revenue analysis in **Exhibit 21-5** demonstrates that the special order should be accepted.

Exhibit 21-5	Special Order Differential Analysis		
Increase in sales revenue (300 units × $400)			$120,000
Increase in variable production costs:			
Direct material (300 units × $233)	(69,900)		
Direct labor (300 units × $100)	(30,000)		
Variable manufacturing overhead (300 units × $20)	(6,000)		
Total increase in production costs (300 units × $353). . .		(105,900)	
Cost of special attachment		(1,500)	
Total differential cost			(107,400)
Net advantage in accepting special order			$ 12,600

The differential costs of accepting the order consist of the variable production costs and the additional cost of the attachment needed to affix the private brand. Actually, with any price higher than $358 ($107,400 total differential costs ÷ 300 units), Fezzari would earn a profit on the order.

Note that excess production capacity is significant to the special order decision. Without sufficient excess capacity, the additional production would probably cause additional amounts of fixed costs to be incurred or the loss of productive capacity for Fezzari's normal bike production. In addition, Fezzari management would also want to consider the opportunity cost of utilizing the available production capacity for this special order, because accepting the order would limit Fezzari's ability to meet increased demand for a higher-margin bike. Also note that although the $1,500 special attachment in this example is a fixed cost, it is relevant to this decision because it differs between alternatives.

YOUR TURN! 21.1

The solution is on page 981.

Current sales are 50,000 units at $25 per unit. Production capacity is 80,000 units. Variable costs are $14 per unit. Fixed costs are $400,000. A special order for 10,000 units at $20 each is received. It will require the purchase of new equipment for $40,000. The equipment will have a salvage value of $5,000 at the end of the contract. Should the offer be accepted?

TAKEAWAY 21.3

The Special Order rule of thumb: ACCEPT the special order IF incremental revenues exceed incremental costs (assuming there are no qualitative factors deemed to outweigh the qualitative analysis).

Additional Decision Factors

Specific qualitative factors that should be considered here include ascertaining that (1) the special price does not constitute unfair price discrimination; (2) the special order does not negatively impact the actual or perceived quality of the retail bikes; and (3) the long-term price structure for the product is not adversely affected by the special order. Significant concern in any of these, or other areas, might be a basis for rejecting the special order despite the potential $12,600 profit.

Make or Buy?

Many manufacturing situations require the assembly of large numbers of specially de-signed components and subassemblies. Usually, the manufacturer must choose between making these components and subassemblies and buying them from outside suppliers. In each situation, management should evaluate the relative costs of the two choices and buy from outside if the differential cost of buying is less than the differential cost of making the components or subassemblies. Because making a component uses some portion of the firm's manufacturing capacity, we assume that no more attractive use of that capacity is available.

LO3 **Demonstrate** when to make or buy needed parts.

Business Situation

To illustrate the make-or-buy decision, we assume that John Deere manufactures a loader-backhoe with the following costs:

Manufactured Cab:	
Direct material	$3,000
Direct labor.	1,190
Variable manufacturing overhead.	750
Fixed manufacturing overhead.	650
Total cost	$5,590

Investigations by John Deere's purchasing department indicate that the loader-backhoe cab assembly can be purchased in sufficient quantities at a unit price of $5,031, an indicated savings of 10% per unit. At first glance, the opportunity to purchase seems attractive.

Analysis and Recommendation

A review of operations indicates that by purchasing the component, John Deere can re-duce its variable costs of production, but the fixed overhead costs will remain. The fixed overhead costs related to equipment used to manufacture the cabs are an example of a sunk cost. The differential analysis in **Exhibit 21-6** indicates that by purchasing the cab, John Deere's overall costs would increase by $91 per unit. Thus, John Deere should con-tinue to manufacture the cab.

Exhibit 21-6	Make or Buy Differential Analysis		
	Manufacture Cab	Purchase Cab	Increase (Decrease) in Cost if Cab Is Purchased
Cost per unit:			
Direct material	$3,000		$(3,000)
Direct labor.	1,190		(1,190)
Variable manufacturing overhead.	750		(750)
Fixed manufacturing overhead.	650	650	—
Purchase price of components		5,031	5,031
	$5,590	$5,681	$ 91

The following approach to this analysis confirms the more comprehensive one above:

Cost to purchase cab.			$ 5,031
Less costs avoided by purchasing:			
Direct material.		$3,000	
Direct labor		1,190	
Variable manufacturing overhead		750	$ 4,940
Increase in acquisition cost by purchasing . . .			$ 91

Additional Decision Factors

These analyses assume that the manufacturing capacity released by the decision to purchase would not be used. However, should an opportunity arise to use this capacity to generate another product with more than $91 of contribution margin per unit, then the opportunity to purchase the components would be more attractive. However, qualitative factors, such as the effects on employee morale, product quality, and dependability of the supply chain, are also very important. Once a decision is reached based on the quantitative analyses, it should be weighed against these and other qualitative factors that may be important to management.

Dropping Unprofitable Segments

LO4 Demonstrate when to drop an unprofitable product or segment.

SERVICE AND MERCHANDISING

Occasionally, a company's financial reporting system provides its management with segment information that suggests that a particular division, department, office, product, or product line is losing money. In these situations, management should compare the direct segment cost saved to the revenue lost if the segment were to be dropped. The company should drop the segment if the cost saved is greater than the revenue lost.

Business Situation

Assume that EBC's segment financial statements show that the Water/Wastewater segment lost $5,298 for 2016. It would appear that dropping the segment would increase EBC's profit by $5,298, or almost 1% (see **Exhibit 21-7**).

Exhibit 21-7	Segment Income Statement		
	ENVIRONMENTAL BUSINESS CONSULTANTS, LLC **Line of Business Statement** **For the Year Ended December 31, 2016**		
	Solid Waste	**Water/ Wastewater**	**Firm Total**
Gross sales.	$3,676,000	$470,000	$ 4,146,000
Less reimbursable costs	(366,350)	(64,650)	(431,000)
Net sales.	$3,309,650	$405,350	$ 3,715,000
Cost of services	(2,238,787)	(384,713)	(2,623,500)
Gross profit on sales.	$1,070,863	$ 20,637	$ 1,091,500
Direct operating expenses	(166,065)	(25,935)	(192,000)
Line of business contribution	$ 904,798	$ (5,298)	$ 899,500
Common operating expenses			(364,500)
Interest revenue			7,500
Income before tax			$ 542,500

Assume that the Water/Wastewater cost of services includes an office lease expense of $38,625 that would continue even if the business line were discontinued. The rest of the Water/Wastewater cost of services and direct operating expenses are variable in nature and would be eliminated with the dropping of the segment.

Analysis and Recommendation

The differential analysis in **Exhibit 21-8** indicates that EBC's overall income would decrease, rather than increase, by discontinuing the Water/Wastewater.

Exhibit 21-8	Dropping Unprofitable Segment Differential Analysis		
Decrease in net revenue.			$(405,350)
Decrease in expenses:			
Variable cost of goods sold*		$346,088	
Variable direct operating expenses		25,935	$ 372,023
Decrease in total contribution margin (and net income) from discontinuing Water/Wastewater			$ (33,327)

*$384,713 − $38,625

Even though Water/Wastewater reports a $5,298 annual loss, it does generate a contribution margin of $33,327 toward the absorption of fixed costs and expenses. If Water/Wastewater is discontinued, there would be no contribution margin, although $38,625 of fixed cost would remain. This would result in a loss of $38,625, which is $33,327 worse than the current $5,298 loss. Thus, EBC should maintain its Water/Wastewater segment and look for ways to either increase revenue or decrease costs.

Additional Decision Factors

Management must often consider other factors in decisions of this type. Among these are (1) the potential termination of employees and subsequent effects on non-terminated employee morale, and (2) the possible effects on customer patronage (for example, customers of the Solid Waste line of business may go to other firms for all of their consulting services if Water/Wastewater's services are no longer available from the same source). On the other hand, EBC management might also begin to explore other potential services that might generate greater profits than the Water/Wastewater segment.

From a financial point of view, when should an unprofitable segment be dropped?

DECISION TIME 21.2

The solution is on page 981.

TAKEAWAY 21.5

The Dropping an Unprofitable Segment rule of thumb: DROP the segment IF the direct cost savings is greater than the lost revenue (assuming there are no qualitative factors deemed to outweigh the qualitative analysis).

Sell or Process Further?

Firms sometimes face the decision of either selling products at one point in the production sequence or processing them further and selling them at a higher price. Examples are finished versus unfinished furniture, crude oil versus gasoline, and unassembled kits versus assembled units of product. In these process-further decision situations, management should compare the incremental revenue to the additional processing costs and process the products further if the incremental revenue exceeds the incremental processing costs.

LO5 Demonstrate when to sell a product or process it further.

Business Situation

Assume that Sunrise Landscape sells screened topsoil with the following values per yard:

Current sales price (per cubic yard)		$20.00
Costs:		
Direct material.	$5.00	
Direct labor	5.00	
Variable overhead	1.00	
Fixed overhead*	2.50	13.50
Gross margin per unit.		$ 6.50

*Applied at 50% of direct labor costs.

Sunrise has excess productive capacity, which should remain available in the foreseeable future. Consequently, management believes that part of this excess capacity could be used to create a garden mix blended soil (topsoil that has been amended with compost and peat) and sell it at $30.00 per cubic yard to homeowners for their vegetable gardens and planting beds. A study carried out by the company's management indicates that the additional processing will add $5.00 to the direct material cost and $2.00 to the direct labor cost of each unit and that variable overhead will continue to be incurred at 20% of direct labor cost. See **Exhibit 21-9** for the specific steps involved.

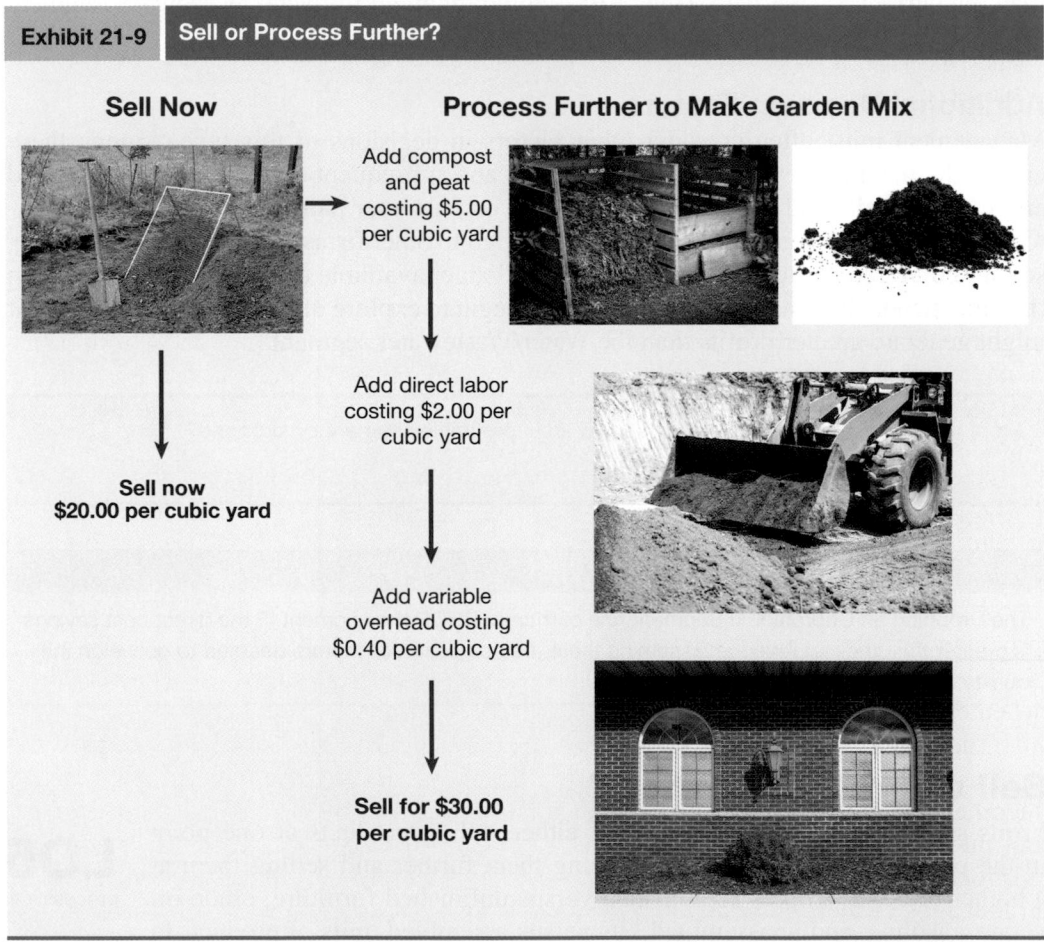

Exhibit 21-9 Sell or Process Further?

Sell Now

Sell now
$20.00 per cubic yard

Process Further to Make Garden Mix

Add compost and peat costing $5.00 per cubic yard

Add direct labor costing $2.00 per cubic yard

Add variable overhead costing $0.40 per cubic yard

Sell for $30.00 per cubic yard

Analysis and Recommendation

The differential analysis in **Exhibit 21-10** supports the proposal to process further:

Exhibit 21-10	Sell or Process Further Differential Analysis	
		Per Cubic Yard
Differential revenue ($30.00 − $20.00)........................		$10.00
Differential cost:		
Direct material...	$5.00	
Direct labor...	2.00	
Variable manufacturing overhead (20% of direct labor).........	0.40	
Fixed manufacturing overhead.............................	—	
Total differential cost		7.40
Excess of differential revenue over differential cost.............		$ 2.60

The per-unit differential analyses indicate that Sunrise will earn an additional $2.60 per cubic yard for every yard of garden mix processed and sold.

Joint Products

Often, the processing of direct material results in two or more products of significant commercial value. Such products derived from a common input are **joint products**, and the related cost of the direct material is a joint product cost. An obvious example of a direct material whose processing results in joint products is crude oil, from which a variety of fuels, solvents, lubricants, and residual petrochemical pitches are derived. Cattle, from which the meat packer obtains many cuts and grades of meat, hides, and other products, are another example.

A.K.A. *Joint product costs are manufacturing costs incurred in producing joint products up to the split-off point.*

It is impossible to allocate a joint product cost among joint products in such a way that management can decide whether to continue production or what price to charge for a joint product. To decide to produce one joint product is to decide to produce all related joint products, even if some are discarded. Therefore, to make informed decisions about joint products, management must compare the total revenue generated by all joint products with their total production costs. The joint costs incurred to the point at which the joint products are separately identified are irrelevant with regard to decisions about whether to sell or process any of the joint products further.

The primary reason for allocating a joint product cost among two or more products is to assign cost to the ending inventories of joint products when determining periodic income. The most popular method of allocating joint product costs for inventory costing purposes is the relative sales value method. This approach uses arithmetic proportions. The total joint product cost is allocated to the various joint products in the proportions of their individual sales values to the total sales value of all joint products at the split-off point—that is, where physical separation takes place. For example, assume that 50,000 55-gallon barrels of crude oil costing $5,000,000 are processed into 800,000 gallons of fuel selling for $3.00 per gallon, 400,000 gallons of lubricants selling for $5.00 per gallon, and 1,000,000 gallons of petrochemical residues selling for $1.50 per gallon. The following calculations illustrate the joint product cost allocation using the relative sales value approach:

Joint Product	Quantity Produced (gallons)	Unit Sales Value	Product Sales Value	Proportion of Total Product Sales Value	Allocated Cost	Quantity Produced (gallons)	Cost per Unit
Fuel........	800,000	$3.00	$2,400,000	40.68%	$2,034,000	800,000	$2.54
Lubricants...	400,000	$5.00	2,000,000	33.90%	1,695,000	400,000	$4.24
Residues....	1,000,000	$1.50	1,500,000	25.42%	1,271,000	1,000,000	$1.27
			$5,900,000	100.00%	$5,000,000		

Note that the relative sales value approach results in assigned unit costs that are the same percentage of the selling price for each product. In our illustration, the cost per unit equals approximately 85% of the sales value per unit.

Exhibit 21-11 illustrates the allocation of the $5,000,000 joint product cost to the three joint products. Note also that each product may then incur additional manufacturing costs before it is completed and ready for sale. For example, in Exhibit 21-11, an additional $206,000 of costs are incurred after the split-off point to finish the production of the fuel. When added to the allocated joint costs, the total cost of the fuel is $2,240,000, or $2.80 per gallon.

Exhibit 21-11	Joint Product Costs

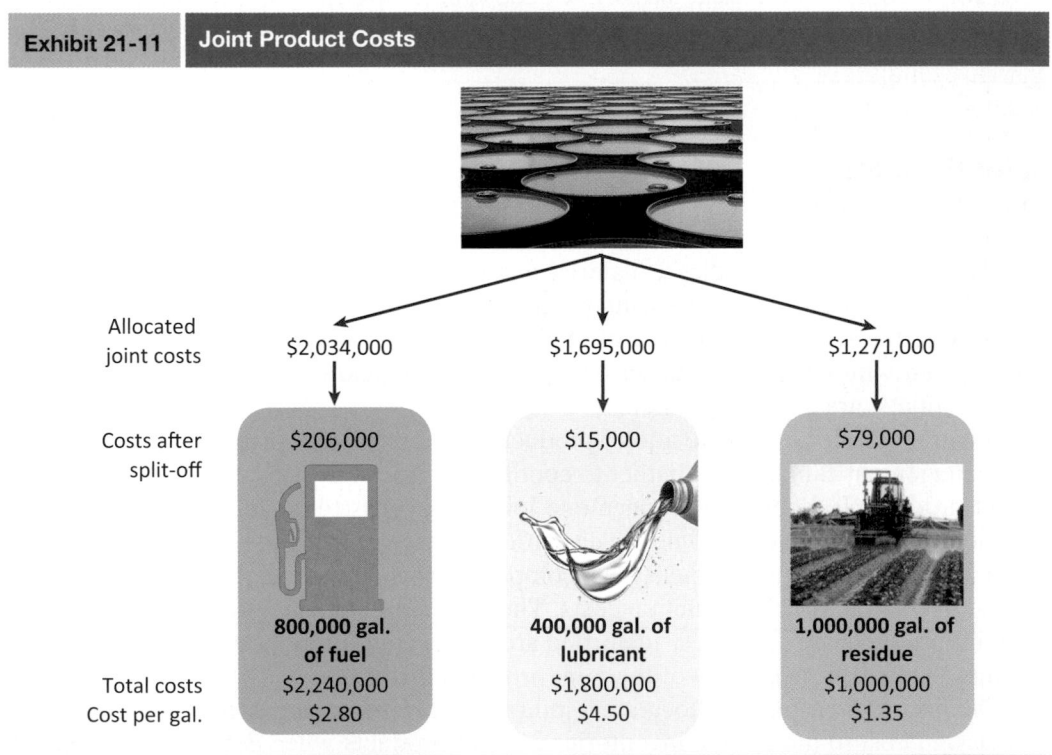

Allocated joint costs	$2,034,000	$1,695,000	$1,271,000
Costs after split-off	$206,000	$15,000	$79,000
	800,000 gal. of fuel	400,000 gal. of lubricant	1,000,000 gal. of residue
Total costs	$2,240,000	$1,800,000	$1,000,000
Cost per gal.	$2.80	$4.50	$1.35

Byproducts

Byproducts have relatively little sales value compared with the other products derived from a particular process. Byproducts are considered incidental to the manufacture of the more important products. For example, the sawdust and shavings generated in a lumber mill or in a furniture manufacturer's cutting department are byproducts.

We may account for byproducts by assigning them a cost equal to their sales value less any disposal costs. This net amount is charged to an inventory account for the byproduct and credited to the work-in-process account that was charged with the original materials. For example, consider a furniture factory in which walnut boards are processed through a cutting and shaping department. In processing $40,000 worth of lumber, 800 bushels of sawdust and shavings are generated, which, after treatment costing $80, can be sold for $1 per bushel. The amount to be charged to the Sawdust and Shavings Inventory account would be $720 [(800 bushels × $1) − $80].

This procedure reduces the costs of the main products by the net amount recovered from byproducts.

Constrained Resources

Because most firms produce several products, management must continually examine operating data and decide which combination of products offers the greatest total long-term profit potential. The decisions related to product emphasis are seldom as simple as determining the most profitable product and confining production to that one product. For example, John Deere faces such operational constraints as limited demand for the most profitable products, the competitive necessity of offering a line of products with a variety of qualities and capacities, and, in seeking better utilization of existing capacity, the need to produce other, less profitable products.

LO6 Demonstrate how to determine which product to produce.

In a **constrained resource** analysis, an important and widely accepted generalization is that the firm optimizes its income when it maximizes the contribution margin earned per unit of constraining resource. The concept of constraining resource stems from the realization that as a firm increases its volume, some resource is eventually exhausted and thus constrains, or limits, the continued expansion of the firm. Which resources are constraining depends on the firm, the operating conditions, and even the products under consideration. Typical examples are key materials, labor skills, machine capacities, and factory floor space or storage space. Simply stated, management has optimized the firm's product mix when it maximizes the contribution margin earned on each unit of the particular resource that limits increased production.

A.K.A. Constrained resources are commonly referred to as *bottlenecks*.

Business Situation

To illustrate constrained resource decisions, assume that John Deere's Waterloo Works Tractor, Cab, and Assembly Operations in Waterloo, Illinois, produces three 6R Series row-crop tractors, the 6140R, the 6150R, and the 6170R. Also assume the operation's constraining resource is its factory machine capacity. John Deere operates at 90% capacity, and management wants to devote the unused capacity to one of the three products. The following data represent John Deere's current operations:

	Products		
	6140R	**6150R**	**6170R**
Per-unit data:			
Sales price	$130,000	$143,000	$150,000
Variable costs.	99,450	109,000	117,000
Contribution margin	$ 30,550	$ 34,000	$ 33,000
Fixed costs*	16,150	18,700	17,850
Net income.	$ 14,400	$ 15,300	$ 15,150
Machine hours required	38	44	42

*Allocated on basis of machine hours at $425 per hour.

Analysis and Recommendation

Intuition suggests that the extra capacity should be devoted either to the 6170R, which has the highest sales price, or to the 6150R, which has the highest per-unit contribution margin and net income. However, an analysis of the contribution margin of each product per unit of constraining resource (machine hour) reveals that the 6140R should receive the added capacity.

Note that fixed costs are allocated among products on the basis of machine hours—the constraining resource in our example. Furthermore, the unit allocations of fixed costs, noted previously, indicate that the 6170R requires 2 fewer machine hours than the 6150R and 4 more than the 6140R. The contribution per unit of machine capacity for each product is shown in **Exhibit 21-12**.

Exhibit 21-12	Constrained Resource Differential Analysis		
		Products	
	6140R	**6150R**	**6170R**
Contribution margin per unit	$30,550	$34,000	$33,000
Divided by machine hours required	38	44	42
Contribution margin per machine hour (the constraining resource).	$ 804	$ 773	$ 786

Use of the remaining capacity generates a greater contribution margin if devoted to the 6140R. As this example illustrates, in deciding how to utilize the constraining resource, management should use contribution margin per unit of constraining resource, rather than the relative sales prices, unit contribution margins, or even unit profit of various products.

YOUR TURN! 21.2

The solution is on page 981.

Product A requires 2 machine hours per unit, has a unit contribution margin of $15, and a contribution margin ratio of 60%. Product B requires 1 machine hour per unit, has a unit contribution margin of $12, and a contribution margin ratio of 40%. Which product should be emphasized if machine hours are limited?

TAKEAWAY 21.7

The Constrained Resource rule of thumb: MAXIMIZE the contribution margin per unit of scarce resource (assuming there are no qualitative factors deemed to outweigh the qualitative analysis).

SERVICE INDUSTRY IN FOCUS

SERVICE AND MERCHANDISING

Environmental Business Consultants, LLC (EBC) has been approached by Terrabean Coffee, a large retail coffee company with 5,000 shops across North America, to manage Terrabean Coffee's waste disposal and recycling services under a 3-year contract. It is unlikely that the contract would be extended beyond the initial 3-year term. Terrabean has asked EBC to provide these services at a discounted average hourly billing rate of $60 per hour.

In order to take on this major new contract, EBC would need to establish a call center to receive calls from the 5,000 shops and coordinate the appropriate response. The call center would be in a leased office space at a cost of $3,000 per month, including utilities. Additional capital, including office furniture, computers, and phones, would be purchased at a total cost of $35,000. The office furniture, computers, and phones are expected to have a value of $5,000 at the end of the contract and would not be of use to EBC in its regular business. The call center would be managed by a current EBC consultant that normally bills 1,800 hours per year at a rate of $125 per hour. An additional ten call center employees would be hired at an average hourly wage of $25, plus benefits equal to

50% of the hourly wage. Each employee would be expected to work 2,000 hours per year. EBC expects to bill Terrabean 20,000 hours per year for the call center under the contract.

Required

1. Determine whether EBC should accept this new contract offer from Terrabean. Calculate the differential net revenue or cost associated with the contract. (Hint: Don't forget that the call center manager is a current EBC employee and would not be available for any other work.)

2. What other factors should EBC management consider in making the decision?

Solution

1.

Solution	Service Industry in Focus	
Increase in annual revenue (20,000 hours × $60)		$1,200,000
Lost revenue from call center manager (1,800 × $125). . .		(225,000)
Total differential billing revenue		$ 975,000
Increase in costs:		
Direct labor (10 employees × 2,000 hours × $37.50) . . .	$750,000	
Office lease ($3,000 × 12 months).	36,000	
Other capital costs [($35,000 − 5,000)/3 years)]	10,000	
Total differential cost		$ 796,000
Net advantage in accepting contract offer.		$ 179,000

2. EBC management should consider the impact on the ten employees who will need to be hired for the call center. At the end of the contract term, these employees will need to be terminated unless other work can be found.

SUMMARY OF LEARNING OBJECTIVES

Describe management's use of accounting information in the decision-making process. Define relevant costs and describe the use of differential analysis. (p. 950)   LO1

- Top management establishes long-range goals, middle management deals with intermediate goals, and lower management focuses on short-range goals.
- Decision making, which is essentially choosing among alternatives, usually comprises three phases: planning, execution, and evaluation.
- Relevant costs are those that differ between alternatives.
- Differential analysis is the study of those amounts that are expected to differ among alternatives.

Demonstrate when to accept a special order. (p. 955)   LO2

- Management should evaluate special order propositions and accept the special order if incremental revenues exceed incremental costs.
- Management should also consider qualitative factors that could be the basis of rejecting a special order despite a net increase in revenues, such as unfair pricing, impact on quality, and long-term pricing impact.

Demonstrate when to make or buy needed parts. (p. 957)   LO3

- Management should evaluate the relative costs of the two choices and buy from outside if the differential cost of buying is less than the differential cost of making the components or subassemblies.
- Management should also consider qualitative factors such as the effects on employee morale, product quality, and dependability of the supply chain.

LO4   Demonstrate when to drop an unprofitable product or segment. (p. 958)

- Management should compare the direct segment cost saved to the revenue lost if the segment were to be dropped. The company should drop the segment if the cost saved is greater than the revenue lost.
- Management should also consider the potential termination of employees and subsequent effects on non-terminated employee morale, and the possible effects on customer patronage.

LO5   Demonstrate when to sell a product or process it further. (p. 959)

- Management should compare the incremental revenue to the additional processing costs and process the products further if the incremental revenue exceeds the incremental processing costs.
- The joint costs incurred to the point at which the joint products are separately identified are irrelevant with regard to decisions about whether to sell or process any of the joint products further.

LO6   Demonstrate how to determine which product to produce. (p. 963)

- Management should maximize the contribution margin earned on each unit of the particular resource that limits increased production.

KEY TERMS

Constrained resource (p. 963)	**Execution phase** (p. 952)	**Planning phase** (p. 952)
Decision making (p. 951)	**Incremental cost** (p. 955)	**Relevant costs** (p. 953)
Differential analysis (p. 954)	**Joint product costs** (p. 961)	**Sunk cost** (p. 953)
Differential cost (p. 955)	**Joint products** (p. 961)	
Evaluation phase (p. 952)	**Management** (p. 950)	

Assignments with the ⬤ logo in the margin are available in ᵐʸBusinessCourse.
See the Preface of the book for details.

SELF-STUDY QUESTIONS

(Answers to Self-Study Questions are at the end of this chapter.)

LO1   1. **When using differential analysis to analyze two alternatives to the current operation, what factors should *not* be considered?**
   a.   Direct material costs that are different
   b.   Direct labor costs that exist for only one alternative
   c.   Overhead costs that are the same for both alternatives
   d.   Sales commissions that apply to only one alternative

LO2   2. **When considering a special order, management should accept the order if which of the following conditions is met?**
   a.   Incremental costs are greater than incremental revenues.
   b.   There is excess production capacity.
   c.   Incremental costs are less than incremental revenues.
   d.   Employees are willing to work overtime.

LO3   3. **When considering whether to continue to manufacture a part or buy it from an outside supplier, management should buy the part if the**
   a.   incremental cost to buy is less than the incremental cost to manufacture the part.
   b.   equipment used for making the part is fully depreciated.
   c.   equipment used for making the part could be sold.
   d.   incremental cost to buy is less than the total cost to manufacture the part.

LO4   4. **A business segment reports segment revenues of $1.2 million, segment costs of $1.0 million, and allocated corporate overhead costs of $300,000. If management were to drop the segment, overall corporate profits would**
   a.   increase by $100,000.
   b.   decrease by $100,000.
   c.   increase by $200,000.
   d.   decrease by $200,000.

5. **True or false: Costs incurred to the split-off point in the manufacture of joint products are always relevant to the decision of whether to sell the joint products or process them further.**   **LO5**
   a. True
   b. False

QUESTIONS

1. Identify three phases of decision making and briefly discuss the role of each phase in the decision process.   **LO1**
2. Although separate phases of decision making are identifiable, management is usually involved in all phases at the same time. Explain.   **LO1**
3. In the chapter we discuss quantitative methods to assist management in making business decisions. Discuss other common aspects of decision making that are not often subject to quantification.   **LO1**
4. Explain what is meant by the term *differential analysis*.   **LO1**
5. Explain how differential analysis can be applied to the following types of decisions: **LO2, 3, 4, 5, 6**
   a. Accepting special orders
   b. Making or buying product components
   c. Dropping unprofitable segments of the firm
   d. Selling or processing further
   e. Product emphasis
6. Delton Company produces unassembled picture frames at the following average per-unit costs: direct material, $X; direct labor, $Y; and manufacturing overhead, $Z. Delton can assemble the frames at a unit cost of $2.50 and raise the selling price from $11 to $15. What is the apparent advantage or disadvantage of assembling the frames?   **LO5**
7. Explain the concept of *constraining resource*, and present a general rule for optimizing product mixes.   **LO6**
8. "In differential analysis, we can generally count on variable cost being relevant and fixed cost being irrelevant." Comment.   **LO1**
9. If both approaches to a decision lead to the same conclusion, why might differential analysis be considered superior to a comprehensive analysis that reflects all revenue and costs?   **LO1**

EXERCISES—SET A

E21-1A. Dropping Unprofitable Department   Thomas Corporation has four departments, all of which appear to be profitable except department 4. Operating data for 2016 are as follows: **LO4**

SERVICE AND MERCHANDISING

	Total	Departments 1–3	Department 4
Sales.	$950,000	$800,000	$150,000
Cost of sales.	634,000	520,000	114,000
Gross profit.	$316,000	$280,000	$ 36,000
Direct expenses	$144,000	$120,000	$ 24,000
Common expenses	123,000	105,000	18,000
Total expenses.	$267,000	$225,000	$ 42,000
Net income (Loss).	$ 49,000	$ 55,000	$ (6,000)

Required
a. Calculate the gross profit percentage for departments 1–3 combined and for department 4.
b. What effect would elimination of department 4 have had on total firm net income? (Ignore the effect of income tax.)

LO1
E21-2A. Analyzing Operational Changes Operating results for department B of Delta Company during 2016 are as follows:

Sales.	$540,000
Cost of goods sold.	378,000
Gross profit.	$162,000
Direct expenses	$120,000
Common expenses	66,000
Total expenses.	$186,000
Net loss	$ (24,000)

If department B could maintain the same physical volume of product sold while raising selling prices an average of 15% and making an additional advertising expenditure of $45,000, what would be the effect on the department's net income or net loss? (Ignore income tax in your calculations.)

LO1
E21-3A. Analyzing Operational Changes Suppose that department B in Exercise E21-2A could increase physical volume of product sold by 10% if it spent an additional $18,000 on advertising while leaving selling prices unchanged. What effect would this have on the department's net income or net loss? (Ignore income tax in your calculations.)

LO1
E21-4A. Differential Analysis In each of four independent cases, the amount of differential revenue or differential cost is as follows (parentheses indicate decreases):

	1	2	3	4
Increases (decreases) in:				
Revenue	$18,000	$-0-	?	?
Costs.	?	?	($12,000)	$-0-

For each case, determine the missing amount that would be necessary for the net differential amount to be

a. $10,000
b. ($6,000)

Indicate whether your answers reflect increases or decreases.

LO2
E21-5A. Special Order Carson Manufacturing, Inc., sells a single product for $36 per unit. At an operating level of 8,000 units, variable costs are $18 per unit and fixed costs $10 per unit.

Carson has been offered a price of $20 per unit on a special order of 2,000 units by Big Mart Discount Stores, which would use its own brand name on the item. If Carson accepts the order, material cost will be $3 less per unit than for regular production. However, special stamping equipment costing $4,000 would be needed to process the order; the equipment would then be discarded.

Assuming that volume remains within the relevant range, prepare an analysis of differential revenue and costs to determine whether Carson should accept the special order.

LO3
E21-6A. Make or Buy Eastside Company incurs a total cost of $120,000 in producing 10,000 units of a component needed in the assembly of its major product. The component can be purchased from an outside supplier for $11 per unit. A related cost study indicates that the total cost of the component includes fixed costs equal to 50% of the variable costs involved.

a. Should Eastside buy the component if it cannot otherwise use the released capacity? Present your answer in the form of differential analysis.
b. What would be your answer to requirement (a) if the released capacity could be used in a project that would generate $50,000 of contribution margin?

E21-7A. Sell or Process Further Jensen Manufacturing Company makes a partially completed assembly unit   **LO5**
that it sells for $36 per unit. Normally, 42,000 units are sold each year. Variable unit cost data on the
assembly are as follows:

Direct material	$10
Direct labor.	8
Variable manufacturing overhead.	4

The company is now using only 70% of its normal capacity; it could fully use its normal capacity by
processing the assembly further and selling it for $43 per unit. If the company does this, material and
labor costs will each increase by $2 per unit and variable overhead will go up by $1 per unit. Fixed
costs will increase from the current level of $160,000 to $220,000.

Prepare an analysis showing whether Jensen should process the assemblies further.

E21-8A. Joint Cost Cheyenne, Inc. produces three products from a common input. The joint costs for a typi-   **LO5**
cal quarter follow:

Direct materials	$45,000
Direct labor.	55,000
Overhead	60,000

The revenues from each product are as follows:

Product A	$75,000
Product B	$80,000
Product C	$30,000

Management is considering processing Product A beyond the split-off point, which would increase the
sales value of Product A to $116,000. However, to process Product A further means that the company
must rent some special equipment costing $17,500 per quarter. Additional materials and labor also
needed would cost $12,650 per quarter.

Required

a.   What is the gross profit currently being earned by the three products for one quarter?
b.   What is the effect on quarterly profits if the company decides to process Product A further?

E21-9A. Service Emphasis The following analysis of selected data is for each of the two services Gates Cor-   **LO6**
poration provides.

	Service A	Service B
Per-service data at 10,000 services		
Sales price	$26	$22
Service costs:		
Variable.	9	9
Fixed	6	4
Selling and administrative expenses:		
Variable.	5	3
Fixed	3	1

In the Gates operation, labor capacity is the company's constraining resource. Each unit of A requires
3 hours of labor, and each unit of B requires 2 hours of labor. Assuming that all services can be sold
at a normal price, prepare an analysis showing which of the two services should be provided with any
unused productive capacity that Gates might have.

EXERCISES—SET B

LO4   **E21-1B. Dropping Unprofitable Department** Penn Corporation has four departments, all of which appear to be profitable except department 4. Operating data for 2016 are as follows:

**SERVICE AND
MERCHANDISING**

	Total	Departments 1-3	Department 4
Sales....................	$1,052,000	$900,000	$152,000
Cost of sales.............	654,000	540,000	114,000
Gross profit..............	$ 398,000	$360,000	$ 38,000
Direct expenses...........	$ 177,000	$150,000	$ 27,000
Common expenses	140,000	120,000	20,000
Total expenses...........	$ 317,000	$270,000	$ 47,000
Net income (loss)	$ 81,000	$ 90,000	$ (9,000)

a. Calculate the gross profit percentage for departments 1–3 combined and for department 4.
b. What effect would elimination of department 4 have had on total firm net income? (Ignore the effect of income tax.)

LO1   **E21-2B. Analyzing Operational Changes** Operating results for department B of Shaw Company during 2016 are as follows:

Sales...	$800,000
Cost of goods sold...	480,000
Gross profit...	$320,000
Direct expenses...	$215,000
Common expenses	123,000
Total expenses..	$338,000
Net loss	$ (18,000)

If department B could maintain the same physical volume of product sold while raising selling prices an average of 10% and making an additional advertising expenditure of $50,000, what would be the effect on the department's net income or net loss? (Ignore income tax in your calculations.)

LO1   **E21-3B. Analyzing Operational Changes** Suppose that department B in Exercise E21-2B could increase physical volume of product sold by 10% if it spent an additional $40,000 on advertising while leaving selling prices unchanged. What effect would this have on the department's net income or net loss? (Ignore income tax in your calculations.)

LO1   **E21-4B. Differential Analysis** In each of four independent cases, the amount of differential revenue or differential cost is as follows (parentheses indicate decreases):

	1	2	3	4
Increases (decreases) in:				
Revenue	$36,000	$-0-	?	?
Costs............................	?	?	$(20,000)	$-0-

For each case, determine the missing amount that would be necessary for the net differential amount to be

a. $24,000
b. ($16,000)

Indicate whether your answers reflect increases or decreases.

E21-5B. Special Order Northern Company regularly sells its only product for $34 per unit and has a 25% **LO2** profit on each sale. The company has accepted a special order for a number of units, the production of which would use part of its unused capacity. The special order sales price is 50% of the normal price, and the profit margin is only 60% of the regular dollar profit. What, apparently, is

    a.   Northern's profit per unit on the special order?
    b.   Northern's variable cost per unit?
    c.   Northern's average fixed cost per unit on regular sales?

E21-6B. Make or Buy Harper Company incurs a total cost of $252,000 in producing 20,000 units of a com- **LO3** ponent needed in the assembly of its major product. The component can be purchased from an outside supplier for $6 per unit. A related cost study indicates that the total cost of the component includes fixed costs equal to 80% of the variable costs involved.

    a.   Should Harper buy the component if it cannot otherwise use the released capacity? Present your answer in the form of differential analysis.
    b.   What would be your answer to requirement (a) if the released capacity could be used in a project that would generate $15,000 of contribution margin?

E21-7B. Sell or Process Further Turner Manufacturing Company makes a partially completed assembly unit **LO5** that it sells for $50 per unit. Normally, 35,000 units are sold each year. Variable unit cost data on the assembly are as follows:

Direct material	$12
Direct labor.	7
Variable manufacturing overhead.	9

The company is now using only 75% of its normal capacity; it could fully use its normal capacity by processing the assembly further and selling it for $58 per unit. If the company does this, material and labor costs will each increase by $2 per unit and variable overhead will go up by $1 per unit. Fixed costs will increase from the current level of $125,000 to $165,000.

    Prepare an analysis showing whether Turner should process the assemblies further.

E21-8B. Service Emphasis The following analysis of selected data is for each of the two services Rockville **LO6** Corporation provides.

	Service G	Service H
Per-unit data @ 10,000 services		
Sales price	$29	$16
Service costs:		
Variable.	9	7
Fixed	6	4
Selling and administrative expenses:		
Variable.	5	2
Fixed	3	1

In Rockville's operation, labor capacity is the company's constraining resource. Each unit of G requires 3 hours of labor, and each unit of H requires 1 hour of labor. Assuming that all services can be sold at a normal price, prepare an analysis showing which of the two services should be provided with any unused productive capacity that Rockville might have.

PROBLEMS—SET A

LO1 **P21-1A. Analyze Operational Changes** Richmond's is a retail store with eight departments, including a garden department that has been operating at a loss. The following condensed income statement gives the latest year's operating results:

	Garden Department	All Other Departments
Sales.	$336,000	$2,400,000
Cost of sales.	201,600	1,560,000
Gross profit.	$134,400	$ 840,000
Direct expenses	$108,000	$ 273,000
Common expenses	48,000	312,000
Total expenses	$156,000	$ 585,000
Net income (Loss).	$ (21,600)	$ 255,000

Required

a. Calculate the gross profit percentage for the garden department and for the other departments as a group.

b. Suppose that if the garden department were discontinued, the space occupied could be rented to an outside firm for $18,000 per year, and the common expenses of the firm would be reduced by $4,500. What effect would this action have on Richmond's net income? (Ignore income tax in your calculations.)

c. It is estimated that if an additional $6,000 were spent on advertising, prices in the garden center could be raised an average of 5% without a change in physical volume of products sold. What effect would this have on the operating results of the garden department? (Again, ignore income tax in your calculations.)

LO2 **P21-2A. Special Order** Total cost data follow for Glendale Manufacturing Company, which has a normal capacity per period of 8,000 units of product that sell for $60 each. For the foreseeable future, regular sales volume should continue to equal normal capacity.

Direct material	$100,800
Direct labor.	62,400
Variable manufacturing overhead.	46,800
Fixed manufacturing overhead (Note 1).	38,400
Selling expense (Note 2).	35,200
Administrative expense (fixed)	15,000
	$298,600

Notes:

1. Beyond normal capacity, fixed overhead costs increase $1,800 for each 500 units *or fraction thereof* until a maximum capacity of 10,000 units is reached.

2. Selling expenses consist of a 6% sales commission and shipping costs of 80 cents per unit. Glendale pays only three-fourths of the regular sales commission on sales totaling 501 to 1,000 units and only two-thirds the regular commission on sales totaling 1,000 units or more.

Glendale's sales manager has received a special order for 1,200 units from a large discount chain at a price of $36 each, F.O.B. factory. The controller's office has furnished the following additional cost data related to the special order:

1. Changes in the product's design will reduce direct material costs $1.50 per unit.
2. Special processing will add 20% to the per-unit direct labor costs.
3. Variable overhead will continue at the same proportion of direct labor costs.
4. Other costs should not be affected.

Required

a. Present an analysis supporting a decision to accept or reject the special order. (Round computations to the nearest cent.)

b. What is the lowest price Glendale could receive and still make a $3,600 profit before income taxes on the special order?

c. What general qualitative factors should Glendale consider?

P21-3A. Make or Buy Allen Corporation currently makes the nylon convertible top for its main product, a   **LO3**
fiberglass boat designed especially for water skiing. The costs of producing the 1,500 tops needed
each year follow:

Nylon fabric	$270,000
Aluminum tubing	96,000
Frame fittings	24,000
Direct labor.	162,000
Variable manufacturing overhead.	30,000
Fixed manufacturing overhead.	152,000

Dustin Company, a specialty fabricator of synthetic materials, can make the needed tops of comparable quality for $400 each, F.O.B. shipping point. Allen would furnish its own trademark insignia at a unit cost of $16. Transportation in would be $28 per unit, paid by Allen Corporation.

Allen's chief accountant has prepared a cost analysis that shows that only 20% of fixed overhead could be avoided if the tops are purchased. The tops have been made in a remote section of Allen's factory building, using equipment for which no alternate use is apparent in the foreseeable future.

Required

a. Prepare a differential analysis showing whether or not you would recommend that the convertible tops be purchased from Dustin Company.

b. Assuming that the production capacity released by purchasing the tops could be devoted to a subcontracting job for another company that netted a contribution margin of $41,600, what maximum purchase price could Allen Corporation pay for the tops?

c. Identify two important qualitative factors that Allen Corporation should consider in deciding whether to purchase the needed tops.

P21-4A. Dropping Unprofitable Division Based on the following analysis of last year's operations of Bing-   **LO4**
ham, Inc., a financial vice president of the company believes that the firm's total net income could be
increased by $200,000 if its engineering division were discontinued. (Amounts are given in thousands
of dollars.)

	Totals	All Other Divisions	Engineering Division
Sales.	$11,200	$8,000	$ 3,200
Cost of services:			
Variable.	(3,880)	(2,600)	(1,280)
Fixed.	(2,120)	(1,400)	(720)
Gross profit.	$ 5,200	$4,000	$ 1,200
Operating expenses:			
Variable.	(3,000)	(2,000)	(1,000)
Fixed.	(1,600)	(1,200)	(400)
Net income (loss)	$ 600	$ 800	$ (200)

Required

Provide answers for each of the following independent situations:

a. Assuming that total fixed costs and expenses would not be affected by discontinuing the engineering division, prepare an analysis showing why you agree or disagree with the vice president.

b. Assume that discontinuance of the engineering division will enable the company to avoid 20% of the fixed portion of cost of services and 25% of the fixed operating expenses allocated to the engineering division. Calculate the resulting effect on net income.

c. Assume that in addition to the cost avoidance in requirement (b), the capacity released by discontinuance of the engineering division can be used to provide 6,000 new services that would have a variable cost per service of $36 and would require additional fixed costs totaling $68,000. At what unit price must the new service be sold if Bingham is to increase its total net income by $120,000?

LO5   P21-5A. Joint Cost The Sun-Kissed Company manufactures two skin-care lotions, Soft Skin and Silken Skin, out of a joint process. The joint (common) costs incurred are $420,000 for a standard production run that generates 180,000 gallons of Soft Skin and 120,000 gallons of Silken Skin. Additional processing costs beyond the split-off point are $1.40 per gallon for Soft Skin and $0.90 per gallon for Silken Skin. Soft Skin sells for $2.40 per gallon while Silken Skin sells for $3.90 per gallon.

The Best Eastern Hotel chain has asked the Sun-Kissed Company to supply it with 240,000 gallons of Silken Skin at a price of $3.65 per gallon. Best Eastern plans to have the Silken Skin bottled in 1.5-ounce personal-use containers that are supplied in each of its hotel rooms as part of the complimentary personal products for guest use.

If Sun-Kissed accepts the order, it will save $0.05 per gallon in packaging of Silken Skin. There is sufficient excess capacity in Sun-Kissed's production system to handle just one more production run in order to have sufficient Silken Skin for this special order. However, the nature of the joint process always results in 180,000 gallons of Soft Skin and 120,000 gallons of Silken Skin. Also, the market for Soft Skin is saturated; hence, any additional sales of Soft Skin would take place at a price of $1.60 per gallon.

Required
a. What is the profit normally earned on one production run of Soft Skin and Silken Skin?
b. What is the incremental effect on overall income if the Sun-Kissed Company accepts the special order for Silken Skin?

LO6   P21-6A. Product Emphasis Lowell Corporation manufactures both a deluxe and a standard model of a household food blender. Because of limited demand, for several years production has been at 80% of estimated capacity, which is thought to be limited by the number of machine hours available. At current operation levels, a profit analysis for each product line shows the following data:

	Per-Unit Data			
	Deluxe		**Standard**	
Sales price		$216		$84
Production costs:				
Direct material.	$89		$12	
Direct labor	36		23	
Variable manufacturing overhead.	15		11	
Fixed manufacturing overhead*	25	$165	10	$56
Variable operating expenses		18		10
Fixed operating expenses		8		5
Total cost		$191		$71
Operating income.		$ 25		$13

* Assigned on the basis of machine hours at normal capacity.

Management wants to utilize the company's current excess capacity by increasing production.

Required
a. What general decision guideline applies in this situation?
b. Assuming that sufficient units of either product can be sold at current prices to use existing capacity fully and that total fixed cost will not be affected, prepare an analysis showing which product line should be emphasized if net income for the firm is the decision basis.

PROBLEMS—SET B

P21-1B. Analyze Operational Changes The management of Manchester's Department Store is concerned about the operation of its sporting goods department, which has not been very successful. The following condensed income statement gives the latest year's results:

LO1

SERVICE AND
MERCHANDISING

	Sporting Goods Department	All Other Departments
Sales.	$480,000	$2,400,000
Cost of goods sold.	360,000	1,560,000
Gross profit.	$120,000	$ 840,000
Direct expenses	$ 67,500	$ 336,000
Indirect expenses.	48,000	240,000
Total expenses.	$115,500	$ 576,000
Net income.	$ 4,500	$ 264,000

Required

a. Calculate the gross profit percentage for the sporting goods department and for the other departments as a group.

b. It is estimated that if an additional $10,500 were spent on promotion of sporting goods, average prices can be raised 5% without affecting physical volume of goods sold. What effect would this have on the operating results of the sporting goods department? (Ignore the effect of income tax.)

c. Alternatively, it is estimated that physical volume of goods sold could be increased 8% if an additional $15,000 were spent on promotion of sporting goods and prices were not increased. Assuming that operating expenses remain the same, what effect would this have on the operating results of the sporting goods department? (Ignore the effect of income tax.)

P21-2B. Special Order Total cost data follow for Greenfield Manufacturing Company, which has a normal capacity per period of 20,000 units of product that sell for $54 each. For the foreseeable future, regular sales volume should continue to equal normal capacity.

LO2

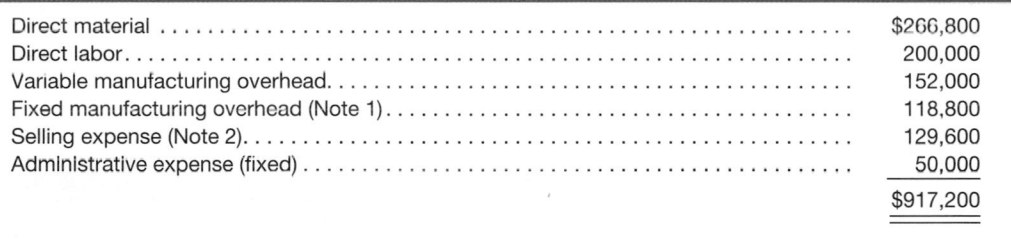

Direct material	$266,800
Direct labor.	200,000
Variable manufacturing overhead.	152,000
Fixed manufacturing overhead (Note 1).	118,800
Selling expense (Note 2).	129,600
Administrative expense (fixed)	50,000
	$917,200

Notes:

1. Beyond normal capacity, fixed overhead costs increase $4,500 for each 1,000 units *or fraction thereof* until a maximum capacity of 24,000 units is reached.

2. Selling expenses consist of a 10% sales commission and shipping costs of $1 per unit. Greenfield pays only one-half of the regular sales commission rates on sales amounting to $3,000 or more.

Greenfield's sales manager has received a special order for 2,500 units from a large discount chain at a price of $44 each, F.O.B. factory. The controller's office has furnished the following additional cost data related to the special order:

1. Changes in the product's design will reduce direct material costs by $4 per unit.
2. Special processing will add 10% to the per-unit direct labor costs.
3. Variable overhead will continue at the same proportion of direct labor costs.
4. Other costs should not be affected.

Required

a. Present an analysis supporting a decision to accept or reject the special order.
b. What is the lowest price Greenfield could receive and still make a profit of $5,000 before income taxes on the special order?
c. What general qualitative factors should Greenfield consider?

LO3  **P21-3B. Make or Buy** Walsh Corporation currently makes the nylon mooring cover for its main product, a fiberglass boat designed for tournament bass fishing. The costs of producing the 2,000 covers needed each year follow:

Nylon fabric	$320,000
Wood battens.	64,000
Brass fittings.	32,000
Direct labor.	128,000
Variable manufacturing overhead.	96,000
Fixed manufacturing overhead.	160,000

Calvin Company, a specialty fabricator of synthetic materials, can make the needed covers of comparable quality for $320 each, F.O.B. shipping point. Walsh would furnish its own trademark insignia at a unit cost of $20. Transportation in would be $16 per unit, paid by Walsh Corporation.

Walsh's chief accountant has prepared a cost analysis that shows that only 30% of fixed overhead could be avoided if the covers are purchased. The covers have been made in a remote section of Walsh's factory building, using equipment for which no alternate use is apparent in the foreseeable future.

Required

a. Prepare a differential analysis showing whether or not you would recommend that the mooring covers be purchased from Calvin Company.
b. Assuming that the production capacity released by purchasing the covers could be devoted to a subcontracting job for another company that netted a contribution margin of $64,000, what maximum purchase price could Walsh pay for the covers?
c. Identify two important qualitative factors that Walsh Corporation should consider in deciding whether to purchase the needed covers.

LO4 **P21-4B. Dropping Unprofitable Division** Based on the following analysis of last year's operations of
SERVICE AND
MERCHANDISING
Groves, Inc., a financial vice president of the company believes that the firm's total net income could be increased by $160,000 if its design division were discontinued. (Amounts are given in thousands of dollars.)

	Totals	All Other Divisions	Design Division
Sales.	$18,800	$14,400	$4,400
Cost of services:			
Variable.	(7,600)	(5,600)	(2,000)
Fixed.	(4,800)	(4,000)	(800)
Gross profit	$ 6,400	$ 4,800	$1,600
Operating expenses:			
Variable.	(3,360)	(2,000)	(1,360)
Fixed.	(1,600)	(1,200)	(400)
Net income (loss)	$ 1,440	$ 1,600	$ (160)

Required

Provide answers for each of the following independent situations:

a. Assuming that total fixed costs and expenses would not be affected by discontinuing the design division, prepare an analysis showing why you agree or disagree with the vice president.
b. Assume that discontinuance of the design division will enable the company to avoid 30% of the fixed portion of cost of services and 40% of the fixed operating expenses allocated to the design division. Calculate the resulting effect on net income.

c. Assume that in addition to the cost avoidance in requirement (b), the capacity released by discontinuance of the design division can be used to provide 6,000 new services that would have a variable cost per service of $60 and would require additional fixed costs totaling $68,000. At what unit price must the new service be sold if Groves is to increase its total net income by $180,000?

P21-5B. Product Emphasis McDermott Corporation manufactures both automatic and manual residential **LO6** water treatment units. Because of limited demand, for several years production has been at 90% of estimated capacity, which is thought to be limited by the number of machine hours available. At current operation levels, a profit analysis for each product line shows the following:

	Per-Unit Data			
	Automatic		**Manual**	
Sales price		$800		$416
Production costs:				
Direct material	$144		$80	
Direct labor	128		64	
Variable manufacturing overhead	64		32	
Fixed manufacturing overhead*	144	$480	72	$240
Variable operating expenses		80		16
Fixed operating expenses		144		96
Total cost		$704		$360
Operating income		$ 96		$ 56

*Assigned on the basis of machine hours at normal capacity.

Management wants to utilize the company's current excess capacity by increasing production.

Required

a. What general decision guideline applies in this situation?
b. Assuming that sufficient units of either product can be sold at current prices to use existing capacity fully and that total fixed cost will not be affected, prepare an analysis showing which product line should be emphasized if net income for the firm is the decision basis.

CERTIFIED MANAGEMENT ACCOUNTANT (CMA®) EXAM SAMPLE QUESTIONS

CMA21-1. Tucariz Company processes Duo into two joint products, Big and Mini. Duo is purchased in 1,000-gallon drums for $2,000. Processing costs are $3,000 to process the 1,000 gallons of Duo into 800 gallons of Big and 200 gallons of Mini. The selling price is $9 per gallon for Big and $4 per gallon for Mini. If the sales value at split-off method is used to allocate joint costs to the final products, the per-gallon cost (rounded to the nearest cent) of producing Big is

a. $5.63 per gallon.
b. $5.00 per gallon.
c. $4.50 per gallon.
d. $3.38 per gallon.

CMA21-2. Current business segment operations for Whitman, a mass retailer, are presented below.

	Merchandise	Automotive	Restaurant	Total
Sales	$500,000	$400,000	$100,000	$1,000,000
Variable costs	300,000	200,000	70,000	570,000
Fixed costs	100,000	100,000	50,000	250,000
Operating income (loss)	$100,000	$100,000	$ (20,000)	$ 180,000

Management is contemplating the discontinuance of the Restaurant segment because "it is losing money." If this segment is discontinued, $30,000 of its fixed costs will be eliminated. In addition,

Merchandise and Automotive sales will decrease 5% from their current levels. What will Whitman's total contribution margin be if the Restaurant segment is discontinued?

a. $160,000
b. $220,000
c. $367,650
d. $380,000

CMA21-3. Johnson Company manufactures a variety of shoes, and has received a special one-time-only order directly from a wholesaler. Johnson has sufficient idle capacity to accept the special order to manufacture 15,000 pairs of sneakers at a price of $7.50 per pair. Johnson's normal selling price is $11.50 per pair of sneakers. Variable manufacturing costs are $5.00 per pair and fixed manufacturing costs are $3.00 a pair. Johnson's variable selling expense for its normal line of sneakers is $1.00 per pair. What would the effect on Johnson's operating income be if the company accepted the special order?

a. Decrease by $60,000
b. Increase by $22,500
c. Increase by $37,500
d. Increase by $52,500

CMA21-4. The loss of a key customer has temporarily caused Bedford Machining to have some excess manufacturing capacity. Bedford is considering the acceptance of a special order, one that involves Bedford's most popular product. Consider the following types of costs.

I. Variable costs of the product
II. Fixed costs of the product
III. Direct fixed costs associated with the order
IV. Opportunity cost of the temporarily idle capacity

Which one of the following combinations of cost types should be considered in the special order acceptance decision?

a. I and II
b. I and IV
c. II and III
d. I, III, and IV

CMA21-5. Refrigerator Company manufactures ice-makers for installation in refrigerators. The costs per unit, for 20,000 units of ice-makers, are as follows.

Direct materials	$ 7
Direct labor	12
Variable overhead	5
Fixed overhead	10
Total costs	$34

Cool Compartments Inc. has offered to sell 20,000 ice-makers to Refrigerator Company for $28 per unit. If Refrigerator accepts Cool Compartments' offer, the facilities used to manufacture ice-makers could be used to produce water filtration units. Revenues from the sale of water filtration units are estimated at $80,000, with variable costs amounting to 60% of sales. In addition, $6 per unit of the fixed overhead associated with the manufacture of ice-makers could be eliminated.

For Refrigerator Company to determine the **most** appropriate action to take in this situation, the total relevant costs of make vs. buy, respectively, are

a. $600,000 vs. $560,000.
b. $648,000 vs. $528,000.
c. $600,000 vs. $528,000.
d. $680,000 vs. $440,000.

EKY21-1. Business Decision Case Marvin Corporation manufactures both an automatic and a manual household dehumidifier. Because of limited demand, for several years production has been at 80% of estimated capacity, which is thought to be limited by the number of machine hours available. At current operation levels, a profit analysis for each product line shows the following:

	Per-unit Data			
	Automatic		**Manual**	
Sales price		$350		$150
Production costs:				
Direct material.	$65		$32	
Direct labor	35		25	
Variable manufacturing overhead.	68		16	
Fixed manufacturing overhead.	50	$218	18	$ 91
Variable operating expenses		52		21
Fixed operating expenses		30		13
Total cost		$300		$125
Operating income.		$ 50		$ 25

Management wants to make use of the company's current excess capacity by increasing production. Each unit of the automatic model requires 2.5 machine hours; the manual model requires 1 machine hour per unit.

Required
Present answers for the following questions in each independent situation:

a. Assume that sufficient units of either product can be sold at current prices to utilize existing capacity fully and that fixed costs will not be affected.
 1. To which product should the excess capacity be devoted if the decision basis is maximization of contribution margin per unit of product?
 2. Prepare an analysis showing which product line should be emphasized if the firm's net income is the decision basis.
 3. What general decision guideline applies in this situation?

b. Suppose the excess capacity represents 10,000 machine hours, which can be used to make 4,000 automatic units or 10,000 manual units or any proportionate combination. The only market available for these extra units is a foreign market in which the sales prices must be reduced by 20% and in which no more than 6,000 units of either model can be sold. All costs will remain the same except that the sales commission of 10% (included in the variable operating expenses) will be avoided. Prepare an analysis showing which product should be emphasized and the effect on the firm's net income.

c. Assume that the excess capacity can be used as indicated in requirement (b) and that the firm's market research department believes that the production available from using the excess capacity exclusively on either model can be sold in the domestic market at regular prices if a promotion campaign costing $225,000 is undertaken for the automatic model or $235,000 for the manual model. Prepare an analysis indicating for which product the campaign should be undertaken.

EKY21-2. Business Decision Case Hall Manufacturing Corporation makes a new high-tech adhesive in a single process that blends and bottles the product, which currently sells for $20 per gallon. Market demand for the product seems good, but management is not satisfied with the product's seemingly low profit margin and has sought your advice.

Because of its concern, management has allocated a $60,000 fund for a program of product promotion or cost reduction, or both. Members of the firm's controller's office and marketing staff have identified the following three possible plans:

1. Plan A: Devote all funds to product promotion, which allows all costs and the sales volume to remain the same, but permits a sales price increase of $3.50 per gallon.
2. Plan B: Spend $32,000 on product promotion and $28,000 on cost reduction techniques, which maintains sales volume, permits a price increase of $2 per gallon, and reduces conversion costs by 10% per gallon.
3. Plan C: Devote all funds to cost reduction efforts. Sales volume and price do not change. For each gallon produced, however, direct material cost decreases 10%, and conversion cost decreases 20%.

The controller's office also provides you with the following operating data for a typical period (all materials are added initially; conversion costs occur evenly throughout the process; the weighted average method is used for process costing):

Beginning work in process (2,500 gallons, 60% processed).....................	$ 32,250
Units started in process (34,000 gallons)	
Ending work in process (3,500 gallons, 60% processed)	
Costs charged to the department:	
Direct material	275,400
Direct labor...	186,390
Manufacturing overhead	156,330
	$650,370

Required
Using the data from this representative production period, analyze the apparent relative benefits derived from each plan and make a recommendation supported by relevant calculations. Assume that sales for each period will equal units completed in that period. *Hint:* You will need to prepare a Production Report, Cost per Equivalent Unit Report, and Production Cost Report to analyze the three plans. These reports were discussed in Chapter 17.

EKY21-3.   Ethics Case Swan Sports manufactures golfing equipment. Traditionally, the company has been busy all year but has noticed that over the past few years business has fallen off in October and November. If new business does not come in this year, the company will have to lay off some long-time employees for those 2 months. Rob Patell, a sales representative, received an order from Better Equipment Co., a competitor. Better Equipment cannot meet a customer's rush order on time and is willing to subcontract the work to Swan Sports on the condition that the Better Equipment Co. name—not Swan Sports' name—appear on all products. The order is at a price substantially below Swan Sports' usual selling price. The only way this order can be produced is to use lower-quality materials than Swan Sports normally uses in its own products.

Rob Patell has recommended to his supervisor that this order be accepted and that lower-quality materials be used. Patell's reasoning includes the following points:

a.   It is clearly a one-time order.
b.   Swan Sports' name will not appear on it.
c.   Workers will not have to be laid off during October and November.

A differential analysis shows that Swan Sports will lose $1,000 on the order.

Required
What should the sales supervisor consider before making a decision?

EKY21-4.   Corporate Social Responsibility The "Corporate Social Responsibility" box in this chapter highlights some early citizenship milestones of John Deere. Go to John Deere's web site and search under the "Our Company" tab for "Citizenship." Under the citizenship page find the link to learning about John Deere's citizenship milestones. Select a more recent time period and read about some of the reported moments that became milestones. Can you think of a good business purpose for these reported achievements, or are they simply things that make John Deere a good corporate citizen?

ANSWERS TO SELF-STUDY QUESTIONS:

1. c, (p. 953)   2. c, (p. 956)   3. a, (pp. 957–958)   4. d, (pp. 958–959)   5. b, (p. 961)

YOUR TURN! SOLUTIONS

Solution 21.1
Yes.

Differential revenue.	$200,000
Differential cost (10,000 × $14) + ($40,000 − $5,000)	175,000
Net increase in profit	$ 25,000

Solution 21.2
Product B. ($12/1 hour is greater than $15/2 hours)

DECISION TIME SOLUTIONS

Solution 21.1
No. Fixed costs that differ among alternatives are relevant.

Solution 21.2
The segment should be dropped if the company will avoid more in fixed costs than it loses in contribution margin.

22

Planning and Budgeting

PAST

Chapter 21 described some of the tools and techniques that management can use in making short-term business decisions.

PRESENT

Chapter 22 discusses the budgeting process, the components of the master budget, and the interrelationships of the individual budgets, and presents an illustration of a budget for a manufacturer and a service company.

FUTURE

Chapter 23 provides an overview of standard costing and variance analysis. Moreover, it describes how standard costs influence financial statements.

LEARNING OBJECTIVES

1. **Describe** the planning process, including strategic planning and operational planning. *(p. 984)*

2. **Discuss** the budgeting process and **summarize** its advantages. **Define** the key elements of effective budgeting. *(p. 987)*

3. **Define** the components of a master budget and **illustrate** the interrelationships of the individual budgets that comprise the master budget. *(p. 991)*

4. **Prepare** individual budgets for a manufacturing and a service company, including the cash budget. *(p. 992)*

5. **Prepare** budgeted financial statements. *(p. 1001)*

MONSANTO

MONSANTO

Monsanto manufactures agricultural products for farmers throughout the world. The company's products include 21 types of conventional and biotech vegetable seeds and herbicides, including Roundup®, to enable farmers to produce more from their land while conserving water and energy. Monsanto's seeds include corn, soybean, cotton, wheat, canola, sorghum, and sugar cane seeds. In some cases, Monsanto uses genetic modification to bring beneficial traits, such as drought tolerance or the ability to ward off pests, to the resulting plant. Its herbicides are used on both farms for agricultural purposes and in industrial and large non-farm areas such as parks, golf courses, and zoos.

Monsanto's business is highly seasonal, with approximately three-fourths of its seed sales occurring during the second and third quarters of its fiscal year, which ends August 31. The seasonality corresponds to the North American purchasing and growing patterns. The season for several of Monsanto's herbicide products is even shorter—about 2 months long. The capital investment required to produce all required product during the 2-month sales period would be substantial—instead, Monsanto must project product demand, produce the product well in advance, and store or ship the products to its distributors, wholesalers, and retailers before the growing season begins each year.

Its business is also influenced by weather. With climate shifts becoming more volatile, planting time may vary by several weeks in a specific location. The combination of seasonality and weather, together with normal economic variability, makes Monsanto's business very challenging to forecast. Because Monsanto must produce its products well in advance of the season, even a small error in forecasting demand for its products can result in either (1) significant inventory left at the end of the season or (2) lost sales due to product shortages.

Historically, sales forecasts were developed by corporate headquarters 6 to 9 months prior to the actual sales period. The manufacturing of finished goods was largely driven by the production of the active ingredients, which were produced year-round. Thus, product was shipped ahead of actual demand because of limited storage capabilities at Monsanto's production facilities. If demand were affected by weather or some other market effect, more product might have been shipped to a particular site than was needed and not enough product might have been shipped to another site. Inaccurate forecasts required costly redistribution of product to match supply with demand.

More recently, Monsanto has attempted to address the uncertainties regarding demand for its products by employing local sales employees to develop more frequent (as often as weekly) forecasts of the local market demand. These forecasts are aggregated into weekly demand forecasts that are used to develop production and distribution plans. Nevertheless, demand uncertainty will always be an issue for Monsanto's management, making the budgeting process a challenge to manage!

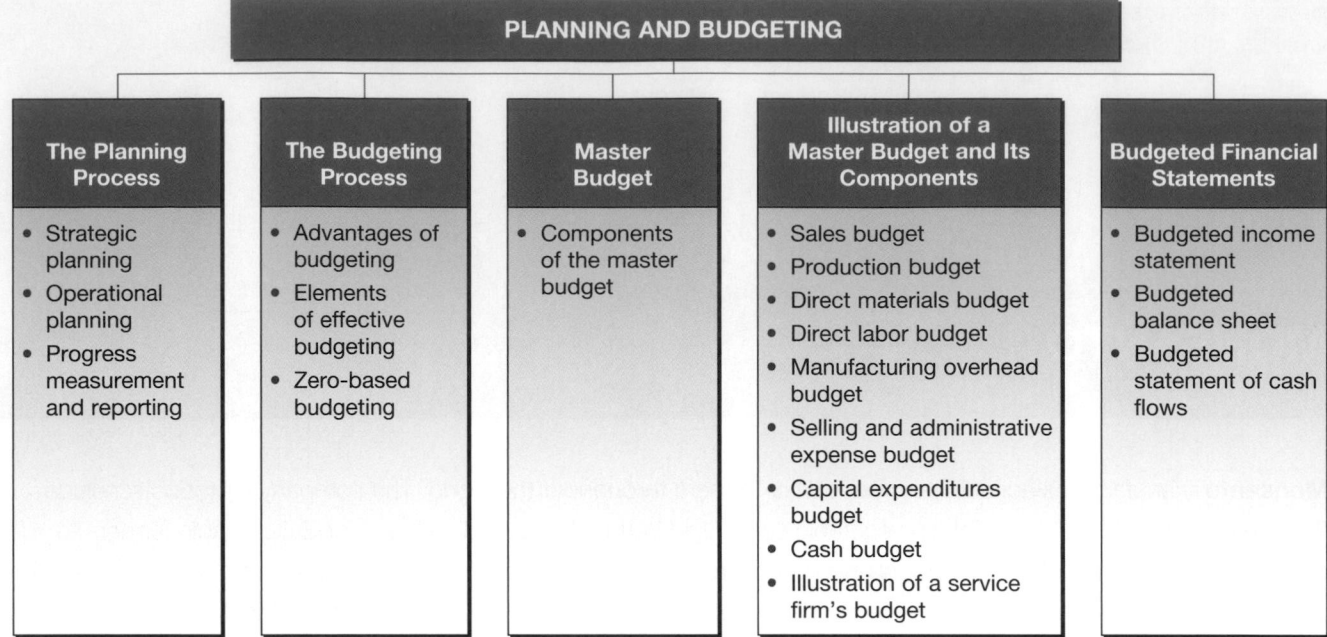

Prediction is very difficult, especially about the future.

NIELS BOHR

Your ability to live within your means over the long term and meet your financial obligations from paycheck to paycheck depends in large part on your ability to accurately identify your income and manage your expenses. If you consistently overestimate your income or underestimate your expenses, you may find yourself getting deeper and deeper into debt. Without a financial plan, or budget, you run the risk of financial hardship or ruin.

Likewise, to be successful, every business needs to produce products or provide services at competitive costs for a growing customer base to ensure that reasonable profits are made to continue to grow the business. Management has a basic responsibility to plan, control, and measure performance and to make decisions. To carry out these responsibilities, management must develop plans and budgets, determine actual operating results, compare actual results to planned results, evaluate differences, and take corrective action to improve operations. This chapter focuses on managerial planning and budgeting.

THE PLANNING PROCESS

LO1 **Describe** the planning process, including strategic planning and operational planning.

All types of organizations—service organizations, merchandising firms, manufacturing companies, government agencies, and not-for-profit entities—can benefit from formalized planning. A formal planning process usually includes strategic planning and operational planning.

A **planning horizon** is the future time span, usually expressed in years, for which a particular plan is developed. Different types of plans have different planning horizons. Typically, longer planning horizons are associated with higher-level planning (such as strategic planning), whereas shorter planning horizons are associated with lower-level planning (such as annual operational planning.) **Exhibit 22-1** is an example of a formal planning process. As illustrated, the planning process begins with the definition of a vision or mission statement. This statement defines what the company is and provides a focus for its strategy and operational planning. The best vision statements are succinct and clear. Monsanto states that it is a sustainable agriculture company that supports farmers, enabling them to produce more from their land while conserving the world's natural resources, such as water and energy.

Exhibit 22-1	Planning Process

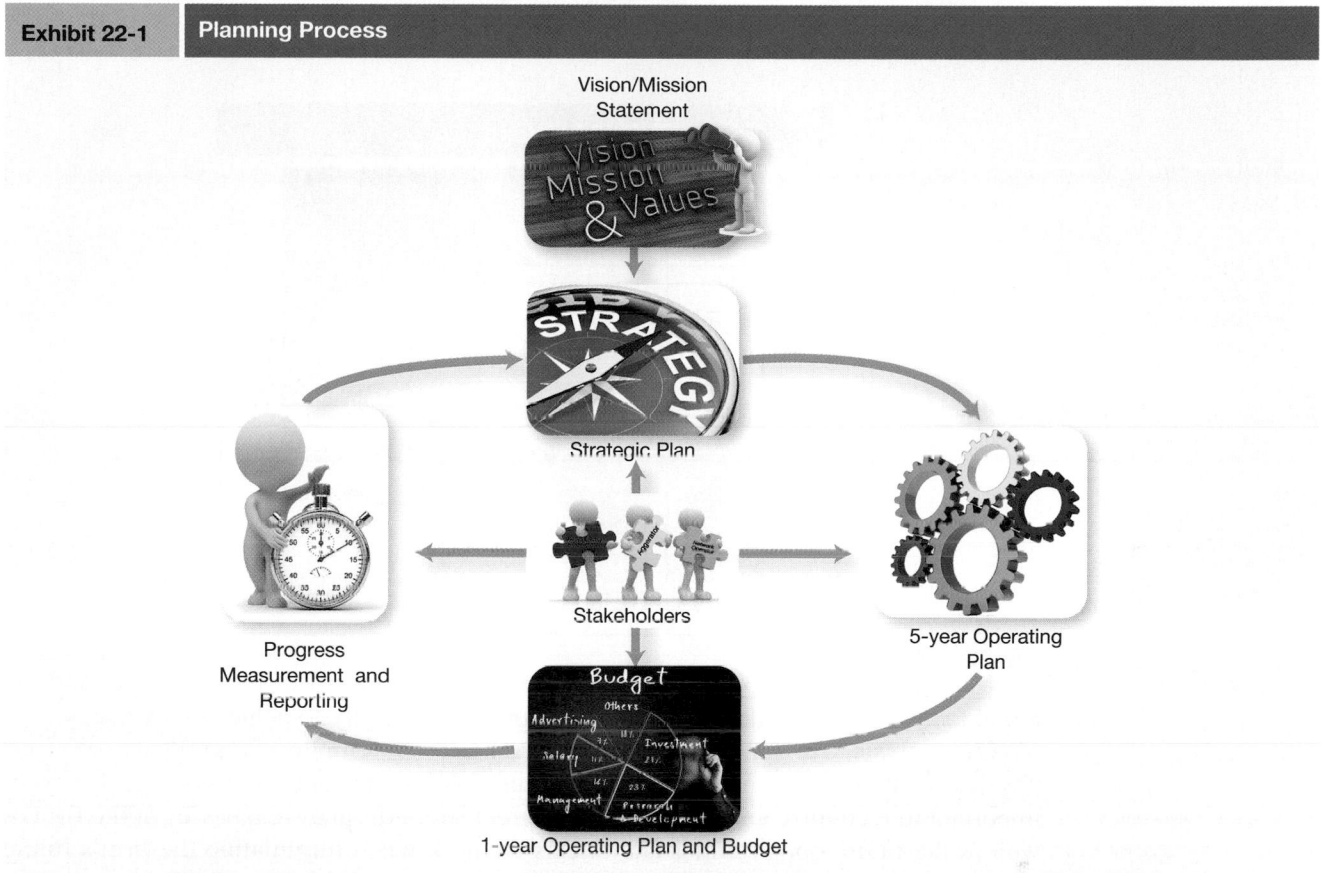

Strategic Plan

Stakeholders

5-year Operating Plan

Progress Measurement and Reporting

1-year Operating Plan and Budget

Vision/Mission Statement

Strategic Planning

Strategic planning is a formal process that addresses and documents the overall mission and long-term goals of the organization based on the vision statement. Management must evaluate and decide what directions the organization should go in the future. Issues to be decided include what basic lines of business to pursue, which geographic markets to establish, what organization structure to develop, where to locate facilities, which means of sales and distribution to use, and how aggressively the organization should grow. For example, Monsanto's strategic plan is to provide healthy and nutritious food for a world population that is growing faster than food production. In keeping with this strategy, Monsanto's management sold its animal agricultural products business (its dairy business) in 2008 to focus on seeds and improving crop productivity.

General Motors Strategic Plans	ACCOUNTING IN PRACTICE

The 2014 **General Motors** annual report included a letter to stockholders from Chief Executive Officer Mary T. Barra highlighting the goal for GM to become the most valued automotive company. It included the following strategic initiatives:

1. Introduce a new mid-sized truck
2. Restore Cadillac to a position of leadership in the global luxury segment
3. Rebuild the Opel brand
4. Expand in China, Brazil and other developing markets
5. Expand ability to offer customers financing and leasing

Management must accumulate and analyze a great deal of information to create an appropriate strategic plan incorporating these decisions. Many companies use a technique such as a **strengths, weaknesses, opportunities, and threats (SWOT) analysis** to begin this accumulation and analysis process. **Exhibit 22-2** illustrates this process in the form of a 2 × 2 matrix.

Exhibit 22-2	SWOT Matrix	
	Helpful	Harmful
Internal	Strengths	Weaknesses
External	Opportunities	Threats

Management uses SWOT analysis to analyze and document those internal and external factors that both help and harm the company's ability to achieve its strategy. The SWOT analysis will specifically address management, employees, products, services, physical facilities, customers, competitors, distribution channels, and systems. It is very important to recognize and document the current strengths and weaknesses of the firm as well as the future opportunities and threats facing it when formulating the firm's future strategic directions.

Management takes the information accumulated during the SWOT analysis, makes assumptions about the economy and the future competitive environment, and formulates management strategies for the entity. A 5- or 10-year planning horizon is typical. These strategies are documented in the strategic plan, which is typically updated and revised annually for changing conditions. Frequently, elements of a SWOT analysis can be seen in the Management's Discussion and Analysis section of a public company's Form 10-K filing with the Securities and Exchange Commission.

YOUR TURN! 22.1

The solution is on page 1023.

Assume you are performing a SWOT analysis for the retail company **Target** and have been assigned to focus on threats to its business. List some threats that could impact the company in coming years.

Operational Planning

Management also prepares operating plans consistent with the strategic plan. **Operational planning** is the process of developing specific goals and objectives for the entity as a whole and its individual departments, formulating an operating plan to accomplish the goals and objectives, and preparing written documentation of the goals and objectives as well as the operating plan. Firms frequently develop a long-term operating plan that covers a 3- to 5-year planning horizon as well as an annual operating plan that covers a 1-year planning horizon. The annual operating plan is typically more detailed than the long-term operating plan.

The annual operating plan projects some of the current operations as they exist and provides for changes in others to reflect management's desires for improvements in the operations. The annual operating plan reflects the strategies, goals, objectives, and action plan documented in the strategic plan and the long-term operating plan. Further, the annual operating plan is usually not in a format that enables management to determine whether the plans are economically feasible. Management tests the economic feasibility of the annual operating plan through the development of the annual operating budget.

For example, Monsanto's 2014 Annual Report[1] identifies plans to improve its vegetable seeds business, in part through strategic acquisitions and continued investment in seeds, genomics, and biotechnology.

Progress Measurement and Reporting

No planning process is complete without an accounting of the progress achieved in pursuing the plans made. A periodic accounting is helpful in measuring progress, holding individuals accountable for aspects of the plan that are within their area of responsibility, and evaluating whether changes need to be made to future plans based on changes in the internal or external environment in which the company operates. This accounting takes many forms, including internal management reports and external reports to owners, creditors, and other stakeholders. For example, Monsanto's external reports include quarterly earnings releases, numerous Securities and Exchange Commission reports, and a corporate sustainability report. Each of these reports highlights different results of Monsanto's operations.

Monsanto's Employee Volunteer Program—Monsantogether	CORPORATE SOCIAL RESPONSIBILITY

This chapter discusses the importance of budgeting to a company's financial performance. A recent *Forbes* article discusses the importance of budgeting for corporate social responsibility success.* The article discusses how doing good through employee volunteering programs leads to the company doing well through increased employee engagement, employee retention, and employee recruitment.

Monsanto appears to agree with what the article author writes. As noted on Monsanto's web site, "Monsanto employees are fighting rural hunger as part of a coordinated volunteer effort in areas where Monsanto employees live and work across the United States. . . . [in two events] 965 Monsanto employees worked more than 3,800 volunteer hours at 96 food bank or food drive locations. The effort is part of an employee volunteer program called Monsantogether, which is focused on enriching the communities where Monsanto employees live and work. Both individual employees and groups of employees can earn money through Monsantogether for qualified non-profit organizations where they volunteer, simply as a result of volunteering a minimum of 20 hours. In 2012, Monsanto awarded more than $225,000 in grants to non-profit organizations based on nearly 50,000 employee volunteer hours. Of that amount, $15,000 was directed toward food banks and food pantries across the U.S. to help address local community needs. The Fighting Rural Hunger volunteer events are part of Monsanto's larger effort to eradicate hunger in rural America through partnerships and philanthropy."

*Ryan Scott, "'Tis the Season to Budget for CSR Success," *Forbes*, November 19, 2012.

THE BUDGETING PROCESS

A **budget** is a detailed plan for the acquisition and use of financial resources during a specific period of time.

Budgeting is the process of developing a formal, written operating plan that presents management's planned actions in financial terms. Budgeting should reflect the conclusions reached in the strategic plan and the operating plan. Two budgets usually result from the budgeting process: the annual operating budget and the capital expenditures budget. We present and discuss the

LO2 Discuss the budgeting process and **summarize** its advantages. **Define** the key elements of effective budgeting.

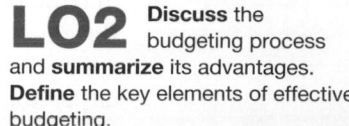

A.K.A. The annual operating budget is also called the master budget.

[1] http://www.monsanto.com/investors/documents/annual%20report/2014/2014_monsanto_annualreport.pdf, page 29.

annual operating budget in this chapter and the capital expenditures budget in Chapter 25. **Exhibit 22-1** presents the sequence for preparing the various types of plans and budgets.

All types of entities can derive benefits from the budgeting process. Although the basic concepts of budgeting apply to all types of entities, the precise budget form will vary among those entities. Budgeting typically incorporates many accounting concepts discussed in previous chapters. In fact, some components of the annual operating budget have familiar accounting formats.

TAKEAWAY 22.1

In practice, budgeting rarely turns out to be 100% accurate. However, it is still an important process because it forces management and other involved parties to consider all aspects of a company and how managerial decisions impact company performance.

Advantages of Budgeting

The use of budgets to manage and control a firm's activities is known as **budgetary control.** Budgetary control involves the steps taken by management to ensure that the goals and objectives established during the planning stage are attained, and to ensure that all segments of the firm operate in a manner consistent with organizational policies. Used properly, a budget can sharpen management's focus, ensure that operating activities will help achieve management's overall strategy, and be useful in evaluating performance.

The annual planning and budgeting process forces management to step back from the daily operations of the entity, examine current operations, decide what improvements are necessary, and formulate plans and budgets that implement the established goals and objectives for the entity. The annual operating budget represents a specific plan for accomplishing these goals and objectives.

A budget can be used to control operations. When a business is large enough to be divided into departments, management needs to ensure that the operation of each department is consistent with the overall plans for the entity as a whole. The budget provides guidance for the departmental managers so their decisions will be consistent with decisions in other departments. For example, the budget provides guidance so the purchasing department buys quantities of material consistent with the factory's budget of units to be manufactured; that budget, in turn, is consistent with the sales department's budget of units to be sold.

TAKEAWAY 22.2

Assume management budgets sales of 10,000 units and has only 1,000 currently on hand. In this scenario, management would not budget production at 2,000 units because that would only leave 3,000 available for sale (1,000 on hand + 2,000 produced). Failure to budget for sufficient production to make 10,000 units available for sale would be considered a lack of consistency among departmental budgets.

Budgets serve as guides and targets to managers when they make decisions and as one basis for performance evaluation. Performance evaluations could be based on comparison of actual results to prior-period results. However, comparison to prior-period results fails to take into account the changes and improvements that have been incorporated into the budget. As a result, the budget is frequently the basis for evaluating performance. Because the budget is used as a basis for evaluating performance, it can also be a motivating factor for individual managers. Assuming that the budget is realistic, it provides a target that each manager will try to attain.

DECISION TIME 22.1

The solution is on page 1023.

What are the advantages of budgeting?

Elements of Effective Budgeting

Even though specific budgeting procedures vary widely among business firms, all entities engaged in comprehensive budgeting should consider the following elements of effective budgeting.

Identifying a **budget director** is vital to effective budgeting. Budget director may be a full-time or part-time position, depending on the size and complexity of the business. The budget director must be well organized and a good communicator, since he or she is responsible for organizing the budgeting process, communicating with the people involved in budgeting, and monitoring the process to ensure that it proceeds on a timely basis.

The **budget committee** generally consists of representatives from all major areas of the firm, such as sales, manufacturing, purchasing, and accounting, and is usually headed by the budget director. The primary functions of the budget committee are to provide central guidance to the budget preparation process, ensure that all departments participate in the process, and evaluate the proposed budget segments for reasonableness.

The task of developing the detailed amounts for the budget is usually not done by the budget director or the budget committee. **Participative budgeting** requires that detailed budget amounts be formulated "from the bottom up." That is, all departments should participate in the development and refinement of the budget amounts so they will be accepted by the departments as reasonable standards of performance. The participants in this process are illustrated in **Exhibit 22-3**.

Exhibit 22-3	Participants in a Participative Budgeting Process

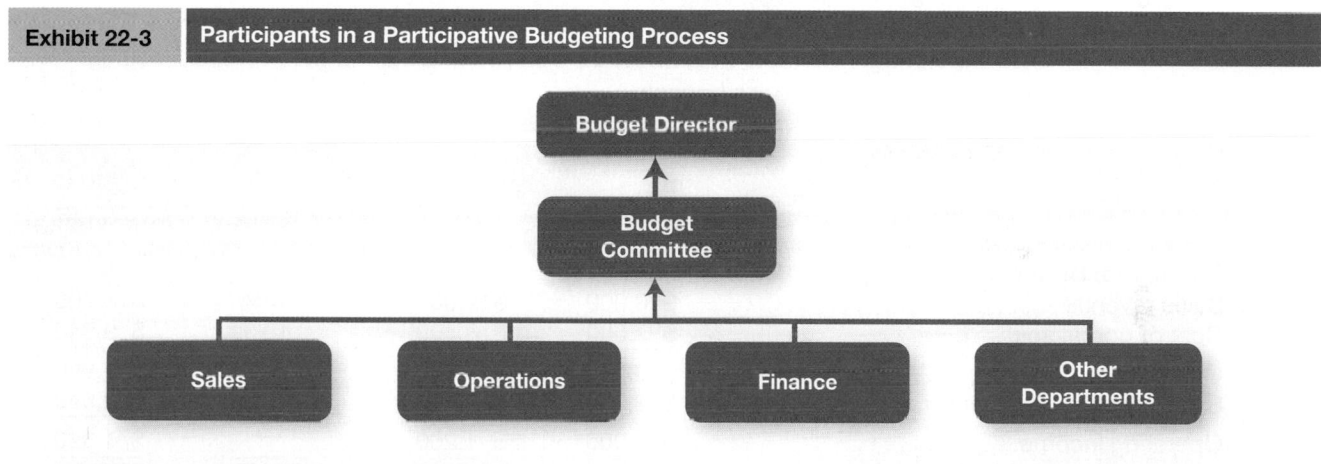

There are advantages to participative budgeting:

1. Individuals at all levels are part of a team.

2. The person in direct contact with the activity is in the best position to make the estimates.

3. A person has ownership of and is therefore more motivated to work at fulfilling a budget that he or she has helped establish.

The **budget period,** the future time span for which the budget is prepared, varies according to the nature of the specific activity involved. Most companies, however, prepare annual operating budgets, which are segmented into quarterly or monthly budgets. Short-term operating budgets covering a month or a quarter may be useful benchmarks as one element of performance evaluations, enabling management to compare budgeted amounts to actual results and initiate corrective action as required.

The capital expenditures budget usually covers a multiyear period, often 3 to 5 years. This longer budget period is necessary because of the long time period required to construct or acquire long-term assets of a unique nature.

A.K.A. Continuous **budgets** are also known as **perpetual** or **rolling budgets**.

Many businesses use **continuous budgeting** techniques for the operating budget. As each monthly or quarterly budget period passes, the oldest month or quarter is removed from the budget and another month or quarter is added to extend the budget to a full year in the future. With this approach, regardless of the time of the year, the budget always covers 12 months or four quarters.

Zero-Base Budgeting

Traditional budgeting procedures typically use an incremental approach to the development of the annual operating budget. For example, the level of each expense for the prior year is used as the starting point for determining the budgeted level for the next year. The person preparing the budget then either adds to or subtracts from the amount in the previous budget. During the budget process, only the increase or decrease is justified to the managers reviewing the proposed budget drafts. The prior year base amount is assumed to be reasonable. For example, the simple traditional budget example in **Exhibit 22-4** shows a budget based on a 10% increase from the current year.

Many organizations—manufacturing companies, merchandising firms, service organizations, governmental agencies, and not-for-profit entities—have experienced increases in their annual operating budgets that they deem to be unacceptable. Some of these organizations have decided to use zero-base budgeting techniques to address this problem. **Zero-base budgeting** requires budget preparers to start at a zero level for every item in the budget and justify every dollar, not just the increases or decreases. In effect, the budget is prepared "from the ground up" as if the entity had just been formed. The simple zero-base budget example in **Exhibit 22-4** shows that the budget is created without reference to the previous year's budgets.

Exhibit 22-4	Traditional Budgeting vs. Zero-Base Budgeting			
	Prior Year	**Current Year**	**Adjustment**	**Budget Year**
Traditional Budgeting				
Sales revenue..........................	$10,000	$12,000	10%	$13,200
Cost of goods sold.....................	$ 7,000	$ 8,400	10%	$ 9,240
Gross profit...........................	$ 3,000	$ 3,600		$ 3,960
Sales, general, & administrative expenses...	$ 2,000	$ 2,400	10%	$ 2,640
Operating income......................	$ 1,000	$ 1,200		$ 1,320
Zero-base Budgeting				
Sales revenue..........................	$ —	$ —	$13,200	$13,200
Cost of goods sold.....................	$ —	$ —	$ 9,240	$ 9,240
Gross profit...........................	$ —	$ —	$ 3,960	$ 3,960
Sales, general, & administrative expenses...	$ —	$ —	$ 2,640	$ 2,640
Operating income......................	$ —	$ —	$ 1,320	$ 1,320

Organizations that have adopted zero-base budgeting use a variety of specific procedures. A common approach is to segment the budget into "decision packages" in which the preparer ranks all of the activities according to their relative importance for each activity. The preparer might note the consequences of not performing the activity, possible alternative activities, and whether there is an external mandate to perform the activity. This approach enables various levels of management to eliminate low-ranking activities until a desired budget level is reached.

Note that zero-base budgeting is a time-consuming and costly process. As a result, many entities that employ the technique usually do not apply it to all portions of the operating budget each year. Some use zero-base budgeting every year but apply the technique to only selected segments of the budget so that all segments will be subjected to the technique once during each 5-year period. Others apply the technique to all segments periodically (such as every third year). As a result, traditional budgeting techniques might be used to prepare budgets for years 1 and 2, with zero-base budgeting used to prepare the budget for year 3.

TAKEAWAY 22.3

Zero-base budgeting requires that a manager:

1. Determine goals, operations, and costs for all activities under his or her jurisdiction.
2. Determine alternative means of conducting the activity.
3. Evaluate the implications of changes in the level of each activity.
4. Establish workload.
5. Rank activities in order of importance.

THE FRAMEWORK OF THE MASTER BUDGET

Master budget is the name given to the comprehensive annual operating budget. The master budget combines and integrates all of the individual, detailed operating budgets for all of the firm's various activities for the year. All amounts in the master budget are usually based on the expected level of operations. The exact structure of the master budget varies according to whether the firm's operations are manufacturing, merchandising, service, or government oriented. In this chapter, we illustrate budgeting and a master budget for Fezzari, the small bicycle manufacturer introduced in Chapter 14. The following budgets constitute Fezzari's master budget:

LO3 **Define** the components of a master budget and **illustrate** the interrelationships of the individual budgets that comprise the master budget.

1. Sales budget
2. Production budget
3. Direct material budget
4. Direct labor budget
5. Manufacturing overhead budget
6. Selling and administrative expense budget
7. Capital expenditures budget
8. Cash budget
9. Budgeted income statement
10. Budgeted balance sheet
11. Budgeted statement of cash flows

Fezzari's master budget includes budgets that are interdependent and must be prepared in a specific sequence. **Exhibit 22-5** presents Fezzari's master budget and the data flows that are necessary between the individual budgets during their preparation.

The sales budget is prepared first. It is based on the sales forecast and typically includes both sales dollars and quantities. As the sales budget feeds into each of the succeeding budgets, the quality of the sales forecast determines the success of the remaining process. Then the production budget is prepared to identify the number of units of each product to be manufactured. Then the direct material budget, the direct labor budget, and the manufacturing overhead budget determine the levels of product cost to be incurred based on the units to be manufactured. The selling and administrative expense budget determines the level of selling and general administrative expense necessary to support the sales budget.

A.K.A. Budgets may be called **pro forma statements**. They are forecasted financial statements instead of actual financial statements.

The cash budget receives input from the budgets established previously as well as the capital expenditures budget and the budgeted income statement. In turn, the cash budget provides inputs to the budgeted balance sheet and the budgeted statement of cash flows. The budgeted balance sheet also receives input from the budgeted income statement and the capital expenditures budget and supplies input to the budgeted income statement. We illustrate these interrelationships in the following example.

Exhibit 22-5	Budgets and Data Flows in Fezzari's Master Budget

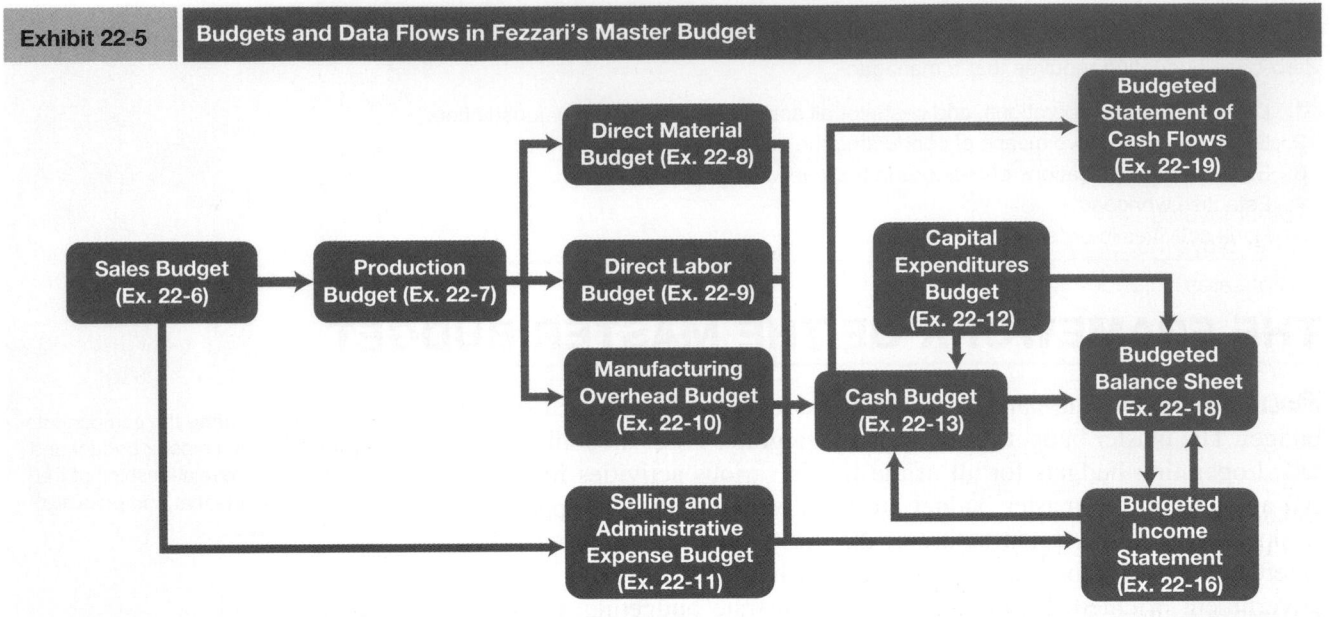

ILLUSTRATION OF A MASTER BUDGET AND ITS COMPONENTS

Sales Budget

LO4 **Prepare** individual budgets for a manufacturing and a service company, including the cash budget.

The **sales budget** provides the basis for all subsequent budgets. Anticipated unit sales volume is based on the **sales forecast**. The sales forecast is the sales department's best estimate of what sales will be for the company and the industry in which it operates. Factors that are evaluated in preparing the sales forecast include prior company sales levels, future pricing policies, market research studies, general economic conditions, specific economic indicators, advertising and promotion plans, and anticipated activities of the competition. Over-estimating sales volume can lead to large unwanted inventories, which in turn result in extra storage costs and possibly sales price reductions when liquidating the excess inventory. Underestimating sales can lead to loss of sales revenue and customer ill will stemming from unfilled orders.

Assume that Fezzari managers are preparing their budget for the upcoming fiscal year. As we have discussed in earlier chapters, Fezzari sells two types of bikes, road and mountain, with several different models of each type. For purposes of this illustration, we will assume that the budget is prepared at the bike-type level, although in reality the budget would be prepared at the model level. Further, assume that Fezzari's management anticipates a 20% growth in sales in the next year.

The estimated unit sales volume of each product is multiplied by planned average unit sales prices to estimate total sales revenue. We present an example of a sales budget in **Exhibit 22-6**. To simplify the presentation of the cash budget, assume all Fezzari's sales are on a cash basis; therefore Fezzari carries no accounts receivable balances. We will demonstrate a sales budget for a service firm with credit sales later in the chapter.

Exhibit 22-6	Sales Budget Illustration

FEZZARI PERFORMANCE BICYCLES
Sales Budget
For the Year Ended December 31, 2016

	Forecast Unit Sales Volume	Average Unit Sales Price	Budgeted Total Sales
Road bicycles.	2,160	$1,250	$2,700,000
Mountain bicycles	3,240	$1,000	3,240,000
Total bicycles	5,400		$5,940,000
Other bicycle accessories			297,000
Total sales revenue			$6,237,000

Production Budget

The **production budget** reflects the quantity of each product to be produced during the budget period. Scheduled production should specifically provide for anticipated sales and desired ending inventories and, of course, consider the beginning inventories of each product. Assume that Fezzari wants to increase its inventory of road bikes from 8 to 12 units and its inventory of mountain bikes from 14 to 18 units. Fezzari's production budget appears in **Exhibit 22-7**. Note that the desired change in inventory of each product is accomplished by scheduling the appropriate production volumes. Because bicycle accessories are not manufactured by Fezzari, but simply purchased from vendors for resale, they are not included in the production budget.

Like Fezzari, many manufacturing companies use the just-in-time approach for finished goods inventory to reduce their inventory carrying costs. When the **just-in-time inventory** approach is used, finished goods are not produced until they are needed for shipment to customers. As a result, the planned ending inventory of finished goods is zero or nearly zero.

Hint: Companies that do not use the just-in-time inventory method often determine required inventory levels based on a percentage of unit sales.

Exhibit 22-7	Production Budget Illustration

FEZZARI PERFORMANCE BICYCLES
Production Budget
For the Year Ended December 31, 2016

	Units of Finished Product	
	Road Bikes	Mountain Bikes
Forecast unit sales	2,160	3,240
Desired ending finished goods inventories	12	18
Quantities to be available	2,172	3,258
Less: beginning finished goods inventories	8	14
Total production to be scheduled	2,164	3,244

This approach is practical only for companies that can forecast their sales very accurately, that do not have highly seasonal demand, and that have highly reliable suppliers of the materials and components needed to manufacture the finished goods. Many companies prefer to maintain a **safety stock** of finished goods inventory so they minimize the

Hint: Running out of an item of inventory not only results in the loss of a current sale, but could also cause the loss of future sales due to negative publicity.

risk of running out of stock. Safety stock is defined as a quantity of inventory maintained to supply unexpected demand or to provide stock when manufacturing is slowed through delays in receipt of materials and components from suppliers.

Direct Material Budget

The quantities of material to be purchased to meet scheduled production and desired ending materials inventory requirements are presented in the **direct material budget**. Any beginning material inventory must be considered in estimating purchases for the budget period. Because Fezzari assembles its bikes only after receiving a customer order, it does not maintain a large inventory of direct materials. The quantities to be acquired are multiplied by the anticipated unit prices to calculate the total dollar amounts of material purchases. In the direct material budget illustrated in **Exhibit 22-8**, we assume that Fezzari uses only two direct materials, a frame and a build kit containing all of the other components, in producing road and mountain bikes. Further, Fezzari targets to have sufficient frames and build kits in ending inventory for 6 road bikes and 10 mountain bikes.

Exhibit 22-8	Direct Materials Budget Illustration		
FEZZARI PERFORMANCE BICYCLES Direct Materials Budget For the Year Ended December 31, 2016			
	Frame	**Build Kit**	**Total**
Direct material required:			
Road bicycles.	2,164	2,164	
Desired ending material inventory	6	6	
Total units of material to be available.	2,170	2,170	
Less: beginning material inventory.	8	8	
Total units of material to be purchased	2,162	2,162	
Average unit purchase price.	$ 325	$ 275	
Total road bike material purchases	$ 702,650	$ 594,550	$1,297,200
Direct material required:			
Mountain bicycles	3,244	3,244	
Desired ending material inventory	10	10	
Total units of material to be available.	3,254	3,254	
Less: beginning material inventory.	14	14	
Total units of material to be purchased	3,240	3,240	
Average unit purchase price.	$ 350	$ 290	
Total mountain bike material purchases	$1,134,000	$ 939,600	$2,073,600
Total material purchases	$1,836,650	$1,534,150	$3,370,800
Add: beginning accounts payable balance . . .			50,000
Less: ending accounts payable balance			(75,000)
Cash budgeted for material purchases			$3,345,800

The just-in-time inventory philosophy may also apply to the materials inventory of manufacturing firms. Under this philosophy, materials and components needed to manufacture finished products would not be received from the suppliers until immediately before they are needed for manufacturing. As a result, the material inventory would be zero or nearly zero. Many firms prefer to carry safety stocks of materials and components to ensure that the manufacturing facility is not slowed or stopped by a supplier missing a scheduled delivery.

The direct materials budget in **Exhibit 22-8** shows the total purchases that are budgeted for 2016. However, because Fezzari purchases these materials on credit from its suppliers, the dollar amount of purchases may not equal the cash that will be expended for materials during 2016. Thus, in preparing the cash budget, an adjustment must be made for the change in the accounts payable balance during the year. **Exhibit 22-8** illustrates how the cash expended for direct materials might be calculated, assuming that the balance in accounts payable was expected to increase from $50,000 to $75,000 in 2016.

The increase in the accounts payable balance of $25,000 over the year means that Fezzari will spend $25,000 less than the total material purchases in cash.

Direct Labor Budget

The **direct labor budget** presents the number of direct labor hours necessary for the production volume planned for the budget period. These hours are multiplied by the applicable hourly labor rates to determine the total dollar amounts of direct labor costs to be budgeted. In the direct labor budget for Fezzari in **Exhibit 22-9**, we have assumed that both road and mountain bikes require the following average hours in the assembly and quality control and packaging departments:

	Assembly Hours	Quality Control and Packaging Hours
Road bikes	5.5	2.0
Mountain bikes.	7.0	2.0

Exhibit 22-9	Direct Labor Budget Illustration

FEZZARI PERFORMANCE BICYCLES
Direct Labor Budget
For the Year Ended December 31, 2016

	Assembly Department	Quality Control and Packaging Department	Total
Direct labor			
Road Bicycles (average 5.5 hours assembly, 2 hours packaging)	11,902[1]	4,328[2]	
Mountain Bicycles (average 7 hours assembly, 2 hours packaging)	22,708[3]	6,488[4]	
Total direct labor hours	34,610	10,816	45,426
Hourly rate for direct labor	$ 25	$ 20	
Total direct labor cost	$865,250	$216,320	$1,081,570

[1] (2,164 bikes × 5.5 hours)
[2] (2,164 bikes × 2 hours)
[3] (3,244 bikes × 7 hours)
[4] (3,244 bikes × 2 hours)

Manufacturing Overhead Budget

Recall from earlier chapters that manufacturing overhead comprises all manufacturing costs that are not direct material or direct labor. Examples of manufacturing overhead are indirect material, indirect labor, supervisory salaries, utilities, depreciation, maintenance, property taxes, and insurance. Because of the variety of cost factors, manufacturing overhead includes both variable and fixed cost elements.

The **manufacturing overhead budget** for Fezzari's Assembly and Packaging departments is shown in **Exhibit 22-10**. Note that the format separates variable and fixed overhead cost elements and presents budgeted overhead costs for the 45,426 direct labor hours expected to be incurred.

Management would determine the budgeted variable costs based on purchase agreements with its vendors (indirect material), labor agreements with its employees (indirect labor), and contracted rates for other services (utilities). Management would determine the budgeted fixed costs based on lease agreements, insurance contracts, local government tax notices, and current levels of equipment. These amounts would not be expected to vary from year to year. Usually, lease agreements are multiyear agreements with fixed rates for each year of the agreement and insurance coverage is adjusted only as manufacturing facilities are expanded. To simplify the presentation of the cash budget, assume that all overhead expenses, except depreciation, are paid in the month they are incurred.

Exhibit 22-10	Manufacturing Overhead Budget Illustration

FEZZARI PERFORMANCE BICYCLES
Manufacturing Overhead Budget
For the Year Ended December 31, 2016

	Variable Cost Per Direct Labor Hour	Total Costs at 45,426 Direct Labor Hours
Variable manufacturing costs		
Indirect material	$0.08	$ 3,634
Indirect labor	$0.78	$ 35,432
Factory utilities	$0.86	$ 39,066
Other	$0.36	$ 16,353
Total variable manufacturing overhead	$2.08	$ 94,485
Fixed manufacturing costs		
Lease expense		$100,000
Insurance		68,000
Property taxes		12,000
Depreciation		45,100
Total fixed manufacturing overhead		225,100
Total manufacturing overhead		$319,585
Less: depreciation		(45,100)
Cash budgeted for manufacturing overhead		$274,485
Direct labor hours		45,426
Budgeted predetermined manufacturing overhead rate (rounded)		*$ 7.0353

* ($319,585/45,426)

As we discussed in **Chapter 16**, the predetermined overhead rate is determined by dividing the total budgeted manufacturing overhead by the budgeted activity level, or direct labor hours in this example. For the year ended December 31, 2016, the total cost formula for overhead at the planned operating volume of 45,426 direct labor hours (DLH) would be as follows:

Total manufacturing overhead cost = $2.08 × DLH + $225,100

Selling and Administrative Expense Budget

The **selling and administrative expense budget** will consist of variable and fixed expenses. The variable selling expenses will typically vary with dollars of sales. To simplify the presentation of the cash budget, assume that selling and administrative expenses, except depreciation, are paid in the month incurred. **Exhibit 22-11** presents Fezzari's selling and administrative expense budget.

Exhibit 22-11	Selling and Administrative Expenses Budget Illustration

FEZZARI PERFORMANCE BICYCLES
Selling and Administrative Expenses Budget
For the Year Ended December 31, 2016

	Percentage of Sales	Total Cost
Selling expenses		
Variable costs:		
Sales commissions	2%	$124,740
Shipping expense	3%	187,110
Fixed costs:		
Advertising expense		120,000
Administrative expenses:		
Fixed costs:		
Executive salaries expense		200,000
Other administrative expenses		
Legal costs		30,000
Accounting costs		95,000
Depreciation		5,000
General liability insurance		15,000
Total selling and administrative expenses		$776,850
Less: depreciation		(5,000)
Cash budgeted for selling and administrative expenses		$771,850

Capital Expenditures Budget

Expenditures for property, plant, and equipment are among a firm's most important transactions. The type of analysis that is undertaken to determine whether a particular item should be acquired is known as capital budgeting and is discussed in detail in Chapter 25. The **capital expenditures budget** lists long-term assets that are planned to be acquired over a multiyear period. **Exhibit 22-12** presents an illustration for Fezzari. We will assume that it is abstracted from the complete capital expenditures budget.

Exhibit 22-12	Capital Expenditures Budget Illustration

FEZZARI PERFORMANCE BICYCLES
Capital Expenditures Budget
For the Year Ended December 31, 2016

	1st Quarter	2nd Quarter	3rd Quarter	4th Quarter	Total
Assembly equipment	$25,000		$25,000		$50,000
Packaging equipment		$10,000			$10,000
Administrative computers				$5,000	$ 5,000
Total	$25,000	$10,000	$25,000	$5,000	$65,000

The capital expenditures budget has an impact on many other budgets. The plant and equipment available at any point in time determine the productive capacity of the firm. Further, depreciation expense in both the overhead budgets and the selling and administrative expense budget is affected by the capital expenditures budget, as are the cash expenditures in the cash budget and the property, plant, and equipment assets on the balance sheet.

Cash Budget

The **cash budget** presents the projected cash flows during the budget period. The budgeted cash flows are separated into two groups, *cash receipts* (inflows of cash) and *cash disbursements* (outflows of cash). *Cash receipts* include cash sales, collections of accounts receivable, sale of investments and unneeded assets, and proceeds from borrowings and stock sales. *Cash disbursements* include payments for manufacturing costs (direct material, direct labor, and manufacturing overhead), payments for selling and administrative expenses, interest expense, capital expenditures (land, buildings, and equipment), income tax payments, and cash dividends.

ACCOUNTING IN PRACTICE	Financing Cash Flows

In practice, the cash budget often includes a separate section for financing activities. This section would provide details of borrowings and repayments, including interest payments.

Much of the information needed to prepare the cash budget is available in the previously prepared budgets. However, because of characteristic time lags between transactions and their related effects on cash, cash budgeting often requires the analysis of other data as well. For example, sales precede collections from customers, purchases precede payments on account, depreciation is not a cash outflow, and prepayments call for cash outlays before the related expenses are recognized. **Exhibit 22-13** shows the cash budget for Fezzari. For simplicity, the cash budget assumes that all sales are made in cash and that all expenses, with the exception of depreciation and direct materials, are paid in cash. We demonstrate the determination of cash from sales when sales are made on account in the following section.

Exhibit 22-13	Cash Budget Illustration

FEZZARI PERFORMANCE BICYCLES
Cash Budget
For the Year Ended December 31, 2016

	Amount	Source
Cash receipts:		
Sales......................	$6,237,000	Exhibit 22-6
Cash disbursements:		
Direct materials...............	(3,345,800)	Exhibit 22-8
Direct labor..................	(1,081,570)	Exhibit 22-9
Manufacturing overhead........	(274,485)	Exhibit 22-10 (excluding depreciation)
Selling and administrative costs...	(771,850)	Exhibit 22-11
Capital expenditures...........	(65,000)	Exhibit 22-12
Interest	(5,000)	Financing budget (not shown)
Income taxes	(240,250)	Exhibit 22-16
Net change in cash.............	$453,045	
Beginning cash................	550,631	
Ending cash	$1,003,676	

What are some examples of noncash expenses excluded from a cash budget?

YOUR TURN! 22.2

The solution is on page 1023.

Illustration of a Service Firm's Budgets

SERVICE AND MERCHANDISING

Assume that Environmental Business Consultants (EBC) has collected the following actual data for February and March 2016 and developed the following forecasted data for the quarter ended June 30, 2016:

1. Actual sales for February and March 2016, were the following:

	Actual Credit Sales
February.	$310,000
March	290,000

2. Forecast sales for the quarter ended June 30, 2016, are as follows:

	Forecast Credit Sales
April	$400,000
May.	350,000
June	380,000

3. The collection of cash from credit sales during the quarter ended June 30, 2016, will follow the same pattern as the previous quarter:

    a. In the month of sale, 10% is collected.

    b. In the month following sale, 50% is collected.

    c. In the second month following sale, 38% is collected. The remaining 2% of accounts receivable are written off as uncollectible.

    Based on the information in items 1–3, the cash collections can be computed as follows:

Month of Credit Sale	Cash Collections from Customers			
	April	May	June	Quarter Total
February	$117,800			
March	$145,000	$110,200		
April	$ 40,000	$200,000	$152,000	
May.		$ 35,000	$175,000	
June			$ 38,000	
Month total	$302,800	$345,200	$365,000	$1,013,000

4. Forecast cash disbursements for the quarter ended June 30, 2016, are as follows:

	Forecast Cash Disbursements		
	April	May	June
Labor	$195,000	$195,000	$195,000
Office lease.	$ 16,875	$ 16,875	$ 16,875
Office supplies	$ 2,000	$ 5,000	$ 3,000
Selling and administrative expenses	31,000	32,000	62,000
Interest expense (on existing debt)	$ 417	$ 417	$ 417
Cash distributions to owners	—	—	100,000

The increase in the selling and administrative expense in June is due to the anticipated payment of employee mid-year bonuses.

5. EBC has a policy of maintaining a cash balance of $500,000. All borrowings and repayments are made at the end of the month and the short-term loan carries an annual interest rate of 6%.

The cash budget for EBC is shown in **Exhibit 22-14**. A three-column format is used so the cash flow of each month of the quarter can be analyzed separately. The starting point in preparing this cash budget is a beginning cash balance for April of $400,000. The cash receipts and cash disbursements for April are then added to the budget. Note that interest is assumed to be paid in the period in which it is incurred. The preliminary ending cash balance of $457,508 is then calculated.

Remember that EBC has a policy of maintaining a cash balance of $500,000. As shown in **Exhibit 22-14**, EBC starts and ends the month of April with a cash balance below this target. To meet its target by the end of April, EBC could budget to borrow $42,492 ($500,000 – $457,508) on a short-term basis. In May, EBC would have sufficient cash to repay this short-term borrowing.

The budgeted ending cash balance for April becomes the budgeted beginning cash balance for May. The procedure described earlier is then repeated for May.

Exhibit 22-14	Service Firm Cash Budget Illustration		

ENVIRONMENTAL BUSINESS CONSULTANTS
Cash Budget
For the Quarter Ended June 30, 2016

	April	May	June
Beginning cash balance.	$400,000	$500,000	$553,204
Cash receipts			
Collections from customers	302,800	345,200	365,000
Cash available	$702,800	$845,200	$918,204
Cash disbursements			
Labor.	$195,000	$195,000	$195,000
Office lease.	16,875	16,875	16,875
Office supplies	2,000	5,000	3,000
Selling and administrative costs.	31,000	32,000	62,000
Interest (on existing debt).	417	629*	417
Cash distributions to owners	—	—	100,000
Total disbursements.	$245,292	$249,504	$377,292
Preliminary ending cash balance	$457,508	$595,696	$540,912
Target cash balance.	$500,000	$500,000	$500,000
Required short-term borrowing (repayment)	42,492	(42,492)	—
Final ending cash balance	$500,000	$553,204	$540,912

* Interest on existing debt.	$417	
Interest on $42,492 short-term borrowing ($42,492 × (6.0%/12)).	212	
Total interest.	$629	

The budgeted ending cash balance for May then becomes the budgeted beginning cash balance for June and the process is repeated again. One additional cash disbursement appears in June: the $100,000 quarterly cash distribution to the owners.

Budgeted Financial Statements

Budgeted Income Statement

The development of the master budget is completed with the preparation of the budgeted financial statements: the budgeted income statement, the budgeted balance sheet, and the budgeted statement of cash flows. The **budgeted income statement** is usually prepared first. In addition to the budgets that were previously prepared, supplemental schedules and worksheets may be needed to prepare the budgeted income statement. Returning to the Fezzari example, one of these supplementary schedules is the schedule of estimated product cost per unit, which is presented in **Exhibit 22-15**. We then use the estimated cost per unit to calculate our budgeted cost of goods sold, which is included in our budgeted income statement (**Exhibit 22-16**).

LO5 **Prepare** budgeted financial statements.

Exhibit 22-15	Estimated Product Cost per Unit Illustration

FEZZARI PERFORMANCE BICYCLES
Estimated Product Cost per Unit
For the Year Ended December 31, 2016

		Cost			
	Quantity	Road Bicycle	Mountain Bicycle	Road Bicycle	Mountain Bicycle
Direct material					
Frame	1.0	× $325.00	$350.00	= $325.00	$350.00
Build kit.	1.0	× 275.00	290.00	= 275.00	290.00

	Cost per unit		Quantity		
Direct labor:					
Assembly	$ 25.00	×	5.5	7.0	= 137.50	175.00
QC and packaging	$ 20.00	×	2.0	2.0	= 40.00	40.00
Manufacturing overhead:					
Combined	$7.0353*	×	7.5	9.0	= 52.76	63.32
Product cost per unit					$830.26	$918.32

* $319,585/45,426 DLH =$7.0353 (rounded) (see Exhibit 22-10)

Exhibit 22-16	Budgeted Income Statement Illustration

FEZZARI PERFORMANCE BICYCLES
Budgeted Income Statement
For the Year Ended December 31, 2016

Sales (from Exhibit 22-6)	$6,237,000
Less: cost of goods sold	
Road bicycles: 2,160 units × $830.26 (from Exhibit 22-15).	1,793,372*
Mountain bicycles: 3,240 units × $918.32 (from Exhibit 22-15)	2,975,349*
Gross profit.	$1,468,279
Less: selling and administrative expense (from Exhibit 22-11)	776,850
Income from operations	$ 691,429
Less: interest expense (from financing budget not shown)	5,000
Income before income taxes	$ 686,429
Less: Income taxes (separate schedule not shown)	240,250
Net income.	$ 446,179

*Difference due to rounding

Budgeted Balance Sheet

The preparation of the **budgeted balance sheet** usually follows the preparation of the budgeted income statement. It is important to note that the budgeted balance sheet is based on the ending balance sheet from the prior year adjusted for budgeted changes. **Exhibit 22-17** presents Fezzari's beginning balance sheet as of December 31, 2015.

Exhibit 22-17	Actual Balance Sheet

FEZZARI PERFORMANCE BICYCLES
Balance Sheet
As of December 31, 2015

Assets

Current assets:

Cash		$550,631
Inventories		33,252
Total current assets		$583,883
Plant assets:		
Equipment	$135,300	
Less: accumulated depreciation	(45,100)	90,200
Total assets		$674,083

Liabilities

Current liabilities

Accounts payable.		50,000
Long-term liabilities:		
Long-term borrowing		83,333
Total liabilities.		$133,333

Stockholders' Equity

Common stock ($1 par value; 10,000 shares authorized and issued) . . .	$10,000	
Paid in capital—excess of par-common stock	90,000	
Total paid-in capital		$100,000
Retained earnings		440,750
Total stockholders' equity		$540,750
Total liabilities and stockholders' equity		$674,083

Exhibit 22-18 presents the budgeted balance sheet for December 31, 2016. This balance sheet reflects the changes in the asset, liability, and equity accounts that result from the budgeted activity for the year. For 2016, Fezzari management has assumed that there will be no additional borrowings or stock sales.

Exhibit 22-18	Budgeted Balance Sheet Illustration

FEZZARI PERFORMANCE BICYCLES
Budgeted Balance Sheet
As of December 31, 2016

Assets			
Current assets:			
Cash		$1,003,676	a
Inventories			
Direct materials	$ 10,000		b
Finished goods	26,493	36,493	c
Total current assets		$1,040,169	
Plant assets:			
Equipment	$200,300		d
Less: accumulated depreciation	(95,200)	105,100	e
Total assets		$1,145,269	
Liabilities			
Current liabilities			
Accounts payable		75,000	
Long-term liabilities:			
Long-term borrowing		83,333	f
Total liabilities		$ 158,333	
Stockholders' Equity			
Common stock ($1 par value; 10,000 shares authorized and issued)	$ 10,000		f
Paid in capital—excess of par-common stock	90,000		f
Total paid-in capital		$ 100,000	
Retained earnings		886,936	g
Total stockholders' equity		$ 986,936	
Total liabilities and stockholders' equity		$1,145,269	

a Beginning cash balance from Exhibit 22-17 plus net cash increase from Exhibit 22-13.
b (6 road bike units × [$325 + $275]) + (10 mountain bike units × [$350 + $290]) = $10,000
c (12 road bike units × $830.26) + (18 units mountain bike units × $918.32) = $26,494. Difference due to rounding.
d Beginning equipment ($135,300) plus budgeted capital purchases from Exhibit 22-12 ($65,000).
e Beginning accumulated depreciation ($45,100) plus current year depreciation from Exhibit 22-10 ($45,100) and Exhibit 22-11 ($5,000).
f No change.
g Beginning retained earnings ($440,750) plus net income from Exhibit 22-16 ($446,179). Difference due to rounding.

Budgeted Statement of Cash Flows

The **budgeted statement of cash flows** follows directly from the cash budget. The dollar amounts will be the same, but the grouping and sequence will usually be different. **Exhibit 22-19** presents Fezzari's budgeted statement of cash flows. Note that this statement groups the cash flows into three sections: cash flows from operating activities, cash flows from investing activities, and cash flows from financing activities.

Exhibit 22-19	Budgeted Statement of Cash Flows Illustration

FEZZARI PERFORMANCE BICYCLES
Budgeted Statement of Cash Flows—Direct Method
For the Period Ended December 31, 2016

Cash flows from operating activities

Cash receipts from customers.........................	$6,237,000	
Cash payments for inventory..........................	(4,701,855)	
Cash paid for selling and administrative expenses........	(771,850)	
Cash paid for interest...............................	(5,000)	
Income tax payment................................	(240,250)	
Net cash provided by operating activities		$ 518,045
Cash flows from investing activities		
Capital expenditures	(65,000)	
Net cash used by investing activities		(65,000)
Cash flows from financing activities		
Net cash provided by financing activities..............		—
Net increase (decrease) in cash......................		$ 453,045
Beginning cash balance.............................		550,631
Ending cash balance		$1,003,676

SERVICES INDUSTRY IN FOCUS

SERVICE AND MERCHANDISING

Refer to the Environmental Business Consultants (EBC) illustration on page 314 in the chapter. Assume that local governments (EBC's target market) are experiencing a sharp reduction in the collection of tax revenues due to a recession in the general economy. EBC anticipates that this will impact the timeliness of payments made by its clients *beginning in April* as shown below:

  a.   In the month of sale, 10% is collected.

  b.   In the month following sale, 30% is collected.

  c.   In the second month following sale, 30% is collected.

  d.   In the third month following sale, 20% is collected. The remaining 10% of accounts receivable will be written off as uncollectible.

Note that payments related to the February and March sales that have yet to be collected will be impacted by the recession also. For example, 10% of the February sales were collected in February, 50% were collected in March, but only 30% will be collected in April (not 38%) and the remaining 10% will be written off. Further, 10% of the March sales were collected in March, but only 30% will be collected in April (not 50%), 30% will be collected in May, and 20% will be collected in June. Assume that all other forecasted data remain the same.

Assume that because of the recession, EBC has temporarily eliminated its policy of maintaining a cash balance of $500,000.

Required

1.   Re-compute the forecasted cash collections for the quarter ended June 30, 2016.

2.   Prepare a new cash budget reflecting these new cash collections.

Solution

1.

Cash Collections from Customers				
Month of Credit Sale	April	May	June	Quarter Total
February.................	$ 93,000			
March...................	$ 87,000	$ 87,000	$ 58,000	
April	$ 40,000	$120,000	$120,000	
May...................		$ 35,000	$105,000	
June			$ 38,000	
Month total.............	$220,000	$242,000	$321,000	$783,000

2.

ENVIRONMENTAL BUSINESS CONSULTANTS Cash Budget For the Quarter Ended June 30, 2016			
	April	May	June
Beginning cash balance....................	$400,000	$374,708	$367,416
Cash receipts			
Collections from customers	220,000	242,000	321,000
Cash available	$620,000	$616,708	$688,416
Cash disbursements			
Labor.......................	$195,000	$195,000	$195,000
Office lease..........................	16,875	16,875	16,875
Office supplies	2,000	5,000	3,000
Selling and administrative expenses	31,000	32,000	62,000
Interest expense (on existing debt).........	417	417	417
Cash distributions to owners	—	—	100,000
Total disbursements......................	$245,292	$249,292	$377,292
Ending cash balance	$374,708	$367,416	$311,124

COMPREHENSIVE PROBLEM

The sales department of Jackson Manufacturing, Inc. has completed the following sales forecast for the months of January through March 20X5 for its only two products: 40,000 units of X1 to be sold at $110 each and 20,000 units of X2 to be sold at $85 each. The desired unit inventories at March 31, 20X5, are 10% of the next quarter's unit sales forecast, which are 50,000 units of X1 and 25,000 units of X2. The January 1, 20X5, unit inventories were 7,000 units of X1 and 1,500 units of X2.

Each unit of X1 requires 4 pounds of material R and 2 pounds of material S for its manufacture; X2 requires 2 pounds of R and 3 pounds of S. The purchase cost of R is $10 per pound and of S is $5 per pound. Materials on hand at January 1, 20X5, were 20,000 pounds of R and 8,000 pounds of S. Desired inventories at March 31, 20X5, are 15,000 pounds of R and 6,000 pounds of S.

Each unit of X1 requires 0.5 hour of direct labor in the factory; each unit of X2 requires 1.0 hour of direct labor. The average hourly rate for direct labor is $12 per hour. Estimated manufacturing overhead cost is $8 per direct labor hour plus $100,000 per month. Selling and administrative expenses are estimated to be 10% of sales revenue plus $200,000 per month.

Cash sales in December 20X4 were $250,000 and credit sales were $2,000,000. Cash sales for the first quarter are estimated to be $200,000 per month. It is forecast that 40% of the credit sales for the quarter ended March 31, 20X5, will occur in January, 30% in February, and 30% in March. Of credit sales (December through March), 40% will be collected as cash in the month of sale and 50% will be collected in the following month. The remainder will be uncollectible.

The January 1, 20X5, cash balance was $60,000. The minimum acceptable cash balance at the end of each month is $50,000. Short-term borrowings are made in multiples of $10,000 with interest charged at the rate of 1% per month. The first interest payment is made the month following the borrowing. Cash disbursements (excluding interest on short-term borrowings) are estimated as follows:

	January	February	March
Manufacturing costs.	$1,200,000	$1,100,000	$1,000,000
Selling and administrative expenses	$ 380,000	$ 400,000	$ 340,000
Interest expense.	$ 100,000	$ 100,000	$ 100,000
Income tax payment.	—	—	200,000
Capital expenditures	100,000	340,000	60,000
Cash dividends.	400,000	—	—

Required

a. Prepare the sales budget for the quarter ended March 31, 20X5.
b. Prepare the production budget for the quarter ended March 31, 20X5.
c. Prepare the direct material budget for the quarter ended March 31, 20X5.
d. Prepare the direct labor budget for the quarter ended March 31, 20X5.
e. Prepare the overhead budget for the quarter ended March 31, 20X5.
f. Prepare a schedule of estimated product cost per unit for the quarter ended March 31, 20X5.
g. Prepare a schedule of cash collected from customers for the quarter ended March 31, 20X5.
h. Prepare the cash budget for the quarter ended March 31, 20X5.

SOLUTION TO COMPREHENSIVE PROBLEM

a.

JACKSON MANUFACTURING, INC.
Sales Budget
For the Quarter Ended March 31, 20X5

Product	Forecasted Unit Sales Volume	Planned Unit Sales Price	Budgeted Total Sales
X1	40,000	$110.00	$4,400,000
X2	20,000	$ 85.00	1,700,000
Total sales revenue.			$6,100,000

b.

JACKSON MANUFACTURING, INC.
Production Budget
For the Quarter Ended March 31, 20X5

	Units of Finished Product	
	X1	X2
Forecast unit sales	40,000	20,000
Desired ending inventories:		
10% × 50,000.	5,000	
10% × 25,000.		2,500
Quantities to be available.	45,000	22,500
Less: Beginning inventories	7,000	1,500
Total production to be scheduled	38,000	21,000

c.

JACKSON MANUFACTURING, INC.
Direct Material Budget
For the Quarter Ended March 31, 20X5

	Material R	Material S
Direct material required:		
Product X1: 38,000 × 4.	152,000	
38,000 × 2.		70,000
Product X2: 21,000 × 2.	42,000	
21,000 × 3.		63,000
Desired ending material inventories.	15,000	6,000
Total pounds of material to be available	209,000	145,000
Less: Beginning material inventories	20,000	8,000
Total pounds of material to be purchased.	189,000	137,000
Unit purchase price	$ 10.00	$ 5.00
Total material purchases	$1,890,000	$685,000

d.

JACKSON MANUFACTURING, INC.
Direct Labor Budget
For the Quarter Ended March 31, 20X5

Direct labor hours required for production:	
Product X1: 38,000 × 0.5 hours	19,000
Product X2: 21,000 × 1.0 hours	21,000
Total direct labor hours required	40,000
Hourly rate for direct labor	$ 12.00
Total direct labor cost	$480,000

e.

JACKSON MANUFACTURING, INC.
Overhead Budget
For the Quarter Ended March 31, 20X5

Total direct labor hours	40,000
Variable manufacturing overhead rate	$ 8.00
Variable manufacturing overhead cost.	$320,000
Fixed manufacturing overhead cost ($100,000 × 3 months).	$300,000
Total manufacturing overhead cost	$620,000

f.

JACKSON MANUFACTURING, INC.
Schedule of Estimated Product Cost Per Unit
For the Quarter Ended March 31, 20X5

	Quantity				
	Product X1	Product X2	Cost	Product X1	Product X2
Direct material:					
Material R.	4	2	$10.00	$40.00	$20.00
Material S.	2	3	$ 5.00	$10.00	$15.00
Direct labor.	0.5	1	$12.00	$ 6.00	$12.00
Manufacturing overhead	0.5	1	*$15.50	$ 7.75	$15.50
Product cost per unit				$63.75	$62.50

*$620,000/40,000 = $15.50 per direct labor hour

g.

JACKSON MANUFACTURING, INC.
Schedule of Cash Collected From Customers
For the Quarter Ended March 31, 20X5

	January	February	March
Cash sales	$ 200,000	$ 200,000	$ 200,000
Credit sales			
December: $2,000,000 × 50%	1,000,000		
January: $2,200,000* × 40%	880,000		
$2,200,000* × 50%		1,100,000	
February: $1,650,000** × 40%		660,000	
$1,650,000** × 50%			825,000
March: $1,650,000** × 40%			660,000
	$1,880,000	$1,760,000	$1,485,000
Total cash collected	$2,080,000	$1,960,000	$1,685,000

*($6,100,000 total sales − $600,000 cash sales) × 40% = $2,200,000
**($6,100,000 total sales − $600,000 cash sales) × 30% = $1,650,000

h.

JACKSON MANUFACTURING, INC.
Cash Budget
For the Quarter Ended March 31, 20X5

	January	February	March
Beginning cash balance	$ 60,000	$ 50,000	$ 69,100
Cash receipts:			
Cash sales	200,000	200,000	200,000
Collections from credit customers	1,880,000	1,760,000	1,485,000
Short-term borrowing	90,000	—	—
Cash available	$2,230,000	$2,010,000	$1,754,100
Cash disbursements:			
Manufacturing costs	$1,200,000	$1,100,000	$1,000,000
Selling and administrative expenses	380,000	400,000	340,000
Interest expense*	100,000	100,900	100,900
Income tax payments	—	—	200,000
Capital expenditures	100,000	340,000	60,000
Cash dividends	400,000	—	—
Total disbursements	$2,180,000	$1,940,900	$1,700,900
Ending cash balance	$ 50,000	$ 69,100	$ 53,200

* For February and March: $100,000 + ($90,000 × 1%) = $100,900

SUMMARY OF LEARNING OBJECTIVES

LO1 Describe the planning process, including strategic planning and operational planning. (p. 984)

- Strategic planning is a formal process that addresses and documents the mission and long-term goals of the organization. SWOT analysis is used to develop and analyze the data needed for this type of planning.
- Operational planning is the development of specific goals and objectives for the entity as a whole and its individual departments, the formulation of a plan of attack to accomplish the goals and objectives, and the written documentation of the goals and objectives and the plan of attack.

LO2 Discuss the budgeting process and summarize its advantages. Define the key elements of effective budgeting. (p. 987)

- Budgeting is the process of developing a formal, written operational plan that presents management's planned actions in financial terms.

■ Two budgets result from the budgeting process: the annual operating budget that covers a 1-year budget period and the capital expenditures budget that covers a multiple-year budget period.

■ Budgets represent a plan for accomplishing goals and objectives. They provide operational guidance to the department managers so they make decisions that are consistent with decisions made in other departments.

■ Because the budget is used as a basis for evaluating performance, it serves as a target for individual managers.

■ A budget director should be identified to organize the budgeting process, communicate with people involved in budgeting, and monitor the budgeting process.

■ A budget committee, consisting of representatives from all major areas of the company, should provide general guidance to the budgeting process and evaluate proposed budget segments for reasonableness.

■ Participative budgeting requires that all departments participate in the development and refinement of the budget amounts so that departmental managers will accept the budget as a reasonable standard of performance.

■ The future time span, for which the budget is prepared, known as the budget period, varies according to the activity involved.

■ The use of budgets to manage and control a firm's activities is known as budgetary control.

■ Zero-base budgeting requires budget preparers to start at a zero level for every item in the budget and justify every dollar, not just the increases or decreases.

Define the components of the master budget and illustrate the interrelationships of the individual budgets that comprise the master budget. (p. 991)   **LO3**

■ The master budget for a manufacturing firm consists of at least the following individual budgets:
  Sales budget
  Production budget
  Direct material budget
  Direct labor budget
  Manufacturing overhead budget
  Selling and administrative expense budget
  Capital expenditures budget
  Cash budget
  Budgeted income statement
  Budgeted balance sheet
  Budgeted statement of cash flows

■ The individual budgets must be prepared in a specific sequence, beginning with the sales budget, to properly reflect the interrelationships among the individual budgets.

Prepare individual budgets for a manufacturing and a service company, including the cash budget. (p. 992)   **LO4**

■ The sales budget is based on the sales forecast.

■ The production budget determines the number of units of each product that should be manufactured during the budget period.

■ The direct material budget displays the amount of each direct material item that should be purchased to supply the budgeted production.

■ The direct labor budget presents the amount of direct labor, by department, that is required to accomplish the budgeted production.

■ The manufacturing overhead budget determines, for each factory department, the amount of variable overhead and the amount of fixed overhead needed to complete the budgeted production.

■ The selling and administrative expense budget accumulates the variable and fixed selling and administrative expenses for the entity. Some of the expenses may vary with sales; others may vary with production.

■ The capital expenditures budget presents the planned expenditures for property, plant, and equipment over an extended budget period, possibly 5 years.

■ The cash budget, usually segmented by month, presents all of the cash receipts and cash disbursements planned for the budget period.

- Much of the information needed to prepare the cash budget comes from previously prepared budgets. However, additional schedules and worksheets are usually needed to place required information in proper form.
- Cash collected from customers from prior credit sales needs careful analysis to take into account timing, cash discounts, and uncollectible accounts.

LO5 **Prepare budgeted financial statements. (p. 1001)**

- The budgeted income statement is prepared for the budget period.
- The budgeted balance sheet is prepared as of the ending date of the budget period.
- The budgeted statement of cash flows is prepared for the budget period, based primarily on data from the cash budget.

KEY TERMS

Budget (p. 987)

Budgetary control (p. 988)

Budget committee (p. 989)

Budget director (p. 989)

Budgeted balance sheet (p. 1002)

Budgeted income statement (p. 1001)

Budgeted statement of cash flows (p. 1003)

Budgeting (p. 987)

Budget period (p. 989)

Capital expenditures budget (p. 997)

Cash budget (p. 998)

Continuous budgeting (p. 990)

Direct labor budget (p. 995)

Direct material budget (p. 994)

Just-in-time inventory (p. 993)

Manufacturing overhead budget (p. 996)

Master budget (p. 991)

Operational planning (p. 986)

Participative budgeting (p. 989)

Planning horizon (p. 984)

Production budget (p. 993)

Safety stock (p. 993)

Sales budget (p. 992)

Sales forecast (p. 992)

Selling and administrative expense budget (p. 997)

Strategic planning (p. 985)

Strengths, weaknesses, opportunities, and threats (SWOT) analysis (p. 986)

Zero-base budgeting (p. 990)

Assignments with the 🔵 logo in the margin are available in BusinessCourse.
See the Preface of the book for details.

SELF-STUDY QUESTIONS

(Answers to Self-Study Questions are at the end of this chapter.)

LO2 **1. If a company uses participative budgeting, which group should prepare the initial set of budget dollar amounts?**

    a. Budget committee   *c.* Top management

    b. Operating department managers   *d.* Accounting department

LO4 **2. Which of the following budgets will typically have the longest budget period?**

    a. Capital expenditures budget   *c.* Sales budget

    b. Cash budget   *d.* Budgeted income statement

LO3 **3. Which of the following budgets should be prepared before all of the others listed below?**

    a. Cash budget   *c.* Manufacturing overhead budget

    b. Direct materials budget   *d.* Production budget

LO4 **4. If the beginning inventory of a company that manufactures only one product is 5,000 units, the sales forecast is 34,000 units sold, and the desired ending inventory is 6,000 units, how many units should be produced?**

    a. 35,000   *c.* 40,000

    b. 33,000   *d.* 39,000

5. Smith Company started business on September 1. Smith had credit sales of $200,000 in September and $300,000 in October. The pattern for collection of cash from customers is expected to be 40% in the month of sale (subject to a 2% cash discount), 50% in the month following the month of sale, and 7% in the second month following the month of sale, with 3% uncollectible. How much cash did Smith Company receive from customers on account during October?   **LO4**
    a. $120,000   *c.* $217,600
    b. $117,600   *d.* $220,000

QUESTIONS

1. What is a planning horizon? How will it differ between strategic planning and operational planning?   **LO1**
2. Describe strategic planning.   **LO1**
3. Describe operational planning.   **LO1**
4. Define budgeting.   **LO2**
5. List and briefly explain four advantages of budgeting.   **LO2**
6. Describe the budget committee.   **LO2**
7. Why is participative budgeting important to the success of the budgeting process?   **LO2**
8. What is meant by continuous budgeting?   **LO2**
9. What is the master budget? List, in the order of preparation, the various budgets that the master budget for a small manufacturing company might comprise.   **LO3**
10. Why do most firms prepare the sales budget first?   **LO3**
11. Beginning finished goods inventory is 10,000 units, anticipated sales volume is 60,000 units, and the desired ending finished goods inventory is 12,000 units. What number of units should be produced?   **LO4**
12. Three pounds of material R (costing $5 per pound) and 4 pounds of material S (costing $7 per pound) are required to make one unit of product T. If management plans to increase the inventory of material R by 500 pounds and reduce the inventory of material S by 800 pounds during a period when 3,000 units of product T are to be produced, what are the budgeted purchase costs of material R and material S?   **LO4**
13. Carroll Manufacturing Company has two labor operations in its factory: machining and assembly. Workers in the machining department are paid $14 per hour; workers in the assembly department are paid $12 per hour. During January, 10,000 units of product A and 20,000 units of product B are to be manufactured. Each unit of A requires 1 hour of machining and 2 hours of assembly; each unit of B requires 3 hours of machining and 1 hour of assembly. What is the total direct labor budget for January?   **LO4**
14. Johnson Manufacturing Company has budgeted 30,000 direct labor hours for March. The budgeted cost formula for monthly manufacturing overhead is $4 per direct labor hour plus $65,000. What is the manufacturing overhead budget for March?   **LO4**
15. A company collects cash from its credit sales in the following pattern: 30% in the month of sale, 50% in the month following the month of sale, and 20% in the second month following the month of sale. What percentage of which months' credit sales will be collected during October?   **LO4**
16. What are the three major groupings of cash flows in the budgeted statement of cash flows?   **LO4**

EXERCISES—SET A

E22-1A. Budgeting Inventories For each independent situation below, determine the amounts indicated by the question marks: **LO4**

	A	B	C	D
Beginning inventory	10,000	?	7,000	?
Produced	40,000	27,000	?	60,000
Available	?	?	26,000	64,000
Sold	45,000	28,000	?	?
Ending inventory	?	10,000	6,000	2,000

LO4 **E22-2A. Budget Preparation** Collins Company is preparing its master budget for April. Use the given estimates to determine the amounts necessary for each of the following requirements. (Estimates may be related to more than one requirement.)

    a. What should total sales revenue be if territories A and B estimate sales of 10,000 and 12,000 units, respectively, and the unit selling price is $40?

    b. If the beginning finished goods inventory is an estimated 2,000 units and the desired ending inventory is 3,000 units, how many units should be produced?

    c. What dollar amount of material should be purchased at $4 per pound if each unit of product requires 3 pounds and beginning and ending materials inventories should be 5,000 and 4,000 pounds, respectively?

    d. How much direct labor cost should be incurred if each unit produced requires 1.5 hours at an hourly rate of $13?

    e. How much manufacturing overhead should be incurred if fixed manufacturing overhead is $50,000 and variable manufacturing overhead is $2.50 per direct labor hour?

LO4 **E22-3A. Budget Preparation** Westport Company is preparing its master budget for May. Use the estimates provided to determine the amounts necessary for each of the following requirements. (Estimates may be related to more than one requirement.)

    a. What should total sales revenue be if territories E and W estimate sales of 50,000 and 100,000 units, respectively, and the unit selling price is $27?

    b. If the beginning finished goods inventory is an estimated 7,000 units and the desired ending inventory is 6,000 units, how many units should be produced?

    c. What dollar amount of material should be purchased at $2 per pound if each unit of product requires 2.5 pounds and beginning and ending materials inventories should be 13,500 and 12,000 pounds, respectively?

    d. How much direct labor cost should be incurred if each unit produced requires 0.5 hours at an hourly rate of $11?

    e. How much manufacturing overhead should be incurred if fixed manufacturing overhead is $45,000 and variable manufacturing overhead is $1.30 per direct labor hour?

LO4 **E22-4A. Budgeting Cash Collections** Spencer Consulting, which invoices its clients on terms 2/10, n/30, had credit sales for May and June of $70,000 and $80,000, respectively. Analysis of Spencer's operations indicates that the pattern of customers' payments on account is as follows (percentages are of total monthly credit sales):

	Receiving Discount	Beyond Discount Period	Totals
In month of sale	50%	20%	70%
In month following sale.	15%	10%	25%
Uncollectible accounts, returns, and allowances.			5%
			$100%

Determine the estimated cash collected on customers' accounts in June.

LO4 **E22-5A. Budgeting Cash Flow** The following various elements relate to Whitfield, Inc.'s cash budget for April of the current year. For each item, determine the amount of cash that Whitfield should receive or pay in April.

    a. At $28 each, unit sales are 5,000 and 6,000 for March and April, respectively. Total sales are typically 40% for cash and 60% on credit; 30% of credit sales are collected in the month of sale, with the balance collected in the following month. Uncollectible accounts are negligible.

    b. Merchandise purchases were $45,000 and $78,000 for March and April, respectively. Typically, 20% of total purchases are paid for in the month of purchase with a 5% cash discount. The balance of purchases is paid for (without discount) in the following month.

    c. Fixed administrative expenses, which total $11,000 per month, are paid in the month incurred. Variable administrative expenses amount to 20% of total monthly sales revenue, one-half of which is paid in the month incurred, with the balance paid in the following month.

d. A store asset originally costing $8,000, on which $6,000 depreciation has been taken, is sold for cash at a loss of $400.

E22-6A. Prepare Cash Budget For 3 Months Brewster Corporation expects the following cash receipts and disbursements during the first quarter of 2016 (receipts exclude new borrowings and disbursements exclude interest payments on borrowings since January 1, 2016):

LO4

	January	February	March
Cash receipts	$260,000	$280,000	$250,000
Cash disbursements	240,000	320,000	260,000

The expected cash balance at January 1, 2016, is $42,000. Brewster wants to maintain a cash balance at the end of each month of at least $40,000. Short-term borrowings at 1% interest per month will be used to accomplish this, if necessary. Borrowings (in multiples of $1,000) will be made at the beginning of the month in which they are needed, with interest for that month paid at the end of the month. Prepare a cash budget for the quarter ended March 31, 2016.

E22-7A. Prepare Cash Budget From Budgeted Transactions Prepare a cash budget for the month ended May 31, 2016. Campton Company anticipates a cash balance of $84,000 on May 1, 2016. The following budgeted transactions for May 2016 present data related to anticipated cash receipts and cash disbursements:

LO4

SERVICE AND MERCHANDISING

1. For May, budgeted cash sales are $60,000 and budgeted credit sales are $500,000. (Credit sales for April were $450,000.) In the month of sale, 40% of credit sales are collected, with the balance collected in the month following sale.
2. Budgeted merchandise purchases for May are $280,000. (Merchandise purchases in April were $240,000.) In the month of purchase, 70% of merchandise purchases are paid for, and the balance is paid for in the following month.
3. Budgeted cash disbursements for salaries and operating expenses for May total $165,000.
4. During May, $25,000 of principal repayment and $4,000 of interest payment are due to the bank.
5. A $20,000 income tax deposit is due to the federal government during May.
6. A new delivery truck will be purchased during May for $6,000 cash and an $8,000 note payable. Depreciation for May will be $500.

Prepare a cash budget for Campton Company for the month of May 2016.

EXERCISES—SET B

E22-1B. Budgeting Inventories For each independent situation below, determine the amounts indicated by the question marks.

LO4

Number of Units	A	B	C	D
Beginning inventory	9,000	?	6,000	?
Produced	15,000	27,000	?	75,000
Available.	?	?	46,000	85,000
Sold	18,000	28,000	?	?
Ending inventory.	?	3,000	8,000	11,000

E22-2B. Budget Preparation Reeves Company is preparing its master budget for July. Use the given estimates to determine the amounts necessary for each of the following requirements. (Estimates may be related to more than one requirement.)

LO4

a. What should total sales revenue be if territories A and B estimate sales of 8,000 and 20,000 units, respectively, and the unit selling price is $50?

b. If the beginning finished goods inventory is an estimated 1,500 units and the desired ending inventory is 2,500 units, how many units should be produced?

  c. What dollar amount of material should be purchased at $3 per pound if each unit of product requires 2 pounds and beginning and ending materials inventories should be 4,000 and 3,000 pounds, respectively?

  d. How much direct labor cost should be incurred if each unit produced requires 1.5 hours at an hourly rate of $14?

  e. How much manufacturing overhead should be incurred if fixed manufacturing overhead is $60,000 and variable manufacturing overhead is $1.50 per direct labor hour?

LO4 **E22-3B. Budget Preparation** Tuttle Company is preparing its master budget for November. Use the estimates provided to determine the necessary amounts for each of the following requirements. (Estimates may be related to more than one requirement.)

  a. What should total sales revenue be if territories N and S estimate sales of 40,000 and 80,000 units, respectively and the unit selling price is $18?

  b. If the beginning finished goods inventory is an estimated 6,000 units and the desired ending inventory is 5,000 units, how many units should be produced?

  c. What dollar amount of material should be purchased at $2 per pound if each unit of product requires 3 pounds and beginning and ending materials inventories should be 12,000 and 10,000 pounds, respectively?

  d. How much direct labor cost should be incurred if each unit produced requires 0.5 hours at an hourly rate of $10?

  e. How much manufacturing overhead should be incurred if fixed manufacturing overhead is $32,000 and variable manufacturing overhead is $1 per direct labor hour?

LO4 **E22-4B. Budgeting Cash Collections** Lowell Consulting, which sells on terms 2/10, n/30, had credit sales for

March and April of $60,000 and $50,000, respectively. Analysis of Lowell's operations indicates that the pattern of customers' payments on account is as follows (percentages are of total monthly credit sales):

	Receiving Discount	Beyond Discount Period	Totals
In month of sale	40%	20%	60%
In month following sale.	15%	20%	35%
Uncollectible accounts, returns, and allowances.			5%
			100%

Determine the estimated cash collected on customers' accounts in April.

LO4 **E22-5B. Budgeting Cash Flow** The following various elements relate to Murphy, Inc.'s cash budget for

October of the current year. For each item, determine the amount of cash that Murphy should receive or pay in October.

  a. At $24 each, unit sales are 10,000 and 12,000 for September and October, respectively. Total sales are typically 30% for cash and 70% on credit; 40% of credit sales are collected in the month of sale, with the balance collected in the following month. Uncollectible accounts are negligible.

  b. Merchandise purchases were $43,000 and $76,000 for September and October, respectively. Typically, 20% of total purchases are paid for in the month of purchase with a 5% cash discount. The balance of purchases is paid for (without discount) in the following month.

  c. Fixed administrative expenses, which total $15,000 per month, are paid in the month incurred. Variable administrative expenses amount to 20% of total monthly sales revenue, 65% of which is paid in the month incurred, with the balance paid in the following month.

  d. Fixed selling expenses, which total $4,200 per month, are paid in the month incurred. Variable selling expenses, which are 5% of total sales revenue, are paid in the month following their incurrence.

LO4 **E22-6B. Prepare Cash Budget For 3 Months** Windsor Corporation expects the following cash receipts and disbursements during the first quarter of 2016 (receipts exclude new borrowings and disbursements exclude interest payments on borrowings since January 1, 2016):

	January	February	March
Cash receipts	$430,000	$440,000	$400,000
Cash disbursements	390,000	520,000	420,000

The expected cash balance at January 1, 2016, is $75,000. Windsor wants to maintain a cash balance at the end of each month of at least $60,000. Short-term borrowings at 1% interest per month will be used to accomplish this, if necessary. Borrowings (in multiples of $1,000) will be made at the beginning of the month in which they are needed, with interest for that month paid at the end of the month.

Prepare a cash budget for the quarter ended March 31, 2016.

E22-7B. Prepare Cash Budget From Budgeted Transactions McCall Company anticipates a cash balance of $100,000 on July 1, 2016. The following budgeted transactions for July 2016 present data related to anticipated cash receipts and cash disbursements: LO4

1. For July, budgeted cash sales are $72,000 and budgeted credit sales are $600,000. (Credit sales for June were $550,000.) In the month of sale, 40% of credit sales are collected, with the balance collected in the month following sale.

2. Budgeted merchandise purchases for July are $340,000. (Merchandise purchases in June were $290,000.) In the month of purchase, 70% of merchandise purchases are paid for, and the balance is paid for in the following month.

3. Budgeted cash disbursements for salaries and operating expenses for July total $200,000.

4. During July, $30,000 of principal repayment and $5,000 of interest payment are due to the bank.

5. A $25,000 income tax deposit is due to the federal government during July.

6. A new delivery truck will be purchased during July for $7,000 cash and a $10,000 note payable. Depreciation for July will be $600.

Prepare a cash budget for McCall Company for the month of July 2016.

PROBLEMS—SET A

P22-1A. Budgeting Cash Whitney's, Inc., sells on terms of 5% discount for "cash and carry" or 2/10, n/30 and estimates its total sales for the second calendar quarter of next year as follows: April, $300,000; May, $240,000; and June, $360,000. An analysis of operations indicates the following customer collection patterns: LO4

	Portions of Total Sales
In month of sale:	
Cash at time of sale	25%
On account, during discount period.	15%
On account, after discount period	10%
In month following sale:	
On account, during discount period.	20%
On account, after discount period	10%
In second month following sale:	
On account, after discount period	15%
Average portion uncollectible.	5%
	100%

Prepare an estimate of the cash to be collected from customers during June.

P22-2A. Preparation of Individual Budgets During the first calendar quarter of 2016, Clinton Corporation is planning to manufacture a new product and introduce it in two regions. Market research indicates that sales will be 6,000 units in the urban region at a unit price of $53 and 5,000 units in the rural region at $48 each. Because the sales manager expects the product to catch on, he has asked for production sufficient to generate a 4,000-unit ending inventory. The production manager has furnished the following estimates related to manufacturing costs and operating expenses: LO4

	Variable (per unit)	Fixed (total)
Manufacturing costs:		
Direct material:		
A (4 lb. @ $3.15/lb.)...	$12.60	—
B (2 lb. @ $4.65/lb.)..	9.30	—
Direct labor (0.5 hr. per unit)......................................	7.50	—
Manufacturing overhead:		
Depreciation	—	$ 7,650
Factory supplies	0.90	4,500
Supervisory salaries	—	28,800
Other...	0.75	22,950
Operating expenses:		
Selling:		
Advertising	—	22,500
Sales salaries and commissions*.............................	1.50	15,000
Other*..	0.90	3,000
Administrative:		
Office salaries	—	2,700
Supplies	0.15	1,050
Other...	0.08	1,950

*Varies per unit sold, not per unit produced.

Required

a. Assuming that the desired ending inventories of materials A and B are 4,000 and 6,000 pounds, respectively, and that work-in-process inventories are immaterial, prepare budgets for the calendar quarter in which the new product will be introduced for each of the following operating factors:

1. Total sales
2. Production
3. Material purchases cost
4. Direct labor costs
5. Manufacturing overhead costs
6. Selling and administrative expenses

b. Using data generated in requirement (a), prepare a budgeted income statement for the calendar quarter. Assume an overall effective income tax rate of 30%.

LO4   **P22-3A. Monthly Cash Budget** Grove, Inc. is a wholesaler for its only product, deluxe wireless electric drills, which sell for $90 each and cost Grove $54 each. On December 1, 2016, Grove's management requested a cash budget for December. The following selected account balances at November 30, 2016, were gathered by the accounting department:

Cash...	$ 135,000
Marketable securities (at cost)...	210,000
Accounts receivable (all trade)...	1,710,000
Inventories (15,000 units)...	810,000
Operating expenses payable	140,400
Accounts payable (all merchandise)....................................	583,200
Note payable (due 12/31/2016)	393,000

Actual sales for the months of October and November were 20,000 and 30,000 units, respectively. Projected unit sales for December and January are 50,000 and 40,000, respectively. Experience indicates that 50% of sales should be collected in the month of sale, 30% in the month following sale, and the balance in the second month following sale. Uncollectible accounts, returns, and allowances are negligible.

Planned purchases should provide ending inventories equal to 30% of next month's unit sales volume. Approximately 70% of the purchases are paid for in the month of purchase and the balance in the following month.

Monthly operating expenses are budgeted at $8.10 per unit sold plus a fixed amount of $189,000 including depreciation of $81,000. Except for depreciation, 60% of operating expenses are paid in the month incurred and the balance in the following month. Interest expense is included in operating expenses.

Special anticipated year-end transactions include the following:

1. Declaration of a $22,500 cash dividend to be paid 2 weeks after the December 20 date of record.
2. Sale of one-half of the marketable securities held on November 30; a gain of $21,000 is anticipated.
3. Pay off the note payable due December 31, 2016.
4. Trade-in of an old computer originally costing $675,000 and now having accumulated depreciation of $540,000 at a gain of $157,500 on a new computer costing $1,350,000. Sufficient cash will be paid at the time of trade-in so that only 50% of the total price will have to be financed.
5. Grove's treasurer has a policy of maintaining a minimum month-end cash balance of $135,000 but wants to raise this to $225,000 at December 31. She has a standing arrangement with the bank to borrow any amount up to a limit of $450,000.

Required
Prepare a cash budget for Grove, Inc., for December 2016.

P22-4A. Budgeting Production and Purchases and Just-In-Time Materials Inventory Hancock Manufacturing, Inc. is preparing budgets for the third quarter of 2016. Hancock produces only one product in its factory. This product requires 5 pounds of material B, 2 pounds of material G, and a component, K, that is purchased from another manufacturer. Hancock operates on a just-in-time basis for material B. As a result, Hancock maintains no inventory of material B. On July 1, 2016, the inventory of material G is expected to be 2,000 pounds and the inventory of component K is expected to be 500 units. Hancock wants the inventories of G and K at September 30, 2016, to be 20% less than the inventories at July 1, 2016. The inventory of finished products at June 30, 2016, is expected to be 1,000 units; the desired inventory at September 30, 2016, is 3,000 units to allow a buildup for heavy sales in the fourth quarter. The sales forecast for the third quarter is 12,000 units at $300 each. Budgeted purchase costs are $10 per pound for B, $7 per pound for G, and $40 per component for K.

LO5

Required
a. Prepare the production budget for Hancock Manufacturing, Inc., for the third quarter of 2016.
b. Prepare the direct material budget for Hancock Manufacturing, Inc., for the third quarter of 2016.

P22-5A. Prepare and Evaluate Budgeted Income Statement Fairfield Stores, a retailer in a shopping mall, prepared the following income statement for its operations for the month just ended:

LO4

SERVICE AND MERCHANDISING

FAIRFIELD STORES		
Income Statement		
for the Month Ended April 30, 2016		
Sales.		$500,000
Cost of goods sold.		240,000
Gross profit.		$260,000
Operating expenses:		
Sales commissions expense	$25,000	
Advertising expense	60,000	
Lease expense	20,000	
Depreciation expense.	10,000	
Salaries expense.	30,000	
Other operating expenses	15,000	160,000
Income before income taxes		$100,000
Income tax expense.		30,000
Net income.		$ 70,000

Sales commissions were 5% of sales. Income taxes were 30% of income before income taxes. Both should continue at the same rate for the remainder of the year.

Fairfield Stores is preparing the budget for the month of May 2016. If no basic changes are made, Fairfield management expects that the income statement would be virtually identical to the one for April. However, Fairfield's management has decided to make some changes in the operations. The plans include the following:

1. Increase advertising expense by 40%.
2. Decrease all selling prices by 10%.
3. Increase the number of units sold by 25% as a result of the first two changes.

Required

a. Prepare a budgeted income statement for the month of May 2016. (Round all amounts on the income statement to the nearest dollar.)

b. Should Fairfield's management make the planned changes?

PROBLEMS—SET B

LO4 **P22-1B. Budgeting Cash** Judson, Inc., sells on terms of 5% discount for "cash and carry" or 2/10, n/30 and estimates its total sales for the second calendar quarter of next year as follows: July, $225,000; August, $150,000; and September, $180,000. An analysis of operations indicates the following customer collection patterns:

	Portions of Total Sales
In month of sale:	
Cash at time of sale	30%
On account, during discount period.	20%
On account, after discount period	10%
In month following sale:	
On account, during discount period.	20%
On account, after discount period	10%
In second month following sale:	
On account, after discount period	7%
Average portion uncollectible.	3%
	100%

Required

Prepare an estimate of the cash to be collected from customers during September.

LO4 **P22-2B. Preparation of Individual Budgets** During the first calendar quarter of 2016, Williams Corporation is planning to manufacture a new product and introduce it in two regions. Market research indicates that sales will be 8,000 units in the urban region at a unit price of $65 and 6,000 units in the rural region at $55 each. Because the sales manager expects the product to catch on, she has asked for production sufficient to generate a 4,000-unit ending inventory. The production manager has furnished the following estimates related to manufacturing costs and operating expenses:

	Variable (per unit)	Fixed (total)
Manufacturing costs:		
Direct material:		
A (2 lb. @ $2.50/lb.).	$ 5	—
B (5 lb. @ $1.40/lb.).	7	—
Direct labor (2 hrs. per unit)	10	—
Manufacturing overhead:		
Depreciation	—	$22,500
Factory supplies	0.55	2,500
Supervisory salaries	—	16,250
Other	0.65	9,200
Operating expenses:		
Selling:		
Advertising	—	12,500
Sales salaries and commissions*	1.25	20,000
Other*	0.50	4,200
Administrative:		
Office salaries	—	15,000
Supplies	0.40	1,200
Other.	0.25	5,000

*Varies per unit sold, not per unit produced.

Required

a. Assuming that the desired ending inventories of materials A and B are 4,000 and 20,000 pounds, respectively, and that work-in-process inventories are immaterial, prepare budgets for the calendar quarter in which the new product will be introduced for each of the following operating factors:

1. Total sales
2. Production
3. Material purchases cost
4. Direct labor costs
5. Manufacturing overhead costs
6. Selling and administrative expenses

b. Using data generated in requirement (a), prepare a budgeted income statement for the calendar quarter. Assume an overall effective income tax rate of 35%. (Round income statement amounts to nearest dollar.)

P22-3B. Monthly Cash Budget Sutter, Inc. is a wholesaler for its only product, deluxe wireless rechargeable electric shavers, which sell for $70 each and cost Sutter $48 each. On June 1, 2016, Sutter's management requested a cash budget for June. The following selected account balances at May 31, 2016, were gathered by the accounting department: **LO5**

Cash.	$ 56,000
Marketable securities (at cost)	160,000
Accounts receivable (all trade)	2,170,000
Inventories (12,000 units)	576,000
Operating expenses payable	196,800
Accounts payable (all merchandise).	902,400
Note payable	600,000

Actual sales for April and May were 30,000 and 50,000 units, respectively. Projected unit sales for June and July are 40,000 and 20,000, respectively. Experience indicates that 50% of sales should be collected in the month of sale, 30% in the month following sale, and the balance in the second month following sale. Uncollectible accounts, returns, and allowances are negligible.

Planned purchases should provide ending inventories equal to 30% of next month's unit sales volume. Approximately 60% of the purchases are paid for in the month of purchase and the balance in the following month.

Monthly operating expenses are budgeted at $9.60 per unit sold plus a fixed amount of $288,000 including depreciation of $112,000. Except for depreciation, 70% of operating expenses are paid in the month incurred and the balance in the following month. Interest expense is included in operating expenses.

Special anticipated June transactions include the following:

1. Declaration of a $60,000 cash dividend to be paid 2 weeks after the June 20 date of record.
2. Sale of all but $40,000 of the marketable securities held on May 31; a gain of $18,000 is anticipated.
3. Payment of $50,000 installment on the note payable.
4. Trade-in of an old company plane originally costing $300,000 and now having accumulated depreciation of $200,000 at a gain of $160,000 on a new plane costing $2,000,000. Sufficient cash will be paid at the time of trade-in so that only 50% of the total price will have to be financed.
5. Sutter's treasurer has a policy of maintaining a minimum month-end cash balance of $40,000 and has a standing arrangement with the bank to borrow any amount up to a limit of $400,000.

Required
Prepare a cash budget for Sutter, Inc., for June 2016.

P22-4B. Budgeting Production and Purchases and Just-In-Time Materials Inventory Central Manufacturing, Inc. is preparing budgets for the second quarter of 2016. Central produces only one product in its factory. This product requires 4 pounds of material C, 3 pounds of material H, and a component, M, that is purchased from another manufacturer. Central operates on a just-in-time basis for material C. As a result, Central maintains no inventory of material C. On April 1, 2016, the inventory of material H is expected to be 3,000 pounds and the inventory of component M is expected to be 600 units. Central wants the inventories of H and M at June 30, 2016, to be 20% less than the inventories at April 1, 2016. The inventory of finished products at March 31, 2016, is expected to be 2,000 units; the desired inventory at June 30, 2016, is 4,000 units to allow a buildup for heavy sales **LO4**

in the third quarter. The sales forecast for the second quarter is 14,000 units at $200 each. Budgeted purchase costs are $5 per pound for C, $6 per pound for H, and $50 per component for M.

Required

a. Prepare the production budget for the second quarter of 2016.

b. Prepare the direct material budget for the second quarter of 2016.

LO5

SERVICE AND MERCHANDISING

P22-5B. Prepare and Evaluate Budgeted Income Statement Medford Stores, a retailer in a shopping mall, prepared the following income statement for its operations for the month just ended:

MEDFORD STORES Income Statement for the Month Ended April 30, 2016		
Sales.		$700,000
Cost of goods sold.		330,000
Gross profit.		$370,000
Operating expenses:		
Sales commissions expense	$35,000	
Advertising expense.	90,000	
Lease expense	50,000	
Depreciation expense.	20,000	
Salaries expense.	40,000	
Other operating expenses	25,000	260,000
Income before income taxes		$110,000
Income tax expense.		33,000
Net income.		$ 77,000

Sales commissions were 5% of sales. Income taxes were 30% of income before income taxes. Both should continue at the same rate for the remainder of the year.

Medford Stores is preparing the budget for the month of May 2016. If no basic changes are made, Medford's management expects that the income statement would be virtually identical to the one for April. However, Medford's management has decided to make some changes in the operations. The plans include the following:

1. Increase advertising expense by 30%.
2. Decrease all selling prices by 10%.
3. Increase the number of units sold by 20% as a result of the first two changes.

Required

a. Prepare a budgeted income statement for the month of May 2016. (Round all amounts on the income statement to the nearest dollar.)

b. Should Medford's management make the planned changes?

CERTIFIED MANAGEMENT ACCOUNTANT (CMA®) EXAM SAMPLE QUESTIONS

CMA22-1. All of the following are advantages of the use of budgets in a management control system, *except* that budgets

a. force management planning.

b. provide performance criteria.

c. promote communication and coordination within the organization.

d. limit unauthorized expenditures.

CMA22-2. Which one of the following items would most likely cause the planning and budgeting system to fail?

a. Lack of historical financial data

b. Lack of input from several levels of management

c. Lack of top management support

d. Lack of adherence to rigid budgets during the year

CMA22-3. Which one of the following statements concerning approaches for the budget development process is **correct**?

    a. The authoritative approach to budgeting discourages strict adherence to strategic organizational goals.

    b. To prevent ambiguity, once departmental budgeted goals have been developed, they should remain fixed even if the sales forecast upon which they are based proves to be wrong in the middle of the fiscal year.

    c. With the information technology available, the role of budgets as an organizational communication device has declined.

    d. Because department managers have the most detailed knowledge about organizational operations, they should use this information as the building blocks of the operating budget.

CMA22-4. What would be the correct chronological order of preparation for the following budgets?

    I. Cost of goods sold budget.

    II. Production budget.

    III. Purchases budget.

    IV. Administrative budget.

    a. I, II, III, IV

    b. III, II, IV, I.

    c. IV, II, III, I.

    d. II, III, I, IV.

CMA22-5. Hannon Retailing Company prices its products by adding 30% to its cost. Hannon anticipates sales of $715,000 in July, $728,000 in August, and $624,000 in September. Hannon's policy is to have on hand enough inventory at the end of the month to cover 25% of the next month's sales. What will be the cost of the inventory that Hannon should budget for purchase in August?

    a. $509,600

    b. $540,000

    c. $560,000

    d. $680,000

EXTENDING YOUR KNOWLEDGE

EYK22-1. **Business Decision Case** The sales department of Donovan Manufacturing, Inc. has completed the following sales forecast for the months of January through March 2016 for its only two products: 50,000 units of J to be sold at $90 each and 30,000 units of K to be sold at $70 each. The desired unit inventories at March 31, 2016, are 10% of the next quarter's unit sales forecast, which are 60,000 units of J and 30,000 units of K. The January 1, 2016, unit inventories were 5,000 units of J and 2,000 units of K.

    Each unit of J requires 3 pounds of material A and 2 pounds of material B for its manufacture; K requires 2 pounds of A and 4 pounds of B. The purchase cost of A is $9 per pound and the purchase cost of B is $5 per pound. Materials A and B on hand at January 1, 2016, were 19,000 pounds of A and 7,000 pounds of B. Desired inventories at March 31, 2016, are 14,000 pounds of A and 8,000 pounds of B.

    Each unit of J requires 0.5 hour of direct labor in the factory; each unit of K requires 1.0 hour of direct labor. The average hourly rate for direct labor is $12 per hour. Estimated manufacturing

LO4

overhead cost is $6 per direct labor hour plus $90,000 per month. Selling and administrative expenses are estimated to be 10% of sales revenue plus $180,000 per month.

Cash sales for the first quarter are estimated to be $300,000 per month. It is forecast that 30% of the credit sales for the quarter ended March 31, 2016, will occur in January, 30% in February, and 40% in March. Of credit sales (December through March), 40% will be collected as cash in the month of sale and 55% will be collected in the following month. The remainder will be uncollectible. Cash collected in January 2016 from December 2015 sales will be $1,050,000.

The January 1, 2016, cash balance was $70,000. The minimum acceptable cash balance at the end of each month is $60,000. Short-term borrowings (6-month term) are made in multiples of $10,000. Interest is charged at the rate of 1% per month on short-term borrowings. The first interest payment is made the month following the borrowing. Cash disbursements (excluding interest on short-term borrowings) are estimated as follows:

	January	February	March
Manufacturing costs.	$1,500,000	$1,300,000	$1,400,000
Selling and administrative expenses	390,000	410,000	400,000
Interest expense.	90,000	90,000	90,000
Income tax payment.	0	0	210,000
Capital expenditures	124,000	110,000	50,000
Cash dividends.	300,000	0	0

Required

a. Prepare the sales budget for the quarter ended March 31, 2016.
b. Prepare the production budget for the quarter ended March 31, 2016.
c. Prepare the direct material budget for the quarter ended March 31, 2016.
d. Prepare the direct labor budget for the quarter ended March 31, 2016.
e. Prepare the manufacturing overhead budget for the quarter ended March 31, 2016.
f. Prepare the selling and administrative expense budget for the quarter ended March 31, 2016.
g. Prepare a schedule of cash collected from customers for the quarter ended March 31, 2016.
h. Prepare the cash budget for the quarter ended March 31, 2016.

LO3

SERVICE AND
MERCHANDISING

EYK22-2. Ethics Case Steve Waller is the corporate accounting manager for Giant Video Stores. As part of the budgeting process for the entire corporation, he has asked the manager of each video store to prepare a store master budget.

The manager of one of the largest stores, Jeff Miller, decides to understate the sales budget and overstate all the budgets related to expenses. Jeff believes this is a more conservative approach than using the estimated numbers he honestly believes will be achieved for the year. He also thinks that the corporate office will look more favorably on his store's actual achievements when they are subsequently compared to this budget.

Jeff has asked Lisa Dorton, his assistant manager, to review the budget before it is submitted. Lisa is aware of the real estimates that Jeff made.

Required

What is the impact of Jeff Miller's budget for the corporation? What ethical issues face Lisa Dorton?

ANSWERS TO SELF-STUDY QUESTIONS:

1. b, (pp. 989–990) 2. a, (pp. 997–998) 3. d, (pp. 991–992) 4. a, (pp. 993–994) 5. c, (p. 999)

DECISION TIME SOLUTION

Solution 22.1

1. It requires management to give priority to planning.
2. It provides a way of formalizing a plan.
3. It provides a benchmark for evaluation.
4. It serves as a motivating factor.
5. It coordinates the entire organization.

YOUR TURN! SOLUTIONS

Solution 22.1

Threats might include the emergence of online retailers such as Amazon.com, increased minimum wages, intense competition from Walmart and other similar retailers, and an economic slowdown in the United States.

Solution 22.2

Depreciation, depletion, amortization, and uncollectible accounts expense

Standard Costing and Variance Analysis

PAST

Chapter 22 discussed the budgeting process, the components of the master budget and interrelationships of the individual budgets, and presented an illustration of a budget for a manufacturer and a service company.

PRESENT

Chapter 23 defines standard costs and standard cost variances: direct material, direct labor, and variable overhead variances.

FUTURE

Chapter 24 introduces flexible budgets and performance evaluation of business segments. In addition, it explores both performance and variance analysis.

LEARNING OBJECTIVES

1. **Define** standard costs and **describe** their use in standard cost accounting. *(p. 1026)*

2. **Develop** an overall understanding of the determination of standard costs for direct material, direct labor, and variable overhead. *(p. 1028)*

3. **Understand** and **calculate** direct materials variances. *(p. 1032)*

4. **Understand** and **calculate** direct labor variances. *(p. 1036)*

5. **Understand** and **calculate** variable overhead variances. *(p. 1039)*

6. **Present** and **illustrate** the use of standard costs in financial statements. *(p. 1041)*

7. Appendix 23A: **Present** journal entries associated with standard costs. *(p. 1043)*

BOEING

Boeing is the world's largest aerospace company and a leading manufacturer of commercial jetliners and defense, space, and security systems. Its products include commercial and military aircraft, satellites, weapons, electronic and defense systems, launch systems, and advanced information and communication systems. Approximately 75% of the world's fleet of commercial jetliners in service, almost 12,000 jets, were made by Boeing (including those made by McDonnell Douglas, which merged with Boeing in 1997). The main commercial jetliner products include the familiar 737, 747, 767, and 777 families of airplanes. New jetliner products under development include the 787 Dreamliner and the 747-8.

The 787 Dreamliner is a new, super-efficient airplane that incorporates advanced composite materials, systems, and an engine that was expected to improve fuel efficiency by 20% over existing small twin-aisle airplanes and reduce maintenance and replacement costs. Boeing's approach to the design and manufacture of the 787 involved significant outsourcing that was intended to reduce the 787's development time from 6 to 4 years and development cost from $10 billion to $6 billion. The customers' travel experience was to be improved also, because the composite material used would allow for increased humidity and pressure and would enable the 787 to fly nonstop between any pair of cities without layovers. Because of these promised improvements, the 787 became the fastest-selling plane in aviation history. The actual results have been not what Boeing executives expected when the development of the 787 began. The first of the 787s was to have been delivered in 2008. Due to a host of management problems, including outsourcing of major components and systems, lack of on-site support for outsourced components, delegation of detailed engineering and procurement to subcontractors, inadequate communication and oversight of foreign suppliers, and other management failures, the first 787 wasn't delivered until 2011. Subsequent operational problems included brake problems, fuel leaks, a cracked windshield, a couple of electrical fires, and an emergency landing followed by the grounding of all 787s that had been delivered. As of early 2013, less than 10% of the planes sold had been delivered.

For products as complex as the 787 aircraft, manufacturers often use a standard costing system. Standard costs are developed for all direct materials, direct labor, and overhead associated with the product. Actual results can

then be compared to the established standard costs to identify where there are significant variances and take appropriate action to improve performance. In its 2013 Annual Report, Boeing reports that the first three flight-test 787s could not be sold due to an inordinate amount of rework and extensive modifications. Boeing included the costs of those three planes in its research and development expense. In effect, Boeing wrote off 100% of the cost of three planes, representing a multibillion-dollar variance!

STANDARD COSTING AND VARIANCE ANALYSIS						
Standard Costs	**Determining Standard Costs**	**Direct Materials Variances**	**Direct Labor Variances**	**Variable Overhead Variances**	**Financial Statements**	**Cost Variance Journal Entries (Appendix 23A)**
• Definition • Uses	• Direct material standards • Direct labor standards • Variable overhead standards • Total standard costs	• Cost variances • Materials price variance • Materials efficiency variance • Fezzari direct materials variances	• Labor rate variance • Labor efficiency variance • Fezzari direct labor variances	• Spending variances • Efficiency variances • Fezzari variable overhead variances	• Standard costs in financial statements	• Raw materials variances • Direct labor variances • Variable overhead variances

STANDARD COSTS

LO1 **Define** standard costs and **describe** their use in standard cost accounting.

Managers follow a cycle of planning (budgeting) before each accounting period and then following up with performance evaluation after the period ends. An important tool that managers use in both the pre-planning phase and in the post-evaluation phase is standard costing. Standard costing consists of setting targets, benchmarks, or goals for performance. In other words, managers define standards or expectations of what they consider to be efficient quantities, costs, and rates they expect to achieve in the production process. After setting these objectives at the beginning of the period (during the budgeting phase), they use them to evaluate performance after the period ends. Specifically, in order to budget expected costs for a period, managers determine how much they "should" spend to produce products or services. Thus, **standard costs** are the costs that should be incurred under normal, efficient operating conditions to produce specific products or to perform specific services. Standards should be attainable through efficient efforts by the typical worker at a task. A complex process, involving engineering specifications, time and motion studies, estimates of supply and demand, and analyses of historical trends, is used to develop standard costs. Standard costs are usually stated per unit of product or service and are useful for a number of purposes, including preparing flexible budgets and master budgets, establishing selling prices, and preparing performance reports.

Standard costs are budgeted costs, the costs that should be incurred during the upcoming year. Obviously, managers use past performance to set standards, but these standards are not intended to simply be a description of past performance, but are intended to be their best projection of *future* performance. In other words, managers want to spend their time looking through the windshield to see where they are going rather than looking at the rearview mirror. Nevertheless, the past is often the best way to project the firm's trajectory for the future. Reasonably attainable levels of efficiency and productivity are used to establish standard costs, so they can serve as a motivating factor and a standard of performance. Typically, standard costs are revised no more frequently than once each year.

Standard costs are usually established prior to the beginning of each year as part of the budgeting process. They should not be updated during the year unless there are major, unexpected changes in vendor costs, wage rates, technology, or product design. One of the important uses of standard costs is to compare them to actual costs to identify significant differences. This comparison process will be most meaningful when the standards used represent the level of efficiency and productivity that was planned during the budgeting process.

Uses of Standard Cost Accounting

Many companies, especially manufacturing firms, adopt **standard cost accounting** for product costs. Although we focus on manufacturing firms in this chapter, it is important to note that standard costing concepts also apply in service companies. The concepts discussed in this chapter relative to labor and overhead apply equally in service and manufacturing environments. When this approach is taken in a manufacturing setting, all inventory accounts—material, work in process, and finished goods—and the cost of goods sold account are stated in terms of standard or predetermined costs rather than actual costs incurred. Specifically, standard costs are used for direct material, direct labor, variable overhead, and fixed overhead. (Fixed overhead standard costs and variances are beyond the scope of this textbook. We will limit our discussion to variable production costs.)

Standard cost accounting can be used with either job order costing or process costing. When standard cost accounting is used, standard costs are carried in the inventory accounts and the cost of goods sold account and the differences between the standard costs and actual costs are recorded as **variances**. Essentially, variances are the deviations from the company's predetermined standards. Thus, variances serve as an important evaluation tool to help managers assess how realistic their budgeted costs determined at the beginning of the period were. Moreover, they allow managers to pinpoint areas for improvement in future periods. **Exhibit 23-1** illustrates how standard costs are set at the beginning of the period. Managers rely on many sources to determine the costs they "should" incur under efficient operating conditions by consulting with engineers regarding historical and projected production rates, past purchase contracts for materials, historical labor rates, and so forth. These standard costs become the basis for the current-period budget. At the end of the period, managers compare the actual costs to the previously defined standard costs to evaluate performance and to help them identify areas for improvement.

Exhibit 23-1	Comparing Standard Cost Budgets to Actual Results

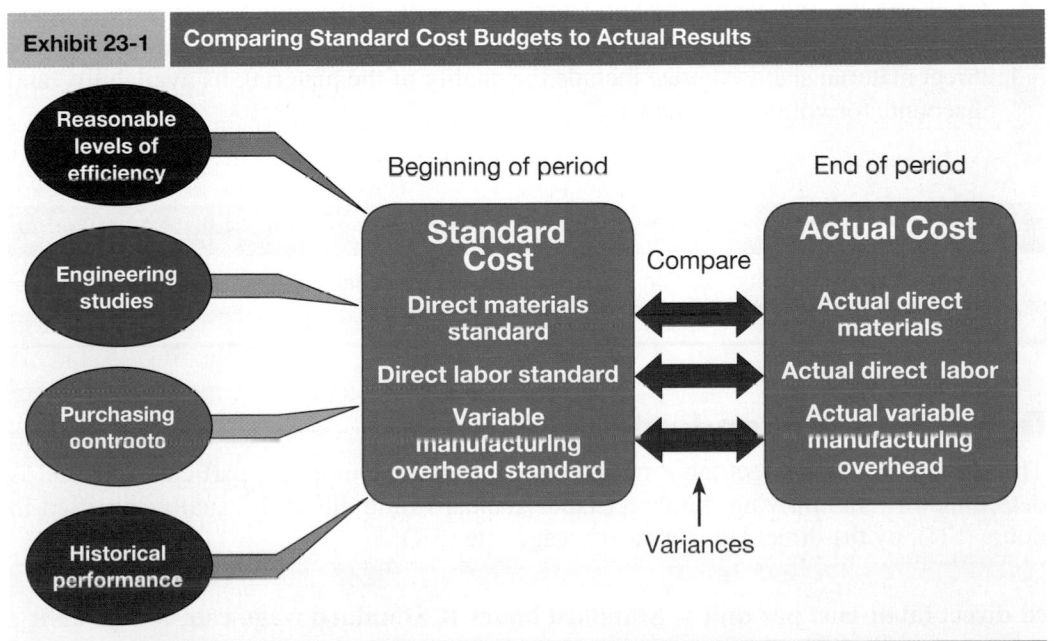

DETERMINING STANDARD COSTS

LO2 **Develop** an overall understanding of the determination of standard costs for direct material, direct labor, and variable overhead.

The development of standard costs per unit of product for all variable inputs requires the use of six components: (1) direct material standard price, (2) direct material standard quantity, (3) direct labor standard rate, (4) direct labor standard time allowed, (5) standard variable overhead rate, and (6) variable overhead standard capacity. The cost-related components are developed and updated as part of the budgeting process, and quantity and capacity standards are usually developed as part of the product design and engineering process. We describe the six standard costing components in the following sections.

Direct Material Standards

Hint: The product of direct material standard price and direct material standard quantity is part of a static budget.

The standard direct material cost to produce a unit of a particular finished product is determined by multiplying the direct material standard quantity (SQ) per unit by the direct material standard price (SP) per unit:

> **Standard direct material cost per unit = Standard quantity × Standard price = SQ × SP**

To illustrate this calculation, consider the fact that each of Boeing's 787 jetliners requires seat-back tray tables. Assume that the standard quantity of seat-back tray tables per 787 is 232. Moreover, assume that Boeing has a supplier that produces the tray tables and that the standard purchase price per tray table is $50. Given this information, the standard direct material cost to provide seat-back tray tables for a Boeing 787 would be calculated as follows:

$$
\begin{aligned}
\text{Standard tray table cost per 787 airplane} &= \text{SQ} \times \text{SP} \\
&= 232 \text{ tables per } 787 \times \$50 \text{ per table} \\
&= \$11{,}600 \text{ per } 787
\end{aligned}
$$

A number of factors affect the direct material standard quantity, including material quality, engineering specifications, the skill of the direct labor workers, and the capabilities of the equipment used to process the material. Factors affecting the direct material standard price include the quality of the material, its availability, and discounts for volume purchases.

ACCOUNTING IN PRACTICE   **Standard Cost of Material**

The standard material cost should be the expected cost of material including delivery costs and net of any discounts.

Direct Labor Standards

The standard cost of direct labor required to produce one unit of a particular product is determined by multiplying the direct labor standard time allowed, usually specified in hours (SH), by the direct labor standard wage rate (SR):

> **Standard direct labor cost per unit = Standard hours × Standard wage rate = SH × SR**

Continuing the Boeing illustration, assume that the standard amount of direct labor needed to install the seat-back tray tables is 8 hours per 787 and that the standard hourly wage rate for direct labor is $30. The resulting standard direct labor cost per 787 is $240:

Standard direct labor cost per 787 =	SH $\times$ SR
=	8 Direct labor hours per 787 $\times$ $30 per direct labor hour
=	$240 per 787

The direct labor standard wage rate represents the expected weighted average of labor rates for all levels of workers who undertake direct labor tasks on the product. The rates for the various levels of workers are set by the company or prescribed by labor contract. Direct labor standard times are based primarily on prior employee performance and current time and motion studies. Moreover, these wage rates include all compensation components guaranteed to employees (such as health insurance, payroll taxes, retirement plans, etc.).

Standard Cost of Labor	ACCOUNTING IN PRACTICE

The direct labor standard time should include an allowance for breaks, personal needs, cleanup, and so on.

Variable Overhead Standards

The standard cost of variable overhead needed to manufacture one unit of a particular product is determined by multiplying the variable overhead standard capacity (SC), by the standard (or predetermined) variable overhead application rate (SR):

$$\text{Standard variable overhead cost per unit} = \frac{\text{Variable overhead}}{\text{standard capacity}} \times \frac{\text{Variable overhead}}{\text{application rate}} = \text{SC} \times \text{SR}$$

Traditionally we separate overhead costs into fixed and variable components. This is necessary because fixed costs hold constant within all production levels within our relevant range. Only the variable component fluctuates in response to changes in volume. Therefore our variable overhead application rate (SR) is the variable portion of the predetermined overhead application rate that was explained in the discussion of job order costing in **Chapter 16**. Recall that the basis for determining the rate can be direct labor hours, direct labor dollars, machine hours, or some other overhead application base. The basis selected should be the best common measure of variable overhead capacity utilized during production.

The variable overhead standard capacity (SC) should be stated in the same terms as the rate (SR). For instance, if the basis for the variable overhead application rate is direct labor hours, then the variable overhead standard capacity allowed will be the number of direct labor hours expected to produce one unit. This will also typically be the same application base used to apply the overhead application rate to production.

In the Boeing illustration, assume that Boeing allocates variable overhead based on direct labor hours and that the standard variable overhead application rate (SR) is calculated to be $50 per direct labor hour and that the variable overhead standard capacity (SC) for installing the seat-back tray tables is 8 direct labor hours per 787 (i.e., the same as the direct labor standard time or SH allowed). The resulting standard variable overhead cost per 787 associated with the tray installation is calculated as follows:

Standard variable overhead cost per 787 =	SC × SR	
	=	8 Direct labor hours per 787 × $50 per direct labor hour
	=	$400 per 787

A.K.A. The *standard variable overhead rate* is also known as the *predetermined variable overhead rate*.

The standard variable overhead rate is based on the expected level of operations. Because a wide variety of cost items is included in variable overhead, many different factors affect the rate. The variable overhead standard capacity is influenced by such factors as prior employee performance, prior machine performance, and current time and motion studies.

TAKEAWAY 23.1

It is good practice for management to understand and utilize standard costs and variances. Establishing standards helps managers track their expectations against actual results for a period. This information can then guide management to a better understanding of costs and the factors that cause cost fluctuations.

Total Standard Costs

Exhibit 23-2 summarizes the relationships described so far. Most firms that use standard costs prepare a summary of the standard product costs for each product that they produce.

Exhibit 23-2	**Standard Cost Summary**
Standard direct material cost per unit . . . . . . =	SQ × SP
Standard direct labor cost per unit . . . . =	SH × SR
Standard variable overhead cost per unit . . . =	SC × SR

Where: SQ = Standard Quantity
SP = Standard Price
SH = Standard Hours
SR = Standard Rate
SC = Standard Capacity

Based on the preceding concepts, Boeing's standard cost summary for seat-back tray tables in a 787 would appear as in **Exhibit 23-3**.

Exhibit 23-3	**Standard Cost Summary**	
	BOEING 787 **Seat-Back Tray Tables**	
Direct material	(232 tables × $50 per table) =	$11,600
Direct labor.	(8 DLH × $30 per DLH) =	240
Variable overhead.	(8 DLH × $50 per DLH) =	400
Total standard product cost per 787		$12,240

Where: DLH = Direct Labor Hours

Standard costs are also used in determining product cost variances. The remaining sections of this chapter deal with the calculation and use of product cost variances.

COST VARIANCES

Standard costs are extremely helpful in budgeting prior to the start of a fiscal period. Moreover, they can also be very useful in evaluating performance at the end of a period. Even in well-managed companies with carefully established and currently maintained cost standards, actual costs will differ from standard costs. The differences, often called *variances*, should be analyzed for indications of their cause so that appropriate action may be taken to prevent them in future periods.

We first provide an overview of each type of variance and then illustrate the calculation of these variances based on the production data for an important Fezzari product. Suppose that during June 2016, Fezzari Bicycles produced 100 Fore CR2 road bikes for which it incurred the following actual costs (assume no beginning or ending work in process inventories):

Direct material:	
Frame	$33,600
Build kit.	31,500
Direct labor:	
Assembly	15,000
Quality control and packaging	5,000
Variable overhead.	1,525
Total actual variable production costs	$86,625

Exhibit 23-4 compares the actual costs with standard costs to produce 100 bikes, and calculates the differences, or variances, for each cost category. We multiply the standard costs by the actual quantity of 100 bikes produced in June. Note that both favorable and unfavorable variances exist and that the overall net variance of $7,315 is unfavorable. To initiate remedial action, management must analyze the variance for each manufacturing cost element to determine the underlying causal factors related to prices paid, quantities used, and productive capacity used.

Exhibit 23-4	Comparison of Standard and Actual Costs			
	FEZZARI PERFORMANCE BICYCLES **Variance Analysis** **June 30, 2016**			
	Actual Costs	**Standard Costs**	**Total Flexible Budget Variances**	
Direct material	$65,100	$60,000	$5,100	Unfavorable*
Direct labor.	20,000	17,750	2,250	Unfavorable
Variable overhead.	1,525	1,560	(35)	Favorable
	$86,625	$79,310	$7,315	Unfavorable

*The total material variance calculated in the next section is not equal to the difference between the total standard costs and total actual costs because the amount purchased is different from the amount used in production. See the chapter discussion for a detailed explanation.

Direct Materials Variances

LO3 Understand and calculate direct materials variances.

We begin our discussion with direct materials variances. Direct materials variances are often slightly more complicated than the other variable manufacturing cost variances simply because the quantity of materials purchased often differs from the quantity used in production during the period. To aid in (1) understanding how variances work, (2) remembering how they are calculated, and (3) visualizing each type of variance, we present each type of variable manufacturing cost variance using a simple "fork diagram." **Exhibit 23-5** provides a simple diagram for materials (assuming the quantity purchased is equal to the quantity used in production).

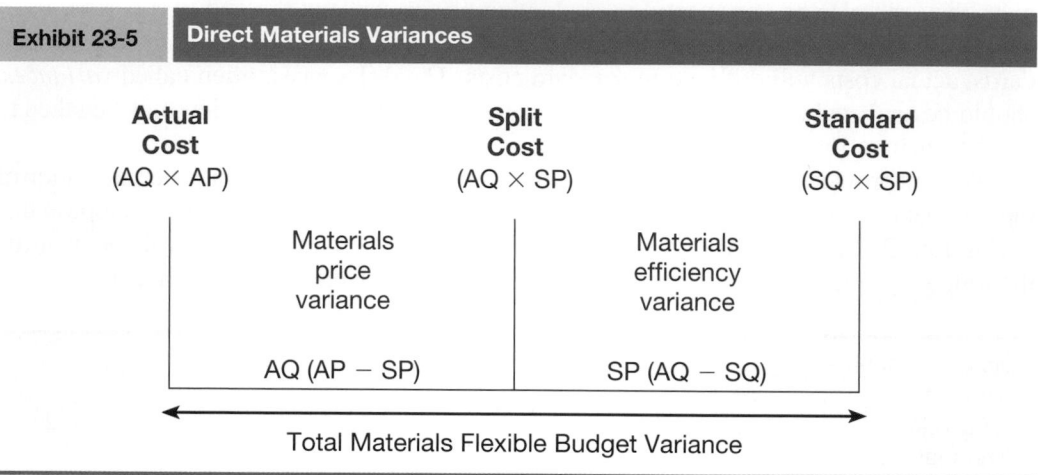

Exhibit 23-5 Direct Materials Variances

Variance analysis simply compares actual costs with standard costs. We place the actual materials cost on the left. How much did we spend to purchase materials? Actual materials purchased equals the actual quantity (AQ) purchased times the actual price per unit (AP). We place the standard cost of materials allowed for this level of production on the far right of the diagram. How much should we have spent on raw materials at this level of production? As explained previously, standard materials cost equals the standard quantity allowed (SQ) for this level of output times the standard price per unit (SP). The total difference between actual and standard costs (as explained in more detail in **Chapter 24**) is called the total materials flexible budget variance. However, there are two reasons we may spend more or less than our standards would indicate. First, we may pay too much or too little when we purchase the materials. Second, we may not use the materials efficiently in the production process. Hence, it is useful to split the total materials flexible budget variance into its two main components: (1) the **materials price variance** and (2) the **materials efficiency variance**. In order to facilitate this analysis, we place a new number in the middle of the diagram (the split cost), which takes the actual quantity purchased (AQ) from the far left of the diagram and multiplies it by the standard price (SP) from the far right of the diagram. This number represents the standard price we should have spent to buy the actual quantity purchased (AQ × SP).

We calculate the materials price variance by subtracting the standard price we should have paid for the actual quantity purchased from our actual purchase price:

$$\text{Materials price variance} = (\text{AQ} \times \text{AP}) - (\text{AQ} \times \text{SP})$$

Using simple algebra, we can factor out the common element in each number (AQ) and rewrite the materials price variance as follows:

$$\text{Materials price variance} = \text{AQ} (\text{AP} - \text{SP})$$

Written this way, we see that the *cause* of this variance is the difference between the actual price paid to purchase materials compared to the standard price management had budgeted at the beginning of the period. If the actual price exceeds the standard price (i.e., we paid too much), the materials price variance will appear as a positive number. Thus, positive price variance is "unfavorable" because it would indicate that we paid too much per unit when we purchased the materials. On the other hand, if the materials price variance is a negative number (i.e., we paid less than our standards had predicted), the variance is "favorable."

We calculate the materials efficiency variance by subtracting the standard materials cost (SQ × SP) from what we should have paid for the actual quantity purchased according to our standards (AQ × SP):

$$\text{Materials efficiency variance} = (\text{AQ} \times \text{SP}) - (\text{SQ} \times \text{SP})$$

Again, we can use basic algebra to factor out the common element (SP) to rewrite the materials efficiency variance to better illustrate what causes the variance:

$$\text{Materials efficiency variance} = \text{SP}\,(\text{AQ} - \text{SQ})$$

When expressed this way, it is clear that, holding the standard price constant, what *causes* the variance is the quantity used. If we do not use the materials efficiently in production, we may spend too much or too little. Similar to what we observe for the materials price variance, if the actual quantity exceeds the standard quantity (i.e., we used too much of the material in producing products during this period), the materials efficiency variance will appear as a positive number, suggesting that we did not use our materials efficiently (thus the variance will be "unfavorable"). On the other hand, if we use less than our budgeted standards would dictate (i.e., the materials efficiency variance is negative), we conclude that we used less than we expected (and we would label this negative number as a "favorable" materials efficiency variance).

When the quantity of materials purchased is exactly equal to the quantity used in production, this simple diagram indicates that the total materials flexible budget variance is equal to the sum of the materials price variance and the materials efficiency variance. However, it is common in practice that companies purchase more or less than they actually use in production. To account for these common differences, **Exhibit 23-6** illustrates how we modify the "fork diagram" for materials to better differentiate between these two quantities because the materials price variance is based on the quantity of materials *purchased*, whereas the materials efficiency variance depends on the amount of materials *used* in the production process. In other words, the split cost number (AQ × SP), the actual quantity at the standard price, must actually be shown twice because the price variance is based on the quantity *purchased*, whereas the efficiency variance is calculated using the actual quantity *used* in the production process. It is easy to make mistakes in calculating variances if you don't pay close attention to which quantity you are referring to! The version of the materials "fork diagram" in **Exhibit 23-6** can help you to avoid these careless errors. We illustrate these calculations next.

| **Managing Variances** | ACCOUNTING IN PRACTICE |

Managers may trade off one variance for another. For example, a manager may decide to use a pre-cut material rather than a bulk material. This usually will result in higher cost (unfavorable price variance) and lower quantities (favorable quantity variance) than budgeted.

Exhibit 23-6	Direct Materials Variances

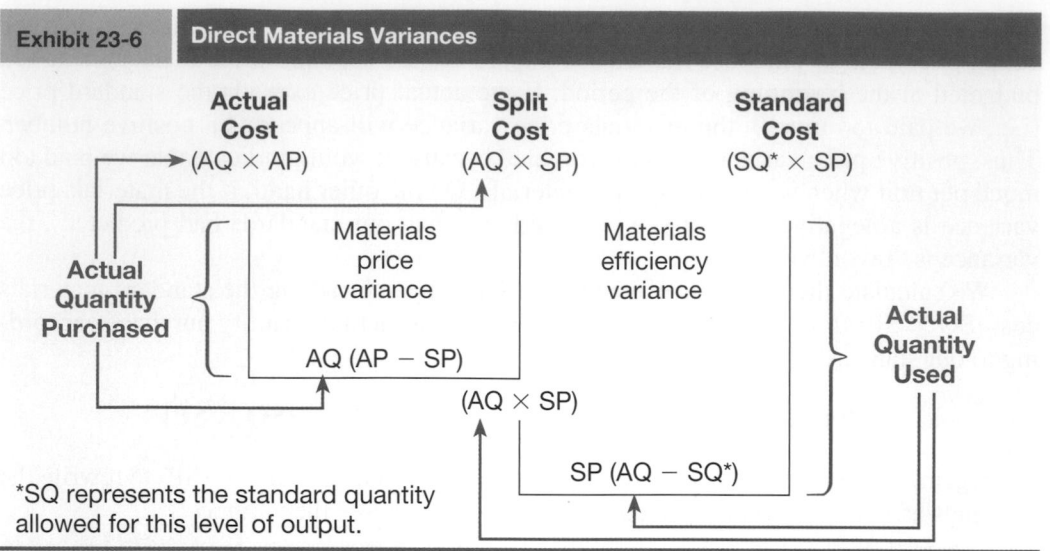

*SQ represents the standard quantity allowed for this level of output.

Fezzari's Direct Materials Variances

We first calculate the materials price variance for frames. Fezzari actually **purchased** 105 frames at a price of $320 per frame and **used** 101 in production during the month. Assume that the standard price is $325 per frame.

The calculations in **Exhibit 23-7** indicate a favorable price variance for frames of $525. This is calculated as the difference between the actual and budgeted price for frames ($320 − $325) multiplied by the number of frames purchased (105). The variance is favorable because Fezzari spent $5 less per frame than anticipated in the budget. However, these calculations also indicate an unfavorable efficiency variance of $325. This is calculated as the budgeted price per frame ($325) multiplied by the difference between the actual number of frames used and the budgeted number of frames used (101 − 100). Fezzari used one more frame than anticipated for this level of production because one bike was damaged beyond repair during production.

Exhibit 23-7	Direct Materials Variances—Frames

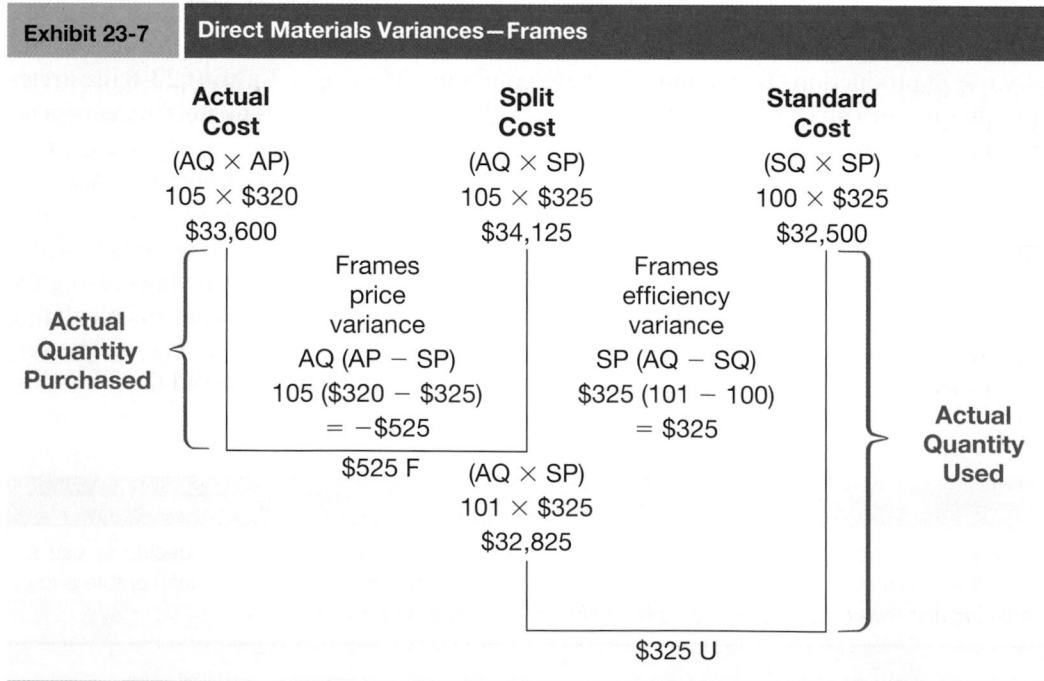

Next, we use the same process to calculate the materials price variance for build kits. Fezzari actually *purchased* 105 build kits at a price of $300 per build kit and *used* 101 in production during the month. Assume that the standard price is $275 per build kit.

Exhibit 23-8	Direct Materials Variances—Build Kits

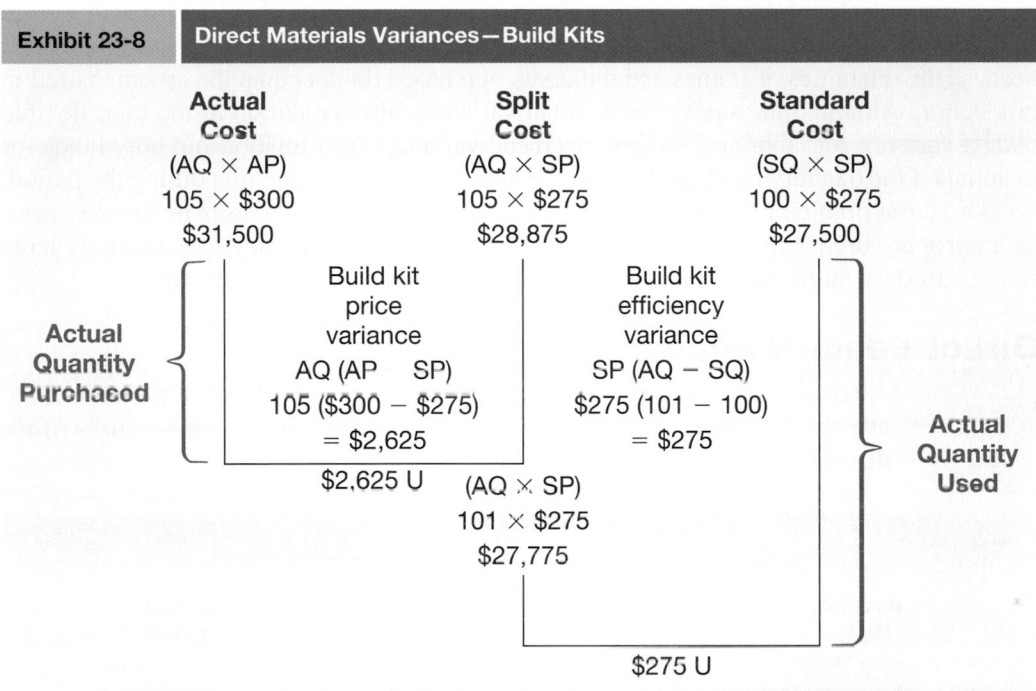

The calculations in **Exhibit 23-8** indicate an unfavorable price variance for build kits of $2,625 (105 build kits × $25 per build kit) because Fezzari spent $25 more per build kit than anticipated in the budget. These calculations also indicate an unfavorable efficiency variance of $275 ($275 × 1 extra build kit). Fezzari used one more build kit than would normally be anticipated for this level of production because one bike was damaged beyond repair during production.

The net materials price variance of $2,100 ($2,625 U − $525 F) is unfavorable because the actual price for build kits was $25 per unit greater than the standard price (even though the price of frames was actually $5 per unit lower than anticipated). Note that for the materials price variance, the quantity represents the number of units purchased, not the number of units manufactured.

The net materials efficiency variance of $600 ($325 U + $275 U) is unfavorable because the actual quantity is greater than the standard quantity (because one frame and one build kit were damaged beyond repair, Fezzari used materials for 101 bikes to only produce 100 usable bikes). Note that for the materials efficiency variance, the quantity represents the number of units issued into production, not the number of units purchased.

A company purchased and used 90,000 feet of material at $2.90 per foot to make 22,000 units of a finished product. The per-unit standard for material is 4 feet @ $3.00 = $12.00. What were the materials price variance and the materials efficiency variance?

YOUR TURN! 23.1

The solution is on page 1058.

Exhibit 23-4 indicates that the total flexible budget variance for direct materials is $5,100 U. However, the sum of the materials price and efficiency variances is only $2,700 U:

Materials price variance	$2,100 U
Materials efficiency variance	600 U
Sum of material variances	$2,700 U

The sum of the material variances does not agree with the total flexible budget variance because the quantities of frames and build kits purchased do not equal the amounts used in production. Although the sums of individual variances always add up to the total flexible budget variance for labor and variable overhead variances, this relationship only holds for materials if the quantity purchased equals the quantity used in production during the period.

The unfavorable price variance may have been caused by increases in supplier prices, improper purchasing, or other factors. The unfavorable efficiency variance may have been caused by inefficient workers, inferior-quality material, or other factors.

Direct Labor Variances

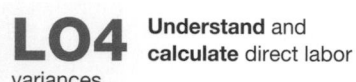

LO4   Understand and calculate direct labor variances.

After learning how to work with materials variances, labor variances are really easy! In order to visualize direct labor variances, we use a similar "fork diagram," as illustrated in **Exhibit 23-9**.

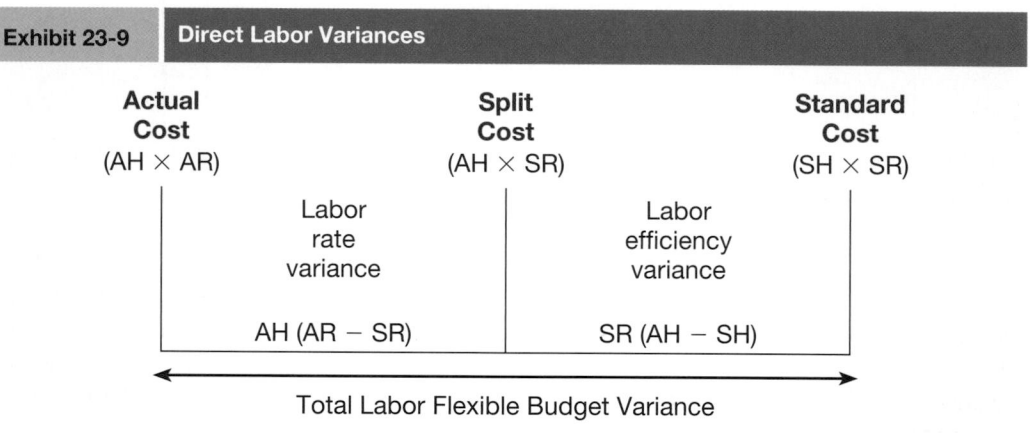

Similar to materials variances, we place the actual direct labor cost on the left. How much did we pay our labor force? Actual labor costs equal the actual number of hours worked (AH) times the actual wage rate (AR). We place the standard direct labor cost on the far right of the diagram. How much should we have paid our employees to produce this level of output? As explained previously, standard labor costs equal the standard number of hours to produce this many units (SH) times the standard hourly wage rate (SR). The total difference between actual and standard costs (as explained in more detail in Chapter 24) is called the total labor flexible budget variance. However, there are two reasons we may spend more or less than our standards would indicate. First, we may pay our employees too much or too little relative to what we expected when we prepared our budget at the beginning of the period. Second, we may not use our workforce efficiently in producing inventory. Similar to what we observed for materials, it is useful to split the total labor flexible budget variance into its two main components: (1) the **labor rate variance** and (2) the **labor efficiency variance**. In order to facilitate this analysis, we place a split cost number in the middle of the diagram, which takes the actual hours worked (AH) from the far left of the diagram and multiplies it by the standard wage rate (SR) from the far right of the diagram. This number represents the standard amount we should have spent to pay our workforce (AH × SR) to produce this level of output.

We calculate the labor rate variance by subtracting the standard price we should have paid our employees for the actual level of production from our actual labor costs:

$$\text{Labor rate variance} = (\text{AH} \times \text{AR}) - (\text{AH} \times \text{SR})$$

Using simple algebra, we can factor out the common element in each number (AH) and rewrite the labor rate variance as follows:

$$\text{Labor rate variance} = \text{AH (AR} - \text{SR)}$$

Written this way, we see that the *cause* of this variance is the difference between the actual wage rate as compared with the standard wage rate management had forecasted at the beginning of the period. If the actual rate exceeds the standard rate (i.e., we paid employees more than expected), the labor rate variance will appear as a positive number. Thus, a positive price variance is "unfavorable" because we paid more than we had budgeted. On the other hand, if the labor rate variance is a negative number (i.e., we paid less than our standards had predicted), the variance is "favorable."

We calculate the labor efficiency variance by subtracting the standard labor cost (SH × SR) from what we should have paid for the actual hours worked according to our standards (AH × SR):

$$\text{Labor efficiency variance} = (\text{AH} \times \text{SR}) - (\text{SH} \times \text{SR})$$

Again, we can use basic algebra to factor out the common element (SR) to rewrite the labor efficiency variance to better illustrate what causes the variance:

$$\text{Labor efficiency variance} = \text{SR (AH} - \text{SH)}$$

When expressed this way, it is clear that holding the standard wage rate constant, what *causes* the variance is the number of hours used. If we do not use our employees efficiently in production, we may spend too much or too little. If the actual number of hours worked exceeds the standard number of hours (i.e., we used too many employee hours), the labor efficiency variance will appear as a positive number, suggesting that we did not use our labor force efficiently (thus the variance will be "unfavorable"). On the other hand, if we use fewer hours than our standards would have predicted (i.e., the labor efficiency variance is negative), we conclude that we were able to use our workers less than we expected (and we would label this negative number as a "favorable" labor efficiency variance).

Fezzari's Direct Labor Variances

We illustrate the calculation of direct labor variances using the Fezzari data presented previously. Specifically, we use the data for the assembly department. Assembly personnel actually worked 750 hours during June at an average rate of $20 per hour. However, the standard number of hours to produce 100 CR2 bikes is 550 hours and the standard wage rate in this department is $25 per hour. Using this information, we can calculate assembly labor variances as illustrated in **Exhibit 23-10**. These calculations indicate a favorable rate variance in the assembly department of $3,750, calculated as 750 hours multiplied by the $5-per-hour difference between the actual and standard rate. The variance is favorable because Fezzari paid an average of $5 less per hour than anticipated in the budget. However, these calculations also indicate an unfavorable efficiency variance of $5,000 ($25 standard rate × 200 extra hours) because Fezzari's assembly crew worked 200 hours more than anticipated for this level of production.

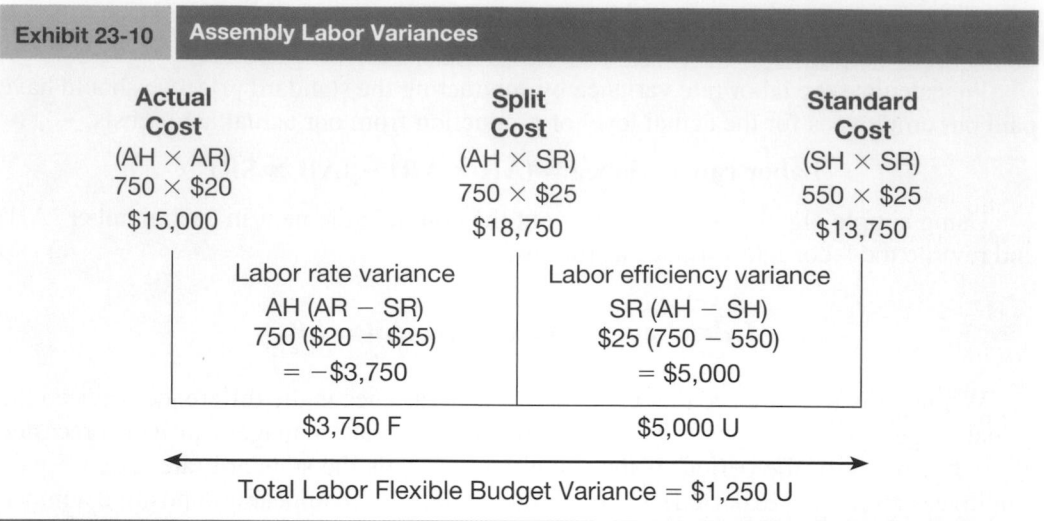

Exhibit 23-10   **Assembly Labor Variances**

	Actual Cost (AH × AR) 750 × $20 $15,000		**Split Cost** (AH × SR) 750 × $25 $18,750		**Standard Cost** (SH × SR) 550 × $25 $13,750

Labor rate variance
AH (AR − SR)
750 ($20 − $25)
= −$3,750

Labor efficiency variance
SR (AH − SH)
$25 (750 − 550)
= $5,000

$3,750 F $5,000 U

Total Labor Flexible Budget Variance = $1,250 U

Next, **Exhibit 23-11** calculates the labor variances for the quality control (QC) and packaging department. Employees in this department actually worked 250 hours during June at an average rate of $20 per hour. Assume that the standard number of hours at this production level is 200 and the standard wage rate is exactly $20 per hour.

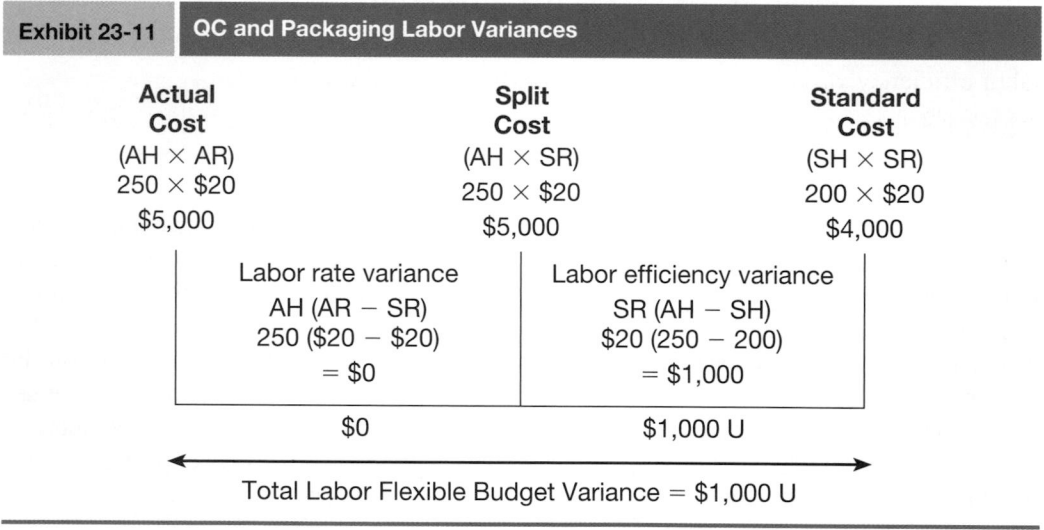

Exhibit 23-11   **QC and Packaging Labor Variances**

	Actual Cost (AH × AR) 250 × $20 $5,000		**Split Cost** (AH × SR) 250 × $20 $5,000		**Standard Cost** (SH × SR) 200 × $20 $4,000

Labor rate variance
AH (AR − SR)
250 ($20 − $20)
= $0

Labor efficiency variance
SR (AH − SH)
$20 (250 − 200)
= $1,000

$0 $1,000 U

Total Labor Flexible Budget Variance = $1,000 U

Because the actual wage rate coincides perfectly with the standard wage rate, there is no labor rate variance. However, these calculations indicate an unfavorable efficiency variance of $1,000 ($20 standard rate × 50 extra hours) because Fezzari's QC and packaging employees worked 50 hours more than anticipated for this level of production.

YOUR TURN! 23.2 The solution is on page 1058.	Actual hours worked were 35,000 at a rate of $7.50 per hour to make 22,000 units of a finished product. The per-unit standard for labor is 1.5 hours @ $7.00 = $10.50. What were the labor rate variance and the labor efficiency variance?

Combining the results for the assembly and the QC and packaging departments, we calculate the following total variances:

Labor rate variance	$3,750 F
Labor efficiency variance	6,000 U
Total flexible budget variance for labor	$2,250 U

Notice that the sum of the labor rate and efficiency variances equals the total flexible budget variance for labor in **Exhibit 23-4**.

Variable Overhead Variances

Variable overhead variances are virtually identical to labor variances. Therefore we can visualize variable overhead variances using the **Exhibit 23-12** "fork diagram" that is very similar to the direct labor diagram. As explained previously, overhead may be applied to product cost based on any application base that represents the "cost driver." Therefore the standard cost of variable overhead needed to manufacture one unit of a particular product, shown on the far right of the diagram, is determined by multiplying the variable overhead standard capacity (SC) of that "cost driver" by the standard (or predetermined) variable overhead application rate (SR). Note that variable overhead items are recorded as "actual" debits to the manufacturing overhead account as they occur. There is no "rate" applied to these actual amounts. The "actual" amount spent, shown on the far left of the diagram, is simply the sum of all indirect variable items (such as indirect materials, indirect labor, etc.). For simplicity, assume that a company uses direct labor hours as that cost driver in developing a predetermined variable overhead application rate.

LO5 Understand and calculate variable overhead variances.

Exhibit 23-12	Variable Overhead Variances

Actual Cost	**Split Cost** (AH × SR)	**Standard Cost** (SH × SR)
	Variable overhead spending variance	Variable overhead efficiency variance
	(Actual − Split)	SR (AH − SH)

Total variable overhead flexible budget variance

In this diagram, the predetermined variable overhead application rate (i.e., the standard rate, SR) is based on direct labor hours. The variable overhead spending variance (i.e., the rate variance) determines whether that predetermined overhead application rate is higher or lower than the standard rate determined by managers in the budgeting process. Similarly, variable overhead efficiency variance is attributable to the use of that overhead application base or "driver." In this diagram, we list the number of direct labor hours as the "cause" of the efficiency variance. Obviously, if some other application base were used to calculate the predetermined overhead application rate, such as machine hours, direct labor dollars, or quality inspections, the efficiency variance would be based on that factor. For example, if we had used the number of inspections as our variable overhead application base, the formula for the variable overhead efficiency variance would be SR (AI − SI), where "AI" would represent the actual number of quality inspections and "SI" would represent the standard number of quality inspections for that production run.

FEZZARI'S VARIABLE OVERHEAD VARIANCES

Fezzari's variable overhead variances result from paying more or less than planned for items that comprise variable overhead (the **variable overhead spending variance**) and from using more or less than the standard amount of capacity (the **variable overhead efficiency variance**).

ACCOUNTING IN PRACTICE	Standard Capacity

The standard capacity allowed for variable overhead and fixed overhead will be stated in terms of a common measure of plant capacity, such as direct labor hours or machine hours. A different measure may be used for variable overhead and fixed overhead.

Assume that Fezzari incurs actual variable overhead during the month of June of $1,525, comprised of the following items:

Indirect material	$ 55
Indirect labor	550
Factory utilities	645
Other	275
Total	$1,525

These items would be recorded as debits to the manufacturing overhead account as incurred:

Manufacturing overhead	1,525	
Raw materials inventory		55
Wages payable		550
Utilities payable		645
Other payables (or cash)		275

Also assume that during its budgeting process for the year, Fezzari decided to allocate variable overhead based on estimated labor hours in the QC and packaging department and that the predetermined overhead application rate is $7.80 per hour. Therefore, the variable overhead variances for Fezzari are computed and recorded as shown in **Exhibit 23-13**. The calculations are similar to those for material and labor, which, like variable overhead, are variable product cost components.

Exhibit 23-13	Variable Overhead Variances

Actual Cost	Split Cost (AH × SR) 250 × $7.80	Standard Cost (SH × SR) 200 × $7.80
$1,525	$1,950	$1,560

Variable overhead spending variance

(Actual − Split)
$1,525 − $1,950
= −$425

Variable overhead efficiency variance

SR (AH − SH)
$7.80 (250 − 200)
= $390

$425 F $390 U

Total variable overhead flexible budget variance= $35 F

The actual variable overhead costs are less than would be projected, based on the actual number of hours worked in this department multiplied by the predetermined (standard) variable overhead application rate. Therefore, the variable overhead spending variance is $425 favorable. The variable overhead efficiency variance is $390 unfavorable simply because employees in the QC and packaging department worked 50 hours more than was anticipated for this level of projection.

The total variable overhead variance would be as follows:

Variable overhead spending variance	$425 F
Variable overhead efficiency variance	390 U
Total variable overhead variance	$ 35 F

Notice that the total variable overhead variance agrees with the amount in **Exhibit 23-4**.

YOUR TURN! 23.3

Actual variable overhead was $63,000. Actual hours were 35,000 to make 22,000 finished products. The per-unit standard for variable overhead is 1.5 hours @ $2.00, or $3.00. What were the variable overhead spending variance and the variable overhead efficiency variance?

The solution is on page 1058.

DECISION TIME 23.1

The following is a list of cost variances a company experienced during the first year of its operations. List reasons why these variances could have occurred.

The solution is on page 1058.

Materials price variance	$4,500 Unfavorable
Materials usage variance	$6,700 Unfavorable
Labor rate variance	$12,000 Favorable
Labor efficiency variance	$9,600 Unfavorable

STANDARD COSTS IN FINANCIAL STATEMENTS

When the standard costs and related variances for direct material, direct labor, and variable overhead are recorded as previously illustrated, the work in process account is debited for each in amounts representing standard quantities and standard prices. All variances—favorable and unfavorable—are carried in separate accounts with appropriate titles. Fezzari records completed production for June in the following entry (assume no beginning or ending work in process inventories):

LO6 Present and Illustrate the use of standard costs in financial statements.

Finished goods inventory (at standard cost)	79,310	
Work in process inventory (at standard cost)		79,310
To record completion of June's production of 100 units at a standard variable unit cost of $793.10 ($60,000 material, $17,750 labor, and $1,560 variable overhead).		

As each month's production is sold, the related amounts of standard costs are transferred from Finished Goods Inventory to Cost of Goods Sold.

Standard costs and related variances are usually reported in financial reports intended only for management's use. **Exhibit 23-14** contains a partial income statement that illustrates how variances might appear on interim financial statements for Fezzari's internal use (amounts are assumed).

Exhibit 23-14	Summary

FEZZARI PERFORMANCE BICYCLES
Partial Income Statement
For the Month Ended June 30, 2016

Sales.	$375,000
Cost of goods sold at standard cost	250,000
Gross profit at standard cost	$125,000
Less: Net unfavorable cost variance	6,500
Gross profit.	$118,500

The total net variance could be broken down into sub-variances or detailed in a schedule of variances accompanying the financial statements.

At year-end, firms commonly close the variance accounts by transferring their balances to Cost of Goods Sold. In effect, this transfer converts Cost of Goods Sold from standard costs to actual costs. If large variances exist at year-end and there is evidence that the standards may not apply, a firm may be justified in allocating all or part of the variances to Work in Process Inventory, Finished Goods Inventory, and Cost of Goods Sold.

SERVICES INDUSTRY IN FOCUS

SERVICE AND MERCHANDISING

Environmental Business Consultants, Inc. (EBC) has hired several new staff members in the last year and has invested considerable effort in training these new employees in the EBC approach to conducting rate review projects. Due to the unique market in which EBC operates, there are not commercial training conferences or online training materials available to provide the necessary training. Therefore, the training is done primarily on the job by EBC managers, resulting in extra hours over what is typically incurred in completing this type of project. EBC management is interested in estimating the cost of this on-the-job training in terms of "lost billings," that is, the billing value of the extra hours incurred by both managers and staff as compared with normal budgeted hours. This is equivalent to the labor efficiency variance.

Assume that for the year just ended, EBC completed 25 rate review projects. The following table shows the normal hourly budget for managers and staff on a rate review project. EBC managers billed a total of 1,200 hours and staff billed a total of 3,500 hours on rate review projects during the year. For the year, managers were billed at a standard rate of $200 per hour and staff were billed at a standard rate of $120 per hour.

	Managers	Staff
Budgeted hours per rate review project.	40	120

Required:
Determine the total labor efficiency variance for both managers and staff for the year.

Solution

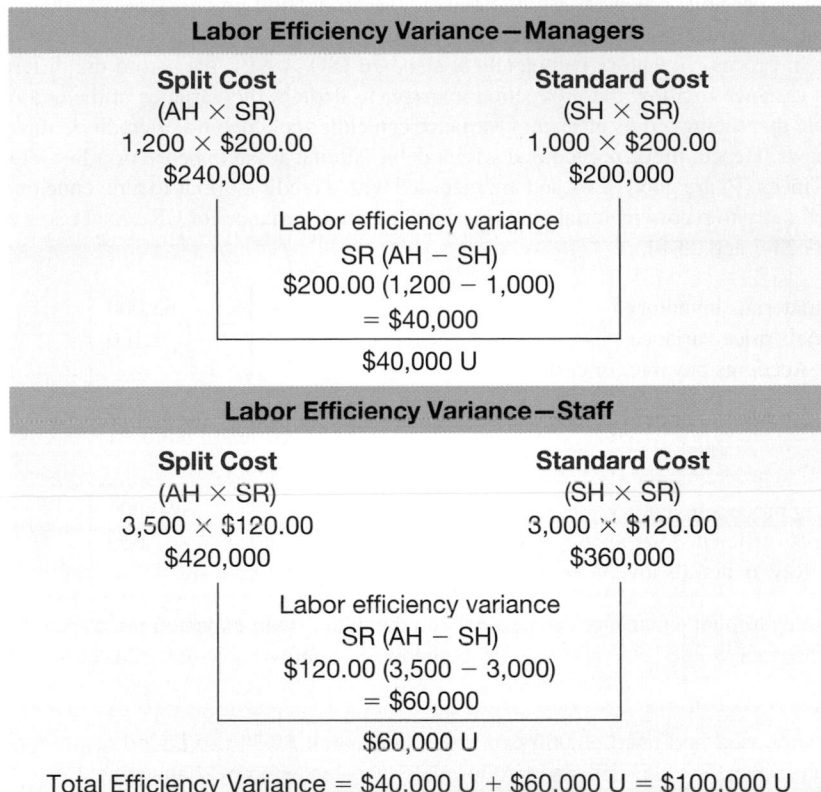

Labor Efficiency Variance—Managers	
Split Cost	**Standard Cost**
(AH × SR)	(SH × SR)
1,200 × $200.00	1,000 × $200.00
$240,000	$200,000

Labor efficiency variance
SR (AH − SH)
$200.00 (1,200 − 1,000)
= $40,000

$40,000 U

Labor Efficiency Variance—Staff	
Split Cost	**Standard Cost**
(AH × SR)	(SH × SR)
3,500 × $120.00	3,000 × $120.00
$420,000	$360,000

Labor efficiency variance
SR (AH − SH)
$120.00 (3,500 − 3,000)
= $60,000

$60,000 U

Total Efficiency Variance = $40,000 U + $60,000 U = $100,000 U

APPENDIX 23A: Cost Variance Journal Entries Illustrated

This appendix illustrates the journal entries used in a standard costing system to record materials, labor, and variable overhead variances based on the Fezzari example used throughout the chapter.

LO7 **Present** journal entries associated with standard costs.

JOURNAL ENTRIES ILLUSTRATED

The materials price variance is recorded in the accounting system at the time materials are purchased. Although the amount paid to suppliers is always the "actual" invoice price, we enter materials into the raw materials inventory account at the standard price:

Raw materials inventory	(AQ × SP)	
Materials price variance	U	or F
Accounts payable (or cash)		(AQ × AP)

Thus, the credit to Accounts Payable (or Cash) is for the actual amount (AQ × AP), whereas the debit to Raw Materials Inventory is for the standard price to purchase the actual quantity acquired (AQ × SP). We record the difference as the raw materials price variance to allow the manager of the purchasing department to explain the variance at the end of the fiscal period. Note that the materials price variance can either be a debit or a credit. Unfavorable variances (U) are bad news. Hence, they are recorded with a debit (similar to an expense or a loss). On the other hand, favorable variances (F) are good news and are recorded with a credit (similar to a revenue or a gain).

The materials efficiency variance is recorded in the accounting records when raw materials are used in production:

Work in process inventory	(SQ × SP)	
Materials efficiency variance	U	or F
Raw materials inventory		(AQ × SP)

We note that when raw materials were purchased, they were recorded at the actual quantity purchased times the standard price per unit. When we use materials in the production process, we take them out of Raw Materials Inventory as the actual quantity used times the standard price per unit (AQ × SP). However, we enter materials into Work in Process Inventory completely at standard (SQ × SP). We record the difference as the materials efficiency variance to allow the production manager to explain the variance at the end of the fiscal period. We again note that the materials efficiency variance can either be a debit or a credit. Unfavorable variances (U) are bad news. Hence, they are recorded with a debit (similar to an expense or a loss). On the other hand, favorable variances (F) are good news and are recorded with a credit (similar to a revenue or a gain).

Fezzari's journal entry to record material purchases and the price variance for CR2 road bikes would be as follows (see Exhibits 23-7 and 23-8):

Raw materials inventory	63,000	
Materials price variance	2,100	
Accounts payable (or cash)		65,100

Moreover, Fezzari's journal entry to record the materials that are used in production for CR2s would be as follows:

Work in process inventory	60,000	
Materials efficiency variance	600	
Raw materials inventory		60,600

The purchasing department's manager can best explain the higher-than-expected prices paid for materials and the production manager would be responsible for explaining the unfavorable materials efficiency variance.

YOUR TURN! 23.4

The solution is on pages 1058–1059.

Truck Company purchased and used 55,000 pounds of material at $5.30 per pound to produce 11,000 units of a finished product. The per-unit standard for material established by management was 4 pounds @ $5.10 = $20.40. What were the materials price and efficiency variances, and what journal entry would management make to record these variances?

We only record one entry in the accounting records relative to direct labor. As employees work directly on our products (or in providing services), we increase Work in Process Inventory and show either a decrease to cash or an increased liability, as follows:

Work in process inventory	(SH × SR)	
Labor rate variance	U	or **F**
Labor efficiency variance	U	or **F**
Wages payable (or cash)		(AH × AR)

Obviously, our employees won't continue working for us if we don't pay them for their services. Moreover, they are not likely to be happy if we tell them, "We're sorry, but your wage rates are higher than our budget anticipated, so we're only going to pay you the standard wage rate." We have to pay our employees whatever wage rate we contracted with them when we hired them (or when they received their last raise). Hence, the credit to Wages Payable (or Cash) must be for the amount the employees actually earned (AH × AR). However, as explained previously, under a standard costing approach, we record manufacturing costs in Work in Process Inventory completely at standard (SH × SR). Thus, the difference between actual and standard costs can be explained by both the labor rate variance and the labor efficiency variance. As explained previously, positive variances are deemed to be "unfavorable" (U) and are recorded with debits, whereas negative variances are deemed to be "favorable" (F) and are recorded with a credit.

The following journal entry records these costs and variances (see Exhibits 23-10 and 23-11):

Work in process inventory	17,750	
Labor efficiency variance	6,000	
Labor rate variance		3,750
Wages payable (or cash)		20,000

The journal entry charges Work in Process Inventory with standard direct labor costs, records the unfavorable labor efficiency variance as a debit and the favorable labor rate variance as a credit, and records the liability for direct labor (or cash) at the amount owed, which is determined using actual hours worked and actual rates paid.

The unfavorable labor efficiency variance might be charged to the production supervisor, who presumably oversees the production teams. The favorable labor rate variance resulted from assigning lower-paid employees to perform the assembly. Other reasons for a favorable labor rate variance include using less overtime or paying decreased labor rates.

Car Company used 23,000 actual direct labor hours at a rate of $3.00 per hour to make 15,000 units of a finished product. The per-unit standard for labor is 2 hours @ 3.50 = $7.00. What were the labor rate and efficiency variances, and what journal entry would management make to record these variances?

YOUR TURN! 23.5

The solution is on page 1059.

Similar to direct labor, we only record one entry in the accounting records relative to the application of variable overhead to units produced. In this example, because we use direct labor hours as the application base in our predetermined variable overhead rate, it would be driven by the actual number of direct labor hours. As employees work directly on our products (or in providing services), we apply more variable overhead to Work in Process Inventory and a corresponding decrease to Manufacturing Overhead, as follows:

Work in process inventory	(SC × SR)	
Variable overhead spending variance	U	or **F**
Variable overhead efficiency variance	U	or **F**
Manufacturing overhead		(AC × AR)

The interpretations of the variable overhead variances are identical to those for the labor variances.

For Fezzari, the general journal entry to record variable overhead costs and variances is as follows (see Exhibit 23-13):

Work in process inventory	1,560	
Variable overhead efficiency variance	390	
Variable overhead spending variance		425
Manufacturing overhead		1,525

This journal entry assumes that no overhead is applied to Work in Process Inventory until the end of the accounting period. When this entry is recorded at period end, all of the efficiency and spending variances are recorded simultaneously. In this example, the "applied overhead" for the entire period is actually $1,950 (250 actual hours worked × 7.80 predetermined overhead rate). If overhead were applied to Work in Process during the period as jobs were completed, the applied overhead for each job would be analogous to smaller pieces of the middle number in the fork diagram (i.e., the credit to Manufacturing Overhead) and a portion of the variable overhead efficiency variance would be recorded with each portion of the overhead applied. The entire variable overhead spending variance would be recorded at the end of the period as the over- or under-applied overhead amount written off to Cost of Goods sold.

This journal entry charges Work in Process Inventory with standard variable overhead costs, and records the unfavorable variable overhead efficiency variance as a debit and the favorable variable overhead spending variance as a credit.

COMPREHENSIVE PROBLEM

Crenshaw Manufacturing, Inc. planned to produce 25,000 units of its only product during the year. The standard cost data for this product are as follows:

	Per Unit
Direct material (3 lbs. @ $2 per lb.).	$ 6
Direct labor (0.5 hr. @ $8 per hr.)	4
Variable overhead (0.5 hr. @ $4 per hr.)	2
Total standard cost per unit	$12

The actual level of production was 24,000 units, with the following actual total costs incurred:

	Total Cost
Direct material (74,000 lbs. @ $1.80)	$133,200
Direct labor (13,000 hrs. @ $8.10)	105,300
Variable overhead.	50,200
Total actual cost.	$288,700

Required

a. Calculate the variances for material, labor, and variable overhead.

b. Is the difference between total actual cost and total standard cost equal to the sum of all the variances? Why?

Solution to Comprehensive Problem

a.

Materials Variances

Actual Cost	Split Cost	Standard Cost
(AQ × AP)	(AQ × SP)	(SQ × SP)
74,000 × $1.80	74,000 × $2.00	72,000 × $2.00
$133,200	$148,000	$144,000

	Materials price variance	Materials efficiency variance
	AQ (AP − SP)	SP (AQ − SQ)
	74,000 ($1.80 − $2.00)	$2.00 (74,000 − 72,000)
	= − $14,800	= $4,000
	$14,800 F	$4,000 U

Labor Variances

Actual Cost	Split Cost	Standard Cost
(AH × AR)	(AH × SR)	(SH × SR)
13,000 × $8.10	13,000 × $8.00	12,000 × $8.00
$105,300	$104,000	$96,000

	Labor rate variance	Labor efficiency variance
	AH (AR − SR)	SR (AH − SH)
	13,000 ($8.10 − $8.00)	$8.00 (13,000 − 12,000)
	= $1,300	= $8,000
	$1,300 U	$8,000 U

Variable Overhead Variances

Actual Cost	Split Cost	Standard Cost
	(AH × SR)	(SH × SR)
(AH × AR)	(13,000 × $4.00)	(12,000 × $4.00)
$50,200	$52,000	$48,000

	Variable overhead spending variance	Variable overhead efficiency variance
	(Actual − Split)	SR (AH − SH)
	($50,200 − $52,000)	$4.00 (13,000 − 12,000)
	= −$1,800	= $4,000
	$1,800 F	$4,000 U

b.

Total actual cost.	$288,700
Total standard cost ($12 X 24,000)	288,000
Total variance	$700 U
Material price variance.	$ 14,800 F
Material quantity variance	4,000 U
Labor rate variance.	1,300 U
Labor efficiency variance	8,000 U
Variable overhead spending variance	1,800 F
Variable overhead efficiency variance	4,000 U
Sum of all variances	$ 700 U

In this example, the difference between total actual cost and total standard cost is equal to the sum of all variances. However, this is only true because, in this example, the amount of direct materials *purchased* is equal to the direct materials *used* in production. If this were not the case, the materials price variance plus the materials efficiency variance would not be equal to the total flexible budget variance for materials. Hence, in a broader sense, it is also true that if the amount of direct materials *purchased* had not been equal to the direct materials *used* in production, the difference between total actual costs and total standard costs would not have been equal to the sum of all of the variances. This is a key concept to remember.

SUMMARY OF LEARNING OBJECTIVES

Define standard costs and their use in standard cost accounting. (p. 1026)   **LO1**

- Standard costs represent the costs per unit that should be incurred during the upcoming year. They are established as part of the budgeting process.

- When standard cost accounting is used, all inventory accounts—material, work in process, and finished goods—and the cost of goods sold account are stated in terms of standard costs. Actual costs are accumulated separately.

Develop an overall understanding of the determination of standard costs for direct material, direct labor, and variable overhead. (p. 1028)   **LO2**

- Six components are required to develop standard variable product costs:
    - Direct material standard price
    - Direct material standard quantity
    - Direct labor standard rate
    - Direct labor standard time allowed
    - Standard variable overhead rate
    - Variable overhead standard capacity

- The standard direct material cost to produce a unit of a particular finished product is determined by multiplying the direct material standard quantity per unit by the direct material standard price per unit.

- The standard cost of direct labor required to produce one unit of a particular product is determined by multiplying the direct labor standard time allowed, usually specified in hours, by the direct labor standard wage rate.

- The standard cost of variable overhead needed to manufacture one unit of a particular product is determined by multiplying the variable overhead standard capacity by the standard (or predetermined) variable overhead application rate.

- A standard cost summary is usually prepared for each product that is manufactured. Standard costs are extremely helpful in budgeting prior to the start of a fiscal period. Moreover, they can also be very useful in evaluating performance at the end of a period.

Understand and calculate direct materials variances. (p. 1032)   **LO3**

- We calculate the materials price variance by subtracting the standard price we should have paid for the actual quantity purchased from our actual purchase price.

- We calculate the materials efficiency variance by subtracting the standard materials cost from what we should have paid according to our standards for the actual quantity purchased.

- Each variance can be either favorable or unfavorable.

LO4 **Understand and calculate direct labor variances. (p. 1036)**

- We calculate the labor rate variance by subtracting the standard price we should have paid our employees for the actual level of production from our actual labor costs.

- We calculate the labor efficiency variance by subtracting the standard labor cost from what we should have paid according to our standards for the actual hours worked.

- Each variance can be either favorable or unfavorable.

LO5 **Understand and calculate variable overhead variances. (p. 1039)**

- The variable overhead "rate" variance (i.e., the spending variance) determines whether the predetermined overhead application rate is higher or lower than the standard rate determined by managers in the budgeting process.

- Similarly, variable overhead efficiency variance is attributable to the use of that overhead application base or "driver."

- Each variance can be either favorable or unfavorable.

LO6 **Present and illustrate the use of standard costs in financial statements. (p. 1041)**

- When the standard costs and related variances for direct material, direct labor, and variable overhead are recorded, the work in process account is debited for each in amounts representing standard quantities and standard prices.

- All variances—favorable and unfavorable—are carried in separate accounts with appropriate titles.

- Standard costs are typically used in financial statements for internal use only by management.

- At year-end, firms commonly close the variance accounts by transferring their balances to Cost of Goods Sold.

- If large variances exist at year-end and there is evidence that the standards may not apply, a firm may be justified in allocating all or part of the variances to Work in Process Inventory, Finished Goods Inventory, and Cost of Goods Sold.

LO7 **Appendix 23A: Present journal entries associated with standard costs. (p. 1043)**

- Illustration of journal entries related to raw materials
- Illustration of journal entries related to direct labor
- Illustration of journal entries related to variable overhead

KEY TERMS

Labor efficiency variance (p. 1036)	Materials price variance (p. 1032)	Variable overhead efficiency variance (p. 1040)
Labor rate variance (p. 1036)	Standard cost accounting (p. 1027)	Variable overhead spending variance (p. 1040)
Materials efficiency variance (p. 1032)	Standard costs (p. 1026)	Variances (p. 1027)

Assignments with the ⬤ logo in the margin are available in BusinessCourse.
See the Preface of the book for details.

SELF-STUDY QUESTIONS

(Answers to Self-Study Questions are at the end of this chapter.)

LO1 1. **When a standard costing system is used, which of the following accounts will be reported at standard costs?**
    a. Accounts payable   *c.* Work in process inventory
    b. Wages payable   *d.* Accounts receivable

LO2 2. **In what terms are standard variable overhead application rates (SR) usually stated?**
    a. Per dollar   *c.* Per unit of product
    b. Per direct labor hour   *d.* Per month

3. **The formula [(Actual Price − Standard Price) × Actual Quantity] can be used to calculate which** LO3
   cost variance?
   a. Variable overhead volume
   b. Labor efficiency
   c. Materials efficiency
   d. Materials price

4. **Which variance considers production capacity not used?** LO5
   a. Variable overhead efficiency
   b. Labor efficiency
   c. Variable overhead spending
   d. Materials efficiency

5. **The gross profit on the interim income statement of a firm using standard costs is computed as:** LO6
   a. Sales less cost of goods sold at standard
   b. Sales less cost of goods sold at standard plus net unfavorable variances
   c. Sales less cost of goods sold at standard less net unfavorable variances
   d. Sales less cost of goods sold at actual

QUESTIONS

1. What is the difference between budgeted costs and standard costs? LO1
2. Define standard costs and describe how they are developed. LO2
3. When should standard costs be established and how often should such standards be changed? LO1
4. "Standard costs can be set too high or too low for motivational purposes." Comment. LO1
5. What is standard cost accounting? LO2
6. A finished product requires 2 pounds of a material costing $6 per pound. What is the standard cost of direct LO2
   material per unit of product?
7. A finished product requires 20 minutes of direct labor to complete each unit. Factory workers are paid $12 LO2
   per hour. What is the standard cost of direct labor per unit of product?
8. Assume that the variable overhead rate for the product described in Question 7 is $9 per hour. What is the LO2
   standard cost of variable overhead per unit of product?
9. Name and briefly describe the two direct material variances. LO3
10. Garcia Company used 6,300 pounds of direct material costing $7.80 per pound for a batch of products that LO3
    should have consumed 6,000 pounds costing $8 per pound. What are the material variances?
11. Name and briefly describe the two direct labor variances. LO4
12. Wong Lee used 1,200 direct labor hours at an average wage rate of $8.70 to manufacture products that LO4
    should have used 1,300 direct labor hours at an average wage rate of $8.50 per hour. What are the labor
    variances?
13. "Total actual cost exactly equals total standard cost, so everything must be okay." Comment. LO1
14. The variable overhead rate is $5 per direct labor hour; 31,000 direct labor hours were used to produce LO5
    7,500 units of product. The standard is 4 direct labor hours per unit. Actual, variable overhead cost was
    $153,000. Determine the variable overhead variances.
15. Who in the firm might be responsible for each of the following variances? LO7
    a. Materials price and efficiency variances
    b. Labor rate and efficiency variances
    c. Variable overhead spending and efficiency variances
16. Briefly explain how standard cost variances are reported on financial statements. LO6

EXERCISES—SET A

E23-1A. Standard Product Costs Deerfield Company manufactures product M in its factory. Production of LO2
M requires 2 pounds of material P, costing $4 per pound and 0.5 hour of direct labor costing, $10 per
hour. The variable overhead rate is $8 per direct labor hour, and the fixed overhead rate is $12 per
direct labor hour. What is the standard product cost for product M?

E23-2A. Material and Labor Variances The following actual and standard cost data for direct material and LO3, 4
direct labor relate to the production of 2,000 units of a product:

	Actual costs	Standard costs
Direct material	3,900 lb. @ $5.30	4,000 lb. @ $5.10
Direct labor	6,200 hrs. @ $8.40	6,000 hrs. @ $8.70

Determine the following variances:

a. Materials price   c. Labor rate

b. Materials efficiency   d. Labor efficiency

LO5 **E23-3A. Variable Overhead Variances** Morgan Tax Company considers 6,000 direct labor hours or 300 tax returns its normal monthly capacity. Its standard variable overhead rate is $5 per direct labor hour. During the current month, $25,400 of variable overhead cost was incurred in working 5,600 direct labor hours to prepare 270 tax returns. Determine the following variances, and indicate whether each is favorable or unfavorable:

a. Variable overhead spending

b. Variable overhead efficiency

LO3, 4, 5 **E23-4A. Material, Labor, and Variable Overhead Variances** The following summarized manufacturing data relate to Thomas Corporation's April operations, during which 2,000 finished units of product were produced. Normal monthly capacity is 1,100 direct labor hours.

	Standard Unit Costs	Total Actual Costs
Direct material:		
Standard (2 lb. @ $9/lb.)	$18	
Actual (4,200 lb. @ $10.20/lb.)		$42,840
Direct labor:		
Standard (0.5 hr. @ $24/hr.)	12	
Actual (950 hrs. @ $23.40/hr.)		22,230
Variable overhead:		
Standard (0.5 hr. @ $6/hr.)	3	
Actual		6,450
Total	$33	$71,520

Determine the materials price and efficiency variances, labor rate and efficiency variances, and variable overhead spending and efficiency variances.

LO3, 4, 5 **E23-5A. Working With Variances** From the following data, determine the total actual costs incurred for direct material, direct labor, and variable overhead.

	Standard Costs	Variances
Direct material	$120,000	
Price variance		$3,000 U
Quantity variance		4,000 F
Direct labor	100,000	
Rate variance		1,400 U
Efficiency variance		1,800 U
Variable overhead	44,000	
Spending variance		1,000 F
Efficiency variance		600 U

EXERCISES—SET B

LO2 **E23-1B. Standard Product Costs** Harrison Company manufactures product Q in its factory. Production of Q requires 3 pounds of material T, costing $7 per pound and 2 hours of direct labor, costing $10 per hour. The variable overhead rate is $6 per direct labor hour, and the fixed overhead rate is $9 per direct labor hour. What is the standard product cost for product Q?

E23-2B. Material and Labor Variances The following actual and standard cost data for direct material and direct labor relate to the production of 2,000 units of a product:

	Actual Costs	Standard Costs
Direct material	4,200 lb. @ $4.90	4,000 lb. @ $5.20
Direct labor	5,700 hrs. @ $9.30	6,000 hrs. @ $9.50

Determine the following variances:

a. Materials price
b. Materials efficiency
c. Labor rate
d. Labor efficiency

E23-3B. Variable Overhead Variances Marshfield Tax Company considers 8,000 direct labor hours or 400 tax returns its normal monthly capacity. Its standard variable overhead rate is $4 per direct labor hour. During the current month, $31,500 of variable overhead cost was incurred in working 7,500 direct labor hours to produce 360 units of product. Determine the following variances, and indicate whether each is favorable or unfavorable:

a. Variable overhead spending
b. Variable overhead efficiency

E23-4B. Material, Labor, and Variable Overhead Variances The following summarized manufacturing data relate to Brown Corporation's May operations, during which 2,000 finished units of product were produced. Normal monthly capacity is 1,100 direct labor hours.

	Standard Unit Costs	Total Actual Costs
Direct material:		
Standard (3 lb. @ $2.00/lb.)	$ 6	
Actual (6,400 lb. @ $2.20/lb.)		$14,080
Direct labor:		
Standard (0.5 hr. @ $14/hr.)	7	
Actual (950 hrs. @ $13.70/hr.)		13,015
Variable overhead:		
Standard (0.5 hr. @ $4/hr.)	2	
Actual		4,300
Total	$15	$31,395

Determine the materials price and efficiency variances, labor rate and efficiency variances, and variable overhead spending and efficiency variances.

E23-5B. Working With Variances From the following data, determine the total actual costs incurred for direct material, direct labor, and variable overhead.

	Standard Costs	Variances
Direct material	$55,000	
Price variance		$1,200 U
Quantity variance		2,200 F
Direct labor	46,000	
Rate variance		500 U
Efficiency variance		800 U
Variable overhead	18,000	
Spending variance		400 F
Efficiency variance		700 U

PROBLEMS—SET A

LO3, 4, 5 **P23-1A. Calculate Variances** The following summary data relate to the operations of Dobson Company for April, during which 9,000 finished units were produced. Normal monthly capacity was 20,000 direct labor hours.

	Standard Unit Costs	Total Actual Costs
Direct material:		
Standard (4 lb. @ $2.20/lb.)	$ 8.80	
Actual (38,000 lb. @ $2.00/lb.)		$ 76,000
Direct labor:		
Standard (2 hrs. @ $11.00/hr.)	22.00	
Actual (18,500 hrs. @ $11.30/hr.)		209,050
Variable overhead:		
Standard (2 hrs. @ $3.00/hr.)	6.00	
Actual		54,900
Total	$36.80	$339,950

Required

Determine the following variances and indicate whether each is favorable or unfavorable:

a. Materials price and efficiency variances
b. Labor rate and efficiency variances
c. Variable overhead spending and efficiency variances

LO3, 4, 5, 6,7 **P23-2A. Variances, Entries, and Income Statement** A summary of Glendale Company's manufacturing variance report for May 2016 follows:

	Total Standard Costs (9,200 units)	Total Actual Costs (9,200 units)	Variances
Direct material	$ 38,640	$ 42,630	$3,990 U
Direct labor........................	193,200	193,120	80 F
Variable overhead..................	23,460	23,230	230 F
Fixed overhead....................	9,660	9,660	
	$264,960	$268,640	$3,680 U

Standard material cost per unit of product is 0.5 pounds at $8.40 per pound, and standard direct labor cost is 1.5 hours at $14.00 per hour. The total actual materials cost represents 4,900 pounds purchased at $8.70 per pound. Total actual labor cost represents 14,200 hours at $13.60 per hour. According to standards, variable overhead rate is applied at $1.70 per direct labor hour (based on a normal capacity of 15,000 direct labor hours or 10,000 units of product). Assume that all fixed overhead is applied to work in progress inventory.

Required

a. Calculate variances for materials price and efficiency, labor rate and efficiency, and variable overhead spending and efficiency.
b. Prepare general journal entries to record standard costs, actual costs, and related variances for material, labor, and overhead.
c. Prepare journal entries to record the transfer of all completed units to Finished Goods Inventory and the subsequent sale of 8,400 units on account at $54 each (assume no beginning finished goods inventory).
d. Prepare a partial income statement (through gross profit on sales) showing gross profit based on standard costs, the incorporation of variances, and gross profit based on actual costs.

P23-3A. Variances and Journal Entries Jacobs Company manufactures a single product and uses a standard costing system. The nature of its product dictates that it be sold in the period it is produced. Thus, no ending work in process or finished goods inventories remain at the end of the period. However, raw materials can be stored and are purchased in bulk when prices are favorable. Per-unit standard product costs are material, $8 (4 pounds); labor, $6 (0.5 hour); and variable overhead, $4 (based on direct labor hours). Budgeted fixed overhead is $54,000.

LO3, 4, 5, 7

Jacobs accounts for all inventories and cost of goods sold at standard cost and records each variance in a separate account. The following data relate to May 2016 when 17,700 finished units were produced.

Required

a. Assume Jacobs purchased 69,000 pounds of raw materials on account at $2.20 per pound and used 67,000 pounds in May's production, prepare a journal entry to record the purchase of raw materials and a separate journal entry to record the use of raw materials in production. Record these entries using standard costs and include the appropriate materials variances.

b. Assuming employees worked 8,900 direct labor hours at an average hourly rate of $11.70, prepare a journal entry to record actual costs, standard costs, and any labor variances.

c. Assuming Jacobs' actual and applied variable overhead was $74,200 and that budgeted and actual fixed overhead incurred was $54,000, prepare a journal entry to record actual and standard overhead costs and any overhead variances.

P23-4A. Variances, Total Overhead Variances, and Variance Reconciliation Milton Company planned to produce 21,000 units of its only product during the year. Milton established the following standard cost data for this product prior to the beginning of the year:

LO3, 4, 5

	Per Unit
Direct material (3 lbs. @ $5.00 per lb.)	$15.00
Direct labor (2 hrs. @ $17.50 per hr.)	35.00
Variable overhead (2 hrs. @ $6 per hr.)	12.00
Total standard cost per unit	$62.00

Total budgeted fixed overhead is $400,000.

Assume that Milton (1) actually produced 22,000 units, (2) used 68,000 pounds of direct materials in production, (3) and incurred the following actual total costs:

	Total Cost
Direct materials purchased (70,000 lbs. @ 4.80)	$ 336,000
Direct labor (43,000 hrs. @ $18.00)	774,000
Variable overhead	262,320
Fixed overhead	400,000
Total actual costs	$1,772,320

Required

a. Calculate the variances for materials, labor, and variable overhead.

b. Does the difference between total actual costs and total standard costs equal the sum of all of the variances? Explain.

PROBLEMS—SET B

LO3, 4, 5

P23-1B. Calculate Variances The following summary data relate to the operations of Randolph Company for July, during which 4,500 finished units were produced:

	Standard Total Unit Costs	Total Actual Costs
Direct material:		
Standard (0.6 lb. @ $9.00/lb.)	$ 5.40	
Actual (3,000 lb. @ $9.40/lb.)		$ 28.200
Direct labor:		
Standard (0.8 hr. @ $12.80/hr.).	10.24	
Actual (3,800 hrs. @ $12.50/hr.)		47,500
Variable overhead:		
Standard (0.8 hr. @ $7.50/hr.).	6.00	
Actual		30,100
Total	$21.64	$105,800

Required

Determine the following variances and indicate whether each is favorable or unfavorable:

a. Materials price variance and efficiency variance
b. Labor rate variance and efficiency variance
c. Variable overhead spending variance and efficiency variance

LO3, 4, 5, 6 ,7

P23-2B. Variances, Entries, and Income Statement A summary of Blake Company's manufacturing variance report for June 2016 follows.

	Total Standard Costs (7,600 units)	Total Actual Costs (7,600 units)	Variances
Direct material	$ 66,880	$ 65,100	$1,780 F
Direct labor.	77,520	82,800	5,280 U
Variable overhead.	34,200	33,000	1,200 F
Fixed overhead.	102,600	102,600	
	$281,200	$283,500	$2,300 U

Standard material cost per unit of product is 4 pounds at $2.20 per pound, and standard direct labor cost is 0.75 hours at $13.60 per hour. Total actual material cost represents 31,000 pounds purchased at $2.10 per pound. Total actual labor cost represents 6,000 hours at $13.80 per hour. According to standards, variable overhead rate is applied at $6 per direct labor hour (based on a normal capacity of 6,000 direct labor hours or 8,000 units of product). Assume that all fixed overhead is applied to work in progress inventory.

Required

a. Calculate variances for materials price and efficiency, labor rate and efficiency, and variable overhead spending and efficiency.
b. Prepare general journal entries to record standard costs, actual costs, and related variances for material, labor, and overhead.
c. Prepare journal entries to record the transfer of all completed units to Finished Goods Inventory and the subsequent sale of 6,400 units on account at $60 each (assume no beginning finished goods inventory).
d. Prepare a partial income statement (through gross profit on sales) showing gross profit based on standard costs, the incorporation of variances, and gross profit based on actual costs.

LO3, 4, 5, 7

P23-3B. Variances and Journal Entries Kent Company manufactures a single product and uses a standard costing system. The nature of its product dictates that it be sold in the period it is produced. Thus, no ending work in process or finished goods inventories remain at the end of the period. However, raw materials can be stored and are purchased in bulk when prices are favorable. Per-unit, standard product costs are material, $6 (0.5 pound); labor, $15 (1.5 hours); and variable overhead, $3 (based on direct labor hours). Budgeted fixed overhead is $96,000.

Kent Company accounts for all inventories and cost of goods sold at standard cost and records each variance in a separate account. The following data relate to June, 2016 when 7,800 finished units were produced.

Required

a.   Assume Kent purchased 4,500 pounds of raw materials on account at $11.60 per pound and used 4,200 pounds in June's production, prepare a journal entry to record the purchase of raw materials and a separate journal entry to record the use of raw materials in production. Record these entries using standard costs and include the appropriate materials variances.

b.   Assuming Kent's employees worked 12,000 direct labor hours at an average hourly rate of $10.50, prepare a journal entry to record actual costs, standard costs, and any labor variances.

c.   Assuming Kent's actual and applied variable overhead was $23,100 and that budgeted and actual fixed overhead incurred was $96,000, prepare a journal entry to record actual and standard overhead costs and any overhead variances.

P23-4B. Variances, Total Overhead Variances, and Variance Reconciliation Sanchez Company planned to   **LO3, 4, 5** produce 10,000 units of its only product during the year. Sanchez established the following standard cost data for this product prior to the beginning of the year:

	Per Unit
Direct material (2 lb. @ $7.50 per lb.)	$15.00
Direct labor (1.5 hrs. @ $13.50 per hr.).	20.25
Variable overhead (1.5 hrs. @ $6 per hr.)	9.00
Total standard cost per unit.	$44.25

Total budgeted fixed overhead is $144,000.

Assume that Sanchez (1) actually produced 9,000 units, (2) used 17,000 pounds of direct materials in production, (3) and incurred the following actual total costs:

	Total Cost
Direct materials purchased (19,000 lb. @ 7.80)	$148,200
Direct labor (14,000 hrs. @ $13.35)	186,900
Variable overhead.	80,250
Fixed overhead.	144,000
Total actual costs	$559,350

Required

a.   Calculate the variances for materials, labor, and variable overhead.

b.   Does the difference between total actual costs and total standard costs equal the sum of all of the variances? Explain.

CERTIFIED MANAGEMENT ACCOUNTANT (CMA®) EXAM SAMPLE QUESTIONS

CMA23-1. Which one of the following statements is correct concerning a flexible budget cost formula? Variable costs are stated

a.   per unit and fixed costs are stated in total.

b.   in total and fixed costs are stated per unit.

c.   in total and fixed costs are stated in total.

d.   per unit and fixed costs are stated per unit.

CMA23-2. Of the following pairs of variances found in a flexible budget report, which pair is most likely to be related?

    a. Materials price variance and variable overhead efficiency variance.

    b. Labor rate variance and variable overhead efficiency variance.

    c. Material usage variance and labor efficiency variance.

    d. Labor efficiency variance and fixed overhead volume variance.

CMA23-3. Lee manufacturing uses a standard cost system with overhead applied based on direct labor hours. The manufacturing budget for the production of 5,000 units for the month of June included 10,000 hours of direct labor at $15 per hour, $150,000. During June, 4,500 units were produced, using 9,600 direct labor hours, incurring $39,360 of variable overhead, and showing a variable overhead efficiency variance of $2,400 unfavorable. The standard variable overhead rate per direct labor hour was

    a. $3.85.

    b. $4.00.

    c. $4.10.

    d. $6.00.

CMA23-4. Marten Company has a cost-benefit policy to investigate any variance that is greater than $1,000 or 10% of budget, whichever is larger. Actual results for the previous month indicate the following.

	Budget	Actual
Raw material.	$100,000	$89,000
Direct labor.	50,000	54,000

The company should investigate

    a. neither the material variance nor the labor variance.

    b. the material variance only.

    c. the labor variance only.

    d. both the material variance and the labor variance.

CMA23-5. Frisco Company recently purchased 108,000 units of raw material for $583,200. Three units of raw materials are budgeted for use in each finished good manufactured, with the raw material standard set at $16.50 for each completed product. Frisco manufactured 32,700 finished units during the period just ended and used 99,200 units of raw material. If management is concerned about the timely reporting of variances in an effort to improve cost control and bottom-line performance, the materials purchase price variance should be reported as

    a. $6,050 unfavorable.

    b. $9,920 favorable.

    c. $10,800 unfavorable.

    d. $10,800 favorable.

EXTENDING YOUR KNOWLEDGE

EYK23-1. **Business Decision Case** Porter Corporation has just hired Bill Harlow as its new controller. Although Harlow has had little formal accounting training, he professes to be highly experienced, having learned accounting "the hard way" in the field. At the end of his first month's work, Harlow prepared the following performance report:

PORTER CORPORATION
Performance Report
for the Month of June, 2015

	Total Actual Costs	Total Budgeted Costs	Variances
Direct material	$216,630	$237,600	$20,970 F
Direct labor.	119,340	132,000	12,660 F
Variable overhead.	63,000	66,000	3,000 F
Fixed overhead.	184,000	184,000	
	$582,970	$619,600	$36,630 F

In his presentation at Porter's month-end management meeting, Harlow indicated that things were going "fantastically." "The figures indicate," he said, "that the firm is beating its budget in all cost categories." This good news made everyone at the meeting happy and furthered Harlow's acceptance as a member of the management team.

After the management meeting, Susan Jones, Porter's general manager, asked you, as an independent consultant, to review Harlow's report. Jones' concern stemmed from the fact that Porter has never operated as favorably as Harlow's report seems to imply, and she cannot explain the apparent significant improvement.

While reviewing Harlow's report, you are provided the following cost and operating data for June: Porter has a monthly normal capacity of 11,000 direct labor hours or 8,800 units of product. Standard costs per unit for its only product are direct material, 3 pounds at $9 per pound; direct labor, 1.25 hours at $12 per hour; and variable overhead rate per direct labor hour of $6. During June, Porter produced 8,000 units of product, using 24,900 pounds of material costing $8.70 each, 10,200 direct labor hours at an average rate of $11.70 each, and incurred variable overhead costs of $63,000 and fixed overhead costs of $184,000.

After reviewing Porter's June cost data, you tell Harlow that his cost report contains a classic budgeting error, and you explain how he can remedy it. In response to your suggestion, Harlow revises his report as follows:

	Total Actual Costs	Total Budgeted Costs	Variances
Direct material	$216,630	$216,000	$ 630 U
Direct labor.	119,340	120,000	660 F
Variable overhead.	63,000	60,000	3,000 U
Fixed overhead.	184,000	184,000	
	$582,970	$580,000	$2,970 U

Harlow's revised report is accompanied by remarks expressing regret at the oversight in the original report.

Required

In your role as consultant,

a. Verify that Harlow's actual cost figures are correct.
b. Identify and explain the classic budgeting error that Harlow apparently incorporated into his original cost report.
c. Explain why Harlow's revised figures could be considered deficient.
d. Further analyze Harlow's revised variances, isolating underlying potential causal factors. How do your analyses indicate bases for concern to management?

EYK23-2. Ethics Case Custom Furniture, manufacturer of handmade furniture, uses standard cost accounting for the company. Standards are developed annually based on input from production workers and supervisors.

The supervisor of the table department has approached several employees that work for him and suggested that the employees overestimate the amount of material (by 20%) and labor (by 30%) involved in producing certain new tables. He states that it is better to overestimate than underestimate costs as the product has never been manufactured in quantity before and it is uncertain what the actual materials and labor will be. In addition, he states that this would result in any variances being favorable to the department.

The employees are not sure what estimates they should discuss with the accounting department. The accounting department wants accurate input that it will adjust for uncertainty.

Required
How would you advise the employees? What ethical issues are involved?

ANSWERS TO SELF-STUDY QUESTIONS:

1. c, (p. 1027)   2. b, (p. 1029)   3. d, (p. 1032)   4. a, (p. 1039)   5. c, (pp. 1041–1042)

DECISION TIME SOLUTION

Solution 23.1

- An unfavorable materials price variance suggests that personnel in the purchasing department paid more for materials than the company's standard costs would normally allow.
- An unfavorable materials efficiency variance would mean that assembly workers used more material (or parts) in production than standards would normally allow.
- A favorable labor rate variance suggests that human resource personnel were able to hire production workers at wage rates below what standards would normally allow.
- An unfavorable labor efficiency variance would indicate that workers spent more time to produce the actual number of outputs than standards would normally allow.

YOUR TURN! SOLUTIONS

Solution 23.1
Materials price variance: AQ (AP − SP) = 90,000 ($2.90 − $3.00) = $9,000 F
Materials efficiency variance: SP (AQ − SQ) = $3.00 [90,000 − (4 × 22,000)] = $6,000 U

Solution 23.2
Labor rate variance: AH (AR − SR) = 35,000 × ($7.50 − $7.00) = $17,500 U
Labor efficiency variance: SR (AH − SH) = $7.00 [35,000 − (1.5 × 22,000)] = $14,000 U

Solution 23.3
Variable overhead spending variance: Actual VOH − (AQ × AR) = $63,000 − (35,000 × $2.00) = $7,000 F
Variable overhead efficiency variance: SR (AH − SH) = $2.00 [35,000 − (1.5 × 22,000)] = $4,000 U

Solution 23.4
Materials price variance: AQ (AP − SP) = 55,000 ($5.30 − $5.10) = $11,000 U
Materials efficiency variance: SP (AQ − SQ) = $5.10 [55,000 − (4 × 11,000)] = $56,100 U

Raw Materials Inventory	280,500	
Materials Price Variance	11,000	
Accounts Payable (or Cash)		291,500

Work in Process Inventory	224,400	
Materials Efficiency Variance	56,100	
Raw Materials Inventory		280,500

Solution 23.5

Labor rate variance: AH (AR − SR) = 23,000 ($3.00 − $3.50) = $11,500 F
Labor efficiency variance: SR (AH − SH) = $3.50 [23,000 − (2 × 15,000)] = $24,500 F

Work in Process Inventory	105,000	
Labor Rate Variance		11,500
Labor Efficiency Variance		24,500
Wages Payable		69,000

24

Flexible Budgets, Segment Reporting, and Performance Analysis

PAST

Chapter 23 defined standard costs and standard cost variances: direct material, direct labor, and variable overhead variances.

PRESENT

Chapter 24 introduces flexible budgets and performance evaluation of business segments. In addition, it explores both performance and variance analysis.

FUTURE

Chapter 25 introduces capital budgeting and illustrates how capital budgeting is used to make capital investment decisions.

LEARNING OBJECTIVES

1. **Describe** a static budget, **illustrate** its use, and **present** an example of a static budget performance report. *(p. 1062)*

2. **Introduce** the flexible budget and **present** an example of a flexible budget performance report. **Explain** how flexible budgeting helps in variance analysis. *(p. 1063)*

3. **Present** an overview of reporting operations for segments of a business. *(p. 1069)*

4. **Construct** a segmented contribution margin income statement. **Identify** the difference between traceable and common fixed costs. *(p. 1072)*

5. **Compute** return on investment, return on sales, return on assets, and residual income for business segments. **Discuss** the importance of each indicator in assessing a company's performance. *(p. 1079)*

6. Appendix 24A: **Determine** the proper transfer price to maximize company profit with and without excess productive capacity. *(p. 1086)*

MICROSOFT CORPORATION

When was the last time you fired up and used your computer? Chances are the software you used was produced by Microsoft Corporation. Microsoft commands a dominating presence in the software industry, boasting a 95% market share in the productivity software market, 75% share in the operating system market, and approximately 75% share in the server software market.[1] Microsoft is a global leader in software production and one of the world's most valuable companies. In Chapter 10 we introduced Microsoft as one of the world's most well-recognized companies. Its early business model was so successful it did not need to issue debt financing until 34 years after the company was founded by Bill Gates in 1975.

While the company has grown significantly since its founding, it has maintained an edge in the software industry through the careful application of managerial accounting concepts. In budgeting sales and production needs for future periods, Microsoft is never 100% accurate in its forecasts, as sales frequently grow more slowly or quickly than expected. To accommodate the fluctuation in sales, the company can find a meaningful method of comparing actual results to budgeted results, with the number of units produced remaining the same for both. In a previous chapter, we presented and discussed the components of the master budget. In this chapter, we will examine flexible budgeting, and the advantages of using flexible budgeting over static budgeting. In addition, we will introduce segment reporting and performance analysis, and explain performance measures that are helpful in assessing the health of a company.

Performance analysis is essential in the management process of any entity. Budgetary control involves the steps taken by management to ensure that the goals and objectives established during the planning stage are attained, and to ensure that all segments of the firm operate in a manner consistent with organizational policies. Budgets should serve as guides or targets for managers when they make decisions because the budget is usually the basis for performance evaluation. Segment reporting allows managers to compare and assess the performance of individual segments or employees across the company by evaluating segments' key performance indicators, such as return on investment, return on sales, return on assets, and residual income. Another and more comprehensive tool used to assess performance is the balanced scorecard, which includes both financial and nonfinancial measures of performance.

---

[1] http://www.forbes.com/sites/greatspeculations/2013/01/09/an-overview-why-microsofts-worth-42/

FLEXIBLE BUDGETS, SEGMENT REPORTING, AND PERFORMANCE ANALYSIS					
Static Budgets	**Flexible Budgets**	**Internal Reporting of Segment Operations**	**Performance Reporting**	**Performance Analysis**	**Transfer Pricing (Appendix 24A)**
• Definition • Uses	• Flexible budgets in a manufacturing environment • Variance analysis of flexible budget differences • Flexible budgets in a service environment	• Decentralized organizations • Segment reporting • Types of business segments	• Departmental operations • Contribution margin income statement • Segment performance evaluation • Service company segment reporting illustration	• Return on investment • Return on sales • Asset utilization • Residual income • Balanced scorecard	• Domestic transfer pricing • International transfer pricing

It is critically important that management have a means of measuring and evaluating the performance of employees, departments, segments, and the overall company to ensure that all are working toward the achievement of the company's strategic vision. In this chapter, we discuss several tools available to assist managers in evaluating performance: flexible budgets, segment reporting, and performance analysis and reporting.

STATIC BUDGETS

LO1 **Describe** a static budget, **illustrate** its use, and **present** an example of a static budget performance report.

The master budget is made up of budgets known as static budgets. A **static budget** is a financial plan developed for a fixed level of operating activity, typically the expected or most likely level. The static budget is the budgeted amount used to calculate the standard costs that we discussed in Chapter 23.

If actual results are compared to a static budget, the variances that result are of little use to management, because the budget is often based on a different level of activity than the actual operations. The following example illustrates this point.

A.K.A. Static budgets are also called *nonmoving* or *stationary budgets*.

Exhibit 24-1 presents a simple static budget for Fezzari's Foré CR1 product line for the 2016 fiscal year. Although Fezzari's management has a target production of 5,000 Foré CR1 road bikes during the year, it anticipates that this may be an aggressive projection.

Exhibit 24-1	Static Budget Illustration

FEZZARI FORÉ CR1 PRODUCT LINE Static Budget for Product Costs For the Year Ended December 31, 2016	
Budgeted units of production	5,000
Budgeted costs:	
Direct material.	$2,500,000
Direct labor	285,000
Manufacturing overhead.	525,000
Total	$3,310,000

Exhibit 24-2 presents a static budget performance report for the CR1 product line for 2016. The static budget performance report compares the *actual* costs to produce 4,800 units with the *budgeted* costs to produce 5,000 units. The performance report accurately reveals that actual units of CR1 production were 200 less than management had budgeted. In a performance report comparing actual costs to budgeted costs, "F" indicates a favorable variance and "U" identifies an unfavorable variance.

Exhibit 24-2	Static Budget Performance Report Illustration

FEZZARI FORÉ CR1 PRODUCT LINE
Static Budget Performance Report
For the Year Ended December 31, 2016

Budgeted units of production	5,000	
Actual units of production	4,800	
Units of production variance	200	U

	Actual Cost Incurred for 4,800 Units	Budget Based on 5,000 Units	Cost Variances	
Direct material	$2,486,400	$2,500,000	$(13,600)	F
Direct labor.	302,400	285,000	17,400	U
Manufacturing overhead	490,000	525,000	(35,000)	F
Total	$3,278,800	$3,310,000	$(31,200)	F

U = Unfavorable
F = Favorable

The static budget performance report, however, provides misleading cost variances. For example, the direct material variance is $13,600 favorable (i.e., the actual cost is less than budgeted cost). This comparison is misleading because the actual cost to produce 4,800 units is being compared to the budgeted cost to produce 5,000 units, not 4,800 units. Moreover, although the total variance is $31,200 favorable, the actual cost per unit is about $683 per unit ($3,278,800/4,800 CR1s), and the budgeted cost per CR1 is only $662 ($3,310,000/5,000 CR1s). Hence, although the cost per unit is actually higher than the budgeted cost per unit, the total static budget variance appears to be favorable simply because the company produced 200 fewer CR1s than it anticipated.

FLEXIBLE BUDGETS

A **flexible budget** is a financial plan in the form of a cost formula or a multiple-column presentation that makes cost projections for various activity levels within a relevant range.

LO2 Introduce the flexible budget and **present** an example of a flexible budget performance report. **Explain** how flexible budgeting helps in variance analysis.

Flexible Budgets in a Manufacturing Environment

Exhibit 24-3 presents a 2016 flexible budget for Fezzari's Foré CR1 product line. The first two columns show the CR1 budgeted per-unit variable costs and budgeted total fixed costs of production. The last three columns present the budget for different levels of production. The middle column is the budget for 5,000 units of production that would be comparable to the static budget in **Exhibit 24-1**. Knowing the per-unit variable costs and the fixed costs of production allows Fezzari management to prepare a budget for any level of production within the relevant range.

Exhibit 24-3	Flexible Budget for Fezzari Foré CR1				

FEZZARI FORÉ CR1 PRODUCT LINE
Flexible Product Costs Budget
For the Year Ended December 31, 2016

	1		2		
	Variable Cost per Unit	**Total Fixed Cost**	**4,500 Units**	**5,000 Units**	**5,500 Units**
Variable costs					
Direct material	$500.00		$2,250,000	$2,500,000	$2,750,000
Direct labor.	57.00		256,500	285,000	313,500
Variable overhead. . . .	60.00		270,000	300,000	330,000
	$617.00		$2,776,500	$3,085,000	$3,393,500
Fixed costs					
Fixed overhead.		$225,000	$ 225,000	$ 225,000	$ 225,000
Total			$3,001,500	$3,310,000	$3,618,500

Exhibit 24-3 demonstrates a number of the characteristics about flexible budgets. First, the flexible budget usually divides costs and expenses into two groups: variable and fixed. Second, the flexible budget typically presents the variable costs and expenses on a per-unit basis and the fixed costs and expenses in total. Third, in using a columnar format, all of the columns are based on levels of activity within the relevant range. It is important to remember that the flexible budget formula is valid only for the range of activity for which it is formulated.

ACCOUNTING IN PRACTICE | **Relevant Range**

To illustrate the concept of relevant range, assume that XYZ Company has one manufacturing building in which it manufactures toys. As long as no more than 10,000 toys are produced, the fixed costs associated with this building belong to one relevant range, 0–10,000 toys. If more than 10,000 toys are produced, XYZ will need an additional building, thus incurring additional fixed costs. The costs will be in a new relevant range.

A flexible budget, prepared with columns representing different projected levels of activity, provides managers with targets for various activity levels. Hence, during the period, a flexible budget can help managers assess the reasonableness of the firm's performance as the period progresses. However, one of the most important uses of the flexible budget comes not during, but *after* the end of the period. The flexible budget formula also allows managers to compare actual costs to budgeted costs based on the actual production level achieved. Specifically, the flexible budget performance report compares actual costs at the actual level of activity to the budgeted costs at the actual level of activity.

Exhibit 24-4 presents Fezzari's 2016 flexible budget performance report for the Foré CR1 product line. This performance report allows managers to evaluate how the company's actual performance compares to budgeted performance (based on the actual level of production) for different products. Specifically, the flexible budget performance report compares actual performance in column A to budgeted performance in column B with a flexible budget (rate or price) variance, as discussed in Chapter 23, for each component of product cost (direct materials, direct labor, variable overhead, and fixed overhead). Further, it compares the flexible budget in column A (based on 4,800 actual units) to the static budget in column C (based on 5,000 budgeted units). These differences are the efficiency variances, as discussed in Chapter 23.

Exhibit 24-4	Flexible Budget Performance Report Illustration

FEZZARI FORÉ CR1 PRODUCT LINE
Flexible Budget Performance Report
For the Year Ended December 31, 2016

Budgeted units of production . . .		5,000			
Actual units of production		4,800			
Units of production variance		200 U			

	A	B	(A-B)	C	(B-C)
	Actual Costs Incurred for 4,800 Units	Flexible Budget Based on 4,800 Units	Price or Rate Variances	Static Budget Based on 5,000 Units	Efficiency Variances
Variable costs:					
Direct material.	$2,486,400	$2,400,000	$86,400 U	$2,500,000	$(100,000) F
Direct labor	302,400	273,600	28,800 U	285,000	(11,400) F
Variable overhead	268,800	288,000	(19,200) F	300,000	(12,000) F
	$3,057,600	$2,961,600	$96,000 U	$3,085,000	$(123,400) F
Fixed costs:					
Fixed overhead	$ 221,200	$ 225,000	$ (3,800) F	$ 225,000	$ —
Total	$3,278,800	$3,186,600	$92,200 U	$3,310,000	$(123,400) F

U = Unfavorable
F = Favorable

In essence, the flexible budget performance report compares "what we actually spent" to "what we should have spent" for the final production level. The flexible performance report is prepared by simply using the flexible budget formula to budget what the company "should have spent" based on the actual level of production (i.e., inserting the actual number of CR1 units produced, 4,800, into the flexible product costs budget).

A comparison of cost variances in the static budget performance report (**Exhibit 24-2**) and the flexible budget performance report (**Exhibit 24-4**) reveals a very different result. The static budget performance report indicates a total favorable cost variance of $31,200, whereas the flexible budget performance report reveals a total unfavorable rate or price variance of $92,200 and a total favorable efficiency variance of $123,400. As explained previously, one reason the budget projections in **Exhibit 24-2** do not provide an accurate depiction of budgeted costs is that the static budget is based on the projected production level (5,000 CR1s) when actual production fell short (4,800 CR1s). Thus, part of the difference in the two comparisons is related to the volume differential (i.e., actual production came up 200 units short of the static budget production level). Clearly, the variances from the flexible budget performance report provide a more complete explanation because they are based on a comparison of what the costs actually were to what the costs should have been at the actual level of activity.

As discussed in Chapter 23, management can delve further into the causes for the overall flexible budget variance (columns A and B) by breaking each component of the variance down into individual price/rate variances. For example, to explain the $86,400 unfavorable price variance for direct materials, price variances could be calculated for *each* direct material used in producing a Foré CR1.

Similarly, labor rate variances would be computed to explain the overall $28,800 unfavorable labor rate variance and the overall $19,200 favorable variable overhead variance.

Management by Exception

Performance reports should incorporate the management-by-exception concept. Variances outside acceptable ranges should be identified so management attention can be directed to those exceptional items.

Flexible Budgets in a Service Environment

SERVICE AND MERCHANDISING

Flexible budgets can be used in a service company just like in a manufacturing firm. For example, Old Rosebud is a 400-acre farm on the outskirts of the Kentucky Bluegrass region that specializes in boarding broodmares and their foals. An economic downturn in the thoroughbred industry has led to a decline in breeding activities. As a consequence, the demand for thoroughbred boarding has decreased, making the boarding business extremely competitive. To meet the competition, in 2016 Old Rosebud planned to entertain clients, advertise, and absorb expenses formerly borne by clients (for example, the company would pay for both veterinary and blacksmith's fees).

Exhibit 24-5 presents the variances between Old Rosebud's actual operating results in 2016 and amounts budgeted for the year. Its budget—like those of most service organizations—was a static budget (i.e., it forecast an expected level of activity). Old Rosebud expected to log 21,900 boarding days, and it budgeted boarding rates at $25 per day per mare.

The variable expenses per mare per day were budgeted as follows:

Feed	$5.00
Veterinary fees	$3.00
Blacksmith fees	$0.30
Supplies	$0.40

All other budgeted expenses were either semi-fixed or fixed.

The static budget in **Exhibit 24-5** can be used to explain only two factors: sales and fixed expenses. As sales volume problems arose during the year, Old Rosebud decided not to replace a farm worker who quit in March. It also developed a new farm brochure and entertained more potential clients. These strategies generated the fixed-expense variances—that is, the differences between the budgeted and actual line item amounts in the income statement.

No sound conclusions can be drawn about either the effect of price changes on the decrease in net income or the expense variances. When sales volume declines, sales revenue and variable expenses may be expected to decrease proportionately. However, the rate of Old Rosebud's decline in the number of boarding days (13%) differs from the rate of decrease in sales revenue (31%) and the rate of decrease in variable expenses (7%).

A plausible interpretation of the variances in **Exhibit 24-5** is that the large variance in net income is caused by a decrease in sales volume. This interpretation follows from the large unfavorable sales revenue variance and the generally favorable expense variances.

Indeed, at first glance, it appears as though expenses are well under control. All variable-expense variances are favorable, and the total of the two unfavorable fixed-expense variances is insignificant in relation to the total sales-revenue variance. The unfavorable advertising and entertainment variances may be interpreted as having prevented the unfavorable net income variance from being even greater. More business might have been lost had Old Rosebud not overspent its budgeted amounts for those items.

Because sales are down and expenses are well under control, this analysis suggests an obvious but faulty remedy: Do more advertising and entertaining.

Exhibit 24-5	Static Budget Illustration—Service

OLD ROSEBUD
Static Budget Income Statement
Year Ended December 31, 2016

	Actual	Static Budget	Variance
Number of mares	62	60	(0) U
Number of boarding days	18,980	21,900	(2,920) U
Sales.	$379,600	$547,500	$(167,900) U
Less variable expenses:			
Feed	104,390	109,500	(5,110) F
Veterinary fees	58,838	65,700	(6,862) F
Blacksmith fees	6,074	6,570	(496) F
Supplies	7,402	8,760	(1,358) F
Total variable expenses	$176,704	$190,530	(13,826) F
Contribution margin	$202,896	$356,970	$(154,074) U
Less fixed expenses:			
Depreciation	$ 45,000	$ 45,000	$ —
Insurance	11,000	11,000	—
Utilities	12,000	14,000	(2,000) F
Repairs and maintenance.	10,000	11,000	(1,000) F
Labor.	88,000	96,000	(8,000) F
Advertisement.	11,000	8,000	3,000 U
Entertainment	8,000	5,000	3,000 U
Total fixed expenses	$185,000	$190,000	$ (5,000) F
Net income.	$ 17,896	$166,970	$(149,074) U

U = Unfavorable
F = Favorable

Exhibit 24-6 compares Old Rosebud's actual operating results with those in a flexible budget for 2016. The flexible budget takes the same budgeted per-unit amounts for sales and variable expenses and applies them to the actual number of boarding days achieved in 2016. Because, by definition, fixed expenses don't vary with volume, they're the same as in the static budget. A budget constructed in this way removes the distortion in the sales-revenue and variable-expense variances of a static budget.

Two surprises are immediately apparent. First, when the unfavorable sales-revenue variance of $167,900 is separated into the unfavorable sales-price ($94,900) and unfavorable sales-volume ($73,000) variances, it becomes clear that the sales-price variance is larger. Further investigation of the sales-price variance revealed that Old Rosebud lost a major client in 2016. Moreover, because of fierce competition, the farm reduced its boarding charges well below $25 per day per mare as the year progressed. As a result, the average boarding rate declined for the year.

The second surprise in **Exhibit 24-6** is that expense control was far worse than analysis of the static budget variance had indicated. All variable-expense variances, except supplies, were unfavorable. The unfavorable feed variance of $9,490 alone accounted for nearly 82% of the net unfavorable variable-expense variances of $11,578. The large feed variance was explained by the drought that hit Kentucky and most of the rest of the nation in 2016. In addition, several recent studies had indicated that copper feed supplements may be necessary to minimize skeletal bone disease in young horses. Old Rosebud incorporated the supplement at an increased cost and continued to feed first-class hay despite the drought.

Exhibit 24-6	Flexible Budget Illustration—Service

OLD ROSEBUD
Flexible Budget Income Statement
Year Ended December 31, 2016

Budgeted number of boarding days ... 21,900
Actual number of boarding days 18,980

	Budget (per mare per day)	Actual	Flexible Budget	Variance	
Number of mares		52	52	0	
Number of boarding days		18,980	18,980	0	
Sales............................	$25.00	$379,600	$474,500	$ (94,900)	U
Less variable expenses:					
Feed	5.00	104,390	94,900	9,490	U
Veterinary fees	3.00	58,838	56,940	1,898	U
Blacksmith fees	0.30	6,074	5,694	380	U
Supplies	0.40	7,402	7,592	(190)	F
Total variable expenses	$ 8.70	$176,704	$165,126	$ 11,578	U
Contribution margin	$16.30	$202,896	$309,374	$(106,478)	U
Less fixed expenses:					
Depreciation		$ 45,000	$ 45,000	$ —	
Insurance		11,000	11,000	—	
Utilities		12,000	14,000	(2,000)	F
Repairs and maintenance..........		10,000	11,000	(1,000)	F
Labor...........................		88,000	96,000	(8,000)	F
Advertisement...................		11,000	8,000	3,000	U
Entertainment		8,000	5,000	3,000	U
Total fixed expenses		$185,000	$190,000	(5,000)	F
Net income......................		$ 17,896	$119,374	$(101,478)	U

U = Unfavorable
F = Favorable

Accurate information about what causes the differences between actual and expected results is a precondition for corrective action. Variance analysis can lead to an accurate analysis. In contrast, a static budget can focus only on sales and fixed expenses that differ from budgeted figures, and not realizing this may lead to faulty analysis of the results. Flexible budget variances aren't misleading because they incorporate actual levels of activity if different from those expected.

For Old Rosebud, the main problem is price—not volume. Had the farm been able to maintain its boarding rates but not the number of boarding days, its actual net income would have been:

Sales revenue...	$474,500
Less total variable expenses	(176,704)
Less total fixed expenses...............................	(185,000)
Net income...	$112,796

This amount is six times greater than the net income of $17,896 actually achieved. The farm needs to develop a strategy that restores boarding rates more than it needs to replace the eight horses it lost.[2]

Microsoft's Corporate Citizenship "Budget"

CORPORATE SOCIAL RESPONSIBILITY

The opening vignette discussed the importance of budgeting to Microsoft's operations, in particular financial measures such as sales. The process of budgeting as discussed in this chapter is applicable to far more than just financial results. Microsoft uses budgets to track revenues and expenses that are eventually communicated to interested parties in its annual financial report. In addition, Microsoft sets goals and tracks these goals with budgeting techniques outlined in this chapter for its annual Citizenship Report. In this report Microsoft highlights its performance in such areas as Ethical Business Conduct and Governance, People, Serving Communities, Human Rights, Responsible Sourcing, and Environmental Sustainability. The report can be found at and downloaded from Microsoft's website under the Corporate Citizenship section at the following link: https://www.microsoft.com/about/corporatecitizenship/en-us/

INTERNAL REPORTING OF SEGMENT OPERATIONS

Decentralized Organizations

LO3 Present an overview of reporting operations for segments of a business.

As businesses grow, management of the organization becomes more and more difficult. Most large businesses are decentralized, meaning that the authority to make decisions is spread throughout the business.

Although decentralization occurs almost out of necessity as businesses grow, there are significant advantages to involving lower-level management in the decision-making process of the business:

1. Delegation of day-to-day operational decisions frees up upper management to focus on strategy and business development.

2. Involvement of lower-level management in running the business provides excellent on-the-job training for those who will eventually become the upper management of the business.

3. Empowering lower-level managers may increase their job satisfaction and motivation to work hard.

4. Because lower-level managers are more familiar with the day-to-day operation of the business, they are more likely to identify and react more quickly to trends in the marketplace.

On the other hand, decentralization can lead to less desirable consequences:

1. Lower-level managers may not be privy to the larger business strategy.

---

[2] SOURCE: Adapted from Hans Sprohge and John Talbott, "New Applications for Variance Analysis," *Journal of Accountancy*, April 1989, pp. 137, 138, 140, 141. Reprinted with permission from the *Journal of Public Accountancy*, copyright © 1989 by the American Institute of Certified Public Accountants, Inc. Opinions of the authors are their own and do not necessarily reflect the policies of the AICPA.

2. Decisions made by lower-level managers may not be consistent with and supportive of goals and objectives of other departments or divisions within the business.

3. Largely autonomous departments or divisions may lead to "silos" within the business, resulting in important operating information or innovative ideas not being shared with other departments or divisions, to the detriment of the business overall.

Segment Reporting

Many business entities are very complex, with diverse divisions and departments in multiple locations. Managers of this type of entity often find it useful to divide the entity into segments to enhance managerial planning and control. Segments usually are based on organizational units (divisions or departments) or areas of economic activity (geographic regions or product lines). Many large companies have found that segmentation by organizational unit is the approach that proves most useful. It is important that the managerial accounting systems and procedures that develop information for planning and control decisions be structured to reflect the segmentation.

Internal reporting of segment operations deals primarily with the measurement of operating performance. As a result, segmented reports usually take the format of a contribution margin income statement. These statements may provide information to answer the following types of questions:

1. What amount does each segment contribute to the sales and operating income of the entity as a whole?

2. How do revenues and expenses for each segment compare to planned or budgeted amounts?

3. What is the rate of profitability of each segment? Should any segment be expanded, reduced, or eliminated?

4. Which areas need corrective action, and what should be done?

5. Where should promotional efforts be directed?

Types of Business Segments

With delegated authority comes accountability. In a decentralized organization, segment managers must demonstrate that the results of their decisions support and are congruent with the overall business strategy of the organization. Portions of a business for which a manager has been given a measure of authority and accountability are often referred to as **responsibility centers**. Depending on the authority delegated, these responsibility centers may be described as cost centers, profit centers, and investment centers. An example of these responsibility centers may be seen in PACCAR, a heavy-duty truck manufacturer.

PACCAR is a Fortune 200 company that designs, manufactures, and distributes trucks and related aftermarket parts that are sold worldwide under the Kenworth, Peterbilt, and DAF nameplates. It ranked as the third-largest manufacturer of medium- and heavy-duty trucks in the world in 2012.

The company has its headquarters in Bellevue, Washington. It began in 1905 as Seattle Car Manufacturing Company, at which time it produced railway and logging equipment. Over time, it expanded through acquisitions of commercial truck manufacturers and parts suppliers. As it grew and became more complex, management organized various business segments or responsibility centers. As described in the following discussion, some of PACCAR's responsibility centers might be considered cost centers, profit centers, or investment centers.

Access the most recent 10-K filing of PACCAR at edgar.sec.gov. What operating segments does PACCAR report (search for the term "segment" under Item 1 of the 10-K filing)?

YOUR TURN! 24.1

The solution is on page 1106.

The manager of a **cost center** is responsible for the costs and expenses of only that segment of the business. He or she has no responsibility for revenue generation. An example of a PACCAR cost center is its Technical Centers, which provide research, development, and testing for new products. The output of these Technical Centers is a service to other PACCAR divisions or segments that is not sold to consumers outside the company. As a result, no revenue is generated directly by these centers.

The manager of a **profit center** is responsible for revenue generation as well as for cost and expense control. An example of a PACCAR profit center is its PACCAR Parts business, which operates a network of parts distribution centers that offer aftermarket support to its truck dealerships and customers throughout the world. PACCAR evaluates the performance of PACCAR Parts on its operating profit or segment contribution margin.

The manager of an **investment center** is responsible for the use of capital (productive assets), along with revenues and costs. The manager is typically evaluated on a measure of return on assets or return on investment. An example of a PACCAR investment center is its PACCAR Mexico (KENMEX) division, which manufactures trucks for Mexico and exports to other countries in a 590,000-square-foot facility.

Managerial reports that measure the operating performance of a business entity and its segments reflect whether the segments are investment, profit, or cost centers. Return on investment, revenue, expenses, and profits are reported for investment centers; revenue, expenses, and profits are reported for profit centers; and only expenses are reported for cost centers. **Exhibit 24-7** illustrates the relationship among the different reporting segments.

Exhibit 24-7	Reporting Segments

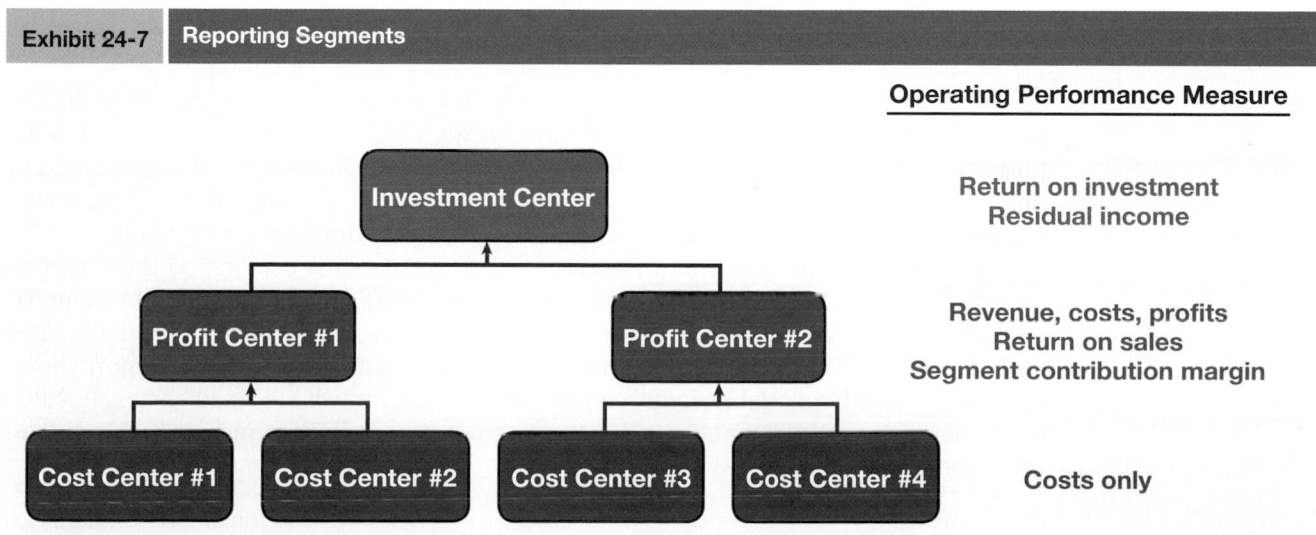

In June 2013, the Securities and Exchange Commission (SEC) charged PACCAR for various accounting deficiencies that obscured the company's financial reporting to investors and regulators from 2008 through 2012. Among the charges was that PACCAR failed to report the operating results of its aftermarket parts business separately from its truck sales business as required under segment reporting requirements. These requirements are intended to allow investors to gain the same insight into the company's operations as its executives.

How significant was this violation of generally accepted accounting principles (GAAP)? In its 2009 annual report, PACCAR reported $68 million in income before taxes for its truck segment. However, had it followed GAAP, it would have reported a $474 million loss in the truck segment and a $542 million profit in its parts segment.

The SEC and PACCAR agreed to a settlement under which, without admitting or denying the charges, PACCAR agreed to the entry of a permanent injunction and the payment of a $225,000 penalty. Michael S. Dicke, associate regional director of the SEC's San Francisco Regional Office said, "Companies must continually and diligently monitor their internal accounting systems to ensure that the information they are providing investors is accurate and consistent with relevant accounting guidance. The deficient controls and procedures at PACCAR caused inconsistencies in its financial reporting and kept investors and regulators from seeing the company through the eyes of management." http://www.sec.gov/News/PressRelease/Detail/PressRelease/1365171575142#.VATK9_IdV8E

TAKEAWAY 24.2

Managers divide complex businesses into segments to enhance planning and control and provide for performance accountability.

PERFORMANCE REPORTING

LO4 Construct a segmented contribution margin income statement. **Identify** the difference between traceable and common fixed costs.

Hint: Direct expenses do not need to be allocated.

Performance reports are usually constructed periodically for each investment, profit, and cost center. They contain different levels of detail for different levels of managerial responsibility. Whereas top managers need highly summarized information, lower-level managers require more detailed, specialized reports.

Exhibit 24-8 presents multilevel performance reports for three successively higher levels of management. The arrows show how the totals from the lower-level reports flow to and are included in the higher-level reports.

Note that in this illustration, all costs from the lower level are included in the upper level. In practice, this may not always be the case—for proper decision-making purposes, only those costs that are directly traceable (see Chapter 15 for a discussion of direct versus indirect costs) to each department should be assigned to that department. Common costs would not be assigned for purposes of performance evaluation.

Also note that the reports in Panels B and C are for cost centers, so these reports only contain cost information. The manager of machining operations and the vice president of operations do not have responsibility for revenue, so revenues are not allocated to their reports. The divisions shown in Panel A are profit centers, so the report shows revenues, traceable variable costs, contribution margin, traceable fixed costs, allocated segment costs, and segment contribution margin in a contribution margin income statement format.

Exhibit 24-8	Segment Performance Reports

Panel A: First-Level Segment Report of Metal Works

METAL WORKS INC.
For the Month of August 20X1
Profit Center

	Divisions		
	Kitchen Cutlery	Hand Tools	Total Company
Sales	$180,000	$340,000	$520,000
Less variable costs.	117,300	248,000	365,300
Contribution margin	$ 62,700	$ 92,000	$154,700
Less traceable fixed costs	39,600*	60,000	99,600
Plant margin	$ 23,100	$ 32,000	$ 55,100
Allocated division costs	8,000	9,000	17,000
Division margin.	$ 15,100	$ 23,000	$ 38,100
Common and unallocated company overhead . . .			22,500
Net income.			$ 15,600

* $39,600 = Fixed manufacturing overhead ($9,600) + Common and unallocated plant overhead ($30,000) from Panel B.

Panel B: Second-Level Segment Report of the Kitchen Cutlery Division

Plant Operations—Kitchen Cutlery
For the Month of August 20X1
Cost Center

	Departments			Total Kitchen Cutlery
	Machining	Fabricating	Assembly	
Variable costs:				
Direct material.	$16,000	$ 25,545	$ 1,295	$ 42,840
Direct labor	18,000	28,739	20,720	67,459
Variable manufacturing overhead.	1,200	1,916	3,885	7,001
Total variable costs.	$35,200	$ 56,200	$ 25,900	$117,300
Fixed manufacturing overhead.	3,000	5,400	1,200	9,600
Total department costs	$38,200	$ 61,600	$ 27,100	$126,900
Common and unallocated plant overhead.				30,000
Total costs				$156,900

Panel C: Third-Level Segment Report of the Kitchen Cutlery Machining Department

Machining Department—Kitchen Cutlery
For the Month of August 20X1
Cost Center

Variable costs:	
Direct material.	$ 16,000
Direct labor	18,000
Variable manufacturing overhead.	1,200
Total variable costs.	$ 35,200
Fixed manufacturing overhead.	3,000
Total department costs	$ 38,200

Departmental Operations

Departmentalization is a common and logical type of segmentation for many firms. In many companies, departments are classified by processes performed. In the previous example, the Kitchen Cutlery division is composed of three segments, or departments: machining, fabricating, and assembly. These departments represent the primary processes performed in making the knives, forks, and spoons that comprise a set of kitchen cutlery.

In other companies, departments might be classified by products sold. The very term *department store* signifies a type of merchandising by product (men's clothing, women's clothing, home furnishings, etc.). Grocery stores are also commonly departmentalized by product groups such as meat, produce, groceries, bakery, and delicatessen. Sometimes departments are classified by type of customer. For example, home improvement centers selling such products as floor coverings, lighting fixtures, and heating and air-conditioning units may separate commercial sales operations from residential sales operations.

The methods of accounting and reporting departmental operating activities depend on the performance measures used and the degree of analysis desired by management. Some firms may desire to identify only contribution margin by department. Others may adopt a more detailed performance measure, such as contribution margin less those fixed costs directly incurred by the department (segment or department income).

Contribution Margin Income Statement

The main reason for analyzing segment contribution margin is that it permits management to review pricing policies and supplier costs. Comparisons can be made among segments to determine areas with high segment contribution margin and areas that may need major promotional efforts. For example, in the Metal Works, Inc. example in **Exhibit 24-8**, the segment report permits a comparison of the Cutlery and Hand Tools divisions (or segments) of the company. Comparisons can also be made with contribution margin achieved in previous periods or with statistics for other firms selling similar products. (These statistics may be obtained from trade association publications and credit agencies.[3]) A very low segment contribution margin may signal a need to investigate purchasing policies or to revise prices.

To obtain contribution margin figures by segment or department, a firm customarily creates a contribution margin income statement. A contribution margin income statement allows managers to identify those costs that are controllable by the segment and for which the segment manager should be held accountable. The use of a contribution margin income statement requires management to segregate those costs that are attributable to the segment from those costs that are attributable to other segments. As shown in Panel A of **Exhibit 24-8**, the attributable costs must be further classified as variable and fixed costs (both traceable to the department and common). Recall that in a contribution margin income statement, cost of goods sold consists of only variable manufacturing costs, all variable costs (both production and selling and administrative) are deducted from sales revenue to compute the contribution margin, and all fixed costs are deducted from contribution margin to compute the division margin. Note that in creating a segment contribution margin income statement, only fixed costs that are traceable to the segment are deducted to arrive at the segment contribution margin.

Segment Performance Evaluation

Department managers should be held responsible only for costs and expenses that they control. Therefore in segment reporting, costs are commonly classified and reported as trace-

---

[3] For example, the Risk Management Association publishes the RMA Annual Statement Studies, which is a source of comparative data drawn from the financial statements of the small- and medium-sized business customers of RMA's member institutions.

able (controlled by the segment) or common (not controlled by the segment). **Traceable expenses** are those operating expenses or costs traceable to and incurred for the benefit of a single department and thus ordinarily controllable by the department. **Common expenses** are those operating expenses or costs incurred for the benefit of multiple departments and thus neither traceable to nor controllable by a specific department. In Panel A of **Exhibit 24-8**, $22,500 of company expenses is determined to be common and unallocated to the Kitchen Cutlery and Hand Tools divisions.

Frequently, costs are considered controllable at one level of management but not at other levels. For example, the vice president of marketing for Metal Works, Inc. may be responsible for decisions related to advertising. Even though the cost of advertising is incurred at the division level (Kitchen Cutlery and Hand Tools), the manager of these divisions should not be held responsible for that expense if the vice president of marketing makes all the decisions relative to that cost or expense. These costs would be included in the common and unallocated company overhead costs shown in Panel A of **Exhibit 24-8**.

TAKEAWAY 24.3

Segment managers should be held responsible for traceable expenses but not common expenses.

SERVICE COMPANY SEGMENT REPORTING ILLUSTRATION

Let's review an example of segment reporting with Environmental Business Consultants (EBC). EBC, which has two offices in northern and southern California, was introduced to you in earlier chapters. Within EBC, each office is considered a department—the word *department* is used interchangeably with *office* in the following discussion.

SERVICE AND MERCHANDISING

Office Margin

EBC maintains its accounting records to produce absorption income statements in accordance with GAAP as required by its bank. However, assume that EBC's management desires a better measure of operating performance. It is then faced with the problem of assigning or *allocating* operating expenses to the offices. If managers desire a measure of office margin, it is necessary to trace the operating expenses to the offices.

Some expenses may be readily identified with the operation of particular offices, but others cannot be. To identify expenses with offices, it is helpful to classify them into traceable and common expenses. For example, payroll expense related to personnel who work exclusively in one office is a traceable expense of that office. Payroll expense related to administrative personnel whose work benefits all offices is a common expense of the offices. EBC also has several common expenses, incurred for the benefit of both offices. Some examples are marketing expenses, some administrative salaries, and a variety of other administrative expenses. These expenses must be fairly assigned, where traceable, to the offices if the measure of office net income is to be meaningful. Note that some general administrative costs such as executive salaries, general accounting expenses, and general legal expenses should not be allocated for purposes of evaluating an office's performance because the office manager has no control over those items.

Assume that EBC management classifies its operating costs as variable or fixed as follows:

Variable Expenses	Amount
Employee bonuses.	$126,000
Marketing expenses.	48,000
Office supplies expense.	64,500
Other general administrative expenses	70,000
Total variable operating expenses	$308,500

Fixed Expenses	Amount
Executive salaries.	$ 844,500
Clerical salaries	217,500
Consultant salaries.	1,050,000
Employee benefits	145,500
Payroll taxes.	123,000
Employee continuing education expenses.	27,000
Office lease expense	202,500
Other general administrative expenses	285,500
Total fixed operating expenses	$2,895,500

In preparing an office income statement, EBC might analyze and assign these expenses as described in the following subsections.

Employee Bonuses

All EBC employees are eligible for bonuses based on the profits earned during the year. Because each employee is assigned to an office, the bonuses for each office can be directly determined from payroll records, which show $96,178 for northern California and $29,822 for southern California.

Marketing Expenses

Of EBC's $48,000 marketing expenses, $28,000 was spent on proposal preparation in northern California, $11,000 on proposal preparation in southern California, $4,000 on attendance at industry trade shows that benefit both markets, and $5,000 on general professional journal advertisements directed at both markets. The latter two amounts are not assigned to the offices because they are considered common expenses, as shown in **Exhibit 24-9**.

Exhibit 24-9	Marketing Expenses Allocation		
	Northern California	Southern California	Firm Total
Proposal preparation	$28,000*	$11,000*	$39,000
Trade shows.			4,000
Advertising.			5,000
			$48,000

* Directly identified

Office Supplies Expenses

Office supplies are purchased by each office as needed, so they are easily traceable to each office. EBC records show that $51,600 and $12,900 of office supplies were purchased by the northern and southern California offices, respectively, during the year.

Other General Administrative Expenses

Other general administrative expenses include the salaries and benefits for the office manager and bookkeeper and other costs associated with billings, collections, and customer inquiries. These costs, both the variable and fixed portions, are considered common costs and are not assigned to the individual offices.

Salaries and Related Benefits

Executive, clerical, and consultant salaries and related employee benefits and taxes are traceable to the office in which the employee works. EBC payroll records show that the total salaries, benefits, and taxes for each office are $1,876,200 and $504,300 for the northern and southern California offices, respectively.

Employee Continuing Education Expenses

All professional consultants are required to complete 40 hours of continuing education (CE) credits each year. As with salaries and related benefits, these costs can be determined directly for each office. The firm's time records show CE expenses of $20,828 for northern California consultants and $6,172 for southern California consultants.

Office Lease Expense

Each of the EBC offices negotiates and pays for its own office space. EBC records show that $154,500 in lease expense was paid by the northern California office and $48,000 was paid by the southern California office.

TAKEAWAY 24.4

Some costs are not large enough to justify being allocated individually. These costs are pooled and allocated together.

Exhibit 24-10 presents a summary of the operating expenses, showing the traceable variable and traceable fixed expenses of each department and common expenses for the firm.

Exhibit 24-10	Operating Expense Assignment			
	Northern California	Southern California	Common	Firm Total
Variable costs				
Employee bonuses.....................	$ 96,178	$ 29,822		$ 126,000
Marketing expenses	28,000	11,000	9,000	48,000
Office supplies expense	51,600	12,900		64,500
Other general administrative expenses			70,000	70,000
Total variable costs	$ 175,778	$ 53,722	$ 79,000	$ 308,500
Fixed costs				
Salaries and benefits	$1,876,200	$504,300		$2,380,500
Employee continuing education expenses...	20,828	6,172		27,000
Office lease expense	154,500	48,000		202,500
Other general administrative expenses			$285,500	285,500
Total fixed costs........................	$2,051,528	$558,472	$285,500	$2,895,500
Total costs	$2,227,306	$612,194	$364,500	$3,204,000

Expense Allocation for Federal Government Grants and Contracts

Organizations, such as universities, that do business with the federal government under grants and contracts must use federal-government-specified allocation methods. The guidelines, known as OMB Circular A-87, establish the principles and standards for determining allowable costs for federal awards carried out through grants, cost reimbursement contracts, and other agreements with state and local governments. Allowable costs must meet certain criteria, including being necessary and reasonable, legally incurred under state or local law, consistent with federal policies and regulations, consistently applied, and adequately documented.

This departmental expense distribution is used to prepare the variable income statement for EBC shown in **Exhibit 24-11**, which extends the departmental operating results through office margin. Note that in this presentation, traceable variable costs are deducted to compute office contribution margin, from which traceable fixed costs are subtracted to compute office margin. Common expenses are not allocated to the individual offices.

Exhibit 24-11	Office Margin Statement

ENVIRONMENTAL BUSINESS CONSULTANTS, LLC
Office Margin Statement
For the Year Ended December 31, 2016

	Northern California	Southern California	Firm Total
Gross sales.	$2,900,000	$1,246,000	$4,146,000
Less reimbursable costs	(344,800)	(86,200)	(431,000)
Net sales.	2,555,200	1,159,800	3,715,000
Traceable variable costs	(175,778)	(53,722)	(229,500)
Office contribution margin	2,379,422	1,106,078	3,485,500
Traceable fixed costs	(2,051,528)	(558,472)	(2,610,000)
Office margin	$ 327,894	$ 547,606	875,500
Common expenses			(364,500)
Operating income.			511,000
Interest revenue			7,500
Income before tax			$ 518,500

Operating statements that extend departmental results to operating or net income measures are often criticized on the grounds that the indirect or common expenses are not controllable at the departmental level and therefore should not be assigned to departments when measuring performance. An additional criticism is that the bases for assignment of common expenses are frequently arbitrary.

In the EBC example, the other general administrative costs, although necessary expenses for the firm overall, are not controllable by the individual office managers. Thus, they should not be allocated to the offices at all. To allocate these costs on some arbitrary basis could lead management to draw incorrect conclusions and make poor business decisions.

Departmental revenue is $600,000 for Company X, and departmental operating income is $350,000. Traceable expenses for this department are as follows:

Direct labor.	$25,000
Other traceable costs.	$40,000
Direct materials	$30,000

Compute common expenses for this department.

YOUR TURN! 24.2

The solution is on page 1106.

PERFORMANCE ANALYSIS

The contribution margin income statement that was discussed in the previous section may be used to evaluate the performance of a profit center. This section addresses evaluation of investment centers.

Managers use a number of methods for evaluating the performance of investment centers. We explore several performance evaluation methods and discuss their relative strengths and weaknesses. To illustrate these different performance methods, we compare hypothetical data for Fezzari's mountain bike and road bike divisions. **Exhibit 24-12** indicates that the mountain bike division earned $2.5 million during 2016, and the road bike division earned $1.7 million. It also shows that the mountain bike division's investment in operating assets is $18.3 million, and the road bike division's investment is $11 million. We use this information to demonstrate the relative pros and cons of the various performance methods.

LO5 Compute return on investment, return on sales, return on assets, and residual income for business segments. **Discuss** the importance of each indicator in assessing a company's performance.

Exhibit 24-12	Performance Analysis

FEZZARI PERFORMANCE BICYCLES
Division Performance
For the Year Ended December 31, 2016

	Divisions	
(in thousands)	Mountain	Road
Sales.	$14,400	$ 7,900
Expenses	(11,900)	(6,200)
Operating income.	$ 2,500	$ 1,700
Asset investment	$18,300	$11,000

We note that one might be tempted to simply compare the operating income numbers of the two divisions and conclude that the mountain bike division is outperforming the road bike division because it has a higher operating income for the period. However, some of the other performance metrics we discuss here may provide different insights.

Return on Investment

One of the problems with simply comparing the net income figures of the two divisions is that they differ in size. One way to "level the playing field" of two divisions of different sizes is to compare the divisions on a relative basis based on a ratio.

One ratio that is useful in comparing the profitability of two divisions is the **return on investment** (ROI) ratio, which is calculated as the operating income number divided by the investment in operating assets:

$$ROI = \frac{\text{Operating income}}{\text{Operating asset investment}}$$

ROI examines the division's operating income as a percentage of the asset base used to generate that income.

Given the information in **Exhibit 24-12**, Fezzari's mountain bike division has an ROI of 13.7% ($2,500/$18,300), and the road bike division has an ROI of 15.5% ($1,700/$11,000). Therefore, the ROI ratio indicates that the road bike division earns a higher rate of return on its investment in assets than the mountain bike division earns on its investment. Thus, Fezzari's division ROI measures indicate that the mountain bike division generates 13.7 cents of profit for every dollar invested in assets, and the road bike division earns 15.5 cents of profit on every dollar invested in its asset base. Therefore, the ROI ratio provides evidence that the road bike division is more profitable on a relative basis, given its investment in assets.

In the 1920s, the DuPont brothers recognized that ROI could be further divided into two ratios, return on sales and asset utilization (or asset turnover), which provided managers additional levers to improve the overall ROI. This has come to be referred to as the **DuPont formula**. The formula for ROI can be expressed as:

$$ROI = \text{Return on sales (ROS)} \times \text{Asset utilization} = \frac{\text{Operating income}}{\text{Sales}} \times \frac{\text{Sales}}{\text{Investment}}$$

Exhibit 24-13 summarizes the calculation of ROI based on the DuPont formula for Fezzari's mountain and road bike divisions. The calculations of Fezzari's return on sales and asset utilization are discussed in the following sections.

Exhibit 24-13	ROI Analysis

FEZZARI PERFORMANCE BICYCLES
DuPont ROI Analysis
For the Year Ended December 31, 2016

	ROS	×	Asset Utilization	=	ROI
Mountain	17.4%	×	78.7%	=	13.7%
Road	21.5%	×	71.8%	=	15.5%*

* Difference due to rounding.

Return on Sales

The **return on sales** (ROS) ratio (the first component of the DuPont ROI formula) is useful in comparing the profitability of two divisions, which is simply calculated as the operating income number divided by sales:

$$ROS = \frac{\text{Operating income}}{\text{Sales}}$$

As shown in **Exhibit 24-13**, Fezzari's mountain bike division has an ROS of 17.4% ($2,500/$14,400), whereas the road bike division has an ROS of 21.5% ($1,700/$7,900). Thus, even though the road bike division has a lower net income than the mountain bike division, it is higher as a percentage of sales. One way of interpreting the ROS ratio is the number of pennies left over from each dollar of sales after covering all costs. Thus, Fezzari's division ROS measures indicate that although the mountain bike division may have a greater operating income number, it does not manage expenses as efficiently as the road bike division, because only 17.4 cents of every sales dollar is left over after covering operating costs, whereas the road bike division generates 21.5 cents of operating income for every sales dollar generated. At least based on this profitability measure, the road bike division is actually relatively more profitable.

Asset Utilization

The **asset utilization** ratio (the second component of the DuPont ROI formula) is used to compare the efficiency with which the divisions are using their operating assets to generate sales. It is calculated as sales divided by the investment in operating assets:

$$\text{Asset utilization} = \frac{\text{Sales}}{\text{Investment}}$$

As shown in **Exhibit 24-13**, Fezzari's mountain bike division has an asset utilization ratio of 78.7% ($14,400/$18,300), and the road bike division has an ROS of 71.8% ($7,900/$11,000). This means that the mountain bike division generates 78.7 cents in sales for every dollar of operating assets, whereas the road bike division generates only 71.8 cents in sales for every dollar of operating assets. The mountain bike division uses its operating assets more efficiently.

Interestingly, the DuPont analysis indicates that the road bike division has higher core profitability but the mountain bike division uses its assets more efficiently. Nevertheless, the result of multiplying the ROS ratio by the asset turnover ratio is that the road bike division has a higher ROI.

Residual Income

Another method for comparing two subsidiary companies or operating divisions is based on **residual income**. Similar to ROI, residual income takes the size of the division into account. However, unlike ROI, residual income is not a ratio; it is defined as the income that is left over after the company or division earns some minimum return on investment. Residual income is based on the idea that owners or investors expect a company to provide a reasonable rate of return on their investment. Investors could invest their money in other types of investments, so they likely have some minimum rate of return (called a hurdle rate) they would like to earn on their investment in the company. Another way of looking at residual income is to calculate the amount of extra income after a division earns a minimum ROI. The formula for residual income is:

Residual income = Net operating income − (Average operating assets × Minimum ROI)

One of many variations of residual income is Economic Value Added (EVA®), which has been trademarked by the consulting firm Stern, Stewart & Co. EVA makes certain adjustments to the calculation of net operating income (e.g., goodwill amortization and other non-cash expenses are added back) and uses the firm's weighted cost of capital as the minimum required return. A detailed discussion of EVA® will be left to a more advanced managerial or finance textbook.

Exhibit 24-14 first assumes that managers or owners expect each division to earn a hurdle rate of 5%. Given the mountain bike division's investment in assets of $18.3 million and the company's desired ROI of $915,000 ($18.3 million × 0.05), it has residual income of $1.59 million. Similarly, the road bike division has a desired ROI of $550,000 ($11.0 million × 0.05) and residual income of $1.15 million. Thus, we would conclude that the mountain bike division generates more residual income than the road bike division.

Exhibit 24-14	Residual Income Analysis		

FEZZARI PERFORMANCE BICYCLES
Residual Income Analysis
For the Year Ended December 31, 2016

		Divisions	
(in thousands)		**Mountain**	**Road**
Net income...		$2,500	$1,700
Required return (5% rate)................................		(915)	(550)
Residual income.....................................		$1,585	$1,150
Net income...		$2,500	$1,700
Required return (12% rate).............................		(2,196)	(1,320)
Residual income.....................................		$ 304	$ 380

On the other hand, what if managers or owners expect each division to earn a hurdle rate of 12%? Given the mountain bike division's investment in assets of $18.3 million and the company's desired ROI of $2.20 million ($18.3 million × 0.12), it has residual income of $304,000. Similarly, the road bike division has a desired ROI of $1.32 million ($11.0 million × 0.12) and residual income of $380,000. Thus, we would conclude that the road bike division's $380,000 of residual income exceeds the mountain bike division's $304,000 of residual income.

How is it possible that the mountain bike division has higher residual income if the required ROI is 5% and the road bike division has a higher residual income when the desired ROI is 12%? The answer is in the size of the asset base. When interest rates are low, it is relatively inexpensive to borrow money to buy assets. However, when interest rates are high, it becomes more costly to borrow money to buy assets. Hence, when the required ROI is low, larger divisions are favored, but when the desired ROI is high, smaller divisions have an advantage.

Balanced Scorecard

One drawback to the performance measures discussed so far is that they focus solely on financial measures. Over time, managers have become more aware of the fact that there are also many *nonfinancial* measures that influence both performance and other major corporate decisions. Thus, in recent years, many companies have begun evaluating performance using the balanced scorecard.[4] The **balanced scorecard** seeks to provide a "balanced view" of company performance by evaluating a company's subunits based on both financial and nonfinancial measures in each of the following areas:

1. Financial performance
2. Customer satisfaction
3. Internal business processes
4. Learning and growth

---

[4] The balanced scorecard originated in the 1990s with Robert Kaplan and David Norton at the Harvard Business School ("Using the Balanced Scorecard as a Strategic Management System," *Harvard Business Review*, January–February 1996, p. 76).

Obviously, financial performance remains perhaps the most important area of focus for most managers, because if a business isn't profitable and if it doesn't generate positive cash flows, it won't survive for long. Examples of financial measures include ratios and other financial statement measures. However, the long-term health of a company depends largely on its ability to attract and retain customers. Hence, the second focus area relates to customer satisfaction. Customer-related performance measures include such factors as the number of customer complaints. A well-run company seeks to achieve the highest level of efficiency. In their quest to maximize financial goals and maintain customer satisfaction, companies constantly seek to improve internal operations to achieve highly efficient processes. Evaluation of internal processes can measure factors such as throughput time and the number of quality inspection failures. Finally, effective organizations recognize that their greatest asset doesn't appear on the balance sheet. A company's employees bring perhaps the greatest value in determining the organization's continued success. Attracting and developing the best people is a constant struggle for any organization and is directly associated with an organization's capacity to grow and improve. Thus, the learning and growth aspect of a business can measure factors such as training and employee development efforts.

Exhibit 24-15 illustrates how Fezzari might evaluate itself based on the objectives it has defined in each of the four areas of focus.

Assume that you are the managing partner of a small CPA firm. You have decided to evaluate the firm's performance using a balanced scorecard. Identify at least one measure that you might use in each of the four areas of the balanced scorecard: financial performance, customer satisfaction, internal business processes, and learning and growth.	**DECISION TIME 24.1** The solution is on page 1106.

TAKEAWAY 24.5

Managers use a variety of measures to evaluate the performance of investment centers, including return on investment, return on sales, asset utilization, residual income, and a balanced scorecard.

Exhibit 24-15	Balanced Scorecard Illustration

FEZZARI PERFORMANCE BICYCLES
Balanced Scorecard
For the Year Ended December 31, 2016

	Objectives	Measures	Targets	Initiatives
Financial	Maximize returns	ROI	14%	
	Profitable growth	Revenue growth	6%	
	Manage operating costs	Operating costs/customer	$1,000	
Customer	Industry-leading customer loyalty	Customer satisfaction survey	90%	Customer loyalty program
Internal Processes	Business growth			
	-Use alliances and joint ventures	% of customers serviced through alliances	10%	
	Customer service excellence			
	-Educate customers	% education plans executed	90%	
	-Effective customer service	Problem resolution cycle time	6 hrs.	Customer service software integration
Learning & Growth	Leading employee satisfaction	Employee satisfaction rating	3 on 5-point scale	Performance compensation link

SERVICE INDUSTRY IN FOCUS

In addition to evaluating its operations by office as shown earlier, EBC also wishes to evaluate the performance of its two lines of business, Solid Waste and Water/Wastewater (Water/WW). EBC management has prepared the following line of business income statement:

ENVIRONMENTAL BUSINESS CONSULTANTS, LLC
Line of Business Statement
For the Year Ended December 31, 2016

	Solid Waste	Water/WW	Firm Total
Gross sales.	$3,676,000	$470,000	$ 4,146,000
Less reimbursable costs	(366,350)	(64,650)	$ (431,000)
Net sales.	$3,309,650	$405,350	$ 3,715,000
Cost of services	(2,256,787)	(390,713)	$(2,647,500)
Gross profit on sales.	$1,052,863	$ 14,637	$ 1,067,500
Operating expenses.			(556,500)
Operating income.			$ 511,000
Interest revenue			7,500
Income before tax			$ 518,500

EBC accountants have provided the following analysis of the cost of services, all of which are considered traceable:

Cost of Services

Solid Waste			Water/WW			
Variable	Fixed	Total	Variable	Fixed	Total	Firm Total
$51,600	$2,205,187	$2,256,787	$12,900	$377,813	$390,713	$2,647,500

In addition, EBC has accumulated the following information regarding the operating expenses. Variable costs are shown in red; fixed costs are shown in black.

Operating Expenses Allocation

	Solid Waste			Water/WW			
	Traceable	Common	Total	Traceable	Common	Total	Firm Total
Employee bonuses.	$109,722	$ —	$109,722	$16,278	$ —	$16,278	$126,000
Proposal preparation	31,400	—	31,400	7,600	—	7,600	39,000
Trade shows.	—	3,000	3,000	—	1,000	1,000	4,000
Advertising	—	4,000	4,000	—	1,000	1,000	5,000
Employee CE expenses	24,943	—	24,943	2,057	—	2,057	27,000
Other general admin. expenses	—	306,849	306,849	—	48,651	48,651	355,500
	$166,065	$313,849	$479,914	$25,935	$50,651	$76,586	$556,500

Required

1. Prepare a line of business contribution margin statement for EBC (similar to **Exhibit 24-11**) that extends the line of business operating results through line of business contribution to common expenses.

2. Comment on the operating results for each line of business. What should EBC management do with regard to the Water/WW business based on these results?

Solution

1.

Solution 1	Service Industry in Focus		

ENVIRONMENTAL BUSINESS CONSULTANTS, LLC
Line of Business Statement
For the Year Ended December 31, 2016

	Solid Waste	Water/WW	Firm Total
Gross sales.	$3,676,000	$470,000	$4,146,000
Less reimbursable costs	(366,350)	(64,650)	(431,000)
Net sales.	$3,309,650	$405,350	$3,715,000
Traceable variable costs	(192,722)*	(36,778)*	(229,500)
Contribution margin	$3,116,928	$368,572	$3,485,500
Traceable fixed costs.	(2,230,130)**	(379,870)**	(2,610,000)
Line of business contribution.	$ 886,798	$ (11,298)	$ 875,500
Common operating expenses			(364,500)
Interest revenue			7,500
Income before tax			$ 518,500

*Solid Waste: $51,600 + $109,722 + $31,400 = $192,722
 Water/WW: $12,900 + $16,278 + $7,600 = $36,778
**Solid Waste: $2,205,187 + $24,943 = $2,230,130
 Water/WW: $377,813 + $2,057 = $379,870

2. The Water/WW line of business has a net loss at the line of business contribution level. It is not covering its own traceable operating costs, let alone contributing to the firm's common operating expenses. EBC management has several possible courses of action to consider:

   a. Determine whether revenues can be increased through higher fees for the service provided. An increase of just over 2.4% (11,298/470,000) would eliminate the loss.

   b. Carefully review the classification of expenses as cost of service and traceable operating expenses. Even a minor misclassification of an expense could make a difference in the reported results.

   c. Consider whether some of the Water/WW traceable expenses could be reduced or eliminated. For example, given these results, perhaps Water/WW employees should not be receiving bonuses.

   d. Consider whether the Water/WW line of business should be spun off or eliminated. This is a major decision with significant implications for EBC and its owners and employees. It may be that the Water/WW line of business provides cross-selling opportunities for the Solid Waste line of business that would have a greater impact on income before tax if eliminated.

APPENDIX 24A: Transfer Pricing

DOMESTIC TRANSFER PRICING

LO6   **Determine** the proper transfer price to maximize company profit with and without excess productive capacity.

Management of a large, complex company usually divides the business into a number of segments. A segment is a logical portion of a business, such as a division or department. When a segment is established as a profit center, the segment's manager is responsible for revenue generation as well as cost and expense control. If the profit center receives products or services from another profit center within the same business or provides products or services to another profit center within the same business, the two profit center managers must agree on a transfer price for the product or service. The **transfer price** is the price that the selling profit center will charge the buying profit center for the product or service provided.

Objectives for Transfer Pricing

Two objectives should be met when establishing transfer prices. First, the transfer price of the product or service transferred should allow both the selling and buying divisions to make a reasonable gross profit. Second, the contribution margin of the entire business should be maximized.

Reasonable Gross Profit

Assume that John Deere Waterloo Works has two operating divisions, the Drivetrain Operations division and the Tractor, Cab, and Assembly Operations division. Top management has decided that the Drivetrain Operations division should sell a particular component to the Tractor, Cab, and Assembly Operations division, which will incorporate the component into the 6170R tractor that it manufactures and sells for $150,000 per unit. The per-unit product costs incurred in this process are the following:

	Drivetrain Operations Division	Tractor, Cab, and Assembly Operations Division
Direct material	$6,250	$62,250
Direct labor.	1,500	27,750
Variable overhead.	1,000	17,000
Fixed overhead.	1,250	17,850
Transfer price of component	?	

A negotiated transfer price below market price can be justified. Expenses may be less when intercompany sales are made, or volume may be large enough to justify quantity discounts.

BUSINESS SITUATION 1:   Assume that the transfer price is established as $10,000, the total absorption product cost of the component in the Drivetrain Operations division ($6,250 + $1,500 + $1,000 + $1,250 = $10,000). The resulting gross profit per unit for the two divisions would be calculated as follows:

	Drivetrain Operations Division	Tractor, Cab, and Assembly Operations Division
Revenue:		
Transfer price	$10,000	
Sales price		$150,000
Cost:		
Transfer price		$10,000
Direct material.	$6,250	62,250
Direct labor	1,500	27,750
Variable overhead	1,000	17,000
Fixed overhead	1,250	17,850
	10,000	$134,850
Gross profit per unit	$ —	$ 15,150

BUSINESS SITUATION 2: Assume that the transfer price is established as $12,000, the price that the Drivetrain Operations division would receive from an outside customer and the cost that the Tractor, Cab, and Assembly Operations division would incur from an outside supplier. The resulting gross profit per unit for the two divisions would be calculated as follows:

	Drivetrain Operations Division	Tractor, Cab, and Assembly Operations Division
Revenue:		
Transfer price	$12,000	
Sales price		$150,000
Cost:		
Transfer price		$12,000
Direct material.	$6,250	62,250
Direct labor	1,500	27,750
Variable overhead.	1,000	17,000
Fixed overhead.	1,250	17,850
	10,000	$136,850
Gross profit per unit	$ 2,000	$ 13,150

In situation 1, the Tractor, Cab, and Assembly Operations division generates a 10.1% gross profit ($15,150/$150,000 = 0.101), and the Drivetrain Operations division generates no gross profit. In situation 2, the Drivetrain Operations division generates a gross profit of $2,000 and the Tractor, Cab, and Assembly division generates a gross profit of $13,150. Situation 1 illustrates a full absorption product cost transfer price, and situation 2 illustrates a market price transfer price. In both situations, total John Deere gross profit per 6170R is $15,150.

Situation 2 meets the first objective—the transfer price of the product or service transferred should allow both the selling and buying divisions to make a reasonable gross profit. In general, a transfer price based on market price, not absorption product cost, will satisfy the objective of reasonable gross profits for both the selling and buying profit centers or divisions.

Maximize Contribution Margin

The second objective—that the contribution margin of the entire business should be maximized—can be met by identifying a proper minimum transfer price and allowing the manager of the buying profit center to decide whether to buy from the selling profit center or from an outside supplier. As shown in **Exhibit 24A-1**, assume the Drivetrain Operations division of John Deere is currently manufacturing and selling only component A to outside customers for $7,500 per unit.

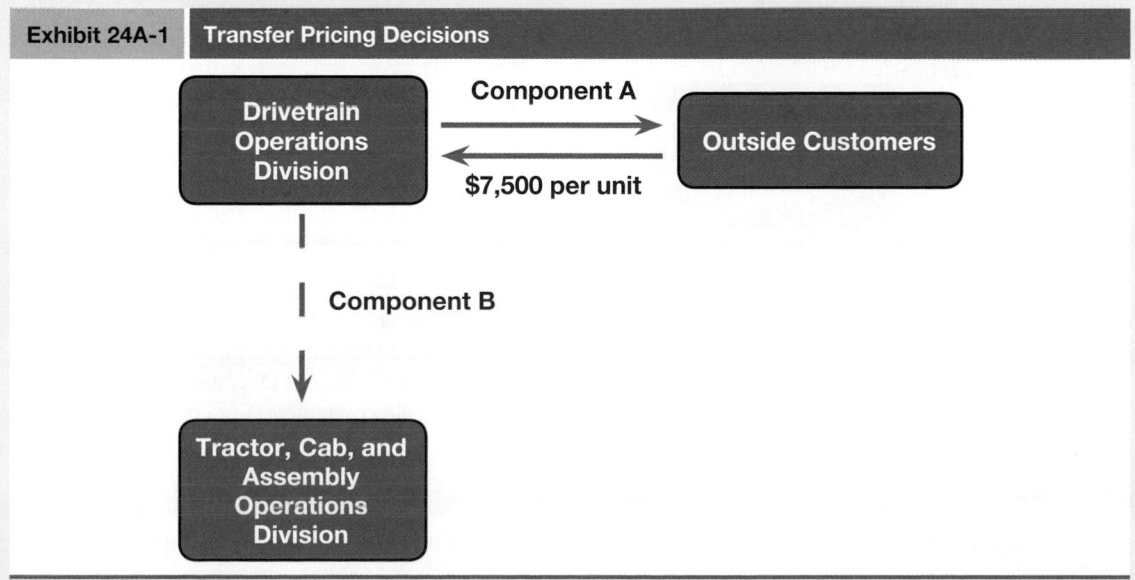

Exhibit 24A-1 | **Transfer Pricing Decisions**

The Tractor, Cab, and Assembly Operations division has proposed that the Drivetrain Operations division begin manufacturing and selling 2,000 units of component B per year to the Tractor, Cab, and Assembly Operations division. The formula for the minimum transfer price for component B is the following:

Product B minimum transfer price	=	Variable cost of product B, per unit	+	Contribution margin lost from not selling product A, per unit of product B

Next we will apply these objectives of transfer pricing to two situations, one in which the supplier does not have any excess capacity and one in which the supplier does have excess capacity.

No Excess Capacity

Assume the Drivetrain Operations division has no excess manufacturing capacity. Therefore, if the Drivetrain Operations division produces component B for the Tractor, Cab, and Assembly Operations division, the Drivetrain Operations division will have to reduce its production and sale of component A to outside customers. Assume that 5,000 fewer units of component A will have to be produced and sold to allow the manufacture of 2,000 units of component B.

The minimum transfer price that the Drivetrain Operations division is willing to accept is one that maintains the contribution margin of the Drivetrain Operations division at its current level. The formula given earlier will generate a transfer price that would allow this to happen. Assume that the variable cost per unit of component A is $5,000, and its selling price is $7,500. The variable cost per unit of component B is $8,750. The total contribution margin that would be given up on 5,000 units of component A is $12,500,000 (5,000 units × [$7,500 − $5,000]). Using the formula, the minimum transfer price for component B is $15,000 ($8,750 + [$12,500,000/2,000 units of B]) (see **Exhibit 24A-2**).

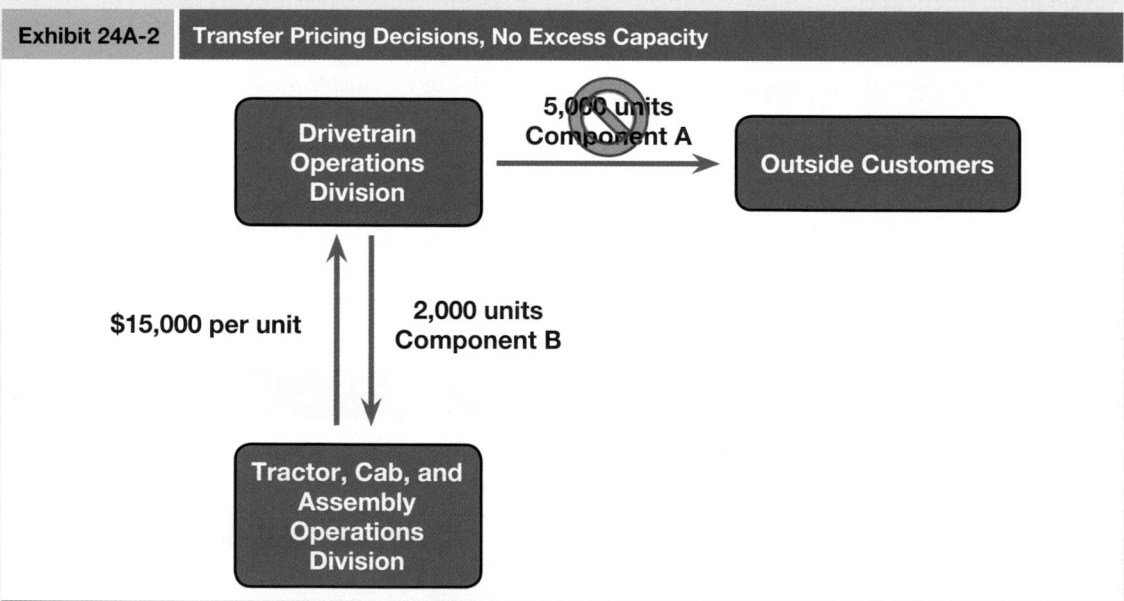

Exhibit 24A-2 | **Transfer Pricing Decisions, No Excess Capacity**

The switch from the production and sale of 5,000 units of component A to 2,000 units of component B would not affect total fixed costs, would create new variable costs of $8,750 per unit, and would eliminate $12,500,000 of contribution margin. The $15,000 transfer price would reimburse the Drivetrain Operations division for the additional variable costs and the lost contribution margin. As a result, the Drivetrain Operations division would generate exactly the same contribution margin whether it produced and sold component A or component B.

TAKEAWAY 24.2

Total gross profit for the firm is unaffected by the transfer price; all transfer prices yield the same total gross profit.

With the transfer price set at $15,000, the Tractor, Cab, and Assembly Operations division is in a position to make a decision that will maximize its contribution margin and the contribution margin of the entire business. Assume that the Tractor, Cab, and Assembly Operations division adds $107,000 of variable cost in addition to the costs of the Drivetrain Operations division and then sells the end product for $150,000. If the Tractor, Cab, and Assembly Operations division can only buy component B from an outside supplier for a price greater than $15,000, then it will choose to buy component B from the Drivetrain Operations division. However, if the product division can buy component B from an outside supplier for a price less than $15,000, then it will choose to buy the component from the outside supplier (see **Exhibit 24A-3**). In either case, the contribution margin of the company as a whole has been maximized.

Exhibit 24A-3	Transfer Pricing Decisions, No Excess Capacity

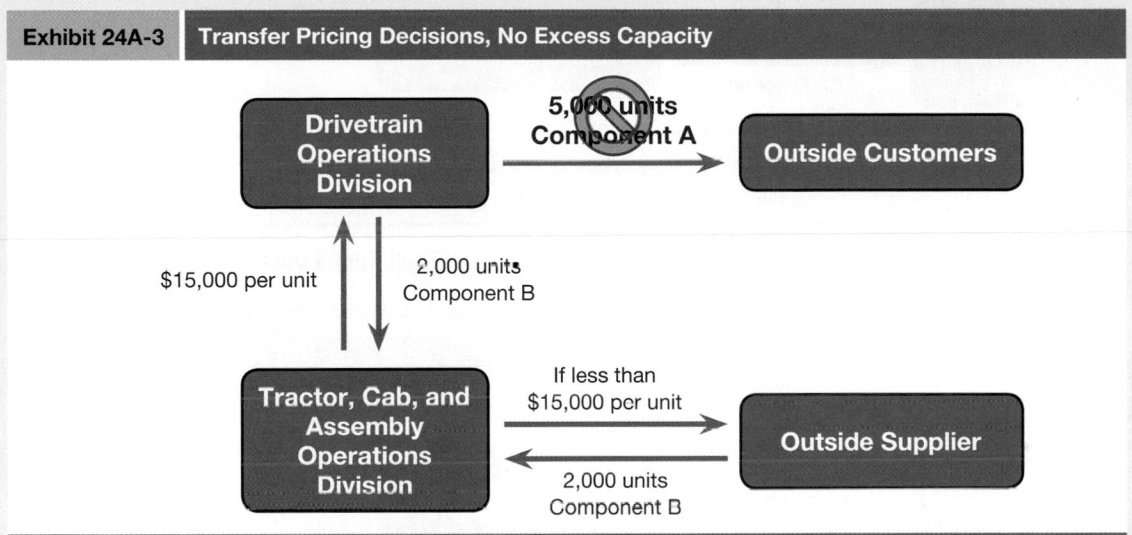

To illustrate, let us assume two situations:
(1) the outside supplier's price is $16,000; and,
(2) the outside supplier's price is $14,000.

BUSINESS SITUATION 1: **Exhibit 24A-4** shows the calculation of the contribution margin for the first situation. If the Tractor, Cab, and Assembly Operations division purchases component B from the Drivetrain Operations division at a per-unit transfer price of $15,000, the Drivetrain Operations division would earn a contribution margin of $12,500,000 and the Tractor, Cab, and Assembly Operations division would earn a contribution margin of $56,000,000 on the sale of the 6170R to its customers, for a total contribution margin of $68,500,000.

Exhibit 24A-4	Transfer Pricing Decisions, No Excess Capacity

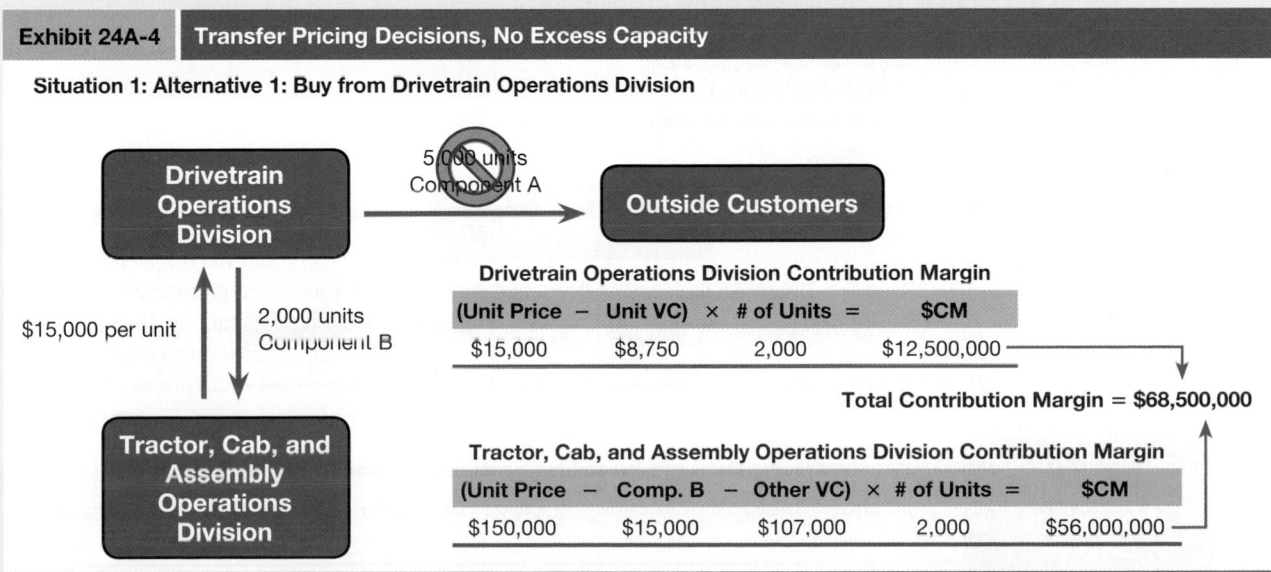

However, **Exhibit 24A-5** shows the calculation of the contribution margin if the Tractor, Cab, and Assembly Operations division purchases component B from outside suppliers at a price of $16,000 per unit. This would allow the Drivetrain Operations division to continue to sell component A to its outside customers at a contribution margin of $12,500,000. The Tractor, Cab, and Assembly Operations division would earn a contribution margin of $54,000,000 on the sale of the 6170R, for a total contribution margin of $66,500,000.

Exhibit 24A-5	Transfer Pricing Decisions, No Excess Capacity

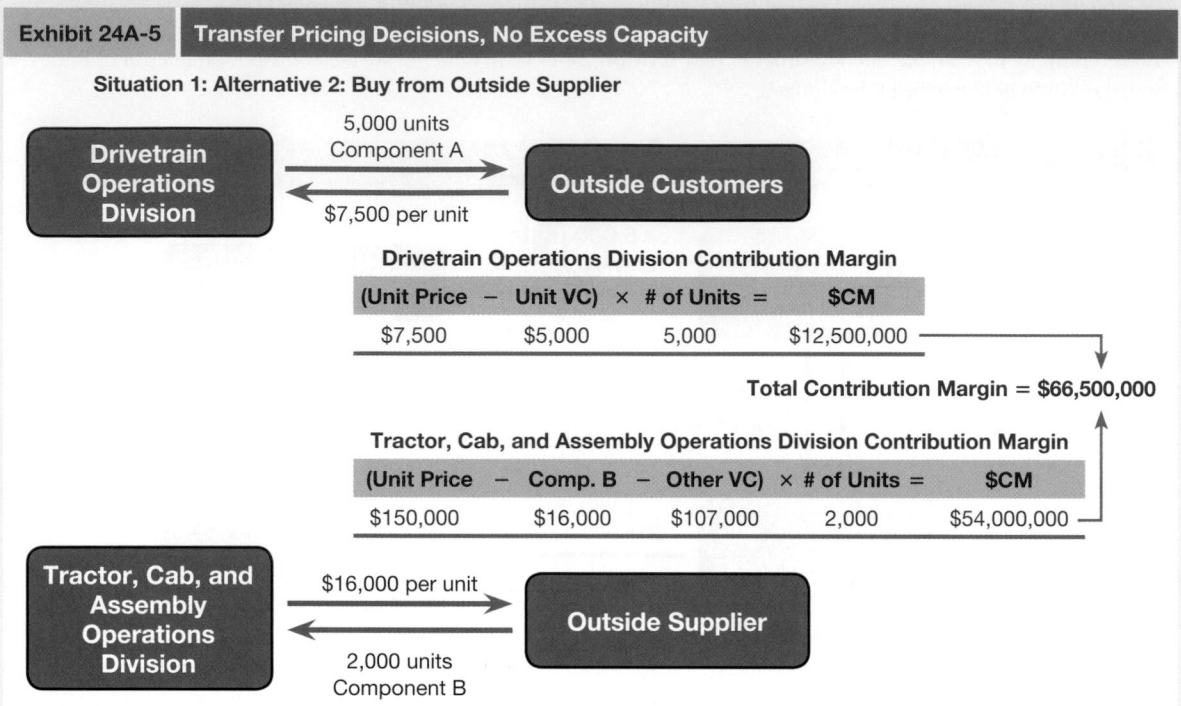

Situation 1: Alternative 2: Buy from Outside Supplier

Drivetrain Operations Division Contribution Margin

(Unit Price	−	Unit VC)	×	# of Units	=	$CM
$7,500		$5,000		5,000		$12,500,000

Total Contribution Margin = $66,500,000

Tractor, Cab, and Assembly Operations Division Contribution Margin

(Unit Price	−	Comp. B	−	Other VC)	×	# of Units	=	$CM
$150,000		$16,000		$107,000		2,000		$54,000,000

A careful study of **Exhibits 24A-4** and **24A-5** shows that John Deere will earn $2,000,000 more in contribution margin by purchasing component B from the Drivetrain Operations division.

BUSINESS SITUATION 2:   **Exhibit 24A-6** shows the calculation of the contribution margin for the second situation. If the Tractor, Cab, and Assembly Operations division purchases component B from the Drivetrain Operations division at a per-unit transfer price of $15,000, the Drivetrain Operations division would earn a contribution margin of $12,500,000 and the Tractor, Cab, and Assembly Operations division would earn a contribution margin of $56,000,000 on the sale of the 6170R to its customers, for a total contribution margin of $68,500,000. This is exactly the same as the first situation.

Exhibit 24A-6	Transfer Pricing Decisions, No Excess Capacity

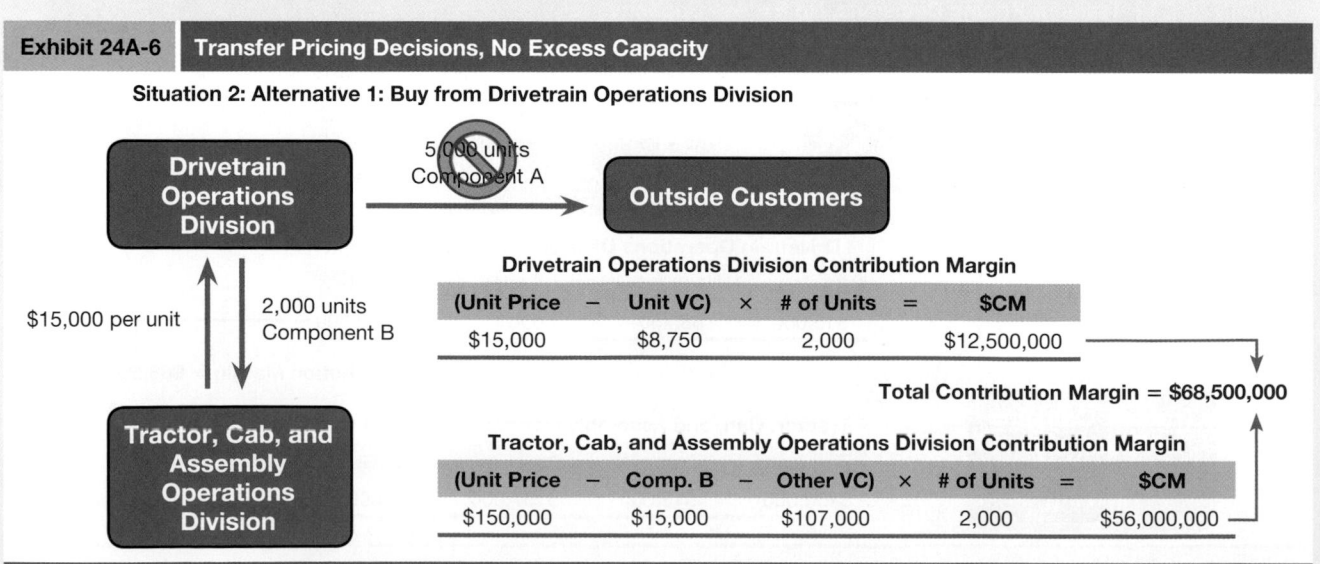

Situation 2: Alternative 1: Buy from Drivetrain Operations Division

Drivetrain Operations Division Contribution Margin

(Unit Price	−	Unit VC)	×	# of Units	=	$CM
$15,000		$8,750		2,000		$12,500,000

Total Contribution Margin = $68,500,000

Tractor, Cab, and Assembly Operations Division Contribution Margin

(Unit Price	−	Comp. B	−	Other VC)	×	# of Units	=	$CM
$150,000		$15,000		$107,000		2,000		$56,000,000

However, **Exhibit 24A-7** shows the calculation of the contribution margin if the Tractor, Cab, and Assembly Operations division purchases component B from outside suppliers at a price of $14,000 per unit. This would allow the Drivetrain Operations division to continue to sell component A to its outside customers at a contribution margin of $12,500,000. The Tractor, Cab, and Assembly Operations division would earn a contribution margin of $58,000,000 on the sale of the 6170R, for a total contribution margin of $70,500,000.

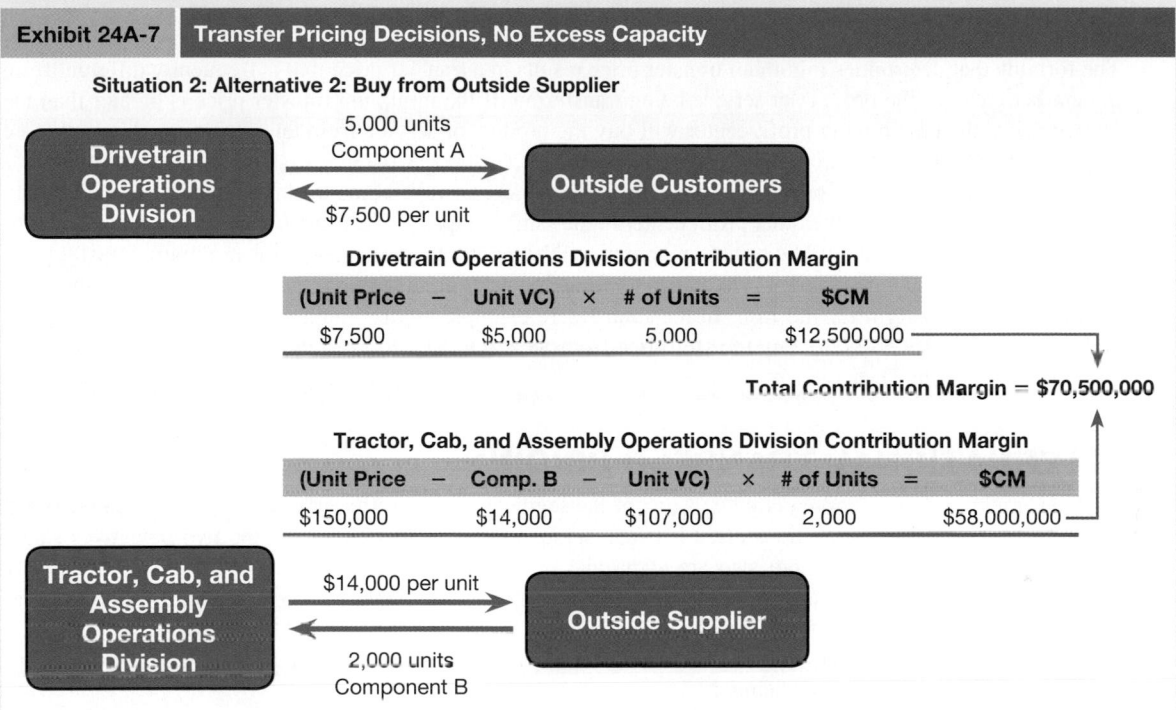

Exhibit 24A-7	Transfer Pricing Decisions, No Excess Capacity

Situation 2: Alternative 2: Buy from Outside Supplier

Drivetrain Operations Division Contribution Margin

(Unit Price	−	Unit VC)	×	# of Units	=	$CM
$7,500		$5,000		5,000		$12,500,000

Total Contribution Margin = $70,500,000

Tractor, Cab, and Assembly Operations Division Contribution Margin

(Unit Price	−	Comp. B	−	Unit VC)	×	# of Units	=	$CM
$150,000		$14,000		$107,000		2,000		$58,000,000

A comparison of **Exhibits 24A-6** and **24A-7** shows that John Deere will earn $2,000,000 more in contribution margin by purchasing component B from the outside supplier.

Excess Capacity

In the John Deere example, we assumed that the Drivetrain Operations division had no excess manufacturing capacity. If we now assume that the Drivetrain Operations division has sufficient capacity to produce and sell the 2,000 units of component B without reducing the production and sale of component A, we will determine a different minimum transfer price. Applying the previous formula for the minimum transfer price, we determine that the minimum transfer price is $8,750 ($8,750 + [$0/2,000]) (see **Exhibit 24A-8**).

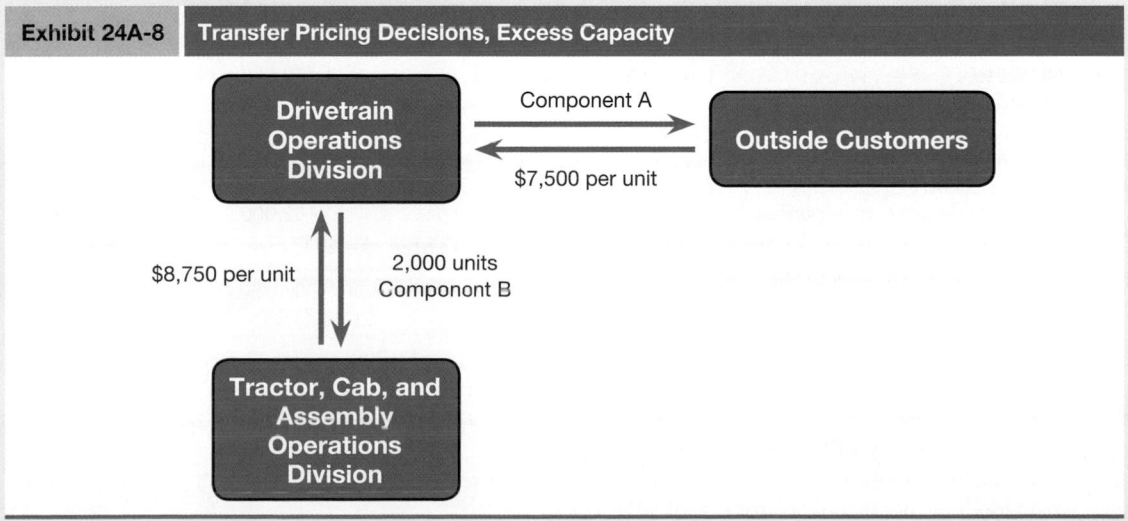

Exhibit 24A-8	Transfer Pricing Decisions, Excess Capacity

In this case, the production and sale of 2,000 units of component B would not affect total fixed costs, would create new variable costs of $8,750 per unit, and would eliminate no contribution margin from the production and sale of component A. The $8,750 transfer price would reimburse the Drivetrain Operations division for the additional variable costs. As a result, the Drivetrain Operations division would generate exactly the same contribution margin whether or not it produced and sold product B.

Negotiated Transfer Prices

The formula that determines minimum transfer price results in a transfer price that is frequently different from the market value of the product or service being transferred. If the minimum transfer price is greater than the market price, then the buying profit center will buy the product or service from an outside supplier and there will be no need for a transfer price.

If the minimum transfer price is less than the market price, however, then the buying profit center will buy the product or service from the other profit center in the same company. The exact transfer price will be negotiated by the two profit centers. The resulting amount will be greater than or equal to the minimum transfer price and less than or equal to the market price. Any negotiated transfer price within this range will result in the same total contribution margin for the firm. In the John Deere example, with a minimum transfer price of $8,750 and a market price of $15,000, any transfer price from $8,750 to $15,000 results in a contribution margin of $12,500,000 for John Deere.

INTERNATIONAL TRANSFER PRICING

Transfer pricing becomes more complex if one of the segments is in a different country than the other. When products or services are being transferred between segments in different countries, the two objectives stated earlier still apply. However, there also are additional objectives that may conflict with the two previously mentioned. The additional objectives include minimization of international income taxes and tariffs and conformance with international trade agreements. These topics are beyond the scope of this introduction to transfer pricing. Intermediate cost accounting textbooks generally provide a more in-depth coverage of these topics related to international transfer pricing.

COMPREHENSIVE PROBLEM

LT Roofing Company sells roofing products through two departments, composite and steel. Operating information for 2016 is as follows:

	Composite Department	Steel Department
Inventory, January 1, 2016.	$ 90,000	$ 39,000
Inventory, December 31, 2016.	75,000	45,000
Net sales.	1,170,000	720,000
Purchases.	726,000	543,000
Purchases returns	42,000	12,000
Purchases discounts	24,000	6,000
Transportation in	27,000	21,000
Traceable department expenses	162,000	84,000

Common operating expenses of the firm were $180,000.

Required

a. Prepare a department income statement showing department contribution to common expenses and net income of the firm. Assume an overall effective income tax rate of 30%. LT uses a periodic inventory system.

b. Calculate the gross profit percentage for each department.

c. If the common expenses were allocated 55% to the composite department and 45% to the steel department, what would the net income be for each department?

Solution

LT ROOFING COMPANY
Department Income Statement
For the Year Ended December 31, 2016

a.

	Composite Department	Steel Department	Total
Net sales.	$1,170,000	$720,000	$1,890,000
Cost of goods sold:			
Inventory, January 1, 2016	90,000	39,000	129,000
Purchases	726,000	543,000	1,269,000
Less: Purchases returns	(42,000)	(12,000)	(54,000)
Purchases discounts	(24,000)	(6,000)	(30,000)
Transportation in	27,000	21,000	48,000
Cost of goods available for sale	$ 777,000	$585,000	$1,362,000
Inventory, December 31, 2016	75,000	45,000	120,000
Cost of goods sold	$ 702,000	$540,000	$1,242,000
Gross profit	$ 468,000	$180,000	$ 648,000
Traceable department expenses	162,000	84,000	246,000
Department margin	$ 306,000	$ 96,000	$ 402,000
Common expenses			180,000
Income before tax			$ 222,000
Income tax expense (30% × $222,000)			66,600
Net income			$ 155,400

b. Gross profit percentages:
    Composite dept.: $468,000/$1,170,000 = 40%
    Steel dept.: $180,000/$720,000 = 25%

c.

	Composite	Steel	Total
Department margin	$ 306,000	$ 96,000	$ 402,000
Common expenses*	99,000	81,000	180,000
Income before tax	$ 207,000	$ 15,000	$ 222,000
Income tax expense (30% × $207,000 and 30% × $15,000)	62,100	4,500	66,600
Net income	$ 144,900	$ 10,500	$ 155,400

* 55% × $180,000 = $99,000
  45% × $180,000 = $81,000

SUMMARY OF LEARNING OBJECTIVES

Describe a static budget, illustrate its use, and present an example of a static budget performance report. (p. 1062)   LO1

- A static budget is a financial plan developed for a fixed level of operating activity, typically the expected or most likely level.
- If actual results are compared to a static budget, the variances that result are of little use to management, because the budget is often based on a different level of activity than the actual operations.

LO2 **Introduce the flexible budget and present an example of a flexible budget performance report. Explain how flexible budgeting helps in variance analysis. (p. 1063)**

- A flexible budget is a financial plan that makes cost projections for various activity levels within a relevant range.
- A flexible budget usually divides costs and expenses into variable and fixed costs.
- A flexible budget performance report compares actual costs to budgeted costs based on the actual production level achieved.

LO3 **Present an overview of reporting operations for segments of a business. (p. 1069)**

- Business segments may consist of organizational units (departments or divisions) or areas of economic activity (product lines or markets).
- A business segment may be an investment center (where management is responsible for the efficient use of capital as well as revenues and expenses), a profit center (where management is responsible for both revenues and expenses), or a cost center (where management is responsible for expenses only).
- Internal reporting of segment operations deals primarily with the measurement of operating performance.
- Accounting and reporting by business segment are indispensable to management and very important to external groups such as investors and creditors.

LO4 **Construct a segmented contribution margin income statement. Identify the difference between traceable and common fixed costs. (p. 1072)**

- Total amounts from lower-level reports flow to and are included in higher-level reports.
- A performance report is usually prepared for each accounting period for each profit center and each cost center.
- Expenses incurred by, or for the benefit of, one business segment are called traceable expenses. Expenses incurred for more than one business segment are called common expenses.
- Reporting for segments of a firm is typically extended to contribution to common expenses. Only traceable expenses are deducted.

LO5 **Compute return on investment, return on sales, return on assets, and residual income for business segments. Discuss the importance of each indicator in assessing a company's performance. (p. 1079)**

- Return on investment is operating income as a percentage of the asset base used to generate that income. It illustrates the amount of profit generated for every dollar invested in the company's asset base.
- The DuPont formula recognizes that ROI can be further divided into two ratios, return on sales and asset utilization.
- Return on sales is operating income as a percentage of sales revenue. It may be interpreted as the number of pennies left over from each dollar of sales after covering all costs.
- Asset utilization is sales divided by the investment in operating assets. It is a measure of a company's efficiency in utilizing its operating assets. It represents the amount of sales per dollar of operating asset.
- Residual income is the income that is left over after the company or division earns some minimum return on investment.
- The balanced scorecard seeks to provide a "balanced view" of company performance by evaluating a company's subunits based on both financial and nonfinancial measures, including financial performance, customer satisfaction, internal business processes, and learning and growth.

LO6 **Determine the proper transfer price to maximize company profit with and without excess productive capacity. (p. 1086)**

- The transfer price of the product or service transferred should allow both the selling and buying divisions to make a reasonable gross profit.
- The negotiated transfer price should maximize the contribution margin of the entire business.
- A transfer price based on market price will satisfy the objective of reasonable gross profits for both the selling and buying profit centers or divisions.

KEY TERMS

Asset utilization (p. 1081)

Balanced scorecard (p. 1082)

Common expenses (p. 1075)

Cost center (p. 1071)

DuPont formula (p. 1080)

Flexible budget (p. 1063)

Investment center (p. 1071)

Performance reports (p. 1072)

Profit center (p. 1071)

Residual income (p. 1081)

Responsibility centers (p. 1070)

Return on investment (p. 1079)

Return on sales (p. 1080)

Static budget (p. 1062)

Traceable expenses (p. 1075)

Transfer price (p. 1086)

Assignments with the ⓶ logo in the margin are available in BusinessCourse.
See the Preface of the book for details.

SELF-STUDY QUESTIONS

(Answers to Self-Study Questions are at the end of this chapter.)

1. The manager of which of the following segments of a business is responsible for revenue generation as well as for cost and expense control?   **LO3**
   - *a.* Cost center
   - *b.* Accounting department
   - *c.* Profit center
   - *d.* Assembly line

2. Which of the following is not considered in determining contribution to common expenses?   **LO4**
   - *a.* Income taxes
   - *b.* Cost of goods sold
   - *c.* Traceable expenses
   - *d.* Net sales

3. In performance reporting (budgeted cost compared to actual cost), which performance report must be prepared first?   **LO4**
   - *a.* Division, consisting of five departments
   - *b.* Region, consisting of three divisions
   - *c.* Department, consisting of four cost centers
   - *d.* Company, consisting of two regions

4. Which of the following is the correct formula for return on sales?   **LO5**
   - *a.* Income/Investment
   - *b.* Investment/Income
   - *c.* Income/Revenue
   - *d.* Revenue/Investment

5. During the past twelve months, the Aaron Corporation had a net income of $50,000. What is the amount of the investment if the return on investment is 20%?   **LO5**
   - *a.* $100,000
   - *b.* $200,000
   - *c.* $250,000
   - *d.* $500,000

QUESTIONS

1. Give examples of segments of business firms segmented by (a) organizational unit and (b) economic activity.   **LO3**

2. Distinguish between a profit center and a cost center.   **LO3**

3. Explain the difference between a static budget and a flexible budget.   **LO1, 2**

4. Explain what is meant by a static budget variance and a flexible budget variance.   **LO1, 2**

5. Distinguish between traceable expenses and common expenses. Which are more likely to be controllable at the department level?   **LO4**

6. If a firm wishes to compare the performance of two divisions, why might divisional operating income be a poor basis for comparison?   **LO5**

LO4   7. Suggest an allocation basis for each of the following traceable expenses of a departmentalized firm that uses a net income measure to determine the profitability of departments:

     a. Janitorial expense
     b. Plant manager's salary
     c. Utilities (heat, light, and air conditioning)
     d. Property taxes

LO4   8. What is meant by departmental contribution to common expenses? What advantages does this measure have over net income in measuring departmental performance?

LO2   9. "The higher the management level receiving reports, the more detailed the reports should be." Comment.

LO4   10. Department B of the local Top Value Store shows a contribution to common expenses of $22,000 and a net loss of $9,000 (before taxes). The firm believes that discontinuing department B will not affect sales, gross profit, or traceable expenses of other departments. If total common expenses remain unchanged, what effect will discontinuing department B have on the income before taxes of the Top Value Store?

LO4   11. Department 2 of Kapp Company has a gross profit of $100,000, representing 40% of net departmental sales. Traceable departmental expenses are $75,000. Management believes that an increase of $6,500 in advertising, coupled with a 5% average increase in sales prices, will permit the physical volume of products sold to remain the same next period but will improve the department's contribution to common expenses. If management's expectations are correct, what will be the effect on this contribution?

LO4   12. Department A of Racine Company has a gross profit of $140,000, representing 35% of net departmental sales. Management believes that an increase of $36,000 in advertising will increase volume of product sold by 20%. Other traceable departmental expenses are $64,000. What effect will this decision have on department A's contribution to common expenses?

LO6   13. What is the maximum amount that one division should pay to another division of the same company for a component needed in manufacturing its product?

LO5   14. What is the primary purpose of the balanced scorecard?

LO5   15. What are the four key performance measures in the balanced scorecard?

EXERCISES—SET A

LO1, 2   **E24-1A. Static and Flexible Budgets** Graham Corporation used the following data to evaluate its current operating system. The company sells items for $10 each and used a budgeted selling price of $10 per unit.

	Actual	Budgeted
Units sold	495,000 units	500,000 units
Variable costs.	$1,250,000	$1,500,000
Fixed costs.	$925,000	$900,000

     a. Prepare the actual income statement, flexible budget, and static budget.
     b. What is the static-budget variance of revenues?
     c. What is the flexible budget variance for variable costs?
     d. What is the flexible budget variance for fixed costs?

LO2   **E24-2A. Using Flexible Budgets** The following summary data are from a performance report for Sterling Company for May, during which 9,600 units were produced. The budget reflects the company's normal capacity of 10,000 units.

	Budget (10,000 Units)	Actual Costs (9,600 Units)	Variances
Direct material	$140,000	$136,800	$3,200 F
Direct labor	280,000	277,200	2,800 F
Variable overhead	96,000	98,400	2,400 U
Fixed overhead	72,000	72,400	400 U
Total	$588,000	$584,800	$3,200 F

a. What is the general implication of the performance report? Why might Sterling question the significance of the report?

b. Revise the performance report using flexible budgeting, and comment on the general implication of the revised report.

E24-3A. Assigning Traceable Fixed Expenses Selected data for Miller Company, which operates three departments, follow: **LO4**

	Department A	Department B	Department C
Inventory	$ 80,000	$288,000	$112,000
Equipment (average cost)	720,000	432,000	288,000
Payroll	405,000	360,000	135,000
Square feet of floor space	18,000	9,000	3,000

During the year, the company's fixed expenses included the following:

Depreciation on equipment	$80,000
Real estate taxes	24,000
Personal property taxes (on inventory and equipment)	38,400
Personnel department expenses	40,000

Assume that the property tax rate is the same for both inventory and equipment. Using the most causally related bases, prepare a schedule assigning the fixed expenses to the three departments. *Hint:* Not all fixed expenses are traceable to the three departments. One of these fixed costs should be considered a common cost and not traceable to the departments.

E24-4A. Return on Investment and Residual Income Johnson Company has two sources of funds: long-term debt and equity capital. Johnson Company has profit centers in the following locations with the following net incomes and total assets: **LO5**

SERVICE AND MERCHANDISING

	Net Income	Assets
Las Vegas	$ 960,000	$ 4,000,000
Dallas	$1,200,000	$ 8,000,000
Tampa	$2,040,000	$12,000,000

a. Calculate ROI for each profit center and rank them from highest to lowest based on ROI.

b. Calculate residual income for each profit center based on a desired ROI of 5% and rank them from highest to lowest based on residual income.

EXERCISES—SET B

E24-1B. Using Flexible Budgets The following summary data are from a performance report for Hyland Company for June, during which 9,600 units were produced. The budget reflects the company's normal capacity of 10,000 units.   **LO2**

	Budget (10,000 Units)	Actual Costs (9,600 Units)	Variances
Direct material	$105,000	$102,600	$2,400 F
Direct labor.	210,000	207,900	2,100 F
Variable overhead.	72,000	73,800	1,800 U
Fixed overhead.	54,000	54,300	300 U
Total	$441,000	$438,600	$2,400 F

a. What is the general implication of the performance report? Why might Hyland question the significance of the report?

b. Revise the performance report using flexible budgeting and comment on the general implication of the revised report.

LO4 **E24-2B. Assigning Traceable Fixed Expenses** Selected data for Colony Company, which operates three departments, follow:

	Department A	Department B	Department C
Inventory.	$ 40,000	$144,000	$ 56,000
Equipment (average cost).	360,000	216,000	144,000
Payroll.	607,500	540,000	202,500
Square feet of floor space	27,000	13,500	4,500

During the year, the company's fixed expenses included the following:

Depreciation on equipment	$60,000
Real estate taxes	18,000
Personal property taxes (on inventory and equipment)	28,800
Personnel department expenses	30,000

Assume that the property tax rate is the same for both inventory and equipment. Using the most causally related bases, prepare a schedule assigning the fixed expenses to the three departments. *Hint:* Not all fixed expenses are traceable to the three departments. One of these fixed costs should be considered a common cost and not traceable to the departments.

LO5  **E24-3B. Return on Investment and Residual Income** The Emergency Medical Services Company has two divisions that operate independently of one another. The financial data for the year 20X5 reported the following results:

	North	South
Sales.	$3,000,000	$2,500,000
Operating income.	750,000	550,000
Taxable income	650,000	375,000
Investment	6,000,000	5,000,000

The company's desired rate of return is 10%. Income is defined as operating income.

a. What are the respective return-on-investment ratios for the North and South divisions?

b. What are the respective residual incomes for the North and South divisions?

c. Which division has the better return on investment and which division has the better residual income figure, respectively?

LO5 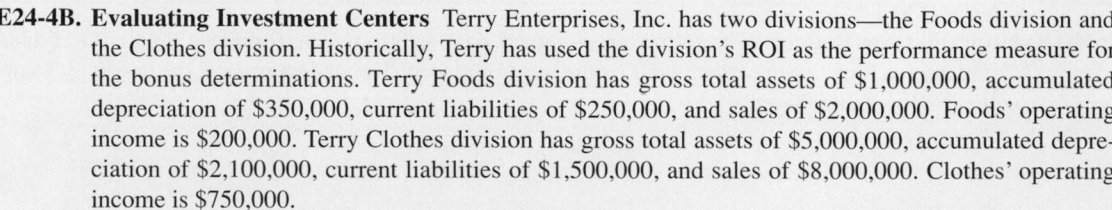 **E24-4B. Evaluating Investment Centers** Terry Enterprises, Inc. has two divisions—the Foods division and the Clothes division. Historically, Terry has used the division's ROI as the performance measure for the bonus determinations. Terry Foods division has gross total assets of $1,000,000, accumulated depreciation of $350,000, current liabilities of $250,000, and sales of $2,000,000. Foods' operating income is $200,000. Terry Clothes division has gross total assets of $5,000,000, accumulated depreciation of $2,100,000, current liabilities of $1,500,000, and sales of $8,000,000. Clothes' operating income is $750,000.

Required

Use the DuPont formula to compute ROI for each division and for Terry Enterprises as a whole. Use operating income and gross total assets as the measures of income and investment. *Hint:* Calculate the ROI for Terry Enterprises (as a whole), to three decimal places.

PROBLEMS—SET A

P24-1A. Flexible Budget Application The polishing department of Taylor Manufacturing Company operated during April 2016 with the following manufacturing overhead cost budget based on 5,000 hours of monthly productive capacity:

LO2

TAYLOR MANUFACTURING COMPANY Polishing Department Overhead Budget (5,000 Hours) for the Month of April 2016		
Variable costs:		
Factory supplies	$100,000	
Indirect labor.	152,000	
Utilities (usage charge)	68,000	
Patent royalties on secret process	296,000	
Total variable overhead.		$ 616,000
Fixed costs:		
Supervisory salaries	$160,000	
Depreciation on factory equipment	144,000	
Factory taxes	48,000	
Factory insurance	32,000	
Utilities (base charge)	80,000	
Total fixed overhead		$ 464,000
Total manufacturing overhead		$1,080,000

The polishing department was operated for 4,600 hours during April and incurred the following manufacturing overhead costs:

Factory supplies.	$ 97,520
Indirect labor	136,160
Utilities (usage factor).	82,800
Utilities (base factor).	96,000
Patent royalties.	280,416
Supervisory salaries	168,000
Depreciation on factory equipment	144,000
Factory taxes	56,000
Factory insurance.	32,000
Total manufacturing overhead incurred	$1,092,896

Required

Using a flexible budgeting approach, prepare a performance report for the polishing department for April 2016, comparing actual overhead costs with budgeted overhead costs for 4,600 hours. Separate overhead costs into variable and fixed components and show the amounts of any variances between actual and budgeted amounts.

LO4 **P24-2A. Departmental Income Statement** Elgin Flooring Company sells floor coverings through two departments, carpeting and hard covering (tile and linoleum). Operating information for 2016 appears below.

	Carpeting Department	Hard Covering Department
Inventory, January 1, 2016...............................	$ 60,000	$ 26,000
Inventory, December 31, 2016...........................	50,000	30,000
Net sales......................................	780,000	480,000
Purchases.....................................	484,000	362,000
Purchases returns	28,000	8,000
Purchases discounts	16,000	4,000
Transportation in	18,000	14,000
Traceable departmental expenses...............	108,000	56,000

Common operating expenses of the firm were $120,000.

Required

a. Prepare a departmental income statement showing departmental contribution to common expenses and net income of the firm. Assume an overall effective income tax rate of 35%. Elgin uses a periodic inventory system.

b. Calculate the gross profit percentage for each department.

c. If the common expenses were allocated 60% to the carpeting department and 40% to the hard covering department, what would the net income be for each department?

LO4 **P24-3A. Departmental Income Statement** The following information was obtained from the ledger of Woodfield Candies, Inc., at the end of 2016:

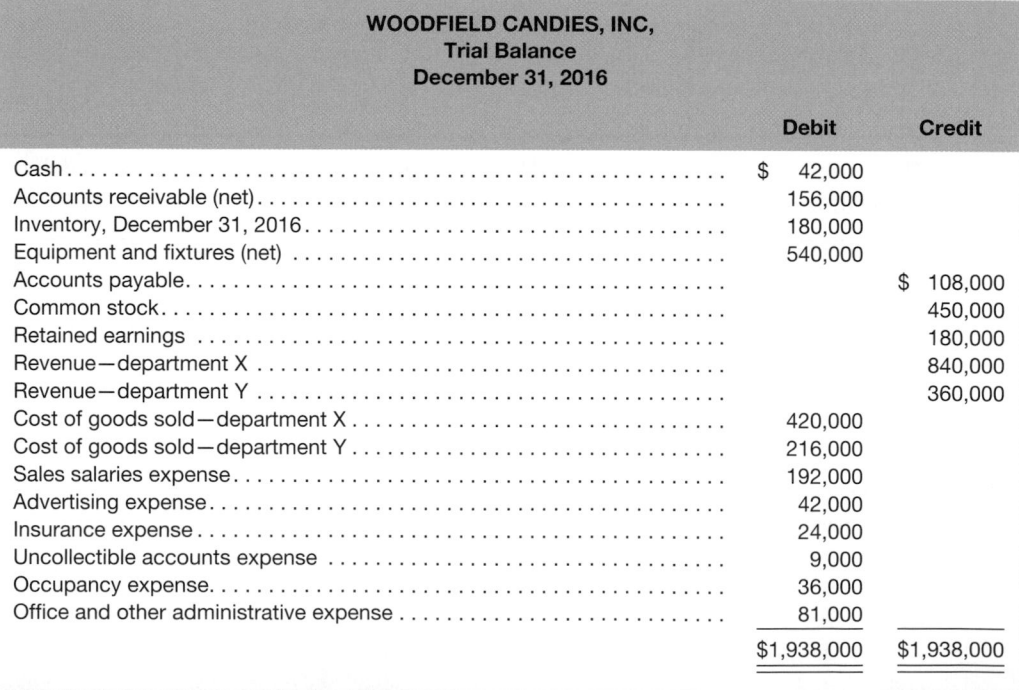

WOODFIELD CANDIES, INC, Trial Balance December 31, 2016		
	Debit	Credit
Cash..	$ 42,000	
Accounts receivable (net).....................................	156,000	
Inventory, December 31, 2016.................................	180,000	
Equipment and fixtures (net)	540,000	
Accounts payable..		$ 108,000
Common stock..		450,000
Retained earnings		180,000
Revenue—department X		840,000
Revenue—department Y		360,000
Cost of goods sold—department X..............................	420,000	
Cost of goods sold—department Y..............................	216,000	
Sales salaries expense.......................................	192,000	
Advertising expense...	42,000	
Insurance expense..	24,000	
Uncollectible accounts expense	9,000	
Occupancy expense...	36,000	
Office and other administrative expense	81,000	
	$1,938,000	$1,938,000

Woodfield analyzes its operating expenses at the end of each period in order to prepare an income statement that will exhibit departmental contribution to common expenses. From payroll records, advertising copy, and other records, the following tabulation was obtained:

	Traceable Expense		Common Expense
	Dept. X	**Dept. Y**	
Sales salaries expense....................................	$147,000	$45,000	
Advertising expense.......................................	18,000	6,000	$18,000
Insurance expense..	15,000	9,000	
Uncollectible accounts expense	6,000	3,000	
Occupancy expense.......................................			36,000
Office and other administrative expense.....................	12,000	9,000	60,000

Required

Prepare a departmental income statement for Woodfield Candies, Inc., showing departmental contribution to common expenses, assuming an overall income tax rate of 35%.

P24-4A. Departmental Contribution to Common Expenses Certain operating information is shown below for Palmer Department Store:

LO4

SERVICE AND MERCHANDISING

	Department A	Department B	All Other Departments
Sales.....................................	$600,000	$900,000	$2,100,000
Traceable expenses.......................	105,000	165,000	600,000
Common expenses	90,000	120,000	300,000
Gross profit percentage....................	30%	40%	50%

The managers are disappointed with the operating results of department A. They do not believe that competition will permit raising prices; however, they believe that spending $21,000 more for promoting this department's products will increase the physical volume of products sold by 20%.

An alternative is to discontinue department A and use the space to expand department B. It is believed that department B's physical volume of products sold can thus be increased 37.5%. Special sales personnel are needed, however, and department B's traceable expenses would increase by $90,000. Neither alternative would appreciably affect the total common departmental expense.

Required

a. Calculate the contribution now being made to common expenses by department A, by department B, and by the combination of other departments.

b. Which of the two alternatives should management choose: increase promotional outlays for department A or discontinue department A and expand department B? Support your answer with calculations.

PROBLEMS—SET B

P24-1B. Flexible Budget Application The cutting department of Liberty Manufacturing Company operated during September 2016 with the following manufacturing overhead cost budget based on 6,000 hours of monthly productive capacity:

LO2

LIBERTY MANUFACTURING COMPANY
Cutting Department
Overhead Budget (6,000 Hours)
for the Month of September 2016

Variable costs:		
Factory supplies	$ 48,000	
Indirect labor.	72,000	
Utilities (usage charge)	36,000	
Patent royalties on secret process.	144,000	
Total variable overhead.		$300,000
Fixed costs:		
Supervisory salaries	$ 96,000	
Depreciation on factory equipment	140,000	
Factory taxes	40,000	
Factory insurance.	24,000	
Utilities (base charge)	32,000	
Total fixed overhead		$332,000
Total manufacturing overhead		$632,000

The cutting department was operated for 5,500 hours during September and incurred the following manufacturing overhead costs:

Factory supplies.	$ 40,400
Indirect labor	67,200
Utilities (usage factor).	38,100
Utilities (base factor).	32,000
Patent royalties.	134,000
Supervisory salaries	96,000
Depreciation on factory equipment	140,000
Factory taxes	43,400
Factory insurance.	27,000
Total manufacturing overhead incurred	$618,100

Required

Using a flexible budgeting approach, prepare a performance report for the cutting department for September 2016, comparing actual overhead costs with budgeted overhead costs for 5,500 hours. Separate overhead costs into variable and fixed components and show the amounts of any variances between actual and budgeted amounts.

LO4 **P24-2B. Departmental Income Statement** Perkins Appliance & Furniture Company has two departments, appliances and furniture. Operating information for 2016 appears below.

	Appliance Department	Furniture Department
Inventory, January 1, 2016.	$ 120,000	$ 90,000
Inventory, December 31, 2016.	75,600	48,000
Net sales.	1,120,000	760,000
Purchases.	640,000	480,000
Purchases discounts	8,000	6,000
Transportation in	18,000	16,000
Traceable departmental expenses.	199,600	82,000

Common operating expenses of the firm were $180,000.

Required

a. Prepare a departmental income statement showing departmental contribution to common expenses and net income of the firm. Assume an overall effective income tax rate of 40%. Perkins uses a periodic inventory system.

b. Calculate the gross profit percentage for each department.

c. If the common expenses were allocated 70% to the appliance department and 30% to the furniture department, what would the net income be for each department?

P24-3B. Departmental Income Statement The following information was obtained from the ledger of Stillwell Emporium, Inc., at the end of 2016:

LO4

STILLWELL EMPORIUM, INC. Trial Balance December 31, 2016		
	Debit	**Credit**
Cash.	$ 18,000	
Accounts receivable (net).	70,000	
Inventory, December 31, 2016.	45,000	
Equipment and fixtures (net)	97,000	
Accounts payable.		$ 34,000
Common stock.		120,000
Retained earnings		30,000
Sales—department a		360,000
Sales—department b		140,000
Cost of goods sold—department a	216,000	
Cost of goods sold—department b	70,000	
Sales salaries expense.	74,000	
Advertising expense.	31,000	
Insurance expense (on merchandise).	10,000	
Uncollectible accounts expense	3,000	
Occupancy expense.	16,000	
Office and other administrative expense	34,000	
	$684,000	$684,000

Stillwell analyzes its operating expenses at the end of each period in order to prepare an income statement that will exhibit departmental contribution to common expenses. From payroll records, advertising copy, and other records, the following tabulation was obtained:

	Traceable Expense		Common Expense
	Dept. A	**Dept. B**	
Sales salaries expense.	$48,000	$20,000	$ 6,000
Advertising expense.	15,000	6,000	10,000
Insurance expense	8,000	2,000	
Occupancy expense.			16,000
Uncollectible accounts expense	2,000	1,000	
Office and other administrative expense	17,000	9,000	8,000

Required

Prepare a departmental income statement for Stillwell Emporium, Inc., showing departmental contribution to common expenses, assuming an overall income tax rate of 30%.

P24-4B. Departmental Contribution to Common Expenses Certain operating information is shown below for Harris Department Store:

LO4

SERVICE AND MERCHANDISING

	Department R	Department S	All Other Departments
Sales.	$320,000	$480,000	$1,120,000
Traceable expenses.	56,000	88,000	320,000
Common expenses	48,000	64,000	160,000
Gross profit percentage	30%	40%	50%

The managers are disappointed with the operating results of department R. They do not believe that competition will permit raising prices; however, they believe that spending $10,000 more for promoting this department's products will increase the physical volume of products sold by 20%.

An alternative is to discontinue department R and use the space to expand department S. It is believed that department S's physical volume of products sold can thus be increased 35%. Special sales personnel are needed, however, and department S's traceable expenses would increase by $48,000. Neither alternative would appreciably affect the total common departmental expense.

Required

a. Calculate the contribution now being made to common expenses by department R, by department S, and by the combination of other departments.

b. Which of the two alternatives should management choose: increase promotional outlays for department R, or discontinue department R and expand department S? Support your answer with calculations.

CERTIFIED MANAGEMENT ACCOUNTANT (CMA®) EXAM SAMPLE QUESTIONS

CMA24-1. Rainbow Inc. recently appointed Margaret Joyce as vice president of finance and asked her to design a new budgeting system. Joyce has changed to a monthly budgeting system by dividing the company's annual budget by twelve. Joyce then prepared monthly budgets for each department and asked the managers to submit monthly reports comparing actual to budget. A sample monthly report for Department A is shown below.

RAINBOW INC. **Monthly Report for Department A**			
	Actual	**Budget**	**Variance**
Units.	1,000	900	100F
Variable production costs			
Direct material.	$ 2,800	$ 2,700	$ 100U
Direct labor	4,800	4,500	300U
Variable factory overhead.	4,250	4,050	200U
Fixed costs			
Depreciation	3,000	2,700	300U
Taxes	1,000	900	100U
Insurance	1,500	1,350	150U
Administration	1,100	990	110U
Marketing	1,000	900	100U
Total costs	$19,450	$18,090	$1,360U

This monthly budget has been imposed from the top and will create behavior problems. All of the following are causes of such problems **except**

a. the use of a flexible budget rather than a fixed budget.

b. top management authoritarian attitude toward the budget process.

c. the inclusion of non-controllable costs such as depreciation.

d. the lack of consideration for factors such as seasonality.

CMA24-2. When compared to static budgets, flexible budgets

a. offer managers a more realistic comparison of budget and actual fixed cost items under their control.

b. provide a better understanding of the capacity variances during the period being evaluated.

c. encourage managers to use less fixed costs items and more variable cost items that are under their control.

d. offer managers a more realistic comparison of budget and actual revenue and cost items under their control.

CMA24-3. Arkin Co.'s controller has prepared a flexible budget for the year just ended, adjusting the original static budget for the unexpected large increase in the volume of sales. Arkin's costs are mostly variable. The controller is pleased to note that both actual revenues and actual costs approximated amounts shown on the flexible budget. If actual revenues and actual costs are compared with amounts shown on the original (static) budget, what variances would arise?

   a.   Both revenue variances and cost variances would be favorable.

   b.   Revenue variances would be favorable and cost variances would be unfavorable.

   c.   Revenue variances would be unfavorable and cost variances would be favorable.

   d.   Both revenue variances and cost variances would be unfavorable.

CMA24-4. Of the following pairs of variances found in a flexible budget report, which pair is **most likely** to be related?

   a.   Material price variance and variable overhead efficiency variance.

   b.   Labor rate variance and variable overhead efficiency variance.

   c.   Material usage variance and labor efficiency variance.

   d.   Labor efficiency variance and fixed overhead volume variance.

CMA24-5. Sara Bellows, manager of the telecommunication sales team, has the following department budget.

Billings—long distance	$350,000
Billings—phone card	75,000
Billings—toll free	265,000

Her responsibility center is **best** described as a

   a.   cost center.

   b.   revenue center.

   c.   profit center.

   d.   investment center.

EXTENDING YOUR KNOWLEDGE

EYK24-1. **Business Decision Case** The monthly sales volume of Shugart Corporation varies from 7,000 units to 9,800 units over the course of a year. Management is currently studying anticipated selling expenses along with the related cash resources that will be needed. Which type of budget (flexible or static) (1) should be used by Shugart in planning, and (2) will provide Shugart the best feedback in performance reports for comparing planned expenditures with actual amounts? When Shugart's CEO asks you why it is advantageous to use a flexible budget instead of a static budget, what is one example you could give him?

EYK24-2. **Ethics Case** CJ Corporation manufactures steel rebar for use in construction. The accounting staff is currently preparing next year's budget. Bob Johnson is new to the firm and is interested in learning how this process occurs. He has lunch with the sales manager and the production manager to discuss further the planning process. Over the course of lunch, Bob discovers that the sales manager adjusts sales projections between a flexible amount and a static amount based on which will reflect the lowest variance from actual results. The production manager does the same for cost estimates. Both managers' year-end bonus is determined based on how low of a variance is achieved. When Bob asks about why they adjust their projections between flexible and static budgets, the response is simply that everyone around here does it.

Required

   a.   What do the sales and production managers hope to accomplish by their methods?

   b.   How might this backfire and work against them?

   c.   Are the actions of the sales and production managers unethical?

ANSWERS TO SELF-STUDY QUESTIONS

1. c, (p. 1071) 2. a, (p. 1075) 3. c, (pp. 1072–1073) 4. c, (p. 1080) 5. c, (p. 1080)

YOUR TURN! SOLUTIONS

Solution 24.1
PACCAR Parts segment, Trucks segment, and Financial Services segment.

Solution 24.2

Revenue	$600,000
Traceable departmental expenses:	
Direct materials.	$30,000
Direct labor	25,000
Other traceable expenses.	40,000
Department contribution	$505,000
Common expenses.	**155,000**
Departmental operating income.	$350,000

DECISION TIME SOLUTION

Solution 24.1

A CPA firm's balanced scorecard might include some of the following measures:

Financial Performance
Segment margin by practice area (tax, audit, consulting)
Average collection period by practice area
Revenue by partner

Customer Satisfaction
Summary of customer satisfaction survey results
Percentage of repeat customers
Average number of years completing customer tax returns

Internal Business Processes
Ratio of new sales to billings for the period
Ratio of chargeable hours to total available hours by staff level
Ratio of billable hours to hours (actually) charged

Learning and Growth
Average number of annual continuing education hours
Partner-to-staff ratio
Average number of community service hours per staff

25 Capital Budgeting

LEARNING OBJECTIVES

1. **Introduce** and **illustrate** the elements of capital budgeting. *(p. 1110)*

2. **Discuss** required rates of return and the time value of money. *(p. 1112)*

3. **Demonstrate** the use of present value factors to perform time value of money calculations. *(p. 1115)*

4. **Explain** and **illustrate** the determination of after-tax cash flows. *(p. 1117)*

5. **Describe** the net present value method of capital expenditure analysis. *(p. 1121)*

6. **Present** the cash payback and average rate of return methods of capital expenditure analysis. *(p. 1128)*

WASTE MANAGEMENT

If you have ever thrown away trash in the United States, there is a greater than 50% chance that either Waste Management (WM) or its chief competitor, Republic Services, Inc., handled the garbage collection. WM is the largest environmental solutions provider in North America, serving more than 20 million customers in the United States and Canada. The company has reason to boast, as it has the largest network of recycling facilities, transfer stations, and landfills in the industry. The network includes 367 collection operations, 355 transfer stations, 273 active landfill disposal sites, 16 waste-to-energy plants, 134 recycling plants, 111 beneficial-use landfill projects, and 6 independent power production plants. It also boasts the largest trucking fleet in the United States. How did WM grow to dominance in this industry?

WM was formed in 1968 and began aggressively purchasing many of the smaller garbage collection companies across the United States. The company went public in 1971 and within a year had made 133 acquisitions, with over $82 million in revenue. In the 1980s, WM continued its aggressive expansion and acquired Service Corporation of America to become the largest waste hauler in the country. Current company projections include managing more than 20 million tons every year by 2020, up from the more than 12 million tons the company handled in 2012.

Behind every capital expenditure at WM is a team dedicated to evaluating new opportunities. With explosive growth and seemingly continuous capital expenditure opportunities, it is no surprise that the company would dedicate a full team to expansion. The current facilities that WM operates require additional capital outlays to upgrade or replace old equipment and buildings and close and maintain old landfills. In addition, expenditures are needed for new equipment and buildings to accommodate the company's growth strategy. When analyzing capital expenditures, the Waste Management team calculates the company's cost of capital to determine whether a proposed project can generate value for shareholders. If the cost of capital cannot be achieved through the cash flows generated by the newly acquired capital, the company rejects the project.

For example, in the early 2000s, a joint-powers authority that included four jurisdictions in northern California issued a request for proposal for garbage and recycling collection services. WM (including its predecessor company) had been providing these services for many decades. When the proposals were received and evaluated, WM's proposal was the most expensive. WM representatives reported that the proposed amount was the amount required to meet the cost of capital threshold established by the corporate office. As a result, the new contract was offered to one of WM's competitors.

```
┌─────────────────────────────────────────────────────────────────────────┐
│                          CAPITAL BUDGETING                                │
└─────────────────────────────────────────────────────────────────────────┘
```

The Elements of Capital Budgeting	Required Rates of Return and the Time Value of Money	Performing Net Present Value Calculations	Measurements of Investments and Returns	Net Present Value Analysis	Other Capital Budgeting Analyses
• Capital budgeting phases • Capital expenditure analysis	• Cost of capital • Time value of money	• Single-sum cash flows • Annuity flows	• Cash flows • After-tax cash flows • Depreciation tax shield • Cash flow illustration • Summary	• Basic steps • Illustration of NPV analysis • Liquidation proceeds • Excess PV index	• Cash payback analysis • Average rate of return analysis

Planning long-term investments in productive assets is known as **capital budgeting**. The term reflects the fact that for most firms the total cost of all attractive investment opportunities exceeds the available investment capital. Thus, management must ration, or budget, investment capital among competing investment proposals. In deciding which new long-term assets to acquire, management must seek investments that promise to optimize return on the funds employed.

Capital budgeting is most valuable for organizations in which managers are responsible for the long-term profitability of their area of concern and are therefore encouraged to develop new products and more efficient production processes. Firms often make their most capable employees responsible for capital budgeting decisions, because such decisions determine how large sums of money are invested and commit the firm for extended future periods. Furthermore, investment decision errors are often difficult and costly to remedy or abandon.

Managers as well as accountants should be familiar with the special analytical techniques that evaluate the relative attractiveness of alternative uses of available capital. In this chapter, we first discuss the nature and procedures of capital budgeting, how required investment earning rates are determined, the time value of money, and the effect of income taxes on capital expenditure decisions. We conclude by illustrating three approaches to capital expenditure analysis: the net present value method, the cash payback method, and the average rate of return method.

ELEMENTS OF CAPITAL BUDGETING

LO1 Introduce and illustrate the elements of capital budgeting.

Capital Budgeting Phases

Capital budgeting has three phases:

1. Identify potential investments,
2. Select investments to be undertaken, and
3. Monitor the selected investments.

Hint: Inventory and other current asset purchases are not capital expenditures, even though they are commonly referred to as working "capital."

Many firms have a capital budgeting calendar calling for consideration of capital expenditure proposals at regular intervals, for example, every 6 months or every year. Proposals are usually examined with respect to (1) compliance with capital budget policies and procedures; (2) aspects of operational urgency, such as the need to replace critical equipment;

(3) established criteria for minimum return on capital investments; and, (4) consistency with the firm's operating policies and long-term goals. Proposals for relatively small cash outlays may require the approval of low-level management only, whereas major proposals are subject to approval at high management levels, perhaps including the board of directors. These major proposals and the decisions based on them profoundly affect a firm's long-term success.

Once approved, capital expenditures should be monitored to ensure that amounts and purposes are consistent with the original proposal. At appropriate intervals, the actual rates of return earned on important expenditures should be compared with projected rates. These periodic reviews encourage those responsible to formulate thorough and realistic proposals, and often provide an incentive for improving overall capital budgeting procedures.

Capital Expenditure Analysis

The scope of capital expenditures varies widely, ranging from the routine replacement of production equipment to the construction of entire manufacturing complexes. Whatever their size, most capital expenditure projects have the three stages shown in **Exhibit 25-1**.

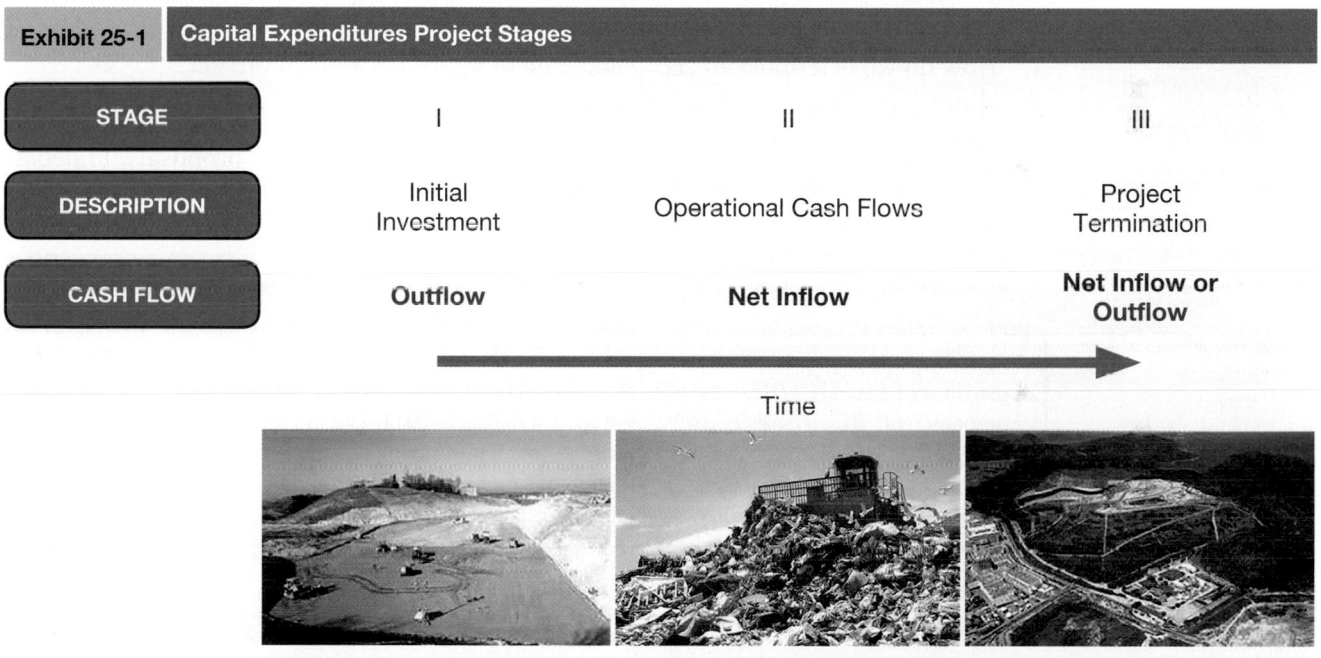

Exhibit 25-1	Capital Expenditures Project Stages		
STAGE	I	II	III
DESCRIPTION	Initial Investment	Operational Cash Flows	Project Termination
CASH FLOW	Outflow	Net Inflow	Net Inflow or Outflow

Time

Initial investment (stage I) consists of a net cash outlay for a project or an asset. Net operational cash flows during the life of the project (stage II) may result from either an excess of periodic cash revenues over related cash expenditures or a periodic saving in some cash expenditure. Finally, the termination of a project (stage III) often results in some amount of liquidation proceeds from the sale of the project capital or could result in some cash outlay for the removal of the project or restoration of the property to its former condition.

For example, the development of a new WM municipal waste landfill (stage I) requires millions of dollars for the purchase of the property, performance of the necessary environmental studies, obtainment of land use approvals and permits, and the development of appropriate access roads, gatehouse and vehicle scales, administrative buildings, security fencing, and environmental protection systems.

Over the life of the landfill (stage II), WM will collect cash fees from users of the landfill and expend cash for the compacting and covering of the trash and the monitoring, collection, and treatment of liquids and methane gas created by the decomposing waste.

Finally, once the landfill reaches its permitted capacity, WM must close the landfill (stage III), applying a final cap on the waste, and then monitor, collect, and treat the liquids and methane gas created by the decomposing waste for a period of 30 to 40 years.

The attractiveness of a particular investment is determined in large part by the quantitative relationship between the cash investment in stage I and the net cash receipts expected in stages II and III. In its simplest form, this relationship is usually expressed as a ratio known as the **rate of return**:

$$\text{Rate of return} = \frac{\text{Returns}}{\text{Investment}}$$

All other things being equal, the higher the expected rate of return, the more attractive the investment opportunity. Proposed investments can be ranked according to their expected rates of return, and capital outlays can be allocated among the most attractive investments. Capital expenditure analysis consists of judging the attractiveness of income-producing or cost-saving opportunities in relation to required investments. The results of this analysis are among the most important input data in capital budgeting decisions.

Three questions are of considerable concern in capital budgeting:

1. How do we determine an acceptable rate of return for a given project?

2. How can we meaningfully compare investments made now with returns to be received in the future?

3. In what terms should investments and returns be measured?

These challenging problems are considered in the following sections of this chapter.

ACCOUNTING IN PRACTICE

Capital Budgeting in Growing a Company

Waste Management's 2014 annual report includes the following on page 67 of the management discussion and analysis (MD&A) section: "We used $1,271 million during 2013 for capital expenditures, compared with $1,510 million in 2012 and $1,324 million in 2011. The increase in capital expenditures in 2012 and 2011 is a result of our increased spending on compressed natural gas vehicles, related fueling infrastructure, and information technology infrastructure and growth initiatives, as well as our taking advantage of the bonus depreciation legislation."

REQUIRED RATES OF RETURN AND THE TIME VALUE OF MONEY

eLectures
MBC

The mix of capital sources (i.e., available cash or proceeds from new debt or equity) that a company uses will depend on market conditions as well as the philosophies of the members of the board of directors and the management team.

Cost of Capital

LO2 Discuss required rates of return and the time value of money.

In determining an acceptable rate of return for a given project, we must consider not only the initial capital outlay, but also all of the costs associated with the acquisition of that capital. The parties providing the funds expect to be reasonably compensated for their use. When the money is borrowed from a bank or through a bond issuance, the interest paid by the firm is a cost of using the funds. When stockholder funds are used, we assume that some combination of dividend payments and increase in the value of the capital stock compensates stockholders for furnishing the investment capital. The cost to the firm of acquiring the funds used in capital investment projects—typically expressed as an annual percentage rate—is called the **cost of capital**.

A firm may acquire capital by issuing preferred or common stock, using retained earnings, borrowing, or some combination of these. Consequently, the overall cost of capital for a given project should reflect the cost rates of the several sources of funds in proportion to the amounts obtained from each source. This is called the **weighted average cost of capital**, or **WACC**.

Assume that a particular company had acquired capital through all four sources and in the proportions and with the cost of capital rates as shown here:

Hint: Because the earnings retained by the firm might otherwise have been distributed to the common shareholders in the form of dividends, firms often use the same cost of capital for retained earnings as is used for common stock.

Source of Capital	Percentage of Total	×	Cost of Capital Rate	=	Weighted Average Cost of Capital Component
Debt	40%	×	8%	=	3.2%
Preferred stock.	10%	×	9%	=	0.9%
Common stock.	20%	×	12%	=	2.4%
Retained earnings	30%	×	12%	=	3.6%
Weighted average cost of capital. .					10.1%

Multiplying the percentage of each capital source by its cost of capital rate provides weighted cost factors whose sum is the weighted average cost of capital. This percentage (in this case, 10.1%) can then be used to compare the attractiveness of proposed investments.

TAKEAWAY 25.1

The cost of capital is calculated based on all sources of financing, including both debt financing and equity financing.

Logically, for a capital investment to be considered favorably by a firm, its expected rate of return must be at least as high as the cost of capital. Therefore, the cost of capital represents a minimum required rate of return, or **hurdle rate**. In other words, a firm whose cost of capital is 10% will ordinarily want to invest only in an asset or project whose expected rate of return is more than 10%. An investment whose return is less than the cost of capital would be economically detrimental, although firms sometimes disregard their cost of capital if qualitative considerations override the quantitative aspects of the decision. Qualitative considerations might include the desire to achieve certain environmental goals, the desire to maintain research leadership in the industry, and the need to maintain full employment of the work force during a business slowdown.

Some firms consider only investments whose rates of return are at least a certain number of percentage points higher than the cost of capital. This **buffer margin** acts as a safety factor, because proposals that project estimated cash inflows and outflows years into the future have a significant amount of uncertainty regarding the amount and timing of those cash flows. Of course, in an environment of limited resources, even proposals whose expected rate of return is higher than the hurdle rate may be rejected if other investment opportunities offer still higher returns.

The following sources of financing, their proportions, and their cost of capital rates are for a merchandising company. Calculate and interpret the WACC for this company.

YOUR TURN! 25.1

The solution is on page 1147.

	Percentage of Total	Cost of Capital Rate
Bank loan	45%	12%
Equity capital	55%	9%

Time Value of Money

We have seen that in determining the desirability of a proposed capital investment, management compares the amount of investment required at the beginning of a project with its expected returns—typically a series of returns extending several years into the future. This comparison, which is so important in capital budgeting decisions, cannot be made properly using the absolute amounts of the future returns because money has a time value. The **time value of money** means that the right to receive an amount of money today is worth more than the right to receive the same amount at some future date, because a current receipt can be invested to earn interest over the intervening period. Thus, if 10% annual interest can be obtained on investments, $100 received today is equal in value to $110 received 1 year from now. One year from now, today's $100 has a future value of $110; conversely, the present value of a $110 receipt expected 1 year from today is $100.

The difference between present and future values is a function of interest rates and time periods. The higher the interest rate or longer the time period involved, the higher the amount by which a future value is reduced, or discounted, in deriving its present value. For example, **Exhibit 25-2** shows just how significant the time value of money can be at various interest rates and time periods. As the table indicates, 5 years from now $100 has a present value of $78, $62, or $50 if the applicable interest rates are 5%, 10%, and 15%, respectively. Note also that the higher the time period or the interest rate, the larger the difference between the future value of $100 and its present value. Comparing a current investment with its future returns without discounting the returns to their present value would substantially overstate the economic significance of the returns. We must therefore recognize the time value of money in capital budgeting procedures.

Exhibit 25-2	Time Value of Money		
Present Value of $100 (Rounded to Nearest Dollar)			
		Rate	
Years	**5%**	**10%**	**15%**
1	$95	$91	$87
2	91	83	76
3	86	75	66
4	82	68	57
5	78	62	50
10	61	39	25
20	38	15	6
30	23	6	2
40	14	2	0
50	9	1	0

Techniques for discounting future cash flows to their present values apply to both cash receipts and cash outlays. In other words, the current value of the right to receive—or the current value of the obligation to pay—a sum in the future is its present value computed at an appropriate interest rate. We maximize our economic position by arranging to receive amounts as early as possible and postponing amounts to be paid as long as possible. These generalizations will be apparent in the capital budgeting illustrations later in the chapter.

PERFORMING NET PRESENT VALUE CALCULATIONS

Appendix 10A introduced time value of money concepts as they relate to the pricing of bonds. The Chapter 10 appendix demonstrated present value calculations using three methods: 1) tables, 2) a financial calculator, 3) and an electronic spreadsheet. In this chapter we will perform net present value calculations using tables to measure capital investments and their related returns. Present value tables provide factors for combinations of time periods and interest rates that may be multiplied by a stream of cash flows or a one-time future cash flow to determine its present value. These tables can be found in Appendix E of the text, along with a more detailed discussion of time value of money concepts. If you would like to review net present value calculations using a financial calculator or an electronic spreadsheet, refer back to Appendix 10A.

LO3 **Demonstrate** the use of present value factors to perform time value of money calculations.

Throughout the chapter, the following abbreviations, related to time value of money calculations, are used:

> **PV = present value at time 0**
> **FV = future value at time n**
> **i = interest at which the amount compounds each period**
> **n = number of periods (time)**
> **PMT = periodic cash flow (payment)**

Single-Sum Cash Flows

Let us first consider how to compute the present value of a single sum cash flow. This calculation will be used to determine the present value of sporadic cash flows when the returns expected on an investment, or the expenditures it requires, are unequal amounts or are expected at irregular intervals during or at the end of the life of the investment.

To illustrate, we assume that an investment project promises a return of $2,000 at the end of 2 years and another $1,000 at the end of 5 years. The desired rate of return is 10% per year. **Exhibit 25-3** illustrates the cash flows on a timeline.

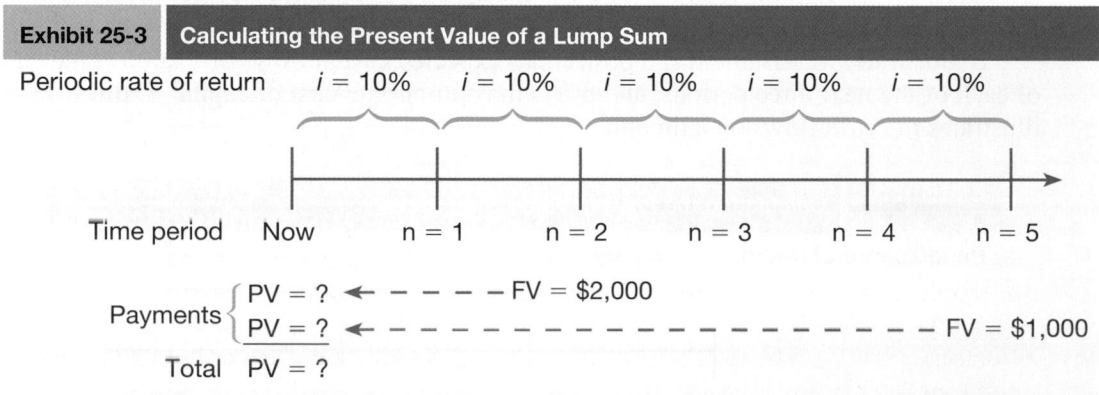

| Exhibit 25-3 | Calculating the Present Value of a Lump Sum |

Hint: *Present values should always be less than future values; otherwise, the calculation was performed incorrectly.*

Using factors from Table III, Present Value of $1, from Appendix E, we calculate the present value of each cash flow separately using the following process.

First, calculate the present value of the $2,000 cash flow. The formula for calculating the present value of a future sum is as follows:

Present value (PV) = Future value (FV) × PV table factor*

PV = $2,000 × 0.82645
PV = $1,652.90

*Because the $2,000 cash flow occurs at the end of Year 2, we use the factor associated with a 10% rate of return and 2 years (0.82645; see Table III in Appendix E).

This value may be interpreted as the amount that, if invested today in an account paying 10% interest, would allow for the withdrawal of $2,000 at the end of 2 years. This can be proved as follows: $1,652.90 invested today would earn $165.29 in interest in the first year, for a total value of $1,818.19 ($1,652.90 + $165.29). This balance would earn $181.82 in interest in the second year, for a total value of $2,000.01 ($1,818.19 + $181.82).

Next, calculate the present value of the $1,000 cash flow:

PV = FV × PV table factor*

PV = $1,000 × 0.62092
PV = $620.92

*Because the $1,000 cash flow occurs at the end of Year 5, we use the factor from a present value table for a single amount associated with a 10% rate of return and 5 years (0.62092; see Table III in Appendix E).

This value may be interpreted as the amount that, if invested today in an account paying 10% interest, would allow for the withdrawal of $1,000 at the end of 5 years.

The total present value of the combined flows is $2,273.82 ($1,652.90 + $620.92). That is, $2,273.82 invested today in an account paying 10% interest would allow withdrawal of $2,000 at the end of 2 years and $1,000 at the end of 5 years.

YOUR TURN! 25.2

The solution is on page 1147.

An investment project promises a return of $2,000 at the end of 3 years and $4,000 at the end of 4 years. If the company's cost of capital is 12%, what is the total present value of these cash flows?

Annuity Flows

Let us next consider how to compute the present value of an annuity. An **annuity** is cash flows that are the same each period over two or more equal periods.

To illustrate, we assume that a project has expected cash inflows of $1,000 at the end of each of the next three periods, and 8% is the appropriate cost of capital. **Exhibit 25-4** illustrates the cash flows on a timeline.

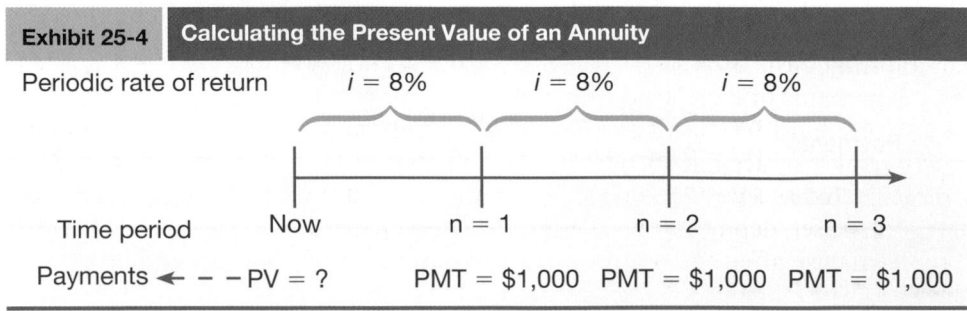

Exhibit 25-4 — Calculating the Present Value of an Annuity

Using factors from Table IV, Present Value of an Ordinary Annuity of $1 per Period, from Appendix E, we calculate the present value of these cash flows using the following formula:

$$\textbf{PV} = \textbf{PMT} \times \textbf{PV table factor*}$$

PV = $1,000 × 2.57710
PV = $2,577.10

*Because the $1,000 cash flow occurs at the end of each year for 3 years, we use the factor associated with an 8% rate of return and 3 years (2.57710; see Table IV in Appendix E).

This value may be interpreted as the amount that, if invested today in an account paying 8% interest annually, would allow for the withdrawal of $1,000 at the end of each year for the next 3 years. This can be proved as follows: $2,577.10 invested today would earn $206.17 ($2,577.10 × 0.08) in interest in the first year, for a total value of $2,783.27 ($2,577.10 + $206.17). A withdrawal of $1,000 would leave a balance of $1,783.27. This balance would earn $142.66 ($1,783.27 × 0.08) in interest in the second year, for a total value of $1,925.93 ($1,783.27 + $142.66). A second withdrawal of $1,000 would leave a balance of $925.93. This balance would earn $74.07 ($925.93 × 0.08) in interest in the third year, for a total value of $1,000 ($925.93 + $74.07), allowing for a third and final withdrawal of $1,000.

Both illustrations assume that all cash flows occur at the end of the periods. This assumption is somewhat simplistic, because cash receipts or cost savings from most industrial investments occur in a steady stream throughout the operating periods. Nevertheless, businesses assume end-of-period cash flows for ease of use. These calculations will understate the present values of flows that are gradual throughout the period, because the present values of cash flows early in the period are higher than similar inflows or outlays at the end of the period. The difference, however, is normally not material.

An investment project promises a return of $5,000 at the end of each of the next 7 years. If the company's cost of capital is 6%, what is the total present value of these cash flows?

YOUR TURN! 25.3

The solution is on page 1147.

MEASUREMENT OF INVESTMENTS AND RETURNS

Cash Flows

When present value analysis is used to make investment decisions, investments and returns must be stated in the form of cash flows. Present value determinations are basically interest calculations, and therefore only money amounts—cash flows—are properly used in interest calculations. Furthermore, only the *incremental* cash flows that will occur if the project is accepted should be considered in the analysis.

LO4 Explain and illustrate the determination of after-tax cash flows.

Typically, financial data available in the accounts are not stated in terms of cash flows because accrual-basis accounting is used. Amounts compiled on the accrual basis must be restated in terms of the appropriate cash flows for capital budgeting purposes. For example, apportioning the cost of an asset over its life through depreciation accounting is an important feature of accrual accounting. When present value analysis is used, the cost of an asset is treated as a cash outlay when the asset is paid for. In measuring future returns related to the asset, depreciation expense does not represent a cash outlay. However, depreciation expense affects cash flows indirectly by reducing cash outlays for income tax payments.

Likewise, earnings from projects should reflect the cash inflows rather than the revenue amounts computed using accrual accounting. The timing of the cash collections is important, too, because the essence of present value analysis is that cash received can be reinvested.

After-Tax Cash Flows

Both federal and state income taxes are important to investment decisions; for some companies, the combined federal and state income tax rate may approach 40%. Generally, income taxes reduce the economic significance of taxable receipts and deductible expenditures.

Exhibit 25-5	Tax Impact on Cash Flows		
		Inflow	**Outflow**
Pre-tax amount.		$40,000	$(15,000)
Income tax rate		40%	40%
Tax benefit/(expense).		(16,000)	6,000
After-tax amount		24,000	(9,000)

As illustrated in **Exhibit 25-5**, assuming a 40% tax rate, a $40,000 before-tax gain (cash inflow) would increase taxable income by $40,000 and income taxes by $16,000 (40% × $40,000), resulting in a $24,000 after-tax cash inflow. A $15,000 before-tax expense would reduce taxable income by $15,000 and income taxes by $6,000 (40% × $15,000), resulting in a $9,000 after-tax cash outflow. In general terms, the formulas for determining after-tax cash flows are as follows:

> **After-tax cash inflow = Pre-tax cash inflow × (1 − tax rate)**
>
> **After-tax cash outflow = Pre-tax cash outflow × (1 − tax rate)**

After-tax cash flows are more relevant than before-tax cash flows because they represent the amounts available to retire debt, finance expansions, or pay dividends. For this reason, investment decision analyses must be formulated in terms of after-tax cash flows.

Depreciation Tax Shield

Depreciation deductions *shield* revenues from taxation and thus reduce the taxes a company must pay. Depreciation creates a tax savings. **Exhibit 25-6** illustrates how to compute the amount of tax savings created by depreciation.

Exhibit 25-6	Tax Impact of Depreciation	
		Inflow
Pre-tax amount.		$30,000
Income tax rate		40%
Tax benefit/(expense).		12,000

To understand this effect, assume that a company had taxable revenues of $30,000 and no expenses. Assuming a 40% tax rate, this company would owe $12,000 in tax ($30,000 × 40%). Now, assume that the company had one deductible expense: depreciation in the amount of $30,000. In this case, the company would owe no taxes, because it can deduct the depreciation expense from its taxable revenue ($30,000 − $30,000 = $0 taxable income). Thus, the depreciation saved the company from having to pay $12,000 in tax. The formula for determining the tax shield is as follows:

> **After-tax depreciation tax shield = Depreciation expense × Tax rate**

Illustration of After-Tax Cash Flows

Thinking in terms of after-tax cash flows represents a significant departure from the accrual-based accounting for revenue and expenses. However, remember that the pre-tax cash flows are available to us in the cash flow statement. We can use our understanding of the cash flow statement to determine the after-tax cash flows needed for capital budgeting and other time value of money analyses.

To explore the relationship between the traditional income statement and the related after-tax cash flows, let's revisit Fezzari's 2016 income statement from Chapter 22. **Exhibit 25-7** shows Fezzari's income statement in column A. Column B identifies the related cash flows from Fezzari's cash flow statement. An understanding of **Exhibit 25-7** will provide a basis for understanding the comprehensive illustration of capital budgeting later in the chapter.

Column A in **Exhibit 25-7** is the traditional income statement, showing that revenue minus operating expenses and income taxes results in a net income of $446,179. For simplicity, we assume that revenue and cash expenses involve no significant accruals and that depreciation is the same on both the books and the tax return. Ordinarily, net income does not represent after-tax cash flows because depreciation expense—a noncash expense—is deducted to derive net income. As indicated in column A of **Exhibit 25-7**, to convert the $446,179 net income to after-tax cash flow, we must add back the depreciation of $45,100, resulting in $491,279 of after-tax cash flow.

Exhibit 25-7	Illustration of Determining After-Tax Cash Flows

Fezzari Performance Bicycles
For the Period Ended December 31, 2016

	A Traditional Income Statement	B Income Statement Cash Inflows (Outflows)	C Individual After-Tax Cash Inflow (Outflow) Effects
Sales.	$6,237,000	$6,237,000	$ 4,054,050
Less: Cost of goods sold (excluding depreciation) . . .	4,723,621	(4,723,621)	$(3,070,354)
Less: Depreciation expense.	45,100		15,785
Gross profit.	$1,468,279		
Less: Selling and administrative expense	776,850	(776,850)	$ (504,952)
Income from operations.	$ 691,429		
Less: Interest expense	5,000	(5,000)	$ (3,250)
Income before income taxes	$ 686,429		
Less: Income taxes	240,250	(240,250)	
Net income.	$ 446,179		
Add back depreciation expense.	45,100		
After-tax cash flow	$ 491,279	$ 491,279	$ 491,279

Column B of **Exhibit 25-7** confirms the $491,279 amount of after-tax cash flow determined in column A. This is accomplished by simply listing the amounts in column A that constitute cash inflows (revenue of $6,237,000) and cash outflows (cash expenses of

$4,723,621, $776,850, and $5,000 and income tax payments of $240,250). Depreciation is excluded because it does not represent a cash payment.

Column C in **Exhibit 25-7** illustrates the determination of the individual amounts of after-tax cash flows for each item on the income statement. We use this approach in the comprehensive illustration of capital budgeting appearing later in the chapter. Amounts in column C are determined as follows (again, a 35% income tax rate is assumed).

Receipt of $6,237,000 cash revenue

Receipt of $6,237,000 cash revenue would, by itself, increase taxable income by $6,237,000, adding $2,182,950 ($6,237,000 × 35%) to income taxes. The $4,054,050 after-tax cash inflow is the difference between the $6,237,000 cash revenue received and the related $2,182,950 increase in income taxes (a cash outflow). Applying the previous formula for an after-tax inflow results in the same amount:

$$\text{After-tax cash inflow} = \text{Pre-tax cash inflow} \times (1 - \text{Tax rate})$$

OR

$$\$4,054,050 = \$6,237,000 \times (1 - 0.35)$$

Payment of $4,723,621 in cash operating expenses

Payment of $4,723,621 in cash operating expenses represents a deductible cash outflow that reduces taxable income by $4,723,621 and thus reduces income taxes by $1,653,267 ($4,723,621 × 35%). The $3,070,354 net cash outflow is the difference between the $4,723,621 actually paid out for expenses and the $1,653,267 of income tax payments avoided by virtue of the tax deductibility of the expenses. Applying the previous formula for an after-tax outflow results in the same amount:

$$\text{After-tax cash outflow} = \text{Pre-tax cash outflow} \times (1 - \text{Tax rate})$$

OR

$$\$3,070,354 = \$4,723,621 \times (1 - 0.35)$$

Hint: The depreciation amount that provides a tax shield is the depreciation deduction on the tax return. Tax depreciation deductions are governed by tax regulations, not by generally accepted accounting principles. Often the periodic tax depreciation will differ from depreciation expense on the income statement (in Exhibit 25-7 we assume that the amounts are equal). When identifying the depreciation tax shield in capital budgeting analysis, then, it is important to use the depreciation amount from the tax return.

Notice that *avoiding a cash outflow* has the same effect on net cash flows as a cash inflow. In other words, total net cash inflows can be increased by adding to cash inflows or by avoiding cash outflows.

Recording $45,100 of depreciation expense

Although depreciation expense is tax deductible, no related cash expenditure occurs during the period. The $45,100 deduction reduces taxable income by $45,100 and income taxes by $15,785 ($45,100 × 35%). Depreciation expense and similar noncash expense deductions are often referred to as *tax shields* because they shield an equal amount of income from whatever income tax rate is applicable.

Payment of $776,850 in cash selling and administrative expenses

Payment of $776,850 in cash selling and administrative expenses represents a deductible cash outflow that reduces taxable income by $776,850 and thus reduces income taxes by $271,898 ($776,850 × 35%). The $504,952 net cash outflow is the difference between the $776,850 actually paid out for expenses and the $271,898 of income tax payments avoided by virtue of the tax deductibility of the expenses. Applying the previous formula for an after-tax outflow results in the same amount:

$$\text{After-tax cash outflow} = \text{Pre-tax cash outflow} \times (1 - \text{Tax rate})$$

OR

$$\$504,952^* = \$776,850 \times (1 - 0.35)$$

* Difference due to rounding.

Payment of $5,000 in cash interest expense

Payment of $5,000 in cash interest expense represents a deductible cash outflow that reduces taxable income by $5,000 and thus reduces income taxes by $1,750 ($5,000 × 35%). The $3,250 net cash outflow is the difference between the $5,000 actually paid out for interest expense and the $1,750 of income tax payments avoided by virtue of the tax deductibility of the expense. Applying the previous formula for an after-tax outflow results in the same amount:

$$\text{After-tax cash outflow} = \text{Pre-tax cash outflow} \times (1 - \text{Tax rate})$$

OR

$$\$3{,}250 = \$5{,}000 \times (1 - 0.35)$$

Combining the after-tax cash flow effect of each individual amount in column C again confirms that net cash inflows total $491,279.

Summary of Concerns Underlying Capital Budgeting

1. The typical investment pattern involves a present investment of funds resulting in anticipated returns, often extending years into the future.

2. The basic question in capital budgeting is whether present investments are justified by related future returns.

3. Because money has a time value, returns that occur in the future must be discounted to their present values for a proper comparison with present investments.

4. To use discounting (interest) calculations properly, we must state amounts in capital budgeting analyses in terms of cash flows.

5. Because income tax rates are substantial, capital budgeting analyses should be formulated in terms of after-tax cash flows.

Thus far in the chapter, we have presented a number of important aspects of capital budgeting as background for the review of several approaches to capital expenditure analysis. These background materials have focused on the analytical concept known as net present value. Accountants generally concede that the net present value approach is conceptually and analytically superior to the other two approaches that we will also illustrate: cash payback and average rate of return.

NET PRESENT VALUE ANALYSIS

Basic Steps

The basic approach to the **net present value method** is shown in **Exhibit 25-8**. Each step described here and used in the example that follows is color coded to correspond to the exhibit. Referring to the items in the exhibit, the steps in the net present value approach are to:

LO5 **Describe** the net present value method of capital expenditure analysis.

Step 1: Determine the amount of the **investment outlay** required in terms of incremental after-tax cash flows.

Step 2: Estimate the amounts and timing of **future operating receipts or cost savings** in terms of incremental after-tax cash flows.

Step 3: Estimate any **incremental after-tax liquidation proceeds** to be received on termination of the project.

Step 4: Discount all future cash flows to their **present value** at an appropriate interest rate, usually the minimum desired rate of return on capital.

Step 5: Subtract the investment outlay from the total present value of future cash flows to determine **net present value.** If net present value is zero or positive (returns equal or exceed investment), then the project's rate of return equals or exceeds the minimum desired rate and should be accepted. Negative net present values indicate that the project's return is less than desired, and the project should be rejected.

ACCOUNTING IN PRACTICE	**Undertaking Negative-NPV Projects**
	There are reasons companies may follow through with a capital investment even though it has a projected negative NPV. Reasons for this include projects that support other projects, hope that the investment will return more than originally expected, response to competition, and response to government regulations. These and other qualitative factors should be considered by management.

Exhibit 25-8	Net Present Value Method Approach

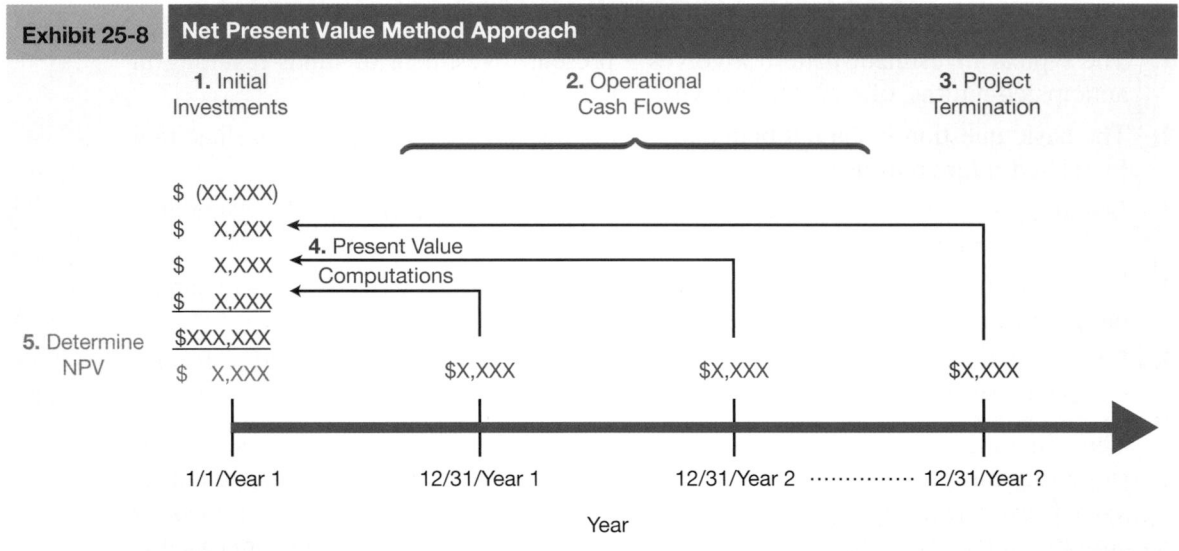

Illustration of Net Present Value Analysis

To illustrate net present value analysis, assume that Fezzari owns its bicycle assembly facility. The building is 30 years old, and its heating, ventilating, and air-conditioning (HVAC) systems are functioning, but significantly out of date. A local HVAC contractor has told Fezzari management that new HVAC technology could significantly reduce Fezzari's monthly utility bill. The HVAC contractor has offered to replace the current HVAC system with a new, state-of-the-art system for an installed price of $150,000. The new system has an expected useful life of 20 years, at which point it will be worthless, but it will save an estimated $22,500 per year in cash utilities expenses during its useful life. Fezzari management has a minimum desired return of 10% on any capital project. Fezzari's tax rate is 35%.

To evaluate the local contractor's proposal, management decides to use a net present value analysis.

Recall that depreciation is based on the depreciation deduction from the tax return. Based on a half-year convention (one-half of the first year's depreciation is recognized in the year of acquisition and disposition), the annual depreciation (rounded to the nearest dollar) would be computed as follows:

Year	Capitalized Cost	Depreciation Rate	Annual Depreciation*
1	$150,000	3.750%	$ 5,625
2	150,000	7.219	10,829
3	150,000	6.677	10,016
4	150,000	6.177	9,266
5	150,000	5.713	8,570
6	150,000	5.285	7,928
7	150,000	4.888	7,332
8	150,000	4.522	6,783
9	150,000	4.462	6,693
10	150,000	4.461	6,692
11	150,000	4.462	6,693
12	150,000	4.461	6,692
13	150,000	4.462	6,693
14	150,000	4.461	6,692
15	150,000	4.462	6,693
16	150,000	4.461	6,692
17	150,000	4.462	6,693
18	150,000	4.461	6,692
19	150,000	4.462	6,693
20	150,000	4.461	6,692
21	150,000	2.231	3,347

*Tax return depreciation, 150% declining balance, half-year convention.

Exhibit 25-9 presents a net present value analysis of the HVAC system as an investment project. Note that the format (including the color coding) follows the analysis outlined in **Exhibit 25-8**: Future returns are stated in terms of after-tax cash flows; then the present values of future cash flows are determined and compared with the investment. The computations shown in **Exhibit 25-9** are explained in the following subsections.

Step 1: Initial investment
The initial investment of $150,000 occurs at the beginning of Year 1, which we identify as Year 0. It is shown in **Exhibit 25-9** as a negative number, signifying that it represents an outflow of cash.

Step 2: Annual cash flows (expense savings)
Cash savings or expense reductions have the same effects as cash revenue, income, or gains. Thus, these amounts are shown as positive amounts, signifying that they represent an inflow of cash. They also have the same consequence of increasing income taxes. In our example, saving $22,500 in cash expenses each year raises taxable income by $22,500, which leads to an increase in taxes of $7,875 ($22,500 × 35%). Thus, the annual after-tax cash flow is $14,625—the $22,500 savings less the $7,875 tax increase.

Annual depreciation tax shield: The depreciation deduction on the tax return shields an equal amount of income from taxes. The avoided taxes are equal to the depreciation deduction multiplied by the applicable tax rate. In our illustration, the annual tax savings from the depreciation tax shield are as follows:

Exhibit 25-9 | Illustration of Net Present Value Analysis: After-Tax Cash Flows (Rounded to Nearest Dollar)

	Present Value	Projected After-Tax Cash Flows												
		Year 0	Year 1	Year 2	Year 3	Year 4	Year 5	Year 6	Year 7	Year 8	Year 9	.....	Year 19	Year 20	Year 21
Initial investment.	$(150,000)	$(150,000)														
Annual cash exp. savings.			$22,500	$22,500	$22,500	$22,500	$22,500	$22,500	$22,500	$22,500	$22,500	$22,500		$22,500	$22,500	—
Less income tax @ 35%.			7,875	7,875	7,875	7,875	7,875	7,875	7,875	7,875	7,875	7,875		7,875	7,875	—
After-tax exp. savings	$124,511		$14,625	$14,625	$14,625	$14,625	$14,625	$14,625	$14,625	$14,625	$14,625	$14,625		$14,625	$14,625	$ —
Tax savings from depr. tax shield:																
Year1	$ 1,790		$ 1,969													
Year2	3,132			$ 3,790												
Year3	2,634				$ 3,506											
Year4	2,215					$ 3,243										
Year5	1,863						$ 3,000									
Year6	1,566							$ 2,775								
Year7	1,317								$ 2,566							
Year8	1,107									$ 2,374						
Year9	994										$ 2,343					
Year10	903															
Year11	821															
Year12	746															
Year13	679															
Year14	617															
Year15	561															
Year16	510															
Year17	464															
Year18	421															
Year19	383													$ 2,343		
Year20	348														$ 2,342	
Year21	158															$1,171
Ttl. PV of future cash flows	$147,740		$16,594	$18,415	$18,131	$17,868	$17,625	$17,400	$17,191	$16,999	$16,968	$16,968		$16,968	$16,967	$1,171
Net present value	$ (2,260)															

Year	Annual Depreciation*	Tax Rate	Tax Shield
1	$ 5,625	35%	$1,969
2	10,829	35	3,790
3	10,016	35	3,506
4	9,266	35	3,243
5	8,570	35	3,000
6	7,928	35	2,775
7	7,332	35	2,566
8	6,783	35	2,374
9	6,693	35	2,343
10	6,692	35	2,342
11	6,693	35	2,343
12	6,692	35	2,342
13	6,693	35	2,343
14	6,692	35	2,342
15	6,693	35	2,343
10	6,692	35	2,342
17	6,693	35	2,343
18	6,692	35	2,342
19	6,693	35	2,343
20	6,692	35	2,342
21	3,347	35	1,171

*Tax return depreciation, 150% declining balance, half-year convention

Step 3: Project termination

For purposes of this illustration, we have assumed that the HVAC system will be worthless at the end of its 20-year life. Thus, there will be no additional incremental cash flow at the end of the project. When the system is replaced, any cost of removing the old system will be added to the cost of the installation of a new HVAC system as part of the initial investment in the new system.

Step 4: Present value calculations

The present value column in **Exhibit 25-9** shows the results of the calculations of the present values of the cash flows discussed earlier. Proper consideration of the required investment involves neither an income tax nor a present value calculation. Fezzari's $150,000 investment itself is not tax deductible; the related depreciation deductions are tax deductible, and are, of course, incorporated into our previous analysis. Because the investment expenditure is immediate, no discounting for present value is required. Thus, $150,000 represents the after-tax present value of the required investment outflow.

The $14,625 saved each year for 20 years can be treated as an annuity. The present value of an annuity of $14,625 for 20 years at 10% is $124,511 (PV = $14,625 × 8.51356).

Because the tax shield amounts differ from year to year based on the tax depreciation deduction, the present value of each year's amount must be computed separately. These amounts are computed using the PV factors as shown below:

Year	Depreciation	PV Factor*	PV
1	$1,969	0.90909	$1,790
2	3,790	0.82645	3,132
3	3,506	0.75131	2,634
4	3,243	0.68301	2,215
5	3,000	0.62092	1,863
6	2,775	0.56447	1,566
7	2,566	0.51316	1,317
8	2,374	0.46651	1,107
9	2,343	0.42410	994
10	2,342	0.38554	903
11	2,343	0.35049	821
12	2,342	0.31863	746
13	2,343	0.28966	679
14	2,342	0.26333	617
15	2,343	0.23939	561
16	2,342	0.21763	510
17	2,343	0.19784	464
18	2,342	0.17986	421
19	2,343	0.16351	383
20	2,342	0.14864	348

* Present value of a single sum payment, over 20 periods, at a 10% discount factor. See Table III in Appendix E.

These amounts are summed to arrive at the total present value of the future cash flows, or $147,740.

Step 5: Net present value calculation

The net present value is calculated by subtracting the initial investment from the total present value of the future cash flows. With its annual savings of cash expense and tax savings from the depreciation tax shield, the $150,000 investment results in future cash flows with a total present value of $147,740 and therefore a net present value of $(2,260). This negative return on the capital invested, adjusted for the time value of money, means that the project will return less than the 10% return sought by Fezzari management.

On the basis of the net present value analysis alone, it would appear that Fezzari management should reject the proposal. However, rather than reject it outright, this analysis may provide a basis for negotiating a better price for the HVAC system, or looking for modifications to the system's features that might result in a lower initial price. For example, Fezzari could pay as much as $147,740 for the system and still attain the desired 10% rate of return. Management may also wish to take a closer look at the anticipated utility savings—for example, the analysis did not include any anticipated increases in the utility costs over the 20-year life of the HVAC system. If utility costs are expected to increase in the future, it may make the anticipated savings even more significant.

DECISION TIME 25.1

The solution is on page 1147.

Mining Equipment Manufacturer is considering the purchase of a new building. The building would require an initial outlay of $350,000. It would be depreciated using the straight-line method over 20 years, with a $15,000 salvage value. The building would generate cash inflows of $47,200/year; the company's income tax rate is 30% and WACC is 8%. Calculate the NPV of this project and decide whether the investment should be undertaken.

Liquidation Proceeds

The amount realized when an asset is liquidated contributes to the relative attractiveness of an investment in capital equipment. Liquidation proceeds on long-lived assets are sometimes disregarded because their occurrence is so far in the future that the amounts are difficult to predict, and their present values tend to be small. When useful lives are short, however, liquidation proceeds may be a deciding factor in the analysis. In our illustration, the HVAC system has a 20-year life with no salvage value. However, assume that as a sales promotion, the manufacturer of the HVAC system guaranteed to buy back the system for $20,000 after 20 years. For tax purposes, salvage value may be ignored in computing depreciation, so the machine is fully depreciated over the 20 years to a zero book value. The HVAC's sale for $20,000, then, creates a $20,000 gain on the tax return ($20,000 sales price − $0 tax book value). The $20,000 gain increases income taxes by $7,000, which is deducted from the sales price of $20,000 to produce a net after-tax cash flow of $13,000 in Year 20. The present value of $13,000 for 20 years at 10% is $1,932.32 ($13,000 × 0.14864; see Table III in Appendix E).

Note that if an asset is sold before the end of its tax depreciation period, a loss may be generated for tax purposes. The loss operates as a tax shield because it shields an equal amount of income from taxes. The tax savings is added to the cash proceeds to determine the net after-tax cash flow.

If a machine with a book value of $10,000 is sold for $7,500 cash, what is the after-tax cash flow from the sale? The income tax rate is 35%.	**YOUR TURN! 25.4** The solution is on page 1147.

The solution is on page 1147.

TAKEAWAY 25.3

Remember that all transactions that relate to an investment, including depreciation and gains or losses on liquidation, are included in an NPV analysis. Although depreciation and gains or losses do not directly impact cash flows, they do have an indirect effect through changing the taxes a company must pay.

Excess Present Value Index

Alternative capital expenditure proposals may be compared in terms of their **excess present value index**, defined as follows:

$$\text{Excess present value index} = \frac{\textbf{Total present value of future cash flows}}{\textbf{Initial investment}}$$

For the investment presented in **Exhibit 25-9**, the excess present value index would be

$$\frac{\$147,740}{\$150,000} = 0.985$$

The higher the ratio of return on investment, the more attractive is the proposal. A ratio below 1.00 means that the project returns less than the target rate of return, and a ratio above 1.00 means that the project return exceeds the target rate of return. Although the excess present value index may be a convenient measure for ranking various proposals, it does not reflect the amount of the investment. Two proposals, requiring initial cash investments of $5,000 and $5,000,000, respectively, could have identical excess present value indexes but could hardly be considered equal investment opportunities.

OTHER CAPITAL BUDGETING ANALYSES

LO6 Present the cash payback and average rate of return methods of capital expenditure analysis.

Cash Payback Analysis

The **cash payback method** is a form of capital expenditure analysis that evaluates investment proposals in terms of the **cash payback period**. The cash payback period is the time in years that it takes net future after-tax cash inflows to equal the original investment.

Assume that Fezzari received a competing proposal for its new HVAC system. Management is considering purchasing either system A or system B, for which the following data are given:

System	Investment Required	Annual Net After-Tax Cash Inflows	Useful Life
A.............................	$150,000	$17,250	20 years
B.............................	115,000	15,000	15 years

For this illustration, we have assumed that the systems will be depreciated on a straight-line basis for tax purposes, making the annual net cash inflows equal over time. The cash payback period is computed as follows:

$$\frac{\text{Original investment}}{\text{Annual net cash inflows}} = \text{Cash payback in years}$$

Thus, for the two systems, we obtain:

$$\text{System A: } \frac{\$150,000}{\$17,250} = \text{8.70-year cash payback}$$

$$\text{System B: } \frac{\$115,000}{\$15,000} = \text{7.67-year cash payback}$$

This analysis shows that system A will pay back its required investment in 8.7 years, and system B will take 7.67 years. Because the decision rule in cash payback analysis states that the shorter the payback period, the better, system B would be considered the better investment.

If annual net cash inflows are not equal, the cash payback period is computed by summing the annual cash inflows until the cumulative amount equals the initial investment. For example, refer back to **Exhibit 25-9**. The investment is expected to generate annual net after-tax cash inflows for 9 years, as follows:

Year	Annual After-Tax Cash Inflows	Cumulative Cash Payback	Amount Required to Reach $150,000
1.....................	$16,594	$ 16,594	$133,406
2.....................	18,415	35,009	114,991
3.....................	18,131	53,140	96,860
4.....................	17,868	71,008	78,992
5.....................	17,625	88,633	61,367
6.....................	17,400	106,033	43,967
7.....................	17,191	123,224	26,776
8.....................	16,999	140,223	9,777
9.....................	16,968	157,191	

As shown in the amount required to reach $150,000 column, the original investment in the HVAC system will be recovered in cash partway through Year 9. The portion of the year required may be computed by dividing the remaining amount needed by the next year's inflow ($9,777/$16,968 = 0.576). The cash payback period, then, is 8.576 years.

Concern for the payback of investments is quite natural because the shorter a project's payback period, the more quickly the funds invested in that project are recovered and available for other investments. In high-risk investments, the payback period indicates how soon a firm is "bailed out" of an investment should projected cash inflows prove inaccurate.

TAKEAWAY 25.4

The cash payback period is important to new companies that are short on cash. A project with a short payback period and a low rate of return might be preferable to another project with a longer payback period and higher rate of return. The company may need a fast recovery of cash.

The cash payback method is considered less sophisticated than net present value analysis. A primary limitation of cash payback analysis is that the relative profitability of various investments is not specifically considered. Note, for example, that in the previous illustration, system B has the better (shorter) cash payback period. However, its useful life, which is ignored in cash payback analysis, indicates that system B will stop generating cash inflows about 7 years beyond payback. In contrast, although system A has a longer payback period, it will generate future cash inflows for over 11 years beyond payback and therefore promises to be more profitable.

Regardless of its failure to consider profitability, cash payback analysis is widely used, probably because of its relative simplicity. It can be useful in conjunction with other analyses or as a preliminary screening device for investment projects under consideration.

Average Rate of Return Analysis

The **average rate of return method** uses accrual accounting information in its calculation, not cash flows. This approach addresses the future impact on the income statement.

This measure is calculated as follows:

$$\text{Average rate of return} = \frac{\text{Average annual net income from investment}}{\text{Average investment}}$$

Note that the focus here is not on after-tax cash flows but on traditional accounting net income.

Assume that system A described earlier requires an initial investment of $150,000, provides $17,250 annual cash inflows from operations, and has a useful life of 20 years. Assuming no salvage value, the accounting annual straight-line depreciation on system A would be ($150,000/20), or $7,500. With an income tax rate of 35%, the average annual net income from the investment would be $6,337, computed as follows:

Cash inflow from operations	$17,250
Depreciation expense	7,500
Pre-tax income from investment	$ 9,750
Income tax expense	3,413
Net income from investment	$ 6,337

Initial outflows:		
Building purchase.		$(2,000,000)
Leasehold improvements		(250,000)
Total initial outflows		$(2,250,000)
Annual cash flows:		
Lease revenue*		$ 120,000
Total annual inflows		$ 120,000
Annual depreciation expense**		$ 75,000
Building useful life (years).		30
Income tax rate		35%
Cost of capital		10%

* 3,000 sq. ft. × $40/sq. ft. per year
** $2,250,000/30 years

Required

Perform a capital expenditure analysis to decide whether EBC should purchase the building, analyzing the net present value as well as payback period and average rate of return.

Solution

Net present value analysis:

Annual after-tax revenues	$120,000 × (1 − 35%)	$ 78,000
Tax shield from depreciation	$75,000 × 35%	26,250
Annual net cash inflows	$78,000 + $26,250	$ 104,250
Present value of the annual cash inflows	($104,250 × 9.42691)	$ 982,756
Net present value		
Initial outflows.		$(2,250,000)
PV of future cash flows.		982,756
NPV.		$(1,267,244)

Cash payback analysis:

Initial cash outflow	$2,250,000
Divided by the annual net cash inflows . . .	$104,250
Payback period	21.58 years

Average rate of return analysis:

Annual revenues.		$ 120,000
Annual expenses		75,000
Average annual net income		45,000
Income tax @ 35%.		15,750
Average after-tax net income.		29,250
Initial investment.		2,250,000
Ending investment		0
Average investment	($2,250,000 + $0)/2	$ 1,125,000
Average rate of return	$29,250/$1,125,000	2.60%

Based on the negative NPV, the long cash payback period and the small average rate of return, EBC should *not* purchase the building for $2,000,000.

COMPREHENSIVE PROBLEM

Carolina Company is evaluating a possible $150,000 investment in equipment that would increase cash flows from operations for 4 years. The equipment will have no salvage value.

The income tax rate is 30%. Carolina uses a 15% hurdle rate when using net present value analysis. Other information regarding the proposal is as follows:

	Year 1	Year 2	Year 3	Year 4
Cash inflow from operations (pre-tax)	$60,000	$87,000	$42,000	$40,000
Depreciation on tax return	50,000	67,000	22,000	11,000
Depreciation in financial statements	37,500	37,500	37,500	37,500
Net income from investment	15,750	34,650	3,150	1,750
PV Factor @ 15%	0.86957	0.75614	0.65752	0.57175

Required

a. What are the annual net after-tax cash inflows from this proposal?
b. Compute the net present value and indicate whether it is positive or negative (round amounts to nearest dollar).
c. Compute the cash payback period.
d. Compute the average rate of return.

Solution

a. We may compute the individual after-tax cash effects by multiplying (1) the cash inflow from operations by 70% (that is, 1 – Income tax rate) and (2) the tax return depreciation by 30% (that is, the income tax rate). Combining the individual after-tax cash effects gives the annual net after-tax cash inflows:

Year 1:	$60,000 × 70% = $42,000
	50,000 × 30% = 15,000
	After-tax cash flow $57,000

Year 3:	$42,000 × 70% = $29,400
	22,000 × 30% = 6,600
	After-tax cash flow $36,000

Year 2:	$87,000 × 70% = $60,900
	67,000 × 30% = 20,100
	After-tax cash flow $81,000

Year 4:	$40,000 × 70% = $28,000
	11,000 × 30% = 3,300
	After-tax cash flow $31,300

Alternatively, we may compute the net after-tax cash inflows by subtracting the cash income tax payments from the cash inflows from operations. The annual cash income tax payments are 30% of the cash inflow from operations less the tax return depreciation.

	Year 1	Year 2	Year 3	Year 4
Cash inflow from operations	$60,000	$87,000	$42,000	$40,000
Cash payment for income taxes	3,000	6,000	6,000	8,700
After-tax cash flows	$57,000	$81,000	$36,000	$31,300

b.

Year	Annual Net After-Tax Cash Inflows	PV Factor	Present Value
1	$57,000	0.86957	$ 49,565
2	81,000	0.75614	61,247
3	36,000	0.65752	23,671
4	31,300	0.57175	17,896
Total present value			152,379
Investment required in equipment			150,000
Net positive present value			$ 2,379

c. The cash payback period is 2 1/3 years, computed as follows:

Year	Annual Net After-Tax Cash Inflows	Cumulative Cash Payback	
1	$57,000	$ 57,000	
2	81,000	138,000	
3	36,000	150,000	(requires 1/3 of $36,000 to reach $150,000)
4	31,300		

d.

Annual net income from investment:		
	Year 1	$15,750
	Year 2	34,650
	Year 3	3,150
	Year 4	1,750
	Total	$55,300

Average annual net income from investment: $55,300/4 = $13,825
Average investment: ($150,000 + $0)/2 = $75,000
Average rate of return: $13,825/$75,000 = 18.4%

SUMMARY OF LEARNING OBJECTIVES

LO1   Introduce and illustrate the elements of capital budgeting. (p. 1110)

- Capital budgeting is the planning of long-lived asset investments. Capital expenditure analysis basically examines how well prospective future returns justify related current investments.
- Most capital expenditures have three stages: (1) initial investment, (2) operational cash flows, and (3) project termination.

LO2   Discuss required rates of return and the time value of money. (p. 1112)

- Cost of capital is a measure of the firm's cost for investment capital; it usually represents the minimum acceptable return for investment opportunities.
- The time value of money concept recognizes that the further into the future cash flows occur, the less current economic worth they have.
- The difference between present and future values is a function of interest rates and time periods.

LO3   Demonstrate the use of present value factors to perform time value of money calculations. (p. 1115)

- Present value factor tables enable us to compute the present values of future cash flows at appropriate interest rates.
- The present value calculations used most frequently in capital budgeting are those for future single-sum flows and end-of-period annuity flows.
- The present value of a single sum calculation is used to determine the present value of sporadic cash flows when the returns expected on an investment, or the expenditures it requires, are unequal amounts or are expected at irregular intervals during or at the end of the life of the investment. The formula for the present value of a single sum is PV = FV × PV table factor.
- The present value of an annuity is used to determine the present value of cash flows that are the same each period over two or more equal periods. The formula for the present value of an annuity is PV = PMT × PV table factor.

LO4   Explain and illustrate the determination of after-tax cash flows. (p. 1117)

- After-tax cash flows probably represent the most relevant measure of the prospective returns of proposed investments.
- We convert cash flows from revenues and expenses into after-tax amounts by multiplying them by (1 − Income tax rate).

- Depreciation deductions shield revenues from taxation, referred to as a tax shield. We convert depreciation deductions into their after-tax cash flow effect by multiplying the deduction by the applicable income tax rate.

Describe the net present value method of capital expenditure analysis. (p. 1121)   **LO5**

- Net present value analysis compares the present value of net future cash flow returns with the investment. Projects having zero or positive net present value are acceptable.

- Alternative investment proposals may be compared in terms of their excess present value index; the higher the index, the more attractive is the proposal.

Present the cash payback and average rate of return methods of capital expenditure analysis. (p. 1128)   **LO6**

- Cash payback analysis measures the time in years necessary for the net future after-tax cash flows to equal the original investment. In this type of analysis, the shorter the payback period, the more attractive is the investment.

- Average rate of return analysis compares the annual average net income with the average investment. The higher this ratio is, the more attractive is the investment.

- Cash payback analysis fails to consider the relative profitability of alternative projects. Average rate of return analysis fails to consider the time value of money.

KEY TERMS

Annuity (p. 1116)	Cash payback period (p. 1128)	Net present value method (p. 1121)
Average rate of return method (p. 1129)	Cost of capital (p. 1113)	Rate of return (p. 1112)
Buffer margin (p. 1113)	Excess present value index (p. 1127)	Time value of money (p. 1114)
Capital budgeting (p. 1110)	Hurdle rate (p. 1113)	Weighted average cost of capital, or WACC (p. 1113)
Cash payback method (p. 1128)		

Assignments with the logo in the margin are available in BusinessCourse.
See the Preface of the book for details.

SELF-STUDY QUESTIONS

(Answers to Self-Study Questions are at the end of this chapter.)

1. **A firm's cost of acquiring the funds for capital investment projects is known as the**   **LO2**
   a. Payback period.
   c. Cost of capital.
   b. Rate of return.
   d. Time value of money.

2. **All other things remaining the same, when the interest rate used to discount future values increases, present values**   **LO2**
   a. Decrease.
   b. Increase in proportion to the interest rate increase.
   c. Remain the same.
   d. Increase but not in proportion to the interest rate increase.

3. **Although depreciation is a noncash expense, it does have an indirect effect on cash flows because it shelters an equal amount of income from income taxes. This feature is known as a**   **LO4**
   a. Buffer margin.
   c. Depreciation flow.
   b. Cash payback.
   d. Tax shield.

4. **Blaine Company is considering four investment proposals, each requiring the same amount of initial cash investment. The excess present value index for each proposal is listed below. Using the index as a selection criterion, identify the index of the most attractive proposal.**   **LO5**
   a. 90
   c. 110
   b. 100
   d. 115

LO6 5. **The primary limitation of the cash payback method is that it**
   a.   Uses before-tax cash flows.
   b.   Identifies the length of time it will take to recover the investment outlay in cash.
   c.   Ignores the profitability of one investment project as compared to another.
   d.   Involves a more sophisticated analysis than the net present value method.

QUESTIONS

LO1 1. What is capital budgeting?

LO1 2. List three reasons why capital budgeting decisions are often important.

LO1 3. What are the three stages typical of most investments in plant and equipment?

LO2 4. Briefly describe the concept of weighted average cost of capital.

LO2 5. In what sense does the cost of capital limit a firm's investment considerations?

LO2 6. A company plans to accumulate 75% of its needed investment capital by issuing bonds having a capital cost percentage of 12%; the balance will be raised by issuing stock having a capital cost percentage of 16%. What would be the weighted average cost of capital for the total amount of capital?

LO2 7. Briefly describe the concept of the time value of money.

LO3 8. You have the right to receive $30,000 at the end of each of the next four years, and money is worth 8%. Using the PV tables, your financial calculator, or Excel, compute the present value of this annuity.

LO3 9. A rich uncle allows you to stipulate which of two ways you receive your inheritance:

   a. $850,000 one year after his death or
   b. $250,000 on his death and $200,000 each year at the end of the first, second, and third years following his death. If money is worth 10%, what is the relative advantage of the more attractive alternative?

LO3 10. You can settle a debt with either a single payment now of $30,000 or with payments of $8,000 at the end of each of the next five years. If money is worth 10%, what is the relative advantage of the most attractive alternative? If money is worth 12%, would your answer change? Why?

LO4 11. Explain how to convert before-tax cash operating expenses and depreciation deductions into after-tax amounts.

LO4 12. What is meant by the term *depreciation tax shield*?

LO3, 5 13. What amounts are compared in net present value analysis? State the related decision rule.

LO5 14. What is an excess present value index?

LO6 15. Define cash payback period, state the related decision rule, and specify an important limitation of this analysis.

LO6 16. Define average rate of return, state the related decision rule, and specify an important limitation of this analysis.

EXERCISES—SET A

LO2 **E25-1A. Weighted Average Cost of Capital** Gardner, Inc., plans to finance its expansion by raising the needed investment capital from the following sources in the indicated proportions and respective capital cost rates:

| | Capital Cost | |
Source	Proportion	Rate
Bonds	40%	13%
Preferred stock	20	9
Common stock	30	12
Retained earnings	10	9
	100%	

Calculate the weighted average cost of capital.

E25-2A. Present Value Computations Assuming that money is worth 10%, compute the present value of

LO3

1. $7,000 received 15 years from today.
2. The right to inherit $1,000,000 14 years from now.
3. The right to receive $1,000 at the end of each of the next six years.
4. The obligation to pay $3,000 at the end of each of the next 10 years.
5. The right to receive $5,000 at the end of the 7th, 8th, 9th, and 10th years from today.

E25-3A. After-Tax Cash Flows For each of the following independent situations, compute the net after-tax cash flow amount by subtracting cash outlays for operating expenses and income taxes from cash revenue. The cash outlay for income taxes is determined by applying the income tax rate to the cash revenue received less the cash and noncash (depreciation) expenses.

LO4

SERVICE AND
MERCHANDISING

	A	B	C
Cash revenue received.	$90,000	$450,000	$220,000
Cash operating expenses paid.	54,000	315,000	145,000
Depreciation on tax return	12,000	30,000	20,000
Income tax rate	40%	30%	20%

E25-4A. After-Tax Cash Flows Using the data in E25-3A, (a) calculate the individual after-tax cash flow effect of each relevant item in each independent situation, and (b) sum the individual after-tax cash flows in each situation to determine the overall net after-tax cash flow.

LO4

SERVICE AND
MERCHANDISING

E25-5A. Depreciation Tax Shields Lincoln Company has purchased equipment for $200,000. After it is fully depreciated, the equipment will have no salvage value. Lincoln may select either of the following depreciation schedules for tax purposes:

LO4

Year	Option 1 Depreciation	Option 2 Depreciation
1.	$40,000	$20,000
2.	64,000	40,000
3.	38,400	40,000
4.	23,040	40,000
5.	23,040	40,000
6.	11,520	20,000

Assuming a 40% tax rate and a 12% desired annual return, compute the total present value of the tax savings provided by these alternative depreciation tax shields. Which depreciation schedule would be more attractive to Lincoln?

E25-6A. Net Present Value Analysis Anderson Company must evaluate two capital expenditure proposals. Anderson's hurdle rate is 12%. Data for the two proposals follow.

LO5

	Proposal X	Proposal Y
Required investment	$120,000	$120,000
Annual after-tax cash inflows.	24,000	
After-tax cash inflows at the end of years 3, 6, 9, and 12		72,000
Life of project	12 years	12 years

Using net present value analysis, which proposal is the more attractive? If Anderson has sufficient funds available, should both proposals be accepted?

E25-7A. Cash Payback Refer to the data in E25-6A. What is the cash payback period for Proposal X? For Proposal Y?

LO6

E25-8A. Average Rate of Return Lakeland Company is considering the purchase of equipment for $150,000. The equipment will expand the Company's production and increase revenue by $40,000 per year. Annual cash operating expenses will increase by $10,000. The equipment's useful life is 10 years with no salvage value. Lakeland uses straight-line depreciation. The income tax rate is 35%. What is the average rate of return on the investment?

LO6

EXERCISES—SET B

LO2 **E25-1B. Weighted Average Cost of Capital** Austin, Inc. plans to finance its expansion by raising the needed investment capital from the following sources in the indicated proportions and respective capital cost rates.

Source	Proportion	Capital Cost Rate
Bonds...	45%	10%
Preferred stock....................................	10	8
Common stock.....................................	25	14
Retained earnings	20	12
	100%	

Calculate the weighted average cost of capital.

LO3 **E25-2B. Present Value Computations** Assuming that money is worth 10%, compute the present value of

1. $6,000 received 15 years from today.
2. The right to inherit $2,000,000 14 years from now.
3. The right to receive $2,000 at the end of each of the next six years.
4. The obligation to pay $1,000 at the end of each of the next 10 years.
5. The right to receive $10,000 at the end of the 7th, 8th, 9th, and 10th years from today.

LO4 **E25-3B. After-Tax Cash Flows** For each of the following independent situations, compute the net after-tax cash flow amount by subtracting cash outlays for operating expenses and income taxes from cash revenue. The cash outlay for income taxes is determined by applying the income tax rate to the cash revenue received less the cash and noncash (depreciation) expenses.

SERVICE AND MERCHANDISING

	A	B	C
Cash revenue received.....................................	$80,000	$400,000	$200,000
Cash operating expenses paid............................	45,000	260,000	120,000
Depreciation on tax return	10,000	25,000	15,000
Income tax rate	30%	40%	20%

LO4 **E25-4B. After-Tax Cash Flows** Using the data in E25-3B, (a) calculate the individual after-tax cash flow effect of each relevant item in each independent situation, and (b) sum the individual after-tax cash flows in each situation to determine the overall net after-tax cash flow.

SERVICE AND MERCHANDISING

LO4 **E25-5B. Depreciation Tax Shields** Mendota Company has purchased equipment for $100,000. After it is fully depreciated, the equipment will have no salvage value. Mendota may select either of the following depreciation schedules for tax purposes:

Year	Option 1 Depreciation	Option 2 Depreciation
1..	$20,000	$10,000
2..	32,000	20,000
3..	19,200	20,000
4..	11,520	20,000
5..	11,520	20,000
6..	5,760	10,000

Assuming a 40% tax rate and a 12% desired annual return, compute the total present value of the tax savings provided by these alternative depreciation tax shields. Which depreciation schedule would be more attractive to Mendota?

LO5 **E25-6B. Net Present Value Analysis** Hermson Company must evaluate two capital expenditure proposals. Hermson's hurdle rate is 12%. Data for the two proposals follow.

	Proposal X	Proposal Y
Required investment	$140,000	$140,000
Annual after-tax cash inflows.	33,000	
After-tax cash inflows at the end of years 3, 6, 9, and 12		99,000
Life of project	12 years	12 years

Using net present value analysis, which proposal do you find to be the more attractive? If Hermson has sufficient funds available, should both proposals be accepted?

E25-7B. Cash Payback Refer to the data in E25-6B. What is the cash payback period for proposal X? for proposal Y?   **LO6**

E25-8B. Average Rate of Return Clancy Company is considering the purchase of equipment for $100,000. The equipment will expand the company's production and increase revenue by $30,000 per year. Annual cash operating expenses will increase by $8,000. The equipment's useful life is 10 years with no salvage value. Clancy uses straight-line depreciation. The income tax rate is 35%. What is the average rate of return on the investment?   **LO6**

PROBLEMS—SET A

P25-1A. After-Tax Cash Flows Below is a list of aspects of various capital expenditure proposals that the capital budgeting team of Anchor, Inc., has incorporated into its net present value analyses during the past year. Unless otherwise noted, the items listed are unrelated to each other. All situations assume a 40% income tax rate and an 11% minimum desired rate of return.   **LO4**

1. Pre-tax savings of $4,000 in cash expenses will occur in each of the next three years.
2. A machine is purchased now for $37,000 cash.
3. A long-haul tractor costing $27,000 will be depreciated $9,000, $12,000, $4,050, and $1,950, respectively, on the tax return over four years.
4. Equipment costing $200,000 will be depreciated over five years on the tax return in the following amounts: $25,000; $50,000; $50,000; $50,000; and $25,000.
5. Pre-tax savings of $8,800 in cash expenses will occur in each of the next six years.
6. Pre-tax savings of $7,000 in cash expenses will occur in the first, third, and fifth years from now.
7. The tractor described in aspect 3 will be sold after four years for $5,000 cash.
8. The equipment described in aspect 4 will be sold after four years for $20,000 cash.

Required
Set up an answer form with the two column headings as shown below. Answer each investment aspect separately. Prepare your calculations on a separate paper and key them to each item. The answer to investment aspect 1 is presented as an example.

Investment Aspect 1	A After-tax Cash Flow Effect(s) Inflows (Outflows)	B Year(s) of Cash Flow
	$2,400	1, 2, 3

Calculations:
1. Pre-tax cash savings		$4,000
Less income tax at 40%.		1,600
After-tax cash inflow.		$2,400

a.   Calculate and record in column A the related after-tax cash flow effect(s). Place parentheses around outflows.
b.   Indicate in column B the timing of each cash flow shown in column A. Use 0 to indicate immediately and 1, 2, 3, 4, and so on for each year involved.

P25-2A. Net Present Value Analysis Champion Company is considering a contract that would require an expansion of its food processing capabilities. The contract covers five years. To provide the required   **LO5**

products, Champion would have to purchase additional equipment for $64,000. Champion estimates the contract will provide annual net cash inflows (before taxes) of $26,000. For tax purposes, the equipment will be depreciated as follows:

Year 1	$ 8,000
Year 2	16,000
Year 3	16,000
Year 4	16,000
Year 5	8,000

Although salvage value is ignored in the tax depreciation calculations, Champion estimates the equipment will be sold for $8,000 after five years.

Required

Assuming a 35% income tax rate and a 10% hurdle rate, compute the net present value of this contract proposal. Using net present value analysis, should Champion accept the contract? (Round amounts to the nearest dollar.)

LO5, 6 **P25-3A. Net Present Value, Cash Payback, and Average Rate of Return Methods** Western Company is evaluating a possible $42,000 investment in special tools that would increase cash flows from operations for four years. The tools will have no salvage value. The income tax rate is 40%. Western uses a 12% hurdle rate when using present value analysis. Other information regarding the proposal is as follows:

	Year 1	Year 2	Year 3	Year 4
Cash inflow from operations (pre-tax)	$15,000	$20,000	$16,500	$12,000
Depreciation on tax return	14,000	18,500	6,500	3,000
Depreciation in financial statements	10,500	10,500	10,500	10,500
Net income from investment	2,700	5,700	3,600	900

Required

a. What are the annual net after-tax cash inflows from this proposal?
b. Compute the net present value and indicate whether it is positive or negative (round amounts to nearest dollar).
c. Compute the excess present value index.
d. Compute the cash payback period.
e. Compute the average rate of return.

LO5, 6 **P25-4A. Excess Present Value Index and Average Rate of Return** Highpoint Company is evaluating five different capital expenditure proposals. The company's hurdle rate for net present value analyses is 12%. A 10% salvage value is expected from each of the investments. Information on the five proposals is as follows:

Proposal	Required Investment	Present Value at 12% of After-tax Cash Flows	Average Annual Net Income from Investment
A	$270,000	$310,030	$37,400
B	200,000	236,780	26,000
C	160,000	173,040	19,200
D	180,000	216,300	27,600
E	128,000	136,990	14,960

Required

a. Compute the excess present value index for each of the five proposals.
b. Compute the average rate of return for each of the five proposals.
c. Assume that Highpoint will commit no more than $500,000 to new capital expenditure proposals. Using the excess present value index, which proposals would be accepted? Using the average rate of return, which proposals would be accepted?

P25-5A. Cash Payback, Average Rate of Return, and Net Present Value Methods Landover Amusement Park is considering the construction of a new facility to house a curved, multistory movie screen. The facility will cost $400,000 and be useful for 10 years, with no salvage value. The facility will be depreciated on a straight-line basis over 10 years on both the books and the tax return. The following annual results are expected if the facility is constructed:

LO5, 6

SERVICE AND MERCHANDISING

Increase in annual cash revenue		$200,000
Increase in expenses:		
Cash operating expenses.	$80,000	
Depreciation	40,000	120,000
Pretax income		$ 80,000
Income tax expense (40%).		32,000
Net income.		$ 48,000

Landover uses a 12% hurdle rate when analyzing capital expenditure proposals using net present value.

Required
a. What are the annual net cash flows (net inflows) from this project?
b. Compute the cash payback period.
c. Compute the average rate of return.
d. Compute the net present value and indicate whether it is positive or negative.
e. Assume that Landover decides to use a 10% hurdle rate when using net present value analysis. Compute the net present value using a 10% hurdle rate and indicate whether it is positive or negative.

P25-6A. Weighted Average Cost of Capital and Net Present Value Analysis Tate Company is considering a proposal to acquire new equipment for its manufacturing division. The equipment will cost $192,000, be useful for four years, and have a $12,000 salvage value. Tate expects annual savings in cash operating expenses (before taxes) of $68,000. For tax purposes, the annual depreciation deduction will be $64,000, $86,000, $28,000, and $14,000, respectively, for the four years (the salvage value is ignored on the tax return). The income tax rate is 40%.

LO2, 5

Tate establishes a hurdle rate for a net present value analysis at the company's weighted average cost of capital plus 1 percentage point. Tate's capital is provided in the following proportions: debt, 60%; common stock, 20%; and retained earnings, 20%. The cost rates for these capital sources are debt, 10%; common stock, 12%; and retained earnings, 13%.

Required
a. Compute Tate's (1) weighted average cost of capital and (2) hurdle rate.
b. Using Tate's hurdle rate, compute the net present value of this capital expenditure proposal. Under net present value analysis, should Tate accept the proposal? (Round amounts to the nearest dollar.)

PROBLEMS—SET B

P25-1B. After-Tax Cash Flows Below is a list of aspects of various capital expenditure proposals that the capital budgeting team of Modern Systems, Inc., has incorporated into its net present value analyses during the past year. Unless otherwise noted, the items listed are unrelated to each other. All situations assume a 30% income tax rate and a 10% minimum desired rate of return.

LO4

1. Pre-tax savings of $5,000 in cash expenses will occur in each of the next three years.
2. A machine is purchased now for $82,000.
3. Special tools costing $45,000 will be depreciated $9,000, $18,000, and $18,000, respectively, on the tax return over a three-year life.
4. A patent purchased for $330,000 will be amortized on a straight-line basis over 15 years on the tax return. No salvage value is expected.
5. Pre-tax savings of $8,000 in cash expenses will occur in each of the next seven years.
6. Pre-tax savings of $5,500 in cash expenses will occur in the first, fourth, and seventh years from now.

7. The special tools described in aspect 3 will be sold after three years for $10,000 cash.

8. A truck with a tax book value of $7,200 after two years will be sold at that time for $4,600.

Required

Set up an answer form with the four column headings as shown below. Answer each investment aspect separately. Prepare your calculations on a separate paper and key them to each item. The answer to investment aspect 1 is presented as an example.

Investment Aspect 1	A After-tax Cash Flow Effect(s) Inflows (Outflows)	B Year(s) of Cash Flow
	$3,500	1, 2, 3
Calculations:		
1. Pre-tax cash savings		$5,000
Less income tax at 30%......................		1,500
After-tax cash inflow.........................		$3,500

a. Calculate and record in column A the related after-tax cash flow effect(s). Place parentheses around outflows.

b. Indicate in column B the timing of each cash flow shown in column A. Use 0 to indicate immediately and 1, 2, 3, 4, and so on for each year involved.

LO5   **P25-2B. Net Present Value Analysis** You have an opportunity to invest in a concession at a world exposition. To use the building and exhibits more fully, the venture is expected to cover a six-year period consisting of a preliminary year, the two years of formal exposition, and a three-year period of reduced operation as a regional exposition.

The terms of the concession agreement specify the following:

1. At inception, a $60,000 deposit is paid to Global Expo, Inc., the promoting organization. This amount is returned in full at the end of the six years if the operator maintains the concession in order and keeps it open during scheduled hours. The deposit is not tax deductible, nor is its return subject to income taxes.

2. The operator must install certain fixtures that will cost $240,000. The fixtures become the property of Global Expo, Inc., at the end of the six years.

After careful investigation and consultation with local experts, you conclude that the following schedule reflects the estimated pre-tax income of the concession (amounts in thousands of dollars):

	Year 1	Year 2	Year 3	Year 4	Year 5	Year 6
Sales (all cash)	$150	$435	$488	$300	$240	$180
Operating expenses:						
Cash	$ 75	$228	$279	$170	$140	$106
Tax depreciation.................	48	77	46	28	28	13
Total expenses	$123	$305	$325	$198	$168	$119
Pre-tax income....................	$ 27	$130	$163	$102	$ 72	$ 61

Required

Assuming an income tax rate of 40% and a desired annual return of 9%, what is the net present value of this investment opportunity? What is the maximum amount that could be invested and still earning a 9% annual return? (Round amounts to the nearest dollar.)

LO5, 6   **P25-3B. Cash Payback, Average Rate of Return, and Net Present Value Methods** At a cash cost of $330,000, Monona, Inc., can acquire equipment that will save $100,000 in annual cash operating expenses. No salvage value is expected at the end of its five-year useful life. Assume the machine will be depreciated over five years on a straight-line basis on both the books and the tax return. The income tax rate is 30% and Monona has a 10% hurdle rate when using a net present value analysis.

Required

a. What are the annual after-tax cash savings in operating expenses?

b. What are the annual tax savings from the depreciation tax shield?

c. Compute the cash payback period.

d. Compute the average rate of return.

e. Compute the net present value and indicate whether it is positive or negative (round amounts to nearest dollar).

f. Compute the excess present value index.

P25-4B. Excess Present Value Index and Average Rate of Return Swanson Corporation is evaluating five different capital expenditure proposals. The company's hurdle rate for net present value analysis is 12%. A 15% salvage value is expected from each of the investments. Information on the five proposals is as follows:

Proposal	Required Investment	Net Present Value	Average Annual Net Income from Investment
A.	$ 50,000	$ 8,996	$ 9,100
B.	80,000	5,812	12,000
C.	110,000	27,034	18,300
D.	150,000	7,544	21,500
E.	72,000	15,822	13,960

Required

a. Compute the excess present value index for each of the five proposals.

b. Compute the average rate of return for each of the five proposals.

c. Assume that Swanson will commit no more than $200,000 to new capital expenditure proposals. Using the excess present value index, which proposals would be accepted? Using the average rate of return, which proposals would be accepted?

P25-5B. Cash Payback, Average Rate of Return, and Net Present Value Methods Lyle Company is considering whether to enter into a franchise agreement that would give the company exclusive distribution rights in a three-state region to a quality line of leisure spas. The franchise agreement will extend eight years and cost $600,000. There is no salvage value. The franchise cost will be amortized on a straight-line basis over eight years on both the books and the tax return. The following annual results are expected if the franchise is acquired:

Increase in annual cash revenue		$230,000
Increase in expenses:		
Cash operating expenses	$95,000	
Amortization	75,000	170,000
Pretax income		$ 60,000
Income tax expense (35%)		21,000
Net income		$ 39,000

Lyle uses a 12% hurdle rate when analyzing capital expenditure proposals using net present value.

Required

a. What are the annual net cash flows (net inflows) from this proposal?

b. Compute the cash payback period.

c. Compute the average rate of return.

d. Compute the net present value and indicate whether it is positive or negative.

e. Assume that Lyle decides to use a 10% hurdle rate when using net present value analysis. Compute the net present value using a 10% hurdle rate and indicate whether it is positive or negative.

P25-6B. Weighted Average Cost of Capital and Net Present Value Analysis Manchester Company is considering a proposal to purchase special equipment at a cost of $640,000. The equipment will be useful for five years and has an expected $60,000 salvage value. Manchester expects annual savings in cash operating expenses (before taxes) of $230,000. For tax purposes, the annual depreciation deduction will be as follows (salvage value is ignored on the tax return):

Year 1	$ 80,000
Year 2	160,000
Year 3	160,000
Year 4	160,000
Year 5	80,000

The income tax rate is 40%.

Manchester establishes a hurdle rate for a net present value analysis at the company's weighted average cost of capital plus 2 percentage points. Manchester's capital is provided in the following proportions: debt, 70%; common stock, 20%; and retained earnings, 10%. The cost rates for these capital sources are debt, 8%; common stock, 12%; and retained earnings, 10%.

Required

a. Compute Manchester's (1) weighted average cost of capital and (2) hurdle rate.

b. Using Manchester's hurdle rate, compute the net present value of this capital expenditure proposal. Under net present value analysis, should Manchester accept the proposal?

CERTIFIED MANAGEMENT ACCOUNTANT (CMA®) EXAM SAMPLE QUESTIONS

CMA25-1. An accountant for Stability Inc. must calculate the weighted average cost of capital of the corporation using the following information.

		Interest Rate
Accounts payable	$35,000,000	0
Long-term debt	10,000,000	8%
Common stock	10,000,000	15%
Retained earnings	5,000,000	18%

What is the weighted average cost of capital of Stability?

a. 6.88%

b. 8.00%

c. 10.25%

d. 12.80%

CMA25-2. Kielly Machines Inc. is planning an expansion program estimated to cost $100 million. Kielly is going to raise funds according to its target capital structure shown below.

Debt	0.30
Preferred stock	0.24
Equity	0.46

Kielly had net income available to common shareholders of $184 million last year of which 75% was paid out in dividends. The company has a marginal tax rate of 40%.

Additional data:

- The before-tax cost of debt is estimated to be 11%.
- The market yield of preferred stock is estimated to be 12%.
- The after-tax cost of common stock is estimated to be 16%.

What is Kielly's weighted average cost of capital?
a. 12.22%
b. 13.00%
c. 13.54%
d. 14.00%

CMA25-3. Which one of the following items is **least** likely to directly impact an equipment replacement capital expenditure decision?

a. The net present value of the equipment that is being replaced.
b. The depreciation rate that will be used for tax purposes on the new asset.
c. The amount of additional accounts receivable that will be generated from increased production and sales.
d. The sales value of the asset that is being replaced.

CMA25-4. Wilcox Corporation won a settlement in a lawsuit and was offered four different payment alternatives by the defendant's insurance company. A review of interest rates indicates that 8% is appropriate for analyzing this situation. Ignoring any tax considerations, which one of the following four alternatives should the controller recommend to Wilcox management?

a. $135,000 now
b. $40,000 per year at the end of each of the next four years
c. $5,000 now and $20,000 per year at the end of each of the next ten years
d. $5,000 now and $5,000 per year at the end of each of the next nine years, plus a lump-sum payment of $200,000 at the end of the tenth year

CMA25-5. The following schedule reflects the incremental costs and revenues for a capital project. The company uses straight-line depreciation. The interest expense reflects an allocation of interest on the amount of this investment, based on the company's weighted average cost of capital.

Revenues		$650,000
Direct costs	$270,000	
Variable overhead.	50,000	
Fixed overhead.	20,000	
Depreciation	70,000	
General & administrative	40,000	
Interest expense.	8,000	
Total costs		458,000
Net profit before taxes		$192,000

The annual cash flow from this investment, before tax considerations, would be
a. $192,000.   c. $262,000.
b. $200,000.   d. $270,000.

EXTENDING YOUR KNOWLEDGE

EYK25-1. Business Decision Case New Haven Corporation recently identified an investment opportunity involving the purchase of a patent that will permit the company to modify its line of CD recorders. The patent's purchase price is $720,000 and the legal protection it provides will last for five more years; there is no salvage value. However, after preparing the capital expenditure analysis below, New Haven's treasurer has recommended to the company's capital budgeting committee that the investment be rejected. Brad Decker, chairperson of the capital budgeting committee, finds it difficult to accept the treasurer's analysis because he "feels intuitively" that the investment is attractive. For this reason, he has retained you to review the treasurer's analysis and recommendation. You are provided with the following data and summary of the treasurer's analysis:

1. Required investment: $720,000 cash for the patent to be amortized on a straight-line basis, five-year useful life, with a zero salvage value.

2. Projected cash revenue and operating expenses:

Year	Cash Revenue	Cash Expenses
1	$ 620,000	$240,000
2	560,000	200,000
3	400,000	170,000
4	250,000	80,000
5	200,000	50,000
	$2,030,000	$740,000

3. Source of capital: New Haven plans to raise 10% of the needed capital by issuing bonds, 30% by issuing stock, and the balance from retained earnings. For these sources, the capital cost rates are 8%, 9%, and 10%, respectively. New Haven has a policy of seeking a return equal to the weighted average cost of capital plus 2.5 percentage points as a "buffer margin" for the uncertainties involved.

4. Income taxes: New Haven has an overall income tax rate of 30%.

5. Treasurer's analysis:

Average cost of capital		
(8% + 9% + 10%)/3 = 9%		
Total cash revenue		$2,030,000
Total cash expenses	$740,000	
Total amortization	720,000	
Total operating expenses		1,460,000
Projected net income over five years		$ 570,000
Average annual income		$ 114,000
Present value of future returns		$ 443,420
Required investment		720,000
Negative net present value		$ (276,580)

Recommendation: Reject investment because of insufficient net present value.

Required

a. Review the treasurer's analysis, identifying any questionable aspects and briefly comment on the apparent effect of each such item on the treasurer's analysis.

b. Prepare your own analysis of the investment, including a calculation of the proper cost of capital and hurdle rates, a net present value analysis of the project, and a brief recommendation to Decker regarding the investment (round amounts to nearest dollar).

c. Because of his concern for the uncertainties of the CD recorder business, Decker also has asked you to provide analyses supporting whether or not your recommendation would change
   1. If estimates of projected cash revenue were reduced by 10%.
   2. If the "buffer margin" were tripled from 2.5% to 7.5%.

EYK25-2.  **Ethics Case** Sandy Williams is the manager of General Company's cutting department, which employs 70 people. The cutting department desperately needs new equipment to increase productivity and thus avoid the layoff of 25 people. This department is one of four departments being considered for new equipment. The budget committee has announced that only one department's capital request will be approved this year.

Williams works up the cost savings from the new machinery and contacts suppliers to learn the equipment's estimated cost. Williams knows that General Company uses the payback method to evaluate capital projects. The estimated costs for the equipment are extremely high, particularly with all the safety shields recommended by the manufacturer. If one of these recommended safety features, electronic safety sensors not on the current equipment, were left off, the cost would be $200,000 less and the payback period would decrease by three years. If only minimum electronic safety sensors required by the union contract were included, the cost would be $70,000 less and the payback period would decrease by one year.

Required

What are the ethical considerations Sandy Williams faces as she prepares the equipment proposal?

ANSWERS TO SELF-STUDY QUESTIONS:

1. c, (p. 1113)   2. a, (p. 1114)   3. d, (p. 1118)   4. d, (p. 1117)   5. c, (p. 1129)

YOUR TURN! SOLUTIONS

Solution 25.1

Bank loan	45% × 12% =	5.40%
Equity capital	55% × 9% =	4.95%
Weighted average cost of capital		10.35%

Solution 25.2

N = 3; i/YR = 12; FV = $2,000; PV = $2,000 × .71178, so PV = $1,423.56.
N = 4; i/YR = 12; FV = $4,000; PV = $4,000 × .63552, so PV = $2,542.08.
Total PV = $3,965.64.

Solution 25.3

N = 7; i/YR = 6; PMT = $5,000; PV = $5,000 × 5.58238, so PV = $27,911.90.

Solution 25.4

Book value	$10,000
Cash selling price	7,500
Loss on sale	$ 2,500
Income tax rate	× 35%
Tax saving	$ 875
Plus: Cash selling price	7,500
After-tax cash flow	$ 8,375

DECISION TIME SOLUTION

Solution 25.1

Depreciation tax shield:
    [($350,000 − $15,000)/20 years] × 0.30 = $5,025

After-tax cash inflow:
    [$47,200 × (1 − 0.30)] = $33,040

Total cash inflow:
    ($5,025 + $33,040) = $38,065

Present value of cash flows:
    N = 20; i/YR = 8; PMT = 38,065; PV = $38,065 × 9.81815, so PV = $373,727.87.

NPV:
    ($350,000) + $373,727.87 = $23,727.87

Because the NPV is positive, the company should purchase the building.

Appendix

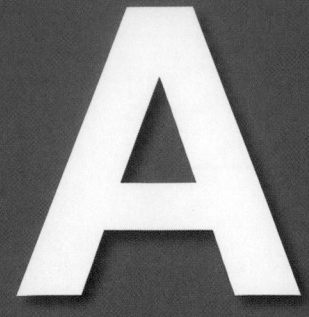

Columbia Sportswear Company

The complete version of Appendix A and Columbia Sportswear's complete 10-K are available on this book's website.

The law requires publicly traded companies to submit an audited annual report to the Securities and Exchange Commission (SEC) within two months of the close of their fiscal year. This annual report is called Form 10-K. Companies also provide their stockholders with an annual report that contains many of the items included in Form 10-K, along with a letter to the shareholders and public relations and marketing material. Although each annual report is different, all annual reports typically include the following elements:

- Letter to the Shareholders
- Management Discussion and Analysis
- Independent Auditor's Report
- Financial Statements
- Notes to Financial Statements
- Report on Internal Control
- Management's Certification of Financial Statements
- Supplemental Information

In addition, many publicly traded companies also provide a voluntary report on their corporate social responsibility commitments. Because this report is voluntary, its content varies to a greater degree from company to company. Most reports, however, discuss the company's commitment in the areas of both social and environmental impact.

The following pages include the financial statements from Columbia Sportswear's 2014 Annual Report. The rest of Appendix A and Columbia's complete 10-K are available on this book's website. Appendix A is organized as follows:

Report of Independent Auditors	A-2
Financial Statements	A-3
Notes to Financial Statements (Notes 1-15)	A-7
Earnings Per Share Data	A-22
Supplemental Information	A-23
Report on Internal Control	A-25

Occasionally, companies restate financial data for previous years, which may cause specific amounts to change in their financial statements. The data in this appendix reflect the financial data presented in Columbia Sportswear's 2014 Annual Report.

REPORT OF INDEPENDENT AUDITORS

Report of Independent Registered Public Accounting Firm

To the Board of Directors and Shareholders
Columbia Sportswear Company
Portland, Oregon

We have audited the accompanying consolidated balance sheets of Columbia Sportswear Company and subsidiaries (the "Company") as of December 31, 2014 and 2013, and the related consolidated statements of operations, comprehensive income, equity, and cash flows for each of the three years in the period ended December 31, 2014. Our audits also included the financial statement schedule listed in the Index at Item 15. These financial statements and financial statement schedule are the responsibility of the Company's management. Our responsibility is to express an opinion on these financial statements and financial statement schedule based on our audits.

We conducted our audits in accordance with the standards of the Public Company Accounting Oversight Board (United States). Those standards require that we plan and perform the audit to obtain reasonable assurance about whether the financial statements are free of material misstatement. An audit includes examining, on a test basis, evidence supporting the amounts and disclosures in the financial statements. An audit also includes assessing the accounting principles used and significant estimates made by management, as well as evaluating the overall financial statement presentation. We believe that our audits provide a reasonable basis for our opinion.

In our opinion, such consolidated financial statements present fairly, in all material respects, the financial position of Columbia Sportswear Company and subsidiaries as of December 31, 2014 and 2013, and the results of their operations and their cash flows for each of the three years in the period ended December 31, 2014, in conformity with accounting principles generally accepted in the United States of America. Also, in our opinion, such financial statement schedule, when considered in relation to the basic consolidated financial statements taken as a whole, presents fairly, in all material respects, the information set forth therein.

We have also audited, in accordance with the standards of the Public Company Accounting Oversight Board (United States), the Company's internal control over financial reporting as of December 31, 2014, based on the criteria established in *Internal Control—Integrated Framework (2013)* issued by the Committee of Sponsoring Organizations of the Treadway Commission, and our report dated February 26, 2015, expressed an unqualified opinion on the Company's internal control over financial reporting.

/s/   DELOITTE & TOUCHE LLP
Portland, Oregon
February 26, 2015

FINANCIAL STATEMENTS

COLUMBIA SPORTSWEAR COMPANY

CONSOLIDATED BALANCE SHEETS

(In thousands)

	December 31,	
	2014	2013
ASSETS		
Current Assets:		
Cash and cash equivalents	$ 413,558	$ 437,489
Short-term investments	27,267	91,755
Accounts receivable, net (Note 6)	344,390	306,878
Inventories	384,650	329,228
Deferred income taxes (Note 11)	57,001	52,041
Prepaid expenses and other current assets	39,175	33,081
Total current assets	1,266,041	1,250,472
Property, plant, and equipment, net (Note 7)	291,563	279,373
Intangible assets, net (Notes 3, 8)	143,731	36,288
Goodwill (Notes 3, 8)	68,594	14,438
Other non-current assets	22,280	25,017
Total assets	$ 1,792,209	$ 1,605,588
LIABILITIES AND EQUITY		
Current Liabilities:		
Accounts payable	$ 214,275	$ 173,557
Accrued liabilities (Note 10)	144,288	120,397
Income taxes payable (Note 11)	14,388	7,251
Deferred income taxes (Note 11)	169	49
Total current liabilities	373,120	301,254
Note payable to related party (Note 22)	15,728	—
Other long-term liabilities (Notes 12, 13)	35,435	29,527
Income taxes payable (Note 11)	9,388	13,984
Deferred income taxes (Note 11)	3,304	7,959
Total liabilities	436,975	352,724
Commitments and contingencies (Note 14)		
Shareholders' Equity:		
Preferred stock; 10,000 shares authorized; none issued and outstanding	—	—
Common stock (no par value); 250,000 shares authorized; 69,828 and 69,190 issued and outstanding (Note 15)	72,700	52,325
Retained earnings	1,255,070	1,157,733
Accumulated other comprehensive income (Note 18)	15,833	35,360
Total Columbia Sportswear Company shareholders' equity	1,343,603	1,245,418
Non-controlling interest (Note 5)	11,631	7,446
Total equity	1,355,234	1,252,864
Total liabilities and equity	$ 1,792,209	$ 1,605,588

See accompanying notes to consolidated financial statements

COLUMBIA SPORTSWEAR COMPANY

CONSOLIDATED STATEMENTS OF OPERATIONS

(In thousands, except per share amounts)

	Year Ended December 31,		
	2014	2013	2012
Net sales	$2,100,590	$1,684,996	$1,669,563
Cost of sales	1,145,639	941,341	953,169
Gross profit	954,951	743,655	716,394
Selling, general and administrative expenses	763,063	625,656	596,635
Net licensing income	6,956	13,795	13,769
Income from operations	198,844	131,794	133,528
Interest income, net	1,004	503	379
Interest expense on note payable to related party (Note 22)	(1,053)	—	—
Other non-operating expense	(274)	(871)	—
Income before income tax	198,521	131,426	133,907
Income tax expense (Note 11)	(56,662)	(37,823)	(34,048)
Net income	141,859	93,603	99,859
Net income (loss) attributable to non-controlling interest	4,686	(738)	—
Net income attributable to Columbia Sportswear Company	$ 137,173	$ 94,341	$ 99,859
Earnings per share attributable to Columbia Sportswear Company (Note 17):			
Basic	$ 1.97	$ 1.37	$ 1.48
Diluted	1.94	1.36	1.46
Weighted average shares outstanding (Note 17):			
Basic	69,807	68,756	67,680
Diluted	70,681	69,434	68,264

See accompanying notes to consolidated financial statements

COLUMBIA SPORTSWEAR COMPANY

CONSOLIDATED STATEMENTS OF CASH FLOWS

(In thousands)

	Year Ended December 31,		
	2014	2013	2012
Cash flows from operating activities:			
Net income	$ 141,859	$ 93,603	$ 99,859
Adjustments to reconcile net income to net cash provided by operating activities:			
Depreciation and amortization	54,017	40,871	40,892
Loss on disposal or impairment of property, plant, and equipment	481	9,344	1,582
Deferred income taxes	(6,978)	8,818	7,140
Stock-based compensation	11,120	8,878	7,833
Excess tax benefit from employee stock plans	(4,927)	(1,532)	(1,016)
Changes in operating assets and liabilities:			
Accounts receivable	(31,478)	27,442	18,166
Inventories	(62,086)	34,089	2,951
Prepaid expenses and other current assets	(4,869)	5,166	(2,025)
Other assets	4,291	(4,215)	(1,259)
Accounts payable	41,941	31,711	(12,330)
Accrued liabilities	35,051	12,210	(5,199)
Income taxes payable	1,166	5,534	(11,052)
Other liabilities	6,195	2,356	3,126
Net cash provided by operating activities	185,783	274,275	148,668
Cash flows from investing activities:			
Acquisition of business, net of cash acquired	(188,467)	—	—
Purchases of short-term investments	(48,243)	(125,390)	(83,969)
Sales of short-term investments	112,895	78,636	42,319
Capital expenditures	(60,283)	(69,443)	(50,491)
Proceeds from sale of property, plant, and equipment	71	111	7,099
Net cash used in investing activities	(184,027)	(116,086)	(85,042)
Cash flows from financing activities:			
Proceeds from credit facilities	52,356	69,136	100,654
Repayments on credit facilities	(52,205)	(69,292)	(100,498)
Proceeds from issuance of common stock under employee stock plans	22,277	19,537	14,600
Tax payments related to restricted stock unit issuances	(3,141)	(2,291)	(1,486)
Excess tax benefit from employee stock plans	4,927	1,532	1,016
Repurchase of common stock	(15,000)	—	(206)
Proceeds from note payable to related party	16,072	—	—
Capital contribution from non-controlling interest	—	8,000	—
Cash dividends paid	(39,836)	(31,298)	(29,780)
Net cash used in financing activities	(14,550)	(4,676)	(15,700)
Net effect of exchange rate changes on cash	(11,137)	(6,805)	1,821
Net increase (decrease) in cash and cash equivalents	(23,931)	146,708	49,747
Cash and cash equivalents, beginning of year	437,489	290,781	241,034
Cash and cash equivalents, end of year	$ 413,558	$ 437,489	$ 290,781
Supplemental disclosures of cash flow information:			
Cash paid during the year for income taxes	$ 53,958	$ 22,771	$ 43,696
Supplemental disclosures of non-cash investing activities:			
Capital expenditures incurred but not yet paid	7,196	5,195	5,313

See accompanying notes to consolidated financial statements

COLUMBIA SPORTSWEAR COMPANY

CONSOLIDATED STATEMENTS OF EQUITY
(In thousands)

| | Columbia Sportswear Company Shareholders' Equity | | | | | |
| | Common Stock | | | Accumulated Other | Non- | |
	Shares Outstanding	Amount	Retained Earnings	Comprehensive Income	Controlling Interest	Total
BALANCE, JANUARY 1, 2012	67,276	$ 3,037	$1,024,611	$ 46,897	$ —	$ 1,074,545
Net income	—	—	99,859	—	—	99,859
Other comprehensive income (loss):						
Unrealized holding losses on available-for-sale securities, net	—	—	—	(7)	—	(7)
Unrealized holding losses on derivative transactions, net	—	—	—	(4,745)	—	(4,745)
Foreign currency translation adjustment, net	—	—	—	4,518	—	4,518
Cash dividends ($0.44 per share)	—	—	(29,780)	—	—	(29,780)
Issuance of common stock under employee stock plans, net	882	13,114	—	—	—	13,114
Tax adjustment from stock plans	—	1,036	—	—	—	1,036
Stock-based compensation expense	—	7,833	—	—	—	7,833
Repurchase of common stock	(8)	(206)	—	—	—	(206)
BALANCE, DECEMBER 31, 2012	68,150	24,814	1,094,690	46,663	—	1,166,167
Net income (loss)	—	—	94,341	—	(738)	93,603
Other comprehensive income (loss):						
Unrealized holding gains on available for sale securities, net	—	—	—	3	—	3
Unrealized holding losses on derivative transactions, net	—	—	—	(1,261)	—	(1,261)
Foreign currency translation adjustment, net	—	—	—	(10,045)	184	(9,861)
Cash dividends ($0.46 per share)	—	—	(31,298)	—	—	(31,298)
Issuance of common stock under employee stock plans, net	1,040	17,246	—	—	—	17,246
Capital contribution from non-controlling interest	—	—	—	—	8,000	8,000
Tax adjustment from stock plans	—	1,387	—	—	—	1,387
Stock-based compensation expense	—	8,878	—	—	—	8,878
BALANCE, DECEMBER 31, 2013	69,190	52,325	1,157,733	35,360	7,446	1,252,864
Net income	—	—	137,173	—	4,686	141,859
Other comprehensive income (loss):						
Unrealized holding gains on available-for-sale securities, net	—	—	—	10	—	10
Unrealized holding gains on derivative transactions, net	—	—	—	7,751	—	7,751
Foreign currency translation adjustment, net	—	—	—	(27,288)	(501)	(27,789)
Cash dividends ($0.57 per share)	—	—	(39,836)	—	—	(39,836)
Issuance of common stock under employee stock plans, net	1,059	19,136	—	—	—	19,136
Tax adjustment from stock plans	—	5,119	—	—	—	5,119
Stock-based compensation expense	—	11,120	—	—	—	11,120
Repurchase of common stock	(421)	(15,000)	—	—	—	(15,000)
BALANCE, DECEMBER 31, 2014	69,828	$ 72,700	$1,255,070	$ 15,833	$ 11,631	$ 1,355,234

See accompanying notes to consolidated financial statements

Appendix

B

Financial Statements for Under Armour

The complete annual report for Under Armour is available on this book's website.

Under Armour, Inc. and Subsidiaries

Consolidated Balance Sheets
(In thousands, except share data)

	December 31, 2014	December 31, 2013
Assets		
Current assets		
Cash and cash equivalents	$ 593,175	$ 347,489
Accounts receivable, net	279,835	209,952
Inventories	536,714	469,006
Prepaid expenses and other current assets	87,177	63,987
Deferred income taxes	52,498	38,377
Total current assets	1,549,399	1,128,811
Property and equipment, net	305,564	223,952
Goodwill	123,256	122,244
Intangible assets, net	26,230	24,097
Deferred income taxes	33,570	31,094
Other long term assets	57,064	47,543
Total assets	$2,095,083	$1,577,741
Liabilities and Stockholders' Equity		
Current liabilities		
Revolving credit facility	$ —	$ 100,000
Accounts payable	210,432	165,456
Accrued expenses	147,681	133,729
Current maturities of long term debt	28,951	4,972
Other current liabilities	34,563	22,473
Total current liabilities	421,627	426,630
Long term debt, net of current maturities	255,250	47,951
Other long term liabilities	67,906	49,806
Total liabilities	744,783	524,387
Commitments and contingencies (see Note 7)		
Stockholders' equity		
Class A Common Stock, $0.0003 1/3 par value; 400,000,000 shares authorized as of December 31, 2014 and 2013; 177,295,988 shares issued and outstanding as of December 31, 2014 and 171,628,708 shares issued and outstanding as of December 31, 2013.	59	57
Class B Convertible Common Stock, $0.0003 1/3 par value; 36,600,000 shares authorized, issued and outstanding as of December 31, 2014 and 40,000,000 shares authorized, issued and outstanding as of December 31, 2013.	12	13
Additional paid-in capital	508,350	397,248
Retained earnings	856,687	653,842
Accumulated other comprehensive income (loss)	(14,808)	2,194
Total stockholders' equity	1,350,300	1,053,354
Total liabilities and stockholders' equity	$2,095,083	$1,577,741

See accompanying notes.

Under Armour, Inc. and Subsidiaries

Consolidated Statements of Income
(In thousands, except per share amounts)

	Year Ended December 31,		
	2014	2013	2012
Net revenues	$3,084,370	$2,332,051	$1,834,921
Cost of goods sold	1,572,164	1,195,381	955,624
Gross profit	1,512,206	1,136,670	879,297
Selling, general and administrative expenses	1,158,251	871,572	670,602
Income from operations	353,955	265,098	208,695
Interest expense, net	(5,335)	(2,933)	(5,183)
Other expense, net	(6,410)	(1,172)	(73)
Income before income taxes	342,210	260,993	203,439
Provision for income taxes	134,168	98,663	74,661
Net income	$ 208,042	$ 162,330	$ 128,778
Net income available per common share			
Basic	$ 0.98	$ 0.77	$ 0.62
Diluted	$ 0.95	$ 0.75	$ 0.61
Weighted average common shares outstanding			
Basic	213,227	210,696	208,686
Diluted	219,380	215,958	212,760

See accompanying notes.

Under Armour, Inc. and Subsidiaries

Consolidated Statements of Stockholders' Equity
(In thousands)

	Class A Common Stock		Class B Convertible Common Stock		Additional Paid-In Capital	Retained Earnings	Accumulated Other Comprehensive Income (Loss)	Total Stockholders' Equity
	Shares	Amount	Shares	Amount				
Balance as of December 31, 2011	161,984	$ 54	45,000	$ 14	$268,172	$366,164	$ 2,028	$ 636,432
Exercise of stock options	2,436	2	—	—	12,370	—	—	12,372
Shares withheld in consideration of employee tax obligations relative to stock-based compensation arrangements	(76)	—	—	—	—	(1,761)	—	(1,761)
Issuance of Class A Common Stock, net of forfeitures	178	—	—	—	3,246	—	—	3,246
Class B Convertible Common Stock converted to Class A Common Stock	2,400	—	(2,400)	—	—	—	—	—
Stock-based compensation expense	—	—	—	—	19,845	—	—	19,845
Net excess tax benefits from stock-based compensation arrangements	—	—	—	—	17,670	—	—	17,670
Comprehensive income	—	—	—	—	—	128,778	340	129,118
Balance as of December 31, 2012	166,922	56	42,600	14	321,303	493,181	2,368	816,922
Exercise of stock options	1,822	—	—	—	12,159	—	—	12,159
Shares withheld in consideration of employee tax obligations relative to stock-based compensation arrangements	(47)	—	—	—	—	(1,669)	—	(1,669)
Issuance of Class A Common Stock, net of forfeitures	332	—	—	—	3,439	—	—	3,439
Class B Convertible Common Stock converted to Class A Common Stock	2,600	1	(2,600)	(1)	—	—	—	—
Stock-based compensation expense	—	—	—	—	43,184	—	—	43,184
Net excess tax benefits from stock-based compensation arrangements	—	—	—	—	17,163	—	—	17,163
Comprehensive income	—	—	—	—	—	162,330	(174)	162,156
Balance as of December 31, 2013	171,629	57	40,000	13	397,248	653,842	2,194	1,053,354
Exercise of stock options	1,454	1	—	—	11,258	—	—	11,259
Shares withheld in consideration of employee tax obligations relative to stock-based compensation arrangements	(95)	—	—	—	—	(5,197)	—	(5,197)
Issuance of Class A Common Stock, net of forfeitures	908	—	—	—	12,067	—	—	12,067
Class B Convertible Common Stock converted to Class A Common Stock	3,400	1	(3,400)	(1)	—	—	—	—
Stock-based compensation expense	—	—	—	—	50,812	—	—	50,812
Net excess tax benefits from stock-based compensation arrangements	—	—	—	—	36,965	—	—	36,965
Comprehensive income (loss)	—	—	—	—	—	208,042	(17,002)	191,040
Balance as of December 31, 2014	177,296	$ 59	36,600	$ 12	$508,350	$856,687	$(14,808)	$1,350,300

See accompanying notes.

Under Armour, Inc. and Subsidiaries

Consolidated Statements of Cash Flows
(In thousands)

	Year Ended December 31,		
	2014	**2013**	**2012**
Cash flows from operating activities			
Net income	$ 208,042	$ 162,330	$128,778
Adjustments to reconcile net income to net cash used in operating activities			
Depreciation and amortization	72,093	50,549	43,082
Unrealized foreign currency exchange rate losses (gains)	11,739	1,905	(2,464)
Loss on disposal of property and equipment	261	332	524
Stock-based compensation	50,812	43,184	19,845
Deferred income taxes	(17,584)	(18,832)	(12,973)
Changes in reserves and allowances	31,350	13,945	13,916
Changes in operating assets and liabilities, net of effects of acquisitions:			
Accounts receivable	(101,057)	(35,960)	(53,433)
Inventories	(84,658)	(156,900)	4,699
Prepaid expenses and other assets	(33,345)	(19,049)	(4,060)
Accounts payable	49,137	14,642	35,370
Accrued expenses and other liabilities	28,856	56,481	21,966
Income taxes payable and receivable	3,387	7,443	4,511
Net cash provided by operating activities	219,033	120,070	199,761
Cash flows from investing activities			
Purchases of property and equipment	(140,528)	(87,830)	(50,650)
Purchase of business	(10,924)	(148,097)	—
Purchases of other assets	(860)	(475)	(1,310)
Change in loans receivable	—	(1,700)	—
Change in restricted cash	—	—	5,029
Net cash used in investing activities	(152,312)	(238,102)	(46,931)
Cash flows from financing activities			
Proceeds from revolving credit facility	—	100,000	—
Payments on revolving credit facility	(100,000)	—	—
Proceeds from term loan	250,000	—	—
Payments on term loan	(13,750)	—	(25,000)
Proceeds from long term debt	—	—	50,000
Payments on long term debt	(4,972)	(5,471)	(44,330)
Excess tax benefits from stock-based compensation arrangements	36,965	17,167	17,868
Proceeds from exercise of stock options and other stock issuances	15,776	15,099	14,776
Payments of debt financing costs	(1,713)	—	(1,017)
Net cash provided by financing activities	182,306	126,795	12,297
Effect of exchange rate changes on cash and cash equivalents	(3,341)	(3,115)	1,330
Net increase in cash and cash equivalents	245,686	5,648	166,457
Cash and cash equivalents			
Beginning of period	347,489	341,841	175,384
End of period	$ 593,175	$ 347,489	$341,841
Non-cash investing and financing activities			
Increase in accrual for property and equipment	$ 4,922	$ 3,786	$ 12,137
Non-cash acquisition of business	11,233	—	—
Other supplemental information			
Cash paid for income taxes	103,284	85,570	57,739
Cash paid for interest, net of capitalized interest	4,146	1,505	3,306

See accompanying notes.

Appendix

C

Financial Statements for LVMH Moet Hennessy - Louis Vuitton

The complete annual report for LVMH Moet Hennessy - Louis Vuitton is available on this book's website.

CONSOLIDATED INCOME STATEMENT

(EUR millions, except for earnings per share)	Notes	2014	2013[1]	2012[1]
Revenue	23-24	30,638	29,016	27,970
Cost of sales		(10,801)	(9,997)	(9,863)
Gross margin		**19,837**	**19,019**	**18,107**
Marketing and selling expenses		(11,744)	(10,767)	(10,013)
General and administrative expenses		(2,373)	(2,212)	(2,151)
Income (loss) from joint ventures and associates	7	(5)	(23)	(19)
Profit from recurring operations	23-24	**5,715**	**6,017**	**5,924**
Other operating income and expenses	25	(284)	(119)	(182)
Operating profit		**5,431**	**5,898**	**5,742**
Cost of net financial debt		(115)	(101)	(138)
Other financial income and expenses		3,062	(97)	126
Net financial income (expense)	26	**2,947**	**(198)**	**(12)**
Income taxes	27	(2,273)	(1,753)	(1,821)
Net profit before minority interests		**6,105**	**3,947**	**3,909**
Minority interests	17	(457)	(511)	(484)
Net profit, Group share		**5,648**	**3,436**	**3,425**
Basic Group share of net earnings per share *(EUR)*	28	**11.27**	**6.87**	**6.86**
Number of shares on which the calculation is based		501,309,369	500,283,414	499,133,643
Diluted Group share of net earnings per share *(EUR)*	28	**11.21**	**6.83**	**6.82**
Number of shares on which the calculation is based		503,861,733	503,217,497	502,229,952

(1) The financial statements as of December 31, 2013 and 2012 have been restated to reflect the retrospective application as of January 1, 2012 of IFRS 11 Joint Arrangements. See Note 1.2.

FINANCIAL STATEMENTS

Consolidated financial statements

CONSOLIDATED BALANCE SHEET

ASSETS (EUR millions)	Notes	2014	2013 [1] [2]	2012 [1]
Brands and other intangible fixed assets	3	13,031	12,596	11,322
Goodwill	4	8,810	9,058	7,709
Property, plant and equipment	6	10,387	9,621	8,694
Investments in joint ventures and associates	7	519	480	483
Non-current available for sale financial assets	8	580	7,080	6,004
Other non-current assets	9	489	457	519
Deferred tax	27	1,436	913	952
Non-current assets		**35,252**	**40,205**	**35,683**
Inventories and work in progress	10	9,475	8,492	7,994
Trade accounts receivable	11	2,274	2,174	1,972
Income taxes		354	223	201
Other current assets	12	1,916	1,856	1,813
Cash and cash equivalents	14	4,091	3,226	2,187
Current assets		**18,110**	**15,971**	**14,167**
Total assets		**53,362**	**56,176**	**49,850**

LIABILITIES AND EQUITY (EUR millions)	Notes	2014	2013 [1] [2]	2012 [1]
Share capital	15.1	152	152	152
Share premium account	15.1	2,655	3,849	3,848
Treasury shares and LVMH-share settled derivatives	15.2	(374)	(451)	(414)
Cumulative translation adjustment	15.4	492	(8)	342
Revaluation reserves		1,019	3,900	2,731
Other reserves		12,171	16,001	14,340
Net profit, Group share		5,648	3,436	3,425
Equity, Group share		**21,763**	**26,879**	**24,424**
Minority interests	17	1,240	1,028	1,084
Total equity		**23,003**	**27,907**	**25,508**
Long-term borrowings	18	5,054	4,149	3,825
Non-current provisions	19	2,291	1,797	1,772
Deferred tax	27	4,392	4,280	3,884
Other non-current liabilities	20	6,447	6,404	5,456
Non-current liabilities		**18,184**	**16,630**	**14,937**
Short-term borrowings	18	4,189	4,674	2,950
Trade accounts payable		3,606	3,297	3,118
Income taxes		549	357	442
Current provisions	19	332	324	335
Other current liabilities	21	3,499	2,987	2,560
Current liabilities		**12,175**	**11,639**	**9,405**
Total liabilities and equity		**53,362**	**56,176**	**49,850**

(1) The financial statements as of December 31, 2013 and 2012 have been restated to reflect the retrospective application as of January 1, 2012 of IFRS 11 Joint Arrangements. See Note 1.2.

(2) The consolidated balance sheet as of December 31, 2013 has been restated to reflect the finalized purchase price allocation for Loro Piana. See Note 2.

CONSOLIDATED STATEMENT OF CHANGES IN EQUITY

(EUR millions)	Number of shares	Share capital	Share premium account	Treasury shares and LVMH-share settled derivatives	Cumulative translation adjustment	Available for sale financial assets	Hedges of future foreign currency cash flows	Vineyard land	Employee benefit commitments	Net profit and other reserves	Group share	Minority interests	Total
							Revaluation reserves					Total equity	
Notes		15.1		15.2	15.4							17	
As of December 31, 2011	**507,815,624**	**152**	**3,801**	**(485)**	**431**	**1,990**	**(15)**	**714**	**(28)**	**15,811**	**22,371**	**1,055**	**23,426**
Gains and losses recognized in equity					(89)	(47)	133	44	(60)	-	(19)	(15)	(34)
Net profit										3,425	3,425	484	3,909
Comprehensive income		-	-	-	(89)	(47)	133	44	(60)	3,425	3,406	469	3,875
Stock option plan and similar expenses										50	50	3	53
(Acquisition)/disposal of treasury shares and LVMH-share settled derivatives				24						(12)	12	-	12
Exercise of LVMH share subscription options	1,344,975		94								94	-	94
Retirement of LVMH shares	(997,250)		(47)	47							-	-	-
Capital increase in subsidiaries											-	8	8
Interim and final dividends paid										(1,447)	(1,447)	(317)	(1,764)
Changes in control of consolidated entities										(12)	(12)	(11)	(23)
Acquisition and disposal of minority interests' shares										(40)	(40)	(25)	(65)
Purchase commitments for minority interests' shares										(10)	(10)	(98)	(108)
As of December 31, 2012	**508,163,349**	**152**	**3,848**	**(414)**	**342**	**1,943**	**118**	**758**	**(88)**	**17,765**	**24,424**	**1,084**	**25,508**
Gains and losses recognized in equity					(350)	912	18	188	51	-	819	21	840
Net profit										3,436	3,436	511	3,947
Comprehensive income		-	-	-	(350)	912	18	188	51	3,436	4,255	532	4,787
Stock option plan and similar expenses										31	31	3	34
(Acquisition)/disposal of treasury shares and LVMH-share settled derivatives				(103)						(7)	(110)	-	(110)
Exercise of LVMH share subscription options	1,025,418		67								67	-	67
Retirement of LVMH shares	(1,395,106)		(66)	66							-	-	-
Capital increase in subsidiaries											-	8	8
Interim and final dividends paid										(1,500)	(1,500)	(228)	(1,728)
Acquisition of a controlling interest in Loro Piana[1]											-	235	235
Changes in control of consolidated entities										1	1	(1)	-
Acquisition and disposal of minority interests' shares										(73)	(73)	(76)	(149)
Purchase commitments for minority interests' shares[1]										(216)	(216)	(529)	(745)
As of December 31, 2013	**507,793,661**	**152**	**3,849**	**(451)**	**(8)**	**2,855**	**136**	**946**	**(37)**	**19,437**	**26,879**	**1,028**	**27,907**
Gains and losses recognized in equity					500	(2,648)	(122)	(15)	(96)	-	(2,381)	108	(2,273)
Net profit										5,648	5,648	457	6,105
Comprehensive income		-	-	-	500	(2,648)	(122)	(15)	(96)	5,648	3,267	565	3,832
Stock option plan and similar expenses										37	37	2	39
(Acquisition)/disposal of treasury shares and LVMH-share settled derivatives				27						(17)	10	-	10
Exercise of LVMH share subscription options	980,323		59								59	-	59
Retirement of LVMH shares	(1,062,271)		(50)	50							-	-	-
Capital increase in subsidiaries											-	3	3
Interim and final dividends paid										(1,579)	(1,579)	(328)	(1,907)
Distribution in kind of Hermès shares. See Note 8.			(1,203)							(5,652)	(6,855)	-	(6,855)
Changes in control of consolidated entities										(5)	(5)	11	6
Acquisition and disposal of minority interests' shares										(2)	(2)	32	30
Purchase commitments for minority interests' shares										(48)	(48)	(73)	(121)
As of December 31, 2014	**507,711,713**	**152**	**2,655**	**(374)**	**492**	**207**	**14**	**931**	**(133)**	**17,819**	**21,763**	**1,240**	**23,003**

[1] The consolidated balance sheet as of December 31, 2013 has been restated to reflect the finalized purchase price allocation for Loro Piana. See Note 2.

Consolidated financial statements

CONSOLIDATED CASH FLOW STATEMENT

(EUR millions)	Notes	2014	2013[1]	2012[1]
I. OPERATING ACTIVITIES AND OPERATING INVESTMENTS				
Operating profit		5,431	5,898	5,742
Income/(loss) and dividends from joint ventures and associates [a]	7	26	49	37
Net increase in depreciation, amortization and provisions		1,895	1,435	1,289
Other computed expenses		(188)	(29)	(59)
Other adjustments		(84)	(76)	(52)
Cash from operations before changes in working capital		7,080	7,277	6,957
Cost of net financial debt: interest paid		(116)	(111)	(152)
Income taxes paid [a]		(1,639)	(1,832)	(1,880)
Net cash from operating activities before changes in working capital		5,325	5,334	4,925
Change in working capital	14.1	(718)	(620)	(810)
Net cash from operating activities		4,607	4,714	4,115
Operating investments	14.2	(1,775)	(1,657)	(1,694)
Net cash from operating activities and operating investments (free cash flow)		2,832	3,057	2,421
II. FINANCIAL INVESTMENTS				
Purchase of non-current available for sale financial assets	8	(57)	(197)	(131)
Proceeds from sale of non-current available for sale financial assets	8	160	38	36
Dividends received [a]	8	69	71	179
Income tax related to financial investments [a]		(237)	(11)	(21)
Impact of purchase and sale of consolidated investments	2.4	(167)	(2,161)	(59)
Net cash from (used in) financial investments		(232)	(2,260)	4
III. TRANSACTIONS RELATING TO EQUITY				
Capital increases of LVMH SE	15.1	59	66	95
Capital increases of subsidiaries subscribed by minority interests	17	3	7	8
Acquisition and disposals of treasury shares and LVMH-share settled derivatives	15.2	1	(113)	5
Interim and final dividends paid by LVMH SE	15.3	(1,619)[b]	(1,501)	(1,447)
Income taxes paid related to interim and final dividends paid [a]		(79)	(137)	(73)
Interim and final dividends paid to minority interests in consolidated subsidiaries	17	(336)	(220)	(314)
Purchase and proceeds from sale of minority interests	2.4	10	(150)	(206)
Net cash from (used in) transactions relating to equity		(1,961)	(2,048)	(1,932)
Change in cash before financing activities		639	(1,251)	493
IV. FINANCING ACTIVITIES				
Proceeds from borrowings		2,407	3,095	1,028
Repayment of borrowings		(2,100)	(1,057)	(1,494)
Purchase and proceeds from sale of current available for sale financial assets	13	(106)	101	(67)
Net cash from (used in) financing activities		201	2,139	(533)
V. EFFECT OF EXCHANGE RATE CHANGES		27	47	(43)
NET INCREASE (DECREASE) IN CASH AND CASH EQUIVALENTS (I+II+III+IV+V)		867	935	(83)
CASH AND CASH EQUIVALENTS AT BEGINNING OF PERIOD	14	2,916	1,981	2,064
CASH AND CASH EQUIVALENTS AT END OF PERIOD	14	3,783	2,916	1,981
TOTAL INCOME TAXES PAID		(1,955)	(1,980)	(1,974)
Transactions included in the table above, generating no change in cash:				
- acquisition of assets by means of finance leases		5	7	5

(a) Restated to reflect the amended presentation of dividends received and income tax paid starting in 2014. See Note 1.4.

(b) The distribution in kind of Hermès shares had no impact on cash, apart from related income tax effects. See Note 8.

(1) The financial statements as of December 31, 2013 and 2012 have been restated to reflect the retrospective application as of January 1, 2012 of IFRS 11 Joint Arrangements. See Note 1.2.

Appendix

D

Accounting for Investments and Consolidated Financial Statements

Appendix D is available on this book's website.

Appendix

Accounting and the Time Value of Money

LEARNING OBJECTIVES

1. **Describe** the nature of interest and **distinguish** between simple and compound interest. *(p. E-2)*

2. **Calculate** future values. *(p. E-3)*

3. **Calculate** present values. *(p. E-6)*

TIME VALUE OF MONEY CONCEPT

LO1 Describe the nature of interest and **distinguish** between simple and compound interest.

Would you rather receive a dollar now or a dollar one year from now? Most people would answer "a dollar now." Intuition tells us that a dollar received now is more valuable than the same amount received sometime in the future. Sound reasons exist, however, for choosing the option of receiving the money sooner rather than later, the most obvious of which concerns risk. Because the future is always uncertain, some event may prevent you from receiving the dollar at a later date. To avoid this risk, we choose the earlier date.

A second reason for choosing the earlier date is that the dollar has a **time value**—that is, the dollar received now could be invested such that one year from now, you could have not only the original dollar but also the interest income on the dollar for the past year. **Interest** is a payment for the use of money, much like a rent payment for the use of an apartment. Interest is calculated by multiplying an interest rate, usually stated as an annual rate, by a principal amount for a period of time. The **principal** amount represents the amount to be repaid. The amount of interest can be computed as either a simple interest amount or a compound interest amount.

Time Value of Money: Simple Interest Model

Simple interest involves calculating interest on only the principal amount owed without considering any interest already earned. Simple interest is calculated using the following well-known formula:

$$\text{Interest} = p \times i \times n$$

where

> p = principal (total amount)
> i = interest rate for one period
> n = time (number of periods)

For example, if you borrow $3,000 for four years at a simple interest rate of six percent annually, the amount of simple interest would total $720, calculated as $3,000 $\times$ .06 $\times$ 4.

Time Value of Money: Compound Interest Model

Compound interest differs from simple interest because it is calculated on both the principal and any previously earned interest that has not been paid. In other words, compound interest involves computing interest on interest, along with the principal amount.

As we can see in **Exhibit E-1**, simple interest only uses the original $3,000 principal to compute the annual interest in each of the four years. In contrast, compound interest uses the entire principal balance, including both the original $3,000 principal and the accumulated interest to date, to compute the next year's interest. This results in increasing interest each year, with the result in **Exhibit E-1** for compound interest yielding a larger ending balance by $67.43.

Because almost all businesses use compound interest, we will assume the use of compound interest in all of the illustrations in this appendix. Simple interest is generally only used in short-term credit arrangements, typically lasting less than a year.

Exhibit E-1	Illustration Comparing Simple Interest to Compound Interest						
	Simple Interest Model				**Compound Interest Model**		
	Interest Calculation	Simple Interest	Principal Balance		Interest Calculation	Compound Interest	Principal Balance
Year 1..	$3,000.00 × 6%	$180.00	$3,180.00		$3,000.00 × 6%	$180.00	$3,180.00
Year 2..	$3,000.00 × 6%	$180.00	$3,360.00		$3,180.00 × 6%	$190.80	$3,370.80
Year 3..	$3,000.00 × 6%	$180.00	$3,540.00		$3,370.80 × 6%	$202.25	$3,573.05
Year 4..	$3,000.00 × 6%	$180.00	$3,720.00		$3,573.05 × 6%	$214.38	$3,787.43
		$720.00 ⟶	$67.43 difference	⟵		$787.43	

FUTURE VALUE OF AN AMOUNT

The **future value** of a single sum is the amount that a specified investment will be worth at a future date if invested at a given rate of compound interest. For example, suppose that we decide to invest $6,000 in a savings account that pays six percent annual interest, and that we intend to leave the principal and interest in the account for five years. Assuming that interest is credited to the account at the end of each year, the balance in the account at the end of five years is determined using the following formula:

LO2   Calculate future values.

$$FV = PV \times (1 + i)^n$$

where

FV = future value of an amount
PV = present value (today's value)
 i = interest rate for one period
 n = number of periods

The future value in this case is $8,029, computed as $[\$6,000 \times (1.06)^5] = (\$6,000 \times 1.33823)$.

It is often easier to solve time value of money problems with the aid of a time diagram, as illustrated in **Exhibit E-2**. Time diagrams are drawn to show the timing of the various cash inflows and outflows. Note in **Exhibit E-2** that our initial $6,000 cash inflow (the amount deposited in a savings account) allows us to withdraw $8,029 (a cash outflow) at the end of five years.

Exhibit E-2	Solving Future Values with the Aid of a Time Diagram

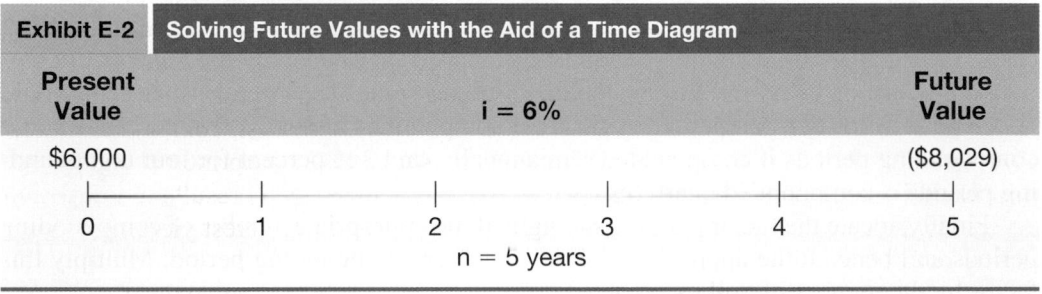

We can also calculate the future value of a single amount with the use of a table like **Table I**, which presents the future value of a single dollar after a given number of time periods. Simply stated, future value tables provide a multiplier for many combinations of time periods and interest rates that, when applied to the dollar amount of a present value, determines its future value.

Table I	Future Value of $1											
Period	**1.0%**	**2.0%**	**3.0%**	**4.0%**	**5.0%**	**6.0%**	**7.0%**	**8.0%**	**9.0%**	**10.0%**	**11.0%**	**12.0%**
1	1.01000	1.02000	1.03000	1.04000	1.05000	1.06000	1.07000	1.08000	1.09000	1.10000	1.11000	1.12000
2	1.02010	1.04040	1.06090	1.08160	1.10250	1.12360	1.14490	1.16640	1.18810	1.21000	1.23210	1.25440
3	1.03030	1.06121	1.09273	1.12486	1.15763	1.19102	1.22504	1.25971	1.29503	1.33100	1.36763	1.40493
4	1.04060	1.08243	1.12551	1.16986	1.21551	1.26248	1.31080	1.36049	1.41158	1.46410	1.51807	1.57352
5	1.05101	1.10408	1.15927	1.21665	1.27628	1.33823	1.40255	1.46933	1.53862	1.61051	1.68506	1.76234
6	1.06152	1.12616	1.19405	1.26532	1.34010	1.41852	1.50073	1.58687	1.67710	1.77156	1.87041	1.97382
7	1.07214	1.14869	1.22987	1.31593	1.40710	1.50363	1.60578	1.71382	1.82804	1.94872	2.07616	2.21068
8	1.08286	1.17166	1.26677	1.36857	1.47746	1.59385	1.71819	1.85093	1.99256	2.14359	2.30454	2.47596
9	1.09369	1.19509	1.30477	1.42331	1.55133	1.68948	1.83846	1.99900	2.17189	2.35795	2.55804	2.77308
10	1.10462	1.21899	1.34392	1.48024	1.62889	1.79085	1.96715	2.15892	2.36736	2.59374	2.83942	3.10585
11	1.11567	1.24337	1.38423	1.53945	1.71034	1.89830	2.10485	2.33164	2.58043	2.85312	3.15176	3.47855
12	1.12683	1.26824	1.42576	1.60103	1.79586	2.01220	2.25219	2.51817	2.81266	3.13843	3.49845	3.89598
13	1.13809	1.29361	1.46853	1.66507	1.88565	2.13293	2.40985	2.71962	3.06580	3.45227	3.88328	4.36349
14	1.14947	1.31948	1.51259	1.73168	1.97993	2.26090	2.57853	2.93719	3.34173	3.79750	4.31044	4.88711
15	1.16097	1.34587	1.55797	1.80094	2.07893	2.39656	2.75903	3.17217	3.64248	4.17725	4.78459	5.47357
16	1.17258	1.37279	1.60471	1.87298	2.18287	2.54035	2.95216	3.42594	3.97031	4.59497	5.31089	6.13039
17	1.18430	1.40024	1.65285	1.94790	2.29202	2.69277	3.15882	3.70002	4.32763	5.05447	5.89509	6.86604
18	1.19615	1.42825	1.70243	2.02582	2.40662	2.85434	3.37993	3.99602	4.71712	5.55992	6.54355	7.68997
19	1.20811	1.45681	1.75351	2.10685	2.52695	3.02560	3.61653	4.31570	5.14166	6.11591	7.26334	8.61276
20	1.22019	1.48595	1.80611	2.19112	2.65330	3.20714	3.86968	4.66096	5.60441	6.72750	8.06231	9.64629
25	1.28243	1.64061	2.09378	2.66584	3.38635	4.29187	5.42743	6.84848	8.62308	10.83471	13.58546	17.00006
30	1.34785	1.81136	2.42726	3.24340	4.32194	5.74349	7.61226	10.06266	13.26768	17.44940	22.89230	29.95992
35	1.41660	1.99989	2.81386	3.94609	5.51602	7.68609	10.67658	14.78534	20.41397	28.10244	38.57485	52.79962
40	1.48886	2.20804	3.26204	4.80102	7.03999	10.28572	14.97446	21.72452	31.40942	45.25926	65.00087	93.05097
50	1.64463	2.69159	4.38391	7.10668	11.46740	18.42015	29.45703	46.90161	74.35752	117.39085	184.56483	289.00219

Future value tables are used as follows. First, determine the number of interest compounding periods involved (five years compounded annually are five periods, five years compounded semiannually are ten periods, five years compounded quarterly are 20 periods, and so on). The extreme left-hand column indicates the number of periods covered in the table.

Second, determine the interest rate per compounding period. Note that interest rates are usually quoted on an annual or *per year* basis. Therefore, only in the case of annual compounding is the quoted interest rate the interest rate per compounding period. In other cases, the rate per compounding period is the annual rate divided by the number of compounding periods in a year. For example, an interest rate of ten percent per year would be ten percent for one compounding period if compounded annually, five percent for two compounding periods if compounded semiannually, and 2 ½ percent for four compounding periods if compounded quarterly.

Finally, locate the factor that is to the right of the appropriate number of compounding periods and beneath the appropriate interest rate per compounding period. Multiply this factor by the number of dollars involved.

Note the logical progression among the various multipliers in **Table I**. All values are 1.0 or greater because the future value is always greater than the $1 present amount if the interest rate is greater than zero. Also, as the interest rate increases (moving from left to right in the table) or the number of periods increases (moving from top to bottom), the multipliers become larger.

Continuing with our example of calculating the future value of a $6,000 savings account deposit earning 6 percent annual compound interest for five years, and using the multipliers from Table I, we solve for the future value of the deposit as follows:

$$\textbf{Principal} \quad \times \quad \textbf{Factor} \quad = \quad \textbf{Future Value}$$
$$\textbf{\$6,000} \quad \times \quad \textbf{1.33823} \quad = \quad \textbf{\$8,029}$$

The factor 1.33823 is in the row for five periods and the column for six percent. Note that this factor is the same as the multiplier we determined using the future value formula in our calculation above.

Suppose, instead, that the interest is credited to the savings account semiannually rather than annually. In this situation, there are ten compounding periods, and we use a three percent rate (one-half the annual rate). The future value calculation using the **Table I** multipliers is as follows:

$$\textbf{Principal} \quad \times \quad \textbf{Factor} \quad = \quad \textbf{Future Value}$$
$$\textbf{\$6,000} \quad \times \quad \textbf{1.34392} \quad = \quad \textbf{\$8,064}$$

FUTURE VALUE OF AN ANNUITY

Using future value tables like **Table I**, we can calculate the future value of any single future cash flow or series of future cash flows. One frequent pattern of cash flows, however, is subject to a more convenient calculation. This pattern, known as an **annuity**, can be described as *equal amounts equally spaced over a period*.

For example, assume that $100 is to be deposited at the end of each of the next three years as an annuity into a savings account. When annuity cash flows occur at the end of each period, the annuity is called an **ordinary annuity**. As shown below in **Exhibit E-3**, the future value of this ordinary annuity can be calculated from **Table I** by calculating the future value of each of the three individual deposits and summing them (assuming eight percent annual interest).

Exhibit E-3	Future Value of an Ordinary Annuity					
Future Deposits (ordinary annuity)				**FV Multiplier (Table I)**		**Future Value**
Year 1	**Year 2**	**Year 3**				
$100			×	1.16640	=	$1.1664
	$100		×	1.08000	=	1.0800
		$100	×	1.00000	=	1.0000
				Total future value		$324.64

Present Value				**Future Value**
	$100	$100		$100
0	1	2		3

Table II, on the other hand, provides a single multiplier for calculating the future value of a series of future cash flows that reflect an ordinary annuity. Referring to **Table II** in the three periods row and the eight percent interest column, we see that the multiplier is 3.24640, equal to the sum of the three future value factors in **Exhibit E-3**. When applied to the $100 annuity amount, the multiplier gives a future value of $324.64, or $100 × 3.2464. As shown above, the same future value is derived from the several multipliers of **Table I**. For annuities of 5, 10, or 20 years, numerous calculations are avoided by using annuity tables like **Table II**.

Table II	Future Value of an Ordinary Annuity of $1 per period											
Period	1%	2%	3%	4%	5%	6%	7%	8%	9%	10%	11%	12%
1	1.00000	1.00000	1.00000	1.00000	1.00000	1.00000	1.00000	1.00000	1.00000	1.00000	1.00000	1.00000
2	2.01000	2.02000	2.03000	2.04000	2.05000	2.06000	2.07000	2.08000	2.09000	2.10000	2.11000	2.12000
3	3.03010	3.06040	3.09090	3.12160	3.15250	3.18360	3.21490	3.24640	3.27810	3.31000	3.34210	3.37440
4	4.06040	4.12161	4.18363	4.24646	4.31013	4.37462	4.43994	4.50611	4.57313	4.64100	4.70973	4.77933
5	5.10101	5.20404	5.30914	5.41632	5.52563	5.63709	5.75074	5.86660	5.98471	6.10510	6.22780	6.35285
6	6.15202	6.30812	6.46841	6.63298	6.80191	6.97532	7.15329	7.33593	7.52333	7.71561	7.91286	8.11519
7	7.21354	7.43428	7.66246	7.89829	8.14201	8.39384	8.65402	8.92280	9.20043	9.48717	9.78327	10.08901
8	8.28567	8.58297	8.89234	9.21423	9.54911	9.89747	10.25980	10.63663	11.02847	11.43589	11.85943	12.29969
9	9.36853	9.75463	10.15911	10.58280	11.02656	11.49132	11.97799	12.48756	13.02104	13.57948	14.16397	14.77566
10	10.46221	10.94972	11.46388	12.00611	12.57789	13.18079	13.81645	14.48656	15.19293	15.93742	16.72201	17.54874
11	11.56683	12.16872	12.80780	13.48635	14.20679	14.97164	15.78360	16.64549	17.56029	18.53117	19.56143	20.65458
12	12.68250	13.41209	14.19203	15.02581	15.91713	16.86994	17.88845	18.97713	20.14072	21.38428	22.71319	24.13313
13	13.80933	14.68033	15.61779	16.62684	17.71298	18.88214	20.14064	21.49530	22.95338	24.52271	26.21164	28.02911
14	14.94742	15.97394	17.08632	18.29191	19.59863	21.01507	22.55049	24.21492	26.01919	27.97498	30.09492	32.39260
15	16.09690	17.29342	18.59891	20.02359	21.57856	23.27597	25.12902	27.15211	29.36092	31.77248	34.40536	37.27971
16	17.25786	18.63929	20.15688	21.82453	23.65749	25.67253	27.88805	30.32428	33.00340	35.94973	39.18995	42.75328
17	18.43044	20.01207	21.76159	23.69751	25.84037	28.21288	30.84022	33.75023	36.97370	40.54470	44.50084	48.88367
18	19.61475	21.41231	23.41444	25.64541	28.13238	30.90565	33.99903	37.45024	41.30134	45.59917	50.39594	55.74971
19	20.81090	22.84056	25.11687	27.67123	30.53900	33.75999	37.37896	41.44626	46.01846	51.15909	56.93949	63.43968
20	22.01900	24.29737	26.87037	29.77808	33.06595	36.78559	40.99549	45.76196	51.16012	57.27500	64.20283	72.05244
25	28.24320	32.03030	36.45926	41.64591	47.72710	54.86451	63.24904	73.10594	84.70090	98.34706	114.41331	133.33387
30	34.78489	40.56808	47.57542	56.08494	66.43885	79.05819	94.46079	113.28321	136.30754	164.49402	199.02088	241.33268
35	41.66028	49.99448	60.46208	73.65222	90.32031	111.43478	138.23688	172.31680	215.71075	271.02437	341.58955	431.66350
40	48.88637	60.40198	75.40126	95.02552	120.79977	154.76197	199.63511	259.05652	337.88245	442.59256	581.82607	767.09142
50	64.46318	84.57940	112.79687	152.66708	209.34800	290.33590	406.52893	573.77016	815.08356	1163.90853	1668.77115	2400.01825

If we decide to invest $50 at the end of each six months for three years at an eight percent annual rate of return, we would use the factor for 6 periods at four percent, as follows:

$$\text{Periodic Payment} \times \text{Factor} = \text{Future Value}$$
$$\$50 \times 6.63298 = \$331.65$$

PRESENT VALUE OF AN AMOUNT

LO3 Calculate present values.

We can generalize that (1) the right to receive an amount of money now—its **present value**—is normally worth more than the right to receive the same amount later—its future value; (2) the longer we must wait to receive an amount, the less attractive the receipt is; and (3) the difference between the present value of an amount and its future value is a function of interest (Principal × Interest Rate × Time). Further, the more risk associated with any situation, the higher the appropriate interest rate.

We support these generalizations with an illustration. What amount should we accept now that would be as valuable as receiving $100 one year from now ($100 represents the future value) if the appropriate interest rate is ten percent? We recognize intuitively that with a ten percent interest rate, we should accept less than $100, or approximately $91.

We base this estimate on the realization that the $100 received in the future must equal the present value (100 percent) plus ten percent interest on the present value. Thus, in our example, the $100 future receipt must be 1.10 times the present value. Dividing $100 by 1.10, we obtain a present value of $90.91. In other words, under the given conditions, we would do as well to accept $90.91 now as to wait one year and receive $100. To confirm the equality of a $90.91 payment now with a $100 payment one year later, we calculate the future value of $90.91 at ten percent for one year as follows:

$$\textbf{\$90.91} \times \textbf{1.10} \times \textbf{1 year} = \textbf{\$100 (rounded)}$$

Thus, we calculate the present value of a future receipt by discounting (deducting an interest factor) the future receipt back to the present at an appropriate interest rate. We present this schematically below:

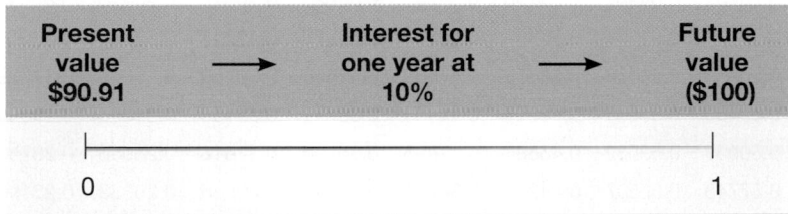

The formula for calculating the present value of a single amount is determined using the following formula:

$$\textbf{PV} = \textbf{FV} \times [\textbf{1} \div (\textbf{1} + \textbf{i})^{\textbf{n}}]$$

where

PV = present value of an amount
FV = future value
  i = interest rate for one period
  n = number of periods

As can be seen from this formula, if either the time period or the interest rate is increased, the resulting present value would decrease. If more than one time period is involved, compound interest calculations are appropriate. **Exhibit E-4** illustrates the calculation of the present value of a single amount.

Exhibit E-4	Present Value of a Single Amount

How much must be deposited in a savings account today in order to have $1,000 in four years if the savings account pays 12 percent annual interest?

$$PV = \$1,000 \times [1 \div (1.12)^4] = (\$1,000 \times 0.63552) = \$636$$

Present Value	←	Discounted for 4 years at 6%	←	Future Value

$636				($1,000)
0	1	2	3	4

Table III can be used to calculate the present value amounts in a manner similar to the way we previously calculated future values using **Tables I** and **II**. As with the future value tables, present value tables provide a multiplier for many combinations of time periods and interest rates that, when applied to the dollar amount of a future cash flow or annuity, determines its present value.

Table III	Present Value of $1											
Period	**1%**	**2%**	**3%**	**4%**	**5%**	**6%**	**7%**	**8%**	**9%**	**10%**	**11%**	**12%**
1	0.99010	0.98039	0.97087	0.96154	0.95238	0.94340	0.93458	0.92593	0.91743	0.90909	0.90090	0.89286
2	0.98030	0.96117	0.94260	0.92456	0.90703	0.89000	0.87344	0.85734	0.84168	0.82645	0.81162	0.79719
3	0.97059	0.94232	0.91514	0.88900	0.86384	0.83962	0.81630	0.79383	0.77218	0.75131	0.73119	0.71178
4	0.96098	0.92385	0.88849	0.85480	0.82270	0.79209	0.76290	0.73503	0.70843	0.68301	0.65873	0.63552
5	0.95147	0.90573	0.86261	0.82193	0.78353	0.74726	0.71299	0.68058	0.64993	0.62092	0.59345	0.56743
6	0.94205	0.88797	0.83748	0.79031	0.74622	0.70496	0.66634	0.63017	0.59627	0.56447	0.53464	0.50663
7	0.93272	0.87056	0.81309	0.75992	0.71068	0.66506	0.62275	0.58349	0.54703	0.51316	0.48166	0.45235
8	0.92348	0.85349	0.78941	0.73069	0.67684	0.62741	0.58201	0.54027	0.50187	0.46651	0.43393	0.40388
9	0.91434	0.83676	0.76642	0.70259	0.64461	0.59190	0.54393	0.50025	0.46043	0.42410	0.39092	0.36061
10	0.90529	0.82035	0.74409	0.67556	0.61391	0.55839	0.50835	0.46319	0.42241	0.38554	0.35218	0.32197
11	0.89632	0.80426	0.72242	0.64958	0.58468	0.52679	0.47509	0.42888	0.38753	0.35049	0.31728	0.28748
12	0.88745	0.78849	0.70138	0.62460	0.55684	0.49697	0.44401	0.39711	0.35553	0.31863	0.28584	0.25668
13	0.87866	0.77303	0.68095	0.60057	0.53032	0.46884	0.41496	0.36770	0.32618	0.28966	0.25751	0.22917
14	0.86996	0.75788	0.66112	0.57748	0.50507	0.44230	0.38782	0.34046	0.29925	0.26333	0.23199	0.20462
15	0.86135	0.74301	0.64186	0.55526	0.48102	0.41727	0.36245	0.31524	0.27454	0.23939	0.20900	0.18270
16	0.85282	0.72845	0.62317	0.53391	0.45811	0.39365	0.33873	0.29189	0.25187	0.21763	0.18829	0.16312
17	0.84438	0.71416	0.60502	0.51337	0.43630	0.37136	0.31657	0.27027	0.23107	0.19784	0.16963	0.14564
18	0.83602	0.70016	0.58739	0.49363	0.41552	0.35034	0.29586	0.25025	0.21199	0.17986	0.15282	0.13004
19	0.82774	0.68643	0.57029	0.47464	0.39573	0.33051	0.27651	0.23171	0.19449	0.16351	0.13768	0.11611
20	0.81954	0.67297	0.55368	0.45639	0.37689	0.31180	0.25842	0.21455	0.17843	0.14864	0.12403	0.10367
25	0.77977	0.60953	0.47761	0.37512	0.29530	0.23300	0.18425	0.14602	0.11597	0.09230	0.07361	0.05882
30	0.74192	0.55207	0.41199	0.30832	0.23138	0.17411	0.13137	0.09938	0.07537	0.05731	0.04368	0.03338
35	0.70591	0.50003	0.35538	0.25342	0.18129	0.13011	0.09366	0.06763	0.04899	0.03558	0.02592	0.01894
40	0.67165	0.45289	0.30656	0.20829	0.14205	0.09722	0.06678	0.04603	0.03184	0.02209	0.01538	0.01075
50	0.60804	0.37153	0.22811	0.14071	0.08720	0.05429	0.03395	0.02132	0.01345	0.00852	0.00542	0.00346

Exhibit E-5 illustrates calculations of present values using the factors in **Table III**.

Exhibit E-5	Present Value of a Single Amount Using Present Value Tables

Calculate the present value of $1,000 four years hence, at twelve percent interest compounded annually:

Number of periods (one year, annually) = 4
Interest rate per period (12%/1) = 12%
Multiplier = 0.63552
Present value = $1,000 × 0.63552 = $636
(This result agrees with our earlier illustration.)

Calculate the present value of $116.99 two years hence, at eight percent compounded semiannually:

Number of periods (two years, semiannually) = 4
Interest rate per period (8%/2) = 4%
Multiplier = 0.85480
Present value = $116.99 × 0.85480 = $100 (rounded)

PRESENT VALUE OF AN ANNUITY

We can also use present value tables like **Table III** to calculate the present value of any single future cash flow or series of future cash flows. For example, assume $100 is to be received at the end of each of the next three years as an annuity. As shown in **Exhibit E-6**, the present value of this ordinary annuity can be calculated from **Table III** by calculating the present value of each of the three individual receipts and summing them (assuming five percent annual interest).

Exhibit E-6	Present Value of an Ordinary Annuity					
Future Receipts (ordinary annuity)				**PV Multiplier (Table I)**		**Future Value**
Year 1	**Year 2**	**Year 3**				
$100			×	0.95238	=	$ 95.24
	$100		×	0.90703	=	90.70
		$100	×	0.86384	=	86.38
				Total present value....		$272.32

Table IV, on the other hand, provides a single multiplier for calculating the present value of a series of future cash flows that represent an ordinary annuity. Referring to **Table IV** in the three periods row and the five percent interest column, we see that the multiplier is 2.72325, equal to the sum of the three present value factors in **Exhibit E-6**. When applied to the $100 annuity amount, the multiplier gives a present value of $272.32.

Table IV	Present Value of an Ordinary Annuity of $1 per period											
Period	**1%**	**2%**	**3%**	**4%**	**5%**	**6%**	**7%**	**8%**	**9%**	**10%**	**11%**	**12%**
1	0.99010	0.98039	0.97087	0.96154	0.95238	0.94340	0.93458	0.92593	0.91743	0.90909	0.90090	0.89286
2	1.97040	1.94156	1.91347	1.88609	1.85941	1.83339	1.80802	1.78326	1.75911	1.73554	1.71252	1.69005
3	2.94099	2.88388	2.82861	2.77509	2.72325	2.67301	2.62432	2.57710	2.53129	2.48685	2.44371	2.40183
4	3.90197	3.80773	3.71710	3.62990	3.54595	3.46511	3.38721	3.31213	3.23972	3.16987	3.10245	3.03735
5	4.85343	4.71346	4.57971	4.45182	4.32948	4.21236	4.10020	3.99271	3.88965	3.79079	3.69590	3.60478
6	5.79548	5.60143	5.41719	5.24214	5.07569	4.91732	4.76654	4.62288	4.48592	4.35526	4.23054	4.11141
7	6.72819	6.47199	6.23028	6.00205	5.78637	5.58238	5.38929	5.20637	5.03295	4.86842	4.71220	4.56376
8	7.65168	7.32548	7.01969	6.73274	6.46321	6.20979	5.97130	5.74664	5.53482	5.33493	5.14612	4.96764
9	8.56602	8.16224	7.78611	7.43533	7.10782	6.80169	6.51523	6.24689	5.99525	5.75902	5.53705	5.32825
10	9.47130	8.98259	8.53020	8.11090	7.72173	7.36009	7.02358	6.71008	6.41766	6.14457	5.88923	5.65022
11	10.36763	9.78685	9.25262	8.76048	8.30641	7.88687	7.49867	7.13896	6.80519	6.49506	6.20652	5.93770
12	11.25508	10.57534	9.95400	9.38507	8.86325	8.38384	7.94269	7.53608	7.16073	6.81369	6.49236	6.19437
13	12.13374	11.34837	10.63496	9.98565	9.39357	8.85268	8.35765	7.90378	7.48690	7.10336	6.74987	6.42355
14	13.00370	12.10625	11.29607	10.56312	9.89864	9.29498	8.74547	8.24424	7.78615	7.36669	6.98187	6.62817
15	13.86505	12.84926	11.93794	11.11839	10.37966	9.71225	9.10791	8.55948	8.06069	7.60608	7.19087	6.81086
16	14.71787	13.57771	12.56110	11.65230	10.83777	10.10590	9.44665	8.85137	8.31256	7.82371	7.37916	6.97399
17	15.56225	14.29187	13.16612	12.16567	11.27407	10.47726	9.76322	9.12164	8.54363	8.02155	7.54879	7.11963
18	16.39827	14.99203	13.75351	12.65930	11.68959	10.82760	10.05909	9.37189	8.75563	8.20141	7.70162	7.24967
19	17.22601	15.67846	14.32380	13.13394	12.08532	11.15812	10.33560	9.60360	8.95011	8.36492	7.83929	7.36578
20	18.04555	16.35143	14.87747	13.59033	12.46221	11.46992	10.59401	9.81815	9.12855	8.51356	7.96333	7.46944
25	22.02316	19.52346	17.41315	15.62208	14.09394	12.78336	11.65358	10.67478	9.82258	9.07704	8.42174	7.84314
30	25.80771	22.39646	19.60044	17.29203	15.37245	13.76483	12.40904	11.25778	10.27365	9.42691	8.69379	8.05518
35	29.40858	24.99862	21.48722	18.66461	16.37419	14.49825	12.94767	11.65457	10.56682	9.64416	8.85524	8.17550
40	32.83469	27.35548	23.11477	19.79277	17.15909	15.04630	13.33171	11.92461	10.75736	9.77905	8.95105	8.24378
50	39.19612	31.42361	25.72976	21.48218	18.25593	15.76186	13.80075	12.23348	10.96168	9.91481	9.04165	8.30450

CALCULATIONS USING A CALCULATOR AND A SPREADSHEET

While present value tables can provide a handy method to solve some time value of money problems, they are not suitable for many real world situations. For example, many real world interest rates are not even integers like those appearing in **Table I** through **Table IV**, nor are many problems limited to the number of time periods appearing in the tables. While it is still possible to solve these problems with the provided formulas, financial calculators and spreadsheet programs provide a much quicker solution. Financial calculators can be distinguished from other calculators by the presence of dedicated keys for present and future values, along with keys for the number of periods, interest rates, and annuity payments. There exists many brands of financial calculators; however, all of them work in much the same way.[1] We illustrate the calculation of bond issuance prices using a calculator and a spreadsheet in Appendix 10A at the end of Chapter 10.

---

[1] It is usually necessary to do some preliminary setup on a financial calculator before performing time value of money calculations. For example, the HP 10BII calculator has a default setting of monthly compounding. This may need to be changed if the problem calls for a different number of compounding periods, such as annual. In addition, the calculator assumes annuity payments occur at the end of each period. This will need to be changed if the problem requires beginning of period payments. See your calculator manual to determine how to make these setting changes.

SUMMARY OF LEARNING OBJECTIVES

LO1   Describe the nature of interest and distinguish between simple and compound interest. (p. E-2)
- Interest is payment for the use of money over time.
- Simple interest is computed only on the principal.
- Compound interest is computed on the accumulated principal including any earned interest that has not been paid.

LO2   Calculate future values. (p. E-3)
- The future value of a single amount is the amount that a specified investment will be worth at a future date if invested at a given rate of compound interest.
- The formula for calculating the future value of a single amount is $PV = FV \times (1 + i)^n$.
- Future value tables provide a multiplier for many combinations of time periods and interest rates that, when applied to the dollar amount of a present value, determines its future value.
- An annuity represents a special case of a pattern of cash flows where the cash flow amounts are of equal amounts and equally spaced over time.
- A separate table is available that provides a multiplier for the future value of an annuity rather than using separate multipliers from the future value of $1 table.

LO3   Calculate present values. (p. E-6)
- The right to receive an amount of money now—its present value—is normally worth more than the right to receive the same amount later—its future value.
- The formula for calculating the present value of a single amount is $PV = FV \times [1 \div (1 + i)^n]$.
- A separate table is available that provides a multiplier for the present value of an annuity rather than using separate multipliers from the present value of $1 table.

GLOSSARY OF KEY TERMS

Annuity (p. E-5)   **Interest** (p. E-2)   **Principal** (p. E-2)
Compound interest (p. E-2)   **Ordinary annuity** (p. E-5)   **Simple interest** (p. E-2)
Future value (p. E-3)   **Present value** (p. E-6)   **Time value** (p. E-2)

Assignments with the logo in the margin are available in ᵐʸBusinessCourse.
See the Preface of the book for details.

SELF-STUDY QUESTIONS

(Answers to Self-Study Questions are at the end of this appendix.)

1. **Calculate the future value of each of the following items.**   **LO2**
   a. $50,000 deposited in a savings account for ten years if the annual interest rate is
      1. Twelve percent compounded annually.
      2. Twelve percent compounded semiannually.
      3. Twelve percent compounded quarterly.
   b. $5,000 received at the end of each year for the next ten years if the money earns interest at the rate of four percent compounded annually.
   c. $3,000 received semiannually for the next five years if the money earns interest at the rate of eight percent compounded semiannually.
   d. $1,000 deposited each year for the next ten years plus a single sum of $15,000 deposited today if the interest rate is ten percent per year compounded annually.

2. **Calculate the present value of each of the following items.**   **LO3**
   a. $90,000 ten years hence if the annual interest rate is
      1. Eight percent compounded annually.
      2. Eight percent compounded semiannually.
      3. Eight percent compounded quarterly.
   b. $1,000 received at the end of each year for the next eight years if money is worth ten percent per year compounded annually.
   c. $600 received at the end of each six months for the next fifteen years if the interest rate is eight percent per year compounded semiannually.
   d. $500,000 inheritance ten years hence if money is worth ten percent per year compounded annually.
   e. $2,500 received each half year for the next ten years plus a single sum of $85,000 at the end of ten years if the interest rate is twelve percent per year compounded semiannually.

EXERCISES—SET A

EE-1A. Simple and Compound Interest   **LO1**
   a. For each of the following notes, calculate the simple interest due at the end of the term.

Note	Principal	Rate	Term
1	$10,000	2%	6 years
2	$10,000	4%	4 years
3	$10,000	6%	3 years

   b. Compute the amount of interest due at the end of the term for each of the above notes assuming interest is compounded annually.

EE-2A. Future Value Computation At the beginning of the year you deposit $3,000 in a savings account.   **LO2**
How much will accumulate in three years if you earn 8% compounded annually?

EE-3A. Future Value Computation You deposit $3,000 at the end of every year for three years. How much   **LO2**
will accumulate in three years if you earn 8% compounded annually?

EE-4A. Present Value Computation You will receive $3,000 in three years. What is the present value if you   **LO3**
can earn 8% interest compounded annually?

EE-5A. Present Value Computation You receive $3,000 at the end of every year for three years. What is the   **LO3**
present value of these receipts if you earn 8% compounded annually?

EE-6A. Future Value Computation What amount will be accumulated in five years if $10,000 is invested   **LO2**
today at 6% interest compounded annually?

LO3 **EE-7A.** **Present Value Computation** You are scheduled to be paid $10,000 in five years. What amount today is equivalent to the $10,000 to be received in five years assuming interest is compounded annually at 6%?

LO2 **EE-8A.** **Future Value Computation** What amount will be accumulated in five years if $10,000 is invested every six months beginning in six months and ending five years from today? Interest will accumulate at an annual rate of 10% compounded semiannually.

LO2 **EE-9A.** **Future Value Computation** You are scheduled to receive $10,000 every six months for ten periods beginning in six months. What amount in five years is equivalent to the future series of payments assuming interest compounds at the annual rate of 8% compounded semiannually?

LO3 **EE-10A.** **Present Value Computation** Zazzi, Inc., believes it will need $100,000 in five years to expand its operations. Zazzi can earn 5%, compounded annually, if it deposits its money right now. How large of a deposit must Zazzi make in order to have the necessary $100,000 in five years?

LO2 **EE-11A.** **Future Value Computation** Peyton Company deposited $10,000 in the bank today, earning 8% interest. Peyton plans to withdraw the money in five years. How much money will be available to withdraw assuming that interest is compounded (a) annually, (b) semiannually, and (c) quarterly?

LO2 **EE-12A.** **Future Value Computation** Sam Smith deposited $5,000 in a savings account today. The deposit will earn interest at the rate of 8%. How much will be available for Sam to withdraw in three years, assuming interest is compounded (a) annually, (b) semiannually, and (c) quarterly?

LO3 **EE-13A.** **Present Value Computation** Pete Frost made a deposit into his savings account three years ago, and earned interest at an annual rate of 8%. The deposit accumulated to $25,000. How much was initially deposited assuming that the interest was compounded (a) annually, (b) semiannually, and (c) quarterly?

LO2 **EE-14A.** **Future Value Computation** Kumari Jennings has decided to start saving for his daughter's college education by depositing $2,500 at the end of every year for 18 years. He has determined that he will be able to earn 6% interest compounded annually. He hopes to have at least $70,000 when his daughter starts college in eighteen years. Will his savings plan be successful?

LO3 **EE-15A.** **Present Value Computation** Kerry Bales won the state lottery and was given four choices for receiving her winnings.

1. Receive $400,000 right now.
2. Receive $432,000 in one year.
3. Receive $40,000 at the end of each year for 20 years.
4. Receive $36,000 at the end of each year for 30 years.

Assuming Kerry can earn interest of 8% compounded annually, which option should Kerry choose?

EXERCISES—SET B

LO1 **EE-1B.** **Simple and Compound Interest**

a. For each of the following notes, calculate the simple interest due at the end of the term.

Note	Principal	Rate	Term
1	$8,000	8%	8 years
2	$8,000	12%	5 years
3	$8,000	4%	2 years

b. Compute the amount of interest due at the end of the term for each of the above notes assuming interest is compounded annually.

EE-2B. **Future Value Computation** At the beginning of the year you deposit $2,500 in a savings account. **LO2** How much will accumulate in four years if you earn 6% compounded annually?

EE-3B. **Future Value Computation** You deposit $2,500 at the end of every year for four years. How much **LO2** will accumulate in four years if you earn 6% compounded annually?

EE-4B. **Present Value Computation** You will receive $2,500 in four years. What is the present value if you **LO3** can earn 6% interest compounded annually?

EE-5B. **Present Value Computation** You receive $2,500 at the end of every year for four years. What is the **LO3** present value of these receipts if you earn 6% compounded annually?

EE-6B. **Future Value Computation** What amount will be accumulated in six years if $5,000 is invested **LO2** today at 5% interest compounded annually?

EE-7B. **Present Value Computation** You are scheduled to be paid $5,000 in eight years. What amount today **LO3** is equivalent to the $5,000 to be received in eight years assuming interest is compounded annually at 6%?

EE-8B. **Future Value Computation** What amount will be accumulated in five years if $3,000 is invested **LO2** every six months beginning in six months and ending five years from today? Interest will accumulate at an annual rate of 4% compounded semiannually.

EE-9B. **Future Value Computation** You are scheduled to receive $5,000 every six months for eight periods **LO2** beginning in six months. What amount in four years is equivalent to the future series of payments assuming interest compounds at the annual rate of 8% compounded semiannually?

EE-10B. **Present Value Computation** Zumi, Inc., believes it will need $150,000 in nine years to expand its **LO3** operations. Zumi can earn 6%, compounded annually, if it deposits its money right now. How large of a deposit must Zumi make in order to have the necessary $150,000 in nine years?

EE-11B. **Future Value Computation** Triton Company deposited $9,500 in the bank today, earning 8% inter- **LO2** est. Triton plans to withdraw the money in five years. How much money will be available to withdraw assuming that interest is compounded (a) annually, (b) semiannually, and (c) quarterly?

EE-12B. **Future Value Computation** Sally Smithton deposited $2,000 in a savings account today. The deposit **LO2** will earn interest at the rate of 12%. How much will be available for Sally to withdraw in three years, assuming interest is compounded (a) annually, (b) semiannually, and (c) quarterly?

EE-13B. **Present Value Computation** Raul Gomez made a deposit into his savings account four years ago, **LO3** and earned interest at an annual rate of 12%. The deposit accumulated to $40,000. How much was initially deposited assuming that the interest was compounded (a) annually, (b) semiannually, and (c) quarterly?

EE-14B. **Future Value Computation** Herman Lee has decided to start saving for his daughter's college edu- **LO2** cation by depositing $3,000 at the end of every year for 18 years. He has determined that he will be able to earn 6% interest compounded annually. He hopes to have at least $90,000 when his daughter starts college in eighteen years. Will his savings plan be successful?

EE-15B. **Present Value Computation** Kelly Zales won the state lottery and was given four choices for receiv- **LO3** ing her winnings.

1. Receive $1,000,000 right now.
2. Receive $1,040,000 in one year.
3. Receive $150,000 at the end of each year for eight years.
4. Receive $57,500 at the end of each year for 30 years.

Assuming Kelly can earn interest of 4% compounded annually, which option should Kelly choose?

ANSWERS TO SELF-STUDY QUESTIONS:

1. *a.* 1. $ 50,000 × 3.10585 = $155,293
      2. $ 50,000 × 3.20714 = $160,357
      3. $ 50,000 × 3.26204 = $163,102
   b. $ 5,000 × 12.00611 = $ 60,031
   c. $ 3,000 × 12.00611 = $ 36,018
   d. $ 1,000 × 15.93742 = $ 15,937
          $ 15,000 × 2.59374 = $ 38,906
                                $ 54,843

2. *a.* 1. $ 90,000 × 0.46319 = $ 41,687
      2. $ 90,000 × 0.45639 = $ 41,075
      3. $ 90,000 × 0.45289 = $ 40,760
   b. $ 1,000 × 5.33493 = $ 5,335
   c. $ 600 × 17.29203 = $ 10,375
   d. $500,000 × 0.38554 = $192,770
   e. $ 2,500 × 11.46992 = $ 28,675
          $ 85,000 × 0.31180 = $ 26,503
                                $ 55,178

Index

A

Abbott Laboratories, 593–594
ABC. *See* activity-based costing (ABC)
ABM. *See* activity-based management
    (ABM)
absorption costing
    defined, 928
    illustration, 929
    uses for, 930
accelerated depreciation method, 433–434
account form, 193
accounting
    accrual basis of, 27, 122–151
    adjusting accounts and, 125–136
    capital market and, 12, 469, 538
    careers in, 22–23
    cash basis of, 27, 122–124, 339–340,
        583
    change in accounting principle and,
        630, 632–633
    cherry picking and, D12
    conceptual framework for, FASB, 11,
        25–28
    defined, 10
    depreciation and, 127–128, 289, 426,
        428, 430–442
    discounts and, 196, 239–244
    double-entry, 62, 337
    ethics and, 8–9. *See also* ethics
    external users and, 6–7
    financial, 7
    Financial Accounting Standards Board
        (FASB) and, 10–11, 25–28,
        582–583, 660–661
    financial reports and, 9–21, 25–27
    forensic, 9, 80, 206, 279, 290, 331, 336,
        355, 391, 440, 490–491, 537, 656,
        657
    GAAP and, 10–12, 26–27. *See also*
        generally accepted accounting
        principles (GAAP)
    importance of, 630
    internal control and, 9, 331, 333–339,
        341–352, 355–357
    internal users and, 6, 8
    International Accounting Standards
        Board (IASB) and, 11–12, 253
    inventory and, 20, 233, 235–237. *See*
        also inventory
    long-lived assets and, 127, 426–431,
        442
    maintaining adequate records for, 335,
        337
    managerial, 8

matching concept and, 384, 400, 431,
    484, 488
merchandising firms and, 195–197,
    234–254
need for skills in, 22
paper trails and, 347
physical control of, 333, 337
purchases of merchandise and,
    237–241, 249–250
purpose of, 10
salaries, 22, 23e
sales of merchandise and, 241–245,
    250–254
summary of significant accounting
    policies and, 659
accounting cycle
    accounting equation and, 13, 60–67
    accrual basis of accounting and, 27,
        122–124, 139, 146–148
    analyzing transactions and, 58e, 61–67
    calendar year and, 61
    employee hires and, 5, 65
    fiscal year and, 61, 472, 484, 549
    issued stock example, 63
    paid cash on dividend, 66
    paid employee wages, 66
    paid rent in advance, 63
    payment received on account, 66
    provided services for customers, 65
    purchased equipment with cash, 64
    purchased office supplies on account,
        63–64
    received customer prepayment, 64–65
    signed bank note in exchange for cash,
        64
accounting entity concept, 27–28, D13
accounting equation, 13
    double–entry accounting and, 62
    expanded, 62, 67e
    general ledger and, 69–78
    information processing and, 61–72
accounting information, 6–10
    constraints on, 27
    principles of, 27–28
    qualitative characteristics of, 25–26,
        26e
accounting in practice
    accounting as an aid to investing, 655
    activity-based costing, 850, 852, 856,
        860
    capital budgeting, 1112, 1122, 1130
    cash equivalents, defined, 579
    cost-volume-profit relationships, 894,
        899, 907
    differential analysis, 954

expense allocation for federal
    government grants and contracts,
    1078
factory supplies vs. indirect materials,
    717
financing cash flows, 998
job order costing, 753, 761, 763
management by exception, 1066
multiple predetermined overhead rates,
    755
relevant range, 1064
SEC EDGAR database, 634
segment reporting, 1072
standard costs, 1028, 1029, 1031
statement of cash flows, 583–584, 594
strategic planning, 985
tracking time, 761
variances, 1033, 1040
accounting period concept, 27, 136
accounting principles, change in, 632–633
accounting software, 59, 61
Accounting Standards Codification
    (FASB), 11
accounting transactions
    accounting equation and, 61–70
    adjusting accounts and, 121, 125–136
    analysis of, 61–70
    cash and, 339–345
    chart of accounts and, 68
    closing process and, 137–140
    debit-credit system and, 66–78
    defined, 62
    employee hires, 65
    explanations of complex or special, 659
    general journal and, 71–72
    general ledger postings and, 72–78
    issued stock, 63, 73
    paid cash dividend, 66, 76
    paid employee wages, 66, 75
    paid rent in advance, 63, 73
    performed services for customers, 65,
        75
    purchased equipment with cash, 64, 74
    purchased office supplies on account,
        63, 73
    received customer prepayment, 64–65,
        74
    received payment on account, 66, 76
    recording, 70–78
    related-party, 659
    signed bank note in exchange for cash,
        64, 74
    source documents and, 71
Accounting Trends and Techniques, 193

accounts
  chart of, 68
  contra, 128, 243
  defined, 68
  normal balance and, 69
  open, 236
  permanent, 137, 139, 144–148
  recoveries of, 390–391
  system of debits and credits, 68–70
  T-account, 70–72, 78, 125, 137–138
  temporary, 137–139, 144–148
  trial balance and, 79–80
  uncollectible, 384–391
  writing off, 385–387, 390, 400
accounts payable
  cash management and, 354
  liabilities and, 13, 192, 470. *See also*
    liabilities
  maintaining adequate records for, 337
accounts receivable
  accrual basis of accounting and, 123,
    138
  aging method and, 387–391
  allowance method and, 384–387
  analysis of, 396–397
  average collection period and, 397,
    648–649
  balance sheet title for, 383
  business decisions and, 13
  Columbia Sportswear Company, 3, 5,
    14–22
  credit card sales and, 392
  credit-collection policy and, 383–384
  credit-granting policy and, 383, 387
  credit scoring systems and, 383–384
  defined, 382
  discounting and, 397
  estimating credit losses and, 387–391
  factoring and, 397
  financial statements and, 191, 365–366,
    642, 646–651
  going concern concept and, 27, 356
  information processing and, 63–69
  interest on, 393–395
  internal control and, 333–338, 341–351
  lapping and, 391
  maintaining adequate records for, 335,
    337
  management of, 396–397
  matching concept and, 384
  merchandising firms and, 195–198,
    241–242, 250–252
  as percentage of assets, 382
  plant assets and, 441–442
  quick ratio and, 647
  sales revenue and, 382–383
  statements of cash flows and, 585–591
  turnover, 396–397, 648
  uncollectible accounts and, 383–391

  writing off accounts and, 385–386,
    390–391
accrual basis of accounting, 27
  adjusted financial statements and,
    133–136
  adjusted trial balance and, 133–136
  adjusting accounts and, 125–132
  balance sheet and, 126–130, 132e, 134,
    135e, 142–148
  closing procedures and, 137–141
  contra accounts and, 128
  depreciation and, 128
  earnings quality and, 140
  expense recognition (matching)
    principle and, 27, 124
  prepaid expenses and, 126
  retained earnings and, 144–148
  revenue recognition principle and,
    122–123
  statement of cash flows and, 135, 584
  statement of stockholders' equity and,
    134, 135e
  unearned revenues and, 126
  worksheets and, 148–151
accrued expenses, 126–132, 469
accrued fees, 131
accrued interest, 131, 395, 429, 472,
  481–482
accrued revenue, 126, 130
accrued wages, 129–130
acid-test ratio, 646
acquisitions, 440, 629
activities
  defined, 848
  financing activities, 580–581
  IFRS alert, 581
  investing activities, 580
  noncash investing and financing, 582
  operating activities, 580, 583
  statement of cash flows classifications,
    579–582
  usefulness of, 581–582
activity-based costing (ABC), 844–861
  activity-based management, 859–860
  benefits of, 852
  changing cost environment, 847–848
  current status of, 860
  customer profitability analysis,
    857–859
  defined, 845
  departmental overhead rates, 772
  illustration, 849
  implementation issues, 855–857
  indirect costs, 846–848
  limitations of, 855
  model, 850–851
  overhead, 852–854
  overview, 848–849
  product costing model, 850–851
  services industry, 860–861

  traditional product costing vs., 851–855
activity-based management (ABM)
  activity-based costing and, 847,
    859–860
  defined, 859
  purpose of, 859
activity basis, 884–885
activity classifications, 579–582
add-on interest method, 471
adjusted trial balance, 133–136, 148–151
adjusting entries, 132e
  accrued expenses, 126
  accrued revenues, 126
  adjusted trial balance, 133–136
  allocating unearned revenue to sales
    revenue, 128–129
  asset allocation to expenses, 125–128
  deferrals, 126
  depreciation, 127–128
  generally accepted accounting
    principles (GAAP) and, 136
  interest on notes receivable, 393–395
  office supplies, 127
  prepaid expenses, 127
  prepaid rent, 127
  recording previously unrecorded
    expenses, 128–129
  recording previously unrecorded sales
    revenues, 129–130
  unadjusted trial balance, 125–127
  unearned revenues, 126
  worksheets and, 148–151
  year-end accounting procedures. *See
    also* journal entries
administrative expense
  after-tax cash flows, 1120
  budget, 997
advance payments, 192, 476
advertising
  accrual basis of accounting and,
    126–127
  internal control and, 336
  merchandising firms and, 196–197, 234
Aetna Inc., D2
affiliate companies, D9
after-tax cash flows, 1118–1121, 1124
aging method, 387–391
aging schedule, 388
AIG, 8
Albertsons, 123
Allen, Paul, 469
allocation of cost
  basis of, 770–771
  service departments, 769
Allowance for Uncollectible Accounts, 385
allowance method, 385–387
alternative career paths, 703–704
Amazon, 11, 492, 695
American Express, 392

Note: Exhibits and notes are included in the index with a corresponding e or n following the page numbers.

American Institute of Certified Public Accountants (AICPA), 9, 10, 23, 705

amortization
  bonds and, 483–484, 494–495
  debt securities and, D5, D7–D8
  description of, 443
  effective interest method and, 483
  expense, 426, 588
  intangible assets and, 426, 446
  straight-line method and, 483, 494–496
  year-end adjustments and, 484

analytical techniques for information sources, 634–635

annual operating budget, 987

annual reports, 20

annuity, E5–E6, E8–E9
  defined, 1116, E5
  future value, E5–E6
  ordinary annuity, E5–E6
  present value of, 1116–1117, E9

Apple
  accounts receivable as percentage of assets, 382
  balance sheet analysis, 198–201
  classified balance sheet and, 190–194
  classified income statement and, 195–197
  Cook and, 61
  generally accepted accounting principles (GAAP) and, 194
  income statement analysis, 201–202
  iTunes and, 201
  Jobs and, 189
  multi-step income statement of, 195–198
  popular products of, 189, 201
  ratio analysis and, 198–199
  single-step income statement of, 195
  statement of cash flows and, 204–206
  statement of stockholders' equity and, 201–202
  stockholders' equity and, 193
  Wayne and, 189
  as win-win company, 189
  Wozniak and, 189

Apple Inc., 711, 727–732

articles of incorporation, 530

articulation, 18

asset management, 6

asset turnover ratio, 446–447, 641–645

asset utilization ratio, 1081

assets, 6. See also accounts receivable
  acquisition information and, 198–199
  balance sheet and, 13–14, 198–200, 585–586
  book value and, 441–442
  classified balance sheet and, 190–193
  cost principle and, 238, 427–429

current/noncurrent classifications and, 191, D12
current ratio and, 199, 490–491, 646–647
debit-credit system and, 68–69
debt-to-total assets ratio and, 200–201
depreciation and, 426, 428, 430–440
in expanded accounting equation, 64e
goodwill and, 445
intangible, 191, 442–445
liquidity and, 191, 193, 198–201, 341, 646–650
long-lived, 426–442
long-term, 191–192
property, plant and equipment, 191
return on assets (ROA), 198, 446–447, 641–645
working capital and, 642e, 646–647

AT&T Inc., 445, 549

auditor's report, 20, 356

audits
  auditor's report, 20
  financial statement, 355
  forensic accounting and, 355
  going concern concept and, 356
  internal, 337–338, 355–357, 391, 440
  operational, 357
  procedures for, 356
  Public Company Accounting Oversight Board (PCAOB) and, 356

authorized shares, 534

automation, factory, 699

available-for-sale securities, D2–D3, D11

average collection period, 396–398, 642e, 648–649

average cost method. See weighted average cost method

average rate of return method, 1129–1131

B

balanced scorecard, 1082–1083

balance sheet
  accounting equation and, 13
  accounts receivable and, 383–387, 396, 400
  accrual basis of accounting and, 126, 132e, 134, 135e, 144–151, 150e
  analysis of, 636–639, 656, 658–661
  assets and, 199–201, 585–586
  bonds payable and, 484
  budgeted, 1002–1003
  cherry picking and, D12
  classified, 190–194
  Columbia Sportswear Company and, 13–14, 19e
  contra-stockholders' equity account and, 541
  current assets and, 190–191
  debt securities and, D5–D7
  debt-to-total assets ratio and, 200

depreciation and, 436–438
description of, 13–14
equity securities and, D9–D11
financial statements and, 13–14, 18–19
horizontal analysis, 637
intangible assets and, 446
internal control and, 339–340, 346–351
inventory and, 275, 286–287, 300–302
leveraging of, 478
liabilities and, 13, 469–471, 475, 478, 484, 486–490, 585–586
liquidity and, 199
long-lived assets and, 427–430
long-term assets and, 191–192
merchandising firms and, 194, 233
notes receivable and, 396–397
off-balance-sheet financing and, 486, 503
overview of, 12–18
Procter & Gamble and, 637e
return on assets and, 446–447
solvency and, 200
statement of cash flows and, 204–205, 578, 584–591
stockholders' equity and, 13, 14e, 536, 538–540, 585–586
uncollectible accounts and, 386
working with, 198–200

Ballmer, Steve, 469

bank notes, 64, 71–72

Bank of America Corporation, 7e, 485

bank reconciliation, 346–351

bank statement, 346–351

bankruptcy, 275

bank-to-bank EFT, 346

bar codes, 239

Barrons magazine, 549

base year, 638–639

Bayer Group, 70

bearers, 393

Bellagio, 381

benchmarking analysis, 199, 203, 245–247

Benford's Law, 331, 336

Best Buy, 275, 293–294, 550

best efforts basis, 538

betterments, 439–440

big data, 701

Big Four, 7

bill of materials, 757–758, 759

Blank, Arthur, 577

Boeing, 1025

bonds payable, D2
  advantages/disadvantages of issuing bonds and, 485–486
  amortization and, 454–499
  balance sheet disclosure for, 484
  bond features and, 478
  bond indenture and, 486
  bond prices and, 479–481, 493–501
  call provision and, 478

Note: Exhibits and notes are included in the index with a corresponding e or n following the page numbers.

bonds payable (*continued*)
  convertible bonds and, 478
  coupon rate and, 479
  debenture bonds and, 478
  discounts and, 480–483, 494–495
  effective interest method and, 496
  face value and, 480–481
  issuance between interest dates and, 480–481
  issue price calculation, 497–499
  market rate of interest and, 480–481
  premiums and, 480–481, 483–484, 495–496
  present value and, 480–481, 493–495, 500–501
  recording, 481–485
  retirement of bonds before maturity and, 484–485
  risk ratings and, 478
  secured bonds and, 478
  selling price calculation, 500–501
  serial bonds and, 478
  sinking fund provision and, 478
  straight-line method and, 483
  term loans and, 485–486
  time value of money and, E2–E10
  types of bonds and, 478
  year-end adjustments and, 483–484
  zero-coupon bonds and, 483
book of original account, 68
book value, 441–442
books, 68
Boston Celtics, 61
bottlenecks, 963
break-even analysis
  basic assumptions, 894
  break-even formula, 895
  break-even point, 893
  cost-volume-profit chart, 893–894
  defined, 884
  multiple products, 905–906
  operating leverage, 902–903
  purpose of, 897
bribes, 8
budget, 336
  annual operating budget, 987
  balance sheet, 1002–1003
  capital expenditures, 997–998
  cash, 998
  continuous (perpetual, rolling), 989–990
  "decision packages," 990
  defined, 987
  direct labor, 995
  direct material, 994–995
  flexible. *See* flexible budget
  income statement, 1001
  manufacturing overhead, 995–996
  master budget, 987, 991–992
  nonmoving, 1062

  operating, 987
  perpetual, 989
  production, 993–994
  sales, 992–993
  selling and administrative expense, 997
  service firm illustration, 999–1000
  standard costs, 1026–1027
  statement of cash flows, 1003–1004
  static, 1062–1063
  stationary, 1062
budget committee, 989
budget director, 989
budget period, 989
budgetary control, 988
budgeted balance sheet, 1002–1003
budgeted income statement, 1001
budgeted statement of cash flows, 1003–1004
budgeting
  advantages of, 988
  capital. *See* capital budgeting
  defined, 987
  elements, 989–990
  participative, 989
  zero-base, 990–991
buffer margin, 1113
business activities, 5–6
business entities, types of, 697–698
Business Ethics magazine, 430
business organization, 4–5
business-to-consumer (B2C) transaction, 235
byproducts, 962–963

C

calendar year, 61, 476
California State Bar Association, 845
call provision, 478
callable preferred stock, 537
Canada, 11, 246
capital
  cost of, 1112–1113
  weighted average cost of capital, 1113
  working capital, 645, 1110
capital budgeting, 1108–1132
  average rate of return analysis, 1129–1131
  capital expenditure analysis, 1111–1112
  cash payback analysis, 1128–1129
  cost of capital, 1112–1113
  defined, 1110
  measurement of investments and returns, 1117–1121
  net present value analysis, 1121–1127
  net present value calculations, 1115–1117
  phases, 1110–1111
  service industry, 1131–1132
  summary of concerns, 1121
  time value of money, 1114

capital expenditures, 439–440
  analysis of, 1111–1112
  budget, 997–998
  project stages, 1111
  stages, 1111–1112
  U.S. business, 1130
capital-intensity ratio, 425
capital leases, 502–503
capital market, preferred shares, 538
careers
  accounting, 22–23
  in managerial accounting, 703–704
carrying value, 128
cash, 578–579
  accounting for, 339–345
  accrual-basis method and, 584
  annuity form of cash flow and, E5–E6
  bank reconciliation and, 346–351
  bank statement and, 346–351
  checks and, 345–346
  controller and, 342–343
  electronic funds transfer (EFT) and, 346
  equivalents and, 578–579
  excess, investment of, 353
  free cash flow and, 592–593
  internal audit and, 343, 345
  internal control of cash receipts transactions and, 341–351
  inventory turnover and, 275
  long-lived asset purchases and, 427–429
  mailroom and, 341–342
  monitoring of, 353–354
  operating activities and, 583–584
  operating cash flow-to-capital expenditures ratio and, 593–594, 652
  operating cash flow-to-current liabilities ratio and, 593, 647–648
  paid-in capital and, 538–540
  paper trails and, 347
  petty cash fund and, 346–347
  principles of effective management of, 353
  quick ratio and, 647
  received from retail sales, 343–345
  received on account, 341–343
  remittance advice and, 341
  remittance list and, 341
  reporting, 339–340
  sources and uses of, 17
  statement of cash flows and, 577–599. *See also* statement of cash flows
  stock dividends and, 543–544
  stock issuances for, 538–540
  treasurer and, 342, 344e, 345
cash basis of accounting, 27, 124
cash budget, 998
cash disbursements, 998

Note: Exhibits and notes are included in the index with a corresponding e or n following the page numbers.

cash discount, 239
cash equivalents, 340, 578–579
   defined, 578, 579
   in the statement of cash flows, 578–579
cash flow
   after-tax, 1118–1121, 1124
   annuity flows, 1116–1117
   discounted cash flow, 1115
   financing cash flows, 998
   present value analysis, 1117–1118
   single-sum, 1115–1116
cash fraud schemes, 206
cash larceny, 206
cash management, 352–353, 578
cash payback method, 1128–1129
cash payback period, 1128
cash receipts, 998
cash registers, 206, 279, 343–345
casino resorts, 381, 396
Central America, 390
certificates of deposit (CDs), 339, 578
certifications, professional, 705
Certified Fraud Examiner (CFE)
   certification, 22
Certified Internal Auditor (CIA)
   certification, 22
Certified Management Accounting (CMA)
   certification, 22, 705
certified public accountants (CPAs), 7, 22,
   355, 705
CH2M Hill, 751
change in accounting principle, 632–633
Charles Schwab Corporation, D2
chart of accounts, 68, 73e
Chase Bank, 392
checks, 206, 345–346, 349
cherry picking, D12
Chevron, 549
China, 390
Chiquita Brands, 584
Circuit City, 275
Circus Circus, 381
Cisco Systems, Inc., 492
Citibank, 200, 236, 292
classified balance sheet, 190e
   account form and, 192
   Apple and, 190–194
   current assets and, 190–191
   current liabilities and, 192
   intangible assets and, 191
   long-term assets and, 191–192
   long-term liabilities and, 193
   property, plant, and equipment, 191
   report form and, 193, 194e
   stockholders' equity and, 193, 194
classified common stock, 535
classified income statement
   Apple and, 195–198
   gross profit and, 195–198
   merchandising firms and, 195–198

closing process
   accrual basis of accounting and,
     137–139
   statement of retained earnings and,
     144–147
   temporary accounts and, 137–139
   trial balance and, 146–147
closing the books, 137, 144–147
CM (credit memo), 347
CMA (Certified Management Accountant),
   705
Coca-Cola Company, 549, 846, 856
COGM. See cost of goods manufactured
   (COGM)
COGS. See cost of goods sold (COGS)
Columbia Sportswear Company, 3, 659,
   660
   accounts receivable of, 20–21
   annual report of, 20
   auditor's report of, 21
   balance sheet of, 13–14, 19e
   description of, 3
   financial statements of, 13–19, 20–21,
     659–660
   Form 10-K and, 20
   income statement of, 15, 18–19
   Management Discussion and Analysis
     (MD&A) and, 20
   notes to financial statements of, 20–21
   retained earnings of, 14c, 16, 19c
   segments and, 660–661
   statement of cash flows of, 17, 19e
   statement of stockholders' equity of,
     16, 19e
combined costs, 719
commercial paper, D2
commitments, 659–660
common expenses, 1075
common shares, 16
common-size financial statement, 639–641
common stock, 16, 64e, D2
common stockholders' equity, 534
company-wide overhead rate, 771
comparability, accounting information,
   26, 27e
comparative financial statement analysis,
   635–639
comparative selected financial data, 661
compound interest, E2, E3e
compound journal entry, 72
comprehensive income, 633
conceptual framework, FASB, 25–27
conflicts of interest, 247
conformity rule, 289
conglomerates, D14
conservatism concept, 292, 437
consignment goods, 278–279
consistency principle, 26, 287, 633, 636,
   638
constrained resources, 963–964

constraints, accounting information, 28
contingency, 660
contingent liabilities, 470–476
continuing education expenses, reporting
   of, 1077
continuous budget, 989–990
contra accounts, 128, 243
contributed capital, 15, 203
contribution margin
   alternative break-even formulas, 897
   analysis, 895–897
   contribution margin ratio, 896
   defined, 896, 898
   income statement, 1074
   transfer pricing objective, 1087–1088
   variable costing, 933
   variable operating income statement,
     895–896
control numbers, 336
controller, 342–343, 344e, 345
controlling securities, D2–D3
conversion costs
   defined, 719
   equivalent unit calculation, 802, 807
convertible bonds, 478
Cook, Tim, 62
copyright, 444
corporate social responsibility (CSR)
   accrual-basis of accounting and, 140
   business decisions and, 15
   decision making, 951
   engineers, shortage of, 754
   environmental issues and, 8, 15, 189,
     204, 294, 396, 430
   environmental performance reporting at
     Apple, 732
   fraud and, 333
   General Mills tried to make a
     difference, 809
   Home Depot values, 591
   information processing and, 70
   Microsoft's corporate citizenship
     budget, 1069
   Monsantogether, 987
   more than the bottom line, 698
   Pampers and UNICEF, 633
   responsible gaming and, 396
   standards of professionalism, 849
   stockholders' equity and, 534
   triple bottom line reporting, 16, 932
   true innovation, 904
   values and, 591
corporations, 529
   acquisitions and, 629
   advantages of, 4–5, 530–532
   alternative organizational forms of, 533
   articles of incorporation and, 530
   best efforts basis and, 538
   capital raising capability of, 532
   cash dividends and, 543–544

Note: Exhibits and notes are included in the index with a corresponding e or n following the page numbers.

corporations (*continued*)

certificates of capital stock and, 530

conglomerates and, D14

continuity of existence of, 531

costs of, 532

defined, 530

disadvantages of, 532

entity concept and, 531

equity ownership and, 532

formation of, 530–533

forward stock split and, 540

going concern concept and, 531

greenmail and, 541

legal issues and, 530–532

limited liability of, 531

mergers and, 629

nature of, 530–533

noncash stock issuances and, 538–539

no-par value stock and, 533–534

Paid-in Capital and, 538–539

parent-subsidiary relationship and, D12–D14

par value stock and, 533–534

personal liability and, 5

regulation of, 533

retained earnings and, 546–547

separate legal entity of, 530

stakeholder responsibilities and, 531e

statement of retained earnings and, 546–547

statement of stockholders' equity and, 546–547

stock dividends and, 544–546

stockholders' equity and, 533–550

stock issuances for cash and, 538–539

stock splits and, 538

supervision of, 533

taxes and, 532

transferability of ownership of, 531

treasury stock and, 534, 540–542

types of capital stock and, 534–537

underwriters and, 537

cost

allocation, 769–771

of capital, 1112–1113

combined, 719

conversion, 719, 802, 807

direct, 714–716

fixed. *See* fixed cost

incremental, 955

indirect, 714–715, 846–848

joint product, 961

mixed, 713–714, 715, 887

opportunity, 953

period costs, 712–713, 715

prime cost, 719

product. *See* product costing

production department, 853

relevant range, 953–955

semi-variable, 713, 887

standard. *See* standard costs

sunk cost, 953, 955

total manufacturing, 722, 724

total standard, 1030

total variable, 886

variable. *See* variable cost

cost accounting systems, 752–754

choosing, 753

job order costing system, 752–753

process costing system, 753

timely product costing, 753–754

cost allocation

basis of, 770–771

service departments, 769

cost behavior analysis, 884–893

activity basis, 884–885

analyzing costs in practice, 892–893

cost behavior patterns, 886–887

cost-volume graphs, 885–886

defined, 884

high-low method of cost behavior analysis, 889–891

least squares regression method of cost behavior analysis, 891–892

scattergraph method of cost behavior analysis, 888–889

cost behavior patterns, 886–887

cost-benefit constraint, 28

cost center

segment organizations, 1071

service department as, 768

cost control, defined, 716

cost drivers, 755, 850–851

cost flows, 236, 729–732

data for illustration of, 281

goods flow and, 281

impacts of assumptions in, 285–286, 300–301

inventory and, 280e, 281, 285–287, 299–300

cost object, defined, 712

cost of goods available for sale, 236, 252, 281, 283

cost of goods manufactured (COGM)

calculation of, 808–809, 821–822

defined, 722

flow through the inventory system, 722–723

cost of goods purchased, 236, 237

cost of goods remaining, 809

cost of goods sold (COGS), 15

analysis of financial statements and, 631, 636–637, 648–650

calculating, 726–727

defined, 723

inventory and, 279–294

merchandising firms and, 195, 198, 236, 240–247

cost of jobs or projects, 715

cost of sales, 242

cost principle, 27, 238, 427–429

cost variances

direct labor variances, 1036–1039

direct materials variances, 1032–1036

standard costs, 1031–1041

variable overhead variances, 1039–1041

cost-volume graphs, 885–886

cost-volume-profit (CVP) analysis, 884

cost-volume-profit chart, 893–894

cost-volume-profit relationships, 882–909

activity basis, 884–885

analyzing costs in practice, 892–893

break-even analysis, 893–895

break-even analysis and multiple products, 905–906

contribution margin analysis, 895–897

cost behavior analysis, 884–887, 888–893

cost behavior patterns, 886–887

cost-volume graphs, 885–886

desired profit, 897–899

high-low method of cost behavior analysis, 889–891

least squares regression method of cost behavior analysis, 891–892

margin of safety, 900

operating leverage, 900–904

planning for profit, 897–907

relevant range, 887–888

retail businesses, 906–907

scattergraph method of cost behavior analysis, 888–889

service industry, 908–909

use of, 904–905

Costco, 382

costing, activity-based. *See* activity-based costing (ABC)

coupon rate, 479

CPA (Certified Public Accountant), 705

Crazy Eddie, 290

credit card fee, 392

credit card sales, 392

credit-collection policy and, 383–384

credit-granting policy, 383–384

credit guarantees, 489

credit lines, 381

credit loss estimation, 387–391

credit period, 239–240

credit scoring systems, 383–384

credit system, 68–69

compound journal entry and, 72

general journal and, 71–78

trial balance, 279

creditors, 5

credits, on bank statement, 348

Crest toothpaste, 629

Crisco, 629

Cummins Inc., 430, 437

cumulative dividends, 536

Note: Exhibits and notes are included in the index with a corresponding e or n following the page numbers.

currency measurement, 10
current assets, 190–191
current liabilities, 192
    accounts payable and, 470
    add-on interest method and, 471
    advance payments–unearned revenue
        and, 476
    current position of long-term debt and,
        472
    generally accepted accounting
        principles (GAAP) and, 471
    income taxes payable and, 475–476
    interest and, 470–472
    interest payable and, 472
    maturity date and, 470
    notes payable and, 470–472
    payroll-related, 472–474
    product warranties and, 476–477
    sales and excise taxes payable and,
        472–473
current portion of long-term debt, 472
current ratio, 302–303, 496–497, 646–647
custodial departments, 342
customer prepayment, 64, 74
customer profitability
    activity-based costing and analysis of,
        857–859
    profitability profile, 857–859
    services industry, 860–861
    trends in tracking, 700–701
CVP (cost-volume-profit) analysis, 884

D

Darden Restaurant Group, 8e
days'-inventory-on-hand ratio, 294
days' sales in inventory, 293–294, 649–650
days' sales outstanding (DSO), 648
DCF (discounted cash flow), 1115
"death spiral" decision, 935
debenture bonds, 478
debit system, 68–69
    compound journal entry and, 72
    general journal and, 71–78
    trial balance, 79–81
debits, on bank statement, 348
debt financing, 5
debt securities, D2–D3
    amortization and, D5, D7–D8
    balance sheet valuation and, D5–D7
    current/noncurrent classifications and,
        D12
    generally accepted accounting
        principles (GAAP) and, D12
    materiality concept and, D5
    purchase of, D4–D5
    recognition of interest income and,
        D5–D6
    sale or redemption at maturity and,
        D7–D8
    unrealized gains and losses, D6–D7

debt-to-equity ratio, 651
debt-to-total assets ratio, 200–201
decentralized organizations, 1069–1070
decision making
    constrained resources, 963–964
    defined, 951
    differential analysis, 953–964
    dropping unprofitable segments,
        958–959
    evaluation phase, 952
    execution phase, 952
    make or buy parts, 957–958
    management responsibilities, 950–951
    planning phase, 952
    quantitative vs. qualitative factors, 954
    relevant costs, 953–955
    sell or process further, 959–963
    service industry, 958–959, 964–965
    special orders, 955–956
"decision packages" for budgets, 990
declining-balance method, 433–435
deferrals, 126
deferred payment purchases, 428
Deferred Revenue, 64, 128
Dell Inc., 276, 294
Del Monte, 234
Deloitte and Touche, 7, 20, 356
Delta Airlines, 7e, 382
departmental operations, 1074
departmental overhead rates, 771–772
deposits in transit, 349
depreciation, 128
    accelerated, 433–434
    allocation vs. valuation and, 431
    annual, 431–435
    calculating expense of, 431–434
    change estimation and, 436–438
    comparison of alternative methods for,
        435–437
    conservatism and, 437
    declining-balance method and,
        433–434
    double declining balance, 433
    expense, 426
    generally accepted accounting
        principles (GAAP) and, 437
    going concern concept and, 433
    impairment losses and, 437–438
    income taxes and, 438
    International Financial Reporting
        Standards (IFRS) and, 438
    long-lived assets and, 426, 428,
        430–440
    matching concept and, 431
    modified accelerated cost recovery
        system (MACRS) and, 438
    nature of, 430–431
    150 percent-declining balance
        depreciation, 433
    revenue expenditures and, 439–440

    straight-line method and, 431–432
    units-of-production method and,
        434–435
depreciation expense as noncash expense,
    588–589
depreciation-per-unit, 434
depreciation tax shield, 1118–1120
desired net income, 898
detection control, 334
differential analysis
    constrained resources, 963–964
    make or buy parts, 957–958
    quantitative vs. qualitative factors, 954
    relevant costs and, 953–955
    special orders, 955–956
differential cost, 955
direct cost
    in manufacturing environment,
        714–715
    in service and merchandising, 715–716
    variable costing, 928
direct labor
    defined, 718
    standard costs, 1028–1029
    variances, 1036–1039
direct labor budget, 995
direct materials
    budget, 994–995
    defined, 718
    equivalent unit calculation, 806
    standard costs, 1028
    variances, 1032–1036
direct method, 583, 585, 597–599
direct write-off method, 400
disclosures
    commitments and, 660
    comparative selected financial data
        and, 661
    contingencies and, 660
    details of reported amounts and,
        659–660
    explanations of complex or special
        transactions and, 659
    financial statement, 658–661
    management discussion and, 661
    parenthetical, 659
    quarterly data and, 661
    segments and, 660–661
    subsequent events and, 661
    summary of significant accounting
        policies and, 659
    supplementary information and, 661
discontinued operations, 632
discount periods, 239–241, 244
discounted cash flow (DCF), 1115
discounting, 395–396
discover, 236, 392
dishonored notes, 394–395
dividend payout ratio, 549–550, 654–655

Note: Exhibits and notes are included in the index with a corresponding e or n following the page numbers.

dividends
  cash, 543–544
  declaration date and, 542–544
  earnings per share (EPS) and, 653–654
  in expanded accounting equation, 62e
  large stock, 545–546
  payment date and, 542
  price-earnings ratio and, 654
  record date and, 542
  small stock, 544–545
  stockholders' equity and, 16
  yield, 548–549, 654–655
DM (debit memo), 347
double-declining balance depreciation, 433
double-entry accounting, 62, 337
DSO (days' sales outstanding), 648
Duke Energy, 7e, 491
Dun & Bradstreet, 634
DuPont formula, 1080

E

earned capital, 16, 203
earnings per share (EPS), 632, 653–654
earnings persistence, 630–634
earnings quality, 140
earnings statement, 14
eBay, 10
Ebbers, Bernard, 80, 440
EC (error correction), 347
Economic Value Added (EVA), 1081
EDGAR database, 634
EDGAR (Electronic Data Gathering,
    Analysis, and Retrieval) system,
    634
effective interest method, 483, 496–497
effective interest rate, 480, 496
effective yield rate, 480
electronic controls, 337
Electronic Data Gathering, Analysis, and
    Retrieval (EDGAR) database, 634
electronic funds transfer (EFT), 346
electronic spreadsheets, 500–501
employee benefits, reporting of, 1077
employee bonuses, reporting of, 1076
employee collusion, 338
employee theft, 279
employer taxes, 474–475
ending work in process inventory, 809
Enron Corporation, 8, 9, 332, 334, 338
entity concept, 531
Environmental Business Consultants, LLC
    budget, 999–1000, 1004–1005
    capital budgeting, 1131–1132
    cost-volume-profit relationships,
        908–909
    decision making, 958–959, 964–965
    job order costing, 772–773
    overview, 702–703
    performance analysis, 1084–1085
    process costing, 812–813

product costing, 733–735
segment reporting, 1075–1079
standard costing, 1042–1043
variable costing, 935–937
environmental issues
  business decisions and, 8, 15
  corporate social responsibility and, 16,
      70, 189, 534
  liabilities and, 469, 488–489, 660
environmental performance reporting at
    Apple, 732
EPS (earnings per share), 632, 653
equipment purchase, 64
equity financing, 5
equity method, D9
equity securities, D2
  accounting guidelines for, D8e
  balance sheet valuation and, D9–D11
  current/noncurrent classifications and,
      D12
  generally accepted accounting
      principles (GAAP) and, D12
  purchase of, D8–D9
  recognition of investment income and,
      D9, D10e
  sale of, D11–D12
equivalent units
  calculation of, 802, 805–807, 818–820
  conversion costs, 807
  defined, 805
  direct materials, 806
  FIFO method, 806
  weighted average method, 806
Ernst & Young, 7
ethics, 8–9, 440, 491
  AIG and, 8
  American Institute of Certified Public
      Accountants (AICPA) and, 9
  Best Buy and, 295
  bonus pressure and, 9
  Business Ethics magazine and, 430
  corporate social responsibility (CSR)
      and, 16, 141, 204, 334, 534
  employee theft and, 279
  Enron and, 8, 9, 332, 334, 338
  environmental issues and, 16, 189, 204,
      294, 469, 487–488, 534, 660
  Financial Accounting Standards Board
      (FASB) and, 10–11, 62, 660–661
  fraud and, 9, 80, 206, 290. *See also*
      fraud
  GAAP and, 10–11. *See also* generally
      accepted accounting principles
      (GAAP)
  IFRS and, 11–12. *See also* International
      Financial Reporting Standards
      (IFRS)
  income tax and, 9
  information confidentiality and, 9

Institute of Management Accountants
    (IMA) and, 9
International Accounting Standards
    Board (IASB) and, 11–12, 62
long-run perspective and, 9
Sarbanes-Oxley Act and, 9, 11–12, 338,
    356
socially responsible investing (SRI)
    and, 204
triple bottom line and, 16
Worldcom and, 8–9, 80, 338, 440
European Union (EU), 11
EVA (Economic Value Added), 1081
evaluation phase of decision making, 952
Excalibur, 381
Excel, 46, 148, 500
excess capacity, 1088–1092
excess present value index, 1127
excise tax payable, 472–473
execution phase of decision making, 952
expense recognition (matching) principle,
    25e, 27, 124, 242
expenses
  administrative, 997, 1120
  allocation for federal government
      grants and contracts, 1078
  amortization, 588
  common, 1075
  continuing education, 1077
  depreciation as noncash expense, 588,
      589
  in expanded accounting equation, 62e
  on income statement, 14–15
  interest. *See* interest expense
  marketing, 1076
  on multi-step income statement,
      195–198
  noncash, 588–589
  office lease, 1077
  office supplies, 1076
  operating, 1120
  other general administrative expenses,
      1077
  reporting of, 1075–1079
  selling, 997, 1120
  traceable, 1075
  types of, 15
external users, 7

F

face value, 479–480, 493–494
factoring, 397–398
factory automation, 699
factory burden, 718
factory overhead, 718
factory supplies, 716–717
Fair Labor Association Workplace Code of
    Conduct, 294
faithful representation, accounting
    information, 25e, 26

Note: Exhibits and notes are included in the index with a corresponding e or n following the page numbers.

Fannie Mae, D2
FCF (free cash flow), 592
Federal Express Corporation, 7e
Federal Insurance Contributions Act
    (FICA), 473
Federal Mogul Corporation, 594
FedEx, 846
feedback data, 953
fees revenue, 65, 68
Fezzari Performance Bicycles
    absorption costing, 928–934
    activity-based costing, 851–854
    budget, 991–998, 1001–1004
    capital budgeting, 1119–1121
    cost-volume-profit relationships,
        885–887, 893–900, 903–905
    differential analysis, 955–956
    flexible budgets, 1063–1065
    job order costing system, 757–767
    overview, 701–702
    performance analysis, 1079–1083
    product cost accumulation, 724–727
    standard costs, 1031–1042
    static budgets, 1062–1063
fidelity bonds, 338
Fidelity Investments, D2
FIFO method
    to calculate equivalent units, 800, 806
    process costing using, 816–822
financial accounting, 7
    defined, 696
    managerial accounting vs., 696–697
Financial Accounting Standards Board
        (FASB)
    Accounting Standards Codification, 11
    business decisions and, 11
    cash flow presentation from operating
        activities, 583
    conceptual framework of, 25–28
    generally accepted accounting
        principles (GAAP) and, 10–11, 26,
        62, 585, 630–631
    liabilities and, 585
    segments and, 660–661
    statement of cash flows and, 582–583,
        585
    supplementary information and, 661
financial calculator, 499–500
financial flexibility, 583
financial pressure, 332–333
financial reporting objectives, 25–26
financial statements, 12–19. See also
        balance sheet; income statement;
        statement of cash flows
    accounting equation and, 13
    accounts receivable turnover and, 648
    accrual basis of accounting and,
        122–124, 129–135
    adjusted trial balance and, 133–135
    analysis limitations, 656

analytical techniques and, 634–635
annual report and, 20–21
articulation and, 18
asset turnover ratio and, 644
audits and, 20, 355–357. See also audits
average collection period and, 648–649
balance sheet and, 13–14. See also
    balance sheet
bank statement and, 347
benchmarking analysis and, 199, 202e,
    245–247
budgeted, 1001–1004
common-size, 639–641
comparative analysis and, 635–639
comparative financial statement
    analysis, 635
conglomerates and, D14
consistency principle and, 633
consolidated, D13–D14
current ratio and, 199–200, 646–647
days' sales in inventory and, 650
debt-to-equity ratio and, 651
disclosures and, 658–661
discontinued operations and, 632
dividend payout ratio and, 549–550
dividend yield and, 548–549, 645–655
earnings per share (EPS) and, 653–654
earnings quality and, 140
expenses and, 14–15
FASB conceptual framework and, 25,
    26e
Form 10-K and, 20
gross profit percentage and, 641–642
horizontal analysis and, 635–639
income statement and, 12, 14–15, 134,
    135e, 630–633. See also income
    statement
information sources and, 634–635
inventory turnover and, 649–650
liabilities and, 13
limitations in analysis of, 656
Management Discussion and Analysis
    (MD&A) and, 21
notes to, 20, 26, 658–661
operating cash flow-to-capital
    expenditures ratio and, 652
operating cash flow-to-current
    liabilities ratio and, 647–648
period-of-time statements, 19
persistent earnings and, 630–633
point-of-time statements, 19
price-earnings ratio and, 654
pro forma, 991
product cost, 730–732
profitability analysis and, 202
quick ratio and, 647
ratio analysis and, 198, 641–655
relations among, 18–19
retained earnings and, 14e, 15–16,
    18–19, 203, 546–547, 633

return on assets (ROA) and, 198–199,
    202, 446–447, 641–655
return on sales and, 202, 641–655
return on stockholders' equity and,
    641–655
sales revenue and, 14
solvency and, 200–201
standard costs, 1041–1042
statement of cash flows and, 12, 17. See
    also statement of cash flows
statement of stockholders' equity and,
    12, 15–16, 134, 135e, 547, 633
stockholders' equity and, 13
summary of significant accounting
    policies and, 659
sustainable earnings and, 630
times-interest-earned ratio and,
    651–652
transitory earnings and, 630
trend analysis and, 199, 636–639
triple bottom line and, 16
vertical analysis and, 635, 640–641
working with, 201–203
financing activities, 5, 6e, 579–581
financing mix, balance sheet and, 14
finished goods, accounting for, 763–765
finished goods inventory, 277, 716
firm liquidity, 646–650
firm profitability, 641–655
firm solvency, 650–652
first-in, first-out (FIFO), equivalent unit
    calculation, 800, 806
first in, first out (FIFO) inventory method
    comparative analysis of costing
        methods and, 285–290, 297–298
    cost flow assumptions and, 285–286
    description of, 282, 283e
    financial statement analysis and,
        632–633, 656
    inventory analysis and, 293–294
    LIFO inventory reserve and, 302–303
fiscal year
    accrual-basis of accounting and, 121
    financial statements and, 61, 202e
    information processing and, 61
    liabilities and, 472, 480
    statement of cash flows and, 579
    stockholders' equity and, 549
fixed assets, 296
fixed cost
    cost behavior patterns, 886–887
    in manufacturing environment, 713,
        714
    operating leverage with, 901
    in service and merchandising, 715
flexible budget
    defined, 1063
    in manufacturing environment,
        1063–1066
    in service environment, 1066–1069

Note: Exhibits and notes are included in the index with a corresponding e or n following the page numbers.

flexible-manufacturing-system automation, 699
F.O.B. (free on board) destination, 238–239, 278
F.O.B. (free on board) shipping point, 238–239, 278
Ford, Henry, production process, 700
Ford Motor Company, 62, 234, 447
forensic accounting, 9, 656
    accounting software and, 490
    audits and, 355
    Benford's Law and, 336
    cash fraud schemes and, 206
    employee theft and, 279
    fraudulent reporting and, 80
    internal controls and, 657
    interrogation skills and, 355
    lapping and, 391
    liabilities and, 491
    surveillance tactics and, 355
Form 10-K, 20
forward stock split, 540
franchises, 444–445
fraud, 656
    accounting for cash and, 338–354
    audits and, 336–338
    Benford's Law and, 336
    cash larceny and, 206
    certification and, 9
    check tampering and, 206
    competent personnel and, 336
    corporate social responsibility (CSR) and, 334
    defined, 334
    employee collusion and, 338
    Enron and, 8, 9, 332, 334, 338
    financial reporting and, 332–338, 355–357, 657
    inconsistencies and, 486
    internal audits and, 334–335, 337–338, 356–357
    internal control and, 9, 332–338, 657
    job rotation and, 336
    lapping and, 391
    legal issues and, 333
    line costs and, 440
    mandatory vacations and, 336
    opportunity and, 333
    passwords and, 279
    pressures and, 332–333, 657
    rationalization and, 333
    reporting and, 80
    Sarbanes-Oxley Act and, 9, 338, 356
    securities, 290
    segregation of duties and, 335
    skimming and, 206
    "tone at the top" and, 333
    triangle of, 332–333
    Worldcom and, 8, 9, 80, 338, 440
free cash flow (FCF), 205–206, 592–593

freight bill, 278
full costing, 928
full disclosure, 27, 287, 487
future operating receipts or cost savings, 1121
future value of an amount, E3–E5
future value of an annuity, E5–E6

G

GAAP. *See* generally accepted accounting principles (GAAP)
Gamble, James, 629
Gannett Co., Inc., 592–593
Gap, 61
Gates, Bill, 469
General Electric (GE), 8e, 445, 479, 850, D13
general journal, 71–72, 77e
    closing process and, 137–139
    compound journal entry and, 72
    cost side, 242
    general ledger posting and, 72–77
    purchase of merchandise and, 237–241
    revenue side, 241
    sales of merchandise and, 241–245
general ledger
    accounts receivable and, 441–442. *See also* accounts receivable
    adjusted trial balance and, 125, 135e
    adjusting entries and, 126, 132
    analyzing transactions and, 72
    defined, 72
    notes receivable and, 382, 393, 396, 660–661
    paid cash dividend, 76
    paid employee wages, 75
    paid rent in advance, 73
    performed services for cash on account, 75
    performed services for customer, 75
    posting journal entries to, 73–76
    purchased office equipment, 74
    purchased office supplies on account, 73
    received customer prepayment, 74
    received payment on account, 76
    signed bank note in exchange for cash, 74
    trial balance, 79–80
    uncollectible accounts and, 383–392, 396
    writing off accounts and, 385–386
General Mills Inc., 797
General Motors (GM), 8e, 382, 927, 985
generally accepted accounting principles (GAAP)
    accounts receivable and, 381, 400
    accrual-basis of accounting and, 135
    adjusting entries and, 135
    Apple and, 194

    balance sheet and, 194
    business decisions and, 10–12, 26–27
    characteristics of accounting information and, 66–67
    collection efforts and, 381
    comprehensive income and, 633
    conglomerates and, D14
    conservatism and, 437
    cost principle and, 27
    debt/equity securities and, D12
    depreciation and, 438
    direct write-off method and, 400
    effective interest method and, 483
    Financial Accounting Standards Board (FASB) and, 11, 62, 542, 585, 660–661
    financial oversight and, 11
    financial statements and, 194, 630–634, 660–661
    global uniformity for, 11
    IFRS and, 12. *See also* International Financial Reporting Standards (IFRS)
    income statement and, 630–632
    information processing and, 62
    intangible assets and, 443
    interest expense and, 471
    inventory and, 284, 288, 293
    liabilities and, 471, 480–481, 486
    long-lived assets and, 438
    materiality concept and, 439
    multiple-step income statement and, 195–197, 632
    notes to financial statements, 24
    persistent earnings, 630
    Public Company Accounting Oversight Board (PCAOB), 11
    reporting standards, 696
    research and development costs and, 443
    statement of cash flows activities, 581
    statement of cash flows and, 578, 581, 587
    stockholders' equity and, 542, 547
    summary of significant accounting policies and, 659
    Tesco PLC and, 632
    unusual item reporting, 631
    U.S. Securities and Exchange Commission (SEC) and, 11
generally accepted auditing standards (GAAS), 11
Gillette, 629
Ginnie Mae, D2
Global Reporting Initiative, 70
going concern concept, 27, 356, 385, 433, 531
goods flow, 267
goods in transit, 281
goodwill, 445

Note: Exhibits and notes are included in the index with a corresponding e or n following the page numbers.

Google, Inc., 491, 535, 695
governance, conflicts of interest and, 247
Governmental Accounting Standards
    Board (GASB), 11n
government grants and contracts, expense
    allocation for, 1078
graphs
    cost-volume, 885–886
    scattergraph method of cost behavior
        analysis, 888–889
greenmail, 541
gross margin, 196, 245, 641–642
gross pay, 473–474
gross profit
    costing methods analysis and, 287–290,
        301–302
    defined, 641
    financial statement analysis and,
        630–632, 636–639, 641, 646,
        660–661
    inventory and, 286–290, 293–294,
        300–302
    merchandising firms and, 195–198,
        245–246
    in multi-step income statement,
        195–198
    percentage, 245, 292, 641–645
    profitability analysis and, 245–247
    Target and Walmart and, 245–247
gross profit on sales, defined, 641

H

Hamilton, Anita, 275n
Harley-Davidson, 584
Head & Shoulders shampoo, 629
health regulations, 8
held-to-maturity securities, D2–D3, D12
Hewlett Packard, 8e, 199–202, 499
high-low method of cost behavior analysis,
    889–891
high-yield bonds, 478
hiring, 65
holding companies, D12
Home Depot, 430, 577, 591
horizontal analysis, 635–639
hurdle rate, 1113

I

IBM, 549, 846
IFRS alerts
    multi-step income statement, 632
    statement of cash flows activities, 581
    statement of cash flows presentation,
        585
Il Giornale, 529
IMA (Institute of Management
    Accountants), 705
impairment losses, 437–438
IN (interest earned), 347
income

cash receipts, 1120
comprehensive, 633
desired net income, 898
residual, 1081–1082
income reconciliation, 932–934
income statement, 201–203
    accounts receivable and, 384, 393–394,
        400
    accrual-basis of accounting and,
        123–132, 134–135, 148–151
    analysis of, 630–634, 636–641, 653
    budgeted, 1001
    change in accounting principle and,
        632–633
    cherry picking and, D12
    classified, 195–198
    Columbia Sportswear Company and,
        15, 18
    comprehensive income and, 633
    consistency principle and, 633
    contribution margin, 1074
    depreciation and, 431, 436–438
    description of, 14–15
    direct method conversion schedule, 597
    discontinued operations and, 632
    expenses and, 14–15
    financial statements and, 12, 14–15,
        18–19
    generally accepted accounting
        principles (GAAP) and, 630–632
    horizontal analysis, 636
    impairment losses and, 437–438, 445
    income tax and, 196, 630–632
    inventory and, 286–287, 293–295,
        301–302
    liabilities and, 471, 488–489, 491–492,
        503
    long-lived assets and, 426, 431,
        436–437, 439
    manufacturing firm, 727
    merchandising firms and, 195–198
    multiple-step, 195–198, 630–632
    net income, 15
    net loss, 15
    persistent earnings, 630–634
    profitability analysis and, 15
    return on assets and, 446–447
    sales revenue and, 14
    single-step, 195, 630
    statement of cash flows and, 578, 580,
        587–591, 597
    stockholders' equity and, 532, 536
    sustainable earnings and, 630
    transitory earnings and, 630
    unusual items and, 631
    variable costing, 930–934
    variable operating, 895–896
    working with, 201–202
income tax

advantages/disadvantages of issuing
    bonds and, 485–486
amounts withheld in payroll and,
    473–475
business organization and, 4–5
contingencies and, 660
corporations and, 4, 5e, 532
current liabilities and, 192
depreciation and, 438
direct write-off method and, 400
dividend yield and, 654–655
ethics and, 9
expenses and, 14–15, 128–129,
    475–476, 632
income before taxes and, 196
income statement and, 630–632
inventory and, 287–288, 299–301
liabilities and, 475–476
modified accelerated cost recovery
    system (MACRS) and, 438
partnership and, 4, 5e
payable, 475–476
sole proprietor and, 4, 5e
statement of cash flows and, 580,
    585–591
stockholders' equity and, 485, 536
times-interest-earned ratio and,
    491–492, 651–652
incremental after-tax liquidation proceeds,
    1121
incremental cost, 955
Indianapolis, City of, 846
indirect cost
    activity-based costing, 846–848
    in manufacturing environment,
        714–715
    in service and merchandising, 715
indirect labor, 718
indirect manufacturing costs, 718
indirect materials, 717–718
indirect method of presenting cash flow
    from operating activities, 583–591
influential securities, D2–D3
information
    accounting cycle and, 61–70
    analytical techniques and, 635–636
    comparability and, 661
    confidentiality and, 9
    debit-credit system and, 68–78
    disclosures and, 658–661
    EDGAR system and, 634
    general ledger postings and, 73–78
    horizontal analysis and, 636–639
    inside, 8
    limitations in analysis of financial
        statements, 656
    management discussion and, 661
    processing of, 58–79
    ratio analysis and, 641–655
    sources of, 634–636

Note: Exhibits and notes are included in the index with a corresponding e or n following the page numbers.

information (*continued*)
  supplementary, 661
  trend analysis and, 639–641
  vertical analysis and, 636, 641–642
initial acquisitions and additions, 440
initial public offering (IPO), 529, D2
Institute of Management Accountants
    (IMA), 9, 705
intangible assets, 191–192, 426
  amortization and, 426, 443–444, 446
  balance sheet presentation and, 446
  copyright, 444
  defined, 442–444
  examples of, 443–445
  franchises, 444–445
  generally accepted accounting
      principles (GAAP) and, 443
  goodwill, 445
  International Financial Reporting
      Standards (IFRS) and, 443
  measurement of, 443
  patents, 444
  quick ratio and, 647
  ratio analysis and, 641–655
  research and development costs and,
      443
  trademarks, 445
  types of, 445
Intel Corporation, 276
interest
  adjusting entries for, 394–395
  advantages/disadvantages of issuing
      bonds and, 485–486
  annuity form of cash flow and, E5–E6
  compound, E2, E3e
  debt securities and, D5, D6e
  effective interest method and, 483
  effective rate and, 483
  future value of single amount and,
      E3–E6
  insurance between interest dates and,
      481–482
  maturity date and, 394
  nature of, E2
  notes receivable and, 393–395
  present value of an amount and, E6–E8
  present value of an annuity and, E8–E9
  principal and, E2
  recognition of interest income and, D5
  recording of, 393–395
  simple, E2, E3e
  times-interest-earned ratio and, 492
  time value of money and, E2–E10
interest coverage ratio, 492, 651
interest expense
  after-tax cash flows, 1121
  cash flow presentation from operating
      activities, 589
  compound interest, E2–E3
  defined, E2

simple interest, E2
  times-interest-earned ratio, 651–652
interest payable
  accrual-basis of accounting and, 130
  add-on interest method and, 471
  bond issue price and, 493–495
  current liabilities and, 472
  liabilities and, 477–485
  maturity date and, 471
  recording, 471–472
  statement of cash flows and, 580
internal audits
  cash and, 342–345
  employee collusion and, 338
  fidelity bond and, 338
  outside independent auditors and, 338
  internal control and, 334, 337, 339,
      355–357, 390–391, 441
  Sarbanes-Oxley Act (SOX) and, 338
internal control
  accounting for cash and, 338–353
  budget development and, 336
  cash receipts transactions and, 340–341
  clear lines of authority and
      responsibility for, 334–335
  competent personnel and, 335
  control numbers and, 336
  defined, 333–334
  detection control and, 334–336
  employee collusion and, 338
  Enron and, 8–9, 332, 334, 338
  failures of, 338–339
  fidelity bonds and, 338
  financial reporting and, 332, 340–341,
      355–357
  forensic accounting and, 657
  fraud and, 10, 332–338, 657
  going concern concept and, 355
  internal audits and, 334, 337–339,
      355–357, 391, 440
  job rotation and, 336
  maintaining adequate records for, 337
  management's responsibility for, 334
  mandatory vacations and, 336
  MICR and, 345–346
  paper trails and, 347
  passwords and, 343
  physical and electronic controls for,
      337
  physical control of assets and, 337
  prevention control and, 334, 336
  proper authorization, 335
  reliability and, 334
  segregation of duties and, 335
Internal Revenue Service (IRS), 289
internal users, 8
International Accounting Standards Board
    (IASB), 62
  business decisions and, 12
  leases and, 502–503

statement of cash flows and, 585
International Financial Reporting
    Standards (IFRS)
  balance sheet and, 191
  business decisions and, 12
  contingent liabilities and, 486
  depreciation and, 438
  financial statements and, 191, 632
  information processing and, 62
  intangible assets and, 443
  inventory and, 293
  last-in, first out (LIFO) methods and,
      292
  leases and, 503
  liabilities and, 479, 486, 500–501
  long-lived assets and, 438
  merchandising firms and, 197
  multiple-step income statement and,
      197, 632
  reporting liabilities and, 479, 480
  statement of cash flows and, 581, 585
  stockholders' equity and, 542, 547
  Tesco PLC and, 194, 632
International Game Technology, 579
International Labor Association, 294
international transfer pricing, 1092
introduction to managerial accounting,
      696–697
Intuit, 59, 61, 490
inventory
  analysis of, 293–295
  balance sheet and, 275, 286–287,
      300–301
  bankruptcy and, 275
  beginning, 236, 281–290
  cash flow and, 275
  cash management and, 353
  categories of, 276–277
  comparative analysis and, 285–290,
      296–303
  conservatism and, 292
  consignment goods and, 279–280
  consistency and, 287
  cost flows and, 280e, 281, 285–286,
      300–301
  costing methods and, 280–290,
      296–303
  days' sales in, 293–294, 649–650
  determining ownership and, 278
  ending, 236, 280, 290
  ending work in process, 809, 822
  factory supplies, 716
  finished goods, 277, 716
  first in, first out (FIFO) method and,
      282–290, 293, 296–303, 633, 656,
      800
  full disclosure and, 287
  goods flow and, 281
  goods in transit and, 278

Note: Exhibits and notes are included in the index with a corresponding e or n following the page numbers.

gross profit and, 195–198, 286–291, 293–294, 300–301
income statement and, 286–287, 293–295, 300–301
income tax and, 287–288, 300–302
information processing and, 61
just-in-case, 277
just-in-time. *See* just-in-time (JIT) inventory
just-in-time manufacturing and, 277
last-in, first-out (LIFO) method and, 283, 286–290, 293–294, 296–297, 656
lower-of-cost-or-market (LCM) method and, 291–293
management concepts for, 277
manufacturing firms, 716–717
manufacturing product cost categories, 717–719
materials, 716
merchandising and service firms, 717, 719
merchandising firms and, 197, 233, 236–245, 249–254, 276–279
net realizable value and, 291
office supplies, 716–717
periodic system for, 236, 249–253, 281
perpetual system for, 233, 236, 251, 296–303
phantom profit and, 288
physical count and, 278–280, 289–290
purchase discounts and, 239–241, 249–250
purchase returns and allowances and, 237–239, 249–250
purchases of merchandise and, 237–241, 249–252
quick response system and, 278
raw materials and, 276–277
sales of merchandise and, 195–198, 241–244, 250–252
shrinkage and, 279–280
specific identification method and, 282, 285, 296–297, 300–302
Target and, 233
transportation costs and, 249
turnover and, 293–295, 650–651
turnover ratio, 649
weighted-average cost method and, 281, 284, 287, 296, 299–302
work in process, 276–277, 716, 809, 822
inventory-on-hand period, 294
inventory overage, 277–280
investing activities
accounting as an aid to investing, 655
included transactions, 580
investment. *See also* stockholders
balance sheet valuation and, D5–D7

bonds payable and, 489. *See also* bonds payable
as business activity, 6
capital-intensity ratio and, 425
categories of, D2–D3
cherry picking and, D12
commercial paper and, D2
common stock and, D2
consolidated financial statements and, D12–D14
current/noncurrent classifications and, D12
debt securities and, D2–D8, D12
equity securities and, D2, D8–D12
of excess cash, 353
financing activities and, 580–581
generally accepted accounting principles (GAAP) and, D12
identifying win-win companies and, 189
income statement and, 630–634
initial public offering (IPO) and, 529, D2
manufacturers and, 425
materiality concept and, D5
noncash, 582
objectivity principle and, D10
parent-subsidiary relationship and, D12–D14
persistent earnings and, 630–634
preferred stock and, D2
purchase and, D4–D5
recognition of interest income and, D5
recognition of investment income and, D9, D10c
return on assets (ROA) and, 198, 446–447, 640–645
statement of cash flows and, 580
sustainable earnings and, 630
time value of money and, E2–E10
trend analysis and, 198–199, 639–641
unrealized gains and losses, D6–D7
investment center, 1071
investment outlay, 1121
invoice price, 239
iPad, 189, 201
iPhone, 189, 201
iPod, 189, 201
issued shares, 534
issued stock, 63–73
iTunes, 201, 883
"I've Got Your Number" (Nigrini), 336

J

J.C. Penney, 549
JIT. *See* just-in-time (JIT) inventory
job order costing
cost accounting systems, 752–754
departmental overhead rates, 771–772
flow of documents, 757–758

manufacturer illustration, 758–767
overview, 798–799
predetermined overhead rates, 755–757
service department accounting, 768–771
service firm illustration, 767–768
service industry, 767–768, 772–773
uses for, 799
job order costing system
defined, 752–753
flow of documents, 757–758
manufacturer illustration, 758–767
purpose of, 757
service firm illustration, 767–768
job order cost sheet, 758
job rotation, 336
Jobs, Steve, 189
John Deere, 949
Johnson & Johnson Company, 10, 396, 491, 543
Johnson Controls, Inc., 548
joint product costs, 961
joint products, 961–962
journal, 71
journal entries, 71
cost variance, 1043–1045
labor, 824–825
process costing, 811–812
product cost, 727–732
journalize, 71, 76–78
Journal of Accountancy, 336
just-in-case inventory, 277
just-in-time (JIT) inventory
defined, 699
minimal inventory levels, 700
overview, 699–700
production budget, 993
purpose of systems, 699–700
just-in-time manufacturing, 277

K

Kali Company, 631e, 632
Kellogg Company, 492
Kentucky Fried Chicken (KFC), 444
KPMG, 7
Krispy Kreme, 121–124

L

labor
accounting for, 761–762, 767
direct. *See* direct labor
direct labor budget, 995
indirect, 718
process costing journal entries, 811, 824–825
product cost flows, 720–721
labor efficiency variance, 1036–1037
labor rate variance, 1036–1037
land expenditures, 429–430
lapping, 391

Note: Exhibits and notes are included in the index with a corresponding e or n following the page numbers.

larceny, 206
large stock dividends, 545–546
last-in, first-out (LIFO) inventory method
 comparative analysis of costing
  methods and, 285–290, 296–303
 conformity rule and, 289
 cost flow assumptions and, 285–286
 description of, 283
 financial statements analysis and, 656
 generally accepted accounting
  principles (GAAP) and, 292
 International Financial Reporting
  Standards (IFRS) and, 292
 LIFO conformity rule, 289
 LIFO inventory reserve, 302–303
lean manufacturing, 700
leasehold, 426e, 502
leasehold improvements, 429–430
leases, 502–503
least squares regression method of cost
 behavior analysis, 891–892
legal capital, 533
legal issues
 business decisions and, 4
 corporations and, 530–532
 financial statements and, 191
 fraud and, 315. See also fraud
 greenmail and, 541
 intangible assets and, 442–443
 lawsuits and, 4, 20, 469, 487, 489e,
  580, 660
 liabilities and, 469, 473–474, 486–487
 long-lived assets and, 429
 parent-subsidiary relationship and,
  D12–D14
lessee, 502
lessor, 502
Levi Strauss, 584
liabilities
 add-on interest method and, 471
 advance payments–unearned revenue
  and, 476
 advantages/disadvantages of issuing
  bonds and, 485–486
 analysis of, 490–491
 balance sheet and, 13, 469–470, 475,
  478, 484, 486–488, 585–586
 bonds payable and, 476–486
 classified balance sheet and, 192–193
 contingent, 466–469
 credit guarantees and, 489
 current, 192, 470–477
 current ratio and, 199, 490–492,
  646–647
 debit-credit system and, 68–69
 debt-to-equity ratio and, 651
 debt-to-total assets ratio and, 200
 defined, 470
 in expanded accounting equation, 62e
 forensic accounting and, 491

full disclosure principle and, 487
generally accepted accounting
 principles (GAAP) and, 471, 480
income taxes payable and, 475–476
interest payable and, 470–472
International Financial Reporting
 Standards (IFRS) and, 480
leases and, 502–503
legal issues and, 469, 473–475,
 486–487, 489e
long-term, 193
maturity date and, 471
measuring unit concept and, 487
notes payable and, 13, 62–67, 470–472,
 581, 659
off-balance-sheet financing and, 486,
 503
operating cash flow-to-current
 liabilities ratio and, 593, 647–648
payroll-related, 473–475
product warranties and, 487–488
quick ratio and, 490–491, 647
reporting, 480
sales and excise taxes payable and,
 472–473
times-interest-earned ratio and,
 491–492
working capital and, 490–491, 646–647
LIFO conformity rule, 289
LIFO inventory reserve, 302–303
Linens n' Things, 275
liquidation proceeds, 1126–1127
liquidity
 current ratio and, 191
 definition of, 191
 financial statements and, 191, 193,
  198–199, 646–652
 internal control and, 341
 liabilities and, 485, 489e
 long-lived assets and, 341
list price, 245
Lockheed Martin Corporation, 594
long-lived assets
 accounting for, 426–428
 acquisition cost of, 426–428
 asset turnover and, 447
 betterments and, 440
 book value and, 441–442
 capital expenditures and, 439–440
 cash purchases and, 428
 deferred payment purchases and, 428
 depreciation and, 426, 428, 430–440
 disposal of, 441–442
 generally accepted accounting
  principles (GAAP) and, 438
 initial acquisitions and additions, 440
 International Financial Reporting
  Standards (IFRS) and, 439
 land expenditures and, 429–430
 leasehold improvements and, 429–430

low-cost items and, 439–440
maintenance and, 439
matching concept and, 431
package purchases and, 428–429
plant assets and, 425–426, 430,
 439–442, 446–447
repairs and, 439
return on assets and, 446–447
revenue expenditures and, 439–440
long-term assets, 191–192
long-term firm solvency analysis, 650–653
 debt-to-equity ratio, 651
 operating-cash-flow-to-capital-
  expenditures ratio, 652–653
 times-interest-earned ratio, 651–652
long-term liabilities, 193
Loss from Doubtful Accounts, 384
Loss from Uncollectible Accounts, 384
lower-of-cost-or-market (LCM) method,
 291–292
Luxor, 381

M

Madoff, Bernard, 9
Madoff Investment Securities LLC, 332
magnetic characters, 345–346
mailrooms, 341–343
make or buy parts, 957–958
maker, 345
management
 by exception, 1066
 cash management, 578
 decision-making, 950–951
 defined, 950
 evaluation phase decisions, 952
 execution phase decisions, 952
 planning phase decisions, 952
 upper, middle, and lower management
  responsibilities, 951
 zero-base budgeting responsibilities,
  991
management discussion and analysis
 (MD&A), 20, 631
 financial statement disclosures, 661
 SEC requirements, 899
managerial accounting, 8
 defined, 696
 financial accounting vs., 696–697
 objectives, 697, 712–716
 overview, 696–697
Mandalay Bay, 381
mandatory vacations, 336
manufacturing
 environmental issues and, 189, 204,
  294, 430, 469, 489–490, 660
 financial statements and, 201–202
 inventory and, 276–277, 285, 294
 just-in-time, 277
 long-lived assets and, 425–426, 430
 merchandising and, 233–235, 237–245

Note: Exhibits and notes are included in the index with a corresponding e or n following the page numbers.

statements of cash flows and, 579, 592–593
stockholders' equity and, 648–649
manufacturing cell, 699
manufacturing firms
combined costs, 719
defined, 697
flexible budgets, 1063–1066
income statement, 727
inventories, 716–717
job order costing, 758–767
process costing, 801
product cost categories, 717–719
product costing, 712–715, 717–719, 753–754
reputable companies, 697–698
manufacturing overhead
budget, 995–996
accounting for, 762–763
as cost of product, 931
defined, 718, 996
examples, 995–996
process costing journal entries, 811–812, 825
product cost flows, 721–722
margin of safety, 900
market rate of interest, 480
marketing expenses, reporting of, 1076
master budget
defined, 987, 991
framework, 991–992
MasterCard, 236, 392
Masterful Merchandising, 708
matching concept, 384, 400, 431, 484, 488
matching principle, 588
materiality concept, 439, 497, D5
materials
accounting for, 759–760, 767
bill of materials, 757–759
direct. See direct materials
indirect, 718
process costing journal entries, 811
requisition, 757–758, 760
materials efficiency variance, 1032
materials inventory, 716
materials price variance, 1032
materials requisition, 757–758, 760
maturity date, 394, 471, D7–D8
maturity value, 459
McAdams Wright Ragen, 486
McDonald's, 134
MD&A. See management discussion and analysis (MD&A)
MeadWestvaco Corporation, 492
measuring unit concept, 487
merchandise inventory, 276–277, 279
merchandising firms. See also service firms
accounting for purchases of merchandise and, 237–241

accounting for sales of merchandise and, 195–198, 241–245
advertising and, 196–197, 235
bar codes and, 239
business-to-consumer transactions and, 235
classified income statements and, 195–197
cost flows and, 236
credit period and, 439
defined, 697
discount periods and, 239–241, 244–245
electronic cash registers and, 337
expenses and, 195–198
inventory and, 197, 233, 236–244, 249–254, 276–277, 279, 717, 719
invoice price and, 239
leasehold improvements and, 429–430
manufacturers and, 233–245
middlemen and, 233
net sales and, 195–196, 244–245
open accounts and, 236
operating cycles of, 235–236
product costing, 715–716, 733–735
profitability analysis and, 245–247
purchase discounts and, 232–234
purchase returns and allowances, 238–239
reputable companies, 697–698
retailers and, 21, 61, 189, 194. See also retailers
sale on account and, 236
sales discounts and, 196, 243–245
sales returns and allowances, 242–243
transportation costs and, 238–239
wholesalers and, 234–236, 249, 276, 346
mergers, 629
Mervyn's, 275
Mexico, 10, 577
MGM Grand Las Vegas, 381
MGM Resorts International, 381, 396
MICR format, 345–346
Microsoft Corporation, 469, 476, 486, 490, 550, 695, 1061
Midas Mufflers, 444
middlemen, 233
military issues, 8
Mirage, The, 381
misleading information, 9
mixed cost
cost behavior patterns, 887
in manufacturing environment, 713–714
in service and merchandising, 715
Model Manufacturing, 708
modified accelerated cost recovery system (MACRS), 438–439
Moet Hennessy-Louis Vuitton, 10

monetary unit concept, 27, 70
Monsanto, 983, 987
Monte Carlo, 381
Moody's Investors, 378, 634
multiple-step income statement, 195–198, 630–632. See also classified income statement

N

n/30 credit period, 239
NASDAQ, 632
negative net present value, 1122
net assets, 13
net book value, 432
net credit period, 239
net earnings, 15
net income 15, 16
net loss, 15
net pay, 473
net present value
annuity flows, 1116–1117
calculations, 1115–1117
present value analysis, 1122
single-sum cash flows, 1115–1116
net present value analysis
basic steps, 1121–1122
excess present value index, 1127
illustration, 1122–1126
liquidation proceeds, 1126–1127
net present value method, 1121
net profit, 15
net realizable value, 291
net revenue, 14
net sales
accounts receivable and, 388, 396–397, 648
business decisions and, 14, 20
classified income statement and, 195–198
estimating credit losses and, 387
financial statements and, 201–202, 636–639, 649
merchandising firms and, 245–246
in multi-step income statement, 195–198
operating revenues and, 446–447
percentage of net sales method and, 387
profitability analysis and, 245–247
New York-New York, 381
New York Stock Exchange (NYSE), 5, 533
Nigrini, Mark, 336
Nikon, 294
nominal rate, 479
noncash expenses, 588–589
noncash investing and financing activities, 582
noncash stock issuances, 539
noncurrent liabilities, 193. See also long-term liabilities
nonmoving budget, 1062

Note: Exhibits and notes are included in the index with a corresponding e or n following the page numbers.

no-par value stock, 533–534
Nordstrom, 236
Norfolk Southern Corporation, 594
notes, to financial statements, 20–21, 26, 658–661
notes payable
    add-on interest method and, 471
    business decisions and, 13
    current liabilities and, 472
    financial statements and, 194, 660–661
    information processing and, 62, 64, 67
    interest and, 470–472
    liabilities and, 470–472
    maturity date and, 471
    recording, 471–472
    statement of cash flows and, 533
notes receivable, 382
    analysis of, 396–397
    average collection period and, 396–397
    bearer and, 393
    determining maturity date for, 394–395
    discounting and, 397
    dishonored notes and, 394–395
    factoring and, 397
    financial statements and, 660–661
    interest on, 393–395
    maker and, 393
    management of, 396–398
    payee and, 393
    promissory note and, 393
    recording of, 394
    reporting on balance sheet, 396
    revenue recognition principle and, 396
NSF (insufficient funds), 339

O

objectives of managerial accounting
    cost control, 716
    manufacturing product costing, 712–715
    overview, 697
    service and merchandising product costing, 715–716
objectivity principle, 582, D9
OD (overdraft), 347
off-balance-sheet financing, 486, 503
office equipment, 64, 74
office lease expense, reporting of, 1077
office margin, reporting of, 1075–1079
office supplies, 716–717, 1076
    on account, 64
on account, goods, 65
150 percent-declining balance depreciation, 433
open account, 236
operating activities, 6, 580, 583–584
    audits and, 356. See also audits
    direct method conversion schedule, 597
    expenses and, 195–198
    leases and, 502–503

operating cash flow-to-capital expenditures ratio, 593–594, 652
operating cash flow-to-current liabilities ratio, 593, 647–649
operating cycle, 190–192, 235–236, 470, 472
operating budget, 987
operating-cash-flow-to-capital-expenditures ratio, 593–594, 652–653
operating-cash-flow-to-current-liabilities ratio, 592–593, 647
operating cycle, 650
operating expense, 1120
operating leverage, 900–904
operational planning, 986–987
opportunity, 333–334
opportunity cost, 953
ordinary annuity, E5–E6
other general administrative expenses, reporting of, 1077
other income and expenses, multi-step income statement, 195–198
outsourcing, 698–699
outstanding checks, 349
outstanding shares, 534
overapplied overhead, 765–767
overhead
    accounting for, 767
    activity-based costing application, 852–854
    departmental overhead rates, 771–772
    disposition of under- and overapplied, 765–767
    manufacturing. See manufacturing overhead
    predetermined overhead rates, 755–757
    understanding of costs, 848
    variable overhead standard costs, 1029–1030
    variable overhead variances, 1039–1041
ownership of inventory, 278

P

PACCAR, 1070–1072
package purchases, 428–429
packaging, accounting for, 763–765
paid cash dividend, 66, 76
Paid-in Capital, 538–540
paid rent in advance, 63
Pampers, 629, 633, 634
Panasonic, 233
paper trails, 347
par value stock, 533
Parakh, Sid, 486
parallel product processing, 801–802
Paramount Pictures, 8e
parent companies, D12–D14
parenthetical disclosures, 658–659

Parmalat SpA, 491
participating preferred stock, 537
participative budgeting, 989
partnerships, 4–5, 530
passwords, 343
patents, 444
payee, 393
payer, 393
payroll-related liabilities
    amounts withheld and, 473–475
    employer taxes and, 474–475
    gross pay and, 473–474
    net pay and, 473–474
    recording, 474–475
Peach Inc., 708–709
P/E multiple, 653, 654
PepsiCo, Inc., 543, 579, 594
percentage of net sales method, 387–388
performance analysis, 1079–1083
    asset utilization, 1081
    balanced scorecard, 1082–1083
    residual income, 1081–1082
    return on investment, 1079–1080
    return on sales, 1080–1081
    service industry, 1084–1085
performance reporting, 1072–1075
    contribution margin income statement, 1074
    departmental operations, 1074
    segment performance evaluation, 1074–1075
performed services, 65, 75
period costs
    defined, 713
    in manufacturing environment, 712–713
    in service and merchandising, 715
periodic inventory system, 236, 249–254, 281
period-in-time statements, 16
permanent accounts, 137, 144–148
permanent earnings, 630
perpetual budget, 989
perpetual inventory system
    cost flow assumptions and, 300–301
    costing methods and, 296–302
    FIFO method and, 282–283, 285–287
    internal control and, 337
    LIFO method and, 283–287
    merchandising firms and, 236, 251
    specific identification and, 282, 285–287
    weighted-average cost method and, 284–287
persistent earnings and the income statement, 630–634
personal liability, 5
per-unit cost determination, 807–808, 820–821
petty cash fund, 346–347

Note: Exhibits and notes are included in the index with a corresponding e or n following the page numbers.

phantom profit, 288
physical controls, 337
physical count of inventory, 278–280,
    289–290
planning
    operational, 986–987
    process of, 984–987
    progress measurement and reporting,
        987
    strategic, 985–986
    SWOT analysis, 986
planning horizon, 984
planning phase of decision making, 952
plant assets
    balance sheet presentation and, 446
    defined, 426
    disposal of, 441–442
    exchange of, 442
    long-lived assets and, 425–426, 430,
        440–442, 447
plant-wide overhead rate, 771
point-in-time statements, 18
pollution. See environmental issues
post-closing trial balance, 138–139,
    146–147
posting, 72–77
PP&E property, plant, and equipment, 6,
    14e, 191, 205e, 426
practical capacity, 855
predetermined manufacturing overhead
    rate, 755
predetermined overhead rates, 755–757
    annual vs. monthly rates, 756–757
    calculation of, 755–756
    multiple rates, 755
predetermined variable overhead rate,
    1030
predictive analysis, 701
preemptive right, 535
preferred stock, 535–538, D2
premiums, 480–481, 483, 496
prepaid rent, 63, 125–128
present value, 479–481, 494–495,
    501–502, E6–E9
    of an amount, E6–E8
    of an annuity, E9
    defined, E6
    future cash flows, 1121
pretax income, 196
prevention control, 334, 335
price-earnings ratio, 653–654
price gouging, 8
prices
    materials price variance, 1032
    price-earnings ratio, 653–654
    setting, 1031
    transfer pricing, 1086–1092
PricewaterhouseCoopers, 7, 338, 491
prime cost, 719
principal, 5

defined, E2
principles
    consistency principle, 633, 636
    matching principle, 588
    objectivity principle, 582
pro forma statements, 991
process costing, 797–813
    characteristics, 800–802
    defined, 753, 799
    journal entries illustrated, 811–812
    reporting standards, 809–811, 822–824
    for service industries, 812–813
    steps. See process costing steps
    uses for, 799
process costing steps, 802–809
    calculate equivalent units, 805–807,
        818–820
    cost of goods manufactured calculation,
        808–809, 821–822
    ending work in process inventory
        calculation, 809, 822
    overview, 802–804, 816–817
    per-unit cost determination, 807–808,
        820–821
    using FIFO method, 816–822
    visualize physical flow of the units,
        804, 817–818
process costing system, 800
Procter & Gamble Company (P&G), 445,
    550, 629
    acquisitions of, 629
    annual performance, 637e
    balance sheet, 637e
    debt-to-equity ratio of, 651
    dividend payout ratio and, 550, 655
    earnings per share (EPS) and, 653–654
    horizontal analysis and, 636–639
    income statement, 636e
    information sources and, 633, 639–641
    operating cash flow-to-capital
        expenditures ratio and, 652
    price-earnings ratio and, 653–654
    ratio analysis and, 641–656
    statement of cash flows, 636e
    trend analysis, 639–641
    vertical analysis and, 631–632
Procter, William, 629
product cost
    accumulation, illustrated, 723–727
    categories, 718
    journal entries, 727–732
    period costs vs., 712–713
    service department costs as, 768–769
product cost flows, 719–723
    cost of goods manufactured, 722–723
    cost of goods sold, 723
    labor, 720–721
    manufacturing overhead, 721–722
    raw materials, 719–720
product cost report, 800, 809–811

product costing
    ABC model, 850–851. See also
        activity-based costing (ABC)
    absorption costing, 928–930
    combined costs, 719
    defined, 712
    in manufacturing environment,
        712–715
    in service and merchandising, 715
    variable costing, 928–929
product warranties, 476 477
production budget, 993–994
production department costs, 853
production order, 757
production processes, multiple, 811
professional certifications, 705
professionalism, standards of, 849
profit center, 1071
profit margin, 246–247, 643, 644
profit, planning for, 897–907
    desired profit, 897–899
    target profits without taxes, 897–899
    target profits with taxes, 899
profitability analysis, 15, 202–203
    asset turnover, 643–644
    gross profit percentage, 641
    return on assets, 644
    return on common stockholders' equity,
        644 645
    return on sales (profit margin), 643
    Target and Walmart, 245–246
promissory notes, 393
proper authorization, 333
property, plant, and equipment, 6, 14e,
    191, 205e, 426
Public Company Accounting Oversight
    Board (PCAOB), 11, 356
purchase, D4–D5
purchase allowances, 238–239, 249
purchase discounts, 239–240, 249–250
purchase returns, 238–239, 249

Q

qualitative characteristics of accounting
    information, 25–26, 27e
quarterly data, 660
QuickBooks, 59, 61, 63, 490
quick ratio, 490–491, 646–648
quick response systems, 277

R

rate of return, 1112
RateFinancials, Inc., 141
ratio analysis, 198
    accounts receivable turnover and, 639
    asset turnover ratio and, 632 637
    average collection period and, 648–649
    current ratio and, 647–648
    days' sales in inventory and, 650
    debt-to-equity ratio and, 651

Note: Exhibits and notes are included in the index with a corresponding e or n following the page numbers.

ratio analysis (*continued*)
  dividend payout ratio and, 655
  dividend yield and, 654–655
  earnings per share (EPS) and, 653–654
  financial ratios for common
      stockholders and, 653–656
  firm profitability and, 642–647
  gross profit percentage and, 642–647
  inventory turnover and, 649–650
  long-term firm solvency and, 651–653
  operating cash flow-to-current
      liabilities ratio and, 592, 648–649,
      652
  price-earnings ratio and, 654
  quick ratio and, 648
  return on assets and, 642–647
  return on sales and, 642–647
  return on stockholders' equity and,
      642–647
  short-term firm liquidity and, 647–652
  times-interest-earned ratio and,
      652–653
  working capital and, 642e, 647–648
rationalization, 333
ratios
  accounts receivable turnover, 648
  acid-test, 646
  asset turnover, 643–644
  asset utilization, 1081
  average collection period, 648–649
  current ratio, 646
  days' sales in inventory, 649–650
  debt-to-equity ratio, 651
  dividend payout ratio, 654–655
  dividend yield, 654
  earnings per share, 653
  financial ratios for common
      stockholders, 653–655
  firm profitability, 641, 643–645
  gross profit percentage, 641
  interest coverage ratio, 651
  inventory turnover, 649
  key financial ratios, 642
  long-term firm solvency, 650–653
  operating-cash-flow-to-capital-
      expenditures ratio, 593–594,
      652–653
  operating-cash-flow-to-current-
      liabilities ratio, 592–593, 647
  price-earnings ratio, 653–654
  quick ratio, 646–647
  return on assets, 644
  return on common stockholders' equity,
      644–645
  return on sales (profit margin), 643
  short-term firm liquidity, 645–650
  stockholder financial ratios, 653–655
  times-interest-earned ratio, 651–652
raw materials inventory, 276, 277e,
      719–720

real rate of interest, 480
receivables. *See* accounts receivable; notes
      receivable
received payment on account, 66, 76
recognition and measurement criteria, 25
recognition of interest income, D5, D6e
reconciled cash balance, 348–349
recording department, 342–343
relevance, 25, 27e
relevant costs, 953–955
relevant range, 887–888, 1064
reliability
  internal control and, 334
  Sarbanes-Oxley Act (SOX) and, 9, 338,
      356
remittance advice, 341
remittance list, 341
rent expense, 127–128, 197, 502–503
report form, 193–194e
reporting
  continuing education expenses, 1077
  employee benefits, 1077
  employee bonuses, 1076
  environmental performance, 732
  of expenses, 1075–1079
  GAAP. *See* generally accepted
      accounting principles (GAAP)
  marketing expenses, 1076
  office lease expense, 1077
  office margin, 1075–1079
  office supplies, 1076
  other general administrative expenses,
      1077
  performance reporting, 1072–1075
  process costing, 809–811, 822–824
  product cost, 800, 809–811
  progress measurement and reporting,
      987
  salaries, 1077
  segments, 1069–1079
  10-K annual report, 634
  10-Q quarterly report, 634
  triple bottom line reporting, 932
research and development costs, 443
residual claim, 13
residual income, 1081–1082
residual value, 430
responsibility centers, 1070–1071
retail business and cost-volume-profit
      analysis, 906–907
retail EFT, 346
retail sales area, 343, 344e
retail sales supervisor, 343–345
retailers, 20
  accounts receivable and, 392
  business-to-consumer transactions and,
      235
  cash accounting and, 342–343
  financial statements and, 189, 194, 632,
      642

information processing and, 62
internal control and, 336, 342–343, 345
inventory and, 275–277, 291–293
liabilities and, 488–489
long-lived assets and, 429–430
merchandising firms and, 234–235,
      239–240
open accounts and, 236
statement of cash flows and, 577
retained earnings
  closing procedures and, 144–148
  Columbia Sportswear Company and,
      14e, 16, 19e
  consistency principle and, 633
  description of, 16
  in expanded accounting equation, 62e
  financial statements and, 14e, 16,
      18–19
  statement of stockholders' equity and,
      546–547
return on assets (ROA), 644
  asset turnover and, 447
  financial statements and, 198, 201,
      642–647
return on common stockholders' equity,
      642–647
return on investment (ROI), 1079–1080
return on sales (ROS) ratio, 643,
      1080–1081
  financial statements and, 201–202, 635,
      642–647
  merchandising firms and, 245–247
revenue. *See* income
revenue expenditures, 439–441
revenue recognition principle, 27,
      122–123, 242, 395
rise over run, 886
ROI (return on investment), 1079–1080
rolling budget, 989
ROS (return on sales), 643, 1080–1081
routing number, 345
RT (returned item), 347

S

S&P 500 Index, 141, 478, 537
safety, 8, 70, 652
safety stocks, 699
Safeway, 123, 190, 281, 293
salaries
  accounting, 22, 23e
  reporting of, 1077
sale of plant assets, 649–650
sale on account, 236
sale on credit, 236
sales
  prices, setting, 1031
  recording, 768
  selling and administrative expenses,
      1120

selling products or processing further, 959–963
sales allowances, 196, 238–239, 243–244
sales budget, 992–993
sales discounts, 196, 239–240, 243–244, 250–251
sales forecast, 992
sales order, 757
sales returns and allowances, 196–197, 242 243, 250
sales revenue, 14, 15
sales tax payable, 472–473
salvage value, 430
Samsung Galaxy, 8e
Sarbanes-Oxley Act (SOX)
    Enron and, 338
    ethics and, 9
    internal control and, 331, 338
    Public Company Accounting Oversight Board (PCAOB) and, 356
    WorldCom and, 338
Satyam Computer Services, 338
SC (service charge), 347
scattergraph method of cost behavior analysis, 888–889
schedule of cost of goods manufactured, 724–726
Schultz, Howard, 529
scrap value, 430
secured bonds, 478
Securities and Exchange Commission (SEC)
    EDGAR database, 634
    management discussion and analysis, 899
    10-K and 10-Q filings, 634
segments, 660–661
    cost center, 1071
    decentralized organizations, 1069 1070
    financial statement disclosures, 660
    internal reporting, 1069–1072
    investment center, 1071
    performance evaluation, 1074–1075
    performance reporting, 1072–1075
    profit center, 1071
    reporting, 1070–1072
    responsibility centers, 1070–1071
    service company reporting illustration, 1075–1079
    unprofitable, 958–959
segregation of duties, 335
selling and administrative expense
    after-tax cash flows, 1120
    budget, 997
semi-variable costs, 713, 887
sequential product processing, 801
serial bonds, 478
service department
    accounting for, 768–771
    as cost centers, 768

costs as product costs, 768–769
service firms. See also merchandising firms
    budget, 999–1000, 1004–1005
    capital budgeting, 1131–1132
    combined costs, 719
    cost analysis, 892–893
    cost-volume-profit analysis, 906–909
    customer profitability analysis, 860 861
    decision making, 958–959, 964–965
    defined, 697
    dropping unprofitable segments, 958–959
    flexible budgets, 1066–1069
    inventories, 717, 719
    job order costing, 767–768, 772–773
    multi-step income statement, 195–198
    performance analysis, 1084–1085
    process costing, 812–813
    product costing, 715–716, 719, 733–735, 754
    reputable companies, 697–698
    segment reporting illustration, 1075–1079
    standard costing, 1042–1043
    variable costing, 935–937
settlement value, 479
shareholders. See stockholders
Sharper Image, 275
short-term firm liquidity analysis, 645–650
    accounts receivable turnover, 648
    average collection period, 648 649
    current ratio, 646
    days' sales in inventory, 649–650
    inventory turnover, 649
    operating-cash-flow-to-current-liabilities ratio, 647
    quick ratio, 646 647
simple interest, E2, E3e
single-step income statement, 195, 630
single-sum cash flows, 1115–1116
sinking fund provision, 478
skimming, 206
small stock dividends, 544–545
socially responsible investing (SRI), 204
social responsibility. See corporate social responsibility
sole proprietorship, 4–5, 530
solvency, 199 200
Sony, 233, 294
source documents, 71
sources of information, 634–635
South America, 390
Southwest Airlines, 476
special orders, 955–956
specific identification method
    comparative analysis of costing methods and, 296–297, 300–301
    description of, 285–286

spreadsheets, 500–501
    to calculate time value of money, E10
stand-alone automation, 699
Standard & Poor's Corporation (S&P), 478
standard costs
    accounting, 1027
    budgets and, 1026–1027
    cost variance journal entries, 1043–1045
    cost variances, 1031–1041
    defined, 1026
    direct labor standards, 1028–1029
    direct labor variances, 1036–1039
    direct material standards, 1028
    direct materials variances, 1032–1036
    financial statements, 1041–1042
    services industry, 1042–1043
    total standard costs, 1030
    variable overhead standards, 1029–1030
    variable overhead variances, 1039 1041
standard variable overhead rate, 1030
Starbucks, 529, 533–534
stated rate, 479
stated value, 479, 534
statement of cash flows, 576–599
    accrual-basis and cash-basis comparison, 584
    accrual basis of accounting and, 135, 594
    activity classifications in, 579–582
    analyzing cash flows and, 592–594
    Apple and, 205–207
    budgeted, 1003–1004
    cash and cash equivalents, 578 579
    cash basis of accounting and, 584
    Columbia Sportswear Company and, 17, 18e
    defined, 578
    description of, 17
    direct method and, 583, 585, 597–599
    Financial Accounting Standards Board (FASB) and, 582–583, 585
    financial analysis and, 638e
    financial flexibility and, 583
    financial statements and, 12, 17–19
    financing activities and, 580–581
    free cash flow and, 205–206, 592–593
    generally accepted accounting principles (GAAP) and, 579, 581
    horizontal analysis, 638
    IFRS alert, 581, 585
    indirect method of preparation, 583–591
    internal control and, 341, 352
    International Accounting Standards Board (IASB) and, 585
    International Financial Reporting Standards (IFRS) and, 581, 585

Note: Exhibits and notes are included in the index with a corresponding e or n following the page numbers.

statement of cash flows (*continued*)
  investing activities and, 580
  matching principle, 588
  noncash investing and financing
    activities, 582
  objectivity principle, 582
  operating activities and, 580, 583–584
  operating-cash-flow-to-capital-
    expenditures ratio, 593–594
  operating-cash-flow-to-current-
    liabilities ratio, 592–593
  preparation of, 584–591
  Procter & Gamble, 636e
  purpose of, 578
  use of, 582–583
statement of financial position, 13
statement of income, 14
statement of operations, 14
statement of retained earnings. *See*
    retained earnings
statement of stockholders' equity
  accrual basis of accounting and, 134,
    135e
  Apple and, 203–204
  Columbia Sportswear Company and,
    16, 18e
  contributed capital and, 16, 203
  earned capital and, 16, 203
  financial statements and, 12, 16, 18–19,
    633
  retained earnings and, 16, 546–547
static budget, 1062–1063
stationary budget, 1062
Steve and Barry's, 275
stockholders, 4
  advantages/disadvantages of issuing
    bonds and, 485–487
  asset distribution preference and, 536
  authorized shares and, 534
  best efforts basis and, 538
  bonds payable and, 476–486
  cash dividends and, 543–544
  common stock and, 534–535, D2
  convertible stocks and, 536–537
  corporations and, 533–534
  coupon rate and, 479
  cumulative dividends and, 536
  debt securities and, D3–D8, D11
  discounts and, 533
  dividend preference and, 535–536
  earnings per share (EPS) and, 653–654
  equity ownership and, 532
  equity securities and, D8–D12
  expanded accounting equation and, 62
  forward stock split and, 540
  greenmail and, 541
  issuance between interest dates and,
    481–482
  issued shares and, 534
  large stock dividends and, 545–546

market rate of interest and, 480–481
noncash stock issuances and, 539
no-par value stock and, 533–534
outstanding shares and, 534
paid cash dividends and, 66
Paid-in Capital and, 538–540
par value stock and, 533–534
parent-subsidiary relationship and,
    D12–D14
personal liability and, 5
preemptive right and, 535
preferred stock and, 535–538, D2
ratio analysis and, 642–657
retirement of bonds before maturity
    and, 584–585
risk ratings and, 478
small stock dividends and, 544–545
stated value and, 534
stock issuances for cash and, 538–539
time value of money and, E2–E10
treasury stock and, 534, 540–542
underwriters and, 538
stockholders' equity, 13
  alternative organization forms and, 533
  analysis of, 548–550
  balance sheet and, 13, 14e, 536,
    538–540, 585–586
  contra-account and, 541
  corporations and, 533–550
  debt-to-equity ratio and, 651
  dividend payout ratio and, 549–550
  dividend yield and, 548–549
  dividends and, 14
  in expanded accounting equation, 62e
  generally accepted accounting
    principles (GAAP) and, 542
  International Financial Reporting
    Standards (IFRS) and, 542
  net income and, 16
  return on, 548–549, 641–646
stockholders, financial ratios for, 653–655
  dividend payout ratio, 654–655
  dividend yield, 654
  earnings per share, 653
  price-earnings ratio, 653–654
straight-line depreciation, 128
straight-line method, 431–432, 494–496
strategic planning, 985–986
strengths, weaknesses, opportunities, and
    threats (SWOT) analysis, 986
subsequent events, 660, 661
subsidiaries, D12–D14
summary of significant accounting
    policies, 659
sunk cost, 953, 955
Superior Services, 708
supplementary information, 661
sustainable earnings, 630

SWOT (strengths, weaknesses,
    opportunities, and threats) analysis,
    986

T

T-accounts, 68, 70, 73–76, 137–140,
    723–724
Target Corporation, 7e, 986
  Business Conduct Guide, 247
  forensic accounting and, 279
  gross profit of, 245–246
  size of, 233
taxes
  after-tax cash flows, 1118–1121, 1124
  depreciation tax shield, 1118–1120
  incremental after-tax liquidation
    proceeds, 1121
  target profits with taxes, 899
  target profits without taxes, 897–899
temporary accounts
  accrual basis of accounting and,
    137–138, 151
  closing procedures and, 137–138,
    145–151
  statement of retained earnings and,
    145–151
  stockholders' equity and, 544
10-K annual report, 634
10-Q quarterly report, 634
term loans, 476–478
Tesco, PLC, 632
Tesla, 894
time clocks, 761
Time magazine, 275
time record, 758, 761
time value of money
  annuity form of cash flow and, E5–E6
  calculations using a calculator and
    spreadsheet, E10
  compound interest and, E2, E3e
  concept, E2–E3
  defined, 1114
  electronic spreadsheets and, E10
  financial calculator and, E10
  future value of an amount, E3–E5
  future value of an annuity, E5–E6
  future value of single amount and,
    E3–E6
  nature of interest and, E2
  overview, 1114
  present value of an amount and, E6–E8
  present value of an annuity and, E9
  simple interest and, E2, E3e
  time value, defined, E2
Time Warner Inc., 7e
timeliness, accounting information, 26e
times-interest-earned ratio, 491–492,
    651–652
Toronto's Hospital for Sick Children, 846
total manufacturing costs, 722, 724

Note: Exhibits and notes are included in the index with a corresponding e or n following the page numbers.

total standard costs, 1030
total variable costs, 886
Toyota Production System, 700
traceable expenses, 1075
trade receivables, 383
trademarks, 445
trading securities, D2–D3
transfer pricing, 1086–1092
   defined, 1086
   international, 1092
   maximize contribution margin,
     1087–1088
   negotiated, 1092
   no excess capacity, 1088–1091
   objectives, 1086
transitory earnings, 630
transportation costs, 237–238, 249
treasurer, 342–343, 344c, 345
treasury bills, 534, 540–542, 578, D2
trend analysis, 198, 639–641
trend percentages, 637–639
trends in business and managerial
    accounting
   big data and predictive analytics, 701
   customer profitability, 700–701
   factory automation, 699
   just-in-time inventory, 699–700
   lean manufacturing, 700
   outsourcing, 698–699
trial balance
   adjusted, 133–136, 148–149
   post-closing, 138–139, 146–147
   unadjusted, 79, 125–126, 133, 149
triple bottom line reporting, 16, 932

U

unadjusted trial balance, 138–139,
    146–147
Uncollectible Accounts Expense, 384
underapplied overhead, 765–767
Under Armour, Inc., 660–661
understandability, accounting information,
    26, 27e
underwriters, 538
Unearned Revenue, 64, 123–128, 476
UNICEF, 633
United Kingdom, 438, 532
United Nations, 16
United Parcel Service (UPS), 7
units-of-production method, 434
unprofitable segments, dropping of,
    958–959
unrealized gains and losses, D6–D7
unusual items, 631
UPS, 846
useful life, 431
U.S. Federal Reserve System, 345
U.S. Postal Service (USPS), 846
U.S. Securities and Exchange Commission
    (SEC)

EDGAR database and, 635
fiscal reports and, 635
Form 10-K and, 20
fraud and, 80, 331
generally accepted accounting
    principles (GAAP) and, 11–12
IFRS and, 12
information sources and, 635, 661
quarterly data and, 661
U.S. Treasury bills, 578, D2

V

variable cost
   in manufacturing environment, 713–714
   operating leverage with, 901
   in service and merchandising, 715
variable costing, 926–937
   absorption costing, 928, 930
   advantages of use, 934–935
   disadvantages of use, 935
   illustration, 929
   income reconciliation, 932–934
   income statement preparation, 930–932
   overview, 928–929
   service industry, 935–937
   triple bottom line reporting, 932
   uses for, 930
variable operating income statement,
    895–896
variable overhead efficiency variance,
    1040
variable overhead spending variance, 1040
variable overhead standard capacity, 1029
variable overhead standard costs,
    1029–1030
variable overhead variances, 1039–1041
variances. See also cost variances
   defined, 1027, 1031
   direct materials, 1032–1036
   managing, 1033
verifiability, accounting information, 26,
    27e
Verizon Communications, 491
vertical analysis of financial statements,
    635, 639–640
vice pressure, 333
Visa, 236, 392
visualizing the physical flow of the units,
    804, 817–818

W

WACC (weighted average cost of capital),
    1113
wages, 66, 75
Wall Street Journal, The, 549
Walmart Corporation, 7c, 245–247, 487,
    549
Waste Management, 1109
Wayne, Ronald, 189
wealth transfer, 535

Websites
   professional certifications, 705
   U.S. SEC EDGAR database, 634
weighted-average cost method
   comparative analysis of costing
     methods and, 285–290, 296–297,
     300–302
   cost flow assumptions and, 281
   description of, 284
   financial statements and, 633
weighted average cost of capital (WACC),
    1113
weighted average method to calculate
    equivalent units, 806
Wells Fargo & Company, 7e
wholesale EFT, 346
wholesalers
   business decisions and, 20
   internal control and, 346
   inventory and, 276
   merchandising firms and, 234–236
"Why Circuit City Busted, While Best Buy
    Boomed" (Hamilton), 275n
Wickes Furniture, 275
win-win companies, 189
working capital, 645, 1110
   financial statements and, 597–598,
     642e, 646–648
   liabilities and, 490–491
   ratio analysis and, 642e, 646–648
   statement of cash flows and, 597
   stockholders' equity and, 544
work in process inventory, 276–277
   ending calculation, 809, 822
   items included, 716
work/life balance, 704
worksheets, 148–151
WorldCom, 8–9, 80, 338, 440
Worthington Industries, 549
Wozniak, Steve, 189
write-offs
   accounts receivable and, 385–386,
     390–391
   intangible assets and, 426, 443–446
   plant assets and, 425–426, 430,
     439–442, 446–447

Z

Zales, 293
zero-base budgeting, 990–991
zero-coupon bonds, 483

Note: Exhibits and notes are included in the index with a corresponding e or n following the page numbers.